Network

Interrupts

A Programmer's Reference to Network APIs

Ralph Brown

Jim Kyle

Addison-Wesley Publishing Company

Reading, Massachusetts   Menlo Park, California   New York
Don Mills, Ontario   Wokingham, England   Amsterdam   Bonn
Sydney   Singapore   Tokyo   Madrid   San Juan
Paris   Seoul   Milan   Mexico City   Taipei

ISBN: 0-201-62664-6

Managing Editor: Amorette Pedersen
Production Editor: Andrew Williams
Set in 10.5 point Galliard by Benchmark Productions, Inc.

1 2 3 4 5 6 7 8 9-MA-9897969594
First Printing, January 1994

Addison-Wesley books are available for bulk purchases by corporations, institutions, and other organizations. For more information please contact the Corporate, Government, and Special Sales Department at (617) 944-3700 x2915.

Table of Contents

CHAPTER 1   **Introduction**   **1**
  Why This Book Exists   1
  Interrupts and the '86 CPU Family   2
  Some Words of Caution   2
  Sample Entry   3
  About The Authors   4
  Acknowledgments   4

CHAPTER 2   **Overview of Interrupt Usage**   **7**

CHAPTER 3   **MS-DOS Network Support**   **21**
  Internal Network Support Functions   63
  MS-DOS Data Structures   75

CHAPTER 4   **BAPI**   **87**

CHAPTER 5   **IPX/SPX**   **91**

CHAPTER 6   **Named Pipes**   **105**

CHAPTER 7   **NDIS**   **109**

CHAPTER 8   **NetBIOS**   **117**

CHAPTER 9   Network Redirector   **123**

CHAPTER 10   Open Data-Link Interface (ODI)   **137**

CHAPTER 11   Packet Driver Specification   **147**

CHAPTER 12   Alloy Multiuser/Network Systems   **157**

CHAPTER 13   APPC/PC   **195**

CHAPTER 14   Banyan VINES   **215**

CHAPTER 15   CD-ROM   **241**

CHAPTER 16   DECnet DOS   **247**

CHAPTER 17   DESQview/X Networking   **255**
   DESQview/X Socket Interrupts   255
   DESQview/X Socket API Functions   258

CHAPTER 18   DRIVEMAP   **275**

CHAPTER 19   LAN Manager   **281**

CHAPTER 20   LANtastic Network Operating System   **295**

CHAPTER 21   Novell NetWare Shell (NETX)   **311**
   Accounting Services   316
   Bindery Services   318
   Connection Services   329
   Directory Services   334
   File Server   347
   File Services   369
   Message Services   373
   Print Services   379
   Queue Services   385
   Synchronization Services   396
   Transaction Tracking System   404
   Workstation Functions   406
   General Functions   409

CHAPTER 22   Novell NetWare Lite   **421**

CHAPTER 23   Novell NetWare Utilities   **427**
   Access Server   427
   TASKID   430
   TBMI   431
   VNETWARE.386   434
   Miscellaneous   435

CHAPTER 24   PC LAN Program   **437**

CHAPTER 25   SK-UPPS Data Link Interface   **441**

CHAPTER 26   SNAP (Simple Network Access Protocol)   **451**

CHAPTER 27   10NET   **457**
10NET Core Functionality   457
10NET Utilities   479

CHAPTER 28   TopWare Network Operating System   **483**

CHAPTER 29   Web for DOS   **497**

CHAPTER 30   Workgroup Connection   **503**

CHAPTER 31   Other Redirectors and Shells   **505**
Generic Network Support   505
Excelan LAN Workplace for DOS   508
INTERLNK   510
Nanosoft TurboNET   511
PC-NET   513
Shamrock Software NET.24   513
SilverNET   515
Miscellaneous   518

CHAPTER 32   Beame and Whiteside BW-TCP and BW-NFS   **525**

CHAPTER 33   FTP Software PC/TCP   **541**
Network Kernel   541
Old-Style Configuration Drivers   558
Printer Redirection   560
Miscellaneous   562

CHAPTER 34   Other TCP/IP Software   **563**
Microsoft LAN Manager TCP/IP   563
Novell NetWare TCP/IP   563
Sun PC-NFS   566
Super-TCP   566
Lanera TCPOpen   570
TelAPI   571

CHAPTER 35   BSD 4.x Unix Sockets   **575**
Overview of Functions, Error Codes, and Structures   575
Socket Functions   579

CHAPTER 36   Windows Sockets   **595**
Overview   595
Socket Functions   599

CHAPTER 38   Network Serial I/O Emulation   **645**
ArtiCom   645
Beame and Whiteside BWCOM14   650
Connection Manager   650
Interconnections Inc. TES   658
Novell NASI/NACS   660
NPC NCSI Extended Serial I/O   661
Telebit ACS Serial I/O   664

CHAPTER 39   Network Remote Control Software   **667**

CHAPTER 40   Da Vinci eMail   **669**

CHAPTER 41   Other Electronic Mail Software   **677**
Shamrock Software EMAIL   677
Workgroup Connection MICRO.EXE   679
Network Courier E-Mail   680

CHAPTER 42   Miscellaneous Networking Calls   **681**
License Service   681
Embedded DOS (STARLITE Architecture)   683
QPC Software PKTINT   684
Miscellaneous   685

Bibliography   **689**
Additional References   692

Index   **693**

CHAPTER 1

Introduction

Welcome to *Network Interrupts*, a comprehensive guide to network-related interrupt calls on IBM PCs and compatible machines. Together with its larger companion book *PC Interrupts*, it forms the most comprehensive reference to IBM PC-related interrupt calls available. However, this book can stand on its own without *PC Interrupts*; it is meant to complement whatever programming books you may already own, including *PC Interrupts* or *Undocumented DOS* (both Addison-Wesley, 1993).

Why This Book Exists

The IBM PC and compatibles form the largest portion of the computer market, and likely will continue to do so into the next century. The MS-DOS operating system for IBM PCs is the most popular ever developed, and the brisk sales of the recently released MS-DOS 6.0 proves that it will remain so for some time. Because the architecture of the IBM PC allows programs to provide services to other programs via software interrupts, and MS-DOS provides a mechanism for retaining programs in memory in order to continue providing such services, hundreds of software vendors have extended the basic set of services in often incompatible ways. As more programs provide additional interrupt calls, the probability of conflict between different programs increases.

Over the years, literally dozens of books have been written which include reference sections detailing the ROM BIOS services built into IBM PCs, and the additional services provided by MS-DOS. Some also cover the Expanded Memory Specification (EMS) services, but few go beyond that; similarly, those books which do cover networking calls are limited to a single networking package. Thus, programmers have been forced to accumulate information about additional interrupt services piecemeal—one document covering one specification, another a second, and an electronic bulletin-board message a third. With such a collection of sources, it can be quite difficult to determine that two programs are incompatible because they expect different services from the same interrupt call.

This book is a comprehensive collection of the varied calls which have been implemented by various networking software over the years. It includes all calls for some three dozen major application programming interfaces and various resident utilities (including undocumented interfaces). Because of the number of different calls covered (over 1400), there is no room for detailed discussions or sample code.

Network Interrupts is designed to be a reference, not a tutorial. It will form a companion to any texts covering the IBM PC, MSDOS, or networking which you may already own. In addition to its main purpose as a programming reference, you may also find it valuable as a tool to help you track down undesirable interactions between various programs running on the same PC. To this end, conflicts are mentioned even where the actual calls involved are described in *PC Interrupts* rather than here.

The material presupposes some familiarity with programming using software interrupts, although there is no need to know a particular programming language. Software interrupts may be invoked from most high-level languages for the IBM PC as well as assembler, and most books on those languages cover interrupts at least briefly.

Interrupts and the '86 CPU Family

While this book is intended as a reference rather than as a tutorial, so many different partial listings of interrupt usage have been published, each using its own vocabulary and assumptions, that it is necessary to take a few pages up front to present an overview of the subject. This section briefly describes the basic interrupt concept as implemented in the Intel 80x86 family of processor.

The Intel 80x86 family of processors all provide the capability of servicing a maximum of 256 distinct interrupt actions, by means of a table of 256 four-byte interrupt vectors. This table occupies the first 1024 bytes of the RAM address space. Each vector consists of a 32-bit address, in standard Segment:Offset format, of the routine that will be called automatically in response to the corresponding interrupt.

The interrupt request that triggers the calling of such a routine can be generated in any of three ways: it can be internally generated by the processor chip itself, it can be created by an external interrupt request signal (called INTR by Intel), or it can be the result of a software interrupt (INT) instruction.

The original members of this processor family, the 8086 and 8088, only dedicated the first five interrupt vectors (INT 00h through INT 04h) to serving internally generated interrupts, although Intel clearly warned all users of the chips that the remaining 27 of the first 32 interrupts were reserved for future use. IBM chose to ignore that warning in the design of the PC, and assigned INT 05h to the print-screen action, while using the upper 24 of the 32 reserved interrupts for communication with hardware devices and BIOS. Of these 24 vectors, the first eight were assigned to deal with external device interrupts (INT 08h through 0Fh, for IRQ0 through IRQ7 respectively). The remaining 16 provided, via software INT requests, standardized interfaces to the BIOS routines.

When the next version of the processor, the 80186, appeared, problems ensued. Trade journals reported that the conflict between IBM's use of the reserved locations, and Intel's subsequent assignment of them, were the reason that no IBM machine used the 80186, but this was never publicly confirmed. However the following chip, the 80286, was more restrained in its assignment of interrupt actions. Subsequent designs have followed its lead; all of the first 32 locations now have internal actions assigned for at least some versions of the processor family, but all remain compatible with MS-DOS usage.

So far as the processor's actions are concerned, there is almost no difference between an interrupt caused by one of the sources and another caused by any other. The only significant difference is that external interrupts automatically disable response to additional external interrupt requests, while software interrupts do not.

Some Words of Caution

Much of the information in this book is undocumented, and has therefore been determined by tracing calls and by trial-and-error experiments. Such undocumented information may be inaccurate, incomplete, highly version-dependent, or have any mix of these attributes. You should take care when attempting to use any calls marked as "internal" or "undocumented", or containing a large amount of italicized text (signifying its questionable or incomplete nature). Further, you should use documented equivalents whenever possible, even if the undocumented call is simpler or faster.

Version information has been included in many function descriptions; note, however, that this information represents only the version limits that we (or our contributors) were able to verify. Especially in the case of third-party software, any function may well have been present but undetected in versions earlier than those listed. And open-ended items such as "Version 2.1+" (meaning "all versions equal to or newer than 2.1") may have a hidden upper limit imposed by changes not reported to us before this information went to press.

Sample Entry

To illustrate some of the aspects of the entries in this book which may not be self-explanatory, we present a mythical function followed by explanations of various parts of the entry.

INT FFh Function 0Fh   *XYZZY models 17 and 23 only*
GET GONKULATOR SETTINGS   *FROB.SYS*

Purpose: Determine the current or default options for the gonkulator.

Registers at call:	Return Registers:
AH = 0Fh	CF clear if successful
AL = subfunction	CX = number of times settings
01h get default settings	have been modified since startup
02h get current settings	ES:DI buffer filled
ES:DI -> settings table (Table 99-2)	CF set on error
	AX = error code (02h,FFh)
	(see Table 99-1)

Details: The link farm directory is the location for the write-only memory, among other things.
Conflicts: DIDDLE.SYS (Chapter 96)
See also: Function 0Eh, DIDDLE.SYS INT FEh Function 02h (Chapter 96), FOO-BAR INT FEh Function FEh (PCI-17)

99-1 Format of settings table:

Offset	Size	Description
00h	WORD	heartbeat frequency in Hertz
02h	BYTE	feeper duration
03h	BYTE	feeper pitch
04h	DWORD	(big-endian) microfortnights between pings
08h	64 BYTEs	link farm directory name

Explanations

Following the heading which indicates the interrupt number, function number, and subfunction number (if applicable) along with the function name, restrictions to particular systems or software, and other limitations such as processor mode, each entry has a number of fields. Both Registers at call and Return Registers may have multiple mutually-exclusive cases, which are indicated by indentation. Thus, for this example, the call modifies CX and the user's buffer if the carry flag is clear on return, but modifies AX instead if the carry flag is set.

The cross-references for *Conflicts* and *See also* indicate which chapter contains the referenced call, unless it is in the current chapter; if it is in *PC Interrupts*, it is marked as PCI-00. Thus, the example has two references to Chapter 96, one to the current chapter, and one to Chapter 17 of *PC Interrupts*. Conflicts specifies calls that use the same interrupt and function; you would look in Chapter 99 for interrupt FFh Function 0Fh (or, in some cases, simply interrupt FFh) in the section for DIDDLE.SYS if the chapter is divided into sections. For *See also*, the interrupt number is omitted if it is the same as the interrupt for the current entry; thus, you would look up interrupt FFh, function 0Eh in the current chapter.

The notation *(big-endian)* indicates that the value is stored with the most-significant byte at the lowest address, which is the reverse of the normal Intel byte-ordering (placing the least-significan byte at the lowest address).

In the various sections and in tables, information which is known to be incomplete or of questionable accuracy is italicized. This generally occurs only for undocumented calls.

About The Authors

Ralf Brown

Ralf Brown is an independent software developer and author who recently received a Ph.D. in Computer Science from Carnegie Mellon University. He has delved into the innards of MSDOS and IBM PC compatibles since early 1984, and is well-known in the on-line community for maintaining the MSDOS Interrupt List and authoring a number of useful free programs. He coauthored *Undocumented DOS* and *PC Interrupts* (Addison-Wesley 1993).

Jim Kyle

Jim Kyle has been a professional writer since 1948, and has published more than a dozen books and hundreds of magazine articles, including coauthoring *Undocumented DOS* and *PC Interrupts* (Addison-Wesley 1993). He has been disassembling operating systems as a hobby since 1970 or so, on mainframes and minicomputers as well as microcomputers. He has been Primary Forum Administrator of the Computer Language forum on CompuServe since 1985. Jim is currently Director, Research Projects, and a co-founder of Automation Resources, Inc., in Oklahoma City, OK.

Acknowledgments

The information in this book has been adapted from a large freely-available electronic listing, known as the MSDOS Interrupt List, maintained by Ralf Brown and updated several times per year. The Interrupt List is available in many places, including but not limited to:

- CompuServe (IBM Programming Forum [GO IBMPRO],Download Library 6)
- Internet
- Internet (oak.oakland.edu and mirror sites such as wuarchive.wustl.edu, where it resides in /mirrors/msdos/info)
- BITNET
- BITNET (any of a number of mailservers, such as LISTSERVPIECS in the United States or TRICKLE@DS0RUS1I in Germany)
- Fidonet
- Fidonet (bulletin boards belonging to the Prorammer's Distribution Network, as well as others)
- other bulletin boards world-wide.

The list is distributed under the filenames INTERrrA through INTERrrD, where rr is the release number (36 for the August, 1993 version to which this edition corresponds). Unlike PC Interrupts, the electronic listing is in purely numerical order and does not contain an index.

Many people have contributed information to the Interrupt List over the years, resulting in a much larger listing than would otherwise have been the case. We gratefully acknowledge the contributions of the following people:

A. Padgett Peterson, **A. Peter Blicher**, **Aaron Emigh**, **Aki Korhonen**, Alex Fedorov, **Alexi Lookin**, Andrea Omodeo, Andrei Tsyganenko, **Andrew Rossmann**, **Andrew Schulman**, Andrew Torda, **Andy Hakim**, **Ari Huttunen**, **Arne Schapers**, **Barry Burke**, Ben Castricum, **Ben Myers**, **Bent Lynggaard**, **Bernd Schemmer**, Bert Baker, **Bill Frolik**, **Bill White**, Bob Aitchison, Bob Fehrenbach, Bob Green, **Bob Jack**, **Boris M. Mostovoy**, **Brad Davis**, Brad Templeton, Brett Warthen, Brian Leeming, Brian Long, Brian McGuinness, Bruce Gingery, Carl Schelin, Carlos Antunes, **Carlos M. de Sousa**, Carlos Rioja, Chris Blum, **Chris Dunford**, **Chris Hall**, **Christian Franke**, **Christopher J. Ambler**, Ciriaco Garcia de Celis, **Clarence A. Dold**, Claude Marche, **Cornel Kaufmann**, **Dan Bodoh**, Dan Crocker, **Dan Davison**, **Dan Fandrich**, **Dan Lanciani**,

Dan Prather, Darryl Gregorash, Dave Andrews, Dave Guggisberg, Dave Kirsch, David Dyck, David Fink, David G. Thomas, **David H. Bennett**, David Herron, **David Maxey**, David Woolley, **Dennis Grinberg**, **Diomidis Spinellis**, Dmitry Ablov, **Dmitry Stefankov**, **Dr. David Bailey**, Drake Koefoed, **Duncan Murdoch**, Eberhard Mattes, **Ed Nather**, Ed Palmer, Edwin Cleton, Edwin Floyd, Erik Liljencrantz, Everett C. Johnson, **Everett Kaser**, **Finn Thoegerson**, Francis Turner, **Francis Turner**, Frank Behrens, **Frank Gladu**, **Frank Klemm**, Frank van der Linden, **Frank Vorstenbosch**, Frank-Christian Kruegel, **Fridrik Skulason**, **Fyodor Evseev**, **G. Adam Stanislav**, **Gary E. Miller**, **Ge van Geldorp**, **Geoff Chappell**, **George L. Fulk**, George Smith, George W. Pogue, Gianni Albóre, Gino Lucrezi, Glen Kriekenbeck, Gordon Edwards, **Grant Echols**, Greg Pasquariello, Guenther Thiele, Harald Langhammer, **Harry Sumar**, Heath Ian Hunnicutt, **Helmut Waelder**, **Herwig Feichtinger**, **Holger Veit**, **Howard Johnson**, **Ian Oliver**, **Igor Sysoev**, Inbar Raz, Ivan Martinez, J. B. Gill, **J. Weaver Jr.**, Jack Alvrus, **Jack Ridgway**, **Jacob Rieper**, James Berry, James Birdsall, James P. Kiely, James West, Jan Ceuleers, **Jan-Pascal van Best**, **Jan-Pieter Cornet**, **Janet Jack**, Janos Haide, **Jean-Francois Larvoire**, Jeff Pipkins, Jens Bleuel, **Jens Vollmar**, Jeremy Laidman, **Jeroen Pluimers**, Jerzy Tarasiuk, **Jim Kyle**, Jim Peterson, Jiri Kuchta, Joe Morris, **Joe Souza**, Johan Zwiekhorst, John B. Thiel, **John Cooper**, **John DesRosiers**, **John Fa'atuai**, **John Howells**, John Jurewicz, **John Lefor**, John Murphy, John Navas, John P. Vias, **John Ruschmeyer**, John Spinks, John Villalovos, John Werner, John.Brennen, Jonathan Story, Jose R. Rodriguez Santia, **Joseph G. Souza**, **Joseph Gil**, Ken Medellin, Kevin Gillett, **Kevin Gillett**, Klaus Fischer, Klaus Hartnegg, **Konstantin Kisurin**, **Krzysztof Halasa**, KUCHTA@dcse.fee.vutbr.cs, **Kyle Rogers**, Leonard Erickson, **Les Moskowitz**, Lewis Paper, Lutz Schroer, Madis Kaal, **Manfred Young**, Marc Scholtis, Marco Lumachi, **Marcus Groeber**, **Mark Aitchison**, Mark Davis, **Mark Livingstone**, Mark Scase, Mark Seiffert, Mark T. Garlanger, Mark T. Vitt, Martin Shipley, Martin Wilde, Martin Winkler, Marty Leisner, **Maxime Dallaire**, **Michael A. Moran**, **Michael A. Shiels**, Michael Bootz, Michael D. Lawler, **Michael D. Shride**, Michael Dickson, Michael Ho, **Michael Hung**, Michael L. Kaufman, Michael S. Stratoti, **Michel Mathieu**, **Mikael Rydberg**, **Mike Baszczak**, **Mike Morearty**, **Mike Weaver**, Mitch Davis, **Morten Welinder**, Naota Kimura, Nelluri Reddy, Nemrod Kedem, Nigel Bree, noesis@ucscb.UCSC.EDU, Norbert Juffa, Norbert Sommer, **Norman Walsh**, Otto J. Makela, Otto-Michael Braun, **Patrick Ibbetson**, Paul Ratcliffe, Paul van Keep, Paul Vojta, Paul Williamson, Pavel Shtemenko, Per-Eric Larsson, Pete Fales, Pete Peterson, **Peter Holzmann**, **Peter Sawatzki**, Peter Singer, **Phil Rea**, **Rainer Schuetze**, **Ralf Brown**, Ralph Heredia, Rehn-Lieh Lin, Rich Goldschmidt, **Richard A. Plinston**, Richard D. Morris, **Richard Hargrove**, **Richard Marks**, **Richard Talon**, **Rick Wagner**, **Rickard Faith**, **Riku Meskanen**, Risto Lankinen, **Rob Luursema**, Robert Chafer, **Robert Goldsmith**, **Robert Seals**, **Robin Walker**, **Roeland Jansen**, **Roger Bowler**, Roman Rutman, Ronald Lokker, **Ross M. Greenberg**, Ross Wentworth, RS Tse, Russ Nelson, Scott C. Pedigo, Sean Lin, Serge Krupa, Serge Pachkovsky, **Serge Pachkovsky**, Sergey Danilov, Sergio Fogel, Shalom Krischer, Simon Phipps, **Skip Gilbrech**, Skule Johansen, Stan Brown, Stefan Gustafsson, **Stephan Wolf**, **Stephen Bean**, **Steve Bromwich**, Steve Grant, Steve Halko, **Stuart R. Kemp**, Sylvan Butler, **Tamura Jones**, Thomas Dwyer, Thomas Hundt, Thomas Lukka, **Tim Farley**, Timo Salmi, **Todor Todorov**, Tom Rawson, Torbjlrn Lindgren, **Urs Zurbuchen**, Victor Poon, **Vincent Broman**, Vsevolod M. Shabad, W.F. Schroeder, **Warner Young**, **Wes Cowley**, Wilbert Van Leijen, **William Peavy**, **Wim Osterholt**, **Wolfgang Lierz**, **Xavier Cabelle**, **Ying-Kuen K. Hwang**, Yousuf Khan

Special thanks also to the following companies for making API information and other materials available at no charge:

Alloy Computer Products, Inc.
1 Brigham Street
Marlborough, MA 01752

NetManage, Inc.
20823 Stevens Creek Blvd
Suite 100
Cupertino, CA 95014

Banyan Systems, Inc.
115 Flanders Road
Westboro, MA 01581

Novell, Inc.
122 East 1700 South
Provo, UT 84601

General Software
P.O. Box 2571
Redmond, WA 98073

Softwarehouse Corporation
326 State Street
Los Altos, CA 94022

Microsoft Corporation
16011 NE 36th Way
Box 97017
Redmond, WA 98073-9717

Tiara Computer Systems, Inc.
1091 Shoreline Blvd
Mountain View, CA 94043

Nanosoft, Inc.
13 Westfield Road
Natick, MA 01760

Webcorp
2750 Bridgeway
Sausalito, CA 94965

Net-Source, Inc.
1265 El Camino Real, Suite 101
Santa Clara, CA 95050

CHAPTER 2

Overview of Interrupt Usage

The brief listings in Tables 2-1 through 2-4 show which chapters describe functions for each of the 256 possible interrupts (where *P-00* or *PCI-00* refers to Chapter 00 in the companion book *PC Interrupts*). Those referenced for more than one chapter or program probably have conflicts under some conditions.

Two areas in particular have a high probability of conflicts. The first is the multiplex interrupt, INT 2Fh (Table 2-2), and the second is the user interrupts, INT 60h to INT 67h.

Interrupt 2Fh is shared by many programs, with the value of AH on call specifying the program which is to handle the call. As more programs use the multiplex interrupt to provide an interface to resident code, the probability of conflicting multiplex numbers (the value in AH) increases. While there is a standardized method for determining whether a particular multiplex number is in use (though not all programs follow the convention), there is no standardized approach for determining whether a specific program is using it. Thus, a program may be fooled into thinking that it is already installed if a different program happens to be using the same multiplex number, or worse yet, make calls which are handled by a program other than the intended one, possibly with disastrous results.

We consider a two-level scanning approach such as that used by Quarterdeck's RPCI (PCI-63) the minimum for avoiding conflicts between programs on INT 2Fh, but recommend using the Alternate Multiplex Interrupt Specification described in Chapter 50 of *PC Interrupts* instead of INT 2Fh. AMIS-compliant TSRs automatically avoid conflicts (including hotkey conflicts) and provide standardized calls for removal and popup while imposing an overhead of less than 100 bytes in the resident code; they may also be removed in any order.

One problem caused by the lack of a written specification for INT 2Fh usage is that not all programs use the convention of returning AL=FFh when called with AL=00h, and many that do support the convention also modify other registers—including segment registers or BP—even without the presence of "magic" values on entry. Therefore, any program which searches a range of multiplex numbers must be prepared for all registers except SS:SP to be destroyed by an attempted installation check.

The user interrupts 60h to 67h do not have a convention for an installation-check call, and thus require a different approach. However, the user interrupts are rarely chained, so a check whether the vector is 0000h:0000h suffices to determine if a particular interrupt is available. To determine whether the vector is in use by the program making the installation check, the usual approach is to place a signature immediately prior to or immediately following the interrupt handler address, since there are no safe calls which can be made—the vector may not even point at code! Table 2-3 lists programs we have identified as using this group of interrupts, but like Table 2-2, it is almost certain to be incomplete.

A final area of conflict needs to be mentioned here, as it is the reason so few programs use interrupts 86h through F0h. These vectors are used by the BASIC interpreter in the ROM of genuine IBM machines to allow extensions and tracing. The BASIC.COM and BASICA.COM extensions to the ROM Cassette BASIC set these vectors to handlers inside themselves at startup, but never restore them. Thus, any resident programs which have hooked any of these interrupts will lose them if the user runs an interpreted BASIC program. Worse, the vectors will be pointing at whatever code or data happens to have been loaded into those locations since BASIC terminated, virtually guaranteeing a system crash.GWBASIC (the version for those without an IBM ROM containing BASIC), on the other hand, only uses interrupts EFh and F0h, and restores those on exit.

2-1 Overview of Interrupt Usage

INT	Usage
00h	Divide Error (PCI-3), Zenith ROM Debugger (PCI-57)
01h	Single-Step/Debugging Exceptions (PCI-3)
02h	Non-Maskable Interrupt (PCI-3)
03h	Breakpoint (PCI-3); Columbia ROM Debugger, Soft-ICE (PCI-57)
04h	Overflow Detected (PCI-3)
05h	Bounds Exceeded (PCI-3), Print Screen (PCI-4), PSPS (PCI-15)
06h	Invalid Opcode (PCI-3), HP 95LX (PCI-7)
07h	Coprocessor Not Present (PCI-3)
08h	Double Fault, IRQ0 (PCI-3)
09h	Coprocessor Protection Violation, IRQ1 (PCI-3)
0Ah	Invalid TSS, IRQ2 (PCI-3)
0Bh	Segment Not Present, IRQ3 (PCI-3); HP 95LX (PCI-7)
0Ch	IBM System 36/38 Workstation Emulation (Chapter 37); Stack Violation, IRQ4 (PCI-3)
0Dh	General Protection Violation, IRQ5 (PCI-3); HP 95LX (PCI-7)
0Eh	Page Fault, IRQ6 (PCI-3); HP 95LX (PCI-7)
0Fh	IRQ7 (PCI-3), HP 95LX (PCI-7)
10h	Alloy MW386 (Chapter 12); 3270PC (Chapter 37); Coprocessor Error (PCI-3); AX PC Video (PCI-6); Corona/Cordata BIOS (PCI-7); BIOS Video, Chips&Technologies Extended BIOS, Compaq Extensions, Everex Extended Video BIOS, HP Vectra Extended BIOS, EGA Register Interface Library, BIOS Window Extension, Compaq ADAPT.COM, M10_SCR, Hercules GRAFIX, SCROLOCK, UltraVision, Netroom SCRNCLK, MSHERC, Realtek RTVGA, Direct Graphics Interface Standard, SCREENR, Show Partner F/X, VUIMAGE (PCI-8); SuperVGA Video, Cirrus Logic BIOS, VESA SuperVGA BIOS, SOLLEX SuperVGA (PCI-9); FASTBUFF (PCI-13); FRIEZE (PCI-15); Tinytalk Personal (PCI-23); GO32 DOS extender (PCI-37); TopView, DESQview Video (PCI-44); Carbon Copy Plus (PCI-58); CU Writer (PCI-66)
11h	Alignment Check (PCI-3), Get Equipment List (PCI-4), SDLP (PCI-11), BNU FOSSIL (PCI-12), Blank-It screen blanker (PCI-14), Back&Forth (PCI-49), Borland C++ IDE (PCI-54), RainbowFAX (PCI-64)
12h	Get Memory Size (PCI-4), KEYBUI (PCI-13), Back&Forth (PCI-49), Borland C++ IDE (PCI-54), PARKER (PCI-66)
13h	Beame&Whiteside BWLPD (Chapter 32); Disk I/O, ESDI Hard Disk, Priam EDVR.SYS, SWBIOS, Western Digital SuperBIOS (PCI-10); Adaptec AHA-154x BIOS, Future Domain SCSI (PCI-11); FAST! disk cache, HyperDisk, IBMCACHE.SYS, NOW! disk cache, QUICKCACHE II, Super PC-Kwik (PCI-17); ScanBoot, VSAFE/VWATCH (PCI-59)
14h	3com BAPI (Chapter 4); Alloy MW386 (Chapter 12); TelAPI (Chapter 34); ARTICOM, Beame&Whiteside BWCOM14, Connection Manager, Interconnections Inc. TES (Chapter 38); Video FOSSIL (PCI-8); Serial I/O, COMM-DRV, COURIERS.COM,

	Digiboard DigiCHANNEL, IBM/Yale EBIOS, FOSSIL, MBBIOS, MX5 Extended FOSSIL, TSRCOMM (PCI-12); Keyboard FOSSIL (PCI-13); ASAP (PCI-23); MultiDOS Plus IODRV (PCI-45); PC-MOS/386 $serial.sys (PCI-49)
15h	ABIOS, Cassette I/O, OS hooks, BIOS System functions, keyboard intercept, joystick, extended memory access, PS/2 DMA control, PS/2 Device Descriptor Tables (PCI-4); EISA System ROM (PCI-5); Compaq extensions, HP 95LX, Phoenix 386 BIOS (PCI-7); Amstrad PC1512 (Chapters 7 and 21); ESDI disk formatting (PCI-10); PRINT (PCI-15); Advanced Power Management specification (PCI-19); PS/2 Pointing Device interface (PCI-21); Far East MS-DOS (PCI-24); Rational Systems DOS/16M and DOS/4G (PCI-35); Tandon Memory Mapper (PCI-42); DESQview, TopView, DESQview/X (PCI-44); MultiDOS Plus (PCI-45); VMiX (PCI-46); Omniview multitasker (PCI-49); Microsoft TSR Specification (PCI-51)
16h	PC Tools DRIVEMAP (Chapter 18); Shamrock Software EMAIL (Chapter 41); Keyboard (PCI-4); AX PC keyboard (PCI-6); Compaq extensions, HP HIL Vectras (PCI-7); EGAPAL and VGAPAL (PCI-8); FAKEY.COM, M16_KBD.COM, STACKEY.COM, TEXTCAP (PCI-13); Netroom CACHECLK (PCI-17); Netroom (PCI-41); CPTASK (PCI-49); Swap Utilities, TSRBONES, TurboPower TSRs (PCI-51); Paint Tools PTxxx.COM (PCI-54); pcANYWHERE (PCI-58); PC Tools CPSCHED/DESKTOP/PCShell/PCRUN (PCI-61); Norton Guides (PCI-62); APCAL, AT.COM, CALCULATOR, FastJuice, JORJ, MAKEY.COM, PC Magazine PUSHDIR, SCOUT, TMED, Borland Turbo Lightning, WATCH.COM, Microsoft Word (PCI-66)
17h	Alloy networks (Chapter 12); Shamrock Software NET.24 (Chapter 31); AX PC Printer (PCI-6); FLASHUP.COM, SPEEDSCR.COM (PCI-8); BIOS Printer Services, Emulaser ELTSR, INSET, NorthNet JetStream, LPTx, PC-MOS/386 print spooler, PC Paint Plus, PC Magazine PCSpool, T2PS (PCI-15)
18h	Diskless Boot hook (PCI-4), NEC PC-9800 (PCI-6)
19h	Bootstrap Loader (PCI-4)
1Ah	SNAP (Chapter 26); BIOS Time Services (PCI-4); Intel PCI BIOS, PCMCIA Socket Services (PCI-5); NEC PC-9800 (PCI-6); AT&T 6300 (PCI-7); Disk Spool II, Emulaser ELSPL (PCI-15); Microsoft Real-Time Compression Interface (PCI-16); PCjr sound, SND, Tandy digital sound (PCI-22); DATEFIX, RighTime, Word Perfect interface (PCI-66)
1Bh	Control-Break handler (PCI-4)
1Ch	System Timer Tick (PCI-4)
1Dh	Video Parameter Tables (PCI-4)
1Eh	Diskette Parameters (PCI-10)
1Fh	8x8 Graphics Font (PCI-8)
20h	MS-DOS Program Termination (PCI-24), Minix (PCI-49), COMTROL Hostess (PCI-57)
21h	DOS network support (Chapter 3), Named Pipes interface (Chapter 6), NDIS (Chapter 7), Alloy NTNX (Chapter 12), Banyan VINES (Chapter 14), LAN Manager (Chapter 19), LANtastic (Chapter 20), Novell NetWare (Chapter 21), 10NET (Chapter 27), Topware Network Operating System (Chapter 28), WORKGRP.SYS (Chapter 30), CBIS PowerLAN (Chapter 31), LANstep (Chapter 31), BW-TCP (Chapter 32), FTPSOFT.DOS (Chapter 33), PC/TCP (Chapter 33), Sun PC-NFS (Chapter 34), IBM System 36/38 Workstation Emulation (Chapter 37), Attachmate Extra (Chapter 37); PGS1600.DEV, Compaq AG1024.SYS (PCI-8); xDISK (PCI-10); ASPI, ASPITAPE.SYS, ST-01 SCSI.SYS (PCI-11); CED, DOSED, WCED (PCI-13); CUBIT, DBLSPACE.BIN, DIET, Diet Disk, DUBLDISK.SYS, NewSpace, PCMANAGE/DCOMPRES, Stacker (PCI-16); COMBI-disk, Super PC-Kwik, SMARTDRV.SYS (PCI-17); FARTBELL (PCI-22); MS-DOS (PCI-24);

European MS-DOS (PCI-25); DR-DOS/Novell DOS, Concurrent DOS, DR Multiuser DOS, OS/2 Family API, OS/2 Virtual DOS Machine (PCI-26); CD-ROM device driver, SHARE (PCI-27); Intel Code Builder, Phar Lap 386|DOS-Extender, FlashTek X-32VM (PCI-33); OS/286 and OS/386 (PCI-34); DOS/4GW (PCI-35); AI Architects, GO32 (PCI-37); QEMM-386 (PCI-39); 386MAX (PCI-40); The Last Byte, Memory Managers, Microsoft EMM386.EXE (PCI-42); DESQview (PCI-44); CTask, DoubleDOS, Headroom, PC-Mix, PC-MOS/386, Software Carousel (PCI-49); COMTROL Hostess, StopPrg, Turbo Debugger hardware breakpoints (PCI-57); pcANYWHERE IV/LAN (PCI-58); Virus, F-Prot, FLU_SHOT+, VDEFEND/VSAFE/VWATCH (PCI-59); DOS-UP.SYS, HOOKROM.SYS (PCI-63); SoftLogic Data Guardian, ELRES, IBM Genie, PCW Weather Card, SCROLLit, TAME, Trusted Access, WATCH.COM, WILDUNIX (PCI-66)

22h	Program Termination Address (PCI-24), COMTROL Hostess (PCI-57)
23h	Control-C/Control-Break Handler (PCI-24), COMTROL Hostess (PCI-57)
24h	Critical Error Handler (PCI-24)
25h	Stacker (PCI-16), PC-CACHE.SYS (PCI-17), Absolute Disk Read (PCI-24)
26h	Absolute Disk Write (PCI-24), COMTROL Hostess (PCI-57)
27h	Terminate and Stay Resident (PCI-24), COMTROL Hostess (PCI-57)
28h	DOS Idle (PCI-24)
29h	Fast Console Output (PCI-24)
2Ah	Network (Chapter 3), NetBIOS (Chapter 8), LANtastic (Chapter 20), Novell NetWare Lite (Chapter 22), PC Network (Chapter 24), PC/TCP PREDIR (Chapter 33), IBM 3270 Emulation Program (Chapter 37), PRINT (PCI-15)
2Bh	reserved by MS-DOS (PCI-24)
2Ch	reserved by MS-DOS (PCI-24), STARLITE architecture (PCI-26), Cloaking API (PCI-32)
2Dh	reserved by MS-DOS (PCI-24), Alternate Multiplex Interrupt Specification (PCI-50) and AMIS TSRs: Burnout Plus (PCI-14), dLite (PCI-16), RATSR (PCI-58), RAMLIGHT (PCI-66), Screen Thief (PCI-66)
2Eh	COMMAND.COM back door, 4DOS SHELL2E.COM (PCI-28); Windows NT native API (PCI-43)
2Fh	Multiplex Interrupt—see Table 2-2
30h	DOS CP/M entry point (PCI-24)
31h	DOS CP/M entry point (PCI-24), DOS Protected-Mode Interface (PCI-30), Netroom3 DPMI.EXE (PCI-41), Virus (PCI-59)
32h	reserved by MS-DOS (PCI-24), Virus (PCI-59)
33h	Mouse, Smooth Mouse Driver (PCI-21); Switch-It (PCI-49)
34h-37h	Floating Point emulation (PCI-54)
38h	PC-MOS/386 (PCI-49), Floating Point emulation (PCI-54)
39h-3Eh	Floating Point emulation (PCI-54)
3Fh	Overlay manager, MS Dynamic Link Library manager (PCI-54)
40h	Acorn BBC Master 512, Zenith Z100 (PCI-7); Floppy Diskette services (PCI-10)
41h	Acorn BBC Master 512, Zenith Z100 (PCI-7); Hard Disk 0 parameter table (PCI-10); MS Windows debugging kernel (PCI-57)
42h	Acorn BBC Master 512, Zenith Z100 (PCI-7); EGA-relocated INT 10h services (PCI-8); Western Digital SuperBIOS (PCI-10)
43h	Acorn BBC Master 512, Zenith Z100 (PCI-7); EGA+ character table (PCI-8)
44h	Novell NetWare (Chapter 21); IBM 3270-PC HLLAPI (Chapter 37); Acorn BBC Master 512, Zenith Z100 (PCI-7); PCjr BIOS character font (PCI-8); Virus (PCI-59)
45h	Acorn BBC Master 512, Zenith Z100 (PCI-7)
46h	Acorn BBC Master 512, Zenith Z100 (PCI-7); Hard Disk 1 parameter table (PCI-10)

47h	Acorn BBC Master 512, Zenith Z100 (PCI-7); Western Digital SuperBIOS (PCI-10); SQL Base (Chatper 54)
48h	Watstar PC Network (Chapter 42); Acorn BBC Master 512, Zenith Z100 (PCI-7); Western Digital SuperBIOS (PCI-10); PCjr keyboard translation (PCI-13); Compaq UILIB.EXE (PCI-54)
49h	Watstar PC Network (Chapter 42); Acorn BBC Master 512, Zenith Z100 (PCI-7); Texas Instruments PC video (PCI-8); PCjr scan-code translation table (PCI-13); MAGic (PCI-23)
4Ah	User Alarm Handler (PCI-4); Acorn BBC Master 512, Zenith Z100 (PCI-7)
4Bh	Acorn BBC Master 512, Zenith Z100 (PCI-7); Common Access Method SCSI interface, IBM SCSI interface (PCI-11); Virtual DMA Specification (PCI-18)
4Ch	Acorn BBC Master 512, Zenith Z100 (PCI-7)
4Dh	Acorn BBC Master 512 (PCI-7)
4Eh	Zenith Z100 (PCI-7), TI Professional PC disk (PCI-10)
4Fh	Zenith Z100 (PCI-7), Common Access Method SCSI interface (PCI-11)
50h	IBM 3278 emulation relocated IRQ0 (Chapter 37), TIL Xpert AIM (Chapter 42), OS/2 relocated IRQ0 (PCI-26), DESQview relocated IRQ0 (PCI-44), Vanderaart Text Windows (PCI-66), PC Thuis Shell (PCI-66)
51h	IBM 3278 emulation relocated IRQ1 (Chapter 37), OS/2 relocated IRQ1 (PCI-26), DESQview relocated IRQ1 (PCI-44)
52h	IBM 3278 emulation relocated IRQ2 (Chapter 37), OS/2 relocated IRQ2 (PCI-26), DESQview relocated IRQ2 (PCI-44)
53h	WEB (Chapter 29), IBM 3278 emulation relocated IRQ3 (Chapter 37), OS/2 relocated IRQ3 (PCI-26), DESQview relocated IRQ3 (PCI-44)
54h	IBM 3278 emulation relocated IRQ4 (Chapter 37), OS/2 relocated IRQ4 (PCI-26), DESQview relocated IRQ4 (PCI-44)
55h	IBM 3278 emulation relocated IRQ5 (Chapter 37), OS/2 relocated IRQ5 (PCI-26), DESQview relocated IRQ5 (PCI-44)
56h	IBM 3278 emulation relocated IRQ6 (Chapter 37), OS/2 relocated IRQ6 (PCI-26), DESQview relocated IRQ6 (PCI-44)
57h	IBM 3278 emulation relocated IRQ7 (Chapter 37), OS/2 relocated IRQ7 (PCI-26), DESQview relocated IRQ7 (PCI-44)
58h	DESQview relocated IRQ8 (PCI-44), DoubleDOS relocated IRQ0 (PCI-49)
59h	GSS Computer Graphics Interface (PCI-8), DESQview relocated IRQ9 (PCI-44), DoubleDOS relocated IRQ1 (PCI-49)
5Ah	Cluster Adapter (Chapter 42), DESQview relocated IRQ10 (PCI-44), DoubleDOS relocated IRQ2 (PCI-49)
5Bh	AT&T Starlan Extended NetBIOS (Chapter 8), Alloy NTNX (Chapter 12), ISOLAN Multi Protocol Software (Chapter 31), Cluster Adapter (Chapter 42), Microsoft Network Transport Layer (Chapter 42), DESQview relocated IRQ11 (PCI-44), DoubleDOS relocated IRQ3 (PCI-49), SitBack (PCI-66)
5Ch	NetBIOS (Chapter 8), TOPS (Chapter 31), ATALK.SYS (Chapter 31), IBM 802.2 interface (Chapter 31), $25 LAN (Chapter 31), DESQview relocated IRQ12 (PCI-44), DoubleDOS relocated IRQ4 (PCI-49)
5Dh	DESQview relocated IRQ13 (PCI-44), DoubleDOS relocated IRQ5 (PCI-49)
5Eh	DESQview relocated IRQ14 (PCI-44), DoubleDOS relocated IRQ6 (PCI-49)
5Fh	HP 95LX Graphics Primitives (PCI-20), DESQview relocated IRQ15 (PCI-44), DoubleDOS relocated IRQ7 (PCI-49)
60h-67h	reserved for user interrupts—see Table 2-3
68h	APPC/PC (Chapter 13), Sangoma CCPOP 3270 (Chapter 37)

69h	DECnet DOS (Chapter 16), 10NET SYSSVC.COM (Chapter 27), Zenith AT BIOS (PCI-7), ISR.COM (PCI-57)
6Ah	DECnet DOS (Chapter 16), Super-TCP kernel (Chapter 34), OPTHELP (PCI-66)
6Bh	DECnet DOS (Chapter 16), TelAPI (Chapter 34), Novell NASI/NACS (Chapter 38), NCSI (Chapter 38), Virus (PCI-59), Tandy Schoolmate Plus (PCI-66)
6Ch	DECnet DOS (Chapter 16), Convertible System Resume Vector (PCI-4), DOS 3.2 Realtime Clock update (PCI-24)
6Dh	DECnet DOS (Chapter 16); VGA internal, ATI VGA Wonder, Trident SVGA (PCI-9)
6Eh	DECnet DOS (Chapter 16)
6Fh	10NET (Chapter 27), Novell NetWare 3270 API (Chapter 37), HP HIL Vectras (PCI-7), MS Windows (PCI-43)
70h	IRQ8 Real-Time Clock (PCI-3), Virus (PCI-59)
71h-76h	IRQ9 to IRQ14 (PCI-3)
77h	IRQ15, Compaq Power Conservation (PCI-3)
78h	ADP-60 IDE controller (PCI-10); TARGA.DEV (PCI-11); DBOS DOS Extender, GO32 (PCI-37); AutoCAD Device Interface (PCI-66)
79h	ADP-60 IDE adapter (PCI-10); AVATAR.SYS (PCI-13); DBOS DOS Extender, GO32 (PCI-37); AutoCAD Device Interface (PCI-66)
7Ah	Novell NetWare (Chapter 21), TopWare Network Operating System (Chapter 28), IBM 3270 Workstation Program (Chapter 37), X.PC Packet (Chapter 42), PRINDIR (PCI-15), GO32 (PCI-37), AutoCAD Device Interface (PCI-66), Canon IX-30F Image Scanner (PCI-66)
7Bh	Eicon Access (Chapter 37), GO32 (PCI-37), Btrieve (PCI-54), AutoCAD Device Interface (PCI-66)
7Ch	SK-UPPS (Chapter 25), PRINDIR (PCI-15), GO32 (PCI-37), REXX88PC (PCI-66)
7Dh	SCSILink (PCI-11), GO32 (PCI-37), HyperPAD (PCI-66), YTERM (PCI-66)
7Eh	GO32 (PCI-37), XLOAD (PCI-41), DIP, Ltd. ROM Library (PCI-66), YTERM (PCI-66)
7Fh	see Table 2-4
80h	QPC Software PKTINT (Chapter 42), SoundBlaster SBFM driver (PCI-22), reserved for BASIC (PCI-54), Q-PRO (PCI-66)
81h	IBM Token Ring Adapter (Chapter 42), reserved for BASIC (PCI-54)
82h	IBM Token Ring Adapter (Chapter 42), reserved for BASIC (PCI-54)
83h-85h	reserved for BASIC (PCI-54)
86h	NetBIOS (Chapter 8), APL*PLUS/PC (PCI-53), IBM ROM BASIC (PCI-54)
87h	APL*PLUS/PC (PCI-53), IBM ROM BASIC (PCI-54), Virus (PCI-59)
88h	APL*PLUS/PC (PCI-53), IBM ROM BASIC (PCI-54)
89h	IBM ROM BASIC (PCI-54)
8Ah	APL*PLUS/PC (PCI-53), IBM ROM BASIC (PCI-54)
8Bh	APL*PLUS/PC (PCI-53), IBM ROM BASIC (PCI-54), Virus (PCI-59)
8Ch	APL*PLUS/PC (PCI-53), IBM ROM BASIC (PCI-54)
8Dh-8Fh	IBM ROM BASIC (PCI-54)
90h	APL*PLUS/PC (PCI-53), IBM ROM BASIC (PCI-54)
91h	IBM Token Ring Adapter (Chapter 42), IBM ROM BASIC (PCI-54)
92h	Sangoma X.25 interface (Chapter 37), DaVinci eMail Dispatcher (Chapter 40), IBM ROM BASIC (PCI-54)
93h	IBM Token Ring Adapter (Chapter 42), IBM ROM BASIC (PCI-54)
94h	PCM driver (PCI-22), Media Vision PCM.COM (PCI-22), IBM ROM BASIC (PCI-54)
95h	APL*PLUS/PC (PCI-53), IBM ROM BASIC (PCI-54)
96h-9Bh	IBM ROM BASIC (PCI-54)

9Ch-9Fh   IBM ROM BASIC (PCI-54), Virus (PCI-59)
A0h   APL*PLUS/PC (PCI-53), IBM ROM BASIC (PCI-54)
A1h-A3h   IBM ROM BASIC (PCI-54)
A4h   IBM ROM BASIC (PCI-54), Right Hand Man (PCI-66)
A5h-B2h   IBM ROM BASIC (PCI-54)
B3h   IBM ROM BASIC (PCI-54), ZIPKEY (PCI-60)
B4h   IBM ROM BASIC (PCI-54), StackMan (PCI-66)
B5h   Netroom NETSWAP4 (PCI-41), IBM ROM BASIC (PCI-54), StackMan (PCI-66)
B6h-BDh   IBM ROM BASIC (PCI-54)
BEh   DESQview/X (PCI-44), IBM ROM BASIC (PCI-54)
BFh-C5h   IBM ROM BASIC (PCI-54)
C6h-CFh   APL*PLUS/PC (PCI-53), IBM ROM BASIC (PCI-54)
D0h   APL*PLUS/PC (PCI-53), IBM ROM BASIC (PCI-54), NJFRERAM (PCI-66)
D1h-D3h   APL*PLUS/PC (PCI-53), IBM ROM BASIC (PCI-54)
D4h   PC-MOS/386 (PCI-49), APL*PLUS/PC (PCI-53), IBM ROM BASIC (PCI-54)
D5h-D7h   APL*PLUS/PC (PCI-53), IBM ROM BASIC (PCI-54)
D8h-DBh   APL*PLUS/PC (PCI-53), IBM ROM BASIC (PCI-54), Screen Thief (PCI-66)
DCh   APL*PLUS/PC (PCI-53), IBM ROM BASIC (PCI-54), Screen Thief (PCI-66),
          PC/370 (PCI-66)
DDh-DEh   APL*PLUS/PC (PCI-53), IBM ROM BASIC (PCI-54), Screen Thief (PCI-66)
DFh   Victor 9000 (PCI-7), APL*PLUS/PC (PCI-53), IBM ROM BASIC (PCI-54), Screen
          Thief (PCI-66)
E0h   DR Multiuser DOS (PCI-48), APL*PLUS/PC (PCI-53), IBM ROM BASIC (PCI-54),
          Virus (PCI-59)
E1h-E2h   PC Cluster (Chapter 31), IBM ROM BASIC (PCI-54)
E3h   IBM ROM BASIC (PCI-54)
E4h   IBM ROM BASIC (PCI-54), Logitech Modula (PCI-54)
E5h-EBh   IBM ROM BASIC (PCI-54)
ECh   Alloy NTNX (Chapter 12), Exact (PCI-54), IBM ROM BASIC (PCI-54)
EDh-EEh   IBM ROM BASIC (PCI-54)
EFh   BASIC (PCI-54), GEM (PCI-54)
F0h   BASIC, BASICA (PCI-54)
F1h   reserved for user interrupt: AQUEDUCT/PIPELINE (PCI-12), SPEECH.COM
          (PCI-22), Virus (PCI-59)
F2h   reserved for user interrupt: ICCTSR (PCI-8), SPEECH.COM (PCI-22)
F3h   reserved for user interrupt: ICCTSR (PCI-8), SoundBlaster (PCI-22)
F4h   reserved for user interrupt: DoubleDOS (PCI-49)
F5h   reserved for user interrupt: DoubleDOS (PCI-49)
F6h   reserved for user interrupt: DoubleDOS (PCI-49)
F7h   reserved for user interrupt: DoubleDOS (PCI-49), FSBBS (PCI-66)
F8h   reserved for user interrupt: DoubleDOS (PCI-49)
F9h   reserved for user interrupt: DoubleDOS (PCI-49)
FAh   reserved for user interrupt: DoubleDOS (PCI-49)
FBh   reserved for user interrupt: DoubleDOS (PCI-49)
FCh   reserved for user interrupt: DoubleDOS (PCI-49)
FDh   reserved for user interrupt: TFPCX (PCI-12), DoubleDOS (PCI-49)
FEh   destroyed by return from protected mode (PCI-4), DoubleDOS (PCI-49), Turbo
          Debugger (PCI-57)

FFh destroyed by return from protected mode (PCI-4), Z100 Warm Boot (PCI-7), QEMM-386 (PCI-39), Virus (PCI-59)

2-2 INT 2Fh Multiplex Number Usage

Program	Chapter	Low	Default	High	Selection
Ross Wentworth POPUP library	P-51	00h	N/A	FFh	compile-time
CiriSOFT University of Valladolid TSRs	P-51	00h	00h	FFh	automatic
PRINT.COM	P-15	00h		.	fixed
PSPRINT	P-15	00h		.	fixed
PRINT.COM	P-15	01h		.	fixed
PC LAN Program redirector	24	02h		.	fixed
Critical Error Message Expansion	P-27	.	05h	.	fixed
ASSIGN	P-27	.	06h	.	fixed
DRIVER.SYS support	P-24	.	08h	.	fixed
SuperStor Pro SSTORDRV.SYS	P-16	.	10h	.	fixed
DR-DOS SHARE support	P-26	.	10h	.	fixed
SHARE	P-27	.	10h	.	fixed
MSCDEX	P-27	.	11h	.	fixed
Network Redirector interface	9	.	11h	.	fixed
LAN Manager	19	.	11h	.	fixed
MS-DOS Network Redirector support	3	.	12h	.	fixed
DR-DOS video memory space control	P-26	.	12h	.	fixed
DOS 3.2+ disk handler addresses	P-24	.	13h	.	fixed
MS-NET	31	.	13h	.	fixed
European MS-DOS POPUP	P-25	.	14h	.	fixed
DR-DOS NLSFUNC	P-26	.	14h	.	fixed
MS-DOS NLSFUNC	P-27	.	14h	.	fixed
PC-DOS 4.00 GRAPHICS.COM	P-27	.	15h	.	fixed
CD-ROM	15	.	15h	.	fixed
MS Windows DOS-app interface	P-43	.	16h	.	fixed
DOS Protected-Mode Interface (DPMI)	P-30	.	16h	.	fixed
MS Windows WINOLDAP API	P-43	.	17h	.	fixed
MS-Manager	P-66	.	18h	.	fixed
DOS 4.x SHELLB.COM	P-27	.	19h	.	fixed
ANSI.SYS	P-27	.	1Ah	.	fixed
ANSIPLUS.SYS	P-8	.	1Ah	.	fixed
AVATAR.SYS	P-8	.	1Ah	.	fixed
AVATAR Serial Dispatcher	P-12	.	1Ah	.	fixed
XMA2EMS.SYS	P-27	.	1Bh	.	fixed
DR-DOS GRAFTABL	P-26	.	23h	.	fixed
DR-DOS TaskMAX	P-47	.	27h	.	fixed
Gammafax DOS Dispatcher	P-64	.	2Ah	.	fixed
Kingswood TSR interface	P-51	.	39h	.	fixed
Kingswood TSR Windows	P-66	.	39h	.	fixed
OS/2 compatibility box	P-26	.	40h	.	fixed
Phar Lap 286|DOS-Extender Lite	P-33	.	0h	.	fixed
Windows callouts	P-43	.	40h	.	fixed

LAN Manager					
MINIPOP/NETPOPUP	19	.	41h	.	fixed
LAN Manager messenger service	19	.	42h	.	fixed
DOS Protected Mode Services					
(DPMS)	P-31	.	43h	.	fixed
Extended Memory Specification					
(XMS)	P-38	.	43h	.	fixed
HIMEM.SYS	P-42	.	43h	.	fixed
DOS Extender Support	P-37	.	44h	.	fixed
Microsoft Profiler	P-56	.	45h	.	fixed
DOS 5+ kernel	P-24	.	46h	.	fixed
Windows/286 DOS Extender	P-37	.	46h	.	fixed
F-PROT v1.x	P-59	.	46h	.	fixed
MS Windows v3.x installation check	P-43	.	46h	.	fixed
unknown	P-66	.	47h	.	fixed
DOSKEY	P-13	.	48h	.	fixed
PCED	P-13	.	48h	.	fixed
unknown	P-66	.	49h	.	fixed
DoubleSpace	P-16	.	4Ah	.	fixed
Microsoft Real-Time Compression					
I'face	P-16	.	4Ah	.	fixed
SMARTDRV	P-17	.	4Ah	.	fixed
Floppy-Disk Change notification	P-24	.	4Ah	.	fixed
HMA allocation	P-24	.	4Ah	.	fixed
Diskless Boot memory sizing	P-27	.	4Ah	.	fixed
PROTMAN support	P-27	.	4Ah	.	fixed
DOSSHELL Task Switching API	P-49	.	4Ah	.	fixed
MS Windows WIN.COM	P-43	.	4Bh	.	fixed
DOS Task Switcher interface	P-49	.	4Bh	.	fixed
LAN Manager NETWKSTA.EXE	19	.	4Bh	.	fixed
Advanced Power Management	P-19	.	4Ch	.	fixed
Kana Kanji Converter	P-66	.	4Dh	.	fixed
SilverNET	31	.	4Eh	.	fixed
POWER.EXE	P-19	.	53h	.	fixed
POWER.EXE	P-19	.	54h	.	fixed
TesSeRact RAM-resident interface	P-51	.	54h	.	fixed
COMMAND.COM interface	P-28	.	55h	.	fixed
INTERLNK	31	.	56h	.	fixed
Iomega Corp.	P-10	.	57h	.	fixed
PC Tools VDEFEND/VSAFE					
/VWATCH/DATAMON	P-59	.	62h	.	fixed
SCRNSAV2.COM	P-14	.	64h	.	fixed
License Service API	42	.	70h	.	fixed
SRDISK	P-10	.	72h	.	fixed
Novell NetWare IPX/SPX	5	.	7Ah	.	fixed
Novell NetWare utilities	23	.	7Ah	.	fixed
LAN HiJack	39	.	7Ah	.	fixed
Jim Harper's CD-ROM redirector	P-11	.	7Fh	.	fixed
FaxBIOS	P-64	.	80h	.	fixed

ASCII	P-66	.	80h	.	fixed
EASY-NET	31	.	80h	.	fixed
Nanosoft TurboNET server	31	.	80h	.	fixed
Nanosoft TurboNET redirector	31	.	81h	.	fixed
RESPLAY	P-22	.	82h	.	fixed
Nanosoft CAPDOS	P-57	.	82h	.	fixed
Codeview for Windows	P-57	.	86h	.	fixed
WHOA!	P-66	.	89h	.	fixed
RAID	P-66	.	90h	.	fixed
PC Tools DRIVEMAP	18	.	92h	.	fixed
Courier LAN E-Mail	41	.	92h	.	fixed
InnerMission	P-14	.	93h	.	fixed
Workgroup Connection MICRO.EXE	41	.	94h	.	fixed
Courier LAN E-Mail OPERATOR.EXE	41	.	9Ch	.	fixed
INTMON	P-57	.	9Eh	.	fixed
INTCFG	P-57	.	9Fh	.	fixed
Ergo DOS Extenders	P-34	.	A1h	.	fixed
Biologic HRAMDEV.SYS	P-42	.	A1h	.	fixed
Futurus Team	P-66	.	A4h	.	fixed
METZTSR.COM	P-66	80h	A9h	FFh	switch
VIDCLOCK	P-66	.	AAh	.	fixed
Btrieve Multi-User	P-54	.	ABh	.	fixed
DOS 4.01+ GRAPHICS.COM	P-27	.	ACh	.	fixed
DR-DOS KEYB	P-26	.	ADh	.	fixed
MS-DOS DISPLAY.SYS	P-27	.	ADh	.	fixed
MS-DOS KEYB	P-27	.	ADh	.	fixed
COMMAND.COM installable commands	P-28	.	AEh	.	fixed
MS-DOS GRAFTABL	P-27	.	B0h	.	fixed
IBM PC3270 Emulation Program	37	.	B4h	.	fixed
APPEND	P-27	.	B7h	.	fixed
10NET installation check	27	.	B8h	.	fixed
Network	31	.	B8h	.	fixed
DOS LAN Requester	31	.	B8h	.	fixed
PC Network	24	.	B9h	.	fixed
Media Vision MVSOUND.SYS	P-22	.	BCh	.	fixed
EGA.SYS	P-43	.	BCh	.	fixed
REDVIEW	P-66	.	BEh	.	fixed
PC LAN Program REDIRIFS	24	.	BFh	.	fixed
WANG_ER.COM	P-10	C0h	C0h	FFh	automatic
ASPIHOOK.SYS	P-11	C0h	C0h	FFh	automatic
After Dark AD-DOS	P-14	C0h	C0h	FFh	automatic
Explosiv	P-14	C0h	C0h	C9h	config
VGAsave	P-14	C0h	C0h	FFh	automatic
Cove Software QMR	P-21	C0h	C0h	FFh	automatic
MTEZ XpressFax	P-64	C0h	C0h	FFh	automatic
FN32	P-66	.	C0h	.	fixed

Novell ODI Link Support Layer (LSL)	10	C0h	C0h	FFh	automatic
Smart Prompt (SMARTPMT)	P-17	.	C6h	.	fixed
ThunderByte	P-59	.	C9h	.	fixed
StackMan	P-66	.	C9h	.	fixed
TBSCANX	P-59	.	CAh	.	fixed
FAXPLUS FAXTSR	P-64	.	CAh	.	fixed
THELP v3.0	P-66	.	CAh	.	fixed
Comwave Microfax Specification	P-64	.	CBh	.	fixed
MTEZ XpressFax CASMGR	P-64	.	CBh	.	fixed
Communicating Appliations Specification	P-65	.	CBh	.	fixed
Intel SatisFAXtion CASMGR	P-65	.	CBh	.	fixed
PC-Kwik programs	P-17	.	CCh	.	fixed
LaserPort interface	P-15	.	CDh	.	fixed
SWELL.EXE	P-49	.	CDh	.	fixed
Intel Image Processing Interface	P-55	.	CDh	.	fixed
TEMPLEXX	P-13	.	CFh	.	fixed
ZWmous	P-21	.	D0h	.	fixed
MDEBUG display driver	P-57	01h	D0h	FEh	config,API
Lotus CD/Networker	15	.	D0h	.	fixed
MDEBUG command driver	P-57	02h	D1h	FFh	config,API
Quarterdeck RPCI	P-63	C0h	D2h	FFh	automatic
PCL-838.EXE	P-66	.	D2h	.	fixed
LapLink Quick Connect	P-12	.	D3h	.	fixed
TeleReplica	P-58	.	D3h	.	fixed
4DOS (4DOS.COM, KSTACK.COM)	P-28	.	D4h	.	fixed
HEART.COM	P-57	.	D6h	.	fixed
VEDIT VSWAP	P-66	.	D6h	.	fixed
Banyan VINES	14	.	D7h	.	fixed
Novell NetWare Lite	22	.	D8h	.	fixed
TRAP.COM	P-57	.	DAh	.	fixed
ZyXEL ZFAX	P-64	.	DAh	.	fixed
Beame&Whiteside BWSNMP	32	.	DAh	.	fixed
GOLD.COM	P-66	.	DCh	.	fixed
xDISK	P-10	.	DDh	.	fixed
CappaCom programs	P-51	.	DDh	.	fixed
DESQview External Device Interface	P-44	C0h	DEh	FFh	automatic
HyperWare programs (HyperDisk, etc.)	P-17	C0h	DFh	FFh	automatic
StuffIt	P-13	.	E0h	.	fixed
SETDRVER.COM	P-66	.	E0h	.	fixed
Phantom of the Keyboard II	P-13	.	E1h	.	fixed
ANARKEY	P-13	C0h	E3h	FFh	switch
NDOS	P-28	.	E4h	.	fixed
Phar Lap DOS Extenders	P-33	.	EDh	.	fixed
GRIDLOC	P-66	.	EEh	.	fixed
XVIEW	P-66	.	EEh	.	fixed
WEB	29	.	EEh	.	fixed

4MAP	P-13	.	F0h	.	fixed
MIN-MEM	P-66	.	F1h	.	fixed
DOS Extender installation check	P-37	.	F1h	.	fixed
WINX	P-43	.	F2h	.	fixed
AUTOPARK	P-66	.	F7h	.	fixed
SuperStor Pro 2XON	P-16	.	F8h	.	fixed
SoundBlaster speech driver	P-22	.	FBh	.	fixed
AutoBraille	P-23	.	FBh	.	fixed
Borland DOS Extenders (DPMILOAD, etc.)	P-36	.	FBh	.	fixed
Borland TDX	P-57	.	FBh	.	fixed
Jot-It!	P-66	.	FBh	.	fixed
Norton Utilities	P-62	.	FEh	.	fixed
Sun PC-NFS	34	.	FEh	.	fixed
Topware Network Operating System	28	.	FFh	.	fixed
BMB Compuscience Canada Utilities	P-51	00h	FFh	FFh	automatic

2-3 User Interrupt Usage

Program	Chapter	60h	61h	62h	63h	64h	65h	66h	67h	Selection
SYS_PROF	P-56	D	.	.	.	.	.	.	.	fixed
Zero Bug virus	P-59	D	.	.	.	.	.	.	.	fixed
3com	31	D	.	.	.	.	.	.	.	fixed
Excelan LAN Workplace for DOS 3.5	31	D	.	.	.	.	.	.	.	fixed
AccessDOS	P-23	D	a	a	a	a	a	a	.	automatic
Nabbit	P-66	D	a	a	a	a	a	a	.	automatic
Banyan VINES	14	D	a	a	a	a	a	a	.	automatic
Tangram Arbiter	37	D	a	a	a	a	a	a	.	config
INTRSPY/CMDSPY	P-57	D	a	a	a	a	a	a	a	automatic
Buffit	P-66	D	a	a	a	a	a	a	a	automatic
PC-IPC	P-66	D	a	a	a	a	a	a	a	switch
PC/370	P-66	D	a	a	a	a	a	a	a	patch
FTP Packet Driver Specification	11	D	a	a	a	a	a	a	a	automatic
MDEBUG	P-57	D	a	a	a	a	a	a	a	config/autodetect
Atari Portfolio	P-7	D	D	.	.	.	.	.	.	fixed
HP 95LX System Manager	P-20	D	D	.	.	.	.	.	.	fixed
JPI TopSPEED Modula-2	P-54	D	D	.	.	.	.	.	.	fixed
Adaptec and OMTI controller drive 0	P-10	D	D	D	D	.	.	.	.	fixed
SEMTEX/Screen Trasher virus	P-59	.	D	.	.	.	.	.	.	fixed
OPTIMA/ET-3000 Zoom TSR	P-8	a	D	a	a	a	a	a	a	config/autodetect
FTP Software PC/TCP kernel	33	a	D	a	a	a	a	a	a	config/autodetect
TCPOpen kernel	34	a	D	a	a	a	a	a	a	config
Sangoma CCIP (CCPOP 3270)	37	.	D	.	.	.	.	.	D	fixed

HP 95LX calculator	P-20	.	.	D	.	.	.	.	.	fixed
Cswitch	P-49	.	.	D	.	.	.	.	.	fixed
FastGraph/Light FGD RIVER	P-52	.	.	D	.	.	.	.	.	fixed
MS SQL Server/Sybase DBLIBRARY	P-54	.	.	D	.	.	.	.	.	fixed
PC Tools COMMUTE	P-58	.	.	D	.	.	.	.	.	fixed
BW-TCP hardware driver (ETHDEV.SYS)	32	a	a	D	a	a	a	.	.	config
4+Power Floppy Controller	P-10	.	.	.	D	.	.	.	.	fixed
HP 100LX memory mapping	P-20	.	.	.	D	.	.	.	.	fixed
Kofax KF9X00 image manipulation card	P-66	.	.	.	D	.	.	.	.	fixed
DESQview/X Socket API	17	.	.	.	D	.	.	.	.	fixed
BW-TCP TCP/IP stack	32	.	a	a	D	a	a	a	.	config
Oracle SQL Protected Mode Executive	P-54	.	.	.	D	D	.	.	.	fixed
Extended Batch Language	P-66	.	.	.	.	D	.	.	.	fixed
Novell NetWare Low-Level API	21	.	.	.	.	D	.	.	.	fixed
BW-NFS BWRPC	32	.	.	a	a	D	a	a	a	config
Data General DG10 MicroECLIPSE	P-66	.	.	.	.	D	D	D	.	fixed
Adaptec controllers drive 1	P-10	.	.	.	.	D	D	D	D	fixed
Pdisk hard drive information	P-10	.	.	.	.	D	D	D	D	fixed
EZRECV	P-12	.	.	.	.	.	D	.	.	fixed
Ad Lib SOUND.COM	P-22	.	.	.	.	.	D	.	.	fixed
Media Vision FM.COM	P-22	.	.	.	.	.	D	.	.	fixed
SD.COM	P-66	.	.	.	.	.	D	.	.	fixed
FTP Software NDIS-Packet Driver adapter	7	.	.	.	.	.	D	.	.	fixed
Nanosoft TurboNET	31	.	.	.	.	.	.	D	.	fixed
Microsoft Windows VITD.386	P-43	.	.	.	.	.	.	D	.	fixed
Bitfax Scheduler	P-64	.	.	.	.	.	.	D	.	fixed
IBMSND driver	P-22	.	.	.	.	.	.	D	.	fixed
IBM Digitized Sound Package MIDI driver	P-22	.	.	.	.	.	.	D	.	fixed
PenDOS	P-66	.	.	.	.	.	.	D	.	fixed
MicroHelp Stay-Res	P-51	.	.	.	.	.	.	D	.	fixed
Virtual Control Program Interface	P-29	.	.	.	.	.	.	.	D	fixed

Expanded Memory Specification (EMS)	P-38	.	.	.	.	.	.	D	fixed
Quarterdeck QEMM installation check	P-39	.	.	.	.	.	.	D	fixed
Qualitas 386MAX MEMLIMIT	P-40	.	.	.	.	.	.	D	fixed
Netroom RM386	P-41	.	.	.	.	.	.	D	fixed
MICEMM	P-41	.	.	.	.	.	.	D	fixed
Compaq CEMM	P-42	.	.	.	.	.	.	D	fixed
Microsoft EMM386.EXE	P-42	.	.	.	.	.	.	D	fixed
Nanosoft MD386	P-42	.	.	.	.	.	.	D	fixed
Quadtel QMAPS	P-42	.	.	.	.	.	.	D	fixed
PC-NET	31	.	.	.	.	.	.	D	fixed
Newkey	P-13	a	a	a	a	a	a	a	D	automatic
CUCKOO	P-66	a	a	a	a	a	a	a	D	automatic

Key: D = default interrupt, **a** = alternate, **.** = not usable by program, **P-00** = Chapter 00 in *PC Interrupts*

2-4 INT 7Fh Usage

Chapter	Program
12	Alloy 386/MultiWare (MW386), NTNX, and ANSK
21	NetWare 2.x File Server
31	Convergent Technologies ClusterShare CTOS Access Vector
37	HLLAPI
38	Telebit ACS Serial I/O
PCI-8	Halo88
PCI-8	HDILOAD 8514/A controller interface
PCI-8	IBM 8516 Touch Screen Device Driver
PCI-8	IBM XGA
PCI-12	TIGA Communications Driver
PCI-37	GO32 DOS Extender
PCI-49	MultiLink Advanced
PCI-54	Btrieve Multi-User
PCI-66	Canon IXHND2 Scanner Interface
PCI-66	YTERM

CHAPTER 3

MS-DOS Network Support

MS-DOS has had built-in networking support as of version 3. This support manifests itself in four areas: user-level DOS calls, internal support calls, internal data areas, and the network redirector interface (discussed in Chapter 9). User-level calls consist primarily of file and record locking, and the addition of new network-related error codes. An entire set of internal support calls was added to ease the job of network redirectors, and the internal data areas were expanded and fixed; where the data areas of previous MS-DOS versions varied radically from OEM to OEM, they are virtually identical across all releases of a particular version since 3.0. Further, it is no possible to directly retrieve the address of the internal data where it was previously necessary to hard-code the address based on the version and OEM.

3-1 Extended MS-DOS error codes:

00h	(0)	no error
01h	(1)	function number invalid
02h	(2)	file not found
03h	(3)	path not found
04h	(4)	too many open files (no handles available)
05h	(5)	access denied
06h	(6)	invalid handle
07h	(7)	memory control block destroyed
08h	(8)	insufficient memory
09h	(9)	memory block address invalid
0Ah	(10)	environment invalid (usually >32K in length)
0Bh	(11)	format invalid
0Ch	(12)	access code invalid
0Dh	(13)	data invalid
0Eh	(14)	reserved
0Fh	(15)	invalid drive
10h	(16)	attempted to remove current directory
11h	(17)	not same device
12h	(18)	no more files

---DOS 3+---

13h	(19)	disk write-protected
14h	(20)	unknown unit
15h	(21)	drive not ready
16h	(22)	unknown command
17h	(23)	data error (CRC)
18h	(24)	bad request structure length

19h	(25)	seek error
1Ah	(26)	unknown media type (non-DOS disk)
1Bh	(27)	sector not found
1Ch	(28)	printer out of paper
1Dh	(29)	write fault
1Eh	(30)	read fault
1Fh	(31)	general failure
20h	(32)	sharing violation
21h	(33)	lock violation
22h	(34)	disk change invalid
23h	(35)	FCB unavailable
24h	(36)	sharing buffer overflow
25h	(37)	(DOS 4+) code page mismatch
26h	(38)	(DOS 4+) cannot complete file operation (out of input)
27h	(39)	(DOS 4+) insufficient disk space
28h-31h		reserved
32h	(50)	network request not supported
33h	(51)	remote computer not listening
34h	(52)	duplicate name on network
35h	(53)	network name not found
36h	(54)	network busy
37h	(55)	network device no longer exists
38h	(56)	network BIOS command limit exceeded
39h	(57)	network adapter hardware error
3Ah	(58)	incorrect response from network
3Bh	(59)	unexpected network error
3Ch	(60)	incompatible remote adapter
3Dh	(61)	print queue full
3Eh	(62)	queue not full
3Fh	(63)	not enough space to print file
40h	(64)	network name was deleted
41h	(65)	network: Access denied
42h	(66)	network device type incorrect
43h	(67)	network name not found
44h	(68)	network name limit exceeded
45h	(69)	network BIOS session limit exceeded
46h	(70)	temporarily paused
47h	(71)	network request not accepted
48h	(72)	network print/disk redirection paused
49h	(73)	network software not installed
		(LANtastic) invalid network version
4Ah	(74)	unexpected adapter close
		(LANtastic) account expired
4Bh	(75)	(LANtastic) password expired
4Ch	(76)	(LANtastic) login attempt invalid at this time
4Dh	(77)	(LANtastic v3+) disk limit exceeded on network node
4Eh	(78)	(LANtastic v3+) not logged in to network node
4Fh	(79)	reserved
50h	(80)	file exists

51h	(81)	reserved
52h	(82)	cannot make directory
53h	(83)	fail on INT 24h
54h	(84)	(DOS 3.3+) too many redirections
55h	(85)	(DOS 3.3+) duplicate redirection
56h	(86)	(DOS 3.3+) invalid password
57h	(87)	(DOS 3.3+) invalid parameter
58h	(88)	(DOS 3.3+) network write fault
59h	(89)	(DOS 4+) function not supported on network
5Ah	(90)	(DOS 4+) required system component not installed
64h	(100)	(MSCDEX) unknown error
65h	(101)	(MSCDEX) not ready
66h	(102)	(MSCDEX) EMS memory no longer valid
67h	(103)	(MSCDEX) not High Sierra or ISO-9660 format
68h	(104)	(MSCDEX) door open

INT 21h Function 3Dh   *DOS 2+*
"OPEN" - OPEN EXISTING FILE

Registers at call: **Return Registers:**
AH = 3Dh   CF clear if successful
AL = access and sharing modes   AX = file handle
  see Table 3-2)   CF set on error
DS:DX -> ASCIZ filename   AX = error code (01h,02h,03h,04h,05h,0Ch,
CL = attribute mask of files to look for   56h) (see Table 3-1)
  (server call only)

Details: The file pointer is set to the start of the file. File handles which are inherited from a parent also inherit sharing and access restrictions. Files may be opened even if given the hidden or system attributes. Under the FlashTek X-32 DOS extender, the pointer is in DS:EDX.

DR-DOS checks the system password or explicitly supplied password at the end of the filename against the reserved field in the directory entry before allowing access.

Sharing modes are effective on local drives only if SHARE is loaded.

Conflicts: JD-448 virus (PCI-59)

See also: Function 5D00h; INT 2Fh Function 1226h (below); Network Redirector INT 2Fh Function 1116h (Chapter 9); MS-DOS Functions 0Fh, 3Ch, and 4301h (PCI-24)

3-2 Bitfields for access and sharing modes:

bits 2-0   access mode
           000 read only
           001 write only
           010 read/write
           011 (DOS 5+ internal) passed to redirector on EXEC to allow case-sensitive filenames
bit 3   reserved (0)
bits 6-4   sharing mode (DOS 3+)
           000 compatibility mode
           001 "DENYALL" prohibit both read and write access by others
           010 "DENYWRITE" prohibit write access by others
           011 "DENYREAD" prohibit read access by others
           100 "DENYNONE" allow full access by others
           111 network FCB (only available during server call)
bit 7   inheritance
           if set, file is private to current process and will not be inherited by child processes

3-3 File sharing behavior:

First Open		Compatib. R W RW	Deny All R W RW	Deny Write R W RW	Deny Read R W RW	Deny None R W RW
Compat	R	Y Y Y	N N N	1 N N	N N N	1 N N
	W	Y Y Y	N N N	N N N	N N N	N N N
	RW	Y Y Y	N N N	N N N	N N N	N N N
Deny All	R	C C C	N N N	N N N	N N N	N N N
	W	C C C	N N N	N N N	N N N	N N N
	RW	C C C	N N N	N N N	N N N	N N N
Deny Write	R	2 C C	N N N	Y N N	N N N	Y N N
	W	C C C	N N N	N N N	Y N N	Y N N
	RW	C C C	N N N	N N N	N N N	Y N N
Deny Read	R	C C C	N N N	N Y N	N N N	N Y N
	W	C C C	N N N	N N N	N Y N	N Y N
	RW	C C C	N N N	N N N	N N N	N Y N
Deny None	R	2 C C	N N N	Y Y Y	N N N	Y Y Y
	W	C C C	N N N	N N N	Y Y Y	Y Y Y
	RW	C C C	N N N	N N N	N N N	Y Y Y

(Second and subsequent Opens span the Deny All, Deny Write, Deny Read, Deny None column groups.)

Legend: Y = open succeeds

N = open fails with error code 05h

C = open fails, INT 24h generated

1 = open succeeds if file read-only, else fails with error code

2 = open succeeds if file read-only, else fails with INT 24h

INT 21h Function 41h   *DOS 2+*
"UNLINK" - DELETE FILE

Registers at call:
AH = 41h
DS:DX -> ASCIZ filename (no
  wildcards, but see below)
CL = attribute mask for deletion
(server call only, see below)

Return Registers:
CF clear if successful
  AX destroyed (DOS 3.3) AL seems to be drive
    of deleted file
CF set on error
  AX = error code (02h,03h,05h) (see Table 3-1)

Details: Under DOS 3.1+, wildcards are allowed if this function is invoked via Function 5D00h (Server Call), in which case the filespec must be canonical (as returned by Function 60h), and only files matching the attribute mask in CL are deleted.

DR-DOS 5.0-6.0 returns error code 03h if invoked via Function 5D00h.

DOS does not erase the file's data; it merely becomes inaccessible because the FAT chain for the file is cleared.

Deleting a file which is currently open may lead to filesystem corruption. Unless SHARE is loaded, DOS does not close the handles referencing the deleted file, thus allowing writes to a non-existent file. Under DRDOS and DR Multiuser DOS, this function will fail if the file is currently open.

Under the FlashTek X-32 DOS extender, the pointer is in DS:EDX

BUG: DR-DOS 3.41 crashes if called via Function 5D00h.
Conflicts: SoftLogic Data Guardian (PCI-66)
See also: Functions 5D00h, and 60h; Novell NetWare Function F244h (Chapter 21); Network Redirector INT 2Fh Function 1113h (Chapter 9); MS-DOS Functions 13h and 4301h (PCI-24); Novell DOS Function 4380h (PCI-26)

INT 21h Function 52h	*DOS 2+ internal*
"SYSVARS" - GET LIST OF LISTS	*Undocumented*

Registers at call: **Return Registers:**
AH = 52h   ES:BX -> DOS list of lists (see Table 3-4)
Details: On return, ES points at the DOS data segment (see also INT 2Fh Function 1203h below).

This function is partially supported by the OS/2 v1.1 compatibility box (however, most pointers are FFFFh:FFFFh, LASTDRIVE is FFh, and the NUL header "next" pointer is FFFFh:FFFFh).
Conflicts: Leapfrog virus (Chapter 59)
See also: INT 2Fh Function 1203h (below)

3-4 Format of List of Lists:

Offset	Size	Description
-24	WORD	(DOS 3.1+) contents of CX from INT 21/AX=5E01h
-22	WORD	(DOS v?+) LRU counter for FCB caching
-20	WORD	(DOS v?+) LRU counter for FCB opens
-18	DWORD	(DOS v?+) address of OEM function handler (see INT 21h Function F8h, PCI-24) FFFFh:FFFFh if not installed or not available
-14	WORD	(DOS v?+) offset in DOS CS of code to return from INT 21h call
-12	WORD	(DOS 3.1+) sharing retry count (see Function 440Bh, PCI-24)
-10	WORD	(DOS 3.1+) sharing retry delay (see Function 440Bh, PCI-24)
-8	DWORD	(DOS 3+) pointer to current disk buffer
-4	WORD	(DOS 3+) pointer in DOS data segment of unread CON input When CON is read via a handle, DOS reads an entire line, and returns the requested portion, buffering the rest for the next read. 0000h indicates no unread input.
-2	WORD	segment of first memory control block
00h	DWORD	pointer to first Drive Parameter Block (see Tables 3-48 and 3-49)
04h	DWORD	pointer to first System File Table (see Tables 3-15 to 3-18)
08h	DWORD	pointer to active CLOCK$ device's header (most recently loaded driver with CLOCK bit set)
0Ch	DWORD	pointer to active CON device's header (most recently loaded driver with STDIN bit set)
---DOS 2.x---		
10h	BYTE	number of logical drives in system
11h	WORD	maximum bytes/block of any block device
13h	DWORD	pointer to first disk buffer (see Table 3-24)
17h 18	BYTEs	actual NUL device driver header (not a pointer!) NUL is always the first device on DOS's linked list of device drivers. (see Table 3-21)
---DOS 3.0---		
10h	BYTE	number of block devices
11h	WORD	maximum bytes/block of any block device

13h	DWORD	pointer to first disk buffer (see Table 3-25)
17h	DWORD	pointer to array of current directory structures (see Table 3-19)
1Bh	BYTE	value of LASTDRIVE command in CONFIG.SYS (default 5)
1Ch	DWORD	pointer to STRING= workspace area
20h	WORD	size of STRING area (the x in STRING=x from CONFIG.SYS)
22h	DWORD	pointer to FCB table
26h	WORD	the y in FCBS=x,y from CONFIG.SYS
28h	18 BYTEs	actual NUL device driver header (not a pointer!) NUL is always the first device on DOS's linked list of device drivers. (see Table 3-21)

---DOS 3.1-3.3---

10h	WORD	maximum bytes per sector of any block device
12h	DWORD	pointer to first disk buffer in buffer chain (see Table 3-25)
16h	DWORD	pointer to array of current directory structures (see Table 3-19)
1Ah	DWORD	pointer to system FCB tables (see Table 3-14)
1Eh	WORD	number of protected FCBs (the y in the CONFIG.SYS FCBS=x,y)
20h	BYTE	number of block devices installed
21h	BYTE	number of available drive letters (largest of 5, installed block devices, and CONFIG.SYS LASTDRIVE=). Also size of current directory structure array.
22h	18 BYTEs	actual NUL device driver header (not a pointer!) NUL is always the first device on DOS's linked list of device drivers. (see Table 3-21)
34h	BYTE	number of JOIN'ed drives

---DOS 4.x---

10h	WORD	maximum bytes per sector of any block device
12h	DWORD	pointer to disk buffer info record (see Tables 3-26, 3-27, and 3-31)
16h	DWORD	pointer to array of current directory structures (see Table 3-19)
1Ah	DWORD	pointer to system FCB tables (see Table 3-18)
1Eh	WORD	number of protected FCBs (the y in the CONFIG.SYS FCBS=x,y) (always 00h for DOS 5.0)
20h	BYTE	number of block devices installed
21h	BYTE	number of available drive letters (largest of 5, installed block devices, and CONFIG.SYS LASTDRIVE=). Also size of current directory structure array.
22h	18 BYTEs	actual NUL device driver header (not a pointer!) NUL is always the first device on DOS's linked list of device drivers. (see Table 3-21)
34h	BYTE	number of JOIN'ed drives
35h	WORD	pointer within IBMDOS code segment to list of special program names (see Table 3-37) (always 0000h for DOS 5.0)
37h	DWORD	pointer to FAR routine for resident IFS utility functions may be called by any IFS driver which does not wish to service functions 20h or 24h-28h itself
3Bh	DWORD	pointer to chain of IFS (installable file system) drivers
3Fh	WORD	the x in BUFFERS x,y (rounded up to multiple of 30 if in EMS)
41h	WORD	number of lookahead buffers (the y in BUFFERS x,y)
43h	BYTE	boot drive (1=A:)
44h	BYTE	flag: 01h to use DWORD moves (80386+), 00h otherwise

INT 21h Function 52h

45h	WORD	extended memory size in KB

---DOS 5.0-6.0---

10h	39 BYTEs	as for DOS 4.x (see above)
37h	DWORD	pointer to SETVER program list or 0000h:0000h
3Bh	WORD	(DOS=HIGH) offset in DOS CS of function to fix A20 control when executing special .COM format
3Dh	WORD	PSP of most-recently EXECed program if DOS in HMA, 0000h if low
3Fh	8 BYTEs	as for DOS 4.x (see above)

3-5 Format of memory control block (see Tables 3-7 and 3-8):

Offset	Size	Description
00h	BYTE	block type: 5Ah if last block in chain, otherwise 4Dh
01h	WORD	PSP segment of owner or special value (see Table 3-6)
03h	WORD	size of memory block in paragraphs
05h	3 BYTEs	unused by MS-DOS (386MAX) if locked-out block, region start/prev region end

---DOS 2.x,3.x---

08h	8 BYTEs	unused

---DOS 4+ ---

08h	8 BYTEs	ASCII program name if PSP memory block or DR-DOS UMB, else garbage null-terminated if less than 8 characters

Notes: Under DOS 3.1+, the first memory block is the DOS data segment, containing installable drivers, buffers, etc. Under DOS 4+ it is divided into subsegments, each with its own memory control block (see Table 3-9), the first of which is at offset 0000h.

For DOS 5+, blocks owned by DOS may have either "SC" or "SD" in bytes 08h and 09h. "SC" is system code or locked-out inter-UMB memory, "SD" is system data, device drivers, etc.

Some versions of DR-DOS use only seven characters of the program name, placing a NUL in the eighth byte.

3-6 Special MCB owner values:

0000h	free
0006h	DR-DOS XMS UMB
0007h	DR-DOS excluded upper memory ("hole")
0008h	belongs to DOS
FFFAh	386MAX UMB control block (see Table 40-11)
FFFDh	386MAX locked-out memory
FFFEh	386MAX UMB (immediately follows its control block)
FFFFh	386MAX 6.01 device driver

3-7 Format of MS-DOS 5+ UMB control block:

Offset	Size	Description
00h	BYTE	type: 5Ah if last block in chain, 4Dh otherwise
01h	WORD	first available paragraph in UMB if control block at start of UMB, 000Ah if control block at end of UMB
03h	WORD	length in paragraphs of following UMB or locked-out region
05h	3 BYTEs	unused
08h	8 BYTEs	block type name: "UMB" if start block, "SM" if end block in UMB

3-8 Format of STARLITE (General Software's Embedded DOS) memory control block:

Offset	Size	Description
00h	BYTE	block type: 5Ah if last block in chain, otherwise 4Dh
01h	WORD	PSP segment of owner, 0000h if free, 0008h if belongs to DOS
03h	WORD	size of memory block in paragraphs
05h	BYTE	unused
06h	WORD	segment address of next memory control block (0000h if last)
08h	WORD	segment address of previous memory control block or 0000h
0Ah	6 BYTEs	reserved

3-9 Format of DOS 4+ data segment subsegment control blocks:

Offset	Size	Description
00h	BYTE	subsegment type (blocks typically appear in this order)
		"D" device driver
		"E" device driver appendage
		"I" IFS (Installable File System) driver
		"F" FILES= control block storage area (for FILES>5)
		"X" FCBS= control block storage area, if present
		"C" BUFFERS EMS workspace area (if BUFFERS /X option used)
		"B" BUFFERS= storage area
		"L" LASTDRIVE= current directory structure array storage area
		"S" STACKS= code and data area, if present (see Table 3-10)
		"T" INSTALL= transient code
01h	WORD	paragraph of subsegment start (usually the next paragraph)
03h	WORD	size of subsegment in paragraphs
05h	3 BYTEs	unused
08h	8 BYTEs	for types "D" and "I", base name of file from which the driver was loaded (unused for other types)

3-10 Format of data at start of STACKS code segment (if present):

Offset	Size	Description
00h	WORD	*unknown*
02h	WORD	number of stacks (the x in STACKS=x,y)
04h	WORD	size of stack control block array (should be 8*x)
06h	WORD	size of each stack (the y in STACKS=x,y)
08h	DWORD	pointer to STACKS data segment
0Ch	WORD	offset in STACKS data segment of stack control block array
0Eh	WORD	offset in STACKS data segment of last element of that array
10h	WORD	offset in STACKS data segment of the entry in that array for the next stack to be allocated (initially same as value in 0Eh and works its way down in steps of 8 to the value in 0Ch as hardware interrupts pre-empt each other)

Note: The STACKS code segment data may, if present, be located as follows:

DOS 3.2: The code segment data is at a paragraph boundary fairly early in the IBMBIO segment (seen at 0070:0190h)

DOS 3.3: The code segment is at a paragraph boundary in the DOS data segment, which may be determined by inspecting the segment pointers of the vectors for those of interrupts 02h, 08h-0Eh, 70h, 72-77h which have not been redirected by device drivers or TSRs.

INT 21h Function 52h

DOS 4+   Identified by sub-segment control block type "S" within the DOS data segment.

See also: STACKMAN INT B4h

3-11 Format of array elements in STACKS data segment:

Offset	Size	Description
00h	BYTE	status: 00h=free, 01h=in use, 03h=corrupted by overflow of higher stack.
01h	BYTE	not used
02h	DWORD	previous SS:SP
06h	WORD	pointer to word at top of stack (new value for SP). The word at the top of the stack is preset to point back to this control block.

3-12 DOS 3.1+ SHARE.EXE hooks:

(offsets from first system file table—pointed at by ListOfLists+04h)

Offset	Size	Description
-3Ch	DWORD	pointer to *unknown* FAR routine

Note: not called by MS-DOS 3.3, set to 0000h:0000h by SHARE 3.3+

-38h   DWORD   pointer to FAR routine called on opening file

Call: internal DOS location (see Tables 3-39 and 3-41) points at name of file just opened

Returns:
CF clear if successful
CF set on error
          AX = DOS error code (24h) (see Table 3-1)

-34h   DWORD   pointer to FAR routine called on closing file

Call: ES:DI -> system file table entry for file

-30h   DWORD   pointer to FAR routine to close all files for given computer (called by Function 5D03h)

-2Ch   DWORD   pointer to FAR routine to close all files for given process (called by Function 5D04h)

-28h DWORD   pointer to FAR routine to close file by name (called by Function 5D02h)

Call: DS:SI -> DOS parameter list (see Table 3-38)
          DPL's DS:DX -> name of file to close.

Returns:
CF clear if successful
CF set on error
          AX = DOS error code (03h) (see Table 3-1)

-24h   DWORD   pointer to FAR routine to lock region of file

Call: BX = file handle
          CX:DX = starting offset
          SI:AX = size

Returns:
CF set on error
          AL = DOS error code (21h) (see Table 3-1)

Details: This function is not called if the file is marked as remote.

-20h   DWORD   pointer to FAR routine to unlock region of file

Call: BX = file handle
          CX:DX = starting offset
          SI:AX = size

Returns:
CF set on error

AL = DOS error code (21h) (see Table 3-1)

Details: This function is not called if the file is marked as remote.

-1Ch   DWORD   pointer to FAR routine to check if file region is locked

          Call: ES:DI -> system file table entry for file

          CX = length of region from current position in file

          Returns:

          CF set if any portion of region locked

          AX = 0021h

-18h   DWORD   pointer to FAR routine to get open file list entry (called by Function 5D05h)

          Call: DS:SI -> DOS parameter list (see Table 3-38)

          DPL's BX = index of sharing record

          DPL's CX = index of SFT in SFT chain of sharing record

          Returns:

          CF set on error or not loaded

          AX = DOS error code (12h) (see Table 3-1)

          CF clear if successful

          ES:DI -> filename

          CX = number of locks owned by specified SFT

          BX = network machine number

          DX destroyed

-14h   DWORD   pointer to FAR routine for *updating FCB from SFT*

          Call: DS:SI -> unopened FCB

          ES:DI -> system file table entry

          Returns:

          BL = *C0h*

Details: This function copies the following fields from SFT to FCB: starting cluster of file (0Bh->1Ah), sharing record offset (33h->1Ch), and file attribute (04h->1Eh)

-10h   DWORD   pointer to FAR routine to *get first cluster of FCB file*

          Call: ES:DI -> system file table entry

          DS:SI -> FCB

          Returns:

          CF set if SFT closed or sharing record offsets mismatched

          CF clear if successful

          BX = starting cluster number from FCB

-0Ch   DWORD   pointer to FAR routine to close file if duplicate for process

          Call: DS:SI -> system file table

          Returns:

          AX = number of handle in JFT which already uses SFT

Details: This function is called during the open/create of a file. If the SFT was opened with inheritance enabled and sharing mode 111, this function does something to all other SFTs owned by the same process which have the same file open mode and sharing record

-08h   DWORD   pointer to FAR routine for closing file

Details: This function closes various handles referring to the file most-recently opened

-04h   DWORD   pointer to FAR routine to update directory info in related SFT entries

          Call: ES:DI -> system file table entry for file (see Tables 3-17 and 3-18)

          AX = subfunction (apply to each related SFT)

          00h: update time stamp (offset 0Dh) and date stamp (offset 0Fh)

          01h: update file size (offset 11h) and starting cluster (offset 0Bh).

          Sets last-accessed cluster fields to start of file if file never accessed

          02h: as function 01h, but last-accessed fields always changed

03h: do both functions 00h and 02h

Details: This function follows the pointer at offset 2Bh in system file table entries. It is a NOP if the file was opened with no-inherit or via FCB.

Details: Most of the above hooks (except -04h, -14h, -18h, and -3Ch) assume either that SS=DOS DS or SS=DS=DOS DS and directly access DOS-internal data

3-13 Format of sharing record:

Offset	Size	Description
00h	BYTE	flag: 00h free block, 01h allocated block, FFh end marker
01h	WORD	size of block
03h	BYTE	checksum of pathname (including NUL)
		if sum of ASCII values is N, checksum is (N/256 + N%256)
04h	WORD	offset in SHARE's DS of first Record Lock Record (see Table 3-14)
06h	DWORD	pointer to start of system file table chain for file
0Ah	WORD	unique sequence number
0Ch	varies	ASCIZ full pathname

3-14 Format of Record Lock Record (SHARE.EXE):

Offset	Size	Description
00h	WORD	offset in SHARE's DS of next lock table in list or 0000h
02h	DWORD	offset in file of start of locked region
06h	DWORD	offset in file of end of locked region
0Ah	DWORD	pointer to System File Table entry for this file
0Eh	WORD	PSP segment of lock's owner

---DOS 5+ ---

Offset	Size	Description
10h	WORD	lock type: (00h lock all, 01h lock writes only)

3-15 Format of DOS 2.x system file tables:

Offset	Size	Description
00h	DWORD	pointer to next file table (offset FFFFh if last)
04h	WORD	number of files in this table
06h	28h bytes per file	

Offset	Size	Description
00h	BYTE	number of file handles referring to this file
01h	BYTE	file open mode (see Table 3-2)
02h	BYTE	file attribute
03h	BYTE	drive (0 = character device, 1 = A, 2 = B, etc)
04h	11 BYTEs	filename in FCB format (no path,no period,blank-padded)
0Fh	WORD	*unknown*
11h	WORD	*unknown*
13h	DWORD	*file size*
17h	WORD	file date in packed format (see Table 3-54)
19h	WORD	file time in packed format (see Table 3-55)
1Bh	BYTE	device attribute (see Table 3-22)

---character device---

Offset	Size	Description
1Ch	DWORD	pointer to device driver

---block device---

Offset	Size	Description
1Ch	WORD	starting cluster of file
1Eh	WORD	relative cluster in file of last cluster accessed

Offset	Size	Description
20h	WORD	absolute cluster number of current cluster

22h	WORD	*unknown*
24h	DWORD	*current file position*

3-16 Format of DOS 3.0 system file tables and FCB tables:

Offset	Size	Description
00h	DWORD	pointer to next file table (offset FFFFh if last)
04h	WORD	number of files in this table
06h	38h bytes per file	

Offset	Size	Description
00h-1Eh as for DOS 3.1+ (see Table 3-17)		
1Fh	WORD	byte offset of directory entry within sector
21h	11 BYTEs	filename in FCB format (no path/period, blank-padded)
2Ch	DWORD	(SHARE.EXE) pointer to previous SFT sharing same file
30h	WORD	(SHARE.EXE) network machine number which opened file (Windows Enhanced mode DOSMGR uses the virtual machine ID as the machine number; see INT 2F/AX=1683h)
32h	WORD	PSP segment of file's owner (first three entries for AUX/CON/PRN contain segment of IO.SYS startup code)
34h	WORD	(SHARE.EXE) offset in SHARE code seg of share record
36h	WORD	*apparently always 0000h*

3-17 Format of DOS 3.1-3.3x, DR-DOS 5.0-6.0 system file tables and FCB tables:

Offset	Size	Description
00h	DWORD	pointer to next file table (offset FFFFh if last)
04h	WORD	number of files in this table
06h	35h bytes per file	

Offset	Size	Description
00h	WORD	number of file handles referring to this file
02h	WORD	file open mode (see Table 3-2) bit 15 set if this file opened via FCB
04h	BYTE	file attribute (see Table 3-53)
05h	WORD	device info word (see Table 3-54) bit 15 set if remote file bit 14 set means do not set file date/time on closing bit 12 set means don't inherit on EXEC bits 5-0 drive number for disk files
07h	DWORD	pointer to device driver header if character device else pointer to DOS Drive Parameter Block (see Table 3-49)
0Bh	WORD	starting cluster of file
0Dh	WORD	file time in packed format (see Table 3-55) not used for character devices in DR-DOS
0Fh	WORD	file date in packed format (see Table 3-56) not used for character devices in DR-DOS
11h	DWORD	file size
---system file table---		
15h	DWORD	current offset in file (may be larger than size of file; INT 21h Function 42h does not check new position)
---FCB table---		
15h	WORD	counter for last I/O to FCB
17h	WORD	counter for last open of FCB

INT 21h Function 52h

(these are separate to determine the times of the latest I/O and open)

19h	WORD	relative cluster within file of last cluster accessed
1Bh	WORD	absolute cluster number of last cluster accessed
		0000h if *file never read or written*
1Dh	WORD	number of sector containing directory entry
1Fh	BYTE	number of dir entry within sector (byte offset/32)
20h	11 BYTEs	filename in FCB format (no path/period, blank-padded)
2Bh	DWORD	(SHARE.EXE) pointer to previous SFT sharing same file
2Fh	WORD	(SHARE.EXE) network machine number which opened file
		(Windows Enhanced mode DOSMGR uses the virtual machine ID as the machine number; see INT 2Fh Function 1683h in Chapter 43)
31h	WORD	PSP segment of file's owner (see Table 3-57) (first three entries for AUX/CON/PRN contain segment of IO.SYS startup code)
33h	WORD	offset within SHARE code segment of sharing record (see Table 3-13)
		0000h = none

3-18 Format of DOS 4.0-6.0 system file tables and FCB tables:

Offset	Size	Description
00h	DWORD	pointer to next file table (offset FFFFh if last)
04h	WORD	number of files in this table
06h	3Bh bytes per file	

Offset	Size	Description
00h	WORD	number of file handles referring to this file
		FFFFh if in use but not referenced
02h	WORD	file open mode (see Table 3-2)
		bit 15 set if this file opened via FCB
04h	BYTE	file attribute (see Table 3-53)
05h	WORD	device info word (see also Table 3-54)
		bit 15 set if remote file
		bit 14 set means do not set file date/time on closing
		bit 13 set if named pipe
		bit 12 set if no inherit
		bit 11 set if network spooler
		bit 7 set if device, clear if file (only if local)
		bits 6-0 as for Function 4400h
07h	DWORD	pointer to device driver header if character device
		else pointer to DOS Drive Parameter Block (see Table 3-49) or REDIR data
0Bh	WORD	starting cluster of file (local files only)
0Dh	WORD	file time in packed format (see Table 3-55)
0Fh	WORD	file date in packed format (see Table 3-56)
11h	DWORD	file size
15h	DWORD	current offset in file (SFT)
		LRU counters (FCB table, two WORDs)

---local file---

19h	WORD	relative cluster within file of last cluster accessed
1Bh	DWORD	number of sector containing directory entry
1Fh	BYTE	number of dir entry within sector (byte offset/32)

---network redirector---

| 19h | DWORD | pointer to REDIRIFS record |
| 1Dh | 3 BYTEs | *unknown* |

20h	11 BYTEs	filename in FCB format (no path/period, blank-padded)
2Bh	DWORD	(SHARE.EXE) pointer to previous SFT sharing same file
2Fh	WORD	(SHARE.EXE) network machine number which opened file (Windows Enhanced mode DOSMGR uses the virtual machine ID as the machine number; see INT 2Fh Function 1683h in Chapter 43)
31h	WORD	PSP segment of file's owner (see Table 3-57) (first three entries for AUX/CON/PRN contain segment of IO.SYS startup code)
33h	WORD	offset within SHARE.EXE code segment of sharing record (see Table 3-13) 0000h = none
35h	WORD	(local) absolute cluster number of last cluster accessed (redirector) *unknown*
37h	DWORD	pointer to IFS driver for file, 0000000h if native DOS

3-19 Format of current directory structure (CDS) (array, LASTDRIVE entries):

Offset	Size	Description
00h	67 BYTEs	ASCIZ path in form X:\PATH (local) or \\MACH\PATH (network)
43h	WORD	drive attributes (see also note below and Function 5F07h)

    bit 15: uses network redirector
    bit 14: physical drive
    bit 13: JOIN'ed
    bit 12: SUBST'ed
    bit

} invalid if 00, installable file system if 11 path above is true path that would be needed if not under SUBST or JOIN 7: remote drive hidden from redirector's assign-list and exempt from network connection make/break commands; set

| 45h | DWORD | pointer to Drive Parameter Block for drive (see Table 3-49) |

---local drives---

49h	WORD	starting cluster of current directory 0000h = root, FFFFh = never accessed
4Bh	WORD	*apparently always FFFFh*
4Dh	WORD	*apparently always FFFFh*

---network drives---

| 49h | DWORD | pointer to redirector or REDIRIFS record, or FFFFh:FFFFh (DOS 4 only) available for use by IFS driver |
| 4Dh | WORD | stored user data from INT 21h Function 5F03h |

| 4Fh | WORD | offset in current directory path of backslash corresponding to root directory for drive this value specifies how many characters to hide from the "CHDIR" and "GETDIR" calls; normally set to 2 to hide the drive letter and colon, SUBST, JOIN, and networks change it so that only the appropriate portion of the true path is visible to the user. |

---DOS 4+ ---

| 51h | BYTE | (DOS 4 only, remote drives) device type 04h network drive |

52h	DWORD	pointer to IFS driver (DOS 4) or redirector block (DOS 5+) for this drive, 00000000h if native DOS
56h	WORD	available for use by IFS driver

Notes: The path for invalid drives is normally set to X:\, but may be empty after JOIN x: /D in DR-DOS 5.0 or NET USE x: /D in older LAN versions.

Normally, only one of bits 13&12 may be set together with bit 14, but DR-DOS 5.0 uses other combinations for bits 15-12 (see Table 3-20).

3-20 Format of DR-DOS 5.0-6.0 current directory structure entry (array):

Offset	Size	Description
00h	67 BYTEs	ASCIZ pathname of actual root directory for this logical drive
43h	WORD	drive attributes
		1000h SUBSTed drive
		3000h JOINed drive
		4000h physical drive
		5000h ASSIGNed drive
		7000h JOINed drive
		8000h network drive
45h	BYTE	physical drive number (0=A:) if this logical drive is valid
46h	BYTE	*apparently flags for JOIN and ASSIGN*
47h	WORD	cluster number of start of parent directory (0000h = root)
49h	WORD	entry number of current directory in parent directory
4Bh	WORD	cluster number of start of current directory
4Dh	WORD	used for media change detection (details not available)
4Fh	WORD	cluster number of SUBST/JOIN "root" directory
		0000h if physical root directory

3-21 Format of device driver header:

Offset	Size	Description
00h	DWORD	pointer to next driver, offset=FFFFh if last driver
04h	WORD	device attributes (see Table 3-22)
06h	WORD	device strategy entry point
		call with ES:BX -> request header (see Table 3-59)
08h	WORD	device interrupt entry point
---character device---		
0Ah	8 BYTEs	blank-padded character device name
---block device---		
0Ah	BYTE	number of subunits (drives) supported by driver
0Bh	7 BYTEs	unused

12h	WORD	(CD-ROM driver) reserved, must be 0000h
		appears to be another device chain
14h	BYTE	(CD-ROM driver) drive letter (must initially be 00h)
15h	BYTE	(CD-ROM driver) number of units
16h	6 BYTEs	(CD-ROM driver) signature 'MSCDnn' where 'nn' is version (currently '00')

3-22 Bitfields for device attributes:

bit 15	device type (clear = block device, set = character device)
bit 14	IOCTL supported (see Functions 4402h to 4405h, PCI-24)
bit 13	(block) non-IBM format
	(DOS 3+ character) output until busy supported

bit 12   (block) network/remote device
bit 11   (DOS 3+) OPEN/CLOSE/RemMedia calls supported
bit 10   reserved
bit 9   (block) *direct I/O not allowed* (set by DOS 3.3 DRIVER.SYS)
bit 8   (block) *unknown* (set by DOS 3.3 DRIVER.SYS for "new" drives)
bit 7   (DOS 5+) Generic IOCTL check call supported (command 19h) (see Functions 4410h and 4411h, PCI-24)
bit 6   (DOS 3.2+) Generic IOCTL call supported (command 13h) (see Functions 440Ch and 440Dh, PCI-24)
bit 5   reserved
bit 4   (character) device is special (supports fast console output INT 29h)
bit 3   (character) device is CLOCK$ (all reads/writes use transfer record described below)
bit 2   (character) device is NUL
bit 1   (DOS 3.31+ block) driver supports 32-bit sector addressing
          (character) device is standard output
bit 0   (character) device is standard input

Note: For European MS-DOS 4.0, bit 11 also indicates that bits 8-6 contain a version code (000 = DOS 3.0,3.1; 001 = DOS 3.2, 010 = European DOS 4.0).

3-23 Format of CLOCK$ transfer record:

Offset	Size	Description
00h	WORD	number of days since 1-Jan-1980
02h	BYTE	minutes
03h	BYTE	hours
04h	BYTE	hundredths of second
05h	BYTE	seconds

3-24 Format of DOS 2.x disk buffer:

Offset	Size	Description
00h	DWORD	pointer to next disk buffer, offset = FFFFh if last least-recently used buffer is first in chain
04h	BYTE	drive (0=A, 1=B, etc.), FFh if not in use
05h	3 BYTEs	*unused* (seems always to be 00h 00h 01h)
08h	WORD	logical sector number
0Ah	BYTE	number of copies to write (1 for non-FAT sectors)
0Bh	BYTE	sector offset between copies if multiple copies to be written
0Ch	DWORD	pointer to DOS Drive Parameter Block (see Table 3-49)
10h		buffered data

3-25 Format of DOS 3.x disk buffer:

Offset	Size	Description
00h	DWORD	pointer to next disk buffer, offset = FFFFh if last least-recently used buffer is first in chain
04h	BYTE	drive (0=A,1=B, etc.), FFh if not in use
05h	BYTE	buffer flags (see Table 3-30)
06h	WORD	logical sector number
08h	BYTE	number of copies to write (1 for non-FAT sectors)
09h	BYTE	sector offset between copies if multiple copies to be written
0Ah	DWORD	pointer to DOS Drive Parameter Block (see Table 3-49)
0Eh	WORD	*unused* (almost always 0)
10h		buffered data

3-26 Format of DOS 4.00 (pre UR 25066) disk buffer info:

Offset	Size	Description
00h	DWORD	pointer to array of disk buffer hash chain heads (see Table 3-28)
04h	WORD	number of disk buffer hash chains (referred to as NDBCH below)
06h	DWORD	pointer to lookahead buffer, zero if not present
0Ah	WORD	number of lookahead sectors, else zero (the y in BUFFERS=x,y)
0Ch	BYTE	00h if buffers in EMS (/X), FFh if not
0Dh	WORD	EMS handle for buffers, zero if not in EMS
0Fh	WORD	EMS physical page number used for buffers (usually 255)
11h	WORD	*apparently always 0001h*
13h	WORD	segment of EMS physical page frame
15h	WORD	*apparently always zero*
17h	4 WORDs	*EMS partial page mapping information*

3-27 Format of DOS 4.01 (from UR 25066 Corrective Services Disk on) disk buffer info:

Offset	Size	Description
00h	DWORD	pointer to array of disk buffer hash chain heads (see Table 3-28)
04h	WORD	number of disk buffer hash chains (referred to as NDBCH below)
06h	DWORD	pointer to lookahead buffer, zero if not present
0Ah	WORD	number of lookahead sectors, else zero (the y in BUFFERS=x,y)
0Ch	BYTE	01h, possibly to distinguish from pre-UR 25066 format
0Dh	WORD	*EMS segment for BUFFERS* (only with /XD)
0Fh	WORD	*EMS physical page number of EMS segment above* (only with /XD)
11h	WORD	*EMS segment for unknown item* (only with /XD)
13h	WORD	*EMS physical page number of above* (only with /XD)
15h	BYTE	*number of EMS page frames present* (only with /XD)
16h	WORD	segment of one-sector workspace buffer allocated in main memory if BUFFERS/XS or /XD options in effect, possibly to avoid DMA into EMS
18h	WORD	EMS handle for buffers, zero if not in EMS
1Ah	WORD	EMS physical page number used for buffers (usually 255)
1Ch	WORD	*apparently always 0001h*
1Eh	WORD	segment of EMS physical page frame
20h	WORD	*apparently always zero*
22h	BYTE	00h if /XS, 01h if /XD, FFh if BUFFERS not in EMS

3-28 Format of DOS 4.x disk buffer hash chain head (array, one entry per chain):

Offset	Size	Description
00h	WORD	EMS logical page number in which chain is resident, -1 if not in EMS
02h	DWORD	pointer to least recently used buffer header. All buffers on this chain are in the same segment.
06h	BYTE	number of dirty buffers on this chain
07h	BYTE	reserved (00h)

Notes: Buffered disk sectors are assigned to chain N where N is the sector's address modulo the number of disk buffer chain heads (NDBCH), 0 <= N <= NDBCH-1. Each chain resides completely within one EMS page.

This structure is in main memory even if buffers are in EMS.

3-29 Format of DOS 4.0-6.0 disk buffer:

Offset	Size	Description
00h	WORD	forward ptr, offset only, to next least recently used buffer

02h	WORD	backward ptr, offset only
04h	BYTE	drive (0=A,1=B, etc.) if bit 7 clear
		SFT index if bit 7 set
		FFh if not in use
05h	BYTE	buffer flags (see Table 3-30)
06h	DWORD	logical sector number (local buffers only)
0Ah	BYTE	number of copies to write
		for FAT sectors, same as number of FATs
		for data and directory sectors, usually 1
0Bh	WORD	offset in sectors between copies to write for FAT sectors
0Dh	DWORD	pointer to DOS Drive Parameter Block (see Table 3-49)
11h	WORD	size of data in buffer if remote buffer (see Table 3-30)
13h	BYTE	reserved (padding)
14h		buffered data

Note: For DOS 4.x, all buffered sectors which have the same hash value computed as the sum of high and low words of the logical sector number divided by the number of disk buffer chains) are on the same doubly-linked circular chain; for DOS 5+, only a single circular chain exists.

The links consist of offset addresses only, the segment being the same for all buffers in the chain.

3-30 Bitfields for buffer flags:

bit 7	remote buffer
bit 6	buffer dirty
bit 5	buffer has been referenced (reserved in DOS 5+)
bit 4	search data buffer (only valid if remote buffer)
bit 3	sector in data area
bit 2	sector in a directory, either root or subdirectory
bit 1	sector in FAT
bit 0	reserved

3-31 Format of DOS 5.0-6.0 disk buffer info:

Offset	Size	Description
00h	DWORD	pointer to least-recently-used buffer header (may be in HMA) (see Table 3-29)
04h	WORD	number of dirty disk buffers
06h	DWORD	pointer to lookahead buffer, zero if not present
0Ah	WORD	number of lookahead sectors, else zero (the y in BUFFERS=x,y)
0Ch	BYTE	buffer location
		00h base memory, no workspace buffer
		01h HMA, workspace buffer in base memory
0Dh	DWORD	pointer to one-segment workspace buffer in base memory
11h	3 BYTEs	unused
14h	WORD	*unknown*
16h	BYTE	flag: INT 24h fail while making an I/O status call
17h	BYTE	temp storage for user memory allocation strategy during EXEC
18h	BYTE	counter: number of INT 21h calls for which A20 is off
19h	BYTE	bit flags
		bit 0: *unknown*
		bit 1: SWITCHES=/W specified in CONFIG.SYS (don't load WINA20.SYS when MS Windows 3.0 starts)

		bit 2: in EXEC state (INT 21h Function 4B05h)
1Ah	WORD	offset of unpack code start (used only during INT 21h Function 4B05h)
1Ch	BYTE	bit 0 set if UMB MCB chain linked to normal MCB chain
1Dh	WORD	minimum paragraphs of memory required by program being EXECed
1Fh	WORD	segment of first MCB in upper memory blocks or FFFFh if DOS memory chain in base 640K only (first UMB MCB usually at 9FFFh, locking out video memory with a DOS-owned memory block)
21h	WORD	paragraph from which to start scanning during memory allocation

3-32 Format of IFS driver list:

Offset	Size	Description
00h	DWORD	pointer to next driver header
04h	8 BYTEs	IFS driver name (blank padded), as used by FILESYS command
0Ch	4 BYTEs	*unknown*
10h	DWORD	pointer to IFS utility function entry point (see Table 3-33) call with ES:BX -> IFS request (see Table 3-35)
14h	WORD	offset in header's segment of driver entry point *additional fields, if any, unknown*

3-33 IFS utility function entry point calling convention:

Registers at call:	Return Registers:
AH = 20h miscellaneous functions	
AL = 00h get date	CX = year
	DH = month
	DL = day
AL = 01h get process ID and computer ID	BX = current PSP segment
	DX = active network machine number
AL = 05h get file system info ES:DI -> 16-byte info buffer	buffer filled (see Table 3-34)
AL = 06h get machine name ES:DI -> 18-byte buffer for name	buffer filled with name starting at offset 02h
AL = 08h get sharing retry count	BX = sharing retry count
AL = other	CF set

Registers at call:	Return Registers:
AH = 21h get redirection state	BH = state (00h off, 01h on)
BH = type (03h disk, 04h printer)	

Registers at call:	Return Registers:
AH = 22h *some sort of time calculation*	*unknown*
AL = 00h *unknown*	
nonzero *unknown*	

Registers at call:	Return Registers:
AH = 23h *some sort of time calculation*	*unknown*

Registers at call:	Return Registers:
AH = 24h compare filenames	ZF set if files are same ignoring case and
DS:SI -> first ASCIZ filename	/ vs \
ES:DI -> second ASCIZ filename	

Registers at call:	Return Registers:
AH = 25h normalize filename	filename uppercased, forward slashes changed
DS:SI -> ASCIZ filename	to backslashes
ES:DI -> buffer for result	

Registers at call:	Return Registers:
AH = 26h get DOS stack	DS:SI -> top of stack
	CX = size of stack in bytes

Registers at call:	Return Registers:
AH = 27h increment InDOS flag	nothing

Registers at call:	Return Registers:
AH = 28h decrement InDOS flag	nothing

Note: IFS drivers which do not wish to implement Functions 20h or 24h-28h may pass them on to the default handler pointed at by [ListOfLists+37h].

3-34 IFS File System Info:

Offset	Size	Description
00h	2 BYTEs	unused
02h	WORD	number of SFTs (actually counts only the first two file table arrays)
04h	WORD	number of FCB table entries
06h	WORD	number of proctected FCBs
08h	6 BYTEs	unused
0Eh	WORD	largest sector size supported

3-35 Format of IFS request block:

Offset	Size	Description
00h	WORD	total size in bytes of request
02h	BYTE	class of request
		02h *unknown*
		03h redirection
		04h *unknown*
		05h file access
		06h convert error code to string
		07h *unknown*
03h	WORD	(return) DOS error code
05h	BYTE	(return) IFS driver exit status
		00h success
		01h *unknown*
		02h *unknown*
		03h *unknown*
		04h *unknown*
		FFh internal failure
06h	16 BYTEs	*unknown*
---request class 02h---		
16h	BYTE	function code
		04h *unknown*
17h	BYTE	*unused*
18h	DWORD	pointer to *unknown item*
1Ch	DWORD	pointer to *unknown item*
20h	2 BYTEs	*unknown*
---request class 03h---		
16h	BYTE	function code

17h	BYTE	*unknown*
18h	DWORD	pointer to *unknown item*
1Ch	DWORD	pointer to *unknown item*
22h	WORD	(return) *unknown*
24h	WORD	(return) *unknown*
26h	WORD	(return) *unknown*
28h	BYTE	(return) *unknown*
29h	BYTE	*unused*

---request class 04h---

16h	DWORD	pointer to *unknown item*
1Ah	DWORD	pointer to *unknown item*

---request class 05h---

16h	BYTE	function code

                      01h flush disk buffers
                      02h get disk space
                      03h MKDIR
                      04h RMDIR
                      05h CHDIR
                      06h delete file
                      07h rename file
                      08h search directory
                      09h file open/create
                      0Ah LSEEK
                      0Bh read from file
                      0Ch write to file
                      0Dh lock region of file
                      0Eh commit/close file
                      0Fh get/set file attributes
                      10h printer control
                      11h *unknown*
                      12h process termination
                      13h *unknown*

---class 05h function 01h---

17h	7 BYTEs	*unknown*
1Eh	DWORD	pointer to *unknown item*
22h	4 BYTEs	*unknown*
26h	BYTE	*unknown*
27h	BYTE	*unknown*

---class 05h function 02h---

17h	7 BYTEs	*unknown*
1Eh	DWORD	pointer to *unknown item*
22h	4 BYTEs	*unknown*
26h	WORD	(return) total clusters
28h	WORD	(return) sectors per cluster
2Ah	WORD	(return) bytes per sector
2Ch	WORD	(return) available clusters
2Eh	BYTE	(return) *unknown*
2Fh	BYTE	*unknown*

---class 05h functions 03h,04h,05h---

17h	7 BYTEs	*unknown*
1Eh	DWORD	pointer to *unknown item*
22h	4 BYTEs	*unknown*
26h	DWORD	pointer to directory name

---class 05h function 06h---

17h	7 BYTEs	*unknown*
1Eh	DWORD	pointer to *unknown item*
22h	4 BYTEs	*unknown*
26h	WORD	attribute mask
28h	DWORD	pointer to filename

---class 05h function 07h---

17h	7 BYTEs	*unknown*
1Eh	DWORD	pointer to *unknown item*
22h	4 BYTEs	*unknown*
26h	WORD	attribute mask
28h	DWORD	pointer to source filespec
2Ch	DWORD	pointer to destination filespec

---class 05h function 08h---

17h	7 BYTEs	*unknown*
1Eh	DWORD	pointer to *unknown item*
22h	4 BYTEs	*unknown*
26h	BYTE	00h FINDFIRST
		01h FINDNEXT
28h	DWORD	pointer to FindFirst search data + 01h if FINDNEXT
2Ch	WORD	search attribute if FINDFIRST
2Eh	DWORD	pointer to filespec if FINDFIRST

---class 05h function 09h---

17h	7 BYTEs	*unknown*
1Eh	DWORD	pointer to *unknown item*
22h	DWORD	pointer to IFS open file structure (see Table 3-36)
26h	WORD	*unknown* ⎫ together, specify open vs. create, whether or
28h	WORD	*unknown* ⎭ not to truncate
2Ah	4 BYTEs	*unknown*
2Eh	DWORD	pointer to filename
32h	4 BYTEs	*unknown*
36h	WORD	(call) file attributes
		(return) *unknown*
38h	WORD	(return) *unknown*

---class 05h function 0Ah---

17h	7 BYTEs	*unknown*
1Eh	DWORD	pointer to *unknown item*
22h	DWORD	pointer to IFS open file structure (see Table 3-36)
26h	BYTE	seek type (02h = from end)
28h	DWORD	(call) offset
		(return) new absolute position

---class 05h functions 0Bh,0Ch---

17h	7 BYTEs	*unknown*
1Eh	DWORD	pointer to *unknown item*
22h	DWORD	pointer to IFS open file structure (see Table 3-36)

INT 21h Function 52h

28h	WORD	(call) number of bytes to transfer
		(return) bytes actually transferred
2Ah	DWORD	transfer address

---class 05h function 0Dh---

17h	7 BYTEs	*unknown*
1Eh	DWORD	pointer to *unknown item*
22h	DWORD	pointer to IFS open file structure (see Table 3-36)
26h	BYTE	*file handle*
27h	BYTE	*unused*
28h	WORD	*unknown*
2Ah	WORD	*unknown*
2Ch	WORD	*unknown*
2Eh	WORD	*unknown*

---class 05h function 0Eh---

17h	7 BYTEs	*unknown*
1Eh	DWORD	pointer to *unknown item*
22h	DWORD	pointer to IFS open file structure (see Table 3-36)
26h	BYTE	00h commit file
		01h close file
27h	BYTE	*unused*

---class 05h function 0Fh---

17h	7 BYTEs	*unknown*
1Eh	DWORD	pointer to *unknown item*
22h	4 BYTEs	*unknown*
26h	BYTE	02h GET attributes
		03h PUT attributes
27h	BYTE	*unused*
28h	12 BYTEs	*unknown*
34h	WORD	*search attributes*
36h	DWORD	pointer to filename
3Ah	WORD	(GET) returned *unknown*
3Ch	WORD	(GET) returned *unknown*
3Eh	WORD	(GET) returned *unknown*
40h	WORD	(GET) returned *unknown*
42h	WORD	(PUT) new attributes
		(GET) returned attributes

---class 05h function 10h---

17h	7 BYTEs	*unknown*
1Eh	DWORD	pointer to *unknown*
22h	DWORD	pointer to IFS open file structure (see Table 3-36)
26h	WORD	*unknown*
28h	DWORD	pointer to *unknown*
2Ch	WORD	*unknown*
2Eh	BYTE	*unknown*
2Fh	BYTE	subfunction
		01h get printer setup
		03h *unknown*
		04h *unknown*
		05h *unknown*

		06h *unknown*
		07h *unknown*
		21h set printer setup

---class 05h function 11h---

17h	7 BYTEs	*unknown*
1Eh	DWORD	pointer to *unknown item*
22h	DWORD	pointer to IFS open file structure (see Table 3-36)
26h	BYTE	subfunction
27h	BYTE	*unused*
28h	WORD	*unknown*
2Ah	WORD	*unknown*
2Ch	WORD	*unknown*
2Eh	BYTE	*unknown*
2Fh	BYTE	*unknown*

---class 05h function 12h---

17h	15 BYTEs	*unused*
26h	WORD	PSP segment
28h	BYTE	type of process termination
29h	BYTE	*unused*

---class 05h function 13h---

17h	15 BYTEs	*unused*
26h	WORD	PSP segment

---request class 06h---

16h	DWORD	(return) pointer to string corresponding to error code at 03h
1Ah	BYTE	(return) *unknown*
1Bh	BYTE	unused

---request class 07h---

16h	DWORD	pointer to IFS open file structure (see Table 3-36)
1Ah	BYTE	*unknown*
1Bh	BYTE	*unused*

3-36 Format of IFS open file structure:

Offset	Size	Description
00h	WORD	*unknown*
02h	WORD	device info word
04h	WORD	file open mode
06h	WORD	*unknown*
08h	WORD	file attributes
0Ah	WORD	owner's network machine number
0Ch	WORD	owner's PSP segment
0Eh	DWORD	file size
12h	DWORD	current offset in file
16h	WORD	file time
18h	WORD	file date
1Ah	11 BYTEs	filename in FCB format
25h	WORD	*unknown*
27h	WORD	hash value of SFT address
		(low word of linear address + segment&F000h)
29h	3 WORDs	network info from SFT
2Fh	WORD	*unknown*

INT 21h Function 52h

3-37 Format of one item in DOS 4+ list of special program names:

Offset	Size	Description
00h	BYTE	length of name (00h = end of list)
01h	N BYTEs	name in format name.ext
N	2 BYTEs	DOS version to return for program (major,minor) (see Function 30h in PCI-24 and INT 2Fh Function 122Fh below)

---DOS 4 only---

| N+2 | BYTE | number of times to return fake version number (FFh = always) |

Note: If the name of the executable for the program making the DOS "get version" call matches one of the names in this list, DOS returns the specified version rather than the true version number.

INT 21h Function 56h   *DOS 2+*
"RENAME" - RENAME FILE

Registers at call:
AH = 56h
DS:DX -> ASCIZ filename of existing file (no
   wildcards, but see below)
ES:DI -> ASCIZ new filename (no wildcards)
CL = attribute mask (server call only, see below)

Return Registers:
CF clear if successful
CF set on error
   AX = error code (02h,03h,05h,11h)
(see Table 3-1)

Details: This function allows files to be moved between directories on the same logical volume. It does not set the archive attribute, which results in incremental backups not backing up the file under its new name.

Open files should not be renamed.

DOS 3+ allows renaming of directories.

DOS 3.1+ allows wildcards if invoked via Function 5D00h, in which case error 12h (no more files) is returned on success, and both source and destination specs must be canonical (as returned by Function 60h). Wildcards in the destination are replaced by the corresponding character of each source file being renamed. Under DOS 3.x, the call will fail if the destination wildcard is *.* or equivalent; under DR-DOS 5.0, the call will fail if any wildcards are used. When invoked via Function 5D00h, only those files matching the attribute mask in CL are renamed.

Under the FlashTek X-32 DOS extender, the old-name pointer is in DS:EDX and the new-name pointer is in ES:EDI (DS must equal ES)

BUG: Under DR-DOS 3.41, this function will generate a new directory entry with the new name (including any wildcards) which can only be removed with a sector editor when invoked via Function 5D00h.

See also: Functions 5D00h and 60h, MS-DOS Functions 17h and 4301h (PCI-24)

INT 21h Function 5Ch   *DOS 3+*
"FLOCK" - RECORD LOCKING

Registers at call:
AH = 5Ch
AL = subfunction
   00h lock region of file
   01h unlock region of file
BX = file handle
CX:DX = start offset of region within file
SI:DI = length of region in bytes

Return Registers:
CF clear if successful
CF set on error
   AX = error code (01h,06h,21h,24h) (see Table 3-1)

Details: An error is returned unless SHARE or a network is installed.

An unlock call must specify the same region as some prior lock call.

Locked regions become entirely inaccessible to other processes.

Duplicate handles created with Functions 45h or 46h inherit locks, but handles inherited by child processes (see Function 4Bh in *PC Interrupts*) do not.

Under DR-DOS 3.41 and 5.0, if a process opens a file without the no-inherit flag and then starts a child, any locks set by the parent are ignored, and the child will only get an error if it tries to lock an area previously locked by the parent process.

See also: NetWare Functions BCh and BEh (Chapter 21), Network Redirector INT 2Fh Functions 110Ah and 110Bh (Chapter 9), MS-DOS Function 440Bh (PCI-24)

INT 21h Function 5D00h
SERVER FUNCTION CALL
DOS 3.1+ internal
Undocumented

Registers at call:
AX = 5D00h
DS:DX -> DOS parameter list (see Table 3-38)
DPL contains all register values for a call to INT 21h

Return Registers:
as appropriate for function being called

Details: This function does not check AH; out of range values will crash the system.

The requested function executes using the specified computer ID and process ID.

Sharing delay loops are skipped and a special sharing mode is enabled to handle FCBs opened across the network. Wildcards are enabled for DELETE (Function 41h) and RENAME (Function 56h) under MS-DOS; under DR-DOS 3.41, wildcards corrupt the filesystem; and under DR-DOS 5.0-6.0, the call returns error code 03h due to improper support for the server function call (see below). An extra file attribute parameter is enabled for OPEN (Function 3Dh), DELETE (Function 41h), and RENAME (Function 56h).

Functions which take filenames require canonical names (as returned by Function 60h); this is apparently to prevent multi-hop file forwarding

BUGS: The OS/2 2.0 DOS Boot Session incorrectly maps DOS drive letters, seemingly ignoring HPFS drives.

DR-DOS 5.0-6.0 merely recursively call INT 21h after loading the registers from the DPL, leading to problems for peer-to-peer networks.

See also: Functions 3Dh, 41h, 56h, and 60h

3-38 Format of DOS parameter list:

Offset	Size	Description
00h	WORD	AX
02h	WORD	BX
04h	WORD	CX
06h	WORD	DX
08h	WORD	SI
0Ah	WORD	DI
0Ch	WORD	DS
0Eh	WORD	ES
10h	WORD	reserved (0)
12h	WORD	computer ID (0 = current system)
14h	WORD	process ID (PSP segment on specified computer)

Note: Under Windows Enhanced mode, the computer ID is normally the virtual machine ID (see INT 2Fh Function 1683h in PCI-43), though this can reportedly be changed by setting UniqueDOSPSP= in SYSTEM.INI.

INT 21h Function 5D01h
COMMIT ALL FILES FOR SPECIFIED COMPUTER/PROCESS
DOS 3.1+ internal
Undocumented

Registers at call:
AX = 5D01h

DS:DX -> DOS parameter list (see Table 3-38), only
   computer ID and process ID fields used

Return Registers:
CF set on error
      AX = error code (see Table 3-1)
CF clear if successful

Details: This function flushes all buffers and updates the directory entries for each file which has been modified; for remote files, it calls INT 2Fh Function 1107h.

The computer ID and process ID are stored but ignored under DOS 3.3.

This call is not supported by DR-DOS 3.41 and 5.0; it returns error code 01h.

See also: Network Redirector INT 2Fh Function 1107h (Chapter 9), MS-DOS Functions 0Dh and 68h (PCI-24)

INT 21h Function 5D02h
SHARE.EXE - CLOSE FILE BY NAME

DOS 3.1+ internal
Undocumented

Registers at call:
AX = 5D02h
DS:DX -> DOS parameter list (see Table 3-38), only
   fields DX, DS, computer ID, and process ID used
DPL's DS:DX -> ASCIZ name of file to close

Return Registers:
CF set on error
      AX = error code (see Table 3-1)
CF clear if successful

Details: This function returns an error unless SHARE is loaded, as it calls [SysFileTable-28h] (see Table 3-12).

The filename must be canonical and fully-qualified, such as returned by Function 60h.

This function is not supported by DR-DOS 3.41 and 5.0; they return error code 01h.

See also: Functions 5D03h, 5D04h, and 60h; MS-DOS Function 3Eh (PCI-24)

INT 21h Function 5D03h
SHARE.EXE - CLOSE ALL FILES FOR GIVEN COMPUTER

DOS 3.1+ internal
Undocumented

Registers at call:
AX = 5D03h
DS:DX -> DOS parameter list (see
   Table 3-38), only computer ID used

Return Registers:
CF set on error
      AX = error code (see Table 3-1)
CF clear if successful

Details: This function returns an error unless SHARE is loaded, as it calls [SysFileTable-30h] (see Table 3-12).

This function is not supported by DR-DOS 3.41 and 5.0; they return error code 01h.

See also: Functions 5D02h and 5D04h

INT 21h Function 5D04h
SHARE.EXE - CLOSE ALL FILES FOR GIVEN PROCESS

DOS 3.1+ internal
Undocumented

Registers at call:
AX = 5D04h
DS:DX -> DOS parameter list (see Table 3-38), only
   computer ID and process ID fields used

Return Registers:
CF set on error
      AX = error code (see Table 3-1)
CF clear if successful

Details: This function returns an error unless SHARE is loaded, as it calls [SysFileTable-2Ch] (see Table 3-12).

This function is not supported by DR-DOS 3.41 and 5.0; they return error code 01h.

See also: Functions 5D02h and 5D03h, Network Redirector INT 2Fh Function 111Dh (Chapter 9)

INT 21h Function 5D05h
SHARE.EXE - GET OPEN FILE LIST ENTRY

DOS 3.1+ internal
Undocumented

Registers at call:
AX = 5D05h
DS:DX -> DOS parameter list (see
   Table 3-38)
DPL's BX = index of sharing record
   (see Table 3-13)

DPL's CX = index of SFT in sharing
   record's SFT list

Return Registers:
CF clear if successful
        ES:DI -> ASCIZ filename
        BX = network machine number of SFT's owner
        CX = number of locks held by SFT's owner
CF set if either index out of range
        AX = 0012h (no more files)

Details: This function returns an error unless SHARE is loaded, as it calls [SysFileTable-18h] (see Table 3-12).

    Filenames are always canonical and fully-qualified, such as returned by Function 60h.

    This function is not supported by DR-DOS 3.41 and 5.0, but does not return an error.

See also: Functions 5Ch and 60h

INT 21h Function 5D06h
GET ADDRESS OF DOS SWAPPABLE DATA AREA
DOS 3.0+ internal
Undocumented

Registers at call:
AX = 5D06h

Return Registers:
CF set on error
        AX = error code (see Table 3-1)
CF clear if successful
        DS:SI -> nonreentrant data area (see Tables 3-39 and 3-41)
        CX = size in bytes of area which must be swapped while in DOS
        DX = size in bytes of area which must always be swapped

Details: The Critical Error flag is used in conjunction with the InDOS flag (see Tables 3-39 and 3-41, and Function 34h in PCI-24) to determine when it is safe to enter DOS from a TSR.

    Setting the Critical Error flag allows the use of Functions 50h and 51h from INT 28h under DOS 2.x by forcing use of the correct stack.

    Swapping the data area allows reentering DOS unless DOS is in a critical section delimited by INT 2Ah Function 80h and INT 2Ah Functions 81h or 82h.

    Under DOS 4.0, Function 5D0Bh should be used instead of this function.

    SHARE and other DOS utilities consult the byte at offset 04h in the DOS data segment (see INT 2Fh Function 1203h below) to determine the SDA format in use: 00h = DOS 3.x (Table 3-39), 01h = DOS 4.0-6.0 (Table 3-41), other = error.

    DR-DOS 3.41+ supports this function, but the SDA format beyond the first 18h bytes is completely different from MS-DOS.

See also: Function 5D0Bh; INT 2Ah Functions 80h, 81h, and 82h

3-39 Format of DOS 3.10-3.30 Swappable Data Area:

Offset	Size	Description
-31	BYTE	(DOS 3.30) current switch character
-28	BYTE	(DOS 3.30) incremented on each INT 21h Function 5E01h call
-27	16 BYTEs	(DOS 3.30) machine name set by INT 21h Function 5E01h
-11	5 WORDs	zero-terminated list of offsets which need to be patched to enable critical-section calls (see INT 2Ah Function 80h)
-1	BYTE	unused padding
---start of actual SDA---		
00h	BYTE	critical error flag ("ErrorMode")
01h	BYTE	InDOS flag (count of active INT 21h calls)
02h	BYTE	drive on which current critical error occurred, or FFh (DR-DOS sets to drive number during INT 24h, 00h otherwise)
03h	BYTE	locus of last error
04h	WORD	extended error code of last error
06h	BYTE	suggested action for last error

07h	BYTE	class of last error
08h	DWORD	ES:DI pointer for last error
0Ch	DWORD	current DTA
10h	WORD	current PSP
12h	WORD	stores SP across an INT 23h
14h	WORD	return code from last process termination (zeroed after reading with Function 4Dh)
16h	BYTE	current drive
17h	BYTE	extended break flag

---remainder need only be swapped if in DOS---

18h	WORD	value of AX on call to INT 21h
1Ah	WORD	PSP segment for sharing/network
1Ch	WORD	network machine number for sharing/network (0000h = us)
1Eh	WORD	first usable memory block found when allocating memory
20h	WORD	best usable memory block found when allocating memory
22h	WORD	last usable memory block found when allocating memory
24h	WORD	memory size in paragraphs (used only during initialization)
26h	WORD	last entry checked during directory search
28h	BYTE	flag: INT 24h returned Fail
29h	BYTE	flags: allowable INT 24h actions (passed to INT 24h in AH)
2Ah	BYTE	directory flag (00h directory, 01h file)
2Bh	BYTE	flag: FFh if Ctrl-Break termination, 00h otherwise
2Ch	BYTE	flag: allow embedded blanks in FCB
2Dh	BYTE	padding (unused)
2Eh	BYTE	day of month
2Fh	BYTE	month
30h	WORD	year - 1980
32h	WORD	number of days since 1-1-1980
34h	BYTE	day of week (0 = Sunday)
35h	BYTE	flag: console swapped during read from device
36h	BYTE	flag: safe to call INT 28h if nonzero
37h	BYTE	flag: if nonzero, INT 24h Abort turned into INT 24h Fail (set only during process termination)
38h	26 BYTEs	device driver request header (see Table 3-59)
52h	DWORD	pointer to device driver entry point (used in calling driver)
56h	22 BYTEs	device driver request header for I/O calls
6Ch	14 BYTEs	device driver request header for disk status check
7Ah	DWORD	*pointer to device I/O buffer*
7Eh	WORD	*unknown*
80h	WORD	*unknown*
82h	BYTE	type of PSP copy (00h=simple for INT 21h Function 26h, FFh=make child)
83h	BYTE	padding (unused)
84h	3 BYTEs	24-bit user number (see Function 30h, PCI-24)
87h	BYTE	OEM number (see Function 30h, PCI-24)
88h	WORD	offset to error code conversion table for INT 25/INT 26h
8Ah	6 BYTEs	CLOCK$ transfer record (see Table 3-23)
90h	BYTE	device I/O buffer for single-byte I/O functions
91h	BYTE	*padding* (unused)
92h	128 BYTEs	buffer for filename

INT 21h Function 5D06h

112h	128 BYTEs	buffer for filename
192h	21 BYTEs	findfirst/findnext search data block (see Table 3-62)
1A7h	32 BYTEs	directory entry for found file (see Table 3-63)
1C7h	81 BYTEs	copy of current directory structure for drive being accessed
218h	11 BYTEs	FCB-format filename for device name comparison
223h	BYTE	terminating NUL for above filename
224h	11 BYTEs	wildcard destination specification for rename (FCB format)
22Fh	BYTE	terminating NUL for above spec
230h	BYTE	*unknown*
231h	WORD	destination file/directory starting sector
233h	5 BYTEs	*unknown*
238h	BYTE	extended FCB file attribute
239h	BYTE	type of FCB (00h regular, FFh extended)
23Ah	BYTE	directory search attributes
23Bh	BYTE	file open/access mode
23Ch	BYTE	file found/delete flag
		bit 0: file found
		bit 4: file deleted
23Dh	BYTE	flag: device name found on rename, or file not found
23Eh	BYTE	splice flag (file name and directory name together)
23Fh	BYTE	flag indicating how DOS function was invoked
		(00h = direct INT 20/INT 21h, FFh = server call Function 5D00h)
240h	BYTE	sector position within cluster
241h	BYTE	flag: translate sector/cluster (00h no, 01h yes)
242h	BYTE	flag: 00h if read, 01h if write
243h	BYTE	current working drive number
244h	BYTE	cluster factor
245h	BYTE	flag: cluster split mode
246h	BYTE	line edit (Function 0Ah) insert mode flag (nonzero = on)
247h	BYTE	canonicalized filename referred to existing file/dir if FFh
248h	BYTE	volume ID flag
249h	BYTE	type of process termination (00h-03h) (see Function 4Dh in PCI-24)
24Ah	BYTE	file create flag (00h = no)
24Bh	BYTE	value with which to replace first byte of deleted file's name
		(normally E5h, but 00h as described under INT 21h Function 13h)
24Ch	DWORD	pointer to Drive Parameter Block for critical error invocation
		temp: used during process termination
250h	DWORD	pointer to stack frame containing user registers on INT 21h
254h	WORD	stores SP across INT 24h
256h	DWORD	pointer to DOS Drive Parameter Block for *unknown drive*
25Ah	WORD	saving partial cluster number
25Ch	WORD	temp: sector of work current cluster
25Eh	WORD	high part of cluster number (only low byte referenced)
260h	WORD	*temporary*
262h	BYTE	Media ID byte returned by Functions 1Bh and 1Ch
263h	BYTE	padding (unused)
264h	DWORD	pointer to device header
268h	DWORD	pointer to current SFT
26Ch	DWORD	pointer to current directory structure for drive being accessed

INT 21h Function 5D06h

270h	DWORD	pointer to caller's FCB
274h	WORD	number of SFT to which file being opened will refer
276h	WORD	temporary storage for file handle
278h	DWORD	pointer to a JFT entry in process handle table (see Table 3-57)
27Ch	WORD	offset in DOS DS of first filename argument
27Eh	WORD	offset in DOS DS of second filename argument
280h	WORD	offset of last component in pathname or FFFFh
282h	WORD	offset of transfer address to add
284h	WORD	last relative cluster within file being accessed
286h	WORD	temp: absolute cluster number being accessed
288h	WORD	directory sector number
28Ah	WORD	*current cluster number*
28Ch	WORD	*current offset in file DIV bytes per sector*
28Eh	WORD	current sector number
290h	WORD	current byte offset within sector
292h	DWORD	current offset in file
296h	DWORD	temp: file byte count
29Ah	WORD	temp: file byte count
29Ch	WORD	free file cluster entry
29Eh	WORD	last file cluster entry
2A0h	WORD	next file cluster number
2A2h	DWORD	number of bytes appended to file
2A6h	DWORD	pointer to current work disk buffer
2AAh	DWORD	pointer to working SFT
2AEh	WORD	used by INT 21h dispatcher to store caller's BX
2B0h	WORD	used by INT 21h dispatcher to store caller's DS
2B2h	WORD	temporary storage while saving/restoring caller's registers
2B4h	DWORD	pointer to prev call frame (offset 250h) if INT 21h reentered also switched to for duration of INT 24h
2B8h	21 BYTEs	FindFirst search data for source file(s) of a rename operation (see Table 3-62)
2CDh	32 BYTEs	directory entry for file being renamed (see Table 3-63)
2EDh	331 BYTEs	critical error stack
403h	35 BYTEs	scratch SFT
438h	384 BYTEs	disk stack (functions greater than 0Ch, INT 25h, INT 26h)
5B8h	384 BYTEs	character I/O stack (functions 01h through 0Ch)
---DOS 3.2,3.3x only---		
738h	BYTE	device driver lookahead flag (usually printer) (see Function 64h in PCI-24)
739h	BYTE	volume change flag
73Ah	BYTE	flag: virtual open
73Bh	BYTE	*unknown*

INT 21h Function 5D07h   *DOS 3.1+ network*
GET REDIRECTED PRINTER MODE   *Undocumented*

Registers at call: Return Registers:
AX = 5D07h   DL = mode
                                         00h redirected output is combined
                                         01h redirected output in separate print jobs

See also: Functions 5D08h and 5D09h, Network Redirector INT 2Fh Function 1125h (Chapter 9)

INT 21h Function 5D08h
SET REDIRECTED PRINTER MODE
DOS 3.1+ network
Undocumented

Registers at call: Return Registers:
AX = 5D08h   none
DL = mode
    00h redirected output is combined
    01h redirected output placed in separate jobs, start new print job now
See also: Functions 5D07h and 5D09h, Network Redirector INT 2Fh Function 1125h (Chapter 9)

INT 21h Function 5D09h
FLUSH REDIRECTED PRINTER OUTPUT
DOS 3.1+ network
Undocumented

Registers at call: Return Registers:
AX = 5D09h   none
Details: This call forces redirected printer output to be printed, and starts a new print job.
    This function is also supported by 10Net, which calls it Terminate All Spool Jobs, and does not flush output if in "combine" mode.
See also: Functions 5D07h and 5D08h, Network Redirector INT 2Fh Function 1125h (Chapter 9)

INT 21h Function 5D0Ah
SET EXTENDED ERROR INFORMATION
DOS 3.1+

Registers at call: Return Registers:
AX = 5D0Ah   nothing. The next call to Function 59h will return
DS:DX -> 11-word DOS parameter   values from fields AX,BX,CX, DX,DI, and ES in the
  list (see Table 3-38)   corresponding registers (see Tables 3-1 and 3-50 to
                                                 3-52).

Details: This function was undocumented prior to the release of MS-DOS 5.0. The *MS-DOS Programmer's Reference* incorrectly states that this call was introduced in DOS 4, and fails to mention that the ERROR structure passed to this function is a DOS parameter list.
    BUG: DR-DOS 3.41 and 5.0 read the value for ES from the DS field of the DPL; fortunately, MS-DOS ignores the DS field, allowing a generic routine which sets both DS and ES fields to the same value.
See also: Function 59h (PCI-24)

INT 21h Function 5D0Bh
GET DOS SWAPPABLE DATA AREAS
DOS 4.x only internal
Undocumented

Registers at call: Return Registers:
AX = 5D0Bh   CF set on error
                                                 AX = error code (see Table 3-1)
                                             CF clear if successful
                                                 DS:SI -> swappable data area list (see Table 3-40)
Details: Copying and restoring the swappable data areas allows DOS to be reentered unless it is in a critical section delimited by calls to INT 2Ah Function 80h and INT 2Ah Functions 81h or 82h.
    SHARE and other DOS utilities consult the byte at offset 04h in the DOS data segment (see INT 2Fh Function 1203h below) to determine the SDA format in use: 00h = DOS 3.x (Table 3-39), 01h = DOS 4.0-6.0 (Table 3-41), other = error.
    DOS 5+ use the SDA format listed below, but revert back to the DOS 3.x call for finding the SDA (see Function 5D06h).
See also: Function 5D06h; INT 2Ah Functions 80h, 81h, and 82h; INT 2Fh Function 1203h (below)

3-40 Format of DOS 4.x swappable data area list:

Offset	Size	Description
00h	WORD	count of data areas
02h	N BYTEs	"count" copies of data area record

Offset	Size	Description
00h	DWORD	address
04h	WORD	length and type
		bit 15 set if swap always, clear if swap in DOS
		bits 14-0: length in bytes

3-41 Format of DOS 4.0-6.0 swappable data area:

Offset	Size	Description
-31	BYTE	current switch character (ignored by DOS 5+)
-28	BYTE	incremented on each INT 21h Function 5E01h call
-27	16 BYTEs	machine name set by INT 21h Function 5E01h
-11	5 WORDs	zero-terminated list of offsets which need to be patched to enable critical-section calls (see INT 2Ah Function 80h) (all offsets are 0D0Ch, but this list is still present for DOS 3.x compatibility)
-1	BYTE	unused padding

---start of actual SDA---

Offset	Size	Description
00h	BYTE	critical error flag ("ErrorMode")
01h	BYTE	InDOS flag (count of active INT 21h calls)
02h	BYTE	drive on which current critical error occurred or FFh
03h	BYTE	locus of last error
04h	WORD	extended error code of last error
06h	BYTE	suggested action for last error
07h	BYTE	class of last error
08h	DWORD	ES:DI pointer for last error
0Ch	DWORD	current DTA
10h	WORD	current PSP
12h	WORD	stores SP across an INT 23h
14h	WORD	return code from last process termination (cleared after reading with Function 4Dh)
16h	BYTE	current drive
17h	BYTE	extended break flag
18h	BYTE	flag: code page switching
19h	BYTE	flag: copy of previous byte in case of INT 24h Abort

---remainder need only be swapped if in DOS---

Offset	Size	Description
1Ah	WORD	value of AX on call to INT 21h
1Ch	WORD	PSP segment for sharing/network
1Eh	WORD	network machine number for sharing/network (0000h = us)
20h	WORD	first usable memory block found when allocating memory
22h	WORD	best usable memory block found when allocating memory
24h	WORD	last usable memory block found when allocating memory
26h	WORD	memory size in paragraphs (used only during initialization)
28h	WORD	last entry checked during directory search
2Ah	BYTE	flag: nonzero if INT 24h Fail
2Bh	BYTE	flags: allowable INT 24h responses (passed to INT 24h in AH)
2Ch	BYTE	flag: do not set directory if nonzero

INT 21h Function 5D0Bh

2Dh	BYTE	flag: program aborted by ^C
2Eh	BYTE	flag: allow embedded blanks in FCB
2Fh	BYTE	padding (unused)
30h	BYTE	day of month
31h	BYTE	month
32h	WORD	year - 1980
34h	WORD	number of days since 1-1-1980
36h	BYTE	day of week (0 = Sunday)
37h	BYTE	flag: console swapped during read from device
38h	BYTE	flag: safe to call INT 28h if nonzero
39h	BYTE	flag: abort currently in progress, turn INT 24h Abort into Fail
3Ah	30 BYTEs	device driver request header (see Table 3-59) for device calls
58h	DWORD	pointer to device driver entry point (used in calling driver)
5Ch	22 BYTEs	device driver request header for I/O calls
72h	14 BYTEs	device driver request header for disk status check
80h	DWORD	pointer to device I/O buffer
84h	WORD	*unknown*
86h	WORD	*unknown* (0)
88h	BYTE	type of PSP copy (00h=simple for INT 21h Function 26h, FFh=make child)
89h	DWORD	start offset of file region to lock/unlock
8Dh	DWORD	length of file region to lock/unlock
91h	BYTE	padding (unused)
92h	3 BYTEs	24-bit user number (see Function 30h, PCI-24)
95h	BYTE	OEM number (see Function 30h, PCI-24)
96h	6 BYTEs	CLOCK$ transfer record (see Table 3-23)
9Ch	BYTE	*device I/O buffer for single-byte I/O functions*
9Dh	BYTE	*padding*
9Eh	128 BYTEs	buffer for filename
11Eh	128 BYTEs	buffer for filename
19Eh	21 BYTEs	findfirst/findnext search data block (see Table 3-62)
1B3h	32 BYTEs	directory entry for found file (see Table 3-63)
1D3h	88 BYTEs	copy of current directory structure for drive being accessed
22Bh	11 BYTEs	FCB-format filename for device name comparison
236h	BYTE	terminating NUL for above filename
237h	11 BYTEs	wildcard destination specification for rename (FCB format)
242h	BYTE	terminating NUL for above spec
243h	BYTE	*unknown*
244h	WORD	*unknown*
246h	5 BYTEs	*unknown*
24Bh	BYTE	extended FCB file attributes
24Ch	BYTE	type of FCB (00h regular, FFh extended)
24Dh	BYTE	directory search attributes
24Eh	BYTE	file open/access mode
24Fh	BYTE	*unknown* flag bits
250h	BYTE	flag: device name found on rename, or file not found
251h	BYTE	*splice flag* (file name and directory name together)
252h	BYTE	flag indicating how DOS function was invoked (00h = direct INT 20/INT 21h, FFh = server call Function 5D00h)

INT 21h Function 5D0Bh

253h	BYTE	*unknown*
254h	BYTE	*unknown*
255h	BYTE	*unknown*
256h	BYTE	*unknown*
257h	BYTE	*unknown*
258h	BYTE	*unknown*
259h	BYTE	*unknown*
25Ah	BYTE	canonicalized filename referred to existing file/dir if FFh
25Bh	BYTE	*unknown*
25Ch	BYTE	type of process termination (00h-03h)
25Dh	BYTE	*unknown*
25Eh	BYTE	*unknown*
25Fh	BYTE	*unknown*
260h	DWORD	pointer to Drive Parameter Block for critical error invocation
264h	DWORD	pointer to stack frame containing user registers on INT 21h
268h	WORD	*stores SP*
26Ah	DWORD	pointer to DOS Drive Parameter Block for *unknown drive*
26Eh	WORD	segment of disk buffer
270h	WORD	*unknown*
272h	WORD	*unknown*
274h	WORD	*unknown*
276h	WORD	*unknown*
278h	BYTE	Media ID byte returned by Functions 1Bh and 1Ch
279h	BYTE	*unknown* (apparently not referenced, may be padding)
27Ah	DWORD	pointer to *unknown item*
27Eh	DWORD	pointer to current SFT
282h	DWORD	pointer to current directory structure for drive being accessed
286h	DWORD	pointer to caller's FCB
28Ah	WORD	SFT index to which file being opened will refer
28Ch	WORD	temporary storage for file handle
28Eh	DWORD	pointer to a JFT entry in process handle table (see Table 3-57)
292h	WORD	offset in DOS DS of first filename argument
294h	WORD	offset in DOS DS of second filename argument
296h	WORD	*unknown*
298h	WORD	*unknown*
29Ah	WORD	*unknown*
29Ch	WORD	*unknown*
29Eh	WORD	*unknown*
2A0h	WORD	*unknown*
2A2h	WORD	*directory cluster number*
2A4h	DWORD	*unknown*
2A8h	DWORD	*unknown*
2ACh	WORD	*unknown*
2AEh	DWORD	*offset in file*
2B2h	WORD	*unknown*
2B4h	WORD	bytes in partial sector
2B6h	WORD	number of sectors
2B8h	WORD	*unknown*
2BAh	WORD	*unknown*

2BCh	WORD	*unknown*
2BEh	DWORD	number of bytes appended to file
2C2h	DWORD	pointer to *unknown* disk buffer
2C6h	DWORD	pointer to *unknown* SFT
2CAh	WORD	used by INT 21h dispatcher to store caller's BX
2CCh	WORD	used by INT 21h dispatcher to store caller's DS
2CEh	WORD	temporary storage while saving/restoring caller's registers
2D0h	DWORD	pointer to prev call frame (offset 264h) if INT 21h reentered
		also switched to for duration of INT 24h
2D4h	WORD	open mode/action for INT 21h Function 6C00h
2D6h	BYTE	*unknown* (set to 00h by INT 21h dispatcher, 02h when a read is
		performed, and 01h or 03h by INT 21h Function 6C00h)
2D7h	WORD	*apparently unused*
2D9h	DWORD	stored ES:DI for Function 6C00h
2DDh	WORD	extended file open action code (see Function 6C00h in PCI-24)
2DFh	WORD	extended file open attributes (see Function 6C00h)
2E1h	WORD	extended file open file mode (see Function 6C00h)
2E3h	DWORD	pointer to filename to open (see Function 6C00h)
2E7h	WORD	*unknown*
2E9h	WORD	*unknown*
2EBh	BYTE	*unknown*
2ECh	WORD	stores DS during call to [List-of-Lists + 37h]
2EEh	WORD	*unknown*
2F0h	BYTE	*unknown*
2F1h	WORD	*unknown* bit flags
2F3h	DWORD	pointer to user-supplied filename
2F7h	DWORD	pointer to *unknown item*
2FBh	WORD	stores SS during call to [List-of-Lists + 37h]
2FDh	WORD	stores SP during call to [List-of-Lists + 37h]
2FFh	BYTE	flag, nonzero if stack switched in calling [List-of-Lists+37h]
300h	21 BYTEs	FindFirst search data for source file(s) of a rename operation (see Table 3-62)
315h	32 BYTEs	directory entry for file being renamed (see Table 3-63)
335h	331 BYTEs	critical error stack
480h	384 BYTEs	disk stack (functions greater than 0Ch, INT 25h, INT 26h)
600h	384 BYTEs	character I/O stack (functions 01h through 0Ch)
780h	BYTE	device driver lookahead flag (usually printer) (see Function 64h in PCI-24)
781h	BYTE	volume change flag
782h	BYTE	flag: virtual open
783h	BYTE	*unknown*
784h	WORD	*unknown*
786h	WORD	*unknown*
788h	WORD	*unknown*
78Ah	WORD	*unknown*

INT 21h Function 5E00h   *DOS 3.1+ network*
GET MACHINE NAME

Registers at call: **Return Registers:**
AX = 5E00h   CF clear if successful
DS:DX -> 16-byte buffer for ASCIZ   CH = validity
  machine name   00h name invalid

nonzero valid
          CL = NetBIOS number for machine name
          DS:DX buffer filled with blank-paded name
    CF set on error
        AX = error code (01h) (see Table 3-1)

Details: This function is supported by the OS/2 v1.3+ compatibility box and PC-NFS.
Conflicts: 10NET (Chapter 27)
See also: Function 5E01h

INT 21h Function 5E01h   *DOS 3.1+ network*
SET MACHINE NAME

Registers at call: **Return Registers:**
AX = 5E01h   none
CH = operation
    00h undefine name (make it invalid)
    nonzero define name
CL = name number
DS:DX -> 15-character blank-padded
ASCIZ name
Conflicts: 10NET (Chapter 27)
See also: Function 5E00h

INT 21h Function 5E02h   *DOS 3.1+ network*
SET NETWORK PRINTER SETUP STRING

Registers at call: **Return Registers:**
AX = 5E02h   CF clear if successful
BX = redirection list index (see Function 5F02h)   CF set on error
CX = length of setup string   AX = error code (01h) (see Table 3-1)
DS:SI -> setup string
Details: This function is also supported by 10NET v5.0.
See also: Function 5E03h, Network Redirector INT 2Fh Function 111Fh (Chapter 9)

INT 21h Function 5E03h   *DOS 3.1+ network*
GET NETWORK PRINTER SETUP STRING

Registers at call: **Return Registers:**
AX = 5E03h   CF clear if successful
BX = redirection list index (see Function 5F02h)   CX = length of setup string
ES:DI -> 64-byte buffer for setup string   ES:DI buffer filled
                                       CF set on error
                                       AX = error code (01h) (see Table 3-1)

Details: This function is also supported by 10NET v5.0, but 10NET is documented as using DS:SI instead of ES:DI.
See also: Function 5E02h, Network Redirector INT 2Fh Function 111Fh (Chapter 9)

INT 21h Function 5E04h   *DOS 3.1+ network*
SET PRINTER MODE

Registers at call: **Return Registers:**
AX = 5E04h   CF set on error
BX = redirection list index (see Function 5F02h)   AX = error code (see Table 3-1)
DX = mode   CF clear if successful
    bit 0: set if binary, clear if text (tabs expanded to blanks)
Details: This function calls INT 2Fh Function 111Fh with 5E04h on top of the stack.
Conflicts: 10NET (Chapter 27)

See also: Function 5E05h, Network Redirector INT 2Fh Function 111Fh (Chapter 9)

INT 21h Function 5E05h
GET PRINTER MODE
DOS 3.1+ network

Registers at call:
AX = 5E05h
BX = redirection list index (see
    Function 5F02h)

Return Registers:
CF set on error
    AX = error code (see Table 3-1)
CF clear if successful
    DX = printer mode
        bit 0: set if binary, clear if text (tabs expanded to blanks)

Details: This function calls INT 2Fh Function 111Fh with 5E05h on top of the stack.
Conflicts: 10NET (Chapter 27)
See also: Function 5E04h, Network Redirector INT 2Fh Function 111Fh (Chapter 9)

INT 21h Function 5F00h
GET REDIRECTION MODE
DOS 3.1+ network

Registers at call:
AX = 5F00h
BL = redirection type
    03h printer
    04h disk drive

Return Registers:
CF set on error
    AX = error code (see Table 3-1)
CF clear if successful
    BH = redirection state (00h off, 01h on)

Details: This function calls INT 2Fh Function 111Eh with 5F00h on top of the stack.
See also: Function 5F01h, Network Redirector INT 2Fh Function 111Eh (Chapter 9)

INT 21h Function 5F01h
SET REDIRECTION MODE
DOS 3.1+ network

Registers at call:
AX = 5F01h
BL = redirection type
    03h printer
    04h disk drive
BH = redirection state (00h off, 01h on)

Return Registers:
CF set on error
    AX = error code (see Table 3-1)
CF clear if successful

Details: When redirection is off, the local device (if any) rather than the remote device is used.
    This function calls INT 2Fh Function 111Eh with 5F01h on top of the stack.
See also: Function 5F00h, Network Redirector INT 2Fh Function 111Eh (Chapter 9)

INT 21h Function 5F02h
GET REDIRECTION LIST ENTRY
DOS 3.1+ network

Registers at call:
AX = 5F02h
BX = zero-based redirection list index
CX = 0000h (LANtastic)
DS:SI -> 16-byte buffer for ASCIZ
    local device name
ES:DI -> 128-byte buffer for ASCIZ
    network name

Return Registers:
CF clear if successful
    BH = device status (00h valid, 01h invalid)
    BL = device type
        03h printer
        04h disk drive
    CX = user data previously set with Function 5F03h
    DS:SI and ES:DI buffers filled
    DX,BP destroyed
CF set on error
    AX = error code (01h,12h) (see Table 3-1)

Details: This function is passed through to INT 2Fh Function 111Eh by the DOS kernel, with 5F02h on top of the stack.
    Error code 12h is returned if BX is greater than the size of the list.
    This function is also supported by Banyan VINES, PC-NFS, LANtastic, and 10NET.

See also: Function 5F03h, Network Redirector INT 2Fh Function 111Eh (Chapter 9)

INT 21h Function 5F03h   *DOS 3.1+ network*
REDIRECT DEVICE
Registers at call: **Return Registers:**
AX = 5F03h   CF clear if successful
BL = device type   CF set on error
   03h printer   AX = error code (01h,03h,05h,08h,0Fh,12h) (see Table 3-1)
   04h disk drive
CX = user data to save
   0000h for LANtastic
   4E57h ("NW") for NetWare 4.0 requester
DS:SI -> ASCIZ local device name (16 bytes max)
ES:DI -> ASCIZ network name + ASCIZ password (128 bytes max total)
Details: If the device is a disk drive, DS:SI must point at either a null string or a string consisting the drive letter followed by a colon; if a null string, the network attempts to access the destination without redirecting a local drive.

    The DOS kernel calls INT 2Fh Function 111Eh with 5F03h on top of the stack.

    This function is also supported by Banyan VINES, LANtastic, and 10NET.

See also: Functions 5F02h and 5F04h, Network Redirector INT 2Fh Function 111Eh (Chapter 9)

INT 21h Function 5F04h   *DOS 3.1+ network*
CANCEL REDIRECTION
Registers at call: **Return Registers:**
AX = 5F04h   CF clear if successful
DS:SI -> ASCIZ local device   CF set on error
   name or path   AX = error code (01h,03h,05h,08h,0Fh,12h) (see Table 3-1)
CX = 4E57h ("NW") for NetWare 4.0 requester
Details: The DS:SI string must be either a local device name, a drive letter followed by a colon, or a network directory beginning with two backslashes.

    The DOS kernel calls INT 2Fh Function 111Eh with 5F04h on top of the stack.

    This function is also supported by Banyan VINES, LANtastic, and 10NET.

See also: Function 5F03h, Network Redirector INT 2Fh Function 111Eh (Chapter 9)

INT 21h Function 5F05h   *DOS 4+ network*
GET EXTENDED REDIRECTION LIST ENTRY
Registers at call: **Return Registers:**
AX = 5F05h   CF set on error
BX = redirection list index   AX = error code (see Table 3-1)
DS:SI -> buffer for ASCIZ   CF clear if successful
   source device name   AX = server's network process ID handle (10NET)
ES:DI -> buffer for destination   BH = device status flag (bit 0 clear if valid)
   ASCIZ network path   BL = device type (03h if printer, 04h if drive)
                              CX = stored parameter value (user data) from Function 5F03h
                              BP = NETBIOS local session number
                              DS:SI buffer filled
                              ES:DI buffer filled
Details: The local session number (LSN) allows sharing the redirector's session number. However, if an error is caused on the NETBIOS LSN, the redirector may be unable to correctly recover from errors.

    The DOS kernel calls INT 2Fh Function 111Eh with 5F05h on top of the stack.

    This function is also supported by DR-DOS 5.0 and 10NET v5.0.

Conflicts: Embedded DOS (Chapter 42)
See also: Function 5F06h, Network Redirector INT 2Fh Function 111Eh (Chapter 9)

INT 21h Function 5F06h
Network
GET FULL REDIRECTION LIST
Undocumented

Registers at call: **Return Registers:**
AX = 5F06h   *unknown*
others, if any, unknown

Details: This function is similar to Functions 5F02h and 5F05h, but also returns redirections excluded from those calls for various reasons.

The DOS kernel simply calls INT 2Fh Function 111Eh with 5F06h on top of the stack.

Conflicts: Embedded DOS (Chapter 42)
See also: Function 5F05h, Network Redirector INT 2Fh Function 111Eh (Chapter 9)

INT 21h Function 5F07h
DOS 5+
ENABLE DRIVE

Registers at call: **Return Registers:**
AX = 5F07h   CF clear if successful
DL = drive number (0=A:)   CF set on error
                                             AX = error code (0Fh) (see Table 3-1)

Details: This function simply sets the "valid" bit in the drive's CDS.

Conflicts: Embedded DOS (Chapter 42)
See also: Functions 52h and 5F08h

INT 21h Function 5F08h
DOS 5+
DISABLE DRIVE

Registers at call: **Return Registers:**
AX = 5F08h   CF clear if successful
DL = drive number (0=A:)   CF set on error
                                             AX = error code (0Fh) (see Table 3-1)

Details: This function simply clears the "valid" bit in the drive's CDS.

Conflicts: Embedded DOS (Chapter 42)
See also: Functions 52h and 5F07h

INT 21h Function 60h
DOS 3.0+
"TRUENAME" - CANONICALIZE FILENAME OR PATH

Purpose: Determine the canonical name of the specified filename or path, corresponding to the undocumented TRUENAME command in COMMAND.COM.

Registers at call: **Return Registers:**
AH = 60h   CF set on error
DS:SI -> ASCIZ filename   AX = error code
  or path   02h invalid component in directory path or drive letter only
ES:DI -> 128-byte buffer   03h malformed path or invalid drive letter
  for canonicalized name   ES:DI buffer unchanged
                                CF clear if successful
                                  AH = 00h
                                  AL = destroyed (00h or 5Ch or last character of current directory
                                  on drive)
                                  buffer filled with qualified name of form D:\PATH\FILE.EXT or
                                  \\MACHINE\PATH\FILE.EXT

Details: The input path need not actually exist.

Letters are uppercased, forward slashes converted to backslashes, asterisks converted to appropriate number of question marks, and file and directory names are truncated to 8.3 if necessary. (DR-DOS 3.41 and 5.0 do not expand asterisks).

'.' and '..' in the path are resolved.

Filespecs on local drives always start with "d:", those on network drives always start with "\\".

If path string is on a JOINed drive, the returned name is the one that would be needed if the drive were not JOINed; similarly for a SUBSTed, ASSIGNed, or network drive letter. Because of this, it is possible to get a qualified name that is not legal under the current combination of SUB-STs, ASSIGNs, JOINs, and network redirections.

Under DOS 3.3 through 6.00, a device name is translated differently if the device name does not have an explicit directory or the directory is \DEV (relative directory DEV from the root directory works correctly). In these cases, the returned string consists of the unchanged device name and extension appended to the string X:/ (forward slash instead of backward slash as in all other cases) where X is the default or explicit drive letter.

Functions which take pathnames require canonical paths if invoked via INT 21h Function 5D00h.

This function is supported by the OS/2 v1.1 compatibility box.

NetWare 2.1x does not support characters with the high bit set; early versions of NetWare 386 support such characters except in this call. In addition, NetWare returns error code 3 for the path "X:\"; one should use "X:\." instead.

For DOS 3.3-6.0, the input and output buffers may be the same, as the canonicalized name is built in an internal buffer and copied to the specified output buffer as the very last step.

For DR DOS 6.0, this function is not automatically called when on a network. Device drivers reportedly cannot make this call from their INIT function. Using the same pointer for both input and output buffers is not supported in the April 1992 and earlier versions of DR DOS.

See also: INT 2Fh Function 1221h, LANtastic Function 5FB3h (Chapter 20), Network Redirector INT 2Fh Function 1123h (Chapter 9)

INT 2Ah Function 00h   *Network*
INSTALLATION CHECK

Registers at call: **Return Registers:**
AH = 00h   AH nonzero if installed
                                    CF set if NetWare v2.15 NetBIOS emulator installed

Details: This function is also supported by Lantastic, NetWare, 10NET, etc.
Conflicts: AT&T Starlan (Chapter 8)
See also: AT&T Starlan Function 0000h (Chapter 8), NetBIOS INT 5Ch (Chapter 8)

INT 2Ah Function 0300h   *Network*
CHECK DIRECT I/O

Registers at call: **Return Registers:**
AX = 0300h   CF clear if direct physical addressing (INT 13h, INT
DS:SI -> ASCIZ device name (may be   25h) permissible
  full path or only drive specifier— CF set if access via files only
  must include the colon)

Details: Do not use direct disk accesses if this function returns CF set or the device is redirected (INT 21h Function 5F02h).

This function may take some time to execute. It is called by the DOS kernel on INT 25h and INT 26h.

This function is also supported by Lantastic, NetWare, 10NET, etc.
See also: INT 21h Function 5F02h, INT 13h (PCI-10), INT 25h (PCI-24), INT 26h (PCI-24)

INT 2Ah Function 06h
NETWORK PRINT-STREAM CONTROL
NETBIOS, LANtastic

Registers at call:
AH = 06h
AL = new mode
    01h set concatenation mode (all printer output put in
      one job)
    02h set truncation mode (default); printer open/close starts new print job
    03h flush printer output and start new print job

Return Registers:
CF set on error
  AX = error code
CF clear if successful

Details: Subfunction 03h is equivalent to Ctrl/Alt/keypad-*.
    This function is also supported by LANtastic, NetWare, 10NET, etc., but LANtastic v4.x no longer supports this call.
See also: INT 21h Functions 5D08h and 5D09h, Network Redirector INT 2Fh Function 1125h (Chapter 9)

INT 2Ah Function 80h
BEGIN DOS CRITICAL SECTION
NETWORK
Undocumented Callout

Registers at call:
AH = 80h
AL = critical section number (00h-0Fh)
    01h DOS kernel, SHARE.EXE, DOSMGR
        apparently for maintaining the integrity of DOS/SHARE/NET data structures
    02h DOS kernel, DOSMGR
        ensures that no multitasking occurs while DOS is calling an installable device driver
    05h network redirector
    06h DOS 4.x only IFSFUNC
    08h ASSIGN.COM
    0Ah MSCDEX
    0Fh IBM PC LAN server (while intercepting INT 10h Functions 06h,07h,0Eh)

Return Registers:
none

Details: This function is normally hooked to avoid interrupting a critical section, rather than called. The handler should ensure that none of the critical sections are reentered, usually by suspending a task which attempts to reenter an active critical section.
    The DOS kernel does not invoke critical sections 01h and 02h unless it is patched. DOS 3.1+ contains a zero-terminated list of words beginning at offset -11 from the Swappable Data Area (see Table 3-39); each word contains the offset within the DOS data segment of a byte which must be changed from C3h (RET) to 50h (POP AX) under DOS 3.x or from 00h to a nonzero value under DOS 4+ to enable use of critical sections. For DOS 4.0-6.0, all words in this list point at the byte at offset 0D0Ch.
See also: Functions 81h, 82h, and 8700h; INT 21h Functions 5D06h and 5D0Bh

INT 2Ah Function 81h
END DOS CRITICAL SECTION
NETWORK
Undocumented Callout

Registers at call:
AH = 81h
AL = critical section number (00h-0Fh) (see Function 80h)

Return Registers:
none

Details: This function is normally hooked rather than called. The handler should reawaken any tasks which were suspended due to an attempt to enter the specified critical section.
See also: Functions 80h, 82h, and 8700h

INT 2Ah Function 82h
END DOS CRITICAL SECTIONS 0 THROUGH 7
NETWORK
Undocumented Callout

Registers at call:
AH = 82h

Return Registers:

Details: This function is called by DOS's INT 21h function dispatcher for function 00h and functions greater than 0Ch (except 59h), and on process termination. The handler should reawaken any tasks which were suspended due to an attempt to enter one of the critical sections 0 through 7.
See also: Function 81h

INT 2Ah Function 84h   *NETWORK*
KEYBOARD BUSY LOOP   *Undocumented Callout*

Registers at call:	Return Registers:
AH = 84h	none

Details: This function is similar to DOS's INT 28h, and is called from inside the DOS keyboard input loop (i.e. INT 21h Functions 07h or 08h, PCI-24) to allow the network software to process requests.
See also: INT 28h (PCI-24)

INT 2Ah Function 8700h   *PRINT*
BEGIN BACKGROUND PRINTING   *Undocumented Callout*

Purpose: This call is used to inform interested programs that PRINT is about to start its background processing, and allow those programs to postpone the processing if necessary.

Registers at call:	Return Registers:
AX = 8700h	CF clear if OK to print in background now
CF clear	CF set if background printing not allowed at this time

Details: When PRINT gains control and wants to begin printing, it calls this function. If CF is clear on return, PRINT begins its background processing, and calls Function 8701h when it is done. If CF is set on return, PRINT will relinquish control immediately, and will not call Function 8701h.

PCVENUS (an early network shell by IBM and CMU) hooks this call to prevent background printing while its own code is active.
See also: Functions 80h, 81h, and 8701h

INT 2Ah Function 8701h   *PRINT*
END BACKGROUND PRINTING   *Undocumented Callout*

Purpose: This call is used to inform interested programs that PRINT has completed its background processing.

Registers at call:	Return Registers:
AX = 8701h	none

Details: This function is called by PRINT after it has performed some background printing; it is not called if Function 8700h returned with CF set.
See also: Function 8700h

Internal Network Support Functions

The functions in this section provide support for any network redirectors which may be loaded, as well as other add-on modules to the kernel such as SHARE and NLSFUNC. Most of the INT 2Fh Function 12xxh calls may only be invoked while a DOS function call is already in progress, and are thus of limited use to most applications.

INT 2Fh Function 0500h   *DOS 3+ CRITICAL ERROR HANDLER*
INSTALLATION CHECK   *Undocumented Callout*

Purpose: Determine whether a critical error message override is installed.

Registers at call:	Return Registers:
AX = 0500h	AL = status
	00h not installed, OK to install
	01h not installed, can't install
	FFh installed

See also: Function 05h below, INT 24h (Chapter 24)

INT 2Fh Function 05h
EXPAND ERROR INTO STRING

DOS 3+ CRITICAL ERROR HANDLER
Undocumented Callout

Registers at call:
AH = 05h
---DOS 3.x---
AL = extended error code (nonzero)
---DOS 4+ ---
AL = error type
   01h DOS extended error code
   02h parameter error
BX = error code

Return Registers:
CF clear if successful
   ES:DI -> ASCIZ error message (read-only)
  AL = completion state
     00h message requires completion with device
      name, drive, etc.
     01h message is complete as returned
CF set if error code can't be converted to string
  AX,DI,ES destroyed
other flags corrupted

Details: This function is called at the start of COMMAND.COM's default critical error handler if installed by a user program, allowing partial or complete overriding of the default error messages.

    Subfunction 02h is called by many DOS 4 external programs.

    DR-DOS's COMMAND.COM appends additional information ("0 files copied") to the returned string.

See also: Functions 0500h and 122Eh, INT 24h (PCI-24)

INT 2Fh Functions 11xxh
NETWORK REDIRECTOR INTERFACE—see Chapter 9

DOS 3+ internal
Undocumented Callout

Details: The DOS kernel calls these functions to perform various operations on drives it recognizes as network drives rather than local drives.

INT 2Fh Function 1200h
INSTALLATION CHECK

DOS 3+ internal
Undocumented

Registers at call:
AX = 1200h

Return Registers:
AL = FFh (for compatibility with other INT 2Fh functions)

INT 2Fh Function 1201h
CLOSE CURRENT FILE

DOS 3+ internal
Undocumented

Registers at call:
AX = 1201h
SS = DOS DS (must be using a DOS internal stack)
SDA current SFT pointer -> SFT of file to close

Return Registers:
CF set on error
CX new reference count of SFT
ES:DI -> SFT for file
BX may return a value

Details: See Tables 3-39 and 3-41 for the format of the SDA (Swappable Data Area), and Tables 3-15 through 3-18 for the SFT (System File Table) format.

See also: Function 1227h, Network Redirector Function 1106h (Chapter 9), MS-DOS INT 21h Function 3Eh (PCI-24)

INT 2Fh Function 1202h
GET INTERRUPT ADDRESS

DOS 3+ internal
Undocumented

Registers at call:
AX = 1202h
STACK: WORD vector number

Return Registers:
ES:BX -> interrupt vector
STACK unchanged

INT 2Fh Function 1203h
GET DOS DATA SEGMENT

DOS 3+ internal
Undocumented

Registers at call:
AX = 1203h

Return Registers:
DS = data segment of IBMDOS.COM/MSDOS.SYS

Details: For DOS prior to version 5.0, the data segment is the same as the code segment.

INT 2Fh Function 1204h
NORMALIZE PATH SEPARATOR
DOS 3+ internal
Undocumented

Registers at call:
AX = 1204h
STACK: WORD   character to normalize

Return Registers:
AL = normalized character (forward slash turned to backslash, all others unchanged)
ZF set if path separator
STACK unchanged

INT 2Fh Function 1205h
OUTPUT CHARACTER TO STANDARD OUTPUT
DOS 3+ internal
Undocumented

Registers at call:
AX = 1205h
STACK: WORD character to output

Return Registers:
STACK unchanged

Details: This function can only be called from within DOS, such as from a network redirector which has been called by the DOS kernel.

INT 2Fh Function 1206h
INVOKE CRITICAL ERROR
DOS 3+ internal
Undocumented

Registers at call:
AX = 1206h
DI = error code
BP:SI -> device driver header
SS = DOS DS (must be using a DOS internal stack)
STACK: WORD value to be passed to INT 24h in AX

Return Registers:
AL = 0-3 for Abort, Retry, Ignore, Fail
STACK unchanged

See also: INT 24h

INT 2Fh Function 1207h
MAKE DISK BUFFER MOST-RECENTLY USED
DOS 3+ internal
Undocumented

Purpose: Move the indicated buffer to the end of the disk buffer chain (least-recently used is first); under DOS 3.3, the buffer is then moved to the start of the disk buffer chain if it was marked unused.

Registers at call:
AX = 1207h
DS:DI -> disk buffer

Return Registers:
none

Details: This function only can be called from within DOS; it is nearly the same as Function 120Fh.

See also: Function 120Fh

INT 2Fh Function 1208h
DECREMENT SFT REFERENCE COUNT
DOS 3+ internal
Undocumented

Registers at call:
AX = 1208h
ES:DI -> System File Table entry

Return Registers:
AX = original value of reference count

Details: If the reference count was 1, it is set to FFFFh since 0 indicates that the SFT is not in use. It is the caller's responsibility to set the reference count to zero after cleaning up.

This function is used by network redirectors such as MSCDEX.

See also: Network Redirector Function 1106h (Chapter 9)

INT 2Fh Function 1209h
FLUSH AND FREE DISK BUFFER
DOS 3+ internal
Undocumented

Registers at call:
AX = 1209h
DS:DI -> disk buffer

Return Registers:
disk buffer marked unused, contents written to disk if buffer dirty

Details: This function can only be called from within DOS.
See also: Functions 120Eh and 1215h

INT 2Fh Function 120Ah   *DOS 3+ internal*
PERFORM CRITICAL ERROR INTERRUPT   *Undocumented*

Registers at call: **Return Registers:**
AX = 120Ah   AL = user response (0=ignore, 1=retry, 2=abort, 3=fail)
DS = SS = DOS DS (must be using a   CF clear if retry, set otherwise
   DOS internal stack)   STACK unchanged
STACK: WORD extended error code

Details: This function can only be called during a DOS function call, as it uses various fields in the SDA to set up the registers for the INT 24h. It reportedly sets the current DPB's first root directory sector to 1.
See also: INT 24h

INT 2Fh Function 120Bh   *DOS 3+ internal*
SIGNAL SHARING VIOLATION TO USER   *Undocumented*

Registers at call: **Return Registers:**
AX = 120Bh   CF clear if operation should be retried
ES:DI -> system file table entry for   CF set if operation should not be retried
   previous open of file   AX = error code (20h) (see Table 3-1)
STACK: WORD extended error code   STACK unchanged
(should be 20h—sharing violation)

Details: This function can only be called during a DOS function call. It should only be called if an attempt was made to open an already-open file contrary to the sharing rules.

This function invokes INT 24h if the SFT file was opened via FCB or in compatibility mode with inheritance allowed.

INT 2Fh Function 120Ch   *DOS 3+ internal*
OPEN DEVICE AND SET SFT OWNER/MODE   *Undocumented*

Registers at call: **Return Registers:**
AX = 120Ch   ES, DI, AX destroyed
SDA current SFT pointer -> SFT for file
DS = DOS DS
SS = DOS DS (must be using a DOS internal stack)

Details: This function invokes the "device open" call on the device driver for the specified SFT. It also changes the owner of the last-accessed SFT to the calling process if it was opened via FCB.

This function is called by network redirectors such as MSCDEX.

INT 2Fh Function 120Dh   *DOS 3+ internal*
GET DATE AND TIME   *Undocumented*

Registers at call: **Return Registers:**
AX = 120Dh   AX = current date in packed format (see Table 3-55)
SS = DOS DS (must be using a DOS   DX = current time in packed format (see Table 3-56)
   internal stack)
See also: INT 21h Functions 2Ah and 2Ch (PCI-24)

INT 2Fh Function 120Eh   *DOS 3+ internal*
MARK ALL DISK BUFFERS UNREFERENCED   *Undocumented*

Registers at call: **Return Registers:**
AX = 120Eh   DS:DI -> first disk buffer
SS = DOS DS (must be using a DOS internal stack)
Details: This function clears the "referenced" flag on all disk buffers.

In MS-DOS 5+, this function has become essentially a NOP, invoking the same code used by Function 1224h (SHARING DELAY).

See also: Functions 1209h and 1210h, MS-DOS INT 21h Function 0Dh (PCI-24)

INT 2Fh Function 120Fh
MAKE BUFFER MOST RECENTLY USED
DOS 3+ internal
Undocumented

Purpose: Move the indicated buffer to the end of the disk buffer chain (least-recently used is first); under DOS 3.3, the buffer is then moved to the start of the disk buffer chain if it was marked unused.

Registers at call:
AX = 120Fh
DS:DI -> disk buffer
SS = DOS DS (must be using a DOS internal stack)

Return Registers:
DS:DI -> next buffer in buffer list

Details: This function is the same as Function 1207h except that it returns a pointer to the buffer following the specified buffer in the buffer chain.

See also: Function 1207h

INT 2Fh Function 1210h
FIND UNREFERENCED DISK BUFFER
DOS 3+ internal
Undocumented

Registers at call:
AX = 1210h
DS:DI -> first disk buffer to check

Return Registers:
ZF clear if found
        DS:DI -> first unreferenced disk buffer
ZF set if not found

Details: In MS-DOS 5+, this has become essentially a NOP, invoking the same code used by Function 1224h (SHARING DELAY).

See also: Function 120Eh

INT 2Fh Function 1211h
NORMALIZE ASCIZ FILENAME
DOS 3+ internal
Undocumented

Registers at call:
AX = 1211h
DS:SI -> ASCIZ filename to normalize
ES:DI -> buffer for normalized filename

Return Registers:
destination buffer filled with uppercase filename,
  with slashes turned
to backslashes

See also: Functions 121Eh and 1221h

INT 2Fh Function 1212h
GET LENGTH OF ASCIZ STRING
DOS 3+ internal
Undocumented

Registers at call:
AX = 1212h
ES:DI -> ASCIZ string

Return Registers:
CX = length of string

See also: Function 1225h

INT 2Fh Function 1213h
UPPERCASE CHARACTER
DOS 3+ internal
Undocumented

Registers at call:
AX = 1213h
STACK: WORD character to convert to uppercase

Return Registers:
AL = uppercase character
STACK unchanged

INT 2Fh Function 1214h
COMPARE FAR POINTERS
DOS 3+ internal
Undocumented

Registers at call:
AX = 1214h
DS:SI = first pointer
ES:DI = second pointer

Return Registers:
ZF set if pointers are equal, ZF clear if not equal

INT 2Fh Function 1215h
FLUSH BUFFER

DOS 3+ internal
Undocumented

Registers at call:
AX = 1215h
DS:DI -> disk buffer
SS = DOS DS (must be using a DOS internal stack)
STACK: WORD   drives for which to skip buffer

Return Registers:
STACK unchanged

Details: This function can only be called from within DOS.
   The word on the stack specifies that DOS is to ignore the buffer if its drive is the same as the high byte, or the two bytes differ and the buffer is for a drive *other* than that given in low byte.
See also: Function 1209h

INT 2Fh Function 1216h
GET ADDRESS OF SYSTEM FILE TABLE ENTRY

DOS 3+ internal
Undocumented

Registers at call:
AX = 1216h
BX = system file table entry number

Return Registers:
CF clear if successful
    ES:DI -> system file table entry
CF set if BX greater than FILES=

Details: This function is supported by DR-DOS 5+.
See also: Function 1220h

INT 2Fh Function 1217h
GET CURRENT DIRECTORY STRUCTURE FOR DRIVE

DOS 3+ internal
Undocumented

Registers at call:
AX = 1217h
SS = DOS DS (must be using a DOS internal stack)
STACK: WORD   drive (0 = A:, 1 = B:, etc)

Return Registers:
CF set on error
    (drive > LASTDRIVE)
CF clear if successful
    DS:SI -> current directory structure for specified drive
STACK unchanged

See also: Function 1219h

INT 2Fh Function 1218h
GET CALLER'S REGISTERS

DOS 3+ internal
Undocumented

Registers at call:
AX = 1218h

Return Registers:
DS:SI -> saved caller's
AX,BX,CX,DX,SI,DI,BP,DS,ES (on stack)

Details: This function is only valid while within a DOS call.

INT 2Fh Function 1219h
SET DRIVE

DOS 3+ internal
Undocumented

Registers at call:
AX = 1219h
SS = DOS DS (must be using a DOS internal stack)
STACK: WORD drive (0 = default, 1 = A:, etc)

Return Registers:
unknown
STACK unchanged

Details: This function calls Function 1217h. It builds a current directory structure if inside a server call (INT 21h Function 5D00h, above).
See also: Functions 1217h and 121Fh

INT 2Fh Function 121Ah
GET FILE'S DRIVE

DOS 3+ internal
Undocumented

Registers at call:
AX = 121Ah
DS:SI -> filename

Return Registers:
AL = drive (0 = default, 1 = A:, etc, FFh = invalid)
DS:SI -> filename without leading X: (if present)

See also: INT 21h Function 60h (above), INT 21h Function 19h (PCI-24)

INT 2Fh Function 121Bh
SET YEAR/LENGTH OF FEBRUARY

DOS 3+ internal
Undocumented

Registers at call:
AX = 121Bh
CL = year - 1980
DS = DOS data segment
See also: INT 21h Function 2Bh (PCI-24)

Return Registers:
AL = number of days in February

INT 2Fh Function 121Ch
CHECKSUM MEMORY

DOS 3+ internal
Undocumented

Registers at call:
AX = 121Ch
DS:SI -> start of memory to checksum
CX = number of bytes
DX = initial checksum
SS = DOS DS (must be using a DOS internal stack)

Return Registers:
AX, CX destroyed
DX = checksum
DS:SI -> first byte after checksummed range

Details: This function is used by DOS to determine the day count since 1/1/80 given a date. It is supported by DR-DOS 5.0+.
See also: Function 121Dh

INT 2Fh Function 121Dh
SUM MEMORY

DOS 3+ internal
Undocumented

Registers at call:
AX = 121Dh
DS:SI -> memory to add up
CX = 0000h
DX = limit

Return Registers:
AL = byte which exceeded limit
CX = number of bytes before limit exceeded
DX = remainder after adding first CX bytes
DS:SI -> byte beyond the one which exceeded the limit

Details: This function is used by DOS to determine the year or month given day count since 1/1/80. It is supported by DR-DOS 5.0+.
See also: Function 121Ch

INT 2Fh Function 121Eh
COMPARE FILENAMES

DOS 3+ internal
Undocumented

Registers at call:
AX = 121Eh
DS:SI -> first ASCIZ filename
ES:DI -> second ASCIZ filename

Return Registers:
ZF set if filenames equivalent, ZF clear if not

Details: This function is supported by DR-DOS 5.0+.
See also: Functions 1211h and 1221h

INT 2Fh Function 121Fh
BUILD CURRENT DIRECTORY STRUCTURE

DOS 3+ internal
Undocumented

Registers at call:
AX = 121Fh
SS = DOS DS (must be using a DOS
  internal stack)
STACK: WORD drive letter

Return Registers:
ES:DI -> current directory structure (will be
  overwritten by next call)
STACK unchanged

INT 2Fh Function 1220h
GET JOB FILE TABLE ENTRY

DOS 3+ internal
Undocumented

Registers at call:
AX = 1220h
BX = file handle

Return Registers:
CF set on error
    AL = 6 (invalid file handle)

CF clear if successful

ES:DI -> JFT entry for file handle in current process

Details: The byte pointed at by ES:DI contains the number of the SFT entry for the file handle, or FFh if the handle is not open.

This function is supported by DR-DOS 5.0+.

See also: Functions 1216h and 1229h

INT 2Fh Function 1221h
CANONICALIZE FILE NAME

DOS 3+ internal
Undocumented

Registers at call:
AX = 1221h
DS:SI -> file name to be fully qualified
ES:DI -> 128-byte buffer for resulting canonical file name
SS = DOS DS (must be using a DOS internal stack)

Return Registers:
(see INT 21h Function 60h)

Details: This call is identical to INT 21h Function 60h; see that entry for details.

See also: INT 21h Function 60h (above), Network Redirector Function 1123h (Chapter 9)

INT 2Fh Function 1222h
SET EXTENDED ERROR INFORMATION

DOS 3+ internal
Undocumented

Registers at call:
AX = 1222h
SS = DOS data segment
SS:SI -> 4-byte records

    BYTE error code, FFh = last record
    BYTE error class, FFh = don't change
    BYTE suggested action, FFh = don't change
    BYTE error locus, FFh = don't change
SDA error code set (see Tables 3-39 and 3-41)

Return Registers:
SI destroyed
SDA error class, error locus, and suggested action fields set

Details: This function can only be called from within DOS.

See also: Function 122Dh, INT 21h Function 5D0Ah (above), INT 21h Function 59h (PCI-24)

INT 2Fh Function 1223h
CHECK IF CHARACTER DEVICE

DOS 3+ internal
Undocumented

Registers at call:
AX = 1223h
DS = DOS DS
SS = DOS DS (must be using a DOS
  internal stack)
SDA+218h (DOS 3.10-3.30) = eight-character blank-padded name
SDA+22Bh (DOS 4.0-6.0) = eight-character blank-padded name

Return Registers:
CF set if no character device by that name found
CF clear if found
  BH = low byte of device attribute word

Details: This function can only be called from within a DOS call.

See also: INT 21h Functions 5D06h and 5D0Bh (above)

INT 2Fh Function 1224h
SHARING RETRY DELAY

DOS 3+ internal
Undocumented

Registers at call:
AX = 1224h
SS = DOS DS (must be using a DOS
  internal stack)

Return Registers:
after delay set by INT 21h Function 440Bh, unless
  in server call (INT 21h Function 5D00h)

Details: Delay is dependent on the processor speed, and is skipped entirely if inside a server call.

See also: INT 21h Function 52h, INT 21h Function 440Bh (PCI-24), FastGraph/Light INT 62h Function 0097h (PCI-52)

INT 2Fh Function 1225h
GET LENGTH OF ASCIZ STRING
DOS 3+ internal
Undocumented

Registers at call:
AX = 1225h
DS:SI -> ASCIZ string

Return Registers:
CX = length of string

Details: This function is supported by DR-DOS 5.0+.
See also: Function 1212h

INT 2Fh Function 1226h
OPEN FILE
DOS 3.3+ internal
Undocumented

Registers at call:
AX = 1226h
CL = access mode
DS:DX -> ASCIZ filename
SS = DOS DS (must be using a DOS internal stack)

Return Registers:
CF set on error
    AL = error code (see Table 3-1)
CF clear if successful
    AX = file handle

Details: This function can only be called from within a DOS call. It is equivalent to INT 21h Function 3Dh.

This function is used by NLSFUNC to access COUNTRY.SYS when invoked by the DOS kernel.
See also: Function 1227h, INT 21h Function 3Dh (above)

INT 2Fh Function 1227h
CLOSE FILE
DOS 3.3+ internal
Undocumented

Registers at call:
AX = 1227h
BX = file handle
SS = DOS DS (must be using a DOS internal stack)

Return Registers:
CF set on error
    AL = 06h invalid file handle
CF clear if successful

Details: This function can only be called from within a DOS call. It is equivalent to INT 21h Function 3Eh.

This function is used by NLSFUNC to access COUNTRY.SYS when invoked by the DOS kernel.
See also: Functions 1201h and 1226h, Network Redirector Function 1106h (Chapter 9), MS-DOS INT 21h Function 3Eh (PCI-24)

INT 2Fh Function 1228h
MOVE FILE POINTER
DOS 3.3+ internal
Undocumented

Registers at call:
AX = 1228h
BP = 4200h, 4201h, 4202h (see INT 21h Function 42h)
BX = file handle
CX:DX = offset in bytes
SS = DOS DS (must be using a DOS internal stack)

Return Registers:
as for INT 21h Function 42h

Details: This function is equivalent to INT 21h Function 42h, but may only be called from inside a DOS function call. It sets the user stack frame pointer to a dummy buffer, moves BP to AX, performs the LSEEK, and then restores the frame pointer.

This function is used by NLSFUNC to access COUNTRY.SYS when invoked by the DOS kernel.
See also: INT 21h Function 42h (PCI-24)

INT 2Fh Function 1229h
READ FROM FILE
DOS 3.3+ internal
Undocumented

Registers at call: Return Registers:
AX = 1229h   as for INT 21h Function 3Fh
BX = file handle
CX = number of bytes to read
DS:DX -> buffer
SS = DOS DS (must be using a DOS internal stack)
Details: This function is equivalent to INT 21h Function 3Fh, but may only be called when already inside a DOS function call. It is used by NLSFUNC to access COUNTRY.SYS when invoked by the DOS kernel.
See also: Function 1226h, MS-DOS INT 21h Function 3Fh (PCI-24)

INT 2Fh Function 122Ah
SET FASTOPEN ENTRY POINT
DOS 3.3+ internal
Undocumented

Registers at call: Return Registers:
AX = 122Ah   CF set if specified entry point already set
BX = entry point to set (0001h or 0002h)
DS:SI -> FASTOPEN entry point (entry point not set if SI = FFFFh for DOS 4+)
Details: The entry point number in BX is ignored under DOS 3.30. Both entry points are set to same handler by DOS 4.01; DOS 5.0 and 6.0 only set entry point 1.

3-42 DOS 3.30+ FASTOPEN calling convention:
Registers at call: Return Registers:
AL = 01h Lookup   CF set on error or not installed
     CX = *unknown*, seems to be offset
     DI = *unknown*, seems to be offset
     SI = offset in DOS DS of filename
AL = 02h insert file into FASTOPEN cache
AL = 03h delete file from FASTOPEN cache
     SI = offset in DOS DS of filename
AL = 04h purge FASTOPEN cache
     AH = subfunction (00h,01h,02h)
     ES:DI -> *unknown item*
     CX = *unknown* (subfunctions 01h and 02h only)
Note: Function 03h calls Function 01h first.

3-43 PC-DOS 4.01 FASTOPEN is additionally calling convention:
Registers at call: Return Registers:
AL = 04h *unknown*   *unknown*
     AH = 03h
     others, if any, unknown
AL = 05h *unknown*
AL = 0Bh *unknown*
AL = 0Ch *unknown*
AL = 0Dh *unknown*
AL = 0Eh *unknown*
AL = 0Fh *unknown*
AL = 10h *unknown*

3-44 MS-DOS 5.0-6.0 FASTOPEN is additionally calling convention:
Registers at call:
AL = 04h purge FASTOPEN cache

Return Registers:
unknown

AH = 03h
   others, if any, unknown
AL = 05h *unknown*
   DL = drive (00h = A:)
   others, if any, unknown
AL = 06h *unknown*
   others, if any, unknown

INT 2Fh Function 122Bh
IOCTL

DOS 3.3+ internal
Undocumented

Registers at call:
AX = 122Bh
BP = 44xxh
SS = DOS DS (must be using a DOS internal stack)
additional registers as appropriate for INT 21h Function 44xxh

Return Registers:
as for INT 21h Function 44h

Details: This function is equivalent to INT 21h Function 44h, but may only be called when already inside a DOS function call. It sets the user stack frame pointer to a dummy buffer, moves BP to AX, performs the IOCTL, and then restores the frame pointer.

    This function is used by NLSFUNC in accessing COUNTRY.SYS when invoked by the DOS kernel.

See also: INT 21h Function 44h (PCI-24)

INT 2Fh Function 122Ch
GET DEVICE CHAIN

DOS 3.3+ internal
Undocumented

Registers at call:
AX = 122Ch

Return Registers:
BX:AX -> header of second device driver (NUL is first) in driver chain

Details: Although this function exists in DR-DOS 5.0, it returns 0000h:0000h.

See also: INT 21h Function 52h (above)

INT 2Fh Function 122Dh
GET EXTENDED ERROR CODE

DOS 3.3+ internal
Undocumented

Registers at call:
AX = 122Dh

Return Registers:
AX = current extended error code

See also: Function 1222h, INT 21h Function 59h (PCI-24)

INT 2Fh Function 122Eh
GET OR SET ERROR TABLE ADDRESSES

DOS 4+ internal
Undocumented

Registers at call:
AX = 122Eh
DL = subfunction
    00h get standard DOS error table

    01h set standard DOS error table
       ES:DI -> error table

    02h get parameter error table (errors 00h-0Ah)

    03h set parameter error table
       ES:DI -> error table

Return Registers:

ES:DI -> error table
      (DOS 4: errors 00h-12h,50h-5Bh)
      (DOS 5: errors 00h-26h,4Fh,51h-59h)

ES:DI -> error table

Registers at call:	Return Registers:
AX = 122Eh	
DL = subfunction	

04h get critical/SHARE error table (errors 13h-2Bh)   ES:DI -> error table

05h set critical/SHARE error table
     ES:DI -> error table

06h get *unknown* error table   ES:DI -> error table or
                                                  0000h:0000h

07h set *unknown* error table
     ES:DI -> error table

08h get error message retriever (see Table 3-46)

                                      ES:DI -> FAR procedure to
09h set *unknown* error table   fetch error message
     ES:DI -> error table

Details: If the returned segment on a "get" is 0001h, then the offset specifies the offset of the error message table within COMMAND.COM, and the procedure returned by DL=08h should be called.

DOS 5+ COMMAND.COM does not allow setting any of the addresses (calls with DL odd are ignored); they are always returned with segment 0001h.

For DOS 5.0, the standard and critical/SHARE error tables are combined into a single error table.

See also: Function 0500h, MS-DOS INT 21h Function 59h (PCI-24)

3-45 Format of DOS 4.x error table:

Offset	Size	Description
00h	BYTE	FFh
01h 2	BYTEs	04h,00h (*DOS version*)
03h	BYTE	number of error headers following
04h	2N WORDs	table of all error headers for table

	Offset	Size	Description
	00h	WORD	error message number
	02h	WORD	offset of error message from start of header
			error messages are count byte followed by msg

Note: DOS 5 error tables consist of one word per error number; each word contains either the offset of a counted string or 0000h.

3-46 Error retrieval function calling convention:

Registers at call:	Return Registers:
AX = error number	ES:DI -> error message (counted string)
DI = offset of error table	

Details: This function needs to access COMMAND.COM if the messages were not loaded into memory permanently with /MSG; the caller should assume that the returned message will be overwritten by the next call of the function.

This function is supported by DR-DOS 5.0.

3-47 Values for parameter errors:

01h	Too many parameters
02h	Required Parameter missing
03h	Invalid switch

04h	Invalid keyword
06h	Parameter value not in allowed range
07h	Parameter value not allowed
08h	Parameter value not allowed
09h	Parameter format not correct
0Ah	Invalid parameter
0Bh	Invalid parameter combination

INT 2Fh Function 122Fh
SET DOS VERSION NUMBER TO RETURN

DOS 4.x internal
Undocumented

Purpose: Specify the version number that the DOS "get version" call should return, similar to the fake version numbers implemented by MS-DOS 5+ SETVER.

Registers at call:
AX = 122Fh
DX = DOS version number (0000h = return true DOS version)

Return Registers:
none

Details: Not available under DR-DOS 5.0 or 6.0.
See also: INT 21h Functions 30h and 3306h (PCI-24)

MS-DOS Data Structures

This section contains data structures related to calls not discussed in this chapter (see *PC Interrupts* for detailed coverage) which are referenced from functions that are discussed above.

3-48 Format of DOS 1.1 and MS-DOS 1.25 drive parameter block:

Offset	Size	Description
00h	BYTE	sequential device ID
01h	BYTE	logical drive number (0=A:)
02h	WORD	bytes per sector
04h	BYTE	highest sector number within a cluster
05h	BYTE	shift count to convert clusters into sectors
06h	WORD	starting sector number of first FAT
08h	BYTE	number of copies of FAT
09h	WORD	number of directory entries
0Bh	WORD	number of first data sector
0Dh	WORD	highest cluster number (number of data clusters + 1)
0Fh	BYTE	sectors per FAT
10h	WORD	starting sector of directory
12h	WORD	address of allocation table

Note: The DOS 1.0 table is the same except that the first and last fields are missing; see Table 3-49 for the DOS 2+ version.

3-49 Format of DOS 2+ Drive Parameter Block:

Offset	Size	Description
00h	BYTE	drive number (00h = A:, 01h = B:, etc.)
01h	BYTE	unit number within device driver
02h	WORD	bytes per sector
04h	BYTE	highest sector number within a cluster
05h	BYTE	shift count to convert clusters into sectors
06h	WORD	number of reserved sectors at beginning of drive
08h	BYTE	number of FATs
09h	WORD	number of root directory entries
0Bh	WORD	number of first sector containing user data
0Dh	WORD	highest cluster number (number of data clusters + 1)

16-bit FAT if greater than 0FF6h, else 12-bit FAT

0Fh	BYTE	number of sectors per FAT
10h	WORD	sector number of first directory sector
12h	DWORD	address of device driver header
16h	BYTE	media ID byte
17h	BYTE	00h if disk accessed, FFh if not
18h	DWORD	pointer to next DPB

---DOS 2.x---

1Ch	WORD	cluster containing start of current directory, 0000h=root, FFFFh = unknown
1Eh	64 BYTEs	ASCIZ pathname of current directory for drive

---DOS 3.x---

1Ch	WORD	cluster at which to start search for free space when writing
1Eh	WORD	number of free clusters on drive, FFFFh = unknown

---DOS 4.0-6.0---

0Fh	WORD	number of sectors per FAT
11h	WORD	sector number of first directory sector
13h	DWORD	address of device driver header
17h	BYTE	media ID byte
18h	BYTE	00h if disk accessed, FFh if not
19h	DWORD	pointer to next DPB
1Dh	WORD	cluster at which to start search for free space when writing, usually the last cluster allocated
1Fh	WORD	number of free clusters on drive, FFFFh = unknown

3-50 Values for Error Class:

01h	out of resource (storage space or I/O channels)
02h	temporary situation (file or record lock)
03h	authorization (denied access)
04h	internal (system software bug)
05h	hardware failure
06h	system failure (configuration file missing or incorrect)
07h	application program error
08h	not found
09h	bad format
0Ah	locked
0Bh	media error
0Ch	already exists
0Dh	unknown

3-51 Values for Suggested Action:

01h	retry
02h	delayed retry
03h	prompt user to reenter input
04h	abort after cleanup
05h	immediate abort
06h	ignore
07h	retry after user intervention

3-52 Values for Error Locus:

01h	unknown or not appropriate
02h	block device (disk error)

INT 2Fh Function 122Fh

03h   network related
04h   serial device (timeout)
05h   memory related

3-53 Bitfields for file attributes:

bit 7   shareable (Novell NetWare)
bit 6   unused
bit 5   archive
bit 4   directory
bit 3   volume label
         execute-only (Novell NetWare)
bit 2   system
bit 1   hidden
bit 0   read-only

3-54 Bitfields for device information word:

character device

bit 14   device driver can process IOCTL requests (see Function 4402h in PCI-24)
bit 13   output until busy supported
bit 11   driver supports OPEN/CLOSE calls
bit 7   set (indicates device)
bit 6   EOF on input
bit 5   raw (binary) mode
bit 4   device is special (uses INT 29h)
bit 3   clock device
bit 2   NUL device
bit 1   standard output
bit 0   standard input

disk file

bit 15   file is remote (DOS 3+)
bit 14   don't set file date/time on closing (DOS 3+)
bit 11   media not removable
bit 8   (DOS 4 only) generate INT 24h if no disk space on write or read past end of file
bit 7   clear (indicates file)
bit 6   file has not been written
bits 5-0 drive number (0 = A:)

3-55 Bitfields for file time:

bits 15-11   hours (0-23)
bits 10-5   minutes
bits 4-0   seconds/2

3-56 Bitfields for file date:

bits 15-9   year - 1980
bits 8-5   month
bits 4-0   day

3-57 Format of PSP:

Offset	Size	Description
00h	2 BYTEs	INT 20h instruction for CP/M CALL 0 program termination. The CDh 20h here is often used as a signature for a valid PSP.
02h	WORD	segment of first byte beyond memory allocated to program

04h	BYTE	unused filler
05h	BYTE	CP/M CALL 5 service request (FAR JMP to 000C0h, see INT 30h below)
		BUG: (DOS 2-6) PSPs created by INT 21h Function 4Bh point at 000BEh
06h	WORD	CP/M compatibility—size of first segment for .COM files
08h	2 BYTEs	remainder of FAR JMP at 05h
0Ah	DWORD	stored INT 22h termination address
0Eh	DWORD	stored INT 23h control-Break handler address
12h	DWORD	DOS 1.1+ stored INT 24h critical error handler address
16h	WORD	segment of parent PSP
18h	20 BYTEs	DOS 2+ Job File Table, one byte per file handle, FFh = closed
2Ch	WORD	DOS 2+ segment of environment for process
2Eh	DWORD	DOS 2+ process's SS:SP on entry to last INT 21h call
32h	WORD	DOS 3+ number of entries in JFT (default 20)
34h	DWORD	DOS 3+ pointer to JFT (default PSP:0018h)
38h	DWORD	DOS 3+ pointer to previous PSP (default FFFFFFFFh in 3.x) used by SHARE in DOS 3.3
3Ch	BYTE	apparently unused by DOS versions <= 6.00
3Dh	BYTE	apparently used by some versions of APPEND
3Eh	BYTE	(Novell NetWare) flag: next byte initialized if CEh
3Fh	BYTE	(Novell NetWare) Novell task number if previous byte is CEh
40h	2 BYTEs	DOS 5+ version to return on INT 21h Function 30h (SETVER)
42h	WORD	(MSWin3) selector of next PSP (PDB) in linked list Windows keeps a linked list of Windows programs only
44h	4 BYTEs	unused by DOS versions <= 6.00
48h	BYTE	(MSWindows3) bit 0 set if non-Windows application (WINOLDAP)
49h	7 BYTEs	unused by DOS versions <= 6.00
50h	3 BYTEs	DOS 2+ service request (INT 21h/RETF instructions)
53h	2 BYTEs	unused in DOS versions <= 6.00
55h	7 BYTEs	unused in DOS versions <= 6.00; can be used to make first FCB into an extended FCB
5Ch	16 BYTEs	first default FCB, filled in from first commandline argument overwrites second FCB if opened
6Ch	16 BYTEs	second default FCB, filled in from second commandline argument overwrites beginning of commandline if opened
7Ch	4 BYTEs	unused
80h	128 BYTEs	commandline and default DTA the command tail is a BYTE for the length of the tail, N BYTEs for the tail, followed by a BYTE containing 0Dh

Notes: In DOS v3+, the limit on simultaneously open files may be increased by allocating memory for a new open file table, filling it with FFh, copying the first 20 bytes from the default table, and adjusting the pointer and count at 34h and 32h. However, DOS will only copy the first 20 file handles into a child PSP (including the one created on EXEC).

Network redirectors based on the original MS-Net implementation use values of 80h-FEh in the open file table to indicate remote files; Novell NetWare reportedly also uses values of 80h-FEh.

MS-DOS 5.00 incorrectly fills the FCB fields when loading a program high; the first FCB is empty and the second contains the first parameter.

Some DOS extenders place protected-mode values in various PSP fields such as the "parent" field, which can confuse PSP walkers. Always check either for the CDh 20h signature or that the suspected PSP is at the beginning of a memory block which owns itself (the preceding paragraph should be a valid MCB with "owner" the same as the suspected PSP).

Novell NetWare updates the fields at offsets 3Eh and 3Fh without checking that a legal PSP segment is current; see Function 50h for further discussion.

3-58 Device driver command codes:

00h	INIT
01h	MEDIA CHECK (block devices)
02h	BUILD BPB (block devices)
03h	IOCTL INPUT
04h	INPUT
05h	NONDESTRUCTIVE INPUT, NO WAIT (character devices)
06h	INPUT STATUS (character devices)
07h	INPUT FLUSH (character devices)
08h	OUTPUT
09h	OUTPUT WITH VERIFY
0Ah	OUTPUT STATUS (character devices)
0Bh	OUTPUT FLUSH (character devices)
0Ch	IOCTL OUTPUT
0Dh	(DOS 3+) DEVICE OPEN
0Eh	(DOS 3+) DEVICE CLOSE
0Fh	(DOS 3+) REMOVABLE MEDIA (block devices)
10h	(DOS 3+) OUTPUT UNTIL BUSY (character devices)
11h	(European 4.0) STOP OUTPUT (console screen drivers)
12h	(European 4.0) RESTART OUTPUT (console screen drivers)
13h	(DOS 3.2+) GENERIC IOCTL
15h	(European MS-DOS 4.0) RESET UNCERTAIN MEDIA FLAG
17h	(DOS 3.2+) GET LOGICAL DEVICE
18h	(DOS 3.2+) SET LOGICAL DEVICE
19h	(DOS 5+) CHECK GENERIC IOCTL SUPPORT
80h	(CD-ROM) READ LONG
81h	(CD-ROM) reserved
82h	(CD-ROM) READ LONG PREFETCH
83h	(CD-ROM) SEEK
84h	(CD-ROM) PLAY AUDIO
85h	(CD-ROM) STOP AUDIO
86h	(CD-ROM) WRITE LONG
87h	(CD-ROM) WRITE LONG VERIFY
88h	(CD-ROM) RESUME AUDIO

3-59 Format of device driver request header:

Offset	Size	Description
00h	BYTE	length of request header
01h	BYTE	subunit within device driver
02h	BYTE	command code (see Table 3-58)
03h	WORD	status (filled in by device driver)
		bit 15: error
		bits 14-11: reserved
		bit 10: *unknown*, set by DOS kernel on entry to some driver calls
		bit 9: busy

bit 8: done (may be clear on return under European MS-DOS 4.0)

bits 7-0: error code if bit 15 set (see Table 3-60)

---DOS---

05h	4BYTEs	reserved (unused in DOS 2.x and 3.x)
09h	DWORD	(European MS-DOS 4.0 only) pointer to next request header in device's request queue
		(other versions) reserved (unused in DOS 2.x and 3.x)

---STARLITE (Embedded DOS)---

05h	DWORD	pointer to next request header
09h 4	BYTEs	reserved

---command code 00h---

0Dh	BYTE	(return) number of units
0Eh	DWORD	(call) pointer to DOS device helper function (see PCI-24) (European MS-DOS 4.0 only)
		(call) pointer past end of memory available to driver (DOS 5+)
		(return) address of first free byte following driver
12h	DWORD	(call) pointer to commandline arguments
		(return) pointer to BPB array (block drivers) or 0000h:0000h (character drivers)
16h	BYTE	(DOS 3+) drive number for first unit of block driver (0=A)

---European MS-DOS 4.0---

17h	DWORD	pointer to function to save registers on stack

---DOS 5+ ---

17h	WORD	(return) error-message flag
		0001h MS-DOS should display error message on initialization failure

---command code 01h---

0Dh	BYTE	media descriptor
0Eh	BYTE	returned status
		00h don't know, 01h media unchanged, FFh media has been changed
0Fh	DWORD	(return, DOS 3+) pointer to previous volume ID if OPEN/CLOSE/RM bit in device header is set and disk changed

---command code 02h---

0Dh	BYTE	media descriptor
0Eh	DWORD	transfer address
		pointer to scratch sector if NON-IBM FORMAT bit in device header set
		pointer to first FAT sector otherwise
12h	DWORD	pointer to BPB (set by driver) (see Table 3-61)

---command codes 03h,0Ch--- (see also INT 21h Functions 4402h and 4403h in PCI-24)

0Dh	BYTE	media descriptor (block devices only)
0Eh	DWORD	transfer address
12h	WORD	(call) number of bytes to read/write
		(return) actual number of bytes read or written

---command codes 04h,08h,09h---

0Dh	BYTE	media descriptor (block devices only)
0Eh	DWORD	transfer address
12h	WORD	byte count (character devices) or sector count (block devices)
14h	WORD	starting sector number (block devices only)
16h	DWORD	(DOS 3+) pointer to volume ID if error 0Fh returned

1Ah	DWORD	(DOS 4+) 32-bit starting sector number (block devices with device attribute word bit 1 set only) if starting sector number above is FFFFh (see Table 3-22)

---**command code 05h**---

0Dh	BYTE	byte read from device if BUSY bit clear on return

---**command codes 06h,07h,0Ah,0Bh,0Dh,0Eh,0Fh**---

no further fields

---**command code 10h**---

0Dh	BYTE	unused
0Eh	DWORD	transfer address
12h	WORD	(call) number of bytes to write
		(return) actual number of bytes written

---**command codes 11h,12h**---

0Dh	BYTE	reserved

---**command code 15h**---

no further fields

---**command codes 13h,19h**---

0Dh	BYTE	category code
		00h unknown
		01h COMn:
		03h CON
		05h LPTn:
		07h mouse (European MS-DOS 4.0)
		08h disk
		9Eh (STARLITE) Media Access Control driver
0Eh	BYTE	function code
		00h (STARLITE) MAC Bind request
0Fh	WORD	copy of DS at time of IOCTL call (apparently unused in DOS 3.3)
		SI contents (European MS-DOS 4.0)
11h	WORD	offset of device driver header
		DI contents (European MS-DOS 4.0)
13h	DWORD	pointer to parameter block from INT 21h Functions 440Ch or 440Dh

---**command codes 80h,82h**---

0Dh	BYTE	addressing mode
		00h HSG (default)
		01h Phillips/Sony Red Book
0Eh	DWORD	transfer address (ignored for command 82h)
12h	WORD	number of sectors to read
		(if 0 for command 82h, request is an advisory seek)
14h	DWORD	starting sector number
		logical sector number in HSG mode
		frame/second/minute/unused in Red Book mode
		(HSG sector = minute * 4500 + second * 75 + frame - 150)
18h	BYTE	data read mode
		00h cooked (2048 bytes per frame)
		01h raw (2352 bytes per frame, including EDC/ECC)
19h	BYTE	interleave size (number of sectors stored consecutively)
1Ah	BYTE	interleave skip factor (# sectors between consec portions)

---command code 83h---

0Dh	BYTE	addressing mode (see above)
0Eh	DWORD	transfer address (ignored)
12h	WORD	number of sectors to read (ignored)
14h	DWORD	starting sector number (see also above)

---command code 84h---

0Dh	BYTE	addressing mode (see above)
0Eh	DWORD	starting sector number (see also above)
12h	DWORD	number of sectors to play

---command codes 85h,88h---

no further fields

---command codes 86h,87h---

0Dh	BYTE	addressing mode (see above)
0Eh	DWORD	transfer address (ignored in write mode 0)
12h	WORD	number of sectors to write
14h	DWORD	starting sector number (see also above)
18h	BYTE	write mode
		00h mode 0 (write all zeros)
		01h mode 1 (default) (2048 bytes per sector)
		02h mode 2 form 1 (2048 bytes per sector)
		03h mode 2 form 2 (2336 bytes per sector)
19h	BYTE	interleave size (number of sectors stored consecutively)
1Ah	BYTE	interleave skip factor (# sectors between consec portions)

3-60 Values for error code:

00h	write-protect violation
01h	unknown unit
02h	drive not ready
03h	unknown command
04h	CRC error
05h	bad drive request structure length
06h	seek error
07h	unknown media
08h	sector not found
09h	printer out of paper
0Ah	write fault
0Bh	read fault
0Ch	general failure
0Dh	reserved
0Eh	(CD-ROM) media unavailable
0Fh	invalid disk change

3-61 Format of BIOS Parameter Block:

Offset	Size	Description
00h	WORD	number of bytes per sector
02h	BYTE	number of sectors per cluster
03h	WORD	number of reserved sectors at start of disk
05h	BYTE	number of FATs
06h	WORD	number of entries in root directory
08h	WORD	total number of sectors

for DOS 4+, set to zero if partition >32M, then set DWORD at 15h to actual number of sectors

0Ah	BYTE	media ID byte
0Bh	WORD	number of sectors per FAT

---DOS 3+---

0Dh	WORD	number of sectors per track
0Fh	WORD	number of heads
11h	DWORD	number of hidden sectors
15h	11 BYTEs	reserved

---DOS 4+ ---

15h	DWORD	total number of sectors if word at 08h contains zero
19h	6 BYTEs	*unknown*
1Fh	WORD	number of cylinders
21h	BYTE	device type
22h	WORD	device attributes (removable or not, etc)

---DR-DOS 5+ ---

15h	DWORD	total number of sectors if word at 08h contains zero
19h	6 BYTEs	reserved

---European MS-DOS 4.00---

15h	DWORD	total number of sectors if word at 08h contains zero (however, this DOS version does not actually implement >32M partitions)

3-62 Format of FindFirst data block:

Offset	Size	Description

---**PC-DOS 3.10, PC-DOS 4.01, MS-DOS 3.2/3.3/5.0**---

00h	BYTE	drive letter (bits 0-6), remote if bit 7 set
01h	11 BYTEs	search template
0Ch	BYTE	search attributes

---**DOS 2.x** (*and some DOS 3.x*)---

00h	BYTE	search attributes
01h	BYTE	drive letter
02h	11 BYTEs	search template

---**WILDUNIX.COM**---

00h	12 BYTEs	15-character wildcard search pattern and drive letter (packed)
0Ch	BYTE	search attributes

---**DOS 2.x and most 3.x**---

0Dh	WORD	entry count within directory
0Fh	DWORD	*pointer to DTA*
13h	WORD	cluster number of start of parent directory

---**PC-DOS 4.01, MS-DOS 3.2/3.3/5.0**---

0Dh	WORD	entry count within directory
0Fh	WORD	cluster number of start of parent directory
11h	4 BYTEs	reserved

---**all versions, documented fields**---

15h	BYTE	attribute of file found
16h	WORD	file time (see Table 3-55)
18h	WORD	file date (see Table 3-56)
1Ah	DWORD	file size
1Eh	13 BYTEs	ASCIZ filename+extension

3-62 Format of directory entry:

Offset	Size	Description
00h	8 BYTEs	blank-padded filename
08h	3 BYTEs	blank-padded file extension
0Bh	BYTE	attributes
0Ch	10 BYTEs	reserved (used by DR-DOS to store the file password)
16h	WORD	time of creation or last update (see Table 24-96)
18h	WORD	date of creation or last update (see Table 24-97)
1Ah	WORD	starting cluster number
1Ch	DWORD	file size

3-63 Format of File Control Block:

Offset	Size	Description
-7	BYTE	extended FCB if FFh
-6	5 BYTEs	reserved
-1	BYTE	file attribute if extended FCB
00h	BYTE	drive number (0 = default, 1 = A, etc.)
01h	8 BYTEs	blank-padded file name
09h	3 BYTEs	blank-padded file extension
0Ch	WORD	current block number
0Eh	WORD	logical record size
10h	DWORD	file size
14h	WORD	date of last write (see Table 3-56)
16h	WORD	time of last write (see Table 3-55) (DOS 1.1+)
18h	8 BYTEs	reserved (see Tables 3-64 to 3-68)
20h	BYTE	record within current block
21h	DWORD	random access record number (if record size is > 64 bytes, high byte is omitted)

Note: To use an extended FCB, you must specify the address of the FFh flag at offset -7, rather than the address of the drive number field.

3-64 Format of reserved field for DOS 1.0:

Offset	Size	Description
16h	WORD	location in directory (if high byte = FFh, low byte is device ID)
18h	WORD	number of first cluster in file
1Ah	WORD	current absolute cluster number on disk
1Ch	WORD	current relative cluster number within file (0 = first cluster of file, 1 = second cluster, etc.)
1Eh	BYTE	dirty flag (00h = not dirty)
1Fh	BYTE	unused

3-65 Format of reserved field for DOS 1.10-1.25:

Offset	Size	Description
18h	BYTE	bit 7: set if logical device bit 6: not dirty bits 5-0: disk number or logical device ID
19h	WORD	starting cluster number on disk
1Bh	WORD	current absolute cluster number on disk
1Dh	WORD	current relative cluster number within file
1Fh	BYTE	unused

INT 2Fh Function 122Fh

3-66 Format of reserved field for DOS 2.x:

Offset	Size	Description
18h	BYTE	bit 7: set if logical device
		bit 6: *set if open*
		bits 5-0: *unknown*
19h	WORD	starting cluster number on disk
1Bh	WORD	*unknown*
1Dh	BYTE	*unknown*
1Eh	BYTE	*unknown*
1Fh	BYTE	*unknown*

3-67 Format of reserved field for DOS 3.x:

Offset	Size	Description
18h	BYTE	number of system file table entry for file
19h	BYTE	attributes
		bits 7,6: 00 = SHARE.EXE not loaded, disk file
		01 = SHARE.EXE not loaded, character device
		10 = SHARE.EXE loaded, remote file
		11 = SHARE.EXE loaded, local file or device
		bits 5-0: low six bits of device attribute word

---SHARE.EXE loaded, local file---

1Ah	WORD	starting cluster of file on disk
1Ch	WORD	(DOS 3.x) offset within SHARE of sharing record (see AH=52h)
1Eh	BYTE	file attribute
1Fh	BYTE	*unknown*

---SHARE.EXE loaded, remote file---

1Ah	WORD	number of sector containing directory entry
1Ch	WORD	relative cluster within file of last cluster accessed
1Eh	BYTE	absolute cluster number of last cluster accessed
1Fh	BYTE	*unknown*

---SHARE.EXE not loaded---

1Ah	BYTE	(low byte of device attribute word AND 0Ch) OR open mode
1Bh	WORD	starting cluster of file
1Dh	WORD	number of sector containing directory entry
1Fh	BYTE	number of directory entry within sector

Note: If the FCB was opened on a character device, the DWORD at 1Ah is set to the address of the device driver header, and then the BYTE at 1Ah is overwritten.

3-68 Format of reserved field for DOS 5.0:

Offset	Size	Description
18h	BYTE	number of system file table entry for file
19h	BYTE	attributes
		bits 7,6: 00 = SHARE.EXE not loaded, disk file
		01 = SHARE.EXE not loaded, character device
		10 = SHARE.EXE loaded, remote file
		11 = SHARE.EXE loaded, local file or device
		bits 5-0: low six bits of device attribute word

---SHARE.EXE loaded, local file---

| 1Ah | WORD | starting cluster of file on disk |
| 1Ch | WORD | unique sequence number of sharing record |

1Eh	BYTE	file attributes
1Fh	BYTE	*unused*

---SHARE.EXE loaded, remote file---

1Ah	WORD	network handle
1Ch	DWORD	network ID

---SHARE not loaded, local device---

1Ah	DWORD	pointer to device driver header
1Eh	2 BYTEs	*unused*

---SHARE not loaded, local file---

1Ah	BYTE	extra info
		bit 7: read-only attribute from SFT
		bit 6: archive attribute from SFT
		bits 5-0: high bits of sector number
1Bh	WORD	starting cluster of file
1Dh	WORD	low word of sector number containing directory entry
1Fh	BYTE	number of directory entry within sector

CHAPTER 4

BAPI

3com's Bridge Application Program Interface is a set of functions which makes many of the details of LAN communications transparent.

INT 14h Function A0h   *3com BAPI SERIAL I/O*
CONNECT TO PORT

Registers at call: **Return Registers:**
AH = A0h   AH = return code (00h,04h-06h,08h,0Ah-0Ch)
ES:BX -> ASCIZ internet host name   (see Table 4-1)
  CX = length of name   CL = session ID
Details: Novell TELAPI.EXE returns AH=09h (not supported) and CL=00h.
Conflicts: Interconnections, Inc. TES (Chapter 38)
See also: Functions A1h, A2h, A5h, and AF00h

4-1 BAPI return codes:

00h	successful
01h	no characters written
02h	no characters read
03h	no such session
04h	clearinghouse name not found
05h	no response from host
06h	no more sessions available
07h	session aborted
08h	invalid clearinghouse name
09h	not supported
0Ah	internal (general) network error
0Bh	out of memory
0Ch	invalid IP address

INT 14h Function A1h   *3com BAPI SERIAL I/O*
DISCONNECT FROM PORT

Registers at call: **Return Registers:**
AH = A1h   AH = return code (00h,03h,07h,0Ah,0Bh)
DH = session ID (00h for external   (see Table 4-1)
  session managment)   AL destroyed (Novell TELAPI.EXE)
Conflicts: Interconnections, Inc. TES (Chapter 38)
See also: Function A0h

INT 14h Function A2h
WRITE CHARACTER
3com BAPI SERIAL I/O

Registers at call:
AH = A2h
AL = character
DH = session ID (00h for external
  session managment)
Conflicts: Interconnections, Inc. TES (Chapter 38)
See also: Functions A0h, A3h, and A4h

Return Registers:
AH = return code (00h,01h,03h,07h,0Ah,0Bh)
  (see Table 4-1)

INT 14h Function A3h
READ CHARACTER
3com BAPI SERIAL I/O

Registers at call:
AH = A3h
DH = session ID (00h for external
  session managment)
Conflicts: Interconnections, Inc. TES (Chapter 38)
See also: Functions A0h, A2h, A5h, and A7h

Return Registers:
AH = return code (00h,02h,03h,07h,0Ah,0Bh)
  (see Table 4-1)
AL = character read or 00h if none available

INT 14h Function A4h
WRITE BLOCK
3com BAPI SERIAL I/O

Registers at call:
AH = A4h
CX = length of buffer in bytes
DH = session ID (00h for external
  session managment)
ES:BX -> buffer containing data
Conflicts: Interconnections, Inc. TES (Chapter 38)
See also: Functions A0h and A5h, FOSSIL Function 19h (PCI-12), COURIERS Function 86h
(PCI-12)

Return Registers:
AH = return code (00h,01h,03h,07h,0Ah,0Bh)
  (see Table 4-1)
CX = number of bytes actually sent

INT 14h Function A5h
READ BLOCK
3com BAPI SERIAL I/O

Registers at call:
AH = A5h
CX = length of buffer
DH = session ID (00h for external
  session managment)
ES:BX -> buffer for data
Conflicts: Interconnections, Inc. TES (Chapter 38)
See also: Functions A0h, A3h, A4h, and A7h; FOSSIL Function 18h (PCI-12); COURIERS
Function 83h (PCI-12); EBIOS Function FF02h (PCI-12)

Return Registers:
AH = return code (00h,02h,03h,07h,0Ah,0Bh)
  (see Table 4-1)
CX = number of bytes actually read

INT 14h Function A6h
SEND SHORT BREAK
3com BAPI SERIAL I/O

Purpose: Generate a short break signal; if data delivery was turned off by the break, wait for the
host to turn it on again.
Registers at call:
AH = A6h
DH = session ID (00h for external
  session managment)
Conflicts: Interconnections, Inc. TES (Chapter 38)

Return Registers:
AH = return code (00h,03h,07h,0Ah,0Bh)
  (see Table 4-1)

See also: Function A0h, FOSSIL Function 1Ah (PCI-12), COURIERS Function 8Ah (PCI-12), EBIOS Function FAh (PCI-12)

INT 14h Function A7h *3com BAPI SERIAL I/O*
READ STATUS
Registers at call: Return Registers:
AH = A7h   AH = return code (00h,03h,07h,0Ah,0Bh)
DH = session ID (00h for external   (see Table 4-1)
  session managment)   CX = number of bytes available for reading
Details: Novell TELAPI.EXE v4.01 always returns either 0 or 1 bytes available.
Conflicts: Interconnections, Inc. TES (Chapter 38)
See also: Function A5h

INT 14h Function AF00h *3com BAPI SERIAL I/O*
INSTALLATION CHECK
Registers at call: Return Registers:
AX = AF00h   AX = AF01h if installed
BX = AAAAh   BH = protocol type (if BX=AAAAh on entry)
                                             01h NetManage TCP/IP
                                         BL = version for protocol type
                                           (if BX=AAAAh on entry)
Details: Early versions of the BAPI and the ROM BIOS simply destroy AX; this behavior is used to determine whether the newer functions (Functions B0h, B1h, etc.) are available.
See also: Function A0h

INT 14h Function B0h *3com BAPI SERIAL I/O*
EN/DISABLE "ENTER COMMAND MODE" (ECM) CHARACTER
Registers at call: Return Registers:
AH = B0h   AH = return code (00h,07h,0Ah) (see Table 4-1)
AL = new state (00h disabled,
  01h enabled)
Details: Disabling the ECM character allows applications to send data which includes the ECM character.
See also: Functions AF00h, B1h, and B2h

INT 14h Function B1h *3com BAPI SERIAL I/O*
ENTER COMMAND MODE
Purpose: Provide a means for the application or terminal emulator to perform the same action normally caused by the ECM character.
Registers at call: Return Registers:
AH = B1h   AH = return code (00h,07h,0Ah) (see Table 4-1)
See also: Functions B0h and B2h

INT 14h Function B2h *3com BAPI SERIAL I/O*
GET ECM WATCH STATE
Purpose: Determine whether the ECM character is enabled.
Registers at call: Return Registers:
AH = B2h   AH = return code (00h,07h,0Ah) (see Table 4-1)
                                       AL = watch flag (00h disabled, 01h enabled)

See also: Functions B0h and B1h

INT 14h Function B3h   *3com BAPI SERIAL I/O*
GET/SET CONFIGURATION INFO

Registers at call: **Return Registers:**
AH = B3h   AH = return code (00h,03h,09h-0Bh)
AL = direction (00h get, 01h set)   (see Table 4-1)
DH = session ID (00h for external   **---if AL=00h---**
  session managment)   CX = configuration item value (see above)
DL = configuration item
  (00h = end-of-line mapping)
CX = new configuration item value
  (if AL=01h)
    ---if DL=00h---
  CH = application EOL type
    (app to Telnet client)
        01h application will send lone CR
        02h application will send CR-? pair
  CL = driver EOL type (Telnet client
    to Telnet server)
        01h driver should send CR-NUL pair
        02h driver should send CR-LF pair
See also: Function B2h

CHAPTER 5

IPX/SPX

The Internetwork Packet Exchange (IPX) protocol is the lowest layer of a Novell NetWare system, and is now supported by numerous other networking packages. IPX is a datagram protocol, and makes no guarantees that packets will be delivered in order, or even delivered at all. Sitting on top of IPX, the Sequenced Packet Exchange (SPX) protocol provides reliable connections with in-order packet delivery.

INT 2Fh Function 7A00h *Novell NetWare*
LOW-LEVEL API (IPX) INSTALLATION CHECK

Registers at call: Return Registers:
AX = 7A00h   AL = status
         00h not installed
         FFh installed
            ES:DI -> FAR entry point for routines
              accessed exclusively through INT 7Ah
              in NetWare versions through 2.0a.
              Call with same values as INT 7Ah

Conflicts: none known, but see Table 2-2
See also: INT 64h, INT 7Ah, Novell TBMI Function 7AFFh Subfunction 0000h (Chapter 23), NetWare Lite Function D800h (Chapter 22)

INT 64h *Novell NetWare to v2.0a*
LOW-LEVEL API

Details: This interrupt is equivalent to INT 7Ah for NetWare versions through 2.0a only; later versions do not use this interrupt for IPX/SPX access, instead getting an entry point from INT 2Fh Function 7A00h.
Conflicts: see Table 2-3
See also: INT 2Fh Function 7A00h, INT 7Ah

INT 7Ah *Novell NetWare*
LOW-LEVEL API - Notes

Details: This interrupt is used for IPX/SPX access in NetWare versions through 2.0a; in later versions, you should use INT 2Fh Function 7A00h to get an entry point even though INT 7Ah still exists. For both INT 7Ah and the FAR entry point, BX contains the function number; IPX is sometimes called internally with BX bit 15 set.
Conflict: TopWare Network Operating System (Chapter 28), IBM 3270 Workstation Program (Chapter 37), X.PC Packet (Chapter 42), PRINDIR (PCI-15), GO32 (PCI-37), AutoCAD Device Interface (PCI-66), Canon IX-30F Image Scanner (PCI-66)
See also: INT 2Fh Function 7A00h, INT 64h, INT 7Ah Function 0000h

INT 7Ah Function 0000h   *IPX Driver*
OPEN SOCKET

Registers at call: Return Registers:
BX = 0000h   AL = return code
AL = socket longevity   00h success
   00h open until close or terminate   DX = socket number
   FFh open until close   FEh socket table full
DX = socket number (high byte in DL)   FFh socket already open
   0000h dynamic allocation
   else socket to open (see Table 5-1)

Details: TSRs which need to use sockets should set AL to FFh, non-resident programs should normally use AL=00h. IPX can be configured to support up to 150 open sockets on a workstation, and defaults to 20.

   This function is supported by Advanced NetWare 1.02+.

Conflict: TopWare Network Operating System (Chapter 28), IBM 3270 Workstation Program (Chapter 37), X.PC Packet (Chapter 42), PRINDIR (PCI-15), GO32 (PCI-37), AutoCAD Device Interface (PCI-66), Canon IX-30F Image Scanner (PCI-66)

See also: Functions 0001h and 0004h

5-1 Values for socket number:

0451h	File Service (NetWare Core Protocol)
0452h	Service Advertising Protocol
0453h	Routing Information Packet
0455h	NetBIOS Packet
0456h	diagnostics
0457h	server serial numbers (labeled "Copy Protection" by Lanalyzer)
4000h-7FFFh	used for dynamic allocation
4444h	Brightwork Development's SiteLock server
5555h	Brightwork Development's SiteLock client (workstation)
8000h-FFFFh	assigned by Novell

Note: SiteLock is an application metering product using IPX to communicate between the application and the license server.

INT 7Ah Function 0001h   *IPX Driver*
CLOSE SOCKET

Registers at call: Return Registers:
BX = 0001h   none
DX = socket number (high byte in DL)

Details: This function also cancels events set by any Event Control Blocks for the socket. The program must close all open sockets before terminating. This function is supported by Advanced NetWare 1.02+.

Conflict: TopWare Network Operating System (Chapter 28), IBM 3270 Workstation Program (Chapter 37), X.PC Packet (Chapter 42), PRINDIR (PCI-15), GO32 (PCI-37), AutoCAD Device Interface (PCI-66), Canon IX-30F Image Scanner (PCI-66)

See also: Function 0000h

INT 7Ah Function 0002h   *IPX Driver*
GET LOCAL TARGET

Registers at call: Return Registers:
BX = 0002h   AL = return code
ES:SI -> target internetwork address (see Table 5-15)   00h success
ES:DI -> 6-byte buffer for local target   CX = expected one-way transfer

time (clock ticks) for a 576-
byte packet
ES:DI -> local target
FAh unsuccessful (no path to
destination)

Details: The internetwork address consists of a 4-byte network address followed by a 6-byte node address. The local target is only a 6-byte node address. If the target is in the same network, the local target is just the node address of target; otherwise, the local target is the node address of the bridge that leads to the target.

This function may be called from inside IPX and AES Event Service Routines, but not from other interrupt handlers.

This function is supported by Advanced NetWare 1.02+.

Conflict: TopWare Network Operating System (Chapter 28), IBM 3270 Workstation Program (Chapter 37), X.PC Packet (Chapter 42), PRINDIR (PCI-15), GO32 (PCI-37), AutoCAD Device Interface (PCI-66), Canon IX-30F Image Scanner (PCI-66)

See also: Function 0009h

INT 7Ah Function 0003h   *IPX Driver*
SEND PACKET

Registers at call: **Return Registers:**
BX = 0003h   none
ES:SI -> Event Control Block (see Table 5-2)

Details: This function returns immediately; IPX attempts to send the packet in the background.

This function is supported by Advanced NetWare 1.02+.

This function is nearly identical to Function 000Fh, except that it always copies the source address into the IPX header assumed to be at the beginning of the first fragment.

Conflict: TopWare Network Operating System (Chapter 28), IBM 3270 Workstation Program (Chapter 37), X.PC Packet (Chapter 42), PRINDIR (PCI-15), GO32 (PCI-37), AutoCAD Device Interface (PCI-66), Canon IX-30F Image Scanner (PCI-66)

See also: Functions 0004h and 000Fh, NetWare INT 21h Function EEh (Chapter 21)

5-2 Format of Event Control Block:

Offset	Size	Description
00h	DWORD	Link
04h	DWORD	pointer to Event Service Routine (00000000h if none)
08h	BYTE	in-use flag (see Table 5-4)
09h	BYTE	completion code (see Table 5-5)
0Ah	WORD	(big-endian) socket number (see Table 5-1)
0Ch	4 BYTES IPX	workspace
10h	12 BYTES	driver workspace
1Ch	6 BYTES	immediate local node address
22h	WORD	fragment count
24h	varies	fragment descriptors

Offset	Size	Description
00h	DWORD	pointer to fragment data
04h	WORD	size of fragment in bytes

Notes: The Event Service Routine is a far procedure that is called when the ECB has been handled. On call, the in-use flag is zero if the ECB has been handled, non-zero otherwise. If the flag is zero, the completion code holds the result of the event.

The first fragment should start with an IPX header. All fragments are concatenated and sent in one piece.

The node address FFh FFh FFh FFh FFh FFh broadcasts to all nodes.

5-3 Format of AES-ECB:

Offset	Size	Description
00h	DWORD	Link
04h	DWORD	ESR address
08h	BYTE	in use flag (see Table 5-4)
09h	5 BYTEs	AES workspace

5-4 Values for ECB in-use flag:

00h	available
E0h	AES temporary
F6h	\ special IPX/SPX processing for v3.02+
F7h	/
F8h	IPX in critical section
F9h	SPX listening
FAh	processing
FBh	holding
FCh	AES waiting
FDh	AES couting down delay time
FEh	awaiting packet reception
FFh	sending packet

5-5 Values for ECB completion code:

00h	success
ECh	remote terminated connection without acknowledging packet
EDh	abnormal connection termination
EEh	invalid connection ID
EFh	SPX connection table full
F9h	event should not be cancelled
FAh	cannot establish connection with specified destination
FCh	cancelled
FDh	malformed packet
FEh	packet undeliverable
FFh	physical error

5-6 Event Service Routine calling convention:

Registers at call: **Return Registers:**
AL = caller's identity (00h = AES, FFh = IPX)   none
ES:SI -> event control block
interrupts disabled

5-7 Format of IPX header:

Offset	Size	Description
00h	WORD	(big-endian) checksum
02h	WORD	(big-endian) length in bytes of total packet
04h	BYTE	transport control
05h	BYTE	packet type (see Table 5-8)
06h	10 BYTES	destination internetwork address
10h	WORD	(big-endian) destination socket
12h	10 BYTES	source internetwork address
1Ch	WORD	(big-endian) source socket

INT 7Ah Function 0003h

5-8 Values for IPX packet type:

00h	unknown packet type
01h	routing information packet
02h	echo packet
03h	error packet
04h	packet exchange packet (always use this one)
05h	SPX packet
11h	NetWare Core Protocol
14h	Propagated Packet (for NetWare), NetBIOS name packet
15h-1Eh	experimental protocols

5-9 Format of Service Advertising Protocol Service Query Packet:

Offset	Size	Description
00h	30 BYTEs	IPX header
1Eh	WORD	(big-endian) query type
		0001h general find service
		0003h find nearest server
20h	WORD	(big-endian) server type (see NetWare INT 21h Function E3h, Chapter 21)

5-10 Format of Service Advertising Protocol Server Identification Packet:

Offset	Size	Description
00h	30 BYTEs	IPX header
1Eh	WORD	(big-endian) response type
		0002h general service
		0004h nearest service
20h	64N BYTEs	server entries (1-7) (see Table 5-11)

5-11 Format of SAP server entry:

Offset	Size	Description
00h	WORD	(big-endian) server type (see NetWare INT 21h Function E3h, Chapter 21)
02h	48 BYTEs	ASCIZ server name
32h	2 WORDs	(big-endian) network number
34h	3 WORDs	(big-endian) node number
3Ch	WORD	(big-endian) socket number
3Eh	WORD	(big-endian) number of hops between caller and server

5-12 Format of Routing Information Protocol packet:

Offset	Size	Description
00h	30 BYTEs	IPX header
1Eh	WORD	operation (0001h request, 0002h response)
20h	8N BYTEs	network entries (1-50) (see Table 5-13)

5-13 Format of Routing Information Protocol network entry:

Offset	Size	Description
00h	DWORD	network number (FFFFFFFFh = general request)
04h	WORD	(response) number of hops
06h	WORD	(response) number of clock ticks to reach destination

INT 7Ah Function 0004h   *IPX Driver*
LISTEN FOR PACKET

Purpose: This function provides IPX with an ECB for receiving an IPX packet, but does not wait for a packet to arrive.

Registers at call:
BX = 0004h
ES:SI -> Event Control Block (see Table 5-2)

Return Registers:
AL = status
   00h successful
   FFh no listening socket for packet

Details: The application must open a socket and initialize the ECB's ESR address, socket number, fragment count, and fragment descriptor fields before invoking this function.

There is no limit on the number of ECBs which may simultaneously be listening on a socket.

This function is supported by Advanced NetWare 1.02+.

Conflict: TopWare Network Operating System (Chapter 28), IBM 3270 Workstation Program (Chapter 37), X.PC Packet (Chapter 42), PRINDIR (PCI-15), GO32 (PCI-37), AutoCAD Device Interface (PCI-66), Canon IX-30F Image Scanner (PCI-66)

See also: Functions 0000h and 0003h

INT 7Ah Function 0005h
SCHEDULE IPX EVENT
IPX Driver

Registers at call:
BX = 0005h
AX = delay time in clock ticks
ES:SI -> Event Control Block (see Table 5-2)

Return Registers:
none

Details: This function is supported by Advanced NetWare 1.02+.

Conflict: TopWare Network Operating System (Chapter 28), IBM 3270 Workstation Program (Chapter 37), X.PC Packet (Chapter 42), PRINDIR (PCI-15), GO32 (PCI-37), AutoCAD Device Interface (PCI-66), Canon IX-30F Image Scanner (PCI-66)

See also: Functions 0006h, 0007h, and 0008h

INT 7Ah Function 0006h
CANCEL EVENT
IPX Driver

Registers at call:
BX = 0006h
ES:SI -> Event Control
  Block (see Table 5-2)

Return Registers:
AL = return code
  00h success
  F9h event in use
  FCh event cancelled
  FFh unsuccessful, event not in use, or unrecognized ECB flag

Details: One can not cancel packets which the node's driver has already sent.

This function is supported by Advanced NetWare 1.02+.

Conflict: TopWare Network Operating System (Chapter 28), IBM 3270 Workstation Program (Chapter 37), X.PC Packet (Chapter 42), PRINDIR (PCI-15), GO32 (PCI-37), AutoCAD Device Interface (PCI-66), Canon IX-30F Image Scanner (PCI-66)

See also: Function 0005h

INT 7Ah Function 0007h
SCHEDULE SPECIAL EVENT
IPX Driver

Registers at call:
BX = 0007h
AX = delay time
ES:SI -> Event Control Block (see Table 5-2)

Return Registers:
none

Details: This function is supported by Advanced NetWare 1.02+.

Conflict: TopWare Network Operating System (Chapter 28), IBM 3270 Workstation Program (Chapter 37), X.PC Packet (Chapter 42), PRINDIR (PCI-15), GO32 (PCI-37), AutoCAD Device Interface (PCI-66), Canon IX-30F Image Scanner (PCI-66)

See also: Function 0006h

INT 7Ah Function 0008h   *IPX Driver*
GET INTERVAL MARKER
Registers at call: **Return Registers:**
BX = 0008h   AX = interval marker in clock ticks
Details: This function may be used to measure the time elapsed between two events, up to one hour.
       This function is supported by Advanced NetWare 1.02+.
Conflict: TopWare Network Operating System (Chapter 28), IBM 3270 Workstation Program (Chapter 37), X.PC Packet (Chapter 42), PRINDIR (PCI-15), GO32 (PCI-37), AutoCAD Device Interface (PCI-66), Canon IX-30F Image Scanner (PCI-66)
See also: Function 0005h

INT 7Ah Function 0009h   *IPX Driver*
GET INTERNETWORK ADDRESS
Registers at call: **Return Registers:**
BX = 0009h   ES:SI buffer filled
ES:SI -> buffer for own internetwork address (see Table 5-14)   SI destroyed
Details: This function is supported by Advanced NetWare version 1.02+.
Conflict: TopWare Network Operating System (Chapter 28), IBM 3270 Workstation Program (Chapter 37), X.PC Packet (Chapter 42), PRINDIR (PCI-15), GO32 (PCI-37), AutoCAD Device Interface (PCI-66), Canon IX-30F Image Scanner (PCI-66)
See also: Functions 0002h and 000Bh

5-14 Format of internetwork address:

Offset	Size	Description
00h	4 BYTEs	(big-endian) network number
04h	6 BYTEs	(big-endian) node number within network

INT 7Ah Function 000Ah   *IPX Driver*
RELINQUISH CONTROL
Purpose: This call indicates that the application is idle and permits the IPX driver to do some work.
Registers at call: **Return Registers:**
BX = 000Ah   none
Details: This function is supported by Advanced NetWare version 1.02+.
Conflict: TopWare Network Operating System (Chapter 28), IBM 3270 Workstation Program (Chapter 37), X.PC Packet (Chapter 42), PRINDIR (PCI-15), GO32 (PCI-37), AutoCAD Device Interface (PCI-66), Canon IX-30F Image Scanner (PCI-66)
See also: INT 15h Function 1000h (PCI-44), INT 21h Function 89h (PCI-25), INT 2Fh Function 1680h (PCI-43)

INT 7Ah Function 000Bh   *IPX Driver*
DISCONNECT FROM TARGET
Registers at call: **Return Registers:**
BX = 000Bh   none
ES:SI -> internetwork address (see Table 5-15)
Details: This function permits the network software on the remote machine to remove any virtual connection with the calling machine. It should only be used in point-to-point networks.
       This function should never be called from within an Event Service Routine.
       This function is supported by Advanced NetWare version 1.02+.

Conflict: TopWare Network Operating System (Chapter 28), IBM 3270 Workstation Program (Chapter 37), X.PC Packet (Chapter 42), PRINDIR (PCI-15), GO32 (PCI-37), AutoCAD Device Interface (PCI-66), Canon IX-30F Image Scanner (PCI-66)

See also: Functions 0002h and 0009h

5-15 Format of internetwork address:

Offset	Size		Description
00h	4	BYTEs	(big-endian) destination network
04h	6	BYTEs	(big-endian) destination node
0Ah	2	BYTEs	(big-endian) destination socket

INT 7Ah Function 000Ch
INITIALIZE NETWORK ADDRESS

IPX Driver
Undocumented

Registers at call:
BX = 000Ch
CX:DX = global network address (see Table 5-15)
ES:DI -> "OSINCRITICALSECTION" flag
DS:SI -> current mode for socket

Return Registers:
none

Details: The address cannot be changed once it has been initialized.
Conflict: TopWare Network Operating System (Chapter 28), IBM 3270 Workstation Program (Chapter 37), X.PC Packet (Chapter 42), PRINDIR (PCI-15), GO32 (PCI-37), AutoCAD Device Interface (PCI-66), Canon IX-30F Image Scanner (PCI-66)

INT 7Ah Function 000Dh
IPX GET PACKET SIZE

IPX Driver
Undocumented

Registers at call:
BX = 000Dh

Return Registers:
AX = maximum packet size
CX = retry count

Conflict: TopWare Network Operating System (Chapter 28), IBM 3270 Workstation Program (Chapter 37), X.PC Packet (Chapter 42), PRINDIR (PCI-15), GO32 (PCI-37), AutoCAD Device Interface (PCI-66), Canon IX-30F Image Scanner (PCI-66)
See also: Function 001Ah

INT 7Ah Function 000Eh
TERMINATE SOCKETS

IPX Driver
Undocumented

Registers at call:
BX = 000Eh

Return Registers:
none

Details: This function terminates all sockets opened with the current mode; this may be intended for future enhancements as the socket mode never changes in NetWare v2.15.
Conflict: TopWare Network Operating System (Chapter 28), IBM 3270 Workstation Program (Chapter 37), X.PC Packet (Chapter 42), PRINDIR (PCI-15), GO32 (PCI-37), AutoCAD Device Interface (PCI-66), Canon IX-30F Image Scanner (PCI-66)

INT 7Ah Function 000Fh
SEND PACKET

IPX Driver
Undocumented

Registers at call:
BX = 000Fh
ES:SI -> Event Control Block (see Table 5-2)

Return Registers:
none

Details: This function is nearly identical to Function 0003h, but does not copy address into the first fragment.

Conflict: TopWare Network Operating System (Chapter 28), IBM 3270 Workstation Program (Chapter 37), X.PC Packet (Chapter 42), PRINDIR (PCI-15), GO32 (PCI-37), AutoCAD Device Interface (PCI-66), Canon IX-30F Image Scanner (PCI-66)
See also: Function 0003h

INT 7Ah Function 0010h   *SPX Driver*
INSTALLATION CHECK

Registers at call:	Return Registers:
BX = 0010h	AL = FFh if SPX loaded
AL = 00h	BH = SPX major version
	BL = SPX minor version
	CX = maximum SPX connections
	DX = SPX connections available

Details: This function is supported by Advanced NetWare version 2.1+.
Conflict: TopWare Network Operating System (Chapter 28), IBM 3270 Workstation Program (Chapter 37), X.PC Packet (Chapter 42), PRINDIR (PCI-15), GO32 (PCI-37), AutoCAD Device Interface (PCI-66), Canon IX-30F Image Scanner (PCI-66)
See also: Function 0015h

INT 7Ah Function 0011h   *SPX Driver*
ESTABLISH SPX CONNECTION

Purpose: Attempt to establish a connection with a listening socket.

Registers at call:	Return Registers:
BX = 0011h	AL = status
AL = retry count	00h attempting to contact destination socket
AH = watchdog flag	EFh local connection table full
ES:SI -> Event Control Block (see Table 5-2)	FDh buffer size not 42 or fragment count not 1
	FFh sending socket not open
	DX = assigned connection ID number

Details: There should always be at least two SPX ECB's listening to a socket, so that NetWare can perform its internal packet exchanges.

The first fragment should start with a SPX header. Fill in all destination addresses.

This function is supported by Advanced NetWare version 2.1+.

Conflict: TopWare Network Operating System (Chapter 28), IBM 3270 Workstation Program (Chapter 37), X.PC Packet (Chapter 42), PRINDIR (PCI-15), GO32 (PCI-37), AutoCAD Device Interface (PCI-66), Canon IX-30F Image Scanner (PCI-66)
See also: Functions 0000h, 0012h, 0013h, 0014h, and 0015h

5-16 Format of SPX header:

Offset	Size	Description
00h	WORD	(big-endian) checksum
02h	WORD	(big-endian) length in bytes of total packet
04h	BYTE	transport control
05h	BYTE	packet type (see Table 5-8)
06h	10 BYTEs	destination internet address
10h	WORD	(big-endian) destination socket
12h	10 BYTEs	source internet address
1Ch	WORD	(big-endian) source socket
1Eh	BYTE	connection control (see Table 5-17)
1Fh	BYTE	datastream type
		FEh terminate connection request packet
		FFh terminate connection acknowledgement packet

		other user-defined, ignored by SPX
20h	WORD	(big-endian) source connection ID
22h	WORD	(big-endian) destination connection ID
24h	WORD	(big-endian) sequence number
26h	WORD	(big-endian) acknowledge number
28h	WORD	(big-endian) allocation number

5-17 Bitfield for connection control:

bits 3-0	*unused*
bit 4	end of message
bit 5	reserved
bit 6	acknowledgement required
bit 7	system packet

INT 7Ah Function 0012h
LISTEN FOR SPX CONNECTION
SPX Driver

Registers at call:
BX = 0012h
AH = watchdog flag
    00h disabled, 01h enabled
AL = retry count (00h = default)
ES:SI -> Event Control Block (see Table 5-2)

Return Registers:
none

Details: There should always be at least two SPX ECB's listening to a socket, so that NetWare can perform its internal packet exchanges.
    This function is supported by Advanced NetWare version 2.1+.
Conflict: TopWare Network Operating System (Chapter 28), IBM 3270 Workstation Program (Chapter 37), X.PC Packet (Chapter 42), PRINDIR (PCI-15), GO32 (PCI-37), AutoCAD Device Interface (PCI-66), Canon IX-30F Image Scanner (PCI-66)
See also: Functions 0011h, 0013h, and 0014h

INT 7Ah Function 0013h
TERMINATE SPX CONNECTION
SPX Driver

Registers at call:
BX = 0013h
DX = connection ID to terminate
ES:SI -> Event Control Block (see Table 5-2)

Return Registers:
none

Details: This function is supported by Advanced NetWare version 2.1+.
Conflict: TopWare Network Operating System (Chapter 28), IBM 3270 Workstation Program (Chapter 37), X.PC Packet (Chapter 42), PRINDIR (PCI-15), GO32 (PCI-37), AutoCAD Device Interface (PCI-66), Canon IX-30F Image Scanner (PCI-66)
See also: Functions 0011h, 0012h, and 0014h

INT 7Ah Function 0014h
ABORT SPX CONNECTION
SPX Driver

Registers at call:
BX = 0014h
DX = connection ID to terminate

Return Registers:
none

Details: This function is supported by Advanced NetWare version 2.1+.
    This function does not tell the other side that the connection has been terminated. It also aborts any outstanding Establish Connection, Terminate Connection, and Send Sequenced Packet commands.

Conflict: TopWare Network Operating System (Chapter 28), IBM 3270 Workstation Program (Chapter 37), X.PC Packet (Chapter 42), PRINDIR (PCI-15), GO32 (PCI-37), AutoCAD Device Interface (PCI-66), Canon IX-30F Image Scanner (PCI-66)
See also: Functions 0011h and 0013h

INT 7Ah Function 0015h   *SPX Driver*
GET SPX CONNECTION STATUS

Registers at call: **Return Registers:**
BX = 0015h   AL = return code
DX = connection ID   00h connection still valid
ES:SI -> status buffer (see Table 5-18)   ES:SI -> status buffer filled
                                              EEh no such connection

Details: This function is supported by Advanced NetWare version 2.1+.
Conflict: TopWare Network Operating System (Chapter 28), IBM 3270 Workstation Program (Chapter 37), X.PC Packet (Chapter 42), PRINDIR (PCI-15), GO32 (PCI-37), AutoCAD Device Interface (PCI-66), Canon IX-30F Image Scanner (PCI-66)
See also: Functions 0010h and 0011h

5-18 Format of status buffer:

Offset	Size	Description
00h	BYTE	connection state
		01h waiting to establish connection
		02h starting (attempting to create connection)
		03h connection established
		04h terminating
01h	BYTE	watchdog flag
		bit 0: used internally by SPX
		bit 1: SPX watchdog is monitoring connection
		bits 2-7 used internally by SPX
02h	WORD	(big-endian) source connection ID
04h	WORD	(big-endian) destination connection ID
06h	WORD	(big-endian) sequence number of next packet sent
08h	WORD	(big-endian) acknowledge number, expected sequence number of next received packet
0Ah	WORD	(big-endian) maximum sequence number remote SPX may send without ACK from local SPX
0Ch	WORD	(big-endian) remote acknowledge number, next sequence number remote SPX expects to receive
0Eh	WORD	(big-endian) remote allocation number, maximum sequence number local SPX may send
10h	WORD	(big-endian) connection socket
12h	6 BYTEs	immediate node address—bridge on local network to destination
18h	10 BYTEs	destination internetwork address (see Table 5-15)
22h	WORD	(big-endian) retransmit count
24h	WORD	(big-endian) estimated roundtrip delay
26h	WORD	(big-endian) retransmitted packets
28h	WORD	(big-endian) suppressed packets
2Ah	12 BYTEs	*unknown* (v2.15)

INT 7Ah Function 0016h
SEND SPX PACKET
SPX Driver

Registers at call: **Return Registers:**

BX = 0016h   none

DX = connection ID

ES:SI -> Event Control Block (see Table 5-2)

Details: This function is supported by Advanced NetWare version 2.1+.

CX may need to be 0001h.

Conflict: TopWare Network Operating System (Chapter 28), IBM 3270 Workstation Program (Chapter 37), X.PC Packet (Chapter 42), PRINDIR (PCI-15), GO32 (PCI-37), AutoCAD Device Interface (PCI-66), Canon IX-30F Image Scanner (PCI-66)

See also: Functions 0011h and 0017h

INT 7Ah Function 0017h
LISTEN FOR SPX PACKET
SPX Driver

Registers at call: **Return Registers:**

BX = 0017h   none

DX = connection ID (unused in NetWare v2.15)

ES:SI -> Event Control Block (see Table 5-2)

Details: This function is supported by Advanced NetWare version 2.1+.

CX may need to be 0001h.

Conflict: TopWare Network Operating System (Chapter 28), IBM 3270 Workstation Program (Chapter 37), X.PC Packet (Chapter 42), PRINDIR (PCI-15), GO32 (PCI-37), AutoCAD Device Interface (PCI-66), Canon IX-30F Image Scanner (PCI-66)

See also: Functions 0011h and 0016h

INT 7Ah Function 0018h
ADD DIAGNOSTIC ELEMENT
IPX Driver
Undocumented

Registers at call: **Return Registers:**

BX = 0018h   none

ES:SI -> diagnostic element (see Table 5-19) to be added to Diagnostic Queue

Details: This function is supported on file servers only under Advanced NetWare v2.15; v3.02 also supports it on workstations.

Conflict: TopWare Network Operating System (Chapter 28), IBM 3270 Workstation Program (Chapter 37), X.PC Packet (Chapter 42), PRINDIR (PCI-15), GO32 (PCI-37), AutoCAD Device Interface (PCI-66), Canon IX-30F Image Scanner (PCI-66)

See also: Function 0019h

5-19 Format of diagnostic element:

Offset	Size	Description
00h	DWORD	pointer to next diagnostic element
04h	DWORD	pointer to function for *unknown purpose*
08h	DWORD	pointer to function for *unknown purpose*

INT 7Ah Function 0019h
CANCEL DIAGNOSTIC ELEMENT
IPX Driver
Undocumented

Registers at call: **Return Registers:**

BX = 0019h   none

ES:SI -> diagnostic element (see Table 5-19) to be removed

Details: This function is supported on file servers only under Advanced NetWare v2.15; v3.02 also supports it on workstations.

Conflict: TopWare Network Operating System (Chapter 28), IBM 3270 Workstation Program (Chapter 37), X.PC Packet (Chapter 42), PRINDIR (PCI-15), GO32 (PCI-37), AutoCAD Device Interface (PCI-66), Canon IX-30F Image Scanner (PCI-66)
See also: Function 0018h

INT 7Ah Function 001Ah
GET DRIVER PACKET SIZE LIMIT
IPX Driver
Undocumented

Registers at call:
BX = 001Ah

Return Registers:
AX = packet size with preamble
CX = IPX retry count

Details: This function is supported on file servers only under Advanced NetWare v2.15; v3.02 also supports it on workstations.
Conflict: TopWare Network Operating System (Chapter 28), IBM 3270 Workstation Program (Chapter 37), X.PC Packet (Chapter 42), PRINDIR (PCI-15), GO32 (PCI-37), AutoCAD Device Interface (PCI-66), Canon IX-30F Image Scanner (PCI-66)
See also: Function 000Dh

INT 7Ah Function 001Bh
UNKNOWN FUNCTION
IPX Driver
Undocumented

Registers at call:
BX = 001Bh
others, if any, unknown

Return Registers:
unknown

Details: This function is supported on file servers only under Advanced NetWare v2.15; v3.02 also supports it on workstations.
Conflict: TopWare Network Operating System (Chapter 28), IBM 3270 Workstation Program (Chapter 37), X.PC Packet (Chapter 42), PRINDIR (PCI-15), GO32 (PCI-37), AutoCAD Device Interface (PCI-66), Canon IX-30F Image Scanner (PCI-66)

CHAPTER 6

Named Pipes

Named pipes, which can be created on client/server network configurations, allow applications to send and receive streams of data from other applications running on different computers in the network. The applications open, read, and write to named pipes as if they were files. This means an application can read and write variable amounts of data as needed.

The Named Pipe interface was introduced by LAN Manager but has since been adopted by most other major networking products, such as Novell NetWare's DOS Named Pipe Extender (DOSNP), Banyan VINES, OS/2 Virtual DOS Machines, Windows NT, and others.

INT 21h Function 5F32h   *Named Pipes*
LOCAL DosQNmPipeInfo - QUERY NAMED PIPE INFORMATION   *(partially doc.)*

Registers at call: **Return Registers:**
AX = 5F32h   CF clear if successful
BX = handle   _PIPEINFO structure filled in
CX = size of _PIPEINFO structure   CF set on error
DX = level (must be 0001h)   AX = error code
DS:SI -> _PIPEINFO structure (see Table 6-1)
See also: Functions 5F33h and 5F34h

6-1 Format of _PIPEINFO structure:

Offset	Size	Description
00h	WORD	size of outgoing buffer
02h	WORD	size of incoming buffer
04h	BYTE	maximum number of instances allowed
05h	BYTE	current number of instances
06h	BYTE	length of the name (including terminating NUL)
07h	N BYTEs	name

INT 21h Function 5F33h   *Named Pipes*
LOCAL DosQNmPHandState - GET INFORMATION FOR HANDLE   *(partially doc.)*

Registers at call: **Return Registers:**
AX = 5F33h   CF clear if successful
BX = handle   AH = pipe mode bit mask (see Table 6-2)
                                                         AL = maximum number of instances
                                                 CF set on error
                                                         AX = error code

See also: Functions 5F32h and 5F34h

6-2 Bitfields for pipe mode:

bit 7   set if nonblocking, clear if blocking
bit 6   set if server end, clear if client end
bit 2   set if write in message mode, clear if write in byte mode
bit 0   set if read in message mode, clear if read in byte mode

---

INT 21h Function 5F34h
LOCAL DosSetNmPHandState - SET STATE FOR PIPE HANDLE

Named Pipes
(partially doc.)

Registers at call:
AX = 5F34h
BX = handle
CX = pipe mode bit mask
    bit 15: set if nonblocking, clear if blocking
    bit 8: set if read in message mode, clear if read
       in byte mode
See also: Functions 5F32h, 5F33h, and 5F36h

Return Registers:
CF clear if successful
CF set if error
    AX = error code

INT 21h Function 5F35h
LOCAL DosPeekNmPipe - PEEK AT PENDING INPUT FOR PIPE

Named Pipes
(partially doc.)

Registers at call:
AX = 5F35h
BX = handle
CX = buffer length
DS:SI -> buffer

Return Registers:
CF clear if successful
    CX = bytes read
    SI = bytes left in the pipe
    DX = bytes left in the current message
    DI = pipe status
        0001h disconnected
        0002h listening
        0003h connected
        0004h closing
CF set if error
    AX = error code

See also: Functions 5F38h and 5F39h, LAN Manager Function 5F51h (Chapter 19)

INT 21h Function 5F36h
LOCAL DosTransactNmPipe

Named Pipes
(partially doc.)

Registers at call:
AX = 5F36h
BX = handle
CX = in buffer length
DS:SI -> in buffer
DX = out buffer length
ES:DI -> out buffer
See also: Functions 5F34h and 5F37h

Return Registers:
CF clear if successful
    CX = bytes read
CF set on error
    AX = error code

INT 21h Function 5F37h
DosCallNmPipe

Named Pipes
(partially doc.)

Registers at call:
AX = 5F37h
DS:SI -> DosCallNmPipe stack frame (see Table 6-3)

Return Registers:
CF clear if successful
    CX = bytes read
CF set on error
    AX = error code

See also: Functions 5F36h and 5F38h

6-3 Format of DosCallNmPipe stack frame:

Offset	Size	Description
00h	DWORD	timeout
04h	DWORD	pointer to bytes-read WORD (not used!)
08h	WORD	out buffer length
0Ah	DWORD	address of out buffer
0Eh	WORD	in buffer length
10h	DWORD	address of in buffer
14h	DWORD	address of pipe name

INT 21h Function 5F38h   *Named Pipes*
LOCAL DosWaitNmPipe - WAIT UNTIL PIPE INSTANCE AVAILABLE   *(partially doc.)*

Registers at call: **Return Registers:**
AX = 5F38h   CF clear if successful
DS:DX -> pipe name   CF set if error
BX:CX = timeout value   AX = error code

Details: When a client gets a return code of ERROR_PIPE_BUSY on attempting to open a pipe, it should issue this call to wait until the pipe instance becomes available again; on return from this call, the client must attempt to open the pipe once again.
See also: Functions 5F37h and 5F39h

INT 21h Function 5F39h   *Named Pipes*
LOCAL DosRawReadNmPipe - RAW INPUT FROM PIPE   *Undocumented*

Registers at call: **Return Registers:**
AX = 5F39h   CF clear if successful
BX = handle   CX = bytes read
CX = buffer length   CF set if error
DS:DX -> buffer   AX = error code

Details: This function is not documented in the LAN Manager Toolkit.
See also: Functions 5F35h and 5F3Ah, LAN Manager INT 2Fh Function 1186h (Chapter 19)

INT 21h Function 5F3Ah   *Named Pipes*
LOCAL DosRawWriteNmPipe - RAW OUTPUT TO PIPE   *Undocumented*

Registers at call: **Return Registers:**
AX = 5F3Ah   CF clear if successful
BX = handle   CX = bytes written
CX = buffer length   CF set if error
DS:DX -> buffer   AX = error code

Details: This function is not documented in the LAN Manager Toolkit.
See also: Functions 5F39h and 5F3Bh, LAN Manager INT 2Fh Function 118Fh (Chapter 19)

CHAPTER 7

NDIS

In 1989, Microsoft and 3Com jointly developed the Network Device Interface Specification (NDIS) to define a software interface for use by network transport protocols to communicate with the network adapter card. Prior to NDIS (and competing specifications such as Novell's ODI and FTP Software's packet drivers), many transport protocols were tied to specific network adapter cards. Each card vendor had to create proprietary drivers to support a variety of network operating system environments.

Originally designed for LAN Manager, NDIS drivers can now be used by a variety of networking packages, and form the hardware abstraction layer of Windows NT's built-in networking.

INT 21h Function 4402h	*NDIS v2.0.1*
PROTOCOL MANAGER	

Registers at call:	Return Registers:
AX = 4402h	CF clear if successful
BX = file handle for device	AX = number of bytes actually read
"PROTMAN$"	CF set on error
CX = 000Eh (size of request block)	AX = error code (01h,05h,06h,0Dh) (see Table 3-1)
DS:DX -> request block (see Tables 7-1	
to 7-10)	

See also: FTPSOFT.DOS Function 4402h (Chapter 33)

7-1 Format of request block for GetProtocolManagerInfo:

Offset	Size	Description
00h	WORD	01h
02h	WORD	returned status (see Table 7-11)
04h	DWORD	returned pointer to structure representing parsed user configuration
08h	DWORD	unused
0Ch	WORD	returned BCD version of NDIS on which Protocol Manager is based

7-2 Format of request block for RegisterModule:

Offset	Size	Description
00h	WORD	02h
02h	WORD	returned status (see Table 7-11)
04h	DWORD	pointer to module's common characteristics table (see Table 7-12)
08h	DWORD	pointer to list of modules to which the module is to be bound
0Ch	WORD	unused

7-3 Format of request block for BindAndStart:

Offset	Size	Description
00h	WORD	03h
02h	WORD	returned status (see Table 7-11)
04h	DWORD	caller's virtual address in FailingModules structure
08h	DWORD	unused
0Ch	WORD	unused

7-4 Format of request block for GetProtocolManagerLinkage:

Offset	Size	Description
00h	WORD	04h
02h	WORD	returned status (see Table 7-11)
04h	DWORD	returned dispatch point
08h	DWORD	unused
0Ch	WORD	returned protocol manager DS

Note: the dispatch point may be called as follows instead of using this IOCTL:

Registers at call:			Return Registers:
STACK:	WORD	protocol manager DS	AX = returned status
	DWORD	pointer to request block	STACK popped

7-5 Format of request block for GetProtocolIniPath:

Offset	Size	Description
00h	WORD	05h
02h	WORD	returned status (see Table 7-11)
04h	DWORD	pointer to a buffer for the ASCIZ pathname of PROTOCOL.INI
08h	DWORD	unused
0Ch	WORD	buffer length

7-6 Format of request block for RegisterProtocolManagerInfo:

Offset	Size	Description
00h	WORD	06h
02h	WORD	returned status (see Table 7-11)
04h	DWORD	pointer to structure containing parsed user configuration file
08h	DWORD	unused
0Ch	WORD	length of structure

7-7 Format of request block for InitAndRegister:

Offset	Size	Description
00h	WORD	07h
02h	WORD	returned status (see Table 7-11)
04h	DWORD	unused
08h	DWORD	poitner to ASCIZ name of the module to be prebind initialized
0Ch	WORD	unused

7-8 Format of request block for UnbindAndStop:

Offset	Size	Description
00h	WORD	08h
02h	WORD	returned status (see Table 7-11)
04h	DWORD	failing modules as for BindAndStart
08h	DWORD	if not 0000h:0000h, pointer to ASCIZ name of module to unbind if 0000h:0000h, terminate a set of previously dynamically ound protocol modules
0Ch	WORD	unused

7-9 Format of request block for BindStatus:

Offset	Size	Description
00h	WORD	09h
02h	WORD	returned status (see Table 7-11)
04h	DWORD	must be 0000h:0000h
		on return, points to root tree
08h	DWORD	0000h:0000h
0Ch	WORD	unused under DOS

7-10 Format of request block for RegisterStatus:

Offset	Size	Description
00h	WORD	0Ah
02h	WORD	returned status (0000h, 0008h, 002Ch) (see Table 7-11)
04h	DWORD	0000h:0000h
08h	DWORD	pointer to 16-byte ASCIZ module name
0Ch	WORD	0000h

Note: This function is not supported by the 10NET v5.0 PROTMAN$ driver.

7-11 Values for status code:

0000h	success
0001h	wait for release—protocol has retained control of the data buffer
0002h	request queued
0003h	frame not recognized
0004h	frame rejected
0005h	frame should be forwarded
0006h	out of resource
0007h	invalid parameter
0008h	invalid function
0009h	not supported
000Ah	hardware error
000Bh	transmit error
000Ch	unrecognized destination
000Dh	buffer too small
0020h	already started
0021h	binding incomplete
0022h	driver not initialized
0023h	hardware not found
0024h	hardware failure
0025h	configuration failure
0026h	interrupt conflict
0027h	MAC incompatible
0028h	initialization failed
0029h	no binding
002Ah	network may be disconnected
002Bh	incompatible OS version
002Ch	already registered
002Dh	path not found
002Eh	insufficient memory
002Fh	info not found
00FFh	general failure

F000h-FFFFh reserved for vendor-specific codes, treated as general failure

7-12 Format of common characteristics table:

Offset	Size	Description
00h	WORD	size of table in bytes
02h	BYTE	NDIS major version
03h	BYTE	NDIS minor version
04h	WORD	reserved
06h	BYTE	module major version
07h	BYTE	module minor version
08h	DWORD	module function flag bits
		bit 0: binding at upper boundary supported
		bit 1: binding at lower boundary supported
		bit 2: dynamically bound
		bits 3-31 reserved, must be 0
0Ch	16 BYTEs	ASCIZ module name
1Ch	BYTE	upper boundary protocol level (see Table 7-13)
1Dh	BYTE	upper boundary interface type
		for MACs: 1 = MAC
		for data links and transports: to be defined
		for session: 1 = NCB
		any level: 0 = private (ISV-defined)
1Eh	BYTE	lower boundary protocol level (see Table 7-13)
1Fh	BYTE	lower boundary interface type
		same as offset 1Dh
20h	WORD	module ID filled in by protocol manager
22h	WORD	module DS
24h	DWORD	system request entry point
28h	DWORD	pointer to service-specific characteristics
		0000h:0000h if none
2Ch	DWORD	pointer to service-specific status, or 0000h:0000h if none
30h	DWORD	pointer to upper dispatch table (see Table 7-14)
		0000h:0000h if none
34h	DWORD	pointer to lower dispatch table (see Table 7-14)
		0000h:0000h if none
38h	2 DWORDs	reserved, must be 0

Note: For compatibility with NDIS 1.x.x, a major version of 00h is interpreted as 01h.

7-13 Values for boundary protocol level:

00h	physical
01h	Media Access Control
02h	Data link
03h	network
04h	transport
05h	session
FFh	not specified

7-14 Format of dispatch table:

Offset	Size	Description
00h	DWORD	pointer to common characteristics table (see Table 7-12)
04h	4 BYTEs	*unknown*
08h	DWORD	pointer to *unknown* function (called with 12 bytes of stack arguments)

0Ch	DWORD	pointer to *unknown* function (called with 10 bytes of stack arguments)
10h	DWORD	pointer to *unknown* function (called with 16 bytes of stack arguments)
14h	DWORD	pointer to *unknown* function (called with 4 bytes of stack arguments)
18h	DWORD	pointer to *unknown* function (called with 18 bytes of stack arguments)
1Ch	DWORD	pointer to *unknown* function (called with 12 bytes of stack arguments)

7-15 Format of MAC Service-Specific Characteristics Table:

Offset	Size	Description
00h	WORD	length of table in bytes
02h	16 BYTEs	ASCIZ MAC type name, "802.3", "802.4", "802.5", "802.6", "DIX", "DIX+802.3", "APPLETALK", "ARCNET", "FDDI", "SDLC", "BSC", "HDLC", or "ISDN"
12h	WORD	length of station addresses in bytes
14h	16 BYTEs	permanent station address
24h	16 BYTEs	current station address
34h	DWORD	current functional adapter address (00000000h if none)
38h	DWORD	pointer to multicast address list
3Ch	DWORD	link speed in bits/sec
40h	DWORD	service flags (see Table 7-16)
44h	WORD	maximum frame size which may be both sent and received
46h	DWORD	total transmit buffer capacity in bytes
4Ah	WORD	transmit buffer allocation block size in bytes
4Ch	DWORD	total receive buffer capacity in bytes
50h	WORD	receive buffer allocation block size in bytes
52h	3 BYTEs	IEEE vendor code
55h	BYTE	vendor adapter code
56h	DWORD	pointer to ASCIZ vendor adapter description
5Ah	WORD	IRQ used by adapter
5Ch	WORD	transmit queue depth
5Eh	WORD	maximum supported number of data blocks in buffer descriptors
60h	N BYTEs	vendor-specific info

7-16 Bitfields for service flags:

bit 0	supports broadcast
bit 1	supports multicast
bit 2	supports functional/group addressing
bit 3	supports promiscuous mode
bit 4	station address software settable
bit 5	statistics always current
bit 6	supports InitiateDiagnostics
bit 7	supports loopback
bit 8	MAC does primarily ReceiveChain indications instead of ReceiveLookahead indications
bit 9	supports IBM source routing
bit 10	supports MAC reset
bit 11	supports Open/Close adapter
bit 12	supports interrupt request
bit 13	supports source routing bridge
bit 14	supports GDT virtual addresses (OS/2 version)
bit 15	multiple TransferDatas allowed durign a single indication
bit 16	MAC normally sets FrameSize = 0 in ReceiveLookahead
bit 17-31	reserved, must be 0

7-17 Format of NetBIOS Service-Specific Characteristics Table

Offset	Size	Description
00h	WORD	length of table in bytes
02h	16 BYTEs	ASCIZ type name of NetBIOS module
12h	WORD	NetBIOS module code
14h	N BYTEs	vendor-specific info

7-18 Format of MAC Service-Specific Status Table:

Offset	Size	Description
00h	WORD	length of table in bytes
02h	DWORD	seconds since 0:00 1/1/70 when diagnostics last run (FFFFFFFFh = never)
06h	DWORD	MAC status bits (see Table 7-19)
0Ah	WORD	current packet filter flags bit 0: directed/multicast or group/functional bit 1: broadcast bit 2: promiscuous bit 3: all source routing bits 4-15: reserved, must be zero
0Ch	DWORD	pointer to media-specific status table or 0000h:0000h
10h	DWORD	seconds past 0:00 1/1/70 of last ClearStatistics
14h	DWORD	total frames received (FFFFFFFFh = not counted)
18h	DWORD	frames with CRC error (FFFFFFFFh = not counted)
1Ch	DWORD	total bytes received (FFFFFFFFh = not counted)
20h	DWORD	frames discarded—no buffer space (FFFFFFFFh = not counted)
24h	DWORD	multicast frames received (FFFFFFFFh = not counted)
28h	DWORD	broadcast frames received (FFFFFFFFh = not counted)
2Ch	DWORD	frames with errors (FFFFFFFFh = not counted)
30h	DWORD	overly large frames (FFFFFFFFh = not counted)
34h	DWORD	frames less than minimum size (FFFFFFFFh = not counted)
38h	DWORD	multicast bytes received (FFFFFFFFh = not counted)
3Ch	DWORD	broadcast bytes received (FFFFFFFFh = not counted)
40h	DWORD	frames discarded—hardware error (FFFFFFFFh = not counted)
44h	DWORD	total frames transmitted (FFFFFFFFh = not counted)
48h	DWORD	total bytes transmitted (FFFFFFFFh = not counted)
4Ch	DWORD	multicast frames transmitted (FFFFFFFFh = not counted)
50h	DWORD	broadcast frames transmitted (FFFFFFFFh = not counted)
54h	DWORD	broadcast bytes transmitted (FFFFFFFFh = not counted)
58h	DWORD	multicast bytes transmitted (FFFFFFFFh = not counted)
5Ch	DWORD	frames not transmitted—timeout (FFFFFFFFh = not counted)
60h	DWORD	frames not transmitted—hardware error (FFFFFFFFh = not countd)
64h	N BYTEs	vendor-specific info

7-19 Bitfields for MAC status bits:

bits 0-2   operational status
        000 hardware not installed
        001 hardware failed startup diagnostics
        010 hardware configuration problem
        011 hardware fault
        100 operating marginally due to soft faults
        101 reserved
        110 reserved
        111 hardware fully operational
bit 3   MAC bound
bit 4   MAC open
bit 5   diagnostics in progress
bits 6-31 reserved

INT 65h
POST PROCESSING INTERRUPT

FTP Software NDIS-Packet Driver adapter

Conflicts: see Table 2-3

CHAPTER 8

NetBIOS

NetBIOS, the Network Basic Input/Output System, is a high-level interface developed by Sytek, Inc., and first introduced in 1984 with IBM's PC Network adapter card. This made NetBIOS the standard session-layer interface for a large body of network-aware applications. NetBIOS, however, includes both session and transport layer peer-to-peer protocols. If two stations run NetBIOS implementations (such as IBM NetBIOS protocol and Xerox XNS protocol) that differ at the transport layer, the machines will not be able to communicate.

Many current networking products either use NetBIOS as the session layer or provide NetBIOS emulation, including MS-Net, Windows NT, Novell NetWare/Netware Lite and LAN Workplace for DOS, AT&T Starlan, and OS/2. In non-MS-DOS environments, NetBIOS is typically called via a function call (**NetBiosSubmit** for OS/2) rather than an interrupt, but the Network Command Block remains unchanged.

INT 2Ah Function 0000h   *AT&T Starlan Extended NetBIOS (var length names)*
INSTALLATION CHECK

Registers at call:	Return Registers:
AX = 0000h	AH = DDh

Conflicts: MS-DOS (Chapter 3)
See also: INT 5Bh, INT 2Ah Function 00h (Chapter 3)

INT 2Ah Function 01h   *NETWORK (Microsoft, LANtastic)*
EXECUTE NetBIOS REQUEST, NO ERROR RETRY

Registers at call:
AH = 01h
ES:BX -> Network Control Block
   (see Table 8-4)

Return Registers:
AL = NetBIOS error code
AH = status
      00h successful, 01h error

See also: Functions 04h and 0500h, INT 5Bh, INT 5Ch

INT 2Ah Function 02h   *NETWORK (Microsoft)*
SET NET PRINTER MODE

Registers at call:
AH = 02h
others, if any, unknown

Return Registers:
unknown

INT 2Ah Function 04h   *NETWORK (Microsoft, LANtastic)*
EXECUTE NetBIOS REQUEST

Registers at call:
AH = 04h
AL = error retry
    00h automatically retry request on

errors 09h, 12h, and 21h
    01h no retry
    02h *unknown*
ES:BX -> Network Control Block
  (see Table 8-4)

Return Registers:
AX = 0000h if successful
AH = 01h on error
    AL = error code

Details: This function invokes either INT 5Bh or INT 5Ch as appropriate.
    This function is also supported by Lantastic, NetWare, 10NET, etc.
    The Advanced NetWare v2.15 NetBIOS emulator returns CF clear if succesful, set on error.
See also: Functions 01h and 0500h, INT 5Bh, INT 5Ch

INT 2Ah Function 0500h
GET NETWORK RESOURCE AVAILABILITY
NETWORK (Microsoft, LANtastic)

Registers at call:
AX = 0500h

Return Registers:
AX reserved
BX = number of network names available
CX = number of network control blocks available
DX = number of network sessions available

Details: This function is also supported by Lantastic, NetWare, 10NET, etc.
See also: Functions 01h and 04h, INT 5Ch

INT 5Bh
INTERFACE
AT&T Starlan Extended NetBIOS (variable length names)

Registers at call:
ES:BX -> Network Control Block
  (see Table 8-1)

Return Registers:
AL = status (see Table 8-3)

Conflicts: Alloy NTNX (Chapter 12), ISOLAN Multi Protocol Software (Chapter 31), Cluster Adapter (Chapter 42), Microsoft Network Transport Layer (Chapter 42), DESQview relocated IRQ11 (PCI-44), DoubleDOS relocated IRQ3 (PCI-49), SitBack (PCI-66)
See also: INT 5Ch

8-1 Format of Network Control Block:

Offset	Size	Description	
00h	BYTE	ncb_command (see Tables 8-2 and 8-5)	
01h	BYTE	ncb_retcode	
02h	BYTE	ncb_lsn	
03h	BYTE	ncb_num	
04h	DWORD	pointer to ncb_buffer	
08h	WORD	ncb_length	
0Ah	16 BYTEs	ncb_callname	
1Ah	16 BYTEs	ncb_name	
2Ah	BYTE	ncb_rto	
2Bh	BYTE	ncb_sto	
2Ch	DWORD	pointer to ncb_post	/* int (far *ncb_post)(); */
30h	BYTE	ncb_lana_num	
31h	BYTE	ncb_cmd_cplt	
32h	DWORD	pointer to ncb_vname	
36h	BYTE	ncb_vnamelen	
37h	9 BYTEs	ncb_reserve	

Note: Fields 00h-31h are the same as for a standard NetBIOS NCB (see Table 8-4).

8-2 Values for ncb_command field:

same as for INT 5Ch (Table 8-5), except
70h   send net Break

INT 5Ch
NetBIOS INTERFACE

Registers at call: **Return Registers:**
ES:BX -> network control block   AL = status (see Table 8-3)
  (NCB) (see Table 8-4)
Details: The Sytek PCnet card uses DMA channel 3.
Conflicts: TOPS (Chapter 31), ATALK.SYS (Chapter 31), IBM 802.2 interface (Chapter 31),
$25 LAN (Chapter 31), DESQview relocated IRQ12 (PCI-44), DoubleDOS relocated IRQ4
(PCI-49)
See also: INT 2Ah Functions 01h and 04h, INT 5Bh

8-3 Values for NetBIOS status:

00h	successful
01h	bad buffer size
03h	invalid NETBIOS command
05h	timeout
06h	receive buffer too small
07h	No-ACK command failed
08h	bad session number
09h	LAN card out of memory
0Ah	session closed
0Bh	command has been cancelled
0Dh	name already exists
0Eh	local name table full
0Fh	name still in use, can't delete
11h	local session table full
12h	remote PC not listening
13h	bad NCB_NUM field
14h	no answer to CALL or no such remote
15h	name not in local name table
16h	duplicate name
17h	bad delete
18h	abnormal end
19h	name error, multiple identical names in use
1Ah	bad packet
21h	network card busy
22h	too many commands queued
23h	bad LAN card number
24h	command finished while cancelling
26h	command can't be cancelled
30h	name defined by another process (OS/2)
34h	NetBIOS environment not defined, must issue reset (OS/2)
35h	required operating system resources exhausted (OS/2)
36h	maximum applications exceeded (OS/2)
37h	no SAPs available for NetBIOS (OS/2)
38h	requested resources not available (OS/2)

40h	Lana System Error
41h	Lana Remote Hot Carrier
42h	Lana Local Hot Carrier
43h	Lana No Carrier Detected
44h	unusual network condition
45h-4Dh	hardware error
4Eh	token ring is broken
4Fh	token ring error
50h	adapter malfunction
F7h	error in explicit INITIALIZE
F8h	error in implicit OPEN
F9h	TOKREUI internal error
FAh	hardware adapter testing
FBh	NetBIOS emulator not found
FCh	OPEN or OPEN_SAP failure
FDh	unexpected adapter closure
FFh	NetBIOS busy (command pending)

8-4 Format of Network Control Block:

Offset	Size	Description
00h	BYTE	command code (see Table 8-5)
01h	BYTE	return code
02h	BYTE	local session number (LSN)
03h	BYTE	"ncb_num" datagram table entry from ADD NAME
04h	DWORD	pointer to I/O buffer
08h	WORD	length of data in buffer
0Ah	16 BYTEs	remote system to call
1Ah	16 BYTEs	network name of local machine
2Ah	BYTE	receive timeout in 1/2 seconds
2Bh	BYTE	send timeout in 1/2 seconds
2Ch	DWORD	pointer to FAR post handler /* int (far *ncb_post)(); */
30h	BYTE	network adapter number on which to execute command
		00h-03h IBM NetBIOS specs
		F0h-FFh Eicon NABios interface (see also Eicon INT 7Bh in Chapter 37)
31h	BYTE	command completion code (see Table 8-3)
32h	14 BYTEs	reserved for network card

8-5 Values for command code field in NCB (OR with 80h for non-waiting call):

10h	start session with NCB_NAME name (call)
11h	listen for call
12h	end session with NCB_NAME name (hangup)
14h	send data via NCB_LSN
15h	receive data from a session
16h	receive data from any session
17h	send multiple data buffers
20h	send unACKed message (datagram)
21h	receive datagram
22h	send broadcast datagram
23h	receive broadcast datagram
30h	add name to name table
31h	delete name from name table
32h	reset adapter card and tables

33h	get adapter status (see Table 8-7)
34h	status of all sessions for name (see Table 8-8)
35h	cancel
36h	add group name to name table
48h	send data and receive data (LAN Manager NETBEUI.DOS)
70h	unlink from IBM remote program (no F0h function)
71h	send data without ACK
72h	send multiple buffers without ACK
72h	Ungermann-Bass Register (conflicts with above function)
73h	Ungermann-Bass SendNmc
74h	Ungermann-Bass Callniu
75h	Ungermann-Bass Calladdr
76h	Ungermann-Bass Listenaddr
77h	Ungermann-Bass SendPkt
78h	find name
78h	Ungermann-Bass RcvPkt (conflicts with above function)
79h	token-ring protocol trace
79h	Ungermann-Bass SendAttn (conflicts with above function)
7Ah	Ungermann-Bass RcvAttn
7Bh	Ungermann-Bass Listenniu
7Ch	Ungermann-Bass RcvRaw
7Dh	Ungermann-Bass SendNmc2
7Fh	Beame&Whiteside BWNB installation check (returns with return code and completion code both set to 03h, while invalid functions return only return code field set to 03h)
C0h	gather-send (LAN Manager HPFS386 NetBEUI)
C1h	scatter-receive (LAN Manager HPFS386 NetBEUI)
C2h	scatter-receive-any (LAN Manager HPFS386 NetBEUI)

8-6 Format of structure "name":

Offset	Size	Description
00h	16 BYTEs	"nm_name" symbolic name
10h	BYTE	"nm_num" number associated with name
11h	BYTE	nm_status

8-7 Format of structure "astatus":

Offset	Size	Description
00h	6 BYTEs	as_id
06h	BYTE	as_jumpers
07h	BYTE	as_post
08h	BYTE	as_major
09h	BYTE	as_minor
0Ah	WORD	as_interval
0Ch	WORD	as_crcerr
0Eh	WORD	as_algerr
10h	WORD	as_colerr
12h	WORD	as_abterr
14h	DWORD	as_tcount
18h	DWORD	as_rcount
1Ch	WORD	as_retran
1Eh	WORD	as_xresrc

20h	8 BYTEs	as_res0
28h	WORD	as_ncbfree
2Ah	WORD	as_ncbmax
2Ch	WORD	as_ncbx
2Eh	4 BYTEs	as_res1
32h	WORD	as_sespend
34h	WORD	as_msp
36h	WORD	as_sesmax
38h	WORD	as_bufsize
3Ah	WORD	as_names
3Ch	16 name structures ("as_name")	

8-8 Format of structure "sstatus":

Offset	Size	Description
00h	BYTE	number of sessions being reported
01h	BYTE	number of sessions with this name
02h	BYTE	number of outstanding receive datagrams
03h	BYTE	number of outstanding ReceiveAnys
04h	var	session structures (see Table 8-9)

8-9 Format of structure "session":

Offset	Size	Description
00h	BYTE	local session number
01h	BYTE	state
		01h listen pending
		02h call pending
		03h session established
		04h hangup pending
		05h hangup done
		06h session aborted
02h	16 BYTEs	local name
12h	16 BYTEs	remote name
22h	BYTE	number of outstanding receives
23h	BYTE	number of outstanding sends/chainsends

INT 86h   *NetBIOS*
ORIGINAL INT 18h

Details: Some implementations of NetBIOS reportedly relocate INT 18h here.
Conflicts: APL*PLUS/PC (PCI-53), IBM ROM BASIC (PCI-54)
See also: INT 18h

CHAPTER 9

Network Redirector

The network redirector interface was introduced in MS-DOS version 3 to permit transparent support of network devices. Those devices which are internally marked as local continue to be handled by DOS as in previous versions, but remote (i.e., network) devices cause DOS to invoke various functions of the network redirector interface to perform those portions of the operation which it can not do itself on non-local devices. For example, setting the file pointer with LSEEK consists merely of setting a variable in the file's System File Table entry, unless the seek is from the end of the file; in that case, the network redirector is invoked because another process may have changed the size of the file.

While the few networking packages which predate DOS 3 of necessity all used a 'shell' approach (intercepting INT 21h calls for network devices before they reached DOS), more recent software generally uses the network redirector interface. In fact, even the most recent version of a package which formerly used the shell approach—Novell NetWare—has now switched to the network redirector. The redirector interface has the advantage that a smaller number of generally simpler functions need to be implemented (compared to the shell approach) because MS-DOS itself does some preprocessing.

INT 2Fh Function 1100h   *NETWORK REDIRECTOR*
INSTALLATION CHECK   *Callout*

Registers at call: **Return Registers:**
AX = 1100h   AL = status
                              00h not installed, OK to install
                              01h not installed, not OK to install
                              FFh installed
                                    AH = product identifier (ad hoc by various manufacturers)
                                               00h if PC Tools v8 DRIVEMAP
                                               42h ('B') for Beame&Whiteside BWNFS v3.0a
                                               6Eh ('n') for NetWare Lite v1.1 CLIENT

Details: This function is called by the DOS 3.1+ kernel.

In DOS 4.x only, the 11xxh calls are all in IFSFUNC.EXE, not in the PC LAN Program redirector; DOS 5+ moves the calls back into the redirector.

The PC Network 1.00 redirector (renamed to PC LAN Program in 1.1-1.3) only supports Functions 1100h to 1127h.

Conflicts: CD-ROM (Chapter 15)

INT 2Fh Function 1101h   *NETWORK REDIRECTOR*
REMOVE REMOTE DIRECTORY   *Undocumented Callout*

Registers at call:
AX = 1101h

Return Registers:
CF set on error
    AX = DOS error code (see Table 3-1)
CF clear if successful

SS = DOS DS
SDA first filename pointer ->
fully-qualified directory name
SDA CDS pointer -> current directory
    structure for drive with directory

Details: This function is called by the DOS 3.1+ kernel.
See also: Functions 1103h and 1105h, INT 21h Function 60h (Chapter 3), INT 21h Function 3Ah (PCI-24)

INT 2Fh Function 1102h
REMOVE REMOTE DIRECTORY

IFSFUNC.EXE (DOS 4.x only)
Undocumented Callout

Registers at call:
AX = 1102h
SS = DOS DS
SDA first filename pointer ->
fully-qualified directory name
SDA CDS pointer -> current directory
    structure for drive with directory

Return Registers:
CF set on error
    AX = DOS error code (see Table 3-1)
CF clear if successful

Details: This call appears to be identical to Function 1101h; Microsoft internal documentation calls this function "SEQ_RMDIR".
See also: Function 1101h

INT 2Fh Function 1103h
MAKE REMOTE DIRECTORY

NETWORK REDIRECTOR
Undocumented Callout

Registers at call:
AX = 1103h
SS = DOS DS
SDA first filename pointer -> fully-qualified
    directory name
SDA CDS pointer -> current directory structure for drive with dir

Return Registers:
CF set on error
    AX = DOS error code (see Table 3-1)
CF clear if successful

Details: This function is called by the DOS 3.1+ kernel.
See also: Functions 1101h and 1105h, INT 21h Function 60h (Chapter 3), INT 21h Function 39h (PCI-24)

INT 2Fh Function 1104h
MAKE REMOTE DIRECTORY

IFSFUNC.EXE (DOS 4.x only)
Undocumented Callout

Registers at call:
AX = 1104h
SS = DOS DS
SDA first filename pointer -> fully-qualified
    directory name
SDA CDS pointer -> current directory structure for drive with directory

Return Registers:
CF set on error
    AX = DOS error code (see Table 3-1)
CF clear if successful

Details: This call appears to be identical to Function 1103h.
See also: Function 1103h

INT 2Fh Function 1105h
CHDIR

NETWORK REDIRECTOR
Undocumented Callout

Registers at call:
AX = 1105h
SS = DOS DS
SDA first filename pointer -> fully-qualified
    directory name
SS:BX -> fully-qualified directory name

SDA CDS pointer -> current directory structure for drive with directory

Return Registers:
CF set on error
    AX = DOS error code (see Table 3-1)
CF clear if successful
    CDS updated with new path

Details: This function is called by the DOS 3.1+ kernel.

The directory string in the CDS should not have a terminating backslash unless the current directory is the root.

See also: Functions 1101h and 1103h, INT 21h Function 60h (Chapter 3), INT 21h Function 3Bh (PCI-24)

INT 2Fh Function 1106h
CLOSE REMOTE FILE

Registers at call:
AX = 1106h
BX = device info word from SFT
ES:DI -> SFT
    SFT DPB field -> DPB of drive
      containing file

Return Registers:
CF set on error
    AX = DOS error code (see Table 3-1)
CF clear if successful
    SFT updated (redirector must decrement open count, which may be done with INT 2Fh Function 1208h)

Details: This function is called by the DOS 3.1+ kernel.
See also: Function 1116h; Functions 1201h, 1208h, and 1227h (Chapter 3); INT 21h Function 3Eh (PCI-24)

INT 2Fh Function 1107h
COMMIT REMOTE FILE

Registers at call:
AX = 1107h
ES:DI -> SFT
    SFT DPB field -> DPB of drive
      containing file

Return Registers:
CF set on error
    AX = DOS error code (see Table 3-1)
CF clear if successful
    all buffers for file flushed
    directory entry updated

Details: This function is called by the DOS 3.1+ kernel.
See also: INT 21h Function 5D01h (Chapter 3), INT 21h Function 68h (PCI-24)

INT 2Fh Function 1108h
READ FROM REMOTE FILE

Registers at call:
AX = 1108h
ES:DI -> SFT
    SFT DPB field -> DPB of drive
      containing file
CX = number of bytes
SS = DOS DS
SDA DTA field -> user buffer

Return Registers:
CF set on error
    AX = DOS error code (see Table 3-1)
CF clear if successful
    CX = number of bytes read
    (0000h = end of file)
    SFT updated

Details: This function is called by the DOS 3.1+ kernel.
See also: Function 1109h, Function 1229h (Chapter 3), INT 21h Function 5D06h (Chapter 3), INT 21h Function 3Fh (PCI-24)

INT 2Fh Function 1109h
WRITE TO REMOTE FILE

Registers at call:
AX = 1109h

ES:DI -> SFT
    SFT DPB field -> DPB of drive
       containing file
CX = number of bytes
SS = DOS DS
SDA DTA field -> user buffer

Return Registers:
CF set on error
    AX = DOS error code (see Table 3-1)
CF clear if successful
    CX = number of bytes written
    SFT updated

Details: This function is called by the DOS 3.1+ kernel.
See also: Functions 1107h and 1108h, INT 21h Function 5D06h (Chapter 3), MS-DOS INT 21h Function 40h (PCI-24)

INT 2Fh Function 110Ah
LOCK REGION OF FILE
NETWORK REDIRECTOR (DOS 3.x only)
Undocumented Callout

Registers at call:
AX = 110Ah
BX = file handle
CX:DX = starting offset
SI = high word of size
STACK: WORD low word of size
ES:DI -> SFT
    SFT DPB field -> DPB of drive containing file
SS = DOS DS

Return Registers:
CF set on error AL = DOS error code (see Table 3-1)
STACK unchanged

Details: This function is called by the DOS 3.10-3.31 kernel. The redirector is expected to resolve lock conflicts.
See also: Function 110Bh, INT 21h Function 5Ch (Chapter 3)

INT 2Fh Function 110Ah
LOCK/UNLOCK REGION OF FILE
NETWORK REDIRECTOR (DOS 4+)
Undocumented Callout

Registers at call:
AX = 110Ah
BL = function (00h lock, 01h unlock)
DS:DX -> parameter block (see Table 9-1)
ES:DI -> SFT
    SFT DPB field -> DPB of drive containing file
SS = DOS DS

Return Registers:
CF set on error
    AL = DOS error code (see Table 3-1)

Details: This function is called by the DOS 4.0+ kernel. The redirector is expected to resolve lock conflicts.
See also: Function 110Bh, INT 21h Function 5Ch (Chapter 3)

9-1 Format of parameter block:

Offset	Size	Description
00h	DWORD	start offset
04h	DWORD	size of region

INT 2Fh Function 110Bh
UNLOCK REGION OF FILE
NETWORK REDIRECTOR (DOS 3.x only)
Undocumented Callout

Registers at call:
AX = 110Bh
BX = file handle
CX:DX = starting offset
SI = high word of size
STACK: WORD low word of size
ES:DI -> SFT for file
    SFT DPB field -> DPB of drive containing file

Return Registers:
CF set on error
    AL = DOS error code (see Table 3-1)
STACK unchanged

Details: This function is called by the MS-DOS 3.1-3.31 kernel; DOS 4.0+ calls Function 110Ah instead.
See also: Function 110Ah, INT 21h Function 5Ch (Chapter 3)

INT 2Fh Function 110Ch
GET DISK INFORMATION
NETWORK REDIRECTOR
Undocumented Callout

Registers at call:
AX = 110Ch
ES:DI -> current directory structure for desired drive

Return Registers:
AL = sectors per cluster
AH = media ID byte
BX = total clusters
CX = bytes per sector
DX = number of available clusters

Details: This function is called by the DOS 3.1+ kernel.
See also: INT 21h Function 36h (PCI-24)

INT 2Fh Function 110Dh
SET REMOTE FILE'S ATTRIBUTES
IFSFUNC.EXE (DOS 4.x only)
Undocumented Callout

Registers at call:
AX = 110Dh
SDA first filename pointer -> name of file
others, if any, unknown

Return Registers:
unknown

Details: This function is similar to Function 110Eh.
See also: Function 110Eh

INT 2Fh Function 110Eh
SET REMOTE FILE'S ATTRIBUTES
NETWORK REDIRECTOR
Undocumented Callout

Registers at call:
AX = 110Eh
SS = DOS DS
SDA first filename pointer -> fully-qualified name of file
SDA CDS pointer -> current directory structure for drive
   with file
STACK: WORD new file attributes

Return Registers:
CF set on error
   AX = DOS error code (see
   Table 3-1)
CF clear if successful
STACK unchanged

Details: This function is called by the DOS 3.1+ kernel.
See also: Functions 110Dh and 110Fh, INT 21h Function 60h (Chapter 3), INT 21h Function 4301h (PCI-24)

INT 2Fh Function 110Fh
GET REMOTE FILE'S ATTRIBUTES AND SIZE
NETWORK REDIRECTOR
Undocumented Callout

Registers at call:
AX = 110Fh
SS = DOS DS
SDA first filename pointer -> fully-qualified
   name of file
SDA CDS pointer -> current directory
   structure for drive with file

Return Registers:
CF set on error
   AX = DOS error code (see Table 3-1)
CF clear if successful
   AX = file attributes
   BX:DI = file size

Details: This function is called by the DOS 3.1+ kernel.
See also: Function 110Eh, INT 21h Function 60h (Chapter 3), INT 21h Function 4300h (PCI-24)

INT 2Fh Function 1110h
GET REMOTE FILE'S ATTRIBUTES AND SIZE
IFSFUNC.EXE (DOS 4.x only)
Undocumented Callout

Registers at call:
AX = 1110h

SDA first filename pointer -> name of file
others, if any, unknown

Return Registers:
unknown

Details: This call appears to be similar to Function 110Fh.
See also: Function 110Eh

INT 2Fh Function 1111h
RENAME REMOTE FILE

NETWORK REDIRECTOR
Undocumented Callout

Registers at call:
AX = 1111h
SS = DS = DOS DS
SDA first filename pointer = offset of
    fully-qualified old name

Return Registers:
CF set on error
    AX = DOS error code (see Table 3-1)
CF clear if successful

SDA second filename pointer = offset of fully-qualified new name
SDA CDS pointer -> current directory structure for drive with file
Details: This function is called by the DOS 3.1+ kernel.
See also: Function 1112h, INT 21h Functions 56h and 60h (Chapter 3)

INT 2Fh Function 1112h
RENAME REMOTE FILE

IFSFUNC.EXE (DOS 4.x only)
Undocumented Callout

Registers at call:
AX = 1112h
SS = DS = DOS DS
SDA first filename pointer -> name of file
others, if any, unknown

Return Registers:
unknown

Details: This call is similar to Function 1111h.
See also: Function 1111h

INT 2Fh Function 1113h
DELETE REMOTE FILE

NETWORK REDIRECTOR
Undocumented Callout

Registers at call:
AX = 1113h
SS = DS = DOS DS
SDA first filename pointer -> fully-qualified
    filename in DOS DS

Return Registers:
CF set on error
    AX = DOS error code (see Table 3-1)
CF clear if successful

SDA CDS pointer -> current directory structure for drive with file
Details: This function is called by the DOS 3.1+ kernel.
    The filespec may contain wildcards.
See also: Function 1114h, INT 21h Functions 41h and 60h (Chapter 3)

INT 2Fh Function 1114h
DELETE REMOTE FILE

IFSFUNC.EXE (DOS 4.x only)
Undocumented Callout

Registers at call:
AX = 1114h
SDA first filename pointer -> name of file
others, if any, unknown

Return Registers:
unknown

Details: This call is similar to Function 1113h.
See also: Function 1113h

INT 2Fh Function 1115h
OPEN REMOTE FILE

IFSFUNC.EXE (DOS 4.x only)
Undocumented Callout

Registers at call:
AX = 1115h
SS = DOS DS

ES:DI -> SFT *unknown*
others, if any, unknown

Return Registers:
unknown

Details: This call is similar to Function 1116h.
See also: Functions 1116h and 112Eh

INT 2Fh Function 1116h
OPEN EXISTING REMOTE FILE

NETWORK REDIRECTOR
Undocumented Callout

Registers at call:
AX = 1116h
ES:DI -> uninitialized SFT
SS = DOS DS
SDA first filename pointer ->
    fully-qualified name of file to open
STACK: WORD file access and sharing
modes (see Table 3-2)

Return Registers:
CF set on error
    AX = DOS error code (see Table 3-1)
CF clear if successful
    SFT filled (except handle count, which DOS
        manages itself)
STACK unchanged

Details: This function is called by the DOS 3.1+ kernel.
See also: Functions 1106h, 1115h, 1117h, 1118h, and 112Eh; INT 21h Functions 3Dh and 60h
(Chapter 3)

INT 2Fh Function 1117h
CREATE/TRUNCATE REMOTE FILE

NETWORK REDIRECTOR
Undocumented Callout

Registers at call:
AX = 1117h
ES:DI -> uninitialized SFT
SS = DOS DS
SDA first filename pointer ->
    fully-qualified name of file to open
SDA CDS pointer -> current directory
    structure for drive with file
STACK: WORD file creation mode
        low byte = file attributes (see Table 3-53)
        high byte = 00h normal create, 01h create new file

Return Registers:
CF set on error
    AX = DOS error code (see Table 3-1)
CF clear if successful
    SFT filled (except handle count, which DOS
        manages itself)
STACK unchanged

Details: This function is called by the DOS 3.1+ kernel.
See also: Functions 1106h, 1116h, 1118h, and 112Eh; INT 21h Function 60h (Chapter 3); INT
21h Function 3Ch (PCI-24)

INT 2Fh Function 1118h
CREATE/TRUNCATE FILE WITHOUT CDS

NETWORK REDIRECTOR
Undocumented Callout

Registers at call:
AX = 1118h
ES:DI -> uninitialized SFT
SS = DOS DS
SDA first filename pointer -> fully-qualified name of file
STACK: WORD file creation mode
        low byte = file attributes (see Table 3-53)
        high byte = 00h normal create, 01h create new file

Return Registers:
unknown
STACK unchanged

Details: This function is called by the DOS 3.1+ kernel when creating a file on a drive for which
the SDA CDS pointer has offset FFFFh.
See also: Functions 1106h, 1116h, 1117h, and 112Eh; INT 21h Function 60h (Chapter 3)

INT 2Fh Function 1119h
FIND FIRST FILE WITHOUT CDS

NETWORK REDIRECTOR
Undocumented Callout

Registers at call:
AX = 1119h
SS = DOS DS
DS = DOS DS
[DTA] = uninitialized 21-byte
   findfirst search data (see Table 3-62)
SDA first filename pointer -> fully-qualified
   search template
SDA search attribute = attribute mask for search

Return Registers:
CF set on error
   AX = DOS error code (see Table 3-1)
CF clear if successful
   [DTA] = updated findfirst search data (bit 7 of
      first byte must be set)
   [DTA+15h] = standard directory entry for file

Details: This function is called by the DOS 3.1+ kernel.
   DOS 4.x IFSFUNC returns CF set, AX=0003h.
See also: Function 111Ah and 111Bh

INT 2Fh Function 111Ah
FIND NEXT FILE WITHOUT CDS

IFSFUNC.EXE (DOS 4.x only)
Undocumented Callout

Registers at call:
AX = 111Ah
others, if any, unknown

Return Registers:
CF set
   AX = error code (03h for DOS 4.01 IFSFUNC)

Details: Use Function 111Ch for DOS 5+.
See also: Functions 1119h and 111Ch

INT 2Fh Function 111Bh
FINDFIRST

NETWORK REDIRECTOR
Undocumented Callout

Registers at call:
AX = 111Bh
SS = DS = DOS DS
[DTA] = uninitialized 21-byte findfirst
   search data (see Table 3-62)
SDA first filename pointer ->
   fully-qualified search template
SDA CDS pointer -> current directory structure for drive with file
SDA search attribute = attribute mask for search

Return Registers:
CF set on error
   AX = DOS error code (see Table 3-1)
CF clear if successful
   [DTA] = updated findfirst search data (bit 7 of
      first byte must be set)
   [DTA+15h] = standard directory entry for file

Details: This function is called by the DOS 3.1+ kernel.
See also: Functions 1119h and 111Ch, INT 21h Function 60h (Chapter 3), INT 21h Function 4Eh (PCI-24)

INT 2Fh Function 111Ch
FINDNEXT

NETWORK REDIRECTOR
Undocumented Callout

Registers at call:
AX = 111Ch
SS = DS = DOS DS
ES:DI -> CDS
[DTA] = 21-byte findfirst
   search data (see Table 3-62)

Return Registers:
CF set on error
   AX = DOS error code (see Table 3-1)
CF clear if successful
   [DTA] = updated findfirst search data (bit 7 of first byte
      must be set)
   [DTA+15h] = standard directory entry for file

Details: This function is called by the DOS 3.1+ kernel.
See also: Functions 1119h and 111Bh, INT 21h Function 4Fh (PCI-24)

INT 2Fh Function 111Dh
CLOSE ALL REMOTE FILES FOR PROCESS (ABORT)

Registers at call:
AX = 111Dh
SS = DOS DS
DS may contain a value

Return Registers:
unknown

Details: This function is used when a process is aborted. It is called by the DOS 3.1+ kernel.

This function closes all FCBs opened by process.

See also: INT 21h Function 5D04h

INT 2Fh Function 111Eh
DO REDIRECTION

Registers at call:
AX = 111Eh
SS = DOS DS
STACK: WORD function to execute
   (see Tables 9-2 to 9-8)
other registers as appropriate

Return Registers:
CF clear if successful
CF set on error
   AX = error code (see Table 3-1)
STACK unchanged
other registers as appropriate for function

Details: This function is called by the DOS 3.1+ kernel on INT 21h Function 5Fh (including LAN Manager calls), pushing the supplied AX onto the stack.

The PC Network 1.00 redirector does not support function 5F06h.

See also: INT 21h Functions 5F00h, 5F01h, 5F02h, 5F03h, 5F04h, 5F05h, and 5F06h (Chapter 3)

9-2 Redirector "get redirection mode" calling convention:

Registers at call:
STACK: WORD   5F00h
BL = type (03h printer, 04h disk)

Return Registers:
CF clear if successful
   BH = state (00h off, 01h on)
CF set on error
   AX = error code (see Table 3-1)
STACK unchanged

9-3 Redirector "set redirection mode" calling convention:

Registers at call:
STACK: WORD   5F01h
BL = type (03h printer, 04h disk)
BH = state (00h off, 01h on)

Return Registers:
CF clear if successful
CF set on error
   AX = error code (see Table 3-1)
STACK unchanged

9-4 Redirector "get redirection list entry" calling convention:

Registers at call:
STACK: WORD   5F02h
BX = redirection list index
DS:SI -> 16-byte local device
   name buffer
ES:DI -> 128-byte network name buffer

Return Registers:
CF clear if successful
CF set on error
   AX = error code (see Table 3-1)
STACK unchanged
must set user's BX to device type and CX to stored parameter
   value, using Function 1218h (Chapter 3) to get the stack
   frame address

9-5 Redirector "redirect device" calling convention:

Registers at call:
STACK: WORD   5F03h
BL = device type (see INT 21h Function 5F03h above)

CX = stored parameter value
DS:SI -> ASCIZ source device name
ES:DI -> destination ASCIZ network path + ASCIZ
    passwd

Return Registers:
CF clear if successful
CF set on error
    AX = error code (see Table 3-1)
STACK unchanged

9-6 Redirector "cancel redirection" calling convention:

Registers at call:
STACK: WORD   5F04h
DS:SI -> ASCIZ device name or network path

Return Registers:
CF clear if successful
CF set on error
    AX = error code (see Table 3-1)
STACK unchanged

9-7 Redirector "get redirection list extended entry" calling convention:

Registers at call:
STACK: WORD   5F05h
BX = redirection list index
DS:SI -> buffer for ASCIZ source device name
ES:DI -> buffer for destination ASCIZ network
    path

Return Registers:
CF clear if successful
    BH = status flag
    BL = type (03h printer, 04h disk)
    CX = stored parameter value
    BP = NETBIOS local session number
CF set on error
    AX = error code (see Table 3-1)
STACK unchanged

9-8 Redirector Function 5F06h calling convention:

Registers at call:
STACK: WORD   5F06h
others, if any, unknown

Return Registers:
CF clear if successful
    others, if any, unknown
CF set on error
    AX = error code (see Table 3-1)
STACK unchanged

Note: Function 5F06h is similar to Function 5F05h, "get redirection list extended entry".

INT 2Fh Function 111Fh	*NETWORK REDIRECTOR*
PRINTER SETUP	*Undocumented Callout*

Registers at call:
AX = 111Fh
STACK: WORD function
           5E02h set printer setup
           5E03h get printer setup
           5E04h set printer mode
           5E05h get printer mode
other registers as appropriate (see Chapter 3)

Return Registers:
CF clear if successful
    other registers as appropriate
CF set on error
    AX = error code (see Table 3-1)
STACK unchanged

Details: This function is called by the DOS 3.1+ kernel on most INT 21h Function 5Exxh functions, pushing the supplied AX onto the stack before calling.
See also: INT 21h Functions 5E02h, 5E03h, 5E04h, and 5E05h (Chapter 3)

INT 2Fh Function 1120h	*NETWORK REDIRECTOR*
FLUSH ALL DISK BUFFERS	*Undocumented Callout*

Registers at call:
AX = 1120h
DS = DOS DS
others, if any, unknown

Return Registers:
CF clear (successful)

Details: This function is called by the DOS 3.1+ kernel. It uses the CDS array pointer and LASTDRIVE= entries in the DOS list of lists.

See also: INT 21h Function 5D01h (Chapter 3), INT 21h Function 0Dh (PCI-24)

INT 2Fh Function 1121h
SEEK FROM END OF REMOTE FILE
NETWORK REDIRECTOR
Undocumented Callout

Registers at call:
AX = 1121h
CX:DX = offset (in bytes) from end
ES:DI -> SFT
    SFT DPB field -> DPB of drive with file
SS = DOS DS

Return Registers:
CF set on error
    AL = DOS error code (see Table 3-1)
CF clear if successful
    DX:AX = new file position

Details: This function is called by the DOS 3.1+ kernel.
See also: Function 1228h, INT 21h Function 42h (PCI-24)

INT 2Fh Function 1122h
PROCESS TERMINATION HOOK
NETWORK REDIRECTOR
Undocumented Callout

Registers at call:
AX = 1122h
SS = DOS DS
others, if any, unknown

Return Registers:
unknown

Details: This function is called by the DOS 3.1+ kernel.

INT 2Fh Function 1123h
QUALIFY REMOTE FILENAME
NETWORK REDIRECTOR
Undocumented Callout

Registers at call:
AX = 1123h
DS:SI -> ASCIZ filename to canonicalize
ES:DI -> 128-byte buffer for qualified name

Return Registers:
CF set if not resolved

Details: This function is called by the MS-DOS 3.1+ kernel, but is not called by DR-DOS 5.0 unless the filename matches the name of a character device.

    This function is called first when DOS attempts to resolve a filename (unless inside a Function 5D00h server call); if this call fails, DOS resolves the name locally.

    See INT 21h Function 60h in Chapter 3 for details on canonicalization.
See also: Function 1221h, INT 21h Function 60h (Chapter 3)

INT 2Fh Function 1124h
TURN OFF REMOTE PRINTER
NETWORK REDIRECTOR
Undocumented Callout

Registers at call:
AX = 1124h
ES:DI -> SFT
SS = DOS DS
others, if any, unknown

Return Registers:
CX = *unknown*

Details: This function is called by the MS-DOS 3.1+ kernel if Function 1126h returns CF set.
See also: Function 1126h

INT 2Fh Function 1125h
REDIRECTED PRINTER MODE
NETWORK REDIRECTOR
Undocumented Callout

Registers at call:
AX = 1125h
STACK: WORD subfunction
        5D07h get print stream state
        5D08h set print stream state
           DL = new state
        5D09h finish print job

Return Registers:
CF clear if successful
    DL = current state (subfunction 5D07h only)
CF set on error
    AX = error code (see Table 3-1)
STACK unchanged

Details: This function is called by the DOS 3.1+ kernel.

See also: INT 21h Functions 5D07h, 5D08h, and 5D09h (Chapter 3)

INT 2Fh Function 1126h
REMOTE PRINTER ECHO ON/OFF

NETWORK REDIRECTOR
Undocumented Callout

Registers at call:
AX = 1126h
ES:DI -> *SFT for file handle 4*
SS = *DOS DS*
others, if any, unknown

Return Registers:
CF set on error

Details: This function is called by the DOS 3.1+ kernel when print echoing (^P, ^PrtSc) changes state and STDPRN has bit 11 of the device information word in the SFT set.
See also: Function 1124h

INT 2Fh Functions 1127h to 1129h
UNUSED FUNCTIONS

IFSFUNC.EXE (DOS 4.x only)
Undocumented Callout

Registers at call:
AX = 1127h to 1129h

Return Registers:
CF set
          AX = 0001h (invalid function) (see Table 3-1)

INT 2Fh Function 112Ah
CLOSE ALL FILES FOR PROCESS

IFSFUNC.EXE (DOS 4.x only)
Undocumented Callout

Registers at call:
AX = 112Ah
DS = DOS DS
others, if any, unknown

Return Registers:
unknown

Details: This call does something to each IFS driver.

INT 2Fh Function 112Bh
GENERIC IOCTL

IFSFUNC.EXE (DOS 4.x only)
Undocumented Callout

Registers at call:
AX = 112Bh
SS = DOS DS
CX = function/category
DS:DX -> parameter block
STACK: WORD value of AX on entry to INT 21h (440Ch or 440Dh)
others, if any, unknown

Return Registers:
CF clear if successful
CF set on error
          AX = DOS error code (see Table 3-1)

Details: This function is called by the DOS 4.0 kernel.

INT 2Fh Function 112Ch
"UPDATE_CB" - UNKNOWN

NETWORK REDIRECTOR (DOS 4+)
Undocumented Callout

Registers at call:
AX = 112Ch
SS = DOS DS
SDA current SFT pointer -> SFT for file
others, if any, unknown

Return Registers:
CF set on error

Details: This function is called by SHARE in DOS 5.0-6.0.

INT 2Fh Function 112Dh
EXTENDED ATTRIBUTES

IFSFUNC.EXE (DOS 4.x only)
Undocumented Callout

Registers at call:
AX = 112Dh
ES:DI -> SFT for file
SS = DOS DS
BL = subfunction (value of AL on INT 21h)

02h get extended attributes
03h get extended attribute properties
04h set extended attributes

else *unknown*

Return Registers:
DS = DOS DS

CF clear

CX = *unknown* (00h or 02h for DOS 4.01)

Details: This function is called by the DOS 4.0 kernel on INT 21h Functions 5702h,5703h,and 5704h.
See also: INT 21h Functions 5702h, 5703h, and 5704h (PCI-24), INT 21h Function 6Eh (PCI-24)

INT 2Fh Function 112Eh
EXTENDED OPEN/CREATE FILE

NETWORK REDIRECTOR (DOS 4+)
Undocumented Callout

Registers at call:
AX = 112Eh
SS = DS = DOS DS
ES:DI -> uninitialized SFT for file
STACK: WORD file attribute for created/truncated file
          low byte = file attributes
          high byte = 00h normal create/open, 01h
             create new file
SDA first filename pointer -> fully-qualified filename
SDA extended file open action = action code (see
    INT 21h Function 6C00h in PCI-24)
SDA extended file open mode = open mode for file (see INT 21h Function 6C00h)

Return Registers:
CF set on error
    AX = error code
CF clear if successful
    CX = result code
       01h file opened
       02h file created
       03h file replaced (truncated)
    SFT initialized (except handle count,
       which DOS manages itself)

Details: This function is called by the DOS 4+ kernel.
See also: Functions 1115h, 1116h, and 1117h; INT 21h Function 6C00h (PCI-24)

INT 2Fh Function 112Fh
IFS IOCTL

IFSFUNC.EXE (DOS 4.x only)
Undocumented Callout

Registers at call:
AX = 112Fh
SS = DOS DS
STACK: WORD function in low byte
                00h *unknown*
                      DS:SI -> *Current Directory Structure*
                      CL = drive (1=A:)
                01h *unknown*
                      DS:SI -> *unknown*
                      CL = *file handle*
                02h *unknown*
                      DS:SI -> *Current Directory Structure*
                      DI = *unknown*
                      CX = drive (1=A:)

Return Registers:
CF clear if successful
CF set on error
    AX = DOS error code (see Table 3-1)

others, if any, unknown
Details: This function is called by the DOS 4.0 kernel.
See also: INT 21h Function 6Bh (PCI-24)

INT 2Fh Function 1130h
GET IFSFUNC SEGMENT

IFSFUNC.EXE (DOS 4.x only)
Undocumented Callout

Registers at call:
AX = 1130h

Return Registers:
ES = CS of resident IFSFUNC

CHAPTER 10

Open Data-Link Interface (ODI)

The Open Data-Link Interface (ODI) standard was created jointly by Apple and Novell to permit any ODI-compliant network adapter card to be used with any ODI-compliant protocol stack. Novell's drivers first shipped in late 1990 as part of NetWare, Version 3.11.

INT 2Fh Function C000h
LSL.COM
INSTALLATION CHECK

Registers at call:
AX = C000h

Return Registers:
AL = FFh if installed
    DX:BX -> FAR entry point (see Table 10-1)
    ES:SI -> signature string "LINKSUP$"

Details: LSL.COM may use any multiplex number between C0h and FFh; it searches for itself in that range, and installs using the first free multiplex number in the range if not already loaded.

On return, ES = DX for LSL v1.10; LSL makes use of this in its search for a previous installation.

Conflicts: see Table 2-2

10-1 LSL entry point calling convention:

Registers at call:
BX = 0001h "Request MLID Registration"
ES:SI -> *unknown item*
others, if any, unknown

Return Registers:
AX = completion code (see Table 10-2)
DS:DI -> LSL information block

Registers at call:
BX = 0002h get support entry points
ES:SI -> buffer for entry point record
(see Table 10-3)

Return Registers:
ES:SI buffer filled

Registers at call:
BX = 0003h "Request MLID
(Multiple Link Interface Driver) API
entry point"

Return Registers:
ES:SI -> MLID API entry point (call with
BX=function 00h-10h, not range-checked)

Details: LSL v1.10 executes Function 0003h for all other values of BX.

See *Novell LAN Driver Developer's Guide, Volume III* for details of Function 0001h.

10-2 Values for completion code:

0000h	successful
8001h	out of resources
8002h	bad parameter
8003h	no more items
8004h	item not present

8005h	failed
8006h	receive overflow
8007h	canceled
8008h	bad command
8009h	duplicate entry
800Ah	no such handler
800Bh	no such driver

10-3 Format of entry point record:

Offset	Size	Description
00h	DWORD	pointer to protocol support entry point in LSL (see Table 10-4)
04h	DWORD	pointer to general support entry point in LSL (see Table 10-5)

10-4 Protocol support entry point calling convention:

Registers at call:
BX = function number

Return Registers:
AX = completion code (see Table 10-2)
ZF set if successful
SS:SP, DS, BP preserved; most other registers
    may be destroyed

0000h *unknown*
0001h *unknown*
0002h *unknown*
0003h "ScheduleAESEvent"
    ES:SI -> AES ECB to be scheduled   ES,SI preserved
        (see Table 10-8)

Registers at call:
BX = function number

Return Registers:
AX = completion code (see Table 10-2)
ZF set if successful
SS:SP, DS, BP preserved; most other registers
    may be destroyed

0004h "CancelAESEvent"
    ES:SI -> ECB to be cancelled   ES,SI preserved
        (see Table 10-8)

0005h "GetIntervalMarker"   DX:AX = current interval marker in milliseconds
                             all other registers preserved

0006h "RegisterStack"   BX = assigned Stack ID if AX=0000h
    AX = logical board number
    ES:SI -> bound stack info structure
        (see Table 10-17)

Registers at call:
BX = function number
    0007h "DeRegisterStack"
        AX = protocol stack's assigned Stack ID
    0008h "RegisterDefaultStack"
        AX = logical board number
        ES:SI -> stack info structure (see Table
10-17)
    0009h "DeRegisterDefaultStack"
        AX = logical board number
    000Ah "RegisterPrescanStack"

AX = logical board number
ES:SI -> stack info structure (see
    Table 10-17)
000Bh "DeRegisterPrescanStack"
    AX = logical board number
Registers at call:
BX = function number

Return Registers:
AX = completion code (see Table 10-2)
ZF set if successful
SS:SP, DS, BP preserved; most other
    registers may be destroyed

Return Registers:
AX = completion code (see Table 10-2)
ZF set if successful
SS:SP, DS, BP preserved; most other
    registers may be destroyed

000Ch "SendPacket"
    ES:SI -> send ECB
000Dh *unknown*
000Eh *unknown*
000Fh *unknown*
0010h "GetStackIDFromName"
    ES:SI -> counted NUL-terminated
        protocol name (max 15 characters)
Registers at call:
BX = function number

interrupts disabled

BX = Stack ID if AX=0000h

Return Registers:
AX = completion code (see Table 10-2)
ZF set if successful
SS:SP, DS, BP preserved; most other
    registers may be destroyed

0011h "GetPIDFromStackIDBoard"
    AX = Stack ID for protocol
    CX = logical board number
    ES:SI -> 6-byte buffer for protocol ID
0012h "GetMLIDControlEntry"
    AX = logical board number

Registers at call:
BX = function number

ES:SI -> MLID control handler
    (see Table 10-6) if AX=0000h
Return Registers:
AX = completion code (see Table 10-2)
ZF set if successful
SS:SP, DS, BP preserved; most other
    registers may be destroyed

0013h "GetProtocolControlEntry"
    AX = Stack ID or
        FFFEh Prescan stack
            CX = logical board number
        FFFFh default protocol
            CX = logical board number
0014h "GetLSLStatistics"

ES:SI -> protocol stack control entry
    point if AX=0000h (see Table 10-7)

AX = 0000h (successful)
ZF set
ES:SI -> LSL statistics table (see
    Table 10-10)

Registers at call:
BX = function number
0015h "BindStack"
    AX = protocol stack's assigned Stack ID

CX = logical board number
0016h "UnbindStack"
    AX = protocol stack's assigned
      Stack ID
    CX = logical board number
0017h "AddProtocolID"
    AX = frame type ID code
    ES:SI -> 6-byte protocol ID
    CX:DI -> counted NUL-terminated
      short protocol name (max 15
      characters)

Return Registers:
AX = completion code (see Table 10-2)
ZF set if successful
SS:SP, DS, BP preserved; most other registers
may be destroyed

Registers at call:
BX = function number

Return Registers:
AX = completion code, except Function 001Ah
(see
   Table 10-2)
ZF set if successful
SS:SP, DS, BP preserved; most other registers
may
   be destroyed

0018h "RelinquishControl"

0019h "GetLSLConfiguration"

after LSL performs any necessary background
   processing

001Ah "GetTickMarker"

AX = 0000h (successful)
ZF set
ES:SI -> LSL configuration table (see Table 10-9)

AX = number of 55ms ticks since LSL loaded
BX destroyed

10-5 General support entry point calling convention:

Registers at call:
BX = function number
   0000h "Allocate Memory" (obsolete)
   0001h "Free Memory" (obsolete)
   0002h "Realloc Memory" (obsolete)
   0003h "Memory Statistics" (obsolete)
   0004h "Add Memory To Pool"
(obsolete)

Return Registers:
AX = 8008h (BAD_COMMAND)
ZF clear
SS:SP, DS, BP preserved

Registers at call:
BX = function number

Return Registers:
AX = completion code (see Table 10-2)
ZF set if successful
SS:SP, DS, BP preserved

   0005h "AddGeneralService"
      ES:SI -> General Service Control
        Block (see Table 10-19)
   0006h "RemoveGeneralService"
      ES:SI -> General Service Control
        Block (see Table 10-19)
   0007h "GetNETcfgPath"

AX = 0000h (successful)
DS:DX -> ASCIZ pathname for NET.CFG

Registers at call:
BX = function number

Return Registers:
AX = completion code (see Table 10-2)
ZF set if successful
SS:SP, DS, BP preserved

0008h *unknown* (in LSL 1.10)

AX = 0000h
ES:SI -> *unknown* (a 22-byte data area)

000Ah "GetCriticalSectionStatus"

BX = total outstanding calls to
"StartCriticalSection"

000Bh "ServiceEvents"
        interrupts disabled

interrupts disabled

Registers at call:
BX = function number

Return Registers:
AX = completion code (see Table 10-2)
ZF set if successful
SS:SP, DS, BP preserved

0010h "GetStackECB"
        DS:DI -> Lookahead structure
            (see Table 10-20)   interrupts disabled
8000h-FFFFh reserved for user
    general service providers

ES:SI -> ECB if successful (AX=0000h,ZF set)
interrupts disabled

10-6 MLID control handler calling convention:

Registers at call:
AX = logical board number
BX = function number

Return Registers:
AX = completion code (see Table 10-2)
ZF set if successful

0000h "GetMLIDConfiguration"

ES:SI -> MLID's configuration table if successful
    (see Table 10-12)

0001h "GetMLIDStatistics"

ES:SI -> MLID's statistics table if successful (see
    Table 10-16)

Registers at call:
AX = logical board number
BX = function number
    0002h "AddMulticastAddress"
        ES:SI -> 6-byte multicast address
            to add
    0003h "DeleteMulticastAddress"
        ES:SI -> 6-byte multicast address
            to delete
    0005h "MLIDShutdown"
        CX = type
            0000h permanent (also
                deregisters from LSL)
            other temporary (shutdown
                hardware only)
    0006h "MLIDReset" reinitialize
    board / restart from temporary
    shutdown

Return Registers:
AX = completion code (see Table 10-2)
ZF set if successful

Registers at call:
AX = logical board number
BX = function number
   0007h "Create Connection"
     (obsolete?)
       others, if any, unknown
   0008h "Delete Connection"
     (obsolete?)
       others, if any, unknown
   0009h "SetLookAheadSize"
     CX = requested lookahead size
       (00h-80h)
   0010h "PromiscuousChange"
     CX = what to receive promiscuously
       bit 0: MAC frames
       bit 1: non-MAC frames
   0011h "RegisterReceiveMonitor"
     CX = subfunction
       0000h disable receive monitoring
       else enable receive monitoring
          ES:SI -> monitor receive routine
          ES:DI -> monitor transmit routine
   0012h "Driver Poll" (obsolete?)
     unknown

Return Registers:
AX = completion code (see Table 10-2)
ZF set if successful

Details: Not all boards/MLIDs support function 0010h; see bit 13 in the MLID mode flags field of the MLID's configuration table (Table 10-13).

10-7 protocol stack control entry point calling convention:

Registers at call:
BX = function number

0000h "GetProtocolStackConfiguration"

0001h "GetProtocolStackStatistics"

0002h "BindToMLID"
     CX = board number to bind to
     ES:SI -> implementation-dependant
       parameter string
0003h "UnBindFromMLID"
     CX = board number from which
       protocol should unbind
     ES:SI -> optional implementation-dependant
       parameter string
0004h "MLIDDeRegistered"
     CX = board number that has de-registered
       from LSL

Return Registers:
AX = status
     0000h successful
     else implementation-dependant
       error codes
ZF set if successful
SS:SP, DS, BP preserved

ES:SI -> protocol stack's configuration
   table (see Table 10-12)

ES:SI -> protocol stack's statistics table
   (see Table 10-11)

10-8 Format of AES ECB:

Offset	Size	Description
00h	DWORD	"AESLink" pointer used by LSL for list management
04h	DWORD	number of milliseconds to wait
08h	DWORD	"AESStatus" (is set to 00000000h when AES ESR is invoked)
0Ch	DWORD	pointer to function to be invoked when time expires
		ES:SI will point to this structure on entry; DS, BP, and SS:SP must be preserved.

See also: Table 5-3

10-9 Format of LSL Configuration Table:

Offset	Size	Description
00h	BYTE	major version of configuration table
01h	BYTE	minor version of configuration table (decimal, 0-99)
02h	8 BYTEs	reserved
0Ah	BYTE	LSL major version (decimal)
0Bh	BYTE	LSL minor version (decimal, 0-99)

--- LSL 1.0x ---

Offset	Size	Description
0Ch	14 BYTEs	reserved

--- LSL 1.10+ ---

Offset	Size	Description
0Ch	WORD	maximum number of boards which LSL can handle
0Eh	WORD	maximum number of protocol IDs which LSL can handle
10h	12 BYTES	reserved

10-10 Format of LSL Statistics Table:

Offset	Size	Description
00h	BYTE	major version of statistics table format
01h	BYTE	minor version of statistics table format (decimal, 0-99)
02h	WORD	"GenericCounters" number of counters in static portion of table
04h	DWORD	"ValidCountersMask" bit mask indicating which generic counters are actually used. Bit 31 = TotalTxPackets, bit 30 is the next field, etc.
08h	DWORD	"TotalTxPackets" total SendPacket requests made
0Ch	DWORD	reserved
10h	DWORD	reserved
14h	DWORD	"AESEventsCount" number of completed AES events
18h	DWORD	"PostponedEvents" number of events postponed due to critical sections inside the MLIDs
1Ch	DWORD	"CancelAESFailures" number of times CancelAESEvent failed
20h	DWORD	reserved
24h	DWORD	reserved
28h	DWORD	"TotalRxPackets" total number of GetStackECB requests
2ch	DWORD	"UnclaimedPackets" total number of packets not consumed by a protocol stack
30h	WORD	"NumberCustom" number of custom variables that follow
32h	N DWORDs	custom counters
	N DWORDs	pointer to CustomCounterStrN (one per custom counter)
	var	length-prepended and NULL terminated string for Counter 0
	...	
	var	Length-prepended and NULL terminated string for Counter N-1

10-11 Format of Protocol Stack Statistics Table:

Offset	Size	Description
00h	BYTE	statistics table major version
01h	BYTE	statistics table minor version (decimal, 0-99)
02h	WORD	number of generic counters following
04h	DWORD	"ValidCountersMask" (bitmask, bit 31 is TotalTxPackets)
08h	DWORD	TotalTxPackets
0ch	DWORD	TotalRxPackets
10h	DWORD	IgnoredRxPackets
14h	WORD	number of custom counters
16h	N DWORDs	custom counters
	N DWORDs	pointer to CustomCounterStrN (one per custom counter)
	var	length-prepended and NULL terminated string for Counter 0
	...	
	var	length-prepended and NULL terminated string for Counter N-1

10-12 Format of Protocol Stack Configuration Table:

Offset	Size	Description
00h	BYTE	configuration table major version
01h	BYTE	configuration table minor version (decimal, 0-99)
02h	DWORD	pointer to counted NUL-terminated long descriptive name for protocol
06h	DWORD	pointer to counted NUL-terminated short name for protocol (15 characters)
0Ah	BYTE	protocol stack major version
0Bh	BYTE	protocol stack minor version (decimal, 0-99)
0Ch	16 BYTEs	reserved for future use

10-13 Format of MLID Configuration Table:

Offset	Size	Description
00h	26 BYTEs	signature 'HardwareDriverMLID' (8 spaces on end)
1Ah	BYTE	configuration table major version
1Bh	BYTE	configuration table minor version (decimal, 0-99)
1Ch	6 BYTEs	node address
22h	WORD	MLID mode flags (see Table 10-14)
24h	WORD	board number
26h	WORD	board instance (if more than one of same board installed)
28h	WORD	maximum packet size
2Ah	WORD	BestDataSize
2Ch	WORD	WorstDataSize
2Eh	DWORD	pointer to counted NUL-terminated long name for NIC
32h	DWORD	pointer to counted NUL-terminated short name for NIC (8 characters max)
36h	DWORD	pointer to counted NUL-terminated Frame and Media type
3Ah	WORD	reserved (0000h)
3Ch	WORD	frame type ID
3Eh	WORD	TransportTime (milliseconds)
40h	DWORD	pointer to SourceRouteHandler for TokenRing (Used by ROUTE.COM)
44h	WORD	lookahead size
46h	WORD	line speed (Mbps if high bit clear, else Kbps)
48h	WORD	QueueDepth
4Ch	6 BYTEs	reserved (0)
54h	BYTE	driver major version

55h	BYTE	driver minor version (decimal, 0-99)
56h	WORD	flags

bits 10-9: specialized multicast support

        00 = Group addressing is default for medium

        01 = Invalid

        10 = Filter group address in MLID.

        11 = Adapter filters group address.

bit 2: supports Micro Channel cards

bit 1: supports ISA cards

bit 0: supports EISA cards

58h	WORD	send retries
5Ah	DWORD	ConfigTableLink
5Eh	WORD	MLID sharing flags (see Table 10-15)
60h	WORD	slot number
62h	WORD	I/O address 1
64h	WORD	I/O range 1
66h	WORD	I/O address 2
68h	WORD	I/O range 2
6Ah	DWORD	memory address 1
6Eh	WORD	memory size 1
70h	DWORD	memory address 2
74h	WORD	memory size 2
76h	BYTE	interrupt line 1
77h	BYTE	interrupt line 2
78h	BYTE	DMA line 1
79h	BYTE	DMA line 2

10-14 Bitfields for MLID mode flags:

bit 15	MLID supports Octet Bit Reversal
bit 14	node address is non-canonical
bit 13	promiscuous mode is supported
bit 12-8	reserved
bit 7	LDataSize field in LookAhead structure supported
bit 6	raw send supported
bit 5	MLID needs to be polled by LSL
bit 4	reserved (0)
bit 3	multicasting is supported
bit 2	not currently used by DOS ODI, set to 0
bit 1	network card uses DMA
bit 0	RealDriverBit, always set to 1

10-15 Bitfields for MLID sharing flags:

bit 8	NIC can share DMA2
bit 7	NIC can share DMA1
bit 6	NIC can share IRQ2
bit 5	NIC can share IRQ1
bit 4	NIC can share Memory2
bit 3	NIC can share Memory1
bit 2	NIC can share IO2
bit 1	NIC can share IO1
bit 0	MLID is currently shut down

10-16 Format of MLID Statistics Table:

Offset	Size	Description
00h	BYTE	driver statistics table major version
01h	BYTE	driver statistics table minor version (decimal, 0-99)
02h	WORD	number of generic counters (typically 13)
04h	DWORD	"ValidCountersMask" (bit mask, bit 31 is TotalTxCount)
08h	DWORD	TotalTxCount
0Ch	DWORD	TotalRxCount
10h	DWORD	NoECBAvailableCount
14h	DWORD	TxTooBigCount
18h	DWORD	TxTooSmallCount
1ch	DWORD	RxOverflowCount
20h	DWORD	RxTooBigCount
24h	DWORD	RxTooSmallCount
28h	DWORD	TxMiscCount
2ch	DWORD	RxMiscCount
30h	DWORD	TxRetryCount
34h	DWORD	RxChecksumErrorCount
38h	DWORD	RxMismatchCount
3Ch	WORD	number of custom counters
3Eh	N DWORDs	custom counters
	N DWORDs	pointer to CustomCounterStrN (one per custom counter)
	var	length-prepended and NULL terminated string for Counter 0
	...	
	var	length-prepended and NULL terminated string for Counter N-1

10-17 Format of bound stack info structure:

Offset	Size	Description
00h	DWORD	pointer to protocol stack's short name (counted, NUL-terminated)
04h	DWORD	pointer to receive handler
08h	DWORD	pointer to control handler

10-18 Format of stack info structure:

Offset	Size	Description
00h	DWORD	pointer to receive handler
04h	DWORD	pointer to control handler

10-19 Format of General Service Control Block:

Offset	Size	Description
00h	DWORD	pointer to next GSCB (maintained internally by LSL)
04h	DWORD	address of entry point for general service handler
08h	WORD	command code for this general service (8000h-FFFFh)

Note: The control block must not be altered or deallocated until the general service is removed.

10-20 FoErmat of Lookahead structure:

Offset	Size	Description
00h	DWORD	pointer to Media header
04h	DWORD	pointer to lookahead buffer
08h	WORD	length of lookahead buffer
0Ah	6 BYTEs	protocol ID
10h	WORD	logical board number
12h	WORD	lookahead size

CHAPTER 11

Packet Driver Specification

PC/TCP is the flagship product of the FTP Software Group, founded by some of the MIT alumni who first demonstrated TCP/IP on DOS-based PCs. The Wakefield, Mass., company also published the packet-driver specifications so network interface card manufacturers could supply debugged drivers.

To side-step interrupt conflicts, the packet driver specification permits use of a wide range of interrupt vectors (20h through FFh for version 1.10 and higher). The handler for the interrupt will start with a 3-byte jump instruction, followed by the ASCIZ signature string "PKT DRVR" (the terminating NUL is significant). To find the interrupt being used by the driver, an application should scan through interrupt vectors 20h through FFh (60h through 80h for drivers predating v1.10 of the specification) until it finds one with the "PKT DRVR" string. As with all programs using interrupts in the range 60h to 67h, there are numerous potential conflicts with other programs, which are listed in Table 2-2; since the range which is scanned is so large, there are also many conflicts with programs which are listed in Table 2-1.

Packet driver functions 80h to FFh have been reserved for user-defined additions. The only such addition known at the time of writing was Function E9h, used by Crynwr Software and described at the end of this chapter.

INT 60h Function 01FFh   *FTP Packet Driver*
GET DRIVER INFO   *Basic Function*

Registers at call: **Return Registers:**
AX = 01FFh   CF set on error
BX = handle returned by function 02h   DH = error code (see Table 11-1)
                                       CF clear if successful
                                              BX = version
                                              CH = network interface class (see Table 11-2)
                                              DX = interface type (see Table 11-2)
                                              CL = number
                                              DS:SI -> name
                                              AL = driver functions supported
                                                   01h basic
                                                   02h basic and extended
                                                   05h basic and high-performance
                                                   06h basic, high-performance, and extended
                                                   FFh not installed

Details: The handle in BX is optional for drivers written to version 1.07 or higher of the packet driver specification.
Conflicts: see Table 2-3

11-1 Values for error code:

01h	"BAD_HANDLE"	invalid handle number
02h	"NO_CLASS"	no interfaces of the specified class found
03h	"NO_TYPE"	no interfaces of the specified type found
04h	"NO_NUMBER"	no interfaces of the specified number found
05h	"BAD_TYPE"	bad packet type
06h	"NO_MULTICAST"	interface does not support multicast messages
07h	"CANT_TERMINATE"	this packet driver cannot terminate
08h	"BAD_MODE"	invalid receiver mode
09h	"NO_SPACE"	insufficient space
0Ah	"TYPE_INUSE"	type accessed but never released
0Bh	"BAD_COMMAND"	bad command
0Ch	"CANT_SEND"	packet could not be sent
0Dh	"CANT_SET"	hardware address could not be changed
0Eh	"BAD_ADDRESS"	hardware address has a bad length or format
0Fh	"CANT_RESET"	could not reset interface

11-2 Values for Network Interface classes/types:

Class 01h	Ethernet/IEEE 802.3
01h	3COM 3C500/3C501
02h	3COM 3C505
03h	MICOM-Interlan NI5010
04h	BICC Data Networks 4110
05h	BICC Data Networks 4117
06h	MICOM-Interlan NP600
08h	Ungermann-Bass PC-NIC
09h	Univation NC-516
0Ah	TRW PC-2000
0Bh	MICOM-Interlan NI5210
0Ch	3COM 3C503
0Dh	3COM 3C523
0Eh	Western Digital WD8003
0Fh	Spider Systems S4
10h	Torus Frame Level
11h	10Net Communications
12h	Gateway PC-bus
13h	Gateway AT-bus
14h	Gateway MCA-bus
15h	IMC PCnic
16h	IMC PCnic II
17h	IMC PCnic 8-bit
18h	Tigan Communications
19h	Micromatic Research
1Ah	Clarkson "Multiplexor"
1Bh	D-Link 8-bit
1Ch	D-Link 16-bit
1Dh	D-Link PS/2
1Eh	Research Machines 8
1Fh	Research Machines 16
20h	Research Machines MCA

INT 60h Function 01FFh

21h	Radix Microsystems EXM1 16-bit
22h	Interlan Ni9210
23h	Interlan Ni6510
24h	Vestra LANMASTER 16-bit
25h	Vestra LANMASTER 8-bit
26h	Allied Telesis PC/XT/AT
27h	Allied Telesis NEC PC-98
28h	Allied Telesis Fujitsu FMR
29h	Ungermann-Bass NIC/PS2
2Ah	Tiara LANCard/E AT
2Bh	Tiara LANCard/E MC
2Ch	Tiara LANCard/E TP
2Dh	Spider Communications SpiderComm 8
2Eh	Spider Communications SpiderComm 16
2Fh	AT&T Starlan NAU
30h	AT&T Starlan-10 NAU
31h	AT&T Ethernet NAU
32h	Intel smart card
33h	Xircom Packet Adapter
34h	Aquila Ethernet
35h	Novell NE1000
36h	Novell NE2000
37h	SMC PC-510
38h	AT&T Fiber NAU
39h	NDIS to Packet Driver adapter
3Ah	Racal-InterLan ES3210
3Bh	General Systems ISDN simulated Ethernet
3Ch	Hewlett-Packard
3Dh	IMC EtherNic-8
3Eh	IMC EtherNic-16
3Fh	IMC EtherNic-MCA
40h	NetWorth EtherNext
41h	Dataco Scanet
42h	DEC DEPCA
43h	C-Net
44h	Gandalf LANLine
45h	Apricot built-in
46h	David Systems Ether-T
47h	ODI to Packet Driver adapter
48h	AMD Am21110-16
49h	Intel ICD Network controller family
4Ah	Intel ICD PCL2
4Bh	Intel ICD PCL2A
4Ch	AT&T LANPacer
4Dh	AT&T LANPacer+
4Eh	AT&T EVB
4Fh	AT&T StarStation
50h	SLIP simulated ethernet
51h	Racal-Interlan NIA310

52h	Racal-Interlan NISE
53h	Racal-Interlan NISE30
54h	Racal-Interlan NI6610
55h	Ethernet over IP/UDP
56h	ICL EtherTeam 16
57h	David Systems
58h	NCR WaveLAN
59h	Thomas Contrad TC5045
5Ah	Russ Nelson's Parallel Port driver
5Bh	Intell EtherExpress 16
5Ch	IBMTOKEN
5Dh	Zenith Z-Note
5Eh	3Com 3C509
5Fh	Mylex LNE390
60h	Madge Smart Ringnode
61h	Novell NE2100
62h	Allied Telesis 1500
63h	Allied Telesis 1700
64h	Fujitsu EtherCoupler
Class 02h	**ProNET-10**
01h	Proteon p1300
02h	Proteon p1800
Class 03h	**IEEE 802.5/ProNet-4 (without expanded RIFs)**
01h	IBM Token-Ring Adapter
02h	Proteon p1340
03h	Proteon p1344
04h	Gateway PC-bus
05h	Gateway AT-bus
06h	Gateway MCA-bus
07h	Madge board
39h	NDIS to Packet Driver adapter
47h	ODI to Packet Driver adapter
Class 04h	**Omninet**
Class 05h	**Appletalk**
01h	ATALK.SYS adapter
Class 06h	**Serial Line**
01h	Clarkson 8250-SLIP
02h	Clarkson "Multiplexor"
03h	Eicon Technologies
Class 07h	**StarLAN (subsumed by Ethernet class)**
Class 08h	**ARCnet**
01h	Datapoint RIM
Class 09h	**AX.25**
01h	Ottawa PI card
02h	Eicon Technologies
Class 0Ah	**KISS**
Class 0Bh	**IEEE 802.3 with 802.2 headers**
types same as for class 01h	
Class 0Ch	**FDDI with 802.2 headers**

INT 60h Function 01FFh

01h	Western Digital
02h	Frontier Technology
Class 0Dh	**Internet X.25**
01h	Western Digital
02h	Frontier Technology
03h	Emerging Technologies
04h	The Software Forge
05h	Link Data Intelligent X.25
06h	Eicon Technologies
Class 0Eh	**N.T. LANSTAR (encapsulating DIX Ethernet)**
01h	NT LANSTAR/8
02h	NT LANSTAR/MC
Class 0Fh	**SLFP (MIT serial specification)**
01h	MERIT
Class 10h	**PPP (Point-to-Point Protocol)**
01h	8250/16550 UART
02h	Niwot Networks synch
03h	Eicon Technologies
Class 11h	**802.5 with expanded RIFs**

types same as for class 3
Class 12h   reserved for LCP/NCPs
Note: Class and type numbers are cleared through FTP Software.

INT 60h Function 02h   *FTP Packet Driver*
ACCESS TYPE   *Basic Function*

Registers at call:	**Return Registers:**
AH = 02h	CF set on error
AL = interface class	DH = error code (see Table 11-1)
BX = interface type	CF clear if successful
DL = interface number	AX = handle
DS:SI -> type	
CX = length of type (0000h for all packets)	
ES:DI -> receiver	

Conflicts: see Table 2-3
See also: Function 03h

11-3 Receiver calling convention (when a packet is received):

Registers at call: **Return Registers:**
AX = subfunction   (subfunction 00h only)
    00h get packet buffer   ES:DI -> packet buffer
        DX = lookahead length (v1.10+)   0000h:0000h means throw away packet
        DS:SI -> lookahead buffer if DX   CX = size of buffer (v1.10+), may be
          nonzero (v1.10+)   smaller than incoming data
        DI = error flags (class dependent) (v1.10+)
    01h copy completed
        DS:SI -> buffer
        CX = bytes actually copied (v1.10+)
BX = handle
CX = buffer length

INT 60h Function 03h
RELEASE TYPE

FTP Packet Driver
Basic Function

Registers at call:
AH = 03h
BX = handle

Return Registers:
CF set on error
    DH = error code (see Table 11-1)
CF clear if successful

Conflicts: see Table 2-3
See also: Function 02h

INT 60h Function 04h
SEND PACKET

FTP Packet Driver
Basic Function

Registers at call:
AH = 04h
DS:SI -> buffer
CX = length

Return Registers:
CF set on error
    DH = error code (see Table 11-1)
CF clear if successful

Details: The buffer may be modified immediately upon return from this call.
Conflicts: see Table 2-3
See also: Function 0Bh

INT 60h Function 05h
TERMINATE DRIVER FOR HANDLE

FTP Packet Driver
Basic Function

Registers at call:
AH = 05h
BX = handle (optional for v1.10+)

Return Registers:
CF set on error
    DH = error code (see Table 11-1)
CF clear if successful

Conflicts: see Table 2-3

INT 60h Function 06h
GET ADDRESS

FTP Packet Driver
Basic Function

Purpose: Copy the local net address associated with the handle into the specified buffer.

Registers at call:
AH = 06h
BX = handle (optional for v1.10+)
ES:DI -> buffer for address
CX = length

Return Registers:
CF set on error
    DH = error code (see Table 11-1)
CF clear if successful
    CX = length
    ES:DI buffer filled

Conflicts: see Table 2-3

INT 60h Function 07h
RESET INTERFACE

FTP Packet Driver
Basic Function

Registers at call:
AH = 07h
BX = handle (optional for v1.10+)

Return Registers:
CF set on error
    DH = error code (see Table 11-1)
CF clear if successful

Conflicts: see Table 2-3

INT 60h Function 0Ah
GET PARAMETERS

FTP Packet Driver v1.09+
High-Performance Function

Registers at call:
AH = 0Ah

Return Registers:
CF set on error
    DH = error code (0Bh) (see Table 11-1)
CF clear if successful
    ES:DI -> parameter table (see Table 11-4)

Conflicts: see Table 2-3

11-4 Format of parameter table:

Offset	Size	Description
00h	BYTE	major revision of packet driver specification to which driver conforms
01h	BYTE	minor revision of packet driver specification
02h	BYTE	length of this structure in bytes
03h	BYTE	length of a MAC-layer address
04h	WORD	maximum transfer unit, including MAC headers
06h	WORD	buffer size for multicast addr
08h	WORD	number of receive buffers (one less than back-to-back MTU receives)
0Ah	WORD	number of transmit buffers
0Ch	WORD	interrupt number to hook for post-EOI processing, 00h=none

---

INT 60h Function 0Bh *FTP Packet Driver 1.09*
ASYNCHRONOUS SEND PACKET *High-Performance Function*

Registers at call: **Return Registers:**
AH = 0Bh CF set on error
DS:SI -> buffer DH = error code (0Bh,0Ch) (see Table 11-1)
CX = length of buffer CF clear if successful
ES:DI -> FAR function to call when buffer becomes available

Details: Unlike Function 04h, the buffer is not available for modification as soon as the call returns; the buffer may be queued by the driver and not processed until later.

This function has been dropped from v1.10+ of the specification and replaced by Function 0Ch.

Conflicts: see Table 2-3
See also: Functions 04h and 0Ch

11-5 Completion function calling convention:

Registers at call: **Return Registers:**
AX = result none
    00h copy OK
    nonzero error
ES:DI -> buffer passed to INT 60h
Function 0Bh call

INT 60h Function 0Ch *FTP Packet Driver 1.10+*
ASYNCHRONOUS SEND PACKET *High-Performance Function*

Registers at call: **Return Registers:**
AH = 0Ch CF set on error
ES:DI -> pointer to IOCB (see Table 11-6) DH = error code (see Table 11-1)
    CF clear if successful

Conflicts: see Table 2-3
See also: Functions 04h and 0Bh

11-6 Format of IOCB:

Offset	Size	Description
00h	DWORD	pointer to buffer
04h	WORD	length of buffer
06h	BYTE	flags
		bit 0: packet driver is finished with IOCB
		bit 1: application requests upcall when driver completes
07h	DWORD	function address for upcall
0Bh	4 BYTEs	future gather write

| 0Fh | BYTE | *unknown* |
| 10h | 8 BYTEs | private driver workspace |

11-7 Completion function calling convention:

Registers at call:
ES:DI -> IOCB passed to INT 60h
Function 0Ch

Return Registers:
none

INT 60h Function 0Dh
DROP PACKET FROM QUEUE

FTP Packet Driver 1.10+
High-Performance Function

Registers at call:
AH = 0Dh
ES:DI -> IOCB (see Table 11-6)

Return Registers:
CF set on error
    DH = error code (see Table 11-1)
CF clear if successful

Conflicts: see Table 2-3
See also: Function 0Ch

INT 60h Function 14h
SET RECEIVE MODE

FTP Packet Driver
Extended Function

Registers at call:
AH = 14h
BX = handle (optional for v1.10+)
CX = mode (see Table 11-8)
Conflicts: see Table 2-3
See also: Function 15h

Return Registers:
CF set on error
    DH = error code (01h,08h) (see Table 11-1)
CF clear if successful

11-8 Values for receive mode:

01h	turn off receiver
02h	receive only packets sent to this interface
03h	mode 2 plus broadcast packets
04h	mode 3 plus limited multicast packets
05h	mode 3 plus all multicast packets
06h	all packets (promiscuous mode)
07h	raw mode for serial line only (v1.10+)

INT 60h Function 15h
GET RECEIVE MODE

FTP Packet Driver
Extended Function

Registers at call:
AH = 15h
BX = handle (optional for v1.10+)

Return Registers:
CF set on error
    DH = error code (01h) (see Table 11-1)
CF clear if successful
    AX = mode (see Table 11-8)

Conflicts: see Table 2-3
See also: Function 14h

INT 60h Function 16h
SET MULTICAST LIST

FTP Packet Driver
Extended Function

Registers at call:
AH = 16h
ES:DI -> multicast list
CX = length of list in bytes
Conflicts: see Table 2-3
See also: Function 17h

Return Registers:
CF set on error
    DH = error code (06h,09h,0Eh) (see Table 11-1)
CF clear if successful

INT 60h Function 17h
GET MULTICAST LIST

Registers at call:
AH = 17h

Return Registers:
CF set on error
    DH = error code (06h,09h) (see Table 11-1)
CF clear if successful
    ES:DI -> multicast addresses (do not modify)
    CX = bytes of multicast addresses currently in use

Conflicts: see Table 2-3
See also: Function 16h

INT 60h Function 18h
GET STATISTICS

Registers at call:
AH = 18h
BX = handle (optional for v1.10+)

Return Registers:
CF set on error
    DH = error code (01h) (see Table 11-1)
CF clear if successful
    DS:SI -> statistics (see Table 11-9)

11-9 Format of statistics:

Offset	Size	Description
00h	DWORD	packets in
04h	DWORD	packets out
08h	DWORD	bytes in
0Ch	DWORD	bytes out
10h	DWORD	errors in
14h	DWORD	errors out
18h	DWORD	packets dropped

INT 60h Function 19h
SET NETWORK ADDRESS

Registers at call:
AH = 19h
ES:DI -> address
CX = length of address

Return Registers:
CF set on error
    DH = error code (0Dh,0Eh) (see Table 11-1)
CF clear if successful
    CX = length

Conflicts: see Table 2-3

INT 60h Function 1Ah
SEND RAW BYTES

Registers at call:
AH = 1Ah
DS:SI -> buffer
CX = length of buffer
Conflicts: see Table 2-3
See also: Function 1Ch

Return Registers:
CF set on error
    DH = error code (see Table 11-1)
CF clear if successful

INT 60h Function 1Bh
FLUSH RAW BYTES RECEIVED

Registers at call:
AH = 1Bh

Return Registers:
CF set on error
    DH = error code (see Table 11-1)
CF clear if successful

Conflicts: see Table 2-3
See also: Function 1Ch

INT 60h Function 1Ch
FETCH RAW BYTES RECEIVED

Registers at call:
AH = 1Ch
DS:SI -> buffer
CX = length of buffer
DX = timeout in clock ticks
Conflicts: see Table 2-3
See also: Functions 1Ah and 1Bh

Return Registers:
CF set on error
    DH = error code (see Table 11-1)
CF clear if successful
    CX = number of bytes transferred to buffer

INT 60h Function E9h
Crynwr Software - AUTOSELECT TRANSCEIVER

Registers at call:
AH = E9h
others, if any, unknown
Conflicts: see Table 2-3

Return Registers:
unknown

CHAPTER 12

Alloy Multiuser/Network Systems

One of the first mini-network solutions for small office use was the Alloy network system, which originally made it possible to add a "dumb terminal" to a PC as an additional, independently operating, console. From this beginning, the system has evolved into a true networking solution based on a host-slave relationship rather than peer-to-peer or server-oriented operation. The three

Alloy Computer Products, Inc. systems described here are the Alloy NetWare Support Kit (ANSK), Novell-Type Network Executive (NTNX), and 386/MultiWare (MW386).

This chapter describes all interrupt functions that are unique to the Alloy systems; however, Alloy also shares a number of functions with Novell networks, which are described in Chapter 21, and it shares three functions with PC-Net, which are described in Chapter 31.

INT 10h Function 8Bh
Alloy MW386

FORCE WORKSTATION SCREEN UPDATE

Registers at call:　　　　　　　　　**Return Registers:**
AH = 8Bh　　　　　　　　　　　　　　none
Conflicts: none known
See also: Functions 92h and 93h

INT 10h Function 90h
Alloy MW386

GET PHYSICAL WORKSTATION DISPLAY MODE

Registers at call:　　　　　　　　**Return Registers:**
AH = 90h　　　　　　　　　　　　　AL = current video mode (see Function 00h in PCI-8)
Conflicts: none known
See also: Function 91h

INT 10h Function 91h
Alloy MW386

GET PHYSICAL WORKSTATION ADAPTER TYPE

Registers at call:　　　　　　　　**Return Registers:**
AH = 91h　　　　　　　　　　　　　AL = video adapter type (see Table 12-1)
Details: Types less than 80h do not imply that the current user is on the host.
Conflicts: none known
See also: Function 90h

12-1 Values for video adapter type:

00h	monochrome
01h	Hercules monochrome graphics
02h	CGA
03h	EGA

04h	VGA
80h	monochrome text terminal
81h	Hercules graphics terminal
82h	color graphics terminal

INT 10h Function 92h   *Alloy MW386*
INHIBIT WORKSTATION SCREEN UPDATES
Registers at call: **Return Registers:**
AH = 92h   none
Details: The terminal will be updated even when screen updates are inhibited if TTY output is used.
Conflicts: none known
See also: Function 8Bh

INT 10h Function 93h   *Alloy MW386*
REDRAW SCREEN
Registers at call: **Return Registers:**
AH = 93h   none
Conflicts: none known
See also: Function 8Bh, TopView Function FFh (PCI-44)

INT 14h Function 20h   *Alloy MW386*
ATTACH LOGICAL COMMUNICATIONS PORT TO PHYSICAL PORT
Registers at call: **Return Registers:**
AH = 20h   AX = status
AL = logical port (01h COM1, 02h COM2)   0000h successful
DX = physical port number   FFFFh failed
Conflicts: FOSSIL (PCI-12), MultiDOS Plus (PCI-45), PC-MOS/386 (PCI-49)
See also: Functions 21h, 22h, and 23h; INT 17h Function 8Bh

INT 14h Function 21h   *Alloy MW386 v1.x only*
RELEASE PHYSICAL COMMUNICATIONS PORT
Registers at call: **Return Registers:**
AH = 21h   AX = status
DX = physical port number   0000h successful
                                              FFFFh failed
Conflicts: FOSSIL (PCI-12), MultiDOS Plus (PCI-45), PC-MOS/386 (PCI-49)
See also: Functions 20h and 22h

INT 14h Function 22h   *Alloy MW386 v2+*
RELEASE LOGICAL COMMUNICATIONS PORT
Registers at call: **Return Registers:**
AH = 22h   AX = status (0000h successful)
AL = logical port (01h COM1, 02h COM2)
Conflicts: MultiDOS Plus (PCI-45), PC-MOS/386 (PCI-49)
See also: Functions 20h and 21h

INT 14h Function 23h   *Alloy MW386 v2+*
GET PORT NUMBER FROM LOGICAL PORT ID
Registers at call: **Return Registers:**
AH = 23h   AL = MW386 port mode (see Table 12-2)
AL = logical port (01h COM1, 02h COM2)   CX = MW386 port number
DH = user ID   DH = owner's user ID
DL = process ID (DH,DL both FFh for   DL = owner's task ID
  current task)

Conflicts: MultiDOS Plus (PCI-45), PC-MOS/386 (PCI-49)
See also: Function 20h, INT 17h Function 8Bh

12-2 Bitfields for MW386 port mode:

bit 0	port is shared (spooler only)
bit 1	port is spooled instead of direct (spooler only)
bit 2	port is assigned as logical COM device, not in spooler
bit 3	port is free

INT 14h Function 24h   *Alloy MW386 v2+*
CHANGE PHYSICAL PORT PARAMETERS

Registers at call:	Return Registers:
AH = 24h	AH = 00h
CX = physical I/O port number	
DS:DX -> configuration table (see	
Table 12-3)	

Details: Invalid port numbers are merely ignored.
Conflicts: MultiDOS Plus (PCI-45), PC-MOS/386 (PCI-49)
See also: INT 17h Function 96h

12-3 Format of configuration table:

Offset	Size	Description
00h	BYTE	baud rate (see Table 12-4)
01h	BYTE	data bits (00h=5, 01h=6, 02h=7, 03h=8)
02h	BYTE	parity (00h none, 01h odd, 02h even)
03h	BYTE	stop bits (00h=1, 01h=2)
04h	BYTE	receive flow control
		00h none, 01h XON/XOFF, 02h DTR/DSR, 03h XPC, 04h RTS/CTS
05h	BYTE	transmit flow control (as for receive)

12-4 Values for baud rate:

00h	38400
01h	19200
02h	9600
03h	7200
04h	4800
05h	3600
06h	2400
07h	2000
08h	1200
09h	600
0Ah	300
0Bh	150
0Ch	134.5

INT 17h Function 81h   *Alloy NTNX, MW386*
CANCEL JOBS FOR CURRENT USER

Purpose: Cancel the last N printouts for the current task.

Registers at call:	Return Registers:
AH = 81h	AL = status (see Table 12-5)
AL = 00h (NTNX compatibility mode)	
CL = number of jobs to cancel	

Conflicts: none known
See also: Function 82h

12-5 Values for print spooler status:

00h	success
01h-7Fh	warning
80h	general failure
81h	host overloaded (NTNX only)
82h	module busy (NTNX only)
83h	host busy (NTNX only)
84h	re-entry flag set
85h	invalid request
86h	invalid printer
87h	invalid process ID
89h	access denied
8Ah	option not available for given port type
8Bh	option not available for given task type
91h	printer busy
C2h	file not found
C3h	path not found
C4h	file access failure

INT 17h Function 82h   *Alloy NTNX, MW386*
CANCEL ALL JOBS FOR CURRENT USER

Registers at call: **Return Registers:**
AH = 82h   AL = status (see Table 12-5)
AL = 00h (NTNX compatibility mode)
Conflicts: none known
See also: Function 81h

INT 17h Function 83h   *Alloy NTNX, MW386*
SET NUMBER OF COPIES

Registers at call: **Return Registers:**
AH = 83h   AL = status (see Table 12-5)
AL = mode
    00h NTNX compatibility
        CL = number of copies (max 99, default 1)
    02h MW386 v2+
        BX = logical device number
            00h-03h = LPT1-LPT4
            04h-07h = COM1-COM4
        CX = number of copies
Details: In NTNX compatibility mode, this function only affects LPT1.
Conflicts: none known

INT 17h Function 84h   *Alloy NTNX, MW386*
GENERATE PRINT BREAK

Registers at call:
AH = 84h
AL = mode
    00h NTNX compatibility
    02h MW386 v2+

Return Registers:

BX = logical device number   none
    00h-03h = LPT1-LPT4
    04h-07h = COM1-COM4

Details: This function closes the spool file and tells the spooler to queue the print job (LPT1 only under MW386 in NTNX compatibility mode).

Conflicts: Japanese printer (PCI-6)

INT 17h Function 87h   *Alloy NTNX*
SET INDOS POINTER

Registers at call: **Return Registers:**
AH = 87h   BX,CX destroyed
AL = 00h
CX:BX -> buffer for user-written printer drivers

Details: This function must be executed before the printer is enabled.

Conflicts: none known

See also: Function 8Ah

INT 17h Function 88h   *Alloy NTNX, MW386*
REMOVE PRINTER FROM SPOOLER

Purpose: Remove the specified printer from the spooler's list of printers.

Registers at call: **Return Registers:**
AH = 88h   AH = status (see Table 12-5)
AL = mode
    00h NTNX compatibility
        DX = NTNX printer number (see Table 12-6)
    01h MW386
        DX = MW386 printer number

Conflicts: none known

See also: Functions 89h and 8Bh

12-6 Values for NTNX printer number:

00h	host LPT1
01h	host LPT2
02h	host LPT3
03h	host LPT4
04h	host COM1
05h	host COM2
06h	user's logical COM2
07h	user's terminal AUX port
08h	user's logical COM1 (MW386 only)

INT 17h Function 89h   *Alloy NTNX, MW386*
ADD PRINTER TO SPOOLER

Purpose: Add the specified printer to the spooler's list of available printers.

Registers at call: **Return Registers:**
AH = 89h   AL = status (see Table 12-5)
AL = mode
    00h NTNX compatibility
        DX = NTNX printer number (see Table 12-6)
    01h MW386
        DX = MW386 printer number

Conflicts: none known

See also: Functions 88h and 8Bh

INT 17h Function 8Ah
ACTIVATE USER-WRITTEN PRINTER DRIVER

Alloy NTNX

Registers at call:
AH = 8Ah
others, if any, unknown
Conflicts: none known
See also: Function 92h

Return Registers:
unknown

INT 17h Function 8Bh
GET PHYSICAL DEVICE NUMBER FROM NAME

Alloy MW386

Registers at call:
AH = 8Bh
DS:DX -> ASCIZ printer name

Return Registers:
AL = status (see also Table 12-5)
   00h successful
      DX = physical device number

Conflicts: none known
See also: Functions 89h and 8Ch, INT 14h Function 20h

INT 17h Function 8Ch
GET DEVICE NAME FROM PHYSICAL DEVICE NUMBER

Alloy MW386

Registers at call:
AH = 8Ch
DX = physical device number
ES:DI -> 17-byte buffer for ASCIZ device name
Conflicts: none known
See also: Functions 88h and 8Bh

Return Registers:
AL = status (see also Table 12-5)
   00h successful
      ES:DI buffer filled

INT 17h Function 8Dh
RESET SPOOLER

Alloy NTNX, MW386

Registers at call:
AH = 8Dh
AL = 00h

Return Registers:
AL = status (see Table 12-5)

Details: This function clears all buffers and resets the spooler to boot-up values. MW386 supports this function for compatibility only; it is a NOP.
Conflicts: none known

INT 17h Function 8Eh
GET INT 28h ENTRY POINT

Alloy NTNX

Registers at call:
AH = 8Eh
AL = 00h
Conflicts: none known
See also: Function 8Fh

Return Registers:
CX:BX -> INT 28h entry point

INT 17h Function 8Fh
GET DOS INTERCEPT ENTRY POINT

Alloy NTNX

Registers at call:
AH = 8Fh
AL = 00h
Conflicts: none known
See also: Function 8Eh

Return Registers:
CX:BX -> DOS intercept routine

INT 17h Function 90h
SPOOL FILE BY NAME
Alloy NTNX, MW386

Registers at call:
AH = 90h
AL = mode
    00h NTNX compatibility
        DL = printer code (FFh=current) (NTNX, MW386 v1.x only)
        DH = number of copies (FFh=current) (NTNX, MW386 v1.x only)
    02h MW386 v2+
        BX = logical device number
            00h-03h = LPT1-LPT4
            04h-07h = COM1-COM4
CX:SI -> ASCIZ pathname

Return Registers:
AL = status (see Table 12-5)

Details: In mode 00h, the file is always sent to logical LPT1.
Conflicts: none known
See also: Function A0h

INT 17h Function 91h
GET USER NUMBER AND CURRENT PRINTER
Alloy NTNX, MW386

Registers at call:
AH = 91h
AL = mode

    00h NTNX compatibility

    01h MW386

    02h MW386 v2+
        BX = logical device number
        00h-03h = LPT1-LPT4
        04h-07h = COM1-COM4

Return Registers:
AL = status (see Table 12-5)
CX = user number (00h = host)

DX = currently selected printer number (00h-08h)

DX = physical device number of currently selected printer

DX = physical device number

Conflicts: none known
See also: Function 8Ch

INT 17h Function 92h
CHECK PRINTER DRIVER
Alloy NTNX

Registers at call:
AH = 92h
AL = 00h
CL = 00h

Return Registers:
CL = driver state
    01h initialized
    80h not initialized
AX = function status (see Table 12-5)

Conflicts: none known
See also: Function 8Ah

INT 17h Function 94h
SELECT PRINTER
Alloy NTNX, MW386

Registers at call:
AH = 94h
AL = mode
    00h NTNX compatibility
        DX = NTNX printer number (see Table 12-6)
    01h MW386

Return Registers:
DX = MW386 printer number   AL = status (see Table 12-5)
02h MW386 v2+
BX = logical printer number
DX = MW386 printer number

Details: Modes 00h and 01h affect only logical LPT1.
Conflicts: none known
See also: Functions 8Bh and 95h

INT 17h Function 95h   *Alloy NTNX, MW386*
GET CURRENT PRINTER

Registers at call: **Return Registers:**
AH = 95h   AL = status (see Table 12-5)
AL = mode

    00h NTNX compatibility   DX = NTNX printer number (see Table 12-6)
                        (FFFFh if current printer not compatible with NTNX)

    01h MW386   DX = MW386 printer number

    02h MW386 v2+   DX = MW386 printer number (FFFFh = none)
        BX = logical device number
            00h-03h = LPT1-LPT4
            04h-07h = COM1-COM4
Details: Modes 00h and 01h return the printer number for logical LPT1 only.
Conflicts: none known
See also: Function 94h

INT 17h Function 96h   *Alloy NTNX*
SET SERIAL PORT PARAMETERS

Registers at call: **Return Registers:**
AH = 96h   AX = 0000h
AL = 00h
Details: The documentation states that this is a NOP, doing only XOR AX,AX before returning.
Conflicts: none known
See also: INT 14h Function 24h

INT 17h Function 97h   *Alloy NTNX, MW386*
SET DATA DRIVEN PRINT BREAK

Registers at call: **Return Registers:**
AH = 97h   AL = status (see Table 12-5)
AL = mode
    00h NTNX compatibility
    02h MW386 v2+
        BX = logical device number
            00h-03h = LPT1-LPT4
            04h-07h = COM1-COM4
CH,CL,DH = three character break sequence
DL = subfunction
    00h set break string
    else reset break
Details: Mode 00h affects only logical LPT1.

When the break string is encountered, the spool file will be closed and queued for printing automatically.

The break string is not permanently saved, and will be reset each time MW386 or the user is rebooted.

Conflicts: none known
See also: Function 9Bh

INT 17h Function 98h
RESTART PRINTER
Alloy NTNX, MW386

Registers at call:
AH = 98h
AL = 00h
DL = printer number (FFh=current)

Return Registers:
AL = status
    00h successful
    01h incorrect printer
    02h task not found

Details: MW386 supports this function for compatibility only; it is a NOP.
Conflicts: none known

INT 17h Function 99h
GET/SET PRINTER MODE
Alloy NTNX, MW386

Registers at call:
AH = 99h
AL = mode
    00h NTNX compatibility
        DL = NTNX printer number (see Table 12-6)
            (FFh = task's current logical LPT1)
        DH = mode
            bit 0: get mode if 1, set mode if 0
            bit 1: private ("attached")
            bit 2: direct instead of spooled
            bits 3-7 reserved (0)
    01h MW386
        DX = MW386 printer number
        CL = mode (as for DH above)

Return Registers:
AL = status (see Table 12-5)
DH = mode (bits 1 and 2 set as at left)
DL = printer owner's user number if not spooled

Conflicts: none known

INT 17h Function 9Ah
SET TAB EXPANSION
Alloy NTNX, MW386

Registers at call:
AH = 9Ah
AL = mode
    00h NTNX compatibility
        DX = NTNX printer number (see Table 12-6)
            (FFFFh = current logical LPT1)
    01h MW386
        DX = MW386 printer number
CL = tab length (00h = no expansion, 01h-63h = spaces per tab)

Return Registers:
AL = status (see Table 12-5)

Details: Beginning with MW386 v2.0, tab expansion is set on a per-printer basis rather than a per-user basis; NTNX and MW386 v1.x ignore DX.
Conflicts: none known
See also: Function A4h

INT 17h Function 9Bh
SET PRINT BREAK TIMEOUT
Alloy NTNX, MW386

Registers at call:
AH = 9Bh
AL = mode
    00h NTNX compatibility
        CX = timeout value in clock ticks (1/18 sec) (00h = never)
    01h MW386
        CX = timeout value in seconds (00h = never)
    02h MW386 v2+
        BX = logical device number
            00h-03h = LPT1-LPT4
            04h-07h = COM1-COM4
        CX = timeout value in seconds (00h = never)

Return Registers:
AL = status (see Table 12-5)

Details: Modes 00h and 01h affect only the current logical LPT1.
    If no data is sent to a printer for the specified amount of time, the spool file will be closed and queued for printing automatically.
Conflicts: none known
See also: Function 97h

INT 17h Function A0h
SPOOL COPY OF FILE
Alloy MW386

Registers at call:
AH = A0h
AL = mode
    00h NTNX compatibility
        DX = *unknown* (NTNX, MW386 v1.x only)
    02h MW386 v2+
        BX = logical device number
            00h-03h = LPT1-LPT4
            04h-07h = COM1-COM4
CX:SI -> ASCIZ pathname

Return Registers:
AL = status (see Table 12-5)

Details: This function makes a copy of the specified file in the spooler's directory, allowing the original file to be modified or deleted while the copy is printed.
    In mode 00h, the file is printed on logical LPT1.
Conflicts: none known
See also: Function 90h

INT 17h Function A4h
ENABLE/DISABLE FORM FEED
Alloy MW386

Registers at call:
AH = A4h
AL = new state
    00h form feed after end of print job disabled
    01h form feed enabled

Return Registers:
AL = status (see Table 12-5)

Details: This function only affects the current logical LPT1.
Conflicts: none known
See also: Functions 9Ah and A6h, NTNX Host INT 7Fh Function 05h

INT 17h Function A6h
ENABLE/DISABLE BANNER PAGE

Alloy MW386

Registers at call:
AH = A6h
AL = new state
    00h banner page before print job disabled
    01h banner page enabled

Return Registers:
AL = status (see Table 12-5)

Details: This function only affects the current logical LPT1.
Conflicts: none known
See also: Function A4h

INT 17h Function A7h
GET/SET SPOOL FLAGS

Alloy MW386 v2+

Registers at call:
AH = A7h
AL = spool flags
    bit 0: banner page enabled (see Function A4h)
    bit 1: form feed enabled (see Function A6h)
    bits 2-6: reserved (0)
    bit 7: set flags if 1, get flags if 0
BX = logical device number
    00h-03h = LPT1-LPT4
    04h-07h = COM1-COM4

Return Registers:
AL = status (see Table 12-5)

Details: The documentation does not state which register contains the result of a **get** call.
Conflicts: none known
See also: Functions A4h and A6h

INT 17h Function A8h
DEFINE TEMPORARY FILENAME

Alloy MW386

Registers at call:
AH = A8h
CX:SI -> ASCIZ filename without extension (max 8 chars)

Return Registers:
AL = status (see Table 12-5)

Details: This function allows applications to specify the banner page filename for spool files collected from the application's printer output.
Conflicts: none known
See also: Function A9h

INT 17h Function A9h
CHANGE TEMPORARY SPOOL DRIVE

Alloy MW386

Registers at call:
AH = A9h
AL = new spool drive (2=C:,3=D:,etc)

Return Registers:
AL = status (see Table 12-5)

Details: This function does not remove the previous spooling directory since jobs may be pending.
Conflicts: none known
See also: Function A8h

INT 17h Function AAh
GET REAL-TIME PRINTER STATUS

Alloy MW386 v2+

Registers at call:
AH = AAh
AL = mode

00h NTNX
    DX = NTNX printer number
    (see Table 12-6)
01h MW386
    DX = MW386 printer number

Return Registers:
AH = instantaneous printer status
    00h printer ready
    01h not ready
    12h off line
    13h out of paper
    14h general device failure
    15h device timeout
    16h bad device number

Conflicts: none known

INT 17h Function AFh
CHECK SPOOLER
                                                  Alloy MW386

Registers at call:
AH = AFh

Return Registers:
AX = 55AAh if spooler available

Conflicts: none known

INT 5Bh
UNKNOWN
                                              used by Alloy NTNX

INT 7Fh
INSTALLATION CHECK
          Alloy 386/MultiWare (MW386), Novell-Type Network Executive (NTNX)

Details: The words at C800h:0000h and C800h:0002h will both be 584Eh if the MW386 multi-tasking system is present (i.e. signature "NXNX").

    NTNX allows its API to be placed on a different interrupt than 7Fh at load time.

    To determine the actual vector used, open the device "SPOOLER" with INT 21h Function 3D02h, place it in RAW mode with INT 21h Function 4400h and INT 21h Function 4401h, then read one byte which will be the actual interrupt number being used; the other interrupts may be found with INT 7Fh Function 09h Subfunction 03h.

Conflicts: see Table 2-4

INT 7Fh
INSTALLATION CHECK
                          Alloy NetWare Support Kit (ANSK) v2.2+

Details: A program may determine that it is running on an ANSK Slave by checking the five bytes at F000h:0000h for the ASCIZ signature "ANSK"; this address is RAM, and should not be written. However, the above check will not work on Slaves with <1MB RAM or those using the SLIM.SYS device driver.

Conflicts: see Table 2-4

INT 7Fh Function 00h
SEMAPHORE LOCK AND WAIT
                                    Alloy NTNX, MW386

Registers at call:
AH = 00h
DS:DX -> ASCIZ semaphore name (max 64 bytes)

Return Registers:
AL = status (see Table 12-7)
AH = semaphore owner if status=02h

Conflicts: see Table 2-4

See also: Functions 01h, 02h, and 41h; PC-NET INT 67h Function 00h (Chapter 31)

12-7 Values for status:

00h	successful
01h	invalid function
02h	semaphore already locked
03h	unable to lock/unlock semaphore
04h	semaphore space exhausted
05h	host/target PC did not respond (NTNX)

INT 7Fh Function 01h　　　　　　　　　　　　　*Alloy NTNX, MW386*
SEMAPHORE LOCK
Registers at call:　　　　　　　　　　**Return Registers:**
AH = 01h　　　　　　　　　　　　　　AL = status (see Table 12-7)
DS:DX -> ASCIZ semaphore name (max 64 bytes)　　AH = semaphore owner if status=02h
Conflicts: see Table 2-4
See also: Functions 00h, 02h, and 41h

INT 7Fh Function 02h　　　　　　　　　　　　　*Alloy NTNX, MW386*
RELEASE SEMAPHORE
Registers at call:　　　　　　　　　　**Return Registers:**
AH = 02h　　　　　　　　　　　　　　AL = status (see Table 12-7)
DS:DX -> ASCIZ semaphore name (max 64 bytes)　　AH = semaphore owner if status=02h
Conflicts: see Table 2-4
See also: Functions 00h, 01h, and 42h

INT 7Fh Function 03h　　　　　　　　　*Alloy ANSK, NTNX, MW386*
GET USER NUMBER
Registers at call:　　　　　　　**Return Registers:**
AH = 03h　　　　　　　　　　　AL = user number
　　　　　　　　　　　　　　　AH = machine number (MW386)
Details: This function call is the recommended method for a CPU-bound process to prevent its priority from being lowered.
Conflicts: see Table 2-4
See also: Functions 04h, 05h, and A1h

INT 7Fh Function 04h　　　　　　　　　　　　　*Alloy NTNX, MW386*
GET NUMBER OF USERS
Registers at call:　　　　　　**Return Registers:**
AH = 04h　　　　　　　　　AL = total number of users on currrent machine (MW386)
　　　　　　　　　　　　AL = number of slaves on system (NTNX)

Conflicts: see Table 2-4
See also: Function 03h

INT 7Fh Function 05h　　　　　　　　　　　　　*Alloy NTNX (Host)*
LOCK/UNLOCK SYSTEM, SPOOLER CONTROL
Registers at call:　　　　　　**Return Registers:**
AH = 05h　　　　　　　　　none
AL = function
　　00h lock system (disable slave services)
　　01h unlock system
　　02h enable spooler
　　03h disable spooler
　　04h enable slave timer update
　　05h disable slave timer update
　　06h enable form feeds
　　07h disable form feeds
Conflicts: see Table 2-4
See also: INT 17h Function A4h

INT 7Fh Function 05h
GET USER PARAMETERS

Alloy NTNX (Slave), MW386

Registers at call:
AH = 05h
DX:DI -> buffer for user information record (see Table 12-8)

Return Registers:
DX:DI buffer filled

Details: MW386 provides this function for backward compatibility only, and sets many of the fields to zero because they are meaningless under MW386.

This function has no effect when called by the host (user 0).

Conflicts: see Table 2-4
See also: Function 03h

12-8 Format of user information record:

Offset	Size	Description
00h	WORD	segment of video RAM
02h	WORD	segment of secondary copy of video RAM
04h	WORD	offset of screen update flag (see INT 10h Function 8Bh)
		flag nonzero if update needed
06h	WORD	video NMI enable port (not used by MW386, set to 0000h)
08h	WORD	video NMI disable port (not used by MW386, set to 0000h)
0Ah	BYTE	processor type
		00h 8088
		01h V20
		02h 8086
		03h V30
		06h 80386
0Bh	WORD	multitasking flag (00h = single tasking, 01h = multitasking)
		(not used by MW386, set to 0000h)
0Dh	WORD	offset of terminal driver (not used by MW386, set to 0000h)
0Fh	BYTE	port for console I/O (not used by MW386, set to 0000h)
10h	WORD	offset of processor communication busy flag
		bit 7 set when slave communicating with host
12h	WORD	pointer to FAR NX system call (not used by MW386, set to 0000h)
14h	WORD	offset of 16-byte user configuration record (see Function 38h)
16h	WORD	offset of command/status word
18h	WORD	offset of screen valid flag (see INT 10h Function 93h)
		nonzero if screen must be repainted
1Ah	WORD	offset of screen repaint flag
1Ch	WORD	pointer to NEAR NX system call (not used by MW386, set to 0000h)
1Eh	WORD	offset for intercept flags (not used by MW386, set to 0000h)
		intercept flag = FFh if MS-DOS intercepts should be disabled
20h	WORD	offset of terminal lock flag (see INT 10h Function 92h)
		lock flag = FFh if background screen updates should be suspended
22h	26 BYTEs	reserved

INT 7Fh Function 06h
GET SHARED DRIVE INFO

Alloy NTNX (Host)

Registers at call:
AH = 06h
AL = drive number (1=A:, 2=B:, etc)
ES:DI -> drive information record (see Table 12-9)

Return Registers:
AX = status
   0000h successful
     ES:DI buffer filled
   0001h not shared drive

Conflicts: see Table 2-4

12-9 Format of drive information record:

Offset	Size	Description
00h	WORD	segment of drive IO-REQUEST structure (MS-DOS DPB)
02h	WORD	segment of allocation map (owner table)
		one byte per FAT entry, containing user ID owning that entry
04h	WORD	segment of master FAT for drive (copy of FAT on disk)
06h	WORD	pointer to configuration file
08h	WORD	total number of clusters
0Ah	WORD	bytes per sector
0Ch	WORD	sectors per cluster
0Eh	BYTE	FAT type (0Ch = 12-bit, 10h = 16-bit)

INT 7Fh Function 06h   *Alloy NTNX (Slave)*
ALLOCATE FREE CLUSTER ON SHARED DRIVE

Registers at call:
AH = 06h
DL = drive number (1=A:,2=B:,etc)
CX = number of clusters to allocate

Return Registers:
AH = status
    00h successful
        CX = number of clusters still free
    10h invalid shared drive request
        CL = first and second shared drives
    11h invalid cluster count (must be 01h-FFh)

Conflicts: see Table 2-4

INT 7Fh Function 07h   *Alloy NTNX, MW386*
GET LIST OF SHARED DRIVES

Registers at call:
AH = 07h

Return Registers:
ES:DI -> shared drive list (see Table 12-10)

Details: MW386 considers all fixed disks to be shared drives; only C and D will be returned as shared.
Conflicts: see Table 2-4

12-10 Format of shared drive list:

Offset	Size	Description
00h	BYTE	string length
01h	BYTE	number of shared drives
02h N	BYTEs	one byte per shared drive

INT 7Fh Function 08h   *Alloy NTNX (Host)*
GET INTERRUPT VECTORS

Registers at call:
AH = 08h
CL = function
    00h get original interrupt vector
    01h get Network Executive interrrupt
AL = interrupt number
DX:SI -> DWORD to hold interrupt vector

Return Registers:
AL = status
    00h successful
    01h interrupt vector not used by network
      executive
    02h invalid subfunction

Details: The network executive uses interrupts 02h, 08h, 09h, 0Fh, 10h, 13h, 16h-19h, 1Ch, 20h, 28h, 2Ah, 2Fh, 5Bh, 67h, 7Fh, ECh, and F0h-FFh.
Conflicts: see Table 2-4
See also: Function 09h Subfunction 03h, MS-DOS INT 21h Function 35h (PCI-24)

INT 7Fh Function 08h, Subfunction 02h
SET MESSAGE DISPLAY TIMEOUT
Alloy NTNX

Registers at call:
AH = 08h
CL = 02h
DX = timeout in seconds
Conflicts: see Table 2-4

Return Registers:
AL = status
   00h successful
   02h invalid subfunction

INT 7Fh Function 09h
ENABLE/DISABLE MUD FILE CHECKING
Alloy NTNX

Registers at call:
AH = 09h
CL = function
   00h enable checking of RTNX.MUD file
   01h disable RTNX.MUD checking
Conflicts: see Table 2-4

Return Registers:
none

INT 7Fh Function 09h, Subfunction 02h
SWITCH HOST TO DEDICATED MODE
Alloy NTNX

Registers at call:
AH = 09h
CL = 02h

Return Registers:
none

Details: In dedicated mode, the host will only poll for I/O requests from the slave processors, and not provide workstation services.
Conflicts: see Table 2-4

INT 7Fh Function 09h, Subfunction 03h
GET ALTERNATE INTERRUPT
Alloy NTNX, MW386

Registers at call:
AH = 09h
CL = 03h
AL = default interrupt number (67h,7Fh,etc)
Conflicts: see Table 2-4
See also: Function 08h

Return Registers:
CL = actual interrupt which handles specified interrupt's calls

INT 7Fh Function 0Ah, Subfunction 00h
GET SYSTEM FLAGS
Alloy NTNX

Registers at call:
AH = 0Ah
CL = 00h
ES:DI -> buffer for system flags (see Table 12-11)

Return Registers:
ES:DI buffer filled

Details: On a slave, only the NX_Busy flag is returned. All three flags are at fixed positions, so this function only needs to be called once.
   An interrupt handler should only perform DOS or device accesses when all three flags are 00h.
Conflicts: see Table 2-4

12-11 Format of system flags:

Offset	Size	Description
00h	DWORD	pointer to NX_Busy flag (nonzero when communicating with users)
04h	DWORD	pointer to device driver busy flag
08h	DWORD	pointer to InTimer flag

INT 7Fh Function 0Bh, Subfunction 02h
Alloy NTNX (Host)
SET/RESET GRAPHICS DOS ON SLAVE

Registers at call:
AH = 0Bh
CL = 02h
AL = slave ID number
CH = DOS to activate
    00h graphics DOS
    01h character DOS
Conflicts: see Table 2-4

Return Registers:
AL = status
    00h successful
    01h nothing done, proper DOS type already loaded

INT 7Fh Function 10h, Subfunction 00h
Alloy NTNX, MW386
CHANNEL CONTROL - OPEN CHANNEL

Registers at call:
AH = 10h
CL = 00h
AL = channel number
DX:DI -> channel buffer

Return Registers:
AL = status (00h-03h,0Dh) (see Table 12-12)

Details: This function may not be invoked from within a hardware interrupt handler.
Conflicts: see Table 2-4
See also: Function 10h Subfunctions 01h and 04h, Function 14h Subfunction 02h

12-12 Values for status:

00h	successful
01h	busy
02h	channel range error (not 00h-3Fh)
03h	invalid subfunction
0Ah	channel not open
0Ch	channel already locked
0Dh	unable to open

INT 7Fh Function 10h, Subfunction 01h
Alloy NTNX, MW386
CHANNEL CONTROL - CLOSE CHANNEL

Registers at call:
AH = 10h
CL = 01h
AL = channel number

Return Registers:
AL = status (00h-03h,0Ah) (see Table 12-12)

Details: This function may not be invoked from within a hardware interrupt handler.
Conflicts: see Table 2-4
See also: Function 10h Subfunctions 00h and 05h

INT 7Fh Function 10h, Subfunction 02h
Alloy NTNX, MW386
CHANNEL CONTROL - LOCK CHANNEL

Registers at call:
AH = 10h
CL = 02h
AL = channel number

Return Registers:
AL = status (00h-03h,0Ah,0Ch) (see Table 12-12)

Details: This function may not be invoked from within a hardware interrupt handler.
Conflicts: see Table 2-4
See also: Function 10h Subfunctions 03h, 06h, and 08h

INT 7Fh Function 10h, Subfunction 03h   *Alloy NTNX, MW386*
CHANNEL CONTROL - UNLOCK CHANNEL

Registers at call: Return Registers:
AH = 10h   AL = status (00h-03h,0Ah) (see Table 12-12)
CL = 03h
AL = channel number

Details: This function should only be used on channels locked with Function 10h Subfunction 02h, not on those locked by receipt of a datagram. It may not be invoked from within a hardware interrupt handler.
Conflicts: see Table 2-4
See also: Function 10h Subfunctions 02h, 04h, and 09h

INT 7Fh Function 10h, Subfunction 04h   *Alloy NTNX, MW386*
CHANNEL CONTROL - RELEASE BUFFER

Registers at call: Return Registers:
AH = 10h   AL = status (00h-03h) (see Table 12-12)
CL = 04h
AL = channel number

Details: This function unlocks buffer after a received datagram has been processed. It may not be invoked from within a hardware interrupt handler.
Conflicts: see Table 2-4
See also: Function 10h Subfunction 00h

INT 7Fh Function 10h, Subfunction 05h   *Alloy NTNX, MW386*
CHANNEL CONTROL - CLOSE ALL CHANNELS

Registers at call: Return Registers:
AH = 10h   AL = status (00h-03h) (see Table 12-12)
CL = 05h

Details: This function clears all pending datagrams and clears the buffer pointers before closing the channels. It may not be invoked from within a hardware interrupt handler.
Conflicts: see Table 2-4
See also: Function 10h Subfunction 01h

INT 7Fh Function 10h, Subfunction 06h   *Alloy NTNX, MW386*
CHANNEL CONTROL - LOCK ALL OPEN CHANNELS

Registers at call: Return Registers:
AH = 10h   AL = status (00h-03h) (see Table 12-12)
CL = 06h

Details: This function may not be invoked from within a hardware interrupt handler.
Conflicts: see Table 2-4
See also: Function 10h Subfunctions 02h and 08h

INT 7Fh Function 10h, Subfunction 07h   *Alloy NTNX, MW386*
CHANNEL CONTROL - UNLOCK ALL LOCKED IDLE CHANNELS

Registers at call: Return Registers:
AH = 10h   AL = status (00h-03h) (see Table 12-12)
CL = 07h

Details: This function unlocks all locked channels which have no pending datagrams. It may not be invoked from within a hardware interrupt handler.
Conflicts: see Table 2-4
See also: Function 10h Subfunctions 03h and 09h

INT 7Fh Function 10h, Subfunction 08h
Alloy NTNX, MW386
CHANNEL CONTROL - LOCK MULTIPLE CHANNELS

Registers at call:
AH = 10h
CL = 08h
DX = maximum channel number to lock

Return Registers:
AL = status (00h-03h) (see Table 12-12)

Details: This function locks channels numbered 00h through the value in DX. It may not be invoked from within a hardware interrupt handler.
Conflicts: see Table 2-4
See also: Function 10h Subfunctions 02h, 06h, and 09h

INT 7Fh Function 10h, Subfunction 09h
Alloy NTNX, MW386
CHANNEL CONTROL - UNLOCK MULTIPLE CHANNELS

Registers at call:
AH = 10h
CL = 09h
DX = maximum channel number to unlock

Return Registers:
AL = status (00h-03h) (see Table 12-12)

Details: This function unlocks channels numbered 00h through the value in DX. It may not be invoked from within a hardware interrupt handler.
Conflicts: see Table 2-4
See also: Function 10h Subfunctions 03h, 07h, and 08h

INT 7Fh Function 11h
Alloy NTNX, MW386
SEND DATAGRAM

Registers at call:
AH = 11h
DX:SI -> request block (see Table 12-14)

Return Registers:
AL = status (see Table 12-13)

Details: If the wildcard channel FFh is used, the actual channel number will be filled in.
Conflicts: see Table 2-4
See also: Function 12h

12-13 Values for status:

00h	successful
01h	busy
02h	channel range error (not 00h-3Fh)
03h	invalid subfunction
0Ah	packet too large (or <2 bytes if NTNX)
0Bh	can't send packet to itself
0Ch	invalid number of destinations
0Dh	destination channel number out of range
0Eh	destination user is busy
0Fh	destination user has locked channel
10h	channel not open
11h	no datagram server on destination (NTNX)

12-14 Format of request block:

Offset	Size	Description
00h	DWORD	pointer to packet to send
04h	WORD	packet size in bytes (1-4096)
06h	BYTE	number of destinations for packet (max 1Fh)
07h	31 BYTEs	destination user IDs (FFh = broadcast to all except sender)
26h	31 BYTEs	destination channels (FFh = first available channel)
45h	31 BYTEs	return destination statuses

INT 7Fh Function 12h
ACKNOWLEDGE DATAGRAM
Alloy NTNX, MW386

Registers at call:
AH = 12h
AL = channel number being acknowledged
DI:DX = 32-bit status to return to sender

Return Registers:
AL = status (see Table 12-15)

Details: This function also unlocks the channel, allowing the next datagram to be received.
Conflicts: see Table 2-4
See also: Function 11h, Function 15h Subfunction 04h

12-15 Values for status:

00h	successful
01h	busy
02h	channel range error (not 00h-3Fh)
03h	invalid subfunction
0Ah	channel not open
0Bh	no message in channel
0Ch	destination slave busy—retry (NTNX)
0Dh	destination user not active
0Eh	destination slave not active (NTNX)
0Fh	destination disabled datagram service

INT 7Fh Function 13h, Subfunction 00h
RESET USER DATAGRAMS
Alloy NTNX, MW386

Purpose: This function clears all pending datagrams and removes all channels opened in NTNX compatibility mode.

Registers at call:
AH = 13h
CL = 00h

Return Registers:
none

Conflicts: see Table 2-4

INT 7Fh Function 14h, Subfunction 00h
SET RECEIVE ISR
Alloy NTNX, MW386

Registers at call:
AH = 14h
CL = 00h
DX:DI -> application FAR receive service routine (see Table 12-16)

Return Registers:
AL = status (00h-03h) (see Table 12-15)

Conflicts: see Table 2-4
See also: Function 14h Subfunctions 01h and 03h

12-16 Service routine calling convention:

Registers at call:
DH = sender ID
DL = channel with datagram interrupts disabled

Return Registers:
AL = response code
    00h leave buffer locked, set channel status, and repeat call later
    01h release channel buffer
    02h change buffer pointer to DX:DI
AH,CX,DX,DI,SI may be destroyed

INT 7Fh Function 14h, Subfunction 01h
SET ACKNOWLEDGE ISR
Alloy NTNX, MW386

Registers at call:
AH = 14h
CL = 01h
DX:DI -> application FAR acknowledge service routine (see Table 12-17)

Return Registers:
AL = status (00h-03h) (see Table 12-15)

Details: The service routine will be called as soon as an acknowledgment arrives.
Conflicts: see Table 2-4
See also: Function 12h, Function 14h Subfunctions 00h and 04h, Function 15h Subfunction 04h

---

12-17 Service routine calling convention:

Registers at call:
DS:SI -> acknowledge
   structure (see Table 12-21)

Return Registers:
AL = response code
   00h application busy, network executive should call again later
   01h acknowledge accepted
AH,DX,SI may be destroyed

INT 7Fh Function 14h, Subfunction 02h
SET CHANNEL BUFFER POINTER
Alloy NTNX, MW386

Registers at call:
AH = 14h
CL = 02h
AL = channel number
DX:DI -> receive buffer

Return Registers:
AL = status (00h-03h) (see Table 12-15)

Details: This function may be called from within a receive ISR or when a datagram is pending.
Conflicts: see Table 2-4
See also: Function 10h Subfunction 00h, Function 14h Subfunction 00h

---

INT 7Fh Function 14h, Subfunction 03h
GET RECEIVE ISR
Alloy NTNX, MW386

Registers at call:
AH = 14h
CL = 03h

Return Registers:
DX:DI -> current receive ISR

Conflicts: see Table 2-4
See also: Function 14h Subfunctions 00h and 04h

INT 7Fh Function 14h, Subfunction 04h
GET ACKNOWLEDGE ISR
Alloy NTNX, MW386

Registers at call:
AH = 14h
CL = 04h

Return Registers:
DX:DI -> current acknowledge ISR

Conflicts: see Table 2-4
See also: Function 14h Subfunctions 01h and 03h

INT 7Fh Function 14h, Subfunction 05h
GET BUSY POINTER
Alloy NTNX (Host), MW386

Registers at call:
AH = 14h
CL = 05h
DX:DI -> buffer for busy structure (see Table 12-18)

Return Registers:
DX:DI buffer filled

Conflicts: see Table 2-4

12-18 Format of busy structure:

Offset	Size	Description
00h	DWORD	pointer to busy flag byte
04h	WORD	fixed port address (FF00h)

INT 7Fh Function 15h, Subfunction 00h
GET CHANNEL STATUS

Alloy NTNX, MW386

Registers at call:
AH = 15h
CL = 00h
AL = channel number
DX:DI -> status structure (see Table 12-19)
Conflicts: see Table 2-4
See also: Function 15h Subfunction 01h

Return Registers:
AL = status (00h-03h) (see Table 12-15)

12-19 Format of status structure:

Offset	Size	Description
00h	BYTE	channel status
		bit 0: channel open
		bit 1: channel buffer contains received data
		bit 7: channel locked
01h	BYTE	sender ID

INT 7Fh Function 15h, Subfunction 01h
GET NEXT FULL CHANNEL

Alloy NTNX, MW386

Registers at call:
AH = 15h
CL = 01h
DX:DI -> full-channel structure

Return Registers:
AL = status
00h successful
01h busy
0Ah no datagrams available

Details: MW386 v1.0 returns the lowest channel with a datagram; newer
versions and NTNX return the oldest datagram.
Conflicts: see Table 2-4
See also: Function 15h Subfunction 00h

12-20 Format of full-channel structure:

Offset	Size	Description
00h	BYTE	number of channel with oldest datagram
01h	BYTE	sender ID

INT 7Fh Function 15h, Subfunction 02h
GET MAXIMUM NUMBER OF CHANNELS

Alloy NTNX, MW386

Registers at call:
AH = 15h
CL = 02h

Return Registers:
AH = number of channels available (40h for MW386)

Details: The application may always assume at least 32 channels available.
Conflicts: see Table 2-4
See also: Function 15h Subfunction 03h

INT 7Fh Function 15h, Subfunction 03h
GET MAXIMUM PACKET SIZE

Alloy NTNX, MW386

Registers at call:
AH = 15h

CL = 03h
DX:DI -> WORD for return value
Conflicts: see Table 2-4
See also: Function 15h Subfunction 02h

Return Registers:
buffer WORD filled with maximum packet size
(4096 for MW386)

INT 7Fh Function 15h, Subfunction 04h   *Alloy NTNX, MW386*
GET AND CLEAR ACKNOWLEDGE STATUS

Registers at call:
AH = 15h
CL = 04h
DX:DI -> status structure (see Table 12-21)

Return Registers:
AL = status
   00h successful
      DX:DI structure filled
   01h busy
   0Ah no acknowledgement has arrived

Conflicts: see Table 2-4
See also: Function 12h, Function 14h Subfunction 01h

12-21 Format of status structure:

Offset	Size	Description
00h	BYTE	sender ID
01h	BYTE	channel number
02h	4 BYTEs	receiver status (see Table 12-15)

INT 7Fh Function 16h   *Alloy NTNX, MW386*
DIRECT MEMORY TRANSFER

Registers at call:
AH = 16h
DX:SI -> transfer structure (see Table 12-22)

Return Registers:
AL = status
   00h successful
   0Ah source or destination out of range
   0Bh transfer kernal busy—try again

Details: This call transfers memory contents directly between users; both source and destination user IDs may differ from the caller's ID.
   No segment wrap is allowed.
Conflicts: see Table 2-4

12-22 Format of transfer structure:

Offset	Size	Description
00h	WORD	bytes to transfer
02h	BYTE	source ID
		FEh = caller
03h	DWORD	source address
07h	BYTE	destination ID
		FFh = all slaves except caller
		FEh = caller
08h	DWORD	destination address

INT 7Fh Function 21h   *Alloy NTNX, MW386*
SEND MESSAGE OR COMMAND TO USER(S)

Registers at call:
AH = 21h
AL = sender's user ID
DS:DX -> control packet (see Table 12-23)

Return Registers:
none

Details: Messages or commands are ignored if disabled by the destination user.
Conflicts: see Table 2-4

See also: Function 22h

12-23 Format of control packet:

Offset	Size	Description
00h	BYTE	packet type
		00h message
		01h NTNX command
		02h MW386 command
01h	BYTE	destination user ID or 'A' for all users
02h	62 BYTEs	ASCIZ message (packet type 00h)
		BIOS keycodes terminated by NUL byte (type 01h) or word (02h)

Note: A maximum of 16 keycodes will be processed for NTNX and MW386 commands.

INT 7Fh Function 22h   *Alloy NTNX*
GET MESSAGE

Registers at call: **Return Registers:**
AH = 22h   pending messages displayed on user's screen
Conflicts: see Table 2-4
See also: Function 21h

INT 7Fh Function 24h   *Alloy NTNX, MW386*
ATTACH OR RELEASE DRIVE FOR LOW-LEVEL WRITE ACCESS

Registers at call: **Return Registers:**
AH = 24h   AX = status
CL = function   00h successful
   00h attach   01h invalid request
   01h release   02h already attached
CH = drive (0=A:,1=B:,etc)   03h not attached
                                     04h lock table full

Details: Only drives on the current machine may be attached.
Conflicts: see Table 2-4

INT 7Fh Function 24h   *Alloy NTNX*
ATTACH/RELEASE HOST PROCESSOR

Registers at call: **Return Registers:**
AH = 24h   AX = status
CL = function   00h successful
   02h attach host   01h invalid request
   03h release host   02h already attached
                                     03h not attached
                                     04h lock table full

Details: The host processor may be attached in order to perform I/O via the host.
Conflicts: see Table 2-4

INT 7Fh Function 25h, Subfunction 00h   *Alloy ANSK, NTNX, MW386*
GET NETWORK EXECUTIVE VERSION

Registers at call: **Return Registers:**
AH = 25h   AH = version suffix letter
CL = 00h   CH = major version number
                                  CL = minor version number

Conflicts: see Table 2-4
See also: Function 25h Subfunction 01h

INT 7Fh Function 25h, Subfunction 01h
Alloy ANSK, NTNX, MW386
GET NETWORK EXECUTIVE TYPE

Registers at call:
AH = 25h
CL = 01h

Return Registers:
CL = type
    00h RTNX
    01h ATNX
    02h NTNX
    03h BTNX
    04h MW386
    05h ANSK

Conflicts: see Table 2-4
See also: Function 25h Subfunction 00h

INT 7Fh Function 26h, Subfunction 00h
Alloy NTNX, MW386
GET NTNX FILE MODE

Registers at call:
AH = 26h
CL = 00h

Return Registers:
AX = file mode bits (see Table 12-24)

Details: MW386 does not support file modes, and always returns AX=001Fh.
Conflicts: see Table 2-4
See also: Function 26h Subfunctions 01h to 05h, Function 26h Subfunction 06h

12-24 Bitfields for file mode bits:

bit 0   directory protection enabled
bit 1   extended open enabled
bit 2   flush on every disk write
bit 3   flush on every disk write in locked interval
bit 4   flush on reads from simultaneously opened file

INT 7Fh Function 26h, Subfunctions 01h to 05h
Alloy NTNX
SET FILE I/O CHECKING LEVEL

Registers at call:
AH = 26h
CL = check type to set/reset
    01h directory protection
    02h extended open
    03h flush on every disk write
    04h flush on disk write if any lock set during write
    05h flush on all reads if file written
AL = new state (00h off, 01h on)

Return Registers:
none

Conflicts: see Table 2-4
See also: Function 26h Subfunctions 00h and 06h

INT 7Fh Function 26h, Subfunction 06h
Alloy NTNX
CANCEL FLUSH ON WRITE

Registers at call:
AH = 26h
CL = 06h

Return Registers:
none

Details: This function cancels the flags set by Function 26h Subfunctions 03h and 04h.
Conflicts: see Table 2-4
See also: Function 26h Subfunction 00h

INT 7Fh Function 30h
GET PORT INFORMATION
Alloy MW386

Registers at call:
AH = 30h
CX = MW386 port number

Return Registers:
AL = FFh if port not found
    else
    AL = driver unit number
    BL = port mode
    BH = port type
        02h remote
    DH = owner's machine ID
    DL = owner's user ID

Conflicts: see Table 2-4
See also: INT 17h Function 8Bh

INT 7Fh Function 31h
CHECK PORT ASSIGNMENT
Alloy MW386 v1.x only

Registers at call:
AH = 31h
others, if any, unknown
Conflicts: see Table 2-4

Return Registers:
unknown

INT 7Fh Function 37h
GET SEMAPHORE TABLE
Alloy NTNX (Host)

Registers at call:
AH = 37h
Conflicts: see Table 2-4

Return Registers:
ES:AX -> semaphore table

INT 7Fh Function 37h
DUMP STRING TO TERMINAL
Alloy ANSK, NTNX (Slave)

Registers at call:
AH = 37h
DS:DX -> ASCIZ string to display
Details: If the string is empty, a terminal update will be forced.
Conflicts: see Table 2-4

Return Registers:
none

INT 7Fh Function 38h
SET NEW TERMINAL DRIVER
Alloy NTNX (Slave), MW386

Registers at call:
AH = 38h
AL = new terminal driver number
    FFh dummy driver
    FEh current driver
    FDh load new driver
        DS:SI -> new driver
Conflicts: see Table 2-4
See also: Function 39h

Return Registers:
none

INT 7Fh Function 39h
SET TERMINAL DRIVER FOR ANOTHER USER
Alloy MW386

Registers at call:
AH = 39h
AL = new terminal driver number
DL = user number (FFh = caller)
DH = machine number if DL <> FFh

Return Registers:
CF set if invalid user number
CF clear if successful

Details: This function only is available to supervisors. The new driver number will not take effect until the user is rebooted.
Conflicts: see Table 2-4
See also: Function 38h

INT 7Fh Function 3Ah   *Alloy MW386*
GET TERMINAL PARAMETERS

Registers at call:	Return Registers:
AH = 3Ah	CF clear if successful
DL = user number (FFh = caller)	AH = terminal driver number
DH = machine number	AL = baud rate (00h = 38400, 01h = 19200, etc.)
	CL = parity (00h none, 01h even, 02h odd)
	CH = handshaking (00h none, 01h XON/XOFF,
	02h DTR/DSR, 03h XPC)
	CF set if invalid user number

Conflicts: see Table 2-4
See also: Function 3Bh

INT 7Fh Function 3Bh   *Alloy MW386*
SET TERMINAL PARAMETERS

Registers at call:
AH = 3Bh
AL = baud rate (00h = 38400, 01h = 19200, etc)
CL = parity (00h none, 01h even, 02h odd)
CH = handshaking (00h none, 01h XON/XOFF, 02h DTR/DSR, 03h XPC)
DL = user number (FFh = caller)
DH = machine number for user

Return Registers:
CF set if invalid user number

Details: This function is only available to supervisors. The new parameters will take effect immediately if the user's terminal has not been started, else Function 3Dh must be called to post the changes.
Conflicts: see Table 2-4
See also: Functions 3Ah and 3Dh

INT 7Fh Function 3Ch   *Alloy MW386*
ENABLE/DISABLE AUTOBAUD DETECT

Registers at call:
AH = 3Ch
AL = new state
    00h disabled, 01h enabled
DL = user number (FFh = caller)
DH = machine number for user

Return Registers:
CF set if invalid user number

Details: This function is only available to supervisors.
Conflicts: see Table 2-4
See also: Function 3Dh

INT 7Fh Function 3Dh   *Alloy MW386*
POST TERMINAL CONFIGURATION CHANGES

Registers at call:
AH = 3Dh

Return Registers:
none

Details: This function should be called whenever a program changes the terminal type or its parameters.
Conflicts: see Table 2-4
See also: Function 3Bh

INT 7Fh Function 41h   *Alloy NTNX*
LOCK FILE FOR USER

Purpose: Request exclusive read/write access to file.

Registers at call:	Return Registers:
AH = 41h	AL = status
AL = user ID	00h successful
DS:DX -> ASCIZ filename	01h invalid function
	02h already locked
	03h unable to lock
	04h lock table full

Conflicts: see Table 2-4
See also: Functions 00h, 41h, and 42h

INT 7Fh Function 41h   *Alloy MW386*
LOCK SEMAPHORE FOR USER

Registers at call:	Return Registers:
AH = 41h	AL = status
AL = user ID	00h successful
DS:DX -> ASCIZ semaphore name	01h invalid function
	02h semaphore already locked
	03h unable to lock semaphore
	04h semaphore space exhausted

Conflicts: see Table 2-4
See also: Functions 00h and 42h

INT 7Fh Function 42h   *Alloy NTNX*
UNLOCK FILE FOR USER

Registers at call:	Return Registers:
AH = 42h	AL = status
AL = user ID	00h successful
DS:DX -> ASCIZ filename	01h invalid function
	02h already locked
	03h unable to lock
	04h lock table full

Conflicts: see Table 2-4
See also: Functions 00h, 41h, and 42h

INT 7Fh Function 42h   *Alloy MW386*
UNLOCK SEMAPHORE FOR USER

Registers at call:	Return Registers:
AH = 42h	AL = status
AL = user ID	00h successful
DS:DX -> ASCIZ semaphore name	01h invalid function
	03h unable to unlock semaphore

Conflicts: see Table 2-4
See also: Functions 02h, 41h, and 42h

INT 7Fh Function 4Eh   *Alloy MW386 v2+*
SET ERROR MODE

Registers at call:
AH = 4Eh
AL = error mode flags

bit 0: display critical disk errors
bit 1: display sharing errors
DX = 4E58h ("NX")
Conflicts: see Table 2-4
See also: Function 4Fh

Return Registers:
AL = status
    00h successful

INT 7Fh Function 4Fh   *Alloy MW386 v2+*
SET FCB MODE

Registers at call:
AH = 4Fh
AL = FCB mode
    02h read/write compatibility
    42h read/write shared
DX = 4E58h ("NX")
Conflicts: see Table 2-4

Return Registers:
AL = status
    00h successful

INT 7Fh Function 81h   *Alloy NTNX*
ATTACH DEVICE FOR USER

Registers at call:
AH = 81h
AL = user ID
DS:DX -> ASCIZ device name
Conflicts: see Table 2-4
See also: Function 82h

Return Registers:
none

INT 7Fh Function 82h   *Alloy NTNX*
RELEASE DEVICE FOR USER

Registers at call:
AH = 82h
AL = user ID
DS:DX -> ASCIZ device name
Conflicts: see Table 2-4
See also: Function 81h

Return Registers:
none

INT 7Fh Function A0h   *Alloy MW386*
GET USER NAME

Registers at call:
AH = A0h
DL = user number (FFh = caller)
DH = machine number for user
ES:DI -> 17-byte buffer for ASCIZ user name
Conflicts: see Table 2-4
See also: Functions 03h and A1h

Return Registers:
CF set if invalid user number

INT 7Fh Function A1h   *Alloy MW386*
GET MACHINE, USER, AND PROCESS NUMBER

Registers at call:
AH = A1h

Return Registers:
AL = process number
DL = user number
DH = machine number

Conflicts: see Table 2-4
See also: Functions 03h, A0h, and A2h

INT 7Fh Function A2h   *Alloy MW386*
GET USER PRIVILEGE LEVEL

Registers at call: Return Registers:
AH = A2h   CF clear if successful
DL = user number (FFh = caller)   AL = privilege level
DH = machine number for user   00h supervisor
                                              01h high
                                              02h medium
                                              03h low
                                      CF set if invalid user number

Conflicts: see Table 2-4
See also: Functions A1h and A3h

INT 7Fh Function A3h   *Alloy MW386*
GET USER LOGIN STATE

Registers at call: Return Registers:
AH = A3h   CF clear if successful
DL = user number   AL = login state
DH = machine number for user   00h never logged in
                                              01h currently logged out
                                              03h currently logged in
                                      CF set if invalid user number or user not active

Conflicts: see Table 2-4
See also: Function A2h

INT 7Fh Function A4h   *Alloy MW386*
VERIFY USER PASSWORD

Registers at call: Return Registers:
AH = A4h   AL = 00h if accepted else invalid password
DS:DX -> ASCIZ password (null-padded to 16 bytes)
Conflicts: see Table 2-4

INT 7Fh Function A500h   *Alloy MW386*
GET USER STATUS

Registers at call: Return Registers:
AX = A500h   CF clear if successful
DI = machine number and user number   BX = user flags
                                                  bit 5: allow messages
                                          CL = scan code for task manager hotkey
                                          CH = scan code for spooler hotkey
                                          DL = scan code for task swapper hotkey
                                          DH = modifier key status
                                      CF set if invalid user number

Conflicts: see Table 2-4
See also: Function A501h

INT 7Fh Function A501h   *Alloy MW386*
SET USER STATUS

Registers at call:
AX = A501h
BX = user flags (see Function A500h)
CL = scan code for task manager hotkey
CH = scan code for spooler hotkey
DL = scan code for task swapper hotkey

DH = modifier key status
DI = machine number and user number

Return Registers:
CF set if invalid user number

Details: The caller must have supervisor privilege to set another user's status.
Conflicts: see Table 2-4
See also: Function A500h

INT 7Fh Function B0h
RELEASE ALL SEMAPHORES FOR USER
Alloy NTNX, MW386

Registers at call:
AH = B0h
AL = user number
DS = code segment

Return Registers:
none

Details: MW386 ignores AL and DS; it releases all semaphores locked using INT 67h or INT 7Fh locking functions.
Conflicts: see Table 2-4
See also: Functions B1h, B2h, B3h, and B4h

INT 7Fh Function B1h, Subfunction 00h
RELEASE NORMAL SEMAPHORES FOR USER
Alloy NTNX, MW386

Registers at call:
AH = B1h
AL = (bits 7-5) 000
    (bits 4-0) user ID

Return Registers:
none

Details: MW386 ignores AL; it releases all semaphores locked using INT 67h or INT 7Fh locking functions.
Conflicts: see Table 2-4
See also: Functions B0h, B2h, B3h, and B4h

INT 7Fh Function B2h, Subfunction 01h
RELEASE MESSAGES FOR USER
Alloy NTNX

Registers at call:
AH = B2h
AL = (bits 7-5) 001
    (bits 4-0) user ID

Return Registers:
none

Conflicts: see Table 2-4
See also: Functions B0h, B1h, B3h, and B4h

INT 7Fh Function B3h, Subfunction 02h
RELEASE FILES FOR USER
Alloy NTNX

Registers at call:
AH = B3h
AL = (bits 7-5) 010
    (bits 4-0) user ID

Return Registers:
none

Conflicts: see Table 2-4
See also: Functions B0h, B1h, B2h, and B4h

INT 7Fh Function B4h
RELEASE DEVICES FOR USER
Alloy NTNX

Registers at call:
AH = B4h
AL = user ID

Return Registers:
none

Conflicts: see Table 2-4
See also: Functions B0h, B1h, B2h, and B3h

INT 7Fh Function C3h   *Alloy MW386*
WRITE BYTE TO TERMINAL AUX PORT
Registers at call: Return Registers:
AH = C3h   CF clear if successful
AL = byte to write   CF set on error
Conflicts: see Table 2-4
See also: Function C6h

INT 7Fh Function C5h   *Alloy MW386*
CHANGE CONSOLE MODE
Registers at call: Return Registers:
AH = C5h   CF clear if successful
AL = new console mode   AL = prior console mode
    00h keyboard indirect   CF set on error (caller is not remote user)
    01h keyboard direct
    02h data handshake enforced
    03h no data handshake
Details: Modes 2 and 3 may be used for input through the console port; no video output should be performed in these modes.
Conflicts: see Table 2-4

INT 7Fh Function C6h   *Alloy MW386*
WRITE BYTE TO CONSOLE PORT
Registers at call: Return Registers:
AH = C6h   CF clear if successful
AL = byte to write   CF set on error (caller is not remote user)
Details: Any terminal driver data translation will be bypassed.
Conflicts: see Table 2-4
See also: Functions C3h and C7h

INT 7Fh Function C7h   *Alloy MW386*
READ CONSOLE DATA BYTE
Registers at call: Return Registers:
AH = C7h   CF clear if successful
        AL = byte read
        CF set on error (no data available or caller is not remote user)
Details: This function may be used to read data after placing console in mode 2 or 3 (see Function C5h).
Conflicts: see Table 2-4
See also: Functions C5h, C6h, and C8h

INT 7Fh Function C8h   *Alloy MW386*
READ CONSOLE DATA INTO BUFFER
Registers at call: Return Registers:
AH = C8h   CF clear if successful
AL = maximum bytes to read   CX = number of bytes read
ES:DI -> buffer for console data   CF set on error (caller is not remote user)
Conflicts: see Table 2-4
See also: Function C7h

INT 7Fh Function CFh
Alloy NTNX
REBOOT USER PROCESSOR

Registers at call: **Return Registers:**
AH = CFh   none
DS:DX -> ASCIZ string containing user number to be reset
Conflicts: see Table 2-4
See also: Function D6h

INT 7Fh Function D6h
Alloy MW386
RESET NETWORK EXECUTIVE

Registers at call: **Return Registers:**
AH = D6h   never returns if succesful
DS:DX -> reset packet (see Table 12-25)
Details: All users will be shut down immediately if successful.
Conflicts: see Table 2-4
See also: Function CFh

12-25 Format of reset packet:

Offset	Size	Description
00h	DWORD	reset code (60606060h)
04h 16	BYTEs	ASCIZ supervisor password padded with nulls

INT 7Fh Function D7h
Alloy MW386
POST EVENT

Registers at call: **Return Registers:**
AH = D7h   none
AL = user number (if local event)
DX = event number
Conflicts: see Table 2-4

INT 7Fh Function D8h
Alloy MW386
FLUSH DISK BUFFERS

Purpose: Force all disk buffers to be written out immediately.
Registers at call: **Return Registers:**
AH = D8h   CF set on error
Conflicts: see Table 2-4
See also: Network Redirector INT 2Fh Function 1120h (Chapter 9), MS-DOS INT 21h Functions 0Dh and 5D01h (PCI-24)

INT 7Fh Function DBh
Alloy MW386 v2+
GET MW386 INVOCATION DRIVE

Registers at call: **Return Registers:**
AH = DBh   AL = drive from which MW386 was started (2=C:,3=D:,etc)
Conflicts: see Table 2-4

INT 7Fh Function E0h
Alloy MW386
CREATE DOS TASK

Registers at call: **Return Registers:**
AH = E0h   CF clear if successful
AL = memory size (00h=128K, 01h=256K, 02h=384K,   AL = task create ID
  03h=512K, 04h=640K)   CF set on error
DS:DX -> ASCIZ task name (max 16 bytes)
Details: Only foreground DOS tasks can use this function.

Conflicts: see Table 2-4
See also: Functions E1h, E2h, E3h, E6h, and E7h

INT 7Fh Function E1h
GET DOS TASK PID FROM CREATE ID

Alloy MW386

Registers at call:
AH = E1h
AL = create ID (from Function E0h)

Return Registers:
AL = DOS process number
CL = memory size (00h=128K, 01h=256K,
    02h=384K, 03h=512K, 04h=640K)

Details: This function should not be called immediately after creating a new DOS task, since the new task is being initialized by a concurrent process.
Conflicts: see Table 2-4
See also: Functions E0h and E2h

INT 7Fh Function E2h
SWITCH TO NEW DOS TASK

Alloy MW386

Registers at call: **Return Registers:**
AH = E2h   CF set on error (invalid process number or caller not foreground task)
AL = DOS process number (from Function E1h)
Details: The specified task becomes the foreground task and the current task is placed in the background.
    This function may only be called by a foreground task.
Conflicts: see Table 2-4
See also: Functions E0h and E1h

INT 7Fh Function E3h
CHANGE NAME OF DOS TASK

Alloy MW386

Registers at call: **Return Registers:**
AH = E3h   CF set on error (invalid process number)
---v1.x---
AL = user number
---v2+---
BH = user number
BL = task number

DS:DX -> ASCIZ task name
Conflicts: see Table 2-4
See also: Functions E0h, E4h, and E5h

INT 7Fh Function E4h
GET TASK NAME FROM PROCESS NUMBER

Alloy MW386

Registers at call: **Return Registers:**
AH = E4h   CF clear if successful
---v1.x---   CL = memory size (00h=128K, 01h=256K, 02h=384K,
AL = user number   03h=512K, 04h=640K)
---v2+---   DX = task flags
BH = user number   bit 7: MS-DOS process
BL = task number   ES:DI buffer filled
---   CF set on error (invalid process number)
ES:DI -> buffer for task name
Conflicts: see Table 2-4
See also: Functions E3h and E5h

INT 7Fh Function E5h
Alloy MW386
GET PROCESS NUMBER FROM TASK NAME

Registers at call:
AH = E5h
DS:DX -> ASCIZ task name
BH = user number

Return Registers:
CF clear if successful
   AL = DOS process number
   CL = memory size (00h=128K, 01h=256K, 02h=384K, 03h=512K, 04h=640K)
   CF set on error (no match for name)

Conflicts: see Table 2-4
See also: Functions E3h and E4h

INT 7Fh Function E6h
Alloy MW386
GET NUMBER OF AVAILABLE USER TASKS

Registers at call:
AH = E6h

Return Registers:
AX = number of processes available to current user

Conflicts: see Table 2-4
See also: Function E0h

INT 7Fh Function E7h
Alloy MW386
REMOVE DOS TASK

Registers at call:
AH = E7h
AL = DOS process number

Return Registers:
CF set on error (invalid process number or first process)

Details: This function can only be called by a foreground task.
Conflicts: see Table 2-4
See also: Function E0h

INT 7Fh Function E8h
Alloy MW386
DOS TASK DELAY

Registers at call:
AH = E8h
CX = delay time in milliseconds

Return Registers:
none

Details: A delay of 0 may be used to surrender the current time slice.
Conflicts: see Table 2-4
See also: TopView INT 15h Function 1000h (PCI-44), INT 1Ah Function FF01h, DoubleDOS INT 21h Function EEh (PCI-49), MS Windows INT 2Fh Function 1680h (Chapter 43)

INT 7Fh Function F0h
Alloy MW386
RESTRICT DIRECTORY TO GROUP

Registers at call:
AH = F0h
AL = group number
DS:DX -> ASCIZ directory name

Return Registers:
CF clear if successful
   AX = status
      0002h directory not found
      0003h directory not found
      0005h directory in use, cannot be restricted
      02xxh restricted to group xxh
   CF set on error

Details: The restriction on the directory may be removed by calling this function with group 0, then using Function F1h to assign the directory to group 0.
Conflicts: see Table 2-4
See also: Functions F1h, F2h, and F3h

INT 7Fh Function F1h
ASSIGN DIRECTORY TO GROUP

Alloy MW386

Registers at call:	Return Registers:
AH = F1h	none
AL = group number	
DS:DX -> ASCIZ directory name	

Details: This function performs permanent assignment to a group; no immediate action is taken unless the directory has been restricted with Function F0h.

This function may be used to restrict a nonexistent directory.

Conflicts: see Table 2-4

See also: Function F0h

INT 7Fh Function F2h
READ RESTRICTED DIRECTORY ENTRY

Alloy MW386

Registers at call:	Return Registers:
AH = F2h	CF clear if successful
CX = entry number	buffer filled with 63-byte directory info and 1-byte group number
ES:DI -> 64-byte buffer	CF set on error (invalid entry)

Conflicts: see Table 2-4

See also: Functions F0h and F3h

INT 7Fh Function F3h
READ RESTRICTED DIRECTORY ENTRY FOR GROUP

Alloy MW386

Registers at call:	Return Registers:
AH = F3h	CF clear if successful
AL = group number	CX = next entry number
CX = entry number	buffer filled with 63-byte directory info and 1-byte group number
ES:DI -> 64-byte buffer	CF set on error (no more matching entries)

Details: This call is similar to Function F2h, but only returns directories belonging to the specified group.

Conflicts: see Table 2-4

See also: Function F2h

INT 7Fh Function F8h
ASSIGN USER TO GROUP

Alloy MW386

Registers at call:	Return Registers:
AH = F8h	CF clear if successful
AL = group number	CF set on error (user already in maximum number of groups)
DL = user number	
DH = machine number (currently 00h)	

Details: Each user is allowed eight group assignments.

Conflicts: see Table 2-4

See also: Functions F9h and FAh

INT 7Fh Function F9h
REMOVE USER FROM GROUP

Alloy MW386

Registers at call:	Return Registers:
AH = F9h	CF set if failed
AL = group number	
DL = user number	
DH = machine number (currently 00h)	

Conflicts: see Table 2-4

See also: Functions F8h and FAh

INT 7Fh Function FAh   *Alloy MW386*
GET USER GROUP LIST

Registers at call: **Return Registers:**
AH = FAh   CX = number of groups
DL = user number   ES:DI buffer filled with group numbers
DH = machine number (currently 00h)
ES:DI -> 16-byte buffer for group list
Conflicts: see Table 2-4
See also: Functions F8h and F9h

INT 7Fh Function FBh   *Alloy MW386*
ASSIGN GROUP NAME

Registers at call: **Return Registers:**
AH = FBh   none
CL = group number
ES:DI -> ASCIZ group name (max 17 bytes)
Conflicts: see Table 2-4
See also: Function FCh

INT 7Fh Function FCh   *Alloy MW386*
GET GROUP NAME

Registers at call: **Return Registers:**
AH = FCh   ES:DI buffer filled
CL = group number
ES:DI -> 17-byte buffer for ASCIZ name
Details: If the group has not been named, "(unnamed)" is returned.
Conflicts: see Table 2-4
See also: Function FBh

INT ECh   *used by Alloy NTNX*
UNKNOWN
Conflicts: Exact (PCI-54), IBM ROM BASIC (PCI-54)

CHAPTER 13

APPC/PC

IBM's Advanced Program-to-Program Communication is one protocol within the Systems Network Architecture; it is roughly equivalent to the OSI's "session layer" and according to company press releases of the time, is the communications bases for all future applications and system products. APPC/PC is the software package for personal ocmputers that implements one end of the APPC protocol; the mainframe end of the link is handled by LU 6.2.

APPC/PC never really established itself in the PC world despite its official blessing, but its interface will be of interest to all programmers faced with a need to communicate with IBM mainframes.

INT 68h Function 01h, Subfunction 1B00h   *APPC/PC*
NETWORK DEVICE CONTROL - DISPLAY

Registers at call: **Return Registers:**
AH = 01h   control block updated
DS:DX -> control block (see Table 13-1)
Conflicts: Sangoma CCPOP (Chapter 37)
See also: Function 01h Subfunctions 2000h and 2B00h

13-1 Format of control block for Subfunction 1B00h:

Offset	Size	Description
00h	12 BYTEs	reserved
0Ch	WORD	1B00h (verb "DISPLAY")
0Eh	6 BYTEs	00h
14h	DWORD	(big-endian) return code (see Table 13-2)
18h	WORD	00h
1Ah	8 BYTEs	(big-endian) logical unit ID
22h	8 BYTEs	(big-endian) partner logical unit name
2Ah	8 BYTEs	(big-endian) mode name
32h	BYTE	logical unit session limit
33h	BYTE	partner logical unit session limit
34h	BYTE	node maximum negotiable session limit
35h	BYTE	current session limit
36h	BYTE	minimum negotiated winner limit
37h	BYTE	maximum negotiated loser limit
38h	BYTE	active session count
39h	BYTE	active CONWINNER session count
3Ah	BYTE	active CONLOSER session count
3Bh	BYTE	session termination count

| 3Ch | BYTE | bit 7: SESSION_TERMINATION_TARGET_DRAIN |
| | | bit 6: SESSION_TERMINATION_SOURCE_DRAIN |

13-2 Values for return code:

00000000h	successful
00000001h	BAD_TP_ID
00000002h	BAD_CONV_ID
00000003h	bad logical unit ID
00000008h	no physical unit attached
00000110h	bad state
000001B1h	BAD_PART_LUNAME
000001B2h	bad mode name
00000201h	physical unit already active
00000211h	logical unit already active
00000212h	BAD_PART_SESS
00000213h	BAD_RU_SIZES
00000214h	BAD_MODE_SESS
00000216h	BAD_PACING_CNT
00000219h	EXTREME_RUS
0000021Ah	SNASVCMG_1
00000223h	SSCP_CONNECTED_LU
00000230h	invalid change
00000243h	too many TPs
00000272h	adapter close failure
00000281h	GET_ALLOC_BAD_TYPE
00000282h	unsuccessful
00000283h	DLC failure
00000284h	unrecognized DLC
00000286h	duplicate DLC
00000301h	SSCP_PU_SESSION_NOT_ACTIVE
00000302h	data exceeds RU size
00000401h	invalid direction
00000402h	invalid type
00000403h	segment overlap
00000404h	invalid first character
00000405h	table error
00000406h	conversion error
F0010000h	APPC disabled
F0020000h	APPC busy
F0030000h	APPC abended
F0040000h	incomplete

INT 68h Function 01h, Subfunction 2000h
NETWORK DEVICE CONTROL - ATTACH PHYSICAL UNIT

APPC/PC

Registers at call:
AH = 01h
DS:DX -> control block (see Table 13-3)
Conflicts: Sangoma CCPOP (Chapter 37)
See also: Function 01h Subfunctions 2100h and 2B00h

Return Registers:
control block updated

13-3 Format of control block for Subfunction 2000h:

Offset	Size	Description
00h	12 BYTEs	reserved
0Ch	WORD	2000h (verb "Attach Physical Unit")
0Eh	6 BYTEs	00h
14h	DWORD	(big-endian) return code (see Table 13-2)
18h	WORD	00h
1Ah	BYTE	version
1Bh	BYTE	release
1Ch	8 BYTEs	(big-endian) net name
24h	8 BYTEs	(big-endian) physical unit name
2Ch	8 BYTEs	00h
34h	DWORD	pointer to SYSTEM_LOG_EXIT routine, FFFFFFFFh=don't log errors (see also Table 13-10)
38h	DWORD	00h
3Ch	BYTE	00h RETURN_CONTROL: COMPLETE 01h RETURN_CONTROL: INCOMPLETE

INT 68h Function 01h, Subfunction 2100h
NETWORK DEVICE CONTROL - ATTACH LOGICAL UNIT

APPC/PC

Registers at call: **Return Registers:**
AH = 01h   control block updated
DS:DX -> control block (see Table 13-4)
Conflicts: Sangoma CCPOP (Chapter 37)
See also: Function 01h Subfunctions 2000h, 2200h, and 2B00h

13-4 Format of control block for Subfunction 2100h:

Offset	Size	Description
00h	12 BYTEs	reserved
0Ch	WORD	2100h (verb "Attach Logical Unit")
0Eh	6 BYTEs	00h
14h	DWORD	(big-endian) return code (see Table 13-2)
18h	WORD	70 offset to partner logical unit record
1Ah	8 BYTEs	(big-endian) logical unit name
22h	8 BYTEs	(big-endian) logical unit ID
2Ah	BYTE	logical unit local address
2Bh	BYTE	logical unit session limit
2Ch	DWORD	pointer to CREATE_TP_EXIT routine, FFFFFFFFh = reject incoming ALLOCATEs 00000000h = queue ALLOCATEs
30h	DWORD	00h
34h	DWORD	pointer to SYSTEM_LOG_EXIT routine, FFFFFFFFh=don't log errors
38h	DWORD	00h
3Ch	BYTE	maximum TPs
3Dh	BYTE	queue depth
3Eh	DWORD	pointer to LU_LU_PASSWORD_EXIT routine, FFFFFFFFh=no password exit
42h	DWORD	00h
46h	WORD	total length of partner records
48h	var	array of partner logical unit records (see Table 13-5)

13-5 Format of partner logical unit record:

Offset	Size	Description
00h	WORD	length of this partner logical unit record
02h	WORD 42	offset to mode records
04h	8 BYTEs	(big-endian) partner logical unit name
0Ch	BYTE	partner logical unit security capabilities
		bit 7: already verified
		bit 6: conversation level security
		bit 5: session level security
0Dh	BYTE	partner logical unit session limit
0Eh	WORD	partner logical unit maximum MC_SEND_LL
10h	8 BYTEs	(big-endian) partner logical unit DLC name
18h	BYTE	partner logical unit adapter number
19h	17 BYTEs	(counted string) partner logical unit adapter address
2Ah	WORD	total length of mode records
2Ch	16N BYTEs	array of mode records (see Table 13-6)

13-6 Format of mode record:

Offset	Size	Description
00h	WORD 16	length of this mode record
02h	8 BYTEs	(big-endian) mode name
0Ah	WORD	RU_SIZE high bound
0Ch	WORD	RU_SIZE low bound
0Eh	BYTE	mode maximum negotiable session limit
0Fh	BYTE	pacing size for receive

Note: Routines defined by LU_LU_PASSWORD_EXIT, CREATE_TP_EXIT, and SYSTEM_LOG_EXIT pointers are called by pushing the DWORD pointer to the verb on the stack and then performing a FAR call.

13-7 Format of ACCESS_LU_LU_PW verb:

Offset	Size	Description
00h	12 BYTEs	reserved
0Ch	WORD	1900h (verb "ACCESS_LU_LU_PW")
0Eh	8 BYTEs	(big-endian) logical unit ID
16h	8 BYTEs	(big-endian) logical unit name
1Eh	8 BYTEs	(big-endian) partner logical unit name
26h	17 BYTEs	(counted string) partner fully qualified logical unit name
37h	BYTE	password available (0=no, 1=yes)
38h	8 BYTEs	password

13-8 Format of CREATE_TP verb:

Offset	Size	Description
00h	12 BYTEs	reserved
0Ch	WORD	2300h (verb "CREATE_TP")
0Eh	6 BYTEs	00h
14h	DWORD	(big-endian) sense code (see Table 13-9)
18h	8 BYTEs	(big-endian) TP ID
20h	8 BYTEs	(big-endian) logical unit ID
28h	DWORD	(big-endian) conversation ID
2Ch	BYTE	0 basic conversation, 1 mapped conversation
2Dh	BYTE	0 no sync level, 1 confirm

INT 68h Function 01h, Subfunction 2100h

2Eh	BYTE	reserved
2Fh	65 BYTEs	(counted string) transaction program name
70h	6 BYTEs	00h
76h	WORD	length of ERROR_LOG_DATA to return
78h	DWORD	pointer to ERROR_LOG_DATA buffer
7Ch	8 BYTEs	(big-endian) partner logical unit name
84h	18 BYTEs	(counted string) partner fully qualified logical unit name
96h	8 BYTEs	(big-endian) mode name
9Eh	12 BYTEs	00h
AAh	11 BYTEs	(counted string) password
B5h	11 BYTEs	(counted string) user ID
C0h	BYTE	0 verification should be performed
		1 already verified

13-9 Values for sense code:

00000000h	Ok
080F6051h	SECURITY_NOT_VALID
084B6031h	TP_NOT_AVAIL_RETRY
084C0000h	TP_NOT_AVAIL_NO_RETRY
10086021h	TP_NAME_NOT_RECOGNIZED
10086034h	CONVERSATION_TYPE_MISMATCH
10086041h	SYNC_LEVEL_NOT_SUPPORTED

13-10 Format of SYSLOG verb:

Offset	Size	Description
00h	12 BYTEs	reserved
0Ch	WORD	2600h (verb "SYSLOG")
0Eh	10 BYTEs	00h
18h	WORD	(big-endian) type
1Ah	DWORD	(big-endian) subtype
1Eh	DWORD	pointer to ADDITIONAL_INFO
22h	DWORD	(big-endian) conversation ID
26h	8 BYTEs	(big-endian) TP ID
2Eh	8 BYTEs	(big-endian) physical unit or logical unit name
36h	WORD	length of data
38h	DWORD	pointer to data
3Ch	BYTE	00h

INT 68h Function 01h, Subfunction 2200h
NETWORK DEVICE CONTROL - DETACH LOGICAL UNIT   *APPC/PC*

Registers at call: **Return Registers:**
AH = 01h   control block updated
DS:DX -> control block (see Table 13-11)
Conflicts: Sangoma CCPOP (Chapter 37)
See also: Function 01h Subfunctions 2000h, 2100h, and 2700h

13-11 Format of control block for Subfunction 2200h:

Offset	Size	Description
00h	12 BYTEs	reserved
0Ch	WORD	2200h (verb "Detach Logical Unit")
0Eh	6 BYTEs	00h

14h	DWORD	(big-endian) return code (see Table 13-2)
18h	8 BYTEs	(big-endian) logical unit ID
20h	BYTE	00h

INT 68h Function 01h, Subfunction 2700h
NETWORK DEVICE CONTROL - DETACH PHYSICAL UNIT

APPC/PC

Registers at call:
AH = 01h
DS:DX -> control block (see Table 13-12)
Conflicts: Sangoma CCPOP (Chapter 37)
See also: Function 01h Subfunctions 2000h, 2100h, and 2200h

Return Registers:
control block updated

13-12 Format of control block for Function 2700h:

Offset	Size	Description
00h	12 BYTEs	reserved
0Ch	WORD	2700h (verb "Detach Physical Unit")
0Eh	6 BYTEs	00h
14h	DWORD	(big-endian) return code (see Table 13-2)
18h	BYTE	type (00h hard, 01h soft)

INT 68h Function 01h, Subfunction 2B00h
NETWORK DEVICE CONTROL - ACTIVATE DLC

APPC/PC

Registers at call:
AH = 01h
DS:DX -> control block (see Table 13-13)
Conflicts: Sangoma CCPOP (Chapter 37)
See also: Function 01h Subfunctions 1B00h and 2000h

Return Registers:
control block updated

13-13 Format of control block for Subfunction 2B00h:

Offset	Size	Description
00h	12 BYTEs	reserved
0Ch	WORD	2B00h (verb "Activate DLC")
0Eh	6 BYTEs	00h
14h	DWORD	(big-endian) return code (see Table 13-2)
18h	8 BYTEs	(big-endian) DLC name
20h	BYTE	adapter number

INT 68h Function 02h, Subfunction 0100h
CONNECTION CONTROL - ALLOCATE

APPC/PC

Registers at call:
AH = 02h
DS:DX -> control block (see Table 13-14)
Conflicts: Sangoma CCPOP (Chapter 37)
See also: Function 02h Subfunction 0500h

Return Registers:
control block updated

13-14 Format of control block for Subfunction 0100h:

Offset	Size	Description
00h	12 BYTEs	reserved
0Ch	WORD	0100h (verb "Allocate" or "MC_Allocate")
0Eh	BYTE	1 if MC_ (mapped conversation) form of verb
		0 if basic verb
0Fh	5 BYTEs	reserved (0)
14h	WORD	(big-endian) primary return code (see Table 13-15)

16h	DWORD	(big-endian) error code (see Table 13-16)
1Ah	8 BYTEs	(big-endian) TP_ID
22h	DWORD	(big-endian) conversation ID
26h	BYTE	(MC_Allocate only) 0 basic conversation, 1 mapped conversation
27h	BYTE	SYNC_LEVEL (00h none, 01h confirm)
28h	WORD	0000h
2Ah	BYTE	00h RETURN_CONTROL: when session allocated
		01h RETURN_CONTROL: immediate
		02h RETURN_CONTROL: when session free
2Bh	8 BYTEs	00h
33h	8 BYTEs	(big-endian) partner logical unit name
3Bh	8 BYTEs	(big-endian) mode name
43h	65 BYTEs	(counted string) TP name
84h	BYTE	security (00h none, 01h same, 02h pgm)
85h	11 BYTEs	00h
90h	11 BYTEs	(counted string) password
9Bh	11 BYTEs	(counted string) user ID
A6h	WORD	PIP_DATA length
A8h	DWORD	pointer to PIP_DATA

13-15 Values for primary return code:

0000h	successful
0001h	parameter check
0002h	state check
0003h	allocation error
0005h	deallocate abended
0006h	deallocate abended program
0007h	deallocate abended SVC
0008h	deallocate abended timer
0009h	deallocate normal return
000Ah	data posting blocked
000Bh	posting not active
000Ch	PROG_ERROR_NO_TRUNC
000Dh	PROG_ERROR_TRUNC
000Eh	PROG_ERROR_PURGING
000Fh	CONV_FAILURE_RETRY
0010h	CONV_FAILURE_NO_RETRY
0011h	SVC_ERROR_NO_TRUNC
0012h	SVC_ERROR_TRUNC
0013h	SVC_ERROR_PURGING
0014h	unsuccessful
0018h	CNOS partner logical unit reject
0019h	conversation type mixed
F001h	APPC disabled
F002h	APPC busy
F003h	APPC abended
F004h	incomplete

13-16 Values for error code:

0001h	bad TP ID
0002h	bad conversation ID
0004h	allocation error, no retry
0005h	allocation error, retry
0006h	data area crosses segment boundary
0010h	bad TPN length
0011h	bad CONV length
0012h	bad SYNC level
0013h	bad security selection
0014h	bad return control
0015h	SEC_TOKENS too big
0016h	PIP_LEN incorrect
0017h	no use of SNASVCMG
0018h	unknown partner mode
0031h	confirm: SYNC_NONE
0032h	confirm: bad state
0033h	confirm: NOT_LL_BDY
0041h	confirmed: bad state
0051h	deallocate: bad type
0052h	deallocate: flush bad state
0053h	deallocate: confirm bad state
0055h	deallocate: NOT_LL_BDY
0057h	deallocate: log LL_WRONG
0061h	flush: not send state
0091h	post on receipt: invalid length
0092h	post on receipt: not in receive state
0093h	post on receipt: bad fill
00A1h	prepare to receive:invalid type
00A2h	prepare to receive: unfinished LL
00A3h	prepare to receive: not in send state
00B1h	receive and wait: bad state
00B2h	receive and wait: NOT_LL_BDY
00B5h	receive and wait: bad fill
00C1h	receive immediate: not in receive state
00C4h	receive immediate: bad fill
00E1h	request to send: not in receive state
00F1h	send data: bad LL
00F2h	send data: not in send state
0102h	send error: log LL wrong
0103h	send error: bad type
0121h	test: invalid type
0122h	test: not in receive state

INT 68h Function 02h, Subfunction 0300h   *APPC/PC*
CONNECTION CONTROL - CONFIRM

Registers at call: **Return Registers:**
AH = 02h   control block updated
DS:DX -> control block (see Table 13-17)
Conflicts: Sangoma CCPOP (Chapter 37)

See also: Function 02h Subfunction 0400h

13-17 Format of control block for Subfunction 0300h:

Offset	Size	Description
00h	12 BYTEs	reserved
0Ch	WORD	0300h (verb "Confirm" or "MC_Confirm")
0Eh	BYTE	1 if MC_ (mapped conversation) form of verb
		0 if basic verb
0Fh	5 BYTEs	reserved (0)
14h	WORD	(big-endian) primary return code (see Table 13-15)
16h	DWORD	(big-endian) error code (see Table 13-16)
1Ah	8 BYTEs	(big-endian) TP_ID
22h	DWORD	(big-endian) conversation ID
26h	BYTE	request to send received (0=no, 1=yes)

INT 68h Function 02h, Subfunction 0400h
CONNECTION CONTROL - CONFIRMED

Registers at call: Return Registers:
AH = 02h   control block updated
DS:DX -> control block (see Table 13-18)
Conflicts: Sangoma CCPOP (Chapter 37)
See also: Function 02h Subfunction 0300h

13-18 Format of control block for Subfunction 0400h:

Offset	Size	Description
00h	12 BYTEs	reserved
0Ch	WORD	0400h (verb "Confirmed" or "MC_Confirmed")
0Eh	BYTE	1 if MC_ (mapped conversation) form of verb
		0 if basic verb
0Fh	5 BYTEs	reserved (0)
14h	WORD	(big-endian) primary return code (see Table 13-15)
16h	DWORD	(big-endian) error code (see Table 13-16)
1Ah	8 BYTEs	(big-endian) TP_ID
22h	DWORD	(big-endian) conversation ID

INT 68h Function 02h, Subfunction 0500h
CONNECTION CONTROL - DEALLOCATE

Registers at call: Return Registers:
AH = 02h   control block updated
DS:DX -> control block (see Table 13-19)
Conflicts: Sangoma CCPOP (Chapter 37)
See also: Function 02h Subfunctions 0100h and 0300h

13-19 Format of control block for Subfunction 0500h:

Offset	Size	Description
00h	12 BYTEs	reserved
0Ch	WORD	0500h (verb "Deallocate" or "MC_Deallocate")
0Eh	BYTE	1 if MC_ (mapped conversation) form of verb
		0 if basic verb
0Fh	5 BYTEs	reserved (0)
14h	WORD	(big-endian) primary return code (see Table 13-15)
16h	DWORD	(big-endian) error code (see Table 13-16)

1Ah	8 BYTEs	(big-endian) TP_ID
22h	DWORD	(big-endian) conversation ID
26h	BYTE	00h
27h	BYTE	type
		00h SYNC_LEVEL
		01h FLUSH
		02h ABEND_PROC
		03h ABEND_SVC
		04h ABEND_TIMER
		05h ABEND
28h	WORD	(MC_Deallocate only) length of error log data
2Ah	DWORD	(MC_Deallocate only) pointer to error log data

INT 68h Function 02h, Subfunction 0600h
CONNECTION CONTROL - FLUSH
APPC/PC

Registers at call:
AH = 02h
DS:DX -> control block (see Table 13-20)
Conflicts: Sangoma CCPOP (Chapter 37)
See also: Function 02h Subfunction 0300h

Return Registers:
control block updated

13-20 Format of control block for Subfunction 0600h:

Offset	Size	Description
00h	12 BYTEs	reserved
0Ch	WORD	0600h (verb "Flush" or "MC_Flush")
0Eh	BYTE	1 if MC_ (mapped conversation) form of verb
		0 if basic verb
0Fh	5 BYTEs	reserved (0)
14h	WORD	(big-endian) primary return code (see Table 13-15)
16h	DWORD	(big-endian) error code (see Table 13-16)
1Ah	8 BYTEs	(big-endian) TP_ID
22h	DWORD	(big-endian) conversation ID

INT 68h Function 02h, Subfunction 0700h
CONNECTION CONTROL - GET ATTRIBUTES
APPC/PC

Registers at call:
AH = 02h
DS:DX -> control block (see Table 13-21)
Conflicts: Sangoma CCPOP (Chapter 37)
See also: Function 02h Subfunction 0300h

Return Registers:
control block updated

13-21 Format of control block for Subfunction 0700h:

Offset	Size	Description
00h	12 BYTEs	reserved
0Ch	WORD	0700h (verb "Get_Attributes" or "MC_Get_Attributes")
0Eh	BYTE	1 if MC_ (mapped conversation) form of verb
		0 if basic verb
0Fh	5 BYTEs	reserved (0)
14h	WORD	(big-endian) primary return code (see Table 13-15)
16h	DWORD	(big-endian) error code (see Table 13-16)
1Ah	8 BYTEs	(big-endian) TP_ID
22h	DWORD	(big-endian) conversation ID

26h	8 BYTEs	(big-endian) logical unit ID
2Eh	BYTE	00h
2Fh	BYTE	SYNC_LEVEL (0=none, 1=confirm)
30h	8 BYTEs	(big-endian) mode name
38h	8 BYTEs	(big-endian) own net name
40h	8 BYTEs	(big-endian) own logical unit name
48h	8 BYTEs	(big-endian) partner logical unit name
50h	18 BYTEs	(counted string) partner's fully qualified logical unit name
62h	BYTE	00h
63h	11 BYTEs	(counted string) user ID

INT 68h Function 02h, Subfunction 0800h
CONNECTION CONTROL - GET CONVERSATION TYPE

Registers at call:
AH = 02h
DS:DX -> control block (see Table 13-22)
Conflicts: Sangoma CCPOP (Chapter 37)
See also: Function 02h Subfunction 0300h

Return Registers:
control block updated

13-22 Format of control block for Subfunction 0800h:

Offset	Size	Description
00h	12 BYTEs	reserved
0Ch	WORD	0800h (verb "Get_Type")
0Eh	BYTE	1 if MC_ (mapped conversation) form of verb
		0 if basic verb
0Fh	5 BYTEs	reserved (0)
14h	WORD	(big-endian) primary return code (see Table 13-15)
16h	DWORD	(big-endian) error code (see Table 13-16)
1Ah	8 BYTEs	(big-endian) TP_ID
22h	DWORD	(big-endian) conversation ID
26h	BYTE	(return) type (0=basic conversation, 1=mapped conversation)

INT 68h Function 02h, Subfunction 0900h
CONNECTION CONTROL - POST ON RECEIPT

Registers at call:
AH = 02h
DS:DX -> control block (see Table 13-23)
Conflicts: Sangoma CCPOP (Chapter 37)
See also: Function 02h Subfunction 0A00h

Return Registers:
control block updated

13-23 Format of control block for Subfunction 0900h:

Offset	Size	Description
00h	12 BYTEs	reserved
0Ch	WORD	0900h (verb "Post_on_Receipt")
0Eh	BYTE	1 if MC_ (mapped conversation) form of verb
		0 if basic verb
0Fh	5 BYTEs	reserved (0)
14h	WORD	(big-endian) primary return code (see Table 13-15)
16h	DWORD	(big-endian) error code (see Table 13-16)
1Ah	8 BYTEs	(big-endian) TP_ID
22h	DWORD	(big-endian) conversation ID
26h	WORD	maximum length
28h	BYTE	fill (0=buffer, 1=LL)

INT 68h Function 02h, Subfunction 0A00h
CONNECTION CONTROL - PREPARE TO RECEIVE

APPC/PC

Registers at call:
AH = 02h
DS:DX -> control block (see Table 13-24)
Conflicts: Sangoma CCPOP (Chapter 37)
See also: Function 02h Subfunctions 0900h and 0B00h

Return Registers:
control block updated

13-24 Format of control block for Subfunction 0A00h:

Offset	Size	Description
00h	12 BYTEs	reserved
0Ch	WORD	0A00h (verb "Prepare_to_Receive" or "MC_Prepare_to_Receive")
0Eh	BYTE	1 if MC_ (mapped conversation) form of verb
		0 if basic verb
0Fh	5 BYTEs	reserved (0)
14h	WORD	(big-endian) primary return code (see Table 13-15)
16h	DWORD	(big-endian) error code (see Table 13-16)
1Ah	8 BYTEs	(big-endian) TP_ID
22h	DWORD	(big-endian) conversation ID
26h	BYTE	type (0=SYNC_LEVEL, 1=FLUSH)
27h	BYTE	locks (0=short, 1=long)

INT 68h Function 02h, Subfunction 0B00h
CONNECTION CONTROL - RECEIVE AND WAIT

APPC/PC

Registers at call:
AH = 02h
DS:DX -> control block (see Table 13-25)
Conflicts: Sangoma CCPOP (Chapter 37)
See also: Function 02h Subfunctions 0C00h and 0F00h

Return Registers:
control block updated

13-25 Format of control block for Subfunction 0B00h:

Offset	Size	Description
00h	12 BYTEs	reserved
0Ch	WORD	0B00h (verb "Receive_and_Wait" or "MC_Receive_and_Wait")
0Eh	BYTE	1 if MC_ (mapped conversation) form of verb
		0 if basic verb
0Fh	5 BYTEs	reserved (0)
14h	WORD	(big-endian) primary return code (see Table 13-15)
16h	DWORD	(big-endian) error code (see Table 13-16)
1Ah	8 BYTEs	(big-endian) TP_ID
22h	DWORD	(big-endian) conversation ID
26h	BYTE	type of information received (see Table 13-26)
27h	BYTE	(MC_Receive_and_Wait only) fill (0=buffer, 1=LL)
28h	BYTE	Request_to_Send_Received (0=no, 1=yes)
29h	WORD	maximum length
2Bh	WORD	data length
2Dh	DWORD	pointer to data

13-26 Values for type of information received:

00h	data
01h	data complete

02h   data incomplete
03h   confirm
04h   confirm send
05h   confirm deallocate
06h   send

INT 68h Function 02h, Subfunction 0C00h   *APPC/PC*
CONNECTION CONTROL - RECEIVE IMMEDIATE
Registers at call: **Return Registers:**
AH = 02h   control block updated
DS:DX -> control block (see Table 13-27)
Conflicts: Sangoma CCPOP (Chapter 37)
See also: Function 02h Subfunctions 0B00h and 0F00h

13-27 Format of control block for Subfunction 0C00h:

Offset	Size	Description
00h	12 BYTEs	reserved
0Ch	WORD	0C00h (verb "Receive_Immediate" or "MC_Receive_Immediate")
0Eh	BYTE	1 if MC_ (mapped conversation) form of verb
		0 if basic verb
0Fh	5 BYTEs	reserved (0)
14h	WORD	(big-endian) primary return code (see Table 13-15)
16h	DWORD	(big-endian) error code (see Table 13-16)
1Ah	8 BYTEs	(big-endian) TP_ID
22h	DWORD	(big-endian) conversation ID
26h	BYTE	type of information received (see Table 13-26)
27h	BYTE	(MC_Receive_Immediate only) fill (0=buffer, 1=LL)
28h	BYTE	Request_to_Send_Received (0=no, 1=yes)
29h	WORD	maximum length
2Bh	WORD	data length
2Dh	DWORD	pointer to data

INT 68h Function 02h, Subfunction 0E00h   *APPC/PC*
CONNECTION CONTROL - REQUEST TO SEND
Registers at call: **Return Registers:**
AH = 02h   control block updated
DS:DX -> control block (see Table 13-28)
Conflicts: Sangoma CCPOP (Chapter 37)
See also: Function 02h Subfunctions 0F00h and 1000h

13-28 Format of control block for Subfunction 0E00h:

Offset	Size	Description
00h	12 BYTEs	reserved
0Ch	WORD	0E00h (verb "Request_to_Send" or "MC_Request_to_Send")
0Eh	BYTE	1 if MC_ (mapped conversation) form of verb
		0 if basic verb
0Fh	5 BYTEs	reserved (0)
14h	WORD	(big-endian) primary return code (see Table 13-15)
16h	DWORD	(big-endian) error code (see Table 13-16)
1Ah	8 BYTEs	(big-endian) TP_ID
22h	DWORD	(big-endian) conversation ID

INT 68h Function 02h, Subfunction 0F00h
CONNECTION CONTROL - SEND DATA

APPC/PC

Registers at call:
AH = 02h
DS:DX -> control block (see Table 13-29)
Conflicts: Sangoma CCPOP (Chapter 37)
See also: Function 02h Subfunctions 0E00h and 1000h

Return Registers:
control block updated

13-29 Format of control block for Subfunction 0F00h:

Offset	Size	Description
00h	12 BYTEs	reserved
0Ch	WORD	0F00h (verb "Send_Data" or "MC_Send_Data")
0Eh	BYTE	1 if MC_ (mapped conversation) form of verb
		0 if basic verb
0Fh	5 BYTEs	reserved (0)
14h	WORD	(big-endian) primary return code (see Table 13-15)
16h	DWORD	(big-endian) error code (see Table 13-16)
1Ah	8 BYTEs	(big-endian) TP_ID
22h	DWORD	(big-endian) conversation ID
26h	BYTE	request to send received (0=no, 1=yes)
27h	BYTE	00h
28h	WORD	data length
2Ah	DWORD	pointer to data

INT 68h Function 02h, Subfunction 1000h
CONNECTION CONTROL - SEND ERROR

APPC/PC

Registers at call:
AH = 02h
DS:DX -> control block (see Table 13-30)
Conflicts: Sangoma CCPOP (Chapter 37)
See also: Function 02h Subfunction 0F00h

Return Registers:
control block updated

13-30 Format of control block for Subfunction 1000h:

Offset	Size	Description
00h	12 BYTEs	reserved
0Ch	WORD	1000h (verb "Send_Error" or "MC_Send_Error")
0Eh	BYTE	1 if MC_ (mapped conversation) form of verb
		0 if basic verb
0Fh	5 BYTEs	reserved (0)
14h	WORD	(big-endian) primary return code (see Table 13-15)
16h	DWORD	(big-endian) error code (see Table 13-16)
1Ah	8 BYTEs	(big-endian) TP_ID
22h	DWORD	(big-endian) conversation ID
26h	BYTE	request to send received (0=no, 1=yes)
27h	BYTE	type (0=program, 1=SVC)
28h	DWORD	00h
2Ch	WORD	(MC_Send_Error only) LOG_DATA length
2Eh	DWORD	(MC_Send_Error only) pointer to LOG_DATA

INT 68h Function 02h, Subfunction 1200h
CONNECTION CONTROL - TEST

Registers at call:
AH = 02h
DS:DX -> control block (see Table 13-31)
Conflicts: Sangoma CCPOP (Chapter 37)
See also: Function 02h Subfunction 1300h

Return Registers:
control block updated

13-31 Format of control block for Subfunction 1200h:

Offset	Size	Description
00h	12 BYTEs	reserved
0Ch	WORD	1200h (verb "Test" or "MC_Test")
0Eh	BYTE	1 if MC_ (mapped conversation) form of verb
		0 if basic verb
0Fh	5 BYTEs	reserved (0)
14h	WORD	(big-endian) primary return code (see Table 13-15)
16h	DWORD	(big-endian) error code (see Table 13-16)
1Ah	8 BYTEs	(big-endian) TP_ID
22h	DWORD	(big-endian) conversation ID
26h	BYTE	(MC_Test only) test (0=posted, 1=request_to_send received)

Note: Error code has different interpretations for:
    0 posted data
    1 posted not data (primary return code = 0)
    1 bad TP_ID (primary return code = 1)

INT 68h Function 02h, Subfunction 1300h
CONNECTION CONTROL - WAIT

Registers at call:
AH = 02h
DS:DX -> control block (see Table 13-32)
Conflicts: Sangoma CCPOP (Chapter 37)
See also: Function 02h Subfunction 1200h

Return Registers:
control block updated

13-32 Format of control block for Subfunction 1300h:

Offset	Size	Description
00h	12 BYTEs	reserved
0Ch	WORD	1300h (verb "Wait")
0Eh	BYTE	1 if MC_ (mapped conversation) form of verb
		0 if basic verb
0Fh	5 BYTEs	reserved (0)
14h	WORD	(big-endian) primary return code (see Table 13-15)
16h	DWORD	(big-endian) error code (see Table 13-16)
1Ah	8 BYTEs	(big-endian) TP_ID
22h	DWORD	(big-endian) conversation ID
26h	BYTE	number of conversations to wait on

Note: Error codes have interpretations as for Function 02h Subfunction 1200h.

INT 68h Function 03h, Subfunction 2400h
TP STARTED

Registers at call:
AH = 03h
DS:DX -> control block (see Table 13-33)

Return Registers:
control block updated

Conflicts: Sangoma CCPOP (Chapter 37)

13-33 Format of control block for Subfunction 2400h:

Offset	Size	Description
00h	12 BYTEs	reserved
0Ch	WORD	2400h (verb "TP Started")
0Eh	6 BYTEs	00h
14h	DWORD	(big-endian) return code (see Table 13-2)
18h	WORD	00h
1Ah	8 BYTEs	(big-endian) logical unit ID
22h	8 BYTEs	(big-endian) TP ID

INT 68h Function 03h, Subfunction 2800h
GET ALLOCATE

APPC/PC

Registers at call:
AH = 03h
DS:DX -> control block (see Table 13-34)

Return Registers:
control block updated

Conflicts: Sangoma CCPOP (Chapter 37)

13-34 Format of control block for Subfunction 2800h:

Offset	Size	Description
00h	12 BYTEs	reserved
0Ch	WORD	2800h (verb "Get ALLOCATE")
0Eh	6 BYTEs	00h
14h	DWORD	(big-endian) return code (see Table 13-2)
18h	WORD	00h
1Ah	8 BYTEs	(big-endian) logical unit ID
22h	BYTE	type (00h dequeue, 01h test)
23h	DWORD	pointer to CREATE_TP record (see Table 13-8)

INT 68h Function 03h, Subfunction 2A00h
CHANGE LOGICAL UNIT

APPC/PC

Registers at call:
AH = 03h
DS:DX -> control block (see Table 13-35)

Return Registers:
control block updated

Conflicts: Sangoma CCPOP (Chapter 37)

13-35 Format of control block for Subfunction 2A00h:

Offset	Size	Description
00h	12 BYTEs	reserved
0Ch	WORD	2A00h (verb "Change Logical Unit")
0Eh	6 BYTEs	00h
14h	DWORD	(big-endian) return code (see Table 13-2)
18h	WORD	00h
1Ah	8 BYTEs	(big-endian) logical unit ID
22h	DWORD	pointer to CREATE_TP_EXIT routine FFFFFFFFh reject incoming ALLOCATEs 00000000h queue ALLOCATEs
26h	DWORD	00000000h
2Ah	DWORD	pointer to SYSTEM_LOG_EXIT routine, FFFFFFFFh= don't log errors
2Eh	DWORD	00000000h

32h	BYTE	maximum TPs
33h	BYTE	00h stop QUEUE_ALLOCATEs
		01h resume QUEUE_ALLOCATEs
34h	DWORD	pointer to LU_LU_PASSWORD_EXIT routine, FFFFFFFFh
= no exit		
38h	DWORD	00000000h

INT 68h Function 04h
TRANSACTION PROCESSING

Registers at call:
AH = 04h
DS:DX -> control block (see Table 13-36)
Conflicts: Sangoma CCPOP (Chapter 37)

Return Registers:
control block updated

13-36 Format of control block for Subfunctions 2500h and 2900h:

Offset	Size	Description
00h	12 BYTEs	reserved
0Ch	WORD	verb (action)
		2500h TP_ENDED
		2900h TP_VALID
0Eh	6 BYTEs	00h
14h	DWORD	(big-endian) return code (see Table 13-2)
18h	WORD	00h
1Ah	8 BYTEs	(big-endian) TP_ID
22h	DWORD	pointer to CREATE_TP record (see Table 13-8; only if verb = 2900h)

INT 68h Function 05h
TRANSFER MESSAGE DATA

Registers at call:
AH = 05h
DS:DX -> control block (see Table 13-37)
Conflicts: Sangoma CCPOP (Chapter 37)

Return Registers:
control block updated

13-37 Format of control block for Subfunction 1C00h:

Offset	Size	Description
00h	12 BYTEs	reserved
0Ch	WORD	1C00h (verb "Transfer Message Data")
0Eh	BYTE	00h user defined
		01h NMVT
		02h alert subvectors
		03h PDSTATS subvectors
0Fh	5 BYTEs	00h
14h	DWORD	(big-endian) return code (see Table 13-2)
18h	12 BYTEs	00h
24h	BYTE	if bit 0 clear, add correlation subvector
		if bit 1 clear, add product set ID subvector
		if bit 2 clear, do SYSLOG
		if bit 3 clear, send SSCP_PU_SESSION
25h	BYTE	00h
26h	WORD	length of data
28h	N BYTEs	data

INT 68h Function 06h   *APPC/PC*
CHANGE NUMBER OF SESSIONS

Registers at call: Return Registers:
AH = 06h   control block updated
DS:DX -> control block (see Table 13-38)
Conflicts: Sangoma CCPOP (Chapter 37)

13-38 Format of control block for Subfunction 1500h:

Offset	Size	Description
00h	12 BYTEs	reserved
0Ch	WORD	1500h (verb "Change Number of Sessions")
0Eh	6 BYTEs	00h
14h	WORD	(big-endian) primary return code (see Table 13-15)
16h	DWORD	(big-endian) secondary return code (see Tables 13-2 and 13-39)
1Ah	8 BYTEs	(big-endian) logical unit ID
22h	8 BYTEs	blanks
2Ah	8 BYTEs	(big-endian) partner logical unit name
32h	8 BYTEs	(big-endian) mode name
3Ah	BYTE	bit 7: use MODE_NAME_SELECT_ALL rather than MODE_NAME
		bit 6: set negotiable values
3Bh	BYTE	partner logical unit mode session limit
3Ch	BYTE	minimum CONWINNERS_SOURCE
3Dh	BYTE	maximum CONWINNERS_TARGET
3Eh	BYTE	automatic activation
3Fh	BYTE	00h
40h	BYTE	bit 7: drain target
		bit 6: drain source
		bit 5: target responsible, not source

13-39 Values for secondary return code (see also Table 13-2):

0000h	accepted
0001h	negotiated
0003h	bad logical unit ID
0004h	allocation failure, no retry
0005h	allocation failure, retry
0151h	can't raise limits
0153h	all modes must reset
0154h	bad SNASVCMG limits
0155h	minimum greater than total
0156h	mode closed (primary return code = 1)
	CNOS mode closed (primary return code = 18h)
0157h	bad mode name (primary return code = 1)
	CNOS bad mode name (primary return code = 18h)
0159h	reset SNA drains
015Ah	single not SRC response
015Bh	bad partner logical unit
015Ch	exceeds maximum allowed
015Dh	change SRC drains
015Eh	logical unit detached
015Fh	CNOS command race reject

INT 68h Function 07h
PASSTHROUGH
APPC/PC

Registers at call:
AH = 07h
DS:DX -> control block (format depends on
  application subsystem)
Conflicts: Sangoma CCPOP (Chapter 37)
See also: Function FFh

Return Registers:
control block updated

INT 68h Function FAh
ENABLE/DISABLE APPC
APPC/PC

Registers at call:
AH = FAh
AL bit 0 = new state
      0 enable, 1 disable
Conflicts: Sangoma CCPOP (Chapter 37)
See also: Function FDh

Return Registers:
none

INT 68h Function FBh
CONVERT
APPC/PC

Registers at call:
AH = FBh
DS:DX -> control block (see Table 13-40)
Conflicts: Sangoma CCPOP (Chapter 37)

Return Registers:
control block updated

13-40 Format of control block for Subfunction 1A00h:

Offset	Size	Description
00h	12 BYTEs	reserved
0Ch	WORD	1A00h (verb "CONVERT")
0Eh	6 BYTEs	00h
14h	DWORD	(big-endian) return code
18h	BYTE	conversion
		00h ASCII to EBCDIC
		01h EBCDIC to ASCII
19h	BYTE	character set
		00h AE
		01h A
		02h G
1Ah	WORD	length of string to convert
1Ch	DWORD	pointer to source
20h	DWORD	pointer to target

INT 68h Function FCh
ENABLE/DISABLE MESSAGE TRACING
APPC/PC

Registers at call:
AH = FCh
AL = new state
     00h disable tracing
     01h enable tracing
         DX = number of bytes to keep (0=all)
Conflicts: Sangoma CCPOP (Chapter 37)
See also: Functions FDh and FEh

Return Registers:

INT 68h Function FDh
ENABLE/DISABLE API VERB TRACING

APPC/PC

Registers at call:
AH = FDh
AL = new state
    00h disabled, 01h enabled
Conflicts: Sangoma CCPOP (Chapter 37)
See also: Functions FAh, FCh, and FEh

Return Registers:
none

INT 68h Function FEh
SET TRACE DESTINATION

APPC/PC

Registers at call:
AH = FEh
AL = trace destinations (see Table 13-41)
DS:DX -> trace stats record if AL bit 0 set
Conflicts: Sangoma CCPOP (Chapter 37)
See also: Functions FCh and FDh

Return Registers:
none

13-41 Bitfields for trace destinations:

bit 0	storage (DS:DX -> trace stats record)
bit 1	display
bit 2	file (trace written to file OUTPUT.PC)
bit 3	printer

13-42 Format of Trace Statistics Record:

Offset	Size	Description
00h	DWORD	pointer to storage trace buffer
04h	WORD	max number of 80-byte records in trace
06h	WORD	(high-order byte first!) current record number (must init to 0)
08h	DWORD	(high-order byte first!) number of records written (init to 0)
0Ch	DWORD	reserved

Note: Do not move the record while a trace is active.

INT 68h Function FFh
SET PASSTHROUGH

APPC/PC

Registers at call:
AH = FFh
DS:DX -> passthrough exit routine
Conflicts: Sangoma CCPOP (Chapter 37)
See also: Function 07h

Return Registers:

CHAPTER 14

Banyan VINES

The **VI**rtual **NE**twork **S**oftware package from Banyan Systems, Inc. is one of the major players in the large-network competition. This system was one of the first to offer full interconnectoin between such diverse operating systems as MS-DOS and Unix, and because of this found early acceptance by large corporations.

For compatibility, VINES provides a number of functions from other networking software; those are merely pointed out here and are described in full in other chapters.

Although the majority of the API is listed under INT 61h, VINES can use any interrupt from 60h through 66h. The Banyan interrupt handler is identified by the string "BANV" in the four bytes immediately preceding the interrupt handler.

INT 21h Function 4310h *Banyan VINES 2.1+*
GET EXTENDED FILE ATTRIBUTES

Registers at call:	Return Registers:
AX = 4310h	CF clear if successful
DS:DX -> ASCIZ filename	CH = attributes (see Function 4311h)
	CF set on error
	AX = error code (01h,02h,03h,05h) (see Table 3-1)

Details: The filename may be a directory but must be on a VINES file service.
Conflicts: none known
See also: Function 4311h, NetWare Function B6h (Chapter 21), Network Redirector INT 2Fh Function 110Fh (Chapter 9), MS-DOS Function 4300h (PCI-24)

INT 21h Function 4311h *Banyan VINES 2.1+*
SET EXTENDED FILE ATTRIBUTES

Registers at call:	Return Registers:
AX = 4311h	CF clear if successful
CH = new attributes	CF set on error
bit 7: unused	AX = error code (01h,02h,03h,05h) (see Table 3-1)
bit 6: shareable	
bit 5: execute-only	
bits 4-0: unused	
DS:DX -> ASCIZ filename	

Details: The filename may be a directory but must be on a VINES file service.
Conflicts: none known
See also: Function 4310h, Network Redirector INT 2Fh Function 110Eh (Chapter 9), MS-DOS Function 4301h (PCI-24), DR-DOS Function 4305h (PCI-26)

INT 21h Functions D0h to D5h
LOGICAL RECORD LOCKING AND UNLOCKING
Banyan VINES

These functions are identical to Novell NetWare's implementation and are described in Chapter 21.

INT 21h Functions D8h and D9h
RESOURCE ALLOCATION
Banyan VINES

These functions are identical to Novell NetWare's implementation and are described in Chapter 21.

INT 21h Function DCh
GET STATION NUMBER
Banyan VINES

This function are identical to Novell NetWare's implementation and are described in Chapter 21.

INT 21h Function E7h
GET FILE SERVER DATE AND TIME
Banyan VINES

This function are identical to Novell NetWare's implementation and are described in Chapter 21.

INT 2Fh Function D701h, Subfunction 0000h
GET BANV INTERRUPT NUMBER
Banyan VINES v4+

Registers at call:
AX = D701h
BX = 0000h

Return Registers:
AX = 0000h if installed
BX = interrupt number (60h to 66h), nonzero if not present

Details: If AX is nonzero on return, VINES 3.x or earlier may be installed, thus it is necessary to examine the four bytes preceding the handlers for INT 60h through INT 66h for the string "BANV".

Conflicts: none, but see Table 2-2
See also: Functions D702h, D703h, and D704h

INT 2Fh Function D702h
PCPRINT interface
Banyan VINES v4+
Undocumented

Registers at call:
AX = D702h
BX = function
others, if any, unknown

Return Registers:
unknown

Conflicts: none, but see Table 2-2
See also: Functions D701h and D703h, INT 61h Function 0005h

INT 2Fh Function D703h
MAIL interface
Banyan VINES v4+
Undocumented

Registers at call:
AX = D703h
BX = function
others, if any, unknown

Return Registers:
unknown

Conflicts: none, but see Table 2-2
See also: Functions D702h and D704h

INT 2Fh Function D704h
StreetTalk Directory Assistance interface
Banyan VINES v4+
Undocumented

Registers at call:
AX = D704h
BX = function
others, if any, unknown

Return Registers:
unknown

Conflicts: none, but see Table 2-2
See also: Function D703h, INT 61h Function 0007h

INT 60h Function 0Ch
GET STATION ADDRESS
Banyan VINES, 3com

Registers at call:
AH = 0Ch

Return Registers:
AL = status
    00h successful
        ES:SI -> 6-byte station address
    02h semaphore service is unavailable

Conflicts: see Table 2-3

INT 60h Functions 11h to 13h
SEMAPHORE LOCKING AND UNLOCKING
Banyan VINES

These functions are identical to the 3com implementation and are described in Chapter 31.

INT 61h Function 0001h, Subfunction 0001h
"Sosock" - OPEN COMMUNICATIONS SOCKET
Banyan VINES

Registers at call:
AX = 0001h
DS:DX -> communications control block (see Table 14-2)

Return Registers:
AX = status (see Table 14-1)

Details: BANYAN can use any interrupt from 60h through 66h. The Banyan interrupt handler is identified by the string "BANV" in the four bytes immediately preceding the interrupt handler.

Conflicts: see Table 2-3

See also: Function 0001h Subfunctions 0002h and 0008h, DESQview/X INT 15 Function DE2Eh (Chapter 17)

14-1 Values for status:

0000h	successful
0001h	service not installed
0002h	invalid service ID
0003h	-000Ah reserved for BANV interface errors
0097h	invalid socket identifier
0098h	resource already in use
009Bh	destination node unreachable
009Ch	message overflow
009Dh	destination socket nonexistent
009Eh	address family does not exist
009Fh	socket type does not exist
00A0h	protocol does not exist
00A1h	no more sockets available
00A2h	no more buffer space available
00A3h	timeout
00A5h	resource not available
00A6h	internal communication failure
00B1h	resource disconnect

14-2 Format of control block for Subfunction 0001h:

Offset	Size	Description
00h	WORD	0001h (function number)
02h	WORD	pointer to argument block (see Table 14-3)
04h	WORD	error return code
06h 4	BYTEs	reserved

14-3 Format of argument block for Subfunction 0001h:

Offset	Size	Description
00h	WORD	pointer to 2-byte buffer for socket identifier
02h	WORD	address family
		0003h Banyan
04h	WORD	socket type
		in address family 0003h
		0001h IPC socket
		0002h SPP socket
06h	WORD	protocol number
		FFFFh default
08h	WORD	pointer to 16-byte buffer for socket address
0Ah	WORD	local port number
		0000h if service should assign transient port number
		0001h to 01FFh well-known port number (assigned by Banyan)

14-4 Format of IPC port:

Offset	Size	Description
00h	WORD	address family (always 0003h for Banyan ports)
04h 4	BYTEs	network number (server's serial number)
06h	WORD	subnet number (0001h = server, 8000h-FFFEh = PC)
08h	WORD	port ID (0001h-01FFh for "well-known" ports)
0Ah	BYTE	hop count
0Bh	5 BYTEs	filler

INT 61h Function 0001h, Subfunction 0002h
"Sosend" - INITIATE OUTPUT EVENT

Banyan VINES

Registers at call: **Return Registers:**
AX = 0001h   AX = status (see Table 14-1)
DS:DX -> communications control block (see Table 14-5)
Conflicts: see Table 2-3
See also: Function 0001h Subfunctions 0001h and 0005h

14-5 Format of control block for Subfunction 0002h:

Offset	Size	Description
00h	WORD	0002h
02h	WORD	pointer to argument block (see Table 14-6)
04h	WORD	error return code (00h,97h,A2h,A3h,A5h,A6h,B1h) (see Table 14-1)
06h	4 BYTEs	reserved

14-6 Format of argument block for Subfunction 0002h:

Offset	Size	Description
00h	WORD	routine metric
02h	WORD	error return code (see Table 14-1)
04h	WORD	socket identifier
06h	WORD	pointer to send buffer
08h	WORD	length of send buffer
0Ah	WORD	flags (see Table 14-9)
0Ch	16 BYTEs	socket address (see Table 14-8)
1Ch	WORD	timeout value in multiples of 200ms
1Eh	WORD	connection identifier

20h	WORD	type of request
		0001h send message
		0002h establish a virtual connection
		0003h terminate a virtual connection

14-7 Format of buffer descriptor:

Offset	Size	Description
00h	WORD	data segment
02h	WORD	buffer pointer
04h	WORD	buffer length
06h	WORD	character count

14-8 Format of socket address for unreliable datagrams:

Offset	Size	Description
00h	WORD 0003h	address family
02h	DWORD FFFFFFFFh	network number
06h	WORD FFFFh	subnet number
08h	WORD	local port number
0Ah	BYTE 00h-0Fh	hop count
0Bh	5 BYTEs 0000h	filler

14-9 Bitfields for connection flags:

bit 0	asynchronous request
bit 1	reliable message (subfunction 0002h only)
bit 2	flush receive buffer on overflow (subfunction 0003h only)
bit 3	end of user message received
bit 4	vectored request (if set, send/receive buffer contains buffer descriptors)
bit 5	connection-specific receive
bit 6	change to connection-specific receive mode

INT 61h Function 0001h, Subfunction 0003h   *Banyan VINES*
"Sorec" - *RECEIVE INPUT EVENT NOTIFICATION*

Registers at call: **Return Registers:**
AX = 0001h   AX = status (00-0Ah,97h,A2h,A3h) (see Table 14-1)
DS:DX -> communications control block (see Table 14-10)
Conflicts: see Table 2-3
See also: Function 0001h Subfunction 0002h

14-10 Format of control block for Subfunction 0003h:

Offset	Size	Description
00h	WORD	0003h
02h	WORD	pointer to argument block (see Table 14-11)
04h	WORD	error return code (00h,97h,A2h,A3h,A5h,A6h,B1h) (see Table 14-1)
06h 4	BYTEs	reserved

14-11 Format of argument block for Subfunction 0003h:

Offset	Size	Description
00h	WORD	character count
02h	WORD	error return code (see Table 14-1)
04h	WORD	socket identifier
06h	WORD	pointer to receive buffer
08h	WORD	length of receive buffer
0Ah	WORD	flags (see Table 14-9)

0Ch	16 BYTEs	socket address
1Ch	WORD	timeout value in multiples of 200ms
1Eh	WORD	connection identifier
20h	WORD	type of response
		0001h message received
		0002h virtual connection established
		0003h virtual connection terminated

14-12 Format of buffer descriptor:

Offset	Size	Description
00h	WORD	data segment
02h	WORD	buffer pointer
04h	WORD	buffer length
06h	WORD	character count

INT 61h Function 0001h, Subfunction 0004h   Banyan VINES
"Soclose" - CLOSE A SOCKET

Registers at call: **Return Registers:**
AX = 0001h   AX = status (00h-0Ah,97h) (see Table 14-1)
DS:DX -> communications control block (see Table 14-13)
Conflicts: see Table 2-3
See also: Function 0001h Subfunction 0001h, DESQview/X INT 15h Function DE2Eh (Chapter 17)

14-13 Format of control block for Subfunction 0004h:

Offset	Size	Description
00h	WORD	0004h
02h	WORD	pointer to argument block (see Table 14-14)
04h	WORD	error return code (see Table 14-1)
06h 4	BYTEs	reserved

14-14 Format of argument block for Subfunction 0004h:

Offset	Size	Description
00h	WORD	socket identifier

INT 61h Function 0001h, Subfunction 0005h   Banyan VINES
"Sowait" - WAIT FOR ASYNCHRONOUS EVENT COMPLETION

Purpose: Return results for all asynchronous operations invoked from the data segment used for this call.
Registers at call: **Return Registers:**
AX = 0001h   AX = status (00h-0Ah,A2h,A3h) (see Table 14-1)
DS:DX -> communications control block (see Table 14-15)
Conflicts: see Table 2-3
See also: Function 0001h Subfunctions 0002h and 0009h

14-15 Format of control block for Subfunction 0005h:

Offset	Size	Description
00h	WORD	0005h
02h	WORD	pointer to argument block (see Table 14-16)
04h	WORD	error return code (see Table 14-1)
06h 4	BYTEs	reserved

14-16 Format of argument block for Subfunction 0005h:

Offset	Size	Description
00h	WORD	pointer to WORD event pointer
02h	WORD	timeout in multiples of 200ms, FFFFh = infinite

INT 61h Function 0001h, Subfunction 0008h   *Banyan VINES*
"Sosession" - REGISTER APPLICATION WITH COMMUNICATIONS SERVICE

Registers at call: **Return Registers:**
AX = 0001h   AX = status (00h,A2h) (see Table 14-1)
DS:DX -> communications control block (see Table 14-17)
Conflicts: see Table 2-3
See also: Function 0001h Subfunctions 0001h and 0009h

14-17 Format of control block for Subfunction 0008h:

Offset	Size	Description
00h	WORD	0008h
02h	WORD	process type
		0001h transient process
		0002h resident process
04h	WORD	error return code (see Table 14-1)
06h	4 BYTEs	reserved

INT 61h Function 0001h, Subfunction 000Bh   *Banyan VINES*
"Soint" - SET USER COMPLETION FUNCTION

Registers at call: **Return Registers:**
AX = 0001h   AX = status (00h-0Ah,A2h) (see Table 14-1)
DS:DX -> communications control block (see Table 14-18)
Details: The FAR user function is invoked with SS,DS, and ES set to the segment of the control block, and with the stack containing:

DWORD	return address	
WORD	argument pointer ("sosend" or "sorec" argument block)	
WORD	error return code	
	0000h	argument pointer is valid
	00A3h	timeout.

Conflicts: see Table 2-3
See also: Function 0001h Subfunctions 0005h and 0008h

14-18 Format of control block for Subfunction 000Bh:

Offset	Size	Description
00h	WORD	000Bh
02h	WORD	pointer to argument block (see Table 14-19)
04h	WORD	error return code
06h 2	BYTEs	reserved
08h	WORD	user CS register

14-19 Format of argument block for Subfunction 000Bh:

Offset	Size	Description
00h	WORD	pointer to user interrupt function
02h	WORD	pointer to user stack
04h	WORD	initial timeout value in multiples of 200ms, FFFFh = infinite

INT 61h Function 0002h
3270 INTERFACE

Banyan VINES

Registers at call: **Return Registers:**
AX = 0002h   AX = status (see Table 14-21)
BH = function (see Table 14-20)
DS:CX -> argument block (except BH=00h,1Ah) (see Tables 14-22 to 14-37)
Details: Either 3270/SNA or 3270/BSC interface may use AX=0002h, depending on which is loaded first. The other interface will use AX=000Ah.

Status codes greater than 63h indicate an inconsistency in the 3270/SNA or 3270/BSC resident driver, which must be reloaded by the user.
Conflicts: see Table 2-3

14-20 Values for 3270 interface functions:

00h	"pi2reset"	reset 3270/SNA or 3270/BSC driver
02h	"pi2bsc"	(3270/BSC only)
03h	"pi2get"	get information stored in 3270 resident driver
04h	"pi2put"	store information in 3270 resident driver
05h	"pi2gcur"	get current screen position
07h	"pi2sdat"	send data keystroke
08h	"pi2scom"	send command keystroke
0Ah	"pi2field"	get field info for arbitrary screen positions
0Fh	"pi2stat"	get logical unit/device status
12h	"pi2nlus"	determine logical unit/device assignment
13h	"pi2gate"	specifies comm port address to gateway service
14h	"pi2attach"	attach a logical unit/device
15h	"pi2sdev"	save logical unit/device info in resident driver (not supported in >3.0)
16h	"pi2gdev"	get device information (not supported in >3.0)
17h	"pi2luinfo"	get info about specific logical unit/device
18h	"pi2gerr"	get finer error detail
19h	"pi2dhold"	(3270/SNA only) holds a 3270 device
1Ah	"pi2shut"	release memory-resident module
1Ch	"pi2sprof"	save profile info in res driver (not supported in >3.0)
1Dh	"pi2gprof"	get prevsly stored profile info (not supported in >3.0)

14-21 Values for status:

0000h	successful
000Bh	invalid parameter or data does not fit data area
000Ch	another code path currently active in resident driver
000Dh	operation currently not allowed
0032h	encountered connection disconnect error
0033h	encountered "sosend" completion error
0034h	encountered "sosend" communication error
0035h	attach request refused. extended error info via "pi2gerr":
	01h resource unavailable
	02h invalid type
	03h version mismatch
	04h invalid logical unit number
	05h error during ARL processing
	06h no access for user
0071h	encountered "sosock" error

0072h	encountered unrecognizable error
0073h	encountered "sowait" error (extended info via "pi2gerr")
0074h	encountered invalid type-of-request on "sowait"
0075h	encountered "sorec" error (extended info via "pi2gerr")
0076h	encountered "sorec" completion error (ext info via "pi2gerr")
0077h	encountered connection request
0078h	encountered unrecognizable data
0079h	encountered unknown connection ID (ext info via "pi2gerr")

14-22 Format of argument block for Functions 03h,04h:

Offset	Size	Description
00h	WORD	size of data area (max 256)
02h	N BYTEs	data area

14-23 Format of argument block for Function 05h:

Offset	Size	Description
00h	WORD	logical unit/device number
02h	WORD	pointer to WORD buffer for cursor index
04h	WORD	pointer to BYTE buffer for current field attribute

14-24 Format of argument block for Function 07h:

Offset	Size	Description
00h	WORD	logical unit/device number
02h	WORD	ASCII data byte
04h	WORD	pointer to WORD count of characters which will need updating

14-25 Format of argument block for Function 08h:

Offset	Size	Description
00h	WORD	logical unit/device number
02h	WORD	keystroke (see Table 14-26)

14-26 Values for keystroke:

0000h	Enter
0001h	Clear
0002h	PA1
0003h	PA2
0004h	PA3
0005h	PF1
...	
001Ch	PF24
001Dh	CSELECT (cursor select)
001Eh	Insert
001Fh	Delete
0020h	EOField
0021h	EINPUT (erase input)
0022h	Reset
0023h	Attention
0024h	SysReq
0025h	Duplicate
0026h	Fieldmark
0027h	Home
0028h	NextLine

0029h	Tab
002Ah	BackTab
002Bh	cursor up
002Ch	cursor down
002Dh	cursor right
002Eh	cursor left
002Fh	double cursor right
0030h	double cursor left
0031h	PRINT
0032h	CANCEL
0033h	Backspace

14-27 Format of argument block for Function 0Ah:

Offset	Size	Description
00h	WORD	logical unit/device number
02h	WORD	screen index
04h	WORD	pointer to WORD buffer for field length
06h	WORD	pointer to WORD buffer for offset in screen of field start

14-28 Format of argument block for Function 0Fh:

Offset	Size	Description
00h	WORD	logical unit/device number
02h	WORD	clear mask (clear these bits of status after returning status)
04h	WORD	pointer to WORD buffer for device status (see Table 14-29)

14-29 Bitfields for device status:

bit 10	status modified
bit 9	buffer modified
bit 8	set cursor
bit 5	sound alarm
bits 1-0	size of print line for printer logical units

	00	unformatted line
	01	40-character line
	10	64-character line
	11	80-character line

14-30 Format of argument block for Function 12h:

Offset	Size	Description
00h	WORD	pointer to WORD buffer for number of logical units or devices
02h	WORD	pointer to WORD buffer for version number
04h	WORD	pointer to 64-byte buffer for logical unit/device list

14-31 Format of argument block for Function 13h:

Offset	Size	Description
00h	16 BYTEs	communications port address (see Tables 14-4 and 14-8)

14-32 Format of argument block for Function 14h:

Offset	Size	Description
00h	WORD	logical unit/device number
		0000h attach any free device of the specified type
02h	WORD	logical unit/device type
		(3270/SNA) 01h, 02h, or 03h

INT 61h Function 0002h

(3270/BSC) 02h display
(3270/BSC) 03h printer

Offset	Size	Description
04h	WORD	pointer to WORD buffer for attached logical unit/device number

14-33 Format of argument block for Function 16h:

Offset	Size	Description
00h	WORD	pointer to 18-byte buffer for device block (see Table 14-38)
		first WORD must be set to desired logical unit/device number

14-34 Format of argument block for Function 17h:

Offset	Size	Description
00h	WORD	logical unit/device number
02h	WORD	pointer to information block in caller's DS (see Table 14-39)

14-35 Format of argument block for Function 18h:

Offset	Size	Description
00h	WORD	pointer to WORD buffer for major error code
02h	WORD	pointer to WORD buffer for minor error code

14-36 Format of argument block for Function 19h:

Offset	Size	Description
00h	WORD	logical unit/device number

14-37 Format of argument block for Functions 1Ch,1Dh:

Offset	Size	Description
00h	WORD	pointer to profile block in caller's DS (see Table 14-42)

14-38 Format of device block, argument block for Function 15h:

Offset	Size	Description
00h	WORD	logical unit/device number
02h	WORD	logical unit/device type
04h	WORD	display model number
06h	WORD	numeric checking
08h	WORD	status line
0Ah	BYTE	unprotected normal field attribute
0Bh	BYTE	unprotected intensified field attribute
0Ch	BYTE	protected normal field attribute
0Dh	BYTE	protected intensified field attribute
0Eh	WORD	reserved
10h	WORD	printer port number

14-39 Format of information block:

Offset	Size	Description
00h	WORD	device model number
02h	DWORD	screen buffer pointer
06h	DWORD	status line pointer (see Table 14-40)
0Ah	DWORD	reserved

14-40 Format of status line:

Offset	Size	Description
00h	BYTE	comm line status (00h inactive, 01h active)
01h	BYTE	activation level
		01h physical unit activated
		02h logical unit also activated

		03h session is bound
02h	BYTE	data traffic state (00h inactive, 01h active)
03h	BYTE	screen ownership
		00h SLU->PLU sessoin owns screen
		01h SLU->SSCP session owns screen
04h	BYTE	keyboard status (see Table 14-41)
05h	BYTE	insert mode (01h if in insert mode)
06h	BYTE	numeric (01h if current screen buffer is numeric only)
07h	BYTE	printer status
		00h printer not assigned
		01h printer is inactive
		02h printer error
		03h currently printing
		04h printer is busy
		05h printer is very busy
08h	BYTE	printer assignment
09h	BYTE	maximum size of network name
0Ah	N BYTEs	ASCIZ network name
	BYTE	maximum size of message window
	M BYTEs	null-terminated message window
	BYTE	code set (00h EBCDIC, 01h ASCII)
	M BYTEs	extended attributes
		01h extended attributes are in effect (stored at screen+1920)
		each extended attribute specifies
		bits 0,1: 00=normal, 01=blink, 10=reverse, 11=underscor
		bits 2-4: 000=default, 001=blue, 010=red, 011=pink, 100=green,
		101=turquoise, 110=yellow, 111=white
	BYTE	extended color (01h if other than base color is in effect)

14-41 Values for keyboard status:

00h	UNLOCK	ready to accept data
01h	TIME	aid was struck
02h	SYSTEM	received response no restore
03h	FUNCTION	unavailable keyboard function
04h	INPUT	not currently used
05h	ENDFIELD	field filled in insert mode
06h	PROTECTED	attempt to enter in protected field
07h	NUMERIC	attempt to enter in numeric field
08h	PROGRAM	error in outbound data stream

14-42 Format of profile block:

Offset	Size	Description
00h	64 BYTEs	gateway service name
40h	16 BYTEs	gateway comm port address
50h	WORD	primary logical unit number
52h	WORD	secondary logical unit type
54h	WORD	secondary logical unit number
56h	WORD	printer assignment
58h	50 BYTEs	keyboard definitions filename

INT 61h Function 0002h

INT 61h Function 0003h, Subfunction 00h   *Banyan VINES*
ASYNC TERMINAL EMULATION - INITIALIZE USER BUFFER POINTER INFO

Registers at call: **Return Registers:**
AX = 0003h   AX = status (see Table 14-43)
DS:BX -> argument block (see Table 14-44)
Conflicts: see Table 2-3
See also: Function 0003h Subfunctions 06h, 08h and 0Dh

14-43 Values for status:

0000h	successful
000Bh	invalid session ID
000Ch	session not active
000Dh	invalid request type
000Eh	invalid parameters
000Fh	out of heap space
0010h	timeout on send
0011h	Banyan communications error
0012h	session not waiting for host
0013h	session is active
0014h	duplicate suspend session request
0015h	no session suspended
0016h	ring data buffer full
0017h	printer error encountered
0018h	Banyan communications error
0019h	unable to make connection
001Ah	no ring buffer specified at startup
001Bh	service is down
001Ch	invalid service name
001Dh	service is closed
001Eh	invalid connection name
001Fh	max session limit reached for service
0020h	access rights list for connection/dialout does not include this user
0021h	service not responding
0022h	missing telephone number

14-44 Format of argument block:

Offset	Size	Description
00h	BYTE	session ID (00h)
01h	BYTE	00h (function "initialize user buffer pointer information area")
02h	WORD	pointer to user buffer pointer info area in caller's current DS (see Table 14-45)

14-45 Format of user buffer pointer info area:

Offset	Size	Description
00h	WORD	flags
		0000h don't read interface's data buffer
		0001h read data buffer
02h	DWORD	pointer to ring buffer
06h	WORD	length of ring buffer
08h	WORD	ring buffer offset to last byte read by caller
0Ah	DWORD	pointer to WORD containing offset of last byte in ring buffer filled

0Eh	DWORD	pointer to screen buffer
12h	DWORD	pointer to field containing cursor position
16h	DWORD	pointer to terminal status area (see Table 14-46)

14-46 Format of terminal status area:

Offset	Size	Description
00h	BYTE	status of session: 4Eh=oNline, 46h=oFfline, 57h=Waiting
01h	BYTE	terminal type (00h=VT100, 01h=TTY, 02h=VT52, 03h=IBM3101)
02h	BYTE	current keypad mode (VT100,VT52 only)
		4Eh ("N") numeric mode
		41h ("A") application mode
03h	4 BYTEs	current state of LEDs (VT100 only): 00h off, 01h on
07h	WORD	line error count
09h	WORD	primary error code (see Table 14-47)
0Bh	WORD	secondary error code

14-47 Values for primary error code:

0000h	no error
0001h	unable to make connection
0002h	communications error, restart session
0003h	asynchronous terminal emulation service unavailable
0004h	lost carrier
0005h	all matching lines busy
0006h	no lines defined for connection name
0007h	no dial lines available on server
0008h	no matching dial lines available
0009h	out of heap space
000Ah	service error encountered
000Bh	timed out waiting to connect
000Ch	communications error
000Dh	communications error
000Eh	host wants file transferred to/from PC
000Fh	host software changed session parameter
0010h	host software changed tap settings
0011h	host software changed LED indicator
0012h	host software changed display background (secondary error code 00h for white on black, 01h for black on white)
0013h	host software changed display option (secondary error code 00h for off, 01h for on)
0014h	communications error
0015h	communications error
0016h	unable to make connection
0017h	unable to make connection

INT 61h Function 0003h, Subfunction 01h   *Banyan VINES*
ASYNC TERMINAL EMULATION - SEND TO HOST

Registers at call:	Return Registers:
AX = 0003h	AX = status (see Table 14-43)
DS:BX -> argument block (see Table 14-48)	

Conflicts: see Table 2-3
See also: Function 0003h Subfunctions 00h, 02h and 14h

14-48 Format of argument block:

Offset	Size	Description
00h	BYTE	session ID (00h)
01h	BYTE	01h (function "send to host")
02h	BYTE	type
		00h ASCII byte
		01h ASCII string
		02h terminal function code
		03h up arrow
		04h down arrow
		05h left arrow
		06h right arrow
		07h break
03h	N BYTEs	type-specific info (see Table 14-49)

14-49 Format of type-specific info:

Offset	Size	Description
---ASCII byte---		
03h	BYTE	byte to send to host
---ASCII string---		
03h	WORD	length of string
05h	WORD	pointer to string
---terminal function code (VT52/VT100)---		
03h	BYTE	function code
		00h keypad 0
		01h keypad 1
		...
		09h keypad 9
		0Ah keypad -
		0Bh keypad ,
		0Ch keypad .
		0Dh keypad ENTER
		0Eh PF1
		0Fh PF2
		10h PF3
		11h PF4
---terminal function code (IBM3101)---		
03h	BYTE	function code
		00h PF1
		...
		07h PF8
		08h Home

INT 61h Function 0003h, Subfunction 02h
ASYNC TERMINAL EMULATION - "CONTROL MONITOR"

Banyan VINES

Registers at call:
AX = 0003h
DS:BX -> argument block (see Table 14-50)
Conflicts: see Table 2-3
See also: Function 0003h Subfunctions 03h and 05h

Return Registers:
AX = status (see Table 14-43)

14-50 Format of argument block:

Offset	Size	Description
00h	BYTE	session ID (00h)
01h	BYTE	02h (function "control monitor")
02h	BYTE	display flag
		00h don't display data received from host
		01h display data

INT 61h Function 0003h, Subfunction 03h   *Banyan VINES*
ASYNC TERMINAL EMULATION - "FLOW CONTROL DATA"

Purpose: This function permits the caller to freeze/unfreeze the display and the ring buffer.

Registers at call:
AX = 0003h
DS:BX -> argument block (see Table 14-51)
Conflicts: see Table 2-3
See also: Function 0003h Subfunctions 02h and 06h

Return Registers:
AX = status (see Table 14-43)

14-51 Format of argument block:

Offset	Size	Description
00h	BYTE	session ID (00h)
01h	BYTE	03h (function "flow control data")
02h	BYTE	flow control flag
		00h allow characters to be put into display or ring buffer
		01h don't place any more characters into display or ring buffer

---

INT 61h Function 0003h, Subfunction 04h   *Banyan VINES*
ASYNC TERMINAL EMULATION - END ACTIVE SESSION

Registers at call:
AX = 0003h
DS:BX -> argument block (see Table 14-52)
Conflicts: see Table 2-3
See also: Function 0003h Subfunctions 0Ah, 0Dh, and 0Fh

Return Registers:
AX = status (see Table 14-43)

14-52 Format of argument block:

Offset	Size	Description
00h	BYTE	session ID (00h)
01h	BYTE	04h (function "end active session")

INT 61h Function 0003h, Subfunction 05h   *Banyan VINES*
ASYNC TERMINAL EMULATION - SET SESSION PARAMETER

Registers at call:
AX = 0003h
DS:BX -> argument block (see Table 14-53)
Conflicts: see Table 2-3
See also: Function 0003h Subfunctions 00h, 06h, and 08h

Return Registers:
AX = status (see Table 14-43)

14-53 Format of argument block:

Offset	Size	Description
00h	BYTE	session ID (00h)
01h	BYTE	05h (function "set session parameter")
02h	BYTE	parameter number (see Table 14-54)
03h	BYTE	new parameter value

14-54 Values for parameter number:

00h	line speed (00h=any, 01h=50, 02h=110, 03h=134.5, 04h=150, 05h=300, 06h=600, 07h=1200, 08h=2400, 09h=4800, 0Ah=9600)
01h	parity (00h=none, 01h=odd, 02h=even)
02h	duplex (00h=full, 01h=half)
03h	character size (00h=7 bits, 01h=8 bits)
04h	stop bits (00h=1, 01h=2)
05h	XON/XOFF flow control (00h=no, 01h=yes)
07h	intercharacter delay in tenths of a second
08h	interline delay in tenths of a second
09h	auto linefeed (00h=no, 01h=yes)
0Ah	filter control characters (00h=no, 01h=yes)
0Bh	terminal type (00h=VT100, 01h=glassTTY, 02h=VT52, 03h=IBM3101)
0Ch	auto wrap (00h=no, 01h=yes)
0Dh	cursor shape (00h=underscore, 01h=block)
0Eh	character set (00h=UK, 01h=US ASCII)
0Fh	printer port (00h=LPT1, 01h=LPT2, 02h=LPT3)

INT 61h Function 0003h, Subfunction 06h   *Banyan VINES*
ASYNC TERMINAL EMULATION - GET SESSION PARAMETER

Registers at call: **Return Registers:**
AX = 0003h   AX = status (see Table 14-43)
DS:BX -> argument block (see Table 14-55)
Conflicts: see Table 2-3
See also: Function 0003h Subfunctions 00h, 05h, and 07h

14-55 Format of argument block:

Offset	Size	Description
00h	BYTE	session ID (00h)
01h	BYTE	06h (function "get session parameter")
02h	BYTE	parameter number (see Table 14-54)
03h	BYTE	(return) current parameter value

INT 61h Function 0003h, Subfunction 07h   *Banyan VINES*
ASYNC TERMINAL EMULATION - SET TAB SETTINGS

Registers at call: **Return Registers:**
AX = 0003h   AX = status (see Table 14-43)
DS:BX -> argument block (see Table 14-56)
Conflicts: see Table 2-3
See also: Function 0003h Subfunctions 05h and 08h

14-56 Format of argument block:

Offset	Size	Description
00h	BYTE	session ID (00h)
01h	BYTE	07h (function "set tab settings")
02h	WORD	pointer to 80-byte buffer in caller's current DS each byte = 00h if no tab, 01h if tab at that position

INT 61h Function 0003h, Subfunction 08h   *Banyan VINES*
ASYNC TERMINAL EMULATION - GET TAB SETTINGS

Registers at call: **Return Registers:**
AX = 0003h   AX = status (see Table 14-43)
DS:BX -> argument block (see Table 14-57)

Conflicts: see Table 2-3
See also: Function 0003h Subfunctions 06h and 07h

14-57 Format of argument block:

Offset	Size	Description
00h	BYTE	session ID (00h)
01h	BYTE	08h (function "get tab settings")
02h	WORD	pointer to 80-byte buffer in caller's current DS
		each byte set to 00h if no tab, 01h if tab at that position

---

INT 61h Function 0003h, Subfunction 09h

Banyan VINES

ASYNC TERMINAL EMULATION - REFRESH EMULATION SCREEN

Registers at call:
AX = 0003h
DS:BX -> argument block (see Table 14-58)
Conflicts: see Table 2-3
See also: Function 0003h Subfunctions 00h and 0Bh

Return Registers:
AX = status (see Table 14-43)

14-58 Format of argument block:

Offset	Size	Description
00h	BYTE	session ID (00h)
01h	BYTE	09h (function "refresh emulation screen")

INT 61h Function 0003h, Subfunction 0Ah

Banyan VINES

ASYNC TERMINAL EMULATION - SUSPEND SESSION TEMPORARILY

Registers at call:
AX = 0003h
DS:BX -> argument block (see Table 14-59)
Conflicts: see Table 2-3
See also: Function 0003h Subfunctions 04h, 09h, 0Bh, and 0Dh

Return Registers:
AX = status (see Table 14-43)

14-59 Format of argument block:

Offset	Size	Description
00h	BYTE	session ID (00h)
01h	BYTE	0Ah (function "suspend session temporarily")
02h	WORD	size of session information to be saved
04h	WORD	pointer to buffer in caller's DS

INT 61h Function 0003h, Subfunction 0Bh

Banyan VINES

ASYNC TERMINAL EMULATION - RESUME SUSPENDED SESSION

Registers at call:
AX = 0003h
DS:BX -> argument block (see Table 14-60)
Conflicts: see Table 2-3
See also: Function 0003h Subfunctions 09h and 0Ah

Return Registers:
AX = status (see Table 14-43)

14-60 Format of argument block:

Offset	Size	Description
00h	BYTE	session ID (00h)
01h	BYTE	0Bh (function "restore previously suspended session")
02h	WORD	size of buffer into which session info is restored
04h	WORD	pointer to buffer in caller's DS

INT 61h Function 0003h, Subfunction 09h

INT 61h Function 0003h, Subfunction 0Ch
ASYNC TERMINAL EMULATION - SET SCROLL LOCK CHECKING
Banyan VINES

Registers at call:
AX = 0003h
DS:BX -> argument block (see Table 14-61)
Conflicts: see Table 2-3
See also: Function 0003h Subfunction 00h

Return Registers:
AX = status (see Table 14-43)

14-61 Format of argument block:

Offset	Size	Description
00h	BYTE	session ID (00h)
01h	BYTE	0Ch (function "set state of scroll lock checking")
02h	BYTE	check_scroll_lock flag
		00h off
		01h on (display of host data stopped while ScrollLock on)

INT 61h Function 0003h, Subfunction 0Dh
ASYNC TERMINAL EMULATION - EXIT EMULATION
Banyan VINES

Registers at call:
AX = 0003h
DS:BX -> argument block (see Talbe 14-62)
Conflicts: see Table 2-3
See also: Function 0003h Subfunctions 04h and 0Ah

Return Registers:
AX = status (see Table 14-43)

14-62 Format of argument block:

Offset	Size	Description
00h	BYTE	session ID (00h)
01h	BYTE	0Dh (function "exit emulation")

INT 61h Function 0003h, Subfunction 0Eh
ASYNC TERMINAL EMULATION - INTERRUPT ON CHARACTER FROM HOST
Banyan VINES

Registers at call:
AX = 0003h
DS:BX -> argument block (see Table 14-63)
Conflicts: see Table 2-3
See also: Function 0003h Subfunctions 00h and 14h

Return Registers:
AX = status (see Table 14-43)

14-63 Format of argument block:

Offset	Size	Description
00h	BYTE	session ID (00h)
01h	BYTE	0Eh (function "interrupt on character from host")
02h	DWORD	pointer to routine to be called (0000h:0000h = don't call)
06h	DWORD	stack pointer to use when call is made

INT 61h Function 0003h, Subfunction 0Fh
ASYNC TERMINAL EMULATION - START A SESSION
Banyan VINES

Registers at call:
AX = 0003h
DS:BX -> argument block (see Table 14-64)
Conflicts: see Table 2-3
See also: Function 0003h Subfunctions 04h and 0Bh

Return Registers:
AX = status (see Table 14-43)

14-64 Format of argument block:

Offset	Size	Description
00h	BYTE	session ID (00h)
01h	BYTE	0Fh (function "start a session")
02h	WORD	pointer to information area in caller's current DS (see Table 14-65)

14-65 Format of information area:

Offset	Size	Description
00h	WORD	length of service name
02h	WORD	pointer to service name in caller's DS
04h	BYTE	type of connection (00h=connection name, 01h=dialout)
05h	WORD	length of connection name/telephone number
07h	WORD	pointer to connection name/telephone number

INT 61h Function 0003h, Subfunction 10h
ASYNC TERMINAL EMULATION - START/STOP PRINTING

Banyan VINES

Registers at call:
AX = 0003h
DS:BX -> argument block (see Table 14-66)
Conflicts: see Table 2-3
See also: Function 0003h Subfunctions 06h and 13h

Return Registers:
AX = status (see Table 14-43)

14-66 Format of argument block:

Offset	Size	Description
00h	BYTE	session ID (00h)
01h	BYTE	10h (function "start/stop printing of data received from host)
02h	WORD	print capture flag (00h=off, 01h=on)

INT 61h Function 0003h, Subfunction 11h
ASYNC TERMINAL EMULATION - GET FILE TRANSFER PARAMETERS

Banyan VINES

Registers at call:
AX = 0003h
DS:BX -> argument block (see Table 14-67)
Conflicts: see Table 2-3
See also: Function 0003h Subfunctions 00h and 12h

Return Registers:
AX = status (see Table 14-43)

14-67 Format of argument block:

Offset	Size	Description
00h	BYTE	session ID (00h)
01h	BYTE	11h (function "get file transfer parameters")
02h	WORD	pointer to buffer for parameters in caller's current DS (see Table 14-68)

14-68 Format of file transfer parameters:

Offset	Size	Description
00h	BYTE	protocol flag (00h none, 01h Kermit)
01h	BYTE	direction flag (00h send, 01h receive)
02h	BYTE	length of null-terminated PC filename
03h	DWORD	pointer to null-terminated PC filename
07h	BYTE	length of null-terminated host filename
08h	DWORD	pointer to null-terminated host filename

INT 61h Function 0003h, Subfunction 12h   *Banyan VINES*
ASYNC TERMINAL EMULATION - GET CONNECTION INFORMATION

Registers at call: **Return Registers:**
AX = 0003h   AX = status (see Table 14-43)
DS:BX -> argument block (see Table 14-69)
Conflicts: see Table 2-3
See also: Function 0003h Subfunctions 11h and 15h

14-69 Format of argument block:

Offset	Size	Description
00h	BYTE	session ID (00h)
01h	BYTE	12h (function "get connection information")
02h	WORD	offset of buffer for connection information (see Table 14-70)

14-70 Format of connection information:

Offset	Size	Description
00h	WORD	(return) length of service name
02h	WORD	pointer to 64-byte buffer for service name
04h	BYTE	type of connection (00h connection name, 01h dialout)
05h	WORD	length of connection name/telephone number
07h	WORD	pointer to 64-byte buffer for name/telephone number
09h	BYTE	(return) server line number being used

INT 61h Function 0003h, Subfunction 13h   *Banyan VINES*
ASYNC TERMINAL EMULATION - START/STOP TRACING TRAFFIC

Registers at call: **Return Registers:**
AX = 0003h   AX = status (see Table 14-43)
DS:BX -> argument block (see Table 14-71)
Conflicts: see Table 2-3
See also: Function 0003h Subfunctions 00h and 0Eh

14-71 Format of argument block:

Offset	Size	Description
00h	BYTE	session ID (00h)
01h	BYTE	13h (function "start/stop tracing data traffic in session")
02h	BYTE	trace flag (00h=off, 01h=on)

INT 61h Function 0003h, Subfunction 14h   *Banyan VINES*
ASYNC TERMINAL EMULATION - INTERRUPT ON HOST MESSAGE

Registers at call: **Return Registers:**
AX = 0003h   AX = status (see Table 14-43)
DS:BX -> argument block (see Table 14-72)
Conflicts: see Table 2-3
See also: Function 0003h Subfunction 0Eh

14-72 Format of argument block:

Offset	Size	Description
00h	BYTE	session ID (00h)
01h	BYTE	14h (function "interrupt on message from host")
02h	DWORD	pointer to routine to be called (0000h:0000h = don't call)
06h	DWORD	stack pointer to use when call is made

INT 61h Function 0003h, Subfunction 15h
ASYNC TERMINAL EMULATION - RESET ERROR
Banyan VINES

Registers at call:
AX = 0003h
DS:BX -> argument block (see Table 14-73)
Conflicts: see Table 2-3
See also: Function 0003h Subfunctions 00h and 12h

Return Registers:
AX = status (see Table 14-43)

14-73 Format of argument block:

Offset	Size	Description
00h	BYTE	session ID (00h)
01h	BYTE	15h (function "reset error")

INT 61h Function 0004h
GET SERVER SERIAL NUMBER
Banyan VINES

Registers at call:
AX = 0004h
DS:DX -> request block (see Table 14-74)

Return Registers:
AX = status
   0000h server ID returned in request block
   000Fh invalid drive
   0015h drive not ready

Conflicts: see Table 2-3

14-74 Format of request block:

Offset	Size	Description
00h	WORD	0008h
02h	WORD	drive number (0=default, 1=A, ...)
04h 6	BYTEs	buffer for server ID

INT 61h Function 0005h
PRINTER CONTROL
Banyan VINES

Registers at call:
AX = 0005h
DS:DX -> request block (see Table 14-75)

Return Registers:
AX = status
   0000h successful
   0001h network software not installed or incompatible

Conflicts: see Table 2-3
See also: INT 2Fh Function D702h

14-75 Format of request block:

Offset	Size	Description
00h	WORD	function
		0201h "endspool" all data for a print job has been sent
		0205h "getactive" get currently active printer port
02h	WORD	number of active port (1-3)
04h	WORD	*unknown* (0 for function 0201h, 3 for function 0205h)
06h	WORD	0000h

INT 61h Function 0007h, Subfunction 0002h
GET PORTS FOR A SERVICE
Banyan VINES

Registers at call:
AX = 0007h
BX = 0002h
DS:DX -> StreetTalk service name
DS:DI -> port record block (see Table 14-77)

Return Registers:
AX = status (see Table 14-76)

Conflicts: see Table 2-3
See also: Function 0007h Subfunction 0004h

14-76 Values for status:

0000h	successful
0001h	PC network software not installed or incompatible
03E9h	incorrect name syntax
03EAh	organization name too long
03EBh	group name too long
03ECh	item name too long
03EDh	StreetTalk name too long
03F3h	organization not found
03F4h	group not found
03F5h	StreetTalk name not found
03F8h	not a StreetTalk name
0409h	modify access denied
040Dh	appropriate StreetTalk name unavailable

14-77 Format of port record block:

Offset	Size	Description
00h	WORD	number of 17-byte elements
02h 17	BYTEs	element: byte 00h = input port type, bytes 01h-10h = port (see Tables 14-4 and 14-8)

INT 61h Function 0007h, Subfunction 0004h
SET PORTS FOR A SERVICE
Banyan VINES

Registers at call:
AX = 0007h
BX = 0004h
DS:DX -> StreetTalk name of service
DS:DI -> port record block (see Table 14-77)
Conflicts: see Table 2-3
See also: Function 0007h Subfunction 0002h

Return Registers:
AX = status (see Table 14-76)

INT 61h Function 0007h, Subfunction 0005h
GET USER NAME
Banyan VINES

Registers at call:
AX = 0007h
BX = 0005h
DS:DX -> 64-byte buffer for user's StreetTalk name

Return Registers:
AX = status
    0000h successful
    0001h network software not installed
        or incompatible

Details: If no user is logged in, the first byte of the returned name will be 00h.
Conflicts: see Table 2-3
See also: Function 0007h Subfunction 0007h

INT 61h Function 0007h, Subfunction 0006h
TRANSLATE ERROR INTO ASCII STRING
Banyan VINES

Registers at call:
AX = 0007h
BX = 0006h
SI = error code (>100)
DS:DX -> 80-byte buffer for error text
Conflicts: see Table 2-3

Return Registers:
AX = status
    0000h successful
    0001h network software not installed or incompatible

INT 61h Function 0007h, Subfunction 0007h
VERIFY EXISTENCE OF NAME AND RETURN CANONICAL FORM
Banyan VINES

Registers at call:
AX = 0007h
BX = 0007h
DS:DX -> NiceName block (see Table 14-78)
Conflicts: see Table 2-3
See also: Function 0007h Subfunctions 0005h and 0008h

Return Registers:
AX = status (see Table 14-76)

14-78 Format of NiceName block:

Offset	Size	Description
00h	WORD	type of name
		0064h (100) organization
		00C8h (200) group
		012Ch (300) item
02h	WORD	pointer to ASCIZ input name
04h	WORD	pointer to 64-byte buffer for output name

INT 61h Function 0007h, Subfunction 0008h
ENUMERATE StreetTalk NAMES
Banyan VINES

Registers at call:
AX = 0007h
BX = 0008h
DS:DX -> enumerate block (see Table 14-79)

Return Registers:
AX = status
  0000h successful
  0411h all matching names have been returned
  0412h some groups unavailable, all
    available matches returned

Details: Each program using this call should continue until a nonzero status is returned; otherwise, some resources will not be freed for several hours.
Conflicts: see Table 2-3
See also: Function 0007h Subfunction 0007h

14-79 Format of enumerate block:

Offset	Size	Description
00h	WORD	return code
02h	WORD	pointer to pattern string
04h	WORD	enumerate type
		0064h (100) organization
		00C8h (200) group
		012Ch (300) item
06h	WORD	enumerate class
		0000h unspecified (return all matching items)
		0001h user names
		0002h service names
		0003h list names
		0004h nicknames
08h	WORD	pointer to category criteria block (see Table 14-80) or 0000h
0Ah	WORD	pointer to array of 64-byte returned names
0Ch	WORD	number of names returned
0Eh 6	BYTEs	reserved for subsequent enumerated calls (set to zeros on first call)

14-80 Format of category criteria block:

Offset	Size	Description
00h	WORD	exclude flag
		0000h return only items with the specified categories
		0001h return all items except those with the given categories
02h	WORD	number of categories
04h	WORD	category 1 value
06h	WORD	category 2 value
		...

14-81 Values for common service categories:

0002h	file service
0003h	print service
0004h	mail service
0005h	StreetTalk
0006h	time service
0008h	semaphore service
0009h	3270/SNA service
000Ah	asynchronous terminal emulation service
000Ch	NETBIOS service
000Dh	PC-based service

INT 61h Function 0008h, Subfunction 0002h
POST MESSAGE ON LOCAL DISPLAY

Banyan VINES

@BOLDTAG = **Purpose:** Queue up to three messages to be displayed on the bottom line.

Registers at call:
AX = 0008h
BX = 0002h
CX = flags
   bit 0: message will remain on screen
     until user presses ^X
   bit 1: ring bell after displaying message
   bit 2: blink
DS:DX -> ASCIZ string to display (only first 80 characters used)

Return Registers:
AX = status
   0000h successful
   000Bh message display function currently busy
   000Ch message queue full

Conflicts: see Table 2-3
See also: Function 0008h Subfunction 0003h

INT 61h Function 0008h, Subfunction 0003h
INTERCEPT VINES 25th-LINE MESSAGES AT LOCAL PC

Banyan VINES

Registers at call:
AX = 0008h
BX = 0003h
DS:DX -> request block (see Table 14-82)

Return Registers:
AX = status
   0000h successful
   0001h network software not installed or
     incompatible

Details: The message handler should not call BIOS or DOS functions, and should either call the next handler or simply return.

To stop intercepting messages, set the previous and next request blocks to point at each other.
Conflicts: see Table 2-3
See also: Function 0008h Subfunction 0002h

14-82 Format of request block:

Offset	Size	Description
00h	DWORD	pointer to user-written message handler
04h	DWORD	pointer to next request block (filled in by VINES)
08h	DWORD	pointer to previous request block (filled in by VINES)
0Ch	DWORD	pointer to message storage area (filled by VINES) (see Table 14-83)

14-83 Format of message storage area:

Offset	Size	Description
00h	16 BYTEs	IPC port of message sender (see Table 14-4)
10h	BYTE	message flags
11h	WORD	reserved
13h	BYTE	length of message
14h	80 BYTEs	message text

INT 61h Function 000Ah
SECONDARY 3270 INTERFACE
Banyan VINES

Registers at call:
AX = 000Ah

Return Registers:
none

Details: Either 3270/SNA or 3270/BSC interface will use AX=000Ah, depending on which is loaded second. The first interface loaded will use AX=0002h.

Conflicts: see Table 2-3

See also: INT 61h Function 0002h

INT 61h Function 01h
CHECK SERVICE
Banyan VINES

Registers at call:
AH = 01h
AL = service ID (see Table 14-84)

Return Registers:
AX = status
   0000h installed
   0001h not installed
   0002h invalid ID

Conflicts: see Table 2-3

14-84 Values for service ID:

01h	communications
02h	primary 3270 emulation
03h	asynchronous terminal emulation
04h	file deflection
07h	StreetTalk
08h	environment
0Ah	secondary 3270 emulation
0Bh	semaphore service
0Ch	3270 emulation active status
0Dh	3270 keyboard interrupt simulator

INT 61h Function 02h
GET REVISION NUMBER
Banyan VINES

Registers at call:
AH = 02h
DS:DX -> 2-byte buffer for result

Return Registers:
AX = 0000h installed
   DS:DX buffer contains revision number as
   10000d*major_ver + 100d*minor_ver + patch_revision

Conflicts: see Table 2-3

CHAPTER 15

CD-ROM

The Microsoft CD Extensions (MSCDEX) software is an extender that makes a CD-ROM drive appear to be a logical DOS partition. As a result, the CD-ROM drive can be used just as if it were a high-capacity floppy drive with fast data transfer. MSCDEX must be customized for each specific drive with which it is used, and so is usually bundled with the hardware rather than being provided separately.

INT 2Fh Function 1500h
INSTALLATION CHECK   *CD-ROM*

Registers at call: Return Registers:
AX = 1500h   BX = number of CD-ROM drive letters used
BX = 0000h   CX = starting drive letter (0=A:)

Details: This installation check *does not* follow the format used by other software. It also conflicts with the DOS 4.00 GRAPHICS.COM installation check.
Conflicts: PC-DOS 4.00 GRAPHICS (PCI-27)
See also: CD/Networker INT 2Fh Function D000h

INT 2Fh Function 1501h
GET DRIVE DEVICE LIST   *CD-ROM*

Registers at call: Return Registers:
AX = 1501h   buffer filled, for each drive letter:
ES:BX -> buffer to hold drive letter list   BYTE subunit number in driver
  (5 bytes per drive letter)   DWORD address of device driver header
Conflicts: none known

INT 2Fh Function 1502h
GET COPYRIGHT FILE NAME   *CD-ROM*

Registers at call: Return Registers:
AX = 1502h   CF set if drive is not a CD-ROM drive
ES:BX -> 38-byte buffer for name of copyright file   AX = 000Fh (invalid drive)
CX = drive number (0=A:)   CF clear if successful
Conflicts: none known
See also: Function 1503h

INT 2Fh Function 1503h
GET ABSTRACT FILE NAME   *CD-ROM*

Registers at call: Return Registers:
AX = 1503h   CF set if drive is not a CD-ROM drive
ES:BX -> 38-byte buffer for name of abstract file   AX = 000Fh (invalid drive)
CX = drive number (0=A:)   CF clear if successful

Conflicts: none known
See also: Functions 1502h and 1504h

INT 2Fh Function 1504h   *CD-ROM*
GET BIBLIOGRAPHIC DOCUMENTATION FILE NAME

Registers at call: **Return Registers:**
AX = 1504h   CF set if drive is not a CD-ROM drive
ES:BX -> 38-byte buffer for name of   AX = 000Fh (invalid drive)
  bibliographic documentation file   CF clear if successful
CX = drive number (0=A:)
Conflicts: none known
See also: Functions 1502h and 1503h

INT 2Fh Function 1505h   *CD-ROM*
READ VTOC

Registers at call: **Return Registers:**
AX = 1505h   CF set on error
ES:BX -> 2048-byte buffer   AX = error code (0Fh invalid drive, 15h not ready)
CX = drive number (0=A:)   CF clear if successful
DX = sector index (0=first volume   AX = volume descriptor type (01h=standard,
  descriptor,1=second,...)   FFh=terminator, 00h=other)
Conflicts: none known

INT 2Fh Function 1506h   *CD-ROM*
TURN DEBUGGING ON

Registers at call: **Return Registers:**
AX = 1506h   none
BX = debugging function to enable
Details: This function is reserved for development.
Conflicts: none known
See also: Function 1507h

INT 2Fh Function 1507h   *CD-ROM*
TURN DEBUGGING OFF

Registers at call: **Return Registers:**
AX = 1507h   none
BX = debugging function to disable
Details: This function is reserved for development.
Conflicts: none known
See also: Function 1506h

INT 2Fh Function 1508h   *CD-ROM*
ABSOLUTE DISK READ

Registers at call: **Return Registers:**
AX = 1508h   CF set on error
ES:BX -> buffer   AL = error code (0Fh invalid drive, 15h not ready)
CX = drive number (0=A:)   CF clear if successful
SI:DI = starting sector number
DX = number of sectors to read
Conflicts: none known
See also: Function 1509h

INT 2Fh Function 1509h
ABSOLUTE DISK WRITE
CD-ROM

Registers at call:
AX = 1509h
ES:BX -> buffer
CX = drive number (0=A:)
SI:DI = starting sector number
DX = number of sectors to write

Return Registers:
none

Details: This function corresponds to INT 26h (see PCI-24) and is currently reserved and non-functional.
Conflicts: none known
See also: Function 1508h

INT 2Fh Function 150Ah
RESERVED
CD-ROM

Registers at call:
AX = 150Ah

Return Registers:
none

Conflicts: none known

INT 2Fh Function 150Bh
DRIVE CHECK
CD-ROM v2.00+

Registers at call:
AX = 150Bh
CX = drive number (0=A:)

Return Registers:
BX = ADADh if MSCDEX.EXE installed
   AX = result
      0000h if drive not supported
      nonzero if supported

Conflicts: none known
See also: Function 150Dh

INT 2Fh Function 150Ch
GET MSCDEX.EXE VERSION
CD-ROM v2.00+

Registers at call:
AX = 150Ch

Return Registers:
BH = major version
BL = minor version

Details: MSCDEX.EXE versions prior to 2.00 return BX=0000h.
Conflicts: none known

INT 2Fh Function 150Dh
GET CD-ROM DRIVE LETTERS
CD-ROM v2.00+

Registers at call:
AX = 150Dh
ES:BX -> buffer for drive letter list
  (1 byte per drive)

Return Registers:
buffer filled with drive numbers (0=A:). Each byte
  corresponds to the drive in the same position for
  Function 1501h

Conflicts: none known
See also: Function 150Bh

INT 2Fh Function 150Eh
GET/SET VOLUME DESCRIPTOR PREFERENCE
CD-ROM v2.00+

Registers at call:
AX = 150Eh
CX = drive number (0=A:)
BX = subfunction

00h get preference
  DX = 0000h
01h set preference
  DH = volume descriptor
    preference
      01h = primary
      02h = supplementary
  DL = supplementary volume
  descriptor preference
      01h = shift-Kanji

Return Registers:
CF set on error
    AX = error code (15=invalid drive, 1=invalid
       function)
CF clear if successful

DX = current preference settings

Conflicts: none known

INT 2Fh Function 150Fh
GET DIRECTORY ENTRY

CD-ROM v2.00+

Registers at call:
AX = 150Fh
CL = drive number (0=A:)
CH bit 0 = copy flag
    clear if direct copy
    set if copy to structure which removes
       ISO/High Sierra differences
ES:BX -> ASCIZ path name
SI:DI -> buffer for directory entry
  (see Tables 15-1 and 15-2)
        minimum 255 bytes for direct copy

Return Registers:
CF set on error
    AX = error code
CF clear if succesful
    AX = disk format (0=High Sierra, 1=ISO 9660)

Conflicts: none known

15-1 Format of directory entry (direct copy):

Offset	Size	Description
00h	BYTE	length of directory entry
01h	BYTE	length of XAR in Logical Block Numbers
02h	DWORD	LBN of data, Intel (little-endian) format
06h	DWORD	LBN of data, Motorola (big-endian) format
0Ah	DWORD	length of file, Intel format
0Eh	DWORD	length of file, Motorola format

---High Sierra---

12h	6 BYTEs	date and time
18h	BYTE	bit flags
19h	BYTE	reserved

---ISO 9660---

12h	7 BYTEs	date and time
19h	BYTE	bit flags

---both formats---

1Ah	BYTE	interleave size
1Bh	BYTE	interleave skip factor
1Ch	WORD	volume set sequence number, Intel format
1Eh	WORD	volume set sequence number, Motorola format
20h	BYTE	length of file name
21h	N BYTEs	file name
	BYTE	(optional) padding if filename is odd length
	N BYTEs	system data

15-2 Format of directory entry (canonicalized):

Offset	Size	Description
00h	BYTE	length of XAR in Logical Block Numbers
01h	DWORD	Logical Block Number of file start
05h	WORD	size of disk in logical blocks
07h	DWORD	file length in bytes
0Bh	7 BYTEs	date and time
12h	BYTE	bit flags
13h	BYTE	interleave size
14h	BYTE	interleave skip factor
15h	WORD	volume set sequence number
17h	BYTE	length of file name
18h	38 BYTEs	ASCIZ filename
3Eh	WORD	file version number
40h	BYTE	number of bytes of system use data
41h	220 BYTEs	system use data

INT 2Fh Function 1510h   *CD-ROM v2.10+*
SEND DEVICE DRIVER REQUEST

Registers at call: **Return Registers:**
AX = 1510h   request header updated
CX = CD-ROM drive letter (0 = A,
  1 = B, etc)
ES:BX -> CD-ROM device driver
  request header (see Table 3-59)
Conflicts: none known

INT 2Fh Function D000h   *Lotus CD/Networker*
INSTALLATION CHECK

Registers at call: **Return Registers:**
AX = D000h   AL = FFh if CD/Networker TSR is loaded
                                                      BX = 4D44h ("MD") signature
                                                      CX = Windows mode word (from INT 2Fh
                                                          Function 1600h) at time of TSR load
                                                      DX = bitmap identifying all loaded CD/Networker TSRs.
Details: INT 2Fh Function D0h is used by CD/Networker to communicate between a resident redirector TSR and a transient program that controls the TSR's CD-ROM drive emulation (volume attachments, caching, etc). At present there is only one CD/Networker TSR; the bitmap always = 4.
Conflicts: ZWmous (PCI-21), MDEBUG (PCI-57); see also Table 2-2
See also: Function D002h, INT 2Fh Function 1500h

INT 2Fh Function D002h   *Lotus CD/Networker*
GET DATA AREA

Registers at call: **Return Registers:**
AX = D002h   ES:DI -> data area owned by TSR
BX = 4D44h
DX = bitmap identifying one loaded CD/Networker TSR
Details: The format of the data area changes with each minor revision, so it can not be counted on.
Conflicts: ZWmous (PCI-21), MDEBUG (PCI-57); see also Table 2-2
See also: Function D000h

CHAPTER 16

DECnet DOS

DECnet is Digital Equipment Corporation's trademark for their communications protocol and line of networking products that are compatible with Ethernet. Originally introduced with the VAX 11/780, DECnet became the basis for all of Digital's network products. When the company actively entered the MS-DOS arena in mid-1989, it moved to integrate DECnet with existing standards, and the result was DECnet DOS.

INT 69h Function 0100h   *DECnet DOS CTERM*
INSTALLATION CHECK

Registers at call: **Return Registers:**
AX = 0100h   AL = FFh if present
Conflicts: Zenith AT BIOS (PCI-07)
See also: Function 010Fh

INT 69h Function 0101h   *DECnet DOS CTERM*
SEND BYTE

Registers at call: **Return Registers:**
AX = 0101h   AH >= 80h on error
BL = character
DX = session handle
Conflicts: Zenith AT BIOS (PCI-07)
See also: Function 0102h

INT 69h Function 0102h   *DECnet DOS CTERM*
READ BYTE

Registers at call: **Return Registers:**
AX = 0102h   AH >= 80h on error
DX = session handle   AH < 80h if successful
                                                 AL = character

Conflicts: Zenith AT BIOS (PCI-07)
See also: Function 0101h

INT 69h Function 0103h   *DECnet DOS CTERM*
STATUS

Registers at call: **Return Registers:**
AX = 0103h   AH status flags
DX = session handle   bit 7 session has been aborted
                                               bit 6 DECnet error
                                               bit 1 trace data available

bit 0 receive data available
AL = reason code if DECnet error (see Table 16-1)

Conflicts: Zenith AT BIOS (PCI-07)
See also: Function 0104h

16-1 Values for reason code:

00h	normal disconnect
01h	unknown message from host
02h	protocol violation from host
03h	could not process the initiate message
04h	error receiving message from host
05h	error sending message to host
06h	error checking for message from host
07h	remote system does not support CTERM
08h	remote system does not support correct protocol version
09h	did not receive BIND message from host
0Ah	could not send BIND message to host
0Bh	no more sessions available
0Ch	session does not exist
0Dh	not enough memory to complete operation
0Eh	connection has broken

INT 69h Function 0104h   *DECnet DOS CTERM*
DECnet STATUS

Registers at call:
AX = 0104h
DX = session handle

Return Registers:
AX = reason code (see Table 16-1)

Details: Use this call when Function 0103h returns a DECnet error.
Conflicts: Zenith AT BIOS (PCI-07)
See also: Function 0103h

INT 69h Function 0105h   *DECnet DOS CTERM*
OPEN SESSION

Registers at call:
AX = 0105h
DS:BX -> ASCIZ node name
ES:DX -> buffer for session control
   block (see Table 16-7)

Return Registers:
AX <= 0 on error
AX > 0 session handle

Conflicts: Zenith AT BIOS (PCI-07)
See also: Functions 0103h, 0106h, and 010Ah

INT 69h Function 0106h   *DECnet DOS CTERM*
CLOSE SESSION

Registers at call:
AX = 0106h
DX = session handle

Return Registers:
AH = status
   00h good close
   other error code (see Table 16-1)

Conflicts: Zenith AT BIOS (PCI-07)
See also: Functions 0103h and 0105h

INT 69h Function 010Ah   *DECnet DOS CTERM*
GET SESSION CONTROL BLOCK SIZE
Registers at call: **Return Registers:**
AX = 010Ah   AX = length of session control block in bytes
Conflicts: Zenith AT BIOS (PCI-07)
See also: Function 0105h

INT 69h Function 010Bh   *DECnet DOS CTERM*
GET DECnet SOCKET
Registers at call: **Return Registers:**
AX = 010Bh   AX > 0 DECnet socket for the session
DX = session handle   AX = 0000h if no match for handle
Conflicts: Zenith AT BIOS (PCI-07)

INT 69h Function 010Fh   *DECnet DOS CTERM*
DEINSTALL CTERM
Registers at call: **Return Registers:**
AX = 010Fh   AH = status
                                             00h succesful uninstall
                                             other error code (see Table 16-1)
Details: CTERM must have been the last TSR loaded in order to deinstall it.
Conflicts: Zenith AT BIOS (PCI-07)
See also: Function 0100h

INT 69h Function 0Ah   *DECnet DOS 2.1+*
DATA LINK LAYER
Registers at call: **Return Registers:**
AH = 0Ah   AX = status (see Table 16-3)
AL = function (see Table 16-2)
ES:BX -> Datalink Communication Block
Conflicts: Zenith AT BIOS (PCI-07)
See also: INT 6Dh

16-2 Values for function:

00h	initialize
01h	open portal
02h	close portal
03h	enable multicast address
04h	disable multicast address
05h	transmit
06h	request transmit buffer
07h	deallocate transmit buffer
08h	read channel status
09h	read datalink portal list
0Ah	read information about a datalink portal
0Bh	read and/or clear counters
0Ch	request to boot from a network server
0Dh	enable Ethernet channel
0Eh	disable Ethernet channel
0Fh	start MOP/send a System ID message
10h	stop MOP
11h	get DECPARM

12h	set DECPARM
13h	external loopback

16-3 Values for status:

00h	successful
01h	hardware failed to initialize
02h	channel state was not off (must be off to execute that command)
03h	channel state is off (must be on to execute that command)
04h	address not set
05h	hardware missing
06h	buffer too small
07h	no more buffers available
08h	no more resources available
09h	promiscuous receiver active
0Ah	non exclusive
0Bh	unrecognized portal
0Ch	protocol type in use
0Dh	not a valid Multicast address
0Eh	outstanding calls
0Fh	hardware doesn't support receiving bad frames
10h	none outstanding
11h	no events
12h	broken
13h	buffer quota exceeded
14h	already initialized
15h	loopback failure

16-4 Format of Datalink Communication Block

Offset	Type	Description
00h	WORD	portal ID
02h	6 BYTEs	source address
08h	6 BYTEs	destination address
0Eh	DWORD	buffer pointer
12h	WORD	buffer length
14h	WORD	operation
16h	BYTE	pad flag (used on open)
		00h no pad
		01h pad
17h	BYTE	mode flag (used on open)
		00h 802.3
		01h Ethernet
		02h promiscuous
18h	DWORD	line status change function
1Ch	DWORD	received data function
20h	DWORD	transmitted data function
24h	BYTE	maximum outstanding transmits/receives
25h	2 BYTEs	protocol type
27h	WORD	buffers lost

INT 69h Function 0Ah

INT 6Ah   *DECnet DOS*
LOCAL AREA TRANSPORT PROGRAM

Details: The installation check consists of testing for a signature area immediately preceding the interrupt handler.

See also: INT 6Bh, INT 6Dh

16-5 Format of signature area:

Offset	Size	Description
-5	BYTE	major version number
-4	BYTE	minor version number
-3	3 BYTEs	signature (ASCII "LAT")

INT 6Ah Function 01h   *DECnet DOS LOCAL AREA TRANSPORT*
SEND BYTE

Registers at call: **Return Registers:**
AH = 01h   AH >= 80h on error
DH = FFh
AL = character
DL = handle

Conflicts: Super-TCP (Chapter 34), OPTHELP (PCI-66)

See also: Function 02h

INT 6Ah Function 02h   *DECnet DOS LOCAL AREA TRANSPORT*
READ BYTE

Registers at call: **Return Registers:**
AH = 02h   AH < 80h if successful
DH = FFh   AL = character
DL = handle   AH >= 80h on error

Conflicts: Super-TCP (Chapter 34), OPTHELP (PCI-66)

See also: Function 01h

INT 6Ah Function 03h   *DECnet DOS LOCAL AREA TRANSPORT*
STATUS

Registers at call: **Return Registers:**
AH = 03h   AH = status flags (see Table 16-6)
DH = FFh
DL = handle

Conflicts: Super-TCP (Chapter 34), OPTHELP (PCI-66)

16-6 Bitfields for status flags:

bit 5	transmit buffer empty
bit 3	session in start state
bit 2	session not active
bit 1	unable to queue transmit data
bit 0	receive data available

INT 6Ah Function D0h   *DECnet DOS LOCAL AREA TRANSPORT*
OPEN SESSION

Registers at call:
AH = D0h
DH = FFh
AL = password flag
    FFh no password

0Fh   password at ES:DI
ES:BX -> LAT session control block
   (see Table 16-7)
ES:DI -> 16-byte blank-padded
   password

Return Registers:
AH = 00h success
   DL = handle

Conflicts: Super-TCP (Chapter 34), OPTHELP (PCI-66)
See also: Function D000h

16-7 Format of LAT Session Control Block:

Offset	Size	Description
00h	18 BYTEs	service name
12h	18 BYTEs	node name (future use)
24h	18 BYTEs	port name (future use)
36h	DWORD	address of session stopped post routine
3Ah	DWORD	address of service table overflow post routine
3Eh	DWORD	address of transmit post routine
42h	DWORD	address of receive post routine
46h	WORD	session status
		04h circuit failure
		08h stop slot received
48h	WORD	slot state (LAT driver use)
4Ah	WORD	local credits (LAT driver use)
4Ch	DWORD	pointer to VCB (LAT driver use)
50h	WORD	backward slot (LAT driver use)
52h	WORD	forward slot (LAT driver use)
54h	WORD	remote slot ID (LAT driver use)
56h	WORD	local slot ID (LAT driver use)
58h	WORD	slot byte count (LAT driver use)
5Ah	BYTE	remote credits (LAT driver use)
5Bh	255 BYTEs	transmitted data slot
15Ah	BYTE	number of receive data slots (4 recommended)
15Bh	BYTE	number of occupied slots
15Ch	BYTE	index of next receive slot to use
15Dh	BYTE	index of current receive slot
15Eh	WORD	pointer to first received character
160h	N WORDs	pointers to receive slots (buffers); each is 259 bytes

Note: The caller should set the post routines to 0000h:0000h if polled operation will be used.

INT 6Ah Function D000h
CLOSE SESSION
                                      DECnet DOS LOCAL AREA TRANSPORT

Registers at call:
AX = D000h
DH = FFh
DL = handle

Return Registers:
AX = status
   0000h successful
   0001h no such session
   0002h session not running, try again later

Conflicts: Super-TCP (Chapter 34), OPTHELP (PCI-66)
See also: Function D0h

INT 6Ah Function D100h
SEND BREAK

DECnet DOS LOCAL AREA TRANSPORT

Registers at call:
AX = D100h
DH = FFh
DL = handle

Return Registers:
AX = 0000h if successful
AH bit 7 set if unable to send break

Conflicts: Super-TCP (Chapter 34), OPTHELP (PCI-66)

INT 6Ah Function D300h
RESET LAT COUNTERS

DECnet DOS LOCAL AREA TRANSPORT

Registers at call:
AX = D300h
DH = FFh

Return Registers:
none

Conflicts: Super-TCP (Chapter 34), OPTHELP (PCI-66)
See also: Function D400h

INT 6Ah Function D400h
COPY LAT COUNTERS

DECnet DOS LOCAL AREA TRANSPORT

Registers at call:
AX = D400h
DH = FFh
CX = buffer size
ES:BX -> buffer for LAT counters

Return Registers:
AX = status
    0000h counters copied into buffer
    FFFFh buffer too small

Conflicts: Super-TCP (Chapter 34), OPTHELP (PCI-66)
See also: Function D300h

INT 6Ah Function D500h
GET NEXT LAT SERVICE NAME

DECnet DOS LOCAL AREA TRANSPORT

Registers at call:
AX = D500h
DH = FFh
ES:BX -> 17-byte buffer for name

Return Registers:
AH = 00h if successful ES:BX buffer filled
AX = FFFFh if end of table or no name available

Details: Use this function to get the names of the hosts on the network. Successive calls are necessary to get all names.
Conflicts: Super-TCP (Chapter 34), OPTHELP (PCI-66)
See also: Function D600h

INT 6Ah Function D600h
LAT SERVICE TABLE RESET

DECnet DOS LOCAL AREA TRANSPORT

Registers at call:
AX = D600h
DH = FFh

Return Registers:
AX = number of service table entries
BX = status
    0000h service table has not overflowed
    FFFFh service table has overflowed

Conflicts: Super-TCP (Chapter 34), OPTHELP (PCI-66)
See also: Function D500h

INT 6Bh
PORT DRIVER

DECnet DOS

Details: The installation check consists of testing for a signature area (see Table 16-8) immediately preceding the interrupt handler.
See also: INT 6Ah, INT 6Ch

16-8 Format of signature area:

Offset	Size	Description
-5	BYTE	major version number
-4	BYTE	minor version number
-3	3 BYTEs	signature (ASCII "PDV")

INT 6Ch
DECnet DOS network scheduler
API

Details: The installation check consists of testing for a signature area (see Table 16-9) immediately preceding the interrupt handler.

This interrupt is also supported by DEC Pathworks for DOS.

See also: INT 6Bh, INT 6Dh, INT 6Eh

16-9 Format of signature area:

Offset	Size	Description
-5	BYTE	major version number
-4	BYTE	minor version number
-3	3 BYTEs	signature (ASCII "SCH")

INT 6Dh
DECnet DOS (before 2.1)
DATA LINK LAYER PROGRAM

Registers at call: **Return Registers:**
AH = function   *unknown*
others, if any, unknown

Details: The installation check consists of testing for a signature area (see Table 16-10) immediately preceding the interrupt handler.

See also: INT 69h Function 0Ah, INT 6Ch, INT 6Eh

16-10 Format of signature area:

Offset	Size	Description
-5	BYTE	major version number
-4	BYTE	minor version number
-3	3 BYTEs	signature (ASCII "SCH")

INT 6Eh
DECnet DOS
DECnet NETWORK PROCESS API

Details: This is the main DECnet DOS access, and is described in Digital Equipment Corp. manual AA-EB46B-TV ("DECnet-DOS Programmer's Reference Manual").

There is a signature/data area (see Table 16-11) immediately prior to the interrupt handler which may be used as an installation check.

16-11 Format of signature area:

Offset	Size	Description
-5	BYTE	major version number
-4	BYTE	minor version number
-3	3 BYTEs	signature (ASCII "DNP")

CHAPTER 17

DESQview/X Networking

DESQview/X is Quarterdeck Office Systems' marriage of its DESQview multitasker for DOS with the Unix-originated X Windows graphical interface. Since one of its major selling points is the ability to support networked execution with a program's output displayed on a machine other than the one on which it is executing, DESQview/X contains a significant networking API. Between its built-in sockets driver (SOCKET.DVR) and the Network Manager, DESQview/X shields programs using its own API from the enormous differences in interfaces between the various TCP/IP protocol stacks DESQview/X supports (see Chapters 32 through 34).

DESQview versions 2.50-2.52 are distributed as part of DESQview/X v1.0x, and DESQview v2.53 is distributed as part of DESQview/X v1.10.

DESQview/X Socket Interrupts

INT 15h Function 112Dh   *DESQview v2.50+*
GET/SET SOCKET HANDLER—Identical to Function DE2Dh below

INT 15h Function 112Eh   *DESQview v2.50+*
SOCKET API – Identical to Function DE2Eh below

INT 15h Function DE2Dh   *DESQview v2.50+*
GET/SET SOCKET HANDLER   *Undocumented*

Registers at call: Return Registers:
AX = DE2Dh   DX:BX -> socket handler
CX = direction
    FFFFh set socket handler
        DX:BX -> FAR function for socket
        interface (must be of the format
        described under INT 63h below)
    other get socket handler
Details: The "set" subfunction is normally called only by SOCKET.DVR.
See also: Function DE2Eh, INT 63h

INT 15h Function DE2Eh   *DESQview v2.50+*
SOCKET API   *Undocumented*

Registers at call: Return Registers:
AX = DE2Eh   CX = size of socket record in bytes
DX:BX -> socket record (see Table 17-2) or   DX:BX -> socket record which was used
    0000h:0000h to create a new socket record
Details: Socket records are allocated from DESQview common memory.

For Unix compatibility, each socket and connection on a socket is allocated a DOS file handle (referencing an SFT for NUL) which is used on various calls to specify which of possibly multiple connections is to be operated upon.

See also: Function DE2Dh, INT 63h, Banyan VINES INT 61h Function 0001h (Chapter 14)

17-1 Values for function number:

0000h	*initialize socket*
0001h	"gethostname"
0002h	"ioctl" check for input
0003h	"sleep" delay for specified period
0004h	"htons" convert word to network (big-endian) byte order
0005h	"select"
0006h	"bsd_close"/"so_close" close socket
0007h	NOP
0008h	"connect" initiate connection on socket
0009h	"recv"/"recvfrom" read from socket
000Ah	"socket"
000Bh	*unknown*
000Ch	"gethostbyname"
000Dh	"send"/"sendto" write to socket
000Eh	*unknown* (does something to all connections for process)
000Fh	"getpid" get process identifier
0010h	"gettimeofday"
0011h	"bind" assign name to socket
0012h	"listen" listen for connections on socket
0013h	"accept" accept connection on socket
0014h	connect to X server
0015h	"gethostbyaddr" get host information for an address
0016h	"getprotobyname"
0017h	"getprotobynumber"
0018h	"getservbyname"
0019h	"getservbyport"
001Ah	"getsockname" determine name bound to socket
001Bh	"getpeername" get name of connected peer
001Ch	"getsockopt"/"setsockopt"
001Dh	"so_exit" close all sockets for calling process
001Eh	"issock" determine whether file handle references socket
001Fh	"so_attach" reattach previously detached socket
0020h	"so_detach" temporarily detach socket
0021h	get DESQview directory
0022h	"NewProc" start new application (see Function 102Ch in PCI-44)
0023h	"so_linkup"
0024h	canonicalize filename
0025h	indirect INT 15h call
0026h	Network Manager interface
0027h	"so_unlink" close connection from "so_linkup"
0028h	"raisepriority"
0029h	"lowerpriority"
002Ah	*unknown*
FFFFh	"NetExit" (appears to be a NOP)

INT 15h Function DE2Eh

17-2 Format of socket record header:

Offset	Size	Description
00h	WORD	signature F0ADh
02h	WORD	function number (see Table 17-1)
04h	WORD	returned error code (see Table 17-3)
06h	WORD	*maximum message size* (usually 0400h)
08h	WORD	PSP segment to use or 0000h if socket not valid
0Ah	WORD	scratch space (JFT size)
0Ch	DWORD	scratch space (JFT address)
10h	DWORD	mailbox handle (initialized by function 0000h)
14h	DWORD	timer object handle (initialized by function 0000h)

.comment snake this table into two columns

17-3 Values for error code:

0000h	successful
0009h	"BADF" bad file handle
000Ch	"ENOMEM" out of memory
000Eh	"EFAULT" bad address
0016h	"EINVAL" invalid argument
0018h	"EMFILE" too many open files
0020h	*"EPIPE" broken pipe*
0023h	"EWOULDBLOCK" operation cannot be completed at this time
0024h	"EINPROGRESS" operation now in progress
0026h	"ENOTSOCK" socket invalid
0028h	"EMSGSIZE" message too long to send atomically
002Ch	"ESOCKTNOSUPPORT" socket type not supported
002Fh	"EAFNOSUPPORT" address family not supp. by protocol fam.
0031h	"EDOM" argument too large
0038h	"EISCONN" socket is already connected
0039h	"ENOTCONN" socket is not connected

17-4 Format of Socket Context Record:

Offset	Size	Description
00h	DWORD	pointer to next Socket Context Record, 0000h:0000h if last
04h	WORD	SFT index for socket, 00FFh if not connected, FFFFh if detached
06h	WORD	PSP segment of owner or 0000h
08h	WORD	mapping context of owning window (see Function 1016h in PCI-44)
0Ah	2 BYTEs	*unknown*
0Ch	WORD	address family
0Eh	WORD	socket type
10h	WORD	protocol
12h	WORD	socket state
		0001h created
		0002h bound
		0003h *listening*
		0005h connected
14h	DWORD	timer object handle
18h	DWORD	object handle (*mailbox*)
1Ch	DWORD	object handle of parent of above object or 0000h:0000h
20h	DWORD	pointer to *unknown item* or 0000h

INT 15h Function DE2Eh

24h	6 BYTEs	*unknown*
2Ah	WORD	file handle for socket or FFFFh
2Ch	2 BYTEs	*unknown*
2Eh	WORD	nonzero if socket nonblocking
---network connections only---		
30h	2 BYTEs	*unknown*
32h	WORD	*unknown*
34h	4 BYTEs	(big-endian) IP address of remote
38h	6 BYTEs	*unknown*

INT 63h
SOCKET API

Details: Parameters are passed by *patching* the data field immediately following the entry point, as detailed below; the preferred method for calling the socket API is via INT 15h Function DE2Eh.

The installation check consists of testing for the (lowercase) string "dvxunix" at offset 9 from the interrupt handler start.

Conflicts: see Table 2-3
See also: INT 15h Function DE2Eh, INT BEh (PCI-44)

17-5 Format of interrupt handler entry:

Offset	Size	Description
00h	3 BYTEs	near jump or short jump + NOP to actual interrupt handler
03h	WORD	offset from following pointer for initial top of local stack
05h	DWORD	pointer to argument/stack block (see INT 15h Function DE2Eh)
09h	7 BYTEs	signature "dvxunix"

DESQview/X Socket API Functions

The functions in this section are all invoked through INT 15h Function DE2Eh.

Most of them correspond directly to BSD Unix sockets calls, which are detailed in Chapter 35.

Registers at call:	Return Registers:
AX = 112Eh or DE2Eh	CX = size of socket record in bytes
DX:BX -> socket record	DX:BX -> socket record which was used

SOCKET API Function 0000h
INITIALIZE SOCKET

See also: Socket Functions 000Ah, 001Dh, and FFFFh

17-6 Format of socket record for socket initialization:

Offset	Size	Description
00h	WORD	signature F0ADh
02h	WORD	0000h (function number)
04h	WORD	returned error code (see Table 17-3)
06h	WORD	*maximum message size* (usually 0400h)
08h	WORD	PSP segment to use or 0000h if socket not valid
0Ah	WORD	scratch space (JFT size)
0Ch	DWORD	scratch space (JFT address)
10h	DWORD	mailbox handle (initialized by this function)
14h	DWORD	timer object handle (initialized by this function)
18h	WORD	(return) *unknown*

SOCKET API Function 0001h
"gethostname" - GET NAME OF HOST ON WHICH PROGRAM IS RUNNING

See also: Socket Functions 000Ch and 0015h

17-7 Format of socket record for "gethostname":

Offset	Size	Description
00h	WORD	signature F0ADh
02h	WORD	0001h (function number)
04h	WORD	returned error code (see Table 17-3)
06h	WORD	*maximum message size* (usually 0400h)
08h	WORD	PSP segment to use or 0000h if socket not valid
0Ah	WORD	scratch space (JFT size)
0Ch	DWORD	scratch space (JFT address)
10h	DWORD	mailbox handle (initialized by function 0000h)
14h	DWORD	timer object handle (initialized by function 0000h)
18h	WORD	(return) *status*
1Ah	128 BYTEs	(return) ASCIZ hostname (empty string if not on network)
9Ah	WORD	maximum length of hostname to return

SOCKET API Function 0002h
IOCTL - CHECK FOR INPUT/SET BLOCKING STATE

DESQview/X
Undocumented

Purpose: Determine whether input is available for the given socket, or specify whether calls to read from the socket should block if no input is available.

17-8 Format of socket record for Function 0002h:

Offset	Size	Description
00h	WORD	signature F0ADh
02h	WORD	0002h (function number)
04h	WORD	returned error code (see Table 17-3)
06h	WORD	*maximum message size* (usually 0400h)
08h	WORD	PSP segment to use or 0000h if socket not valid
0Ah	WORD	scratch space (JFT size)
0Ch	DWORD	scratch space (JFT address)
10h	DWORD	mailbox handle (initialized by function 0000h)
14h	DWORD	timer object handle (initialized by function 0000h)
18h	WORD	(return) status
1Ah	WORD	socket's file handle
1Ch	WORD	IOCTL function
		05h "FIONREAD" determine available input
		06h "FIONBIO" set blocking state of socket
1Eh	WORD	(return, subfunction 05h) number of bytes available for reading
		(call, subfunction 06h) 0000h blocking, nonzero nonblocking

SOCKET API Function 0003h
"sleep" - DELAY EXECUTION FOR SPECIFIED PERIOD

DESQview/X
Undocumented

17-9 Format of socket record for "sleep":

Offset	Size	Description
00h	WORD	signature F0ADh
02h	WORD	0003h (function number, see Table 17-1)
04h	WORD	returned error code (see Table 17-3)
06h	WORD	*maximum message size* (usually 0400h)
08h	WORD	PSP segment to use or 0000h if socket not valid
0Ah	WORD	scratch space (JFT size)
0Ch	DWORD	scratch space (JFT address)

Offset	Size	Description
10h	DWORD	mailbox handle (initialized by function 0000h)
14h	DWORD	timer object handle (initialized by function 0000h)
18h	2 BYTEs	unused
1Ah	WORD	delay time in seconds

SOCKET API Function 0004h   *DESQview/X*
"htons" - CONVERT WORD TO NETWORK (BIG-ENDIAN) BYTE ORDER   *Undocumented*

17-10 Format of socket record for "htons":

Offset	Size	Description
00h	WORD	signature F0ADh
02h	WORD	0004h (function number)
04h	WORD	returned error code (see Table 17-3)
06h	WORD	*maximum message size* (usually 0400h)
08h	WORD	PSP segment to use or 0000h if socket not valid
0Ah	WORD	scratch space (JFT size)
0Ch	DWORD	scratch space (JFT address)
10h	DWORD	mailbox handle (initialized by function 0000h)
14h	DWORD	timer object handle (initialized by function 0000h)
18h	WORD	(return) result in network (big-endian) byte order
1Ah	WORD	value to convert to network byte order

SOCKET API Function 0005h   *DESQview/X*
"select" - DETERMINE WHICH SOCKETS HAVE ACTIVITY   *Undocumented*

17-11 Format of socket record for "select":

Offset	Size	Description
00h	WORD	signature F0ADh
02h	WORD	0005h (function number)
04h	WORD	returned error code (see Table 17-3)
06h	WORD	*maximum message size* (usually 0400h)
08h	WORD	PSP segment to use or 0000h if socket not valid
0Ah	WORD	scratch space (JFT size)
0Ch	DWORD	scratch space (JFT address)
10h	DWORD	mailbox handle (initialized by function 0000h)
14h	DWORD	timer object handle (initialized by function 0000h)
18h	WORD	(return) *number of handles meeting the specified conditions*
1Ah	WORD	*number of file handles in each bitset*
1Ch	DWORD	*bitset of socket handles to check for readability*
20h	DWORD	*bitset of socket handles to check for writability*
24h	DWORD	*bitset of socket handles to check for errors*
28h	WORD	timeout in *unknown units* or 0000h to block until some socket is ready
2Ah	DWORD	*unknown*
2Eh	DWORD	*unknown*

SOCKET API Function 0006h   *DESQview/X*
"bsd_close"/"so_close" - CLOSE SOCKET   *Undocumented*
See also: Socket Functions 0008h, 000Ah, and 0013h

17-12 Format of socket record for "bsd_close":

Offset	Size	Description
00h	WORD	signature F0ADh

02h	WORD	0006h (function number, see Table 17-1)
04h	WORD	returned error code (see Table 17-3)
06h	WORD	*maximum message size* (usually 0400h)
08h	WORD	PSP segment to use or 0000h if socket not valid
0Ah	WORD	scratch space (JFT size)
0Ch	DWORD	scratch space (JFT address)
10h	DWORD	mailbox handle (initialized by function 0000h)
14h	DWORD	timer object handle (initialized by function 0000h)
18h	WORD	(return) status: 0000h if successful, FFFFh on error
1Ah	WORD	socket's file handle

SOCKET API Function 0008h
"connect" - INITIATE CONNECTION ON SOCKET

DESQview/X
Undocumented

See also: Socket Functions 0006h, 000Ah, and 0013h

17-13 Format of socket record for "connect":

Offset	Size	Description
00h	WORD	signature F0ADh
02h	WORD	0008h (function number)
04h	WORD	returned error code (see Table 17-3)
06h	WORD	*maximum message size* (usually 0400h)
08h	WORD	PSP segment to use or 0000h if socket not valid
0Ah	WORD	scratch space (JFT size)
0Ch	DWORD	scratch space (JFT address)
10h	DWORD	mailbox handle (initialized by function 0000h)
14h	DWORD	timer object handle (initialized by function 0000h)
18h	WORD	(return) status: 0000h if successful, FFFFh on error
1Ah	WORD	socket's file handle
1Ch	WORD	0001h if socket name specified, 0000h if not
1Eh	WORD	length of socket name
20h	N BYTEs	name of socket to which to connect

SOCKET API Function 0009h
"recv"/"recvfrom" - READ FROM SOCKET

DESQview/X
Undocumented

See also: Socket Functions 0002h, 000Dh, and 0012h

17-14 Format of socket record for "recv"/"recvfrom":

Offset	Size	Description
00h	WORD	signature F0ADh
02h	WORD	0009h (function number)
04h	WORD	returned error code (see Table 17-3)
06h	WORD	*maximum message size* (usually 0400h)
08h	WORD	PSP segment to use or 0000h if socket not valid
0Ah	WORD	scratch space (JFT size)
0Ch	DWORD	scratch space (JFT address)
10h	DWORD	mailbox handle (initialized by function 0000h)
14h	DWORD	timer object handle (initialized by function 0000h)
18h	WORD	(return) number of bytes actually read, 0000h if connection closed, or FFFFh on error
1Ah	WORD	socket's file handle
1Ch	WORD	number of bytes to read

1Eh	WORD	flags
20h	WORD	0000h if no source address desired
		0001h if source address is to be stored (datagram sockets)
22h	WORD	length of source address
24h	110 BYTEs	source address
92h	1K BYTEs	buffer for data to be read

SOCKET API Function 000Ah
"socket" - CREATE NEW SOCKET

DESQview/X
Undocumented

See also: Socket Functions 0000h, 0006h, 0008h, and 0012h

17-15 Format of socket record for "socket":

Offset	Size	Description
00h	WORD	signature F0ADh
02h	WORD	000Ah (function number, see Table 17-1)
04h	WORD	returned error code (see Table 17-3)
06h	WORD	*maximum message size* (usually 0400h)
08h	WORD	PSP segment to use or 0000h if socket not valid
0Ah	WORD	scratch space (JFT size)
0Ch	DWORD	scratch space (JFT address)
10h	DWORD	mailbox handle (initialized by function 0000h)
14h	DWORD	timer object handle (initialized by function 0000h)
18h	WORD	(return) socket's file handle or FFFFh on error
1Ah	WORD	address family (0001h,0002h)
1Ch	WORD	socket type
1Eh	WORD	protocol

SOCKET API Function 000Bh
UNDETERMINED FUNCTION

DESQview/X
Undocumented

17-16 Format of socket record for Function 000Bh:

Offset	Size	Description
00h	24 BYTEs	common header (see Table 17-2)
18h	WORD	(return) 0001h if *unknown* or FFFFh on error
1Ah	WORD	socket's file handle
1Eh	WORD	(call) *unknown*

SOCKET API Function 000Ch
"gethostbyname" - GET INFORMATION ABOUT SPECIFIED MACHINE

DESQview/X
Undocumented

See also: Socket Functions 0001h, 0016h, and 0018h

17-17 Format of socket record for "gethostbyname":

Offset	Size	Description
00h	WORD	signature F0ADh
02h	WORD	000Ch (function number)
04h	WORD	returned error code (see Table 17-3)
06h	WORD	*maximum message size* (usually 0400h)
08h	WORD	PSP segment to use or 0000h if socket not valid
0Ah	WORD	scratch space (JFT size)
0Ch	DWORD	scratch space (JFT address)
10h	DWORD	mailbox handle (initialized by function 0000h)
14h	DWORD	timer object handle (initialized by function 0000h)

18h	128 BYTEs	buffer containing ASCIZ hostname
		special case if empty string or "unix"
98h	?	*'struct hostent'*
A2h	?	(return) *unknown*

SOCKET API Function 000Dh
"send"/"sendto" - WRITE DATA TO SOCKET

DESQview/X
Undocumented

See also: Socket Functions 0008h, 0009h, 0013h

17-18 Format of socket record for "send"/"sendto":

Offset	Size	Description
00h	WORD	signature F0ADh
02h	WORD	000Dh (function number, see Table 17-1)
04h	WORD	returned error code (see Table 17-3)
06h	WORD	*maximum message size* (usually 0400h)
08h	WORD	PSP segment to use or 0000h if socket not valid
0Ah	WORD	scratch space (JFT size)
0Ch	DWORD	scratch space (JFT address)
10h	DWORD	mailbox handle (initialized by function 0000h)
14h	DWORD	timer object handle (initialized by function 0000h)
18h	WORD	(return) number of bytes actually written or FFFFh on error
1Ah	WORD	socket's file handle
1Ch	WORD	number of bytes to write
1Eh	WORD	*number of bytes to follow in subsequent writes*
20h	WORD	flags
22h	WORD	0000h if no destination specified, 0001h if destination is present
24h	WORD	*unknown*
26h	WORD	length of destination address
28h	110 BYTEs	destination address
96h	1K BYTEs	buffer containing data to be written

SOCKET API Function 000Eh
UNDETERMINED FUNCTION

DESQview/X
Undocumented

17-19 Format of socket record for Function 000Eh:

Offset	Size	Description
00h	24 BYTEs	common header (see Table 17-2)

SOCKET API Function 000Fh
"getpid" - GET PROCESS IDENTIFIER

DESQview/X
Undocumented

17-20 Format of socket record for "getpid":

Offset	Size	Description
00h	WORD	signature F0ADh
02h	WORD	000Fh (function number)
04h	WORD	returned error code (see Table 17-3)
06h	WORD	*maximum message size* (usually 0400h)
08h	WORD	PSP segment to use or 0000h if socket not valid
0Ah	WORD	scratch space (JFT size)
0Ch	DWORD	scratch space (JFT address)
10h	DWORD	mailbox handle (initialized by function 0000h)
14h	DWORD	timer object handle (initialized by function 0000h)
18h	DWORD	(return) DESQview task handle of calling process

SOCKET API Function 0010h
"gettimeofday"

17-21 Format of socket record for "gettimeofday":

Offset	Size	Description
00h	WORD	signature F0ADh
02h	WORD	0010h (function number, see Table 17-1)
04h	WORD	returned error code (see Table 17-3)
06h	WORD	*maximum message size* (usually 0400h)
08h	WORD	PSP segment to use or 0000h if socket not valid
0Ah	WORD	scratch space (JFT size)
0Ch	DWORD	scratch space (JFT address)
10h	DWORD	mailbox handle (initialized by function 0000h)
14h	DWORD	timer object handle (initialized by function 0000h)
18h	DWORD	(return) current time
1Ch	DWORD	(return) *unknown*

SOCKET API Function 0011h
"bind" - ASSIGN NAME TO SOCKET

See also: Socket Functions 0008h, 000Ah, 0012h, and 001Ah

17-22 Format of socket record for "bind":

Offset	Size	Description
00h	24 BYTEs	common header (see Table 17-1)
18h	WORD	(return) status: 0000h if successful, FFFFh on error
1Ah	WORD	socket's file handle
1Ch	WORD	length of name
1Eh	N BYTEs	buffer for socket name

SOCKET API Function 0012h
"listen" - AWAIT INCOMING CONNECTIONS

See also: Socket Functions 0008h, 000Ah, and 0013h

17-23 Format of socket record for "listen":

Offset	Size	Description
00h	WORD	signature F0ADh
02h	WORD	0012h (function number)
04h	WORD	returned error code (see Table 17-3)
06h	WORD	*maximum message size* (usually 0400h)
08h	WORD	PSP segment to use or 0000h if socket not valid
0Ah	WORD	scratch space (JFT size)
0Ch	DWORD	scratch space (JFT address)
10h	DWORD	mailbox handle (initialized by function 0000h)
14h	DWORD	timer object handle (initialized by function 0000h)
18h	WORD	(return) status: 0000h if successful, FFFFh on error
1Ah	WORD	socket's file handle
1Ch	WORD	maximum backlog of pending connections allowed on socket

SOCKET API Function 0013h
"accept" - ACCEPT CONNECTION ON SOCKET

See also: Socket Functions 0006h, 0008h, 000Ah, and 0012h

17-24 Format of socket record for "accept":

Offset	Size	Description
00h	24 BYTEs	common header (see Table 17-2)
18h	WORD	(return) file handle for new connection or FFFFh on error
1Ah	WORD	listen()ing socket's file handle
1Ch	WORD	(call) length of buffer for connecting entity's address
		(return) actual length of address
1Eh	N BYTEs	buffer for connecting entity's address

SOCKET API Function 0014h
CONNECT TO X SERVER

DESQview/X
Undocumented

See also: Socket Function 0008h

17-25 Format of socket record for Function 0014h:

Offset	Size	Description
00h	WORD	signature F0ADh
02h	WORD	0014h (function number)
04h	WORD	returned error code (see Table 17-3)
06h	WORD	*maximum message size* (usually 0400h)
08h	WORD	PSP segment to use or 0000h if socket not valid
0Ah	WORD	scratch space (JFT size)
0Ch	DWORD	scratch space (JFT address)
10h	DWORD	mailbox handle (initialized by function 0000h)
14h	DWORD	timer object handle (initialized by function 0000h)
18h	WORD	(return) socket's file handle or FFFFh on error
1Ah	4 BYTEs	(return) *unknown*
1Eh	WORD	(return) *unknown*
20h	WORD	(return) *unknown*
22h	256 BYTEs	ASCIZ X display name
122h	*unknown*	

SOCKET API Function 0015h
"gethostbyaddr" - GET HOST INFORMATION FOR SPECIFIED ADDRESS

DESQview/X
Undocumented

See also: Socket Functions 0001h, 0016h, 0018h, and 001Bh

17-26 Format of socket record for "gethostbyaddr":

Offset	Size	Description
00h	WORD	signature F0ADh
02h	WORD	0015h (function number, see Table 17-1)
04h	WORD	returned error code (see Table 17-3)
06h	WORD	*maximum message size* (usually 0400h)
08h	WORD	PSP segment to use or 0000h if socket not valid
0Ah	WORD	scratch space (JFT size)
0Ch	DWORD	scratch space (JFT address)
10h	DWORD	mailbox handle (initialized by function 0000h)
14h	DWORD	timer object handle (initialized by function 0000h)
18h	WORD	(call) *type of address* (test for 0001h seen)
1Ah	WORD	(call) length of buffer for host address
1Ch	110 BYTEs	buffer containing host address
8Ah	WORD	(return) offset of *official host name*
8Ch	WORD	(return) offset of *alias list*

8Eh	WORD	(return) *address type*
90h	WORD	(return) *length of an address in bytes*
92h	WORD	(return) *offset of address*
9Ah	N BYTES	(return) buffer for hostname, alias list, and host address

---

SOCKET API Function 0016h   *DESQview/X*
"getprotobyname" - GET INFORMATION ABOUT NETWORK PROTOCOL *Undocumented*
See also: Socket Functions 0017h and 0018h

17-27 Format of socket record for "getprotobyname":

Offset	Size	Description
00h	24 BYTES	common header (see Table 17-2)
18h	?	*buffer for protocol name*
98h	*unknown*	

SOCKET API Function 0017h   *DESQview/X*
"getprotobynumber" - GET INFORMATION ABOUT NETWORK PROTOCOL *Undocumented*
See also: Socket Functions 0016h and 0019h

17-28 Format of socket record for "getprotobynumber":

Offset	Size	Description
00h	WORD	signature F0ADh
02h	WORD	0017h (function number)
04h	WORD	returned error code (see Table 17-3)
06h	WORD	*maximum message size* (usually 0400h)
08h	WORD	PSP segment to use or 0000h if socket not valid
0Ah	WORD	scratch space (JFT size)
0Ch	DWORD	scratch space (JFT address)
10h	DWORD	mailbox handle (initialized by function 0000h)
14h	DWORD	timer object handle (initialized by function 0000h)
18h	WORD	(call) *protocol number*
1Ah	WORD	(return) *unknown* or 0001h

SOCKET API Function 0018h   *DESQview/X*
"getservbyname" - GET INFORMATION ABOUT A SERVICE   *Undocumented*
See also: Socket Functions 0016h and 0019h

17-29 Format of socket record for "getservbyname":

Offset	Size	Description
00h	24 BYTES	common header (see Table 17-2)
18h	128 BYTES	buffer containing *unknown data*
98h	128 BYTES	buffer containing *unknown data*
118h	WORD	(return) *unknown*

SOCKET API Function 0019h   *DESQview/X*
"getservbyport" - GET INFORMATION ABOUT A SERVICE   *Undocumented*

17-30 Format of socket record for "getservbyport":

Offset	Size	Description
00h	WORD	signature F0ADh
02h	WORD	0019h (function number)
04h	WORD	returned error code (see Table 17-3)
06h	WORD	*maximum message size* (usually 0400h)

08h	WORD	PSP segment to use or 0000h if socket not valid
0Ah	WORD	scratch space (JFT size)
0Ch	DWORD	scratch space (JFT address)
10h	DWORD	mailbox handle (initialized by function 0000h)
14h	DWORD	timer object handle (initialized by function 0000h)
18h	WORD	*length of name*
1Ah	128 BYTEs	*buffer for name*
9Ah	WORD	(return) *unknown*

SOCKET API Function 001Ah
"getsockname" - DETERMINE NAME BOUND TO SOCKET

See also: Socket Functions 000Ah and 0011h

DESQview/X
Undocumented

17-31 Format of socket record for "getsockname":

Offset	Size	Description
00h	WORD	signature F0ADh
02h	WORD	001Ah (function number)
04h	WORD	returned error code (see Table 17-3)
06h	WORD	*maximum message size* (usually 0400h)
08h	WORD	PSP segment to use or 0000h if socket not valid
0Ah	WORD	scratch space (JFT size)
0Ch	DWORD	scratch space (JFT address)
10h	DWORD	mailbox handle (initialized by function 0000h)
14h	DWORD	timer object handle (initialized by function 0000h)
18h	WORD	(return) 0000h if successful, FFFFh on error
1Ah	WORD	socket's file handle
1Ch	WORD	(call) length of buffer for socket name
		(return) actual length of socket name
1Eh	N BYTEs	buffer for socket name

SOCKET API Function 001Bh
"getpeername" - GET NAME OF CONNECTED PEER

See also: Socket Functions 0008h and 0013h

DESQview/X
Undocumented

17-32 Format of socket record for "getpeername":

Offset	Size	Description
00h	24 BYTEs	common header (see Table 17-2)
18h	WORD	(return) status: 0000h if successful, FFFFh on error
1Ah	WORD	socket's file handle
1Ch	WORD	(call) size of buffer for name
		(return) actual size of name
1Eh	N BYTEs	buffer for peer's name

SOCKET API Function 001Ch
"getsockopt"/"setsockopt" - GET/SET SOCKET OPTIONS

See also: Socket Function 000Ah

DESQview/X
Undocumented

17-33 Format of socket record for "getsockopt"/"setsockopt":

Offset	Size	Description
00h	WORD	signature F0ADh
02h	WORD	001Ch (function number)
04h	WORD	returned error code (see Table 17-3)

06h	WORD	*maximum message size* (usually 0400h)
08h	WORD	PSP segment to use or 0000h if socket not valid
0Ah	WORD	scratch space (JFT size)
0Ch	DWORD	scratch space (JFT address)
10h	DWORD	mailbox handle (initialized by function 0000h)
14h	DWORD	timer object handle (initialized by function 0000h)
18h	WORD	(return) status: 0000h if successful, FFFFh on error
1Ah	WORD	direction: 0000h to get, 0001h to set
1Ch	WORD	socket's file handle
1Eh	WORD	option level
20h	WORD	option name
22h	WORD	(call) length of buffer for option value
		(return) actual length of option value
24h	N BYTEs	buffer for option value

SOCKET API Function 001Dh
"so_exit" - CLOSE ALL SOCKETS FOR CALLING PROCESS

DESQview/X
Undocumented

See also: Socket Functions 0006h, 0008h, 000Ah, and 0012h

17-34 Format of socket record for "so_exit":

Offset	Size	Description
00h	WORD	signature F0ADh
02h	WORD	001Dh (function number)
04h	WORD	returned error code (see Table 17-3)
06h	WORD	*maximum message size* (usually 0400h)
08h	WORD	PSP segment to use or 0000h if socket not valid
0Ah	WORD	scratch space (JFT size)
0Ch	DWORD	scratch space (JFT address)
10h	DWORD	mailbox handle (initialized by function 0000h)
14h	DWORD	timer object handle (initialized by function 0000h)

SOCKET API Function 001Eh
"issock" - DETERMINE WHETHER FILE HANDLE REFERENCES SOCKET

DESQview/X
Undocumented

See also: Socket Function 000Ah

17-35 Format of socket record for "issock":

Offset	Size	Description
00h	24 BYTEs	common header (see Table 17-2)
18h	WORD	(return) status: *0000h or 0001h*
1Ah	WORD	file handle which may or may not be a socket

SOCKET API Function 001Fh
"so_attach" - REATTACH PREVIOUSLY DETACHED SOCKET

DESQview/X
Undocumented

See also: Socket Functions 0008h, 0013h, and 0020h

17-36 Format of socket record for "so_attach":

Offset	Size	Description
00h	24 BYTEs	common header (see Table 17-2)
18h	WORD	(return) file handle or FFFFh on error
1Ah	DWORD	(call) pointer to Socket Context Record (see Table 17-4) of a previously detached socket

SOCKET API Function 0020h
"so_detach" - TEMPORARILY DETACH SOCKET

DESQview/X
Undocumented

See also: Socket Functions 0008h, 0013h, and 001Fh

17-37 Format of socket record for "so_detach":

Offset	Size	Description
00h	WORD	signature F0ADh
02h	WORD	0020h (function number)
04h	WORD	returned error code (see Table 17-3)
06h	WORD	*maximum message size* (usually 0400h)
08h	WORD	PSP segment to use or 0000h if socket not valid
0Ah	WORD	scratch space (JFT size)
0Ch	DWORD	scratch space (JFT address)
10h	DWORD	mailbox handle (initialized by function 0000h)
14h	DWORD	timer object handle (initialized by function 0000h)
18h	WORD	(return) status: 0000h if successful or FFFFh on error
1Ah	WORD	socket's file handle
1Ch	DWORD	(return) pointer to Socket Context Record (see Table 17-4) for the file handle

SOCKET API Function 0021h
GET DESQview DIRECTORY

DESQview/X
Undocumented

17-38 Format of socket record for Function 0021h:

Offset	Size	Description
00h	24 BYTEs	common header (see Table 17-2)
18h	64 BYTEs	buffer for DESQview startup directory (see Function DE25h in PCI-44)

SOCKET API Function 0022h
"NewProc" - START NEW APPLICATION

DESQview/X
Undocumented

17-39 Format of socket record for "NewProc":

Offset	Size	Description
00h	24 BYTEs	common header (see Table 17-2)
18h	DWORD	(return) task handle of new application
1Ch	WORD	size of .DVP data
1Eh	129 BYTEs	*unknown ASCIZ data*
9Fh	N BYTEs	.DVP data (see Function 102Ch in PCI-44)

SOCKET API Function 0023h
"so_linkup"

DESQview/X
Undocumented

See also: Socket Function 0027h

17-40 Format of socket record for "so_linkup":

Offset	Size	Description
00h	WORD	signature F0ADh
02h	WORD	0023h (function number, see Table 17-1)
04h	WORD	returned error code (see Table 17-3)
06h	WORD	*maximum message size* (usually 0400h)
08h	WORD	PSP segment to use or 0000h if socket not valid
0Ah	WORD	scratch space (JFT size)
0Ch	DWORD	scratch space (JFT address)
10h	DWORD	mailbox handle (initialized by function 0000h)
14h	DWORD	timer object handle (initialized by function 0000h)

Offset	Size	Description
18h	WORD	(return) *unknown* or FFFFh on error
1Ah	WORD	*socket's file handle*

SOCKET API Function 0024h
CANONICALIZE FILENAME

17-41 Format of socket record for Function 0024h:

Offset	Size	Description
00h	24 BYTEs	common header (see Table 17-2)
18h	WORd	(return) DOS error code (see Table 3-1) 0000h if successful
1Ah	129 BYTEs	ASCIZ filename/pathname
11Bh	129 BYTEs	ASCIZ canonicalized filename/pathname (see INT 21h Function 60h in Chapter 3)

SOCKET API Function 0025h
INDIRECT INT 15h CALL

17-42 Format of socket record for Function 0025h:

Offset	Size	Description
00h	24 BYTEs	common header (see Table 17-2)
18h	WORD	value of AX
1Ah	WORD	value of BX
1Ch	WORD	(call) value of CX for call if AH value other than 12h (call) number of stack parameters if AH value is 12h (return) returned CX for calls other than INT 15h Function 12h
1Eh	WORD	value of DX
20h	WORD	value of DI
22h	WORD	value of SI
24h	WORD	value of DS
26h	WORD	value of ES
28h	WORD	(return) value of FLAGS after call
2Ah	N DWORDs	(call) stack parameters for INT 15h Function 12h call (return) stack results from INT 15h Function 12h call

SOCKET API Function 0026h
Network Manager Interface

17-43 Format of socket record for Function 0026h:

Offset	Size	Description
00h	WORD	signature F0ADh
02h	WORD	0026h (function number, see Table 17-1)
04h	WORD	returned error code (see Table 17-3)
06h	WORD	*maximum message size* (usually 0400h)
08h	WORD	PSP segment to use or 0000h if socket not valid
0Ah	WORD	scratch space (JFT size)
0Ch	DWORD	scratch space (JFT address)
10h	DWORD	mailbox handle (initialized by function 0000h)
14h	DWORD	timer object handle (initialized by function 0000h)
18h	WORD	(call) Network Manager subfunction (see Table 17-44) (return) *status*
1Ah	WORD	(call) size of parameter data

		(return) size of returned data
1Ch N	BYTEs	(call) parameter data required by call (see Table 17-45 to 17-59)
		(return) result data (see Tables 17-55 to 17-59)

17-44 Values for Network Manager subfunction:

0004h	*"so_exit"*
0005h	"gethostbyname"
0006h	"gethostname"
0009h	"socket"
000Dh	"gethostbyaddr"
000Fh	"getprotobyname"
0010h	get protocol name for protocol number
0011h	"getservbyname"
0012h	"getservbyport"
0013h	*"getsockname"*
0016h	*unknown*
0017h	kill Network Manager
0018h	*"getpeername"*
0019h	*unknown* (called by socket function 0000h)
001Ah	*unknown*
001Bh	"so_linkup"
001Dh	get network services
001Fh	"getpwuid"
0020h	"getpwnam"
0021h	"getpwvar"
0022h	"crypt"
0023h	"so_unlink"
0024h	"getlogin"
0028h	"sethostent"
0029h	"gethostent"
002Ah	"soaddhost"
002Bh	"soupdatehost"
002Ch	"sodeletehost"
002Dh	"setservent"
002Eh	"getservent"
002Fh	"setpwent"
0030h	"getpwent"
0031h	*unknown*
0032h	*unknown*
0033h	*unknown*
0034h	get IP network number
0035h	*unknown* (pops up Network Manager window)
0037h	*unknown*
0038h	get machine name and IP address
0039h	*unknown*

17-45 Format of Subfunction 000Fh ("getprotobyname") data:

Offset	Size	Description
00h	8 BYTEs	(return) *unknown*

17-46 Format of Subfunction 0010h ("getprotobynumber") data:

Offset	Size	Description
00h	2 BYTEs	(return) *unknown*
02h	WORD	(return) protocol number
04h	WORD	(call) protocol number for which to get name
06h	WORD	(return) *unknown*
08h	var	(return) ASCIZ protocol name
N	var	(return) ASCIZ protocol name

17-47 Format of Subfunction 0011h ("getservbyname") data:

Offset	Size	Description
00h	8 BYTEs	*unknown*
08h	var	(return) ASCIZ protocol name
	var	(return) *unknown* ASCIZ name
	var	(return) *unknown* ASCIZ name

17-48 Format of Subfunction 0012h ("getservbyport") data:

Offset	Size	Description
00h	8 BYTEs	(return) *unknown*

17-49 Format of Subfunction 0013h ("getsockname") data:

Offset	Size	Description
00h	116 BYTEs	(return) *unknown*

17-50 Format of Subfunction 0016h data:

Offset	Size	Description
00h	4 BYTEs	(return) *unknown*

17-51 Format of Subfunction 0018h ("getpeername") data:

Offset	Size	Description
00h	116 BYTEs	(return) *unknown*

17-52 Format of Subfunction 0019h data:

Offset	Size	Description
00h	4 BYTEs	(return) *unknown*
04h	DWORD	(return) *unknown task handle*

17-53 Format of Subfunction 001Ah data:

Offset	Size	Description
00h	38 BYTEs	(return) *unknown*

17-54 Format of Subfunction 001Bh ("so_linkup") data:

Offset	Size	Description
00h	10 BYTEs	(return) *unknown*

17-55 Format of Subfunction 001Dh return data [array]:

Offset	Size	Description
00h	WORD	*unknown* or FFFFh if end of array
02h	7 BYTEs	*unknown*
09h	27 BYTEs	ASCIZ name of service

17-56 Format of Subfunction 0024h ("getlogin") return data:

Offset	Size	Description
00h	var	ASCIZ username

17-57 Format of Subfunction 0030h ("getpwent") data:

Offset	Size	Description
00h	WORD	(call) UID or 0000h for current user
		(return) *unknown*
02h	WORD	(return) UID
04h	6 BYTEs	(return) *unknown*
0Ah	var	(return) ASCIZ username
	var	(return) ASCIZ encrypted password
	var	(return) ASCIZ initial ("home") directory

17-58 Format of Subfunction 0034h data:

Offset	Size	Description
00h	1-3 BYTEs	IP network number of caller's machine (low byte first)

17-59 Format of Subfunction 0038h return data:

Offset	Size	Description
00h	BYTE	*unknown*
01h	4 BYTEs	IP address
05h	var	ASCIZ machine name
	unknown	

SOCKET API Function 0027h
DESQview/X
Undocumented

"so_unlink" - CLOSE CONNECTION FROM "so_linkup"

See also: Socket Function 0023h

17-60 Format of socket record for Function 0027h:

Offset	Size	Description
00h	24 BYTEs	common header (see Table 17-2)
18h	WORD	(return) status: 0000h if successful, FFFFh on error
1Ah	WORD	socket's file handle

SOCKET API Functions 0028h and 0029h
DESQview/X
Undocumented

RAISE/LOWER PRIORITY

17-61 Format of socket record for Functions 0028h and 0029h:

Offset	Size	Description
00h	WORD	signature F0ADh
02h	WORD	function number
		0028h raise priority
		0029h lower priority
04h	WORD	returned error code (see Table 17-3)
06h	WORD	*maximum message size* (usually 0400h)
08h	WORD	PSP segment to use or 0000h if socket not valid
0Ah	WORD	scratch space (JFT size)
0Ch	DWORD	scratch space (JFT address)
10h	DWORD	mailbox handle (initialized by function 0000h)
14h	DWORD	timer object handle (initialized by function 0000h)
18h	WORD	(call) file handle for which to set priority low/high
		FFFFh to change calling task's priority

SOCKET API Function 002Ah
UNDETERMINED FUNCTION

17-62 Format of socket record for Function 002Ah:

Offset	Size	Description
00h	24 BYTEs	common header (see Table 17-2)

CHAPTER 18

DRIVEMAP

DRIVEMAP is a redirector included with Central Point Software's PC Tools version 8 which allows drives on computers connected over the parallel or serial ports to appear as local drives.

INT 16h Function FF70h   *PC Tools v8+ DRIVEMAP*
API   *Undocumented*

Registers at call: **Return Registers:**
AX = FF70h
BX = function (0000h-0002h)
    0000h installation check   AX = 0000h if installed
        CX = 4C69h ('Li')   CX = 4350h ('CP')
        DX = 6E6Bh ('nk')   DH = major version
                                DL = minor version

    0001h *unknown*   AX = *unknown*
        DL = *unknown*   DH = *unknown*

    0002h *unknown*   AX = *unknown* or FFFEh/FFFFh on error
        BX = *unknown*   DL = *unknown*
        DX = *unknown*

BUG: This call will branch to random locations for BX values other than those listed above for v8.0 because a) the incorrect register is range-tested, resulting in BX=0003h-5CD6h being accepted as valid function numbers, and b) the conditional which branches on invalid function numbers jumps to the following instruction, becoming a NOP.
Conflicts: OPTIMA Zoom TSR (PCI-9), KBUF (PCI-13)
See also: INT 2Fh Function 9203h

INT 2Fh Function 9200h   *PC Tools v8.0 DRIVEMAP*
BUG   *Undocumented*

Registers at call: **Return Registers:**
AX = 9200h   none
BUG: This call jumps to data because the jump table entry is 0000h.
Details: DRIVEMAP returns AX=FFFFh if AX does not contain a valid function number on entry.
Conflicts: Couriers LAN E-Mail (Chapter 41); see also Table 2-2

INT 2Fh Function 9201h
CHECK IF MAPPED DRIVE

PC Tools v8.0 DRIVEMAP
Undocumented

Registers at call:
AX = 9201h
DL = drive number (01h = A:, etc.)

Return Registers:
AL = 92h if mapped drive
AH may be destroyed (v8.0 DRIVEMAP
 returns AX=0000h if not mapped)

Conflicts: Couriers LAN E-Mail (Chapter 41); see also Table 2-2
See also: Functions 9204h and 920Bh

INT 2Fh Function 9202h
UNINSTALL

PC Tools v8.0 DRIVEMAP
Undocumented

Registers at call:
AX = 9202h
BX = caller's CS

Return Registers:
AX = status
 0000h failed
 nonzero successful

Conflicts: Couriers LAN E-Mail (Chapter 41); see also Table 2-2
See also: Function 9204h

INT 2Fh Function 9203h
GET VERSION

PC Tools v8.0 DRIVEMAP
Undocumented

Registers at call:
AX = 9203h

Return Registers:
AH = major version
AL = minor version
CX = segment of resident code

Details: The DRIVEMAP included with PC Tools v8.0 is version 1.00.
Conflicts: Couriers LAN E-Mail (Chapter 41); see also Table 2-2
See also: Function 9204h, INT 16h Function FF70h

INT 2Fh Function 9204h
INSTALLATION CHECK

PC Tools v8.0 DRIVEMAP
Undocumented

Registers at call:
AX = 9204h

Return Registers:
AX = 9200h if installed
 BL = *unknown*
 CX = segment of resident code

Conflicts: Couriers LAN E-Mail (Chapter 41); see also Table 2-2
See also: Functions 9201h, 9202h, and 9203h

INT 2Fh Function 9205h
SET UNKNOWN VALUE

PC Tools v8.0 DRIVEMAP
Undocumented

Registers at call:
AX = 9205h
BX = *unknown* to set

Return Registers:
CX = new value of *unknown*

Conflicts: Couriers LAN E-Mail (Chapter 41); see also Table 2-2

INT 2Fh Function 9206h
UNDETERMINED FUNCTION

PC Tools v8.0 DRIVEMAP
Undocumented

Registers at call:
AX = 9206h
others, if any, unknown

Return Registers:
unknown

Conflicts: Couriers LAN E-Mail (Chapter 41); see also Table 2-2

INT 2Fh Function 9207h   *PC Tools v8.0 DRIVEMAP*
GET UNKNOWN VALUE   *Undocumented*

Registers at call: Return Registers:
AX = 9207h   AX = *unknown*
others, if any, unknown
Conflicts: Couriers LAN E-Mail (Chapter 41); see also Table 2-2

INT 2Fh Function 9208h   *PC Tools v8.0 DRIVEMAP*
UNDETERMINED FUNCTION   *Undocumented*

Registers at call: Return Registers:
AX = 9208h   *unknown*
others, if any, unknown
Conflicts: Couriers LAN E-Mail (Chapter 41); see also Table 2-2

INT 2Fh Function 9209h   *PC Tools v8.0 DRIVEMAP*
UNDETERMINED FUNCTION   *Undocumented*

Registers at call: Return Registers:
AX = 9209h   AX = *unknown*
others, if any, unknown   BX = *unknown*
          CX = *unknown*
          DX = *unknown*
Conflicts: Couriers LAN E-Mail (Chapter 41); see also Table 2-2

INT 2Fh Function 920Ah   *PC Tools v8.0 DRIVEMAP*
UNDETERMINED FUNCTION   *Undocumented*

Registers at call: Return Registers:
AX = 920Ah   AX = *unknown* or FFFBh on error
BX = *unknown*
Conflicts: Couriers LAN E-Mail (Chapter 41); see also Table 2-2

INT 2Fh Function 920Bh   *PC Tools v8.0 DRIVEMAP*
SET DRIVE MAPPING   *Undocumented*

Registers at call: Return Registers:
AX = 920Bh   AX = *unknown* or FFF8h on error
BL = drive letter (41h ['A'] = A:, etc)
CX = *unknown* (0000h removes mapping)
Conflicts: Couriers LAN E-Mail (Chapter 41); see also Table 2-2
See also: Functions 9201h and 920Dh

INT 2Fh Function 920Ch   *PC Tools v8.0 DRIVEMAP*
UNDETERMINED FUNCTION   *Undocumented*

Registers at call: Return Registers:
AX = 920Ch   AX = *unknown* (0002h)
others, if any, unknown   CX = *unknown* (0000h)
Conflicts: Couriers LAN E-Mail (Chapter 41); see also Table 2-2

INT 2Fh Function 920Dh   *PC Tools v8.0 DRIVEMAP*
GET DRIVE TYPE   *Undocumented*

Registers at call: Return Registers:
AX = 920Dh   AX = type flags
BL = drive letter (41h ['A'] = A:, etc)   bit 0: *unknown*
          bit 1: available
          bit 5: local

BX = *unknown*
CX = segment of resident code
(apparently an unintended side effect)

Conflicts: Couriers LAN E-Mail (Chapter 41); see also Table 2-2
See also: Function 9218h, INT 16h Function FF70h

INT 2Fh Function 920Eh
SET LPT MAPPING

PC Tools v8.0 DRIVEMAP
Undocumented

Registers at call:
AX = 920Eh
BX = port number (0-2)
CX = *unknown* (0000h to unmap)

Return Registers:
unknown

Conflicts: Couriers LAN E-Mail (Chapter 41); see also Table 2-2

INT 2Fh Function 920Fh
GET UNKNOWN DATA

PC Tools v8.0 DRIVEMAP
Undocumented

Registers at call:
AX = 920Fh
ES:DI -> 3-byte buffer for *unknown*

Return Registers:
CX = 0000h
ES:DI buffer filled

Conflicts: Couriers LAN E-Mail (Chapter 41); see also Table 2-2

INT 2Fh Function 9210h
UNDETERMINED FUNCTION

PC Tools v8.0 DRIVEMAP
Undocumented

Registers at call:
AX = 9210h
others, if any, unknown

Return Registers:
unknown

Conflicts: Couriers LAN E-Mail (Chapter 41); see also Table 2-2

INT 2Fh Function 9211h
GET UNKNOWN DATA

PC Tools v8.0 DRIVEMAP
Undocumented

Registers at call:
AX = 9211h
ES:DI -> 8-word buffer for *unknown*

Return Registers:
CX = 0000h
ES:DI buffer filled

Conflicts: Couriers LAN E-Mail (Chapter 41); see also Table 2-2

INT 2Fh Function 9212h
CRITICAL SECTION

PC Tools v8.0 DRIVEMAP
Undocumented

Registers at call:
AX = 9212h
BX = phase
    0000h *leave critical section*
    nonzero *enter critical section*

Return Registers:
none

Conflicts: Couriers LAN E-Mail (Chapter 41); see also Table 2-2

INT 2Fh Function 9213h
UNDETERMINED FUNCTION

PC Tools v8.0 DRIVEMAP
Undocumented

Registers at call:
AX = 9213h
BX = function number (0000h-000Bh)
others, if any, unknown

Return Registers:
unknown

Conflicts: Couriers LAN E-Mail (Chapter 41); see also Table 2-2

INT 2Fh Function 9214h
GET UNKNOWN DATA
PC Tools v8.0 DRIVEMAP
Undocumented

Registers at call:
AX = 9214h
ES:DI -> 6-word buffer for *unknown*

Return Registers:
CX = 0000h
AX = *unknown*
ES:DI buffer filled

Conflicts: Couriers LAN E-Mail (Chapter 41); see also Table 2-2

INT 2Fh Function 9215h
GET UNKNOWN DATA
PC Tools v8.0 DRIVEMAP
Undocumented

Registers at call:
AX = 9215h
ES:DI -> 100-word buffer for *unknown*

Return Registers:
CX = 0000h
ES:DI buffer filled

Conflicts: Couriers LAN E-Mail (Chapter 41); see also Table 2-2

INT 2Fh Function 9216h
UNDETERMINED FUNCTION
PC Tools v8.0 DRIVEMAP
Undocumented

Registers at call:
AX = 9216h
ES:DI -> *unknown*

Return Registers:
unknown

Conflicts: Couriers LAN E-Mail (Chapter 41); see also Table 2-2

INT 2Fh Function 9217h
UNDETERMINED FUNCTION
PC Tools v8.0 DRIVEMAP
Undocumented

Registers at call:
AX = 9217h
DS:SI -> 25-word buffer containing
unknown

Return Registers:
unknown

Conflicts: Couriers LAN E-Mail (Chapter 41); see also Table 2-2

INT 2Fh Function 9218h
GET LPT TYPE
PC Tools v8.0 DRIVEMAP
Undocumented

Registers at call:
AX = 9218h
BX = *port number*

Return Registers:
AX = *unknown*
BX = *unknown* (0000h)
CX = *unknown* (0000h)

Conflicts: Couriers LAN E-Mail (Chapter 41); see also Table 2-2

INT 2Fh Function 9219h
UNDETERMINED FUNCTION
PC Tools v8.0 DRIVEMAP
Undocumented

Registers at call:
AX = 9219h
others, if any, unknown

Return Registers:
unknown

Conflicts: Couriers LAN E-Mail (Chapter 41); see also Table 2-2

INT 2Fh Function 921Ah
UNDETERMINED FUNCTION
PC Tools v8.0 DRIVEMAP
Undocumented

Registers at call:
AX = 921Ah
others, if any, unknown

Return Registers:
AH = *unknown*
AL = *unknown*
BX = *unknown*

Conflicts: Couriers LAN E-Mail (Chapter 41); see also Table 2-2

INT 2Fh Function 921Bh
UNDETERMINED FUNCTION

PC Tools v8.0 DRIVEMAP
Undocumented

Registers at call:
AX = 921Bh
others, if any, unknown

Return Registers:
AX = *unknown*
CX = segment of resident code (apparently an
unintended side effect)

Conflicts: Couriers LAN E-Mail (Chapter 41); see also Table 2-2

INT 2Fh Function 921Ch
UNDETERMINED FUNCTION

PC Tools v8.0 DRIVEMAP
Undocumented

Registers at call:
AX = 921Ch
others, if any, unknown

Return Registers:
unknown

Conflicts: Couriers LAN E-Mail (Chapter 41); see also Table 2-2

INT 2Fh Function 921Dh
GET UNKNOWN VALUE

PC Tools v8.0 DRIVEMAP
Undocumented

Registers at call:
AX = 921Dh

Return Registers:
AX = *unknown*

Conflicts: Couriers LAN E-Mail (Chapter 41); see also Table 2-2

INT 2Fh Function 921Eh
UNDETERMINED FUNCTION

PC Tools v8.0 DRIVEMAP
Undocumented

Registers at call:
AX = 921Eh
others, if any, unknown

Return Registers:
unknown

Details: This function sets two variables to 24h each.
Conflicts: Couriers LAN E-Mail (Chapter 41); see also Table 2-2
See also: INT 16h Function FF70h

CHAPTER 19

LAN Manager

Microsoft's LAN Manager is designed to support client-server programming, but also provides all of the facilities of standard PC networks. Its API provides a set of function calls (nearly 130 of them) to issue network requests. Almost any network task that can be done from the command line or by using LAN Manager's full-screen interface can also be done through in-line code via the API.

INT 21h Function 5F30h   *LAN Manager Enhanced DOS*
UNDETERMINED FUNCTION   *Undocumented*

Registers at call: **Return Registers:**
AX = 5F30h   *unknown*
others, if any, unknown

INT 21h Function 5F3Bh   *LAN Manager Enhanced DOS*
NetHandleSetInfo   *(partially doc.)*

Registers at call: **Return Registers:**
AX = 5F3Bh   CF clear if successful
BX = handle   CX = total bytes available
CX = handle_info_1 structure length   CF set if error
   or sizeof DWORD   AX = error code
DI = parameter number to set
    0000h all
    0001h number of milliseconds
    0002h number of characters
DS:DX -> handle_info_1 structure
  (DI=0000h) (see Table 19-1)
    or DWORD (DI=0001h or 0002h)
SI = level of information (0001h)
Conflicts: none known
See also: Function 5F3Ch

19-1 Format of handle_info_1 structure:

Offset	Size	Description
00h	DWORD	number of milliseconds which workstation collects data before it sends the data to the named pipe
04h	DWORD	number of characters which workstation collects before it sends the data to the named pipe

INT 21h Function 5F3Ch
NetHandleGetInfo

LAN Manager Enhanced DOS
(partially doc.)

Registers at call:
AX = 5F3Ch
BX = handle
CX = length of handle_info_1 structure
DS:DX -> handle_info_1 structure
  (see Table 19-1)
SI = level of information (must be 0001h)
Conflicts: none known
See also: Function 5F3Bh

Return Registers:
CF clear if successful
    CX = total bytes available
CF set if error
    AX = error code

INT 21h Function 5F3Dh
WRITE MAILSLOT

LAN Manager Enhanced DOS
Undocumented

Registers at call:
AX = 5F3Dh
others, if any, unknown
Conflicts: none known

Return Registers:
unknown

INT 21h Function 5F3Eh
LOCAL NetSpecialSMB

LAN Manager Enhanced DOS
(partially doc.)

Registers at call:
AX = 5F3Eh
others, if any, unknown
Details: This function is not documented anywhere in the LAN Manager 2.x Toolkit but was documented in LAN Manager 1.x manuals.
Conflicts: none known

Return Registers:
unknown

INT 21h Function 5F3Fh
REMOTE API CALL

LAN Manager Enhanced DOS
Undocumented

Registers at call:
AX = 5F3Fh
CX = api number
ES:DI -> data descriptor
ES:SI -> parameter descriptor
ES:DX -> auxiliary descriptor (if DX nonzero)
others, if any, unknown
Conflicts: none known

Return Registers:
unknown

INT 21h Function 5F40h
LOCAL NetMessageBufferSend

LAN Manager Enhanced DOS
(partially doc.)

Registers at call:
AX = 5F40h
DS:DX -> NetMessageBufferSend
  parameter structure (see Table 19-2)
Conflicts: none known

Return Registers:
AX = error code

19-2 Format of NetMessageBufferSend parameter structure:

Offset	Size	Description
00h	DWORD	pointer to recipient name (name for specific user, name* for domain name wide, * for broadcast)
04h	DWORD	pointer to buffer
08h	WORD	length of buffer

INT 21h Function 5F41h
LOCAL NetServiceEnum

Registers at call:
AX = 5F41h
BL = level of detail (0000h, 0001h or 0002h)
CX = buffer length
ES:DI -> buffer of service_info_0, service_info_1,
  or service_info_2 (see Tables 19-3 to 19-5)
Conflicts: none known

Return Registers:
CF clear if successful
    CX = entries read
    DX = total available
CF set on error
    AX = error code

19-3 Format of service_info_0 structure:

Offset	Size	Description
00h	16 BYTEs	name

19-4 Format of service_info_1 structure:

Offset	Size	Description
00h	16 BYTEs	name
10h	WORD	status bitmask (see Table 19-6)
12h	DWORD	status code (see Table 19-7)
		(also see *Microsoft LAN Manager Programmer's Reference*)
16h	WORD	process ID

19-5 Format of service_info_2 structure:

Offset	Size	Description
00h	16 BYTEs	name
10h	WORD	status bitmask (see Table 19-6)
12h	DWORD	status code (see Table 19-7)
16h	WORD	process ID
18h	64 BYTEs	text

19-6 Bitfields for status bitmask:

bits 0,1   00 uninstall
            01 install pending
            10 uninstall pending
            11 installed
bits 2,3   00 active
            01 Continue pending
            10 Pause pending
            11 paused
bit 4   uninstallable
bit 5   pausable
bit 8   disk redirector paused
bit 9   spooled device redirector paused (printing)
bit 10   communication device redirector paused

19-7 Values for status code:

high word
3051   Bad parameter value
3052   A parameter is missing
3053   An unknown parameter was specified
3054   The resource is insufficient
3055   Configuration is faulty

3056	An MS-DOS or MS OS/2 error occured
3057	An internal error occured
3058	An ambiguous parameter name was given
3059	A duplicate parameter exists
3060	The service was terminated by NetSeviceControl when it did not respond
3061	The service program file could not be executed
3062	The subservice failed to start
3063	There is a conflict in the value or use of these parameters
3064	There is a problem with the file

low word

3070	There is insufficient memory
3071	There is insufficeient disk space
3072	Unable to create thread
3073	Unable to create process
3074 .	A security failure occured
3075	There is bad or missing default path
3076	Network software is not installed
3077	Server software is not installed
3078	The server could not access the UAS database
3079	The action requires user-level security
3080	The log directory is invalid
3081	The LAN group specified could not be used
3082	The computername is being used as a message alias on another computer
3083	The workstation failed to announce the servername
3084	The user accounts system is not configured properly

INT 21h Function 5F42h
LOCAL NetServiceControl

LAN Manager Enhanced DOS
(partially doc.)

Registers at call:
AX = 5F42h
DH = opcode
    00h interrogate status
    01h pause
    02h continue
    03h uninstall
DL = argument
    01h disk resource
    02h print resource
    04h communications resource (not implemented for DOS)
ES:BX -> NetServiceControl parameter structure (see Table 19-8)
Conflicts: none known

Return Registers:
CF clear if successful
CF set on error
    AX = error code

19-8 Format of NetServiceControl parameter structure:

Offset	Size	Description
00h	DWORD	pointer to service name
04h	WORD	result buffer size
06h	DWORD	pointer to result buffer as service_info_2 structure

INT 21h Function 5F43h
LOCAL DosPrintJobGetId

LAN Manager Enhanced DOS
(partially doc.)

Registers at call:
AX = 5F43h
BX = handle of remote print job
CX = size of PRIDINFO struture
ES:DI -> PRIDINFO structure (see Table 19-9)
Conflicts: none known

Return Registers:
CF clear if successful
  PRIDINFO filled in
CF set on error
  AX = error code

19-9 Format of PRIDINFO structure:

Offset	Size	Description
00h	WORD	job id
02h	16 BYTEs	server name
12h	13 BYTEs	queue name
1Fh	1 BYTE	pad

INT 21h Function 5F44h
LOCAL NetWkstaGetInfo

LAN Manager Enhanced DOS
(partially doc.)

Registers at call:
AX = 5F44h
BX = information level (00h, 01h, or 0Ah)
CX = buffer size
ES:DI = buffer in which to store info
Conflicts: none known
See also: Functions 5F45h and 5F49h

Return Registers:
AX = error code
DX = amount of buffer used (or required)

INT 21h Function 5F45h
LOCAL NetWkstaSetInfo

LAN Manager Enhanced DOS
(partially doc.)

Registers at call:
AX = 5F45h
BX = level (0000h or 0001h)
CX = buffer size
DX = parameter to set
ES:DI -> buffer
Conflicts: none known
See also: Function 5F44h

Return Registers:
CF clear if successful
CF set if error
  AX = error code

INT 21h Function 5F46h
LOCAL NetUseEnum

LAN Manager Enhanced DOS
(partially doc.)

Registers at call:
AX = 5F46h
BX = level (0000h or 0001h)
CX = size of buffer
ES:DI -> buffer of use_info_0 or use_info_1 structures
  (see Tables 19-10 and 19-11)
Conflicts: none known
See also: Functions 5F47h, 5F48h, and 5F4Ch

Return Registers:
CF clear if successful
  CX = entries read
  DX = total available entries
CF set if error
  AX = error code

19-10 Format of use_info_0 structure:

Offset	Size	Description
00h	9 BYTEs	local device name
09h	BYTE	padding
0Ah	DWORD	pointer to remote device name in UNC form \\server\share

19-11 Format of use_info_1 structure:

Offset	Size	Description
00h	9 BYTEs	Local device name
09h	BYTE	padding
0Ah	DWORD	pointer to remote device name in UNC form \\server\share
0Eh	DWORD	pointer to password
12h	WORD	ignored
14h	WORD	use type (-1 wildcard, 0 disk, 1 print, 2 com, 3 ipc)
16h	WORD	ignored
18h	WORD	ignored

INT 21h Function 5F47h
LOCAL NetUseAdd

LAN Manager Enhanced DOS
(partially doc.)

Registers at call:
AX = 5F47h
BX = level (0001h)
CX = size of use_info_1 structure
ES:DI -> use_info_1 structure (see Table 19-11)
Conflicts: none known
See also: Functions 5F46h and 5F48h

Return Registers:
CF clear on success
CF set on error
   AX = error code

INT 21h Function 5F48h
LOCAL NetUseDel

LAN Manager Enhanced DOS
(partially doc.)

Registers at call:
AX = 5F48h
BX = force level
   0000h no force
   0001h force
   0002h lots of force
ES:DI -> buffer as either the local device name or UNC remote name
Conflicts: none known
See also: Functions 5F46h, 5F48h, and 5F49h

Return Registers:
CF clear on success
CF set on error
   AX = error code

INT 21h Function 5F49h
NetUseGetInfo

LAN Manager Enhanced DOS
(partially doc.)

Registers at call:
AX = 5F49h
DS:DX -> NetUseGetInfo parameter
  structure (see Table 19-12)

Conflicts: none known
See also: Functions 5F44h and 5F47h

Return Registers:
CF clear on success
   DX = total available
CF set on error
   AX = error code

19-12 Format of NetUseGetInfo parameter structure:

Offset	Size	Description
00h	DWORD	pointer to either the local device name or UNC remote name
04h	WORD	level of information (0000h or 0001h)
06h	DWORD	pointer to buffer of use_info_0 or use_info_1 structures
0Ah	WORD	length of buffer

INT 21h Function 5F4Ah
LOCAL NetRemoteCopy

LAN Manager Enhanced DOS
(partially doc.)

Registers at call:
AX = 5F4Ah
DS:DX -> NetRemoteCopy parameter
structure (see Table 19-13)
Conflicts: none known
See also: Function 5F4Bh

Return Registers:
CF clear if successful
CF set on error
    AX = error code

19-13 Format of NetRemoteCopy parameter structure:

Offset	Size	Description
00h	DWORD	pointer to source name as UNC
04h	DWORD	pointer to destination name as UNC
08h	DWORD	pointer to source password
0Ch	DWORD	pointer to destination password
10h	WORD	destination open bitmap
		if destination path exists
		0000h open fails
		0001h file is appended
		0002h file is overwritten
		if destination path doesn't exist
		0000h open fails
		0010h file is created
12h	WORD	copy control bitmap (see Table 19-14)
14h	DWORD	pointer to copy_info buffer
18h	WORD	length of copy_info buffer

19-14 Bitfields for copy control:

bit 0	destination must be a file
bit 1	destination must be a directory
bit 2	destination is opened in ascii mode instead of binary
bit 3	source is opened in ascii mode instead of binary
bit 4	verify all write operations

INT 21h Function 5F4Bh
LOCAL NetRemoteMove

LAN Manager Enhanced DOS
(partially doc.)

Registers at call:
AX = 5F4Bh
DS:DX -> NetRemoteMove parameter structure

Return Registers:
CF clear if successful
CF set on error
    AX = error code

Conflicts: none known
See also: Function 5F4Ah

19-15 Format of NetRemoteMove parameter structure:

Offset	Size	Description
00h	DWORD	pointer to source name as UNC
04h	DWORD	pointer to destination name as UNC
08h	DWORD	pointer to source password
0Ch	DWORD	pointer to destination password
10h	WORD	destination open bitmap
		if destination path exists

		0000h open fails
		0001h file is appended
		0002h file is overwritten
		if destination path doesn't exist
		0000h open fails
		0010h file is created
12h	WORD	move control bitmap
		0001h destination must be a file
		0002h destination must be a directory
14h	DWORD	pointer to move_info buffer
18h	WORD	length of move_info buffer

INT 21h Function 5F4Ch
LOCAL NetServerEnum

LAN Manager Enhanced DOS
(partially doc.)

Registers at call:
AX = 5F4Ch
BX = level (0000h or 0001h)
CX = buffer length
ES:DI -> buffer in which to store
  information

Return Registers:
CF clear if successful
  ES:DI -> server_info_X structures (depending
    on level) (see Tables 19-16 and 19-17)
  BX = entries read
  CX = total entries available
CF set on error
  AX = error code

Details: This function is also supported by the Novell DOS Named Pipe Extender. It has been obseleted by NetServerEnum2.
Conflicts: none known
See also: Function 5F53h

19-16 Format of server_info_0 structure:

Offset	Size	Description
00h	16 BYTEs	name

19-17 Format of server_info_1 structure:

Offset	Size	Description
00h	16 BYTEs	name
10h	BYTE	major version in lower nibble
11h	BYTE	minor version
12h	DWORD	server type bitmask (see Table 19-18)
16h	DWORD	pointer to comment string

19-18 Bitfields for server type:

bit 0	workstation
bit 1	server
bit 2	SQL server
bit 3	primary domain controller
bit 4	backup domain controller
bit 5	time server
bit 6	Apple File Protocol (AFP) server
bit 7	Novell server
bit 8	Domain Member (v2.1+)
bit 9	Print Queue server (v2.1+)
bit 10	Dialin server (v2.1+)
bit 11	Unix server (v2.1+)

INT 21h Function 5F4Dh
DosMakeMailslot
LAN Manager Enhanced DOS
(partially doc.)

Registers at call:
AX = 5F4Dh
BX = message size
CX = mailslot size (must be bigger than message
  size by at least 1–minimum 1000h, maximum
  FFF6h–and buffer must be 9 bytes bigger than this)
DS:SI -> name
ES:DI -> memory buffer
Conflicts: none known
See also: Functions 5F4Eh, 5F4Fh, 5F50h, and 5F51h

Return Registers:
CF clear if successful
  AX = handle
CF set on error
  AX = error code

INT 21h Function 5F4Eh
DosDeleteMailslot
LAN Manager Enhanced DOS
(partially doc.)

Registers at call:
AX = 5F4Eh
BX = handle

Return Registers:
CF clear if successful
      ES:DI -> memory to be freed (allocated
          during DosMakeMailslot)
CF set on error
      AX = error code

Conflicts: none known
See also: Functions 5F4Dh and 5F4Fh

INT 21h Function 5F4Fh
DosMailslotInfo
LAN Manager Enhanced DOS
(partially doc.)

Registers at call:
AX = 5F4Fh
BX = handle

Return Registers:
CF clear if successful
      AX = maximum message size
      BX = mailslot size
      CX = next message size
      DX = next message priority
      SI = number of messages waiting
CF set on error
      AX = error code

Conflicts: none known
See also: Functions 5F4Dh, 5F4Eh, and 5F50h

INT 21h Function 5F50h
DosReadMailslot
LAN Manager Enhanced DOS
(partially doc.)

Registers at call:
AX = 5F50h
BX = handle
DX:CX = timeout
ES:DI -> buffer

Return Registers:
CF clear if successful
      AX = bytes read
      CX = next item's size
      DX = next item's priority
CF set on error
      AX = error code

Conflicts: none known
See also: Function 5F4Dh, 5F4Fh, 5F51h, and 5F52h

INT 21h Function 5F51h
DosPeekMailslot

LAN Manager Enhanced DOS
(partially doc.)

Registers at call:
AX = 5F51h
BX = handle
ES:DI -> buffer

Return Registers:
CF clear if successful
    AX = bytes read
    CX = next item's size
    DX = next item's priority
CF set on error
    AX = error code

Conflicts: none known
See also: Function 5F35h, 5F4Fh, 5F50h, and 5F52h

INT 21h Function 5F52h
DosWriteMailslot

LAN Manager Enhanced DOS
(partially doc.)

Registers at call:
AX = 5F52h
BX = class
CX = length of buffer
DX = priority
ES:DI -> DosWriteMailslot parameter
  structure (see Table 19-19)
DS:SI -> mailslot name

Return Registers:
CF clear if successful
CF set on error
    AX = error code

Conflicts: none known
See also: Functions 5F4Fh, 5F50h, and 5F51h

19-19 Format of DosWriteMailslot parameter structure:

Offset	Size	Description
00h	DWORD	timeout
04h	DWORD	pointer to buffer

INT 21h Function 5F53h
NetServerEnum2

LAN Manager Enhanced DOS
(partially doc.)

Registers at call:
AX = 5F53h
DS:SI -> NetServerEnum2 parameter
  structure (see Table 19-20)

Return Registers:
CF clear if successful
    BX = entries read
    CX = total entries available
CF set on error
    AX = error code

Conflicts: none known
See also: Function 5F4Ch

19-20 Format of NetServerEnum2 parameter structure:

Offset	Size	Description
00h	WORD	level (0000h or 0001h)
02h	DWORD	pointer to buffer for array of *server_info_* structures
06h	WORD	length of buffer
08h	DWORD	server type bitmask (see Table 19-21)
0Ch	DWORD	pointer to Domain name (may be 0000h:0000h for all local domains)

19-21 Bitfields for server type:

bit 0	workstation
bit 1	server
bit 2	SQL server

bit 3   primary domain controller
bit 4   backup domain controller
bit 5   time server
bit 6   Apple File Protocol (AFP) server
bit 7   Novell server
bit 8   Domain Member (v2.1+)
bit 9   Print Queue server (v2.1+)
bit 10   Dialin server (v2.1+)
bit 11   Unix server (v2.1+)
Note: Set all bits (FFFFFFFFh) for All Types.

19-22 Format of server_info_0 structure:

Offset	Size	Description
00h	16 BYTEs	name

19-23 Format of server_info_1 structure:

Offset	Size	Description
00h	16 BYTEs	name
10h	BYTE	major version in lower nibble
11h	BYTE	minor version
12h	DWORD	server type (bits 0-11) (see Table 19-21)
16h	DWORD	pointer to comment string

INT 21h Function 5F55h
KILL ALL CONNECTIONS

LAN Manager Enhanced DOS
Undocumented

Registers at call:
AX = 5F55h
BX = *unknown*

Return Registers:
CF clear if successful
CF set on error
          AX = error code

Conflicts: none known

INT 2Fh Function 1180h
UNDETERMINED FUNCTION

LAN Manager Enhanced DOS Services

Registers at call:
AX = 1180h
others, if any, unknown
Conflicts: none known

Return Registers:
unknown

INT 2Fh Function 1182h
INSTALL SERVICE

LAN Manager Enhanced DOS Services

Registers at call:
AX = 1182h
others, if any, unknown
Conflicts: none known

Return Registers:
unknown

INT 2Fh Function 1184h
UNDETERMINED FUNCTION

LAN Manager Enhanced DOS

Registers at call:
AX = 1184h
others, if any, unknown
Conflicts: none known

Return Registers:
unknown

INT 2Fh Function 1186h
DosReadAsynchNmPipe
LAN Manager Enhanced DOS

Registers at call:
AX = 1186h
DS:SI -> stack frame (see Table 19-24)

Return Registers:
CF clear if successful
CF set if error
    AX = error code

Details: LAN Manager enhanced mode adds features beyond the standard redirector file/printer services.

Conflicts: none known

See also: Functions 118Fh, 1190h, and 1191h; INT 21h Function 5F39h

19-24 Format of DosReadAsynchNmPipe stack frame:

Offset	Size	Description
00h	DWORD	pointer to number of bytes read
04h	WORD	size of buffer
06h	DWORD	pointer to buffer
0Ah	DWORD	pointer to return code
0Eh	DWORD	function to call on completion as function(char far *buffer)
12h	WORD	handle

INT 2Fh Function 118Ah
STREAM ENCRYPTION SERVICE
LAN Manager 2.0+ ENCRYPT.EXE

Registers at call:
AX = 118Ah
BX = function (0000h or 0001h)

Return Registers:
CF clear if successful
    AX = 1100h success
CF set if error
    AX = 0001h, etc.

Conflicts: none known

See also: Functions 1186h, 41h, 42h, and 4Bh

INT 2Fh Functions 118Bh, 118Ch, and 118Eh
UNDETERMINED FUNCTIONS
LAN Manager Enhanced DOS

Registers at call:
AX = 118Bh, 118Ch, and 118Eh
others, if any, unknown

Return Registers:
unknown

Conflicts: none known

INT 2Fh Function 118Fh
DosWriteAsynchNmPipe
LAN Manager Enhanced DOS

Registers at call:
AX = 118Fh
DS:SI -> stack frame (see Table 19-25)

Return Registers:
CF clear if successful
CF set if error
    AX = error code

Conflicts: none known

See also: Functions 1186h and 1191h, INT 21h Function 5F3Ah

19-25 Format of DosReadAsynchNmPipe stack frame:

Offset	Size	Description
00h	DWORD	pointer to number of bytes read
04h	WORD	Size of buffer
06h	DWORD	pointer to buffer
0Ah	DWORD	pointer to return code
0Eh	DWORD	function to call on completion as function(char far *buffer)
12h	WORD	handle

INT 2Fh Function 1190h
DosReadAsynchNmPipe2

LAN Manager Enhanced DOS

Registers at call:
AX = 1190h
DS:SI -> stack frame (see Table 19-26)

Return Registers:
CF clear if successful
CF set if error
    AX = error code

Conflicts: none known
See also: Functions 1186h and 1191h

19-26 Format of DosReadAsynchNmPipe2 stack frame:

Offset	Size	Description
00h	DWORD	pointer to number of bytes read
04h	WORD	size of buffer
06h	DWORD	pointer to buffer
0Ah	DWORD	pointer to return code
0Eh	DWORD	function to call on completion as function(char far *buffer)
12h	WORD	handle
14h	DWORD	*unknown*

INT 2Fh Function 1191h
DosWriteAsynchNmPipe2

LAN Manager Enhanced DOS

Registers at call:
AX = 1191h
DS:SI -> stack frame (see Table 19-27)

Return Registers:
CF clear if successful
CF set if error
    AX = error code

Conflicts: none known
See also: Functions 118Fh and 1190h, INT 21h Function 5F3Ah

19-27 Format of DosReadAsynchNmPipe2 stack frame:

Offset	Size	Description
00h	DWORD	pointer to number of bytes read
04h	WORD	size of buffer
06h	DWORD	pointer to buffer
0Ah	DWORD	pointer to return code
0Eh	DWORD	function to call on completion as function(char far *buffer)
12h	WORD	handle
14h	DWORD	*unknown*

INT 2Fh Function 4100h
INSTALLATION CHECK

LAN Manager 2.0+ MINIPOP/NETPOPUP

Registers at call:
AX = 4100h

Return Registers:
CF clear if successful
    AL = FFh
CF set on error
    AX = *unknown*

Details: MINIPOP and NETPOPUP provide a network message popup service.
Conflicts: none known
See also: Functions 118Ah, 4103h, 4104h, 42h, and 4Bh

INT 2Fh Functions 4103h and 4104h
UNDETERMINED FUNCTIONS

LAN Manager 2.0+ MINIPOP/NETPOPUP

Registers at call:
AX = 4103h and 4104h

Return Registers:
unknown

Conflicts: none known
See also: Function 4100h

INT 2Fh Function 42h
MESSENGER SERVICE
LAN Manager 2.0 MSRV.EXE

Registers at call: **Return Registers:**
AH = 42h   *unknown*
others, if any, unknown
Conflicts: none known
See also: Functions 118Ah, 4100h, and 4Bh

INT 2Fh Function 4Bh
NETWORK WORKSTATION REDIRECTOR
LAN Manager 2.0 NETWKSTA.EXE

Registers at call: **Return Registers:**
AH = 4Bh   *unknown*
others, if any, unknown
Conflicts: DOS Task Switcher (PCI-49)
See also: Functions 118Ah, 4100h, and 42h

CHAPTER 20

LANtastic Network Operating System

LANtastic is a low-cost network by Artisoft, Inc. for a small to medium number of machines.

INT 21h Function 5F80h *LANtastic*
GET LOGIN ENTRY

Registers at call:
AX = 5F80h
BX = login entry index (0-based)
ES:DI -> 16-byte buffer for machine
name

Return Registers:
CF clear if successful
buffer filled with machine name ("\\" prefix removed)
DL = adapter number (v3+)
CF set on error
AX = error code

Details: The login entry index corresponds to the value BX used in Function 5F83h.
See also: Function 5F83h

INT 21h Function 5F81h *LANtastic*
LOGIN TO SERVER

Registers at call:
AX = 5F81h
ES:DI -> ASCIZ login path followed
immediately by ASCIZ password
BL = adapter number
FFh try all valid adapters
00h-07h try only specified adapter

Return Registers:
CF clear if successful
CF set on error
AX = error code

Details: The login path is of the form "\\machine\username".
If no password is used, the string at ES:DI must be terminated with three NULs for compatibility with LANtastic v3.0.
See also: Functions 5F82h and 5F84h

INT 21h Function 5F82h *LANtastic*
LOGOUT FROM SERVER

Registers at call:
AX = 5F82h
ES:DI -> ASCIZ server name (in form
"\\machine")

Return Registers:
CF clear if successful
CF set on error
AX = error code

See also: Functions 5F81h, 5F88h, and 5FCBh

INT 21h Function 5F83h *LANtastic*
GET USERNAME ENTRY

Registers at call:
AX = 5F83h

BX = login entry index (0-based)
ES:DI -> 16-byte buffer for username
 currently logged into

Return Registers:
CF clear if successful
   DL = adapter number (v3+)
CF set on error
   AX = error code

Details: The login entry index corresponds to the value BX used in Function 5F80h.
See also: Function 5F80h

INT 21h Function 5F84h
GET INACTIVE SERVER ENTRY
LANtastic

Registers at call:
AX = 5F84h
BX = server index not currently logged
 into
ES:DI -> 16-byte buffer for server
 name which is available for logging
 in ("\\" prefix omitted)
See also: Function 5F81h

Return Registers:
CF clear if successful
   DL = adapter number to non-logged-in server is on
CF set on error
   AX = error code

INT 21h Function 5F85h
CHANGE PASSWORD
LANtastic

Registers at call:
AX = 5F85h
ES:DI -> buffer containing
 "\\machine\oldpassword" 00h
 "newpassword" 00h

Return Registers:
CF clear if successful
CF set on error
   AX = error code

Details: The caller must be logged into the named machine. This function is illegal for group accounts.

INT 21h Function 5F86h
DISABLE ACCOUNT
LANtastic

Registers at call:
AX = 5F86h
ES:DI -> ASCIZ machine name and
 password in form
 "\\machine\password"

Return Registers:
CF clear if successful
CF set on error
   AX = error code

Details: The caller must be logged into the named machine and concurrent logins set to 1 by NET_MGR. The system manager is the only one who can re-enable the account.

INT 21h Function 5F87h
GET ACCOUNT
LANtastic v3+

Registers at call:
AX = 5F87h
DS:SI -> 128-byte buffer for account
 information (see Table 20-1)
ES:DI -> ASCIZ machine name in
 form "\\machine"

Return Registers:
CF clear if successful
CF set on error
   AX = error code
BX destroyed

Details: The caller must be logged into the specified machine.

20-1 Format of user account structure:

Offset	Size	Description
00h	16 BYTEs	blank-padded username (zero-padded for v4.x)
10h	16 BYTEs	reserved (00h)
20h	32 BYTEs	user description

40h	BYTE	privilege bits (see Table 20-2)
41h	BYTE	maximum concurrent users
42h	42 BYTEs	bit map for disallowed half hours, beginning on Sunday (bit set if half-hour not an allowed time)
6Ch	WORD	internal (0002h)
6Eh	2 WORDs	last login time
72h	2 WORDs	account expiration date (MS-DOS-format year/month:day)
76h	2 WORDs	password expiration date (0 = none)
7Ah	BYTE	number of days to extend password after change (1-31) 00h if no extension required

---v3.x---

| 7Bh | 5 BYTEs | reserved |

---v4.x---

7Bh	BYTE	storage for first letter of user name when deleted (first character is changed to 00h when deleting account)
7Ch	BYTE	extended privileges
7Dh	3 BYTEs	reserved

20-2 Bitfields for privilege bits:

bit 7	bypass access control lists
bit 6	bypass queue protection
bit 5	treat as local process
bit 4	bypass mail protection
bit 3	allow audit entry creation
bit 2	system manager
bit 0	user cannot change password

LANtastic v4.0+

INT 21h Function 5F88h
LOGOUT FROM ALL SERVERS
Registers at call:
AX = 5F88h

Return Registers:
CF clear if successful
CF set on error
    AX = error code

See also: Function 5F82h

LANtastic

INT 21h Function 5F97h
COPY FILE
Registers at call:
AX = 5F97h
CX:DX = number of bytes to copy
(FFFFFFFFh = entire file)
SI = source file handle
DI = destination file handle

Return Registers:
CF clear if successful
    DX:AX = number of bytes copied
CF set on error
    AX = error code

Details: The copy is performed by the file server.

LANtastic

INT 21h Function 5F98h
SEND UNSOLICITED MESSAGE
Registers at call:
AX = 5F98h
DS:SI -> message buffer (see Table 20-3)

Return Registers:
CF clear if successful
CF set on error
    AX = error code

Details: Versions prior to 4.1 return no errors.

See also: Function 5F99h

20-3 Format of message buffer:

Offset	Size	Description
00h	BYTE	reserved
01h	BYTE	message type
		00h general
		01h server warning
		02h-7Fh reserved
		80h-FFh user-defined
02h	16 BYTEs	ASCIZ destination machine name
12h	16 BYTEs	ASCIZ server name which user must be logged into
22h	16 BYTEs	ASCIZ user name
32h	16 BYTEs	ASCIZ originating machine name (filled in when received)
42h	80 BYTEs	message text

INT 21h Function 5F99h
GET LAST RECEIVED UNSOLICITED MESSAGE   *LANtastic*

Registers at call:
AX = 5F99h
ES:DI -> messsage buffer (see Table 20-3)

Return Registers:
CF clear if successful
CF set on error
    AX = error code

See also: Function 5F98h

INT 21h Function 5F9Ah
GET MESSAGE PROCESSING FLAGS   *LANtastic*

Registers at call:
AX = 5F9Ah

Return Registers:
CF clear if successful
    DL = bits describing processing for received
        unsolicited messages (see Table 20-4)
CF set on error
    AX = error code

See also: Functions 5F9Bh, 5F9Ch, and 5F9Dh

20-4 Bitfields for message processing flags:

bit 0 beep before message is delivered
bit 1 deliver message to message service
bit 2 pop up message automatically (v3+)

INT 21h Function 5F9Bh
SET MESSAGE PROCESSING FLAGS   *LANtastic*

Registers at call:
AX = 5F9Bh
DL = unsolicited message processing
  flags (see Table 20-4)
See also: Functions 5F9Ah and 5F9Eh

Return Registers:
CF clear if successful
CF set on error
    AX = error code

INT 21h Function 5F9Ch
POP UP LAST RECEIVED MESSAGE   *LANtastic v3+*

Registers at call:
AX = 5F9Ch
CX = time to leave on screen in clock ticks

DH = 0-based screen line on which to place
    message

Return Registers:
CF clear if successful
CF set on error
        AX = error code (0Bh)

Details: The original screen contents are restored when the message is removed.
        The message will not appear, and an error will be returned, if the screen is in a graphics mode.
See also: Function 5F9Ah

INT 21h Function 5F9Dh   *LANtastic v4.1+*
GET REDIRECTOR CONTROL BITS
Registers at call:
AX = 5F9Dh

Return Registers:
DL = redirector control bits
        bit 7: set to notify on print job completion

See also: Functions 5F9Ah and 5F9Eh

INT 21h Function 5F9Eh   *LANtastic v4.1+*
SET REDIRECTOR CONTROL BITS
Registers at call:
AX = 5F9Eh
DL = redirector control bits (see
    Function 5F9Dh)

Return Registers:
none

See also: Functions 5F9Bh and 5F9Dh

INT 21h Function 5FA0h   *LANtastic*
GET QUEUE ENTRY
Registers at call:
AX = 5FA0h
BX = queue entry index (0000h is first entry)
DS:SI -> buffer for queue entry (see Table 20-5)
ES:DI -> ASCIZ server name in form "\\name"

Return Registers:
CF clear if successful
CF set on error
        AX = error code
BX = entry index for next queue entry
        (BX-1 is current index)

See also: Functions 5FA1h and 5FA2h

20-5 Format of queue entry:

Offset	Size	Description
00h	BYTE	status of entry (see Table 20-6)
01h	DWORD	size of spooled file
05h	BYTE	type of entry (see Table 20-7)
06h	BYTE	output control
		bit 6: don't delete (for mail)
		bit 5: mail file contains voice mail (v3+)
		bit 4: mail message has been read
		bit 3: response has been requested for this mail
07h	WORD	number of copies
09h	DWORD	sequence number of queue entry
0Dh	48 BYTEs	pathname of spooled file
3Dh	16 BYTEs	user who spooled file
4Dh	16 BYTEs	name of machine from which file was spooled
5Dh	WORD	date file was spooled (see Table 3-56)
5Fh	WORD	time file was spooled (see Table 3-55)
61h	17 BYTEs	ASCIZ destination device or user name
72h	48 BYTEs	comment field

20-6 Values for status of entry:

00h	empty
01h	being updated
02h	being held
03h	waiting for despool
04h	being despooled
05h	canceled
06h	spooled file could not be accessed
07h	destination could not be accessed
08h	rush job

20-7 Values for type of entry:

00h	printer queue file
01h	message
02h	local file
03h	remote file
04h	to remote modem
05h	batch processor file

INT 21h Function 5FA1h
SET QUEUE ENTRY
LANtastic

Registers at call:
AX = 5FA1h
BX = handle of opened queue entry
DS:SI -> queue entry (see Table 20-5)

Return Registers:
CF clear if successful
CF set on error
   AX = error code

Details: The only queue entry fields which may be changed are output control, number of copies, destination device, and comment.

    The handle in BX is that from a create or open call (INT 21h Functions 3Ch and 3Dh in Chapter 3 and PCI-24) on the file "\\server\\@@MAIL" or "\\server\@ame" (for printer queue entries).

See also: Functions 5FA0h, 5FA2h, and 5FA9h

INT 21h Function 5FA2h
CONTROL QUEUE
LANtastic

Registers at call:
AX = 5FA2h
BL = control command (see Table 20-8)
DX = physical printer number
  (commands 00h-05h)
    00h-02h LPT1-LPT3
    03h,04h COM1,COM2
  other all printers
CX:DX = sequence number to control
  (commands 06h-09h)
ES:DI -> ASCIZ server name in form
"\\machine"

Return Registers:
CF clear if successful
CF set on error
   AX = error code

20-8 Values for control command:

00h	start despooling (privileged)
01h	halt despooling (privileged)
02h	halt despooling at end of job (privileged)
03h	pause despooler at end of job (privileged)

04h	print single job (privileged)
05h	restart current job (privileged)
06h	cancel the current job
07h	hold queue entry
08h	release a held queue entry
09h	make queue entry a rushed job (privileged)

INT 21h Function 5FA3h
GET PRINTER STATUS
LANtastic v3+

Registers at call:
AX = 5FA3h
BX = physical printer number (00h-02h =
  LPT1-LPT3, 03h-04h = COM1-COM2)
DS:SI -> buffer for printer status (see Table 20-9)
ES:DI -> ASCIZ server name in form
  "\\machine"

Details: You must be logged in to the specified server.

Return Registers:
CF clear if successful
CF set on error
    AX = error code
BX = next physical printer number

20-9 Format of printer status:

Offset	Size	Description
00h	BYTE	printer state
		bit 7: printer paused
		bits 6-0: 0 printer disabled
		1 will stop at end of job
		2 print multiple jobs
01h	WORD	queue index of print job being despooled
		FFFFh if not despooling—ignore all following fields
03h	WORD	actual characters per second being output
05h	DWORD	number of characters actually output so far
09h	DWORD	number of bytes read from spooled file so far
0Dh	WORD	copies remaining to print

INT 21h Function 5FA4h
GET STREAM INFORMATION
LANtastic v3+

Registers at call:
AX = 5FA4h
BX = 0-based stream index number
DS:SI -> buffer for stream information
  (see Table 20-10)
ES:DI -> ASCIZ machine name in
  form "\\machine"

See also: Function 5FA5h

Return Registers:
CF clear if successful
CF set on error
    AX = error code
BX = next stream number

20-10 Format of stream information:

Offset	Size	Description
00h	BYTE	queueing of jobs for logical printer (0=disabled, other=enabled)
01h	11 BYTEs	logical printer resource template (may contain ? wildcards)

INT 21h Function 5FA5h
SET STREAM INFO
LANtastic v3+

Registers at call:
AX = 5FA5h
BX = 0-based stream index number

DS:SI -> buffer containing stream information
(see Table 20-10)
ES:DI -> ASCIZ machine name in form
"\\machine"
See also: Function 5FA4h

Return Registers:
CF clear if successful
CF set on error
    AX = error code

INT 21h Function 5FA7h   *LANtastic*
CREATE USER AUDIT ENTRY

Registers at call:
AX = 5FA7h
DS:DX -> ASCIZ reason code (max 8 bytes)
DS:SI -> ASCIZ variable reason string (max
    128 bytes)
ES:DI -> ASCIZ machine name in form
    "\\machine"

Return Registers:
CF clear if successful
CF set on error
    AX = error code

Details: You must be logged in to the specified server and have the "U" privilege to execute this call.

INT 21h Function 5FA9h   *LANtastic v4.1+*
SET EXTENDED QUEUE ENTRY

Registers at call:
AX = 5FA9h
BX = handle of opened queue entry
DS:SI -> queue entry (see Table 20-5)

Return Registers:
CF clear if successful
CF set on error
    AX = error code

Details: This call functions exactly the same as Function 5FA1h except that the spooled filename is also set. This call supports direct despooling.
See also: Function 5FA1h

INT 21h Function 5FB0h   *LANtastic*
GET ACTIVE USER INFORMATION

Registers at call:
AX = 5FB0h
BX = server login entry index
DS:SI -> buffer for active user entry (see
    Table 20-11)
ES:DI -> ASCIZ machine name in form
    "\\server"

Return Registers:
CF clear if successful
CF set on error
    AX = error code
BX = next login index

See also: Function 5FB2h

20-11 Format of active user entry:

Offset	Size	Description
00h	WORD	virtual circuit number
02h	BYTE	login state (see Table 20-12)
03h	BYTE	last command issued (see Table 20-13)
04h	5 BYTEs	number of I/O bytes (40-bit unsigned number)
09h	3 BYTEs	number of server requests (24-bit unsigned)
0Ch	16 BYTEs	name of user who is logged in
1Ch	16 BYTEs	name of remote logged in machine
2Ch	BYTE	extended privileges (*v4+*)
		bit 0: user cannot change his password
2Dh	WORD	time left in minutes (0000h = unlimited) (*v4+*)

20-12 Bitfields for login state:

bit 0	fully logged in
bit 1	remote program load login
bit 2	user has system manager privileges
bit 3	user can create audit entries
bit 4	bypass mail protection
bit 5	treat as local process
bit 6	bypass queue protection
bit 7	bypass access control lists

20-13 Values for last command:

00h	login
01h	process termination
02h	open file
03h	close file
04h	create file
05h	create new file
06h	create unique file
07h	commit data to disk
08h	read file
09h	write file
0Ah	delete file
0Bh	set file attributes
0Ch	lock byte range
0Dh	unlock byte range
0Eh	create subdirectory
0Fh	remove subdirectory
10h	rename file
11h	find first matching file
12h	find next matching file
13h	get disk free space
14h	get a queue entry
15h	set a queue entry
16h	control the queue
17h	return login information
18h	return link description
19h	seek on file
1Ah	get server's time
1Bh	create audit entry
1Ch	open file in multitude of modes
1Dh	change password
1Eh	disable account
1Fh	local server file copy

---v3+---

20h	get username from account file
21h	translate server's logical path
22h	make indirect file
23h	get indirect file contents
24h	get physical printer status
25h	get logical print stream info
26h	set logical print stream info

27h get user's account record
---v4+---
28h request server shutdown
29h cancel server shutdown
2Ah stuff server's keyboard
2Bh write then commit data to disk
2Ch set extended queue entry
2Dh terminate user from server
2Eh enable/disable logins
2Fh flush server caches
30h change username
31h get extended queue entry (same as get queue, but can return named fields blanked)

INT 21h Function 5FB1h
GET SHARED DIRECTORY INFORMATION
LANtastic

Registers at call:	Return Registers:
AX = 5FB1h	CF clear if successful
DS:SI -> 64-byte buffer for link description	CX = access control list privileges for requesting user (see Table 20-14)
ES:DI -> ASCIZ machine and shared directory name in form	CF set on error
"\\machine\shared-resource"	AX = error code

.comment snake this table into two columns

20-14 Bitfields for access control list:

bit 4 (I) allow expansion of indirect files
bit 5 (A) allow attribute changing
bit 6 (P) allow physical access to device
bit 7 (E) allow program execution
bit 8 (N) allow file renaming
bit 9 (K) allow directory deletion
bit 10   (D) allow file deletion
bit 11   (L) allow file/directory lookups
bit 12   (M) allow directory creation
bit 13   (C) allow file creation
bit 14   (W) allow open for write and writing
bit 15   (R) allow open for read and reading

INT 21h Function 5FB2h
GET USERNAME FROM ACCOUNT FILE
LANtastic v3+

Registers at call:	Return Registers:
AX = 5FB2h	CF clear if successful
BX = username entry index (0 for first)	CF set on error
DS:SI -> 16-byte buffer for username	AX = error code
ES:DI -> ASCIZ server name in form	BX = next queue entry index
"\\machine"	

See also: Function 5FB0h

INT 21h Function 5FB3h
TRANSLATE PATH
LANtastic v3+

Registers at call:
AX = 5FB3h

DS:SI -> 128-byte buffer for ASCIZ result
ES:DI -> full ASCIZ path, including server name
DX = types of translation to be performed
     bit 0: expand last component as indirect file
     bit 1: return actual path relative to server's physical disk

Return Registers:
CF clear if successful
CF set on error
    AX = error code

Details: This function always expands any indirect files along the path.
See also: Function 5FB4h, MS-DOS INT 21h Function 60h (Chapter 3)

INT 21h Function 5FB4h   *LANtastic v3+*
CREATE INDIRECT FILE

Registers at call:
AX = 5FB4h
DS:SI -> 128-byte buffer containing ASCIZ contents of indirect file
ES:DI -> full ASCIZ path of indirect file to create, including machine name

Return Registers:
CF clear if successful
CF set on error
    AX = error code

Details: The contents of the indirect file may be any valid server-relative path.
See also: Functions 5FB3h and 5FB5h

INT 21h Function 5FB5h   *LANtastic v3+*
GET INDIRECT FILE CONTENTS

Registers at call:
AX = 5FB5h
DS:SI -> 128-byte buffer for ASCIZ indirect file contents
ES:DI -> full ASCIZ path of indirect file

Return Registers:
CF clear if successful
CF set on error
    AX = error code

See also: Function 5FB4h

INT 21h Function 5FB6h   *LANtastic v4.1+*
SET AUTO-LOGIN DEFAULTS

Registers at call:
AX = 5FB6h
ES:DI -> pointer to ASCIZ default user name, immediately followed by ASCIZ password
BL = adapter number to use for default login attempt
    FFh try all valid adapters
    00h-05h try adapter 0-5 explicitly

Return Registers:
CF clear if successful
CF set on error
    AX = error code

Details: Call this function with ES:DI pointing at two nulls to disable auto-login.
See also: Function 5FB7h

INT 21h Function 5FB7h   *LANtastic v4.1+*
GET AUTO-LOGIN DEFAULTS

Registers at call:
AX = 5FB7h

ES:DI -> pointer to 16-byte buffer to store ASCIZ auto-login user name

Return Registers:
CF clear if successful
    DL = adapter number used for default login attempt
        FFh all valid adapters will be tried
        00h-05h specified adapter will be tried explicitly
CF set on error
    AX = error code

See also: Functions 5F81h and 5FB6h

INT 21h Function 5FC0h   *LANtastic*
GET TIME FROM SERVER

Registers at call:
AX = 5FC0h
DS:SI -> time block (see Table 20-15)
ES:DI -> ASCIZ server name from which to get time

See also: Function E7h

Return Registers:
CF clear if successful
CF set on error
    AX = error code

20-15 Format of time block:

OffsetSizeDescription
00hWORDyear
02hBYTEday
03hBYTEmonth
04hBYTEminutes
05hBYTEhour
06hBYTEhundredths of second
07hBYTEsecond

INT 21h Function 5FC8h   *LANtastic v4.0+*
SCHEDULE SERVER SHUTDOWN

Registers at call:
AX = 5FC8h
ES:DI -> ASCIZ server name in form
"\\machine"
DS:SI -> ASCIZ reason string (80 characters)
CX = number of minutes until shutdown (0 = immediate)
DX = option flags (see Table 20-16)
See also: Function 5FC9h

Return Registers:
CF clear if successful
CF set on error
    AX = error code

20-16 Bitfields for option flags:

bit 0auto reboot
bit 1do not notify users
bit 2halt after shutdown
bit 3shutdown due to power fail (used by UPS)
bits 4-7reserved
bits 8-14user definable
bit 15reserved

INT 21h Function 5FC9h   *LANtastic v4.0+*
CANCEL SERVER SHUTDOWN

Registers at call:
AX = 5FC9h

ES:DI -> ASCIZ server name in form "\\machine"

Return Registers:
CF clear if successful
CF set on error
        AX = error code

Details: You must have the "S" privilege to use this call.
See also: Function 5FC8h

INT 21h Function 5FCAh
STUFF SERVER KEYBOARD BUFFER

Registers at call:
AX = 5FCAh
ES:DI -> ASCIZ server name in form "\\machine"
DS:SI -> ASCIZ string to stuff (128 bytes)

Return Registers:
CF clear if successful
CF set on error
        AX = error code

Details: You must have the "S" privilege to use this call.
   The maximum number of characters that can be stuffed is determined by the server's RUN BUFFER SIZE.
See also: INT 16h Function 05h

INT 21h Function 5FCBh
TERMINATE USER

Registers at call:
AX = 5FCBh
ES:DI -> ASCIZ server name in form "\\machine"
DS:SI -> blank-padded username (a null char = wildcard)
DS:DX -> blank-padded machine name (a null char = wildcard)
CX = minutes until termination (0 = immediate)

Return Registers:
CF clear if successful
CF set on error
        AX = error code

Details: You must have the "S" privilege to use this call. You cannot log yourself out using this call.
See also: Function 5F82h

INT 21h Function 5FCCh
GET/SET SERVER CONTROL BITS

Registers at call:
AX = 5FCCh
ES:DI -> ASCIZ server name in form "\\machine"
CX = bit values (value of bits you want to set) (see at right)
DX = bit mask (bits you are interested in, 0 = get only) (see at right)

Return Registers:
CF clear if successful
        CX = control bits after call
                bit 0: disable logins
CF set on error
        AX = error code

Details: You must have the "S" privilege to set bits, anyone can get the current value.

INT 21h Function 5FCDh
FLUSH SERVER CACHES

Registers at call:
AX = 5FCDh

ES:DI -> ASCIZ server name in form
"\\machine"

Return Registers:
CF clear if successful
CF set on error
        AX = error code

Details: You must have the "S" privilege to use this call.

INT 21h Function 5FD0h
GET REDIRECTED PRINTER TIMEOUT

Registers at call:
AX = 5FD0h

Return Registers:
CF clear if successful
        CX = redirected printer timeout in clock ticks of
55ms
                0000h if timeout disabled
CF set on error
        AX = error code

See also: Function 5FD1h

INT 21h Function 5FD1h
SET REDIRECTED PRINTER TIMEOUT

Registers at call:
AX = 5FD1h
CX = printer timeout in clock ticks of
55ms, 0000h to disable timeouts
See also: Function 5FD0h

Return Registers:
CF clear if successful
CF set on error
        AX = error code

INT 21h Function 5FE0h
GET DOS SERVICE VECTOR

Registers at call:
AX = 5FE0h

Return Registers:
CF clear if successful
        ES:BX -> current FAR service routine
CF set on error
        AX = error code

Details: The service routine is called by the LANtastic redirector whenever DOS may safely be
called, permitting external TSRs and drivers to hook into LANtastic's DOS busy flag checking.
See also: Function 5FE1h, INT 2Ah Function 84h (Chapter 3), INT 28h (PCI-24)

INT 21h Function 5FE1h
SET DOS SERVICE VECTOR

Registers at call:
AX = 5FE1h
ES:BX -> FAR routine to call when
DOS services are available
Details: The new handler must chain to the previous handler as its first action.
See also: Function 5FE0h

Return Registers:
CF clear if successful
CF set on error
        AX = error code

INT 21h Function 5FE2h
GET MESSAGE SERVICE VECTOR

Registers at call:
AX = 5FE2h

Return Registers:
CF clear if successful
        ES:BX -> current FAR message service routine
CF set on error
        AX = error code

See also: Functions 5FE0h and 5FE3h

INT 21h Function 5FE3h
SET MESSAGE SERVICE VECTOR

Registers at call:
AX = 5FE3h
ES:BX -> FAR routine for processing
network messages

Return Registers:
CF clear if successful
CF set on error
     AX = error code

Details: The handler must chain to the previous handler as its first action. On invocation, ES:BX points at the just-received message.

See also: Function 5FE2h

CHAPTER 21

Novell NetWare Shell (NETX)

In the world of network operation, Novell NetWare appears to hold a position similar to that held by MS-DOS with respect to operating systems. While NetWare is by no means the only networking system available (as the rest of this book shows), it is the accepted standard to which all others are compared.

It should come as no surprise, then, to find that the interrupt functions used by NetWare provide a multitude of services, or that some other networking systems (such as Alloy's NTNX and Banyan VINES) have also adopted certain NetWare interrupt functions. This chapter lists the calls provided by the NetWare shell NETX, which is commonly considered to *be* the NetWare API by programmers; an overview of these functions is shown in Table 21-1. The NetWare Lite API (which differs from the regular NetWare's API) is covered in Chapter 22, and additional functions provided by other parts of NetWare such as utility programs are listed in Chapter 23. The low-level "raw" network interfaces used by NetWare, IPX and SPX, have now been adopted by a number of other networking programs, and are discussed in Chapter 5.

A note about version numbers: NetWare 4.0 and 4.6 are old versions that predate the current Advanced NetWare, which is commonly called just "NetWare". This has become a particularly confusing problem with the recent release of Advanced NetWare 4.0. In this chapter, "DOS Requester" refers to the 1993 Advanced NetWare 4.0, while all other unqualified references to "NetWare 4.0" apply to the old version 4.0 from the early 1980's.

21-1 Overview of NetWare Functions:

AH/Subfn	Description	Section
B4h	AttachHandle	General Functions
B5h	Task Mode Control	General Functions
B6h	Extended File Attributes	File Services
B7h	HoldFileModeSet	General Functions
B800h	Get Default Capture Flags	Print Services
B801h	Set Default Capture Flags	Print Services
B802h	Get Specific Capture Flags	Print Services
B803h	Set Specific Capture Flags	Print Services
B804h	Get Default Local Printer	Print Services
B805h	Set Default Local Printer	Print Services
B806h	Set Capture Print Queue	Print Services
B807h	Set Capture Print Job	Print Services
B808h	Get Banner User Name	Print Services
B809h	Set Banner User Name	Print Services
B9h	SpecialAtttachableFunction	General Functions
BAh	ReturnCommandComPointers	General Functions

BBh	Set End of Job Status	Workstation Functions
BCh	Log Physical Record	Synchronization Services
BDh	Release Physical Record	Synchronization Services
BEh	Clear Physical Record	Synchronization Services
BFh	Log/Lock Record (FCB)	Synchronization Services
C0h	Release Record (FCB)	Synchronization Services
C1h	Clear Record (FCB)	Synchronization Services
C2h	Lock Physical Record Set	Synchronization Services
C3h	Release Physical Record Set	Synchronization Services
C4h	Clear Physical Record Set	Synchronization Services
C500h	Open Semaphore	Synchronization Services
C501h	Examine Semaphore	Synchronization Services
C502h	Wait on Semaphore	Synchronization Services
C503h	Signal Semaphore	Synchronization Services
C504h	Close Semaphore	Synchronization Services
C6h	Get or Set Lock Mode	Synchronization Services
C700h	Begin Transaction	Transaction Tracking System
C701h	End Transaction	Transaction Tracking System
C702h	Installation Check	Transaction Tracking System
C703h	Abort Transaction	Transaction Tracking System
C704h	Transaction Status	Transaction Tracking System
C705h	Get Application Thresholds	Transaction Tracking System
C706h	Set Application Thresholds	Transaction Tracking System
C707h	Get Workstation Thresholds	Transaction Tracking System
C708h	Set Workstation Thresholds	Transaction Tracking System
C8h	Begin Logical File Locking	Synchronization Services
C9h	End Logical File Locking	Synchronization Services
CAh	Log/Lock Personal File (FCB)	Synchronization Services
CBh	Lock File Set	Synchronization Services
CCh	Release File (FCB)	Synchronization Services
CDh	Release File Set	Synchronization Services
CEh	Clear File (FCB)	Synchronization Services
CFh	Clear File Set	Synchronization Services
D0h	Log Logical Record	Synchronization Services
D1h	Lock Logical Record Set	Synchronization Services
D2h	Release Logical Record	Synchronization Services
D3h	Release Logical Record Set	Synchronization Services
D4h	Clear Logical Record	Synchronization Services
D5h	Clear Logical Record Set	Synchronization Services
D6h	End of Job	Workstation Functions
D7h	System Logout	Connection Services
D8h	Allocate Resource	General Functions
D9h	Deallocate Resource	General Functions
DAh	Get Volume Information with Number	Directory Services
DBh	Get Number of Local Drives	Workstation Functions
DCh	Get Connection Number	Connection Services
DDh	Set NetWare Error Mode	Workstation Functions
DEh/0xh	Set Broadcast Mode	Message Services
DEh/04h	Get Broadcast Mode	Message Services

DEh/05h	Disable Shell Timer Interrupt Checks	General Functions
DEh/06h	Enable Shell Timer Interrupt Checks	General Functions
DFh/00h	Start LPT Capture	Print Services
DFh/01h	End LPT Capture	Print Services
DFh/02h	Cancel LPT Capture	Print Services
DFh/03h	Flush LPT Capture	Print Services
DFh/04h	Start Specific LPT Capture	Print Services
DFh/05h	End Specific LPT Capture	Print Services
DFh/06h	Cancel Specific LPT Capture	Print Services
DFh/07h	Flush Specific LPT Capture	Print Services
E0h/0xh	Print Spooling	Print Services
E0h/09h	Specify Capture File	Print Services
E1h/00h	Send Broadcast Message	Message Services
E1h/01h	Get Broadcast Message	Message Services
E1h/02h	Disable Station Broadcasts	Message Services
E1h/03h	Enable Station Broadcasts	Message Services
E1h/04h	Send Personal Message	Message Services
E1h/05h	Get Personal Message	Message Services
E1h/06h	Open Message Pipe	Message Services
E1h/07h	Close Message Pipe	Message Services
E1h/08h	Check Pipe Status	Message Services
E1h/09h	Broadcast to Console	Message Services
E2h/00h	Set Directory Handle	Directory Services
E2h/01h	Get Directory Path	Directory Services
E2h/02h	Scan Directory Information	Directory Services
E2h/03h	Get Effective Directory Rights	Directory Services
E2h/04h	Modify Maximum Rights Mask	Directory Services
E2h/05h	Get Volume Number	Directory Services
E2h/06h	Get Volume Name	Directory Services
E2h/0Ah	Create Directory	Directory Services
E2h/0Bh	Delete Directory	Directory Services
E2h/0Ch	Scan Directory for Trustees	Directory Services
E2h/0Dh	Add Trustee to Directory	Directory Services
E2h/0Eh	Delete Trustee from Directory	Directory Services
E2h/0Fh	Rename Directory	Directory Services
E2h/10h	Purge Erased Files	File Services
E2h/11h	Restore Erased File	File Services
E2h/12h	Allocate Permanent Directory Handle	Directory Services
E2h/13h	Allocate Temporary Directory Handle	Directory Services
E2h/14h	Deallocate Directory Handle	Directory Services
E2h/15h	Get Volume Information with Handle	Directory Services
E2h/16h	Allocate Special Temp Directory Handle	Directory Services
E2h/17h	Save Directory Handle	Directory Services
E2h/18h	Restore Directory Handle	Directory Services
E2h/19h	Set Directory Information	Directory Services
E2h/1Ah	Get Path from Directory Entry	File Server
E3h/00h	Login	Connection Services
E3h/01h	Change Password	Connection Services
E3h/02h	Map User to Station Set	Connection Services

E3h/03h	Map Object to Number	Connection Services
E3h/04h	Map Number to Object	Connection Services
E3h/05h	Get Station's Logged Information	Connection Services
E3h/06h	Get Station's Root Mask	Connection Services
E3h/07h	Map Group Name to Number	Connection Services
E3h/08h	Map Number to Group Name	Connection Services
E3h/09h	Get Memberset M of Group G	Connection Services
E3h/0Ah	Enter Login Area	Connection Services
E3h/0Ch	Verify Network Serial Number	General Functions
E3h/0Dh	Log Network Message	Message Services
E3h/0Eh	Get Disk Utilization	File Server
E3h/0Fh	Scan File Information	File Services
E3h/10h	Set File Information	File Services
E3h/11h	Get File Server Information	File Server
E3h/12h	Get Serial Number	General Functions
E3h/13h	Get Internet Address	Connection Services
E3h/14h	Login to File Server	Connection Services
E3h/15h	Get Object Connection Numbers	Connection Services
E3h/16h	Get Connection Information	Connection Services
E3h/32h	Create Bindery Object	Bindery Services
E3h/33h	Delete Bindery Object	Bindery Services
E3h/34h	Rename Bindery Object	Bindery Services
E3h/35h	Get Bindery Object ID	Bindery Services
E3h/36h	Get Bindery Object Name	Bindery Services
E3h/37h	Scan Bindery Object	Bindery Services
E3h/38h	Change Bindery Object Security	Bindery Services
E3h/39h	Create Property	Bindery Services
E3h/3Ah	Delete Property	Bindery Services
E3h/3Bh	Change Property Security	Bindery Services
E3h/3Ch	Scan Property	Bindery Services
E3h/3Dh	Read Propery Value	Bindery Services
E3h/3Eh	Write Property Value	Bindery Services
E3h/3Fh	Verify Bindery Object Password	Bindery Services
E3h/40h	Change Bindery Object Password	Bindery Services
E3h/41h	Add Bindery Object to Set	Bindery Services
E3h/42h	Delete Bindery Object from Set	Bindery Services
E3h/43h	Is Bindery Object in Set?	Bindery Services
E3h/44h	Close Bindery	Bindery Services
E3h/45h	Open Bindery	Bindery Services
E3h/46h	Get Bindery Access Level	Bindery Services
E3h/47h	Scan Bindery Object Trustee Paths	Directory Services
E3h/64h	Create Queue	Queue Services
E3h/65h	Destroy Queue	Queue Services
E3h/66h	Read Queue Current Status	Queue Services
E3h/67h	Set Queue Current Status	Queue Services
E3h/68h	Create Queue Job and File	Queue Services
E3h/69h	Close File and Start Queue Job	Queue Services
E3h/6Ah	Remove Job from Queue	Queue Services
E3h/6Bh	Get Queue Job List	Queue Services

E3h/6Ch	Read Queue Job Entry	Queue Services
E3h/6Dh	Change Queue Job Entry	Queue Services
E3h/6Eh	Change Queue Job Position	Queue Services
E3h/6Fh	Attach Queue Server to Queue	Queue Services
E3h/70h	Detach Queue Server from Queue	Queue Services
E3h/71h	Service Queue Job and Open File	Queue Services
E3h/72h	Finish Servicing Queue Job and File	Queue Services
E3h/73h	Abort Servicing Queue Job and File	Queue Services
E3h/74h	Change to Client Rights	Queue Services
E3h/75h	Restore Queue Server Rights	Queue Services
E3h/76h	Read Queue Server Current Status	Queue Services
E3h/77h	Set Queue Server Current Status	Queue Services
E3h/78h	Get Queue Job's File Size	Queue Services
E3h/96h	Get Account Status	Accounting Services
E3h/97h	Submit Account Charge	Accounting Services
E3h/98h	Submit Account Hold	Accounting Services
E3h/99h	Submit Account Note	Accounting Services
E3h/C8h	Check Console Privileges	File Server
E3h/C9h	Get File Server Description Strings	File Server
E3h/CAh	Set File Server Date and Time	File Server
E3h/CBh	Disable File Server Login	File Server
E3h/CCh	Enable File Server Login	File Server
E3h/CDh	Get File Server Login Status	File Server
E3h/CEh	Purge All Erased Files	File Services
E3h/CFh	Disable Transaction Tracking	File Server
E3h/D0h	Enable Transaction Tracking	File Server
E3h/D1h	Send Console Broadcast	File Server
E3h/D2h	Clear Connection Number	File Server
E3h/D3h	Down File Server	File Server
E3h/D4h	Get File System Statistics	File Server
E3h/D5h	Get Transaction Tracking Statistics	File Server
E3h/D6h	Get Disk Cache Statistics	File Server
E3h/D7h	Get Drive Mapping Table	File Server
E3h/D8h	Get Physical Disk Statistics	File Server
E3h/D9h	Get Disk Channel Statistics	File Server
E3h/DAh	Get Connection's Task Information	File Server
E3h/DBh	Get Connection's Open File	File Server
E3h/DCh	Get Connections Using a File	File Server
E3h/DDh	Get Physical Record Locks by Conn/File	File Server
E3h/DEh	Get Physical Record Locks by File	File Server
E3h/DFh	Get Logical Records by Connection	File Server
E3h/E0h	Get Logical Record Information	File Server
E3h/E1h	Get Connection's Semaphores	File Server
E3h/E2h	Get Semaphore Information	File Server
E3h/E3h	Get LAN Driver's Configuration Info	File Server
E3h/E5h	Get Connection's Usage Statistics	File Server
E3h/E6h	Get Bindery Object's Disk Space Left	File Server
E3h/E7h	Get File Server LAN I/O Statistics	File Server
E3h/E8h	Get File Server Miscellaneous Info	File Server

E3h/E9h	Get Volume Information	Directory Services
E4h	Set File Attributes (FCB)	Directory Services
E5h	Update File Size (FCB)	Directory Services
E6h	Copy File to File (FCB)	General Functions
E7h	Get File Server Date and Time	File Server
E8h	Set FCB Re-Open Mode	General Functions
E900h	Get Directory Handle	Directory Services
E905h	Map a Fake Root Directory	Directory Services
E906h	Delete Fake Root Directory	Directory Services
E907h	Get Relative Drive Depth	Directory Services
E908h	Set Show Dots	Directory Services
EAh	Return Shell Version	General Functions
EBh	Log File	Synchronization Services
ECh	Release File	Synchronization Services
EDh	Clear File	Synchronization Services
EEh	Get Physical Station Address	Connection Services
EF00h	Get Drive Handle Table	Workstation Functions
EF01h	Get Drive Flag Table	Workstation Functions
EF02h	Get Drive Connection ID Table	Workstation Functions
EF03h	Get Connection ID Table	Workstation Functions
EF04h	Get File Server Name Table	Workstation Functions
F000h	Set Preferred Connection ID	Workstation Functions
F001h	Get Preferred Connection ID	Workstation Functions
F002h	Get Default Connection ID	Workstation Functions
F003h	Get LPT Capture Status	Print Services
F004h	Set Primary Connection ID	Workstation Functions
F005h	Get Primary Connection ID	Workstation Functions
F1h	File Server Connection	Connection Services
F21xh	Multiplexor	General Functions
F244h	Erase Files	File Services
F3h	File Server File Copy	File Services

Accounting Services

21-2 Values for Accounting Services function status:

00h	successful
C0h	no account privileges
C1h	no account balance
C2h	credit limit exceeded
C3h	too many holds on account

INT 21h Function E3h, Subfunction 96h *Advanced NetWare 2.1+*
GET ACCOUNT STATUS *Accounting Services*

Registers at call: **Return Registers:**
AH = E3h AL = status (00h,C0h,C1h) (see Table 21-2)
DS:SI -> request buffer (see Table 21-3)
ES:DI -> reply buffer (see Table 21-4)
Conflicts: OS/286 and OS/386 (PCI-34), DoubleDOS (PCI-49)
See also: Function E3h Subfunctions 97h, 98h, and 99h

21-3 Format of request buffer:

Offset	Size	Description
00h	WORD	length of following data (max 33h)
02h	BYTE	96h (subfunction "Get Account Status")
03h	WORD	(big-endian) type of bindery object
05h	BYTE	length of object name (01h to 2Fh)
06h	N BYTEs	object name

21-4 Format of reply buffer:

Offset	Size	Description
00h	WORD	(call) length of following buffer space
02h	DWORD	(big-endian) account balance
06h	DWORD	(big-endian) credit limit
		signed number indicating lowest allowable account balance
0Ah	120 BYTEs	reserved
82h	DWORD	(big-endian) object ID, server 1
86h	DWORD	(big-endian) hold amount, server 1
	...	
F8h	DWORD	(big-endian) object ID, server 16
FCh	DWORD	(big-endian) hold amount, server 16

Note: The reply buffer lists the servers which have placed holds on a portion of the account balance, and the amount reserved by each.

INT 21h Function E3h, Subfunction 97h	*Advanced NetWare 2.1+*
SUBMIT ACCOUNT CHARGE	*Accounting Services*

Registers at call:
AH = E3h
DS:SI -> request buffer (see Table 21-5)
ES:DI -> reply buffer (see Table 21-6)

Return Registers:
AL = status (00h,C0h-C2h) (see Table 21-2)

Conflicts: OS/286 and OS/386 (PCI-34), DoubleDOS (PCI-49)
See also: Function E3h Subfunctions 96h and 98h

21-5 Format of request buffer:

Offset	Size	Description
00h	WORD	length of following data (max 13Fh)
02h	BYTE	97h (subfunction "Submit Account Charge")
03h	WORD	(big-endian) service type
05h	DWORD	(big-endian) amount to be charged to account
09h	DWORD	(big-endian) amount of prior hold to be cancelled
0Dh	WORD	(big-endian) type of bindery object
0Fh	WORD	(big-endian) type of comment
		8000h-FFFFh reserved for experimental use
11h	BYTE	length of object's name
12h	N BYTEs	object name
	BYTE	length of comment
	N BYTEs	comment

21-6 Format of reply buffer:

Offset	Size	Description
00h	WORD	0000h (no data returned)

INT 21h Function E3h, Subfunction 98h
SUBMIT ACCOUNT HOLD

Advanced NetWare 2.1+
Accounting Services

Registers at call:
AH = E3h
DS:SI -> request buffer (see Table 21-7)
ES:DI -> reply buffer (see Table 21-8)
Conflicts: OS/286 and OS/386 (PCI-34), DoubleDOS (PCI-49)
See also: Function E3h Subfunctions 96h and 97h

Return Registers:
AL = status (00h,C0h-C3h) (see Table 21-2)

21-7 Format of request buffer:

Offset	Size	Description
00h	WORD	length of following data (max 37h)
02h	BYTE	98h (subfunction "Submit Account Hold")
03h	DWORD	(big-endian) amount of account balance to reserve
07h	WORD	(big-endian) type of bindery object
09h	BYTE	length of object's name
0Ah	N BYTEs	object name

21-8 Format of reply buffer:

Offset	Size	Description
00h	WORD	0000h (no data returned)

INT 21h Function E3h, Subfunction 99h
SUBMIT ACCOUNT NOTE

Advanced NetWare 2.1+
Accounting Services

Registers at call:
AH = E3h
DS:SI -> request buffer (see Table 21-9)
ES:DI -> reply buffer (see Table 21-10)
Conflicts: OS/286 and OS/386 (PCI-34), DoubleDOS (PCI-49)
See also: Function E3h Subfunction 96h

Return Registers:
AL = status (00h,C0h) (see Table 21-2)

21-9 Format of request buffer:

Offset	Size	Description
00h	WORD	length of following data (max 137h)
02h	BYTE	99h (subfunction "Submit Account Note")
03h	WORD	(big-endian) type of service
05h	WORD	(big-endian) type of bindery object
07h	WORD	(big-endian) type of comment
		8000h-FFFFh reserved for experimental use
09h	BYTE	length of object's name
0Ah	N BYTEs	object name
	BYTE	length of comment
	N BYTEs	comment

21-10 Format of reply buffer:

Offset	Size	Description
00h	WORD	0000h (no data returned)

Bindery Services

21-11 Values for Bindery Service status:

00h	successful
96h	server out of memory

E8h	not item property
E9h	member already exists
EAh	member does not exist
EBh	not a group property
ECh	no such segment
EDh	property already exists
EEh	object already exists
EFh	invalid name
F0h	wildcard not allowed
F1h	invalid bindery security level
F3h	not permitted to rename object
F4h	not permitted to delete objects
F5h	not permitted to create objects
F6h	not permitted to delete properties
F7h	not permitted to create properties
F8h	not permitted to write property
F9h	not permitted to read property
FBh	no such property
FCh	no such object
FEh	server bindery locked
FFh	bindery failure

INT 21h Function E3h, Subfunction 32h *Advanced NetWare 1.0+, Alloy NTNX*
CREATE BINDERY OBJECT *Bindery Services*

Registers at call: **Return Registers:**
AH = E3h   AL = status (see Table 21-11)
DS:SI -> request buffer (see Table 21-12)
ES:DI -> reply buffer (see Table 21-13)
Conflicts: OS/286 and OS/386 (PCI-34), DoubleDOS (PCI-49)
See also: Function E3h Subfunctions 33h, 34h, 38h, and 39h

21-12 Format of request buffer:

Offset	Size	Description
00h	WORD	length of following data (max 35h)
02h	BYTE	32h (subfunction "Create Bindery Object")
03h	BYTE	object flag
		00h static
		01h dynamic
04h	BYTE	object security levels
05h	WORD	(big-endian) type of object
07h	BYTE	length of object's name
08h	N BYTEs	object's name

21-13 Format of reply buffer:

Offset	Size	Description
00h	WORD	0000h (no data returned)

INT 21h Function E3h, Subfunction 33h *Advanced NetWare 1.0+, Alloy NTNX*
DELETE BINDERY OBJECT *Bindery Services*
Registers at call:
AH = E3h

DS:SI -> request buffer (see Table 21-14)
ES:DI -> reply buffer (see Table 21-15)

Return Registers:
AL = status (see Table 21-11)

Conflicts: OS/286 and OS/386 (PCI-34), DoubleDOS (PCI-49)
See also: Function E3h Subfunctions 32h and 34h

21-14 Format of request buffer:

Offset	Size	Description
00h	WORD	length of following data (max 33h)
02h	BYTE	33h (subfunction "Delete Bindery Object")
03h	WORD	(big-endian) type of object
05h	BYTE	length of object's name (01h-2Fh)
06h	N BYTEs	object's name

21-15 Format of reply buffer:

Offset	Size	Description
00h	WORD	(call) 0000h (no data returned)

INT 21h Function E3h, Subfunction 34h   *Advanced NetWare 1.0+, Alloy NTNX*
RENAME BINDERY OBJECT   *Bindery Services*

Registers at call:
AH = E3h
DS:SI -> request buffer (see Table 21-16)
ES:DI -> reply buffer (see Table 21-17)

Return Registers:
AL = status (see Table 21-11)

Conflicts: OS/286 and OS/386 (PCI-34), DoubleDOS (PCI-49)
See also: Function E3h Subfunctions 32h and 33h

21-16 Format of request buffer:

Offset	Size	Description
00h	WORD	length of following data (max 63h)
02h	BYTE	34h (subfunction "Rename Bindery Object")
03h	WORD	(big-endian) type of object
05h	BYTE	length of object's name (01h-2Fh)
06h	N BYTEs	object's name
	BYTE	length of new name (01h-2Fh)
	N BYTEs	new name

21-17 Format of reply buffer:

Offset	Size	Description
00h	WORD	(call) 0000h (no data returned)

INT 21h Function E3h, Subfunction 35h   *Advanced NetWare 1.0+, Alloy NTNX*
GET BINDERY OBJECT ID   *Bindery Services*

Registers at call:
AH = E3h
DS:SI -> request buffer (see Table 21-18)
ES:DI -> reply buffer (see Table 21-19)

Return Registers:
AL = status (00h,96h,FCh,FEh,FFh)
  (see Table 21-11)

Details: The requesting workstation must be logged into the file server with read access to the bindery object.
Conflicts: OS/286 and OS/386 (PCI-34), DoubleDOS (PCI-49)
See also: Function E3h Subfunctions 36h and 44h

21-18 Format of request buffer:

Offset	Size	Description
00h	WORD	length of following data (max 33h)

02h	BYTE	35h (subfunction "Get Bindery Object ID")
03h	WORD	(big-endian) type of object
05h	BYTE	length of object's name
06h	N BYTEs	object's name

21-19 Format of reply buffer:

Offset	Size	Description
00h	WORD	(call) 0036h (length of following buffer space)
02h	DWORD	(big-endian) object ID
06h	WORD	(big-endian) type of object
08h	48 BYTEs	object name

INT 21h Function E3h, Subfunction 36h
GET BINDERY OBJECT NAME

Advanced NetWare 1.0+, Alloy NTNX
Bindery Services

Registers at call:
AH = E3h
DS:SI -> request buffer (see Table 21-20)
ES:DI -> reply buffer (see Table 21-21)

Return Registers:
AL = status (00h,96h,EFh,F0h,FCh,FEh,FFh)
(see Table 21-11)

Details: The requesting workstation must be logged into the file server with read access to the bindery object.
Conflicts: OS/286 and OS/386 (PCI-34), DoubleDOS (PCI-49)
See also: Function E3h Subfunctions 35h and 44h

21-20 Format of request buffer:

Offset	Size	Description
00h	WORD	0005h (length of following data)
02h	BYTE	36h (subfunction "Get Bindery Object Name")
03h	DWORD	(big-endian) object ID

21-21 Format of reply buffer:

Offset	Size	Description
00h	WORD	(call) 0036h (length of following buffer space)
02h	DWORD	(big-endian) object ID
06h	WORD	(big-endian) type of object
08h	48 BYTEs	object name

INT 21h Function E3h, Subfunction 37h
SCAN BINDERY OBJECT

Advanced NetWare 1.0+, Alloy NTNX
Bindery Services

Registers at call:
AH = E3h
DS:SI -> request buffer (see Table 21-22)
ES:DI -> reply buffer (see Table 21-23)

Return Registers:
AL = status (00h,96h,EFh,F0h,FCh,FEh,FFh)
(see Table 21-11)

Details: The requesting workstation must be logged into the file server with read access to the bindery object.
Conflicts: OS/286 and OS/386 (PCI-34), DoubleDOS (PCI-49)
See also: Function E3h Subfunctions 32h, 33h, 38h, and 3Ch

21-22 Format of request buffer:

Offset	Size	Description
00h	WORD	length of following data (max 37h)
02h	BYTE	37h (subfunction "Scan Bindery Object")
03h	DWORD	(big-endian) last object ID
07h	WORD	(big-endian) type of object

Offset	Size	Description
09h	BYTE	length of object's name
0Ah	N BYTEs	object's name

21-23 Format of reply buffer:

Offset	Size	Description
00h	WORD	(call) 0039h (length of following buffer space)
02h	DWORD	(big-endian) object ID
		FFFFFFFFh for first call
06h	WORD	(big-endian) type of object
08h	48 BYTEs	object name (counted string)
38h	BYTE	object flag (00h static, 01h dynamic)
39h	BYTE	object's security levels
3Ah	BYTE	object properties flag (00h no, FFh yes)

INT 21h Function E3h, Subfunction 38h
CHANGE BINDERY OBJECT SECURITY

Advanced NetWare 1.0+, Alloy NTNX
Bindery Services

Registers at call:
AH = E3h
DS:SI -> request buffer (see Table 21-24)
ES:DI -> reply buffer (see Table 21-25)
Conflicts: OS/286 and OS/386 (PCI-34), DoubleDOS (PCI-49)
See also: Function E3h Subfunctions 32h and 3Bh

Return Registers:
AL = status
(00h,96h,F0h,F1h,FBh,FCh,FEh,FFh)
(see Table 21-11)

21-24 Format of request buffer:

Offset	Size	Description
00h	WORD	length of following data (max 34h)
02h	BYTE	38h (subfunction "Change Bindery Object Security")
03h	BYTE	new security levels
04h	WORD	(big-endian) type of object
06h	BYTE	length of object's name (01h-2Fh)
07h	N BYTEs	object name

21-25 Format of reply buffer:

Offset	Size	Description
00h	WORD	(call) 0000h (no data returned)

INT 21h Function E3h, Subfunction 39h
CREATE PROPERTY

Advanced NetWare 1.0+, Alloy NTNX
Bindery Services

Registers at call:
AH = E3h
DS:SI -> request buffer (see Table 21-26)
ES:DI -> reply buffer (see Table 21-27)
Conflicts: OS/286 and OS/386 (PCI-34), DoubleDOS (PCI-49)
See also: Function E3h Subfunctions 32h and 3Bh

Return Registers:
AL = status (see Table 21-11)

21-26 Format of request buffer:

Offset	Size	Description
00h	WORD	length of following data (max 45h)
02h	BYTE	39h (subfunction "Create Property")
03h	WORD	(big-endian) type of object
05h	BYTE	length of object's name (01h-2Fh)
06h	N BYTEs	object's name
	BYTE	property flags

	BYTE	property security levels
	BYTE	length of property's name (01h-0Fh)
	N BYTEs	property's name

21-27 Format of reply buffer:

Offset	Size	Description
00h	WORD	(call) 0000h (no data returned)

INT 21h Function E3h, Subfunction 3Ah   *Advanced NetWare 1.0+, Alloy NTNX*
DELETE PROPERTY   *Bindery Services*

Registers at call: **Return Registers:**
AH = E3h   AL = status (see Table 21-11)
DS:SI -> request buffer (see Table 21-28)
ES:DI -> reply buffer (see Table 21-29)
Conflicts: OS/286 and OS/386 (PCI-34), DoubleDOS (PCI-49)
See also: Function E3h Subfunctions 32h and 39h

21-28 Format of request buffer:

Offset	Size	Description
00h	WORD	length of following data (max 43h)
02h	BYTE	3Ah (subfunction "Delete Property")
03h	WORD	(big-endian) type of object
05h	BYTE	length of object's name (01h-2Fh)
06h	N BYTEs	object's name
	BYTE	length of property's name (01h-0Fh)
	N BYTEs	property's name

21-29 Format of reply buffer:

Offset	Size	Description
00h	WORD	(call) 0000h (no data returned)

INT 21h Function E3h, Subfunction 3Bh   *Advanced NetWare 1.0+, Alloy NTNX*
CHANGE PROPERTY SECURITY   *Bindery Services*

Registers at call: **Return Registers:**
AH = E3h   AL = status
DS:SI -> request buffer (see Table 21-30)   (00h,96h,F0h,F1h,FBh,FCh,FEh,FFh)
ES:DI -> reply buffer (see Table 21-31)   (see Table 21-11)
Conflicts: OS/286 and OS/386 (PCI-34), DoubleDOS (PCI-49)
See also: Function E3h Subfunction 38h

21-30 Format of request buffer:

Offset	Size	Description
00h	WORD	length of following data (max 44h)
02h	BYTE	3Bh (subfunction "Change Property Security")
03h	WORD	(big-endian) type of object
05h	BYTE	length of object's name (01h-2Fh)
06h	N BYTEs	object name
	BYTE	new property security levels
	BYTE	length of property's name
	N BYTEs	property name

21-31 Format of reply buffer:

Offset	Size	Description
00h	WORD	(call) 0000h (no data returned)

INT 21h Function E3h, Subfunction 3Ch
SCAN PROPERTY

Advanced NetWare 1.0+, Alloy NTNX
Bindery Services

Registers at call:
AH = E3h
DS:SI -> request buffer (see Table 21-32)
ES:DI -> reply buffer (see Table 21-33)

Return Registers:
AL = status (00h,96h,F1h,FBh,FCh,FEh,FFh)
  (see Table 21-11)

Conflicts: OS/286 and OS/386 (PCI-34), DoubleDOS (PCI-49)
See also: Function E3h Subfunctions 37h and 3Bh

21-32 Format of request buffer:

Offset	Size	Description
00h	WORD	length of following data (max 47h)
02h	BYTE	3Ch (subfunction "Scan Property")
03h	WORD	(big-endian) type of object
05h	BYTE	length of object's name (01h-2Fh)
06h	N BYTEs	object name
	DWORD	(big-endian) sequence number FFFFFFFFh for first call
	BYTE	length of property's name (01h-0Fh)
	N BYTEs	property's name

21-33 Format of reply buffer:

Offset	Size	Description
00h	WORD	(call) 0018h (length of following results buffer)
02h	16 BYTEs	property name
12h	BYTE	property flags
13h	BYTE	property security levels
14h	DWORD	(big-endian) sequence number
18h	BYTE	property value flag (00h no, FFh yes)
19h	BYTE	more properties (00h no, FFh yes)

INT 21h Function E3h, Subfunction 3Dh
READ PROPERTY VALUE

Advanced NetWare 1.0+, Alloy NTNX
Bindery Services

Purpose: Retrieve one 128-byte segment of the specified property's value.
Registers at call:
AH = E3h
DS:SI -> request buffer (see Table 21-34)
ES:DI -> reply buffer (see Table 21-35)

Return Registers:
AL = status (see Table 21-11)

Conflicts: OS/286 and OS/386 (PCI-34), DoubleDOS (PCI-49)
See also: Function E3h Subfunctions 39h, 3Ch, and 3Eh

21-34 Format of request buffer:

Offset	Size	Description
00h	WORD	length of following data (max 44h)
02h	BYTE	3Dh (subfunction "Read Property Value")
03h	WORD	(big-endian) type of object
05h	BYTE	length of object's name (01h-2Fh)
06h	N BYTEs	object name
	BYTE	segment number (01h on first call, increment until done)
	BYTE	length of property's name (01h-0Fh)
	N BYTEs	property name

21-35 Format of reply buffer:

Offset	Size	Description
00h	WORD	(call) 0082h (length of following results buffer)
02h	128 BYTEs	property's value
82h	BYTE	more segments (00h no, FFh yes)
83h	BYTE	property's flags

INT 21h Function E3h, Subfunction 3Eh
WRITE PROPERTY VALUE

Advanced NetWare 1.0+, Alloy NTNX
Bindery Services

Registers at call:
AH = E3h
DS:SI -> request buffer (see Table 21-36)
ES:DI -> reply buffer (see Table 21-37)

Return Registers:
AL = status (see Table 21-11)

Conflicts: OS/286 and OS/386 (PCI-34), DoubleDOS (PCI-49)
See also: Function E3h Subfunctions 39h, 3Ch, and 3Eh

21-36 Format of request buffer:

Offset	Size	Description
00h	WORD	length of following data (max C5h)
02h	BYTE	3Eh (subfunction "Write Property Value")
03h	WORD	(big-endian) type of object
05h	BYTE	length of object's name (01h-2Fh)
06h	N BYTEs	object name
	BYTE	segment number (01h on first call, increment until done)
	BYTE	erase remaining segments (00h no, FFh yes)
	BYTE	length of property's name (01h-0Fh)
	N BYTEs	property name
	128 BYTEs	property value segment

21-37 Format of reply buffer:

OffsetSizeDescription
00hWORD(call) 0000h (no data returned)

INT 21h Function E3h, Subfunction 3Fh
VERIFY BINDERY OBJECT PASSWORD

Advanced NetWare 1.0+, Alloy NTNX
Bindery Services

Registers at call:
AH = E3h
DS:SI -> request buffer (see Table 21-38)
ES:DI -> reply buffer (see Table 21-39)

Return Registers:
AL = status (see also Table 21-11)
   FFh bindery failure: no such object, bad
   password, no password for object, or
   invalid old password

Conflicts: OS/286 and OS/386 (PCI-34), DoubleDOS (PCI-49)
See also: Function E3h Subfunction 40h

21-38 Format of request buffer:

Offset	Size	Description
00h	WORD	length of following data (max 133h)
02h	BYTE	3Fh (subfunction "Verify Bindery Object Password")
03h	WORD	(big-endian) type of object
05h	BYTE	length of object's name (01h-2Fh)
06h	N BYTEs	object name
	BYTE	length of password (00h-7Fh)
	N BYTEs	password

21-39 Format of reply buffer:

Offset	Size	Description
00h	WORD	(call) 0000h (no data returned)

INT 21h Function E3h, Subfunction 40h   *Advanced NetWare 1.0+, Alloy NTNX*
CHANGE BINDERY OBJECT PASSWORD   *Bindery Services*

Registers at call:

AH = E3h
DS:SI -> request buffer (see Table 21-40)
ES:DI -> reply buffer (see Table 21-41)
Conflicts: OS/286 and OS/386 (PCI-34), DoubleDOS (PCI-49)
See also: Function E3h Subfunctions 3Fh and 41h

Return Registers:

AL = status (00h,96h,F0h,FBh,FCh,FEh,FFh)
(see Table 21-11)

21-40 Format of request buffer:

Offset	Size	Description
00h	WORD	length of following data (max 133h)
02h	BYTE	40h (subfunction "Change Bindery Object Password")
03h	WORD	(big-endian) type of object
05h	BYTE	length of object's name (01h-2Fh)
06h	N BYTEs	object name
	BYTE	length of old password (00h-7Fh)
	N BYTEs	old password
	BYTE	length of new password (00h-7Fh)
	N BYTEs	new password

21-41 Format of reply buffer:

Offset	Size	Description
00h	WORD	(call) 0000h (no data returned)

INT 21h Function E3h, Subfunction 41h   *Advanced NetWare 1.0+, Alloy NTNX*
ADD BINDERY OBJECT TO SET   *Bindery Services*

Purpose: Add the specified object to a set property.

Registers at call:

AH = E3h
DS:SI -> request buffer (see Table 21-42)
ES:DI -> reply buffer (see Table 21-43)
Conflicts: OS/286 and OS/386 (PCI-34), DoubleDOS (PCI-49)
See also: Function E3h Subfunctions 40h, 42h, and 43h

Return Registers:

AL = status
(00h,96h,E9h-EBh,F0h,F8h,F9h,FBh,FCh,FEh,
FFh) (see Table 21-11)

21-42 Format of request buffer:

Offset	Size	Description
00h	WORD	length of following data (max 75h)
02h	BYTE	41h (subfunction "Add Bindery Object to Set")
03h	WORD	(big-endian) type of object
05h	BYTE	length of object's name
06h	N BYTEs	object name
	BYTE	length of property name (01h-0Fh)
	N BYTEs	property name
	WORD	(big-endian) type of member object
	BYTE	length of member object's name
	N BYTEs	member object's name

21-43 Format of reply buffer:

Offset	Size	Description
00h	WORD	(call) 0000h (no data returned)

INT 21h Function E3h, Subfunction 42h   *Advanced NetWare 1.0+, Alloy NTNX*
DELETE BINDERY OBJECT FROM SET   *Bindery Services*

Purpose: Delete the specified object from a set property.

Registers at call:	Return Registers:
AH = E3h	AL = status
DS:SI -> request buffer (see Table 21-44)	(00h,96h,E9h-EBh,F0h,F8h,F9h,FBh,FCh,FEh,
ES:DI -> reply buffer (see Table 21-45)	FFh) (see Table 21-11)

Conflicts: OS/286 and OS/386 (PCI-34), DoubleDOS (PCI-49)
See also: Function E3h Subfunctions 40h, 42h, and 43h

21-44 Format of request buffer:

Offset	Size	Description
00h	WORD	length of following data (max 75h)
02h	BYTE	42h (subfunction "Delete Bindery Object from Set")
03h	WORD	(big-endian) type of object
05h	BYTE	length of object's name
06h	N BYTEs	object name
	BYTE	length of property name (01h-0Fh)
	N BYTEs	property name
	WORD	(big-endian) type of member object
	BYTE	length of member object's name
	N BYTEs	member object's name

21-45 Format of reply buffer:

Offset	Size	Description
00h	WORD	(call) 0000h (no data returned)

INT 21h Function E3h, Subfunction 43h   *Advanced NetWare 1.0+, Alloy NTNX*
IS BINDERY OBJECT IN SET   *Bindery Services*

Purpose: Determine whether the specified object is a member of the given set property.

Registers at call:	Return Registers:
AH = E3h	AL = status
DS:SI -> request buffer (see Table 21-46)	(00h,96h,E9h-EBh,F0h,F8h,F9h,FBh,FCh,FEh,
ES:DI -> reply buffer (see Table 21-47)	FFh) (see Table 21-11)

Details: The caller must have read access to the property.
Conflicts: OS/286 and OS/386 (PCI-34), DoubleDOS (PCI-49)
See also: Function E3h Subfunctions 41h and 42h

21-46 Format of request buffer:

Offset	Size	Description
00h	WORD	length of following data (max 75h)
02h	BYTE	43h (subfunction "Is Bindery Object In Set")
03h	WORD	(big-endian) type of object
05h	BYTE	length of object's name
06h	N BYTEs	object's name
	BYTE	length of property's name
	N BYTEs	property's name
	WORD	(big-endian) type of member object
	BYTE	length of member object's name
	N BYTEs	member object's name

21-47 Format of reply buffer:

Offset	Size	Description
00h	WORD	(call) 0000h (no data returned)

INT 21h Function E3h, Subfunction 44h
CLOSE BINDERY

Advanced NetWare 1.0+, Alloy NTNX
Bindery Services

Registers at call:
AH = E3h
DS:SI -> request buffer (see Table 21-48)
ES:DI -> reply buffer (see Table 21-49)
Conflicts: OS/286 and OS/386 (PCI-34), DoubleDOS (PCI-49)
See also: Function E3h Subfunction 45h

Return Registers:
AL = status
 00h successful

21-48 Format of request buffer:

Offset	Size	Description
00h	WORD	0001h (length of following data)
02h	BYTE	44h (subfunction "Close Bindery")

21-49 Format of reply buffer:

Offset	Size	Description
00h	WORD	(call) 0000h (no data returned)

INT 21h Function E3h, Subfunction 45h
OPEN BINDERY

Advanced NetWare 1.0+, Alloy NTNX
Bindery Services

Registers at call:
AH = E3h
DS:SI -> request buffer (see Table 21-50)
ES:DI -> reply buffer (see Table 21-51)
Details: The bindery may only be opened by the supervisor or an object with equivalent privileges.
Conflicts: OS/286 and OS/386 (PCI-34), DoubleDOS (PCI-49)
See also: Function E3h Subfunction 44h

Return Registers:
AL = status
 00h successful

21-50 Format of request buffer:

Offset	Size	Description
00h	WORD	0001h (length of following data)
02h	BYTE	45h (subfunction "Open Bindery")

21-51 Format of reply buffer:

Offset	Size	Description
00h	WORD	(call) 0000h (no data returned)

INT 21h Function E3h, Subfunction 46h
GET BINDERY ACCESS LEVEL

Advanced NetWare 1.0+, Alloy NTNX
Bindery Services

Registers at call:
AH = E3h
DS:SI -> request buffer (see Table 21-52)
ES:DI -> reply buffer (see Table 21-53)
Conflicts: OS/286 and OS/386 (PCI-34), DoubleDOS (PCI-49)

Return Registers:
AL = status
 00h successful

21-52 Format of request buffer:

Offset	Size	Description
00h	WORD	0001h (length of following data)
02h	BYTE	46h (subfunction "Get Bindery Access Level")

21-53 Format of reply buffer:

Offset	Size	Description
00h	WORD	0005h (length of following buffer)
02h	BYTE	security levels
03h	DWORD	(big-endian) object ID

Connection Services

INT 21h Function D7h
SYSTEM LOGOUT

NetWare 4.0+, Advanced NetWare 1.0+, Alloy NTNX
Connection Services

Purpose: This function closes the caller's open files, logs it out from all file servers, detaches the workstation from all non-default file servers, and maps a drive to the default server's SYS:LOGIN directory.

Registers at call:
AH = D7h

Return Registers:
AL = error code

See also: Function D6h, Function E3h Subfunction 14h, Function F1h

---

INT 21h Function DCh
GET CONNECTION NUMBER

Novell NetWare and others
Connection Services

Registers at call:
AH = DCh

Return Registers:
AL = logical connection number
    00h if NetWare not loaded or this machine is a
      non-dedicated server
CX = station number in ASCII (CL = first digit)

Details: This function is supported by NetWare 4.0+, Advanced NetWare 1.0+, Banyan VINES, and Alloy NTNX.

The station number is only unique for those PCs connected to the same semaphore service.

Conflicts: PCMANAGE/DCOMPRES (PCI-16)

INT 21h Function E3h
CONNECTION CONTROL

NetWare 4.0+, Advanced NetWare 1.0+, Alloy NTNX

Registers at call:
AH = E3h
DS:SI -> request buffer (see Table 21-54)
ES:DI -> reply buffer (see Table 21-55)

Return Registers:
AL = status
    00h successful
    else error code

Conflicts: OS/286 and OS/386 (PCI-34), DoubleDOS (PCI-49)

See also: Function E3h Subfunctions 0Ah, 32h, 64h, and C8h

21-54 Format of request buffer:

Offset	Size	Description
00h	WORD	length of following data
02h	BYTE	subfunction number
		00h login
		01h change password
		02h map user to station set
		03h map object to number
		04h map number to object
		05h get station's logged information
		06h get station's root mask (obsolete)
		07h map group name to number
		08h map number to group name

09h get memberset M of group G
03h   var   depends on subfunction

Notes: The above subfunctions are not described in *NetWare System Calls--DOS*. See separate entries for other subfunctions.

21-55 Format of reply buffer:

Offset	Size	Description
00h	WORD	(call) length of following buffer space for results
02h	var	depends on subfunction

21-56 Format of object property:

Offset	Size	Description
00h	1-16 BYTEs	property name
		well-known properties:
		ACCOUNT_BALANCE
		ACCOUNT_SERVERS
		GROUP_MEMBERS
		GROUPS_I'M_IN
		IDENTIFICATION user's name
		LOGIN_CONTROL
		NET_ADDRESS
		OPERATORS
		PASSWORD
		SECURITY_EQUALS
	N BYTE	flags
		bit 0: property is dynamic
		bit 1: property is a set rather than an item
	N+1 BYTE	security levels (see Table 21-57)
	unknown	

21-57 Values for security levels:

00h	"anyone" everyone may access
01h	"logged" only logged-in clients may access
02h	"object" only clients logged-in with object's name, type, and password
03h	"supervisor" only clients logged-in with supervisor privileges
04h	"NetWare" only NetWare may access

Note: The above values are stored in a nybble; the high half-byte is write access and the low half-byte is read access.

21-58 Values for object type:

0000h	unknown
0001h	user
0002h	user group
0003h	print queue
0004h	file server
0005h	job server
0006h	gateway
0007h	print server
0008h	archive queue
0009h	archive server
000Ah	job queue

000Bh	administration
0026h	remote bridge server
0047h	advertising print server
0048h-8000h reserved	
FFFFh	wild (used only for finding objects)

INT 21h Function E3h, Subfunction 0Ah
ENTER LOGIN AREA

Novell NetWare and others
Connection Services

Purpose: Change the login directory for the calling workstation.

Registers at call:
AH = E3h
DS:SI -> request buffer (see Table 21-59)
ES:DI -> reply buffer (see Table 21-60)

Return Registers:
AL = status
  00h successful

Details: This function is supported by NetWare 4.0+, Advanced NetWare 1.0+, and Alloy NTNX.

Conflicts: OS/286 and OS/386 (PCI-34), DoubleDOS (PCI-49)

See also: Function D7h, Function E3h Subfunction 14h

21-59 Format of request buffer:

Offset	Size	Description
00h	WORD	length of following data (max 102h)
02h	BYTE	0Ah (subfunction "Enter Login Area")
03h	BYTE	number of local drives
04h	BYTE	length of subdirectory name (00h-FFh)
05h	N BYTEs	name of subdirectory under SYS:LOGIN where to find the login utility

21-60 Format of reply buffer:

Offset	Size	Description
00h	WORD	(call) 0000h (no data returned)

INT 21h Function E3h, Subfunction 13h
GET INTERNET ADDRESS

Advanced NetWare 1.0+, Alloy NTNX
Connection Services

Registers at call:
AH = E3h
DS:SI -> request buffer (see Table 21-61)
ES:DI -> reply buffer (see Table 21-62)

Return Registers:
AL = status
  00h successful

Conflicts: OS/286 and OS/386 (PCI-34), DoubleDOS (PCI-49)

See also: Function DCh, Function E3h Subfunction 16h, Function EEh

21-61 Format of request buffer:

Offset	Size	Description
00h	WORD	0002h (length of following data)
02h	BYTE	13h (subfunction "Get Internet Address")
03h	BYTE	logical connection number (01h-64h)

21-62 Format of reply buffer:

Offset	Size	Description
00h	WORD	(call) 000Ch (length of following results buffer)
02h	4 BYTEs	network number
06h	6 BYTEs	physical node address
0Ch	2 BYTEs	socket number

INT 21h Function E3h, Subfunction 14h   *Advanced NetWare 1.0+, Alloy NTNX*
LOGIN TO FILE SERVER   *Connection Services*

Purpose: This function retrieves a list indicating the connection numbers under which a bindery object is logged into the default file server.

Registers at call:	Return Registers:
AH = E3h	AL = status
DS:SI -> request buffer (see Table 21-63)	00h successful
ES:DI -> reply buffer (see Table 21-64)	

Conflicts: OS/286 and OS/386 (PCI-34), DoubleDOS (PCI-49)
See also: Functions D7h and F1h

21-63 Format of request buffer:

Offset	Size	Description
00h	WORD	length of following data (max B3h)
02h	BYTE	14h (subfunction "Login To File Server")
03h	WORD	(big-endian) type of object
05h	BYTE	length of object's name (01h-2Fh)
06h	N BYTEs	object's name
	BYTE	length of password
	N BYTEs	password

21-64 Format of reply buffer:

Offset	Size	Description
00h	WORD	(call) 0000h (no data returned)

INT 21h Function E3h, Subfunction 15h   *Advanced NetWare 1.0+, Alloy NTNX*
GET OBJECT CONNECTION NUMBERS   *Connection Services*

Purpose: This function retrieves a list indicating the connection numbers under which a bindery object is logged into the default file server.

Registers at call:	Return Registers:
AH = E3h	AL = status
DS:SI -> request buffer (see Table 21-65)	00h successful
ES:DI -> reply buffer (see Table 21-66)	

Conflicts: OS/286 and OS/386 (PCI-34), DoubleDOS (PCI-49)
See also: Function DCh, Function E3h Subfunction 16h

21-65 Format of request buffer:

Offset	Size	Description
00h	WORD	length of following data (max 33h)
02h	BYTE	15h (subfunction "Get Object Connection Numbers")
03h	WORD	(big-endian) type of object
05h	BYTE	length of object's name (01h-2Fh)
06h	N BYTEs	object's name

21-66 Format of reply buffer:

Offset	Size	Description
00h	WORD	(call) length of following results buffer (max 65h)
v02h	BYTE	number of connections
03h	N BYTEs	connection list

INT 21h Function E3h, Subfunction 16h
GET CONNECTION INFORMATION

Advanced NetWare 1.0+, Alloy NTNX
Connection Services

Registers at call:
AH = E3h
DS:SI -> request buffer (see Table 21-67)
ES:DI -> reply buffer (see Table 21-68)
Conflicts: OS/286 and OS/386 (PCI-34), DoubleDOS (PCI-49)
See also: Functions D7h and DCh, Function E3h Subfunction 14h

Return Registers:
AL = status
    00h successful

21-67 Format of request buffer:

Offset	Size	Description
00h	WORD	0002h (length of following data)
02h	BYTE	16h (subfunction "Get Connection Information")
03h	BYTE	logical connection number (01h-64h)

21-68 Format of reply buffer:

Offset	Size	Description
00h	WORD	(call) 003Eh (length of following results buffer)
02h	DWORD	(big-endian) object ID for object logged in on the connection 00000000h if no object logged in
06h	WORD	(big-endian) type of object
08h	48 BYTEs	name of object
38h	7 BYTEs	login time (see Table 21-69)

Note: Much of the Novell documentation incorrectly states the reply buffer length as 3Fh instead of 40h, which corresponds to a results length of 3Dh (61) bytes instead of the correct 3Eh (62) bytes.

21-69 Format of login time:

Offset	Size	Description
00h	BYTE	year (80-99 = 1980-1999, 00-79 = 2000-2079)
01h	BYTE	month (1-12)
02h	BYTE	day (1-31)
03h	BYTE	hour (0-23)
04h	BYTE	minute (0-59)
05h	BYTE	second (0-59)
06h	BYTE	day of week (0 = Sunday)

INT 21h Function EEh
GET PHYSICAL STATION ADDRESS

NetWare 4.6+, Advanced NetWare 1.0+, Alloy NTNX
Connection Services

Registers at call:
AH = EEh
Conflicts: DoubleDOS (PCI-49), Virus (PCI-59)
See also: Function E3h Subfunction 13h

Return Registers:
CX:BX:AX = six-byte physical address

INT 21h Function F1h
FILE SERVER CONNECTION

Advanced NetWare 1.0+
Connection Services

Registers at call:
AH = F1h
AL = subfunction
        00h attach to file server
                DL = preferred file server (01h-08h)
        01h detach from file server

DL = connection ID
02h logout from file server
    DL = connection ID

Return Registers:
AL = status (see Table 21-70)

Conflicts: DoubleDOS (PCI-49), Virus (PCI-59)
See also: Function D7h, Function E3h Subfunction 14h

21-70 Values for status:

00h	successful
F8h	already attached to server
F9h	connection table full
FAh	no more server slots
FCh	unknown file server
FEh	server bindery locked
FFh	no response from server, or connection does not exist

Directory Services

21-71 Values for status:

00h	successful
84h	not permitted to create
8Ah	not permitted to delete
8Bh	not permitted to rename
8Ch	not permitted to modify
96h	server out of memory
98h	nonexistent volume
9Bh	invalid directory handle
9Ch	invalid path
9Eh	invalid filename
9Fh	directory currently in use
A0h	directory not empty
F0h	wildcard not allowed
F1h	invalid bindery security level
FCh	no such bindery object
FEh	server bindery locked
FFh	bindery failure

INT 21h Function DAh　　　　　　　　　　　NetWare 4.0+, Advanced NetWare 1.0+
GET VOLUME INFORMATION WITH NUMBER　　　　　　　　　*Directory Services*

Registers at call:　　　　　　　　**Return Registers:**
AH = DAh　　　　　　　　　　　　　　AL = 00h
DL = volume number
ES:DI -> reply buffer (see Table 21-72)
Details: Operator console rights are not required to make this call.

The reported total blocks and total unused blocks include the Hot Fix Table; the NetWare shell's implementation of INT 21h Function 36h will report values larger than 268MB as 268MB.
Conflicts: Viruses (PCI-59)
See also: Function E2h Subfunction 15h, Function E3h Subfunction E9h, MS-DOS Function 36h (PCI-24)

21-72 Format of reply buffer:

Offset	Size	Description
00h	WORD	(big-endian) sectors/block

02h	WORD	(big-endian) total blocks on volume
04h	WORD	(big-endian) unused blocks
06h	WORD	(big-endian) total directory entries
08h	WORD	(big-endian) unused directory entries
0Ah	16 BYTEs	volume name, null padded
1Ah	WORD	(big-endian) removable flag, 0000h = not removable

INT 21h Function E2h, Subfunction 00h
SET DIRECTORY HANDLE

Novell NetWare and others
Directory Services

Purpose: Set the target handle to reference the directory specified by the source handle and the source path; both handles must refer to the same file server.

Registers at call:
AH = E2h
DS:SI -> request buffer (see Table 21-73)
ES:DI -> reply buffer (see Table 21-74)

Return Registers:
AL = status (00h,98h,9Bh,9Ch) (see Table 21-71)

Details: This function is supported by NetWare 4.0+, Advanced NetWare 1.0+, and Alloy NTNX. The target handle is not changed if this function fails.

Conflicts: OS/286 and OS/386 (PCI-34), DoubleDOS (PCI-49)

See also: Function E2h Subfunctions 01h, 12h, and 13h

21-73 Format of request buffer:

Offset	Size	Description
00h	WORD	length of following data (max 103h)
02h	BYTE	00h (subfunction "Set Directory Handle")
03h	BYTE	directory handle of target
04h	BYTE	directory handle of source
05h	BYTE	length of source directory path (01h-FFh)
06h	N BYTEs	source directory path

21-74 Format of reply buffer:

Offset	Size	Description
00h	WORD	(call) 0000h (no results returned)

INT 21h Function E2h, Subfunction 01h
GET DIRECTORY PATH

Novell NetWare and others
Directory Services

Registers at call:
AH = E2h
DS:SI -> request buffer (see Table 21-75)
ES:DI -> reply buffer (see Table 21-76)

Return Registers:
AL = status (00h,9Bh) (see Table 21-71)

Details: This function is supported by NetWare 4.0+, Advanced NetWare 1.0+, and Alloy NTNX.

Conflicts: OS/286 and OS/386 (PCI-34), DoubleDOS (PCI-49)

See also: Function E2h Subfunctions 02h, 03h, and 1Ah; Function E9h

---

21-75 Format of request buffer:

Offset	Size	Description
00h	WORD	0002h (length of following data)
02h	BYTE	01h (subfunction "Get Directory Path")
03h	BYTE	directory handle

21-76 Format of reply buffer:

Offset	Size	Description
00h	WORD	(call) length of following data buffer
02h	BYTE	length of directory path (01h-FFh)
03h	N BYTEs	full directory path including volume

INT 21h Function E2h, Subfunction 02h
SCAN DIRECTORY INFORMATION

Novell NetWare and others
Directory Services

Purpose: Get information about the first or next subdirectory of the specified directory.

Registers at call:
AH = E2h
DS:SI -> request buffer (see Table 21-77)
ES:DI -> reply buffer (see Table 21-78)

Return Registers:
AL = status (00h,98h,9Bh,9Ch) (see Table 21-71)

Details: This function is supported by NetWare 4.0+, Advanced NetWare 1.0+, and Alloy NTNX.
Conflicts: OS/286 and OS/386 (PCI-34), DoubleDOS (PCI-49)
See also: Function E2h Subfunctions 01h, 03h, and 19h

21-77 Format of request buffer:

Offset	Size	Description
00h	WORD	length of following data (max 104h)
02h	BYTE	02h (subfunction "Scan Directory Information")
03h	BYTE	directory handle
04h	WORD	(big-endian) subdirectory number
		0000h for first call, returned subdirectory number + 1 on next call
06h	BYTE	length of directory path
07h	N BYTEs	directory path

21-78 Format of reply buffer:

Offset	Size	Description
00h	WORD	(call) 001Ch (length of following data buffer)
02h	16 BYTEs	subdirectory name
12h	DWORD	(big-endian) date and time of creation (see Table 21-79)
16h	DWORD	(big-endian) object ID of owner
1Ah	BYTE	maximum directory rights (see Table 21-82)
1Bh	BYTE	unused
1Ch	WORD	(big-endian) subdirectory number

21-79 Bitfields for date and time:

bits 31-25	year-1980
bits 24-21	month
bits 20-16	day
bits 15-11	hour
bits 10-5	minute
bits 4-0	second

INT 21h Function E2h, Subfunction 03h
GET EFFECTIVE DIRECTORY RIGHTS

Novell NetWare and others
Directory Services

Registers at call:
AH = E2h
DS:SI -> request buffer (see Table 21-80)
ES:DI -> reply buffer (see Table 21-81)

Return Registers:
AL = status (00h,98h,9Bh) (see Table 21-71)

Details: This function is supported by NetWare 4.0+, Advanced NetWare 1.0+, and Alloy NTNX.
Conflicts: OS/286 and OS/386 (PCI-34), DoubleDOS (PCI-49)
See also: Function E2h Subfunctions 01h and 02h

21-80 Format of request buffer:

Offset	Size	Description
00h	WORD	length of following data (max 102h)

02h	BYTE	03h (subfunction "Get Effective Directory Rights")
03h	BYTE	directory handle
04h	BYTE	length of directory path (00h-FFh)
05h	N BYTEs	directory path

21-81 Format of reply buffer:

Offset	Size	Description
00h	WORD	(call) 0001h (length of following data buffer)
02h	BYTE	effective directory rights (see Table 21-82)

21-82 Bitfields for directory rights:

bit 0	reading allowed
bit 1	writing allowed
bit 2	opens allowed
bit 3	file creation allowed
bit 4	deletion allowed
bit 5	"parental" may create/delete subdirectories and grant/revoke trustee rights
bit 6	directory search allowed
bit 7	file attributes may be changed

INT 21h Function E2h, Subfunction 04h
MODIFY MAXIMUM RIGHTS MASK

Novell NetWare and others
Directory Services

Registers at call:
AH = E2h
DS:SI -> request buffer (see Table 21-83)
ES:DI -> reply buffer (see Table 21-84)

Return Registers:
AL = status (00h,8Ch,98h,9Ch) (see
   Table 21-71)

Details: This function is supported by NetWare 4.0+, Advanced NetWare 1.0+, and Alloy NTNX.
Conflicts: OS/286 and OS/386 (PCI-34), DoubleDOS (PCI-49)
See also: Function E2h Subfunctions 03h, 0Ah, and 0Dh

21-83 Format of request buffer:

Offset	Size	Description
00h	WORD	length of following data (max 104h)
02h	BYTE	04h (subfunction "Modify Maximum Rights Mask")
03h	BYTE	directory handle
04h	BYTE	rights to grant (see Table 21-82)
05h	BYTE	rights to revoke (see Table 21-82)
06h	BYTE	length of directory path (00h-FFh)
07h	N BYTEs	directory path

Note: The rights specified at offset 05h are revoked first, and then the rights specified at offset 04h are added to the resulting rights mask.

21-84 Format of reply buffer:

Offset	Size	Description
00h	WORD	(call) 0000h (no results returned)

INT 21h Function E2h, Subfunction 05h
GET VOLUME NUMBER

Novell NetWare and others
Directory Services

Registers at call:
AH = E2h
DS:SI -> request buffer (see Table 21-85)
ES:DI -> reply buffer (see Table 21-86)

Return Registers:
AL = status (00h,98h) (see Table 21-71)

Details: This function is supported by NetWare 4.0+, Advanced NetWare 1.0+, and Alloy NTNX.

Conflicts: OS/286 and OS/386 (PCI-34), DoubleDOS (PCI-49)
See also: Function DAh; Function E2h Subfunctions 02h, 05h, and 15h; Function E3h Subfunction E9h

21-85 Format of request buffer:

Offset	Size	Description
00h	WORD	length of following data (max 12h)
02h	BYTE	05h (subfunction "Get Volume Number")
03h	BYTE	length of volume name (01h-10h)
04h	N BYTEs	volume name

21-86 Format of reply buffer:

Offset	Size	Description
00h	WORD	(call) 0001h (length of following results buffer)
02h	BYTE	volume number

INT 21h Function E2h, Subfunction 06h
GET VOLUME NAME
Novell NetWare and others
Directory Services

Registers at call:
AH = E2h
DS:SI -> request buffer (see Table 21-87)
ES:DI -> reply buffer (see Table 21-88)

Return Registers:
AL = status (00h,98h) (see Table 21-71)

Details: This function is supported by NetWare 4.0+, Advanced NetWare 1.0+, and Alloy NTNX.
Conflicts: OS/286 and OS/386 (PCI-34), DoubleDOS (PCI-49)
See also: Function DAh; Function E2h Subfunctions 02h, 05h, 15h, and 1Ah; Function E3h Subfunction E9h

21-87 Format of request buffer:

Offset	Size	Description
00h	WORD	0002h (length of following data)
02h	BYTE	06h (subfunction "Get Volume Name")
03h	BYTE	volume number

21-88 Format of reply buffer:

Offset	Size	Description
00h	WORD	(call) 0011h (length of following results buffer)
02h	BYTE	length of volume name
03h	16 BYTEs	NUL-padded volume name

INT 21h Function E2h, Subfunction 0Ah
CREATE DIRECTORY
Novell NetWare and others
Directory Services

Registers at call:
AH = E2h
DS:SI -> request buffer (see Table 21-89)
ES:DI -> reply buffer (see Table 21-90)

Return Registers:
AL = status (00h,84h,98h,FCh) (see Table 21-71)

Details: This function is supported by NetWare 4.0+, Advanced NetWare 1.0+, and Alloy NTNX.
Conflicts: OS/286 and OS/386 (PCI-34), DoubleDOS (PCI-49)
See also: Function E2h Subfunctions 0Bh and 0Fh, MS-DOS Function 39h (PCI-24)

21-89 Format of request buffer:

Offset	Size	Description
00h	WORD	length of following data (max 103h)
02h	BYTE	0Ah (subfunction "Create Directory")
03h	BYTE	directory handle

Offset	Size	Description
04h	BYTE	maximum directory rights (see Table 21-82)
05h	BYTE	length of directory path (00h-FFh)
06h	N BYTEs	directory path

21-90 Format of reply buffer:

Offset	Size	Description
00h	WORD	(call) 0000h (no data returned)

INT 21h Function E2h, Subfunction 0Bh
DELETE DIRECTORY

Novell NetWare and others
Directory Services

Registers at call:
AH = E2h
DS:SI -> request buffer (see Table 21-91)
ES:DI -> reply buffer (see Table 21-92)

Return Registers:
AL = status (00h,8Ah,98h,9Bh,9Ch,9Fh,A0h)
   (see Table 21-71)

Details: This function is supported by NetWare 4.0+, Advanced NetWare 1.0+, and Alloy NTNX.
Conflicts: OS/286 and OS/386 (PCI-34), DoubleDOS (PCI-49)
See also: Function E2h Subfunctions 0Ah and 0Fh, MS-DOS Function 3Ah (PCI-24)

21-91 Format of request buffer:

Offset	Size	Description
00h	WORD	length of following data (max 103h)
02h	BYTE	0Bh (subfunction "Delete Directory")
03h	BYTE	directory handle
04h	BYTE	unused
05h	BYTE	length of directory path (00h-FFh)
06h	N BYTEs	directory path

21-92 Format of reply buffer:

Offset	Size	Description
00h	WORD	(call) 0000h (no data returned)

INT 21h Function E2h, Subfunction 0Ch
SCAN DIRECTORY FOR TRUSTEES

Advanced NetWare 1.0+, Alloy NTNX
Directory Services

Registers at call:
AH = E2h
DS:SI -> request buffer (see Table 21-93)
ES:DI -> reply buffer (see Table 21-94)

Return Registers:
AL = status
   00h successful
   9Ch no more trustees

Conflicts: OS/286 and OS/386 (PCI-34), DoubleDOS (PCI-49)
See also: Function E2h Subfunctions 0Dh and 0Eh, Function E3h Subfunction 47h

21-93 Format of request buffer:

Offset	Size	Description
00h	WORD	length of following data (max 103h)
02h	BYTE	0Ch (subfunction "Scan Directory For Trustees")
03h	BYTE	directory handle
04h	BYTE	sequence number
		00h on first call, increment for each subsequent call
05h	BYTE	length of directory path (00h-FFh)
06h	N BYTEs	directory path

21-94 Format of reply buffer:

Offset	Size	Description
00h	WORD	(call) 0031h (length of following results buffer)
02h	16 BYTEs	directory name

12h	4 BYTEs	date and time of creation
16h	DWORD	(big-endian) object ID of owner
1Ah	5 DWORDs	(big-endian) object IDs of Trustees 0 through 4
		00000000h = end of group
2Eh	5 BYTEs	directory rights for Trustees 0 through 4 (see Table 21-82)

INT 21h Function E2h, Subfunction 0Dh
ADD TRUSTEE TO DIRECTORY

Novell NetWare and others
Directory Services

Registers at call:
AH = E2h
DS:SI -> request buffer (see Table 21-95)
ES:DI -> reply buffer (see Table 21-96)

Return Registers:
AL = status (00h,8Ch,FCh) (see Table 21-71)

Details: This function is supported by NetWare 4.0+, Advanced NetWare 1.0+, and Alloy NTNX.
Conflicts: OS/286 and OS/386 (PCI-34), DoubleDOS (PCI-49)
See also: Function E2h Subfunctions 0Ch and 0Eh, Function E3h Subfunction 47h

21-95 Format of request buffer:

Offset	Size	Description
00h	WORD	length of following data (max 107h)
02h	BYTE	0Dh (subfunction "Add Trustee To Directory")
03h	BYTE	directory handle
04h	DWORD	(big-endian) object ID of trustee
08h	BYTE	trustee directory rights (see Table 21-82)
09h	BYTE	length of directory path (00h-FFh)
0Ah	N BYTEs	directory path

21-96 Format of reply buffer:

Offset	Size	Description
00h	WORD	(call) 0000h (no data returned)

INT 21h Function E2h, Subfunction 0Eh
DELETE TRUSTEE FROM DIRECTORY

Novell NetWare and others
Directory Services

Registers at call:
AH = E2h
DS:SI -> request buffer (see Table 21-97)
ES:DI -> reply buffer (see Table 21-98)

Return Registers:
AL = status (00h,98h,9Bh,9Ch) (see Table 21-71)

Details: This function is supported by NetWare 4.0+, Advanced NetWare 1.0+, and Alloy NTNX.
Conflicts: OS/286 and OS/386 (PCI-34), DoubleDOS (PCI-49)
See also: Function E2h Subfunctions 0Ch and 0Dh

21-97 Format of request buffer:

Offset	Size	Description
00h	WORD	length of following data (max 107h)
02h	BYTE	0Eh (subfunction "Delete Trustee From Directory")
03h	BYTE	directory handle
04h	DWORD	(big-endian) object ID of trustee
08h	BYTE	unused
09h	BYTE	length of directory path (00h-FFh)
0Ah	N BYTEs	directory path

21-98 Format of reply buffer:

Offset	Size	Description
00h	WORD	(call) 0000h (no data returned)

INT 21h Function E2h, Subfunction 0Fh
RENAME DIRECTORY

Novell NetWare and others
Directory Services

Registers at call:
AH = E2h
DS:SI -> request buffer (see Table 21-99)
ES:DI -> reply buffer (see Table 21-100)

Return Registers:
AL = status (00h,8Bh,9Bh,9Ch,9Eh) (see
     Table 21-71)

Details: This function is supported by NetWare 4.0+, Advanced NetWare 1.0+, and Alloy NTNX.
    The directories SYS:LOGIN, SYS:MAIL, and SYS:PUBLIC must not be renamed.
Conflicts: OS/286 and OS/386 (PCI-34), DoubleDOS (PCI-49)
See also: Function E2h Subfunctions 0Ah and 0Bh, MS-DOS Function 56h (Chapter 3)

21-99 Format of request buffer:

Offset	Size	Description
00h	WORD	length of following data (max 111h)
02h	BYTE	0Fh (subfunction "Rename Directory")
03h	BYTE	directory handle
04h	BYTE	length of directory path (00h-FFh)
05h	N BYTEs	directory path
	BYTE	length of new directory name (01h-0Eh)
	N BYTEs	new directory name

21-100 Format of reply buffer:

Offset	Size	Description
00h	WORD	(call) 0000h (no data returned)

INT 21h Function E2h, Subfunction 12h
ALLOCATE PERMANENT DIRECTORY HANDLE

Novell NetWare and others
Directory Services

Registers at call:
AH = E2h
DS:SI -> request buffer (see Table 21-101)
ES:DI -> reply buffer (see Table 21-102)

Return Registers:
AL = status (00h,98h,9Ch) (see Table 21-71)

Details: This function is supported by NetWare 4.0+, Advanced NetWare 1.0+, and Alloy NTNX.
Conflicts: OS/286 and OS/386 (PCI-34), DoubleDOS (PCI-49)
See also: Function E2h Subfunctions 00h, 13h, and 14h

21-101 Format of request buffer:

Offset	Size	Description
00h	WORD	length of following data (max 103h)
02h	BYTE	12h (subfunction "Alloc Permanent Directory Handle")
03h	BYTE	directory handle
04h	BYTE	drive ('A'-'Z')
05h	BYTE	length of directory path
06h	N BYTEs	directory path

21-102 Format of reply buffer:

Offset	Size	Description
00h	WORD	(call) 0002h (size of following results buffer)
02h	BYTE	new directory handle
03h	BYTE	effective directory rights (see Table 21-82)

INT 21h Function E2h, Subfunction 13h *Novell NetWare and others*
ALLOCATE TEMPORARY DIRECTORY HANDLE *Directory Services*
Registers at call: Return Registers:
AH = E2h AL = status (00h,98h,9Ch) (see Table 21-71)
DS:SI -> request buffer (see Table 21-103)
ES:DI -> reply buffer (see Table 21-102)
Details: This function is supported by NetWare 4.0+, Advanced NetWare 1.0+, and Alloy NTNX.
    This call is the same as Function E2h Subfunction 12h except that the directory handle will be
automatically deallocated when the calling application executes an End of Job call (Function D6h)
or terminates.
Conflicts: OS/286 and OS/386 (PCI-34), DoubleDOS (PCI-49)
See also: Function D6h; Function E2h Subfunctions 00h, 12h, 14h, and 16h

21-103 Format of request buffer:

Offset	Size	Description
00h	WORD	length of following data (max 103h)
02h	BYTE	13h (subfunction "Alloc Temporary Directory Handle")
03h	BYTE	directory handle
04h	BYTE	drive ('A'-'Z')
05h	BYTE	length of directory path
06h	N BYTEs	directory path

INT 21h Function E2h, Subfunction 14h *Novell NetWare and others*
DEALLOCATE DIRECTORY HANDLE *Directory Services*
Registers at call: Return Registers:
AH = E2h AL = status (00h,9Bh) (see Table 21-71)
DS:SI -> request buffer (see Table 21-104)
ES:DI -> reply buffer (see Table 21-105)
Details: This function is supported by NetWare 4.0+, Advanced NetWare 1.0+, and Alloy NTNX.
Conflicts: OS/286 and OS/386 (PCI-34), DoubleDOS (PCI-49)
See also: Function E2h Subfunctions 12h and 13h

21-104 Format of request buffer:

Offset	Size	Description
00h	WORD	0002h (length of following data)
02h	BYTE	14h (subfunction "Deallocate Directory Handle")
03h	BYTE	directory handle

21-105 Format of reply buffer:

Offset	Size	Description
00h	WORD	(call) 0000h (no returned data)

INT 21h Function E2h, Subfunction 15h *Novell NetWare and others*
GET VOLUME INFORMATION WITH HANDLE *Directory Services*
Registers at call: Return Registers:
AH = E2h AL = status
DS:SI -> request buffer (see Table 21-106) 00h successful
ES:DI -> reply buffer (see Table 21-107)
Details: This function is supported by NetWare 4.0+, Advanced NetWare 1.0+, and Alloy NTNX.
Conflicts: OS/286 and OS/386 (PCI-34), DoubleDOS (PCI-49)
See also: Function DAh; Function E2h Subfunctions 02h, 06h, and 19h; Function E3h Subfunction E9h

21-106 Format of request buffer:

Offset	Size	Description
00h	WORD	0002h (length of following data)
02h	BYTE	15h (subfunction "Get Volume Info With Handle")
03h	BYTE	directory handle

21-107 Format of reply buffer:

Offset	Size	Description
00h	WORD	(call) 001Ch (length of following results buffer)
02h	WORD	(big-endian) sectors per block
04h	WORD	(big-endian) total blocks on volume
06h	WORD	(big-endian) blocks available on volume
08h	WORD	(big-endian) total directory slots
0Ah	WORD	(big-endian) directory slots available
0Ch	16 BYTEs	NUL-padded volume name
1Ch	WORD	(big-endian) flag: volume removable if nonzero

INT 21h Function E2h, Subfunction 16h
ALLOCATE SPECIAL TEMP DIRECTORY HANDLE
Advanced NetWare 1.0+, Alloy NTNX
(part. doc.) Directory Services

Registers at call:
AH = E2h
DS:SI -> request buffer (see Table 21-108)
ES:DI -> reply buffer

Return Registers:
AL = status

Details: This function is not described in *NetWare System Calls--DOS*.
Conflicts: OS/286 and OS/386 (PCI-34), DoubleDOS (PCI-49)
See also: Function E2h Subfunctions 13h and 14h

21-108 Format of request buffer:

Offset	Size	Description
00h	WORD	length of following data
02h	BYTE	16h (subfunction "Allocate Special Temporary Directory Handle")
	unknown	

INT 21h Function E2h, Subfunction 17h
SAVE DIRECTORY HANDLE
Advanced NetWare 2.0+, Alloy NTNX
Directory Services

Registers at call:
AH = E2h
DS:SI -> request buffer (see Table 21-109)
ES:DI -> reply buffer (see Table 21-110)

Return Registers:
AL = status
   00h successful
   else network error code

Conflicts: OS/286 and OS/386 (PCI-34), DoubleDOS (PCI-49)
See also: Function E2h Subfunctions 12h and 17h

21-109 Format of request buffer:

Offset	Size	Description
00h	WORD	0002h (length of following data)
02h	BYTE	18h (subfunction "Restore Directory Handle")
03h	BYTE	directory handle

21-110 Format of reply buffer:

Offset	Size	Description
00h	WORD	(call) 0010h (length of following results buffer)
02h	16 BYTEs	save buffer

INT 21h Function E2h, Subfunction 18h
RESTORE DIRECTORY HANDLE

Advanced NetWare 2.0+, Alloy NTNX
Directory Services

Purpose: Restore a previously saved directory handle to reproduce an executing environment, possibly on a different execution site.

Registers at call:
AH = E2h
DS:SI -> request buffer (see Table 21-111)
ES:DI -> reply buffer (see Table 21-112)

Return Registers:
AL = status
  00h successful
  else network error code

Conflicts: OS/286 and OS/386 (PCI-34), DoubleDOS (PCI-49)
See also: Function E2h Subfunctions 12h and 17h

21-111 Format of request buffer:

Offset	Size	Description
00h	WORD	0011h (length of following data)
02h	BYTE	18h (subfunction "Restore Directory Handle")
03h	16 BYTEs	save buffer

21-112 Format of reply buffer:

Offset	Size	Description
00h	WORD	(call) 0002h (length of following results buffer)
02h	BYTE	new directory handle
03h	BYTE	effective rights (see Table 21-82)

INT 21h Function E2h, Subfunction 19h
SET DIRECTORY INFORMATION

Advanced NetWare 1.0+, Alloy NTNX
Directory Services

Registers at call:
AH = E2h
DS:SI -> request buffer (see Table 21-113)
ES:DI -> reply buffer (see Table 21-114)

Return Registers:
AL = status (00h,9Bh,9Ch) (see Table 21-71)

Conflicts: OS/286 and OS/386 (PCI-34), DoubleDOS (PCI-49)
See also: Function E2h Subfunctions 02h and 0Fh

21-113 Format of request buffer:

Offset	Size	Description
00h	WORD	length of following data (max 10Bh)
02h	BYTE	19h (subfunction "Set Directory Information")
03h	BYTE	directory handle
04h	DWORD	(big-endian) date and time of creation
08h	DWORD	(big-endian) object ID of owner
0Ch	BYTE	maximum directory rightes (see Table 21-82)
0Dh	BYTE	length of directory path
0Eh	N BYTEs	directory path

21-114 Format of reply buffer:

Offset	Size	Description
00h	WORD	(call) 0000h (no results returned)

INT 21h Function E3h, Subfunction 47h
SCAN BINDERY OBJECT TRUSTEE PATHS

Advanced NetWare 1.0+, Alloy NTNX
Directory Services

Purpose: Iterate through the directories to which an object is a trustee.

Registers at call:
AH = E3h
DS:SI -> request buffer (see Table 21-115)
ES:DI -> reply buffer (see Table 21-116)

Return Registers:
AL = status (00h,96h,F0h,F1h,FCh,FEh,FFh)
(see Table 21-71)

Conflicts: OS/286 and OS/386 (PCI-34), DoubleDOS (PCI-49)
See also: Function E2h Subfunctions 0Ch, 0Dh, and 0Eh

21-115 Format of request buffer:

Offset	Size	Description
00h	WORD	0008h (length of following data)
02h	BYTE	47h (subfunction "Scan Bindery Object Trustee Paths")
03h	BYTE	volume number (00h-1Fh)
04h	WORD	(big-endian) last sequence number (FFFFh on first call)
06h	DWORD	(big-endian) object ID

21-116 Format of reply buffer:

Offset	Size	Description
00h	WORD	(call) length of following results buffer (max 107h)
02h	WORD	(big-endian) next sequence number
04h	DWORD	(big-endian) object ID
08h	BYTE	trustee directory rights (see Table 21-82)
09h	BYTE	length of trustee path
0Ah	N BYTEs	trustee path

INT 21h Function E3h, Subfunction E9h
GET VOLUME INFORMATION

Advanced NetWare 2.1+
Directory Services

Registers at call:
AH = E3h
DS:SI -> request buffer (see Table 21-117)
ES:DI -> reply buffer (see Table 21-118)

Return Registers:
AL = status
  00h successful

Conflicts: OS/286 and OS/386 (PCI-34), DoubleDOS (PCI-49)
See also: Function DAh, Function E2h Subfunction 15h

21-117 Format of request buffer:

Offset	Size	Description
00h	WORD	0002h (length of following data)
02h	BYTE	E9h (subfunction "Get Volume Information")
03h	BYTE	directory handle

21-118 Format of reply buffer:

Offset	Size	Description
00h	WORD	(call) 0028h (length of following results buffer)
02h	DWORD	(big-endian) elapsed system time
06h	BYTE	volume number
07h	BYTE	logical drive number
08h	WORD	(big-endian) sectors per block
0Ah	WORD	(big-endian) starting block
0Ch	WORD	(big-endian) total blocks on volume
0Eh	WORD	(big-endian) blocks available on volume
10h	WORD	(big-endian) total directory slots
12h	WORD	(big-endian) directory slots available
14h	WORD	(big-endian) maximum directory entries actually used
16h	BYTE	flag: volume hashed if nonzero
17h	BYTE	flag: volume cached if nonzero
18h	BYTE	flag: volume removable if nonzero
19h	BYTE	flag: volume mounted if nonzero
1Ah	16 BYTEs	NUL-padded volume name

INT 21h Function E4h
SET FILE ATTRIBUTES (FCB)

Novell NetWare
Obsolete

Registers at call:
AH = E4h
CL = file attributes (see Table 21-119)
DX:DX -> FCB (see Table 3-63)

Return Registers:
AL = error code

Details: This function was added in NetWare 4.0, but was removed some time prior to Advanced NetWare 2.15, and is no longer listed in current Novell documentation.
Conflicts: OS/286 and OS/386 (PCI-34), DoubleDOS (PCI-49), Virus (PCI-59)
See also: Function 4301h

21-119 Bitfields for file attributes:

bit 0   read only
bit 1   hidden
bit 2   system
bit 7   shareable

INT 21h Function E5h
UPDATE FILE SIZE (FCB)

Novell NetWare
Obsolete

Registers at call:
AH = E5h
DS:DX -> FCB (see Table 3-63)

Return Registers:
AL = (unreliable) return code

Details: This function was added in NetWare 4.0, but was removed some time prior to Advanced NetWare 2.15, and is no longer listed in current Novell documentation.
    On success, NetWare sets AL to zero; on errors it restores AL.
Conflicts: OS/286 and OS/386 (PCI-34), DoubleDOS (PCI-49)

INT 21h Function E900h
GET DIRECTORY HANDLE

NetWare 4.0+, Advanced NetWare 1.0+, Alloy NTNX
Directory Services

Registers at call:
AX = E900h
DX = drive number to check (0 = A:, ...,
    25 = Z:, 26 ... 31)

Return Registers:
AL = directory handle
AH = flags (drive not mapped if none set)
    bit 0: permanent handle
    bit 1: temporary handle
    bit 7: mapped to local drive

Conflicts: OS/286 and OS/386 (PCI-34), DoubleDOS (PCI-49)
See also: Function E2h Subfunctions 00h, 01h, and 0Ah

INT 21h Function E905h
MAP A FAKE ROOT DIRECTORY

Novell NetWare shell 3.01

Registers at call:
AX = E905h
BL = drive number (0=default, 1=A:, ...)
DS:DX -> ASCIZ path for fake root (may
    include server name or be empty)

Return Registers:
CF set on error
    AL = error code (03h,0Fh,11h) (see Table 3-1)
CF clear if successful

Details: If the drive is not currently mapped, a drive mapping will be created.
Conflicts: OS/286 and OS/386 (PCI-34), DoubleDOS (PCI-49)
See also: Function E906h

INT 21h Function E906h
DELETE FAKE ROOT DIRECTORY
Novell NetWare shell 3.01

Registers at call:
AX = E906h
BL = drive number (0=default, 1=A:, ...)
Details: The specified drive remains mapped.
Conflicts: OS/286 and OS/386 (PCI-34), DoubleDOS (PCI-49)
See also: Function E905h

INT 21h Function E907h
GET RELATIVE DRIVE DEPTH
Novell NetWare shell 3.01

Registers at call:
AX = E907h
BL = drive number (0=default, 1=A:, ...)

Return Registers:
AL = number of directories below the fake root
FFh if no fake root assigned

Conflicts: OS/286 and OS/386 (PCI-34), DoubleDOS (PCI-49)
See also: Function E905h

INT 21h Function E908h
SET SHOW DOTS
Novell NetWare shell 3.01

Registers at call:
AX = E908h
BL = 00h don't return '.' or '..' during
directory scans
= nonzero directory scans will return '.' or
'..' entries

Return Registers:
BL = previous show-dots setting

Conflicts: OS/286 and OS/386 (PCI-34), DoubleDOS (PCI-49)

File Server

21-120 Values for File Server function status:
00h	successful
98h	nonexistent volume
C6h	no console rights
F2h	not permitted to read object

INT 21h Function E2h, Subfunction 1Ah
GET PATH FROM DIRECTORY ENTRY
Novell NetWare and others
File Server

Registers at call:
AH = E2h
DS:SI -> request buffer (see Table 21-121)
ES:DI -> reply buffer (see Table 21-122)

Return Registers:
AL = status
00h successful

Details: This function is supported by NetWare 4.0+, Advanced NetWare 1.0+, and Alloy NTNX.
Conflicts: OS/286 and OS/386 (PCI-34), DoubleDOS (PCI-49)
See also: Function E2h Subfunctions 01h and 06h, Function E3h Subfunction D7h

21-121 Format of request buffer:
Offset	Size	Description
00h	WORD	0004h (length of following data)
02h	BYTE	1Ah (subfunction "Get Path From Directory Entry")
03h	BYTE	volume number (00h-1Fh)
04h	WORD	(big-endian) directory entry number

21-122 Format of reply buffer:

Offset	Size	Description
00h	WORD	(call) size of following results record (max 200h)
02h	256 BYTEs	path

INT 21h Function E3h, Subfunction 0Eh
GET DISK UTILIZATION

Advanced NetWare 2.1+
File Server

Registers at call:
AH = E3h
DS:SI -> request buffer (see Table 21-123)
ES:DI -> reply buffer (see Table 21-124)
Details: The caller must have bindery object read privileges.
Conflicts: OS/286 and OS/386 (PCI-34), DoubleDOS (PCI-49)
See also: Function E3h Subfunctions 11h, D6h, D9h, E6h, and E9h

Return Registers:
AL = status (00h,98h,F2h) (see Table 21-120)

21-123 Format of request buffer:

Offset	Size	Description
00h	WORD	0005h (length of following data)
02h	BYTE	0Eh (subfunction "Get Disk Utilization")
03h	BYTE	volume number (00h-1Fh)
04h	DWORD	(big-endian) object ID

21-124 Format of reply buffer:

Offset	Size	Description
00h	WORD	(call) 000Bh (size of following results buffer)
02h	BYTE	volume number (00h-1Fh)
03h	DWORD	(big-endian) object ID
07h	WORD	(big-endian) directories used by object
09h	WORD	(big-endian) files created by object
0Bh	WORD	(big-endian) disk blocks used by object-created files

---

INT 21h Function E3h, Subfunction 11h
GET FILE SERVER INFORMATION

Advanced NetWare 2.1+
File Server

Purpose: Determine the version of software installed on the file server and how it is configured.
Registers at call:
AH = E3h
DS:SI -> request buffer (see Table 21-125)
ES:DI -> reply buffer (see Table 21-126)
Conflicts: OS/286 and OS/386 (PCI-34), DoubleDOS (PCI-49)
See also: Function E3h Subfunctions 0Eh, 12h, CDh, D3h, and E7h; Function E7h

Return Registers:
AL = status
    00h successful

21-125 Format of request buffer:

Offset	Size	Description
00h	WORD	0001h (length of following data)
02h	BYTE	11h (subfunction "Get File Server Information")

21-126 Format of reply buffer:

Offset	Size	Description
00h	WORD	(call) 0080h (size of following results buffer)
02h	48 BYTEs	server's name
32h	BYTE	NetWare version
33h	BYTE	NetWare subversion (0-99)
34h	WORD	(big-endian) number of connections supported

| 36h | WORD | (big-endian) number of connections in use |
| 38h | WORD | (big-endian) maximum connected volumes |

---**Advanced NetWare 2.1+** ---

3Ah	BYTE	operating system revision number
3Bh	BYTE	fault tolerance (SFT) level
3Ch	BYTE	TTS level
3Dh	WORD	(big-endian) maximum simultaneously-used connections
3Fh	BYTE	accounting version
40h	BYTE	VAP version
41h	BYTE	queueing version
42h	BYTE	print server version
43h	BYTE	virtual console version
44h	BYTE	security restrictions level
45h	BYTE	internetwork bridge version
46h	60 BYTEs	reserved

INT 21h Function E3h, Subfunction C8h
CHECK CONSOLE PRIVILEGES
Advanced NetWare 2.1+
File Server

Purpose: Determine whether the caller is a console operator.

Registers at call:
AH = E3h
DS:SI -> request buffer (see Table 21-127)
ES:DI -> reply buffer (see Table 21-128)

Return Registers:
AL = status (00h,C6h) (see above)

Details: NetWare determines console privileges by checking the file server's OPERATOR property for the caller's object ID.

Conflicts: OS/286 and OS/386 (PCI-34), DoubleDOS (PCI-49)

See also: Function E3h Subfunctions C9h and D1h

21-127 Format of request buffer:

Offset	Size	Description
00h	WORD	0001h (length of following data)
02h	BYTE	C8h (subfunction "Check Console Privileges")

21-128 Format of reply buffer:

Offset	Size	Description
00h	WORD	(call) 0000h (no results returned)

INT 21h Function E3h, Subfunction C9h
GET FILE SERVER DESCRIPTION STRINGS
Advanced NetWare 2.1+
File Server

Registers at call:
AH = E3h
DS:SI -> request buffer (see Table 21-129)
ES:DI -> reply buffer (see Table 21-130)

Return Registers:
AL = status
  00h successful

Details: The calling workstation must be attached to the file server.

Conflicts: OS/286 and OS/386 (PCI-34), DoubleDOS (PCI-49)

See also: Function E3h Subfunctions 11h, CDh, and E8h

21-129 Format of request buffer:

Offset	Size	Description
00h	WORD	0001h (length of following data)
02h	BYTE	C9h (subfunction "Get File Server Description Strings")

21-130 Format of reply buffer:

Offset	Size	Description
00h	WORD	(call) 0200h (size of following results buffer)
02h	var	ASCIZ name of company distributing this copy of NetWare
	var	ASCIZ version and revision
	9 BYTEs	ASCIZ revision date (mm/dd/yy)
	var	ASCIZ copyright notice

INT 21h Function E3h, Subfunction CAh   *Advanced NetWare 2.1+*
SET FILE SERVER DATE AND TIME   *File Server*

Registers at call: **Return Registers:**
AH = E3h   AL = status (00h,C6h) (see Table 21-120)
DS:SI -> request buffer (see Table 21-130)
ES:DI -> reply buffer (see Table 21-131)
Details: The calling workstation must have console operator privileges.
Conflicts: OS/286 and OS/386 (PCI-34), DoubleDOS (PCI-49)
See also: Function E3h Subfunction C8h, Function E7h, MS-DOS Functions 2Bh and 2Dh (PCI-24)

21-131 Format of request buffer:

Offset	Size	Description
00h	WORD	0007h (length of following data)
02h	BYTE	CAh (subfunction "Set File Server Date And Time")
03h	BYTE	year (00-79 = 2000-2079, 80-99 = 1980-1999)
04h	BYTE	month (1-12)
05h	BYTE	day (1-31)
06h	BYTE	hour (0-23)
07h	BYTE	minute
08h	BYTR	second

21-132 Format of reply buffer:

Offset	Size	Description
00h	WORD	(call) 0000h (no results returned)

INT 21h Function E3h, Subfunction CBh   *Advanced NetWare 2.1+*
DISABLE FILE SERVER LOGIN   *File Server*

Registers at call: **Return Registers:**
AH = E3h   AL = status (00h,C6h) (see Table 21-120)
DS:SI -> request buffer (see Table 21-133)
ES:DI -> reply buffer (see Table 21-134)
Details: The calling workstation must have console operator privileges.
Conflicts: OS/286 and OS/386 (PCI-34), DoubleDOS (PCI-49)
See also: Function E3h Subfunctions C8h, CCh, and D3h

21-133 Format of request buffer:

Offset	Size	Description
00h	WORD	0001h (length of following data)
02h	BYTE	CBh (subfunction "Disable File Server Login")

21-134 Format of reply buffer:

Offset	Size	Description
00h	WORD	(call) 0000h (no results returned)

INT 21h Function E3h, Subfunction CCh
ENABLE FILE SERVER LOGIN

Advanced NetWare 2.1+
File Server

Registers at call:
AH = E3h
DS:SI -> request buffer (see Table 21-135)
ES:DI -> reply buffer (see Table 21-136)

Return Registers:
AL = status (00h,C6h) (see Table 21-120)

Details: The calling workstation must have console operator privileges.
Conflicts: OS/286 and OS/386 (PCI-34), DoubleDOS (PCI-49)
See also: Function E3h Subfunctions C8h and CBh

21-135 Format of request buffer:

Offset	Size	Description
00h	WORD	0001h (length of following data)
00h	BYTE	CCh (subfunction "Enable File Server Login")

21-136 Format of reply buffer:

Offset	Size	Description
00h	WORD	(call) 0000h (no results returned)

INT 21h Function E3h, Subfunction CDh
GET FILE SERVER LOGIN STATUS

Advanced NetWare 2.1+
File Server

Registers at call:
AH = E3h
DS:SI -> request buffer (see Table 21-137)
ES:DI -> reply buffer (see Table 21-138)

Return Registers:
AL = status
  00h successful
  C6h no console rights

Details: The calling workstation must have console operator privileges.
Conflicts: OS/286 and OS/386 (PCI-34), DoubleDOS (PCI-49)
See also: Function E3h Subfunctions C8h, CBh, and CCh

21-137 Format of request buffer:

Offset	Size	Description
00h	WORD	0001h (length of following data)
00h	BYTE	CDh (subfunction "Get File Server Login Status")

21-138 Format of reply buffer:

Offset	Size	Description
00h	WORD	(call) 0001h (size of following results buffer)
00h	BYTE	login state (00h disabled, 01h enabled)

INT 21h Function E3h, Subfunction CFh
DISABLE TRANSACTION TRACKING

Advanced NetWare 2.1+
File Server

Registers at call:
AH = E3h
DS:SI -> request buffer (see Table 21-139)
ES:DI -> reply buffer (see Table 21-140)

Return Registers:
AL = status
  00h successful
  C6h no console rights

Details: The calling workstation must have console operator privileges.
Conflicts: OS/286 and OS/386 (PCI-34), DoubleDOS (PCI-49)
See also: Function E3h Subfunctions C8h and D0h

21-139 Format of request buffer:

Offset	Size	Description
00h	WORD	0001h (length of following data)
00h	BYTE	CFh (subfunction "Disable Transaction Tracking")

21-140 Format of reply buffer:

Offset	Size	Description
00h	WORD	(call) 0000h (no results returned)

INT 21h Function E3h, Subfunction D0h
Advanced NetWare 2.1+
ENABLE TRANSACTION TRACKING
File Server

Purpose: Restart transaction tracking after being stopped either explicitly by Function E3h Subfunction CFh or automatically due to a full transaction volume.

Registers at call:
AH = E3h
DS:SI -> request buffer (see Table 21-141)
ES:DI -> reply buffer (see Table 21-142)

Return Registers:
AL = status
  00h successful
  C6h no console rights

Details: The calling workstation must have console operator privileges.
Conflicts: OS/286 and OS/386 (PCI-34), DoubleDOS (PCI-49)
See also: Function E3h Subfunctions C8h and CFh

21-141 Format of request buffer:

Offset	Size	Description
00h	WORD	0001h (length of following data)
00h	BYTE	D0h (subfunction "Enable Transaction Tracking")

21-142 Format of reply buffer:

Offset	Size	Description
00h	WORD	(call) 0000h (no results returned)

INT 21h Function E3h, Subfunction D1h
Advanced NetWare 2.1+
SEND CONSOLE BROADCAST
File Server

Registers at call:
AH = E3h
DS:SI -> request buffer (see Table 21-143)
ES:DI -> reply buffer (see Table 21-144)

Return Registers:
AL = status
  00h successful
  C6h no console rights

Details: The calling workstation must have console operator privileges.

The broadcast message will not be received by workstations which have disabled broadcasts with Function E1h Subfunction 02h.
Conflicts: OS/286 and OS/386 (PCI-34), DoubleDOS (PCI-49)
See also: Function E1h Subfunctions 02h and 09h, Function E3h Subfunctions C8h and D3h

21-143 Format of request buffer:

Offset	Size	Description
00h	WORD	length of following data (max A2h)
00h	BYTE	D1h (subfunction "Send Console Broadcast")
03h	BYTE	number of connections to receive message
		00h = all, else specific list below
04h	N BYTEs	connection list
	BYTE	length of message (max 3Ch)
	N BYTEs	message

21-144 Format of reply buffer:

Offset	Size	Description
00h	WORD	(call) 0000h (no results returned)

INT 21h Function E3h, Subfunction D2h
CLEAR CONNECTION NUMBER

Advanced NetWare 2.1+
File Server

Purpose: Close the open files and release all file locks for a connection, abort transactions if a TTS file server, and detach from the file server.

Registers at call:
AH = E3h
DS:SI -> request buffer (see Table 21-145)
ES:DI -> reply buffer (see Table 21-146)

Return Registers:
AL = status
00h successful
C6h no console rights

Details: The caller must have SUPERVISOR privileges.
Conflicts: OS/286 and OS/386 (PCI-34), DoubleDOS (PCI-49)
See also: Function E3h Subfunctions C9h and D1h

21-145 Format of request buffer:

Offset	Size	Description
00h	WORD	0002h (length of following data)
00h	BYTE	D2h (subfunction "Clear Connection Number")
03h	BYTE	connection number

21-146 Format of reply buffer:

Offset	Size	Description
00h	WORD	(call) 0000h (no results returned)

INT 21h Function E3h, Subfunction D3h
DOWN FILE SERVER

Advanced NetWare 2.1+
File Server

Purpose: Take down the file server.

Registers at call:
AH = E3h
DS:SI -> request buffer (see Table 21-147)
ES:DI -> reply buffer (see Table 21-148)

Return Registers:
AL = status
00h successful
C6h no console rights
FFh files open

Details: The calling workstation must have SUPERVISOR privileges.
Conflicts: OS/286 and OS/386 (PCI-34), DoubleDOS (PCI-49)
See also: Function E3h Subfunctions C8h, CBh, CFh, and D1h

21-147 Format of request buffer:

Offset	Size	Description
00h	WORD	0002h (length of following data)
00h	BYTE	D3h (subfunction "Down File Server")
03h	BYTE	flag: force down even when files open if nonzero

21-148 Format of reply buffer:

Offset	Size	Description
00h	WORD	(call) 0000h (no results returned)

INT 21h Function E3h, Subfunction D4h
GET FILE SYSTEM STATISTICS

Advanced NetWare 2.1+
File Server

Registers at call:
AH = E3h
DS:SI -> request buffer (see Table 21-149)
ES:DI -> reply buffer (see Table 21-150)

Return Registers:
AL = status
00h successful
C6h no console rights

Details: The calling workstation must have console operator privileges.
Conflicts: OS/286 and OS/386 (PCI-34), DoubleDOS (PCI-49)
See also: Function E3h Subfunctions 0Eh, C8h, D9h, E7h, and E8h

21-149 Format of request buffer:

Offset	Size	Description
00h	WORD	0001h (length of following data)
00h	BYTE	D4h (subfunction "Get File System Statistics")

21-150 Format of reply buffer:

Offset	Size	Description
00h	WORD	(call) 0028h (size of following results buffer)
00h	DWORD	(big-endian) clock ticks since system started
06h	WORD	(big-endian) maximum open files set by configuration
08h	WORD	(big-endian) maximum files open concurrently
0Ah	WORD	(big-endian) current number of open files
0Ch	DWORD	(big-endian) total files opened
10h	DWORD	(big-endian) total file read requests
14h	DWORD	(big-endian) total file write requests
18h	WORD	(big-endian) current changed FATs
1Ah	WORD	(big-endian) total changed FATs
1Ch	WORD	(big-endian) number of FAT write errors
1Eh	WORD	(big-endian) number of fatal FAT write errors
20h	WORD	(big-endian) number of FAT scan errors
22h	WORD	(big-endian) maximum concurrently-indexed files
24h	WORD	(big-endian) current number of indexed files
26h	WORD	(big-endian) number of attached indexed files
28h	WORD	(big-endian) number of indexed files available

INT 21h Function E3h, Subfunction D5h
GET TRANSACTION TRACKING STATISTICS

Advanced NetWare 2.1+
File Server

Registers at call:
AH = E3h
DS:SI -> request buffer (see Table 21-151)
ES:DI -> reply buffer (see Table 21-152)

Return Registers:
AL = status
  00h successful
  C6h no console rights

Details: The calling workstation must have console operator privileges.
Conflicts: OS/286 and OS/386 (PCI-34), DoubleDOS (PCI-49)
See also: Function E3h Subfunctions C8h, CFh, D0h, and E8h

21-151 Format of request buffer:

Offset	Size	Description
00h	WORD	0001h (length of following data)
00h	BYTE	D5h (subfunction "TTS Get Statistics")

21-152 Format of reply buffer:

Offset	Size	Description
00h	WORD	(call) length of following results buffer (max 1BCh)
00h	DWORD	(big-endian) clock ticks since system started
06h	BYTE	transaction tracking supported if nonzero (all following fields are invalid if zero)
07h	BYTE	transaction tracking enabled
08h	WORD	(big-endian) transaction volume number
0Ah	WORD	(big-endian) maximum simultaneous transactions configured
0Ch	WORD	(big-endian) maximum simultaneous transactions since startup
0Eh	WORD	(big-endian) current transactions in progress

10h	DWORD	(big-endian) total transactions performed
14h	DWORD	(big-endian) total write transactions
18h	DWORD	(big-endian) total transactions backed out
1Ch	WORD	(big-endian) number of unfilled backout requests
1Eh	WORD	(big-endian) disk blocks used for transaction tracking
20h	DWORD	(big-endian) blocks allocated for tracked-file FATs
24h	DWORD	(big-endian) number of file size changes during a transaction
28h	DWORD	(big-endian) number of file truncations during a transaction
2Ch	BYTE	number of records following
2Dh	Active Transaction Records [array]	

Offset	Size	Description
00h	BYTE	logical connection number
01h	BYTE	task number

INT 21h Function E3h, Subfunction D6h
GET DISK CACHE STATISTICS

Advanced NetWare 2.1+
File Server

Registers at call:
AH = E3h
DS:SI -> request buffer (see Table 21-153)
ES:DI -> reply buffer (see Table 21-154)

Return Registers:
AL = status
  00h successful
  C6h no console rights

Details: The calling workstation must have console operator privileges.
Conflicts: OS/286 and OS/386 (PCI-34), DoubleDOS (PCI-49)
See also: Function E3h Subfunctions C8h, D5h, D8h, D9h, and E6h

---

21-153 Format of request buffer:

Offset	Size	Description
00h	WORD	0001h (length of following data)
00h	BYTE	D6h (subfunction "Get Disk Cache Statistics")

21-154 Format of reply buffer:

Offset	Size	Description
00h	WORD	(call) 004Eh (length of following results buffer)
00h	DWORD	(big-endian) clock ticks since system started
06h	WORD	(big-endian) number of cache buffers
08h	WORD	(big-endian) size of cache buffer in bytes
0Ah	WORD	(big-endian) number of dirty cache buffers
0Ch	DWORD	(big-endian) number of cache read requests
10h	DWORD	(big-endian) number of cache write requests
14h	DWORD	(big-endian) number of cache hits
18h	DWORD	(big-endian) number of cache misses
1Ch	DWORD	(big-endian) number of physical read requests
20h	DWORD	(big-endian) number of physical write requests
24h	WORD	(big-endian) number of physical read errors
26h	WORD	(big-endian) number of physical write errors
28h	DWORD	(big-endian) cache get requests
2Ch	DWORD	(big-endian) cache full write requests
30h	DWORD	(big-endian) cache partial write requests
34h	DWORD	(big-endian) background dirty writes
38h	DWORD	(big-endian) background aged writes
3Ch	DWORD	(big-endian) total cache writes
40h	DWORD	(big-endian) number of cache allocations

44h	WORD	(big-endian) thrashing count
46h	WORD	(big-endian) number of times LRU block was dirty
48h	WORD	(big-endian) number of reads on cache blocks not yet filled by writes
4Ah	WORD	(big-endian) number of times a fragmented write occurred
4Ch	WORD	(big-endian) number of cache hits on unavailable block
4Eh	WORD	(big-endian) number of times a cache block was scrapped

INT 21h Function E3h, Subfunction D7h
GET DRIVE MAPPING TABLE
Advanced NetWare 2.1+
File Server

Registers at call:
AH = E3h
DS:SI -> request buffer (see Table 21-155)
ES:DI -> reply buffer (see Table 21-156)

Return Registers:
AL = status
  00h successful
  C6h no console rights

Details: The calling workstation must have console operator privileges.
Conflicts: OS/286 and OS/386 (PCI-34), DoubleDOS (PCI-49)
See also: Function E3h Subfunctions C8h, D6h, D9h, E6h, and E9h

21-155 Format of request buffer:
Offset	Size	Description
00h	WORD	0001h (length of following data)
00h	BYTE	D7h (subfunction "Get Drive Mapping Table")

21-156 Format of reply buffer:
Offset	Size	Description
00h	WORD	(call) 00ECh (length of following results buffer)
00h	DWORD	(big-endian) clock tick elapsed since system started
06h	BYTE	fault tolerance (SFT) level
07h	BYTE	number of logical drives attached to server
08h	BYTE	number of physical drives attached to server
09h	5 BYTEs	disk channel types (00h none, 01h XT, 02h AT, 03h SCSI, 04h disk coprocessor drive, 32h-FFh value-added drive types)
0Eh	WORD	(big-endian) number of outstanding controller commands
10h	32 BYTEs	drive mapping table (FFh = no such drive)
30h	32 BYTEs	drive mirror table (secondary physical drive, FFh = none)
50h	32 BYTEs	dead mirror table (last drive mapped to, FFh if never mirrored)
70h	BYTE	physical drive being remirrored (FFh = none)
71h	BYTE	reserved
72h	DWORD	(big-endian) remirrored block
76h	60 BYTEs	SFT error table (internal error counters)

INT 21h Function E3h, Subfunction D8h
GET PHYSICAL DISK STATISTICS
Advanced NetWare 2.1+
File Server

Registers at call:
AH = E3h
DS:SI -> request buffer (see Table 21-157)
ES:DI -> reply buffer (see Table 21-158)

Return Registers:
AL = status
  00h successful
  C6h no console rights

Details: The calling workstation must have console operator privileges.
Conflicts: OS/286 and OS/386 (PCI-34), DoubleDOS (PCI-49)
See also: Function E3h Subfunctions C8h, D9h, and E9h

21-157 Format of request buffer:

Offset	Size	Description
00h	WORD	0002h (length of following data)
00h	BYTE	D8h (subfunction "Get Physical Disk Statistics")
03h	BYTE	physical disk number

21-158 Format of reply buffer:

Offset	Size	Description
00h	WORD	(call) 005Dh (size of following results record)
00h	DWORD	(big-endian) clock ticks since system started
06h	BYTE	physical disk channel
07h	BYTE	flag: drive removable if nonzero
08h	BYTE	physical drive type
09h	BYTE	drive number within controller
0Ah	BYTE	controller number
0Bh	BYTE	controller type
0Ch	DWORD	(big-endian) size of drive in 4K disk blocks
10h	WORD	(big-endian) number of cylinders on drive
12h	BYTE	number of heads
13h	BYTE	number of sectors per track
14h	64 BYTEs	ASCIZ drive make and model
54h	WORD	(big-endian) number of I/O errors
56h	DWORD	(big-endian) start of Hot Fix table
5Ah	WORD	(big-endian) size of Hot Fix table
5Ch	WORD	(big-endian) number of Hot Fix blocks available
5Eh	BYTE	flag: Hot Fix disabled if nonzero

INT 21h Function E3h, Subfunction D9h
GET DISK CHANNEL STATISTICS

Advanced NetWare 2.1+
File Server

Registers at call:
AH = E3h
DS:SI -> request buffer (see Table 21-159)
ES:DI -> reply buffer (see Table 21-160)

Return Registers:
AL = status
  00h successful
  C6h no console rights

Details: The calling workstation must have console operator privileges.
Conflicts: OS/286 and OS/386 (PCI-34), DoubleDOS (PCI-49)
See also: Function E3h Subfunctions C8h, D8h, E6h, and E9h

21-159 Format of request buffer:

Offset	Size	Description
00h	WORD	0002h (length of following data)
00h	BYTE	D9h (subfunction "Get Disk Channel Statistics")
03h	BYTE	channel number

21-160 Format of reply buffer:

Offset	Size	Description
00h	WORD	(call) 00A8h (size of following results record)
00h	DWORD	(big-endian) clock ticks since system started
06h	WORD	(big-endian) channel run state (see Table 21-161)
08h	WORD	(big-endian) channel synchronization state (see Table 21-162)
0Ah	BYTE	driver type
0Bh	BYTE	major version of driver

0Ch	BYTE	minor version of driver
0Dh	65 BYTEs	ASCIZ driver description
4Eh	WORD	(big-endian) first I/O address used
50h	WORD	(big-endian) length of first I/O address
52h	WORD	(big-endian) second I/O address used
54h	WORD	(big-endian) length of second I/O address
56h	3 BYTEs	first shared memory address
59h	2 BYTEs	length of first shared memory address
5Bh	3 BYTEs	second shared memory address
5Eh	2 BYTEs	length of second shared memory address
60h	BYTE	first interrupt number in-use flag
61h	BYTE	first interrupt number used
62h	BYTE	second interrupt number in-use flag
63h	BYTE	second interrupt number used
64h	BYTE	first DMA channel in-use flag
65h	BYTE	first DMA channel used
66h	BYTE	second DMA channel in-use flag
67h	BYTE	second DMA channel used
68h	BYTE	flags
69h	BYTE	reserved
6Ah	80 BYTEs	ASCIZ configuration description

21-161 Values for channel run state:

0000h	running
0001h	being stopped
0002h	stopped
0003h	nonfunctional

21-162 Values for channel synchronization state:

0000h	not in use
0002h	used by NetWare, no other requests
0004h	used by NetWare, other requests
0006h	in use, not needed by NetWare
0008h	in use, needed by NetWare
000Ah	channel released, NetWare should use it

INT 21h Function E3h, Subfunction DAh
GET CONNECTION'S TASK INFORMATION

Advanced NetWare 2.1+
File Server

Registers at call:
AH = E3h
DS:SI -> request buffer (see Table 21-163)
ES:DI -> reply buffer (see Table 21-164)

Return Registers:
AL = status
  00h successful
  C6h no console rights

Details: The calling workstation must have console operator privileges.
Conflicts: OS/286 and OS/386 (PCI-34), DoubleDOS (PCI-49)
See also: Function E3h Subfunctions C8h, DBh, DFh, E1h, and E5h

21-163 Format of request buffer:

Offset	Size	Description
00h	WORD	0003h (length of following data)
00h	BYTE	DAh (subfunction "Get Connection's Task Information")
03h	WORD	(big-endian) logical connection number

21-164 Format of reply buffer:

Offset	Size	Description
00h	WORD	(call) size of following results record (max 1FEh)
00h	BYTE	lock status of connection (see Table 21-165)
03h	var	Lock Status Information (see Table 21-166)
	N BYTE	number of records following
N+1		Active Task Information Records [array]

Offset	Size	Description
00h	BYTE	task number (01h-FFh)
01h	BYTE	task state
		01h in TTS explicit transaction
		02h in TTS implicit transaction
		04h shared fileset lock active

21-165 Values for lock status of connection:

00h	no locks
01h	waiting on physical record lock
00h	waiting on file lock
03h	waiting on logical record lock
04h	waiting on semaphore

21-166 Format of Lock Status Information:

Offset	Size	Description
---lock status 00h---		
---lock status 01h---		
00h	BYTE	number of waiting task
01h	DWORD	start address
05h	DWORD	end address
09h	BYTE	volume number
0Ah	WORD	directory entry number
0Ch	14 BYTEs	ASCIZ filename
---lock status 02h---		
00h	BYTE	number of waiting task
01h	BYTE	volume number
00h	WORD	directory entry number
04h	14 BYTEs	ASCIZ filename
---lock status 03h---		
00h	BYTE	number of waiting task
01h	BYTE	length of record name
00h	N BYTEs	ASCIZ record name
---lock status 04h---		
00h	BYTE	number of waiting task
01h	BYTE	length of semaphore's name
00h	N BYTEs	ASCIZ semaphore name

INT 21h Function E3h, Subfunction DBh
GET CONNECTION'S OPEN FILES

Advanced NetWare 2.1+
File Server

Registers at call:
AH = E3h
DS:SI -> request buffer (see Table 21-167)
ES:DI -> reply buffer (see Table 21-168)

Return Registers:
AL = status
  00h successful
  C6h no console rights

Details: The calling workstation must have console operator privileges.
Conflicts: OS/286 and OS/386 (PCI-34), DoubleDOS (PCI-49)
See also: Function E2h Subfunction 1Ah; Function E3h Subfunctions C8h, DAh, DCh, and DFh
See also: Function E3h Subfunction E1h

21-167 Format of request buffer:

Offset	Size	Description
00h	WORD	0005h (length of following data)
00h	BYTE	DBh (subfunction "Get Connection's Open Files")
03h	WORD	(big-endian) logical connection number
05h	WORD	(big-endian) last record seen (0000h on first call)

21-168 Format of reply buffer:

Offset	Size	Description
00h	WORD	(call) size of following results record (max 1FEh)
00h	WORD	next request record (place in "last record" field on next call)
		0000h if no more records
04h	BYTE	number of records following
05h	var	array of File Information Records (see Table 21-169)

21-169 Format of File Information Record:

Offset	Size	Description
00h	BYTE	task number
01h	BYTE	lock flags (see Table 21-170)
00h	BYTE	access flags (see Table 21-171)
03h	BYTE	lock type
		00h no lock
		FEh file lock
		FFh locked by Begin Share File Set
04h	BYTE	volume number (00h-1Fh)
05h	WORD	(big-endian) directory entry
07h	14 BYTEs	ASCIZ filename

21-170 Bitfields for lock flags:

bit 0	file is locked
bit 1	file opened Shareable
bit 2	logged
bit 3	file opened Normal
bit 6	TTS holding lock
bit 7	Transaction Flag set on file

21-171 Bitfields for access flags:

bit 0	file open for reading by calling station
bit 1	file open for writing by calling station
bit 2	deny reads by other stations
bit 3	deny writes by other stations
bit 4	file detached
bit 5	TTS Holding Detach
bit 6	TTS Holding Open

INT 21h Function E3h, Subfunction DCh *Advanced NetWare 2.1+*
GET CONNECTIONS USING A FILE *File Server*

Registers at call: Return Registers:
AH = E3h   AL = status
DS:SI -> request buffer (see Table 21-172)   00h successful
ES:DI -> reply buffer (see Table 21-173)   C6h no console rights
Details: The calling workstation must have console operator privileges.
Conflicts: OS/286 and OS/386 (PCI-34), DoubleDOS (PCI-49)
See also: Function E3h Subfunctions C8h, DAh, DBh, DFh, and E1h

21-172 Format of request buffer:

Offset	Size	Description
00h	WORD	length of following data (max 104h)
00h	BYTE	DCh (subfunction "Get Connections Using a File")
03h	WORD	(big-endian) last record (0000h on first call)
05h	BYTE	directory handle
06h	BYTE	length of file path
07h	N BYTEs	ASCIZ file path

21-173 Format of reply buffer:

Offset	Size	Description
00h	WORD	(call) size of following results record (max 1FEh)
00h	WORD	(big-endian) count of tasks which have opened or logged file
04h	WORD	(big-endian) count of tasks which have opened file
06h	WORD	(big-endian) count of opens for reading
08h	WORD	(big-endian) count of opens for writing
0Ah	WORD	(big-endian) deny read count
0Ch	WORD	(big-endian) deny write count
0Eh	WORD	next request record (place in "last record" field on next call) 0000h if no more records
10h	BYTE	locked flag 00h not locked exclusively else locked exclusively
11h	BYTE	number of records following
12h	var	array of File Usage Information Records (see Table 21-174)

21-174 Format of File Usage Information Record:

Offset	Size	Description
00h	WORD	(big-endian) logical connection number
00h	BYTE	task number
03h	BYTE	lock flags (see Table 21-170)
04h	BYTE	access flags (see Table 21-171)
05h	BYTE	lock type 00h no lock FEh file lock FFh locked by Begin Share File Set

INT 21h Function E3h, Subfunction DDh *Advanced NetWare 2.1+*
GET PHYSICAL RECORD LOCKS BY CONNECTION AND FILE *File Server*
Registers at call:
AH = E3h

DS:SI -> request buffer (see Table 21-175)
ES:DI -> reply buffer (see Table 21-176)

Return Registers:
AL = status
  00h successful
  C6h no console rights
  FFh file not open

Details: The calling workstation must have console operator privileges.
Conflicts: OS/286 and OS/386 (PCI-34), DoubleDOS (PCI-49)
See also: Function E3h Subfunctions C8h, DEh, and DFh

21-175 Format of request buffer:

Offset	Size	Description
00h	WORD	0016h (length of following data)
00h	BYTE	DDh (subfunction "Get Physical Record Locks by Connection and File")
03h	WORD	(big-endian) logical connection number
05h	WORD	(big-endian) last record seen (0000h on first call)
07h	BYTE	volume number (00h-1Fh)
08h	WORD	(big-endian) directory handle
0Ah	14 BYTEs	ASCIZ filename

21-176 Format of reply buffer:

Offset	Size	Description
00h	WORD	(call) size of following results record (max 1FEh)
00h	WORD	next request record (place in "last record" on next call) 0000h if no more records
04h	BYTE	number of physical record locks
05h	BYTE	number of records following
06h	var	array of Physical Record Lock Info records (see Table 21-177)

21-177 Format of Physical Record Lock Info:

Offset	Size	Description
00h	BYTE	task number
01h	BYTE	lock status (see Table 21-178)
00h	DWORD	(big-endian) starting offset of record in file
06h	DWORD	(big-endian) ending offset of record in file

21-178 Bitfields for lock status:

bit 0	exclusive lock
bit 1	shareable lock
bit 2	logged
bit 6	lock held by TTS

INT 21h Function E3h, Subfunction DEh
GET PHYSICAL RECORD LOCKS BY FILE

Advanced NetWare 2.1+
File Server

Registers at call:
AH = E3h
DS:SI -> request buffer (see Table 21-179)
ES:DI -> reply buffer (see Table 21-180)

Return Registers:
AL = status
  00h successful
  C6h no console rights
  FFh file not open

Details: The calling workstation must have console operator privileges.
Conflicts: OS/286 and OS/386 (PCI-34), DoubleDOS (PCI-49)
See also: Function E3h Subfunctions C8h, DDh, and DFh

21-179 Format of request buffer:

Offset	Size	Description
00h	WORD	length of following data (max 104h)
00h	BYTE	DEh (subfunction "Get Physical Record Locks by File")
03h	WORD	(big-endian) last record seen (0000h on first call)
05h	BYTE	directory handle
06h	BYTE	length of filename
07h	N BYTEs	ASCIZ filename

21-180 Format of reply buffer:

Offset	Size	Description
00h	WORD	(call) size of following results record (max 1FEh)
00h	WORD	next request record (place in "last record" on next call) 0000h if no more records
04h	BYTE	number of physical record locks
05h	BYTE	number of records following
06h	var	array of Physical Record Lock Info records (see Table 21-181)

21-181 Format of Physical Record Lock Info:

Offset	Size	Description
00h	WORD	(big-endian) number of tasks logging record
00h	WORD	(big-endian) number of tasks with shareable lock
04h	DWORD	(big-endian) starting offset of record in file
08h	DWORD	(big-endian) ending offset of record in file
0Ch	WORD	(big-endian) logical connection number
0Eh	BYTE	task number
0Fh	BYTE	lock type
		00h none
		FEh file lock
		FFh Begin Share File Set lock

INT 21h Function E3h, Subfunction DFh   *Advanced NetWare 2.1+*
GET LOGICAL RECORDS BY CONNECTION   *File Server*

Registers at call: **Return Registers:**
AH = E3h   AL = status
DS:SI -> request buffer (see Table 21-182)   00h successful
ES:DI -> reply buffer (see Table 21-183)   C6h no console rights
Details: The calling workstation must have console operator privileges.
Conflicts: OS/286 and OS/386 (PCI-34), DoubleDOS (PCI-49)
See also: Function E3h Subfunctions C8h, DDh, E0h, and E2h

21-182 Format of request buffer:

Offset	Size	Description
00h	WORD	0005h (length of following data)
00h	BYTE	DFh (subfunction "Get Logical Records By Connection")
03h	WORD	(big-endian) logical connection number
05h	WORD	(big-endian) last record seen (0000h on first call)

21-183 Format of reply buffer:

Offset	Size	Description
00h	WORD	(call) size of following results record (max 1FEh)
00h	WORD	next request record (place in "last record" field on next call)

		0000h if no more locked records
09h	BYTE	number of records following
0Ah	var	array of Logical Lock Information Records (see Table 21-184)

21-184 Format of Logical Lock Information Record:

Offset	Size	Description
00h	BYTE	task number
01h	BYTE	lock status (see Table 21-178)
00h	BYTE	length of logical lock's name
03h	N BYTEs	logical lock's name

INT 21h Function E3h, Subfunction E0h
GET LOGICAL RECORD INFORMATION
Advanced NetWare 2.1+
File Server

Registers at call:
AH = E3h
DS:SI -> request buffer (see Table 21-185)
ES:DI -> reply buffer (see Table 21-186)

Return Registers:
AL = status
  00h successful
  C6h no console rights

Details: The calling workstation must have console operator privileges.
Conflicts: OS/286 and OS/386 (PCI-34), DoubleDOS (PCI-49)
See also: Function E3h Subfunctions C8h, DDh, DFh, and E2h

21-185 Format of request buffer:

Offset	Size	Description
00h	WORD	length of following data (max 67h)
00h	BYTE	E0h (subfunction "Get Logical Record Information")
03h	WORD	(big-endian) last record seen (0000h on first call)
05h	BYTE	length of logical record's name
06h	N BYTEs	logical record's name

21-186 Format of reply buffer:

Offset	Size	Description
00h	WORD	(call) size of following results record (max 200h)
00h	WORD	(big-endian) number of logical connections logging the record
04h	WORD	(big-endian) number of logical connections with shareable lock
06h	WORD	(big-endian) next request record (place in "last record" field on next call)
08h	BYTE	locked exclusively if nonzero
09h	BYTE	number of records following
0Ah	var	array of Task Information Records (see Table 21-187)

21-187 Format of Task Information Record:

Offset	Size	Description
00h	WORD	(big-endian) logical connection number
00h	BYTE	task number
03h	BYTE	lock status (see Table 21-178)

INT 21h Function E3h, Subfunction E1h
GET CONNECTION'S SEMAPHORES
Advanced NetWare 2.1+
File Server

Registers at call:
AH = E3h
DS:SI -> request buffer (see Table 21-188)
ES:DI -> reply buffer (see Table 21-189)

Return Registers:
AL = status
  00h successful
  C6h no console rights

Details: The calling workstation must have console operator privileges.
Conflicts: OS/286 and OS/386 (PCI-34), DoubleDOS (PCI-49)

See also: Function E3h Subfunctions C8h, DBh, DFh, and E2h

21-188 Format of request buffer:

Offset	Size	Description
00h	WORD	0005h (length of following data)
00h	BYTE	E1h (subfunction "Get Connection's Semaphores")
03h	WORD	(big-endian) logical connection number
05h	WORD	(big-endian) last record seen (0000h on first call)

21-189 Format of reply buffer:

Offset	Size	Description
00h	WORD	(call) size of following results record (max 1FEh)
00h	WORD	next request record (place in "last record" field on next call)
04h	BYTE	number of records following
05h	var	array of Semaphore Information Records (see Table 21-190)

21-190 Format of Semaphore Information Record:

Offset	Size	Description
00h	WORD	(big-endian) open count
00h	BYTE	semaphore value (-128 to 127)
03h	BYTE	task number
04h	BYTE	lock type
05h	BYTE	length of semaphore's name
06h	N BYTEs	semaphore's name
	14 BYTEs	filename

INT 21h Function E3h, Subfunction E2h	*Advanced NetWare 2.1+*
GET SEMAPHORE INFORMATION	*File Server*

Registers at call:
AH = E3h
DS:SI -> request buffer (see Table 21-191)
ES:DI -> reply buffer (see Table 21-192)

Return Registers:
AL = status
  00h successful
  C6h no console rights

Details: The calling workstation must have console operator privileges.
Conflicts: OS/286 and OS/386 (PCI-34), DoubleDOS (PCI-49)
See also: Function E3h Subfunctions C8h and E1h

21-191 Format of request buffer:

Offset	Size	Description
00h	WORD	length of following data (max 83h)
00h	BYTE	E2h (subfunction "Get LAN Driver's Configuration Information")
03h	WORD	(big-endian) last record seen (0000h on first call)
05h	BYTE	length of semaphore's name (01h-7Fh)
06h	N BYTEs	semaphore's name

21-192 Format of reply buffer:

Offset	Size	Description
00h	WORD	(call) size of following results buffer (max 1FEh)
00h	WORD	next request record (place in "last record" on next call) 0000h if no more
04h	WORD	(big-endian) number of logical connections opening semaphore
06h	BYTE	semaphore value (-127 to 128)
07h	BYTE	number of records following
08h	var	array of Semaphore Information records (see Table 21-193)

21-193 Format of Semaphore Information:

Offset	Size	Description
00h	WORD	(big-endian) logical connection number
00h	BYTE	task number

INT 21h Function E3h, Subfunction E3h   *Advanced NetWare 2.1+*
GET LAN DRIVER'S CONFIGURATION INFORMATION   *File Server*

Registers at call: **Return Registers:**
AH = E3h   AL = status
DS:SI -> request buffer (see Table 21-194)   00h successful
ES:DI -> reply buffer (see Table 21-195)   C6h no console rights
Details: The calling workstation must have console operator privileges.
Conflicts: OS/286 and OS/386 (PCI-34), DoubleDOS (PCI-49)
See also: Function E3h Subfunctions C8h, E7h, and E8h

21-194 Format of request buffer:

Offset	Size	Description
00h	WORD	0002h (length of following data)
00h	BYTE	E3h (subfunction "Get LAN Driver's Configuration Information")
03h	BYTE	LAN board (00h-03h)

21-195 Format of reply buffer:

Offset	Size	Description
00h	WORD	(call) 00ACh (size of following results buffer)
00h	4 BYTEs	network number
06h	6 BYTEs	node number
0Ch	BYTE	LAN driver installed (00h no--remaining fields invalid)
0Dh	BYTE	option number selected at configuration time
0Eh	160 BYTEs	configuration text
		ASCIZ hardware type
		ASCIZ hardware settings

INT 21h Function E3h, Subfunction E5h   *Advanced NetWare 2.1+*
GET CONNECTION'S USAGE STATISTICS   *File Server*

Registers at call: **Return Registers:**
AH = E3h   AL = status
DS:SI -> request buffer (see Table 21-196)   00h successful
ES:DI -> reply buffer (see Table 21-197)   C6h no console rights
Details: One must have console operator privileges to get statistics for logical connections other
than one's own.
Conflicts: OS/286 and OS/386 (PCI-34), DoubleDOS (PCI-49)
See also: Function E3h Subfunctions C8h, DAh, DBh, and E1h

21-196 Format of request buffer:

Offset	Size	Description
00h	WORD	0003h (length of following data)
00h	BYTE	E5h (subfunction "Get Connection's Usage Statistics")
03h	WORD	(big-endian) logical connection number

21-197 Format of reply buffer:

Offset	Size	Description
00h	WORD	(call) 0014h (size of following results record)
00h	DWORD	(big-endian) clock ticks since server started

06h	6 BYTEs	bytes read
0Ch	6 BYTEs	bytes written
12h	DWORD	(big-endian) total request packets

INT 21h Function E3h, Subfunction E6h
GET BINDERY OBJECT DISK SPACE LEFT

Advanced NetWare 2.1+
File Server

Registers at call:
AH = E3h
DS:SI -> request buffer (see Table 21-198)
ES:DI -> reply buffer (see Table 21-199)

Return Registers:
AL = status
   00h successful
   C6h no console rights

Details: One must have console operator privileges to get the free space for other bindery objects.
Conflicts: OS/286 and OS/386 (PCI-34), DoubleDOS (PCI-49)
See also: Function E3h Subfunctions C8h, E8h, and E9h

21-198 Format of request buffer:

Offset	Size	Description
00h	WORD	0005h (length of following data)
00h	BYTE	E6h (subfunction "Get Bindery Object Disk Space Left")
03h	DWORD	(big-endian) object ID

21-199 Format of reply buffer:

Offset	Size	Description
00h	WORD	(call) 000Fh (size of following results buffer)
00h	DWORD	(big-endian) clock ticks elapsed since server started
06h	DWORD	(big-endian) object ID
0Ah	DWORD	(big-endian) 4K disk blocks available to user
0Eh	BYTE	restrictions (00h enforced, FFh not enforced)

INT 21h Function E3h, Subfunction E7h
GET FILE SERVER LAN I/O STATISTICS

Advanced NetWare 2.1+
File Server

Registers at call:
AH = E3h
DS:SI -> request buffer (see Table 21-200)
ES:DI -> reply buffer (see Table 21-201)

Return Registers:
AL = status
   00h successful

Conflicts: OS/286 and OS/386 (PCI-34), DoubleDOS (PCI-49)
See also: Function E3h Subfunctions 0Eh, 11h, D3h, and E8h; Function E7h

21-200 Format of request buffer:

Offset	Size	Description
00h	WORD	0001h (length of following data)
00h	BYTE	E7h (subfunction "Get File Server LAN I/O Statistics")

21-201 Format of reply buffer:

Offset	Size	Description
00h	WORD	(call) 0042h (size of following results buffer)
00h	DWORD	(big-endian) clock ticks since system started
06h	WORD	(big-endian) total routing buffers
08h	WORD	(big-endian) maximum routing buffers used
0Ah	WORD	(big-endian) current routing buffers used
0Ch	DWORD	(big-endian) total file service packets
10h	WORD	(big-endian) number of file service packets buffered
12h	WORD	(big-endian) number of invalid connection packets
14h	WORD	(big-endian) packets with bad logical connection numbers

16h	WORD	(big-endian) number of packets received during processing
18h	WORD	(big-endian) number of requests reprocessed
1Ah	WORD	(big-endian) packets with bad sequence numbers
1Ch	WORD	(big-endian) number of duplicate replies sent
1Eh	WORD	(big-endian) number of acknowledgements sent
20h	WORD	(big-endian) number of packets with bad request types
22h	WORD	(big-endian) requests to attach to ws for which a request is being processed
24h	WORD	(big-endian) requests to attach from ws which is already attaching
26h	WORD	(big-endian) number of forged detach requests
28h	WORD	(big-endian) detach requests with bad connection number
2Ah	WORD	(big-endian) requests to detach from ws for which requests pending
2Ch	WORD	(big-endian) number of cancelled replies
2Eh	WORD	(big-endian) packets discarded due to excessive hop count
30h	WORD	(big-endian) packets discarded due to unknown net
32h	WORD	(big-endian) incoming packets discarded for lack of DGroup buffer
34h	WORD	(big-endian) outgoing packets discarded due to lack of buffer
36h	WORD	(big-endian) received packets destined for B,C, or D side drivers
38h	DWORD	(big-endian) number of NetBIOS packets propagated through net
3Ch	DWORD	(big-endian) total number of non-file-service packets
40h	DWORD	(big-endian) total number of routed packets

INT 21h Function E3h, Subfunction E8h   *Advanced NetWare 2.1+*
GET FILE SERVER MISCELLANEOUS INFORMATION   *File Server*

Registers at call: **Return Registers:**
AH = E3h   AL = status
DS:SI -> request buffer (see Table 21-202)   00h successful
ES:DI -> reply buffer (see Table 21-203)   C6h no console rights
Conflicts: OS/286 and OS/386 (PCI-34), DoubleDOS (PCI-49)
See also: Function E3h Subfunctions 0Eh, 11h, CDh, and E7h

21-202 Format of request buffer:

Offset	Size	Description
00h	WORD	0001h (length of following data)
00h	BYTE	E8h (subfunction "Get File Server Misc Information")

21-203 Format of reply buffer:

Offset	Size	Description
00h	WORD	(call) size of following results buffer (max 0048h)
00h	DWORD	(big-endian) clock ticks since system started
06h	BYTE	CPU type
		00h Motorola 68000
		01h Intel 8086, 8088, or V20
		02h Intel 80286+
07h	BYTE	reserved
08h	BYTE	number of service processes in server
09h	BYTE	server utilization in percent
0Ah	WORD	(big-endian) maximum bindery objects set by configuration
		0000h = unlimited
0Ch	WORD	(big-endian) maximum number of bindery objects used
0Eh	WORD	(big-endian) current number of bindery objects in use
10h	WORD	(big-endian) total server memory in KB

12h	WORD	(big-endian) wasted server memory in KB normally 0000h
14h	WORD	number of records following (01h-03h)
16h	var	array of Dynamic Memory Information records (see Table 21-204)

21-204 Format of Dynamic Memory Information:

Offset	Size	Description
00h	DWORD	(big-endian) total dynamic space
04h	DWORD	(big-endian) maximum dynamic space used
08h	DWORD	(big-endian) current dynamic space usage

INT 21h Function E7h
GET FILE SERVER DATE AND TIME
Novell NetWare and others
File Server

Registers at call:
AH = E7h
DS:DX -> date/time buffer (see Table 21-205)

Return Registers:
AL = error code
  00h successful
  FFh unsuccessful

Details: This function is supported by NetWare 4.0+, Advanced NetWare 1.0+, Alloy NTNX, and Banyan VINES.
Conflicts: OS/286 and OS/386 (PCI-34), Virus (PCI-59)
See also: Function E3h Subfunction CAh, LANtastic Function 5FC0h (Chapter 20), MS-DOS Functions 2Ah and 2Ch (PCI-24)

21-205 Format of date/time buffer:

Offset	Size	Description
00h	BYTE	year (80-99 = 1980-1999, 0-79 = 2000-2079)
01h	BYTE	month (1=Jan)
00h	BYTE	day
03h	BYTE	hours
04h	BYTE	minutes
05h	BYTE	seconds
06h	BYTE	day of week (0 = Sunday) (Novell and NTNX only)

File Services

21-206 Values for File Services error code:

00h	successful
89h	not permitted to search directory
8Ch	caller lacks privileges
98h	nonexistent volume
9Bh	invaid directory handle
9Ch	invalid path
C6h	no console rights
FEh	not permitted to search directory
FFh	file not found

INT 21h Function B6h
EXTENDED FILE ATTRIBUTES
Advanced NetWare 2.1+
File Services

Registers at call:
AH = B6h
AL = subfunction
    00h get extended file attributes

01h set extended file attributes
CL = new attributes (see Table 21-207)
DS:DX -> ASCIZ pathname (max 255 bytes)

Return Registers:
CF set on error
AL = error code (8Ch,FEh,FFh) (see Table 21-206)
CF clear if successful
AL = 00h (success)
CL = current extended file attributes (see Table 21-207)

See also: Function E3h Subfunction 0Fh, MS-DOS Function 4300h (PCI-24)

21-207 Bitfields for extended file attributes:
bits 2-0   search mode (executables only)
000 none (use shell's default search)
001 search on all opens without path
010 do not search
011 search on read-only opens without path
100 reserved
101 search on all opens
110 reserved
111 search on all read-only opens
bit 3   reserved
bit 4   transactions on file tracked
bit 5   file's FAT indexed
bit 6   read audit (to be implemented)
bit 7   write audit (to be implemented)

INT 21h Function E2h, Subfunction 10h   *Novell NetWare and others*
PURGE ERASED FILES   *File Services*

Purpose: Purges files marked for deletion on the file server by the calling workstation.

Registers at call:
AH = E2h
DS:SI -> request buffer (see Table 21-208)
ES:DI -> reply buffer (see Table 21-209)

Return Registers:
AL = status (see Table 21-206)

Details: This function is supported by NetWare 4.0+, Advanced NetWare 1.0+, and Alloy NTNX.
Conflicts: OS/286 and OS/386 (PCI-34), DoubleDOS (PCI-49)
See also: Function E2h Subfunction 11h, Function E3h Subfunction CEh, Function F244h, MS-DOS Function 41h (Chapter 3), MS-DOS Function 13h (PCI-24)

21-208 Format of request buffer:
Offset	Size	Description
00h	WORD	0001h (length of following data)
00h	BYTE	10h (subfunction "Purge Erased Files")

21-209 Format of reply buffer:
Offset	Size	Description
00h	WORD	(call) 0000h (no results returned)

INT 21h Function E2h, Subfunction 11h   *Novell NetWare and others*
RESTORE ERASED FILE   *File Services*

Purpose: Restores one file marked for deletion which has not yet been purged.
Registers at call:
AH = E2h

DS:SI -> request buffer (see Table 21-210)
ES:DI -> reply buffer (see Table 21-211)

Return Registers:
AL = status (00h,98h,FFh) (see also
   Table 21-206)
     FFh no more erased files

Details: This function is supported by NetWare 4.0+, Advanced NetWare 1.0+, and Alloy NTNX.
Conflicts: OS/286 and OS/386 (PCI-34), DoubleDOS (PCI-49)
See also: Function E2h Subfunction 10h, Function E3h Subfunction CEh, Function F244h, MS-DOS Function 41h (Chapter 3), MS-DOS Function 13h (PCI-24)

21-210 Format of request buffer:

Offset	Size	Description
00h	WORD	length of following data (max 13h)
00h	BYTE	11h (subfunction "Restore Erased File")
03h	BYTE	directory handle or 00h
04h	BYTE	length of volume name
05h	N BYTEs	volume name (including colon)

Note: If both a directory handle and a volume name are specified, the volume name overrides the handle.

21-211 Format of reply buffer:

Offset	Size	Description
00h	WORD	(call) 001Eh (size of following results buffer)
00h	15 BYTEs	ASCIZ name of erased file
11h	15 BYTEs	ASCIZ name under which file was restored

INT 21h Function E3h, Subfunction 0Fh   *Advanced NetWare 1.0+, Alloy NTNX*
SCAN FILE INFORMATION   *File Services*

Registers at call:
AH = E3h
DS:SI -> request buffer (see Table 21-212)
ES:DI -> reply buffer (see Table 21-213)

Return Registers:
AL = status (00h,89h,FFh) (see also Table
21-206)
   FFh no more matching files

Conflicts: OS/286 and OS/386 (PCI-34), DoubleDOS (PCI-49)
See also: Function B6h, Function E3h Subfunction 10h

21-212 Format of request buffer:

Offset	Size	Description
00h	WORD	length of following data (max 105h)
00h	BYTE	0Fh (subfunction "Scan File Information")
03h	WORD	(big-endian) sequence number
		FFFFh on first call
05h	BYTE	directory handle or 00h
06h	BYTE	search attributes (see Table 3-53)
07h	BYTE	length of filespec
08h	N BYTEs	ASCIZ uppercase filespec

21-213 Format of reply buffer:

Offset	Size	Description
00h	WORD	(call) 005Eh (size of following results buffer)
00h	WORD	next sequence number (place in request buffer for next call)
04h	14 BYTEs	ASCIZ filename
12h	BYTE	file attributes (see Table 3-53)
13h	BYTE	extended file attributes (see Table 21-207)
14h	DWORD	(big-endian) file size in bytes

18h	WORD	(big-endian) file's creation date (see Table 3-56)
1Ah	WORD	(big-endian) date of last access (see Table 3-56)
1Ch	DWORD	(big-endian) date and time of last update (see Table 21-79)
20h	DWORD	(big-endian) object ID of owner
24h	DWORD	(big-endian) date and time last archived (see Table 21-79)
28h	55 BYTEs	reserved

Note: The official documentation erroneously lists the field at offset 04h as 15 bytes and thus shifts the remaining fields by one byte.

INT 21h Function E3h, Subfunction 10h   *Advanced NetWare 1.0+, Alloy NTNX*
SET FILE INFORMATION   *File Services*
    .idnex NetWare;file owner

Registers at call: **Return Registers:**
AH = E3h   AL = status
DS:SI -> request buffer (see Table 21-214)   00h successful
ES:DI -> reply buffer (see Table 21-215)

Details: The caller must have modify privileges on the directory containing the file.
Conflicts: OS/286 and OS/386 (PCI-34), DoubleDOS (PCI-49)
See also: Function B6h, Function E3h Subfunction 0Fh

21-214 Format of request buffer:

Offset	Size	Description
00h	WORD	length of following data (max 151h)
00h	BYTE	10h (subfunction "Set File Information")
03h	BYTE	file attributes (see Table 3-53)
04h	BYTE	extended file attributes (see Table 21-207)
05h	4 BYTEs	reserved
09h	WORD	(big-endian) file's creation date (see Table 3-56)
0Bh	WORD	(big-endian) date of last access (see Table 3-56)
0Dh	DWORD	(big-endian) date and time of last update (see Table 21-79)
11h	DWORD	(big-endian) object ID of owner
15h	DWORD	(big-endian) date and time last archived (see Table 21-79)
19h	56 BYTEs	reserved
51h	BYTE	directory handle or 00h
52h	BYTE	search attributes (see Table 3-53)
53h	BYTE	length of filename
54h	N BYTEs	filename

21-215 Format of reply buffer:

Offset	Size	Description
00h	WORD	(call) 0000h (no results returned)

INT 21h Function E3h, Subfunction CEh   *Novell NetWare and others*
PURGE ALL ERASED FILES   *File Services*

Purpose: All files marked for deletion on the file server are purged, regardless of which workstation actually erased them.

Registers at call: **Return Registers:**
AH = E3h   AL = status
DS:SI -> request buffer (see Table 21-216)   00h successful
ES:DI -> reply buffer (see Table 21-217)   C6h no console rights

Details: This function is supported by NetWare 4.0+, Advanced NetWare 1.0+, and Alloy NTNX.
The calling workstation must have console operator privileges.

Conflicts: OS/286 and OS/386 (PCI-34), DoubleDOS (PCI-49)
See also: Function E2h Subfunction 10h, Function E3h Subfunction C8h, Function F244h, MS-DOS Function 13h (PCI-24)

21-216 Format of request buffer:

Offset	Size	Description
00h	WORD	0001h (length of following data)
00h	BYTE	CEh (subfunction "Purge All Erased Files")

21-217 Format of reply buffer:

Offset	Size	Description
00h	WORD	(call) 0000h (no results returned)

INT 21h Function F244h   *Novell NetWare*
ERASE FILES   *File Services*

Registers at call: **Return Registers:**
AX = F244h   AL = status (00h,98h,9Bh,9Ch,FFh) (see also
DS:SI -> request buffer (see Table 21-218)   Table 21-206)
ES:DI -> reply buffer (*ignored*)   FFh no files found
Details: This function only marks the file for deletion; use Function E2h Subfunction CEh to actually delete all marked files.
Conflicts: DoubleDOS (PCI-49), Virus (PCI-59)
See also: Function E2h Subfunction 0Bh, Function E3h Subfunction CEh, MS-DOS Function 41h (Chapter 3), MS-DOS Function 13h (PCI-24)

21-218 Format of request buffer:

Offset	Size	Description
00h	BYTE	directory handle
01h	BYTE	search attributes (see Table 3-53)
00h	BYTE	length of filespec
03h	N BYTEs	ASCIZ filespec (may include wildcards)

INT 21h Function F3h   *Advanced NetWare 2.0+*
FILE SERVER FILE COPY   *File Services*

Registers at call: **Return Registers:**
AH = F3h   AL = status/error code
ES:DI -> request buffer (see Table 21-219)   CX:DX = number of bytes copied
Details: Both source and destination files must be on the same file server.
Conflicts: DoubleDOS (PCI-49), Virus (PCI-59)
See also: Functions 3Ch and 3Fh

21-219 Format of request buffer:

Offset	Size	Description
00h	WORD	source file handle (as returned by Functions 3Ch or 3Dh; see Chapter 3 and PCI-24)
00h	WORD	destination file handle
04h	DWORD	starting offset in source
08h	DWORD	starting offset in destination
0Ch	DWORD	number of bytes to copy

Message Services

21-220 Values for Message Services status:

00h	successful
FCh	full message queue
FEh	I/O error or out of dynamic workspace

INT 21h Function DEh
SET BROADCAST MODE

NetWare 4.0+, Advanced NetWare 1.0+
Message Services

Registers at call:
AH = DEh
DL = broadcast mode
    00h receive server and workstation
      broadcasts (default)
    01h receive server broadcasts, discard
      user messages
    02h store server broadcasts for retrieval
    03h store all broadcasts for retrieval

Return Registers:
AL = new broadcast mode

Conflicts: Viruses (PCI-59)

INT 21h Function DEh, Subfunction 04h
GET BROADCAST MODE

NetWare 4.0+, Advanced NetWare 1.0+
Message Services

Registers at call:
AH = DEh
DL = 04h

Return Registers:
AL = current broadcast mode
    00h receive server and workstation broadcasts
      (default)
    01h receive server broadcasts, discard user
      message
    02h store server broadcasts for retrieval
    03h store all broadcasts for retrieval

Conflicts: Viruses (PCI-59)

INT 21h Function E1h, Subfunction 00h
SEND BROADCAST MESSAGE

NetWare 4.0+, Advanced NetWare 1.0+
Message Services

Registers at call:
AH = E1h
DS:SI -> request buffer (see Table 21-221)
ES:DI -> reply buffer (see Table 21-222)

Return Registers:
AL = status (see Table 21-220)

Conflicts: OS/286 and OS/386 (PCI-34), DoubleDOS (PCI-49), "Mendoza"/"Fu Manchu" virus (PCI-59)
See also: Function DEh Subfunction 00h to 04h; Function E1h Subfunctions 01h, 04h, and 09h

21-221 Format of request buffer:

Offset	Size	Description
00h	WORD	length of following data (max 9Eh)
00h	BYTE	00h (subfunction "Send Broadcast Message")
03h	BYTE	number of connections (01h-64h)
04h	N BYTEs	list of connections to receive broadcast message
	BYTE	length of message (01h-37h)
	N BYTEs	broadcast message (no control characters or characters above 7Eh)

21-222 Format of reply buffer:

Offset	Size	Description
00h	WORD	(call) size of following results buffer (max 65h)
00h	BYTE	number of connections
03h	N BYTEs	list of per-connection results
		00h successful
		FCh message rejected due to lack of buffer space
		FDh invalid connection number
		FFh blocked (see also Function E1h Subfunction 02h)

INT 21h Function E1h, Subfunction 01h
GET BROADCAST MESSAGE

NetWare 4.0+, Advanced NetWare 1.0+
Message Services

Registers at call:
AH = E1h
DS:SI -> request buffer (see Table 21-223)
ES:DI -> reply buffer (see Table 21-224)

Return Registers:
AL = status (00h,FCh,FEh) (see Table 21-220)

Conflicts: OS/286 and OS/386 (PCI-34), DoubleDOS (PCI-49), "Mendoza"/"Fu Manchu" virus (PCI-59)
See also: Function DEh Subfunction 04h; Function E1h Subfunctions 00h, 05h, and 09h

21-223 Format of request buffer:

Offset	Size	Description
00h	WORD	0001h (length of following data)
00h	BYTE	01h (subfunction "Get Broadcast Message")

21-224 Format of reply buffer:

Offset	Size	Description
00h	WORD	(call) size of following results buffer (max 38h)
00h	BYTE	length of message (00h-37h)
		00h if no broadcast messages pending
03h	N BYTEs	message (no control characters or characters above 7Eh)

INT 21h Function E1h, Subfunctions 02h and 03h
ENABLE/DISABLE BROADCAST MESSAGES

Novell NetWare
Message Services

Registers at call:
AH = E1h
DS:SI -> request buffer (see Table 21-225)
ES:DI -> reply buffer

Return Registers:
AL = status (see Table 21-220)

Details: These functions are supported by NetWare 4.0+ but are not listed in *NetWare System Calls--DOS*; they may be obsolete.
Conflicts: OS/286 and OS/386 (PCI-34), DoubleDOS (PCI-49), "Mendoza"/"Fu Manchu" virus (PCI-59)
See also: Function E1h Subfunctions 00h, 04h, and 09h

21-225 Format of request buffer:

Offset	Size	Description
00h	WORD	length of following data (max 9Eh)
00h	BYTE	subfunction
		02h disable station broadcasts
		03h enable station broadcasts
03h	*unknown*	

21-226 Format of reply buffer:

Offset	Size	Description
00h	WORD	(call) size of following results buffer
00h	*unknown*	

INT 21h Function E1h, Subfunction 04h
SEND PERSONAL MESSAGE

NetWare 4.0+, Advanced NetWare 1.0+
Message Services

Registers at call:
AH = E1h
DS:SI -> request buffer (see Table 21-227)
ES:DI -> reply buffer (see Table 21-228)

Return Registers:
AL = status (00h,FEh) (see Table 21-220)

Details: Message pipes use CPU time on the file server; IPX, SPX, or NetBIOS connections should be used for peer-to-peer communications as these protocols do not use file server time.
Conflicts: OS/286 and OS/386 (PCI-34), DoubleDOS (PCI-49), "Mendoza"/"Fu Manchu" virus (PCI-59)
See also: Function E1h Subfunctions 00h, 05h, 06h, and 08h

21-227 Format of request buffer:

Offset	Size	Description
00h	WORD	length of following data (max E5h)
00h	BYTE	04h (subfunction "Send Personal Message")
03h	BYTE	number of connections (01h-64h)
04h	N BYTEs	list of connections to receive broadcast message
	BYTE	length of message (01h-7Eh)
	N BYTEs	message (no control characters or characters > 7Eh)

21-228 Format of reply buffer:

Offset	Size	Description
00h	WORD	(call) size of following results buffer (max 65h)
00h	BYTE	number of connections
03h	N BYTEs	list of per-connection results
		00h successful
		FCh message rejected because queue is full (contains 6 msgs)
		FDh incomplete pipe
		FFh failed

INT 21h Function E1h, Subfunction 05h
GET PERSONAL MESSAGE

NetWare 4.0+, Advanced NetWare 1.0+
Message Services

Purpose: Return the oldest message in the default file server's message queue for the calling workstation.

Registers at call:
AH = E1h
DS:SI -> request buffer (see Table 21-229)
ES:DI -> reply buffer (see Table 21-230)

Return Registers:
AL = status (00h,FEh) (see Table 21-220)

Conflicts: OS/286 and OS/386 (PCI-34), DoubleDOS (PCI-49), "Mendoza"/"Fu Manchu" virus (PCI-59)
See also: Function E1h Subfunctions 01h, 04h, 06h, and 08h

21-229 Format of request buffer:

Offset	Size	Description
00h	WORD	0001h (length of following data)
00h	BYTE	05h (subfunction "Get Personal Message")

21-230 Format of reply buffer:

Offset	Size	Description
00h	WORD	(call) size of following results buffer (max 80h)
00h	BYTE	connection number of sending station
03h	BYTE	length of message (00h-7Eh)
		00h if no personal messages pending
04h	N BYTEs	message (no control characters or characters > 7Eh)

INT 21h Function E1h, Subfunction 06h
OPEN MESSAGE PIPE

NetWare 4.0+, Advanced NetWare 1.0+
Message Services

Registers at call:
AH = E1h
DS:SI -> request buffer (see Table 21-231)
ES:DI -> reply buffer (see Table 21-232)

Return Registers:
AL = status (00h,FEh) (see Table 21-220)

Conflicts: OS/286 and OS/386 (PCI-34), DoubleDOS (PCI-49), "Mendoza"/"Fu Manchu" virus (PCI-59)

See also: Function E1h Subfunctions 04h, 07h, and 08h

21-231 Format of request buffer:

Offset	Size	Description
00h	WORD	length of following data (max 66h)
00h	BYTE	06h (subfunction "Open Message Pipe")
03h	BYTE	number of pipes to open (01h-64h)
04h	N BYTEs	list of connection numbers

21-232 Format of reply buffer:

Offset	Size	Description
00h	WORD	(call) size of following results buffer (max 65h)
00h	BYTE	number of connections
03h	N BYTEs	list of results
		00h successful
		FEh incomplete (target half not yet created)
		FFh failed

INT 21h Function E1h, Subfunction 07h
CLOSE MESSAGE PIPE

NetWare 4.0+, Advanced NetWare 1.0+
Message Services

Registers at call:
AH = E1h
DS:SI -> request buffer (see Table 21-233)
ES:DI -> reply buffer (see Table 21-234)

Return Registers:
AL = status (00h,FCh,FEh) (see Table 21-220)

Conflicts: OS/286 and OS/386 (PCI-34), DoubleDOS (PCI-49), "Mendoza"/"Fu Manchu" virus (PCI-59)

See also: Function E1h Subfunctions 05h, 06h, and 08h

21-233 Format of request buffer:

Offset	Size	Description
00h	WORD	length of following data (max 66h)
00h	BYTE	07h (subfunction "Close Message Pipe")
03h	BYTE	number of pipes to close (01h-64h)
04h	N BYTEs	list of connection numbers

21-234 Format of reply buffer:

Offset	Size	Description
00h	WORD	(call) size of following results buffer (max 65h)
00h	BYTE	number of connections
03h	N BYTEs	list of results
		00h successful
		FDh failed
		FFh no such pipe

INT 21h Function E1h, Subfunction 08h
CHECK PIPE STATUS

NetWare 4.0+, Advanced NetWare 1.0+
Message Services

Registers at call:
AH = E1h
DS:SI -> request buffer (see Table 21-235)
ES:DI -> reply buffer (see Table 21-236)

Return Registers:
AL = status (00h,FCh,FEh) (see Table 21-220)

Conflicts: OS/286 and OS/386 (PCI-34), DoubleDOS (PCI-49), "Mendoza"/"Fu Manchu" virus (PCI-59)
See also: Function E1h Subfunctions 05h, 06h, and 07h

21-235 Format of request buffer:

Offset	Size	Description
00h	WORD	length of following data (max 66h)
00h	BYTE	08h (subfunction "Check Pipe Status")
03h	BYTE	number of pipes to monitor (01h-64h)
04h	N BYTEs	list of connection numbers

21-236 Format of reply buffer:

Offset	Size	Description
00h	WORD	(call) size of following results buffer (max 65h)
00h	BYTE	number of connections
03h	N BYTEs	list of pipe statuses
		00h open
		FEh incomplete
		FFh closed

INT 21h Function E1h, Subfunction 09h
BROADCAST TO CONSOLE

NetWare 4.0+, Advanced NetWare 1.0+
Message Services

Purpose: Send a one-line message to the system console on the default file server.

Registers at call:
AH = E1h
DS:SI -> request buffer (see Table 21-237)
ES:DI -> reply buffer (see Table 21-238)

Return Registers:
AL = status (00h,FCh,FEh) (see Table 21-220)

Conflicts: OS/286 and OS/386 (PCI-34), DoubleDOS (PCI-49), "Mendoza"/"Fu Manchu" virus (PCI-59)
See also: Function DEh Subfunction 04h, Function E1h Subfunctions 00h and 01h, Function E3h Subfunction D1h

21-237 Format of request buffer:

Offset	Size	Description
00h	WORD	length of following data (max 3Eh)
00h	BYTE	09h (subfunction "Broadcast to Console")
03h	BYTE	length of message (01h-3Ch)
04h	N BYTEs	message (no control characters or characters > 7Eh)

21-238 Format of reply buffer:

Offset	Size	Description
00h	WORD	(call) 0000h (no results returned)

INT 21h Function E3h, Subfunction 0Dh
LOG NETWORK MESSAGE

Novell NetWare and others
Message Services

Purpose: Append a line to the default file server's NET$LOG.MSG file.

Registers at call:
AH = E3h
DS:SI -> request buffer (see Table 21-239)
ES:DI -> reply buffer (see Table 21-240)

Return Registers:
AL = status
    00h successful

Details: This function is supported by NetWare 4.0+, Advanced NetWare 1.0+, and Alloy NTNX.
Conflicts: OS/286 and OS/386 (PCI-34), DoubleDOS (PCI-49)
See also: Function E1h Subfunction 09h

21-239 Format of request buffer:

Offset	Size	Description
00h	WORD	length of following data (max 52h)
00h	BYTE	0Dh (subfunction "Log Network Message")
03h	BYTE	length of message (01h-50h)
04h	N BYTEs	message (no control characters or characters > 7Eh)

Print Services

INT 21h Function B800h   *Advanced NetWare 2.0+*
GET DEFAULT CAPTURE FLAGS   *Print Services*

Registers at call:
AX = B800h
CX = size of reply buffer (01h-3Fh)
ES:BX -> reply buffer for capture flags table
    (see Table 21-240)

Return Registers:
AL = status
    00h successful

Conflicts: Attachmate Extra (Chapter 37)
See also: Functions B801h and B802h, Function DFh Subfunctions 00h and 04h

21-240 Format of capture flags table:

Offset	Size	Description
00h	BYTE	status (used internally, should be set to 00h)
01h	BYTE	print flags
		bit 2: print capture file if interrupted by loss of connection
		bit 3: no automatic form feed after print job
		bit 6: printing control sequences interpreted by print service
		bit 7: print banner page before capture file
00h	BYTE	tab size (01h-12h, default 08h)
03h	BYTE	printer number on server (00h-04h, default 00h)
04h	BYTE	number of copies to print (00h-FFh, default 01h)
05h	BYTE	form type required in printer (default 00h)
06h	BYTE	reserved
07h	13 BYTEs	text to be placed on banner page
14h	BYTE	reserved
15h	BYTE	default local printer (00h = LPT1)
16h	WORD	(big-endian) timeout in clock ticks for flushing capture file on inactivity, or 0000h to disable timeout
18h	BYTE	flush capture file on LPT close if nonzero
19h	WORD	(big-endian) maximum lines per page
1Bh	WORD	(big-endian) maximum characters per line
1Dh	13 BYTEs	name of form required in printer
2Ah	BYTE	LPT capture flag
		00h inactive, FFh LPT device is being captured

2Bh	BYTE	file capture flag
		00h if no file specified, FFh if capturing to file
2Ch	BYTE	timing out (00h if no timeout in effect, FFh if timeout counter running)
2Dh	DWORD	(big-endian) address of printer setup string
31h	DWORD	(big-endian) address of printer reset string
35h	BYTE	target connection ID
36h	BYTE	capture in progress if FFh
37h	BYTE	job queued for printing if FFh
38h	BYTE	print job valid if FFh
39h	DWORD	bindery object ID of print queue if previous byte FFh
3Dh	WORD	(big-endian) print job number (1-999)

INT 21h Function B801h
SET DEFAULT CAPTURE FLAGS

Advanced NetWare 2.0+
Print Services

Registers at call:
AX = B801h
CX = size of buffer (01h-3Fh)
ES:BX -> buffer containing capture flags table
  (see Table 21-240)

Return Registers:
AL = status
   00h successful

Conflicts: Attachmate Extra (Chapter 37)
See also: Functions B800h and B803h, Function DFh Subfunctions 00h and 04h

---

INT 21h Function B802h
GET SPECIFIC CAPTURE FLAGS

Advanced NetWare 2.1+
Print Services

Registers at call:
AX = B802h
CX = size of reply buffer (01h-3Fh)
DH = LPT port (00h-02h)
ES:BX -> reply buffer for capture flags
  table (see Table 21-240)

Return Registers:
AL = status
   00h successful

Conflicts: Attachmate Extra (Chapter 37)
See also: Functions B800h and B803h, Function DFh Subfunctions 00h and 04h

---

INT 21h Function B803h
SET SPECIFIC CAPTURE FLAGS

Advanced NetWare 2.1+
Print Services

Registers at call:
AX = B803h
CX = size of buffer (01h-3Fh)
DH = LPT port (00h-02h)
ES:BX -> buffer containing capture flags table
(see Table 21-240)

Return Registers:
AL = status
   00h successful

Conflicts: Attachmate Extra (Chapter 37)
See also: Functions B800h and B803h, Function DFh Subfunctions 00h and 04h

---

INT 21h Function B804h
GET DEFAULT LOCAL PRINTER

Advanced NetWare 2.1+
Print Services

Registers at call:
AX = B804h

Return Registers:
DH = default LPT port (00h-02h)

Conflicts: Attachmate Extra (Chapter 37)
See also: Functions B800h and B805h, Function DFh Subfunction 00h

INT 21h Function B805h
SET DEFAULT LOCAL PRINTER
Advanced NetWare 2.1+
Print Services

Registers at call:
AX = B805h
DH = new default LPT port (00h-02h)

Return Registers:
AL = status
  00h successful

Conflicts: Attachmate Extra (Chapter 37)
See also: Functions B800h and B804h, Function DFh Subfunction 00h

INT 21h Function B806h
SET CAPTURE PRINT QUEUE
Advanced NetWare 2.1+
Print Services

Purpose: Specify the print queue on which a print job is to be placed the next time a capture is started on the given printer port.

Registers at call:
AX = B806h
DH = LPT port (00h-02h)
BX:CX = print queue's object ID

Return Registers:
AL = status
  00h successful
  FFh job already set

Conflicts: Attachmate Extra (Chapter 37)
See also: Functions B801h, B807h, and E009h

INT 21h Function B807h
SET CAPTURE PRINT JOB
Advanced NetWare 2.1+
Print Services

Purpose: Specify the capture file and print job to be used for subsequent output to the given printer port.

Registers at call:
AX = B807h
DH = LPT port (00h-02h)
BX = job number (see Table 21-256)
SI:DI:CX = NetWare file handle (see
  Table 21-256)

Return Registers:
AL = status
  00h successful
  FFh job already queued

Conflicts: Attachmate Extra (Chapter 37)
See also: Functions B801h, B806h, and E009h; Function E3h Subfunction 68h

INT 21h Function B808h
GET BANNER USER NAME
Advanced NetWare 2.1+
Print Services

Purpose: Get the user name which is printed on the banner page.

Registers at call:
AX = B808h
ES:BX -> 12-byte buffer for user name

Return Registers:
AL = status
  00h successful

Details: The default name is the user's login name.
Conflicts: Attachmate Extra (Chapter 37)
See also: Function B809h

INT 21h Function B809h
SET BANNER USER NAME
Advanced NetWare 2.1+
Print Services

Purpose: Specify the user name which is printed on the banner page.

Registers at call:
AX = B809h
ES:BX -> 12-byte buffer containing user name

Return Registers:
AL = status
  00h successful

Details: The default name is the user's login name.
Conflicts: Attachmate Extra (Chapter 37)
See also: Function B808h

INT 21h Function DFh, Subfunction 00h
START LPT CAPTURE

Novell NetWare and others
Print Services

Purpose: This function redirects the default LPT to a capture file on the file server.

Registers at call:
AH = DFh
DL = 00h

Return Registers:
AL = status
    00h successful

Details: This function is supported by NetWare 4.0+, Advanced NetWare 1.0+, and Alloy NTNX; under NTNX, it sends a print break (see INT 17h Function 84h).

A print job is queued when the first character of output is captured.

Conflicts: Software Carousel (PCI-49)

See also: Functions B800h and B804h; Function DFh Subfunctions 01h, 02h, 03h, and 04h; Function F003h

INT 21h Function DFh, Subfunction 01h
END LPT CAPTURE

Novell NetWare and others
Print Services

Purpose: Stop redirecting the default LPT, close the capture file, and release the job in the print queue for printing.

Registers at call:
AH = DFh
DL = 01h

Return Registers:
AL = status
    00h successful

Details: This function is supported by NetWare 4.0+, Advanced NetWare 1.0+, and Alloy NTNX; under NTNX, it sends a print break (see INT 17h Function 84h in Chapter 12).

After this call, the default LPT defaults to local printing.

Conflicts: Software Carousel (PCI-49)

See also: Function DFh Subfunctions 00h, 02h, 03h, and 05h

INT 21h Function DFh, Subfunction 02h
CANCEL LPT CAPTURE

Novell NetWare and others
Print Services

Purpose: This function ends the capture of the default LPT, removes the job from the print queue, and deletes the capture file unless it is a permanent capture file.

Registers at call:
AH = DFh
DL = 02h

Return Registers:
AL = status
    00h successful

Details: This function is supported by NetWare 4.0+, Advanced NetWare 1.0+, and Alloy NTNX; under NTNX, it sends a print break (see INT 17h Function 84h in Chapter 12).

After this call, the default LPT defaults to local printing.

Conflicts: Software Carousel (PCI-49)

See also: Function DFh Subfunctions 00h and 06h

INT 21h Function DFh, Subfunction 03h
FLUSH LPT CAPTURE

Novell NetWare and others
Print Services

Purpose: This function closes the current capture file for the default LPT and starts printing it if it is not a permanent capture file.

Registers at call:
AH = DFh
DL = 03h

Return Registers:
AL = status
    00h successful

Details: This function is supported by NetWare 4.0+, Advanced NetWare 1.0+, and Alloy NTNX; under NTNX, it sends a print break (see INT 17h Function 84h in Chapter 12).

If more data is sent to the LPT port after this call, a new capture file will be opeend.

Conflicts: Software Carousel (PCI-49)

See also: Function DFh Subfunctions 00h, 01h, 02h, and 07h

INT 21h Function DFh, Subfunction 04h
START SPECIFIC LPT CAPTURE
Advanced NetWare 2.1+
Print Services

Purpose: This function redirects the specified LPT to a capture file on the file server.

Registers at call: **Return Registers:**
AH = DFh   AL = status
DL = 04h   00h successful
DH = LPT port (00h-02h)

Details: A print job is queued when the first character of output is captured.

Conflicts: Software Carousel (PCI-49)

See also: Function B800h; Function DFh Subfunctions 00h, 05h, 06h, and 07h; Function F003h

INT 21h Function DFh, Subfunction 05h
END SPECIFIC LPT CAPTURE
Advanced NetWare 2.1+
Print Services

Purpose: Stop redirecting the specified LPT, close the capture file, and release the job in the print queue for printing.

Registers at call: **Return Registers:**
AH = DFh   AL = status
DL = 05h   00h successful
DH = LPT port (00h-02h)

Details: After this call, the specified LPT defaults to local printing.

Conflicts: Software Carousel (PCI-49)

See also: Function DFh Subfunctions 01h, 04h, 06h, and 07h

INT 21h Function DFh, Subfunction 06h
CANCEL SPECIFIC LPT CAPTURE
Advanced NetWare 2.1+
Print Services

Purpose: This function ends the capture of the specified LPT, removes the job from the print queue, and deletes the capture file unless it is a permanent capture file.

Registers at call: **Return Registers:**
AH = DFh   AL = status
DL = 06h   00h successful
DH = LPT port (00h-02h)

Details: After this call, the specified LPT defaults to local printing.

Conflicts: Software Carousel (PCI-49)

See also: Function DFh Subfunctions 02h, 04h, 05h, and 07h

INT 21h Function DFh, Subfunction 07h
FLUSH SPECIFIC LPT CAPTURE
Advanced NetWare 2.1+
Print Services

Purpose: This function closes the current capture file for the specified LPT and starts printing it if it is not a permanent capture file.

Registers at call: **Return Registers:**
AH = DFh   AL = status
DL = 07h   00h successful
DH = LPT port (00h-02h)

Details: If more data is sent to the LPT port after this call, a new capture file will be opeend.

Conflicts: Software Carousel (PCI-49)

See also: Function DFh Subfunctions 03h, 04h, 05h, and 06h

INT 21h Function E0h
PRINT SPOOLING
Novell NetWare, Alloy NTNX

Registers at call:
AH = E0h

DS:SI -> request buffer (see Table 21-241)   **Return Registers:**
ES:DI -> reply buffer   AL = status

Details: This function was added in NetWare 4.0, but is no longer listed in current Novell documentation and may no longer be supported.
Conflicts: Digital Research DOS Plus (PCI-26), OS/286 and OS/386 (PCI-34), DoubleDOS (PCI-49), Viruses (PCI-59)
See also: AH-E3h Subfunction 68h

21-241 Format of request buffer:

Offset	Size	Description
00h	WORD	length of following data
00h	BYTE	subfunction
		00h spool data to a capture file
		01h close and queue capture file
		02h set spool flags
		03h spool existing file
		04h get spool queue entry
		05h remove entry from spool queue
03h		*others, if any, unknown*

INT 21h Function E0h, Subfunction 06h　　　　*Novell NetWare and others*
GET PRINTER STATUS　　　　　　　　　　　　　　　　*Print Services*

Purpose: Get current state of specified printer attached to the server.

Registers at call:	**Return Registers:**
AH = E0h	AL = status
DS:SI -> request buffer (see Table 21-242)	00h successful
ES:DI -> reply buffer (see Table 21-243)	FFh no such printer

Details: This function is supported by NetWare 4.0+, Advanced NetWare 1.0+, and Alloy NTNX.
Conflicts: Digital Research DOS Plus (PCI-26), OS/286 and OS/386 (PCI-34), DoubleDOS (PCI-49), Viruses (PCI-59)

21-242 Format of request buffer:

Offset	Size	Description
00h	WORD	0002h (length of following data)
00h	BYTE	06h (subfunction "Get Printer Status")
03h	BYTE	printer number (00h-04h)

21-243 Format of reply buffer:

Offset	Size	Description
00h	WORD	(call) 0004h (size of following results buffer)
00h	BYTE	flag: 00h printer active, FFh printer halted
03h	BYTE	flag: 00h printer online, 01h printer offline
04h	BYTE	current form type
05h	BYTE	target printer number (00h-04h)
		same as number in request buffer unless rerouted by server console

---

INT 21h Function E0h, Subfunction 09h　　　　*Novell NetWare and others*
SPECIFY CAPTURE FILE　　　　　　　　　　　　　　*Print Services*

Purpose: Create a permanent capture file for the next print capture to be started.

Registers at call:	**Return Registers:**
AH = E0h	AL = status
DS:SI -> request buffer (see Table 21-244)	00h successful
ES:DI -> reply buffer (see Table 21-245)	9Ch invalid path

Details: This function is supported by NetWare 4.0+, Advanced NetWare 1.0+, and Alloy NTNX.
 The caller must have read, write, and create rights for the directory containing the capture file.
Conflicts: Digital Research DOS Plus (PCI-26), OS/286 and OS/386 (PCI-34), DoubleDOS (PCI-49), Viruses (PCI-59)

21-244 Format of request buffer:

Offset	Size	Description
00h	WORD	length of following data (max 102h)
00h	BYTE	09h (subfunction "Specify Capture File")
03h	BYTE	directory handle or 00h
04h	BYTE	length of filename
05h	N BYTEs	name of capture file

21-245 Format of reply buffer:

Offset	Size	Description
00h	WORD	(call) 0000h (no results returned)

INT 21h Function F003h *Advanced NetWare 1.0+*
GET LPT CAPTURE STATUS *Print Services*

Registers at call:	Return Registers:
AX = F003h	AH = status
	00h not active
	FFh active
	AL = connection ID (01h-08h)

Conflicts: DoubleDOS (PCI-49), Virus (PCI-59)
See also: Functions B800h and B804h, Function DFh Subfunctions 00h and 04h

Queue Services

21-246 Values for Queue Services status:

00h	successful
96h	server out of memory
99h	directory full
9Bh	invalid directory handle
9Ch	invalid path
D0h	queue error
D1h	no such queue
D2h	no server for queue
D3h	no queue rights
D4h	queue full
D5h	no queue job
D6h	no job rights
D7h	queue servicing error
D9h	station is not a server
DAh	queue halted
DBh	too many queue servers
EDh	property already exists
EEh	object already exists
EFh	invalid name
F0h	wildcard not allowed
F1h	invalid bindery security level
F5h	not permitted to create object

F7h	not permitted to create property
FCh	no such object
FEh	server bindery locked
FFh	bindery failure

INT 21h Function E3h, Subfunction 64h
CREATE QUEUE

Advanced NetWare 2.1+
Queue Services

Registers at call:
AH = E3h
DS:SI -> request buffer (see Table 21-247)
ES:DI -> reply buffer (see Table 21-248)

Return Registers:
AL = status
(00h,96h,99h,9Bh,9Ch,EDh-F1h,F5h,F7h,FCh,
    FEh,FFh) (see Table 21-246)

Details: The caller must be on a workstation with SUPERVISOR privileges.
Conflicts: OS/286 and OS/386 (PCI-34), DoubleDOS (PCI-49)
See also: Function E3h Subfunctions 65h, 66h, 68h, and 6Bh

21-247 Format of request buffer:

Offset	Size	Description
00h	WORD	length of following data (max ABh)
00h	BYTE	64h (subfunction "Create Queue")
03h	WORD	(big-endian) queue type
05h	BYTE	length of queue's name (01h-2Fh)
06h	N BYTEs	queue's name
	BYTE	directory handle or 00h
	BYTE	length of path name (01h-76h)
	N BYTEs	path name of directory in which to create queue subdirectory

21-248 Format of reply buffer:

Offset	Size	Description
00h	WORD	(call) 0004h (size of following results buffer)
00h	DWORD	(big-endian) object ID of queue

INT 21h Function E3h, Subfunction 65h
DESTROY QUEUE

Advanced NetWare 2.1+
Queue Services

Purpose: Abort all active jobs, detach all job servers, remove all job entries, delete all job files, remove the queue object and its properties from the bindery, and delete the queue's subdirectory.
Registers at call:
AH = E3h
DS:SI -> request buffer (see Table 21-249)
ES:DI -> reply buffer (see Table 21-250)

Return Registers:
AL = status (00h,96h,9Ch,D0h,D1h,FFh)
    (see also Table 21-246)
    FFh hardware failure

Details: The caller must have SUPERVISOR privileges.
Conflicts: OS/286 and OS/386 (PCI-34), DoubleDOS (PCI-49)
See also: Function E3h Subfunctions 64h, 66h, 68h, 6Ah, and 70h

21-249 Format of request buffer:

Offset	Size	Description
00h	WORD	0005h (length of following data)
00h	BYTE	65h (subfunction "Destroy Queue")
03h	DWORD	(big-endian) object ID of queue

21-250 Format of reply buffer:

Offset	Size	Description
00h	WORD	(call) 0000h (no results returned)

INT 21h Function E3h, Subfunction 66h
READ QUEUE CURRENT STATUS

Advanced NetWare 2.1+
Queue Services

Registers at call:
AH = E3h
DS:SI -> request buffer (see Table 21-251)
ES:DI -> reply buffer (see Table 21-252)

Return Registers:
AL = status
(00h,96h,9Ch,D1h-D3h,F1h,FCh,FEh,FFh)
(see Table 21-246)

Details: The caller must be on a workstation which is security-equivalent to a member of the queue's Q_USERS or Q_OPERATORS properties.
Conflicts: OS/286 and OS/386 (PCI-34), DoubleDOS (PCI-49)
See also: Function E3h Subfunctions 64h, 67h, 6Fh, and 76h

21-251 Format of request buffer:

Offset	Size	Description
00h	WORD	0005h (length of following data)
00h	BYTE	66h (subfunction "Read Queue Current Status")
03h	DWORD	(big-endian) object ID of queue

21-252 Format of reply buffer:

Offset	Size	Description
00h	WORD	(call) 0085h (size of following results)
00h	DWORD	(big-endian) object ID of queue
06h	BYTE	status of queue
		bit 0: operator disabled addition of new jobs
		bit 1: operator refuses additional job servers attaching
		bit 2: operator disabled job servicing
07h	BYTE	number of jobs in queue (00h-FAh)
08h	BYTE	number of servers attached to queue (00h-19h)
09h	25 DWORDs	list of object IDs of attached servers
6Dh	25 BYTEs	list of attached servers' stations
86h	BYTE	(call) maximum number of servers to return

INT 21h Function E3h, Subfunction 67h
SET QUEUE CURRENT STATUS

Advanced NetWare 2.1+
Queue Services

Registers at call:
AH = E3h
DS:SI -> request buffer (see Table 21-253)
ES:DI -> reply buffer (see Table 21-254)

Return Registers:
AL = status
(00h,96h,9Ch,D0h,D1h,D3h,FEh,FFh)
(see Table 21-246)

Details: The caller must have operator privileges.
Conflicts: OS/286 and OS/386 (PCI-34), DoubleDOS (PCI-49)
See also: Function E3h Subfunctions 64h, 66h, 6Fh, and 76h

21-253 Format of request buffer:

Offset	Size	Description
00h	WORD	0006h (length of following data)
00h	BYTE	67h (subfunction "Set Queue Current Status")
03h	DWORD	(big-endian) object ID of queue
07h	BYTE	queue status
		bit 0: operator disabled addition of new jobs
		bit 1: operator refuses additional job servers attaching
		bit 2: operator disabled job servicing

21-254 Format of reply buffer:

Offset	Size	Description
00h	WORD	(call) 0000h (no results returned)

INT 21h Function E3h, Subfunction 68h
CREATE QUEUE JOB AND FILE
Advanced NetWare 2.1+
Queue Services

Registers at call:
AH = E3h
DS:SI -> request buffer (see Table 21-255)
ES:DI -> reply buffer (see Table 21-256)

Return Registers:
AL = status
(00h,96h,99h,9Ch,D0h-D4h,DAh,EDh,EFh-F1h, F7h,FCh,FEh,FFh) (see Table 21-246)

Details: The caller must be on a workstation which is security-equivalent to a member of the queue's Q_USER property.
Conflicts: OS/286 and OS/386 (PCI-34), DoubleDOS (PCI-49)
See also: Function E0h; Function E3h Subfunctions 69h, 6Ah, and 6Eh

21-255 Format of request buffer:

Offset	Size	Description
00h	WORD	0107h (length of following data)
00h	BYTE	68h (subfunction "Close File and Start Queue Job")
03h	DWORD	(big-endian) object ID of queue
07h	BYTE	client station
08h	BYTE	client task number
09h	DWORD	(big-endian) object ID of client
0Dh	DWORD	(big-endian) object ID of target server
		FFFFFFFFh if any server acceptable
11h	6 BYTEs	target execution time (year,month,day,hour,minute,second)
		FFFFFFFFFFFFh to execute as soon as possible
17h	6 BYTEs	job entry time (year,month,day,hour,minute,second)
1Dh	WORD	(big-endian) job number
1Fh	WORD	(big-endian) job type
21h	BYTE	job position
22h	BYTE	job control flags
23h	14 BYTEs	ASCIZ job file name
31h	6 BYTEs	job file handle
37h	BYTE	server station
38h	BYTE	server task number
39h	DWORD	(big-endian) object ID of server
3Dh	50 BYTEs	ASCIZ job description string
6Fh	152 BYTEs	client record area

21-256 Format of reply buffer:

Offset	Size	Description
00h	WORD	(call) 0036h (size of following results buffer)
00h	BYTE	client station
03h	BYTE	client task number
04h	DWORD	(big-endian) object ID of client
08h	DWORD	(big-endian) object ID of target server
0Ch	6 BYTEs	target execution time (year,month,day,hour,minute,second)
12h	6 BYTEs	job entry time (year,month,day,hour,minute,second)
18h	WORD	(big-endian) job number
1Ah	WORD	(big-endian) job type

1Ch	BYTE	job position
1Dh	BYTE	job control flags
1Eh	14 BYTEs	ASCIZ job file name
2Ch	6 BYTEs	job file handle
32h	BYTE	server station
33h	BYTE	server task number
34h	DWORD	(big-endian) object ID of server or 00000000h

INT 21h Function E3h, Subfunction 69h
CLOSE FILE AND START QUEUE JOB

Advanced NetWare 2.1+
Queue Services

Registers at call:
AH = E3h
DS:SI -> request buffer (see Table 21-257)
ES:DI -> reply buffer (see Table 21-258)

Return Registers:
AL = status
(00h,96h,D0h,D1h,D3h,D5h,D6h,FEh,FFh)
  (see Table 21-246)

Details: The caller must be on the workstation which created the job.
Conflicts: OS/286 and OS/386 (PCI-34), DoubleDOS (PCI-49)
See also: Function E3h Subfunctions 68h, 6Ah, and 6Eh

21-257 Format of request buffer:

Offset	Size	Description
00h	WORD	0007h (length of following data)
00h	BYTE	69h (subfunction "Close File and Start Queue Job")
03h	DWORD	(big-endian) object ID of queue
07h	WORD	(big-endian) job number

21-258 Format of reply buffer:

Offset	Size	Description
00h	WORD	(call) 0000h (no results returned)

INT 21h Function E3h, Subfunction 6Ah
REMOVE JOB FROM QUEUE

Advanced NetWare 2.1+
Queue Services

Registers at call:
AH = E3h
DS:SI -> request buffer (see Table 21-259)
ES:DI -> reply buffer (see Table 21-260)

Return Registers:
AL = status
(00h,96h,D0h,D1h,D5h,D6h,FEh,FFh)
  (see Table 21-246)

Details: The caller must have created the job or be an operator.
Conflicts: OS/286 and OS/386 (PCI-34), DoubleDOS (PCI-49)
See also: Function E3h Subfunctions 68h, 6Ah, and 6Eh

21-259 Format of request buffer:

Offset	Size	Description
00h	WORD	0007h (length of following data)
00h	BYTE	6Ah (subfunction "Remove Job From Queue")
03h	DWORD	(big-endian) object ID of queue
07h	WORD	(big-endian) job number

21-260 Format of reply buffer:

Offset	Size	Description
00h	WORD	(call) 0000h (no results returned)

INT 21h Function E3h, Subfunction 6Bh
GET QUEUE JOB LIST

Advanced NetWare 2.1+
Queue Services

Registers at call:
AH = E3h

DS:SI -> request buffer (see Table 21-261)
ES:DI -> reply buffer (see Table 21-262)

Return Registers:
AL = status
(00h,96h,9Ch,D0h-D3h,FCh,FEh,FFh)
   (see Table 21-246)

Details: The caller must be on a workstation which is security-equivalent to a member of the Q_USERS or Q_OPERATORS properties.
Conflicts: OS/286 and OS/386 (PCI-34), DoubleDOS (PCI-49)
See also: Function E3h Subfunctions 68h, 6Ah, and 6Eh

21-261 Format of request buffer:

Offset	Size	Description
00h	WORD	0005h (length of following data)
00h	BYTE	6Bh (subfunction "Get Queue Job List")
03h	DWORD	(big-endian) object ID of queue

21-262 Format of reply buffer:

Offset	Size	Description
00h	WORD	(call) size of following results buffer (max 1F6h)
00h	WORD	(big-endian) job count
04h	N WORDs	(big-endian) list of job numbers by position in queue
	WORD	maximum job numbers

INT 21h Function E3h, Subfunction 6Ch
READ QUEUE JOB ENTRY

Advanced NetWare 2.1+
Queue Services

Registers at call:
AH = E3h
DS:SI -> request buffer (see Table 21-263)
ES:DI -> reply buffer (see Table 21-264)

Return Registers:
AL = status
(00h,96h,D0h-D3h,D5h,FCh,FEh,FFh)
   (see Table 21-246)

Details: The caller must be on a workstation which is security-equivalent to a member of the Q_USERS, Q_OPERATORS, or Q_SERVERS properties.
Conflicts: OS/286 and OS/386 (PCI-34), DoubleDOS (PCI-49)
See also: Function E3h Subfunctions 68h, 6Ah, and 6Eh

21-263 Format of request buffer:

Offset	Size	Description
00h	WORD	0007h (length of following data)
00h	BYTE	6Ch (subfunction "Read Queue Job Entry")
03h	DWORD	(big-endian) object ID of queue
07h	WORD	(big-endian) job number

21-264 Format of reply buffer:

Offset	Size	Description
00h	WORD	(call) 0100h (size of following results)
00h	BYTE	client station number
03h	BYTE	client task number
04h	DWORD	object ID of client
08h	DWORD	(big-endian) object ID of target server
		FFFFFFFFh if any server acceptable
0Ch	6 BYTEs	target execution time (year,month,day,hour,minute,second)
		FFFFFFFFFFFFh if serviced as soon as possible
12h	6 BYTEs	job entry time (year,month,day,hour,minute,second)
18h	WORD	(big-endian) job number
1Ah	WORD	(big-endian) job type

1Ch	BYTE	job position
1Dh	BYTE	job control flags (see Table 21-265)
1Eh	14 BYTEs	ASCIZ job filename
2Ch	6 BYTEs	job file handle
32h	BYTE	server station
33h	BYTE	server task number
34h	DWORD	object ID of server
38h	50 BYTEs	ASCIZ job description string
6Ah	152 BYTEs	client record area

21-265 Bitfields for job control flags:

bit 3 job will be serviced automatically if connection broken
bit 4 job remains in queue after server aborts job
bit 5 client has not filled associated job file
bit 6 User Hold—job advances, but cannot be serviced until this bit is cleared by user or operator
bit 7 Operator Hold—job advances, but cannot be serviced until this bit is cleared by an operator

---

INT 21h Function E3h, Subfunction 6Dh
CHANGE QUEUE JOB ENTRY

Advanced NetWare 2.1+
Queue Services

Registers at call:
AH = E3h
DS:SI -> request buffer (see Table 21-266)
ES:DI -> reply buffer (see Table 21-267)

Return Registers:
AL = status
(00h,96h,D0h,D1h,D5h,D7h,FEh,FFh)
  (see Table 21-246)

Details: The caller must be an operator or the user who created the job.
Conflicts: OS/286 and OS/386 (PCI-34), DoubleDOS (PCI-49)
See also: Function E3h Subfunctions 68h, 6Ah, 6Ch, and 6Eh

21-266 Format of request buffer:

Offset	Size	Description
00h	WORD	0105h (length of following data)
00h	BYTE	6Dh (subfunction "Change Queue Job Entry")
03h	DWORD	(big-endian) object ID of queue
07h	BYTE	client station number
08h	BYTE	client task number
09h	DWORD	(big-endian) object ID of client
0Dh	DWORD	(big-endian) object ID of target server
11h	6 BYTEs	target execution time (year,month,day,hour,minute,second)
17h	6 BYTEs	job entry time (year,month,day,hour,minute,second)
1Dh	WORD	(big-endian) job number
1Fh	WORD	(big-endian) job type
21h	BYTE	job position
22h	BYTE	job control flags (see Table 21-265)
23h	14 BYTEs	ASCIZ job filename
31h	6 BYTEs	job file handle
37h	BYTE	server station
38h	BYTE	server task number
39h	DWORD	object ID of server
3Dh	50 BYTEs	ASCIZ job description string
6Fh	152 BYTEs	client record area

21-267 Format of reply buffer:

Offset	Size	Description
00h	WORD	(call) 0000h (no results returned)

INT 21h Function E3h, Subfunction 6Eh
CHANGE QUEUE JOB POSITION
Advanced NetWare 2.1+
Queue Services

Registers at call:
AH = E3h
DS:SI -> request buffer (see Table 21-268)
ES:DI -> reply buffer (see Table 21-269)

Return Registers:
AL = status
(00h,96h,D0h,D1h,D5h,D6h,FEh,FFh)
  (see Table 21-246)

Details: The caller must be an operator.

If the specified position is greater than the number of jobs in the queue, the job is placed at the end of the queue.

Conflicts: OS/286 and OS/386 (PCI-34), DoubleDOS (PCI-49)

See also: Function E3h Subfunctions 68h, 6Ah, 6Ch, and 6Dh

21-268 Format of request buffer:

Offset	Size	Description
00h	WORD	0008h (length of following data)
00h	BYTE	6Eh (subfunction "Change Queue Job Position")
03h	DWORD	(big-endian) object ID of queue
07h	WORD	(big-endian) job number
09h	BYTE	new position in queue (01h-FAh)

21-269 Format of reply buffer:

Offset	Size	Description
00h	WORD	(call) 0000h (no results returned)

INT 21h Function E3h, Subfunction 6Fh
ATTACH QUEUE SERVER TO QUEUE
Advanced NetWare 2.1+
Queue Services

Purpose: Attach the calling job server to the specified queue.

Registers at call:
AH = E3h
DS:SI -> request buffer (see Table 21-270)
ES:DI -> reply buffer (see Table 21-271)

Return Registers:
AL = status
(00h,96h,9Ch,D0h,D1h,D3h,DAh,DBh,FEh,FFh)
  (see also Function E3h Subfunction 64h)
    FFh bindery failure, or no such property, or no
      such member

Details: A queue may have up to 25 job servers attached.

The calling workstation must be security-equivalent to a member of the queue's Q_SERVERS property.

Conflicts: OS/286 and OS/386 (PCI-34), DoubleDOS (PCI-49)

See also: Function E3h Subfunctions 70h, 71h, 72h, 73h, and 76h

21-270 Format of request buffer:

Offset	Size	Description
00h	WORD	0005h (length of following data)
00h	BYTE	6Fh (subfunction "Attach Queue Server To Queue")
03h	DWORD	(big-endian) object ID of queue

21-271 Format of reply buffer:

Offset	Size	Description
00h	WORD	(call) 0000h (no results returned)

INT 21h Function E3h, Subfunction 70h
DETACH QUEUE SERVER FROM QUEUE

Advanced NetWare 2.1+
Queue Services

Purpose: Remove the calling job server from the specified queue's list of servers.

Registers at call:	Return Registers:
AH = E3h	AL = status
DS:SI -> request buffer (see Table 21-272)	(00h,96h,9Ch,D0h,D1h,D2h,FEh,FFh)
ES:DI -> reply buffer (see Table 21-273)	(see Table 21-246)

Details: The caller must have previously attached itself to the queue.
Conflicts: OS/286 and OS/386 (PCI-34), DoubleDOS (PCI-49)
See also: Function E3h Subfunctions 6Fh, 72h, 73h, and 76h

21-272 Format of request buffer:

Offset	Size	Description
00h	WORD	0005h (length of following data)
00h	BYTE	70h (subfunction "Detach Queue Server From Queue")
03h	DWORD	(big-endian) object ID of queue

21-273 Format of reply buffer:

Offset	Size	Description
00h	WORD	(call) 0000h (no results returned)

INT 21h Function E3h, Subfunction 71h
SERVICE QUEUE JOB AND OPEN FILE

Advanced NetWare 2.1+
Queue Services

Registers at call:	Return Registers:
AH = E3h	AL = status
DS:SI -> request buffer (see Table 21-274)	(00h,96h,9Ch,D0h,D1h,D3h,D5h,D9h,DAh,FEh,
ES:DI -> reply buffer (see Table 21-256)	FFh) (see Table 21-246)

Details: The caller must be on a workstation which is security-equivalent to a member of the queue's Q_USERS, Q_OPERATORS, or Q_SERVERS properties.
Conflicts: OS/286 and OS/386 (PCI-34), DoubleDOS (PCI-49)
See also: Function E3h Subfunctions 6Fh, 72h, 73h, and 76h

21-274 Format of request buffer:

Offset	Size	Description
00h	WORD	0007h (length of following data)
00h	BYTE	71h (subfunction "Service Queue Job and Open File")
03h	DWORD	(big-endian) object ID of queue
07h	WORD	(big-endian) target job type
		FFFFh any

INT 21h Function E3h, Subfunction 72h
FINISH SERVICING QUEUE JOB AND FILE

Advanced NetWare 2.1+
Queue Services

Purpose: Inform the Queue Management System (QMS) that the queue server has completed a job.

Registers at call:	Return Registers:
AH = E3h	AL = status (00h,96h,D0h,D1h,D6h) (see Table
DS:SI -> request buffer (see Table 21-275)	21-246)
ES:DI -> reply buffer (see Table 21-276)	

Details: The caller must be a job server which has previously obtained a job for servicing.
Conflicts: OS/286 and OS/386 (PCI-34), DoubleDOS (PCI-49)
See also: Function E3h Subfunctions 6Fh, 71h, 73h, and 76h

21-275 Format of request buffer:

Offset	Size	Description
00h	WORD	000Bh (length of following data)
00h	BYTE	72h (subfunction "Finish Servicing Queue Job and File")
03h	DWORD	(big-endian) object ID of queue
07h	WORD	(big-endian) job number
09h	DWORD	(big-endian) charge

21-276 Format of reply buffer:

Offset	Size	Description
00h	WORD	(call) 0000h (no results returned)

INT 21h Function E3h, Subfunction 73h
ABORT SERVICING QUEUE JOB AND FILE

Advanced NetWare 2.1+
Queue Services

Purpose: Inform the Queue Management System (QMS) that the queue server is unable to service a previously-accepted job.

Registers at call:
AH = E3h
DS:SI -> request buffer (see Table 21-277)
ES:DI -> reply buffer (see Table 21-278)

Return Registers:
AL = status (00h,96h,D0h,D1h,D6h,D9h)
  (see Table 21-246)

Conflicts: OS/286 and OS/386 (PCI-34), DoubleDOS (PCI-49)
See also: Function E3h Subfunctions 6Fh, 71h, 72h, and 76h

21-277 Format of request buffer:

Offset	Size	Description
00h	WORD	0007h (length of following data)
00h	BYTE	73h (subfunction "Abort Servicing Queue Job and File")
03h	DWORD	(big-endian) object ID of queue
07h	WORD	(big-endian) job number

21-278 Format of reply buffer:

Offset	Size	Description
00h	WORD	(call) 0000h (no results returned)

INT 21h Function E3h, Subfunction 74h
CHANGE TO CLIENT RIGHTS

Advanced NetWare 2.1+
Queue Services

Purpose: Temporarily assume the login identity of the client submitting the job being serviced.

Registers at call:
AH = E3h
DS:SI -> request buffer (see Table 21-279)
ES:DI -> reply buffer (see Table 21-280)

Return Registers:
AL = status (00h,96h,D0h,D1h,D5h,D9h)
  (see Table 21-246)

Details: The caller must be a job server which has obtained a job for servicing.
Conflicts: OS/286 and OS/386 (PCI-34), DoubleDOS (PCI-49)
See also: Function E3h Subfunction 75h

21-279 Format of request buffer:

Offset	Size	Description
00h	WORD	0007h (length of following data)
00h	BYTE	74h (subfunction "Change To Client Rights")
03h	DWORD	(big-endian) object ID of queue
07h	WORD	(big-endian) job number

21-280 Format of reply buffer:

Offset	Size	Description
00h	WORD	(call) 0000h (no results returned)

INT 21h Function E3h, Subfunction 75h   *Advanced NetWare 2.1+*
RESTORE QUEUE SERVER RIGHTS   *Queue Services*

Purpose: Restore server's own identity after assuming the login identity of the client submitting the job being serviced.

Registers at call: **Return Registers:**
AH = E3h   AL = status
DS:SI -> request buffer (see Table 21-281)   (00h,96h,9Ch,D0h,D1h,D3h,D5h,D9h,DAh,FEh,
ES:DI -> reply buffer (see Table 21-282)   FFh) (see Table 21-246)

Details: The caller must be a job server which has previously changed its identity.
Conflicts: OS/286 and OS/386 (PCI-34), DoubleDOS (PCI-49)
See also: Function E3h Subfunction 74h

21-281 Format of request buffer:

Offset	Size	Description
00h	WORD	0001h (length of following data)
00h	BYTE	75h (subfunction "Change To Client Rights")

21-282 Format of reply buffer:

Offset	Size	Description
00h	WORD	(call) 0000h (no results returned)

INT 21h Function E3h, Subfunction 76h   *Advanced NetWare 2.1+*
READ QUEUE SERVER CURRENT STATUS   *Queue Services*

Registers at call: **Return Registers:**
AH = E3h   AL = status
DS:SI -> request buffer (see Table 21-283)   (00h,96h,9Ch,D1h-D3h,F1h,FCh,FEh,FFh)
ES:DI -> reply buffer (see Table 21-284)   (see Table 21-246)

Details: The caller must be on a workstation which is security-equivalent to a member of the Q_USERS or Q_OPERATORS properties.
Conflicts: OS/286 and OS/386 (PCI-34), DoubleDOS (PCI-49)
See also: Function E3h Subfunctions 68h, 6Ch, 6Fh, 77h, and 78h

21-283 Format of request buffer:

Offset	Size	Description
00h	WORD	000Ah (length of following data)
00h	BYTE	76h (subfunction "Read Queue Server Current Status")
03h	DWORD	(big-endian) object ID of queue
07h	DWORD	(big-endian) object ID of server
0Bh	BYTE	server station

21-284 Format of reply buffer:

Offset	Size	Description
00h	WORD	(call) 0040h (size of following results)
00h	64 BYTEs	server status record (format depends on server)
		first four bytes should contain estimated "price" for an average job

---

INT 21h Function E3h, Subfunction 77h   *Advanced NetWare 2.1+*
SET QUEUE SERVER CURRENT STATUS   *Queue Services*

Registers at call:
AH = E3h

DS:SI -> request buffer (see Table 21-285)
ES:DI -> reply buffer (see Table 21-286)

Return Registers:
AL = status (00h,96h,9Ch,D0h,D1h,FEh,FFh)
    (see Table 21-246)

Details: The caller must be a job server which has attached itself to the queue.
Conflicts: OS/286 and OS/386 (PCI-34), DoubleDOS (PCI-49)
See also: Function E3h Subfunctions 68h, 6Ch, 6Fh, 76h, and 78h

21-285 Format of request buffer:

Offset	Size	Description
00h	WORD	0045h (length of following data)
00h	BYTE	77h (subfunction "Set Queue Server Current Status")
03h	DWORD	(big-endian) object ID of queue
00h	64 BYTEs	server status record (format depends on server)
		first four bytes should contain estimated "price" for an average job

21-286 Format of reply buffer:

Offset	Size	Description
00h	WORD	(call) 0000h (no results returned)

INT 21h Function E3h, Subfunction 78h
GET QUEUE JOB'S FILE SIZE

Advanced NetWare 2.1+
Queue Services

Registers at call:
AH = E3h
DS:SI -> request buffer (see Table 21-287)
ES:DI -> reply buffer (see Table 21-288)

Return Registers:
AL = status (see also Table 21-246)
    00h successful

Details: The caller must be on a workstation which is security-equivalent to a member of the queue's Q_USERS, Q_OPERATORS, or Q_SERVERS properties.
Conflicts: OS/286 and OS/386 (PCI-34), DoubleDOS (PCI-49)
See also: Function E3h Subfunctions 68h, 6Ch, and 71h

21-287 Format of request buffer:

Offset	Size	Description
00h	WORD	0007h (length of following data)
00h	BYTE	78h (subfunction "Get Queue Job's File Size")
03h	DWORD	(big-endian) object ID of queue
07h	WORD	(big-endian) job number

21-288 Format of reply buffer:

Offset	Size	Description
00h	WORD	(call) 000Ah (size of following results)
00h	DWORD	(big-endian) object ID of queue
06h	WORD	(big-endian) job number
08h	DWORD	(big-endian) size of job file in bytes

Synchronization Services

21-289 Values for Synchronization Services status:

00h	successful
96h	no dynamic memory for file
FEh	timed out
FFh	failed

INT 21h Function BCh
LOG PHYSICAL RECORD
NetWare 4.6+, Advanced NetWare 1.0+, Alloy NTNX
Synchronization Services

Purpose: Add the specified physical record to the log table, optionally locking it.

Registers at call:
AH = BCh
AL = flags
      bit 0: lock as well as log record
      bit 1: non-exclusive lock
BX = file handle
CX:DX = starting offset in file
SI:DI = length of region to lock
BP = timeout in timer ticks (1/18 sec)
         0000h = don't wait if already locked

Return Registers:
AL = status (see Table 21-289)

See also: Functions BDh, BEh, BFh, C2h, and D0h; MS-DOS Function 5Ch (Chapter 3)

INT 21h Function BDh
RELEASE PHYSICAL RECORD
NetWare 4.6+, Advanced NetWare 1.0+, Alloy NTNX
Synchronization Services

Purpose: Unlock the specified physical record but do not remove it from log table.

Registers at call:
AH = BDh
BX = file handle
CX:DX = starting offset in file
SI:DI = length of record

Return Registers:
AL = status
      00h successful
      FFh record not locked

See also: Functions BCh, BEh, C0h, C3h, and D2h

INT 21h Function BEh
CLEAR PHYSICAL RECORD
NetWare 4.6+, Advanced NetWare 1.0+, Alloy NTNX
Synchronization Services

Purpose: Unlock the physical record and remove it from the log table.

Registers at call:
AH = BEh
BX = file handle
CX:DX = starting offset within file
SI:DI = record length in bytes

Return Registers:
AL = status
      00h successful
      FFh specified record not locked

Conflicts: Viruses (PCI-59)

See also: Functions BCh, BDh, C1h, C4h, and D4h; MS-DOS Function 5Ch (Chapter 3)

INT 21h Function BFh
LOG/LOCK RECORD (FCB)
Novell NetWare, Alloy NTNX
Obsolete

Registers at call:
AH = BFh
AL = flags
      bit 0: lock as well as log record
      bit 1: non-exclusive lock
DS:DX -> opened FCB (see Table 3-63)
BX:CX = offset
BP = lock timeout in timer ticks (1/18 sec)
  if AL nonzero
SI:DI = length

Return Registers:
AL = error code (see Table 21-289)

Details: This function was added in NetWare 4.6, but was removed some time prior to Advanced NetWare 2.15, and is no longer listed in current Novell documentation.

See also: Functions BCh, C0h, and C2h

INT 21h Function C0h   *Novell NetWare, Alloy NTNX*
RELEASE RECORD (FCB)   *Obsolete*
Purpose: Unlocks the record but does not remove it from the log table.
Registers at call: **Return Registers:**
AH = C0h   AL = error code (see above)
DS:DX -> non-extended FCB (see Table 3-63)
BX:CX = offset
Details: This function was added in NetWare 4.6, but was removed some time prior to Advanced
NetWare 2.15, and is no longer listed in current Novell documentation.
Conflicts: Viruses (PCI-59)
See also: Functions BDh, BFh, C1h, and C3h

INT 21h Function C1h   *Novell NetWare, Alloy NTNX*
CLEAR RECORD (FCB)   *Obsolete*
Purpose: Unlocks the record and removes it from the log table.
Registers at call: **Return Registers:**
AH = C1h   AL = error code (see Table 21-289)
DS:DX -> opened FCB (see Table 3-63)
BX:CX = offset
Details: This function was added in NetWare 4.6, but was removed some time prior to Advanced
NetWare, and is no longer listed in current Novell documentation.
Conflicts: "Solano" virus (PCI-59)
See also: Functions BEh, C0h, and C4h

INT 21h Function C2h   *NetWare 4.6+, Advanced NetWare 1.0+, Alloy NTNX*
LOCK PHYSICAL RECORD SET   *Synchronization Services*
Purpose: Attempt to lock all physical records listed in the log table.
Registers at call: **Return Registers:**
AH = C2h   AL = status (00h,FEh,FFh) (see Table 21-289)
AL = flags
      bit 1: non-exclusive lock
BP = lock timeout in timer ticks (1/18 sec)
   0000h = no wait
Details: Status FFh will be returned if one or more physical records have been exclusively locked
by another process.
Conflicts: "Scott's Valley" virus (PCI-59)
See also: Functions BFh, C3h, and D1h

INT 21h Function C3h   *NetWare 4.6+, Advanced NetWare 1.0+, Alloy NTNX*
RELEASE PHYSICAL RECORD SET   *Synchronization Services*
Purpose: Unlock all currently-locked physical records in the log table, but do not remove them
from the table.
Registers at call: **Return Registers:**
AH = C3h   none
Conflicts: Virus (PCI-59)
See also: Functions BDh, C0h, C2h, C4h, and D3h

INT 21h Function C4h   *NetWare 4.6+, Advanced NetWare 1.0+, Alloy NTNX*
CLEAR PHYSICAL RECORD SET   *Synchronization Services*
Purpose: Unlock all physical records in the log table and remove them from the log table.
Registers at call: **Return Registers:**
AH = C4h   none
See also: Functions BEh, C1h, and D5h

INT 21h Function C500h   *NetWare 4.6+, Advanced NetWare 1.0+, Alloy NTNX*
OPEN SEMAPHORE   *Synchronization Services*
Registers at call: **Return Registers:**
AX = C500h   AL = status
DS:DX -> semaphore name (counted   00h successful
   string, max 127 bytes)   BL = number of processes having semaphore
CL = initial value for semaphore   open
                                                         CX:DX = semaphore handle
                                                    FEh invalid name length
                                                    FFh invalid semaphore value
Details: The semaphore's value is incremented by Function C503h and decremented by Function
C502h.
See also: Functions C501h, C502h, C503h, and C504h

INT 21h Function C501h   *NetWare 4.6+, Advanced NetWare 1.0+, Alloy NTNX*
EXAMINE SEMAPHORE   *Synchronization Services*
Registers at call: **Return Registers:**
AX = C501h   AL = status
CX:DX = semaphore handle   00h successful
                                                         CX = semaphore value (-127 to 127)
                                                         DL = count of processes which have the
                                                              semaphore open
                                                    FFh invalid handle

See also: Functions C500h, C502h, and C504h

INT 21h Function C502h   *NetWare 4.6+, Advanced NetWare 1.0+, Alloy NTNX*
WAIT ON SEMAPHORE   *Synchronization Services*
Purpose: Decrement the semaphore's value, optionally waiting until its value becomes positive
before decrementing.
Registers at call: **Return Registers:**
AX = C502h   AL = status
CX:DX = semaphore handle   00h successful
BP = timeout limit in timer ticks   FEh timeout
   (1/18 sec)   FFh invalid handle
          0000h return immediately if
      semaphore already zero or negative
See also: Functions C500h, C501h, and C503h

INT 21h Function C503h   *NetWare 4.6+, Advanced NetWare 1.0+, Alloy NTNX*
SIGNAL SEMAPHORE   *Synchronization Services*
Purpose: Increment the semaphore's value and signal the first process (if any) in the queue wait-
ing on the semaphore.
Registers at call: **Return Registers:**
AX = C503h   AL = status
CX:DX = semaphore handle   00h successful
                                                    01h semaphore value overflowed
                                                    FFh invalid handle

See also: Functions C500h and C502h

INT 21h Function C504h   *NetWare 4.6+, Advanced NetWare 1.0+, Alloy NTNX*
CLOSE SEMAPHORE   *Synchronization Services*
Purpose: Decrement the semaphore's open count, and delete the semaphore if the count reaches
zero.

Registers at call:
AX = C504h
CX:DX = semaphore handle

Return Registers:
AL = status
   00h successful
   FFh invalid handle

See also: Functions C500h and C501h

INT 21h Function C6h
GET OR SET LOCK MODE

NetWare 4.6+, Advanced NetWare 1.0+, Alloy NTNX
Synchronization Services

Registers at call:
AH = C6h
AL = subfunction
   00h set old "compatibility" mode (default)
   01h set new extended locks mode
   02h get lock mode

Return Registers:
AL = current lock mode

Details: The locking mode should be 01h for NetWare 4.61+ and Advanced NetWare 1.0+ locking calls, and 00h for all older calls.
Conflicts: Viruses (PCI-59)
See also: Functions BCh, C4h, and D0h

INT 21h Function C8h
BEGIN LOGICAL FILE LOCKING

Novell NetWare
Obsolete

Purpose: Used to provide TTS support for applications which are not aware of Novell's Transaction Tracking System.

Registers at call:
AH = C8h
if function C6h lock mode 00h:
   DL = mode
      00h no wait
      01h wait
if function C6h lock mode 01h:
   BP = timeout in timer ticks (1/18 sec)

Return Registers:
AL = error code

Details: This function was added in NetWare 4.0, but was removed some time prior to Advanced NetWare 2.15, and is no longer listed in current Novell documentation.
See also: Function C9h

INT 21h Function C9h
END LOGICAL FILE LOCKING

Novell NetWare
Obsolete

Purpose: Used to provide TTS support for applications which are not aware of Novell's Transaction Tracking System.

Registers at call:
AH = C9h

Return Registers:
AL = error code

Details: This function was added in NetWare 4.0, but was removed some time prior to Advanced NetWare 2.15, and is no longer listed in current Novell documentation.
See also: Function C8h

INT 21h Function CAh
LOG/LOCK PERSONAL FILE (FCB)

Novell NetWare, Alloy NTNX
Obsolete

Purpose: Provides file locking support for FCBs.
Registers at call:
AH = CAh
DS:DX -> FCB (see Table 3-63)
if function C6h lock mode 01h:
   AL = log and lock flag

00h log file only
01h lock as well as log file
BP = lock timeout in timer ticks (1/18 sec)

Return Registers:
AL = error code
00h successful
96h no dynamic memory for file
FEh timeout
FFh failed

Details: This function was added in NetWare 4.0, but was removed some time prior to Advanced NetWare 2.15, and is no longer listed in current Novell documentation.
Conflicts: "Piter" virus (PCI-59)
See also: Function CBh

INT 21h Function CBh   *NetWare 4.0+, Advanced NetWare 1.0+, Alloy NTNX*
LOCK FILE SET   *Synchronization Services*

Purpose: Attempt to lock all files listed in the log table.
Registers at call: **Return Registers:**
AH = CBh   AL = status
if function C6h lock mode 00h: 00h successful
    DL = mode   FEh timed out
        00h no wait   FFh failed
        01h wait
if function C6h lock mode 01h:
    BP = lock timeout in timer ticks (1/18 sec)
        0000h = no wait

Details: Status FFh will be returned if one or more of the files have already been exclusively locked by another process.
Conflicts: Viruses (PCI-59)
See also: Functions CAh, CDh, D1h, and EBh

INT 21h Function CCh   *Novell NetWare, Alloy NTNX*
RELEASE FILE (FCB)   *Obsolete*

Purpose: Unlocks file, but does not remove it from the log table or close it.
Registers at call: **Return Registers:**
AH = CCh   none
DS:DX -> FCB (see Table 3-63)

Details: This function was added in NetWare 4.0, but was removed some time prior to Advanced NetWare 2.15, and is no longer listed in current Novell documentation.
Conflicts: "Westwood" virus (PCI-59)
See also: Functions CAh and CDh

INT 21h Function CDh   *NetWare 4.0+, Advanced NetWare 1.0+, Alloy NTNX*
RELEASE FILE SET   *Synchronization Services*

Purpose: Unlock all files listed in the log table, but don't remove them from the table.
Registers at call: **Return Registers:**
AH = CDh   none
Conflicts: "Westwood" virus (PCI-59)
See also: Functions CBh, CCh, CFh, and D3h

INT 21h Function CEh   *Novell NetWare, Alloy NTNX*
CLEAR FILE (FCB)   *Obsolete*

Purpose: Unlocks file and removes it from log table, then closes all opened and logged occurrences.

Registers at call:
AH = CEh
DS:DX -> FCB (see Table 3-63)

Return Registers:
AL = error code

Details: This function was added in NetWare 4.0, but was removed some time prior to Advanced NetWare 2.15, and is no longer listed in current Novell documentation.

See also: Functions CAh, CFh, and EDh

INT 21h Function CFh   *NetWare 4.0+, Advanced NetWare 1.0+, Alloy NTNX*
CLEAR FILE SET   *Synchronization Services*

Purpose: Unlock and remove all files from log table.

Registers at call:
AH = CFh

Return Registers:
AL = 00h

Conflicts: LANstep (Chapter 31)

See also: Functions CAh, CEh, and EBh

INT 21h Function D0h   *Novell NetWare and others*
LOG LOGICAL RECORD   *Synchronization Services*

Purpose: Add the specified logical record name to the log table, and optionally lock the record.

Registers at call:
AH = D0h
DS:DX -> record string (counted string, max
   99 data bytes)
if function C6h lock mode 01h: (Novell,
   NTNX only)
   AL = flags
          bit 0: lock as well as log the record
          bit 1: non-exclusive lock
   BP = lock timeout in timer ticks (1/18 sec)

Return Registers:
AL = status
   00h successful
   96h no dynamic memory for file
   FEh timed out
   FFh unsuccessful

Details: This function is supported by NetWare 4.6+, Advanced NetWare 1.0+, Banyan VINES, and Alloy NTNX.

   Locks on logical record names are advisory and may be ignored by other applications.

Conflicts: "Fellowship" virus (PCI-59)

See also: Functions BCh, D1h, D2h, D4h, and EBh

INT 21h Function D1h   *Novell NetWare and others*
LOCK LOGICAL RECORD SET   *Synchronization Services*

Purpose: Attempt to lock all logical record names listed in the log table.

Registers at call:
AH = D1h
AL = lock type (00h exclusive, 01h shareable)
if function C6h lock mode 00h:
   DL = mode
        00h no wait
        01h wait
if function C6h lock mode 01h: (Novell only)
   BP = lock timeout in timer ticks (1/18 sec)
        0000h no wait

Return Registers:
AL = status
   00h successful
   FEh timed out
   FFh failed

Details: This function is supported by NetWare 4.6+, Advanced Netware 1.0+, Banyan VINES, and Alloy NTNX.

   Status FFh will be returned if one or more logical records have been exclusively locked by another process.

   Locks on logical record names are advisory and may be ignored by other applications.

See also: Functions C2h, CBh, D0h, D3h, and D5h

INT 21h Function D2h   *Novell NetWare and others*
RELEASE LOGICAL RECORD   *Synchronization Services*
Purpose: Unlock the logical record name but do not remove it from the log table.
Registers at call: **Return Registers:**
AH = D2h   AL = status
DS:DX -> semaphore identifier (counted string   00h successful
  up to 99 chars long)   FFh no such record
Details: This function is supported by NetWare 4.0+, Advanced NetWare 1.0+, Banyan VINES, and Alloy NTNX.
    Locks on logical record names are advisory and may be ignored by other applications.
See also: Functions BDh, D0h, D3h, and D4h

INT 21h Function D3h   *Novell NetWare and others*
RELEASE LOGICAL RECORD SET   *Synchronization Services*
Purpose: Unlock all currently-locked logical record names in the log table, but do not remove them from the table.
Registers at call: **Return Registers:**
AH = D3h   none
Details: This function is supported by NetWare 4.0+, Advanced NetWare 1.0+, Banyan VINES, and Alloy NTNX.
    Locks on logical record names are advisory and may be ignored by other applications.
See also: Functions C3h, CDh, D1h, D2h, and D5h

INT 21h Function D4h   *Novell NetWare and others*
CLEAR LOGICAL RECORD   *Synchronization Services*
Purpose: Unlock and remove the logical record name from the log table.
Registers at call: **Return Registers:**
AH = D4h   AL = status
DS:DX -> logical record name (counted string   00h successful
  up to 99 chars long)   FFh no such record name
Details: This function is supported by NetWare 4.0+, Advanced NetWare 1.0+, Banyan VINES, and Alloy NTNX.
    Locks on logical record names are advisory and may be ignored by other applications.
See also: Functions BEh, D0h, D2h, and D5h

INT 21h Function D5h   *Novell NetWare and others*
CLEAR LOGICAL RECORD SET   *Synchronization Services*
Purpose: Unlock and remove all logical record name from the log table.
Registers at call: **Return Registers:**
AH = D5h   AL = status
                                                   00h successful
                                                   FFh no such record name
Details: This function is supported by NetWare 4.0+, Advanced NetWare 1.0+, Banyan VINES, and Alloy NTNX.
    Locks on logical record names are advisory and may be ignored by other applications.
Conflicts: Viruses (PCI-59)
See also: Functions D1h, D3h, and D4h

INT 21h Function EBh   *NetWare 4.6+, Advanced NetWare 1.0+, Alloy NTNX*
LOG FILE   *Synchronization Services*
Purpose: Add the location and size of the specified file to the log table and optionally lock the file.

Registers at call:
AH = EBh
DS:DX -> ASCIZ filename
if function C6h lock mode 01h:
    AL = flags
        00h log file only
        01h lock as well as log file
            BP = lock timeout in timer ticks
              (1/18 second)
                0000h = don't wait if file
                already locked

Return Registers:
AL = error code
    00h successful
    96h no dynamic memory for file
    FEh timed out
    FFh failed

Conflicts: OS/386 (PCI-34), DoubleDOS (PCI-49)
See also: Functions BCh, CAh, D0h, ECh, and EDh

INT 21h Function ECh   *NetWare 4.6+, Advanced NetWare 1.0+, Alloy NTNX*
RELEASE FILE   *Synchronization Services*
Purpose: Unlock the specified file but retain it in the log table.

Registers at call:
AH = ECh
DS:DX -> ASCIZ filename

Return Registers:
AL = status
    00h successful
    FFh file not found

Conflicts: OS/286 and OS/386 (PCI-34), DoubleDOS (PCI-49), "Terror" virus (PCI-59)
See also: Functions CDh, EBh, and EDh

INT 21h Function EDh   *NetWare 4.6+, Advanced NetWare 1.0+, Alloy NTNX*
CLEAR FILE   *Synchronization Services*
Purpose: Unlock the file and remove it from the log table.

Registers at call:
AH = EDh
DS:DX -> ASCIZ filename

Return Registers:
AL = status
    00h successful
    FFh no files found

Conflicts: OS/286 and OS/386 (PCI-34)
See also: Functions CBh, CEh, CFh, EBh, and ECh

Transaction Tracking System

21-290 Values for Transaction Tracking System status:
00h successful
96h out of memory
FDh transaction tracking disabled, no backout
FEh transaction ended, records locked
FFh no explicit transaction active

INT 21h Function C700h   *NetWare 4.0+, Advanced NetWare 1.0+*
BEGIN TRANSACTION   *Transaction Tracking System*

Registers at call:
AX = C700h

Return Registers:
CF clear if successful
    AL = 00h
CF set on error
    AL = error code
        96h out of memory
        FEh implicit transaction already active, converted to explicit
        FFh explicit transaction already active

Conflicts: "MH-757" virus (PCI-59)
See also: Functions C701h, C702h, and C703h

INT 21h Function C701h   *NetWare 4.0+, Advanced NetWare 1.0+*
END TRANSACTION   *Transaction Tracking System*
Registers at call: **Return Registers:**
AX = C701h   AL = status (00h,FDh-FFh) (see also Table 21-290)
                                                 00h successful
                                                          CX:DX = transaction number
                                             CF clear except when AL=FFh

Conflicts: "MH-757" virus (PCI-59)
See also: Functions C700h and C703h

INT 21h Function C702h   *NetWare 4.0+, Advanced NetWare 1.0+*
INSTALLATION CHECK   *Transaction Tracking System*
Purpose: Determine whether the default file server supports TTS.
Registers at call: **Return Registers:**
AX = C702h   AL = status
                                                 00h not available
                                                 01h available
                                                 FDh available but disabled

Conflicts: "MH-757" virus (PCI-59)

INT 21h Function C703h   *NetWare 4.0+, Advanced NetWare 1.0+*
ABORT TRANSACTION   *Transaction Tracking System*
Registers at call: **Return Registers:**
AX = C703h   CF clear if successful
                                                 AL = 00h
                                             CF set on error
                                                 AL = error code (FDh,FEh,FFh) (see Table 21-290)

Conflicts: "MH-757" virus (PCI-59)
See also: Functions C700h, C701h, and C704h

INT 21h Function C704h   *NetWare 4.0+, Advanced NetWare 1.0+*
TRANSACTION STATUS   *Transaction Tracking System*
Purpose: Verify that a transaction has actually been written to disk.
Registers at call: **Return Registers:**
AX = C704h   AL = status
CX:DX = transaction number (see   00h successful
  Function C701h)   FFh not yet written to disk
Details: Transactions are written to disk in the order in which they are ended, but it may take as
much as five seconds for the data to be written.
Conflicts: "MH-757" virus (PCI-59)
See also: Functions C700h, C701h, and C703h

INT 21h Function C705h   *NetWare 4.0+, Advanced NetWare 1.0+*
GET APPLICATION THRESHOLDS   *Transaction Tracking System*
Purpose: Get the per-application limits on record locks allowed before an implicit transaction is
begun.
Registers at call: **Return Registers:**
AX = C705h   AL = status
                                                 00h successful
                                             CL = maximum logical record locks (default 0)
                                             CH = maximum physical record locks (default 0)

Details: If either limit is FFh, implicit transactions are disabled for the corresponding lock type.
Conflicts: "MH-757" virus (PCI-59)
See also: Functions C706h and C707h

INT 21h Function C706h
SET APPLICATION THRESHOLDS

NetWare 4.0+, Advanced NetWare 1.0+
Transaction Tracking System

Purpose: Specify the per-application limits on record locks allowed before an implicit transaction is begun.

Registers at call:	Return Registers:
AX = C706h	AL = status
CL = maximum logical record locks (default 0)	00h successful
CH = maximum physical record locks (default 0)	

Details: If either limit is set to FFh, implicit transactions are disabled for the corresponding lock type.
Conflicts: "MH-757" virus (PCI-59)
See also: Functions C705h and C708h

INT 21h Function C707h
GET WORKSTATION THRESHOLDS

NetWare 4.0+, Advanced NetWare 1.0+
Transaction Tracking System

Purpose: Get the per-workstation limits on record locks allowed before an implicit transaction is begun.

Registers at call:	Return Registers:
AX = C707h	AL = status
	00h successful
	CL = maximum logical record locks (default 0)
	CH = maximum physical record locks (default 0)

Details: If either limit is FFh, implicit transactions are disabled for the corresponding lock type.
Conflicts: "MH-757" virus (PCI-59)
See also: Functions C705h and C708h

INT 21h Function C708h
SET WORKSTATION THRESHOLDS

NetWare 4.0+, Advanced NetWare 1.0+
Transaction Tracking System

Purpose: Specify the per-workstation limits on record locks allowed before an implicit transaction is begun.

Registers at call:	Return Registers:
AX = C708h	AL = status
CL = maximum logical record locks (default 0)	00h successful
CH = maximum physical record locks (default 0)	

Details: If either limit is set to FFh, implicit transactions are disabled for the corresponding lock type.
Conflicts: "MH-757" virus (PCI-59)
See also: Functions C706h and C707h

Workstation Functions

INT 21h Function BBh
SET END OF JOB STATUS

NetWare 4.0+, Advanced NetWare 1.0+, Alloy NTNX
Workstation Functions

Purpose: Specify whether the network shell should automatically generate an End of Job call when the root command processor regains control.

Registers at call:
AH = BBh
AL = new EOJ flag

00h disable EOJs
01h enable EOJs
Conflicts: "Hey You" virus (PCI-59)
See also: Functions 19h and D6h

Return Registers:
AL = old EOJ flag

INT 21h Function D6h
END OF JOB

NetWare 4.0+, Advanced NetWare 1.0+, Alloy NTNX
Workstation Functions

Purpose: Unlocks and clears all locked or logged files and records held by the process(es), closes all files, resets error and lock modes, and releases all network resources.

Registers at call:
AH = D6h
BX = job flag (0000h current job,
  FFFFh all processes on workstation)
See also: Functions BBh and D7h

Return Registers:
AL = error code

INT 21h Function DBh
GET NUMBER OF LOCAL DRIVES

NetWare 4.0+, Advanced NetWare 1.0+, Alloy NTNX
Workstation Functions

Registers at call:
AH = DBh

Return Registers:
AL = number of local disks as set by LASTDRIVE
  in CONFIG.SYS

See also: Function 0Eh

INT 21h Function DDh
SET NetWare ERROR MODE

Advanced NetWare 2.0+
Workstation Functions

Registers at call:
AH = DDh
DL = error mode
  00h invoke INT 24h on critical I/O
    errors (default)
  01h return NetWare extended error
    code in AL
  02h return error code in AL, mapped
    to standard DOS error codes
Conflicts: "Jerusalem"-family viruses (PCI-59)
See also: INT 24h (PCI-24)

Return Registers:
AL = previous error mode

INT 21h Function EF00h
GET DRIVE HANDLE TABLE

Advanced NetWare 1.0+
Workstation Functions

Registers at call:
AX = EF00h

Return Registers:
ES:SI -> network shell's 32-byte drive handle table
AX = 0000h

Details: Each byte in the drive handle table contains the directory handle for the corresponding drive, or 00h if not mapped to a directory.
See also: Functions EF01h, EF02h, EF03h, and EF04h

INT 21h Function EF01h
GET DRIVE FLAG TABLE

Advanced NetWare 1.0+
Workstation Functions

Registers at call:
AX = EF01h

Return Registers:
ES:SI -> network shell's 32-byte drive flag table
  (see Table 21-291)
AX = 0000h

Details: Each byte in the drive flag table corresponds to a drive.
See also: Functions EF00h, EF02h, and EF03h

21-291 Values in drive flag table:

00h	drive is not mapped
01h	permanent network drive
00h	temporary network drive
80h	mapped to local drive
81h	local drive used as permanent network drive
82h	local drive used as temporary network drive

INT 21h Function EF02h   *Advanced NetWare 1.0+*
GET DRIVE CONNECTION ID TABLE   *Workstation Functions*

Registers at call: **Return Registers:**
AX = EF02h   ES:SI -> network shell's 32-byte drive conection ID table
                           AX = 0000h

Details: Each byte in the connection ID table corresponds to a drive and contains either the connection ID (1-8) of the server for that drive or 00h if the drive is not mapped to a file server.
See also: Functions EF01h, EF03h, and F002h

INT 21h Function EF03h   *Advanced NetWare 1.0+*
GET CONNECTION ID TABLE   *Workstation Functions*

Registers at call: **Return Registers:**
AX = EF03h   ES:SI -> network shell's connection ID table
                                 (see Table 21-292)
                           AX = 0000h

See also: Functions EF00h, EF02h, EF04h, and F002h

21-292 Format of connection ID table [one entry of eight-element array]:

Offset	Size	Description
00h	BYTE	in use flag
		E0h AES temporary
		F8h IPX in critical section
		FAh processing
		FBh holding
		FCh AES waiting
		FDh waiting
		FEh receiving
		FFh sending
01h	BYTE	order number assigned to server (1-8)
00h	DWORD	(big-endian) file server's network address
06h	6 BYTEs	(big-endian) file server's node address
0Ch	WORD	(big-endian) socket number
0Eh	WORD	(big-endian) base receive timeout in clock ticks
10h	6 BYTEs	(big-endian) preferred routing node
16h	BYTE	packet sequence number
17h	BYTE	connection number (FFh = no connection)
18h	BYTE	connection status (00h if active)
19h	WORD	(big-endian) maximum receive timeout in clock ticks
1Bh	5 BYTEs	reserved

INT 21h Function EF04h   *Advanced NetWare 1.0+*
GET FILE SERVER NAME TABLE   *Workstation Functions*

Registers at call: **Return Registers:**
AX = EF04h   ES:SI -> network shell's file server name table (see below)
                           AX = 0000h

Details: The name table consists of eight 48-byte entries, each consisting of an ASCIZ server name for the corresponding entry in the connection ID table.
See also: Function EF03h

INT 21h Function F000h   *Advanced NetWare 1.0+*
SET PREFERRED CONNECTION ID   *Workstation Functions*
Registers at call:
AX = F000h
DL = connection ID of prefered file server (1-8) or 00h for none
Details: The preferred connection ID is set to 00h by the shell on EOJ.
Conflicts: DoubleDOS (PCI-49), Virus (PCI-59)
See also: Functions D6h, EF03h, F001h, F002h, and F005h

INT 21h Function F001h   *Advanced NetWare 1.0+*
GET PREFERRED CONNECTION ID   *Workstation Functions*
Registers at call: **Return Registers:**
AX = F001h   AL = connection ID of preferred file server (1-8), 00h if not set
Details: The preferred connection ID is set to 00h by the shell on EOJ.
Conflicts: DoubleDOS (PCI-49), Virus (PCI-59)
See also: Functions D6h, EF03h, F000h, F002h, and F005h

INT 21h Function F002h   *Advanced NetWare 1.0+*
GET DEFAULT CONNECTION ID   *Workstation Functions*
Registers at call: **Return Registers:**
AX = F002h   AL = connection ID of current default file server (1-8)
                                    (see Function EF03h)
Conflicts: DoubleDOS (PCI-49), Virus (PCI-59)
See also: Functions EF03h, F000h, and F004h

INT 21h Function F004h   *Advanced NetWare 2.0+*
SET PRIMARY CONNECTION ID   *Workstation Functions*
Registers at call: **Return Registers:**
AX = F004h   none
DL = connection ID of primary file server
  (1-8) or 00h for none
Conflicts: DoubleDOS (PCI-49), Virus (PCI-59)
See also: Functions D6h, EF03h, F000h, F002h, and F005h

INT 21h Function F005h   *Advanced NetWare 2.0+*
GET PRIMARY CONNECTION ID   *Workstation Functions*
Registers at call: **Return Registers:**
AX = F005h   AL = connection ID of primary file server (1-8), 00h if not set
Details: By default, the primary file server is the one from which the login script executed; it is set to 00h if the workstation is not logged in and when it detaches from its primary file server.
Conflicts: DoubleDOS (PCI-49), Virus (PCI-59)
See also: Functions D6h, EF03h, F000h, F002h, and F004h

General Functions

INT 21h Function B4h   *Novell Netware*
"AttachHandle"   *Undocumented*
Registers at call: **Return Registers:**
AH = B4h   AX = handle or return code
DS:SI -> input buffer (see Table 21-293)

Details: This is an interface provided by NetWare to give DOS file access to NetWare files on non-DOS systems such as Macintosh, OS/2, and Unix.

21-293 Format of input buffer:

Offset	Size	Description
00h	BYTE	"WorkFileServer"
01h	BYTE	access code
00h	DWORD	"OpenHandle"
06h	WORD	"OpenHandleCount"
08h	DWORD	"OpenFileSize"

INT 21h Function B5h   *Novell NetWare shell 3.01*
TASK MODE CONTROL
Purpose: Allows a program to disable the automatic cleanup for programs managing task swapping, etc.

Registers at call:	Return Registers:
AH = B5h	
AL = subfunction	
03h get task mode	AH = 00h
	AL = current task mode byte
04h get task mode pointer	ES:BX -> task mode byte

Details: The task mode byte specifies how task cleanup should be performed, but is declared to be version-dependent.

21-294 Values for task mode byte in version 3.01:

00h-03h	reserved
04h	no task cleanup

INT 21h Function B7h   *Novell NetWare*
"HoldFileModeSet"   *Undocumented Obsolete*

Registers at call:	Return Registers:
AH = B7h	AL = previous value of HoldFileFlag
AL = new value for HoldFileFlag	

Details: This function provided backward compatibility with a bug in early DOS versions and CP/M, but is no longer used or supported.

INT 21h Function B9h   *Novell NetWare*
"SpecialAttachableFunction"   *Undocumented Obsolete*

Registers at call:	Return Registers:
AH = B9h	none
AL = FFh to hook this function	
ES:BX -> function to invoke on	
Function B9h when AL<>FFh	

Details: This function is no longer used or supported by current versions of NetWare.

INT 21h Function BAh   *Novell NetWare*
"ReturnCommandComPointers"   *Undocumented*
Purpose: Used to edit the COMSPEC and PATH variables in the master environment when mapping network drives.

Registers at call:	Return Registers:
AH = BAh	DX = environment segment
	ES:DI -> COMMAND.COM drive

Details: This function was documented in older Novell documents which are no longer available.

INT 21h Function D8h   *Novell NetWare, Banyan VINES*
ALLOCATE RESOURCE   *Obsolete*

Registers at call: **Return Registers:**
AH = D8h   AL = status
DL = resource number   00h successful
                                              FFh unsucessful

Details: This function is no longer used or supported by NetWare, and is not documented in Novell documents.
See also: Function D9h

INT 21h Function D9h   *Novell NetWare, Banyan VINES*
DEALLOCATE RESOURCE   *Obsolete*

Registers at call: **Return Registers:**
AH = D9h   AL = status
DL = resource number   00h successful
                                              FFh unsucessful

Details: This function is no longer used or supported by NetWare, and is not documented in Novell documents.
See also: Function D8h

INT 21h Function DEh, Subfunctions 05h and 06h   *Novell NetWare*
SHELL TIMER INTERRUPT CHECKS   *Obsolete*

Registers at call: **Return Registers:**
AH = DEh   *unknown*
DL = subfunction
    05h disable shell timer interrupt checks
    06h enable shell timer interrupt checks

Details: These functions were added in NetWare 4.0, but are not listed in current Novell documentation and are probably no longer supported.
Conflicts: Viruses (PCI-59)

INT 21h Function E3h, Subfunction 0Ch   *Novell Netware*
VERIFY NETWORK SERIAL NUMBER   *Undocumented*

Registers at call: **Return Registers:**
AH = E3h   AL = status
DS:SI -> request buffer (see Table 21-295)   00h successful
ES:DI -> reply buffer (see Table 21-296)

Details: If the network serial number to be verified is correct, the reply buffer will contain the corresponding application number.
Conflicts: OS/286 and OS/386 (PCI-34), DoubleDOS (PCI-49)
See also: Function E3h Subfunction 12h

21-295 Format of request buffer:

Offset	Size	Description
00h	WORD	0005h (length of following data)
00h	BYTE	0Ch (subfunction "Verify Network Serial Number")
03h	DWORD	(big-endian) network serial number to verify

21-296 Format of reply buffer:

Offset	Size	Description
00h	WORD	(call) 0002h (size of following results buffer)
00h	WORD	(big-endian) application number

INT 21h Function E3h, Subfunction 12h
GET NETWORK SERIAL NUMBER
Advanced NetWare 2.1+

Purpose: Return the serial number and application number for the software installed on the file server.

Registers at call:	Return Registers:
AH = E3h	AL = status
AL = 00h	00h successful
BX = CX = DX = 0000h	
DS:SI -> request buffer (see Table 21-297)	
ES:DI -> reply buffer (see Table 21-298)	

Details: Reportedly, the workstation crashes if AL,BX,CX, and DX are not all zero.

Conflicts: OS/286 and OS/386 (PCI-34), DoubleDOS (PCI-49)

See also: Function E3h Subfunctions 0Ch and 11h

21-297 Format of request buffer:
Offset	Size	Description
00h	WORD	0001h (length of following data)
00h	BYTE	12h (subfunction "Get Serial Number")

21-298 Format of reply buffer:
Offset	Size	Description
00h	WORD	(call) 0006h (size of following results buffer)
00h	4 BYTEs	(big-endian) Netware server serial number
06h	2 BYTEs	(big-endian) Netware application serial number

INT 21h Function E6h
COPY FILE TO FILE (FCB)
Novell NetWare
Obsolete

Registers at call:	Return Registers:
AH = E6h	AL = error code
CX:DX = number of bytes to copy	CX = *unknown*
DS:SI -> opened source FCB	DX = *unknown*
ES:DI -> opened destination FCB	

Details: This function was added in NetWare 4.0, but was removed some time prior to Advanced NetWare 2.15, and is no longer listed in current Novell documentation.

Conflicts: OS/286 and OS/386 (PCI-34)

INT 21h Function E8h
SET FCB RE-OPEN MODE
Novell NetWare, Alloy NTNX
Obsolete

Purpose: This function provided backward compatibility with a bug in CP/M and early DOS versions.

Registers at call:	Return Registers:
AH = E8h	AL = error code
DL = mode	
00h no automatic re-open	
01h auto re-open	

Details: This function was added in NetWare 4.6, but was removed some time prior to Advanced NetWare 2.15, and is no longer listed in current Novell documentation.

Conflicts: OS/286 and OS/386 (PCI-34), DoubleDOS (PCI-49)

INT 21h Function EAh
RETURN SHELL VERSION
NetWare 4.6+, Advanced NetWare 1.0+, Alloy NTNX

Registers at call:
AH = EAh

AL = return version environment string
    00h don't return string
    nonzero return string in 40-byte buffer
      pointed to by ES:DI

Return Registers:
AH = operating system (00h = MS-DOS)
AL = hardware type
    00h IBM PC
    01h Victor 9000
BH = major shell version
BL = minor shell version
CH = (v3.01+) shell type
    00h conventional memory
    01h expanded memory
    02h extended memory
CL = shell revision number
if AL nonzero on entry, buffer filled with three
    null-terminated entries:
        major operating system
        version
        hardware type

Conflicts: OS/286 and OS/386 (PCI-34), DoubleDOS (PCI-49)

INT 21h Function F2h   *Novell NetWare v3.01+ shell*
MULTIPLEXOR   *(partially doc.)*

Registers at call:
AH = F2h
AL = function (see Table 21-299)
CX = length of request buffer in bytes
DX = length of reply buffer in bytes
DS:SI -> request buffer (contents vary
  by function)
ES:DI -> reply buffer (contents vary by
  function)

Return Registers:
AL = status
reply buffer filled as appropriate for function

Details: This is a multiplexor providing a "raw" interface to the underlying NetWare Core Protocol. Many functions which were accessed via a separate AH function in older versions can also be accessed here, but some NetWare 3.x calls appear to be available only here.
Conflicts: DoubleDOS (PCI-49), Virus (PCI-59)
See also: Function F244h

21-299 Values for NetWare Core Protocol functions:

Fnc/Subfn	Description
01h	File Set Lock
00h	File Release Lock
03h	Log File (see INT 21h Function EBh)
04h	Lock File Set (see INT 21h Function CBh)
05h	Release File (see INT 21h Functions CCh and ECh)
06h	Release File Set (see INT 21h Function CDh)
07h	Clear File (see INT 21h Functions CEh and EDh)
08h	Clear File Set (see INT 21h Function CFh)
09h	Log Logical Record (see INT 21h Function D0h)
0Ah	Lock Logical Record Set (see INT 21h Function D1h)
0Bh	Clear Logical Record (see INT 21h Function D4h)
0Ch	Release Logical Record (see INT 21h Function D2h)
0Dh	Release Logical Record Set (see INT 21h Function D3h)
0Eh	Clear Logical Record Set (see INT 21h Function D5h)

0Fh	Allocate Resource (see INT 21h Function D8h)
10h	Deallocate Resource (see INT 21h Function D9h)
11h/0Ah	Get Printer Queue
11h/xxh	print spooling (see INT 21h Functions E0xxh)
12h	Get Volume Info with Number (see INT 21h Function DAh)
13h	Get Station Number (see INT 21h Function ???h)
14h	Get File Server Date and Time (see INT 21h Function E7h)
15h/xxh	(see INT 21h Functions E1xxh)
16h/0Fh	Rename Directory
16h/1Bh	Scan Salvagable Files
16h/1Ch	Recover Salvagable File
16h/1Dh	Purge Salvagable File
16h/1Eh	Scan Dir Entry
16h/1Fh	Get Dir ENtry
16h/20h	Scan Volume for Restrictions
16h/21h	Add User Disk Space Restriction
16h/22h	Clear Volume Restrictions
16h/23h	Scan Dir Restrictions
16h/24h	Set Directory Disk Space Restriction
16h/25h	Set Entry
16h/26h	Scan File or Directory For Extended Trustees
16h/27h	Add Extended Trustee to Directory or File
16h/28h	Scan File Physical
16h/29h	Get Object Disk Restrictions
16h/2Ah	Get Effective Rights
16h/2Bh	Delete Trustee
16h/2Ch	Get Volume Usage
16h/2Dh	Get Dir Info
16h/2Eh	Move Entry
16h/2Fh	Fill Name Space Buffer
16h/30h	Get Name Space Entry
16h/31h	Open Data Stream
16h/32h	Get Object Effective Rights
16h/33h	Get Extended Volume Info
16h/F3h	Map Directory Number to Path
16h/xxh	(see INT 21h Functions E2xxh)
17h/17h	Get Encryption Key
17h/18h	Login Object Encrypted
17h/1Ch	Get Connection Information
17h/1Fh	Get Connection List from Object
17h/48h	Get Bindery Object Access Level
17h/49h	Is Station a Manager?
17h/4Ah	Verify Bindery Object Password Encrypted
17h/4Bh	Change Bindery Object Password Encrypted
17h/4Ch	Get Relation of an Object
17h/D2h	Clear Connection Number (Logout Station)
17h/EBh	Get Connection's Open Files
17h/ECh	Get Connections Using a File
17h/EEh	Get Physical Record Locks by File

17h/F2h	Get Semaphore Information	
17h/F3h	Map Directory Number to Path	
17h/F4h	Convert Path to Directory Entry	
17h/xxh	(see INT 21h Functions E3xxh)	
18h	End of Job (see INT 21h Function D6h)	
19h	Logout (see INT 21h Function D7h)	
1Ah	Log Physical Record (see INT 21h Function BCh)	
1Bh	Lock Physical Record Set (see INT 21h Function C2h)	
1Ch	Release Physical Record (see INT 21h Function BDh)	
1Dh	Release Physical Record Set (see INT 21h Function C3h)	
1Eh	Clear Physical Record (see INT 21h Function BEh)	
1Fh	Clear Physical Record Set (see INT 21h Function C4h)	
20h/xxh	semaphore services (see INT 21h Functions C5xxh)	
21h	Negotiate Buffer	
22h/00h	TTS Is Available (see INT 21h Function C702h)	
22h/01h	TTS Begin Transaction (see INT 21h Function C700h)	
22h/02h	TTS End Transaction (see INT 21h Function C701h)	
22h/03h	TTS Abort Transaction (see INT 21h Function C703h)	
22h/04h	TTS Transaction Status (see INT 21h Function C704h)	
22h/05h	TTS Get Application Thresholds (see INT 21h Function C705h)	
22h/06h	TTS Set Application Thresholds (see INT 21h Function C706h)	
22h/07h	TTS Get Workstation Thresholds (see INT 21h Function C707h)	
22h/08h	TTS Set Workstation Thresholds (see INT 21h Function C708h)	
22h/09h	TTS Get Control Flags	
22h/0Ah	TTS Set Control Flags	
23h/01h	AFP Create Directory	
23h/02h	AFP Create File	
23h/03h	AFP Delete	
23h/04h	AFP Get Entry ID From Name	
23h/05h	AFP Get FIle Infomration	
23h/06h	AFP Get Entry ID From NetWare Handle	
23h/07h	AFP Rename	
23h/08h	AFP Open File Fork	
23h/09h	AFP Set File Information	
23h/0Ah	AFP Scan File Information	
23h/0Bh	AFP Alloc Temporary Dir Handle	
23h/0Ch	AFP Get Entry ID From Path Name	
3Dh	Commit File	
3Eh	File Search Initialize (FindFirst)	
3Fh	File Search Continue (FindNext)	
40h	Search File	
42h	File Close	
43h	File Create	
44h	Erase Files	
45h	File Rename	
46h	Set File Attributes	
47h	Get File Size	
48h	File Read	
49h	File Write	

4Ah	File Server Copy (see INT 21h Function F3h)
4Bh	Set File Time and Date
4Ch	File Open
4Dh	Create New File
4Eh	Allow Task Access to File
4Fh	Set Extended File Attributes (see INT 21h Function B6h)
55h	Get File Bit Map
57h/03h	Scan NS Entry Info
57h/06h	Get NS Entry Info
57h/07h	Set NS Entry DOS Info
57h/0Ch	Allocate Temp NS Dir Handle
57h/13h	Read NS Info
57h/16h	Get Directory Base
57h/17h	Get NS Info
57h/19h	Write NS Info
57h/1Ah	Read Extended NS Info
57h/1Bh	Write Extended NS Infor
57h/1Ch	Get NS Path
58h/01h	Get Volume Audit Statistics
58h/02h	Add Audit Property
58h/03h	Login as Volume Auditor
58h/04h	Change Auditor Password
58h/05h	Check Audit Access
58h/06h	Remove Audit Property
58h/07h	Disable Auditing on Volume
58h/08h	Enable Auditing on Volume
58h/09h	Is User Audited?
58h/0Ah	Read Auditing Bit Map
58h/0Bh	Read Audit Config Header
58h/0Dh	Logout as Volume Auditor
58h/0Eh	Reset Auditing File
58h/0Fh	Reset Audit History File
58h/10h	Write Auditing Bit Map
58h/11h	Write Audit Config Header
58h/13h	Get Auditing Flags
58h/14h	Close Old Auditing File
58h/15h	Delete Old Auditing File
58h/16h	Check Audit Level Two Access
5Ah/01h	Get DM Info
61h	Negotiate LIP Buffer
65h	Packet Burst Connection
7Bh/01h	Get Cache Information
7Bh/02h	Get File Server Information
7Bh/03h	Get NetWare File Systems Information
7Bh/04h	Get User Information
7Bh/05h	Get Packet Burst Information
7Bh/06h	Get IPX/SPX Information
7Bh/07h	Get Garbage Collection Information
7Bh/08h	Get CPU Information

7Bh/09h	Get Volume Switch Information
7Bh/0Ah	Get NLM Loaded List
7Bh/0Bh	Get NLM Information
7Bh/0Ch	Get Directory Cache Information
7Bh/0Dh	Get OS Version Information
7Bh/0Eh	Get Active Connection List by Type
7Bh/0Fh	Get NLM's Resource Tag List
7Bh/14h	Get Active LAN Board List
7Bh/15h	Get LAN Configuration Information
7Bh/16h	Get LAN Common Counters Information
7Bh/17h	Get LAN Custom Counters Information
7Bh/18h	Get LAN Config Strings
7Bh/19h	Get LSL Informatino
7Bh/1Ah	Get LSL Logical Board Statistics
7Bh/1Eh	Get Media Manager Object Information
7Bh/1Fh	Get Media Manager Object List
7Bh/20h	Get Media Manager Object Children List
7Bh/21h	Get Volume Segment List
7Bh/28h	Get Active Protocol Stacks
7Bh/29h	Get Protocol Stack Configuration Information
7Bh/2Ah	Get Protocol Stack Statistics Information
7Bh/2Bh	Get Protocol Stack Custom Information
7Bh/2Ch	Get Protocol Stack Numbers By Media Number
7Bh/2Dh	Get Protocol Stack Numbers By LAN Board Number
7Bh/2Eh	Get Media Name by Media Number
7Bh/2Fh	Get Loaded Media Number List
7Bh/32h	Get General Router and SAP Information
7Bh/33h	Get Network Router Information
7Bh/34h	Get Network Routers Information
7Bh/35h	Get Known Networks Information
7Bh/36h	Get Server Information
7Bh/38h	Get Known Servers Information
7Bh/3Ch	Get Server Set Commands Information
7Bh/3Dh	Get Server Set Categories

INT 2Fh Function 7A20h, Subfunction 0000h   *Novell NetWare*
GET CALL ADDRESS   *Advanced NetWare 4.0 DOS Requester*

Registers at call: **Return Registers:**
AX = 7A20h   AX = 0000h on success
BX = 0000h   ES:BX -> far call address for DOS Requester

Details: The DOS Requester replaces the NetWare Shell (ANETx, NETx) on NetWare LAN's as of the release of Advanced NetWare 4.0 (1993). It is backward compatible with NetWare 2.1x through 3.11 servers as well. Note that there was a NetWare 4.0 in the early 1980's, which can cause confusion.

Conflicts: none, but see Table 2-2

INT 2Fh Function 7A20h, Subfunction 0001h   *Novell NetWare*
GET UNKNOWN ENTRY POINT   *Advanced NetWare 4.0 DOS Requester v1.03*

Registers at call: **Return Registers:**
AX = 7A20h   AX = 0000h (successful)
BX = 0001h   ES:BX -> *unknown* far call address

Conflicts: none, but see Table 2-2

INT 2Fh Function 7A20h, Subfunction 0002h
GET UNKNOWN DATA

Novell NetWare
Advanced NetWare 4.0 DOS Requester v1.03

Registers at call:
AX = 7A20h
BX = 0002h
Conflicts: none, but see Table 2-2

Return Registers:
AX = 0000h (successful)
ES:BX -> *unknown* data

INT 2Fh Function 7A20h, Subfunction 0003h
GET UNKNOWN

Novell NetWare
Advanced NetWare 4.0 DOS Requester v1.03

Registers at call:
AX = 7A20h
BX = 0003h
Conflicts: none, but see Table 2-2

Return Registers:
AX = 0000h (successful)
ES:BX -> *unknown item*

INT 2Fh Function 7A20h, Subfunction 0004h
GET UNKNOWN DATA

Novell NetWare
Advanced NetWare 4.0 DOS Requester v1.03

Registers at call:
AX = 7A20h
BX = 0004h
Conflicts: none, but see Table 2-2

Return Registers:
AX = 0000h (successful)
ES:BX -> *unknown* data (see Table 21-300)

21-300 Format of unknown data:

Offset	Size	Description
00h	DWORD	pointer to *unknown* code
04h	4 BYTEs	*unknown*
08h	DWORD	pointer to *unknown* code
	other fields, if any, unknown	

INT 2Fh Function 7A20h, Subfunction 0005h
GET UNKNOWN ENTRY POINT

Novell NetWare
Advanced NetWare 4.0 DOS Requester v1.03

Registers at call:
AX = 7A20h
BX = 0005h
Conflicts: none, but see Table 2-2

Return Registers:
AX = 0000h (successful)
ES:BX -> *unknown* far call address

INT 2Fh Function 7A20h, Subfunctions 0006h to 0008h
GET UNKNOWN ENTRY POINTS

Novell NetWare
Advanced NetWare 4.0 DOS Requester v1.03

Registers at call:
AX = 7A20h
BX = 0006h to 0008h

Return Registers:
AX = 0000h (successful)
ES:BX -> *unknown* far call address

Details: These Subfunctions are identical to Subfunctions 0080h to 0082h; it is possible that they are accepted because of a lacking range check.
Conflicts: none, but see Table 2-2

INT 2Fh Function 7A20h, Subfunctions 0080h to 0082h
GET UNKNOWN ENTRY POINT

Novell NetWare
Advanced NetWare 4.0 DOS Requester v1.03

Registers at call:
AX = 7A20h
BX = 0080h to 0082h

Return Registers:
AX = 0000h (successful)
ES:BX -> *unknown* far call address

Details: These subfunctions are currently NOPs because each returns the address of a different RETF instruction.
Conflicts: none, but see Table 2-2

INT 2Fh Function 7A80h   *Novell NetWare*
SHELL 3.01d BROADCAST - ABNORMAL EXIT   *Callout*

Purpose: Called on abnormal exit of the NetWare shell to notify other Novell TSRs that it is unsafe to call the shell in the future.

Registers at call:	Return Registers:
AX = 7A80h	none

Details: This function must be passed through so that all interested programs see the exit.

On receiving this call, IPXODI clears an internal pointer to a default value; Novell's NETBIOS.EXE clears its INT 21h pointer to 0000h:0000h and stops calling it.

Conflicts: none, but see Table 2-2
See also: Function 7A81h

INT 2Fh Function 7A81h   *Novell NetWare*
SHELL 3.01d BROADCAST - SET SHELL INT 21h HANDLER   *Callout*

Purpose: The shell calls this function as it loads to allow interested TSRs and drivers to make a local copy of the shell's entry point.

Registers at call:	Return Registers:
AX = 7A81h	none
CX:DX -> shell's INT 21h entry point	

Details: This function must be passed through so that all interested programs see it.
Conflicts: none, but see Table 2-2

INT 2Fh Function 7A85h   *Novell NetWare*
shell 3.01 - BROADCAST INFORM   *Callout*

Registers at call:	Return Registers:
AX = 7A85h	CX = 0000h if broadcast message handled by
CX = broadcast server number	another program
	CX unchanged if broadcast not handled

Conflicts: none, but see Table 2-2

INT 44h   *Novell NetWare*
HIGH-LEVEL LANGUAGE API

Conflicts: IBM 3270PC High-Level Language API (Chapter 37), Acorn BBC Master (PCI-7), Z100 (PCI-7), PCjr Video Data (PCI-8), "Lehigh" virus (PCI-59)

INT 7Fh   *Non-dedicated NetWare 2.x File Server*
ENTER CONSOLE MODE

Details: The installation check consists of checking for the signature "Lynn" in the four bytes preceding the interrupt handler; if present, the current program is running as a DOS task on a non-dedicated NetWare 2.x file server.

Before placing the server into "console" mode, it is recommended that NetWare broadcast messages be disabled with INT 21h Function DE00h.

Conflicts: see Table 2-4
See also: INT 21h Function DE00h

CHAPTER 22

Novell NetWare Lite

NetWare Lite is Novell's entry into the low-end networking market. Despite the name, it has little in common with its older and more advanced sibling NetWare. Most of the functions within this package are undocumented.

NetWare Lite can be configured as a peer-to-peer system or as a client-server system; when configured for peer-to-peer operation, conflicts with serial communications are frequent.

This chapter provides the information we have been able to gather concerning the NetWare Lite API; note that much of the detail remains "unknown."

INT 2Ah Functions D800h and D801h *Novell NetWare Lite*
SERVER - SET/RESET UNKNOWN FLAG *Undocumented*
Purpose: Sets *unknown* flag, and sets *unknown* to initial value.
Registers at call: **Return Registers:**
AX = function none
   D800h set flag
   D801h reset flag
Details: These functions are called by CLIENT.
See also: Functions D850h and D851h

INT 2Ah Function D850h *Novell NetWare Lite*
CLIENT - INCREMENT UNKNOWN COUNTER *Undocumented*
Purpose: Increments an internal byte-sized counter.
Registers at call: **Return Registers:**
AX = D850h none
Details: This call is intercepted by the DV/X v1.10 PEERSERV.DVR.
See also: Function D851h

INT 2Ah Function D851h *Novell NetWare Lite*
CLIENT - RESET UNKNOWN COUNTER *Undocumented*
Purpose: Resets an internal byte-sized counter to zero.
Registers at call: **Return Registers:**
AX = D851h none
Details: This call is intercepted by the DV/X v1.10 PEERSERV.DVR.
See also: Function D850h

INT 2Fh Function D800h *Novell NetWare Lite*
CLIENT.EXE - INSTALLATION CHECK *Undocumented*
Registers at call: **Return Registers:**
AX = D800h AL = FFh if installed
    DX = version number (0100h for v1.0, 0101h for v1.1)

BX = data segment of resident copy
ES:DI -> private API entry point (see Tables 22-1 to 22-23)
SI = segment of resident code

See also: Functions 7A00h and D880h

22-1 CLIENT entry point Function 0000h calling convention:

Registers at call:
BX = 0000h get *unknown values*

Return Registers:
DX = *CLIENT version* (0101h for v1.1)
ES:BX -> *unknown* data

22-2 CLIENT entry point Function 0001h calling convention:

Registers at call:
BX = 0001h *unknown*

Return Registers:
unknown

22-3 CLIENT entry point Function 0002h calling convention:

Registers at call:
BX = 0002h *unknown*

Return Registers:
unknown

22-4 CLIENT entry point Function 0003h calling convention:

Registers at call:
BX = 0003h *unknown*

Return Registers:
unknown

22-5 CLIENT entry point Function 0004h calling convention:

Registers at call:
BX = 0004h *unknown*

Return Registers:
unknown

22-6 CLIENT entry point Function 0005h calling convention:

Registers at call:
BX = 0005h *unknown*
DL = *unknown*
others, if any, unknown

Return Registers:
unknown

22-7 CLIENT entry point "get module name" calling convention:

Registers at call:
BX = 0006h
ES:DI -> 16-byte buffer

Return Registers:
CX = *unknown*
ES:DI filled with "NWLITE_CLIENT"
    00h 00h 00h

22-8 CLIENT entry point Function 0007h calling convention:

Registers at call:
BX = 0007h *unknown*
DX:CX = *unknown*
others, if any, unknown

Return Registers:
unknown

22-9 CLIENT entry point Function 0008h calling convention:

Registers at call:
BX = 0008h *unknown*

Return Registers:
unknown

22-10 CLIENT entry point Function 0009h calling convention:

Registers at call:
BX = 0009h *unknown*
DL = *unknown*
ES:DI -> 16-byte buffer for *unknown data*

Return Registers:
CF clear if successful
    AX = 0000h
    CX = 0000h
    SI,DI destroyed
CF set on error
    AX = error code 4903h

INT 2Fh Function D800h

22-11 CLIENT entry point Function 000Ah calling convention:

Registers at call:
BX = 000Ah *unknown*
AH = subfunction
      00h get *unknown value*
      01h clear/set *unknown* flag
            AL = new state (00h cleared, 01h set)
      02h set *unknownn value*
            DX = new value of *unknown item*

Return Registers:
DX = old value of *unknown*

22-12 CLIENT entry point Function 000Bh calling convention:

Registers at call:
BX = 000Bh *unknown*
AX = *unknown*
others, if any, unknown

Return Registers:
unknown

22-13 CLIENT entry point Function 000Ch calling convention:

Registers at call:
BX = 000Ch *unknown*
AX = *unknown*
others, if any, unknown

Return Registers:
unknown

22-14 CLIENT entry point Function 000Dh calling convention:

Registers at call:
BX = 000Dh *unknown*
AX = *unknown*
others, if any, unknown

Return Registers:
unknown

22-15 CLIENT "Get Original INT 17h" calling convention:

Registers at call:
BX = 000Eh

Return Registers:
CF clear
ES:BX -> original INT 17h

22-16 CLIENT entry point Function 000Fh calling convention:

Registers at call:
BX = 000Fh *unknown*

Return Registers:
unknown

22-17 CLIENT entry point Function 0010h calling convention:

Registers at call:
BX = 0010h *unknown*
AX = *unknown*
others, if any, unknown

Return Registers:
unknown

22-18 CLIENT entry point Function 0011h calling convention:

Registers at call:
BX = 0011h get *unkown value*

Return Registers:
CF clear
DL = *unknown*

22-19 CLIENT entry point Function 0012h calling convention:

Registers at call:
BX = 0012h get *unknown data*
AL = index of *unknown item*
ES:DI -> 10-byte buffer for *unknown item*

Return Registers:
CF clear if successful
      ES:DI buffer filled
      AX,CX destroyed
CF set on error
      AX = error code (4907h if AL out of range)

22-20 CLIENT entry point Function 0013h calling convention:

Registers at call:
BX = 0013h get *unknown values*

Return Registers:
CF clear
DH = *unknown*
DL = *unknown*

22-21 CLIENT entry point Function 0014h calling convention:

Registers at call:
BX = 0014h *unknown*
DL = *unknown*
others, if any, unknown

Return Registers:
CF clear if successful
    unknown
CF set on error
    AX = error code 8056h

22-22 CLIENT entry point Function 0015h calling convention:

Registers at call:
BX = 0015h *unknown*
DX = *unknown*

Return Registers:
ES:DI -> *unknown*

22-23 CLIENT entry point unsupported functions calling convention:

Registers at call:
BX = value not listed in Tables 22-1 to
22-22

Return Registers:
CF set
AX = 0001h (invalid function)

INT 2Fh Function D856h
SERVER - GET UNKNOWN VALUES   *Novell NetWare Lite v1.1*
                                                          Undocumented

Registers at call:
AX = D856h

Return Registers:
AX = *unknown* (0001h for v1.1)
BX = *unknown* (0004h for v1.1)
CX = *unknown* (0F20h for v1.1)
DS = segment of resident code
ES = data segment of resident copy

INT 2Fh Function D880h
SERVER - INSTALLATION CHECK   *Novell NetWare Lite v1.0+*
                                                          Undocumented

Registers at call:
AX = D880h

Return Registers:
AL = FFh if installed
    DX = version number (0100h for v1.0,
       0101h for v1.1)
    BX = data segment of resident copy
    CL = current state (00h SERVER is disabled,
       01h SERVER is active)
    ES:DI -> private API entry point
       (see Tables 22-24 to 22-26)
    SI = *unknown* (offset of configuration info?)

See also: Functions 7A00h and D800h

22-24 SERVER entry point Function 0000h calling convention:

Registers at call:
BX = 0000h *unknown*
others, if any, unknown

Return Registers:
unknown

Details: This function closes open files by calling INT 21h Function 3Eh.

22-25 SERVER "Get Connection Information" calling convention:

Registers at call:
BX = 0001h
DX = connection number (0001h-max connections)
ES:DI -> 28-byte buffer for connection information

Return Registers:
CF clear if successful
    ES:DI buffer filled
CF set on error
    AX = FFFFh

22-26 SERVER entry point unsupported functions calling convention:

Registers at call:
BX = values not listed in Tables 22-24
to 22-25

Return Registers:
CF set
AX = 0001h (invalid function)

INT 2Fh Function D8C0h
NLCACHE - INSTALLATION CHECK

Novell NetWare Lite v1.1
Undocumented

Purpose: NLCACHE is a disk cache included with NetWare Lite.

Registers at call:
AX = D8C0h

Return Registers:
AL = FFh if installed
    CL = cache variant (01h NLCACHEC, 02h NLCACHEX,
       03h NLCACHEM)
    DH = *major version* (01h for v1.1)
    DL = *minor version* (01h for v1.1)
    ES:DI -> private API entry point (see Tables 22-27 and 22-28)

See also: Functions D800h and D880h

22-27 NLCACHE entry point Function 0000h calling convention:

Registers at call:
BX = 0000h *unknown*
others, if any, unknown

Return Registers:
CF clear if successful
    AX = 0000h
    unknown
CF set on error
    AX = error code

22-28 NLCACHE entry point unsupported functions calling convention:

Registers at call:
BX = nonzero

Return Registers:
CF set
AX = 0001h (invalid function)

CHAPTER 23

Novell NetWare Utilities

This chapter covers the calls provided by a variety of add-on programs which are a part of NetWare.

While there are no known direct conflicts with the INT 2Fh Function 7Axxh calls, a few TSRs have a sufficiently large range of allowable multiplex numbers that they could potentially conflict; see Table 2-2 for details.

Access Server

The Access Server provides dial-in access to a NetWare network.

INT 2Fh Function 7AF1h
INSTALLATION CHECK
Access Server Driver

Registers at call:	Return Registers:
AX = 7AF1h	AX <> 7AF1h if present
BL = sequence number (01h first driver, 02h second, 00h no driver)	BH = total number of drivers
	---if BL nonzero on entry---
	AL = number of ports provided by specified driver
	ES:DI -> driver entry point (see Tables 23-1 to 23-10)
	ES:DX -> ID string

23-1 Driver entry point "initialize port" calling convention:

Registers at call:	Return Registers:
AH = 01h	CF clear if successful
AL = port number (00h-0Fh)	CF set on error
ES:BX -> configuration parameter block (see Table 23-14)	
interrupts disabled	

23-2 Driver entry point "get port status" calling convention:

Registers at call:	Return Registers:
AH = 02h	CF clear if successful
AL = port number (00h-0Fh)	BL = transmitter status (see Table 23-11)
interrupts disabled	BH = receiver status (see Table 23-12)
	DL = external status signals (see Table 23-13)
	CF set on error
	interrupts disabled

23-3 Driver entry point "get input from port" calling convention:

Registers at call:
AH = 03h
AL = port number (00h-0Fh)
CX = size of data buffer
ES:BX -> buffer for data
interrupts disabled

Return Registers:
CF clear if successful
CF set on error
interrupts disabled
CX = number of bytes read

Details: The driver will add a NUL to the buffer when a break signal is detected.

23-4 Driver entry point "send output data to port" calling convention:

Registers at call:
AH = 04h
AL = port number (00h-0Fh)
CX = number of bytes to send
ES:BX -> buffer containing data
interrupts disabled

Return Registers:
CF clear if successful
CF set on error
interrupts disabled
CX = number of bytes actually written

23-5 Driver entry point "get I/O character counts" calling convention:

Registers at call:
AH = 05h
AL = port number (00h-0Fh)
interrupts disabled

Return Registers:
CF clear if successful
        BX = number of bytes pending transmission
        CX = number of bytes available for reading
CF set on error
interrupts disabled

23-6 Driver entry point "control XON/XOFF" calling convention:

Registers at call:
AH = 06h
AL = port number (00h-0Fh)
DL = new state (00h software flow
    control disabled, else enabled)
interrupts disabled

Return Registers:
CF clear if successful
CF set on error
interrupts disabled

23-7 Driver entry point "get error counts and statistics" calling convention:

Registers at call:
AH = 07h
AL = port number (00h-0Fh)
ES:BX -> buffer for statistics
    (see Table 23-15)
interrupts disabled

Return Registers:
CF clear if successful
        ES:BX buffer filled
CF set on error
interrupts disabled

23-8 Driver entry point "general request" calling convention:

Registers at call:
AH = 08h
AL = port number (00h-0Fh)
DX = requested operations
        bit 0: flush transmit buffers
        bit 1: flush receive buffers
        bit 4: define XON/XOFF characters
ES:BX -> XON/XOFF characters
    (see Table 23-16) if DX bit 4 set
interrupts disabled

Return Registers:
CF clear if successful
CF set on error
interrupts disabled

23-9 Driver entry point "deadman timer management" calling convention:

Registers at call:
AH = 09h
AL = port number (00h-0Fh)
BX = next time interval in seconds
  (0000h to disable timer)
interrupts disabled

Return Registers:
CF clear
interrupts disabled

23-10 Driver entry point "get buffer sizes" calling convention:

Registers at call:
AH = 0Ah
AL = port number (00h-0Fh)
interrupts disabled

Return Registers:
CF clear if successful
  BX = size of transmit buffer
  CX = size of receive buffer
CF set on error
interrupts disabled

23-11 Values for transmitter status:

00h	uninitialized
01h	ready, not transmitting
02h	transmitting
03h	XOFF received
04h	transmitting, buffer full
05h	XOFF received and buffer full

23-12 Values for receiver status:

00h	uninitialized
01h	ready
02h	receive buffer full, data may have been lost

23-13 Bitfields for external status signals:

bits 7,6	undefined
bit 5	CTS active
bit 4	DSR active
bit 3	DCD active
bits 2,1	undefined
bit 0	ring indicator

23-14 Format of configuration parameter block:

Offset	Size	Description
00h	BYTE	receive baud rate index
		00h 50 bps, 01h 75 bps, 02h 110 bps, 03h 134.5 bps,
		04h 150 bps, 05h 300 bps, 06h 600 bps, 07h 1200 bps,
		08h 1800 bps, 09h 2000 bps, 0Ah 2400 bps, 0Bh 3600 bps,
		0Ch 4800 bps, 0Dh 7200 bps, 0Eh 9600 bps, 0Fh 19200 bps,
		10h 38400 bps, 11h 57600 bps, 12h 115200 bps
01h	BYTE	receive bits per character (0=5 bits..3=8 bits)
02h	BYTE	receive stop bits
03h	BYTE	receive parity

		00h none, 01h odd, 02h even, 03h mark, 04h space
04h	BYTE	transmit baud rate index (same as receive baud rate)
05h	BYTE	transmit bits per character (0=5 bits..3=8 bits)
06h	BYTE	transmit stop bits
07h	BYTE	transmit parity (same as receive parity)
08h	BYTE	DTR state (00h off, 01h on)
09h	BYTE	RTS state (00h off, 01h on)
0Ah	BYTE	flow control
		00h none, 01h XON/XOFF, 02h RTS/CTS, 03h both
0Bh	BYTE	break control (00h off, 01h on)

23-15 Format of statistics:

Offset	Size	Description
00h	BYTE	port number
01h	BYTE	external status signals (see Table 23-13)
02h	BYTE	transmitter status (see Table 23-11)
03h	BYTE	receiver status (see Table 23-12)
04h	DWORD	number of characters received
08h	DWORD	number of characters transmitted
0Ch	WORD	input parity errors
0Eh	WORD	input framing errors
10h	WORD	lost characters due to hardware overrun
12h	WORD	lost characters due to data buffer overrun

Note: The counts are not allowed to wrap around; once a count reaches FFFFh or FFFFFFFFh, it is no longer incremented.

23-16 Format of XON/XOFF characters:

Offset	Size	Description
00h	BYTE	04h (number of bytes following)
01h	BYTE	transmit XON character
02h	BYTE	transmit XOFF character
03h	BYTE	receive XON character
04h	BYTE	receive XOFF character

TASKID

INT 2Fh Function 7A18h	*TASKID v1.0*
INSTALLATION CHECK	*Undocumented*

Registers at call:
AX = 7A18h

Return Registers:
AL = FFh if installed
    BX = configuration flags (see Table 23-17)
    CX = resident code segment

See also: Function 7A10h

23-17 Bitfields for configuration flags:

bit 0	INT 2Fh hooked
bit 3	INT 08h hooked
other	unused

INT 2Fh Function 7A19h
GET INT 08h HANDLERS

Registers at call:
AX = 7A19h

Return Registers:
AL = FFh
DS:DX -> TASKID INT 08h handler
ES:BX -> original INT 08h handler

See also: Function 7A1Ah

INT 2Fh Function 7A1Ah
GET INT 2Fh HANDLERS

Registers at call:
AX = 7A1Ah

Return Registers:
AL = FFh
DX:DX -> TASKID INT 2Fh handler
ES:BX -> original INT 2Fh handler

See also: Functions 7A11h and 7A19h

INT 2Fh Function 7A1Bh
GET DIAGNOSTICS INFORMATION

Registers at call:
AX = 7A1Bh
CX = desired information

   0000h supported functions

   0001h TASKID ID number

   0002h set-ID count

Return Registers:
AL = FFh
BX = highest supported subfunction
   number (0002h)

CX = ID number

CX = ID set count

See also: Functions 7A14h and 7A18h

TBMI

TBMI is the Task-Switched Buffer Manager Interface.

INT 2Fh Function 7A10h
GET TBMI STATUS

Registers at call:
AX = 7A10h

Return Registers:
DH = major TBMI version number
DL = minor TBMI version number (01h for v1.1)
CX = segment address of TBMI resident part
BX = TBMI status word (see Table 23-18)

See also: Functions 7A11h, 7A12h, 7A13h, and 7A14h

23-18 Bitfields for status word:

bit 0	INT 2Fh intercepted by TBMI
bit 1	INT 7Ah intercepted by TBMI
bit 2	INT 64h intercepted by TBMI
bits 3-14	*reserved or unused*
bit 15	outstanding task ID was detected

INT 2Fh Function 7A11h
GET INT 2Fh HANDLERS

TBMI v1.1+
Undocumented

Registers at call: Return Registers:
AX = 7A11h   ES:BX -> old INT 2Fh handler
                                              DS:DX -> TBMI INT 2Fh handler

See also: Functions 7A10h, 7A12h, 7A13h, and 7A1Ah

INT 2Fh Function 7A12h
GET INT 64h HANDLERS

TBMI v1.1+
Undocumented

Registers at call: Return Registers:
AX = 7A12h   ES:BX -> old INT 64h handler
                                              DS:DX -> TBMI INT 64h handler

See also: Functions 7A10h, 7A11h, and 7A13h

INT 2Fh Function 7A13h
GET INT 7Ah HANDLERS

TBMI v1.1+
Undocumented

Registers at call: Return Registers:
AX = 7A13h   ES:BX -> old INT 7Ah handler
                                              DS:DX -> TBMI INT 7Ah handler

See also: Functions 7A10h, 7A11h, and 7A12h

INT 2Fh Function 7A14h
GET STATISTICS

TBMI v1.1+
Undocumented

Registers at call: Return Registers:
AX = 7A14h   BX = maximum supported subfunction (000Ch)
CX = statistic to retrieve

0000h *available diagnostic functions*   CX = *maximum available function* (000Ch for v2.0)

0001h buffers in use   CX = TBMI buffers currently in use

0002h maximum buffers used   CX = maximum number of buffers ever in use

0003h unavailable buffers   CX = count of unavailable TBMI buffers

0004h old interrupt usage   CX = TBMI accesses to intercepted old vectors
                                              INT 2Fh, INT 64h, and INT 7Ah
0005h far call usage
                                         CX = TBMI accesses to IPX/SPX far call handler
0006h task buffering   (not including internal accesses)

0007h current task ID   CX = TBMI task buffering status (*enabled/disabled*
                                              or disable/enable switch count)
0008h outstanding ID count
                                         CX = TBMI current task ID number
0009h configured ECBs   (0000h if *unknown*)

000Ah configured data ECBs   CX = number of outstanding TBMI IDs

000Bh configured sockets   CX = number of TBMI Event
                                              Control Blocks configured
000Ch current sockets

CX = number of TBMI data ECBs configured

CX = number of TBMI sockets configured (from NETCFG)

CX = number of TBMI sockets currently in use

See also: Function 7A10h

INT 2Fh Function 7A15h
RESET UNKNOWN VARIABLE

TBMI v1.1 only
Obsolete Undocumented

Purpose: Set *unknown* to its default value.

Registers at call:	Return Registers:
AX = 7A15h	BX = new value of *unknown*

Details: This call is a NOP under TBMI v2.0 (TBMI2).
See also: Function 7A17h

INT 2Fh Function 7A16h
UNDETERMINED FUNCTION

TBMI v1.1 only
Obsolete Undocumented

Registers at call:	Return Registers:
AX = 7A16h	*unknown*
CX = *unknown*	
others, if any, unknown	

Details: This call is a NOP under TBMI v2.0 (TBMI2).

INT 2Fh Function 7A17h
UNDETERMINED FUNCTION

TBMI v1.1 only
Obsolete Undocumented

Registers at call:	Return Registers:
AX = 7A17h	BX = old value of *unknown*
others, if any, unknown	CX = new value of *unknown*

Details: This call is a NOP under TBMI v2.0 (TBMI2).
See also: Function 7A15h

INT 2Fh Function 7A1Ch
UNDETERMINED FUNCTION

TBMI v1.1+
Undocumented

Registers at call:	Return Registers:
AX = 7A1Ch	AX = 70FFh
BP = *unknown*	
CX:DX = *unknown*	

INT 2Fh Function 7A1Dh
UNDETERMINED FUNCTION

TBMI v1.1+
Undocumented

Registers at call:	Return Registers:
AX = 7A1Dh	ES = *unknown*
others, if any, unknown	SI destroyed
	others, if any, unknown

INT 2Fh Function 7A1Eh
UNDETERMINED FUNCTION

TBMI v1.1+
Undocumented

Registers at call:	Return Registers:
AX = 7A1Eh	*unknown*
ES:SI -> *unknown*	
others, if any, unknown	

INT 2Fh Function 7A4Dh
UNDETERMINED FUNCTION
Novell Netware

Registers at call:
AX = 7A4Dh
BX = 0001h
ES:DI -> *unknown*

Return Registers:
AL = FFh if *unknown*
    ES:DI -> *unknown*

Details: This function is called by NETBIOS.EXE v3.01.

INT 2Fh Function 7AFFh, Subfunction 0000h
INSTALLATION CHECK
TBMI v1.1+

Registers at call:
AX = 7AFFh
BX = 0000h
CX = 4E65h ("Ne")
DX = 7457h ("tW")
ES:DI -> IPX/SPX special handler
  (*XMS/EMS*)

Return Registers:
AL = FFh if installed
    CX = configured sockets (14h)
    DS:SI -> data table *unknown*
    ES:DI -> IPX far call handler

Details: For IPX/SPX this call reportedly returns DS:DI pointing to the table of pointers to service events queue head and tail.
    This function is also supported by IPXODI.
See also: Function 7AFFh Subfunction 0001h

INT 2Fh Function 7AFFh, Subfunction 0001h
INSTALLATION CHECK
TBMI v1.1+, shell v3.01d

Registers at call:
AX = 7AFFh
BX = 0001h
CX = 4E65h ("Ne")
DX = 7457h ("tW")

Return Registers:
AL = FFh if installed
    CX = *unknown* (8000h)
    SI = *unknown* (or pointer to *unknown item*) (0002h)
    ES:DI -> IPX far call handler
    ES:DX -> 6-byte data area *unknown*

Details: This function is also supported by IPXODI.
See also: Function 7AFFh Subfunction 0000h

VNETWARE.386

VNETWARE.386 is a virtual device driver which provides support for Novell NetWare under Microsoft Windows. See Chapter 43 in *PC Interrupts* for a more detailed discussion of virtual device driver calls.

INT 21h Function B500h
GET INSTANCE DATA
VNETWARE.386
Undocumented

Registers at call:
AX = B500h

Return Registers:
ES:BX -> data
CX = length

See also: Functions B501h and B502h

INT 21h Function B501h
END VIRTUAL MACHINE
VNETWARE.386
Undocumented

Registers at call:
AX = B501h
See also: Functions B500h and B502h

Return Registers:

INT 21h Function B502h
START VIRTUAL MACHINE

Registers at call: **Return Registers:**
AX = B502h   none
See also: Functions B500h and B501h

INT 21h Function B505h
SET VIRTUAL MACHINE ID

Registers at call: **Return Registers:**
AX = B505h   *unknown*
others, if any, unknown
See also: Functions B502h and B506h

INT 21h Function B506h
GET VIRTUAL MACHINE SUPPORT LEVEL

Registers at call: **Return Registers:**
AX = B506h   AX = *unknown* (0002h)
See also: Function B505h

Miscellaneous

This section describes the interrupts associated with the utilities that implement NETBIOS operation, and the Named Pipes feature.

INT 2Fh Function 7A90h
INSTALLATION CHECK

Registers at call: **Return Registers:**
AX = 7A90h   AL = 00h if present
                              BX = *unknown*
                              CX = PSP segment of NETBIOS resident code

See also: Function 7AFEh

INT 2Fh Function 7AF0h
INSTALLATION CHECK

Purpose: DOSNP.EXE provides "named pipes" (see Chapter 6) support for DOS workstations running NetWare.
Registers at call: **Return Registers:**
AX = 7AF0h   AL = FFh if present
                              ES = 7AF0h
                              CX = PSP segment of resident code

INT 2Fh Function 7AFEh
INSTALLATION CHECK

Purpose: DOSNP.EXE provides "named pipes" (see Chapter 6) support for DOS workstations running NetWare.
Registers at call: **Return Registers:**
AX = 7AFEh   AL = FFh if present
                              ES = *data* segment of DOSNP

Details: The NetWare shell calls this function and refuses to load if DOSNP is present.
See also: Function 7A90h

CHAPTER 24

PC LAN Program

PC Network was an early networking package which was renamed the IBM PC Local Area Network Program (PC LAN Program) as of v1.10. This chapter describes the interrupts used by both.

INT 2Ah Function 07h　　　　　　　　　　　　　　　　　　　　　　*PC Network v1.00*
RECEIVER.COM - UNDETERMINED FUNCTION　　　　　　　　　　　*Undocumented*

Registers at call:　　　　　　　　　　**Return Registers:**
AH = 07h　　　　　　　　　　　　　　　　*unknown*
others, if any, unknown
See also: Function 86h

INT 2Ah Function 7802h　　　　　　　　　　　　　　　　　　*PC LAN Program v1.31+*
GET LOGGED ON USER NAME

Registers at call:　　　　　　　　　　**Return Registers:**
AX = 7802h　　　　　　　　　　　　　　　AL = 00h if no user logged on to Extended Services
ES:DI -> 8-byte buffer to be filled　　　　AL nonzero if user logged on to Extended Services
　　　　　　　　　　　　　　　　　　　　　　buffer at ES:DI filled with name, padded to
　　　　　　　　　　　　　　　　　　　　　　8 chars with blanks.

INT 2Ah Function 86h　　　　　　　　　　　　　　　　　　　　　　*PC Network v1.00*
RECEIVER.COM - UNDETERMINED FUNCTION　　　　　　　　　　　*Undocumented*

Registers at call:　　　　　　　　　　**Return Registers:**
AH = 86h　　　　　　　　　　　　　　　　*unknown*
others, if any, unknown
See also: Functions 07h and C4h

INT 2Ah Function 89h　　　　　　　　　　　　　　　　　　　　　　*PC Network v1.00*
RECEIVER.COM - UNDETERMINED FUNCTION　　　　　　　　　　　*Undocumented*

Registers at call:　　　　　　　　　　**Return Registers:**
AH = 89h　　　　　　　　　　　　　　　　*unknown*
AL = *unknown* (ASSIGN uses 08h)
others, if any, unknown

INT 2Ah Function C4h　　　　　　　　　　　　　　　　　　　　　　*PC Network v1.00*
RECEIVER.COM - UNDETERMINED FUNCTION　　　　　　　　　　　*Undocumented*

Registers at call:
AH = C4h
AL = subfunction
　　　07h *unknown*
　　　08h *unknown*

Return Registers:
unknown

BX = *unknown*
others, if any, unknown
See also: Function 86h

INT 2Ah Function E0h
UNDETERMINED FUNCTION

PC Network 1.00
Undocumented

Registers at call:
AH = E0h
AL = *subfunction* (01h,02h, maybe others)
others, if any, unknown

Return Registers:
unknown

Details: Called by the PC Network v1.00 NET.COM, a shell program from which others are run.

INT 2Fh Function 0200h
REDIR/REDIRIFS - INSTALLATION CHECK

PC LAN Program
Undocumented

Purpose: Determine whether the PC LAN Program redirector is installed.

Registers at call:
AX = 0200h

Return Registers:
AL = FFh if installed

Conflicts: none known, but see Table 2-2 for potential conflicts
See also: Functions 0201h and 0203h

INT 2Fh Function 0201h
REDIR/REDIRIFS - UNDETERMINED FUNCTION

PC LAN Program
Undocumented

Registers at call:
AX = 0201h

Return Registers:
none

Details: This function is called by the DOS 3.3+ PRINT.COM.
   Function 0202h appears to be the opposite function; these functions are supposedly used to signal opening and closing of printers.
Conflicts: none known, but see Table 2-2 for potential conflicts
See also: Function 0202h

INT 2Fh Function 0202h
REDIR/REDIRIFS - UNDETERMINED FUNCTION

PC LAN Program
Undocumented

Registers at call:
AX = 0202h
others, if any, unknown

Return Registers:
none

Details: This function is called by the DOS 3.3+ PRINT.COM. Function 0201h appears to be the opposite function; these functions are supposedly used to signal opening and closing of printers.
Conflicts: none known, but see Table 2-2 for potential conflicts
See also: Function 0201h

INT 2Fh Function 0203h
UNDETERMINED FUNCTION

PC LAN PROGRAM REDIR/REDIRIFS internal
Undocumented

Registers at call:
AX = 0203h

Return Registers:
none

Details: This function is called by the DOS 3.3+ PRINT.COM. Function 0204h appears to be the opposite function; these functions are supposedly used to signal opening and closing of printers.
Conflicts: none known, but see Table 2-2 for potential conflicts
See also: Functions 0200h and 0204h

INT 2Fh Function 0204h
UNDETERMINED FUNCTION

PC LAN PROGRAM REDIR/REDIRIFS internal
Undocumented

Registers at call:
AX = 0204h
others, if any, unknown

Return Registers:
none

Details: This function is called by the DOS 3.3+ PRINT.COM.

Function 0203h appears to be the opposite function; these functions are supposedly used to signal opening and closing of printers.

Conflicts: none known, but see Table 2-2 for potential conflicts

See also: Functions 0200h and 0203h

INT 2Fh Functions 02xxh   *PC LAN PROGRAM REDIR/REDIRIFS internal*
UNDETERMINED FUNCTION   *Undocumented*

Registers at call: **Return Registers:**
AX = 02xxh   *unknown*
others, if any, unknown

Conflicts: none known, but see Table 2-2 for potential conflicts

---

INT 2Fh Function B80Ah   *PC Network 1.00*
UNDETERMINED FUNCTION

Registers at call: **Return Registers:**
AX = B80Ah   *unknown*
others, if any, unknown

Details: This function is called by RECEIVER (equivalent to NetWare Lite's SERVER).

Conflicts: none known, but see Table 2-2 for potential conflicts

---

INT 2Fh Function B900h   *PC Network*
RECEIVER.COM - INSTALLATION CHECK

Registers at call: **Return Registers:**
AX = B900h   AL = status
                                                00h not installed
                                                FFh installed

Conflicts: none known, but see Table 2-2 for potential conflicts

---

INT 2Fh Function B901h   *PC Network*
GET RECEIVER.COM INT 2Fh HANDLER ADDRESS

Purpose: Allows more efficient execution by letting the caller bypass any other INT 2Fh handlers which have been added since RECEIVER.COM was installed.

Registers at call: **Return Registers:**
AX = B901h   AL = *unknown*
                                             ES:BX -> RECEIVER.COM INT 2Fh handler

Conflicts: none known, but see Table 2-2 for potential conflicts

---

INT 2Fh Function B903h   *PC Network*
GET RECEIVER.COM POST ADDRESS

Registers at call: **Return Registers:**
AX = B903h   ES:BX -> POST handler

Conflicts: none known, but see Table 2-2 for potential conflicts

See also: Function B904h, Function B803h (Chapter 31)

INT 2Fh Function B904h   *PC Network*
SET RECEIVER.COM POST ADDRESS

Registers at call: **Return Registers:**
AX = B904h   none
ES:BX -> new POST handler

Conflicts: none known, but see Table 2-2 for potential conflicts

See also: Function B903h, Function B804h (Chapter 31)

INT 2Fh Function B905h
PC Network
RECEIVER.COM - GET FILENAME

Registers at call:　　　　　　　　　**Return Registers:**
AX = B905h　　　　　　　　　　　　　buffers filled from RECEIVER.COM internal buffers
DS:BX -> 128-byte buffer for filename 1
DS:DX -> 128-byte buffer for filename 2

Details: The use of the filenames is unknown, but one appears to be for storing messages.
Conflicts: none known, but see Table 2-2 for potential conflicts
See also: Function B906h

INT 2Fh Function B906h
PC Network
RECEIVER.COM - SET FILENAME

Registers at call:　　　　　　　　　**Return Registers:**
AX = B906h　　　　　　　　　　　　　RECEIVER.COM internal buffers filled
DS:BX -> 128-byte buffer for filename 1　　　from user buffers
DS:DX -> 128-byte buffer for filename 2

Details: The use of the filenames is unknown, but one appears to be for storing messages.
Conflicts: none known, but see Table 2-2 for potential conflicts
See also: Function B905h

INT 2Fh Function B908h
PC Network
RECEIVER.COM - UNLINK KEYBOARD HANDLER

Registers at call:　　　　　　　　　**Return Registers:**
AX = B908h　　　　　　　　　　　　　none
ES:BX -> INT 09h handler RECEIVER
　should call after it finishes INT 09h

Details: This call replaces the address to which RECEIVER.COM chains on an INT 09h without preserving the original value. This allows a prior handler to unlink, but does not allow a new handler to be added such that RECEIVER gets the INT 09h first.
Conflicts: none known, but see Table 2-2 for potential conflicts
See also: Function B808h (Chapter 31)

INT 2Fh Function BF00h
PC LAN Program
REDIRIFS.EXE - INSTALLATION CHECK

Registers at call:　　　　　　　　　**Return Registers:**
AX = BF00h　　　　　　　　　　　　　AL = FFh if installed

Conflicts: none known, but see Table 2-2 for potential conflicts

INT 2Fh Function BF01h
PC LAN Program
Undocumented
REDIRIFS.EXE - UNDETERMINED FUNCTION

Registers at call:　　　　　　　　　**Return Registers:**
AX = BF01h　　　　　　　　　　　　　*unknown*
others, if any, unknown

Conflicts: none known, but see Table 2-2 for potential conflicts

INT 2Fh Function BF80h
PC LAN Program
REDIR.SYS - SET REDIRIFS ENTRY POINT

Registers at call:　　　　　　　　　**Return Registers:**
AX = BF80h　　　　　　　　　　　　　AL = FFh if installed
ES:DI -> FAR entry point to IFS　　　　　ES:DI -> internal workspace
　handler in REDIRIFS

Details: All future IFS calls to REDIR.SYS are passed to the ES:DI entry point.
Conflicts: none known, but see Table 2-2 for potential conflicts

CHAPTER 25

SK-UPPS Data Link Interface

SK-UPPS is the Schneider & Koch Universal Portable Protocol Stack, which provides an API on top of its Data Link Interface (DLI), allowing the use of any of several network transport layers; this product is called SK-PASSPORT in the USA.

The installation check consists of testing for the ASCII signature string "UPPS_DLI" immediately preceding the interrupt handler. To find the service interrupt being used by the driver (the default is INT 7Ch), an application should scan through the interrupt table until it finds an interrupt vector with the "UPPS_DLI" string. There may be more than one DLI loaded, each having its own service interrupt.

On the default of INT 7Ch, all of the functions described in this chapter conflict with PRINDIR (PCI-15), GO32 (PCI-37), and the IBM REXXPC command language (PCI-66).

INT 7Ch Function 0000h   *SK-UPPS Data Link Interface*
GET DRIVER VERSION

Registers at call:	Return Registers:
AX = 0000h	AH = major DLI version
	AL = minor DLI version
	DX = OEM signature (see Table 25-1)
	CL = DLI 2.8+ topology: 1=Ethernet, 2=FDDI, 3=Token-Ring

See also: Functions 0002h, 000Bh, 000Dh, and 000Eh

25-1 OEM signatures (defined by SK):

0001h	experimental
3343h	3COM
4942h	IBM
4943h	Intellicom
494Eh	Intel
4B4Fh	Kodiak
4D41h	Madge
4E45h	Novell
4F43h	Olicom
5349h	Siemens
534Bh	Schneider & Koch (SysKonnect)
5744h	Western Digital

INT 7Ch Function 0001h   *SK-UPPS Data Link Interface*
DOWN (UNINSTALL) DRIVER

Registers at call:	Return Registers:
AX = 0001h	AX = completion code (see Table 25-2)

Details: The DLI will refuse to unload if there are any protocols (see Function 0007h) or clients (see Function 0010h) active.

25-2 Completion codes:

0000h	successful
0005h	invalid multicast
0006h	buffer too small
0007h	no buffers left
0008h	no resources left
000Bh	illegal protocol ID
000Ch	protocol in use
000Dh	no multicast address
000Fh	protocols active
0010h	clients active
001Bh	invalid mode
001Ch	mode not supported
FFFFh	unknown service

INT 7Ch Function 0002h
GET DRIVER STATUS
SK-UPPS Data Link Interface

Registers at call:
AX = 0002h
ES:DI -> Status Information Block
  (SIB) (see Table 25-14)

Return Registers:
AX = completion code (see Table 25-2)

Details: GET DRIVER INFO (Function 000Eh) should be used instead of this one.
See also: Functions 0000h, 000Bh, 000Dh, and 000Eh

INT 7Ch Function 0003h
CHANGE DRIVER ADDRESS
SK-UPPS Data Link Interface

Registers at call:
AX = 0003h
ES:DI -> new node address (6 bytes)

Return Registers:
AX = completion code (see Table 25-2)

Details: The DLI will refuse to change the address if any protocols (see Function 0007h) are active.
See also: Functions 0001h and 000Eh

INT 7Ch Function 0004h
REQUEST BUFFER
SK-UPPS Data Link Interface

Registers at call:
AX = 0004h
DX = protocol ID (see Table 25-5)

Return Registers:
AX = completion code (see also Table 25-2)
  0000h successful
        ES:BX -> Memory Buffer (Mbuf) (see Table 25-3)

Details: If the DLI has no free Mbufs, it will set an internal flag for the protocol and later call the protocol's Event Upcall with EV_BUFFER_AVAILABLE (see Table 25-10) as soon as an Mbuf becomes available. There will only be one "buffer available" Upcall, even if this function has been called several times before.
See also: Functions 0005h, 0006h, 0012h, and 0013h

25-3 Format of Memory Buffer (Mbuf):

Offset	Size	Description
00h	DWORD	pointer to next Mbuf (linked list)
04h	WORD	offset of actual data within DATA area
06h	2 BYTEs	reserved (currently unused)

08h	WORD	length of actual data found in data area starting at given offset
0Ah	2 BYTEs	reserved (currently unused)
0Ch	DWORD	pointer to data area (size can be obtained via Function 000Eh call)
10h	WORD	protocol ID of protocol currently "owning" the Mbuf
12h	BYTE	IN USE flag; nonzero if Mbuf still in use by DLI (see Function 0006h)
13h	BYTE	receive status (bits 0-7 only; see Table 25-8)

INT 7Ch Function 0005h   *SK-UPPS Data Link Interface*
RELEASE BUFFER

Registers at call: **Return Registers:**
AX = 0005h   none
ES:BX -> Mbuf (see Table 25-3)
See also: Function 0004h

INT 7Ch Function 0006h   *SK-UPPS Data Link Interface*
TRANSMIT FRAME

Registers at call: **Return Registers:**
AX = 0006h   none
ES:BX -> Mbuf (see Table 25-3)
Details: The DLI will send LENGTH bytes found in the Mbuf's data area starting at the specified offset. A complete and valid frame must be stored there. The DLI will only copy the current node address (see Function 0003h) to the source node field of the frame's MAC header. On Ethernet, the DLI will always send a minimum of 60 bytes, regardless of the value found in the LENGTH field.

This function returns immediately; the DLI will call the protocol's Transmit Upcall (see Function 0007h) when the frame has been sent. The Mbuf's IN USE field will be non-zero until the DLI calls the Transmit Upcall.
See also: Functions 0002h, 0004h, and 0013h

25-4 Transmit Upcall calling convention:
Registers at call: **Return Register:**
ES:BX -> Mbuf (NEXT field destroyed)   none
interrupts disabled
Note: On FDDI the bytes of the source and destination node fields in the MAC header have been bit-swapped to physical address format.

INT 7Ch Function 0007h   *SK-UPPS Data Link Interface*
REGISTER PROTOCOL

Registers at call: **Return Registers:**
AX = 0007h   AX = completion code (see Table 25-2)
ES:BX -> Protocol Control Block
   (see Table 25-5)
See also: Functions 0008h and 000Bh

25-5 Format of Protocol Control Block (PCB):

Offset	Size	Description
00h	WORD	(big-endian) protocol type
02h	WORD	protocol mode (see Table 25-6)
04h	DWORD	pointer to Receive Upcall routine
08h	DWORD	pointer to Transmit Upcall routine
0Ch	DWORD	pointer to Event Upcall routine
10h	DWORD	pointer to ASCIZ protocol name (zero if none)
14h	WORD	protocol ID will be returned here (always non-zero)

25-6 Bitfields for protocol mode:

bit 0   promiscuous mode; protocol receives all frames regardless of their destination (PROTOCOL TYPE must be FFFFh)

bit 1   if set, protocol's Event Upcall will be called on entry and exit of the DLI's Interrupt Service Routine (see Table 25-10)

bit 2   DLI 2.2+ hook mode; protocol receives all directed frames destined for this station (PROTOCOL TYPE must be FFFFh)

bit 3   DLI 2.3+ receive error frames (only valid in promiscuous mode (bit 0))

bit 4-5   DLI 2.5+ frame type:

> 00 Ethernet II; specify type code in PROTOCOL TYPE field
> 01 IEEE 802.2; specify Service Access Point (SAP) in MSB (offset 0) of PROCOTOL TYPE field; LSB must be zero
> 10 IEEE 802.2 with SNAP header; specify type code in PROTOCOL TYPE field
> 11 reserved (currently unused)

bit 6   DLI 2.5+ if set, protocol's Event Upcall will be called with event code EV_BUFFER_WANTED, when DLI runs out of Mbufs

bit 7   DLI 2.7+ chain mode; if set, client allows the specified frame type to be shared with other clients

bit 8   DLI 2.8+ receive non-LLC frames rather than LLC frames

bit 9   DLI 2.8+ receive all multicast frames (see also Function 0009h)

bit 10-15 reserved (currently unused; must be zero)

Notes: If PROTOCOL TYPE is FFFFh and neither the "promiscuous" nor the "hook" mode bit is set, the protocol receives all frames that did not match any registered frame type (demultiplexor mode).

Protocols using "promiscuous", "hook" or "chain" mode should always return from the Receive Upcall with the received Mbuf in ES:BX and the Carry Flag set. The DLI will then pass the Mbuf to the FEED BACK BUFFER function (see Function 000Fh).

Some DLIs do not support all or even any of the "promiscuous", "receive non-LLC" and "receive all multicasts" mode bits.

25-7 Receive Upcall calling convention:

Registers at call: **Return Registers:**

ES:BX -> Mbuf   none

AX = receive status (see Table 25-8;
   also stored in Mbuf's RECEIVE
STATUS field)

interrupts disabled

25-8 Bitfields for receive status (reserved bits currently unused and always zero):

bit 0-2   reserved

bit 3   frame check sequence (FCS) error

bit 4   overflow (frame too long)

bit 5   framing error

bit 6   reserved

bit 7   non-LLC frame (see bit 8 of PCB's protocol mode field)

bit 8-15   reserved

Notes: The protocol's Receive Upcall routine will be called whenever a frame matching the specified frame type is received. A received frame is passed to the protocol in the Mbuf's DATA area at OFFSET and its size is LENGTH bytes.

INT 7Ch Function 0007h

The receive status passed to the Receive Upcall in register AL is always zero, except for protocols using "non-LLC" mode (bit 8 of PCB's protocol mode field) or "promiscuous" mode together with "receive error frames" (bits 0 & 3).

Upcalls are FAR routines and must return with a RET FAR. If the Carry Flag is set on return from a Receive or Transmit Upcall, then ES:BX must point to an Mbuf, which the DLI will then pass to the RELEASE BUFFER function (see Function 0005h). See also notes for PROTOCOL MODE.

25-9 Event Upcall calling convention:

Registers at call:
AX = event code (see Table 25-10)

Return Registers:
none

Details: All Event Upcalls may be ignored by the protocol.

25-10 Event codes for Event Upcall:

00h	EV_BUFFER_AVAILABLE	client may now call REQUEST BUFFER (Function 0004h)
01h	EV_ISR_START	start of Interrupt Service Routine
02h	EV_ISR_END	end of ISR (see bit 1 in PCB's protocol mode field)
03h	EV_BUFFER_WANTED	DLI temporarily out of Mbufs
04h	EV_NETWORK_STATUS	DLI 2.8+ network status (DX=status; see Table 25-11)
05h	EV_IO_CONTROL	DLI 2.8+ I/O control (DX=subfunction; see Function 0016h)

25-11 Bitfields for EV_NETWORK_STATUS in register DX:

	Token-Ring	FDDI
bit 15	SIGNAL_LOSS	SIGNAL_LOSS
bit 14	HARD_ERROR	HARD_ERROR
bit 13	SOFT_ERROR	SOFT_ERROR
bit 12	TRANSMIT_BEACON	TRANSMIT_BEACON
bit 11	LOBE_WIRE_FAULT	PATH_TEST_FAILED
bit 10	AUTO_REMOVAL	SELF_TEST_REQUIRED
bit 9	reserved	reserved
bit 8	REMOVE_RECEIVED	REMOTE_DISCONNECT
bit 7	COUNTER_OVERFLOW	reserved
bit 6	SINGLE_STATION	DUPLICATE_ADDRESS
bit 5	RING_RECOVERY	NO_RING_OP_STATUS
bit 4	reserved	VERSION_MISMATCH
bit 3	reserved	STUCK_BYPASS
bit 2	reserved	FDDI_EVENT
bit 1	reserved	RING_OP_CHANGE
bit 0	reserved	reserved

Note: EV_NETWORK_STATUS is not supported on Ethernet

INT 7Ch Function 0008h   *SK-UPPS Data Link Interface*
DISABLE PROTOCOL

Registers at call:
AX = 0008h
BX = protocol ID (see Table 25-5)

Return Registers:
AX = completion code (see Table 25-2)

Details: The DLI will handle any Mbufs given to TRANSMIT FRAME (Function 0006h) as if they had been given to TRANSMIT FRAME RELEASE (Function 0013h).

All multicast addresses registered for this protocol will be disabled.

After this function returns, the protocol's Upcall routines will no longer be called.

See also: Functions 0007h and 000Bh

INT 7Ch Function 0009h
REGISTER MULTICAST
SK-UPPS Data Link Interface

Registers at call:
AX = 0009h
BX = protocol ID (see Table 25-5)
ES:DI -> multicast address (6 bytes)

Return Registers:
AX = completion code (see Table 25-2)

Details: The broadcast address is always enabled.
    Set bit 9 of PCB's protocol mode field in REGISTER PROTOCOL call (Function 0007h) to receive all multicast frames.
See also: Functions 000Ah and 0014h

INT 7Ch Function 000Ah
DISABLE MULTICAST
SK-UPPS Data Link Interface

Registers at call:
AX = 000Ah
BX = protocol ID (see Table 25-5)
ES:DI -> multicast address (6 bytes)
See also: Functions 0009h and 0014h

Return Registers:
AX = completion code (see Table 25-2)

INT 7Ch Function 000Bh
GET PROTOCOL LIST
SK-UPPS Data Link Interface

Registers at call:
AX = 000Bh
ES:DI -> protocol ID buffer
CX = number of 2-byte protocol IDs
    that may be stored in buffer

Return Registers:
AX = completion code (see Table 25-2)
CX = number of active protocols (regardless of value
    returned in AX)
protocol ID buffer filled with active protocol IDs

Details: If the buffer supplied is too small, CX still contains the total number of active protocols and the buffer has been filled to capacity.
See also: Functions 000Ch and 0014h

INT 7Ch Function 000Ch
GET PROTOCOL STATUS
SK-UPPS Data Link Interface

Registers at call:
AX = 000Ch
BX = protocol ID (see Function 000Bh)
ES:DI -> Protocol Status Block (see Table 25-12)
See also: Functions 000Bh and 0014h

Return Registers:
AX = completion code (see Table 25-2)

25-12 Format of Protocol Status Block (PSB):

Offset	Size	Description
00h	DWORD	pointer to ASCIZ protocol name
04h	WORD	protocol mode (see Table 25-6)
06h	WORD	protocol type (see Function 0007h)
08h	WORD	number of registered multicasts (see Functions 0009h and 0014h)

INT 7Ch Function 000Dh
GET DRIVER STATISTICS
SK-UPPS Data Link Interface

Registers at call:
AX = 000Dh
BX = flag: 0=don't clear statistics, 1=clear statistics
ES:DI -> Statistics Data Block (see Table 25-13)
See also: Functions 0002h and 0015h

Return Registers:
AX = completion code (see Table 25-2)

25-13 Format of Statistics Data Block (SDB):

Offset	Size	Description
00h	DWORD	node uptime in ticks (1/18.21 sec.)
04h	DWORD	number of bytes received
08h	DWORD	number of bytes transmitted
0Ch	DWORD	frames received
10h	DWORD	frames transmitted
14h	DWORD	multicast bytes received
18h	DWORD	multicast frames received
1Ch	DWORD	unrecognized frames
20h	WORD	missed frames
22h	WORD	frame check sequence (FCS) errors
24h	WORD	framing errors
26h	WORD	babbling errors
28h	WORD	late collision errors
2Ah	WORD	loss of carrier errors
2Ch	WORD	16 retries failed errors
2Eh	WORD	overflow errors

Note: Fields 26h through 2Ch are always zero, except in some very old versions of the DLI. Use GET MEDIA STATISTICS (Function 0015h) to get more detailed information.

INT 7Ch Function 000Eh   *SK-UPPS Data Link Interface*
DLI 2.5+ - GET DRIVER INFORMATION

Registers at call:
AX = 000Eh
ES:DI -> Driver Information Block
  (see Table 25-14)
BX = offset of 1st field within DIB to
  be returned
CX = number of bytes to be returned
See also: Functions 0000h, 0002h, 000Bh, 000Dh, and 0015h

Return Registers:
AX = completion code (see Table 25-2)
CX = number of bytes copied (regardless of
  value returned in AX)

25-14 Format of Driver Information Block (DIB):

Offset	Size	Description
00h	6 BYTEs	physical node address (from adapter's ROM)
06h	6 BYTEs	current node address (see Function 0003h)
0Ch	BYTE	adapter id (defined by OEM)
0Dh	BYTE	IRQ line (FFh if none)
0Eh	DWORD	pointer to shared memory (zero if none)
12h	DWORD	size of shared memory (zero if none)
16h	WORD	base I/O port (zero if none)
18h	BYTE	DMA line (FFh if none)
19h	BYTE	DLI 2.4+ topology (see Function 0000h)
1Ah	WORD	size of an Mbuf's DATA area (see Table 25-3)
1Ch	2 BYTEs	reserved (currently unused)
1Eh	WORD	total number of Mbufs the DLI has
20h	WORD	maximum number of Mbufs that can be allocated via REQUEST BUFFER (Function 0004h) and SYNC REQUEST BUFFER (Function 0012h)

—**end of Status Information Block returned by GET DRIVER STATUS (Function 0002h)**—

22h	DWORD	pointer to ASCIZ adapter name
26h	WORD	number of I/O ports used (zero if none)
28h	DWORD	line speed in bits/second

INT 7Ch Function 000Fh
FEED BACK BUFFER   *SK-UPPS Data Link Interface*

Registers at call: **Return Registers:**
AX = 000Fh   none
ES:BX -> Mbuf

Details: A protocol may call this function instead of returning the Mbuf directly from the Receive Upcall if it is running in "promiscuous", "hook" or "chain" mode.
See also: Function 0007h

INT 7Ch Function 0010h
CLIENT HOOK   *SK-UPPS Data Link Interface*

Registers at call: **Return Registers:**
AX = 0010h   none

Details: An application having no active protocols may call this function to prevent the DLI from unloading.
See also: Functions 0001h and 0011h

INT 7Ch Function 0011h
CLIENT UNHOOK   *SK-UPPS Data Link Interface*

Registers at call: **Return Registers:**
AX = 0011h   none
See also: Function 0010h

INT 7Ch Function 0012h
SYNC REQUEST BUFFER   *SK-UPPS Data Link Interface*

Registers at call: **Return Registers:**
AX = 0012h   AX = completion code (see Table 25-2)
DX = protocol ID (see Table 25-5)   if AX=0000h: ES:BX -> Mbuf (see Table 25-3)

Details: If the protocol wants to be informed when an Mbuf becomes available, REQUEST BUFFER (Function 0004h) should be used instead.
See also: Functions 0004h, 0005h, 0006h, and 0013h

INT 7Ch Function 0013h
TRANSMIT FRAME RELEASE   *SK-UPPS Data Link Interface*

Registers at call: **Return Registers:**
AX = 0013h   none
ES:BX -> Mbuf (see Table 25-3)

Details: This function returns immediately; the protocol's Transmit Upcall will not be called. The Mbuf may no longer be used by the protocol in any way (i.e. the Mbuf's IN USE field may not be polled).
See also: Functions 0004h and 0013h

INT 7Ch Function 0014h
GET MULTICAST LIST   *SK-UPPS Data Link Interface*

Registers at call: **Return Registers:**
AX = 0014h   AX = completion code (see Table 25-2)
BX = protocol ID (see Function 000Bh)   CX = number of registered multicast addresses for
ES:DI -> multicast address buffer   this protocol (regardless of value returned in AX)
CX = number of 6-byte multicast addresses   multicast address buffer filled with multicast
that may be stored in buffer   addresses registered for this protocol

Details: If the buffer supplied is too small, CX still contains the total number of registered multicast addresses for this protocol and the buffer has been filled to capacity.
See also: Functions 000Bh, 0009h, and 000Ch

INT 7Ch Function 0015h
SK-UPPS Data Link Interface
DLI 2.6+ - GET MEDIA STATISTICS

Registers at call:	Return Registers:
AX = 0015h	AX = completion code (see Table 25-2)
ES:DI -> media-specific statistics buffer (see Table 25-15)	CX = number of bytes copied (regardless of value returned in AX)
BX = offset of 1st field within MSS to be returned	
CX = number of bytes to be returned	

Details: This function is not supported by all DLIs, and will return AX=FFFFh if not supported.
See also: Functions 0000h and 000Dh

25-15 Format of media-specific statistics for Ethernet:

Offset	Size	Description
00h	DWORD	alignment errors
04h	DWORD	frame check sequence (FCS) errors
08h	DWORD	single collision frames
0Ch	DWORD	multiple collision frames
10h	DWORD	signal quality error (SQE) test errors
14h	DWORD	deferred transmissions
18h	DWORD	late collisions
1Ch	DWORD	excessive collisions
20h	DWORD	internal MAC transmit errors
24h	DWORD	carrier sense errors
28h	DWORD	excessive deferrals
2Ch	DWORD	frame too longs
30h	DWORD	in range length errors
34h	DWORD	out of range length fields
38h	DWORD	internal MAC receive errors

25-16 Format of media-specific statistics for FDDI:

Offset	Size	Description
00h	DWORD	SMT operating version id (refer to ANSI 7.1.2.2)
04h	DWORD	SMT CF state: 1=Isolated, 2=Wrap_S, 3=Wrap_A, 4=Wrap_B, 5=Wrap_AB, 6=Thru (refer to ANSI SMT 9.7.4.3)
08h	DWORD	SMT frames sent
0Ch	DWORD	SMT frames received
10h	DWORD	SMT ring up count
14h	6 BYTEs	MAC upstream neighbor
1Ah	6 BYTEs	MAC downstream neighbor
20h	DWORD	MAC frame counter (refer to ANSI MAC 2.2.1)
24h	DWORD	MAC error counter (")
28h	DWORD	MAC lost counter (")
2Ch	BYTE	port 1 link error estimate (ranges from 10^{-4} to 10^{-15} and is reported as the absolute value of the exponent)
2Dh	BYTE	port 2 link error estimate (")
2Eh 2	BYTEs	reserved (currently unused)

| 30h | DWORD | attachment class: 1=single-attachment (S PORT),
2=dual-attachment (A/B PORT pairs), 3=concentrator (M PORTs) |
| 34h | DWORD | attachment optical bypass present: 1=true, 2=false |

25-17 Format of media-specific statistics for Token Ring:

Offset	Size	Description
00h	6 BYTEs	upstream neighbour
06h	WORD	local ring number
08h	DWORD	ring up count
0Ch	DWORD	signal loss errors
10h	DWORD	lobe wire faults
14h	DWORD	ring recovery count
18h	DWORD	line errors
1Ch	DWORD	burst errors
20h	DWORD	ARI/FCI errors
24h	DWORD	lost frame errors
28h	DWORD	receive congestion errors
2Ch	DWORD	frame copied errors
30h	DWORD	token errors
34h	DWORD	DMA bus errors
38h	DWORD	DMA parity errors
3Ch	DWORD	receive overflow errors

INT 7Ch Function 0016h
SK-UPPS Data Link Interface
DLI 2.8+ - DRIVER I/O CONTROL

Registers at call:
AX = 0016h
DX = subfunction; bits 14-15 specify
  direction of I/O:
        00 no data at all (ES:BX undefined)
    01   driver -> application (GET)
        10 application -> driver (SET)
    11   both directions (GET/SET)
ES:BX -> I/O buffer (optional)
CX = size of buffer (if ES:BX valid)

Return Registers:
AX = completion code; defined by OEM

Details: This function is not supported by all DLIs, and will return AX=FFFFh if not supported.
  Subfunction codes are defined by OEMs.
See also: Function 0001h

INT 7Ch Function 0017h
SK-UPPS Data Link Interface
DLI 2.8+ - INTERRUPT REQUEST

Registers at call:
AX = 0017h

Return Registers:
AX = completion code (see Table 25-2)

Details: This function is not supported by all DLIs, and will return AX=FFFFh if not supported.
It must be called with interrupts disabled; when the client re-enables interrupts, an interrupt will
be generated and reported to the client through an Event Upcall (see Function 0007h
[EV_ISR_START/EV_ISR_END]).
See also: Function 0007h

CHAPTER 26

SNAP
(Simple Network Access Protocol)

SNAP.EXE is a TSR written by IBM and Carnegie Mellon University which implements the Simple Network Application Protocol. It is required by PCVENUS (a network shell), which allows the use of the Andrew File System as one or more networked drives.

26-1 Values for SNAP status:

0000h	successful
F830h	"SNAP_ABORTED"
FC04h	"SNAP_SERVERDIED"
FC05h	"SNAP_RESEND"
FC06h	"SNAP_SELECTFAILED"
FC07h	"SNAP_WRONGVERSION"
FC08h	"SNAP_INVALIDACK"
FC09h	"SNAP_TIMEOUT"
FC0Ah	"SNAP_SERVERREJECT"
FC0Bh	"SNAP_NOREPLYDUE"
FC0Ch	"SNAP_NOAUTHENTICATE"/"SNAP_GUARDIAN_ERROR"
FC0Dh	"SNAP_NOINIT"
FC0Eh	"SNAP_SOCKETERROR"
FC0Fh	"SNAP_BUFFERLIMIT"
FC10h	"SNAP_INVALIDCID"
FC11h	"SNAP_INVALIDOP"
FC12h	"SNAP_XMITFAIL"
FC13h	"SNAP_NOMORERETRIES"
FC14h	"SNAP_BADPARMS"
FC15h	"SNAP_NOMEMORY"
FC16h	"SNAP_NOMORECONVS"
FFFFh	failed (invalid function/parameter)

INT 1Ah Function 6108h
SNAP.EXE 3.2+
"SNAP_SENDWITHREPLY" - SEND MESSAGE AND GET REPLY

Registers at call:
AX = 6108h
STACK: WORD conversation ID (0000h-0009h)
        DWORD pointer to message buffer
        WORD length of message
        DWORD pointer to reply buffer
        WORD length of reply buffer

WORD 0000h
(use default "Cparams"
structure)
See also: Function 6205h

Return Registers:
AX = status (see Table 26-1)
STACK unchanged

INT 1Ah Function 6205h   *SNAP.EXE 3.2+*
"SNAP_SENDNOREPLY" - SEND MESSAGE, DON'T AWAIT REPLY

Registers at call:
AX = 6205h
STACK: WORD conversation
ID (0000h-0009h)
DWORD pointer to message
WORD length of message
WORD 0000h
(use default "Cparms" structure)
See also: Function 6108h

Return Registers:
AX = status (see Table 26-1)
STACK unchanged

INT 1Ah Function 6308h   *SNAP.EXE 3.2+*
"SNAP_BEGINCONV" - BEGIN CONVERSATION

Registers at call:
AX = 6308h
STACK: WORD offset of ASCIZ
"guardian"
WORD offset of ASCIZ hostname
WORD offset of ASCIZ server name
WORD offset of ASCIZ userid
WORD offset of ASCIZ password
WORD offset of password length
WORD offset of password type
WORD offset of "Cparms" structure (Table 26-2)

Return Registers:
unknown
STACK unchanged

Details: All stacked offsets are within the SNAP data segment (use Function 6A01h to allocate a buffer).
See also: Functions 6405h and 7202h

26-2 Format of Cparms structure:

Offset	Size	Description
00h	WORD	retry delay in seconds
02h	WORD	timeout delay in seconds
04h	WORD	maximum buffer size
06h	WORD	encryption level

INT 1Ah Function 6405h   *SNAP.EXE 3.2+*
"SNAP_ENDCONV" - END CONVERSATION

Registers at call:
AX = 6405h
STACK: WORD conversation ID
(0000h-0009h)
DWORD pointer to message buffer
WORD length of message
WORD 0000h (use default "Cparms" structure)
See also: Function 6308h

Return Registers:
AX = status (see Table 26-1)
STACK unchanged

INT 1Ah Function 6900h
"SNAP_DATASEG" - GET RESIDENT DATA SEGMENT

Registers at call:
AX = 6900h
See also: Functions 6A01h and 6F01h

Return Registers:
AX = value used for DS by resident code

INT 1Ah Function 6A01h
"SNAP_ALLOC" - ALLOCATE BUFFER IN SNAP DATA SEGMENT

Registers at call:
AX = 6A01h
STACK: WORD number of bytes
              to allocate
See also: Function 6B01h

Return Registers:
AX = offset of allocated buffer or 0000h if out
  of memory
STACK unchanged

INT 1Ah Function 6B01h
"SNAP_FREE" - DEALLOCATE BUFFER IN SNAP DATA SEGMENT

Registers at call:
AX = 6B01h
STACK: WORD offset within SNAP
              data segment of previously
              allocated buffer
Details: This call is a NOP if the specified offset is 0000h.
See also: Function 6A01h

Return Registers:
STACK unchanged

INT 1Ah Function 6C04h
"SNAP_COPYTO" - COPY DATA TO RESIDENT SNAP PACKAGE

Registers at call:
AX = 6C04h
STACK: WORD offset within SNAP
              data segment of destination
              (nonzero)
              WORD segment of source buffer
              WORD offset of source buffer
              WORD number of bytes to copy
See also: Function 6D04h

Return Registers:
AX = offset of byte after last one copied
  to destination
STACK unchanged

INT 1Ah Function 6D04h
"SNAP_COPYFROM" - COPY DATA FROM RESIDENT SNAP PACKAGE

Registers at call:
AX = 6D04h
STACK: WORD offset within SNAP
              data segment of source
              buffer
              WORD segment of destination buffer
              WORD offset of destination buffer
              WORD number of bytes to copy
See also: Function 6C04h

Return Registers:
AX = offset of byte after last one copied from
  source
buffer filled
STACK unchanged

INT 1Ah Function 6E01h
"SNAP_SETDEBUG" - SET UNKNOWN VALUE

Registers at call:
AX = 6E01h
STACK: WORD new value for *unknown*

Return Registers:
AX = old value of *unknown*
STACK unchanged

INT 1Ah Function 6F01h
"SNAP_CHKINSTALL" - INSTALLATION CHECK

SNAP.EXE 3.2+

Registers at call:
AX = 6F01h
STACK: WORD 0000h

Return Registers:
AX = status
   0000h SNAP is resident
   other SNAP not present
STACK unchanged

See also: Functions 6900h and 7400h

INT 1Ah Function 7002h
"SNAP_SETANCHOR"

SNAP.EXE 3.2+

Registers at call:
AX = 7002h
STACK: WORD anchor number
      (0000h-0009h)
      WORD new value for the anchor

Return Registers:
AX = status
   0000h successful
   FFFFh failed (top word on stack not in
      range 00h-09h)
STACK unchanged

See also: Function 7101h

INT 1Ah Function 7101h
"SNAP_GETANCHOR"

SNAP.EXE 3.2+

Registers at call:
AX = 7101h
STACK: WORD anchor number (0000h-0009h)

Return Registers:
AX = anchor's value
STACK unchanged

See also: Function 7002h

INT 1Ah Function 7202h
"SNAP_SETCONVPARMS" - SET CONVERSATION PARAMETERS

SNAP.EXE 3.2+

Registers at call:
AX = 7202h
STACK: WORD conversation ID
      (0000h-0009h)
      WORD offset within resident
      data segment of "Cparms"
      structure (see Table 26-2)

Return Registers:
AX = *status*
STACK unchanged

See also: Function 6308h

INT 1Ah Function 7302h
"SNAP_CLIENTVERSION" - GET VERSION

SNAP.EXE 3.2+

Registers at call:
AX = 7302h
STACK: WORD conversation
      ID (0000h-0009h)
      WORD offset within resident
      data segment of *unknown item*

Return Registers:
AX = *unknown*
others, if any, unknown
STACK unchanged

See also: Function 7400h

INT 1Ah Function 7400h
"SNAP_VERSION" - GET VERSION

SNAP.EXE 3.2+

Registers at call:
AX = 7400h

Return Registers:
AX = version (AH=major, AL=minor)

Details: This call is only valid if SNAP is installed.
See also: Function 7302h, INT 1Ah Function 6F01h

INT 1Ah Function 75h
"SNAP_NOP" - UNDETERMINED FUNCTION   *SNAP.EXE 3.2+*

Registers at call: **Return Registers:**
AH = 75h   AX = *unknown* (0000h)
AL = *unknown*

INT 1Ah Function 76h
"SNAP_802_5" - UNDETERMINED FUNCTION   *SNAP.EXE 3.2+*

Registers at call: **Return Registers:**
AH = 76h   AX = *unknown*
AL = *unknown*

INT 1Ah Function 77h
UNDETERMINED FUNCTION   *SNAP.EXE 3.4*

Registers at call: **Return Registers:**
AH = 77h   *unknown*
AL = *unknown* (at least 01h)   STACK unchanged
STACK: WORD *unknown*
         others, if any, unknown

INT 1Ah Function 7802h
UNDETERMINED FUNCTION   *SNAP.EXE 3.4*

Registers at call: **Return Registers:**
AX = 7802h   *unknown*
STACK: WORD *unknown*   STACK unchanged
         WORD *unknown*

CHAPTER 27

10NET

Tiara Computer Systems 10Net (formerly known as DCA 10Net), also distributed by Sitka Corp. under license from Tiara, is a peer-to-peer entry-level system considered competitive to Artisoft's Lantastic by many reviewers. Versions 4.1 and above are compatible with Windows 3.1. Windows treats them as Microsoft Network-compatible.

10NET Core Functionality

INT 21h Function 5E00h   10NET v5.0
GET MACHINE NAME
Registers at call: **Return Registers:**
AX = 5E00h   CL = redirector's NetBIOS name number
                                               ES:DI -> network node ID

Conflicts: MS-DOS (Chapter 3)
See also: Function 5E01h

INT 21h Function 5E01h   10NET v5.0
GET LOCAL 10NET CONFIGURATION TABLE
Registers at call: **Return Registers:**
AX = 5E01h   none
CX = length of buffer
DS:DX -> buffer for 10Net
configuration table (see Table 27-1)
Conflicts: MS-DOS (Chapter 3). **See also:** Function 5E00h, INT 6Fh Functions 02h and 03h

27-1 Format of 10Net Configuration Table:

Offset	Size	Description
00h	8 BYTEs	user name
08h	15 BYTEs	node ID
17h	3 BYTEs	unique portion of Ethernet address
1Ah	BYTE	Who group number
1Bh	WORD	services mask (see Table 27-3)
1Dh	DWORD	serial number
21h	BYTE	maximum concurrent users with same serial number allowed on net
22h	BYTE	chat mask (see Table 27-4)
23h	BYTE	internal system bits (see Table 27-5)
24h	9 BYTEs	version number in format MM.mm.xxx
2Dh	BYTE	flag: 01h if machine is a PS/2
2Eh	BYTE	flag: 03h if 80386

2Fh	BYTE	spool termination mode: 01h concatenate, 02h truncate (see Function 5D09h in Chapter 3)
30h	WORD	autospool timeout in clock ticks
32h	WORD	monitor timeout in clock ticks
34h	WORD	unused
36h	WORD	chat timeout in clock ticks
38h	WORD	netBIOS session timeout in half-seconds
3Ah	WORD	datagram send timeout in seconds
3Ch	WORD	keyboard value for initiating chat mode
3Eh	WORD	Who timeout in clock ticks
40h	BYTE	flag: 01h if server should process rom NetBIOS Post return
41h	BYTE	flag: 01h if FCBs should be recycled
42h	3 BYTEs	signature "DBG"
45h	BYTE	last interrupt (21h or 6Fh)
46h	BYTE	last INT 21h AH value
47h	BYTE	last INT 6Fh AH value
48h	WORD	last item posted
4Ah	WORD	last item free-posted
4Ch	WORD	last item handled by server
4Eh	WORD	last redirector send NCB
50h	WORD	last redirector receive NCB
52h	4 BYTEs	signature "TABL"
56h	WORD	offset of datagram buffer table header
58h	WORD	offset of chat buffer table header
5Ah	WORD	offset of Raw buffer table header
5Ch	WORD	offset of Workstation buffer table header
5Eh	WORD	offset of server receive-any table header
60h	WORD	offset of Tiny buffer table header
62h	WORD	offset of zero-length buffer table (NCBs)
64h	WORD	offset of Rdr (Redirector Mount) table header
66h	WORD	offset of Ntab (Redirector Session) table header
68h	WORD	offset of FCB table header
6Ah	WORD	offset of user file handle table header
6Ch	WORD	offset of workstation printer RDR extension table header
6Eh	WORD	offset of server shared device table header
70h	WORD	offset of server connection table header
72h	WORD	offset of server login table header
74h	WORD	offset of server file table header
76h	WORD	offset of server shared file table header
78h	WORD	offset of server record lock table header
7Ah	WORD	offset of remote printer claim table header
7Ch	WORD	offset of remote printer device table header
7Eh	WORD	offset of print server mount table header
80h	WORD	offset of print server sessions table header
82h	WORD	offset of print server print job structure table header
84h	WORD	offset of print server pooled device table header
86h	WORD	size of workstation buffer
88h	WORD	size of server receive-any buffer
8Ah	WORD	size of server raw I/O buffer

INT 21h Function 5E01h

8Ch	6 BYTEs	reserved
92h	DWORD	pointer to profile pathname
96h	BYTE	datagram retry count
97h	BYTE	NetBIOS LAN adapter number
98h	6 BYTEs	physical Ethernet address
9Eh	BYTE	NetBIOS server name number
9Fh	BYTE	NetBIOS redirector name number
A0h	BYTE	10Net interrupt number
A1h	BYTE	flag: chat is loaded
A2h	BYTE	flag: INT 6Fh APIs permanently loaded
A3h	BYTE	flag: file security present
A4h	WORD	reserved
A6h	BYTE	fixed mount bitmask for drives A:-H:
A7h	BYTE	reserved
A8h	WORD	10Net system flags (see Table 27-6)
AAh	BYTE	monitor flags (see Table 27-7)
ABh	5 BYTEs	reserved
B0h	WORD	offset of monitor timer block
B2h	WORD	offset of server timer block
B4h	WORD	offset of chat timer block
B6h	WORD	timer chain
B8h	4 BYTEs	signature "TALS"
BCh	WORD	number of 10Net sends
BEh	WORD	number of 10Net receives
C0h	WORD	number of no-buffer conditions
C2h	WORD	number of dropped posted messages
C4h	WORD	number of server NCB errors
C6h	WORD	number of redirector NCB errors
C8h	WORD	number of datagram send/receive errors
CAh	WORD	number of dropped Whos
CCh	WORD	number of dropped submits
CEh	WORD	number of session aborts
D0h	BYTE	number of NetBIOS interface-busy errors
D1h	BYTE	last NetBIOS bad post command
D2h	BYTE	last NetBIOS bad redirector command
D3h	BYTE	do send datagram send/receive error command
D4h	DWORD	pointer to DOS system parameter table
D8h	WORD	number of DOS physical drives
DAh	WORD	offset of DOS PSP field in DOS data segment
DCh	WORD	offset of in-DOS flag in DOS data segment
DEh	WORD	DOS data segment
E0h	WORD	offset of DOS SFT in DOS data segment
E2h	WORD	offset of number-of-physical-units field in DOS data segment
E4h	WORD	10Net code segment
E6h	WORD	10Net data segment
E8h	WORD	10Net common server segment
EAh	WORD	10Net file server segment
ECh	WORD	10Net print server segment
EEh	WORD	10Net remote printer segment

Note: The documentation lists the field at offset D0h as a WORD, but all following offsets are as though it were a BYTE; if it is indeed a WORD, all offsets after D0h must be increased by one byte.

27-2 Format of 10Net Table Header:

Offset	Size	Description
-16	4 BYTEs	table identifier
-12	WORD	peak number of tables allocated
-10	WORD	number of tables currently in use
-8	WORD	total number of tables
-6	WORD	size of each table
-4	WORD	offset of first allocated table
-2	WORD	offset of first free table

27-3 Bitfields for services mask:

bit 0	workstation
bit 1	file server
bit 2	print queue server
bit 3	de-spool server

27-4 Bitfields for chat mask:

bit 0	chat permitted
bit 1	bell enabled
bit 2	chat keyboard initiated
bit 3	in INT 16h handler
bit 4	in Get Input
bit 5	display has timed out
bit 6	chat is idle

27-5 Bitfields for internal system bits:

bit 0	submit permitted
bit 1	submit initiated
bit 2	submit executing
bit 3	internal client call/chat/spool/autospool
bit 4	in spool termination
bit 5	print permitted
bit 6	waiting for keyboard input

27-6 Bitfields for 10Net System Flags:

bit 0	in NetBIOS
bit 1	processing INT 28h
bit 2	is server
bit 3	in net user-DOS function
bit 4	in DOS user-DOS function
bit 5	in net for user non-DOS function
bit 6	in server DOS function
bit 7	in server non-DOS function
bit 8	in terminate
bit 10	in user on server request
bit 13	in DOS for user on server
bit 14	disable critical error handler

27-7 Bitfields for Monitor Flags:

bit 0	waiting for monitor response
bit 4	in monitor get-input routine
bit 5	monitor display timeout
bit 6	sensing for escape key

INT 21h Function 5E04h
INITIATE PRINT JOB

Registers at call:
AX = 5E04h
BX = zero-based redirection list index
   (see Function 5F02h in Chapter 3)
DS:DX -> extended workstation
   printer setup structure
   (see Table 27-8)
Conflicts: MS-DOS (Chapter 3)
See also: Functions 5E05h and 5E06h

Return Registers:
CF clear if successful
CF set on error
   AX = error code (see Table 3-1)

27-8 Format of extended workstation printer setup structure:

Offset	Size	Description
00h	BYTE	notification flags (see Table 27-9)
01h	BYTE	job control mask (see Table 27-10)
02h	WORD	days to retain file
04h	WORD	test print length
06h	BYTE	number of copies to print
07h	BYTE	compression algorithm
08h	BYTE	tab width (00h = don't expand)
09h	BYTE	initiation type (00h normal, 01h non-spooled)
0Ah	38 BYTEs	job start operation notification instructions
30h	32 BYTEs	comment for job
50h	64 BYTEs	output filename or non-spooled file

27-9 Bitfields for notification flags:

bit 0	user at print start
bit 1	operator at start, with reply
bit 2	user at print completion
bit 3	operator at completion, with reply
bit 4	user on queue switch
bit 5	operator on queue switch, with reply
bit 6	user on print error

27-10 Bitfields for job control mask:

bit 0	print banner page
bit 1	eject page at end of job
bit 2	mark as "held" (queue but don't print)
bit 3	rush job (queue at top)
bit 4	overwrite file with zeros before deletion
bit 5	hyperspool if possible

INT 21h Function 5E05h
TERMINATE PRINT JOB
10NET v5.0

Registers at call:
AX = 5E05h
BX = zero-based redirection list index
  (see Function 5F02h in Chapter 3)

Return Registers:
CF clear if successful
CF set on error
  AX = error code (see Table 3-1)

Details: This call resets the spool termination mode to "truncate" (see Function 5D08h in Chapter 3).
Conflicts: MS-DOS (Chapter 3)
See also: Functions 5E04h and 5E06h

INT 21h Function 5E06h
GET/SET 10NET WORKSTATION PRINTER SETUP STRUCTURE
10NET v5.0

Registers at call:
AX = 5E06h
BX = zero-based redirection list index
  (see Function 5F02h in Chapter 3)
CX = operation (06h set, 07h get)
DS:DX -> buffer for setup structure
  (same as first nine bytes of
  workstation printer setup)
  (see Table 27-8)

Return Registers:
CF clear if successful
  DS:DX buffer updated on get
CF set on error
  AX = error code (see Table 3-1)

See also: Functions 5E04h and 5E05h

INT 2Fh Function B800h
INSTALLATION CHECK
10NET

Registers at call:
AX = B800h
CX = F041h

Return Registers:
AL = status
  00h not installed
  nonzero installed
    BX = installed component flags (test in this order!)
      bit 6 server
      bit 2 messenger
      bit 7 receiver
      bit 3 redirector
      bit 1 LANPUP (LANtastic 4.0)
    CX = 10Net data segment
    CX:DX -> 10Net Configuration Table
      (see Table 27-1)

Details: If CX is not F041h on entry, neither CX nor DX will be changed, and this call becomes identical to the standard installation check described in Chapter 31.
Conflicts: network (Chapter 31)
See also: INT 21h Function 5E01h, Function B800h (Chapter 31)

INT 6Fh Function 00h
LOGIN
10NET

Registers at call:
AH = 00h
DS:DX -> login record (see Table 27-11)

Return Registers:
CL = security level
AX = status (see Table 27-12)

Conflicts: Novell NetWare PCOX (Chapter 37)
See also: Functions 01h and 80h, 10MEMMGR INT 21h Function 4402h

27-11 Format of login record:

Offset	Size	Description
00h	8 BYTEs	ser name
08h	8 BYTEs	password
10h	12 BYTEs	name of SuperStation

27-12 Values for status:

0000h	successful	
01FFh	"RTO_NERR"	transmit interrupt lost (time out on response)
02FFh	"NET_NERR"	network (hardware) error
03FFh	"PAS_NERR"	invalid password
04FFh	"LRN_NERR"	local resource not available
05FFh	"SRN_NERR"	server resource not available
06FFh	"LNM_NERR"	already logged in under different name
07FFh	"LSF_NERR"	login security failure (node)
08FFh	"NLI_NERR"	not logged in
09FFh	"DIVZ_NERR"	position calc error
0AFFh	"NT1_NERR"	receive subfunction not = send subfunction (i.e. read,write)
0BFFh	"RFNC_NERR"	request function not in range
0CFFh	"NSFH_NERR"	no more server file handle entries left
0DFFh	"NFTAB_NERR"	no more shared file table entries left
0EFFh	"NUFH_NERR"	no more user file handle entries left
0FFFh	"CHAT_NERR"	chat permit not on
10FFh	"NSRV_NERR"	not a server on request
11FFh	"NOBD_NERR"	no transporter board error
12FFh	"STO_NERR"	time out on send
13FFh	"INF_NERR"	item not found (spool item not on queue)
14FFh	"DACS_NERR"	DOS access incompatible
15FFh	"RLOCK_NERR"	record already locked
16FFh	"IVP_NERR"	invalid parameter
17FFh	"RLTO_NERR"	record lock time out error
18FFh	"CSPL_NERR"	currently spooling to named device
19FFh	"DRP_NERR"	dropped receive message (throttle)
1AFFh	"SOPV_NERR"	open sharing violation
1BFFh	"NTUF_NERR"	no more tuf entries left
1CFFh	"NOWN_NERR"	not file owner on open
1DFFh	"RSEC_NERR"	read security not passed
1EFFh	"WSEC_NERR"	write security not passed
1FFFh	"GSEC_NERR"	group security not passed
20FFh	"SEC1_NERR"	security file failure
21FFh	"ACT1_NERR"	activity file failure
22FFh	"SPL1_NERR"	spool control file failure
23FFh	"NMT_NERR"	device not mounted (spooling)
24FFh	"RSPL_NERR"	spool file has not been terminated
25FFh	"DNSH_NERR"	device not mounted or is not being shared
26FFh	"DUP_NERR"	duplicate node ID
27FFh	"FNF_NERR"	file not found error
28FFh	"NMF_NERR"	no more files
29FFh	"UN_NERR"	unknown internal system error
2AFFh	"QCP_NERR"	print queue is full or corrupted

2BFFh	"IFNC_NERR"	invalid function
2CFFh	"IVH_NERR"	invalid handle
2DFFh	"TOF_NERR"	too many files opened
2EFFh	"PNF_NERR"	path not found
2FFFh	"SACT_NERR"	named file is active

--- **10NET v5.0+** ---

30FFh	"NAK_NERR"	received NAK on send (destination out of buffers)
31FFh	"RENT_NERR"	reentrancy in driver F_SEND
32FFh	"RECV_NERR"	driver could not be put in receive mode
33FFh	"NRLT_NERR"	no more RLTAB entries left
34FFh	"DIAL_NERR"	function requires an unsupported dialect
35FFh	"IVD_NERR"	invalid device
36FFh	"NALV_NERR"	netname access level violated
37FFh	"NPIDNF_NERR"	network path not found
38FFh	"SP_NERR"	server is paused
39FFh	"TMNM_NERR"	too many remote user names
3AFFh	"DUPD_NERR"	duplicate network device
3BFFh	"DIU_NERR"	shared device in use, can't delete
3CFFh	"NNWD_NERR"	network name was deleted
3DFFh	"NPFS_NERR"	not enough space for print file
3EFFh	"NNNF_NERR"	network name not found (can't find the call name)
3FFFh	"NB_NERR"	network busy
40FFh	"NDNLE_NERR"	network device no longer exists
41FFh	"NBCLE_NERR"	NetBIOS command limit exceeded
42FFh	"FINT24_NERR"	Fail on INT 24h
43FFh	"PEXP_NERR"	password expired
44FFh	"NPUP_NERR"	new password error
45FFh	"MAXS_NERR"	maximum allowed disk space exceeded
46FFh	"TDOW_NERR"	time-of-day/day-of-week error

INT 6Fh Function 01h   *10NET*
LOGOFF

Registers at call:
AH = 01h
DS:DX -> superstation ID or nulls
  (12 bytes)
Conflicts: Novell NetWare PCOX (Chapter 37)
See also: Functions 00h and 81h

Return Registers:
CX = number of files closed
AX = status (see also Table 27-12)
       08FFh superstation ID not already logged in

INT 6Fh Function 02h   *10NET*
STATUS OF NODE

Registers at call:
AH = 02h
DS:DX -> 512-byte status record
  (see Table 27-13)
Conflicts: Novell NetWare PCOX (Chapter 37)
See also: INT 21h Function 5E01h

Return Registers:
CF clear if successful
CF set on error
       AX = error code (see Table 27-12)

27-13 Format of node status record:

Offset	Size	Description
00h	8 BYTEs	ser name (0 if none)
08h	BYTE	station type
		00h workstation
		01h superstation
		02h gateway station
		03h gateway active
		04h logged into multiple superstations
		05h reserved
09h	24 BYTEs	list of superstations logged into more than one superstation
21h	12 BYTEs	node ID
2Dh	WORD	message count for this station (send for user node, receive for superstations)

---for superstations only---

Offset	Size	Description
2Fh	WORD	drives allocated (bit 0=A:, bit 1=B:,...)
31h	BYTE	user service flags (see Table 27-14)
32h	BYTE	printers allocated (bit 0=LPT1,...)
33h	BYTE	number of unprinted spool files
34h	BYTE	number of opened files
35h	BYTE	number of logged on nodes
36h	BYTE	primary drive (1=A:)
37h	BYTE	reserved
38h	N BYTEs	list of logged on node IDs (each 12 bytes, max 37 IDs)
1F4h	3 BYTEs	time: sec/min/hrs
1F7h	3 BYTEs	date: day/mon/year-1980

27-14 Bitfields for user service flags:

bit 7	gate
bit 6	print permit on
bit 4	SUBMIT is on
bit 3	mail waiting for node
bit 2	calendar waiting for you
bit 1	news waiting for you
bit 0	mail waiting for you

INT 6Fh Function 03h
GET ADDRESS OF CONFIGURATION TABLE
10NET

Registers at call:
AH = 03h
DS:DI -> node ID (optional)

Return Registers:
ES:BX -> configuration table

Conflicts: Novell NetWare PCOX (Chapter 37)
See also: Function 13h, INT 21h Function 5E01h

27-15 Format of configuration table:

Offset	Size	Description
-41	WORD	local device table address
-39	WORD	extended network error mapping table address
-37	WORD	shared device table address
-35	WORD	mounted device table address
-33	BYTE	receive buffer counter

-32	BYTE	collect buffer counter
-31	WORD	TUF address
-29	BYTE	enable flag
-28	BYTE	FCB keep flag
-27	WORD	reserved

---up to here, 10NET v3.3---

-25	WORD	count of dropped Send6F
-23	WORD	buffer start address
-21	WORD	comm driver base address
-19	WORD	send/receive retry count
-17	BYTE	number of 550ms loops before timeout
-16	WORD	UFH address
-14	WORD	CDIR address
-12	WORD	LTAB address
-10	WORD	SFH address
-8	WORD	FTAB address
-6	WORD	RLTAB address
-4	WORD	SMI address
-2	WORD	NTAB address
00h	WORD	address of first CT_DRV
02h	BYTE	number of DRV entries
03h	8 BYTEs	login name
0Bh	12 BYTEs	node ID (blank-padded)
17h	6 BYTEs	node address
1Dh	BYTE	flag
1Eh	BYTE	CT_CFLG (chat permit)
		bit 1: sound bell
		bit 0: CHAT permit
1Fh	BYTE	CT_PSFLG
		bit 5: PRINT permit
		bit 4: KB initiated
		bit 3: CHAT called FOXPTRM
		bit 2: SUBMIT active
		bit 1: SUBMIT received
		bit 0: SUBMIT permit
20h	BYTE	in 10Net flag
21h	WORD	receive message count
23h	WORD	send message count
25h	WORD	retry count
27h	WORD	failed count
29h	WORD	driver errors
2Bh	WORD	dropped responses/CHATs
2Dh	9 BYTEs	LIST ID/NTAB address (3 entries—LPT1-3)
36h	6 BYTEs	AUX ID/NTAB address (2 entries—COM1-2)
3Ch	BYTE	active CB channel
3Dh	BYTE	received 6F messages on queue
3Eh	9 BYTEs	activity counters for channels 1-9

INT 6Fh Function 03h

---beyond here, 10NET v3.3---

47h	BYTE	bit 0: RS232 gate
		bit 1: Send6F gate (user set)
48h	DWORD	pointer into gate (user set)
4Ch	DWORD	pointer into 10Net send
50h	N WORDs	addresses of timer blocks

INT 6Fh Function 04h
SEND   *10NET*

Registers at call: **Return Registers:**
AH = 04h   CF clear if successful
DS:BX -> send record (see Table 27-16)   CF set on error
DS:DX -> data (max 1024 bytes)   AX = error code (see Table 27-12)
Conflicts: Novell NetWare PCOX (Chapter 37)
See also: Functions 05h, 09h, and 0Ah

27-16 Format of send record:

Offset	Size	Description
00h	12 BYTEs	receiving node's ID
		if first byte has high-order bit set, message is directed to the CT_RGATE vector at the receiver
		if second byte is 00h, first byte is taken as a CB channel number and delivered to all nodes on same channel
0Ch	WORD	length of data at DS:DX

INT 6Fh Function 05h
RECEIVE   *10NET*

Registers at call: **Return Registers:**
AH = 05h   CF clear if successful
CX = number of seconds before timeout   AH = FEh if dequeued message is a CB message
DS:DX -> receive buffer (see Table 27-17)   CF set on error
                                             AX = error code (see Table 27-12)
Conflicts: Novell NetWare PCOX (Chapter 37)
See also: Function 04h

27-17 Format of receive buffer:

Offset	Size	Description
00h	12 BYTEs	sending node's ID
0Ch	WORD	length of message
0Eh	N BYTEs	message (maximum 1024 bytes)

INT 6Fh Function 07h
LOCK HANDLE   *10NET*

Registers at call: **Return Registers:**
AH = 07h   CF clear if successful
BX = file handle   CF set on error
CX:DX = starting offset in file   AX = error code (see also Table 27-12)
SI = record length   0002h file not found
Conflicts: Novell NetWare PCOX (Chapter 37)
See also: Functions 08h and 0Fh, MS-DOS INT 21h Function 5Ch (Chapter 3)

INT 6Fh Function 08h
UNLOCK HANDLE

Registers at call:
AH = 08h
BX = file handle
AL = mode
    00h unlock all
    01h unlock record at CX:DX

Return Registers:
CF clear if successful
CF set on error
    AX = error code (see also Table 27-12)
        0002h file not found

Conflicts: Novell NetWare PCOX (Chapter 37)
See also: Functions 07h and 0Fh, MS-DOS INT 21h Function 5Ch (Chapter 3)

INT 6Fh Function 09h
SUBMIT

Registers at call:
AH = 09h
DS:BX -> submit record (see Table 27-18)

Return Registers:
none

Conflicts: Novell NetWare PCOX (Chapter 37)
See also: Function 04h

27-18 Format of submit record:

Offset	Size	Description
00h	12 BYTEs	destination node ID (must be logged in)
0Ch	WORD	length+2 of following 'command line' text
0Eh	N BYTEs	command line text (<=100 bytes), system adds CR

INT 6Fh Function 0Ah
CHAT

Registers at call:
AH = 0Ah
DS:BX -> control parameters (see Table 27-19)
DS:DX -> chat message (see Table 27-20)

Return Registers:
none

Conflicts: Novell NetWare PCOX (Chapter 37)
See also: Functions 04h and 8Ah

27-19 Format of control parameters:

Offset	Size	Description
00h	8 BYTEs	sender ID, defaults to node's userID if nulls
08h	8 BYTEs	destination user ID, 'EVERYONE' may be used
10h	12 BYTEs	destination node ID

27-20 Format of chat message:

Offset	Size	Description
00h	WORD	length of chat message including this word
02h	N BYTEs	text, max 101 bytes

INT 6Fh Function 0Bh
LOCK SEMAPHORE, RETURN IMMEDIATELY

Registers at call:
AH = 0Bh
AL = drive number or 0
ES:SI = Ethernet address or 0
DS:BX -> 31-byte ASCIZ semaphore name

Return Registers:
AL = status (see Table 27-21)

Details: This function is the same as INT 60h Function 12h.

Conflicts: Novell NetWare PCOX (Chapter 37)
See also: Function 0Ch, INT 60h Function 12h

27-21 Values for status:

00h	successful
01h	semaphore currently locked
02h	server not responding
03h	invalid semaphore name
04h	semaphore list is full
05h	invalid drive ID
06h	invalid Ethernet address
07h	not logged in
08h	write to network failed
09h	semaphore already logged in this CPU

INT 6Fh Function 0Ch
UNLOCK SEMAPHORE
10NET

Registers at call:
AH = 0Ch
AL = drive number or 0
ES:SI = Ethernet address or 0
DS:BX -> 31-byte ASCIZ semaphore name

Return Registers:
AL = status (see also Table 27-21)
    01h semaphore not locked

Details: This function is the same as INT 60h Function 13h.
Conflicts: Novell NetWare PCOX (Chapter 37)
See also: Function 0Bh, INT 60h Function 13h

INT 6Fh Function 0Dh
"WHO" - ENUMERATE USERS ON NETWORK
10NET

Registers at call:
AH = 0Dh
AL = type code
    01h return superstations only
    02h return non-superstations only
    otherwise return all
CX = length of data buffer
DS:DX -> array of records to be filled (see Table 27-22)

Return Registers:
CL = number of records returned
    (responding stations)

Conflicts: Novell NetWare PCOX (Chapter 37)
See also: Functions 16h and 8Dh

27-22 Format of station record:

Offset	Size	Description
00h	12 BYTEs	node ID
0Ch	BYTE	flags
		bit 1: workstation
		bit 2: superstation
		bit 3: xgate
		bit 4: active gate

---if AL = 01h---

0Dh	BYTE	version number
0Eh	WORD	level number of 10Net software in responding node

---if AL = 02h---

0Dh	8 BYTEs	user ID
15h	BYTE	version number
16h	WORD	level number

INT 6Fh Function 0Eh
SPOOL/PRINT

10NET

Registers at call:
AH = 0Eh
DS:DX -> spool/print record
 (see Table 27-24)

Return Registers:
CF clear if successful
CF set on error
      AX = error code (see also Table 27-12)
          17FFh device not mounted
          18FFh already spooling to named device

Conflicts: Novell NetWare PCOX (Chapter 37)

27-23 Values for operation code:

0000h	initiate spool
0001h	abort print
0002h	close spool
0003h	delete spool
0004h	print
0005h	get report info
0006h	set chat template
0007h	queue
0008h	return queue
0009h	queue non-spooled file for printing

27-24 Format of Spool/Print record:

Offset	Size	Description
00h	WORD	operation code (see Table 27-23)
02h	11 BYTEs	file name in FCB format
---if operation code = 00h or 06h---		
0Dh	BYTE	notification flags (see Table 27-25)
0Eh	BYTE	days to keep (FFh=forever)
0Fh	BYTE	bits 0,1: device (1=LPT1)
		bits 4-7: remote drive to store spool file (1=A,...)
10h	WORD	length of following data area
12h	N BYTEs	up to 64 bytes of description
---if operation code = 03h---		
0Dh	8 BYTEs	user ID to associate with filename
---if operation code = 04h---		
0Dh	WORD	block number
0Fh	8 BYTEs	user ID to associate with filename
---if operation code = 05h---		
0Dh	BYTE	RRN to start retrieve
0Eh	BYTE	bits 0,1: local print device (LPTx)
		bit 3: if set, return entries for all users
0Fh	WORD	length of following area
11h	N BYTEs	up to 1500 bytes to receive $SCNTL records returned

---if operation code = 07h---

0Dh	BYTE	queue number
0Eh	BYTE	bits 0,1: local print device (LPTx)
0Fh	WORD	number of bytes of test print to be done
11h	BYTE	code: 01h print device
		02h test print count
		03h prn

---if operation code = 08h---

0Dh	BYTE	queue location or $SCNTL location to start access
		returns next item for access:
		00h-7Fh queued items
		80h-FEh non-queued, non-printed items
		FFh no more items
0Eh	WORD	unused
10h	WORD	length of following area
12h	N BYTEs	up to 64 bytes to receive $SCNTL records

---if operation code = 09h---

0Dh	3 BYTEs	unused
10h	N BYTEs	path to non-spooled file to be queued for printing

27-25 Bitfields for notification flags:

bit 7	queue to top
bit 6	do ID page
bit 5	no form feed
bit 4	reserved
bit 3	explicit queuing only
bit 2	notify at print completion
bit 1	notify server operator, with reply
bit 0	notify at print start

27-26 Format of $SCNTL record:

Offset	Size	Description
00h	8 BYTEs	user ID
08h	11 BYTEs	filename in FCB format
13h	6 BYTEs	node ID
19h	3 BYTEs	creation date
1Ch	BYTE	notification flags (see Table 27-25)
1Dh	BYTE	retention time in days
1Eh	BYTE	printing device (LPTx)
1Fh	3 BYTEs	date last printed (0 = never)
22h	BYTE	device containing spoolfile
23h	WORD	BYTEs to print for test print
25h	WORD	block number to start print
27h	BYTE	reserved

INT 6Fh Function 0Fh   *10NET v5.0*
"RM LOCK" - FILE/RECORD LOCKING

Registers at call: **Return Registers:**
AH = 0Fh   *unknown*
others, if any, unknown

Conflicts: Novell NetWare PCOX (Chapter 37)
See also: Functions 07h and 08h

INT 6Fh Function 10h   10NET
ATTACH/DETACH PRINTER

Registers at call: **Return Registers:**
AH = 10h   none
AL = subfunction
      00h initiate spooling if LPT1 is mounted
      01h terminate spooling if LPT1 is mounted
Conflicts: Novell NetWare PCOX (Chapter 37)
See also: INT 21h Function 5D08h

INT 6Fh Function 11h   10NET
LOCK FCB

Registers at call: **Return Registers:**
AH = 11h   CF clear if successful
AL = mode   CF set on error
      01h sequential   AX = error code (see also Table 27-12)
      02h random   0002h file not found
      03h random block
            CX = number of records
DS:DX -> FCB (see Table 3-63)
Conflicts: Novell NetWare PCOX (Chapter 37)
See also: Function 12h

INT 6Fh Function 12h   10NET
UNLOCK FCB

Registers at call: **Return Registers:**
AH = 12h   CF clear if successful
AL = mode   CF set on error
      00h sequential   AX = error code (see also Table 27-12)
      01h random   0002h file not found
      02h random block
            CX = number of records
DS:DX -> FCB (see Table 3-63)
Conflicts: Novell NetWare PCOX (Chapter 37)
See also: Function 11h

INT 6Fh Function 13h   10NET v3.3+
GET REMOTE CONFIGURATION TABLE ADDRESS

Registers at call: **Return Registers:**
AH = 13h   CF clear if successful
DS:DX -> node ID, 12 bytes blank-padded   ES:BX = configuration table address on
                       given machine
                  CF set on error
                    AX = error code (see Table 27-12)

Conflicts: Novell NetWare PCOX (Chapter 37)
See also: Function 03h

INT 6Fh Function 14h
GET REMOTE MEMORY

Registers at call:
AH = 14h
BX:SI = address of remote memory
CX = length (max 1024 bytes)
DS:DX -> node ID, 12 bytes
  blank-padded
DS:DI -> area to receive remote
  memory image

Return Registers:
CF clear if successful
      CX = amount of memory copied to DS:SI
CF set on error
      AX = error code (see Table 27-12)

INT 6Fh Function 1501h
GET SHARED DEVICE ENTRY

Registers at call:
AX = 1501h
BX = zero-based index
DS:SI -> node ID, 12 bytes
  blank-padded
ES:DI -> 85-byte buffer for shared
  device table entry (see Table 27-27)
Conflicts: Novell NetWare PCOX (Chapter 37)
See also: Functions 1502h, 1503h, and 9501h

Return Registers:
CF clear if successful
      ES:DI buffer contains shared device table
          entry of BXth device
CF set on error
      AX = error code (see Table 27-12)

27-27 Format of shared device table entry:

Offset	Size	Description
00h	8 BYTEs	device
08h	8 BYTEs	alias
10h	64 BYTEs	path
50h	8 BYTEs	password
58h	BYTE	access
59h	4 BYTEs	mask

INT 6Fh Function 1502h
SET SHARED DEVICE ENTRY

Registers at call:
AX = 1502h
DS:SI -> node ID, 12 bytes blank-padded
ES:DI -> valid shared device table entry
Conflicts: Novell NetWare PCOX (Chapter 37)
See also: Functions 1501h, 1503h, and 9502h

Return Registers:
CF clear if successful
CF set on error
      AX = error code (see Table 27-12)

INT 6Fh Function 1503h
DELETE SHARED DEVICE ENTRY

Registers at call:
AX = 1503h
BX = zero-based index
DS:SI -> node ID, 12 bytes blank-padded
Conflicts: Novell NetWare PCOX (Chapter 37)
See also: Functions 1501h, 1502h, and 9503h

Return Registers:
CF clear if successful
CF set on error
      AX = error code (see Table 27-12)

INT 6Fh Function 16h
"GL WHO" - GET USERS

Registers at call: **Return Registers:**
AH = 16h   *unknown*
others, if any, unknown
Conflicts: Novell NetWare PCOX (Chapter 37)
See also: Function 0Dh

INT 6Fh Function 17h
MOUNT

Registers at call: **Return Registers:**
AH = 17h   CF clear if successful
AL = local drive number (0=A:)   CF set on error
BL = remote drive letter or '1'..'3' for   AX = error code (see Table 27-12)
  LPTn or '4' or '5' for COMx
DS:DX -> node ID, 12 bytes
  blank-padded
Conflicts: Novell NetWare PCOX (Chapter 37)
See also: Function 18h

INT 6Fh Function 18h
UNMOUNT

Registers at call: **Return Registers:**
AH = 18h   CF clear if successful
AL = local drive number (0=A:)   CF set on error
BL = type   AX = error code (see Table 27-12)
  00h disk
  01h-03h LPTn
  04h,05h COMx
Conflicts: Novell NetWare PCOX (Chapter 37)
See also: Function 17h

INT 6Fh Function 19h
AUDIT

Registers at call: **Return Registers:**
AH = 19h   *unknown*
others, if any, unknown
Conflicts: Novell NetWare PCOX (Chapter 37)
See also: Function 99h

INT 6Fh Function 1Ah
"BULL" - UNDETERMINED FUNCTION

Registers at call: **Return Registers:**
AH = 1Ah   *unknown*
others, if any, unknown
Conflicts: Novell NetWare PCOX (Chapter 37)

INT 6Fh Function 1Bh
"GMOUNT" - UNDETERMINED FUNCTION

Registers at call: **Return Registers:**
AH = 1Bh   *unknown*
others, if any, unknown
Conflicts: Novell NetWare PCOX (Chapter 37)

INT 6Fh Function 1Ch
"GLOGIN" - GET LOGIN LIST

10NET v5.0
Undocumented

Registers at call: Return Registers:
AH = 1Ch   *unknown*
others, if any, unknown
Conflicts: Novell NetWare PCOX (Chapter 37)

INT 6Fh Function 1Dh
"TABDATA" - UNDETERMINED FUNCTION

10NET v5.0
Undocumented

Registers at call: Return Registers:
AH = 1Dh   *unknown*
others, if any, unknown
Conflicts: Novell NetWare PCOX (Chapter 37)

INT 6Fh Function 1Eh
"SCHED" - UNDETERMINED FUNCTION

10NET v5.0
Undocumented

Registers at call: Return Registers:
AH = 1Eh   *unknown*
others, if any, unknown
Conflicts: Novell NetWare PCOX (Chapter 37)

INT 6Fh Function 1Fh
"WHOAMI" - GET USER INFORMATION

10NET v5.0
Undocumented

Registers at call: Return Registers:
AH = 1Fh   *unknown*
others, if any, unknown
Conflicts: Novell NetWare PCOX (Chapter 37)

INT 6Fh Function 20h
UNDETERMINED FUNCTION

10NET v5.0
Undocumented

Registers at call: Return Registers:
AH = 20h   *unknown*
others, if any, unknown
Conflicts: Novell NetWare PCOX (Chapter 37)

INT 6Fh Function 21h
UNDETERMINED FUNCTION

10NET v5.0
Undocumented

Registers at call: Return Registers:
AH = 21h   *unknown*
others, if any, unknown
Conflicts: Novell NetWare PCOX (Chapter 37)

INT 6Fh Function 22h
UNDETERMINED FUNCTION

10NET v5.0
Undocumented

Registers at call: Return Registers:
AH = 22h   *unknown*
others, if any, unknown
Conflicts: Novell NetWare PCOX (Chapter 37), HP HIL Vectras (PCI-7)

INT 6Fh Function 80h
LOGIN

10NET v5.0

Registers at call:
AH = 80h

DS:DX -> login record
  (see Table 27-28)

Return Registers:
CF clear if successful
    BL = number of days until password expires
      (00h = never)
    CL = security level
CF set on error
    AX = status (see Table 27-12)

See also: Functions 00h and 81h

27-28 Format of login record:

Offset	Size	Description
00h	8 BYTEs	user name
08h	8 BYTEs	password
10h	15 BYTEs	server node ID
1Fh	8 BYTEs	new password
27h	BYTE	invoke mode (00h command line, 01h interactive)

INT 6Fh Function 81h
LOGOUT
10NET v5.0

Registers at call:
AH = 81h
DS:DX -> server node ID
  (DX=0000h for universal logout)

Return Registers:
AX = status (see Table 27-12)

See also: Functions 01h and 80h

INT 6Fh Function 8Ah
CHAT
10NET v5.0

Registers at call:
AH = 8Ah
DS:BX -> chat parameters (see Table 27-29)
DS:DX -> chat message (see Table 27-20)
See also: Function 0Ah

Return Registers:
CF clear if successful
CF set on error
    AX = status (see Table 27-12)

27-29 Format of chat parameters:

Offset	Size	Description
00h	8 BYTEs	sender's user name
08h	8 BYTEs	destination user name
10h	15 BYTEs	destination node (0 if broadcast-style chat)

INT 6Fh Function 8Dh
"WHO" - ENUMERATE USERS ON NETWORK
10NET v5.0

Registers at call:
AH = 8Dh
BX = services mask (see Table 27-3)
CX = length of buffer
DS:DX -> buffer for array of Who data
  structures (see Table 27-30)
See also: Function 0Dh

Return Registers:
CF clear if successful
    CX = number of nodes matching service mask
    DS:DX buffer filled
CF set on error
    AX = status (see Table 27-12)

27-30 Format of Who data structure:

Offset	Size	Description
00h	8 BYTEs	user name
08h	15 BYTEs	node ID
17h	3 BYTEs	unique portion of Ethernet address

1Ah	BYTE	Who group number
1Bh	WORD	services mask (see Table 27-3)
1Dh	DWORD	serial number
21h	BYTE	maximum concurrent users with same serial number allowed on net
22h	BYTE	chat mask (see Table 27-4)
23h	BYTE	internal system bits (see Table 27-5)
24h	9 BYTEs	version number in format MM.mm.xxx
2Dh	BYTE	number of shared directories
2Eh	BYTE	number of shared printer queues

Note: The first 2Dh bytes of the Who structure correspond exactly to the beginning of the 10Net Configuration Table (see Table 27-1).

INT 6Fh Function 9501h   *10NET v5.0*
GET SHARED DEVICE ENTRY

Registers at call: **Return Registers:**
AX = 9501h   CF clear if successful
BX = zero-based index   CF set on error
DS:SI -> server's node ID   AX = status (see Table 27-12)
ES:DI -> buffer for shared device
   structure (see Table 27-31)

See also: Functions 1501h, 9502h, 9503h, and 9504h

27-31 Format of shared device structure:

Offset	Size	Description
00h	8 BYTEs	alias
08h	BYTE	type (02h modem, 03h print queue, 04h directory)
09h	BYTE	access rights
		bit 0: read
		bit 1: write
		bit 2: create
0Ah	8 BYTEs	password
12h	32 BYTEs	comment

---directory---

32h	64 BYTEs	pathname of shared directory

---print queue---

32h	BYTE	notification bit mask (see Table 27-9)
33h	BYTE	job control bit mask (see Table 27-10)
34h	WORD	number of days to retain file
36h	WORD	test print length
38h	BYTE	number of copies to print
39h	BYTE	compression algorithm
3Ah	BYTE	tab width (00h = don't expand)
3Bh	BYTE	priority
3Ch	WORD	time to open queue (FFFFh = always)
3Eh	WORD	time to close queue
40h	WORD	pause following queue switch, in clock ticks
42h	WORD	pause between print jobs, in clock ticks
44h	BYTE	associate queue file existence mask
		bit 0: queue switch file exists
		bit 1: initiate file exists
		bit 2: abort file exists

45h	6 BYTEs	character sequence for page eject
4Bh	BYTE	status of print queue
		bit 0: queue is closed
4Ch	WORD	number of jobs on queue
4Eh	WORD	offset of next print job to be dispatched (FFFFh = none)
50h	BYTE	number of print devices in printer pool
51h	WORD	offset of first print device structure (FFFFh if empty)

INT 6Fh Function 9502h   *10NET v5.0*
SET SHARED DEVICE ENTRY

Registers at call: **Return Registers:**
AX = 9502h   CF clear if successful
DS:SI -> server's node ID   CF set on error
ES:DI -> shared device structure   AX = status (see Table 27-12)
  (see Table 27-31)
See also: Functions 1502h, 9501h, 9503h, and 9504h

INT 6Fh Function 9503h   *10NET v5.0*
DELETE SHARED DEVICE

Registers at call: **Return Registers:**
AX = 9503h   CF clear if successful
BX = zero-based index   CF set on error
DS:SI -> server's node ID   AX = status (see Table 27-12)
See also: Functions 1503h, 9501h, 9502h, and 9504h

INT 6Fh Function 9504h   *10NET v5.0*
ENUMERATE USERS OF SHARED DEVICE

Registers at call: **Return Registers:**
AX = 9504h   CF clear if successful
BX = zero-based shared device index   ES:DI -> node ID of the CX'th user of the
CX = zero-based user index   BX'th device
DS:SI -> server's node ID   CF set on error
                                          AX = status (see Table 27-12)

See also: Functions 9501h, 9502h, and 9503h

INT 6Fh Function 99h   *10NET v5.0*
AUDIT

Registers at call: **Return Registers:**
AH = 99h   CF clear if successful
DS:SI -> server's node ID   CF set on error
ES:DI -> data to be appended to   AX = status (see Table 27-12)
  audit trail file (max 106 bytes)
See also: Functions 19h and 9Ch

INT 6Fh Function 9Ch   *10NET v5.0*
GET LOGIN LIST

Registers at call: **Return Registers:**
AH = 9Ch   CF clear if successful
BX = zero-based index   DS:DI -> BX'th node ID that caller's machine
                                              is logged into
                                      CF set on error
                                          AX = status (see Table 27-12)

10NET Utilities

INT 21h Function 4402h   *10NET v5.0*
10BEUI.DOS - API

Registers at call: **Return Registers:**
AX = 4402h   CF clear if successful
BX = file handle referencing   AX destroyed
  device "10BEUI$"   CF set on error
DS:DX -> parameter record   AX = error code (01h,05h,06h,0Dh) (see Table 3-1)
  (see Table 27-32)
CX ignored
See also: 10MEMMGR Function 4402h, INT 6Fh Function 00h

27-32 Format of parameter record:

Offset	Size	Description
00h	WORD	000Ah (*function number*)
02h	WORD	*unknown*
04h	DWORD	pointer to buffer for *unknown item*
08h	4 BYTEs	*unknown*
0Ch	WORD	transfer size

INT 21h Function 4402h   *10NET v5.0*
10MEMMGR.SYS - API

Registers at call: **Return Registers:**
AX = 4402h   CF clear if successful
BX = file handle referencing device   AX destroyed
  "MEMMGR0$"   CF set on error
DS:DX -> 6-byte buffer for interface   AX = error code (01h,05h,06h,0Dh) (see Table 3-1)
  info (see Table 27-33)
CX ignored
See also: 10BEUI Function 4402h, INT 6Fh Function 00h

27-33 Format of interface info:

Offset	Size	Description
00h	DWORD	address of entry point (see Table 27-34)
04h	WORD	version (0500h for v5.00)

27-34 10MEMMGR entry point calling convention:

Registers at call: **Return Registers:**
AL = 01h *unknown*   CF clear if successful
BX = *unknown*   CF set on error
                                            AX = error code

Registers at call:
AL = 02h and 03h *unknown*
others, if any, unknown
Registers at call: **Return Registers:**
AL = 04h set/restore memory   CF clear if successful
  allocation strategy   CF set on error (if function disabled)
BX = subfunction   various registers destroyed
    0000h set strategy
    0001h restore strategy

Registers at call:
AL = other than above

Return Registers:
CF set
AX = 0000h
BL = 01h

INT 69h Function 4001h   *10NET v5.0*
SYSSVC.COM - UNDETERMINED FUNCTION

Registers at call:
AX = 4001h

Return Registers:
CF clear
AX = 0000h
ES:SI -> *unknown*

Conflicts: Zenith AT BIOS (PCI-7)
Details: INT 69h is the default, and may be set to any interrupt from 60h-7Fh; the signature "SYSV" immediately before the interrupt handler serves as the installation check.
See also: Function 4002h

INT 69h Function 4002h   *10NET v5.0*
SYSSVC.COM - UNDETERMINED FUNCTION

Registers at call:
AX = 4002h
others, if any, unknown
Conflicts: Zenith AT BIOS (PCI-7)

Return Registers:
unknown

INT 69h Function 4101h   *10NET v5.0*
SYSSVC.COM - UNDETERMINED FUNCTION

Registers at call:
AX = 4101h

Return Registers:
CF clear
ES:SI -> *unknown*

Conflicts: Zenith AT BIOS (PCI-7)
See also: Functions 4102h, 4103h, and 4104h

INT 69h Functions 4102h to 4104h   *10NET v5.0*
SYSSVC.COM - UNKNOWN FUNCTIONS

Registers at call:
AX = 4102h to 4104h
others, if any, unknown
Conflicts: Zenith AT BIOS (PCI-7)

Return Registers:
unknown

INT 69h Function 42h   *10NET v5.0*
SYSSVC.COM - UNDETERMINED FUNCTION

Registers at call:
AH = 42h
AL = subfunction (01h-14h)
others, if any, unknown
Conflicts: Zenith AT BIOS (PCI-7)

Return Registers:
unknown

INT 69h Function 43h   *10NET v5.0*
SYSSVC.COM - UNDETERMINED FUNCTION

Registers at call:
AH = 43h
AL = subfunction (01h-05h)
others, if any, unknown
Conflicts: Zenith AT BIOS (PCI-7)

Return Registers:
unknown

INT 69h Function 44h   *10NET v5.0*
SYSSVC.COM - UNDETERMINED FUNCTION

Registers at call: **Return Registers:**
AH = 44h   *unknown*
AL = subfunction (01h-03h)
others, if any, unknown
Conflicts: Zenith AT BIOS (PCI-7)

INT 69h Function 49h   *10NET v5.0*
SYSSVC.COM - BUG

Registers at call: **Return Registers:**
AH = 49h   none
Details: Due to a fencepost error, this function branches to a random location.
Conflicts: Zenith AT BIOS (PCI-7)
See also: Functions 4001h and FFh

INT 69h Function FFh   *10NET v5.0*
SYSSVC.COM - SIGNAL SYSTEM ERROR

Registers at call: **Return Registers:**
AH = FFh   *never returns*
Details: This function displays a "System Error" message and a register dump, then halts the system.
Conflicts: Zenith AT BIOS (PCI-7)
See also: Functions 4001h and 49h

CHAPTER 28

TopWare Network Operating System

TopWare Network Operating System is manufactured by Grand Computer Company.

INT 21h Function FF00h
GET SYSTEM INFORMATION

Registers at call:
AX = FF00h
CL = what to get
    00h user information
    01h drive mapping
    02h printer server(s)
    05h local DOS drive number

Return Registers:
ES:BX -> desired information
    (see Tables 28-1 and 28-2)

Details: This call is only supported on workstations, not on the server.
Conflicts: CED and DOSED (PCI-13), DOS OEM function (PCI-24), DOS/4GW (PCI-35), GO32 (PCI-37), Viruses (PCI-59)
See also: Function FF04h, INT 2Fh Function FF00h

28-1 Format of user information:

Offset	Size	Description
00h	BYTE	node ID
01h	15 BYTEs	user name
10h	WORD	user number
12h	BYTE	group number

28-2 Format of drive mapping [array]:

Offset	Size	Description
00h	BYTE	bits 6-0: drive number (1=A:, etc.)
		bit 7: this is a server drive
01h	3 BYTEs	mapping drive (for example, "C:\")
04h	64 BYTEs	current directory

INT 21h Function FF04h
GET/SET DEFAULT FILE PROTECTION ATTRIBUTES

Registers at call:
AX = FF04h
CL = function
    00h get protections

01h set protections
    BH = read attribute
    BL = write attribute

Return Registers:

BH = read attribute
BL = write attribute

Details: This function is supported only on workstations, not on the server.
Conflicts: CED and DOSED (PCI-13), DOS OEM function (PCI-24), DOS/4GW (PCI-35), GO32 (PCI-37), Viruses (PCI-59)
See also: Function FF00h

INT 21h Function FF80h, Subfunction FFh
SEND MESSAGE
TopWare Network OS v5.10+

Registers at call:
AX = FF80h
DH = FFh
DL = destination address (FFh for broadcast)
CX = message length (max 2000)
DS:SI -> message to be sent (see Table 28-3)

Return Registers:
none

Details: This function is supported on both workstations and the server.
    There is no guarantee that the message will be received correctly, or at all, by the destination.
Conflicts: CED and DOSED (PCI-13), DOS OEM function (PCI-24), DOS/4GW (PCI-35), GO32 (PCI-37), Viruses (PCI-59)

28-3 Format of message:

Offset	Size	Description
00h	BYTE	type code
		07h TopSend
		11h user application
		other reserved for TopWare
01h	var	data

Note: Sending messages with a type code other than 11h will cause unpredictable results.

INT 21h Function FF82h
GET STATION ADDRESS
TopWare Network OS v5.10+

Registers at call:
AX = FF82h

Return Registers:
AL = station address

Details: This function is supported on both workstations and the server.
Conflicts: CED and DOSED (PCI-13), DOS OEM function (PCI-24), DOS/4GW (PCI-35), GO32 (PCI-37), Viruses (PCI-59)
See also: Function FF91h

INT 21h Function FF8Ch
GET STATUS OF TopShow/Emulated FUNCTION
TopWare Network OS v5.10+

Registers at call:
AX = FF8Ch
BL = subfunction
    00h get TopShow status
    FFh get Emulated status

Return Registers:
AL = status
    00h not installed
    01h already installed

Conflicts: CED and DOSED (PCI-13), DOS OEM function (PCI-24), DOS/4GW (PCI-35), GO32 (PCI-37), Viruses (PCI-59)

INT 21h Function FF8Dh
CALL TopShow FUNCTION

Registers at call:
AX = FF8Dh
CH = monochrome flag
  (01h monochrome, 00h not monochrome)
CL = screen mode of station to be viewed
  (see Table 28-4)
BL = graphic page number for monochrome

Return Registers:
AL = status (00h successful, else failed)

Conflicts: CED and DOSED (PCI-13), DOS OEM function (PCI-24), DOS/4GW (PCI-35), GO32 (PCI-37), Viruses (PCI-59)
See also: Functions FF8Eh and FFCFh

28-4 Values for screen mode:

00h	text mode
01h	720x348
02h	640x408
03h	720x352
04h	640x390
05h	reserved

INT 21h Function FF8Eh
CANCEL TopShow FUNCTION

Registers at call:
AX = FF8Eh

Return Registers:
AL = 00h (successful, TopShow removed)

Conflicts: CED and DOSED (PCI-13), DOS OEM function (PCI-24), DOS/4GW (PCI-35), GO32 (PCI-37), Viruses (PCI-59)
See also: Function FF8Dh

INT 21h Function FF91h
GET FILE SERVER STATION NUMBER

Registers at call:
AX = FF91h

Return Registers:
AL = station number of file server

Conflicts: CED and DOSED (PCI-13), DOS OEM function (PCI-24), DOS/4GW (PCI-35), GO32 (PCI-37), Viruses (PCI-59)
See also: Function FF82h

INT 21h Function FF97h
GET MAXIMUM STATION NUMBER

Registers at call:
AX = FF97h

Return Registers:
AL = maximum station number

Conflicts: CED and DOSED (PCI-13), DOS OEM function (PCI-24), DOS/4GW (PCI-35), GO32 (PCI-37), Viruses (PCI-59)
See also: Function FF98h

INT 21h Function FF98h
GET MAXIMUM FILE NUMBER

Registers at call:
AX = FF98h

Return Registers:
AL = maximum file

Conflicts: CED and DOSED (PCI-13), DOS OEM function (PCI-24), DOS/4GW (PCI-35), GO32 (PCI-37), Viruses (PCI-59)
See also: Function FF97h

INT 21h Function FF9Ah
RECEIVE USER-DEFINED PACKETS
TopWare Network OS v5.10+

Registers at call:
AX = FF9Ah
ES:BX -> buffer for user-defined
packet (see Table 28-5)

Return Registers:
none

Conflicts: CED and DOSED (PCI-13), DOS OEM function (PCI-24), DOS/4GW (PCI-35), GO32 (PCI-37), Viruses (PCI-59)

28-5 Format of user-defined packet:

Offset	Size	Description
00h	BYTE	FFh
01h	WORD	(call) length of data field plus 3
		(return) length of received message (0000h if none received)
03h	BYTE	destination ID (FFh for broadcast message)
04h	BYTE	sending station ID
05h	BYTE	type code (11h; all other codes reserved for TopWare)
06h	N BYTEs	received message

INT 21h Function FF9Fh
ENABLE/DISABLE TopTerm SERVICE
TopWare Network OS v5.10+

Registers at call:
AX = FF9Fh
CL = new state (00h disable [disregard
TopTerm packets], 01h enable)

Return Registers:
AL = status (00h successful, FFh failed)

Details: This function is only supported by Workstations, not the server.
Conflicts: CED and DOSED (PCI-13), DOS OEM function (PCI-24), DOS/4GW (PCI-35), GO32 (PCI-37), Viruses (PCI-59)

INT 21h Function FFB0h
GET SPOOLER PRINTING PRIORITY
TopWare Network OS v5.10+

Registers at call:
AX = FFB0h

Return Registers:
AL = priority status (see Table 28-6)

Conflicts: CED and DOSED (PCI-13), DOS OEM function (PCI-24), DOS/4GW (PCI-35), GO32 (PCI-37), Viruses (PCI-59)
See also: Function FFB1h

28-6 Bitfields for printer priority status:

bit 0	LPT1 has high priority
bit 1	LPT2 has high priority
bit 2	LPT3 has high priority

INT 21h Function FFB1h
SET SPOOLER PRINTING PRIORITY
TopWare Network OS v5.10+

Registers at call:
AX = FFB1h
CH = printer number (00h LPT1, 01h
LPT2, 02h LPT3)
CH = new priority (00h normal, 01h high)

Return Registers:
none

Conflicts: CED and DOSED (PCI-13), DOS OEM function (PCI-24), DOS/4GW (PCI-35), GO32 (PCI-37), Viruses (PCI-59)
See also: Function FFB0h

INT 21h Function FFB3h
TopWare Network OS v5.10+
GET DEFAULT START-OF-JOB FORMFEED STATUS

Registers at call:
AX = FFB3h

Return Registers:
AL = starting formfeed status (see Table 28-7)

Conflicts: CED and DOSED (PCI-13), DOS OEM function (PCI-24), DOS/4GW (PCI-35), GO32 (PCI-37), Viruses (PCI-59)
See also: Functions FFB4h and FFC0h

28-7 Bitfields for printer start-of-job formfeed status:

bit 0	LPT1 has formfeed enabled
bit 1	LPT2 has formfeed enabled
bit 2	LPT3 has formfeed enabled

INT 21h Function FFB4h
TopWare Network OS v5.10+
SET DEFAULT START-OF-JOB FORMFEED STATUS

Registers at call:
AX = FFB4h
CH = printer number (00h LPT1, 01h LPT2, 02h LPT3)
CH = new formfeed status (00h off, 01h on)

Return Registers:
none

Conflicts: CED and DOSED (PCI-13), DOS OEM function (PCI-24), DOS/4GW (PCI-35), GO32 (PCI-37), Viruses (PCI-59)
See also: Functions FFB3h and FFC1h

INT 21h Function FFBBh
TopWare Network OS v5.10+
GET PRINTER SERVER STATION ADDRESS

Registers at call:
AX = FFBBh
CH = printer number (00h LPT1, 01h LPT2, 02h LPT3)

Return Registers:
AL = current mapping printer server station number or 00h if local

Conflicts: CED and DOSED (PCI-13), DOS OEM function (PCI-24), DOS/4GW (PCI-35), GO32 (PCI-37), Viruses (PCI-59)
See also: Function FFBCh

INT 21h Function FFBCh
TopWare Network OS v5.10+
CANCEL TopShow FUNCTION

Registers at call:
AX = FFBCh
CH = printer number (00h LPT1, 01h LPT2, 02h LPT3)
CL = printer server station address or 00h for local printer

Return Registers:
AL = status (00h successful, else failed)

Conflicts: CED and DOSED (PCI-13), DOS OEM function (PCI-24), DOS/4GW (PCI-35), GO32 (PCI-37), Viruses (PCI-59)
See also: Function FFBBh

INT 21h Function FFBDh
TopWare Network OS v5.10+
GET CURRENT AUTOPRINT TIME

Registers at call:
AX = FFBDh
CH = printer number (00h LPT1, 01h LPT2, 02h LPT3)

Return Registers:
AX = current AutoPrint timeout in clock ticks

Conflicts: CED and DOSED (PCI-13), DOS OEM function (PCI-24), DOS/4GW (PCI-35), GO32 (PCI-37), Viruses (PCI-59)
See also: Function FFBEh

INT 21h Function FFBEh
SET AUTOPRINT TIME
TopWare Network OS v5.10+

Registers at call:
AX = FFBEh
CH = printer number (00h LPT1,
  01h LPT2, 02h LPT3)
BX = timeout in clock ticks

Return Registers:
none

Conflicts: CED and DOSED (PCI-13), DOS OEM function (PCI-24), DOS/4GW (PCI-35), GO32 (PCI-37), Viruses (PCI-59)
See also: Function FFBDh

INT 21h Function FFBFh
GET LOGON USER INFORMATION
TopWare Network OS v5.10+

Registers at call:
AX = FFBFh
DX:BX -> buffer for logon
  information (see Table 28-8)

Return Registers:
AL = status (00h successful, else failed)
AH = number of logged-in stations

Conflicts: CED and DOSED (PCI-13), DOS OEM function (PCI-24), DOS/4GW (PCI-35), GO32 (PCI-37), Viruses (PCI-59)

28-8 Format of logon information:

Offset	Size	Description
00h	BYTE	station address
01h	15 BYTEs	username

INT 21h Function FFC0h
GET DEFAULT END-OF-JOB FORMFEED STATUS
TopWare Network OS v5.10+

Registers at call:
AX = FFC0h

Return Registers:
AL = ending formfeed status (see Table 28-9)

Conflicts: CED and DOSED (PCI-13), DOS OEM function (PCI-24), DOS/4GW (PCI-35), GO32 (PCI-37), Viruses (PCI-59)
See also: Functions FFB3h and FFC1h

28-9 Bitfields for printer end-of-job formfeed status:

bit 0	LPT1 has formfeed enabled
bit 1	LPT2 has formfeed enabled
bit 2	LPT3 has formfeed enabled

INT 21h Function FFC1h
SET DEFAULT END-OF-JOB FORMFEED STATUS
TopWare Network OS v5.10+

Registers at call:
AX = FFC1h
CH = printer number (00h LPT1,
  01h LPT2, 02h LPT3)
CH = new formfeed status
  (00h off, 01h on)

Return Registers:
none

Conflicts: CED and DOSED (PCI-13), DOS OEM function (PCI-24), DOS/4GW (PCI-35), GO32 (PCI-37), Viruses (PCI-59)
See also: Functions FFB4h and FFC0h

INT 21h Function FFC2h
GET DEFAULT COPIES OF SPOOLING FILE

Registers at call:
AX = FFC2h
CH = printer number (00h LPT1,
   01h LPT2, 02h LPT3)

Return Registers:
AL = default number of copies printed

Conflicts: CED and DOSED (PCI-13), DOS OEM function (PCI-24), DOS/4GW (PCI-35), GO32 (PCI-37), Viruses (PCI-59)
See also: Function FFC7h

INT 21h Function FFC3h
GET SHARING STATUS OF PRINTER SERVER

Registers at call:
AX = FFC3h

Return Registers:
AL = sharing status of printers (see Table 28-10)
   FFh if not a printer server

Conflicts: CED and DOSED (PCI-13), DOS OEM function (PCI-24), DOS/4GW (PCI-35), GO32 (PCI-37), Viruses (PCI-59)

28-10 Bitfields for printer sharing status:
bit 0	LPT1 is shared
bit 1	LPT2 is shared
bit 2	LPT3 is shared

INT 21h Function FFC4h
GET/SET LPT PORT ON PRINT SERVER

Registers at call:
AX = FFC4h
CH = local printer (00h LPT1 ... 02h LPT3)
BL = subfunction
   00h get

Return Registers:

AL = mapped printer port on print server

   01h set
      CL = network printer port (00h LPT1, 01h LPT2, 02h LPT3)
Conflicts: CED and DOSED (PCI-13), DOS OEM function (PCI-24), DOS/4GW (PCI-35), GO32 (PCI-37), Viruses (PCI-59)

INT 21h Function FFC6h
SET DEFAULT PRINT FILE HEADER

Registers at call:
AX = FFC6h
CH = printer number (00h LPT1,
   01h LPT2, 02h LPT3)
CL = header state (00h off, 01h on)

Return Registers:
none

Conflicts: CED and DOSED (PCI-13), DOS OEM function (PCI-24), DOS/4GW (PCI-35), GO32 (PCI-37), Viruses (PCI-59)
See also: Function FFC8h

INT 21h Function FFC7h
SET DEFAULT PRINT COPIES

Registers at call:
AX = FFC7h
CH = printer number (00h LPT1, 01h LPT2, 02h LPT3)
CL = new default number of copies to print

Return Registers:

Conflicts: CED and DOSED (PCI-13), DOS OEM function (PCI-24), DOS/4GW (PCI-35), GO32 (PCI-37), Viruses (PCI-59)
See also: Function FFC2h

INT 21h Function FFC8h *TopWare Network OS v5.10+*
GET DEFAULT PRINT FILE HEADER STATUS

Registers at call: Return Registers:
AX = FFC8h   AL = header status for printers (see Table 28-11)
Conflicts: CED and DOSED (PCI-13), DOS OEM function (PCI-24), DOS/4GW (PCI-35), GO32 (PCI-37), Viruses (PCI-59)
See also: Function FFC6h

28-11 Bitfields for print header status:
bit 0   LPT1 has headers enabled
bit 1   LPT2 has headers enabled
bit 2   LPT3 has headers enabled

INT 21h Function FFC9h *TopWare Network OS v5.10+*
SET PRINTER SHARING

Registers at call: Return Registers:
AX = FFC9h   AL = status (00h successful, FFh not printer server)
CH = printer number (00h LPT1,
   01h LPT2, 02h LPT3)
CL = new sharing state (00h off, 01h on)
Conflicts: CED and DOSED (PCI-13), DOS OEM function (PCI-24), DOS/4GW (PCI-35), GO32 (PCI-37), Viruses (PCI-59)

INT 21h Function FFCAh *TopWare Network OS v5.10+*
MOVE FILE FROM ONE PRINT SERVER TO ANOTHER

Registers at call: Return Registers:
AX = FFCAh   AL = status (00h successful, else failed)
CH = printer number (00h LPT1,
   01h LPT2, 02h LPT3)
CL = original printer server station address
BL = target printer server station address
DS:DX -> filename (12 bytes)
Conflicts: CED and DOSED (PCI-13), DOS OEM function (PCI-24), DOS/4GW (PCI-35), GO32 (PCI-37), Viruses (PCI-59)
See also: Function FFCBh

INT 21h Function FFCBh *TopWare Network OS v5.10+*
DELETE FILE FROM SPOOLING QUEUE

Registers at call: Return Registers:
AX = FFCBh   AL = status (00h successful, else failed)
CH = printer number (00h LPT1,
   01h LPT2, 02h LPT3)
CL = printer server station address
DS:DX -> filename (12 bytes)
Conflicts: CED and DOSED (PCI-13), DOS OEM function (PCI-24), DOS/4GW (PCI-35), GO32 (PCI-37), Viruses (PCI-59)
See also: Function FFCAh

INT 21h Function FFCCh
GET PRINT SERVER'S SPOOLING QUEUE STATUS
TopWare Network OS v5.10+

Registers at call:
AX = FFCCh
CL = printer server station address
BH = start item number of spooling
   file for print server
BL = number of the item to be retrieved
DS:DX -> buffer for queued file information
   (see Table 28-12)

Return Registers:
AL = status
   00h successful
      AH = number of spool files
      DS:DX buffer filled
   nonzero failed

Conflicts: CED and DOSED (PCI-13), DOS OEM function (PCI-24), DOS/4GW (PCI-35), GO32 (PCI-37), Viruses (PCI-59)

28-12 Format of queued file information buffer [16-item array, one element]:

Offset	Size	Description
00h	12 BYTEs	filename
0Ch	DWORD	size
10h	WORD	date
12h	WORD	time
14h	15 BYTEs	username
23h	BYTE	count
24h	BYTE	flag: header
25h	BYTE	print number

INT 21h Function FFCDh
GET STATUS OF ALL PRINT SERVERS
TopWare Network OS v5.10+

Registers at call:
AX = FFCDh
DS:DX -> buffer for server status
   (see Table 28-13)

Return Registers:
AL = status
   00h successful
      AH = number of print servers
   nonzero failed

Conflicts: CED and DOSED (PCI-13), DOS OEM function (PCI-24), DOS/4GW (PCI-35), GO32 (PCI-37), Viruses (PCI-59)

28-13 Format of server status:

Offset	Size	Description
00h	BYTE	station address
01h	15 BYTEs	username
10h	BYTE	flag: 01h printer is shared, 00h sharing disabled
11h	BYTE	number of files pending in queue

INT 21h Function FFCFh
CALL TopLook FUNCTION
TopWare Network OS v5.10+

Registers at call:
AX = FFCFh
DH = page number (0-2, 2 is text mode)
DL = type
      00h look at specific screen
      01h AutoLook on
      FFh AutoLook off
BH = station number wishing to look
BL = station number to be looked at

CH = monochrome flag
   (01h monochrome, 00h not monochrome)
CL = screen mode (see Table 28-4)

Return Registers:
AL = status (00h successful, nonzero failed)

Conflicts: CED and DOSED (PCI-13), DOS OEM function (PCI-24), DOS/4GW (PCI-35), GO32 (PCI-37), Viruses (PCI-59)
See also: Function FF8Dh

INT 21h Function FFD6h   *TopWare Network OS v5.10+*
GET KEYCARD SERIAL NUMBER AND MAXIMUM USERS

Registers at call:
AX = FFD6h
ES:BX -> 12-byte buffer for
   keycard serial number

Return Registers:
CX = maximum number of users
ES:BX buffer filled

Conflicts: CED and DOSED (PCI-13), DOS OEM function (PCI-24), DOS/4GW (PCI-35), GO32 (PCI-37), Viruses (PCI-59)

INT 21h Function FFD7h   *TopWare Network OS v5.10+*
GET NETWORK PROTECTION ATTRIBUTES STATUS

Registers at call:
AX = FFD7h

Return Registers:
AL = status (00h disabled, 01h enabled)

Conflicts: CED and DOSED (PCI-13), DOS OEM function (PCI-24), DOS/4GW (PCI-35), GO32 (PCI-37), Viruses (PCI-59)

INT 21h Function FFE3h, Subfunction 00h   *TopWare Network OS v5.10+*
INITIATE ACCESS TO SPECIFIC PACKET TYPE

Registers at call:
AX = FFE3h
DL = 00h
BX = packet type for Ethernet header
   (IP = 0800h, ARP = 0806h, etc.)
ES:DI -> receive routine
   (see Table 28-15)

Return Registers:
CF clear if successful
   AX = handle number
CF set on error
   DH = error code (03h,05h,09h,0Ah,11h)
   (see Table 28-14)

Conflicts: CED and DOSED (PCI-13), DOS OEM function (PCI-24), DOS/4GW (PCI-35), GO32 (PCI-37), Viruses (PCI-59)
See also: Function FFE3h Subfunction 01h

28-14 Values for error code:

01h	invalid handle
03h	no interfaces of the specified type found
05h	bad packet type
09h	insufficient space
0Ah	type already being accessed
0Ch	unable to send packet (usually hardware error)
11h	invalid function

28-15 Receive routine calling convention:

Registers at call:
AX = function
   0000h request packet buffer
      CX = packet size
   0001h packet copied
      CX = packet size

DS:SI -> copied packet
(same as returned ES:DI above)

Return Registers:

ES:DI -> buffer or 0000h:0000h to
discard packet

INT 21h Function FFE3h, Subfunction 01h   *TopWare Network OS v5.10+*
END ACCESS TO SPECIFIC PACKET TYPE

Registers at call:
AX = FFE3h
DL = 01h
BX = handle returned by
   Function FFE3h Subfunction 00h

Return Registers:
CF clear if successful
CF set on error
   DH = error code (01h,11h) (see Table 28-14)

Details: The specified access handle will no longer be valid after this call.
Conflicts: CED and DOSED (PCI-13), DOS OEM function (PCI-24), DOS/4GW (PCI-35), GO32 (PCI-37), Viruses (PCI-59)
See also: Function FFE3h Subfunctoin 00h

INT 21h Function FFE3h, Subfunction 02h   *TopWare Network OS v5.10+*
SEND PACKET

Registers at call:
AX = FFE3h
DL = 02h
CX = length of data buffer
DS:SI -> buffer containing data

Return Registers:
CF clear if successful
CF set on error
   DH = error code (0Ch,11h) (see Table 28-14)

Conflicts: CED and DOSED (PCI-13), DOS OEM function (PCI-24), DOS/4GW (PCI-35), GO32 (PCI-37), Viruses (PCI-59)

INT 21h Function FFE3h, Subfunction 03h   *TopWare Network OS v5.10+*
GET LOCAL NETWORK INTERFACE ADDRESS

Registers at call:
AX = FFE3h
DL = 03h
ES:DI -> 6-byte buffer for address

Return Registers:
none

Conflicts: CED and DOSED (PCI-13), DOS OEM function (PCI-24), DOS/4GW (PCI-35), GO32 (PCI-37), Viruses (PCI-59)
See also: Function FFE3h Subfunction 00h

INT 2Fh Function FF00h   *Topware Network Operating System*
INSTALLATION CHECK

Registers at call:
AX = FF00h

Return Registers:
AL = status
   00h not installed, OK to install
   01h not installed, not OK to install
   FFh installed

Conflicts: no direct conflicts known, but see Table 2-2
See also: Function FF01h, INT 21h Function FFh, Topware INT 7Ah

---

INT 2Fh Function FF01h   *Topware Network Operating System*
GET VERSION

Registers at call:
AX = FF01h

Return Registers:
AX = version

Conflicts: no direct conflicts known, but see Table 2-2
See also: Function FF00h

INT 2Fh Function FF02h
GET TopNet VERSION STRING
TopWare Network OS v5.10+

Registers at call:
AX = FF02h

Return Registers:
ES:BX -> version string

Conflicts: no direct conflicts known, but see Table 2-2
See also: Functions FF00h and FF01h

INT 2Fh Function FF10h
TopTerm - INSTALLATION CHECK
TopWare Network OS v5.10+

Registers at call:
AX = FF10h

Return Registers:
AL = status (00h not installed, 01h installed)

Conflicts: no direct conflicts known, but see Table 2-2
See also: Functions FF00h, FF11h, FF12h, and FF13h

INT 2Fh Function FF11h
TopTerm - ENABLE KEYBOARD SERVICE
TopWare Network OS v5.10+

Registers at call:
AX = FF11h

Return Registers:
none

Details: This function is only available on workstations, not on the server.
Conflicts: no direct conflicts known, but see Table 2-2
See also: Functions FF10h and FF12h

INT 2Fh Function FF12h
TopTerm - DISABLE KEYBOARD SERVICE
TopWare Network OS v5.10+

Registers at call:
AX = FF12h

Return Registers:
none

Details: This function is only available on workstations, not on the server.
Conflicts: no direct conflicts known, but see Table 2-2
See also: Functions FF10h and FF11h

INT 2Fh Function FF13h
TopTerm - SET INSTALLATION FLAG
TopWare Network OS v5.10+

Registers at call:
AX = FF13h
CL = new state (00h off, 01h on)

Return Registers:
none

Conflicts: no direct conflicts known, but see Table 2-2
See also: Function FF10h

INT 2Fh Function FF14h
START BACKGROUND RECEIVE VIDEO DATA
TopWare Network OS v5.10+

Registers at call:
AX = FF14h

Return Registers:
none

Details: This function is only available on workstations, not on the server.
Conflicts: no direct conflicts known, but see Table 2-2
See also: Functions FF10h and FF15h

INT 2Fh Function FF15h
END BACKGROUND RECEIVE VIDEO DATA
TopWare Network OS v5.10+

Registers at call:
AX = FF15h

Return Registers:
none

Details: This function is only available on workstations, not on the server.
Conflicts: no direct conflicts known, but see Table 2-2
See also: Functions FF10h and FF14h

INT 2Fh Function FF16h   *TopWare Network OS v5.10+*
SET CONTROL NUMBER OF "SHOW" SCREEN
Registers at call: **Return Registers:**
AX = FF16h   none
BL = which to set (00h TopShow,
  FFh TopTerm)
CX = destination screen
     0000h all stations
     0000h-00FFh (TopTerm only)
      send to group CL
     8001h-80FEh send to station CL
Conflicts: no direct conflicts known, but see Table 2-2
See also: Function FF18h

INT 2Fh Function FF18h   *TopWare Network OS v5.10+*
SEND FULL SCREEN OF DATA FOR TopShow
Registers at call: **Return Registers:**
AX = FF18h   none
Conflicts: no direct conflicts known, but see Table 2-2
See also: Functions FF00h, FF16h, and FF27h

INT 2Fh Function FF23h   *TopWare Network OS v5.10+*
CLOSE SPOOL FILES AND START PRINTING
Registers at call: **Return Registers:**
AX = FF23h   none
Conflicts: no direct conflicts known, but see Table 2-2
See also: Function FF00h

INT 2Fh Function FF27h   *TopWare Network OS v5.10+*
GET "SHOW" TYPE
Registers at call: **Return Registers:**
AX = FF27h   AL = type (00h complete version, 01h simple
                              version)
                              BL = "show" functions flag (00h disabled, 01h
                              enabled)
Conflicts: no direct conflicts known, but see Table 2-2
See also: Functions FF16h and FF18h

INT 7Ah   *Topware Network Operating System*
UNDETERMINED FUNCTION   *Undocumented*
Registers at call: **Return Registers:**
AL = *unknown*   *unknown*
others, if any, unknown
Conflicts: no direct conflicts known, but see Table 2-2
See also: INT 21h Function FFh, INT 2Fh Function FF00h

CHAPTER 29

Web for DOS

WEB is an IPX-based peer-to-peer network by Webcorp. Version 4.0, introduced early in 1993, provides seamless networking between MS-DOS- and Microsoft Windows-based microcomputers. A Windows-based interface also provides access to network services for MS-DOS and Windows users. Other capabilities include support for TCP/IP and Novell's Open Data Link Interface (ODI).

INT 2Fh Function EE00h   *WEB v4.02*
INSTALLATION CHECK

Registers at call:	Return Registers:
AX = EE00h	AL = status
	00h not installed
	FFh installed

Conflicts: GRIDLOC (PCI-66), XVIEW (PCI-66); see also Table 2-2
See also: Functions EEx0h and EEF0h

INT 2Fh Functions EEx0h   *WEB v4.02*
WEB MODULE INSTALLATION CHECK

Registers at call:	Return Registers:
AH = EEh	AX = 0000h if installed
AL = module ID (see Table 29-1)	ES:DI -> far entry point for module-specific
	API calls (see Tables 29-2 to 29-6)

Conflicts: GRIDLOC (PCI-66), XVIEW (PCI-66); see also Table 2-2
See also: Function EE00h

29-1 Values for module ID:

10h	server module (SERVER.EXE)
20h	client module (CLIENT.EXE)
30h	mail module (MAIL.EXE)
40h	spooler (PCSPOOL.EXE)
50h	kernel module (KERNEL.EXE)
60h	SAP module (KERNEL.EXE)
70h	resident station manager (SM.EXE)
90h	router module (ROUTER.EXE)

29-2 Server module entry point calling convention:

Registers at call:
BX = function
        0000h remove server module

Return Registers:

0001h create SYSINFO file

AX = status (0000h if successful, else
   WEB error code)

0002h get server object table

0003h get server variables

CX = number of server objects
ES:DI -> server object table

ES:DI -> server variables

Details: The SYSINFO file is used by the station manager when displaying info for a particular station.

Server objects include drives and devices that the server module controls.

29-3 Client module entry point calling convention:

Registers at call: **Return Registers:**
BX = function
   0000h remove client module

AX = status (0000h if successful, else WEB
   error code)

   0001h decrement client-only flag
   0002h increment client-only flag
   0005h set device capture
   0006h clear device capture

Details: Function 0005h decrements the DeviceOutput flag, telling the spooler that it may trap device output again. Function 0006h increments the DeviceOutput flag, telling the spooler that it should not trap device output (this is used internally by the spooler to prevent it from trapping its own output).

Registers at call: **Return Registers:**
BX = function
   0007h get client debug pointer   ES:DI -> client debug data structure (see Table 29-7)

   0008h get root drive   AL = WEB startup drive

   0009h get maximum possible   AL = maximum drive redirections
      drive/device redirections   CH = maximum LPTx redirections
                                        CL = maximum COMx redirections

                                        AX = previous value of Suspend flag
   000Ah suspend client

                                        AX = previous value of Suspend flag
   000Bh resume client

                                        CX = number of structures actually returned
   000Ch get instance data
      CX = maximum number of
         structures in array
      ES:DI -> buffer for array of
         WIN_INSTANCE_DATA
         structures (see Table 29-8)

Details: Function 000Ch is used internally by WEB4WIN.

29-4 Mail module entry point calling convention:

Registers at call:	Return Registers:

BX = function

    0000h remove mail module   AX = status (0000h successful, else WEB error code)

    0001h set mail poll
    0002h set mail notify
    0003h clear mail notify

    0004h check whether new mail   AL = new mail status
       has arrived   00h no new mail since last call
                                  else new mail has arrived

    0005h send notify
        ES:DI -> name of WEB user
            to be notified   ES:DI -> full network path of Post Office
                                  subdirectory
    0006h get post office

Details: Function 0001h schedules the WEB mail module. Functions 0002h and 0003h set and clear the Notify flag, which determines whether the user will be notified when mail is received. Function 0004h also clears the new-mail flag after retrieving it.

29-5 Spooler entry point calling convention:

Registers at call:	Return Registers:

BX = function

    0000h remove PCSpool module   AX = status (0000h successful, else WEB error code)

    0001h set spooler poll

    0002h check spooler changed   AX = 0000h

Details: Function 0001h schedules the WEB spooler. Function 0002h is a NOP in current versions of WEB.

29-6 Kernel entry point calling convention:

Registers at call:

BX = function
    0000h remove kernel module

    0001h set kernel ^S filter
        DL = new state (00h don't filter ^S,
           nonzero do filter)
    0002h get kernel data area

    0003h display dialog box
        CL = dialog box type
            00h password
            01h E-Note received notification
            02h Novell login
            03h general notification
        DL = number of rows to display
        ES:SI -> array of far pointers to rows

Return Registers:

to be displayed

ES:DI -> Pascal-style input buffer AX = status (0000h successful, else WEB error code)

ES:DI -> kernel data area

AX = status (0000h successful, else error code)

Registers at call: **Return Registers:**

BX = function

    0004h kernel service events

    0005h get kernel's in-critical-section ES:DI -> kernel InCriticalSection flag
       flag

    0006h schedule DOS event
       AL = directive
          00h do not ignore WEB
            ExtraBusy flag
          01h ignore ExtraBusy flag
          02h (WEB4WIN) check   AX = status (0000h not busy, else busy)
            that current Windows
            VM is foregrnd VM
       ES:SI -> WEB AES Event
          Control Block (ECB)
          (see Table 29-9)

    0007h check busy
       AL = directive
          00h do not ignore WEB
            ExtraBusy flag
          01h ignore ExtraBusy flag
          02h (WEB4WIN) check
            that current Windows
            VM is foregrnd VM

Details: The WEB Asynchronous Event Scheduler is similar to the one used by IPX; Function 0006h schedules a special ECB to be executed at a later time. Unlike IPX ECBs, the timeout must be set explicitly by the caller. Function 0006h also calls Function 0004h

Registers at call: **Return Registers:**

BX = function

    0008h set keyboard intercept
    0009h get keyboard intercept

    000Ah get dialog flags   ES:DI -> kernel dialog flags (see Table 29-10)

    000Bh get network path   ES:DI -> fully-qualified network path of file where
                             the screen is stored on Dialog calls

Details: Functions 0008h and 0009h are currently NOPs which return immediately.

Registers at call:

BX = function

    000Ch kernel alternate dialog
       CL = dialog box type

Return Registers:

AX = status (0000h successful, else error code)

        00h password
        01h E-Note received
           notification
        02h Novell login
        03h general notification
    DL = number of rows to display
    ES:SI -> array of far pointers to
        rows to be displayed
    ES:DI -> Pascal-style input buffer
000Dh get machine/operating
    system type

AX = machine/operating system type
    01h IBM PC, MS-DOS
    02h IBM PC, DOSV (Japanese)
    03h NEC PC-9800, JDOS (Japanese)
    04h IBM PC, Korean DBC DOS

Details: Function 000Ch is identical to function 0003h except that it does not notify WEB4WIN of the impending dialog request.

29-7 Format of client debug data structure:

Offset	Size	Description
00h	WORD	total files
02h	WORD	files free
04h	WORD	no files
06h	WORD	minimum files
08h	WORD	total FCBs
0Ah	WORD	total safe FCBs
0Ch	WORD	FCBs in use
0Eh	WORD	wrong FCB
10h	WORD	compressed
12h	WORD	retransmits

29-8 Format of WIN_INSTANCE_DATA structure:

Offset	Size	Description
00h	DWORD	real-mode pointer to data to be instanced
04h	WORD	size of data to be instanced

29-9 Format of WEB AES Event Control Block:

Offset	Size	Description
00h	DWORD	link address
04h	WORD	ESR address
08h	BYTE	InUse flag
09h	BYTE	completion code
0Ah	3 BYTEs	reserved
0Dh	WORD	timeout
0Fh	BYTE	IgnoreExtra flag
10h	WORD	PSP
12h	DWORD	DTA
16h	WORD	AX value for DOS critical information
18h	WORD	BX value for DOS critical information
1Ah	WORD	CX value for DOS critical information
1Ch	WORD	DX value for DOS critical information

29-10 Values for kernel dialog flags:
01h　　　dialog will timeout
02h　　　display stars instead of entered keystrokes

INT 2Fh Function EEF0h　　　　　　　　　　　　　　　　　*WEB v4.02*
WEB GENERAL NOTIFICATION　　　　　　　　　　　　　　　*Callout*

Registers at call:	Return Registers:
AX = EEF0h	varies by notification function
BX = notification function ID	
(see Table 29-11)	

Details: The notification functions are used internally by WEB modules to notify other modules and external programs of actions or event, and should never be called by an application.
Conflicts: see Table 2-2
See also: Function EE00h

29-11 Values for Notification Function ID:
00h　　　node added
01h　　　node deleted
02h　　　dial attempt
03h　　　dial failed
04h　　　file close
05h　　　close connection
07h　　　check Windows mode
20h　　　link up
21h　　　link down

INT 53h　　　　　　　　　　　　　　　　　　　　　　　　　*WEB*
API

Registers at call:	Return Registers:
BX = function	AX = *unknown*
0000h *unknown*	0004h *unknown*
AX = *unknown*	0009h *unknown*
	0015h
	AX = *unknown*
	DX = *unknown*
	0017h
	Return Registers:
	unknown

Conflicts: IBM 3278 (Chapter 37), DESQview IRQ3 (PCI-44)
Details: The installation check consists of looking for the signature "WEBCO" immediately prior to the interrupt handler.

　　The above calls are made by Show Partner F/X v3.6 (see INT 10h Function 53h in PCI-8)

CHAPTER 30

Workgroup Connection

WORKGRP.SYS is the portion of the Workgroup Connection from Microsoft which permits communication with PCs running Windows for Workgroups or LAN Manager.

INT 21h Function 3Fh   *WORKGRP.SYS*
GET ENTRY POINT

Registers at call:	Return Registers:
AH = 3Fh	CF clear if successful
BX = file handle for device "NETHLP"	AX = number of bytes actually read
CX = 0008h	(0 if at EOF before call)
DS:DX -> buffer for entry point record	CF set on error
(see Table 30-1)	AX = error code (05h,06h) (see Table 3-1)

See also: Function 4402h, MICRO.EXE INT 2Fh Function 9400h (Chapter 41)

INT 21h Function 4402h   *WORKGRP.SYS*
GET API ENTRY POINT

Registers at call:	Return Registers:
AX = 4402h	CF clear if successful
BX = file handle for device "NETHLP"	AX = number of bytes actually read
CX = 0008h	CF set on error
DS:DX -> buffer for entry point record	AX = error code (see Table 3-1)
(see Table 30-1)	

See also: Function 3Fh

30-1 Format of entry point record:

Offset	Size	Description	
00h	WORD	3633h	} signature
02h	WORD	EF6Fh	
04h	DWORD	address of entry point	

Note: The first four bytes of the buffer must be 6Fh E9h 33h 36h on entry when using IOCTL rather than READ to get the entry point record.

30-2 WORKGRP entry point calling convention:

Registers at call:	Return Registers:
STACK: WORD function number	STACK unchanged
(0000h-0009h)	

30-3 WORKGRP function 00h calling convention:

Registers at call:			**Return Registers:**
STACK:	WORD	0000h	DX:AX -> data table
		(function "get *unknown value*")	

30-4 WORKGRP function 01h calling convention:

Registers at call: **Return Registers:**
STACK: WORD   0001h   STACK: DWORD pointer to *unknown*
       (function "hook *unknown*")   WORD 0001h (function number)

30-5 WORKGRP function 02h calling convention:

Registers at call: **Return Registers:**
STACK: WORD   0002h   *unknown*
      (function "unhook *unknown*")
   others, if any, unknown

30-6 WORKGRP "reenable printer port" calling convention:

Registers at call: **Return Registers:**
STACK: WORD   0003h   *unknown*
      WORD   LPT port number

30-7 WORKGRP "disable printer port" calling convention:

Registers at call: **Return Registers:**
STACK: WORD   0004h   *unknown*
      WORD   LPT port number

30-8 WORKGRP function 05h calling convention:

Registers at call: **Return Registers:**
STACK: WORD   0005h (*unknown* function)   *unknown*
   others, if any, unknown

30-9 WORKGRP function 06h calling convention:

Registers at call: **Return Registers:**
STACK: WORD   0006h (*unknown* function)   STACK unchanged
                                AX = 0000h
                                DX = 0000h

30-10 WORKGRP functions 07h-09h calling convention:

Registers at call: **Return Registers:**
STACK: WORD   0007h-0009h (NOP functions)   STACK unchanged
                                AX = 0001h
                                DX = 0000h

CHAPTER 31

Other Redirectors and Shells

This chapter covers various other networking software whose APIs are not large enough to have warranted separate chapters, as well as some generic support calls which have been adopted by most MS-DOS-based networks.

Generic Network Support

INT 2Fh Function B800h   *network*
INSTALLATION CHECK

Registers at call:	Return Registers:
AX = B800h	AL = status
	00h not installed
	nonzero installed
	BX = installed component flags (test in this order!)
	bit 6 server
	bit 2 messenger
	bit 7 receiver
	bit 3 redirector
	bit 1 LANPUP (LANtastic 4.0)

Details: This function is supported by LAN Manager, LANtastic, NetWare Lite, SilverNET, 10NET, etc.

LANtastic and NetWare Lite use only BL for the return value, preserving BH; LAN Manager and DOS LAN Requester return BH=00h. This permits differentiation between those two groups by setting BH to a nonzero value before the call and checking its value on return, which is important because the two groups return different values for Function B809h (version check).

Conflicts: 10NET (Chapter 27); see also Table 2-2

See also: Function B809h, SilverNET Function 4E53h (below)

INT 2Fh Function B803h   *network*
GET NETWORK EVENT POST HANDLER

Registers at call:	Return Registers:
AX = B803h	ES:BX -> current event post handler (see Table 31-1)

Details: This function is also supported by 10NET v5.0.

Conflicts: none known, but see Table 2-2

See also: Function B804h, Function B903h (Chapter 24)

INT 2Fh Function B804h
network
SET NETWORK EVENT POST HANDLER

Registers at call: **Return Registers:**
AX = B804h   none
CX = (10NET) 0370h if 10Windows
  is hooking post handler
ES:BX -> new event post handler

Details: This call is used in conjunction with Function B803h to hook into the network event post routine.

    This function also is supported by 10NET v5.0.

    The specified handler is called on any network event. Two events are defined: message received and critical network error.

Conflicts: none known, but see Table 2-2

See also: Function B803h, Function B904h (Chapter 24)

31-1 Post routine calling convention:

Registers at call:
AX = 0000h single block message
    DS:SI -> ASCIZ originator name
    DS:DI -> ASCIZ destination name
    ES:BX -> text header (see Table 31-2)
AX = 0001h start multiple message
  block
    CX = block group ID
    DS:SI -> ASCIZ originator name
    DS:DI -> ASCIZ destination name
AX = 0002h multiple block text
    CX = block group ID
    ES:BX -> text header (see Table 31-2)
AX = 0003h end multiple block message
    CX = block group ID
AX = 0004h message aborted due to error
    CX = block group ID
AX = 0101h server received badly formatted network request
AX = 0102h unexpected network error
    ES:BX -> NCB (see INT 5Ch in Chapter 8)
AX = 0103h server received INT 24h error
    other registers as for INT 24h, except AH is in BH

Return Registers:
AX = response code
  0000h user post routine processed message
  0001h PC LAN will process message, but
    message window not displayed
  FFFFh PC LAN will process message
  (code 0101h always returns FFFFh, code
    0103h only 0000h or FFFFh)

31-2 Format of text header:

Offset	Size	Description
00h	WORD	length of text (maximum 512 bytes)
02h	N BYTEs	text of message

Note: All CRLF sequences in the message text are replaced by 14h (Control-T).

INT 2Fh Function B807h
network
GET NetBIOS NAME NUMBER OF MACHINE NAME

Registers at call: **Return Registers:**
AX = B807h   CH = NetBIOS name number of the machine name

Conflicts: none known, but see Table 2-2

See also: MS-DOS INT 21h Function 5E00h (Chapter 3)

INT 2Fh Function B808h
RELINK KEYBOARD HANDLER

network
Undocumented

Registers at call:
AX = B808h
ES:BX -> INT 09h handler network
  should call after it finishes INT 09h

Return Registers:
none

Details: This call replaces the address to which the network software chains on an INT 09h without preserving the original value. This allows a prior handler to unlink, but does not allow a new handler to be added such that the network gets the INT 09h first unless the new handler completely takes over INT 09h and never chains.

  This function is called by the DOS 3.2 KEYBxx.COM.
Conflicts: none known, but see Table 2-2
See also: Function B908h

INT 2Fh Function B809h
VERSION CHECK

LANtastic, NetWare Lite, SilverNET

Registers at call:
AX = B809h

Return Registers:
AH = major version
AL = minor version (decimal)

Details: NetWare Lite returns its own version number rather than a PC LAN Program compatibility version.
Conflicts: PC LAN Program/LAN Manager Function B809h below; see also Table 2-2
See also: Function B800h, Function B809h below, SilverNET Function 4E53h (below)

INT 2Fh Function B809h
VERSION CHECK

PC LAN Program, LAN Manager, 10NET v5.0

Registers at call:
AX = B809h

Return Registers:
AH = minor version (decimal)
AL = major version

Details: This function is also supported in this form by the DOS LAN Requester.
  10NET returns version 1.10 (AX=0A01h) for compatibility.
Conflicts: LANtastic/NetWare Lite Function B809h above; see also Table 2-2
See also: Function B800h, Function B809h above

INT 2Fh Function B80Fh
GET START PARAMETERS

DOS LAN Requester

Registers at call:
AX = B80Fh
CX = size of return data buffer
ES:DI -> return data buffer
  (see Table 31-3)

Return Registers:
AX = status
    00h network started
    nonzero network not started
CX = number of bytes returned in buffer
ES:DI buffer filled

Conflicts: none known, but see Table 2-2

31-3 Format of return data buffer:

Offset	Size	Description
00h	BYTE	major version
01h	BYTE	minor version
02h	WORD	configuration flags given when network was started (see Table 31-4)
04h	15 BYTEs	NET START machine name (space padded)
13h	BYTE	00h
14h	9 BYTEs	NET START domain name (NULL padded)

1Dh	BYTE	00h
1Eh	32 BYTEs	/WRK heuristics string (space padded, not terminated)
3Eh	WORD	/SRV value
40h	WORD	/ASG value
42h	WORD	/NBC value
44h	WORD	/NBS value
46h	WORD	/BBC value
48h	WORD	/BBS value
4Ah	WORD	/PBC value
4Ch	WORD	/PBS value
4Eh	WORD	/PFS value
50h	WORD	/PFT value
52h	WORD	/PWT value
54h	WORD	/KUC value
56h	WORD	/KST value
58h	WORD	/NVS value
5Ah	WORD	/NMS value
5Ch	WORD	/NDB value
5Eh	WORD	/MBI value
60h	BYTE	NetBIOS name number for machine name
61h	BYTE	NetBIOS name number for domain name
62h	WORD	NetBIOS sessions required for configuration
64h	WORD	NetBIOS commands required for configuration
66h	WORD	NetBIOS names required for configuration
68h	128 BYTEs	NET START path (LANROOT)
E8h	BYTE	00h

31-4 Bitfields for configuration flags:

bit 0	/NVS nonzero
bit 1	/NMS nonzero
bit 2	/API
bit 3	/HIM
bit 4	/LIM
bit 5	/ENC
bit 6	/POP
bit 7	/EMS
bit 8	/RPL
bits 9-12	reserved
bit 13	RDR started
bit 14	RCV started
bit 15	User is currently logged on

Excelan LAN Workplace for DOS

INT 60h   *Excelan LAN Workplace for DOS v3.5*
API

Registers at call: **Return Registers:**
ES:BX -> request packet (see Table 31-5)   request packet updated
Conflicts: see Table 2-3

Details: This interrupt is also supported by Beame&Whiteside's BWLWP35 shim, which was used in creating this description.

The installation check consists of testing for the WORD 4142h ('AB') immediately preceding the interrupt handler

BUG: Because BWLWP35 range-checks only the low byte of the function number, and has a fencepost error even in that test, functions 000Bh and XX01h-XX0Bh (XX nonzero) branch to random locations.

See also: INT 2Fh Function 7A40h

31-5 Format of request packet:

Offset	Size	Description
00h	12 BYTEs	*unknown*
0Ch	WORD	(return) error code (see Table 31-6)
0Eh	DWORD	pointer to *unknown* FAR function
12h	WORD	function number
		0001h *unknown*
		0002h NOP
		0003h NOP
		0004h NOP
		0005h *unknown*
		0006h get *unknown* record
		0007h NOP
		0008h reset *unknown*
		0009h NOP
		000Ah set *unknown*
		unknown

---function 01h---

20h	BYTE	(call) subfunction (32h-3Bh)
		3Bh non-blocking I/O request (will be tested every clock tick)
21h	BYTE	(return) error code
		00h successful
		09h invalid connection number
		2Ah bad connection type
		45h *unknown*

---function 01h, subfunction 32h---

3Ah	WORD	(call) connection type (01h stream, 02h datagram)

---function 01h, subfunction 34h---

26h	WORD	(call) *unknown*
28h	WORD	(call) *unknown*
2Ah	WORD	(call) *unknown*

---function 01h, subfunction 35h---

1Ah	WORD	(call) *connection number*
26h	WORD	(return) *unknown*

---function 01h, subfunction 36h---

1Ah	WORD	(call) *connection number*
38h	WORD	*unknown*

---function 01h, subfunction 37h---

24h	WORD	(return) *unknown*
26h	WORD	(return) *unknown*

---**function 01h, subfunction 38h**---

| 1Ah | WORD | (call) *connection number* |

---**function 01h, subfunction 3Ah**---

22h	WORD	(call) *unknown*
		667Eh *unknown*
		667Fh *unknown*
24h	BYTE	(call 667Eh) *unknown*
24h	WORD	(return 667Fh) *unknown*

---**function 01h, subfunction 3Bh**---

| 0Eh | DWORD | (call) -> function to invoke for I/O or 0000h:0000h |

the function is called with

    AX = 0000h

    STACK: DWORD -> request packet

                                WORD 0000h

and should return STACK unchanged

1Ah	WORD	(call) *connection number*
21h	BYTE	(return) set to 01h when I/O becomes possible
22h	BYTE	(call) direction (00h write, 01h read)
34h	DWORD	(return) -> next pending request packet

---**function 05h**---

1Eh	WORD	(call) *unknown*
20h	WORD	(call) *unknown*
34h	DWORD	(call) -> *unknown item*

---**function 06h**---

16h	DWORD	(call) -> buffer for *unknown* record (see Table 31-7)
1Ah	WORD	(call) number of bytes to copy
22h	WORD	(return) number of bytes transferred

---**function 08h**---

| 14h | WORD | (return) *unknown* (0001h) |

---**function 0Ah**---

| 16h | DWORD | (call) -> WORD *unknown* |
| 1Ch | WORD | (call) must be 000Ah for BWLWP35 |

31-6 LAN Workplace error codes:

0000h	successful
002Dh	invalid function
0050h	*unknown*

31-7 Format of *unknown* record:

Offset	Size	Description
00h	WORD	offset of *unknown item*
02h	4 BYTEs	*unknown*
06h	DWORD	IP address (big-endian)
0Ah	6 BYTEs	physical address (big-endian)
	others, if any, unknown	

INTERLNK

INTERLNK is a remote drive access program that redirects drive letters over the serial or parallel port which Microsoft has licensed from Sewell Development Corporation and bundled with MS-

DOS 6.0. Unlike most networking software, INTERLNK is neither a redirector nor a network shell, but instead a device driver which appears to be a regular block device to DOS.

INT 2Fh Function 5600h
INSTALLATION CHECK
INTERLNK

Registers at call:
AX = 5600h
DX = FFFFh
BL = instance number (00h = any,
   01h = first loaded, etc.)
Conflicts: none known, but see Table 2-2
See also: Functions 5601h and 5602h

Return Registers:
AL = FFh if installed
   BL = instance number
   CX = *unknown*
   DX = resident CS

INT 2Fh Function 5601h
CHECK IF REDIRECTED DRIVE
INTERLNK

Registers at call:
AX = 5601h
DX = FFFFh
BH = drive number (0=A:)
Conflicts: none known, but see Table 2-2
See also: Function 5600h

Return Registers:
(as for Function 5600h if redirected drive)

INT 2Fh Function 5602h
GET UNKNOWN VALUE
INTERLNK

Registers at call:
AX = 5602h
DX = FFFFh
Conflicts: none known, but see Table 2-2
See also: Function 5600h

Return Registers:
CX = *unknown*

Nanosoft TurboNET

TurboNET is a NetBIOS-based file redirector and server; a demonstration version may be downloaded from Nanosoft's BBS.

INT 2Fh Function 8000h
INSTALLATION CHECK
TurboNET server

Registers at call:
AX = 8000h

Return Registers:
AL = FFh if installed
   BX = CS of resident code
   CX = *unknown* (03FCh)

Conflicts: EASY-NET (below), FaxBIOS (PCI-64), ASCII (PCI-66); see also Table 2-2
See also: Function 8100h

INT 2Fh Function 8001h
UNDETERMINED FUNCTION
TurboNET server
Undocumented

Registers at call:
AX = 8001h
DS:SI -> 16-byte buffer for *unknown*

Return Registers:
AH = status
   00h successful
   01h error (TurboNET busy)

Details: This function makes NetBIOS calls.
Conflicts: EASY-NET (below), FaxBIOS (PCI-64), ASCII (PCI-66); see also Table 2-2

INT 2Fh Function 8100h
INSTALLATION CHECK
TurboNET redirector
Undocumented

Registers at call:
AX = 8100h

Return Registers:
AL = FFh if installed

Conflicts: none known, but see Table 2-2
See also: Function 8000h

INT 2Fh Function 8101h
UNDETERMINED FUNCTION
TurboNET redirector
Undocumented

Registers at call:
AX = 8101h

Return Registers:
AL = *unknown*
DL = *unknown*

Conflicts: none known, but see Table 2-2

INT 2Fh Function 8102h
UNDETERMINED FUNCTION
TurboNET redirector
Undocumented

Registers at call:
AX = 8102h

Return Registers:
AL = *unknown*
DL = *unknown*

Conflicts: none known, but see Table 2-2

INT 2Fh Function 8103h
GET MACHINE NAME
TurboNET redirector
Undocumented

Registers at call:
AX = 8103h
ES:DI -> 17-byte buffer

Return Registers:
buffer filled

Conflicts: none known, but see Table 2-2

INT 2Fh Function 8104h
UNDETERMINED FUNCTION
TurboNET redirector
Undocumented

Registers at call:
AX = 8104h
BL = *unknown*
BH = *unknown*
CX = *unknown*
DX = *unknown*
DS:SI -> 16-byte buffer containing *unknown*

Return Registers:
AL = 00h *unknown*

Conflicts: none known, but see Table 2-2

INT 2Fh Function 8105h
UNDETERMINED FUNCTION
TurboNET redirector
Undocumented

Registers at call:
AX = 8105h
CX = *unknown* (don't change current value if 0000h)
DX = *unknown* (don't change current value if 0000h)

Return Registers:
AL = 00h successful

Conflicts: none known, but see Table 2-2

INT 66h
NETWORK PROCESSING
TurboNET
Callout

Details: This interrupt is hooked but not used (IRET) by both redirector and server; it is called from the server's INT 28h handler.
Conflicts: see Table 2-3
See also: INT 2Fh Function 8100h

PC-NET

PC-NET was the original IBM LAN package, based on Microsoft's MS-Net and using NetBIOS as its driver interface. Because of the expectation that its API would become standard, several other network programs adopted it, but IBM then moved on to develop the PC LAN Program (Chapter 24).

INT 67h Function 00h   *PC-NET, Alloy NTNX*
LOCK SEMAPHORE AND WAIT
Registers at call: **Return Registers:**
AH = 00h   AL = status (see Table 31-8)
DS:DX -> ASCIZ semaphore name   AH = semaphore owner if status=02h
 (max 64 bytes)
Conflicts: EMS (PCI-38); see also Table 2-3
See also: Functions 01h and 02h, Alloy INT 7Fh Function 00h (Chapter 12)

31-8 Values for status:
00h	successful
01h	invalid function
02h	semaphore already locked
03h	unable to lock semaphore
04h	semaphore space exhausted

INT 67h Function 01h   *PC-NET, Alloy NTNX*
LOCK SEMAPHORE
Registers at call: **Return Registers:**
AH = 01h   AL = status (see Table 31-8)
DS:DX -> ASCIZ semaphore   AH = semaphore owner if status=02h
 name (max 64 bytes)
Conflicts: EMS (PCI-38); see also Table 2-3
See also: Functions 00h and 02h, Alloy INT 7Fh Function 01h (Chapter 12)

INT 67h Function 02h   *PC-NET, Alloy NTNX*
UNLOCK SEMAPHORE
Registers at call: **Return Registers:**
AH = 02h   AL = status (see Table 31-8)
DS:DX -> ASCIZ semaphore   AH = semaphore owner if status=02h
 name (max 64 bytes)
Conflicts: EMS (PCI-38); see also Table 2-3
See also: Functions 00h and 01h, Alloy INT 7Fh Function 02h (Chapter 12)

Shamrock Software NET.24

INT 17h Function 2400h   *Shamrock Software NET.24 v3.11+*
ENABLE/DISABLE API FUNCTIONS
Registers at call: **Return Registers:**
AX = 2400h   DL = 24h if installed
DL = new state   DH = minor version number
 00h disabled   CX = network address of this machine
 01h enabled   AL = status (see Table 31-9)
See also: Function 2403h, INT 16h Function 4500h

31-9 Values for NET.24 status:

00h	successful
01h	timeout
02h	header error
03h	data error
04h	busy
05h	invalid parameters

INT 17h Function 2401h   *Shamrock Software NET.24 v3.11+*
RECEIVE BLOCK, NO HANDSHAKE

Registers at call: **Return Registers:**
AX = 2401h   AL = status (see Table 31-9)
BL = timeout in clock ticks   DX:BX -> receive buffer
See also: Functions 2402h, 2404h, and 2408h

INT 17h Function 2402h   *Shamrock Software NET.24 v3.11+*
TRANSMIT BLOCK, NO HANDSHAKE

Registers at call: **Return Registers:**
AX = 2402h   AL = status (see Table 31-9)
transmit buffer filled (see Function 2403h)
See also: Functions 2401h, 2403h, 2404h, and 2409h

INT 17h Function 2403h   *Shamrock Software NET.24 v3.11+*
GET STATUS AND TRANSMISSION BUFFER

Registers at call: **Return Registers:**
AX = 2403h   AL = status (see Table 31-9)
                                          CX = number of characters in receive ring buffer
                                          DX:BX -> transmit buffer

See also: Functions 2400h and 2402h

INT 17h Function 2404h   *Shamrock Software NET.24 v3.11+*
SEND ACK BLOCK

Registers at call: **Return Registers:**
AX = 2404h   AL = status (see Table 31-9)
BX = target address
See also: Functions 2402h and 2405h

INT 17h Function 2405h   *Shamrock Software NET.24 v3.11+*
SEND NAK BLOCK

Registers at call: **Return Registers:**
AX = 2405h   AL = status (see Table 31-9)
BX = target address
See also: Functions 2402h and 2404h

INT 17h Function 2406h   *Shamrock Software NET.24 v3.11+*
PREPARE CHARACTER-ORIENTED RECEIVE

Registers at call: **Return Registers:**
AX = 2406h   AL = status (see Table 31-9)
See also: Functions 2407h and 240Ah

INT 17h Function 2407h
Shamrock Software NET.24 v3.11+
RECEIVE CHARACTER FROM REMOTE

Registers at call:
AX = 2407h

Return Registers:
AL = status (see also Table 31-9)
    06h end of data
DL = received character

See also: Function 2406h

INT 17h Function 2408h
Shamrock Software NET.24 v3.11+
RECEIVE BLOCK, WITH HANDSHAKE

Registers at call:
AX = 2408h

Return Registers:
AL = status (see also Table 31-9)
    06h end of data
CX = number of bytes in receive buffer
DX:SI -> receive buffer

See also: Functions 2401h, 2405h, and 2409h

INT 17h Function 2409h
Shamrock Software NET.24 v3.11+
TRANSMIT COMMAND, WITH HANDSHAKE

Registers at call:
AX = 2409h
BX = target address
CX = number of data bytes
DL = command code to send
DS:SI -> data bytes for command
See also: Functions 2405h and 2408h

Return Registers:
AL = status (see also Table 31-9)
    03h no response
    06h remote currently unable to perform command

INT 17h Function 240Ah
Shamrock Software NET.24 v3.11+
PREPARE CHARACTER-ORIENTED TRANSMIT

Registers at call:
AX = 240Ah
See also: Functions 2406h, 240Bh, and 240Ch

Return Registers:
AL = status (see Table 31-9)

INT 17h Function 240Bh
Shamrock Software NET.24 v3.11+
TRANSMIT SINGLE CHARACTER TO REMOTE

Registers at call:
AX = 240Bh
DL = character to send

Return Registers:
AL = status (see also Table 31-9)
    03h transmission error
    06h write error

See also: Functions 2407h, 240Ah, and 240Ch

INT 17h Function 240Ch
Shamrock Software NET.24 v3.11+
END CHARACTER-ORIENTED TRANSMIT

Registers at call:
AX = 240Ch

Return Registers:
AL = status (see also Table 31-9)
    03h transmission error
    06h remote breaks connection

See also: Functions 240Ah and 240Bh

SilverNET

SilverNET is an SMB-compatible peer-to-peer NOS for DOS or Windows systems by Net-Source, Inc. of Santa Clara, CA.

INT 2Fh Function 4E53h, Subfunction 00h
INSTALLATION CHECK

Registers at call:
AX = 4E53h ("NS")
BL = 00h
BH = module ID (see Table 31-10)
Conflicts: none known, but see Table 2-2
See also: Function 4E53h Subfunctions 01h and 02h, Functions B800h and B809h (above)

Return Registers:
AX = 0000h if specified module installed
BX = 4E53h if SilverNET installed

31-10 Values for module ID:

01h	SilverCACHE
02h	Workstation
03h	NetBIOS
04h	Peer
20h	NS Share
80h	Netware help TSR

INT 2Fh Function 4E53h, Subfunction 01h
GET RUNTIME PARAMETER

Purpose: Retrieve a word of data from the specified SilverNET module.

Registers at call:
AX = 4E53h ("NS")
BL = 01h
BH = module ID (see Table 31-10)
CX = parameter index (see Tables 31-11 to 31-13)
Conflicts: none known, but see Table 2-2

Return Registers:
AX = WORD value at specified index

31-11 Values for Peer parameter index (* = read-only):

00h	*	maximum outstanding SMB buffers
02h	*	maximum logged-in nodes
04h	*	number of shareable resources
06h	*	number of characters to print per time slice
08h	*	number of printers that can be shared
0Ah	*	number of nodes logged in
0Ch	*	number of files to allow opened
0Eh		how fast to despool (/PSLICE)
10h		audit flag
24h	*	far pointer to resource table (each resource is 96 bytes in length)
32h	*	far pointer to SFT (internal if SilverNET files > CONFIG.SYS files, else DOS SFT)
36h		spool flags
		bit 0: LPT1 needs despooling
		bit 1: LPT2 needs despooling
		bit 2: LPT2 needs despooling
		bit 4: COM1 needs despooling
		bit 5: COM2 needs despooling
		bit 6: COM3 needs despooling

31-12 Values for NS Share parameter index (* = read-only):

00h		version number (high byte = minor, low byte = major)
10h	*	segment of first lock record (other records in consecutive paragraphs) (if PSP field = 0000h, lock record is free)

12h	*	maximum possible number of lock records
14h	*	starting segment of sharing buffer
		(NS Share's sharing records are identical to DOS SHARE—see PCI-24 under INT 21h Function 52h—except that fields which are normally offsets into SHARE are segment numbers)
18h	*	size of sharing buffer in paragraphs
1Ah	*	total free paragraphs in sharing buffer
1Ch	*	current number of shared files
1Eh	*	current number of locked records

31-13 Values for Workstation parameter index (* = read-only):

00h		version number (high byte = minor, low byte = major)
02h	*	size of each network buffer for file operations
04h	*	number of redirector file buffers
06h	*	size of each print cache buffer
08h	*	number of network LPT printers
0Ch		flush time in ticks (idle time on network printer before flushing)
0Eh		(16 WORDs) last active time for each printer
2Eh	*	stub segment if program split into two parts
60h		receive name number for datagram listens
62h	*	18-byte machine name
74h	*	LASTDRIVE (01h = A:, etc.)
7Ch		row number of message box on screen
7Eh		message time in clock ticks
82h	*	number of network adapters in use
84h		station ID broadcast flag (never set on redirectors)
96h	*	NetBIOS names left
98h	*	NCBs left
9Ah	*	sessions left
A2h	*	total number of network printers (LPT+COM)
A4h	*	number of serial network printers
A8h	*	segment containing file cache buffers
AAh	*	segment containing print cache buffers
ACh	*	bytes remaining free in HMA before program loaded
AEh	*	start of free memory in HMA
B2h	*	flag: using HMA

INT 2Fh Function 4E53h, Subfunction 02h   *SilverNET*
SET RUNTIME PARAMETERS

Purpose: Set a WORD value in the specified SilverNET module.

Registers at call: **Return Registers:**
AX = 4E53h ("NS")   none
BL = 02h
BH = module ID (see Table 31-10)
CX = parameter index (see Tables 31-11 to 31-13)
DX = new value for specified parameter

Details: Not all indexed parameters are writable; modifying a read-only parameter can result in system crashes.

Conflicts: none known, but see Table 2-2

See also: Function 4E53h Subfunctions 00h and 01h

Miscellaneous

INT 21h Function 3306h
CBIS POWERLAN
NETWORK REDIRECTOR - UNDETERMINED FUNCTION

Registers at call:
AX = 3306h

Return Registers:
AX = 3306h
BL = *unknown* (usually 00h)
BH = *unknown* (usually 00h or FFh)

Details: This undetermined function is in conflict with the DOS 5+ "get true version" call.
Conflicts: MS-DOS Function 3306h (PCI-24)
See also: MS-DOS Function 3306h (PCI-24)

INT 21h Function CFh
LANstep
UNDETERMINED FUNCTION

Purpose: LANstep is a redesign of the Waterloo Microsystems PORT network.

Registers at call:
AH = CFh
others, if any, unknown

Return Registers:
unknown

Conflicts: Novell NetWare (Chapter 21)

INT 2Ah Function 2001h
MS Networks or NETBIOS
UNDETERMINED FUNCTION

Registers at call:
AX = 2001h
others, if any, unknown

Return Registers:
unknown

Details: This function is intercepted by DESQview 2.x.

INT 2Ah Functions 2002h and 2003h
NETWORK
UNDETERMINED FUNCTIONS

Registers at call:
AX = 2002h and 2003h
others, if any, unknown

Return Registers:
unknown

Details: These functions are called by the MS-DOS 3.30-6.00 APPEND.

INT 2Ah Function C2h
Network
UNDETERMINED FUNCTION
Undocumented

Registers at call:
AH = C2h
AL = subfunction
    07h *unknown*
    08h *unknown*
BX = 0001h
others, if any, unknown

Return Registers:
unknown

Details: This function is called by the DOS 3.30-6.00 APPEND.

INT 2Fh Function 13h
MS-NET
UNDETERMINED FUNCTION
Undocumented

Registers at call:
AH = 13h
others, if any, unknown

Return Registers:
unknown

Details: This function is reportedly used to move (or control the movement of) NCBs.
Conflicts: MS-DOS kernel (PCI-24)

INT 2Fh Function 8000h
INSTALLATION CHECK
Purpose: EASY-NET is a shareware two-machine serial-port network.

Registers at call:	Return Registers:
AX = 8000h	AL = status
	00h not installed
	FFh installed

Conflicts: TurboNET (above), FaxBIOS (PCI-64), ASCII (PCI-66)

INT 5Bh
API

Registers at call:	Return Registers:
ES:BX -> Transfer Control Block	AL = status

Details: This software interface allows multiple protocols/software packages to access a BICC 411x network card.

Conflicts: AT&T Starlan (Chapter 8), Alloy NTNX (Chapter 12), Cluster Adapter (Chapter 42), Microsoft Network Transport Layer Interface (Chapter 42), DESQview IRQ11 (PCI-44), DoubleDOS IRQ3 (PCI-49), SitBack (PCI-66)

31-14 Format of Transfer Control Block:

Offset	Type	Description
00h	BYTE	command code
		B3h Status
		F2h Activate
		F3h Deactivate
		F4h Send Data
01h	BYTE	command identity
02h	BYTE	virtual circuit ID
03h	WORD	buffer length
05h	DWORD	buffer pointer
09h	BYTE	expedited data flag
0Ah	BYTE	cancelable flag
0Bh	16 BYTEs	local network address
1Bh	16 BYTEs	remote network address
2Bh	DWORD	asynchronous notification routine
30h	DWORD	local network number
34h	DWORD	remote network number
38h	BYTE	call timeout
39h	BYTE	not used
3Ah	8 BYTEs	reserved
42h	BYTE	command code extension
43h	WORD	Blue Book MAC type

INT 5Ch
API

Registers at call:	Return Registers:
ES:BX -> Network Control Block	NCB updated

Details: The TOPS card may be configured to use DMA channels 1, 3, or none.

Conflicts: ATALK.SYS below, IBM 802.2 interface below, $25 LAN below, NetBIOS (Chapter 8), DESQview IRQ12 (PCI-44), DoubleDOS IRQ4 (PCI-49)

INT 5Ch
AppleTalk INTERFACE   *ATALK.SYS*

Registers at call: **Return Registers:**
DX:BX -> control block (see Table 31-15)   none

Details: This driver can use any interrupt from 5Ch to 70h. The signature 'AppleTalk' appears 16 bytes prior to the interrupt handler; this serves as the installation check.

Conflicts: TOPS above, IBM 802.2 interface below, $25 LAN below, NetBIOS (Chapter 8), DESQview IRQ12 (PCI-44), DoubleDOS IRQ4 (PCI-49)

31-15 ATALK.SYS command codes:

01h	"AT_INIT"	initialize the driver
02h	"AT_KILL"	
03h	"AT_GETNETINFO"	get current network info including init status
04h	"AT_GETCLOCKTICKS"	
05h	"AT_STARTTIMER"	
06h	"AT_RESETTIMER"	
07h	"AT_CANCELTIMER"	
10h	"LAP_INSTALL"	
11h	"LAP_REMOVE"	
12h	"LAP_WRITE"	
13h	"LAP_READ"	
14h	"LAP_CANCEL"	
20h	"DDP_OPENSOCKET"	
21h	"DDP_CLOSESOCKET"	
22h	"DDP_WRITE"	
23h	"DDP_READ"	
24h	"DDP_CANCEL"	
30h	"NBP_REGISTER"	
31h	"NBP_REMOVE"	
32h	"NBP_LOOKUP"	
33h	"NBP_CONFIRM"	
34h	"NBP_CANCEL"	
35h	"ZIP_GETZONELIST"	
36h	"ZIP_GETMYZONE"	
37h	"ZIP_TAKEDOWN"	
38h	"ZIP_BRINGUP"	
40h	"ATP_OPENSOCKET"	
41h	"ATP_CLOSESOCKET"	
42h	"ATP_SENDREQUEST"	
43h	"ATP_GETREQUEST"	
44h	"ATP_SENDRESPONSE"	
45h	"ATP_ADDRESPONSE"	
46h	"ATP_CANCELTRANS"	
47h	"ATP_CANCELRESPONSE"	
48h	"ATP_CANCELREQUEST"	
50h	"ASP_GETPARMS"	
51h	"ASP_CLOSESESSION"	
52h	"ASP_CANCEL"	
53h	"ASP_INIT"	
54h	"ASP_KILL"	

55h	"ASP_GETSESSION"
56h	"ASP_GETREQUEST"
57h	"ASP_CMDREPLY"
58h	"ASP_WRTCONTINUE"
59h	"ASP_WRTREPLY"
5Ah	"ASP_CLOSEREPLY"
5Bh	"ASP_NEWSTATUS"
5Ch	"ASP_ATTENTION"
5Dh	"ASP_GETSTATUS"
5Eh	"ASP_OPENSESSION"
5Fh	"ASP_COMMAND"
60h	"ASP_WRITE"
61h	"ASP_GETATTENTION"
70h	"PAP_OPEN"
71h	"PAP_CLOSE"
72h	"PAP_READ"
73h	"PAP_WRITE"
74h	"PAP_STATUS"
75h	"PAP_REGNAME"
76h	"PAP_REMNAME"
77h	"PAP_INIT"
78h	"PAP_NEWSTATUS"
79h	"PAP_GETNEXTJOB"
7Ah	"PAP_KILL"
7Bh	"PAP_CANCEL"

31-16 Format of AppleTalk control block:

Offset	Size	Description
00h	WORD	command code (see Table 31-15)
		OR with the following flags
		8000h start command then return
		4000h wait for interrupt service to complete
02h	WORD	returned status
		0000h success (already initialized if function 01h)
04h	DWORD	pointer to completion function
08h	WORD	network number
0Ah	BYTE	node ID

---if general func (01h,03h), control block continues:

0Bh	BYTE	"inf_abridge"
0Ch	WORD	"inf_config"
0Eh	DWORD	pointer to buffer
12h	WORD	buffer size

---if DDP function (20h-24h), control block continues:

0Bh	BYTE	"ddp_addr_socket"
0Ch	BYTE	"ddp_socket"
0Dh	BYTE	"ddp_type"
0Eh	DWORD	pointer to buffer
12h	WORD	buffer size
14h	BYTE	"ddp_chksum"

---if Name Binding Protocol (30h-34h), control block continues:

0Bh	BYTE	"nbp_addr_socket"
0Ch	WORD	"nbp_toget"
0Eh	DWORD	pointer to buffer
12h	WORD	buffer size
14h	BYTE	"nbp_interval"
15h	BYTE	"nbp_retry"
16h	DWORD	"nbp_entptr"

---if AppleTalk Transaction Protocol (42h), control block continues:

0Bh	BYTE	"atp_addr_socket"
0Ch	WORD	"atp_socket"
0Eh	DWORD	pointer to buffer
12h	WORD	buffer size
14h	BYTE	"atp_interval"
15h	BYTE	"atp_retry"
16h	BYTE	ATP flags
		bit 5: exactly one transaction
17h	BYTE	"atp_seqbit"
18h	BYTE	transaction ID
19h	4 BYTEs	ATP user bytes
1Dh	BYTE	number of BDS buffers
1Eh	BYTE	number of BDS responses
1Fh	DWORD	pointer to BDS buffers (see Table 31-18)

31-17 Format of Name Binding Protocol Name-to-Address binding entries for NBP_LOOKUP:

Offset	Size	Description
00h	WORD	"tup_address_network"
02h	BYTE	"tup_address_notid"
03h	BYTE	"tup_address_socket"
04h	BYTE	"tup_enum"
05h	99 BYTEs	name

31-18 Format of BDS entries:

Offset	Size	Description
00h	DWORD	pointer to buffer
04h	WORD	size of buffer
06h	WORD	BDS data size
08h	4 BYTEs	"bds_userbytes"

INT 5Ch
API
IBM 802.2 INTERFACE (LLC)

Registers at call:
ES:BX -> CCB (see Table 31-19)

Return Registers:
none

Conflicts: TOPS above, ATALK.SYS above, $25 LAN below, NetBIOS (Chapter 8), DESQview IRQ12 (PCI-44), DoubleDOS IRQ4 (PCI-49)

31-19 Format of CCB:

Offset	Size	Description
00h	BYTE	adapter
01h	BYTE	command code
02h	BYTE	return code
03h	BYTE	work

04h	DWORD	pointer to *unknown item*
08h	DWORD	pointer to *completion function*
0Ch	DWORD	pointer to *parameters*

INT 5Ch $25 LAN
INSTALLATION CHECK

Details: Current versions only check whether the vector is 0000h:0000h or not. Future versions are supposed to have the signature "NET" in the three bytes preceding the INT 5Ch handler.

Conflicts: TOPS above, ATALK.SYS above, IBM 802.2 interface above, NetBIOS (Chapter 8), DESQview IRQ12 (PCI-44), DoubleDOS IRQ4 (PCI-49)

INT 5Ch Function 04h $25 LAN
CHECK IF CONNECTION ALIVE

Registers at call:
AH = 04h
AL = COM port (0 = default)
CX = wait count in character times (should be at least 100)

Return Registers:
ZF set if link alive

Conflicts: TOPS above, ATALK.SYS above, IBM 802.2 interface above, NetBIOS (Chapter 8), DESQview IRQ12 (PCI-44), DoubleDOS IRQ4 (PCI-49)

INT 60h Function 11h   3com, 10NET, Banyan VINES
LOCK AND WAIT

Registers at call:
AH = 11h
AL = drive number or 0
DX = number of seconds to wait
ES:SI = Ethernet address or 0
DS:BX -> 31-byte ASCIZ semaphore name

Return Registers:
AL = status (see Table 31-20)

Conflicts: see Table 2-3
See also: Functions 12h and 13h

31-20 Values for status:

00h	successful
01h	timeout
02h	server not responding
03h	invalid semaphore name
04h	semaphore list is full
05h	invalid drive ID
06h	invalid Ethernet address
07h	not logged in
08h	write to network failed
09h	semaphore already logged for this CPU

INT 60h Function 12h   3com, 10NET, Banyan VINES
LOCK

Registers at call:
AH = 12h
AL = drive number or 00h
ES:SI = Ethernet address or 0000h:0000h
DS:BX -> 31-byte ASCIZ semaphore name

Return Registers:
AL = status (see also Table 31-20)
  01h semaphore currently locked by another PC

Details: Unlike Function 11h, this function returns immediately.
Conflicts: see Table 2-3
See also: Functions 11h and 13h

INT 60h Function 13h
UNLOCK
3com, 10NET, Banyan VINES

Registers at call:
AH = 13h
AL = drive number or 00h
ES:SI = Ethernet address or 0000h:0000h
DS:BX -> 31-byte ASCIZ semaphore name
Conflicts: see Table 2-3
See also: Functions 11h and 12h

Return Registers:
AL = status (see also Table 31-20)
   01h semaphore not locked

INT 7Fh
ACCESS VECTOR
Convergent Technologies ClusterShare CTOS

Registers at call:
AL = request ID
   01h "Request"/"RequestDirect"
      ES:BX -> pRq
      DX ignored
   04h "Wait"
      ES:BX -> ppMsgRet
      DX = exchange
   05h "AllocExch"
      ES:BX -> pExchRet
   06h "DeAllocExch"
      DX = exchange
   07h "Check"
      ES:BX -> ppMsgRet
      DX = exchange
CX = 4354h ('CT')
Conflicts: see Table 2-4

Return Registers:
AX = status
   0000h successful

INT E1h
Disk Server Information
PC Cluster

Conflicts: IBM ROM BASIC (PCI-54)
See also: INT E2h

INT E2h
UNDETERMINED USAGE
PC Cluster Program

Conflicts: IBM ROM BASIC (PCI-54)

CHAPTER 32

Beame and Whiteside
BW-TCP and BW-NFS

BW-TCP is a TCP/IP protocol stack by Beame & Whiteside Software. BW-NFS adds Network File System support on top of BW-TCP.

The Beame&Whiteside TCP/IP protocol stack uses two consecutive interrupts (62h and 63h by default); the BW-NFS client uses a third consecutive interrupt (64h by default) if it is loaded.

INT 13h Function 4257h   *Beame&Whiteside BWLPD*
INSTALLATION CHECK   *Undocumented*

Purpose: BWLPD is the printer daemon from the BW-NFS package.

Registers at call:	Return Registers:
AX = 4257h ("BW")	BX = 414Ch if installed
DX = 1234h	

See also: BW-TCP INT 62h

INT 21h Function 3Fh   *BW-TCP*
GET DRIVER INFO

Registers at call:
AH = 3Fh
BX = file handle for device "ETHDEV27"
CX = 002Bh
DS:DX -> buffer for driver info
  (see Table 32-1)

Return Registers:
CF clear if successful
  AX = number of bytes actually read
    (0 if at EOF before call)
CF set on error
  AX = error code (05h,06h) (see Table 3-1)

Details: The Beame&Whiteside socket library performs an INT 21h Function 4401h with DX=0060h before making this call to retrieve the driver information; one should also call the private API interrupt with Function 15h.

The installation check for the TCP/IP stack is to test for the existence of the character device UDP-IP10.

See also: BW-TCP INT 62h, INT 63h Function 03h, INT 64h Function 00h, BWCOM14 INT 14h Function 56h (Chapter 38)

32-1 Format of driver info:

Offset	Size	Description
00h	WORD	I/O base address
02h	BYTE	shared memory page (01h = segment 0100h, etc.)
03h	BYTE	interrupt vector for private API
04h	BYTE	IRQ used by board
05h	WORD	size of data buffer
07h	WORD	maximum transfer window
09h	WORD	time zone

0Bh	BYTE	address type (01h user, 04h RARP, 05h BOOTP)
0Ch	DWORD	internet address
10h	WORD	"value"
12h	BYTE	subnet mask
13h	WORD	"ether_pointer"
15h	WORD	offset in device driver of log server records
17h	WORD	offset in device driver of name server records
19h	WORD	offset in device driver of print server records
1Bh	WORD	offset in device driver of time server records
1Dh	WORD	offset in device driver of gateway records
1Fh	WORD	segment address of device driver
21h	BYTE	transfer size
22h	9 BYTEs	network adapter board name
--- 11/21/91 or newer version ---		
23h	BYTE	ETHDEV version (major in high nybble, minor in low nybble)
24h	BYTE	ETHDEV revision
25h	BYTE	TCPIP version (major in high nybble, minor in low nybble)
26h	BYTE	TCPIP revision
27h	BYTE	BWRPC version (major in high nybble, minor in low nybble)
28h	BYTE	BWRPC revision
29h	BYTE	BWNFS version (major in high nybble, minor in low nybble)
2Ah	BYTE	BWNFS revision
2Bh	BYTE	Telnet version (major in high nybble, minor in low nybble)
2Ch	BYTE	Telnet revision
2Dh	BYTE	NETBIOS version (major in high nybble, minor in low nybble)
2Eh	BYTE	NETBIOS revision

Note: For each driver, if the version is 0, the driver is not installed or does not support the version check.

32-2 Format of server records:

Offset	Size	Description
00h	BYTE	number of server records following
01h	N DWORDs	internet addresses of servers

INT 2Fh Function DAB2h   *Beame&Whiteside BWSNMP*
INSTALLATION CHECK   *Undocumented*

Purpose: BWSNMP is part of the BW-NFS package.
Registers at call: **Return Registers:**
AX = DAB2h   AX = 00FFh if installed
                                 BX:CX -> MIB table
Conflicts: TRAP.COM (PCI-57), ZyXEL ZFAX (PCI-64); see also Table 2-2
See also: BW-TCP INT 62h

INT 62h Function 00h   *BW-TCP HARDWARE DRIVER (ETHDEV.SYS)*
GET PHYSICAL HARDWARE ADDRESS

Registers at call: **Return Registers:**
AH = 00h   AX = *length of hardware address*
DS:DX -> 6-byte buffer for address
Details: The Beame&Whiteside TCP/IP protocol stack uses two consecutive interrupts (62h and 63h by default); the BW-NFS client uses a third consecutive interrupt (64h by default) if it is loaded.
Conflicts: see Table 2-3

INT 62h Function 01h *BW-TCP HARDWARE DRIVER (ETHDEV.SYS)*
NOP for ETHDEV.ODI

Registers at call:
AH = 01h

Return Registers:
CF clear if successful
CF set on error
    AL = error code

Conflicts: see Table 2-3

INT 62h Function 02h *BW-TCP HARDWARE DRIVER (ETHDEV.SYS)*
INITIALIZE

Registers at call:
AH = 02h

Return Registers:
CF clear if successful
CF set on error
    AL = error code

Conflicts: see Table 2-3

INT 62h Function 03h *BW-TCP HARDWARE DRIVER (ETHDEV.SYS)*
GET REAL IP ADDRESS

Registers at call:
AH = 03h
DS:SI -> DWORD buffer for IP address

Return Registers:
CF clear if successful
CF set on error
    AL = error code

Conflicts: see Table 2-3

INT 62h Function 04h *BW-TCP HARDWARE DRIVER (ETHDEV.SYS)*
SET UNKNOWN POINTER

Registers at call:
AH = 04h
BX = *unknown*
ES:SI -> FAR routine for *unknown*

Return Registers:
CF clear if successful
CF set on error
    AL = error code

Conflicts: see Table 2-3

INT 62h Functions 05h and 06h *BW-TCP HARDWARE DRIVER (ETHDEV.SYS)*
UNDETERMINED FUNCTIONS

Registers at call:
AH = 05h and 06h
others, if any, unknown

Return Registers:
CF clear if successful
CF set on error
    AL = error code

Conflicts: see Table 2-3

INT 62h Function 07h *BW-TCP HARDWARE DRIVER (ETHDEV.SYS)*
UNDETERMINED FUNCTION

Registers at call:
AH = 07h
DS:SI -> *unknown*

Return Registers:
CF clear if successful
CF set on error
    AL = error code

Conflicts: see Table 2-3

INT 62h Function 08h *BW-TCP HARDWARE DRIVER (ETHDEV.SYS)*
UNDETERMINED FUNCTION

Registers at call:
AH = 08h

CX = *unknown*
ES:SI -> buffer (see Table 32-3)

Return Registers:
CF clear if successful
CF set on error
    AL = error code

Conflicts: see Table 2-3

32-3 Format of buffer:

Offset	Size	Description
00h	6 BYTEs	*hardware address*
06h	6 BYTEs	*unknown*
0Ch	WORD	*unknown*
0Eh	WORD	*unknown*

INT 62h Function 09h
HOOK TIMER INTERRUPT
BW-TCP HARDWARE DRIVER (ETHDEV.SYS)

Registers at call:
AH = 09h

Return Registers:
AX = handler ID if successful

Conflicts: see Table 2-3

INT 62h Function 0Ah
UNHOOK TIMER INTERRUPT
BW-TCP HARDWARE DRIVER (ETHDEV.SYS)

Registers at call:
AH = 0Ah
DX = handler ID

Return Registers:
CF clear if successful
CF set on error
    AL = error code

Conflicts: see Table 2-3

INT 62h Function 0Bh
ADD UNKNOWN ITEM
BW-TCP HARDWARE DRIVER (ETHDEV.SYS)

Registers at call:
AH = 0Bh
AL = *unknown*
DX = *unknown*
BP = *unknown*
ES:SI -> *unknown*

Return Registers:
CF clear if successful
CF set on error
    AL = error code

Conflicts: see Table 2-3

INT 62h Function 0Ch
REMOVE UNKNOWN ITEM
BW-TCP HARDWARE DRIVER (ETHDEV.SYS)

Registers at call:
AH = 0Ch
DX = *unknown*
BP = *unknown*

Return Registers:
CF clear if successful
CF set on error
    AL = error code

Conflicts: see Table 2-3
See also: Function 0Dh

INT 62h Function 0Dh
NOP for ETHDEV.ODI
BW-TCP HARDWARE DRIVER (ETHDEV.SYS)

Registers at call:
AH = 0Dh

Return Registers:
CF clear if successful
CF set on error
    AL = error code

Conflicts: see Table 2-3
See also: Function 0Ch

INT 62h Function 0Eh
BEGIN CRITICAL SECTION
BW-TCP HARDWARE DRIVER (ETHDEV.SYS)

Registers at call:
AH = 0Eh

Return Registers:
CF clear if successful
CF set on error
    AL = error code

Conflicts: see Table 2-3
See also: Functions 0Fh and 10h

INT 62h Function 0Fh
END CRITICAL SECTION
BW-TCP HARDWARE DRIVER (ETHDEV.SYS)

Registers at call:
AH = 0Fh

Return Registers:
CF clear if successful
CF set on error
    AL = error code

Conflicts: see Table 2-3
See also: Functions 0Eh and 10h

INT 62h Function 10h
QUERY CRITICAL SECTION
BW-TCP HARDWARE DRIVER (ETHDEV.SYS)

Registers at call:
AH = 10h

Return Registers:
CF clear if no critical section active
CF set if in critical section

Conflicts: see Table 2-3
See also: Functions 0Fh and 10h

INT 62h Function 11h
SET UNKNOWN POINTER
BW-TCP HARDWARE DRIVER (ETHDEV.SYS)

Registers at call:
AH = 11h
ES:SI -> *unknown*
Conflicts: see Table 2-3

Return Registers:
CF clear

INT 62h Function 12h
GET UNKNOWN VALUE
BW-TCP HARDWARE DRIVER (ETHDEV.SYS)

Registers at call:
AH = 12h

Return Registers:
AX = *unknown* (memory variable incremented after reading)

Conflicts: see Table 2-3

INT 62h Function 13h
UNDETERMINED FUNCTION
BW-TCP HARDWARE DRIVER (ETHDEV.SYS)

Registers at call:
AH = 13h
CX = *unknown*

Return Registers:
CF clear if successful
    AL = 00h
CF set on error
    AL = error code

Conflicts: see Table 2-3

INT 62h Function 14h   *BW-TCP HARDWARE DRIVER (ETHDEV.SYS)*
UNDETERMINED FUNCTION

Registers at call: **Return Registers:**
AH = 14h   CF clear if successful
ES:SI -> *unknown*   AL = 00h
                                                CF set on error
                                                    AL = error code

Conflicts: see Table 2-3

INT 62h Function 15h   *BW-TCP HARDWARE DRIVER (ETHDEV.SYS)*
GET UNKNOWN ITEM

Registers at call: **Return Registers:**
AH = 15h   CF clear if successful
                                                    AX = *unknown (destroyed)*
                                                CF set on error
                                                    AL = error code

Details: Call this function after reading the ETHDEV27 device.
Conflicts: see Table 2-3

INT 62h Function 16h   *BW-TCP HARDWARE DRIVER (ETHDEV.SYS)*
UNDETERMINED FUNCTION

Registers at call: **Return Registers:**
AH = 16h   CF clear if successful
                                                CF set on error
                                                    AL = error code

Conflicts: see Table 2-3

INT 62h Function 17h   *BW-TCP HARDWARE DRIVER (ETHDEV.SYS)*
UNDETERMINED FUNCTION

Registers at call: **Return Registers:**
AH = 17h   Cf clear
DX = segment of *unknown*
Conflicts: see Table 2-3

INT 62h Function 18h   *BW-TCP HARDWARE DRIVER (ETHDEV.SYS)*
ALLOCATE AND MAP EMS FOR DRIVER

Registers at call: **Return Registers:**
AH = 18h   CF clear if successful
                                                CF set on error
                                                    AL = error code

Details: This function calls Function 17h after EMS has been allocated and mapped.
Conflicts: see Table 2-3

INT 62h Function FEh   *BW-TCP HARDWARE DRIVER (ETHDEV.SYS)*
MAP EMS

Registers at call: **Return Registers:**
AH = FEh   CF clear if successful
    00h map in driver's memory   CF set on error
    01h map out driver's memory   AL = error code

Details: This function is supported by at least the SLIP and ODI versions of ETHDEV.SYS.
Conflicts: see Table 2-3
See also: Function FEh, INT 21h Function 3Fh, BW-TCP INT 63h, BW-NFS INT 64h Function FEh

INT 63h Function 00h
SET IP ADDRESS
BW-TCP TCPIP.SYS

Registers at call:
AH = 00h
DS:BX -> DWORD containing IP
  address (big-endian)

Return Registers:
CF clear if successful
CF set on error
AX destroyed

Details: The Beame&Whiteside TCP/IP protocol stack uses two consecutive interrupts (62h and 63h by default); the BW-NFS client uses a third consecutive interrupt (64h by default) if it is loaded.
Conflicts: see Table 2-3
See also: Functions 01h and 02h

INT 63h Function 01h
UNDETERMINED FUNCTION
BW-TCP TCPIP.SYS

Registers at call:
AH = 01h
ES:BX -> *unknown*
others, if any, unknown

Return Registers:
unknown

Conflicts: see Table 2-3
See also: Functions 00h and 02h

INT 63h Function 02h
UNDETERMINED FUNCTION
BW-TCP TCPIP.SYS

Registers at call:
AH = 02h
others, if any, unknown

Return Registers:
unknown

Conflicts: see Table 2-3
See also: Functions 00h and 01h

INT 63h Function 03h
GET IP ADDRESS
BW-TCP TCPIP.SYS

Registers at call:
AH = 03h
DS:SI -> buffer for DWORD IP
  address (big-endian)

Return Registers:
AX destroyed
CF clear if successful
CF set on error

Details: This call may use ARP or RARP to determine the address.
Conflicts: see Table 2-3

INT 63h Function 04h
UNDETERMINED FUNCTION
BW-TCP TCPIP.SYS

Registers at call:
AH = 04h
others, if any, unknown

Return Registers:
unknown

Conflicts: see Table 2-3

INT 63h Function 05h
UNDETERMINED FUNCTION
BW-TCP TCPIP.SYS

Registers at call:
AH = 05h
DS:BX -> *unknown*
ES:SI -> *unknown*

Return Registers:
unknown

Conflicts: see Table 2-3

INT 63h Function 06h   *BW-TCP TCPIP.SYS*
UNDETERMINED FUNCTION

Registers at call: **Return Registers:**
AH = 06h   *unknown*
others, if any, unknown
Conflicts: see Table 2-3

INT 63h Function 07h   *BW-TCP TCPIP.SYS*
UNDETERMINED FUNCTION

Registers at call: **Return Registers:**
AH = 07h   *unknown*
others, if any, unknown
Conflicts: see Table 2-3

INT 63h Function 08h   *BW-TCP TCPIP.SYS*
SET DEFAULT UNKNOWN HANDLER

Registers at call: **Return Registers:**
AH = 08h   CF clear if successful
DS:BX -> DWORD containing IP   CF set on error
  address   *others, if any, unknown*
Conflicts: see Table 2-3

INT 63h Function 09h   *BW-TCP TCPIP.SYS*
INSTALL UNKNOWN HANDLERS

Registers at call: **Return Registers:**
AH = 09h   *unknown*
BL = handler type
ES:SI -> FAR handler of specified type
Conflicts: see Table 2-3
See also: Functions 0Ah and 0Dh

INT 63h Function 0Ah   *BW-TCP TCPIP.SYS*
DELETE UNKNOWN HANDLERS

Registers at call: **Return Registers:**
AH = 0Ah   CF clear if successful
BL = handler type   CF set on error (no handler of specified type
                                installed)

Conflicts: see Table 2-3
See also: Function 09h

INT 63h Function 0Bh   *BW-TCP TCPIP.SYS*
UNDETERMINED FUNCTION

Registers at call: **Return Registers:**
AH = 0Bh   *unknown*
AL = *unknown*
DL = *unknown*
DS:BX -> *unknown*
ES:SI -> *unknown*
Conflicts: see Table 2-3

INT 63h Function 0Ch   *BW-TCP TCPIP.SYS*
UNDETERMINED FUNCTION
Registers at call: **Return Registers:**
AH = 0Ch   *unknown*
others, if any, unknown
Conflicts: see Table 2-3

INT 63h Function 0Dh   *BW-TCP TCPIP.SYS*
INSTALL DEFAULT UNKNOWN HANDLER
Registers at call: **Return Registers:**
AH = 0Dh   *unknown*
others, if any, unknown
Details: If one is not already installed, this function installs a type 06h handler with Function 09h.
Conflicts: see Table 2-3
See also: Function 09h

INT 63h Function 0Eh   *BW-TCP TCPIP.SYS*
CLOSE NETWORK DESCRIPTOR
Registers at call: **Return Registers:**
AH = 0Eh   *unknown*
others, if any, unknown
Conflicts: see Table 2-3
See also: PC/TCP INT 61h Functions 08h, 09h, and 18h (Chapter 33)

INT 63h Function 0Fh   *BW-TCP TCPIP.SYS*
UNDETERMINED FUNCTION
Registers at call: **Return Registers:**
AH = 0Fh   *unknown*
AL = *unknown*
SI = *unknown*
DS:DI -> *unknown*
others, if any, unknown
Conflicts: see Table 2-3

INT 63h Function 10h   *BW-TCP TCPIP.SYS*
UNDETERMINED FUNCTION
Registers at call: **Return Registers:**
AH = 10h   *unknown*
DS:DI -> *unknown*
others, if any, unknown
Conflicts: see Table 2-3

INT 63h Function 11h   *BW-TCP TCPIP.SYS*
UNDETERMINED FUNCTION
Registers at call: **Return Registers:**
AH = 11h   *unknown*
others, if any, unknown
Conflicts: see Table 2-3

INT 63h Function 12h   *BW-TCP TCPIP.SYS*
LISTEN FOR INCOMING CONNECTIONS
Registers at call:
AH = 12h

DS:SI -> *unknown*
ES:BP -> *unknown*
Conflicts: see Table 2-3
See also: INT 61h Function 23h

Return Registers:
unknown

INT 63h Function 13h   *BW-TCP TCPIP.SYS*
NOP
Registers at call: **Return Registers:**
AH = 13h   none
Conflicts: see Table 2-3

INT 63h Function 14h   *BW-TCP TCPIP.SYS*
OPEN NETWORK CONNECTION
Registers at call: **Return Registers:**
AH = 14h   *unknown*
BX = *network descriptor*
DS:SI -> *unknown*
ES:BP -> *unknown*
Conflicts: see Table 2-3
See also: INT 62h Function 13h, PC/TCP INT 61h Function 13h (Chapter 33)

INT 63h Function 15h   *BW-TCP TCPIP.SYS*
UNDETERMINED FUNCTION
Registers at call: **Return Registers:**
AH = 15h   *unknown*
DS:DI -> *unknown*
others, if any, unknown
Conflicts: see Table 2-3

INT 63h Function 16h   *BW-TCP TCPIP.SYS*
RESET NETWORK CONNECTION
Registers at call: **Return Registers:**
AH = 16h   *unknown*
DS:DI -> *unknown*
Details: This function calls Function 17h after preprocessing.
Conflicts: see Table 2-3. **See also:** Function 17h, PC/TCP INT 61h Function 19h (Chapter 33)

INT 63h Function 17h   *BW-TCP TCPIP.SYS*
UNDETERMINED FUNCTION
Registers at call: **Return Registers:**
AH = 17h   *unknown*
DS:DI -> *unknown*
others, if any, unknown
Conflicts: see Table 2-3
See also: Function 18h

INT 63h Function 18h   *BW-TCP TCPIP.SYS*
UNDETERMINED FUNCTION
Registers at call: **Return Registers:**
AH = 18h   *unknown*
DS:DI -> *unknown*
others, if any, unknown
Details: This call is the same as Function 17h, except that it is performed with interrupts disabled.
Conflicts: see Table 2-3
See also: Function 17h

INT 63h Function 13h

INT 63h Function 19h
BW-TCP TCPIP.SYS
WRITE TO THE NETWORK

Registers at call: **Return Registers:**
AH = 19h   BX = number of bytes **not** written
DS:DI -> *unknown*   *others, if any, unknown*
others, if any, unknown

Details: This function calls Function 17h with interrupts disabled and *unknown* set to 01h.
Conflicts: see Table 2-3
See also: Functions 1Ah and 1Bh, PC/TCP INT 61h Function 1Ah (Chapter 33)

INT 63h Function 1Ah
BW-TCP TCPIP.SYS
READ FROM THE NETWORK

Registers at call: **Return Registers:**
AH = 1Ah   CX = number of bytes actually read
CX = maximum number of bytes to read *others, if any, unknown*
ES:BP -> *unknown*
others, if any, unknown
Conflicts: see Table 2-3
See also: Function 19h, PC/TCP INT 61h Function 1Bh (Chapter 33)

INT 63h Function 1Bh
BW-TCP TCPIP.SYS
UNDETERMINED FUNCTION

Registers at call: **Return Registers:**
AH = 1Bh   DX = *unknown*
CX = *unknown*   *others, if any, unknown*
ES:BP -> *unknown*
Conflicts: see Table 2-3

INT 63h Function 1Ch
BW-TCP TCPIP.SYS
UNDETERMINED FUNCTION

Registers at call: **Return Registers:**
AH = 1Ch   *unknown*
DS:DI -> *unknown*
others, if any, unknown
Details: This function calls Function 17h with *unknown*.
Conflicts: see Table 2-3
See also: Function 17h

INT 63h Function 1Dh
BW-TCP TCPIP.SYS
UNDETERMINED FUNCTION

Registers at call: **Return Registers:**
AH = 1Dh   *unknown*
others, if any, unknown
Conflicts: see Table 2-3

INT 63h Function 1Eh
BW-TCP TCPIP.SYS
UNDETERMINED FUNCTION

Registers at call: **Return Registers:**
AH = 1Eh   CF clear if successful
DS:BX -> DWORD containing IP address CF set on error
(big-endian) *others, if any, unknown* *others, if any, unknown*
Conflicts: see Table 2-3

INT 63h Function 1Fh
SET SOCKET UNKNOWN HANDLER
BW-TCP TCPIP.SYS

Registers at call:
AH = 1Fh
BX = socket number
ES:SI -> FAR function for *unknown*
Conflicts: see Table 2-3
See also: Function 20h

Return Registers:
CF clear if successful
CF set on error (out of slots)

INT 63h Function 20h
REMOVE SOCKET UNKNOWN HANDLER
BW-TCP TCPIP.SYS

Registers at call:
AH = 20h
BX = socket number
Conflicts: see Table 2-3
See also: Function 1Fh

Return Registers:
CF clear if successful
CF set on error (not set)

INT 63h Function 21h
UNDETERMINED FUNCTION
BW-TCP TCPIP.SYS

Registers at call:
AH = 21h
ES:SI -> *unknown*
Conflicts: see Table 2-3
See also: PC/TCP INT 61h Function 1Ch (Chapter 33)

Return Registers:
unknown

INT 63h Function 22h
REMOVE UNKNOWN HANDLER
BW-TCP TCPIP.SYS

Registers at call:
AH = 22h
Details: This function decrements a counter if it is not already zero, and calls Function 0Ah with BL=11h if the counter reaches zero.
Conflicts: see Table 2-3

Return Registers:
CF clear

INT 63h Function 23h
UNDETERMINED FUNCTION
BW-TCP TCPIP.SYS

Registers at call:
AH = 23h
DS:BX -> *unknown*
ES:SI -> 6-byte buffer for *unknown*
Conflicts: see Table 2-3

Return Registers:
CF clear if successful
CF set on error

INT 63h Function 24h
GET SOCKET
BW-TCP TCPIP.SYS

Registers at call:
AH = 24h
Conflicts: see Table 2-3
See also: BW-TCP INT 62h,BW-NFS INT 64h

Return Registers:
AX = new socket number (0400h-FFFFh)

INT 63h Function 25h
GET INTERNET ADDRESS
BW-TCP TCPIP.SYS

Registers at call:
AH = 25h
Conflicts: see Table 2-3
See also: Function 26h, PC/TCP INT 61h Function 05h (Chapter 33)

Return Registers:
CL:CH:DL:DH = caller's Internet address

INT 63h Function 26h   *BW-TCP TCPIP.SYS*
SET INTERNET ADDRESS

Registers at call: **Return Registers:**
AH = 26h   none
CL:CH:DL:DH = Internet address
Details: This function sets a different variable than Function 25h returns.
Conflicts: see Table 2-3
See also: Function 25h

INT 63h Function 27h   *BW-TCP TCPIP.SYS*
SET UNKNOWN ITEM

Registers at call: **Return Registers:**
AH = 27h   *unknown*
BX = *unknown*
ES:SI -> *unknown*
Conflicts: see Table 2-3

INT 63h Functions 28h and 29h   *BW-TCP TCPIP.SYS*
UNDETERMINED FUNCTIONS

Registers at call: **Return Registers:**
AH = 28h and 29h   *unknown*
others, if any, unknown
Conflicts: see Table 2-3

INT 64h Function 01h   *BW-NFS BWRPC*
UNDETERMINED FUNCTION   *Undocumented*

Registers at call: **Return Registers:**
AH = 01h   CF clear if successful
ES:BX -> *unknown* (at least 8 bytes)   *unknown*
ES:BP -> DWORD *unknown*   CF set on error
others, if any, unknown   CX = 0000h
Details: The Beame&Whiteside TCP/IP protocol stack uses two consecutive interrupts (62h and
63h by default); the BW-NFS client uses a third consecutive interrupt (64h by default) if it is
loaded.

The BWRPC installation check consists of determining the interrupt vector assigned to it (two
more than the value returned by reading the ETHDEV27 device), and testing whether the word
immediately preceding the interrupt handler is 4257h ('BW').
Conflicts: see Table 2-3
See also: BW-TCP INT 62h,BW-TCP INT 63h

INT 64h Function 02h   *BW-NFS BWRPC*
UNDETERMINED FUNCTION   *Undocumented*

Registers at call: **Return Registers:**
AH = 02h   *unknown*
DS:DI -> *unknown*
Details: This call is passed directly through to INT 62h Function 07h.
Conflicts: see Table 2-3
See also: INT 62h Function 07h

INT 64h Function 03h   *BW-NFS BWRPC*
ADD UNKNOWN ITEM   *Undocumented*

Registers at call:
AH = 03h

AL = *unknown*
BP = *unknown*
ES:SI -> *unknown*

Return Registers:
unknown

Details: This call is passed directly through to INT 62h Function 0Bh.
Conflicts: see Table 2-3
See also: Function 04h, INT 62h Function 0Bh

INT 64h Function 04h   *BW-NFS BWRPC*
REMOVE UNKNOWN ITEM   *Undocumented*

Registers at call:
AH = 04h
BP = *unknown*

Return Registers:
unknown

Details: This call is passed directly through to INT 62h Function 0Ch.
Conflicts: see Table 2-3
See also: Function 03h, INT 62h Function 0Ch

INT 64h Function 05h   *BW-NFS BWRPC*
UNDETERMINED FUNCTION   *Undocumented*

Registers at call:
AH = 05h
CX = *unknown*

Return Registers:
unknown

Details: This call is passed directly through to INT 62h Function 13h.
Conflicts: see Table 2-3
See also: INT 62h Function 13h

INT 64h Function 06h   *BW-NFS BWRPC*
UNDETERMINED FUNCTION   *Undocumented*

Registers at call:
AH = 06h
ES:SI -> *unknown*

Return Registers:
AL = 00h if CF clear

Details: This call is passed directly through to INT 62h Function 14h.
Conflicts: see Table 2-3
See also: INT 62h Function 14h

INT 64h Function 07h   *BW-NFS BWRPC*
GET IP ADDRESS   *Undocumented*

Registers at call:
AH = 07h

Return Registers:
CX:DX = IP address

Conflicts: see Table 2-3

INT 64h Function 10h   *BW-NFS BWRPC*
CALL ETHDEV.SYS   *Undocumented*

Registers at call:
AH = 10h
AL = ETHDEV function number
other registers as appropriate for
  ETHDEV call

Return Registers:
as returned by ETHDEV

Details: This call is passed directly through to INT 62h.
Conflicts: see Table 2-3
See also: various functions of INT 62h above

INT 64h Function 11h
NOP

Registers at call:
AH = 11h
Conflicts: see Table 2-3

Return Registers:
CF clear

INT 64h Function FEh
MAP EMS PAGE FRAME

Registers at call:
AH = FEh
AL = direction
    00h map in driver's memory block
    01h map out driver's memory block

Return Registers:
CF clear if successful
CF set on error
    AL = error code

Details: This call is passed through directly to ETHDEV.SYS (see INT 62h Function FEh).
Conflicts: see Table 2-3
See also: INT 21h Function 3Fh, INT 62h Function FEh, BW-TCP INT 63h

CHAPTER 33

FTP Software PC/TCP

The TCP/IP package from FTP Software Inc. is one of the oldest and most robust TCP/IP implementations. Since the original version, released in 1986, FTP has continued to refine the product, first separating network drivers from the protocol stack (in the process creating the Packet Driver Specification described in Chapter 11) and then offering the first non-Sun implementation of NFS.

Network Kernel

The PC/TCP kernel installation check consists of testing for the signature "TCPTSR" three bytes beyond the start of the interrupt handler. INT 61h as shown in this chapter is the default; PC/TCP v2.05 may be configured to use any interrupt from 20h through E0h. As with any TSR using interrupts in the range 60h to 67h, there are many potential conflicts which are listed in Table 2-3.

INT 61h   *FTP Software PC/TCP*
TCP/IP TSR System Call interface

Registers at call: **Return Registers:**
AH = system call number (see also   CF clear if successful
   entries below)   CF set on error
      01h "pkt_alloc" (v2.05; this is   AL = basic error (see Table 33-1)
        "net_config" in v2.1+)   AH = suberror number (see Tables 33-2 and 33-3)
      02h "pkt_free" (v2.05; this is
        "get_kernel_info" in v2.1+)

BUG: The SLIP kernel for v2.05 bounds-checks the wrong register, so values greater than 54h in AH may crash the system. Other variants of the kernel may have this bug as well.
Conflicts: see Table 2-3
See also: INT 61h Functions 00h, 2Ah, and 54h

33-1 PC/TCP error codes:
00h	"NET_NOERR" successful
01h	"NET_ERR_INUSE" protocol or socket already in use
02h	"NET_DOS_ERR" MS-DOS error (returned as suberror code in AH)
03h	"NET_ERR_NOMEM" out of memory
04h	"NET_ERR_NOTNETCONN" not a network descriptor
05h	"NET_ERR_ILLEGALOP" invalid operation on given kind of network descriptor
06h	"NET_ERR_BADPKT" illegal or corrupted packet
07h	"NET_ERR_NOHOST" no host bound to specified connection
08h	"NET_ERR_CANTOPEN" unable to open file

09h	"NET_ERR_NET_UNREACHABLE" network is unreachable
0Ah	"NET_ERR_HOST_UNREACHABLE" host is unreachable (see subcodes in Table 33-2)
0Bh	"NET_ERR_PROT_UNREACHABLE" protocol is unreachable
0Ch	"NET_ERR_PORT_UNREACHABLE" port is unreachable
0Dh	"NET_ERR_TIMEOUT" operation timed out
0Eh	"NET_ERR_HOSTUNKNOWN" unable to resolve host name
0Fh	"NET_ERR_NOSERVERS" no name servers configured
10h	"NET_ERR_SERVER_ERR" bad reply from name server
	Subcodes: 0= no error, 1 = Host unreachable
11h	"NET_ERR_BADFORMAT" bad format for IP address or field in IP address structure is zero
12h	"NET_ERR_BADARG" invalid argument
13h	"NET_ERR_EOF" foreign host closed its end of connection
14h	"NET_ERR_RESET" connection has been reset
15h	"NET_ERR_WOULDBLOCK" recv() call was done on a non-blocking connection with no data available
16h	"NET_ERR_UNBOUND" insufficient resources to do operation
17h	"NET_ERR_NODESC" could not allocate network descriptor
18h	"NET_ERR_BADSYSCALL" invalid/unsupported kernel call
19h	"NET_ERR_CANTBROADCAST" unable to broadcast
1Ah	"NET_ERR_NOTESTAB" operation illegal because connection not established
1Bh	kernel busy, try again later
1Ch	"NET_ERR_ICMPMESG" an ICMP message was received (not on streams) (see subcodes in Table 33-3)

---v2.1+---

1Dh	"NET_ERR_TERMINATING" internal kernel fatal error
1Eh	"NET_ERR_TAG_LOCKED" not allowed to set this tag (net_config)
1Fh	"NET_ERR_BAD_INTERFACE" non existent interface specified
20h	"NET_ERR_BADCONFIG" kernel cannot run - bad configuration
21h	"NET_ERR_EMM" expanded memory error
22h	"NET_ERR_CANT_SHUTDOWN" cant unload kernel (multitasker running)
23h	"NET_ERR_PARKED_IN" unable to unhook DOS interrupt
24h	"NET_ERR_NOQIOS" ran out of resources; try again later
25h	"NET_ERR_WOULD_TRUNCATE" datagram too large and "don't truncate" was set

33-2 Subcodes for Error 0Ah "NET_ERR_HOST_UNREACHABLE":

00h	no error
01h	host unreachable
02h	ARP failed
03h	hardware failure
04h	link failure
05h	no route
06h	gateway down

33-3 Subcodes for Error 1Ch "NET_ERR_ICMPMESG":

07h	unrecognised
08h	can't fragment
09h	srcr_fail
0Ah	source quench
0Bh	time exceeded

INT 61h

| 0Ch | parameter problem |
| 0Dh | admin_prohib. see also code 0Ah |

INT 61h Function 00h
GET DEBUG INFORMATION

PC/TCP kernel v2.05+
Undocumented

Registers at call:
AH = 00h
DS:SI -> 216-byte buffer for network
   debugging information (see Table 33-4)

Return Registers:
CF clear
AX = 0000h
buffer filled

Details: This call is not documented by FTP, Inc. for any version. Most of the information returned by this call is available via the documented get_kernel_info or net_info commands.

This function is not supported by Beame&Whiteside's BWPCTCP v3.0a shim.

Conflicts: see Table 2-3
See also: PC/TCP INT 61h, INT 61h Function 2Ah

33-4 Format of network debugging information:

Offset	Size	Description
00h	DWORD	number of interrupts
04h	DWORD	receive buffer low-water mark
08h	DWORD	transmit buffer low-water mark
0Ch	DWORD	number of packets received
10h	DWORD	number of packets transmitted
14h	DWORD	total receive errors
18h	DWORD	total transmit errors
1Ch	4 BYTEs	*unknown*
20h	DWORD	receive resets
24h	DWORD	transmit resets
28h	DWORD	number of "runts" received
2Ch	DWORD	number of alignment errors on received packets
30h	DWORD	number of CRC errors on received packets
34h	DWORD	number of parity errors on received packets
38h	DWORD	number of receive overflow errors
3Ch	DWORD	number of oversized packets received
40h	DWORD	number of packets lost due to lack of buffers
44h	DWORD	receive timeouts
48h	32 BYTEs	*unknown*
68h	DWORD	number of transmit collisions
6Ch	DWORD	number of transmit timeouts
70h	DWORD	number of transmit underflows
74h	DWORD	number of lost "crs" on transmit
78h	DWORD	number of times heartbeat failed on transmit
7Ch	24 BYTEs	*unknown*
94h	WORD	free packet buffers
96h	WORD	total packet buffers
98h	WORD	minimum number of packet buffers free since kernel started
9Ah	24 BYTEs	*unknown*
B2h	DWORD	pointer to *TCP connection list*
B6h	DWORD	pointer to *IP routing table*
BAh	30 BYTEs	*unknown*

INT 61h Function 01h, Subfunction 0000h
"net_config" - CONFIGURE RUNNING KERNEL

PC/TCP kernel v2.1+
(partially doc.)

Registers at call:	Return Registers:
AH = 01h	CF clear if successful
BX = 0000h	CF set on error
DH = tag number	AX = error code (see Table 33-1)
DL = device number	

DS:SI -> buffer to send to kernel
ES:DI -> integer containing size of buffer

Details: There are a large number of tags available; the items returned all refer to local kernel configuration, and are not needed in normal use.

This function is not supported by Beame&Whiteside's BWPCTCP v3.0a shim.

Conflicts: see Table 2-3
See also: PC/TCP INT 61h, INT 61h Functions 00h and 02

INT 61h Function 02h
"get_kernel_info" - GET MISCELLANEOUS LOCAL INFO

PC/TCP kernel v2.1+
(partially doc.)

Registers at call:	Return Registers:
AH = 02h	CF clear if successful
BX = 0000h	data loaded into specified buffer, and size
DH = tag number	value altered
DL = device number	CF set on error
DS:SI -> buffer for result (up to 48 bytes	AX = error code (see Table 33-1)
for version <= 2.2)	

ES:DI -> integer containing size of buffer

Details: There are a large number of tags available; the items returned all refer to local kernel configuration, and are not needed in normal use.

This function is not supported by Beame&Whiteside's BWPCTCP v3.0a shim.

Conflicts: see Table 2-3
See also: PC/TCP INT 61h, INT 61h Functions 00h and 01h

INT 61h Function 05h
"get_addr" - GET INTERNET ADDRESS OF NETWORK DESCRIPTOR

PC/TCP kernel v2.05+

Registers at call:	Return Registers:
AH = 05h	CF clear if successful
BX = network descriptor	DX:AX = Internet address of ND
	CF set on error
	AX = error code (see Table 33-1)

Conflicts: see Table 2-3
See also: PC/TCP INT 61h, INT 61h Functions 00h and 16h, BW-TCP INT 63h Function 25h
(Chapter 32)

INT 61h Function 06h
"net_info" - GET INTERFACE STATISTICS

PC/TCP kernel v2.05

Purpose: Returns the statistics relevant to the particular network interface used by the specified network descriptor.

Registers at call:	Return Registers:
AH = 06h	CF clear if successful
BX = network descriptor	buffer filled
(must be allocated and open)	CF set on error
DS:SI -> 38-byte buffer (see Table 33-5)	AX = error code (see Table 33-1)

Conflicts: see Table 2-3
See also: PC/TCP INT 61h, INT 61h Functions 00h and 05h

33-5 Format of buffer:

Offset	Size	Description
00h	WORD	interface class (e.g. 802.3)
02h	WORD	type (manufacturer) of interface
04h	WORD	interface number
06h	DWORD	(big-endian) IP address of interface
0Ah	DWORD	subnet mask
0Eh	WORD	0001h if interface is up
10h	DWORD	total packets received
14h	DWORD	total packets sent
18h	DWORD	receive errors
1Ch	DWORD	send errors
20h	WORD	length of local net address (e.g. 0006h for Ethernet)
22h	DWORD	pointer to local net address

INT 61h Function 07h   *PC/TCP kernel v2.05+*
"net_globalize" - MAKE NET DESCRIPTOR GLOBAL

Registers at call: **Return Registers:**
AH = 07h   CF clear if successful
BX = local network descriptor   AX = global network descriptor
                                       CF set on error
                                       AX = error code (see Table 33-1)
Details: The new network descriptor can be accessed from all processes and is independent of DOS.
     This function is not supported by Beame&Whiteside's BWPCTCP v3.0a shim.
See also: PC/TCP INT 61h; INT 61h Functions 00h, 08h, and 29h
Conflicts: see Table 2-3

INT 61h Function 08h   *PC/TCP kernel v2.05+*
"net_release" - CLOSE A NETWORK DESCRIPTOR

Registers at call: **Return Registers:**
AH = 08h   CF clear if successful
BX = network descriptor   AX = 0000h (BWPCTCP shim)
                                       CF set on error
                                       AX = error code (see Table 33-1)
Details: The descriptor will be closed and resources released. If it is a stream descriptor, the protocol (FIN etc) is completed unless the non-blocking option has been set.
Conflicts: see Table 2-3
See also: PC/TCP INT 61h, INT 61h Functions 00h and 09h, BW-TCP INT 63h Function 0Eh (Chapter 32)

INT 61h Function 09h   *PC/TCP kernel v2.05+*
"net_releaseall" - CLOSE ALL NON-GLOBAL DESCRIPTORS

Registers at call: **Return Registers:**
AH = 09h   CF clear
Details: This call performs Function 08h on every non-global network descriptor. Global descriptors must be released individually.
     INT 61h is the default; PC/TCP v2.05 may be configured to use any interrupt from 20h through E0h.
Conflicts: see Table 2-3
See also: INT 61h Functions 00h and 08h, BW-TCP INT 63h Function 0Eh (Chapter 32)

INT 61h Function 0Ah
"net_send" - UNDETERMINED FUNCTION

Registers at call:
AH = 0Ah
others, if any, unknown

Return Registers:
unknown

Details: This function is described as "unused" in the v2.05 and v2.2 documentation.
  This function is not supported by Beame&Whiteside's BWPCTCP v3.0a shim.
Conflicts: see Table 2-3
See also: Function 0Bh

INT 61h Function 0Bh
"net_sendto" - UNDETERMINED FUNCTION

Registers at call:
AH = 0Bh
others, if any, unknown

Return Registers:
unknown

Details: This function is described as "unused" in the v2.05 and v2.2 documentation.
  This function is not supported by Beame&Whiteside's BWPCTCP v3.0a shim.
Conflicts: see Table 2-3
See also: Function 0Ah

INT 61h Function 0Ch
"net_stat" - GET CONNECTION STATISTICS

Registers at call:
AH = 0Ch
BX = network descriptor or one of
  the following:
    FFFCh for kernel ICMP statistics
    FFFDh for kernel UDP statistics
    FFFEh for kernel IP statistics
    FFFFh for kernel TCP statistics
DS:DX -> 64-byte buffer

Return Registers:
CF clear if successful
  buffer filled
CF set on error
  AX = error code (see Table 33-1)

Details: The fields filled in for a network descriptor depend on the protocol family used by that descriptor's connection.
  This function is not supported by Beame&Whiteside's BWPCTCP v3.0a shim.
Conflicts: see Table 2-3
See also: PC/TCP INT 61h, INT 61h Function 00h

33-6 Format of kernel TCP statistics:

Offset	Size	Description
00h	16 BYTEs	unused
10h	DWORD	bytes sent
14h	DWORD	bytes received
18h	8 BYTEs	unused
20h	DWORD	packets sent
24h	DWORD	packets received
28h	DWORD	bad checksums
2Ch	DWORD	count of window ignored by remote
30h	DWORD	timeouts
34h	DWORD	resets
38h	DWORD	duplicate packets
3Ch	DWORD	retransmits

33-7 Format of kernel IP statistics:

Offset	Size	Description
00h	8 BYTEs	unused
08h	DWORD	invalid IP header length errors
0Ch	DWORD	protocol errors (unwanted packets)
10h	DWORD	duplicate fragments received
14h	DWORD	bad fragments received
18h	DWORD	security errors
1Ch	DWORD	count of bad IP addresses received
20h	DWORD	packets sent
24h	DWORD	packets received
28h	DWORD	bad checksums received
2Ch	DWORD	total IP protocol errors
30h	DWORD	fragmentation errors
34h	DWORD	IP packets discarded + bad security + bad fragments
38h	DWORD	fragments received
3Ch	4 BYTEs	unused

33-8 Format of kernel UDP statistics:

Offset	Size	Description
00h	28 BYTEs	unused
1Ch	DWORD	packets dropped for lack of buffers
20h	DWORD	packets sent
24h	DWORD	packets received
28h	DWORD	bad checksums
2Ch	DWORD	port not listening errors
30h	4 BYTEs	unused
34h	DWORD	truncated receives
38h	8 BYTEs	unused

33-9 Format of kernel ICMP statistics:

Offset	Size	Description
00h	DWORD	"TimeEx" sent
04h	DWORD	"TimeEx" received
08h	DWORD	"ParamProb" sent
0Ch	DWORD	"ParamProb" received
10h	DWORD	redirects received
14h	DWORD	source quenches received
18h	DWORD	ICMP Echo Requests ("ping") sent
1Ch	DWORD	ICMP Echo Requests received
20h	DWORD	packets sent
24h	DWORD	packets received
28h	DWORD	bad packets received
2Ch	DWORD	"DestUn" received
30h	DWORD	packet send errors
34h	DWORD	"DestUn" sent
38h	DWORD	ICMP Echo replies received
3Ch	DWORD	ICMP Echo replies sent

INT 61h Function 0Dh
"is_netnd" - CHECK IF NETWORK DESCRIPTOR VALID

PC/TCP kernel v2.05+

Registers at call:
AH = 0Dh
BX = possible network descriptor

Return Registers:
CF clear if valid
CF set on error
    AX = error code (see Table 33-1)

Conflicts: see Table 2-3
See also: INT 61h Functions 00h, 08h, and 22h

INT 61h Function 0Eh
"net_select" - DETECT READINESS OF NETWORK

PC/TCP kernel v2.05+

Registers at call:
AH = 0Eh
BX = maximum value of network
    descriptor for which to return info
DS:DX -> 32-bit (max) array of bit
    flags for read readiness
ES:DI -> 32-bit (max) array of bit
    flags for write readiness

Return Registers:
CF clear

Details: Bits in the DS:DX buffer are set if the corresponding network descriptor may be read without blocking; bits in the ES:DI buffer are set if the corresponding network descriptor may be written without blocking. This implies that the network descriptor has opened correctly and the protocol initialized.
Conflicts: see Table 2-3
See also: PC/TCP INT 61h, INT 61h Function 00h

INT 61h Function 0Fh
"get_netversion" - GET SOFTWARE VERSION

PC/TCP kernel v2.05+

Registers at call:
AH = 0Fh

Return Registers:
CF clear
AX = version (AH = major, AL = minor)
BX = patch level

Details: Patch levels are no longer used starting with version 2.10; instead, the minor version level is incremented.
    Beame&Whiteside's BWPCTCP v3.0a shim reports version 2.05, but does not set BX.
Conflicts: see Table 2-3
See also: PC/TCP INT 61h, INT 61h Function 00h

INT 61h Function 10h
"net_shutdown" - UNINSTALL

PC/TCP kernel v2.05+

Registers at call:
AH = 10h

Return Registers:
CF clear if successful
CF set on error
    AX = error code (see Table 33-1)

Details: This function is not supported by Beame&Whiteside's BWPCTCP v3.0a shim.
Conflicts: see Table 2-3
See also: PC/TCP INT 61h, INT 61h Function 00h

INT 61h Function 11h
"disable_async" - DISABLE ASYNCHRONOUS HANDLERS

PC/TCP kernel v2.05+

Registers at call:
AH = 11h

Return Registers:
CF clear

AX = previous state
　　0000h async calls were already disabled
　　else async calls were enabled

Conflicts: see Table 2-3
See also: PC/TCP INT 61h, INT 61h Function 12h

INT 61h Function 12h   *PC/TCP kernel v2.05+*
"enable_async" - ENABLE ASYNCHRONOUS HANDLERS

Registers at call:	Return Registers:
AH = 12h	CF clear
	AX = previous state
	0000h async calls were disabled
	else async calls were already enabled

Conflicts: see Table 2-3
See also: PC/TCP INT 61h, INT 61h Function 11h

INT 61h Function 13h   *PC/TCP kernel v2.05*
"net_connect" - OPEN A NETWORK CONNECTION

Registers at call:
AH = 13h
BX = network descriptor (FFFFh for
　automatic net_getdesc)
DX = protocol (see Table 33-10)
DS:SI -> buffer for "addr" structure
　(see Table 33-11)

Return Registers:
CF clear if successful
　AX = network descriptor used or allocated
CF set on error
　AX = error code (see Table 33-1)

Details: This function invokes Function 22h if BX=FFFFh on entry; it also invokes Function 19h in various cases.

This function will wait for protocol on stream connections unless the non-blocking option was set with Function 20h.

Conflicts: see Table 2-3
See also: PC/TCP INT 61h, INT 61h Functions 00h, 18h, and 23h, BW-TCP INT 63h Function 14h (Chapter 32)

33-10 Values for protocol:

0001h	raw net (undocumented)
0002h	raw IP
0003h	datagram (UDP)
0004h	stream (TCP)
0005h	raw ICMP

33-11 Format of structure "addr":

Offset	Size	Description
00h	DWORD	Internet address (network order)
04h	WORD	remote socket number (network order)
06h	WORD　1	ocal socket number (network order) 0000h means "you choose"
08h	BYTE	protocol (see Table 33-10)

INT 61h Ouh Function 14h   *PC/TCP kernel v2.05*
"net_recv" - NO LONGER SUPPORTED

Registers at call:	Return Registers:
AH = 14h	CF set
BX = network descriptor	AX = 0018h (see Table 33-1)

Details: This function displays the error message "Illegal system call! Please upgrade your PCserver software" to standard output. It is not supported by Beame&Whiteside's BWPCTCP v3.0a shim.

Conflicts: see Table 2-3

See also: PC/TCP INT 61h; INT 61h Functions 00h, 0Ah, and 15h

---

INT 61h Function 15h   *PC/TCP kernel v2.05*
"net_recvfrom" - UNDETERMINED FUNCTION

Registers at call:	Return Registers:
AH = 15h	*unknown*

others, if any, unknown

Details: This function is described as "unused" in the v2.2 documentation. It is not supported by Beame&Whiteside's BWPCTCP v3.0a shim.

Conflicts: see Table 2-3

See also: INT 61h Function 0Bh, INT 61h Function 14h

INT 61h Function 16h   *PC/TCP kernel v2.05+*
"net_peer" - GET DATA ON REMOTE PEER

Registers at call:	Return Registers:
AH = 16h	CF clear if successful
BX = network descriptor	buffer filled
DS:DX -> 9-byte buffer for "addr"	CF set on error
structure (see Table 33-11)	AX = error code (see Table 33-1)

Conflicts: see Table 2-3

See also: PC/TCP INT 61h, INT 61h Function 00h

INT 61h Function 17h   *PC/TCP kernel v2.05+*
"net_reconfig" - RE-READ KERNEL CONFIGURATION

Registers at call:	Return Registers:
AH = 17h	CF clear if successful
	CF set on error
	AX = error code (see Table 33-1)

Details: This routine is deprecated in v2.1+ and will eventually be withdrawn; in v2.1+, this function calls Function 01h which should be used instead.

   This function is not supported by Beame&Whiteside's BWPCTCP v3.0a shim.

Conflicts: see Table 2-3

See also: PC/TCP INT 61h, INT 61h Functions 00h and 01h

INT 61h Function 18h   *PC/TCP kernel v2.05+*
"net_eof" - CLOSE TRANSMIT SIDE OF CONNECTION

Registers at call:	Return Registers:
AH = 18h	CF clear if successful
BX = network descriptor	CF set on error
	AX = error code (see Table 33-1)

Details: A TCP "FIN" command is sent and no further data may be transmitted, although the connection remains open.

Conflicts: see Table 2-3

See also: PC/TCP INT 61h, INT 61h Functions 00h and 13h, BW-TCP INT 63h Function 0Eh (Chapter 32)

INT 61h Function 19h   *PC/TCP kernel v2.05+*
"net_abort" - RESET A NETWORK CONNECTION

Purpose: Immediately destroys the specified connection.

Registers at call:
AH = 19h
BX = network descriptor

Return Registers:
CF clear if successful
CF set on error
    AX = error code (see Table 33-1)

Details: Send a TCP "RST" command if a stream connection is open.
Conflicts: see Table 2-3
See also: PC/TCP INT 61h, INT 61h Functions 00h and 24h

INT 61h Function 1Ah   PC/TCP kernel v2.05+
"net_write" - WRITE TO THE NETWORK

Registers at call:
AH = 1Ah
BX = network descriptor
CX = number of bytes to transmit
    (0000h allowed)
DX = send options (see Table 33-12)
DS:SI -> data to be written

Return Registers:
CF clear if successful
    AX = number of bytes actually written
    DX = *unknown*
CF set on error
    AX = error code (see Table 33-1)

Conflicts: see Table 2-3
See also: PC/TCP INT 61h; INT 61h Functions 00h, 1Bh, and 1Ch; BW-TCP INT 63h Functions 19h and 1Bh (Chapter 32)

33-12 Bitfields for send options:

bit 0   signal "URG"ent data
bit 3   attempt rerouting on non-stream calls if first attempt fails
bit 4   send data with PUSH flag (no override of Nagle) (see option 0Ch)
bit 5   fail rather than truncating datagram
bit 6   fail rather than blocking
bit 7   broadcast packet

INT 61h Function 1Bh   PC/TCP kernel v2.05+
"net_read" - READ FROM THE NETWORK

Registers at call:
AH = 1Bh
BX = network descriptor
CX = maximum number of bytes to read
DX = receive options (see Table 33-13)
DS:SI -> buffer for data
ES:DI -> "addr" structure (see Table 33-11) for remote from which to read
        0000h:0000h for any

Return Registers:
CF clear if successful
    AX = number of bytes actually read
    DX = *unknown*
CF set on error
    AX = error code (see Table 33-1)

Conflicts: see Table 2-3
See also: PC/TCP INT 61h; INT 61h Functions 00h, 1Ah, and 1Dh

---

33-13 Bitfields for receive options:

bit 1   do not remove data from queue, just copy it
bit 2   do not copy data, just remove it from queue
bit 5   fail if datagram would be truncated
bit 6   do not block, return error if no data available

Note: A special case exists for UDP: if both bits 1 and 2 are set, return the number of datagrams.

INT 61h Function 1Ch   PC/TCP kernel v2.05+
"net_writeto" - WRITE A DATAGRAM

Registers at call:
AH = 1Ch

BX = network descriptor
CX = number of bytes to transmit
  (0000h allowed)
DX = send options (see Table 33-12)
DS:SI -> data to be written
ES:DI -> "addr" structure
  (see Table 33-11)

Return Registers:
CF clear if successful
  AX = number of bytes actually written
  DX = *unknown*
CF set on error
  AX = error code (see Table 33-1)

Details: This function differs from Function 1Ah in that the address and socket numbers can be overridden.
Conflicts: see Table 2-3
See also: PC/TCP INT 61h; INT 61h Functions 00h, 1Ah, and 1Dh; BW-TCP INT 63h Function 21h (Chapter 32)

INT 61h Function 1Dh
"net_readfrom" - READ A DATAGRAM
PC/TCP kernel v2.05+

Registers at call:
AH = 1Dh
BX = network descriptor
CX = maximum number of bytes to read
DX = receive options (see Table 33-13)
DS:SI -> buffer for received data
ES:DI -> 9-byte buffer containing "addr" structure (see Table 33-11)

Return Registers:
CF clear if successful
  AX = number of bytes read
  DX = *unknown*
CF set on error
  AX = error code (see Table 33-1)

Details: This function can read from any host or a designated host depending on settings in the "addr" structure. It is only for use with datagram or Raw descriptors.
Conflicts: see Table 2-3
See also: PC/TCP INT 61h; INT 61h Functions 00h, 1Bh, and 1Ch

---

INT 61h Function 1Eh
"net_flush" - FLUSH PENDING DATA
PC/TCP kernel v2.05+

Registers at call:
AH = 1Eh
BX = network descriptor

Return Registers:
CF clear if successful
CF set on error
  AX = error code (see Table 33-1)

Details: Bufferred data is transmitted immediately, overriding Nagle's algorithm if necessary.
  This function is not supported by Beame&Whiteside's BWPCTCP v3.0a shim.
Conflicts: see Table 2-3
See also: PC/TCP INT 61h, INT 61h Function 00h

INT 61h Function 1Fh
"net_asynch" - SET UP ASYNCHRONOUS CALL-BACK
PC/TCP kernel v2.05+

Registers at call:
AH = 1Fh
BX = network descriptor
CX = event type (see Table 33-14)
DS:SI -> event handler routine
  (see Table 33-15)
ES:DI = 32-bit hint passed to handler

Return Registers:
CF clear if successful
  DS:DX -> previous handler
CF set on error
  AX = error code (see Table 33-1)

Details: ICMP messages do not trigger events on stream connections.
Conflicts: see Table 2-3
See also: PC/TCP INT 61h, INT 61h Function 00h

33-14 Values for event type:

00h	alarm
01h	open (successfully opened stream connection)
02h	receive (data available)
03h	transmit (ACK received on stream connection)
04h	*transmit flush*
05h	foreign close (remote host closed data connection)
06h	close (local host closed connection and protocol is complete)
07h	error (error code passed to handler as arg)

33-15 Event handler calling convention:

Registers at call: **Return Registers:**
BX = network descriptor   none
CX = event type (see Table 33-14)
DS:DX -> arg
ES:DI = 32-bit hint value
STACK: small stack, possibly the DOS stack

INT 61h Function 20h   *PC/TCP kernel v2.05+*
"set_option" - SET AN OPTION ON A DESCRIPTOR
Registers at call: **Return Registers:**
AH = 20h   CF clear if successful
BX = network descriptor   CF set on error
CX = length of buffer (usually 04h)   AX = error code (see Table 33-1)
DS:DX -> buffer containing option
SI = (ignored by v2.2-)
DI = option to set (see Table 33-16)
Details: Beame&Whiteside's BWPCTCP shim only supports options 01h and 0Bh; all others
return CF clear.
Conflicts: see Table 2-3
See also: PC/TCP INT 61h, INT 61h Functions 00h and 21h

33-16 Values for option to set:

01h	set non-blocking mode if non-zero
02h	timeout of call in milliseconds
03h	user-defined 4-byte magic cookie (not used by kernel)
04h	TCP window or UDP buffer count (WORD, unsigned)
06h	do TCP keep-alives if non-zero
09h	(v2.1+) set IP precedence
0Ah	(v2.1+) set IP type of service
0Bh	use a privileged port if port = 0
0Ch	turn off TCP PUSH bit and don't flush buffer every write (see Function 1Ah)

Note: Use "C" true or false values for boolean options (zero = false, nonzero = true).

INT 61h Function 21h   *PC/TCP kernel v2.05+*
"get_option" - GET OPTIONS APPLIED TO NET DESCR
Registers at call:
AH = 21h
BX = network descriptor
CX = length of buffer
DS:DX -> buffer for return values

SI = 0004h (ignored by v2.2-)
DI = option (see Table 33-16)

Return Registers:
CF clear if successful
      DS:DX -> value (usually 32 bits) returned
            by selected option
CF set on error
      AX = error code (see Table 33-1)

Details: This function is not supported by Beame&Whiteside's BWPCTCP v3.0a shim.
Conflicts: see Table 2-3
See also: PC/TCP INT 61h, INT 61h Functions 00h and 20h

INT 61h Function 22h   PC/TCP kernel v2.05+
"net_getdesc" - ALLOCATE NETWORK DESCRIPTOR   (partially doc.)

Registers at call:
AH = 22h

Return Registers:
CF clear if successful
      AX = network descriptor
CF set on error
      AX = error code (see Table 33-1)

Details: The descriptor will be an integer in the range 00h-1Fh, and a DOS call is made to allocate this as a file descriptor. Hence a number may not refer to a PC/TCP network descriptor and a DOS file handle simultaneously.
Conflicts: see Table 2-3
See also: PC/TCP INT 61h; INT 61h Functions 00h, 13h, and 29h

---

INT 61h Function 23h   PC/TCP kernel v2.05+
"net_listen" - LISTEN FOR INCOMING CONNECTIONS

Registers at call:
AH = 23h
BX = network descriptor or FFFFh to
  allocate descriptor
DX = type of service
DS:SI -> "addr" structure
  (see Table 33-11)

Return Registers:
CF clear if successful
      AX = network descriptor
CF set on error
      AX = error code (see Table 33-1)

Details: The type of service and "addr" structure are as for Function 13h. Any of the fields in the address structure can be zero; normally the local socket number is filled in prior to making the call.
Conflicts: see Table 2-3
See also: PC/TCP INT 61h, INT 61h Functions 00h and 13h, BW-TCP INT 63h Function 12h (Chapter 32)

INT 61h Function 24h   PC/TCP kernel v2.05+
"net_abortall" - RESET ALL NETWORK CONNECTIONS

Registers at call:
AH = 24h

Return Registers:
always successful

Details: This function performs "net_abort" (Function 19h) on all open non-global descriptors.
Conflicts: see Table 2-3
See also: PC/TCP INT 61h, INT 61h Functions 00h and 19h

INT 61h Function 25h   PC/TCP kernel v2.05+
"ad_res_name" - GET HOST NAME GIVEN ADDRESS

Registers at call:
AH = 25h
DX,BX = IP address in network order

CX = length of buffer for name
DS:SI -> buffer for host name

Return Registers:
CF clear if successful buffer filled with ASCIZ
    host name
CF set on error
      AX = error code (see Table 33-1)

Details: This function will use the host table and/or DNS to resolve the address, depending on the kernel's configuration. Use this call for the normal gethostbyaddr function.
Conflicts: see Table 2-3
See also: PC/TCP INT 61h; INT 61h Functions 00h, 26h, and 27h

---

INT 61h Function 26h   *PC/TCP kernel v2.05+*
"ad_htable" - GET HOST NAME FROM LOCAL TABLE

Registers at call:
AH = 26h
DX,BX = IP address in network order
CX = length of buffer
DS:SI -> buffer for host name

Return Registers:
CF clear if successful
    buffer filled with ASCIZ host name
CF set on error
      AX = error code (see Table 33-1)

Details: Normally one would use Function 25h instead of this function.
    This function is not supported by Beame&Whiteside's BWPCTCP v3.0a shim.
Conflicts: see Table 2-3
See also: PC/TCP INT 61h; INT 61h Functions 00h, 25h, and 27h

---

INT 61h Function 27h   *PC/TCP kernel v2.05+*
"ad_domain" - GET HOST NAME FROM DNS

Registers at call:
AH = 27h
DX,BX = IP address in network order
CX = length of buffer
DS:SI -> buffer for host name

Return Registers:
CF clear if successful
    buffer filled with ASCIZ host name
CF set on error
      AX = error code (see Table 33-1)

Details: Normally one would use Function 25h instead of this function.
Conflicts: see Table 2-3
See also: PC/TCP INT 61h; INT 61h Functions 00h, 25h, and 26h

---

INT 61h Function 28h   *PC/TCP kernel v2.05+*
"net_swap" - EXCHANGE TWO NETWORK DESCRIPTORS

Registers at call:
AH = 28h
BX = network descriptor 1
CX = network descriptor 2

Return Registers:
CF clear if successful
CF set on error
      AX = error code (see Table 33-1)

Details: The two descriptors will exchange places; they must both be local or both global.
Conflicts: see Table 2-3
See also: PC/TCP INT 61h, INT 61h Function 00h

INT 61h Function 29h   *PC/TCP kernel v2.05+*
"net_getglobdesc" - ALLOCATE GLOBAL DESCRIPTOR

Registers at call:
AH = 29h

Return Registers:
CF clear if successful
    AX = network descriptor
CF set on error
      AX = error code (see Table 33-1)

Details: Use this function rather than Function 22h to avoid a DOS call by the PC/TCP kernel; the returned descriptor will be >= 40h and cannot be used with "net_select" (Function 0Eh).
Conflicts: see Table 2-3
See also: PC/TCP INT 61h; INT 61h Functions 00h, 07h, and 22h

INT 61h Function 2Ah
GET CONFIGURATION INFORMATION

PC/TCP kernel v2.05+

Registers at call:
AH = 2Ah
DS:SI -> 26-byte buffer for configuration
  information (see Table 33-17)

Return Registers:
CF clear
AX = 0000h
buffer filled

Details: The size of the buffer may vary with kernel version; 26 bytes is the size for versions 2.05 through 2.2.

This function is not supported by Beame&Whiteside's BWPCTCP v3.0a shim.

Conflicts: see Table 2-3
See also: PC/TCP INT 61h, INT 61h Function 00h

33-17 Format of configuration information:

Offset	Size	Description
00h	BYTE	maximum TCP connections available
01h	BYTE	maximum UDP connections available
02h	BYTE	maximum IP connections available
03h	BYTE	maximum Raw Net connections available
04h	BYTE	number of TCP connections currently in use
05h	BYTE	number of UDP connections currently in use
06h	BYTE	number of IP connections currently in use
07h	BYTE	number of Raw Net connections currently in use
08h	WORD	number of local network descriptors active
0Ah	WORD	number of global network descriptors active
0Ch	BYTE	maximum header size on network
0Dh	BYTE	maximum trailer size on network
0Eh	WORD	size of large packet buffer
10h	WORD	number of network interfaces attached
12h	DWORD	milliseconds since kernel started
16h	DWORD	IP broadcast address

INT 61h Function 2Bh

PC/TCP kernel v2.02+

"net_alarm" - SET TIMED ASYNCHRONOUS EVENT

Registers at call:
AH = 2Bh
BX = network descriptor
CX,DX = time before alarm in
  milliseconds
DS:SI -> handler which will receive
  call (see Table 33-15)
ES:DI = 32-bit cookie passed to handler

Return Registers:
CF clear if successful
CF set on error
  AX = error code (see Table 33-1)

Details: This function will cause a NET_AS_ALARM to be generated; it is intended for TSRs, etc. to regain control periodically.

This function is not supported by Beame&Whiteside's BWPCTCP v3.0a shim.

Conflicts: see Table 2-3
See also: PC/TCP INT 61h, INT 61h Function 00h

INT 61h Function 30h

PC/TCP kernel v2.05+

"icmp_ping" - SEND ICMP ECHO REQUEST (PING)

Registers at call:
AH = 30h

BX,DX = IP address of host
CX = length of data to send

Return Registers:
CF clear if successful (i.e. reply received)
CF set on error
        AX = error code (see Table 33-1)

Details: This function is not supported by Beame&Whiteside's BWPCTCP v3.0a shim.
Conflicts: see Table 2-3
See also: PC/TCP INT 61h, INT 61h Function 00h

INT 61h Functions 31h to 33h
NOP for SLIP kernel

PC/TCP kernel v2.05
(partially doc.)

Registers at call:
AH = function
        31h "net_add_route"
        32h "net_del_route"
        33h "net_dump_routes"

Return Registers:
none

Details: These functions are described as "unused" in the v2.2 documentation. They are not supported by Beame&Whiteside's BWPCTCP v3.0a shim.
        The router configuration can be altered using INT 61h Function 01h.
Conflicts: see Table 2-3

INT 61h Function 34h
"icmp_destun" - UNDETERMINED FUNCTION

PC/TCP kernel v2.1+
Undocumented

Registers at call:
AH = 34h
others, if any, unknown

Return Registers:
unknown

Details: This function is described as "reserved" in the v2.2 documentation. It is not supported by Beame&Whiteside's BWPCTCP v3.0a shim.
Conflicts: see Table 2-3

INT 61h Function 50h
"nm_prs_addr" - TRANSLATE NUMERICAL IP ADDRESS

PC/TCP kernel v2.05+

Registers at call:
AH = 50h
DS:DX -> ASCIZ IP address as
        "dotted quad" (max 127 chars)

Return Registers:
CF clear if successful
        DX:AX -> IP address
CF set on error
        AX = error code (see Table 33-1)

Conflicts: see Table 2-3
See also: PC/TCP INT 61h, INT 61h Functions 00h and 54h

INT 61h Function 51h
"nm_htable" - RESOLVE NAME USING HOST TABLE

PC/TCP kernel v2.05+

Registers at call:
AH = 51h
CX = size of destination buffer
DS:DX -> ASCIZ host name
        (max 127 chars)
ES:DI -> destination buffer or
        0000h:0000h

Return Registers:
CF clear if successful
        DX:AX -> IP address of host
        destination buffer filled with canonical host name
CF set on error
        AX = error code (see Table 33-1)

Details: This function calls DOS, and can fail if the DOS call fails.
Conflicts: see Table 2-3
See also: PC/TCP INT 61h, INT 61h Functions 00h and 54h

INT 61h Function 52h   *PC/TCP kernel v2.05+*
"nm_domain" - RESOLVE NAME USING DNS

Registers at call: **Return Registers:**
AH = 52h   CF clear if successful
CX = size of destination buffer   DX:AX -> IP address of host
DS:DX -> ASCIZ host name   destination buffer filled with canonical host name
  (max 127 chars)   CF set on error
ES:DI -> destination buffer or   AX = error code (see Table 33-1)
  0000h:0000h

Details: This function will poll all configured domain name servers if necessary.
Conflicts: see Table 2-3
See also: PC/TCP INT 61h, INT 61h Functions 00h and 54h

INT 61h Function 53h   *PC/TCP kernel v2.05-*
"nm_ien116" - RESOLVE HOST NAME USING IEN116

Registers at call: **Return Registers:**
AH = 53h   CF clear if successful
DS:DX -> ASCIZ name to be resolved   DX:AX -> IP address of host
  (max 127 chars)   CF set on error
                                                 AX = error code (see Table 33-1)

Details: This function is not supported by PC/TCP v2.10+.
Conflicts: see Table 2-3
See also: PC/TCP INT 61h, INT 61h Functions 00h and 54h

INT 61h Function 54h   *PC/TCP kernel v2.05+*
"nm_res_name" - RESOLVE HOST NAME

Registers at call: **Return Registers:**
AH = 54h   CF clear if successful
CX = size of destination buffer   DX:AX -> IP address of host
DS:DX -> ASCIZ host name   destination buffer filled with canonical host name
  (max 127 chars)   CF set on error
ES:DI -> destination buffer or   AX = error code (see Table 33-1)
  0000h:0000h

Details: This function uses all configured methods in turn to resolve the name (numerical, then host table, then DNS, then IEN116)
BUG: The SLIP kernel for v2.05 bounds-checks the wrong register, so values greater than 54h in AH may crash the system. Other variants of the kernel may have this bug as well; it has been fixed in the v2.2 SLIPDRV kernel.
Conflicts: see Table 2-3
See also: PC/TCP INT 61h; INT 61h Functions 00h and 50h to 53h

Old-Style Configuration Drivers

Versions of PC/TCP prior to version 2.10 used a pair of small device drivers to store and retrieve configuration information. Beginning with version 2.10, PC/TCP uses a Windows-style .INI by default, though it may still be configured to use the old-style drivers for compatibility with other software which accesses those drivers to determine the PC/TCP configuration.

INT 21h Function 3Fh   *PC/TCP IPCUST.SYS*
READ CONFIGURATION DATA

Registers at call:
AH = 3Fh
BX = handle for character device "$IPCUST"

CX = number of bytes to read
DS:DX -> buffer for configuration data
  (see Table 33-18)

Return Registers:
CF clear if successful
  AX = number of bytes actually read
CF set on error
  AX = error code (05h,06h) (see Table 3-1)

Details: If less than the entire data is read or written, the next read/write continues where the previous one ended; IOCTL Functions 4402h and 4403h both reset the location at which the next operation starts to zero. The data pointer is also reset to zero if the previous read or write reached or exceeded the end of the data, and when the current function is *read* and the previous was *write* or vice versa.

See also: Functions 40h and 4402h, FTPSOFT.DOS Function 4402h

33-18 Format of configuration data:

Offset	Size	Description
00h	12 BYTEs	IPCUST.SYS device driver header
12h	BYTE	*unknown*
13h	BYTE	*unknown*
14h	WORD	*unknown*
16h	BYTE	bit flags
		bit 0: send BS rather than DEL for BackSpace key
		bit 1: wrap long lines
17h	BYTE	*unknown*
18h	64 BYTEs	ASCIZ hostname
58h	64 BYTEs	ASCIZ domain name
		(fully qualified domain name is hostname.domain-name)
98h	16 BYTEs	ASCIZ username
A8h	64 BYTEs	ASCIZ full name
E8h	64 BYTEs	ASCIZ office address
128h	32 BYTEs	ASCIZ phone number
148h	WORD	offset from GMT in minutes
14Ah	4 BYTEs	ASCIZ timezone name
14Eh	WORD	number of time servers
150h	? DWORDs	(big-endian) IP addresses for time servers
		intervening fields unknown
164h	WORD	number of old-style name servers
166h	3 DWORDs	(big-endian) IP addresses for name servers
172h	WORD	number of domain name servers
174h	3 DWORDs	(big-endian) IP addresses for domain name servers
180h	DWORD	(big-endian) IP address of default gateway
184h	DWORD	(big-endian) IP address of log server
188h	DWORD	(big-endian) IP address of cookie server
18Ch	DWORD	(big-endian) IP address of lpr server
190h	DWORD	(big-endian) IP address of imagen print server
194h	54 BYTEs	*unknown*
1E8h	WORD	TCP default window size in bytes
1EAh	WORD	TCP low window size
1ECh	64 BYTEs	ASCIZ host tabel filename
22Ch	2 BYTEs	*unknown*
22Eh	80 BYTEs	ASCIZ mail relay host name
27Eh	BYTE	*unknown*
27Fh	BYTE	*unknown* bit flags

280h	44 BYTEs	*unknown*
2ACh	WORD	*unknown*
2AEh	202 BYTEs	*unknown*

INT 21h Function 40h   *PC/TCP IPCUST.SYS*
WRITE CONFIGURATION DATA

Registers at call:

AH = 40h

BX = handle for character device
  "$IPCUST"

CX = number of bytes to write

DS:DX -> buffer for configuration
  data (Table 33-18)

Return Registers:

CF clear if successful
  AX = number of bytes actually written

CF set on error
  AX = error code (05h,06h) (see Table 3-1)

Details: If less than the entire data is read or written, the next read/write continues where the previous one ended; IOCTL Functions 4402h and 4403h both reset the location at which the next operation starts to zero. The data pointer is also reset to zero if the previous read or write reached or exceeded the end of the data, and when the current function is *read* and the previous was *write* or vice versa.

See also: Functions 3Fh and 4402h

INT 21h Functions 4402h and 4403h   *PC/TCP IPCUST.SYS*
RESET CONFIGURATION DATA READ POINTER

Registers at call:

AX = 4402h and 4403h

BX = file handle referencing device
  "$IPCUST"

CX, DS:DX ignored

Return Registers:

CF clear if successful
  AX destroyed

CF set on error
  AX = error code (01h,05h,06h,0Dh) (see Table 3-1)

Details: There are a total of 378h bytes of configuration data for IPCUST.SYS version 2.05. If less than the entire data is read or written, the next read/write continues where the previous one ended; this call and Function 4403h both reset the location at which the next operation starts to zero.

See also: Functions 3Fh and 40h

Printer Redirection

PREDIR.EXE is the network printer redirector included as part of the PC/TCP system by FTP Software, Inc.

INT 2Ah Function FF90h   *PC/TCP PREDIR.EXE*
UNDETERMINED FUNCTION

Registers at call:

AX = FF90h

Return Registers:

AX = *unknown*

INT 2Ah Function FF91h   *PC/TCP PREDIR.EXE*
UNDETERMINED FUNCTION

Registers at call:

AX = FF91h

BX = *unknown*

Return Registers:

AX = *status*

INT 2Ah Function FF92h   *PC/TCP PREDIR.EXE*
INSTALLATION CHECK

Registers at call:

AX = FF92h

Return Registers:

AX = 0000h if installed
  BX = redirected printer port (FFFFh if no printers redirected)
  CX = version (CH = major, CL = minor)

INT 2Ah Function FF93h
UNDETERMINED FUNCTION

Registers at call:
AX = FF93h

Return Registers:
AX = *unknown*

INT 2Ah Function FF94h
UNDETERMINED FUNCTION

Registers at call:
AX = FF94h
BX = *unknown*
CX = *unknown*
DX = *unknown*

Return Registers:
AX = *unknown*

INT 2Ah Function FF95h
GET CONFIGURATION STRINGS

Registers at call:
AX = FF95h
CX = what to get
    0000h *unknown* (returned pointer
      to "C:\COMMAND.COM")
    0001h spooling program
    0002h *unknown*
    0003h spool file name
    0004h swap file name

Return Registers:
AX = status
    0000h successful
BX:DX -> ASCIZ configuration string

INT 2Ah Function FF96h
SET PRINT JOB TERMINATION CONFIGURATION

Registers at call:
AX = FF96h
CX = what to set
    0000h *unknown*
    0001h print-on-hotkey state
    0002h print-on-exit state
    0003h print job timeout in clock ticks
    0004h print-on-EOF state
BX = new value (0000h disabled,
  0001h enabled except for timeout)
See also: Function FF97h

Return Registers:
AX = *unknown*

INT 2Ah Function FF97h
GET PRINT JOB TERMINATION CONFIGURATION

Registers at call:
AX = FF97h
CX = what to get
    0000h *unknown*
    0001h print-on-hotkey state
    0002h print-on-exit state
    0003h print job timeout in clock ticks
    0004h print-on-EOF state
See also: Function FF96h

Return Registers:
AX = status
    0000h successful
BX = old value (0000h disabled, 0001 enabled
  except for timeout)

Miscellaneous

INT 21h Function 4402h   *FTPSOFT.DOS v3.1*
GET UNKNOWN ITEM

Purpose: FTPSOFT.DOS is a device driver for Protocol Manager support from FTP Software, Inc.

Registers at call:	Return Registers:
AX = 4402h	CF clear if successful
BX = file handle for device "FTPSOFT$"	buffer filled
CX = size of buffer	CF set on error
DS:DX -> buffer for data (see Table 33-19)	AX = error code (01h,05h,06h,0Dh) (see Table 3-1)

See also: Function 3Fh, NDIS Function 4402h (Chapter 7)

33-19 Format of data:

Offset	Size	Description
00h	WORD	(call) BA98 (if different, no data returned)
02h	DWORD	pointer to NDIS common characteristics table (see Table 7-12)
06h	DWORD	(call) -> new dispatch table (see Table 7-14)
0Ah	DWORD	pointer to 28-byte buffer for *unknown* data
0Eh	DWORD	*unknown*
12h	DWORD	pointer to FAR function to reset dispatch jump table to defaults
16h	BYTE	*unknown*

Note: The addresses in the new dispatch table are copied into an internal jump table which may be reset by calling the function pointed at by offset 12h.

CHAPTER 34

Other TCP/IP Software

This chapter covers a number of other protocol stacks supporting the TCP/IP protocol suite whose APIs are not large enough or too poorly known to warrant their own chapters.

Microsoft LAN Manager TCP/IP

INT 21h Function 4402h   *LAN Manager TCPDRV.DOS*
API

Registers at call:	**Return Registers:**
AX = 4402h	CF clear if successful
BX = file handle for device "TCPDRV$"	AX = number of bytes actually read
CX = 0019h	CF set on error
DS:DX -> buffer containing parameter	AX = error code (see Table 3-1)
block (see Table 34-1)	

34-1 Format of parameter block:

Offset	Size	Description
00h	BYTE	(call) function number (00h, 06h, 07h)
01h	BYTE	(call) 00h
		(return) error code if error, unchanged if call successful
02h	WORD	signature 4354h ('CT')
---**function 00h**---		
04h	DWORD	(call) pointer to *unknown* FAR function
		function is called with ES:BX pointing at device driver request header
		used to invoke this function
08h	4 BYTEs	*unknown*
0Ch	DWORD	(call) pointer to *unknown record*, WORD at offset 22h in record
		is read by TCPDRV.DOS
10h	DWORD	set to address of *unknown buffer* if 0000h:0000h on call
---**function 06h**---		
04h	4 BYTEs	*unknown*
08h	DWORD	(return) pointer to *unknown item*
---**function 07h**---		
04h	DWORD	(return) pointer to *unknown record*

Novell NetWare TCP/IP

Novell's ODI-based TCP/IP protocol stacks are part of the LAN Workplace product line, which is available for MS-DOS, OS/2, and Macintosh platforms.

INT 2Fh Function 7A40h
TCP/IP Protocol Stack - INSTALLATION CHECK
Novell NetWare

Registers at call:
AX = 7A40h

Return Registers:
AX = 7AFFh if installed
    BX = *unknown*
        bit 0: *unknown*
        bit 1: *unknown*
        bits 15-2: *unknown*
    CX = version (CH=major, CL=minor)
    DX = 0000h
    ES:DI -> entry point for TCP/IP stack (see Table 34-2)

Details: Novell's LAN Workplace for DOS TCPIP.EXE also supports this interface.

This function is also supported by the Beame&Whiteside BWLWP40 shim, but it only returns AL and ES:DI, and does not support Function 7A41h through 7A44h.

Conflicts: none known, but see Table 2-2 for potential conflicts

See also: Function 7A41h, Excelan INT 60h

34-2 Entry point calling convention:

Registers at call:
ES:SI -> parameter block (see Table 34-3)
others, if any, unknown

Return Registers:
ES:SI parameter block updated

34-3 Format of parameter block:

Offset	Size	Description
00h	DWORD	*unknown*
04h	WORD	(return) *unknown*
06h	WORD	(return) *unknown*
08h	4 BYTEs	*unknown*
0Ch	BYTE	*flags*
0Dh	7 BYTEs	*unknown*
14h	BYTE	(return) *unknown*
15h	BYTE	(call) *unknown* number, bit 7 set if *unknown condition*
16h	BYTE	*unknown*
17h	BYTE	(return) result or error code
		others, if any, unknown

INT 2Fh Function 7A41h
TCP/IP Protocol Stack - WINDOWS SUPPORT
Novell NetWare

Registers at call:
AX = 7A41h
ES:DI -> FAR entry point for *unknown*
  (will be called with BX=1,2,3,4)

Return Registers:
AX = 7AFFh if supported
    BX = *unknown* (see Function 7A40h)
    CX = version (CH=major, CL=minor)
    DX = 0000h
    ES:SI -> DWORD containing passed value of ES:DI
    ES:DI -> entry point for TCP/IP stack

Details: Novell's LAN Workplace for DOS TCPIP.EXE also supports this interface.

The pointer which is set to ES:DI is cleared to 0000h:0000h when a Windows exit broadcast is received.

Conflicts: none known, but see Table 2-2 for potential conflicts

See also: Function 7A40h

INT 2Fh Function 7A42h
GET UNKNOWN ENTRY POINT
Novell NetWare TCPIP.EXE v4.1

Registers at call:
AX = 7A42h

Return Registers:
AX = 7AFFh if supported
      ES:DI -> *unknown* entry point (see Table 34-4)

34-4 Call entry point with:

Registers at call:
DX = *unknown*
ES:DI -> *unknown data buffer*
  (see Table 34-5)

Return Registers:
AX = 0000h
other registers destroyed

34-5 Format of data buffer:

Offset	Size	Description
00h	WORD	offset of WORD *unknown* or 0000h
02h	WORD	offset of DWORD *unknown* or 0000h
04h	WORD	offset of DWORD *unknown* or 0000h

INT 2Fh Function 7A43h
UNDETERMINED FUNCTION
Novell NetWare TCPIP.EXE v4.1

Registers at call:
AX = 7A43h

Return Registers:
AX = 7AFFh if supported
      DX = offset of *unknown item*

See also: Function 7A44h

INT 2Fh Function 7A44h
UNDETERMINED FUNCTION
Novell NetWare TCPIP.EXE v4.1

Registers at call:
AX = 7A44h
DX = offset of *unknown item*
  (see Function 7A43h)
See also: Function 7A43h

Return Registers:
AX = 7AFFh if supported

INT 2Fh Function 7A4Ch Novell NetWare TCPIP.EXE v4.1
GET UNKNOWN VALUES

Registers at call:
AX = 7A4Ch

Return Registers:
AX = 7AFFh if supported
      BX = *unknown* (0037h)
      CX = *unknown* (001Ch)

INT 2Fh Function 7A4Fh, Subfunction 0001h
INSTALLATION CHECK
Novell NetWare SNMP.EXE

Registers at call:
AX = 7A4Fh
BX = 0001h
See also: Function 7A4Fh Subfunction 0002h

Return Registers:
AX = 7AFFh if installed

INT 2Fh Function 7A4Fh, Subfunction 0002h
UNDETERMINED FUNCTION
Novell NetWare SNMP.EXE

Registers at call:
AX = 7A4Fh
BX = 0002h

Return Registers:
AL = status
    4Fh if failed
    FFh if successful

See also: Function 7A4Fh Subfunction 0001h

Sun PC-NFS

INT 21h Function 44E0h
API

Registers at call:
AX = 44E0h
DS:DX -> *unknown*
SS:BP -> stack frame (see Table 34-6)

Return Registers:
unknown

Details: This function is also supported by Beame&Whiteside's BWPCNFS shim; the description presented here was derived from that shim.

34-6 Format of stack frame:

Offset	Size	Description
00h	WORD	pointer to previous stack frame
02h	DWORD	return address

INT 2Fh Function FE00h, Subfunction 4454h
INSTALLATION CHECK

PC-NFS

Registers at call:
AX = FE00h
BX = 4454h ("DT")
CX = 4B52h ("KR")
DX = 4E4Dh ("NM")

Return Registers:
AL = FFh if installed
BX = 524Eh ("RM")
CX = 4D44h ("MD")
DX = 544Bh ("TK")

Details: DV/X 1.10 DVPCNFS.DVR searches AH=FEh,FFh,C0h-FDh for a valid response.
Conflicts: Norton Utilities (PCI-62); see also Table 2-2. **See also:** Function FE08h

INT 2Fh Function FE00h, Subfunction 4454h
INSTALLATION CHECK

PC-NFS

Registers at call:
AX = FE00h
BX = 4454h ("DT")
CX = 4B52h ("KR")
DX = 544Dh ("TM")

Return Registers:
AL = FFh if installed
BX = 5254h ("RT")
CX = 4D44h ("MD")
DX = 544Bh ("TK")

Details: DV/X 1.10 DVPCNFS.DVR searches AH=FEh,FFh,C0h-FDh for a valid response.
Conflicts: Norton Utilities (PCI-62); see also Table 2-2
See also: Function FE08h

INT 2Fh Function FE08h
GET UNKNOWN ITEM

PC-NFS

Registers at call:
AX = FE08h

Return Registers:
ES:BX -> *unknown*

Details: DV/X 1.10 DVPCNFS.DVR searches AH=FEh,FFh,C0h-FDh for a valid response.
  Both the driver responding to Function FE00h Subfunction 4E4Dh and the one responding to Function FE00h Subfunction 544Dh support this function.
Conflicts: Norton Utilities (PCI-62); see also Table 2-2
See also: Function FE00h Subfunction 4454h

Super-TCP

Super-TCP is a TCP/IP protocol stack by Frontier Technologies Corp.

INT 6Ah Function 0000h
INSTALLATION CHECK

Registers at call:
AX = 0000h

Return Registers:
AX = 4357h ('CW')

Details: An alternate installation check is to test for the ASCIZ signature "FTC Super-TCP" three bytes past the interrupt handler.
Conflicts: DECnet DOS (Chapter 16), OPTHELP (PCI-66)
See also: Functions 0001h, 0002h, 000Fh, and 0010h, PCTCP INT 61h (Chapter 33), BW-TCP INT 62h (Chapter 32)

INT 6Ah Function 0001h	*Super-TCP DOS TSR Kernel v3.57*
UNDETERMINED FUNCTION	*Undocumented*

Registers at call:
AX = 0001h
BH = function number
    01h *unknown*
        DS:SI -> *unknown* record1
        (see Table 34-7)
        ES:DI -> buffer containing *unknown*
    02h *unknown*
        DS:SI -> *unknown* record2 (see Table 34-8)
        ES:DI -> buffer containing *unknown*
    04h *unknown*
        DS:SI -> *unknown* record3 (see Table 34-9)
        BL = subfunction
            01h *unknown*
                ES:DI -> buffer containing *unknown*
            02h *unknown*
                ES:DI -> buffer containing *unknown*
            03h *unknown*
            else Return: AX = 0005h
    05h *unknown*
        DS:SI -> *unknown* record4 (see Table 34-10)
        ES:DI -> buffer containing *unknown*
    06h *unknown*
        BL = subfunction
            01h
                DS:SI -> record5 (see Table 34-11)
            02h
                DS:SI -> record6 (see Table 34-12)
                ES:DI -> *unknown*
            03h
                DS:SI -> record6 (see Table 34-12)
            04h
                DS:SI -> record7 (see Table 34-13)
            else Return: AX = 0005h
    11h *unknown*
        DS:SI -> *unknown* record8 (see Table 34-14)
        ES:DI -> *unknown*

Return Registers:
AX = function status
    0000h successful
    0005h unsupported function
    000Ah out of memory

See also: Function 0000h

34-7 Format of record1:

Offset	Size	Description
00h	4 BYTEs	*unknown*
04h	WORD	size of ES:DI buffer
06h	18 BYTEs	*unknown*

34-8 Format of record2:

Offset	Size	Description
00h	4 BYTEs	*unknown*
04h	WORD	size of ES:DI buffer
06h	12 BYTEs	*unknown*

34-9 Format of record3:

Offset	Size	Description
00h	2 BYTEs	*unknown*
02h	WORD	*unknown*
04h	WORD	size of ES:DI buffer
06h	WORD	*unknown*
08h	WORD	operation number (for function 0401h)
0Ah	DWORD	pointer to *unknown item*
0Eh	WORD	(return) *unknown*
10h	12 BYTEs	*unknown*

34-10 Format of record4:

Offset	Size	Description
00h	4 BYTEs	*unknown*
04h	WORD	size of ES:DI buffer
06h	14 BYTEs	*unknown*

34-11 Format of record5:

Offset	Size	Description
00h	BYTE	*operation* (00h-07h)
01h	BYTE	*unknown*
02h	WORD	(return) *unknown*
04h	DWORD	pointer to *unknown item*
08h	4 BYTEs	*unknown*
0Ch	DWORD	pointer to *unknown* or 0000h:0000h
10h	16 BYTEs	*unknown*
20h	DWORD	*unknown*
24h	4 BYTEs	*unknown*

34-12 Format of record6:

Offset	Size	Description
00h	4 BYTEs	*unknown*
04h	WORD	size of ES:DI buffer
06h	14 BYTEs	*unknown*

34-13 Format of record7:

Offset	Size	Description
00h	WORD	*unknown*
02h	WORD	*unknown*
04h	WORD	*unknown*
06h	40 BYTEs	*unknown*

34-14 Format of record8:

Offset	Size	Description
00h	4 BYTEs	*unknown*
04h	WORD	size of ES:DI buffer

INT 6Ah Function 0001h

06h	6 BYTEs	*unknown*
0Ch	WORD	(return) *unknown*
0Eh	WORD	*operation* (01h-03h)
10h	12 BYTEs	*unknown*

INT 6Ah Function 0002h
UNDETERMINED FUNCTION

Super-TCP DOS TSR Kernel v3.57
Undocumented

Registers at call:
AX = 0002h
BX = *unknown* (zero/nonzero)
CX = *unknown* identifier
  (see Function 0004h)
DS:SI -> 40-byte buffer for *unknown*
  or 0000h:0000h
ES:DI -> buffer for *unknown* or
  0000h:0000h
Conflicts: DECnet DOS (Chapter 16), OPTHELP (PCI-66)

Return Registers:
AX = 0000h (successful) *unknown*
BL = *unknown*
BH = *unknown*
CX = *unknown*
DX = *unknown*

INT 6Ah Function 0003h
GET UNKNOWN DATA AREA

Super-TCP DOS TSR Kernel v3.57
Undocumented

Registers at call:
AX = 0003h

Return Registers:
CX:DX -> data area (see Table 34-15)

Conflicts: DECnet DOS (Chapter 16), OPTHELP (PCI-66)

34-15 Format of data area:

Offset	Size	Description
00h	2 BYTEs	*unknown*
02h	DWORD	original INT 6Ah vector
06h	2 BYTEs	*unknown*
08h	96 BYTEs	array of 16 6-byte *unknown items*
68h	WORD	number of elements of above array in use
6Ah	WORD	*unknown*
		others, if any, unknown

INT 6Ah Function 0004h
ALLOCATE UNKNOWN

Super-TCP DOS TSR Kernel v3.57
Undocumented

Registers at call:
AX = 0004h
CX = size in *unknown*

Return Registers:
AX = 0000h (successful)
CX = DX = *unknown* identifier

Conflicts: DECnet DOS (Chapter 16), OPTHELP (PCI-66)
See also: Functions 0005h and 000Fh

INT 6Ah Function 0005h
FREE/CLOSE UNKNOWN

Super-TCP DOS TSR Kernel v3.57
Undocumented

Registers at call:
AX = 0005h
CX = *unknown* identifier (from
Function 0004h)

Return Registers:
AX = status (0000h successful, FFFFh failed)

Conflicts: DECnet DOS (Chapter 16), OPTHELP (PCI-66)
See also: Functions 0004h and 000Fh

INT 6Ah Function 000Fh
FREE/CLOSE ALL UNKNOWN

Registers at call: **Return Registers:**
AX = 000Fh   AX = 0000h (successful)
Conflicts: DECnet DOS (Chapter 16), OPTHELP (PCI-66)
See also: Functions 0000h, 0004h, and 0005h

INT 6Ah Function 0010h
UNINSTALL

Registers at call: **Return Registers:**
AX = 0010h   AX = status
                                0000h successful
                                0002h can't uninstall, interrupt vector hooked by another program
Details: If AX is not one of the values listed here on entry, Super-TCP returns AX=FFFEh.
Conflicts: DECnet DOS (Chapter 16), OPTHELP (PCI-66)
See also: Function 0000h

Lanera TCPOpen

TCPOpen is a TCP/IP protocol stack by Lanera Corporation.

The interrupt number used by the kernel may be set to any value from 60h through 7Fh (the default as shown here is 61h) via the configuration file. There does not appear to be an installation check, though Function FFFFh can be used to verify that the software is indeed functioning.

INT 61h
API

Registers at call: **Return Registers:**
ES:BX -> request packet (see Table 34-16)   request packet updated
Conflicts: see Table 2-3

34-16 Format of request packet:

Offset	Size	Description
00h	8 BYTEs	*unknown*
08h	WORD	function number (0000h-001Ah or FFF9h-FFFFh)
		FFFFh installation verification
0Ah	WORD	*unknown*
0Ch	2 BYTEs	*unknown*
0Eh	WORD	(return) return code
10h	2 BYTEs	*unknown*
12h	WORD	*unknown*
14h	WORD	(return) 0001h if requested function complete
16h	WORD	(return) *unknown*
18h	6 BYTEs	*unknown*
1Eh	DWORD	pointer to *unknown item*
22h	WORD	*unknown* or 0000h
24h	WORD	(return) *unknown*

34-17 Function FFFFh (installation verification) calling convention:

Registers at call: **Return Registers:**
Request Packet   Request Packet
    offset 08h = FFFFh   offset 10h = BEEFh
                                                     offset 14h = 0001h
                                                     offset 24h = *unknown*

TelAPI

TelAPI is a Novell addition to its TELNET implementation, part of the LAN Workplace product line, which permits third-party software to access internals of the TELNET terminal emulation package.

TelAPI also supports the NASI/NACS interface on INT 6Bh (see Chapter 38).

INT 14h Function 06h
TelAPI
Undocumented

WRITE

Registers at call:
AH = 06h
CX = *number of characters to write*
DX = port number
ES:DI -> *buffer containing data*

Return Registers:
AX = *number of characters actually sent* (negative on error)
CX = *unknown*

Details: Under Novell TELAPI.EXE v4.01, this function and Function 07h are implemented with identical code.
Conflicts: Connection Manager (Chapter 38), FOSSIL (PCI-12), MBBIOS (PCI-12), Multi-DOS Plus IODRV (PCI-45), PC/MOS-386 (PCI-49)
See also: Functions 07h and E0h

INT 14h Function 07h
TelAPI
Undocumented

WRITE

Registers at call:
AH = 07h
CX = *number of characters to write*
DX = port number
ES:DI -> *buffer containing data*

Return Registers:
AX = *number of characters actually sent* (negative on error)
CX = *unknown*

Details: Under Novell TELAPI.EXE v4.01, this function and Function 06h are implemented with identical code.
Conflicts: Connection Manager (Chapter 38), FOSSIL (PCI-12), MBBIOS (PCI-12), Multi-DOS Plus IODRV (PCI-45), PC/MOS-386 (PCI-49)
See also: Functions 06h and E0h

INT 14h Function A8h
Novell TelAPI v4.01

CONNECTION INFORMATION

Registers at call:
AH = A8h
DH = *session ID*
CH = subfunction
   02h *unknown*
   0Dh *unknown*
   0Fh *unknown*
   10h *unknown*
   11h *unknown*
   28h *unknown*

Return Registers:
AH = return code (see Table 4-1)
  00h successful
     CL = *unknown* (0/1/8) (subfunctions 02h,0Dh,0Fh,10h)
     CL = *unknown* (7Fh/FFh) (subfunction 28h)
     CX = *unknown* (subfunction 11h)
  09h not supported (functions other than those at left)

Conflicts: Interconnections TES (Chapter 38)
See also: Function A9h

INT 14h Function A9h
Novell TelAPI v4.01

CONNECTION CONTROL

Registers at call:
AH = A9h
DH = *session ID*

CH = subfunction
  02h *unknown*
  0Dh *unknown*
  0Fh *unknown*
  10h *unknown*
  11h *unknown*
  28h *unknown*

Return Registers:
AH = return code (see Table 4-1)
  09h not supported (functions other than those at left)
others, if any, unknown

Conflicts: none known
See also: Functions A8h and E4h, INT 6Bh Function 0600h

INT 14h Function E0h   *TelAPI*
UNDETERMINED FUNCTION

Registers at call:
AH = E0h
BX = *unknown*
CX:DX = *unknown*
DS:DI -> *unknown*
ES:SI -> *unknown*

Return Registers:
AX = status (0000h,FF37h,etc.)
ES:SI -> *unknown* if *unknown*
others, if any, unknown

Conflicts: MX5 Extended FOSSIL (PCI-12)
See also: Functions ECh and FF00h

INT 14h Function E1h   *TelAPI*
UNDETERMINED FUNCTION

Registers at call:
AH = E1h
BX = connection ID
others, if any, unknown

Return Registers:
AX = status (0000h,FFF7h,maybe others)
others, if any, unknown

See also: Functions E6h and FF00h

INT 14h Function E2h   *TelAPI*
BUFFERED READ

Registers at call:
AH = E2h
BX = connection ID
CX = length of buffer in bytes
ES:SI -> buffer for data

Return Registers:
AX = *number of characters actually read*
  (negative on error)

See also: Functions E6h and FF00h, INT 6Bh Function 01h (Chapter 38)

INT 14h Function E3h   *TelAPI*
BUFFERED WRITE

Registers at call:
AH = E3h
BX = connection ID
CX = length of buffer in bytes
ES:SI -> buffer containing data

Return Registers:
AX = *number of characters actually written*
  (negative on error)

See also: Functions 07h, E6h, and FF00h; INT 6Bh Function 00h (Chapter 38)

INT 14h Function E4h   *TelAPI*
CONNECTION CONTROL

Registers at call:
AH = E4h
BX = connection ID
CX = *unknown*

ES:SI -> 10-byte buffer containing   **Return Registers:**
  unknown   *unknown*
See also: Functions A9h, E6h, and FF00h; INT 6Bh Function 0600h (Chapter 38)

INT 14h Functions E5h and E6h   *TelAPI*
UNDETERMINED FUNCTIONS
Registers at call: **Return Registers:**
AH = E5h and E6h   AX = *status*
See also: Functions E6h and FF00h
Details: Function E6h invokes Function E5h internally.
See also: Function FF00h, INT 6Bh Function 00h, INT 6Bh Function 10h

---

INT 14h Function E7h   *TelAPI*
GET UNKNOWN ITEM
Registers at call: **Return Registers:**
AH = E7h   AX = 0000h (successful)
ES:SI -> 20-byte buffer for *unknown*   ES:SI buffer filled
See also: Function FF00h

INT 14h Function E8h   *TelAPI*
SET UNKNOWN ITEM
Registers at call: **Return Registers:**
AH = E8h   AX = status (0000h,FFFFh)
BX = connection ID
CL = new value for *unknown*
DX = *unknown* (ignored by Novell TELAPI v4.01)
See also: Function FF00h

INT 14h Function E9h   *TelAPI*
UNDETERMINED FUNCTION
Registers at call: **Return Registers:**
AH = E9h   *unknown*
DX = *unknown*
See also: Function FF00h

INT 14h Function EAh   *TelAPI*
GET CONNECTION INFO
Registers at call: **Return Registers:**
AH = EAh   AX = status (0000h,FFFFh,etc.)
BX = connection ID
ES:SI -> buffer for *info*
See also: Function FF00h

INT 14h Function EBh   *TelAPI*
GET UNKNOWN ITEM
Registers at call: **Return Registers:**
AH = EBh   ES:SI buffer filled
ES:SI -> buffer for *unknown*
See also: Function FF00h

INT 14h Function ECh   *TelAPI*
UNDETERMINED FUNCTION
Registers at call:
AH = ECh

BX = *unknown*
CX:DX = *unknown*
DS:DI -> *unknown*
ES:SI -> *unknown*

Return Registers:
AX = status (0000h,FF37h,etc.)
ES:SI -> *unknown* if *unknown*
others, if any, unknown

Details: This function is not supported by the Microdyne TelAPI v3.7.
See also: Functions E0h and FF00h

INT 14h Function EDh   *TelAPI*
UNDETERMINED FUNCTION

Registers at call:
AH = EDh
BX = connection ID

Return Registers:
AX = status (0000h,FFFFh,etc.)

Details: This function is not supported by the Microdyne TelAPI v3.7.
See also: Function FF00h

INT 14h Function FF00h   *TelAPI*
INSTALLATION CHECK

Registers at call:
AX = FF00h

Return Registers:
AL = FFh if installed
AH = 00h for Novell TELAPI.EXE

See also: Function E6h

INT 6Bh Function 08h   *TelAPI*
UNDETERMINED FUNCTION

Registers at call:
AH = 08h

Return Registers:
CF clear
    AL = 00h
    CX = 0000h

Details: This function also clears an *unknown* flag.
Conflicts: DECnet DOS (Chapter 16), "Saddam" virus (PCI-59)
See also: INT 14h Function FF00h

CHAPTER 35

BSD 4.x Unix Sockets

Unlike the other chapters of this book, this chapter and the next do not cover interrupt calls, but rather function libraries which may be called directly from high-level languages.

Sockets were introduced in Berkeley Unix around 1982, and have become a *de facto* standard for network programming. Most TCP/IP implementations for the PC provide a linkable library which includes most or all of the functions described in this chapter. DESQview/X also provides an interrupt-based API which implements these functions and a number of other Unix-compatibility functions (see Chapter 17); Quarterdeck sells API libraries which provide access to these interupt calls from high-level languages.

Overview of Functions, Error Codes, and Structures

35-1 Overview of Sockets functions:

accept	accept an incoming connection on a socket
bind	bind a name to a socket
close	close a descriptor
connect	initiate a connection on a socket
endhostent	signal end of host lookups
endnetent	signal end of network lookups
endprotoent	signal end of protocol lookups
endservent	signal end of service lookups
gethostbyaddr	get information about a host specified by address
gethostbyname	get information about a host specified by name
gethostent	get next host entry
gethostid	get unique identifier of current host
gethostname	get name of current host
getnetbyaddr	get information about a network specified by address
getnetbyname	get information about a network specified by name
getnetent	get next network entry
getpeername	get name of connected peer
getprotobyname	get information about a protocol specified by name
getprotobynumber	get information about a protocol specified by number
getprotoent	get next protocol entry
getservbyname	get information about a service specified by name
getservbyport	get information about a service specified by port number
getservent	get next service entry
getsockname	get socket's assigned name

getsockopt	get options for socket
htonl	convert *long* to network byte order
htons	convert *short* to network byte order
inet_addr	parse dotted numeric string into Internet address
inet_lnaof	extract local network address from Internet address
inet_makeaddr	make Internet address from network number and local address
inet_netof	extract network number from Internet address
inet_network	parse dotted numeric string into Internet network number
inet_ntoa	convert Internet address to dotted numeric string
ioctl	control I/O device
listen	start socket listening for connection attempts
ntohl	convert *long* to host byte order
ntohs	convert *short* to host byte order
recv	receive a message on a connected socket
recvfrom	receive a message on a socket, with originating address
recvmsg	receive a message on a socket
select	syncronous I/O multiplexing
send	transmit a message over a connected socket
sendto	transmit a message to a specified recipient
sendmsg	transmit a message over a socket
sethostent	start host lookups
sethostid	specify unique identifier for current host
sethostname	specify name of current host
setnetent	start network lookups
setprotoent	start protocol lookups
setservent	start service lookups
setsockopt	specify options for socket
socket	create an endpoint for communication
socketpair	create a pair of connected sockets

35-2 Socket error codes (errno):

EBADF	invalid descriptor
EACCESS	access denied
EADDRINUSE	specified address already in use
EADDRNOTAVAIL	specified address not available on caller's machine
EAFNOSUPPORT	specified address family can not be use with socket
EALREADY	previous operation on non-blocking socket has not completed
ECONNREFUSED	connection attempt was refused
EDQUOT	disk quota exceeded
EFAULT	general error
EHOSTDOWN	host is down
EHOSTUNREACH	no route to host
EINVAL	invalid operation or parameter
EINPROGRESS	non-blocking operation can not be completed immediately
EINTR	socket function call was interrupted by a signal
EIO	I/O error
EISCONN	socket is already connected
EISDIR	null pathname specified
ELOOP	too many symbolic links traversed while translating pathname
EMFILE	no more file handles available to process

ENAMETOOLONG	specified name was too long
ENETUNREACH	specified network is not reachable
ENFILE	system file table is full
ENOBUFS	insufficient resources (i.e. buffer space) for operation
ENOENT	path prefix includes non-existent component, or socket does not exist
ENOPROTOOPT	unknown protocol option for specified level
ENOTCONN	socket is not connected
ENOTDIR	path prefix includes non-directory component
ENOTEMPTY	directory is not empty
ENOTSOCK	descriptor references a file instead of a socket
ENOTTY	request does not apply to object referenced by descriptor
EOPNOTSUPP	operation not supported on specified socket
EOPNOSUPPORT	operation not supported
EPERM	privileged operation attempted by other than super-user
EPFNOSUPPORT	protocol family not supported
EPROTONOSUPPORT	specified protocol type or protocol not supported in domain
EREMOTE	too many levels of remote access in path
EROFS	name would reside on read-only filesystem
ESTALE	stale remote file handle
ETIMEDOUT	operation timed out
ETOOMANYREFS	too many references, can not splice
EUSERS	too many users
EWOULDBLOCK	operation can not be completed immediately and socket is marked n on-blocking

35-3 Host lookup error codes (h_errno):

HOST_NOT_FOUND	host is unknown
TRY_AGAIN	temporary error, usually failure to receive a response
NO_RECOVERY	unrecoverable error
NO_ADDRESS	valid name, but no associated IP address; use another type of lookup

35-4 Format of struct hostent:

Type	Name	Description
char *	h_name	host's official name
char **	h_aliases	NULL-terminated alias list
int	h_addrtype	host address type (AF_INET)
int	h_length	length of address
char **	h_addr_list	NULL-terminated list of addresses returned by name server

35-5 Format of struct in_addr:

union S_un
long S_addr
struct S_un_w
unsigned short s_w1, s_w2
struct S_un_b
char s_b1, s_b2, s_b3, s_b4

35-6 Format of struct iovec:

Type	Name	Description
caddr_t	iov_base	base address in memory of scatter/gather area
int	iov_len	length of area

35-7 Format of struct msghdr:

Type	Name	Description
caddr_t	msg_name	optional source/destination address (empty if none)
int	msg_namelen	size of optional address
struct iovec *	msg_iov	scatter/gather array
int	msg_iovlen	number of elements in scatter/gather array
caddr_t	msg_accrights	access rights sent/received
int	msg_accrightslen	length of access rights

35-8 Format of struct netent:

Type	Name	Description
char *	n_name	network's official name
char **	n_aliases	NULL-terminated list of alias names
int	n_addrtype	type of network number (AF_INET)
unsigned long	n_net	network number in host's byte order

35-9 Format of struct protoent:

Type	Name	Description
char *	p_name	protocol's official name
char **	p_aliases	NULL-terminated list of alias names
int	p_proto	protocol number

35-10 Format of struct servent:

Type	Name	Description
char *	s_name	service's official name
char **	s_aliases	NULL-terminated list of alias names
int	s_port	port number for service (network byte order)
char *	s_proto	protocol to use when contacting service

35-11 Format of struct sockaddr:

Type	Name	Description
unsigned short	sa_family	address family
char[14]	sa_data	family-dependent address data (see Tables 35-12 and 35-13)

35-12 Format of struct sockaddr_in (Internet address family):

Type	Name	Description
short	sin_family	protocol family
unsigned short	sin_port	port number
struct in_addr	sin_addr	internet address
char[8]	sin_zero	

35-13 Format of struct sockaddr_un (Unix address family)

Type	Name	Description
short	sun_family	protocol family
char[108]	sun_path	pathname

35-14 Format of struct timeval:

Type	Name	Description
long	tv_sec	seconds
long	tv_usec	microseconds

Socket Functions

accept: accept an incoming connection on a socket
newsock = accept(sock, address, addrlen)

Arguments:
int sock, newsock ;
struct sockaddr *address ;(Table 35-11)
int *addrlen ;
Header Files:
sys/types.h
sys/socket.h
Details: *accept* extracts the first pending connection for *sock* (which was created with *socket*, bound to an address with *bind*, and is awaiting connections with *listen*), creates a new socket with the same properties, and assigns it to a new descriptor *newsock*. If *sock* has been marked non-blocking and no connections are pending, an error is returned; otherwise, *address* and *addrlen* are filled with the address from which the connection is being made (up to the length specified by *addrlen* on entry).

On error, *accept* returns -1 and sets *errno* (see Table 35-2); if successful, it returns a non-negative socket descriptor.
See also: bind, connect, listen, select, socket

bind: bind a name to a socket
status = bind(sock, name, namelength)

Arguments:
int sock, namelength, status ;
struct sockaddr *name ;(Table 35-11)
Header Files:
sys/types.h
sys/socket.h
Details: *bind* assigns a name to a socket with descriptor *sock* which has not previously been named (bound), such as a socket newly created with the *socket* function. The name to be associated with the socket is given in *name*, whose length is *namelength*. Binding a socket for the Unix domain creates a file which must be explicitly deleted with *unlink*.

On error, *bind* returns -1 and sets *errno*; if successful, it returns 0.
See also: socket, getsockname

close: close a descriptor
status = close(descr)

Arguments:
int status, descr ;
Details: *close* removes a descriptor from the per-process reference table, and deletes the underlying object if the last reference has been removed.

Under Unix, both file and socket descriptors may be closed with this call; most PC implementations (being add-ons) provide a socket-closing function with a slightly different name, such as *bsd_close*, to avoid conflicting with the standard function library.
See also: accept, connect, socket, socketpair, closesocket (Chapter 36)

connect: initiate a connection on a socket
status = connect(sock, name, namelength)

Arguments:
int sock, namelength, status ;
struct sockaddr *name ;(Table 35-11)

Header Files:
sys/types.h
sys/socket.h
Details: If the specified socket is a stream socket (created with the SOCK_STREAM option), *connect* attempts to connect to another socket as specified by *name*. If the socket is a datagram socket (SOCK_DGRAM), this call specifies the address to which datagrams are to be sent and the sole address from which they are to be received by the socket.

On error, *connect* returns -1 and sets *errno*; if successful, it returns 0.

See also: accept, getsockname, select, socket

endhostent: signal end of host lookups
endhostent()

Arguments:
none
Header Files:
netdb.h
Details: If *sethostent* has been called specifying *stayopen*, calls to *gethostbyaddr* and *gethostbyname* will query the name server over a TCP connection which remains open until explicitly closed with this function.

When using the local host table /etc/hosts, *endhostent* closes the file.

See also: gethostbyaddr, gethostbyname, sethostent

endnetent: signal end of network lookups
endnetent()

Arguments:
none
Header Files:
netdb.h
Details: This function closes the network database file /etc/networks.
See also: getnetbyaddr, getnetbyname, setnetent

endprotoent: signal end of protocol lookups
endprotoent()

Arguments:
none
Header Files:
netdb.h
Details: This function closes the protocol database file /etc/protocols.
See also: getprotobyname, getprotobynumber, setprotoent

endservent: signal end of service lookups
endservent()

Arguments:
none
Header Files:
netdb.h
Details: This function closes the network services database file /etc/services.
See also: getservbyname, getservbyport, setservent

gethostbyaddr: get information about a host specified by address
hostinfo = gethostbyaddr(address, addrlen, type)

Arguments:
char *address ;

int addrlen, type ;
struct hostent *hostinfo ;(Table 35-4)
Header Files:
netdb.h
Details: Get information about the host with network address *address* (specified in network byte order) from the name server or a line in /etc/hosts (Unix filename). The returned information is stored in a static area and must thus be copied before any subsequent calls.

If *sethostent* has been called specifying *stayopen*, the name server will be queried over a TCP connection which remains open until explicitly closed with *endhostent*.
See also: endhostent, gethostbyname, sethostent

---

gethostbyname: get information about a host specified by name
hostinfo = gethostbyname(name)

Arguments:
char *name ;
struct hostent *hostinfo ;(Table 35-4)
Header Files:
netdb.h
Details: This function gets information about the specified host from the name server or a line in /etc/hosts (Unix filename). The returned information is stored in a static area and must thus be copied before any subsequent calls.

If *sethostent* has been called specifying *stayopen*, the name server will be queried over a TCP connection which remains open until explicitly closed with *endhostent*.
See also: endhostent, gethostbyaddr, sethostent

---

gethostent: get next host entry
hostinfo = gethostent()

Arguments:
struct hostent *hostinfo ;(Table 35-4)
Header Files:
netdb.h
Details: This function retrieves and parses the next line of the local host table /etc/hosts.
See also: endhostent, gethostbyaddr, gethostbyname, sethostent

---

gethostid: get unique identifier of current host
hostid = gethostid()

Arguments:
long hostid ;
Header Files:
none
Details: This function retrieves the 32-bit identifier for the current processor, usually the Internet address.
See also: gethostname, sethostid

---

gethostname: get name of current host
status = gethostname(name, namelength)

Arguments:
char *name ;
int namelength, status ;
Header Files:
none
Details: This function retrieves the standard host name for the current machine, storing the name in *name* (NUL-terminated unless *namelength* is less than the size required to hold the name).

On error, *gethostname* returns -1 and sets *errno*; if successful, it returns 0.
See also: gethostid, sethostname

---

getnetbyaddr: get information about a network specified by address
netinfo = getnetbyaddr(netnumber, type)
Arguments:
int netnumber, type ;
struct netent *netinfo ;(Table 35-8)
Header Files:
netdb.h
Details: This function retrieves information about a network specified by address from the network database file /etc/networks. If *setnetent* was called specifying *stayopen*, the file will remain open between calls.

NULL is returned if no matching entry is found.

The returned information is stored in a static area and must thus be copied before the next call.

See also: endnetent, getnetbyaddr, setnetent

---

getnetbyname: get information about a network specified by name
netinfo = getnetbyname(name)
Arguments:
char *name ;
struct netent *netinfo ;(Table 35-8)
Header Files:
netdb.h
Details: This function retrieves information about a network specified by name from the network database file /etc/networks. If *setnetent* was called specifying *stayopen*, the file will remain open between calls.

NULL is returned if no matching entry is found.

The returned information is stored in a static area and must thus be copied before the next call.

See also: endnetent, getnetbyaddr, setnetent

---

getnetent: get next network entry
netinfo = getnetent()
Arguments:
struct netent *netinfo ;(Table 35-8)
Header Files:
netdb.h
Details: This function retrieves and parses the next line of the network database file /etc/networks. NULL is returned when the end of the file is reached.

The returned information is stored in a static area and must thus be copied before the next call.

See also: endnetent, getnetbyaddr, getnetbyname, setnetent

---

getpeername: get name of connected peer
status = getpeername(sock, name, namelength)
Arguments:
int sock, status ;
struct sockaddr *name ;(Table 35-11)
int *namelength ;

Details: This function returns the name of the machine connected to the specified socket. On entry, *namelength* should contain the size of the buffer *name*; on return, it will have been updated to the actual size of the returned name (which will be truncated if the buffer is too small).

On error, *getpeername* returns -1; if successful, it returns 0.

See also: accept, bind, connect, getsockname, socket

getprotobyname: get information about a protocol specified by name
protoinfo = getprotobyname(name)

Arguments:
char *name ;
struct protoent *protoinfo ;(Table 35-9)

Header Files:
netdb.h

Details: This function retrieves information about a protocol specified by name from the protocol database file /etc/protocols. If *setprotoent* was called specifying *stayopen*, the file will remain open between calls.

NULL is returned if no matching entry is found or an error is encountered.

The returned information is stored in a static area and must thus be copied before the next call.

See also: endprotoent, getprotobynumber, setprotoent

getprotobynumber: get information about a protocol specified by number
protoinfo = getprotobynumber(number)

Arguments:
int number ;
struct protoent *protoinfo ;(Table 35-9)

Header Files:
netdb.h

Details: This function retrieves information about a protocol specified by number from the protocol database file /etc/protocols. If *setprotoent* was called specifying *stayopen*, the file will remain open between calls.

NULL is returned if no matching entry is found or an error is encountered.

The returned information is stored in a static area and must thus be copied before the next call.

See also: endprotoent, getprotobyname, setprotoent

getprotoent: get next protocol entry
protoinfo = getprotoent()

Arguments:
struct protoent *protoinfo ;(Table 35-9)

Header Files:
netdb.h

Details: This function retrieves and parses the next line of the protocol database file /etc/protocols. If *setprotoent* was called specifying *stayopen*, the file will remain open between calls.

NULL is returned when the end of the file is reached or an error is encountered.

The returned information is stored in a static area and must thus be copied before the next call.

See also: endprotoent, getprotobyname, getprotobynumber, setprotoent

getservbyname: get information about a service specified by name
servinfo = getservbyname(name, protocol)

Arguments:
char *name, *protocol ;

struct servent *servinfo ;(Table 35-10)

Header Files:

netdb.h

Details: This function retrieves information about a network service specified by name from the database file /etc/services. If *setservent* was called specifying *stayopen*, the file will remain open between calls.

NULL is returned if no matching entry is found or an error is encountered.

The returned information is stored in a static area and must thus be copied before the next call.

See also: endservent, getservbyport, setservent

---

getservbynumber: get information about a service specified by port number
servinfo = getservbyport(number, protocol)

Arguments:

int number ;

char *protocol ;

struct servent *servinfo ;(Table 35-10)

Header Files:

netdb.h

Details: This function retrieves information about a network service specified by port number from the database file /etc/services. If *setservent* was called specifying *stayopen*, the file will remain open between calls.

NULL is returned if no matching entry is found or an error is encountered.

The returned information is stored in a static area and must thus be copied before the next call.

See also: endservent, getservbyname, setservent

---

getservent: get next network service entry
servinfo = getservent()

Arguments:

struct servent *servinfo ;(Table 35-10)

Header Files:

netdb.h

Details: This function retrieves and parses the next line of the network services database file /etc/services. If *setservent* was called specifying *stayopen*, the file will remain open between calls.

NULL is returned when the end of the file is reached or an error is encountered.

The returned information is stored in a static area and must thus be copied before the next call.

See also: endservent, getservbyname, getservbyport, setservent

---

getsockname: get socket's assigned name
status = getsockname(sock, name, namelength)

Arguments:

int sock, status ;

struct sockaddr *name ;(Table 35-11)

int *namelength ;

Details: This function returns the current name for the socket *sock*. On entry, *namelength* should be set to the size of the buffer *name*; on return, *namelength* will be updated to the actual size of the returned name.

On error, *getsockname* returns -1; if successful, it returns 0.

See also: bind, getpeername, socket

getsockopt: get options for socket
status = getsockopt(sock, level, optname, optval, optlength)

Arguments:
int sock, level, optname, status ;
char *optval ;
int *optlength ;

Header Files:
sys/types.h
sys/socket.h

Details: Determine the current value of an option for socket *sock*, at *level* (SOL_SOCKET for the socket level or the protocol number for any other level). The desired option is specified by *optname* (see Table 35-15), and the current value will be stored in the buffer pointed at by *optval*, up to a maximum of *optlength* characters. On return, *optlength* is updated to indicated the actual amount of data returned.

On error, *getsockopt* returns -1 and sets *errno* (see Table 35-2); if successful, it returns 0.

See also: getprotoent, setsockopt, socket

htonl: convert long to network byte order
netlong = htonl(hostlong)

Arguments:
unsigned long hostlong, netlong ;

Header Files:
sys/types.h
netinet/in.h

Details: The Internet uses big-endian byte ordering (most-significant byte at the lowest address) for all multi-byte quantities; for little-endian machines such as Intel 80x86 processors, this means that data must be byte-swapped before it can be sent over the network. This call will ensure that a 32-bit quantity has the correct byte order for the network (it is a null function if the processor's byte order is the same as the network's).

See also: htons, ntohl, ntohs

htons: convert short to network byte order
netshort = htons(hostshort)

Arguments:
unsigned short hostshort, netshort ;

Header Files:
sys/types.h
netinet/in.h

Details: The Internet uses big-endian byte ordering (most-significant byte at the lowest address) for all multi-byte quantities; for little-endian machines such as Intel 80x86 processors, this means that data must be byte-swapped before it can be sent over the network. This call will ensure that a 16-bit quantity has the correct byte order for the network (it is a null function if the processor's byte order is the same as the network's).

See also: htonl, ntohl, ntohs

inet_addr: parse dotted numeric string into Internet address
address = inet_addr(dotstring)

Arguments:
unsigned long address ;
char *dotstring ;

Header Files:
sys/socket.h

netinet/in.h
arpa/inet.h

Details: This function accepts a numeric string consisting of one to four parts separated by periods and determines the 32-bit Internet address specified by the string. If the numeric strings consists of a single part, it is stored directly; a two-part string is interpreted as an 8-bit network number and a 24-bit local address; a three-part string is interpreted as two 8-bit numbers specifying the network number and a 16-bit local address; finally, a four-part string is interpreted as four 8-bit numbers with the most-significant first. For all formats, the numbers making up each component may be either decimal, octal (leading '0'), or hexadecimal (leading '0x').

On error, *inet_addr* returns -1.

See also: inet_lnaof, inet_makeaddr, inet_netof, inet_network, inet_ntoa

---

inet_lnaof: extract local network address from Internet address
localaddr = inet_lnaof(inetaddr)

Arguments:
int localaddr ;
struct in_addr inetaddr ;

Header Files:
sys/socket.h
netinet.in.h
arpa.inet.h

Details: This function returns the local network address portion of the specified Internet address.

See also: inet_addr, inet_makeaddr, inet_netof, inet_network, inet_ntoa

---

inet_makeaddr: make Internet address from network number and local address
inetaddr = inet_makeaddr(net, localaddr)

Arguments:
int net, localaddr ;
struct in_addr inetaddr ;

Header Files:
sys/socket.h
netinet.in.h
arpa.inet.h

Details: This function builds a complete 32-bit Internet address given a network number and local network address.

See also: inet_addr, inet_lnaof, inet_netof, inet_network, inet_ntoa

---

inet_netof: extract network number from Internet adress
netnumber = inet_netof(inetaddr)

Arguments:
int netnumber ;
struct in_addr inetaddr ;

Header Files:
sys/socket.h
netinet.in.h
arpa.inet.h

Details: This function returns the network number portion of the specified Internet address.

See also: inet_addr, inet_lnaof, inet_makeaddr, inet_network, inet_ntoa

---

inet_network: parse dotted numeric string into Internet network number
netnumber = inet_network(dotstring)

Arguments:
unsigned long netnumber ;

char *dotstring ;
Header Files:
sys/socket.h
netinet.in.h
arpa.inet.h
Details: This function accepts a numeric string consisting of one to four parts separated by periods and determines the Internet network number specified by the string. If the numeric strings consists of a single part, it is stored directly; a two-part string is interpreted as an 8-bit network number and a 24-bit local address; a three-part string is interpreted as two 8-bit numbers specifying the network number and a 16-bit local address; finally, a four-part string is interpreted as four 8-bit numbers with the most-significant first. For all formats, the numbers making up each component may be either decimal, octal (leading '0'), or hexadecimal (leading '0x').

On error, *inet_network* returns -1.
See also: inet_addr, inet_lnaof, inet_makeaddr, inet_netof, inet_ntoa

---

inet_ntoa: convert Internet address to dotted numeric string
dotstring = inet_ntoa(inetaddr)
Arguments:
struct in_addr *inetaddr* ;
char *dotstring ;
Header Files:
sys/socket.h
netinet/in.h
arpa/inet.h
Details: This function returns an ASCII string in '.' notation corresponding to the specified Internet address. The returned string is located in static storage and must be copied before the next call.
See also: inet_addr, inet_lnaof, inet_makeaddr, inet_netof, inet_network

---

ioctl: control I/O device
status = ioctl(descriptor, request, argument)
Arguments:
int descriptor, status ;
unsigned long request ;
char *argument ;
Header Files:
sys/ioctl.h
Details: The *request* parameter implicitly specifies the type of *argument* (which may be an integer rather than a pointer) and whether it is a value or result parameter.

Support for this function varies wildly among PC implementations.

On error, *ioctl* returns -1 and sets *errno* (see Table 35-2); if successful, it returns 0.
See also: setsockopt, socket

---

listen: start socket listening for connection attempts
status = listen(sock, backlog)
Arguments:
int sock, backlog, status ;
Header Files:
none
Details: This function specifies that the socket *sock* (of type SOCK_STREAM or SOCK_SEQPACKET) is willing to accept incoming connections, and queue up to *backlog* pending connection requests. The allowable queue size may silently be limited to less than the requested size.

On error, *listen* returns -1 and sets *errno* (see Table 35-2); if successful, it returns 0.
See also: accept, bind, setsockopt, socket

---

ntohl: convert long to host byte order
hostlong = ntohl(netlong)
Arguments:
unsigned long netlong, hostlong ;
Header Files:
sys/types.h
netinet/in.h
Details: The Internet uses big-endian byte ordering (most-significant byte at the lowest address) for all multi-byte quantities; for little-endian machines such as Intel 80x86 processors, this means that data received from the network must be byte-swapped before it can used by a program. This call will ensure that a 32-bit quantity has the correct byte order for the processor on which the program is running (it is a null function if the processor's byte order is the same as the network's).
See also: htonl, htons, ntohs

---

ntohs: convert short to host byte order
hostshort = ntohs(netshort)
Arguments:
unsigned short netlong, hostlong ;
Header Files:
sys/types.h
netinet/in.h
Details: The Internet uses big-endian byte ordering (most-significant byte at the lowest address) for all multi-byte quantities; for little-endian machines such as Intel 80x86 processors, this means that data received from the network must be byte-swapped before it can used by a program. This call will ensure that a 16-bit quantity has the correct byte order for the processor on which the program is running (it is a null function if the processor's byte order is the same as the network's).
See also: htonl, htons, ntohl

---

recv: receive a message on a connected socket
msglength = recv(sock, buffer, buflength, flags)
Arguments:
int sock, buflength, flags, msglength ;
char *buffer ;
Header Files:
sys/types.h
sys/socket.h
Details: This function attempts to retrieve a message received by the socket *sock* from its connected peer. It waits for a message to arrive unless the socket has been marked non-blocking, in which case it returns the 'error' EWOULDBLOCK when there are no messages available.

The *flags* are formed by OR-ing the appropriate combination of MSG_OOB (1) to process out-of-band data and MSG_PEEK (2) to peek at incoming messages.

On error, *recvN returns -1 and sets errno*; if successful, it returns the length of the received message which was placed in the caller's buffer (message bytes for which there was not enough space are discarded for some socket types).
See also: accept, connect, read, recvfrom, recvmsg, select, send, socket

---

recvfrom: receive a message on a socket, with originating address
msglength = recvfrom(sock, buffer, buflength, flags, from, fromlength)
Arguments:
int sock, buflength, flags, msglength ;

char *buffer ;
struct sockaddr *from ; (Table 35-11)
int *fromlength ;
Header Files:
sys/types.h
sys/socket.h
Details: This function attempts to retrieve a message received by the socket *sock* from the source specified by *from* and *fromlength*, or the socket's connected peer or any source (connectionless protocols only) if *from* is NULL. It waits for a message to arrive unless the socket has been marked non-blocking, in which case it returns the 'error' EWOULDBLOCK when there are no messages available.

The *flags* are formed by OR-ing the appropriate combination of MSG_OOB (1) to process out-of-band data and MSG_PEEK (2) to peek at incoming messages.

On error, *recvfromN returns -1 and sets errno*; if successful, it returns the length of the received message which was placed in the caller's buffer (message bytes for which there was not enough space are discarded for some socket types).
See also: read, recv, recvmsg, select, send, sendto, socket

---

recvmsg: receive a message from a socket
msglength = recvmsg(sock, msg, flags)
Arguments:
int sock, flags, msglength ;
struct msghdr msg[ ] ;(Table 35-7)
Header Files:
sys/types.h
sys/socket.h
Details: Thsi function attempts to retrieve a message received by the socket *sock* from the source specified in the msghdr structure, or the socket's connected peer or any source (connectionless protocols only) if no source address is specified in *msg*.

flags are formed by *oring* the appropriate combination of MSG_OOB (1) to process out-of-band data and MSG_PEEK (2) to peek at incoming messages.

This function waits for a message to arrive unless the socket has been marked non-blocking, in which case it returns the 'error' EWOULDBLOCK when there are no messages available.

On error, *recvmsgN returns -1 and sets errno*; if successful, it returns the length of the received message which was placed in the caller's buffer (message bytes for which there was not enough space are discarded for some socket types).
See also: read, recv, recvfrom, select, send, socket

---

select: synchronous I/O multiplexing
numfound = select(numdescr, readdescr, writedescr, exceptdescr, timeout)
Arguments:
int numfound, numdescr ;
fd_set *readdescr, *writedescr, *exceptdescr ;
struct timeval *timeout ;(Table 35-14)
Header Files:
sys/types.h
sys/time.h
Details: This function examines the indicated descriptor sets (which are bitfields) to determine whether any of them are ready for reading or accepting a connection (*readdescr*), are ready for writing or have established a connection (*writedescr*), or have an exceptional condition pending (*exceptdescr*). On return, *select* overwrites the supplied descriptor sets with subsets containing only those descriptors which are ready for the specified operation.

This function returns when at least one descriptor is ready or the specified timeout expires. It will block indefinitely if *timeout* is NULL; if *timeout* points at a timeval structure whose value is zero, *select* returns immediately (useful for polling). Some implementations may modify *timeout* to indicate the time remaining.

The macros FD_ZERO, FD_SET, FD_CLR, and FD_ISSET are provided for manipulating desriptor sets.

On error, *select* returns -1 and sets *errno*; if successful, it returns the number of descriptors which are ready (0 if the time limit expired).

See also: accept, connect, read (not listed here), recv, send, write (not listed here)

---

send: transmit a message over a connected socket
bytessent = send(sock, msg, msglength, flags)

Arguments:

int sock, msglength, flags, bytessent ;
char *msg ;

Details: This function attempts to transmit a message *msg* of length *msglength* from *sock* to its connected peer.

The *flags* are formed by OR-ing the appropriate combination of MSG_OOB (1) to send out-of-band data and MSG_DONTROUTE (4) to bypass the standard routing algorithm.

On locally-detected errors, *send* returns -1 and sets *errno*; otherwise, it returns the number of characters sent (which may be less than the number requested), even though they may have failed to be delivered.

---

sendto: transmit a message to a specified recipient
bytessent = sendto(sock, msg, msglength, flags, to, tolen)

Arguments:

int sock, msglength, flags, tolen, bytessent ;
char *msg ;
struct sockaddr *to ;(Table 35-11)

Details: This function attempts to transmit a message *msg* of length *msglength* from *sock* to another socket specified by *to* and *tolen*, or to the socket's connected peer if *to* is NULL.

flags are formed by *or*ing the appropriate combination of MSG_OOB (1) to send out-of-band data and MSG_DONTROUTE (4) to bypass the standard routing algorithm.

On locally-detected errors, *sendto* returns -1 and sets *errno*; otherwise, it returns the number of characters sent (which may be less than the number requested), even though they may have failed to be delivered.

---

sendmsg: transmit message over a socket
bytessent = sendmsg(sock, msg, flags)

Arguments:

int sock, flags, bytessent ;
struct msghdr msg[] ;(Table 35-7)

Details: This function attempts to transmit a message from *sock* to another socket specified by *msg*, or to the socket's connected peer no destination address is supplied in the msghdr structure.

flags are formed by *or*ing the appropriate combination of MSG_OOB (1) to send out-of-band data and MSG_DONTROUTE (4) to bypass the standard routing algorithm.

On locally-detected errors, *sendmsg* returns -1 and sets *errno*; otherwise, it returns the number of characters sent, even though they may have failed to be delivered.

---

sethostent: start host lookups
sethostent(stayopen)

Arguments:

int stayopen ;

send: transmit a message over a connected socket

Header Files:

netdb.h

Details: If *stayopen* is non-zero, *gethostbyaddr* and *gethostbyname* will query the name server using a TCP connection which is retained until explicitly closed with *endhostent*.

When using the local host table /etc/hosts, *sethostent* opens and rewinds the file; *stayopen* specifies whether the file is to be kept open between calls to *gethostbyaddr* and gethostbyname.

See also: endhostent, gethostbyaddr, gethostbyname

sethostid: specify unique identifier for current host
sethostid(hostid)

Arguments:

long hostid ;

Header Files:

Details: This function specifies a unique 32-bit identifier for the current processor, normally the Internet address of the machine.

See also: gethostid, sethostname

sethostname: specify name of current host
status = sethostname(name, namelength)

Arguments:

char *name ;

int namelength, status ;

Header Files:

Details: This function sets the standard host name for the current machine; it may only be called by the super-user, and is normally used only when the system is booted.

On error, *sethostname* returns -1 and sets *errno*; if successful, it returns 0.

See also: gethostname, sethostid

setnetent: start network lookups
setnetent(stayopen)

Arguments:

int stayopen ;

Header Files:

netdb.h

Details: This function opens and rewinds the network database file /etc/networks. If *stayopen* is non-zero, the database file will remain open between calls to *getnetbyaddr* and *getnetbyname*, until explicitly closed with *endnetent*.

See also: endnetent, getnetbyaddr, getnetbyname

setprotoent: start protocol lookups
setprotoent(stayopen)

Arguments:

int stayopen ;

Header Files:

netdb.h

Details: This function opens and rewinds the protocol database file /etc/protocols. If *stayopen* is non-zero, the database file will remain open between calls to *getprotobyname* and *getprotobynumber*, until explicitly closed with *endprotoent*.

See also: endprotoent, getprotobyname, getprotobynumber

setservent: start network services lookups
setservent(stayopen)
Arguments:
int stayopen ;
Header Files:
netdb.h
Details: This function opens and rewinds the network services database file /etc/services. If *stayopen* is non-zero, the database file will remain open between calls to *getservbyname* and *getservbyport*, until explicitly closed with *endservent*.
See also: endservent, getservbyname, getservbyport

setsockopt: specify options for socket
status = setsockopt(sock, level, optname, optval, optlength)
Arguments:
int sock, level, optname, optlength, status ;
char *optval ;
Header Files:
sys/types.h
sys/socket.h
Details: Set an option for the socket *sock*, which may exist at multiple protocol levels (the desired one is selected with *level*: SOL_SOCKET for the socket level or the protocol number for any other level). *optname* specifies the option to be modified (see Table 35-15) and *optval* and *optlength* specify the new value for that option.

On error, *setsockopt* returns -1 and sets *errno* (see Table 35-2); if successful, it returns 0.
See also: getsockopt, ioctl, setprotoent, socket

35-15 Socket-level options:

SO_DEBUG	debugging information recorded?
SO_REUSEADDR	local address reused?
SO_KEEPALIVE	connections kept alive with periodic messages?
SO_DONTROUTE	outgoing message routing bypassed?
SO_LINGER	linger on close if data present (see Table 35-16 for value's format)
SO_BROADCAST	permitted to send broadcast messages?
SO_OOBINLINE	is out-of-band data received in band?
SO_SNDBUF	output buffer size
SO_RCVBUF	input buffer size
SO_TYPE	(get only) socket's type
SO_ERROR	(get only) last error on socket, cleared after retrieving

35-16 Format of struct linger:

Type	Name	Description
int	l_onoff	flag specifying whether *linger* is active
int	l_linger	time to linger awaiting data delivery

shutdown: disable sends or receives on a socket
status = shutdown(sock,how)
Arguments:
int sock, how, status ;
Details: This function is used on all types of sockets to disable reception, transmission, or both. If *how* is 0, subsequent receives on the socket *sock* will be disallowed. This has no effect on the lower protocol layers. If *how* is 1, subsequent sends are disallowed, and if *how* is 2, both sends and receives are disallowed. An application should not rely on being able to re-use a socket after it has been shut down.

If no error occurs, *shutdown* returns 0; otherwise, it returns -1 and sets the global variable *errno* to the specific error code (Table 35-2).

See also: accept, connect, socket

---

socket: create an endpoint for communication
sock = socket(domain, type, protocol)

Arguments:

int sock, domain, type, protocol ;

Details: This function creates an endpoint to which communications may be directed, and returns a handle which may be used to reference it. *domain* specifies the communications domain to be used, and thus the protocol family, which may be one of the values in Table 35-17; similarly, *type* specifies the semantics of communications on the socket and *protocol* specifies the exact protocol within the indicated protocol family.

On error, *socket* returns -1 and sets *errno*; if successful, it returns a socket descriptor.

See also: accept, bind, connect, listen, select, setsockopt, socketpair

35-17 Protocol families:

PF_UNIX	Unix-internal protocols
PF_INET	Internet protocols (TCP, UDP, etc.)
PF_NS	Xeros Network Systems protocols
PF_IMPLINK	IMP link layer protocols

35-18 Socket types:

SOCK_STREAM	sequenced, reliable, two-way connection-based stream
SOCK_DGRAM	connectionless unreliable datagrams
SOCK_RAW	internal network protocols and interfaces (super-user only)
SOCK_SEQPACKET	sequenced, reliable, two-way connection-based datagrams (PF_NS only)
SOCK_RDM	

---

socketpair: create a pair of connected sockets
status = socketpair(domain, type, protocol, sockets)

Arguments:

int domain, type, protocol ;

int sockets[2] ;

Details: This function creates a pair of unnamed sockets in the specified domain, type, and protocol (see *socket* above and Tables 35-17 and 35-18). The two sockets are returned in the array *sockets*; they are indistinguishable.

On error, *socketpair* returns -1 and sets *errno* (see Table 35-2); if successful, it returns 0 and fills in *sockets*.

See also: accept, bind, connect, listen, setsockopt, socket

CHAPTER 36

Windows Sockets

Unlike the most of the other chapters of this book, this chapter does not cover interrupt calls, but rather function libraries which are called directly from high-level languages.

As described in Chapter 35, sockets were introduced in Berkeley Unix around 1982, and have become a *de facto* standard for network programming. The Windows Sockets specification (a copyrighted document, owned by the industry group that created it as a joint effort, rather than by any one vendor) was developed to define a programming interface for Microsoft Windows based on the Berkeley socket routines, augmented by Windows-specific extensions designed to make best use of the message-driven Windows architecture.

This chapter briefly describes the functions specified for Windows Sockets Version 1.1, but for full details and validation requirements the official specification is necessary. It is available in electronic form from a variety of sources, including the Microsoft libraries on CompuServe and the Microsoft Developer Network CD-ROM, and through the Internet electronic mail forum winsock@microdyne.com (microdyne.com contains numerous files, including the Windows Socket specification, which are available for anonymous FTP).

The Windows Sockets specification defines an API and requires that any DLL claiming compliance with the specification provide 100 percent of the defined features; partial implementations are not allowed. To use this API, a compliant DLL (provided by the network interface supplier, such as Microsoft's WINSOCK.DLL) is necessary to implement the actual interface with the network hardware and driver(s).

Overview

The API provides a subset of the full Berkeley capabilities described in Chapter 35; these functions are listed in Table 36-1. In addition, the Windows Sockets specification defines the seven "database" routines summarized in Table 36-2. The pointer returned by certain of these functions points to a structure allocated by the Windows Sockets library which is valid only until the next Windows Sockets API call from that thread. Only one copy of this structure exists for each thread, so an application must copy any needed information before issuing other API calls.

Further, the specification provides a number of extensions to the standard set of routines in order to allow message-based, asynchronous access to network events. These extensions, listed in Table 36-3, are recommended for conformance with generally accepted principles of programming for Microsoft Windows applications. The six functions having names that begin with "WSAAsyncGet" provide asynchronous versions of the standard Unix "getXbyY" functions of similar names.

36-1 Overview of Windows Sockets functions:

accept	accept an incoming connection on a socket
bind	bind a name to a socket
closesocketc	lose a descriptor; renamed from Unix "close" to eliminate name collision
connect	initiate a connection on a socket
getsockname	get socket's assigned name
getsockopt	get options for socket
htonl	convert *u_long* to network byte order
htons	convert *u_short* to network byte order
inet_addr	parse dotted numeric string into Internet address
inet_ntoa	convert Internet address to dotted numeric string
ioctlsocket	control I/O device; renamed from "ioctl" for name collision
listen	start socket listening for connection attempts
ntohl	convert *u_long* to host byte order
ntohs	convert *u_short* to host byte order
recv	receive a message on a connected socket
recvfrom	receive a message on a socket, with originating address
select	synchronous I/O multiplexing
send	transmit a message over a connected socket
sendto	transmit a message to a specified recipient
setsockopt	specify options for socket
shutdown	shut down part of full-duplex communication
socket	create an endpoint for communication

36-2 Overview of Windows Sockets database functions:

gethostbyaddr	retrieve name and address corresponding to a network address
gethostbyname	retrieve name and address corresponding to a host name
gethostname	retrieve name of local host
getprotobyname	retrieve protocol name and number corresponding to a protocol name
getprotobynumber	retrieve protocol name and number corresponding to a protocol number
getservbyname	retrieve service name and port corresponding to a service name
getservbyport	retrieve service name and port corresponding to a port

36-3 Overview of Windows-specific functions:

WSAAsyncGetHostByAddr	see text
WSAAsyncGetHostByName	see text
WSAAsyncGetProtoByName	see text
WSAAsyncGetProtoByNumber	see text
WSAAsyncGetServByName	see text
WSAAsyncGetServByPort	see text
WSAAsyncSelect	perform asynchronous version of select()
WSACancelAsyncRequest	cancel outstanding instance of a WSAAsync function
WSACancelBlockingCall	cancel outstanding "blocking" API call
WSACleanup	sign off from underlying Windows Sockets DLL
WSAGetLastError	obtain details of last Windows Sockets API error
WSAIsBlocking	determine if DLL is already blocking a call for this thread
WSASetBlockingHook	"hook" blocking method used by underlying implementation
WSASetLastError	set error to be returned by a subsequent WSAGetLastError()
WSAStartup	initialize underlying DLL
WSAUnhookBlockingHook	restore original blocking function

To simplify re-use of existing Unix sockets based code, a number of standard Unix 'include' files are supported under the Windows Sockets specification. These header files, which must be supplied by any WinSock-compliant package, are *netdb.h*, *arpa/inet.h*, *sys/time.h*, *sys/socket.h*, and *netinet/in.h*. Each of them consists of the following three lines:

```
#ifndef _WINSOCKAPI_
#include <winsock.h>
#endif
```

The file *winsock.h* contains all type and structure definitions, constants, macros, and function prototypes used by Windows Sockets. Programmers are encouraged to ignore the compatibility headers and include *winsock.h* in each source file.

The Windows Sockets API defines its own set of manifest constants for all detected errors. Additionally, the manifest constant SOCKET_ERROR is provided as a signal of API failure. Although use of this constant is not required by the specification, it is recommended. The manifest constants are listed in Table 36-4. Note that the corresponding Unix manifest constants are also defined, for portability of older code.

36-4 Socket error codes:

EADDRINUSE	specified address already in use; same as WSAEADDRINUSE
EADDRNOTAVAIL	specified address not available on caller's machine; same as WSAEADDRNOTAVAIL
EAFNOSUPPORT	specified address family can not be use with socket; same as WSAEAFNOSUPPORT
EALREADY	previous operation on non-blocking socket has not completed; same as WSAEALREADY
ECONNABORTED	connection was aborted due to timeout or other failure; same as WSAECONNABORTED
ECONNREFUSED	connection attempt was refused; same as WSAECONNREFUSED
ECONNRESET	virtual circuit was reset by the remote side; same as WSAECONNRESET
EDESTADDRREQ	destination address is required; same as WSAEDESTADDRREQ
EDQUOT	disk quota exceeded (not expected to occur with DLL)
EHOSTDOWN	host is down (not expected to occur with DLL)
EHOSTUNREACH	no route to host (not expected to occur with DLL)
EINPROGRESS	non-blocking operation can not be completed immediately; same as WSAEINPROGRESS
EISCONN	socket is already connected; same as WSAEISCONN
ELOOP	too many symbolic links traversed while translating pathname; same as WSAELOOP
EMSGSIZE	datagram was too large to fit into the specified buffer and was truncated; same as WSAEMSGSIZE
ENAMETOOLONG	specified name was too long; same as WSAENAMETOOLONG
ENETDOWN	implementation has detected that the network subsystem has failed; same as WSAENETDOWN
ENETRESET	connection must be reset because Windows Sockets implementation dropped it; same as WSAENETRESET
ENETUNREACH	specified network is not reachable; same as WSAENETUNREACH
ENOBUFS	insufficient buffer space for operation; same as WSAENOBUFS
ENOPROTOOPT	unknown protocol option for specified level; same as WSAENOPROTOOPT
ENOTCONN	socket is not connected; same as WSAENOTCONN
ENOTEMPTY	directory is not empty (not expected to occur with DLL)

ENOTSOCK	descriptor references a file instead of a socket; same as WSAENOTSOCK
EOPNOTSUPP	operation not supported on specified socket; same as WSAEOPNOTSUPP
EPFNOSUPPORT	protocol family not supported (not expected to occur with DLL)
EPROCLIM	too many processes (not expected to occur with DLL)
EPROTONOSUPPORT	specified protocol type or protocol not supported in domain; same as WSAEPROTONOSUPPORT
EPROTOTYPE	specified protocol is wrong type for socket; same as WSAEPROTOTYPE
EREMOTE	too many levels of remote access in path (not expected to occur with DLL)
ESHUTDOWN	socket has been shutdown; same as WSAESHUTDOWN
ESOCKTNOSUPPORT	specified socket type not supported in this address family; same as WSAESOCKTNOSUPPORT
ESTALE	stale remote file handle (not expected to occur with DLL)
ETIMEDOUT	operation timed out; same as WSAETIMEDOUT
ETOOMANYREFS	too many references, can not splice (not expected to occur with DLL)
EUSERS	too many users (not expected to occur with DLL)
EWOULDBLOCK	operation can not be completed immediately and socket is marked non-blocking; same as WSAEWOULDBLOCK
WSAEACCES	requested address is a broadcast address, but the appropriate flag was not set
WSAEADDRINUSE	specified address already in use
WSAEADDRNOTAVAIL	specified address not available on caller's machine
WSAEAFNOSUPPORT	specified address family can not be use with socket
WSAEALREADY	previous operation on non-blocking socket has not completed
WSAEBADF	invalid file handle
WSAECONNABORTED	connection was aborted due to timeout or other failure
WSAECONNREFUSED	connection attempt was refused
WSAECONNRESET	virtual circuit was reset by the remote side
WSAEDESTADDRREQ	destination address is required
WSAEDQUOT	disk quota exceeded (not expected to occur with DLL)
WSAEFAULT	argument is too small
WSAEHOSTDOWN	host is down (not expected to occur with DLL)
WSAEHOSTUNREACH	no route to host (not expected to occur with DLL)
WSAEINPROGRESS	non-blocking operation can not be completed immediately
WSAEINTR	blocking call was canceled
WSAEINVAL	*listen* was not invoked prior to *accept*
WSAEISCONN	socket is already connected
WSAELOOP	too many symbolic links traversed while translating pathname
WSAEMFILE	queue is empty upon entry to accept and there are no descriptors available
WSAEMSGSIZE	datagram was too large to fit into specified buffer and was truncated
WSAENAMETOOLONG	specified name was too long
WSAENETDOWN	implementation has detected that the network subsystem has failed
WSAENETRESET	connection must be reset because Windows Sockets implementation dropped it
WSAENETUNREACH	specified network is not reachable
WSAENOBUFS	insufficient buffer space for operation
WSAENOPROTOOPT	unknown protocol option for specified level

WSAENOTCONN	socket is not connected
WSAENOTEMPTY	directory is not empty (not expected to occur with DLL)
WSAENOTSOCK	descriptor references a file instead of a socket
WSAEOPNOTSUPP	operation not supported on specified socket
WSAEPFNOSUPPORT	protocol family not supported (not expected to occur with DLL)
WSAEPROCLIM	too many processes (not expected to occur with DLL)
WSAEPROTONOSUPPORT	specified protocol type or protocol not supported in domain
WSAEPROTOTYPE	specified protocol is wrong type for socket
WSAEREMOTE	too many levels of remote access in path (not expected to occur with DLL)
WSAESHUTDOWN	socket has been shutdown
WSAESOCKTNOSUPPORT	specified socket type not supported in this address family
WSAESTALE	stale remote file handle (not expected to occur with DLL)
WSAETIMEDOUT	operation timed out
WSAETOOMANYREFS	too many references, can not splice (not expected to occur with DLL)
WSAEUSERS	too many users (not expected to occur with DLL)
WSAEWOULDBLOCK	operation cannot be completed immediately and socket is marked non-blocking
WSAHOST_NOT_FOUND	Authoritative: Host not found from *gethostbyname* and *gethostbyaddr*
WSANO_ADDRESS	no address, look for MX record from *gethostbyname* and *gethostbyaddr* (same as WSANO_DATA)
WSANO_DATA	Valid name, no data record of requested type from *gethostbyname* and *gethostbyaddr*
WSANO_RECOVERY	Non recoverable errors, FORMERR, REFUSED, NOTIMP from *gethostbyname* and *gethostbyaddr*
WSANOTINITIALISED	Returned by any function except *WSAStartup* indicating that a successful *WSAStartup* has not yet been performed
WSASYSNOTREADY	Returned by *WSAStartup* indicating that the network subsystem is unusable
WSATRY_AGAIN	Non-Authoritative: Host not found, or SERVERFAIL from *gethostbyname* and *gethostbyaddr*
WSAVERNOTSUPPORTED	Returned by *WSAStartup* indicating that Windows Sockets DLL cannot support application

Socket Functions

The remainder of this chapter summarizes the individual functions of the WinSock API, in alphabetic sequence.

accept: accept an incoming connection on a socket
newsock = accept(s, addr, addrlen)

Prototype:
SOCKET PASCAL FAR accept (SOCKET s, struct sockaddr FAR * addr, int FAR * addrlen);
Arguments:
SOCKET s ;
struct sockaddr FAR *addr ; (Table 36-5)
int FAR *addrlen ;
Header File:
winsock.h

Details: *accept* extracts the first pending connection for the socket *s* (which was created with *socket*, bound to an address with *bind*, and is awaiting connections with *listen*), creates a new socket with the same properties, and assigns it to a new descriptor which it returns as *newsock*. If no connections are pending, and if s has been marked non-blocking, an error is returned; otherwise, the caller is blocked until a connection is present. In any event the original socket remains open.

On error, *accept* returns SOCKET_ERROR. *WSAGetLastError* will retrieve the error code (see Table 36-4); if successful, it returns a value of type SOCKET which is a descriptor for the accepted connection. The integer referred to by *addrlen* initially contains the amount of space pointed to by *addr* (see Table 36-5). On return it will contain the actual length in bytes of the returned address of the connecting entity (as known to the communications layer); however, if either *addr* or *addrlen* are NULL on entry, no information about the remote address of the accepted socket is returned.

See also: bind, connect, listen, select, socket, WSAAsyncSelect

36-5 Format of struct sockaddr:

Type	Name	Description
short	sa_family	address family
char	sa_data[14]	up to 14 bytes of direct address

Note: The exact format of this structure is determined by the address family established when the socket was created.

See also: Table 35-11

bind: bind a name to a socket
status = bind(s, name, namelen)

Prototype:
int PASCAL FAR bind (SOCKET s, const struct sockaddr FAR * name, int namelen);

Arguments:
SOCKET s;
struct sockaddr *name ;(Table 36-5)
int namelength;

Header File:
winsock.h

Details: *bind* assigns a name to a socket with descriptor s which has not previously been named (bound), such as a socket newly created with the *socket* function. The name to be associated with the socket is given in *name*, whose length is *namelength*. On error, bind returns SOCKET_ERROR, and a specific error code may be retrieved by calling WSAGetLastError; if successful, the function returns 0.

See also: connect, listen, getsockname, setsockopt, socket, WSACancelBlockingCall

closesocket: close a descriptor
status = close(s)

Prototype:
int PASCAL FAR closesocket (SOCKET s);

Arguments:
SOCKET s;A descriptor identifying a socket.

Header File:
winsock.h

Details: *closesocket* releases socket descriptor *s*, so that further references to *s* will fail with the error WSAENOTSOCK. If this is the last reference to the underlying socket, the associated naming information and queued data are discarded. If an error occurs, *closesocket* returns the value SOCKET_ERROR; the specific error code may be obtained by calling WSAGetLastError. Otherwise, *closesocket* returns 0.

See also: accept, socket, ioctlsocket, setsockopt, WSAAsyncSelect

bind: bind a name to a socket

connect: initiate a connection on a socket
status = connect(s, name, namelen)
Prototype:
int PASCAL FAR connect (SOCKET s, const struct sockaddr FAR * name, int namelen);
Arguments:
SOCKET s;A descriptor identifying an unconnected socket.
struct sockaddr *name;Peer to which to connect (Table 36-5).
int namelen;The size of the name.
Header File:
winsock.h
Details: This function creates a connection to the socket specified by *s*. If the specified socket is a stream socket (created with the SOCK_STREAM option), *connect* attempts to connect to another socket as specified by *name*. If the socket is a datagram socket (SOCK_DGRAM), this call specifies the address to which datagrams are to be sent and the sole address from which they are to be received by the socket. On error, *connect* returns SOCKET_ERROR; a specific error code may be retrieved by calling WSAGetLastError. If successful, the function returns 0.
See also: accept, bind, getsockname, socket, select, and WSAAsyncSelect

gethostbyaddr: get information about a host specified by address
hostinfo = gethostbyaddr(addr, len, type)
Prototype:
struct hostent FAR * PASCAL FAR gethostbyaddr (const char FAR * addr, int len, int type);
Arguments:
const char FAR * addr;A pointer to an address in network byte order.
int len;The length of the address, which must be 4 for PF_INET addresses.
int type;The type of the address, which must be PF_INET.
Header File:
winsock.h
Details: Get information about the specified host. The returned information is stored in a static structure (Table 36-6) and a pointer to this structure is returned; the data must thus be copied before any subsequent calls since only one copy of the structure is allocated to each thread.

If an error occurs, this function returns a NULL pointer; a specific error number may then be retrieved by calling WSAGetLastError.
See also: gethostbyname, WSAAsyncGetHostByAddr

36-6 Format of struct hostent:

Type	Name	Description
char FAR *	h_name;	official name of the host (PC)
char FAR * FAR *	h_aliases;	NULL-terminated array of alternate names
short	h_addrtype;	type of address returned; for Windows Sockets always PF_INET
short	h_length;	length, in bytes, of each address; for PF_INET, always 4
char FAR * FAR *	h_addr_list;	NULL-terminated list of host addresses, in network byte order

Note: The macro *h_addr* is defined as h_addr_list[0] for compatibility with older Unix software.

gethostbyname: get information about a host specified by name
hostinfo = gethostbyname(name)
Prototype:
struct hostent FAR * PASCAL FAR gethostbyname (const char FAR * name);
Arguments:
char *name;A pointer to the name of the host.
Header File:
winsock.h

Details: This function gets information about the specified host from the name server. As described for *gethostbyaddr*, the information is stored in a static structure (Table 36-6) and must be copied from this structure before any other calls are made.

If an error occurs, this function returns a NULL pointer; a specific error number may then be retrieved by calling WSAGetLastError. Otherwise the function returns a far pointer to the static structure.

See also: gethostbyaddr, WSAAsyncGetHostByName

gethostname: get standard host name for the local machine
status = gethostname(name, namelen)

Prototype:
int PASCAL FAR gethostname (char FAR * name, int namelen);
Arguments:
char *name; pointer to buffer that will receive the host name.
int namelength; size of buffer in bytes.
Header File:
winsock.h
Details: This function retrieves the name of the local host machine, storing the name in *name* (NUL-terminated unless *namelength* is less than the size required to hold the name). The exact form of the returned name depends on the specific Windows Sockets implementation, and may be either a simple host name, or a fully qualified domain name. However, the name returned will always be successfully parsed by *gethostbyname* and *WSAAsyncGetHostByName*.

On error, *gethostname* returns SOCKET_ERROR. A specific error code may then be retrieved by calling WSAGetLastError. If successful, *gethostname* returns 0.

See also: gethostbyname, WSAAsyncGetHostByName

getpeername: get name of connected peer
status = getpeername(s, name, namelen)

Prototype:
int PASCAL FAR getpeername (SOCKET s, struct sockaddr FAR * name, int FAR * namelen);
Arguments:
int s;descriptor identifying a connected socket.
struct sockaddr *name;structure (Table 36-5) which will receive name of peer.
int *namelen;pointer to size of name structure.
Header File:
winsock.h
Details: This function returns the name of the machine connected to the specified socket. On entry, *namelen* should contain the size of the buffer *name*; on return, it will have been updated to the actual size of the returned name (which will be truncated if the buffer is too small).

On error, *getpeername* returns SOCKET_ERROR, and a specific error code may then be retrieved by calling WSAGetLastError; if successful, the function returns 0.

See also: accept, bind, connect, getsockname, socket

getprotobyname: get information about a protocol specified by name
protoinfo = getprotobyname(name)

Prototype:
struct protoent FAR * PASCAL FAR getprotobyname (const char FAR * name);
Arguments:
char *name;pointer to a protocol name.
Header File:
winsock.h

Details: This function retrieves information about a protocol specified by name, into the structure described in Table 36-7. If no error occurs, *getprotobyname* returns a pointer to this structure. Otherwise it returns a NULL pointer and a specific error number may be retrieved by calling *WSAGetLastError*. The structure whose address is returned is stored in a static area and must thus be copied before the next call.

36-7 Format of struct protoent:

Type	Name	Description
char FAR *	p_name;	official name of protocol
char FAR * FAR *	p_aliases;	NULL-terminated array of alternate names
short	p_proto;	protocol number, in host byte order

See also: getprotobynumber, WSAAsyncGetProtoByName

getprotobynumber: get information about a protocol specified by number
protoinfo = getprotobynumber(number)

Prototype:

struct protoent FAR * PASCAL FAR getprotobynumber (int number);

Arguments:

int number;A protocol number, in host byte order.

Header File:

winsock.h

Details: This function retrieves information about a protocol specified by number, into a static structure (Table 36-7). If an error occurs, *getprotobynumber* returns a NULL pointer and a specific error number may be retrieved by calling *WSAGetLastError*. Otherwise the function returns a pointer to the structure. The returned information must be copied before the next call.

See also: getprotobyname, WSAAsyncGetProtoByNumber

getservbyname: get information about a service specified by name
servinfo = getservbyname(name, protocol)

Prototype:

struct servent FAR * PASCAL FAR getservbyname (const char FAR * name, const char FAR * protocol);

Arguments:

char *name;pointer to a service name.

char *protocol ;optional pointer to a protocol name.

Header File:

winsock.h

Details: This function, if successful, returns a pointer to a servent structure (Table 36-8) which contains the name(s) and service number corresponding to the specified service name and, optionally, protocol. If *protocol* is NULL, *getservbyname* returns the first service entry for which *name* matches the s_name or an s_alias. Otherwise *getservbyname* must match both *name* and *protocol* in order to succeed. The returned information is stored in a static area and must thus be copied before the next call. If any error occurs, *getservbyname* returns a NULL pointer. The specific error number may be determined by calling *WSAGetLastError*.

36-8 Format of struct servent:

Type	Name	Description
char FAR *	s_name	official name of service
char FAR * FAR *	s_aliases	NULL-terminated array of alternate names
short	s_port	port number at which service may be contacted, returned in network byte order
char FAR *	s_proto	name of protocol to use when contacting service

See also: getservbyport, WSAAsyncGetServByName

getservbyname: get information about a service specified by name

getservbyport: get information about a service specified by port number
servinfo = getservbyport(portnumber, protocol)

Prototype:

struct servent FAR * PASCAL FAR getservbyport (int port, const char FAR * protocol);

Arguments:

int portnumber;port for a service, in network byte order

char *protocol;optional pointer to a protocol name

struct servent *servinfo ;

Header File:

winsock.h

Details: This function, if successful, returns a pointer to a servent structure (Table 36-8). If *protocol* is NULL, *getservbyport* returns the first service entry for which *portnumber* matches s_port. Otherwise *getservbyport* must match both *portnumber* and *protocol*. The returned information is stored in a static area and must thus be copied before the next call.

If no match can be found, *getservbyport* returns a NULL pointer. The specific error number may be retrieved by calling *WSAGetLastError*.

See also: getservbyname, WSAAsyncGetServByPort

getsockname: get socket's assigned name
status = getsockname(s, name, namelen)

Prototype:

int PASCAL FAR getsockname(SOCKET s, struct sockaddr FAR * name, int FAR * namelen);

Arguments:

SOCKET s ;descriptor identifying a bound socket

struct sockaddr FAR *name ;receives address (name) of the socket

int FAR * namelen ;size of the name buffer

Header File:

winsock.h

Details: This function retrieves the current name for the specified socket descriptor in *name*. It is used on a bound or connected socket specified by the *s* parameter, and returns the local association for that socket. If any error occurs, *getsockname* returns SOCKET_ERROR and a specific error code may be retrieved by calling *WSAGetLastError*. Otherwise, the function returns 0.

The returned information is stored in a static area and must thus be copied before the next call.

See also: bind, getpeername, socket

getsockopt: get options for socket
status = getsockopt(sock, level, optname, optval, optlength)

Prototype:

int PASCAL FAR getsockopt (SOCKET s, int level, int optname, char FAR * optval, int FAR * optlen);

Arguments:

SOCKET s;descriptor identifying a socket

int level;level at which option is defined; must be SOL_SOCKET or IPPROTO_TCP

int optname;socket option for which value is to be retrieved

char *optval;buffer in which to store retrieved value

int *optlen;pointer to size of *optval* buffer

Header File:

winsock.h

Details: This function obtains the current value of an option for socket *s*, at *level* (SOL_SOCKET for the socket level or the protocol number for any other level). The desired option is specified by *optname* (see Table 36-9), and the current value will be stored in the buffer pointed at by *optval*, up to a maximum of *optlength* characters. On return, *optlength* is updated to indicated the actual amount of data returned.

On error, *getsockopt* returns SOCKET_ERROR and the specific error code may be determined by calling *WSAGetLastError*; if successful, it returns 0.

36-9 Socket-level options:

SO_ACCEPTCONN	socket is listening?
SO_BROADCAST	permitted to send broadcast messages?
SO_DEBUG	debugging information recorded?
SO_DONTLINGER	SO_LINGER option disabled?
SO_DONTROUTE	outgoing message routing bypassed?
SO_ERROR	(get only) last error on socket, cleared after retrieving
SO_KEEPALIVE	connections kept alive with periodic messages?
SO_LINGER	linger on close if data present (see Table 36-10 for value's format)
SO_OOBINLINE	is out-of-band data received in band?
SO_RCVBUF	input buffer size
SO_REUSEADDR	local address reused?
SO_SNDBUF	output buffer size
SO_TYPE	(get only) socket's type
TCP_NODELAY	Nagle algorithm disabled?

36-10 Format of struct linger:

Type	Name	Description
int	l_onoff	flag specifying whether *linger* is active
int	l_linger	time to linger awaiting data delivery

See also: setsockopt, socket, WSAAsyncSelect

---

htonl: convert u_long from host to network byte order
netlong = htonl(hostlong)

Prototype:
u_long PASCAL FAR htonl (u_long hostlong);
Arguments:
u_long hostlong;32-bit number in host byte order
Header File:
winsock.h
Details: The Internet uses big-endian byte ordering (most-significant byte at the lowest address) for all multi-byte quantities; for little-endian machines such as Intel 80x86 processors, this means that data must be byte-swapped before it can be sent over the network. This call will ensure that a 32-bit quantity has the correct byte order for the network (it is a null function if the processor's byte order is the same as the network's).
See also: htons, ntohl, ntohs

---

htons: convert u_short to network byte order
netshort = htons(hostshort)

Prototype:
u_short PASCAL FAR htons (u_short hostshort);
Arguments:
u_short hostshort;16-bit number in host byte order
Header File:
winsock.h
Details: The Internet uses big-endian byte ordering (most-significant byte at the lowest address) for all multi-byte quantities; for little-endian machines such as Intel 80x86 processors, this means

that data must be byte-swapped before it can be sent over the network. This call will ensure that a 16-bit quantity has the correct byte order for the network (it is a null function if the processor's byte order is the same as the network's).

See also: htonl, ntohl, ntohs

inet_addr: parse dotted numeric string into Internet address
address = inet_addr(dotstring)

Prototype:

SOCKET PASCAL FAR accept (SOCKET s, struct sockaddr FAR * addr, int FAR * addrlen);

Arguments:

char *dotstring ;string representing Internet address in standard "dot" notation

Header File:

winsock.h

Details: This function accepts a numeric string consisting of one to four parts separated by periods and determines the 32-bit Internet address specified by the string. If the numeric strings consists of a single part, it is stored directly; a two-part string is interpreted as an 8-bit network number and a 24-bit local address; a three-part string is interpreted as two 8-bit numbers specifying the network number and a 16-bit local address; finally, a four-part string is interpreted as four 8-bit numbers with the most-significant first. For all formats, the numbers making up each component may be either decimal, octal (leading '0'), or hexadecimal (leading '0x').

If successful, *inet_addr* returns an unsigned long containing a suitable binary representation of the Internet address given. If the string passed in does not contain a legitimate Internet address, *inet_addr* returns INADDR_NONE.

See also: inet_ntoa

inet_ntoa: convert Internet address to dotted numeric string
dotstring = inet_ntoa(inetaddr)

Prototype:

char FAR * PASCAL FAR inet_ntoa (struct in_addr in);

Arguments:

struct in_addr inetaddr;   structure representing an Internet host address (Table 35-5)

Header File:

winsock.h

Details: This function returns an ASCII string in '.' notation corresponding to the specified Internet address. The returned string is located in static storage and must be copied before the next call.

See also: inet_addr

ioctlsocket: control I/O device
status = ioctlsocket(descriptor, request, argument)

Prototype:

int PASCAL FAR ioctlsocket(SOCKET s, long cmd, u_long FAR * argp);

Arguments:

SOCKET s;descriptor identifying a socket

long cmd;command to perform on the socket

u_long FAR * argp;pointer to a parameter for *cmd*

Header File:

winsock.h

Details: This function may be called for any socket in any state, to get or retrieve associated operating parameters. The allowable values for *cmd* are listed in Table 36-11. If successful the function returns 0; in case of error, the return value is SOCKET_ERROR and the specific error code may be determined by calling *WSAGetLastError*.

See also: getsockopt, setsockopt, socket, WSAAsyncSelect, ioctl (Chapter 35)

36-11 Allowable commands for ioctlsocket:

Command	Description
FIONBIO	Enable or disable non-blocking mode on the socket *s*. *argp* points at an *unsigned long*, which is non-zero if non-blocking mode is to be enabled and zero if it is to be disabled.
FIONREAD	Determine the amount of data which can be read atomically from socket *s*. *argp* points at an *unsigned long* in which *ioctlsocket* stores the result.
SIOCATMARK	Determine whether or not all out-of-band data has been read. *argp* points at a *BOOL* in which *ioctlsocket* stores the result.

listen: start socket listening for connection attempts
status = listen(sock, backlog)

Prototype:
int PASCAL FAR listen (SOCKET s, int backlog);
Arguments:
SOCKET s;descriptor identifying a bound, unconnected socket
int backlog;maximum length to which the queue of pending connections may grow
Header File:
winsock.h
Details: To accept connections, a three-step process is used. A socket is first created with *socket*, a backlog for incoming connections is specified with *listen*, and then the connections are accepted with *accept*. *listen* applies only to sockets of type SOCK_STREAM. Socket *s* is put into "passive" mode: incoming connections are acknowledged and queued, pending acceptance.

On error, *listen* returns SOCKET_ERROR; *WSAGetLastError* may be called to determine the specific error code. If successful, *listen* returns 0.
See also: accept, connect, socket

ntohl: convert u_long to host byte order
hostlong = ntohl(netlong)

Prototype:
u_long PASCAL FAR ntohl (u_long netlong);
Arguments:
u_long netlong;32-bit number in network byte order
Header File:
winsock.h
Details: The Internet uses big-endian byte ordering (most-significant byte at the lowest address) for all multi-byte quantities; for little-endian machines such as Intel 80x86 processors, this means that data received from the network must be byte-swapped before it can used by a program. This call will ensure that a 32-bit quantity has the correct byte order for the processor on which the program is running (it is a null function if the processor's byte order is the same as the network's).
See also: htonl, htons, ntohs

ntohs: convert u_short to host byte order
hostshort = ntohs(netshort)

Prototype:
u_short PASCAL FAR ntohs (u_short netshort);
Arguments:
u_short netshort;16-bit number in network byte order
Header File:
winsock.h
Details: The Internet uses big-endian byte ordering (most-significant byte at the lowest address) for all multi-byte quantities; for little-endian machines such as Intel 80x86 processors, this means

that data received from the network must be byte-swapped before it can used by a program. This call will ensure that a 16-bit quantity has the correct byte order for the processor on which the program is running (it is a null function if the processor's byte order is the same as the network's). **See also:** htonl, htons, ntohl

recv: receive data from a socket
msglength = recv(sock, buffer, buflength, flags)

Prototype:
int PASCAL FAR recv (SOCKET s, char FAR * buf, int len, int flags);
Arguments:
SOCKET s;descriptor identifying a connected socket
char *buffer;buffer for the incoming data
int FAR * buflength;length of *buf*
int flags;specifies the way in which the call is made
Header File:
winsock.h
Details: This function reads incoming data received by the socket *s* from its connected peer. It waits for a message to arrive unless the socket has been marked non-blocking, in which case it returns SOCKET_ERROR and sets the error code retrievable with *WSAGetLastError* to EWOULDBLOCK when there are no messages available.

If no error occurs, *recv* returns the number of bytes received. If the connection has been closed, it returns 0. Otherwise, a value of SOCKET_ERROR is returned, and a specific error code may be retrieved by calling *WSAGetLastError*.

Flags may be used to influence the behavior of the function beyond any options specified for the socket. The *flags* parameter is constructed by OR-ing the values listed in Table 36-12.
See also: accept, connect, read, recvfrom, recvmsg, select, send, socket

36-12 Bit values for flags:

MSG_PEEK	Peek at incoming data (incoming only). Data is copied into buffer but is not removed from input queue
MSG_OOB	Process out-of-band data
MSG_DONTROUTE	Specifies that outgoing data should not be subject to routing. A Windows Sockets supplier may choose to ignore this flag

recvfrom: receive a message on a socket, with originating address
msglength = recvfrom(sock, buffer, buflength, flags, from, fromlength)

Prototype:
int PASCAL FAR recvfrom (SOCKET s, char FAR * buf, int len, int flags, struct sockaddr FAR * from, int FAR * fromlen);
Arguments:
SOCKET s;descriptor identifying a bound socket
char FAR * buf;buffer for incoming data
int len;length of *buf*
int flags;Specifies way in which call is made (Table 36-12)
struct sockaddr *from;optional pointer to buffer (Table 36-5) in which to return source address
int FAR * fromlen;pointer to the size of the *from* buffer
Header File:
winsock.h
Details: This function reads incoming data on a (possibly connected) socket and captures the address from which the data was sent. If *from* is non-NULL and the socket is of type SOCK_DGRAM, the network address of the peer which sent the data is copied to the struct sockaddr specified by *from* and *fromlen* is updated to contain the actual size of the address.

This function waits for a message to arrive unless the socket has been marked non-blocking, in which case it returns SOCKET_ERROR and sets the error code retrievable with *WSAGetLastError* to EWOULDBLOCK when there are no messages available.

If no error occurs, *recv* returns the number of bytes received. If the connection has been closed, it returns 0. Otherwise, a value of SOCKET_ERROR is returned, and a specific error code may be retrieved by calling *WSAGetLastError.*

Flags may be used to influence the behavior of the function beyond any options specified for the socket. The *flags* parameter is constructed by OR-ing the values listed in Table 36-12.

See also: recv, send, socket, WSAAsyncSelect

---

select: determine status of one or more sockets, waiting if necessary
numfound = select(numdescr, readdescr, writedescr, exceptdescr, timeout)

Prototype:
int PASCAL FAR select (int nfds, fd_set FAR * readfds, fd_set FAR * writefds, fd_set FAR * exceptfds, const struct timeval FAR * timeout);

Arguments:
int nfds;argument ignored, included only for compatibility
fd_set FAR * readfds;optional pointer to a set (Table 36-13) of sockets to be checked for readability
fd_set FAR * writefds;optional pointer to a set (Table 36-13) of sockets to be checked for wrotabo;oty
fd_set FAR * exceptfds;optional pointer to a set (Table 36-13) of sockets to be checked for errors
const struct timeval FAR * timeout;optional time limit on wait (Table 36-14)

Header File:
winsock.h

Details: This function determines the status of one or more sockets by checking the indicated descriptor sets to determine whether any of them are ready for reading or accepting a connection (*readdescr*), are ready for writing or have established a connection (*writedescr*), or have an error condition pending (*exceptdescr*).

This function returns when at least one descriptor is ready or the specified timeout expires. It will block indefinitely if *timeout* is NULL; if *timeout* points at a timeval structure whose value is zero, *select* returns immediately (useful for polling). Some implementations may modify *timeout* to indicate the time remaining.

The macros FD_ZERO, FD_SET, FD_CLR, and FD_ISSET are provided in header file *winsock.h* for manipulating desriptor sets, which are represented as arrays of SOCKETs; the last valid entry in each being followed by an element set to INVALID_SOCKET.

If no error occurs, *select* returns the total number of descriptors which are ready and contained in the fd_set structures, or 0 if the time limit expired. In case of error, the function returns SOCKET_ERROR, and *WSAGetLastError* may be used to retrieve a specific error code.

See also: accept, connect, recv, recvfrom, send, WSAAsyncSelect

---

36-13 Format of struct fd_set:

Type	Name	Description
u_short	fd_count;	how many are SET?
SOCKET	fd_array[FD_SETSIZE];	an array of SOCKETs

36-14 Format of struct timeval:

Type	Name	Description
long	tv_sec	seconds
long	tv_usec	microseconds

send: transmit a message over a connected socket
bytessent = send(sock, msg, msglength, flags)
Prototype:
int PASCAL FAR send (SOCKET s, const char FAR * buf, int len, int flags);
Arguments:
SOCKET s;descriptor identifying a connected socket
const char FAR * buf;buffer containing data to be transmitted
int len;length of data in *buf*
int flags;specifies transmission options
Header File:
winsock.h
Details: This function attempts to transmit a message *buf* of length *len* from *sock* to its connected peer. The value of *flags* is formed by OR-ing appropriate bits (Table 36-12) to send out-of-band data or bypass the standard routing algorithm. Successful completion of a *send* does not indicate that data was successfully delivered.

If no locally-detected error occurs, *send* returns the total number of characters sent (which may be less than the number requested), even though they may have failed to be delivered. Otherwise, a value of SOCKET_ERROR is returned, and a specific error code may be retrieved by calling *WSAGetLastError*.

See also: recv, recvfrom, socket, sendto, WSAStartup

sendto: transmit a message to a specified recipient
bytessent = sendto(sock, msg, msglength, flags, to, tolen)
Prototype:
int PASCAL FAR sendto (SOCKET s, const char FAR * buf, int len, int flags, const struct sockaddr FAR * to, int tolen);
Arguments:
SOCKET s;descriptor identifying a socket
const char FAR * buf;buffer containing data to be transmitted
int len;length of data in *buf*
int flags;specifies way in which call is made
struct sockaddr *to;pointer to target socket (Table 36-5)
int tolen;size of address in *to*
Details: This function attempts to transmit a message *buf* of length *len* from *s* to another socket specified by *to* and *tolen*, or to the socket's connected peer if *to* is NULL. Successful completion of *sendto*() does not indicate that the data was successfully delivered. The value of *flags* is formed by OR-ing appropriate bits (Table 36-12) to send out-of-band data or bypass the standard routing algorithm.

If no locally-detected error occurs, *sendto* returns the total number of characters sent (which may be less than the number requested), even though they may have failed to be delivered. Otherwise, a value of SOCKET_ERROR is returned, and a specific error code may be retrieved by calling *WSAGetLastError*.

See also: recv, recvfrom, socket, send, WSAStartup

setsockopt: specify options for socket
status = setsockopt(sock, level, optname, optval, optlength)
Prototype:
int PASCAL FAR setsockopt (SOCKET s, int level, int optname, const char FAR * optval, int optlen);
Arguments:
SOCKET s;descriptor identifying a socket
int level;level at which option is defined

int optname;option for which value is to be set
char FAR * optval;pointer to buffer in which value for requested option is supplied
int optlen;size of *optval* buffer
Header File:
winsock.h
Details: This function sets an option for socket *s*, which may exist at multiple protocol levels (the desired one is selected with *level*: SOL_SOCKET for the socket level or the protocol number for any other level). *optname* specifies the option to be modified (see Table 36-9) and *optval* and *optlen* specify the new value for that option.

If no error occurs, *setsockopt* returns 0. Otherwise, SOCKET_ERROR is returned, and a specific error code may be retrieved by calling *WSAGetLastError*.
See also: bind, getsockopt, ioctlsocket, socket, WSAAsyncSelect

---

shutdown: disable sends or receives on a socket
status = shutdown(sock,how)
Prototype:
int PASCAL FAR shutdown (SOCKET s, int how);
Arguments:
SOCKET s;descriptor identifying a socket
int how;flag specifying operations no longer to be allowed
Header File:
winsock.h
Details: This function is used on all types of sockets to disable reception, transmission, or both. If *how* is 0, subsequent receives on the socket will be disallowed. This has no effect on the lower protocol layers. If *how* is 1, subsequent sends are disallowed.

This function does not block regardless of the SO_LINGER setting on the socket. An application should not rely on being able to re-use a socket after it has been shut down.

If no error occurs, *shutdown* returns 0. Otherwise, a value of SOCKET_ERROR is returned, and a specific error code may be retrieved by calling *WSAGetLastError*.
See also: connect, socket

---

socket: create an endpoint for communication
sock = socket(domain, type, protocol)
Prototype:
SOCKET PASCAL FAR socket (int domain, int type, int protocol);
Arguments:
int domain;address format specification (Table 36-15)
int type;type specification for the new socket (Table 36-16)
int protocol;particular protocol to be used with the socket, or 0 if unspecified
Header File:
winsock.h
Details: This function creates an endpoint to which communications may be directed, and returns a handle which may be used to reference it. *domain* specifies the communications domain to be used, and thus the protocol family, as listed in Table 36-15; similarly, *type* specifies the semantics of communications on the socket and *protocol* specifies the exact protocol within the indicated protocol family.

If no error occurs, *socket* returns a socket descriptor. Otherwise, a value of SOCKET_ERROR is returned, and a specific error code may be retrieved by calling *WSAGetLastError*.
See also: accept, bind, connect, getsockname, getsockopt, ioctlsocket, listen, recv, recvfrom, select, setsockopt, send, sendto, shutdown

36-15 Protocol families:

PF_UNIX   Unix-internal protocols (not supported)
PF_INET   Internet protocols (TCP, UDP, etc.)
PF_NS   Xeros Network Systems protocols (not supported)
PF_IMPLINK IMP link layer protocols (not supported)

36-16 Socket types:

SOCK_STREAM   sequenced, reliable, two-way connection-based stream
SOCK_DGRAM   connectionless unreliable datagrams

WSAAsyncGetHostByAddr: get host information corresponding to an address, asynchronous version

*handle = **WSAAsyncGetHostByAddr**(hWnd, wMsg, addr, len, type, buf, buflen)*

Prototype:
HANDLE PASCAL FAR WSAAsyncGetHostByAddr (HWND hWnd, unsigned int wMsg, const char FAR * addr, int len, int type, char FAR * buf, int buflen);

Arguments:
HWND hWnd;handle of window to receive message on completion
unsigned int wMsg;message to be received when asynchronous request completes
const char FAR * addr;pointer to network byte order network address for the host
int len;length of address, which must be 4 for PF_INET
int type;type of address, which must be PF_INET
char FAR * buf;pointer to data area to receive hostent data
int buflen;size of data area *buf*

Header File:
winsock.h

Details: This function is an asynchronous version of *gethostbyaddr*, and retrieves host name and address information corresponding to a network address. Windows Sockets initiates the operation and returns to the caller immediately, passing back an *asynchronous task handle* by which the application may identify the operation. When the operation is completed, the results (if any) are copied into the buffer provided by the caller and the specified message is sent to the application's window.

If no error occurs, *WSAAsyncGetHostByAddr* returns 0 in the high 16 bits of *lParam* for the completion message. Otherwise, the high 16 bits contain a specific error code (Table 36-4). If the buffer was too small for the data, the low 16 bits of *lParam* contain the size required. The buffer *buf* must be larger than the size of a hostent structure (Table 36-6) because the area supplied is used by Windows Sockets to contain not only a hostent structure but any and all data referenced by members of the structure. A buffer of MAXGETHOSTSTRUCT bytes is recommended.

See also: gethostbyaddr, WSAAsyncGetHostByName, WSACancelAsyncRequest

WSAAsyncGetHostByName: get host information corresponding to a hostname, asynchronous version

*status = **WSAAsyncGetHostByName**(hWnd,wMsg,name,buf,buflen)*

Prototype:
HANDLE PASCAL FAR WSAAsyncGetHostByName (HWND hWnd, unsigned int wMsg, const char FAR * name, char FAR * buf, int buflen);

Arguments:
HWND hWnd;handle of window to receive message on completion
unsigned int wMsg;message to be received when asynchronous request completes
const char FAR * name;pointer to name of host
char FAR * buf;pointer to data area to receive hostent data
int buflen;size of data area *buf*

Header File:
winsock.h

Details: This function is an asynchronous version of *gethostbyname*, and retrieves name and address information corresponding to a hostname. Windows Sockets initiates the operation and returns to the caller immediately, passing back an *asynchronous task handle* which the application may use to identify the operation. When the operation is completed, the results (if any) are copied into the buffer provided by the caller and a message is sent to the application's window.

If no error occurs, *WSAAsyncGetHostByName* returns 0 in the high 16 bits of *lParam* for the completion message. Otherwise, the high 16 bits contain a specific error code (Table 36-4). If the buffer was too small for the data, the low 16 bits of *lParam* contain the size required. The buffer *buf* must be larger than the size of a hostent structure (Table 36-6) because the area supplied is used by Windows Sockets to contain not only a hostent structure but any and all data referenced by members of the structure. A buffer of MAXGETHOSTSTRUCT bytes is recommended.

See also: gethostbyname, WSAAsyncGetHostByAddr, WSACancelAsyncRequest

---

WSAAsyncGetProtoByName: get protocol information corresponding to a protocol name, asynchronous version

status = WSAAsyncGetProtoByName(hWnd,wMsg,name,buf,buflen)

Prototype:
HANDLE PASCAL FAR WSAAsyncGetProtoByName (HWND hWnd, unsigned int wMsg, const char FAR * name, char FAR * buf, int buflen);

Arguments:
HWND hWnd;handle of window to receive message on completion
unsigned int wMsg;message to be received when asynchronous request completes
const char FAR * name;pointer to protocol name to be resolved
char FAR * buf;pointer to data area to receive protoent data
int buflen ;size of data area *buf*

Header File:
winsock.h

Details: This function is an asynchronous version of *getprotobyname*, and retrieves the protocol name and number corresponding to a protocol name. Windows Sockets initiates the operation and returns to the caller immediately, passing back an *asynchronous task handle* with which the application may identify the operation. When the operation is completed, the results (if any) are copied into the buffer provided by the caller and a message is sent to the application's window.

If no error occurs, *WSAAsyncGetProtoByName* returns 0 in the high 16 bits of *lParam* for the completion message. Otherwise, the high 16 bits contain a specific error code (Table 36-4). If the buffer was too small for the data, the low 16 bits of *lParam* contain the size required. The buffer *buf* must be larger than the size of a protoent structure (Table 36-7) because the area supplied is used by Windows Sockets to contain not only a protoent structure but any and all data referenced by members of the structure. A buffer of MAXGETHOSTSTRUCT bytes is recommended.

See also: getprotobyname, WSAAsyncGetProtoByNumber, WSACancelAsyncRequest

---

WSAAsyncGetProtoByNumber: get protocol information corresponding to a protocol number - asynchronous version

status = WSAAsyncGetProtoByNumber(hWnd,wMsg,number,buf,buflen)

Prototype:
HANDLE PASCAL FAR WSAAsyncGetProtoByNumber (HWND hWnd, unsigned int wMsg, int number, char FAR * buf, int buflen);

Arguments:
HWND hWnd;handle of window to receive message on completion
unsigned int wMsg;message to be received when the asynchronous request completes
int number;protocol number to be resolved, in host byte order

char FAR * buf;pointer to data area to receive protoent data
int buflen;size of data area *buf*

Header File:
winsock.h

Details: This function is an asynchronous version of *getprotobynumber*( ), and retrieves the protocol name and number corresponding to a protocol number. Windows Sockets initiates the operation and returns to the caller immediately, passing back an *asynchronous task handle* with which the application may identify the operation. When the operation is completed, the results (if any) are copied into the buffer provided by the caller and a message is sent to the application's window.

If no error occurs, *WSAAsyncGetProtoByNumber* returns 0 in the high 16 bits of *lParam* for the completion message. Otherwise, the high 16 bits contain a specific error code (Table 36-4). If the buffer was too small for the data, the low 16 bits of *lParam* contain the size required. The buffer *buf* must be larger than the size of a protoent structure (Table 36-7) because the area supplied is used by Windows Sockets to contain not only a protoent structure but any and all data referenced by members of the structure. A buffer of MAXGETHOSTSTRUCT bytes is recommended.

See also: getprotobynumber, WSAAsyncGetProtoByName, WSACancelAsyncRequest

WSAAsyncGetServByName: get service information corresponding to a service name and port, asynchronous version

status = WSAAsyncGetServByName(hWnd,wMsg,name,proto,buf,buflen)

Prototype:
HANDLE PASCAL FAR WSAAsyncGetServByName (HWND hWnd, unsigned int wMsg, const char FAR * name, const char FAR * proto, char FAR * buf, int buflen);

Arguments:
HWND hWnd;handle of window to receive message on completion
unsigned int wMsg;message to be received when the asynchronous request completes
const char FAR * name;pointer to a service name
const char FAR * proto;pointer to a protocol name
char FAR * buf;pointer to data area to receive servent data
int buflen;size of data area *buf*

Header File:
winsock.h

Details: This function is an asynchronous version of *getservbyname*, and retrieves service information corresponding to a service name. Windows Sockets initiates the operation and returns to the caller immediately, passing back an *asynchronous task handle* with which the application may identify the operation. When the operation is completed, the results (if any) are copied into the buffer provided by the caller and a message is sent to the application's window.

If no error occurs, *WSAAsyncGetServByName* returns 0 in the high 16 bits of *lParam* for the completion message. Otherwise, the high 16 bits contain a specific error code (Table 36-4). If the buffer was too small for the data, the low 16 bits of *lParam* contain the size required. The buffer *buf* must be larger than the size of a servent structure (Table 36-8) because the area supplied is used by Windows Sockets to contain not only a servent structure but any and all data referenced by members of the structure. A buffer of MAXGETHOSTSTRUCT bytes is recommended.

See also: getservbyname, WSAAsyncGetServByPort, WSACancelAsyncRequest

WSAAsyncGetServByPort: get service information corresponding to a port and protocol, asynchronous version

status = WSAAsyncGetServByPort(hWnd,wMsg,port,proto,buf,buflen)

Prototype:
HANDLE PASCAL FAR WSAAsyncGetServByPort (HWND hWnd, unsigned int wMsg, int port, const char FAR * proto, char FAR * buf, int buflen);

Arguments:
HWND hWnd;handle of window to receive message on completion
unsigned int wMsg;message to be received when the asynchronous request completes
int port;port for the service, in network byte order
const char FAR * proto;pointer to a protocol name
char FAR * buf;pointer to data area to receive servent data
int buflen;size of data area *buf*
Header File:
winsock.h
Details: This function is an asynchronous version of *getservbyport*, and retrieves service information corresponding to a port number. Windows Sockets initiates the operation and returns to the caller immediately, passing back an *asynchronous task handle* with which the application may identify the operation. When the operation is completed, the results (if any) are copied into the buffer provided by the caller and a message is sent to the application's window.

If no error occurs, *WSAAsyncGetServByPort* returns 0 in the high 16 bits of *lParam* for the completion message. Otherwise, the high 16 bits contain a specific error code (Table 36-4). If the buffer was too small for the data, the low 16 bits of *lParam* contain the size required. The buffer *buf* must be larger than the size of a servent structure (Table 36-8) because the area supplied is used by Windows Sockets to contain not only a servent structure but any and all data referenced by members of the structure. A buffer of MAXGETHOSTSTRUCT bytes is recommended.
See also: getservbyport, WSAAsyncGetServByName, WSACancelAsyncRequest

---

WSAAsyncSelect: request event notification for a socket
status = WSAAsyncSelect(s,hWnd,wMsg,lEvent)
Prototype:
int PASCAL FAR WSAAsyncSelect (SOCKET s, HWND hWnd, unsigned int wMsg, long lEvent);
Arguments:
SOCKET s;   descriptor of socket for which event notification is required
HWND hWnd;   handle of window to receive a message when network event occurs
unsigned int wMsg; message to be received when network event occurs
long lEvent;   bitmask specifying network events (Table 36-17) of interest
Header File:
winsock.h
Details: This function requests that the Windows Sockets DLL send a message to window *hWnd* whenever it detects any network events (Table 36-17) specified by *lEvent* on socket *s*. The message to be sent is *wMsg*.

If no error occurs, *WSAAsyncSelect* returns 0 in the high 16 bits of *lParam* for the completion message. Otherwise, the high 16 bits contain a specific error code (Table 36-4). The low 16 bits of *lParam* specify the event or events, using the values of Table 36-17.
See also: select

36-17 Bitflags for WSAAsyncSelect:

Value	Meaning
FD_READ	readiness for reading
FD_WRITE	readiness for writing
FD_OOB	arrival of out-of-band data
FD_ACCEPT	incoming connections
FD_CONNECT	completed connection
FD_CLOSE	socket closure

WSACancelAsyncRequest: cancel an incomplete asynchronous operation
status = WSACancelAsyncRequest(hAsyncTaskHandle)

Prototype:

int PASCAL FAR WSACancelAsyncRequest (HANDLE hAsyncTaskHandle);

Arguments:

HANDLE hAsyncTaskHandle;handle of asynchronous operation to be canceled

Header File:

winsock.h

Details: This function cancels an asynchronous operation initiated by any of the *WSAAsyncGetXByY* functions such as *WSAAsyncGetHostByName*. The operation to be canceled is identified by the *hAsyncTaskHandle* parameter, which should be set to the asynchronous task handle returned by the initiating function.

If no error occurs, *WSACancelAsyncRequest* returns 0 in the high 16 bits of *lParam* for the completion message. Otherwise, the high 16 bits contain a specific error code (Table 36-4).

See also: WSAAsyncGetHostByAddr, WSAAsyncGetHostByName, WSAAsyncGetProtoBy-Number, WSAAsyncGetProtoByName, WSAAsyncGetHostByName, WSAAsyncGetServByPort, WSAAsyncGetServByName, WSACancelBlockingCall

WSACancelBlockingCall: cancel a blocking call currently in progress
status = WSACancelBlockingCall()

Prototype:

int PASCAL FAR WSACancelBlockingCall (void);

Arguments:

Header File:

winsock.h

Details: This function cancels any outstanding blocking operation for this task.

If no error occurs, *WSACancelBlockingCall* returns 0 if the operation was successfully canceled. Otherwise the value SOCKET_ERROR is returned, and a specific error number may be retrieved by calling *WSAGetLastError*.

See also: WSACancelAsyncRequest, WSAIsBlocking

WSACleanup: terminate use of the Windows Sockets DLL
status = WSACleanup()

Prototype:

int PASCAL FAR WSACleanup (void);

Arguments:

Header File:

winsock.h

Details: Any application using Windows Sockets services must successfully complete a call to *WSAStartup* in order to initialize the library. When through with all Windows Sockets services, the application must call *WSACleanup* to allow any allocated resources to be freed. These calls must be paired; every call to *WSAStartup* requires a corresponding call to *WSACleanup*. Only the final call to *WSACleanup* actually releases the resources.

The return value is 0 if the operation succeeds. Otherwise SOCKET_ERROR is returned, and a specific error number may be retrieved by calling *WSAGetLastError*.

See also: WSAStartup

WSAGetLastError: get error code for last operation which failed
status = WSAGetLastError()
Prototype:
int PASCAL FAR WSAGetLastError (void);
Arguments:
none
Header File:
winsock.h
Details: This function returns the code (Table 36-4) of the last network error that occurred; it corresponds to the global variable *errno* under Unix sockets. When a Windows Sockets API function indicates an error has occurred, this function should be called to obtain the error code.
See also: WSASetLastError

WSAIsBlocking: determine if a blocking call is in progress
status = WSAIsBlocking()
Prototype:
BOOL PASCAL FAR WSAIsBlocking (void);
Arguments:
none
Header File:
winsock.h
Details: This function permits a task to determine whether a previous blocking call is still waiting to complete. Its return value is TRUE if an outstanding blocking function is awaiting completion, and FALSE otherwise.
See also: WSACancelBlockingCall, WSASetBlockingHook

WSASetBlockingHook: establishes an application-specific blocking hook function
status = WSASetBlockingHook(lpBlockFunc)
Prototype:
FARPROC PASCAL FAR WSASetBlockingHook (FARPROC lpBlockFunc);
Arguments:
FARPROC lpBlockFunc;pointer to procedure instance address of blocking function to be installed
Header File:
winsock.h
Details: This function installs a new function which Windows Sockets will use to implement blocking socket function calls, replacing the default mechanism provided by the DLL. Requirements for such a function are beyond the scope of this book–refer to the specification for details.

If no error occurs, *WSASetBlockingHook* returns a pointer to the procedure-instance of the previously installed blocking function. Otherwise, a NULL pointer is returned, and the specific error code may be retrieved by calling *WSAGetLastError*.
See also: WSAIsBlocking, WSAUnhookBlockingHook

WSASetLastError: set error code to be retrieved by WSAGetLastError
status = WSASetLastError(iError)
Prototype:
void PASCAL FAR WSASetLastError (int iError);
Arguments:
int iError;error code (Table 36-4) to be returned by next call to *WSAGetLastError*
Header File:
winsock.h

Details: This function sets the error code that will be returned by a subsequent *WSAGetLastError* call. Any subsequent Windows Sockets routine called by the application will override the code as set by this routine.

See also: WSAGetLastError

WSAStartup: initialize Windows Sockets DLL
status = WSAStartup(wVersionRequested,lpWSAData)

Prototype:

int PASCAL FAR WSAStartup (WORD wVersionRequested, LPWSADATA lpWSAData);

Arguments:

WORD wVersionRequested;highest version of Windows Sockets API support that caller can use.
LPWSADATA lpWSAData ;pointer to *WSADATA* data structure (Table 36-18) to receive details of Windows Sockets implementation

Header File:

winsock.h

Details: Any application using Windows Sockets services must successfully complete a call to *WSAStartup* in order to initialize the library. When through with all Windows Sockets services, the application must call *WSACleanup* to allow any allocated resources to be freed. These calls must be paired; every call to *WSAStartup* requires a corresponding call to *WSACleanup*. Only the final call to *WSACleanup* actually releases the resources.

WSAStartup returns zero if successful. Otherwise it returns one of the error codes listed in Table 36-4. The normal mechanism using *WSAGetLastError* to determine the error code cannot be used, since the DLL may not have been able to create the client data area where "last error" information is stored.

The high order byte of *wVersionRequested* specifies the minor version (revision) number and the low-order byte specifies the major version number of the highest version of Windows Sockets API support that the caller will use.

See also: send, sendto, WSACleanup

36-18 Format of struct WSADATA:

Type	Name	Description
WORD	wVersion;	version of Windows Sockets specification that Windows Sockets DLL expects caller to use
WORD	wHighVersion;	highest version of Windows Sockets specification that this DLL can support
char	szDescription[WSADESCRIPTION_LEN+1];	null-terminated ASCII string into which Windows Sockets DLL copies a description of Windows Sockets implementation, including vendor identification
char	szSystemStatus[WSASYSSTATUS_LEN+1];	null-terminated ASCII string into which Windows Sockets DLL copies relevant status or configuration information

unsigned short	iMaxSockets;	maximum number of sockets which a single process can potentially open
unsigned short	iMaxUdpDg;	size in bytes of largest UDP datagram that can be sent or received by a Windows Sockets application
char FAR *	lpVendorInfo;	pointer to a vendor-specific data structure

---

WSAUnhookBlockingHook: restore default blocking hook function
status = WSAUnhookBlockingHook()

Prototype:
int PASCAL FAR WSAUnhookBlockingHook (void);

Arguments:
none

Header File:
winsock.h

Details: This function removes any blocking hook that has been installed and reinstalls the default blocking mechanism. The return value is 0 if the operation succeeds; otherwise, SOCKET_ERROR is returned, and a specific error number may be retrieved by calling *WSAGetLastError*.

See also: WSASetBlockingHook

CHAPTER 37

IBM Mainframe Connectivity

A number of products that provide connectivity between PC's and IBM mainframe systems exist, but most operate simply as terminal emulators and leave it to the mainframe software to handle terminal communications. Two exceptions to the rule are the IBM System 36/38 Workstation emulator and those programs which emulate the IBM 3270 smart terminal.

3270PC

INT 10h Function 3000h
LOCATE 3270PC CONFIGURATION TABLE (INSTALLATION CHECK)

Registers at call: **Return Registers:**
AX = 3000h CX:DX -> 3270PC configuration table (see Table 37-1)
CX = 0000h CX:DX = 0000h:0000h if 3270PC Control Program not active
DX = 0000h
See also: Function 1F01h

37-1 Format of 3270 PC configuration table:

Offset	Size	Description
00h	BYTE	aspect ratio X
01h	BYTE	aspect ratio Y
02h	BYTE	monitor type (see Table 37-2)
03h	BYTE	reserved
04h	BYTE	adapter ID
		00h = 5151/5272 adapter
		04h = 5151/5272 with XGA adapter
		30h = 3295 or 3270PC G/GX adapter
05h	BYTE	reserved
06h	BYTE	function flags 1 (see Table 37-3)
07h	BYTE	function flags 2
		bit 6: GPI graphics supported
08h	WORD	segment address of Control Program Level table (see Table 37-4)
0Ah	10 BYTEs	reserved

37-2 Values for monitor type:

00h	5151 (mono) or 5272 (color)
01h	3295
02h	5151 or 5272 with *XGA* graphics adapter
03h	5279 with 3270PC G adapter

04h	5379 model C01 with 3270PC GX adapter
05h	5379 model M01 with 3270PC GX adapter
07h	non-3270PC with 3270 Workstation Program
FFh	3270PC Control Program not loaded

37-3 Bitfields for function flags 1:

bit 7	mono text, 1 page
bit 6	color text, 1 page
bit 5	color text, 4 pages
bit 4	CGA color graphics
bit 3	720x350 two-color graphics
bit 2	360x350 four-color graphics
bit 1	720x350 eight-color graphics

37-4 Format of Control Program Level table:

Offset	Size	Description
00h	WORD	program version
		02xxh = 3270PC Control Program v2.xx
		03xxh = 3270PC Control Program v3.xx
		04xxh = 3270 Workstation Program v1.xx
02h	BYTE	Control Program ID (00h)
03h	27 BYTEs	Control Program Descriptor ("IBM 3270 PC CONTROL PROGRAM")

INT 44h   IBM 3270-PC High Level Language API
API

Registers at call: Return Registers:
DS:SI -> parameter control block   none
Conflicts: Novell NetWare (Chapter 21), Acorn BBC Master (PCI-7), Z100 (PCI-7), PCjr (PCI-8), "Lehigh" virus (PCI-59)

Attachmate Extra!

Extra! is a 3270 emulator by Attachmate Corporation.

INT 21h Function A0h   Extra!
GET 3270 DISPLAY STATE

Registers at call: Return Registers:
AH = A0h   AL = display status
                                               bit 7: 0=windowed, 1=enlarged
                                               bits 6-3: current screen profile number 0-9
                                               bits 2-0: active window number
                                                   0=PC, 1-4=host B-E, 5-6=notepad F-G
                                           BX = host window status (see Table 37-5)

See also: Function A1h

37-5 Bitfields for host window status:

bit 15	reserved
bit 14	0=host E window installed, 1=not
bit 13	0=host E terminal on, 1=off
bit 12	0=host E window displayed, 1=not
bit 11	reserved
bit 10	0=host D window installed, 1=not
bit 9	0=host D terminal on, 1=off

bit 8   0=host D window displayed, 1=not
bit 7   reserved
bit 6   0=host C window installed, 1=not
bit 5   0=host C terminal on, 1=off
bit 4   0=host C window displayed, 1=not
bit 3   reserved
bit 2   0=host B window installed, 1=not
bit 1   0=host B terminal on, 1=off
bit 0   0=host B window displayed, 1=not

INT 21h Function A1h
SET 3270 DISPLAY STATE
Extra!

Registers at call: **Return Registers:**
AH = A1h   none
AL = set status byte
    bit 7 : 0=windowed, 1=enlarged
    bits 6-3: current screen profile number 0-9
    bits 2-0: active window number
        0=PC, 1-4=host B-E, 5-6=notepad F-G
Conflicts: Virus (PCI-59)
See also: Functions A0h and A2h

INT 21h Function A2h
SET HOST WINDOW STATE
Extra!

Registers at call: **Return Registers:**
AH = A2h   none
AL = set status byte
    bit 7 : 0=power off, 1=power on
    bit 6 : 0=not installed, 1=installed
    bits 5-3: reserved
    bits 2-0: window number
        1-4=host B-E
See also: Function A1h

INT 21h Function A3h
SEND KEYSTROKES TO HOST WINDOW
Extra!

Registers at call: **Return Registers:**
AH = A3h   CX = zero if character sent, non-zero if not
AL = window number (1-4=host B-E)   BX incremented if CX=0
CX = 0001h
DS:BX -> keystroke buffer
DL = buffer type
    00h host function code
    nonzero ASCII character

37-6 Host function codes:

00h=reserved	10h=PF16	20h=Clear	30h=SysRq
01h=PF1	11h=PF17	21h=Print	31h=ErInp
02h=PF2	12h=PF18	22h=Left	32h=ErEof
03h=PF3	13h=PF19	23h=Right	33h=Ident
04h=PF4	14h=PF20	24h=Up	34h=Test
05h=PF5	15h=PF21	25h=Down	35h=Reset

06h=PF6	16h=PF22	26h=Home	36h=DevCncl
07h=PF7	17h=PF23	27h=Fast Left	37h=Dup
08h=PF8	18h=PF24	28h=Fast Right	38h=FldMark
09h=PF9	19h=Alt on	29h=Bksp	39h=Enter
0Ah=PF10	1Ah=Alt off	2Ah=Insert	3Ah=CrSel
0Bh=PF11	1Bh=Shift on	2Bh=Delete	
0Ch=PF12	1Ch=Shift off	2Ch=Backtab	
0Dh=PF13	1Dh=PA1	2Dh=Tab	
0Eh=PF14	1Eh=PA2	2Eh=Newline	
0Fh=PF15	1Fh=PA3	2Fh=Attn	

INT 21h Function A4h
GET HOST WINDOW BUFFER ADDRESS

Extra!

Registers at call:
AH = A4h
AL = window number (1-4=host B-E)
See also: Functions A5h and B8h

Return Registers:
DS:BX -> 3270 display buffer

INT 21h Function A5h
GET HOST WINDOW CURSOR POSITION

Extra!

Registers at call:
AH = A5h
AL = window number (1-4=host B-E)

Return Registers:
BX = cursor position (80 * row + column,
    where 0:0 is upper left)

Details: If the host window is configured with the Extended Attribute (EAB) feature, multiply the cursor position by 2 to obtain the byte offset into the display buffer.
Conflicts: Virus (PCI-59)
See also: Function A4h

INT 21h Function AFh
GET TRANSLATE TABLE ADDRESS

Extra!

Registers at call:
AH = AFh

Return Registers:
DS:BX -> translate tables (see Table 37-7)

37-7 Format of translate tables:

Offset	Size	Description
00h	256 BYTEs	ASCII to 3270 buffer code translate table
100h	256 BYTEs	3270 buffer code to ASCII translate table
200h	256 BYTEs	3270 buffer code to EBCDIC translate table
300h	256 BYTEs	EBCDIC to 3270 buffer code translate table

INT 21h Function B8h
DISABLE HOST BUFFER UPDATES

Extra!

Registers at call:
AH = B8h
AL = window number (1-4=host B-E)
DL = 01h

Return Registers:
none

Details: This function is only valid in CUT mode.
    The next AID keystroke (e.g. Enter) enables host buffer updates.
Conflicts: Novell NetWare (Chapter 21)
See also: Function A4h

HLLAPI

INT 7Fh Function 0104h *HLLAPI/LLAPI*
IBM 3270 High-Level Language API / Rabbit Low Level API
Registers at call: **Return Registers:**
AX = 0104h (HLLAPI gate ID) parameter control block updated
BX = 0000h
DS:SI -> parameter control block (see Table 37-8)
Conflicts: see Table 2-4
See also: HDILOAD Function 0105h (PCI-8)

37-8 Format of parameter control block:

Offset	Size	Description
00h	3 BYTEs	signature = 'PCB'
03h	BYTE	function number (see Table 37-9)
04h	WORD	segment of control string
06h	WORD	offset of control string
08h	WORD	length of control string, unless explicit end-of-string character set
0Ah	BYTE	unused (IBM)
		ControlString[0] (Rabbit)
0Bh	WORD	return code (see Table 37-10)
0Dh	WORD	maximum length of control string (IBM)
		unused (Rabbit)

37-9 Values for HLLAPI function number:

00h	OEM function (Query System for Attachmate Extra!)
01h	Connect presentation space
02h	Disconnect presentation space
03h	Send string of keystrokes as if typed from keyboard
04h	Wait 60s, returns status of presentation space
05h	Copy current presentation space into a user-defined buffer
06h	Search presentation space for first occurrence of a specified string
07h	Query cursor location in current presentation space
08h	Copy part or all of current presentation space into user buffer
09h	Set session parameters; parameters vary by vendor
0Ah	Get info on sessions currently connected
0Bh	Lock current presentation space
0Ch	Unlock previously locked presentation space
0Dh	Return copy of operator info area (OIA) of current presentation space
0Eh	get attribute byte for given position in the current presentation space
0Fh	copy string of characters to the current presentation space
10h	workstation control functions
11h	storage manager functions, intended primarily for BASIC applications (not implemented by Rabbit)
12h	set delay period in half-second intervals
14h	get info on level of workstation support used
15h	reset session parameters to default values
16h	get detailed info on the current session
17h	start host notification to application on presentation sp or OIA update
18h	check host update when host notification enabled

19h	stop host notification
1Eh	search field within current presentation space for string
1Fh	get first positionof a selected field in the current presentation space
20h	get length of specified field
21h	copy string into a specified field
22h	copy specified field into a user-defined buffer
23h	create alternate presentation space (IBM only), don't use with BASIC
24h	switch to alternate presentation space (IBM only), not with BASIC
25h	display cursor in specified area (IBM only), don't use with BASIC
26h	display alternate presentation space (IBM only), don't use with BASIC
27h	delete alternate presentation space (IBM only), don't use with BASIC
28h	set cursor
29h	start Close Intercept
2Ah	query Close Intercept
2Bh	stop Close Intercept
32h	start intercepting keystrokes to allow filtering
33h	get keystrokes after turning on interception
34h	notify operator when keystroke rejected by filter subroutine
35h	stop intercepting keystrokes
5Ah	send file
5Bh	receive file
5Ch	run a program (not implemented by Rabbit)
5Dh	execute DOS command (not implemented by Rabbit)
63h	change presentation space position to PC display row/col or vice versa
65h	connect to Window Services
66h	disconnect from Window Services
67h	set/query window coordinates
68h	set/query window status
69h	change presentation space name
78h	connect Structured Fields
79h	disconnect Structured Fields
7Ah	query size of communications buffer
7Bh	allocate communications buffer
7Ch	free communications buffer
7Dh	get request completion state
7Eh	read Structured Fields
7Fh	write Structured Fields
FFh	Get info on DCA implementation

37-10 Values for LLAPI function number:

80h	initialize LLAPI (internal call)
83h	set Session ID (one-character ID)
84h	read Session ID (one-character ID)
85h	lock 327x keyboard
86h	unlock 327x keyboard
87h	wait for Clear to Send
88h	type ASCII character
89h	type 327x key
8Ah	read keyboard lock state
8Fh	force screen update

INT 7Fh Function 0104h

90h	view session
91h	relinquish (suspend foreground until background becomes idle)
92h	poke screen character
93h	poke translated character
94h	peek screen character
95h	peek translated character
96h	set cursor position
97h	send scan code (Rabbit only)
98h	synchronize (returns after keystroke queue empty)
99h	type PC key (Rabbit only)

37-11 Session Parameters for function 09h:

ASCII	*unknown* (Rabbit only)
ATTRIB	return attributes in hex
NOATTRIB	return attributes as blanks
CONPHYS	make physical connection
CONLOG	only make logical connection
EAB	copy extended attribute bytes along with data
NOEAB	copy data only
ESC=n	set escape character to "n" (default '@')
EOT=n	set end of string character (default 00h)
FPAUSE	full-duration pause
FTNOWAIT	return immediately from functions 5Ah and 5Bh (Rabbit only)
FTWAIT	wait for file transfer to complete (Rabbit only)
IPAUSE	interruptible pause
RABESC	*unknown* (Rabbit only)
NORABESC	*unknown* (Rabbit only)
SCANCODE	*unknown* (Rabbit only)
STRLEN	use explicit string lengths
STREOT	use terminated strings
SRCHALL	search entire presentation space
SRCHFROM	search from specified offset
SRCHFRWD	search forward from position 1
SRCHBKWD	search backward from last position in presentation space
TIMEOUT=n	*unknown* (Rabbit only)
TWAIT	wait specified time for keyboard ready
LWAIT	wait until keyboard ready
NWAIT	no wait
TRON	enable tracing
TROFF	disable tracing
AUTORESET	send reset before sending keys with function 03h
NORESET	don't send reset
QUIET	don't display messages sent with INT 21h Function 09h
NOQUIET	allow messages to be displayed
TIMEOUT=n	set timeout in 30-second intervals, 0 = wait until ^Break
XLATE	translate extended attribute bytes
NOXLATE	don't translate
NEWRET	use HLLAPI v3.0 return code conventions
OLDRET	use HLLAPI v2.0 return code conventions

37-12 Windows HLLAPI return codes:

Code	Description
00h	successful
01h	Presentation Space not connected/requested size unavailable
02h	invalid function or parameter error/invalid block ID
03h	file transfer complete
04h	file transfer complete (segmented)/Presentation Space busy
05h	inhibited or keyboard locked
06h	data truncated
07h	invalid Presentation Space position
08h	operation not available
09h	system error
0Ah	blocking error
0Bh	resource not available
0Ch	session stopped
14h	undefined key combination
15h	OIA updated
16h	Presentation Space updated
17h	both Presentation Space and OIA updated
18h	no such field
19h	no keystrokes available
1Ah	Presentation Space or Operator Information Area changed
1Bh	file transfer aborted
1Ch	zero-length field
1Eh	cursor type invalid
1Fh	keystroke overflow
20h	another application is already connected
22h	message sent to host cancelled
23h	transmission from host cancelled
24h	lost contact with host
25h	function successful
26h	function incomplete
27h	a DDM session is already connected
28h	disconnected, but asynchronous requests still pending
29h	buffer already in use
2Ah	no matching request found
12Dh	invalid function number
12Eh	file not found
131h	access denied
134h	out of memory
136h	environment invalid
137h	format invalid
270Eh (9998)	invalid Presentation Space ID
270Fh (9999)	invalid row or column code

---Windows HLLAPI extensions---

Code	Description
F000h	asynchronous call already in progress
F001h	invalid asynchronous task ID
F002h	blocking call cancelled
F003h	underlying subsystem not started
F004h	unsupported application version

INT 7Fh Function 0104h

IBM 3270 Workstation Program

INT 7Ah Function 04h
IBM 3270 Workstation Program

CREATE A QUEUE

Registers at call:
AH = 04h
unknown

Return Registers:
unknown

Conflicts: IPX/SPX (Chapter 5), TopWare Network OS (Chapter 28), X.PC (Chapter 42), PRINDIR (PCI-15), GO32.EXE (PCI-37), AutoCAD Device Interface (PCI-66)

See also: Function 06h

INT 7Ah Function 06h
IBM 3270 Workstation Program

DELETE A QUEUE

Registers at call:
AH = 06h
unknown

Return Registers:
unknown

Conflicts: IPX/SPX (Chapter 5), TopWare Network OS (Chapter 28), X.PC (Chapter 42), PRINDIR (PCI-15), GO32.EXE (PCI-37), AutoCAD Device Interface (PCI-66)

See also: Function 04h

INT 7Ah Function 09h
IBM 3270 Workstation Program

SESSION SERVICES

Registers at call:
AH = 09h
BX = 8020h (synchronous request)
CX = 0000h
DX = ID of session manager (SESSMGR)
AL = service (see Table 37-13)
ES:DI -> control block

Return Registers:
unknown

Conflicts: IPX/SPX (Chapter 5), TopWare Network OS (Chapter 28), X.PC (Chapter 42), PRINDIR (PCI-15), GO32.EXE (PCI-37), AutoCAD Device Interface (PCI-66)

37-13 Session services:

01h	get session ID
02h	get session info
04h	dettach from session
05h	attach to session
06h	get list of windows available
07h	get environment of window
08h	get 'PIF' (program information file) info
0Ah	get base window ID
0Bh	get cursor info

INT 7Ah Function 09h
IBM 3270 Workstation Program

KEYBOARD SERVICES

Registers at call:
AH = 09h
BX = 8020h (synchronous request)
CX = 0000h
DX = ID of keyboard manager
AL = service (see Table 37-14)
ES:DI -> control block

Return Registers:
unknown

Conflicts: IPX/SPX (Chapter 5), TopWare Network OS (Chapter 28), X.PC (Chapter 42), PRINDIR (PCI-15), GO32.EXE (PCI-37), AutoCAD Device Interface (PCI-66)

37-14 Keyboard services:

01h	connect to keyboard
02h	disconnect from keyboard
03h	read from keyboard
04h	send keystroke to session
05h	disable input
06h	enable input
07h	update status code

INT 7Ah Function 09h
WINDOW SERVICES   *IBM 3270 Workstation Program*

Registers at call: **Return Registers:**
AH = 09h   *unknown*
BX = 8020h (synchronous request)
CX = 00FFh
DX = ID of window service controller (WSCTRL)
AL = service (see Table 37-15)
ES:DI -> control block

Conflicts: IPX/SPX (Chapter 5), TopWare Network OS (Chapter 28), X.PC (Chapter 42), PRINDIR (PCI-15), GO32.EXE (PCI-37), AutoCAD Device Interface (PCI-66)

37-15 Window services:

01h	connect to WS control
02h	disconnect from WS control
03h	add a window
04h	change window's position on screen
05h	change window's size
06h	change window's color
07h	change window's position in the presentation space
08h	hide/unhide toggle
09h	enlarge/reduce toggle
0Ah	change screen background color
0Bh	get window's position on screen
0Ch	get window's size
0Dh	get window's color
0Eh	get window's position in the presentation space
0Fh	determine whether hidden
10h	determine whether enlarged
11h	get background color
12h	get window names
13h	delete all windows from profile
14h	pick active window
15h	redraw screen
16h	redraw window
17h	delete a window from profile
18h	get active window
19h	get active screen
1Ah	get window data
1Bh	change window data
1Ch	select active screen

INT 7Ah Function 09h
PRESENTATION SPACE SERVICES

Registers at call:
AH = 09h
BX = 8020h
CX = 00FFh
DX = ID of PCPSM
AL = service (see Table 37-16)
ES:DI -> control block

Return Registers:
unknown

Conflicts: IPX/SPX (Chapter 5), TopWare Network OS (Chapter 28), X.PC (Chapter 42), PRINDIR (PCI-15), GO32.EXE (PCI-37), AutoCAD Device Interface (PCI-66)

37-16 Presentation Space services:

01h	define presentation space
02h	delete presentation space
03h	display presentation space
04h	position cursor in presentation space
05h	change default presentation space

INT 7Ah Function 09h
3270 EMULATION

Registers at call:
AH = 09h
BX = 8020h
CX = 00FFh
DX = ID of 3270EML
AL = service
    01h connect
    02h disconnect
ES:DI -> control block

Return Registers:
unknown

Conflicts: IPX/SPX (Chapter 5), TopWare Network OS (Chapter 28), X.PC (Chapter 42), PRINDIR (PCI-15), GO32.EXE (PCI-37), AutoCAD Device Interface (PCI-66)

INT 7Ah Function 09h
OPERATOR INFORMATION AREA

Registers at call:
AH = 09h
BX = 8020h
CX = 00FFh
DX = ID of OIAM
AL = service
    01h read Operator Information Area
    02h read OIA subset
ES:DI -> control block

Return Registers:
unknown

Details: The OIA is the 25th line on the Host session.
Conflicts: IPX/SPX (Chapter 5), TopWare Network OS (Chapter 28), X.PC (Chapter 42), PRINDIR (PCI-15), GO32.EXE (PCI-37), AutoCAD Device Interface (PCI-66)

INT 7Ah Function 09h
TRANSLATE DATA

Registers at call:
AH = 09h

BX = 8020h
CX = 00FFh
DX = ID of XLATE
AL = service

>01h translate from host characters to
>ASCII and vice versa (determined
>by control block byte 11)

ES:DI -> control block

Return Registers:
unknown

Conflicts: IPX/SPX (Chapter 5), TopWare Network OS (Chapter 28), X.PC (Chapter 42), PRINDIR (PCI-15), GO32.EXE (PCI-37), AutoCAD Device Interface (PCI-66)

INT 7Ah Function 09h
COPY SERVICE
IBM 3270 Workstation Program

Registers at call:
AH = 09h
BX = 8020h
CX = 00FFh
DX = ID of copy service
AL = service (see Table 37-17)
ES:DI -> control block

Return Registers:
unknown

Conflicts: IPX/SPX (Chapter 5), TopWare Network OS (Chapter 28), X.PC (Chapter 42), PRINDIR (PCI-15), GO32.EXE (PCI-37), AutoCAD Device Interface (PCI-66)

37-17 Copy services:

01h	copy string from one presentation space to another
02h	copy block from one presentation space to another
03h	connect to PC session for copy
04h	disconnect PC session from copy

INT 7Ah Function 09h
Multi-DOS
IBM 3270 Workstation Program

Registers at call:
AH = 09h
BX = 8020h
CX = 00FFh
ES:DI -> control block
DX = ID of INDJQRY: get environment size
DX = ID of INDJASY: request DOS functions from workstation
DX = ID of MEMORY

>AL = function

>>01h allocate memory
>>02h deallocate memory
>>03h modify allocated size

Return Registers:
unknown

Conflicts: IPX/SPX (Chapter 5), TopWare Network OS (Chapter 28), X.PC (Chapter 42), PRINDIR (PCI-15), GO32.EXE (PCI-37), AutoCAD Device Interface (PCI-66)

INT 7Ah Function 09h
HOST SERVICES
IBM 3270 Workstation Program

Registers at call:
AH = 09h
BX = request type (4000h async, 8028h synchronous)
CX = 0000h
DX = ID of MFIC

Return Registers:
none

AL = service (see Table 37-18)
ES:DI -> control block
Conflicts: IPX/SPX (Chapter 5), TopWare Network OS (Chapter 28), X.PC (Chapter 42), PRINDIR (PCI-15), GO32.EXE (PCI-37), AutoCAD Device Interface (PCI-66)

37-18 Host services:

01h	connect to host
02h	disconnect from host
03h	read DFT structured data from host
04h	write DFT structured data to host
05h	create a host buffer

INT 7Ah Function 13h
GET DATA FROM A QUEUE
IBM 3270 Workstation Program

Registers at call:
AH = 13h
others, if any, unknown

Return Registers:
unknown

Conflicts: IPX/SPX (Chapter 5), TopWare Network OS (Chapter 28), X.PC (Chapter 42), PRINDIR (PCI-15), GO32.EXE (PCI-37), AutoCAD Device Interface (PCI-66)

INT 7Ah Function 81h
RESOLVE A GATE NAME
IBM 3270 Workstation Program

Registers at call:
AH = 81h
ES:DI -> 8-char blank-padded gate name
    "SESSMGR ", "KEYBOARD", "WSCTRL ",
       "MFIC ", "PCPSM ", "3270EML ", "COPY ",
       "XLATE ", "OIAM ", "MEMORY ", "INDJQRY ",
      or "INDJASY "

Return Registers:
DX = gate ID

Conflicts: IPX/SPX (Chapter 5), TopWare Network OS (Chapter 28), X.PC (Chapter 42), PRINDIR (PCI-15), GO32.EXE (PCI-37), AutoCAD Device Interface (PCI-66)

INT 7Ah Function 83h
GET COMPLETION RESULTS
IBM 3270 Workstation Program

Registers at call:
AH = 83h
others, if any, unknown

Return Registers:
unknown

Conflicts: IPX/SPX (Chapter 5), TopWare Network OS (Chapter 28), X.PC (Chapter 42), PRINDIR (PCI-15), GO32.EXE (PCI-37), AutoCAD Device Interface (PCI-66)

IBM PC 3270 Emulation Program

INT 2Ah Function 90h
UNDETERMINED FUNCTION
IBM PC 3270 EMULATION PROGRAM
Undocumented

Registers at call:
AH = 90h
unknown

Return Registers:
unknown

Details: The LANtastic redirector and SERVER.EXE use this function with AL=01h, 03h-07h,0Ch-11h.

INT 2Fh Function B400h
INSTALLATION CHECK

Registers at call:
AX = B400h

Return Registers:
AL = FFh if installed

Conflicts: none known, but see Table 2-2

INT 2Fh Function B401h
GET HOST BUFFER ADDRESS

Registers at call:
AX = B401h

Return Registers:
ES -> host screen buffer (PC ASCII format)
ES unchanged if communications not started

Conflicts: none known, but see Table 2-2

INT 2Fh Functions B402h to B405h
UNDETERMINED FUNCTIONS

Registers at call:
AX = B402h to B405h
BX = *unknown*

Return Registers:
unknown

Conflicts: none known, but see Table 2-2

INT 7Ah Functions FE01h and FE02h
INTERNAL SEND/RECEIVE FUNCTIONS

Registers at call:
AX = FE01h and FE02h
unknown

Return Registers:
unknown

Conflicts: IPX/SPX (Chapter 5), TopWare Network OS (Chapter 28), X.PC (Chapter 42), PRINDIR (PCI-15), GO32.EXE (PCI-37), AutoCAD Device Interface (PCI-66)

INT 7Ah Function FF01h
INTERNAL API INITIALIZATION

Registers at call:
AX = FF01h
ES:DI -> API function handler routine

Return Registers:
CX = 1200h

Conflicts: IPX/SPX (Chapter 5), TopWare Network OS (Chapter 28), X.PC (Chapter 42), PRINDIR (PCI-15), GO32.EXE (PCI-37), AutoCAD Device Interface (PCI-66)
See also: Functions FF02h and FF03h

INT 7Ah Function FF02h
INTERNAL API TERMINATION

Registers at call:
AX = FF02h

Return Registers:
CX = 1200h

Conflicts: IPX/SPX (Chapter 5), TopWare Network OS (Chapter 28), X.PC (Chapter 42), PRINDIR (PCI-15), GO32.EXE (PCI-37), AutoCAD Device Interface (PCI-66)
See also: Function FF01h

INT 7Ah Function FF03h
INTERNAL API INITIALIZATION

Registers at call:
AX = FF03h
ES:DI -> send/receive function
handler routine

Return Registers:
CX = 1200h

Conflicts: IPX/SPX (Chapter 5), TopWare Network OS (Chapter 28), X.PC (Chapter 42), PRINDIR (PCI-15), GO32.EXE (PCI-37), AutoCAD Device Interface (PCI-66)
See also: Function FF01h

INT 7Ah Function FF04h   *IBM PC3270 EMUL PROG v3*
UNDETERMINED FUNCTION   *Undocumented*
Registers at call: Return Registers:
AX = FF04h   CX = 1200h
ES:DI -> *unknown*
Conflicts: IPX/SPX (Chapter 5), TopWare Network OS (Chapter 28), X.PC (Chapter 42), PRINDIR (PCI-15), GO32.EXE (PCI-37), AutoCAD Device Interface (PCI-66)

IBM System 36/38 Workstation Emulation

The IBM System 36/38 Workstation emulator makes the PC appear, to a System 36/38, to be nothing more than another workstation. While the emulator program is running, no other DOS applications can be active; for this reason, conflicts between this emulator and other programs are of relatively little importance.

INT 0Ch   *IBM SYSTEM 36/38 WORKSTATION EMULATION*
API POINTER
Details: The IBM System 36/38 emulator may be invoked through a private API, whose entry point address is offset 100h in the segment pointed at by this vector.
Conflicts: IRQ4 (PCI-3), Stack Fault (PCI-3)

37-19 API entry point calling convention:
Registers at call: Return Registers:
AH = function
    03h update screen   *unknown*

    05h select next session   AL = session type code
        AL = session number (00h-03h)   00h not active
                          01h display session
                          02h printer session
                          FEh invalid session number
                DS = requested session's data segment (0 if not active)

37-20 Format of emulator's data area (offset from interrupt handler's segment):

Offset	Size	Description
13Eh	BYTE	bit flags for status line indicators turned on since this byte last zerod
13Fh	BYTE	bit flags for status line indicators turned off since this byte last set to FFh
140h	WORD	offset of EBCDIC to ASCII translation
146h	WORD	offset of EBCDIC screen buffer
148h	WORD	offset of EC (engineering change) level signature
150h	BYTE	"KEYI"
151h	BYTE	5250 key scan code to be sent to remote
15Bh	BYTE	"SYSAV"
15Dh	BYTE	5250 cursor column
15Eh	BYTE	5250 cursor row
167h	BYTE	"DVCTAD"
178h	BYTE	"FLAGS"
184h	BYTE	"SESSNOAD"
193h	BYTE	"STNAD"
198h	BYTE	"NSDS"

INT 21h Function 4402h
VDI.SYS - GET UNKNOWN DATA
IBM SYSTEM 36/38 WORKSTATION EMULATION
Undocumented

Registers at call:
AX = 4402h
BX = handle for character device "GDMS"
CX = number of bytes to read (>= 4)
DS:DX -> buffer for data (see Table 37-21)

Return Registers:
CF set on error
AX = error code (see Table 3-1)
CF clear if successful
AX = number of bytes read

37-21 Format of returned data:

Offset	Size	Description
00h	4 BYTEs	*unknown*
04h	DWORD	pointer to *unknown item*
08h	4 BYTEs	*unknown*

Novell PCOX 3270 PC Terminal Interface

INT 6Fh Function 0000h
ENTER TERMINAL MODE
Novell NetWare PCOX

Registers at call:
AX = 0000h

Return Registers:
AX = status
0000h no action requested
0001h screen save

Conflicts: 10NET (Chapter 27), HP HIL Vectras (PCI-7), MS Windows (PCI-43)

INT 6Fh Function 0001h
RESET INTERFACE AND SET CONFIGURATION PARAMETERS
Novell NetWare PCOX

Registers at call:
AX = 0001h
DX = bitfields
    bits 2-0: model number
    bits 4-3: I/O address
    bits 6-5: DMA channel

Return Registers:
none

Conflicts: 10NET (Chapter 27), HP HIL Vectras (PCI-7), MS Windows (PCI-43)

INT 6Fh Function 0002h
SET DISPLAY PARAMETERS
Novell NetWare PCOX

Registers at call:
AX = 0002h
DX = bitfields
    bits 1-0: OIA mode
    bits 4-2: monitor support

Return Registers:
none

Conflicts: 10NET (Chapter 27), HP HIL Vectras (PCI-7), MS Windows (PCI-43)

INT 6Fh Function 0003h
READ STATUS
Novell NetWare PCOX

Registers at call:
AX = 0003h

Return Registers:
AX = status word (see Table 37-22)

Conflicts: 10NET (Chapter 27), HP HIL Vectras (PCI-7), MS Windows (PCI-43)

INT 6Fh Function 0004h
READ CURSOR POSITION
Novell NetWare PCOX

Registers at call:
AX = 0004h

Return Registers:
AX = cursor position

Conflicts: 10NET (Chapter 27), HP HIL Vectras (PCI-7), MS Windows (PCI-43)

INT 6Fh Function 0005h
Novell NetWare PCOX
GET CHARACTER FROM DEVICE BUFFER
Registers at call: | **Return Registers:**
AX = 0005h
AH = type (00h data, 01h attribute)
DX = new cursor position
AL = data or attribute character
Conflicts: 10NET (Chapter 27), HP HIL Vectras (PCI-7), MS Windows (PCI-43)

INT 6Fh Function 0006h
Novell NetWare PCOX
SEND CHARACTER
Registers at call: | **Return Registers:**
AX = 0006h
none
DH = type (00h ASCII, 01h extended code)
DL = ASCII character or extended code
Conflicts: 10NET (Chapter 27), HP HIL Vectras (PCI-7), MS Windows (PCI-43)

INT 6Fh Function 0007h
Novell NetWare PCOX
SET TIMEOUT
Registers at call: | **Return Registers:**
AX = 0007h
none
DX = timeout in seconds
Conflicts: 10NET (Chapter 27), HP HIL Vectras (PCI-7), MS Windows (PCI-43)

INT 6Fh Function 0008h
Novell NetWare PCOX
WAIT FOR LOCATION TO BE MODIFIED
Registers at call: | **Return Registers:**
AX = 0008h
AX = status (0000h modified, nonzero timeout)
DX = cursor position
Conflicts: 10NET (Chapter 27), HP HIL Vectras (PCI-7), MS Windows (PCI-43)

INT 6Fh Function 0009h
Novell NetWare PCOX
NOP
Registers at call: | **Return Registers:**
AX = 0009h
none
Conflicts: 10NET (Chapter 27), HP HIL Vectras (PCI-7), MS Windows (PCI-43)

INT 6Fh Function 000Ah
Novell NetWare PCOX
RESTORE DISPLAY
Registers at call: | **Return Registers:**
AX = 000Ah
none
Conflicts: 10NET (Chapter 27), HP HIL Vectras (PCI-7), MS Windows (PCI-43)

INT 6Fh Function 000Bh
Novell NetWare PCOX
UPDATE DEVICE BUFFER
Registers at call: | **Return Registers:**
AX = 000Bh
AX = cursor positoin
Conflicts: 10NET (Chapter 27), HP HIL Vectras (PCI-7), MS Windows (PCI-43)

INT 6Fh Function 000Ch
Novell NetWare PCOX
WRITE STRING TO ADD INFORMATION AREA
Registers at call: | **Return Registers:**
AX = 000Ch
none
DS:DX -> string
Conflicts: 10NET (Chapter 27), HP HIL Vectras (PCI-7), MS Windows (PCI-43)

INT 6Fh Function 000Dh
MAINTENANCE OPERATIONS
Novell NetWare PCOX

Registers at call:　　　　　　　　**Return Registers:**
AX = 000Dh　　　　　　　　　　　AX = operation status
DX = maintenance operation code
Conflicts: 10NET (Chapter 27), HP HIL Vectras (PCI-7), MS Windows (PCI-43)

INT 6Fh Function 000Eh
GET CONTROL PROGRAM VERSION
Novell NetWare PCOX

Registers at call:　　　　　　　　**Return Registers:**
AX = 000Eh　　　　　　　　　　　AH = release number (major version)
　　　　　　　　　　　　　　　　AL = level number (minor version)
Conflicts: 10NET (Chapter 27), HP HIL Vectras (PCI-7), MS Windows (PCI-43)
See also: Function 000Fh

INT 6Fh Function 000Fh
GET MICROCODE VERSION
Novell NetWare PCOX

Registers at call:　　　　　　　　**Return Registers:**
AX = 000Fh　　　　　　　　　　　AH = release number (major version)
　　　　　　　　　　　　　　　　AL = level number (minor version)
Conflicts: 10NET (Chapter 27), HP HIL Vectras (PCI-7), MS Windows (PCI-43)
See also: Function 000Eh

INT 6Fh Function 0010h
SAVE OR DISPLAY GRAPHICS
Novell NetWare PCOX

Registers at call:　　　　　　　　**Return Registers:**
AX = 0010h　　　　　　　　　　　AX = return code
BX = length of data buffer　　　　　CX = length of PIF data
CX = subfunction request code
DS:DX -> data buffer
Conflicts: 10NET (Chapter 27), HP HIL Vectras (PCI-7), MS Windows (PCI-43)

INT 6Fh Function 0011h
PERFORM STRUCTURED FIELD OPERATION
Novell NetWare PCOX

Registers at call:　　　　　　　　**Return Registers:**
AX = 0011h　　　　　　　　　　　AX = status word (see Table 37-22)
CX = request number　　　　　　　CX = error number
DS:DX -> parameter list
Conflicts: 10NET (Chapter 27), HP HIL Vectras (PCI-7), MS Windows (PCI-43)

INT 6Fh Function 0012h
SET CURSOR POSITION FOR DIRECT WRITE BUFFER
Novell NetWare PCOX

Registers at call:　　　　　　　　**Return Registers:**
AX = 0012h　　　　　　　　　　　AX = status word (see Table 37-22)
DX = new cursor position
Conflicts: 10NET (Chapter 27), HP HIL Vectras (PCI-7), MS Windows (PCI-43)

INT 6Fh Function 0013h
WRITE DIRECT TO BUFFER
Novell NetWare PCOX

Registers at call:　　　　　　　　**Return Registers:**
AX = 0013h　　　　　　　　　　　AX = status word (see Table 37-22)
DL = character to be written
DH = translation option

Conflicts: 10NET (Chapter 27), HP HIL Vectras (PCI-7), MS Windows (PCI-43)
See also: Functions 0014h, 0015h, 0016h, and 0017h

INT 6Fh Function 0014h   *Novell NetWare PCOX*
WRITE DIRECT TO BUFFER WITHOUT ECHO

Registers at call: **Return Registers:**
AX = 0014h   AX = status word (see Table 37-22)
DL = character to be written
DH = translation option
Conflicts: 10NET (Chapter 27), HP HIL Vectras (PCI-7), MS Windows (PCI-43)
See also: Functions 0013h, 0015h, 0016h, and 0017h

INT 6Fh Function 0015h   *Novell NetWare PCOX*
SET DIRECT WRITE STRING LENGTH

Registers at call: **Return Registers:**
AX = 0015h   none
DX = string value
Conflicts: 10NET (Chapter 27), HP HIL Vectras (PCI-7), MS Windows (PCI-43)
See also: Functions 0013h, 0014h, 0016h, and 0017h

INT 6Fh Function 0016h   *Novell NetWare PCOX*
WRITE STRING DIRECT TO BUFFER

Registers at call: **Return Registers:**
AX = 0016h   AX = status word (see Table 37-22)
DS:DX -> string
Conflicts: 10NET (Chapter 27), HP HIL Vectras (PCI-7), MS Windows (PCI-43)
See also: Functions 0013h, 0014h, 0015h, and 0017h

INT 6Fh Function 0017h   *Novell NetWare PCOX*
WRITE STRING DIRECT TO BUFFER, UNTRANSLATED

Registers at call: **Return Registers:**
AX = 0017h   AX = status word (see Table 37-22)
DS:DX -> string
Conflicts: 10NET (Chapter 27), HP HIL Vectras (PCI-7), MS Windows (PCI-43)
See also: Functions 0013h, 0014h, and 0016h

INT 6Fh Function 0018h   *Novell NetWare PCOX*
GET DIRECT-WRITE CURSOR POSITION

Registers at call: **Return Registers:**
AX = 0018h   AX = cursor position
Conflicts: 10NET (Chapter 27), HP HIL Vectras (PCI-7), MS Windows (PCI-43)
See also: Functions 0019h and 001Ah

INT 6Fh Function 0019h   *Novell NetWare PCOX*
CONVERT ROW/COLUMN TO CURSOR POSITION

Registers at call: **Return Registers:**
AX = 0019h   AX = cursor position
DH = display row (1-43)
DL = display column (1-132)
Conflicts: 10NET (Chapter 27), HP HIL Vectras (PCI-7), MS Windows (PCI-43)
See also: Functions 0018h and 001Ah

INT 6Fh Function 001Ah
CONVERT CURSOR POSITION TO ROW/COLUMN
Novell NetWare PCOX

Registers at call:
AX = 001Ah
DX = cursor position
Conflicts: 10NET (Chapter 27), HP HIL Vectras (PCI-7), MS Windows (PCI-43)
See also: Functions 0018h and 0019h

Return Registers:
AH = display row
AL = display column

INT 6Fh Function 001Bh
FIND NEXT FIELD
Novell NetWare PCOX

Registers at call:
AX = 001Bh
DX = initial cursor position
Conflicts: 10NET (Chapter 27), HP HIL Vectras (PCI-7), MS Windows (PCI-43)
See also: Functions 001Ch, 001Dh, and 001Fh

Return Registers:
AX = field cursor position

INT 6Fh Function 001Ch
FIND PREVIOUS FIELD
Novell NetWare PCOX

Registers at call:
AX = 001Ch
DX = initial cursor position
Conflicts: 10NET (Chapter 27), HP HIL Vectras (PCI-7), MS Windows (PCI-43)
See also: Functions 001Bh, 001Eh, and 0020h

Return Registers:
AX = field cursor position

INT 6Fh Function 001Dh
FIND NEXT UNPROTECTED FIELD
Novell NetWare PCOX

Registers at call:
AX = 001Dh
DX = initial cursor position
Conflicts: 10NET (Chapter 27), HP HIL Vectras (PCI-7), MS Windows (PCI-43)
See also: Functions 001Bh, 001Eh, and 001Fh

Return Registers:
AX = field cursor position

INT 6Fh Function 001Eh
FIND PREVIOUS UNPROTECTED FIELD
Novell NetWare PCOX

Registers at call:
AX = 001Eh
DX = initial cursor position
Conflicts: 10NET (Chapter 27), HP HIL Vectras (PCI-7), MS Windows (PCI-43)
See also: Functions 001Ch, 001Dh, and 0020h

Return Registers:
AX = field cursor position

INT 6Fh Function 001Fh
FIND NEXT PROTECTED FIELD
Novell NetWare PCOX

Registers at call:
AX = 001Fh
DX = initial cursor position
Conflicts: 10NET (Chapter 27), HP HIL Vectras (PCI-7), MS Windows (PCI-43)
See also: Functions 001Bh, 001Dh, and 0020h

Return Registers:
AX = field cursor position

INT 6Fh Function 0020h
FIND PREVIOUS PROTECTED FIELD
Novell NetWare PCOX

Registers at call:
AX = 0020h
DX = initial cursor position

Return Registers:
AX = field cursor position

Conflicts: 10NET (Chapter 27), HP HIL Vectras (PCI-7), MS Windows (PCI-43)
See also: Functions 001Ch, 001Eh, and 001Fh

INT 6Fh Function 0021h
Novell NetWare PCOX
MASKED SEARCH FORWARD

Registers at call:
AX = 0021h
DH = mask
DL = search pattern

Return Registers:
AX = cursor position or 0000h

Conflicts: 10NET (Chapter 27), HP HIL Vectras (PCI-7), MS Windows (PCI-43)
See also: Functions 001Bh and 0022h

INT 6Fh Function 0022h
Novell NetWare PCOX
MASKED SEARCH BACKWARD

Registers at call:
AX = 0022h
DH = mask
DL = search pattern

Return Registers:
AX = cursor position or 0FFFh

Conflicts: 10NET (Chapter 27), HP HIL Vectras (PCI-7), MS Windows (PCI-43)
See also: Functions 001Ch and 0021h

INT 6Fh Function 0023h
Novell NetWare PCOX
FIND FIELD LENGTH

Registers at call:
AX = 0023h
DX = cursor position

Return Registers:
AX = field length

Conflicts: 10NET (Chapter 27), HP HIL Vectras (PCI-7), MS Windows (PCI-43)
See also: Functions 001Bh, 0021h, and 0024h

INT 6Fh Function 0024h
Novell NetWare PCOX
READ FIELD

Registers at call:
AX = 0024h
DS:DX -> buffer for field contents

Return Registers:
AX = status word (see Table 37-22)

Conflicts: 10NET (Chapter 27), HP HIL Vectras (PCI-7), MS Windows (PCI-43)
See also: Functions 001Bh, 0021h, 0023h, 0025h, and 0026h

INT 6Fh Function 0025h
Novell NetWare PCOX
READ SCREEN

Registers at call:
AX = 0025h
DS:DX -> buffer for screen contents

Return Registers:
AX = status word (see Table 37-22)

Conflicts: 10NET (Chapter 27), HP HIL Vectras (PCI-7), MS Windows (PCI-43)
See also: Functions 0024h, 0026h, and 002Ah

INT 6Fh Function 0026h
Novell NetWare PCOX
READ BUFFER UNTRANSLATED

Registers at call:
AX = 0026h
DX = cursor position

Return Registers:
AX = buffer code
CX:BX -> 3278/79 device buffer image

Conflicts: 10NET (Chapter 27), HP HIL Vectras (PCI-7), MS Windows (PCI-43)
See also: Functions 0024h, 0025h, and 002Ah

INT 6Fh Function 0027h
ENABLE/DISABLE KEYBOARD
Novell NetWare PCOX

Registers at call:
AX = 0027h
DL = new state of keyboard breaks
  (00h enabled, 01h disabled)

Return Registers:
none

Conflicts: 10NET (Chapter 27), HP HIL Vectras (PCI-7), MS Windows (PCI-43)

INT 6Fh Function 0028h
SELECT HOST SESSION
Novell NetWare PCOX

Registers at call:
AX = 0028h
DL = session short name

Return Registers:
AX = session information

Conflicts: 10NET (Chapter 27), HP HIL Vectras (PCI-7), MS Windows (PCI-43)
See also: Function 0029h

INT 6Fh Function 0029h
RETRIEVE HOST SESSION NAME
Novell NetWare PCOX

Registers at call:
AX = 0029h
AX = short name (DFT) or 0000h
  (not available, CUT mode)

Return Registers:
none

Conflicts: 10NET (Chapter 27), HP HIL Vectras (PCI-7), MS Windows (PCI-43)
See also: Function 0028h

INT 6Fh Function 002Ah
GET CURRENT DEVICE BUFFER SIZE
Novell NetWare PCOX

Registers at call:
AX = 002Ah

Return Registers:
AX = device buffer size
CX = segment of EAB

Conflicts: 10NET (Chapter 27), HP HIL Vectras (PCI-7), MS Windows (PCI-43)
See also: Functions 0025h and 0026h

INT 6Fh Function 002Bh
ARM MODIFIED LOCATION TRIGGER
Novell NetWare PCOX

Registers at call:
AX = 002Bh
DX = cursor position

Return Registers:
AX = status (0000h not available, 0001h successful)

Conflicts: 10NET (Chapter 27), HP HIL Vectras (PCI-7), MS Windows (PCI-43)

37-22 Bitfields for status word:
bits 0,1	cursor type
bit 2	cursor inhibited
bit 3	display inhibited
bit 4	feature step inhibited
bit 5	480-character format code
bits 6,7	unused
bits 8-10	model number (2-5)
bit 11	unit has been reset by controller (bit cleared after status returned)
bit 12	buffer has been written into (bit cleared after status returned)
bit 13	alarm has been sounded (bit cleared after status returned)
bits 14-15	monitor type (01 mono, 10 color, 11 hybrid)

Sangoma X.25 and CCPOP 3270

INT 61h   *Sangoma CCIP (CCPOP 3270 resident module)*
INTERFACE
Registers at call: **Return Registers:**
BX:DX -> control block   none
Conflicts: see Table 2-3
See also: Sangoma INT 67h

INT 67h   *Sangoma CCPOP 3270 resident module*
UNDETERMINED USE
Conflicts: EMS (PCI-38); see also Table 2-3
See also: INT 61h, INT 68h

INT 68h   *Sangoma CCPOP 3270 resident module*
UNDETERMINED USE
Conflicts: APPC/PC (Chapter 13)
See also: Sangoma INT 67h, Sangoma INT 92h

INT 92h   *Sangoma X.25 INTERFACE PROGRAM*
API
Registers at call: **Return Registers:**
BX:DX -> control block   none
Conflicts: DaVinci eMail Dispatcher (Chapter 40), IBM ROM BASIC (PCI-54)
See also: Sangoma INT 68h

Miscellaneous

INT 50h to INT 57h   *IBM 3278 emulation control program*
RELOCATED IRQ0 THROUGH IRQ7
Conflicts: WEB (Chapter 29), TIL Expert AIM (Chapter 42), OS/2 v1.x (PCI-26), DESQview
(PCI-44), Vanderaart Text Windows (PCI-66)
See also: IBM 3278 INT 51h

INT 60h   *Tangram Arbiter*
API
Details: Arbiter may use any interrupt from 60h to 66h (parameterized).
    Identified by string "@ARB_API" immediately following a short jump at the interrupt handler
address.
    Arbiter makes a PC disk look like a slow disk over an SNA link to an IBM mainframe.
Conflicts: see Table 2-3

INT 7Ah Function FDCBh   *IBM Personal Communications/3270*
INSTALLATION CHECK
Registers at call: **Return Registers:**
AX = FDCBh   DX:AX -> PCS/3270 signature block if loaded (see
                                                Table 37-23)
Conflicts: IPX/SPX (Chapter 5), TopWare Network OS (Chapter 28), X.PC (Chapter 42),
PRINDIR (PCI-15), GO32.EXE (PCI-37), AutoCAD Device Interface (PCI-66)

37-23 Format of signature block:

Offset	Size	Description
04h	WORD	PCS/3270 signature (5741h)
06h	WORD	version (0501h = PCS/3270 v1.0)

INT 7Bh
API   *Eicon Access (3270/5250 gateways)*

Conflicts: GO32 (PCI-37), Btrieve (PCI-54), AutoCAD Device Interface (PCI-66)
See also: NetBIOS INT 5Ch (Chapter 8)

CHAPTER 38

Network Serial I/O Emulation

In order to extend connectivity past the edges of the local network, many systems include capabilities for serial communications to the outside world.

This chapter describes the API's for a number of such programs, including ArtiCom, an asynchronous communications driver by Artisoft; Beame and Whiteside's BWCOM14; Connection Manager by Softwarehouse Corp.; TES, a network serial port emulation program by Interconnections, Inc.; Novell's NetWare Asynchronous Services Interface (NASI) and NetWare Asynchronous Communications Services module (NACS); Ungermann-Bass Net One which uses the NASI API; NPC NCSI, a superset of the NASI calls, and finally Telebit's ACS Serial I/O package.

ArtiCom

ArtiCom is an asynchronous communications driver by Artisoft which works on top of NetBIOS and allows modem/serial-port sharing by programs using INT 14h for serial I/O.

INT 14h Function 8000h *ArtiCom*
INSTALLATION CHECK

Registers at call:
AX = 8000h

Return Registers:
AL = FFh if installed
    BH = major version
    BL = minor version

Details: ArtiCom supports 32 simultaneous COM ports using multiport cards and drivers.
Conflicts: Communication FOSSIL (PCI-12), COURIERS.COM (PCI-12)
See also: Functions 8001h and 8002h, Serial Functions 00h to 05h (PCI-12)

INT 14h Function 8001h *ArtiCom*
UNLOAD ASYNCHRONOUS REDIRECTOR FROM MEMORY

Registers at call:
AX = 8001h

Return Registers:
AX = error code, if error (see Table 38-2)

Conflicts: Communication FOSSIL (PCI-12), COURIERS.COM (PCI-12)
See also: Functions 8000h, 8002h, and 8003h

INT 14h Function 8002h *ArtiCom*
GET ASYNCHRONOUS REDIRECTOR STATUS

Registers at call:
AX = 8002h
ES:DI -> buffer for redirector status
  structure (see Table 38-1)

Return Registers:
AX = error code, if error (see Table 38-2)

Conflicts: Communication FOSSIL (PCI-12), COURIERS.COM (PCI-12)
See also: Functions 8000h and 8003h

38-1 Format of redirector status:

Offset	Size	Description
00h	WORD	redirector major and minor version numbers
02h	WORD	redirectable ports found
04h	WORD	redirectable ports + local ports found
06h	WORD	redirector internal buffer size
08h	WORD	maximum servers maintained
0Ah	WORD	number of adapters found

INT 14h Function 8003h
TRANSLATE ERROR CODE TO ERROR STRING   *ArtiCom*

Registers at call: **Return Registers:**
AX = 8003h   ES:DI -> ASCIZ error text or NULL if unable to translate
CX = error number to translate

Conflicts: Communication FOSSIL (PCI-12), COURIERS.COM (PCI-12)
See also: Function 8000h

38-2 Values for error codes:

00h	"No error"
01h	"An invalid port number was specified"
02h	"Port is already redirected"
03h	"Too many ports redirected"
04h	"Cannot locate the server"
05h	"Server is busy"
06h	"Access denied"
07h	"Resource in use"
08h	"Resource in use - request queued"
09h	"No such resource"
0Ah	"Invalid username/password pair"
0Bh	"Noncompatible version number"
0Ch	"Can't remove from memory"
0Dh	"Bad NETBIOS adapter number"
0Eh	"No more entries in list"
0Fh	"Resource is not available at this time"
10h	"Invalid value to INT 14h call"

INT 14h Function 8004h
ATTACH ASYNCHRONOUS RESOURCE   *ArtiCom*

Registers at call:
AX = 8004h   **Return Registers:**
DX = port to redirect (COM1=0, COM2=1, ...)   AX = error code, if error (see Table 38-2)
CH = attach type
CL = adapter to use for attach, 0FFh to search all
ES:DI -> attachment structure (see Tbale 38-3)

Details: The wildcard '*' is supported in the server and resource fields. If wild cards are used then the first matching available server is attached.
Conflicts: Communication FOSSIL (PCI-12), COURIERS.COM (PCI-12)
See also: Functions 8000h, 8003h, and 8005h

38-3 Format of attachment structure:

Offset	Size	Description
00h	16 BYTEs	server to look for attach

10h	16 BYTEs	attach to resource name
20h	16 BYTEs	username for attach
30h	16 BYTEs	password for username or resource
40h	BYTE	attach type
		00h normal
		01h queue if resource is in use (not yet supported in v1.00)

INT 14h Function 8005h
DETACH ASYNCHRONOUS RESOURCE

Registers at call:
AX = 8005h
DX = port to detach (COM1=0, COM2=1, ...)

Return Registers:
AX = error code, if error (see Table 38-2)

Details: Only a previously attached resource can be detached.
Conflicts: Communication FOSSIL (PCI-12), COURIERS.COM (PCI-12)
See also: Functions 8000h, 8003h, and 8004h

INT 14h Function 8006h
GET RESOURCE INFORMATION

Registers at call:
AX = 8006h
BX = remote port (COM1=0, COM2=1, ...)
CL = adapter number, FFh to try all adapters
ES:DI -> resource information structure
  (see Table 38-4)
DS:SI -> 16 byte server name (see note)

Return Registers:
AX = error code, if error (see Table 38-2)
BX = next remote port, recall to get next resource info

Details: Wild cards are supported in both the resource field and server name string DS:SI. If wild cards used then first matching available resource information is searched. Set the resource field to FFh to return all resources.
Conflicts: Communication FOSSIL (PCI-12), COURIERS.COM (PCI-12)
See also: Functions 8000h, 8002h, 8003h, and 8007h

38-4 Format of resource information structure:

Offset	Size	Description
00h	BYTE	00h = free, else used
01h	16 BYTEs	resource name
11h	16 BYTEs	username of resource user
21h	WORD	amount of time used
23h	WORD	amount of time remaining
53h	48 BYTEs	description of resource
93h	64 BYTEs	initialization string for modem
B3h	32 BYTEs	dial string for modem
D3h	32 BYTEs	hang-up string for modem

INT 14h Function 8007h
GET REDIRECTED PORT INFORMATION

Registers at call:
AX = 8007h
DX = port index (COM1=0, COM2=1, ...)
ES:DI -> buffer for port information structure
  (see Table 38-5)

Return Registers:
CF clear if redirection info returned and port is redirected
CF set if not a redirected port
AX = error code, if error (see Table 38-2)

Conflicts: Communication FOSSIL (PCI-12), COURIERS.COM (PCI-12)
See also: Functions 8000h, 8003h, 8006h, and 8008h

38-5 Format of port information structure:

Offset	Size	Description
00h	16 BYTEs	server name resource is on
10h	BYTE	adapter number server is on
11h	16 BYTEs	resource name
21h	WORD	remote port index, use to get additional information
23h	WORD	buffer size
25h	WORD	baud rate (see Table 38-6)
26h	BYTE	modem status register
27h	BYTE	modem control register
28h	BYTE	line status register
29h	BYTE	line control register
2Ah	BYTE	flow control in use: 0 - NONE, 1 - XON/XOFF, 2 - RTS/CTS
2Bh	WORD	send timeout in ticks
2Dh	WORD	receive timeout in ticks
2Fh	WORD	time used on remote port
31h	WORD	time left before timeout
33h	BYTE	server changes allowed?
34h	WORD	FFFFh (-1) if connection ok, else old port index

38-6 Values for baud rate:

00h	110
01h	150
02h	300
03h	600
04h	1200
05h	2400
06h	4800
07h	9600
08h	19200
09h	38400
0Ah	57600
0Bh	115200
0Ch	134.5
0Dh	1800
0Eh	2000
0Fh	3600
10h	7200

INT 14h Function 8008h
GET AVAILABLE SERVER NAME

ArtiCom

Registers at call:
AX = 8008h
BX = server index (0,1,...)
ES:DI -> server name structure (see Table 38-7)

Return Registers:
AX = error code, if error (see Table 38-2)
BX = next remote port, repeat call to get next available server

Details: The wildcard '*' is supported in the server name field. Set the server name to FFh to search for all servers.
Conflicts: Communication FOSSIL (PCI-12), COURIERS.COM (PCI-12)
See also: Functions 8000h, 8003h, and 8007h

38-7 Format of server name structure:

Offset	Size	Description
00h	16 BYTEs	(call) ASCIZ server name
10h	BYTE	(return) the adapter server is found

ArtiCom

INT 14h Function 8009h
SET SEND AND RECEIVE TIMEOUTS

Registers at call:
AX = 8009h
BX = send timeout in ticks
CX = receive timeout in ticks
DX = port index (COM1=0, COM2=1, ...)
Conflicts: Communication FOSSIL (PCI-12), COURIERS.COM (PCI-12)
See also: Functions 8000h and 800Ah

Return Registers:
none

ArtiCom

INT 14h Function 800Ah
MODIFY FLOW CONTROL

Registers at call:
AX = 800Ah
BL = flow control type (00h none, 01h
   XON/XOFF, 02h RTS/CTS)
DX = port index (COM1=0, COM2=1, ...)
Details: This function may be used on attached ports only.
Conflicts: Communication FOSSIL (PCI-12), COURIERS.COM (PCI-12)
See also: Functions 8000h, 8003h, and 8009h

Return Registers:
AX = error code, if error (see Table 38-2)

ArtiCom

INT 14h Function 8025h
SET INTERNAL SEND/RECEIVE VECTOR

Registers at call:
AX = 8025h
DS:DX -> address of trap function (see
   Table 38-8) to call on read/write
Details: Setting the vector to a user function allows the redirector's activity to be monitored.
Conflicts: Communication FOSSIL (PCI-12), COURIERS.COM (PCI-12)
See also: Functions 8000h and 8035h, MS-DOS INT 21h Function 25h (PCI-24)

Return Registers:
none

38-8 Trap function calling convention:

Registers at call:
AH = operation
    80h reading character
    81h writing character
AL = character

Return Registers:
AX must be preserved
far JUMP to old trap function (see Function 8035h)

ArtiCom

INT 14h Function 8035h
GET INTERNAL SEND/RECEIVE VECTOR

Registers at call:
AX = 8035h

Return Registers:
ES:BX -> address of current send/receive routine
Details: This function returns the address of the routine which is called inside A-REDIR.EXE
each time a character is received or sent on the active COM port.
Conflicts: Communication FOSSIL (PCI-12), COURIERS.COM (PCI-12)
See also: Functions 8000h and 8025h, MS-DOS INT 21h Function 35h (PCI-24)

Beame and Whiteside BWCOM14

BWCOM14 is a network serial port emulator (simulating a Hayes modem connected to the serial port) distributed as part of the Beame and Whiteside BW-NFS package.

INT 14h Function 56h
INSTALLATION CHECK

BWCOM14
Undocumented

Registers at call:
AH = 56h
See also: Functions 57h and 58h

Return Registers:
CX = 0001h if installed

INT 14h Function 57h
INITIALIZE

BWCOM14
Undocumented

Registers at call:
AH = 57h
DL = port number

Return Registers:
AL = initialization status (00h successful, 01h already initialized)
CX = port status (0001h port redirected, 0002h and FFFFh failed)

Details: After this call, all invocations of INT 14h Function 00h-03h for the specified port will be handled by BWCOM14 until Function 58h is called.
See also: Functions 56h and 58h, BIOS Function 00h (PCI-12)

INT 14h Function 58h
SHUTDOWN

BWCOM14
Undocumented

Registers at call:
AH = 58h

Return Registers:
CX = status (0001h successful, 0002h not initialized)

Details: After this call, BWCOM14 will no longer redirect the COM port.
See also: Functions 56h and 57h

Connection Manager

Connection Manager by Softwarehouse Corp. permits the sharing of serial ports over an IPX or NetBIOS-based network.

For functions 00h to 05h, if DX is 0 through 3 on entry, Connection Manager emulates the standard BIOS function (see PCI-12), but redirects the port over the network; if DX is FFFFh, the call is part of the Connection Manager extended API described here; and if DX is any other value, the call is chained to the previous handler.

38-9 Values for return code:

00h	successful
01h	no such connection
02h	invalid connection ID
03h	invalid subvector found
04h	communication error (check BH)
06h	insufficient resources, retry later
FFh	no data available

INT 14h Function 00h
MODIFY DEFAULT CONNECTION PARAMETERS

Connection Manager

Registers at call:
AH = 00h
DX = FFFFh
ES:DI -> vector string specifying new parameters
See also: Functions 04h, 08h, and 0Ah; BIOS Function 00h (PCI-12)

Return Registers:
AH = return code (00h,03h) (see Table 38-9)

INT 14h Function 01h
SEND CHARACTER
Connection Manager

Registers at call:
AH = 01h
DX = FFFFh
BH = character to send

Return Registers:
AH = return code (00h-02h,06h) (see Table 38-9)

Details: This function is provided primarily for compatibility; Function 06h is the preferred function because it provides better performance.
See also: Functions 02h, 06h, and 09h; BIOS Function 01h (PCI-12)

INT 14h Function 02h
RECEIVE CHARACTER
Connection Manager

Registers at call:
AH = 02h
DX = FFFFh

Return Registers:
AH = return code (00h-02h,04h,FFh)
 (see Table 38-9)
BH = line status
AL = received character (if any)

Details: This function is provided primarily for compatibility; Function 07h is the preferred function because it provides better performance.
See also: Functions 02h, 03h, and 06h; BIOS Function 02h (PCI-12)

INT 14h Function 03h
RETURN COMMUNICATION PORT STATUS
Connection Manager

Registers at call:
AH = 03h
DX = FFFFh
AL = connection ID

Return Registers:
AH = return code (00h-02h) (see Table 38-9)
BH = line status (see Table 38-10)
BL = modem status (all other bits clear)
 bit 7 carrier detect
 bit 5 data set ready
 bit 4 clear to send

See also: Functions 00h, 04h, and 0Ah; BIOS Function 03h (PCI-12)

38-10 Bitfields for line status:
bit 7	CTS changed
bit 6	current CTS state
bit 5	timeout
bit 4	break
bit 3	framing error
bit 2	parity error
bit 1	overrun
bit 0	current carrier state (0 active, 1 no carrier)

INT 14h Function 04h
OPEN COMMUNICATION
Connection Manager

Purpose: Initiate a connection to the Connection Server listed in the current Client parameter set.

Registers at call:
AH = 04h
DX = FFFFh
ES:DI -> Connection Request
 protocol vector (see Table 38-11)

Return Registers:
AH = return code
 00h successful
  AL = connection ID
  BH = connection type
   00h direct connection or no dialing
   01h Connection Server dialed phone

01h no response from Connection Server
03h invalid request

Details: All subvectors of the Connection Request vector are optional; if missing, default values are provided by the default connection parameter set.

Conflicts: BIOS Function 04h (PCI-12), MBBIOS (PCI-12), TSRCOMM (PCI-12), MultiDOS Plus (PCI-45)

See also: Functions 00h, 05h, 06h, 07h, 0Ah, and 0Ch

38-11 Format of protocol command vector:

Offset	Size	Description
00h	WORD	(big-endian) total length of command (including this word)
02h	WORD	(big-endian) command code
		EF01h Connection Request
		EF06h Modify Connection Parameters
04h	N BYTEs	list of subvectors (see Table 38-12)
		allowable subvector types are 01h-04h,17h,18h for command code
		EF01h; 03h,04h for command code EF06h

38-12 Values for subvector type code:

01h	Connection ID
02h	Destination ID
03h	Asynchronous line parameters
04h	Data transfer parameters
09h	Line speed
0Ah	Serial coding
0Bh	Packet size
0Ch	Timers
0Dh	Special characters
0Eh	Target ID
0Fh	Telephone number
10h	ASCII destination ID
11h	Parity
12h	Bits per character
13h	Number of stop bits
14h	Packet timer
15h	Intercharacter timer
17h	Flags
18h	Parameter ranges
19h	Flow control

38-13 Format of subvector:

Offset	Size	Description
00h	BYTE	length of subvector
01h	BYTE	type code (see Table 38-13)
02h	N-2 BYTEs	data, which may include subvectors

38-14 Format of Connection ID subvector:

Offset	Size	Description
00h	BYTE	03h (length)
01h	BYTE	01h (subvector "Connection ID")
02h	BYTE	connection ID

INT 14h Function 04h

38-15 Format of Destination ID subvector:

Offset	Size	Description
00h	BYTE	length
01h	BYTE	02h (subvector "Destination ID")
02h	N BYTEs	subvector(s) of type 0Eh, 0Fh, or 10h

38-16 Format of Asynchronous line parameters subvector:

Offset	Size	Description
00h	BYTE	length
01h	BYTE	03h (subvector "Asynchronous line parameters")
02h	N BYTEs	subvector(s) of type 09h, 0Ah, or 19h

38-17 Format of Data transfer parameters subvector:

Offset	Size	Description
00h	BYTE	length
01h	BYTE	04h (subvector "Data transfer parameters")
02h	N BYTEs	subvector(s) of type 0Bh, 0Ch, or 0Dh

38-18 Format of Line speed subvector:

Offset	Size	Description
00h	BYTE	04h (length)
01h	BYTE	09h (subvector "Line speed")
02h	WORD	bit map, highest set bit selects speed
		bit 0: 2400
		bits 1-7: 1800, 1200, 600, 300, 115200, 150, 110 bps
		bits 8-15: 57600, 38400, 19200, 14400, 9600, 7200, 4800, 3600

38-19 Format of Serial coding subvector:

Offset	Size	Description
00h	BYTE	length
01h	BYTE	0Ah (subvector "Serial coding")
02h	N BYTEs	subvector(s) of type 11h, 12h, or 13h

38-20 Format of Packet size subvector:

Offset	Size	Description
00h	BYTE	04h (length)
01h	BYTE	0Bh (subvector "Packet size")
02h	WORD	(big-endian) packet size, 1 to 1024

38-21 Format of Timers subvector:

Offset	Size	Description
00h	BYTE	length
01h	BYTE	0Ch (subvector "Timers")
02h	8 BYTEs	subvector of type 14h or 15h

38-22 Format of Special characters subvector:

Offset	Size	Description
00h	BYTE	length
01h	BYTE	0Dh (subvector "Special characters")
02h	N BYTEs	list of ASCII characters to be used as EOM or EOB

38-23 Format of Target ID:

Offset	Size	Description
00h	BYTE	length
01h	BYTE	0Eh (subvector "Target ID")
02h	N BYTEs	target ID, 1-16 bytes

38-24 Format of Telephone number subvector:

Offset	Size	Description
00h	BYTE	length
01h	BYTE	0Fh (subvector "Telephone number")
02h	N BYTEs	telephone number

38-25 Format of ASCII destination ID subvector:

Offset	Size	Description
00h	BYTE	length
01h	BYTE	10h (subvector "ASCII destination ID")
02h	N BYTEs	destination ID

38-26 Format of Parity subvector:

Offset	Size	Description
00h	BYTE	03h (length)
01h	BYTE	11h (subvector "Parity")
02h	BYTE	parity type
		bit 7: odd
		bit 6: even
		bit 5: mark
		bit 4: space
		bit 3: none

38-27 Format of Bits per character subvector:

Offset	Size	Description
00h	BYTE	03h (length)
01h	BYTE	12h (subvector "Bits per character")
02h	BYTE	bits per character
		bit 7: seven
		bit 6: eight

38-28 Format of Number of stop bits subvector:

Offset	Size	Description
00h	BYTE	03h (length)
01h	BYTE	13h (subvector "Number of stop bits")
02h	BYTE	stop bits
		bit 7: one
		bit 6: 1.5
		bit 5: two

38-29 Format of Packet timer and Intercharacter timer subvectors:

Offset	Size	Description
00h	BYTE	04h (length)
01h	BYTE	subvector type
		14h Packet timer
		15h Intercharacter timer
02h	WORD	(big-endian) unit of value representing 20ms

38-30 Format of Flags subvector:

Offset	Size	Description
00h	BYTE	03h (length)
01h	BYTE	17h (subvector "Flags")
02h	BYTE	flags
		bit 7: queueing requested

38-31 Format of Parameter ranges subvector:

Offset	Size	Description
00h	BYTE	length
01h	BYTE	18h (subvector "Parameter ranges")
02h	N BYTEs	subvector(s) of type 09h, 11h, 12h, or 13h

38-32 Format of Flow control subvector:

Offset	Size	Description
00h	BYTE	length (02h-04h)
01h	BYTE	19h (subvector "Flow control")
02h	BYTE	XOFF character
03h	BYTE	XON character

Details: If the length is 02h, flow control is disabled; if the length is 03h, any character will be accepted as XON after an XOFF.

INT 14h Function 05h
CLOSE COMMUNICATION
Connection Manager

Purpose: Terminate any existing connection to allow another one to be established.

Registers at call:
AH = 05h
DX = FFFFh
AL = connection ID

Return Registers:
AH = return code
  00h successful
  01h no such connection
  02h invalid connection ID
    AL = correct connection ID

Conflicts: BIOS Function 05h (PCI-12), MultiDOS Plus (PCI-45)
See also: Functions 04h and 0Dh

INT 14h Function 06h
SEND CHARACTER BLOCK
Connection Manager

Registers at call:
AH = 06h
DX = FFFFh
AL = connection ID
CX = number of characters to send
ES:DI -> buffer containing data to be sent

Return Registers:
AH = return code (see Table 38-9)

Conflicts: TelAPI (Chapter 34), MultiDOS Plus (PCI-45)
See also: Functions 04h, 07h, and 09h

INT 14h Function 07h
RECEIVE CHARACTER BLOCK
Connection Manager

Registers at call:
AH = 07h
DX = FFFFh
AL = connection ID
BL = flag
  00h wait for data
  nonzero do not wait if no data avaiable
CX = size of receive buffer
ES:DI -> buffer for received characters

Return Registers:
AH = return code (00h-02h,04h,FFh)
  (see Table 38-9)
BH = line status (see Function 03h)
CX = number of characters received

Conflicts: TelAPI (Chapter 34), FOSSIL (PCI-12), MultiDOS Plus (PCI-45)
See also: Functions 01h, 04h, and 06h

INT 14h Function 08h
RETURN DEFAULT CONNECTION PARAMETERS
Connection Manager

Registers at call:
AH = 08h
DX = FFFFh
CX = size of buffer for parameters or
    0000h to get length
ES:DI -> buffer for parameter vector
    (see Tables 38-11 to 38-22)

Return Registers:
AH = return code
    00h successful
        CX = number of bytes required
            (if CX=0000h on entry)
        CX = number of bytes omitted for lack of
            space (if CX nonzero)
    nonzero invalid request

Conflicts: MBBIOS (PCI-12), MultiDOS Plus (PCI-45)
See also: Functions 00h and 0Fh

INT 14h Function 09h
SEND BREAK
Connection Manager

Registers at call:
AH = 09h
DX = FFFFh
AL = connection ID

Return Registers:
AH = return code (00h-02h) (see Table 38-9)

Conflicts: MBBIOS (PCI-12), MultiDOS Plus (PCI-45)
See also: Functions 02h and 03h

INT 14h Function 0Ah
MODIFY ACTIVE CONNECTION PARAMETERS
Connection Manager

Registers at call:
AH = 0Ah
DX = FFFFh
ES:DI -> vector string containing new
    parameters (see Tables 38-11 to
38-22)

Return Registers:
AH = return code (00h-03h,06h) (see Table 38-9)

Details: Any subvectors valid for the Change Parameters command replace the existing values in
the current set.
Conflicts: MBBIOS (PCI-12)
See also: Functions 00h and 0Fh

INT 14h Function 0Bh
PREPARE FOR INBOUND CONNECTION
Connection Manager

Registers at call:
AH = 0Bh
DX = FFFFh
AL = service name
    00h use parameter file or default
    01h use specified name
        ES:DI -> 16-byte blank-padded name
BH = connection notification
    00h program awaiting connection,
        don't notify user
    01h notify user on connecting
BL = connection type
    00h connection will use Connection
        Manager API

Return Registers:
AH = return code (00h-02h) (see Table 38-9)
AL = connection ID if AH=00h

Conflicts: MBBIOS (PCI-12)
See also: Functions 04h, 0Ch, and 10h

INT 14h Function 0Ch
TEST FOR INBOUND CONNECTION REQUEST

Registers at call:
AH = 0Ch
DX = FFFFh
AL = connection ID from Function 0Bh

Return Registers:
AH = return code (00h-03h) (see also Table 38-9)
    03h not prepared for inbound connection
AL = connection ID (if AH=00h) or correct
    connection ID (if AH=02h)

See also: Functions 03h, 04h, and 0Bh

INT 14h Function 0Dh
TERMINATE CONNECTION CLIENT ACTIVITY

Purpose: End all Connection Client TSR activity to allow it to be removed from memory.

Registers at call:
AH = 0Dh
DX = FFFFh

Return Registers:
AH = return code
    00h successful
    nonzero operation not terminated

Conflicts: FOSSIL (PCI-12)
See also: Functions 05h, Function 6Fh Subfunction FFFFh

INT 14h Function 0Eh
SET HARDWARE FLOW STATE

Registers at call:
AH = 0Eh
DX = FFFFh
AL = connection ID from Function 04h
BL = RTS state (00h off, 01h on)
Conflicts: FOSSIL (PCI-12)
See also: Functions 03h and 0Ah

Return Registers:
AH = return code (00h-03h) (see also Table 38-9)
    03h invalid request (BL not 00h or 01h)

INT 14h Function 0Fh
RETURN ACTIVE CONNECTION PARAMETERS

Registers at call:
AH = 0Fh
DX = FFFFh
AL = connection ID
CX = size of buffer or 0000h to get
  length of returned vector
ES:DI -> buffer for connection parameter
  vector (see Tables 38-11 to 38-22)
See also: Functions 08h and 0Ah

Return Registers:
AH = return code (00h-02h,06h) (see Table 38-9)
CX = number of bytes which could not be returned
  because the given buffer was too small

INT 14h Function 10h
QUERY SERVICE NAMES

Purpose: Obtain the names of groups and lines available for connection requests, and the names of active Connection Servers.

Registers at call:
AH = 10h
DX = FFFFh
CL = subfunction
    00h search first
    01h search next
ES:DI -> pattern buffer (see Table 38-33)
See also: Functions 04h and 0Bh

Return Registers:
AH = return code (00h,01h,03h,06h) (see also
  Table 38-9)
    01h no (more) matching names
    03h invalid request
ES:DI buffer filled with reply buffer (see Table
  38-33) containing matched name if AH=00h

38-33 Format of pattern/reply buffer:

Offset	Size	Description
00h	WORD	length of pattern (30h or 32h)
02h	16 BYTEs	server pattern or name
12h	16 BYTEs	group pattern or name
22h	16 BYTEs	line pattern or name
23h	BYTE	(optional) *unknown*
24h	BYTE	(optional, returned) current line status
		00h available
		01h out of service
		02h currently allocated to a connection

Details: The pattern may include '?' wildcard to match any character.

INT 14h Function 6Fh, Subfunction FFFEh
UNDETERMINED FUNCTION

Connection Manager
Undocumented

Registers at call:
AH = 6Fh
BX = FFFEh
others, if any, unknown

Return Registers:
unknown

INT 14h Function 6Fh, Subfunction FFFFh
INSTALLATION CHECK

Connection Manager

Registers at call:
AH = 6Fh
BX = FFFFh
See also: Function 0Dh

Return Registers:
DX:BX -> Connection Manager Communication Table if installed
BX = FFFFh if not installed

Interconnections Inc. TES

TES is a network serial port emulation program by Interconnections, Inc.

INT 14h Function A0h
INSTALLATION CHECK/STATUS REPORT

TES

Registers at call:
AH = A0h
CX = FFFFh

Return Registers:
CF clear if successful
    AX = 5445h ('TE')
    CX <> FFFFh
    DX = port number
CF set on error

Conflicts: BAPI (Chapter 4)
See also: Function A1h

INT 14h Function A1h
GET LIST OF SESSIONS WITH STATUS

TES

Registers at call:
AH = A1h

Return Registers:
CX = number of active sessions
ES:SI -> status array (see Table 38-34)

Conflicts: BAPI (Chapter 4)
See also: Functions A2h and A3h

38-34 Format of status array entry:

Offset	Size	Description
00h	BYTE	status
01h	WORD	offset of name

INT 14h Function A2h
GET LIST OF SERVER NAMES

TES

Registers at call:
AH = A2h

Return Registers:
CX = number of servers
ES:SI -> array of offsets from ES for server names

Conflicts: BAPI (Chapter 4)
See also: Function A1h

INT 14h Function A3h
START A NEW SESSION

TES

Registers at call:
AH = A3h
ES:SI -> *unknown*

Return Registers:
CF clear if successful
    AX = 5445h ('TE')
    CX <> FFFFh
    DX = port number
CF set on error

Conflicts: BAPI (Chapter 4)
See also: Functions A1h, A4h, and A6h

INT 14h Function A4h
HOLD CURRENTLY ACTIVE SESSION

TES

Registers at call:
AH = A4h
unknown
Conflicts: BAPI (Chapter 4)
See also: Functions A3h and A5h

Return Registers:
unknown

INT 14h Function A5h
RESUME A SESSION

TES

Registers at call:
AH = A5h
AL = session number
Conflicts: BAPI (Chapter 4)
See also: Functions A4h and A6h

Return Registers:
unknown

INT 14h Function A6h
DROP A SESSION

TES

Registers at call:
AH = A6h
AL = session number

Return Registers:
AH = status
    00h successful
    else error

Conflicts: BAPI (Chapter 4)
See also: Functions A3h and A5h

INT 14h Function A7h
SWITCH TO NEXT ACTIVE SESSION

TES

Registers at call:
AH = A7h
unknown
Conflicts: BAPI (Chapter 4)
See also: Functions A3h and A5h

Return Registers:
unknown

INT 14h Function A8h
SEND STRING TO COMMAND INTERPRETER

Registers at call:
AH = A8h
AL = 00h no visible response
ES:SI -> ASCIZ command
Conflicts: TelAPI (Chapter 34)

Return Registers:
unknown

Novell NASI/NACS

NASI is Novell's NetWare Asynchronous Services Interface which runs on workstations; NACS is the NetWare Asynchronous Communications Services module which runs on servers. NASI is commonly known as the "generic INT 6Bh" interface.

This interface is also supported by Ungermann-Bass Net One, TelAPI (which is described in more detail in Chapter 34), and NPC NCSI (whose extensions to the NASI/NACS interface are described in the next section).

INT 6Bh Function 0000h
BUFFERED WRITE

Novell NASI/NACS

Registers at call:
AX = 0000h
CX = length
ES:BX -> buffer

Return Registers:
CX = number of bytes written

Details: For TelAPI, nonzero values in AL specify a connection ID.
Conflicts: DECnet DOS (Chapter 16), "Saddam" virus (PCI-59)
See also: Function 0100h, Function 18h, INT 14h Function 19h, INT 14h Function E3h

INT 6Bh Function 0100h
BUFFERED READ

Novell NASI/NACS

Registers at call:
AX = 0100h
CX = length of buffer
ES:BX -> buffer

Return Registers:
CX = number of bytes read

Details: For TelAPI, nonzero values in AL specify a connection ID.
Conflicts: DECnet DOS (Chapter 16), "Saddam" virus (PCI-59)
See also: Function 0000h, Function 19h, INT 14h Function 18h, INT 14h Function E2h, INT 14h Function FF02h

INT 6Bh Function 02h
INSTALLATION CHECK

Novell NASI/NACS

Registers at call:
AH = 02h
AL nonzero

Return Registers:
AL = 00h if present and OK

Conflicts: DECnet DOS (Chapter 16), "Saddam" virus (PCI-59)
See also: Function 0700h

INT 6Bh Function 0600h
CONTROL

Novell NASI/NACS

Registers at call:
AX = 0600h
CX = command
   02h send break
   04h disconnect
   06h hold

Return Registers:
CF clear if successful
   AL = 00h
CF set on error
   AX < 0

Conflicts: DECnet DOS (Chapter 16), "Saddam" virus (PCI-59)

INT 6Bh Function 0700h   *Novell NASI/NACS*
GET STATUS

Registers at call: Return Registers:
AX = 0700h   CH nonzero if connection active
Details: Novell TelAPI returns CX=FF01h and CF clear.
Conflicts: DECnet DOS (Chapter 16), "Saddam" virus (PCI-59)
See also: Function 02h, Function 10h (below)

NPC NCSI Extended Serial I/O

NPC NCSI provides a superset of the NASI calls, and the added functions are described in this section. Much of this expanded interface (Functions 10h to 19h) is also supported by TelAPI, whose own API is described in Chapter 34. The TelAPI implementation of the NCSI API was used in determining the descriptions shown here.

INT 6Bh Function 10h   *NPC NCSI*
GET STATUS

Registers at call: Return Registers:
AH = 10h   CF clear if successful
AL = connection ID (Novell TELAPI.EXE)   CL = *unknown*
CX = *unknown*   CH = *unknown*
                                            CF set on error
                                                unknown

Conflicts: DECnet DOS (Chapter 16), "Saddam" virus (PCI-59)
See also: Functions 12h and 1Fh, NASI Function 0700h (above)

INT 6Bh Function 11h   *NPC NCSI*
ALLOCATE A VIRTUAL CIRCUIT

Registers at call: Return Registers:
AH = 11h   CF clear if successful
unknown   AL = *virtual circuit number* (01h for Novell TELAPI.EXE)
                                        CL = *unknown* (01h for Novell TELAPI.EXE)
                                        CH = *unknown* (01h for Novell TELAPI.EXE)
                                    CF set on error
                                        unknown

Conflicts: DECnet DOS (Chapter 16), "Saddam" virus (PCI-59)
See also: Functions 12h, 15h, 16h, 17h, and 18h

INT 6Bh Function 12h   *NPC NCSI*
VIRTUAL CIRCUIT STATUS

Registers at call: Return Registers:
AH = 12h   *unknown*
AL = virtual circuit number
CL = *unknown*
ES:BX -> *unknown*
Conflicts: DECnet DOS (Chapter 16), "Saddam" virus (PCI-59)
See also: Functions 10h, 15h, 1Ah, 1Bh, and 1Fh

INT 6Bh Function 13h   *NPC NCSI*
SET/RETRIEVE REQUEST/REPLY SERVICE NAME

Registers at call:
AH = 13h
AL = virtual circuit number

CL = direction (00h get, nonzero set)
ES:BX -> buffer for/containing service name
Conflicts: DECnet DOS (Chapter 16), "Saddam" virus (PCI-59)
See also: Functions 14h and 15h

INT 6Bh Function 14h
SET/RETRIEVE SERVICE ADDRESS

NPC NCSI

Registers at call:
AH = 14h
AL = virtual circuit number
ES:BX -> buffer for/containing service address
Details: TelAPI only supports retrieving the address.
Conflicts: DECnet DOS (Chapter 16), "Saddam" virus (PCI-59)
See also: Functions 13h, 15h, and 21h

Return Registers:
unknown

INT 6Bh Function 15h
SET/RETRIEVE VIRTUAL CIRCUIT CONFIGURATION

NPC NCSI

Registers at call:
AH = 15h
AL = virtual circuit number
CL = direction (00h get, nonzero set)
ES:BX -> buffer for/containing virtual circuit
configuration
Conflicts: DECnet DOS (Chapter 16), "Saddam" virus (PCI-59)
See also: Functions 13h and 14h

Return Registers:
unknown

INT 6Bh Function 16h
LOG AND/OR INITIALIZE VIRTUAL CIRCUIT

NPC NCSI

Registers at call:
AH = 16h
unknown

Return Registers:
CF clear if successful
    AL = *virtual circuit number*
CF set on error
    unknown

Details: TelAPI always returns CF clear and AL=00h.
Conflicts: DECnet DOS (Chapter 16), "Saddam" virus (PCI-59)
See also: Functions 11h, 12h, and 17h

INT 6Bh Function 17h
DISCONNECT A VIRTUAL CIRCUIT

NPC NCSI

Registers at call:
AH = 17h
AL = *virtual circuit number*

Return Registers:
CF clear if successful
CF set on error
    unknown

Details: TelAPI always returns CF clear and AL=00h.
Conflicts: DECnet DOS (Chapter 16), "Saddam" virus (PCI-59)
See also: Functions 11h and 16h

INT 6Bh Function 18h
WRITE DATA ON A VIRTUAL CIRCUIT

NPC NCSI

Registers at call:
AH = 18h
AL = virtual circuit number
unknown

Return Registers:
CF clear if successful
CF set on error
unknown

Details: TelAPI always returns CF clear and AL=30h.
Conflicts: DECnet DOS (Chapter 16), "Saddam" virus (PCI-59)
See also: Functions 12h and 19h, NASI Function 0000h (above)

INT 6Bh Function 19h   *NPC NCSI*
READ DATA ON A VIRTUAL CIRCUIT

Registers at call: **Return Registers:**
AH = 19h   *unknown*
AL = virtual circuit number
unknown
Conflicts: DECnet DOS (Chapter 16), "Saddam" virus (PCI-59)
See also: Functions 12h and 18h, NASI Function 0100h (above)

INT 6Bh Function 1Ah   *NPC NCSI*
RECEIVE STATUS

Registers at call: **Return Registers:**
AH = 1Ah   *unknown*
unknown
Conflicts: DECnet DOS (Chapter 16), "Saddam" virus (PCI-59)
See also: Functions 12h and 1Bh

INT 6Bh Function 1Bh   *NPC NCSI*
TRANSMIT STATUS

Registers at call: **Return Registers:**
AH = 1Bh   *unknown*
unknown
Conflicts: DECnet DOS (Chapter 16), "Saddam" virus (PCI-59)
See also: Functions 12h and 1Ah

INT 6Bh Function 1Ch   *NPC NCSI*
RECEIVE BUFFER CONTROL

Registers at call: **Return Registers:**
AH = 1Ch   *unknown*
unknown
Conflicts: DECnet DOS (Chapter 16), "Saddam" virus (PCI-59)
See also: Functions 1Dh and 1Eh

INT 6Bh Function 1Dh   *NPC NCSI*
TRANSMIT BUFFER CONTROL

Registers at call: **Return Registers:**
AH = 1Dh   *unknown*
unknown
Conflicts: DECnet DOS (Chapter 16), "Saddam" virus (PCI-59)
See also: Functions 1Ch and 1Eh

INT 6Bh Function 1Eh   *NPC NCSI*
ISSUE CONTROL REQUEST

Registers at call: **Return Registers:**
AH = 1Eh   *unknown*
unknown
Conflicts: DECnet DOS (Chapter 16), "Saddam" virus (PCI-59)
See also: Functions 1Ch and 1Dh

INT 6Bh Function 1Fh
EXTERNAL STATUS

Registers at call:
AH = 1Fh
unknown

Return Registers:
unknown

Conflicts: DECnet DOS (Chapter 16), "Saddam" virus (PCI-59)
See also: Functions 10h and 12h

INT 6Bh Function 21h
QUERY NAME SERVICE

Registers at call:
AH = 21h
unknown

Return Registers:
unknown

Conflicts: DECnet DOS (Chapter 16), "Saddam" virus (PCI-59)
See also: Function 14h

Telebit ACS Serial I/O

INT 7Fh
API

Registers at call:
ES:SI-> parameter block (see Table 38-35)

Return Registers:
CF set on error
CF clear on success

Details: The signature "PDGATEWRKSTNIF" appears just prior to the interrupt handler; this serves as the installation check
Conflicts: see Table 2-4

38-35 Format of Telebit ACS parameter block:

Offset	Size	Description
00h	BYTE	command code (see Tbale 38-36)
01h	BYTE	gateway number
02h	BYTE	reserved
03h	BYTE	port
04h	17 BYTEs	auxiliary buffer
15h	BYTE	session
16h	WORD	count of bytes passed to API
18h	DWORD	buffer pointer passed to/from API
1Ch	WORD	count of bytes passed from API
1Eh	BYTE	return code (see Table 38-37)

38-36 Command codes:

3Ch	status
3Dh	connect
3Eh	disconnect
3Fh	read
40h	data/command write
41h	clear receive buffer
42h	get configuration
43h	get receiver status
44h	raw write
45h	search servers
46h	set transmit buffer size

38-37 Values for return code:

00h	success
01h	invalid session
05h	servername invalid
06h	netware fileserver bindery is locked
07h	communication server not active
08h	general failure in netware fileserver
09h	not logged into a fileserver
10h	connection table full
11h	no response from communication server
12h	connection attempt terminated abnormally
13h	connection refused—no sessions available
14h	gateway number/port already in use
15h	invalid connection response
16h	port invalid
17h	incorrect version in server response
18h	gateway number/port combination not configured
19h	initialization has not been completed
20h	no more sockets are available
21h	no active poolname
23h	FATAL internal interface error
24h	registration of host workstation failed—name is already in use
25h	registration of host workstation failed—workstation name table full
26h	registration of host workstation failed—only one session may be registered for dial-in
FFh	Telebit ACS API is busy—retry later

CHAPTER 39

Network Remote Control Software

A number of programs allow remote control of a system over a serial port by dialing up a modem (these are discussed in detail in *PC Interrupts* chapter 58). While the newest versions of many of those remote control programs now allow control by another user over a network, they are still primarily geared toward dial-up use. At least one program, however, has been designed specifically for use over a network, and is described here rather than in *PC Interrupts*.

LAN HiJack is a NetWare utility by KDS Software which allows a user to take over control of a workstation remotely; LHR is the program run on the slave workstation.

INT 2Fh Function 7AC1h   *LAN HiJack*
LHR - DISABLE

Registers at call: Return Registers:
AX = 7AC1h   none
Conflicts: none known, but see Table 2-2
See also: Functions 7AC8h, 7AC9h, and 7ACFh

INT 2Fh Function 7AC2h   *LAN HiJack*
LHR - SYNCHRONIZE SHIFT STATES

Registers at call: Return Registers:
AX = 7AC2h   none
Details: This function sets the BIOS keyboard status byte to the value of an internal variable.
Conflicts: none known, but see Table 2-2
See also: Functions 7AC3h and 7ACFh

INT 2Fh Function 7AC3h   *LAN HiJack*
LHR - CLEAR UNKNOWN FLAG

Registers at call: Return Registers:
AX = 7AC3h   none
Conflicts: none known, but see Table 2-2
See also: Functions 7AC2h and 7ACFh

INT 2Fh Function 7AC8h   *LAN HiJack*
LHR - ENABLE FUNCTIONS

Registers at call: Return Registers:
AX = 7AC8h   none
BL = function(s) to enable (see Table 39-1)
Conflicts: none known, but see Table 2-2
See also: Functions 7AC1h, 7AC9h, and 7ACFh

39-1 Bitfields for function(s) to enable/disable:

bit 0   *unknown*
bit 1   remote keyboard enabled
bit 2   support remote's mouse
bits 3-7   unused

INT 2Fh Function 7AC9h   *LAN HiJack*
LHR - DISABLE FUNCTIONS

Registers at call: **Return Registers:**
AX = 7AC9h   none
BL = function(s) to disable (see Table 39-1)
Conflicts: none known, but see Table 2-2
See also: Functions 7AC1h and 7AC8h

INT 2Fh Function 7ACAh   *LAN HiJack*
LHJ - UNDETERMINED FUNCTION

Registers at call: **Return Registers:**
AX = 7ACAh   *unknown*
BL = *unknown*
Conflicts: none known, but see Table 2-2

INT 2Fh Functions 7ACBh and 7ACCh   *LAN HiJack*
LHJ - UNDETERMINED FUNCTIONS

Registers at call: **Return Registers:**
AX = 7ACBh   *unknown*
BX = *unknown*
Details: Function 7ACBh appears to be related to the keyboard, while Function 7ACCh appears to be related to the mouse.
Conflicts: none known, but see Table 2-2

INT 2Fh Function 7ACFh   *LAN HiJack*
LHR - INSTALLATION CHECK

Registers at call: **Return Registers:**
AX = 7ACFh   BX = segment of resident code if installed
BX = 0000h
Conflicts: none known, but see Table 2-2

CHAPTER 40

Da Vinci eMail

DaVinci Systems Corp. of Raleigh, NC, is one of the accepted leaders in the specialized field of network E-mail providers, and their eMail product is the only one of the top three still owned by its originator. This chapter describes its API.

INT 92h Function E1h *Da Vinci eMail Dispatcher*
API OVERVIEW

Registers at call:
AH = E1h
AL = function
BX = stack count (number of words to push)
CX:DX -> stack data (in word-reversed order ready to push)
Details: This function preserves BP, DS, SI, DI; other registers may be destroyed.
Conflicts: Sangoma X.25 interface (Chapter 37), IBM ROM BASIC (PCI-54)

Return Registers:
AX = status (see Table 40-1)

40-1 Values for status:

0001h	success
FF97h	"ERS_NOT_AVAILABLE"
FF99h	"ERS_TOO_MANY_NAMES"
FF9Ah	"ERS_BAD_NAME_PASSWORD"
FFE3h	"ERS_NAME_NOT_FOUND"
FFF8h	"ERS_USE_STRING" (call NetGetError to get error string)
FFFFh	"ERS_NO_SUCH_FILE"

INT 92h Function E100h *Da Vinci eMail Dispatcher*
"NetInitStart" - INITIALIZE DISPATCHER

Registers at call:
AX = E100h
BX = size of parameter block in words (000Ah)
CX:DX -> parameter block (see Table 40-2)
Conflicts: Sangoma X.25 interface (Chapter 37), IBM ROM BASIC (PCI-54)
See also: Functions E101h and E103h

Return Registers:
AX = 0001h success

40-2 Format of parameter block:

Offset	Size	Description
00h	WORD	segment of *unknown item*
02h	WORD	offset of *unknown item*
04h	WORD	high part of long *unknown item*
06h	WORD	low part of long *unknown item*

08h	WORD	high part of long *unknown item*
0Ah	WORD	low part of long *unknown item*
0Ch	WORD	high part of long *unknown item*
0Eh	WORD	low part of long *unknown item*
10h	WORD	high part of long *unknown item*
12h	WORD	low part of long *unknown item*

INT 92h Function E101h
"NetInitCheck"   *Da Vinci eMail Dispatcher*

Registers at call:
AX = E101h
BX = 0000h
CX:DX ignored

Return Registers:
AX = 0001h success

Conflicts: Sangoma X.25 interface (Chapter 37), IBM ROM BASIC (PCI-54)
See also: Functions E100h and E180h

INT 92h Function E102h
"NetCheckDriver" - **GET DRIVER STATUS**   *Da Vinci eMail Dispatcher*

Registers at call:
AX = E102h
BX = 0000h
CX:DX ignored

Return Registers:
AX = 0001h success

Conflicts: Sangoma X.25 interface (Chapter 37), IBM ROM BASIC (PCI-54)
See also: Functions E10Bh and E180h

INT 92h Function E103h
"NetTerminate"   *Da Vinci eMail Dispatcher*

Registers at call:
AX = E103h
BX = 0000h
CX:DX ignored

Return Registers:
AX = status (see Table 40-1)

Conflicts: Sangoma X.25 interface (Chapter 37), IBM ROM BASIC (PCI-54)
See also: Function E100h

INT 92h Function E104h
"NetWhereIs" - **VERIFY NODE ADDRESS FOR USERNAME**   *Da Vinci eMail Dispatcher*

Registers at call:
AX = E104h
BX = 0006h (size of parameter block in words)
CX:DX -> parameter block (see Table 40-3)

Return Registers:
AX = status (see Table 40-1)

Conflicts: Sangoma X.25 interface (Chapter 37), IBM ROM BASIC (PCI-54)
See also: Function E180h

40-3 Format of parameter block:

Offset	Size	Description
00h	WORD	segment of node address buffer
02h	WORD	offset of node address buffer
04h	WORD	segment of uppercase username
06h	WORD	offset of uppercase username
08h	WORD	segment of "DVSEMAIL"
0Ah	WORD	offset of "DVSEMAIL"

INT 92h Function E105h
Da Vinci eMail Dispatcher
"NetOpen" - OPEN A SUBMISSION CHANNEL
Registers at call:
AX = E105h
BX = 0007h (size of parameter block in words)
CX:DX -> parameter block (see Table 40-4)
Conflicts: Sangoma X.25 interface (Chapter 37), IBM ROM BASIC (PCI-54)
See also: Functions E10Ah, E106h, and E108h

Return Registers:
AX = 0000h Error
AX = handle

40-4 Format of parameter block:

Offset	Size	Description
00h	WORD	operation (1 = read, 2 = write)
02h	WORD	segment of uppercase To: username
04h	WORD	offset of uppercase To: username
06h	WORD	segment of "DVSEMAIL"
08h	WORD	offset of "DVSEMAIL"
0Ah	WORD	segment of node address
0Ch	WORD	offset of node address

INT 92h Function E106h
Da Vinci eMail Dispatcher
"NetRead"
Registers at call:
AX = E106h
BX = 0004h (length of parameter block in words)
CX:DX -> parameter block
Conflicts: Sangoma X.25 interface (Chapter 37), IBM ROM BASIC (PCI-54)
See also: Function E108h

Return Registers:
AX = 0001h

INT 92h Function E107h
Da Vinci eMail Dispatcher
"NetGetError"
Registers at call:
AX = E107h
BX = 0002h (length of parameter block in words)
CX:DX -> parameter block
Conflicts: Sangoma X.25 interface (Chapter 37), IBM ROM BASIC (PCI-54)
See also: Functions E109h and E180h

Return Registers:
AX = 0001h

INT 92h Function E108h
Da Vinci eMail Dispatcher
"NetWrite" - WRITE TRANSACTION TO DISPATCHER
Registers at call:
AX = E108h
BX = 0004h (size of parameter block in words)
CX:DX -> parameter block (see Table 40-5)
Details: The command block is written first and then another call is used to write the associated data.
Conflicts: Sangoma X.25 interface (Chapter 37), IBM ROM BASIC (PCI-54)
See also: Function E106h

Return Registers:
AX = amount written

40-5 Format of parameter block:

Offset	Size	Description
00h	WORD	buffer count
02h	WORD	segment of command buffer

| 04h | WORD | offset of command buffer |
| 06h | WORD | handle from NetOpen |

40-6 Format of command buffer:

Offset	Size	Description
00h	BYTE	command
		21h '!' Protocol commands for remote control
		41h 'A' Authorization protocol element
		42h 'B' Return(back) routing information
		Associated data is the From: username
		43h 'C' Carbon Copy list
		Associated data is a comma delimitted list of usernames
		44h 'D' Distribution list
		Associated data is a comma delimitted list of usernames
		45h 'E' Mail end marker
		No associated data
		48h 'H' Mail message header
		Associated data is a message header buffer
		4Dh 'M' Mail message
		Associated data is the body of the message
		4Fh 'O' Object
		50h 'P' Paperclip attachment
		52h 'R' Routing information
		Associated data is the To: username
		53h 'S' Subject
		Associated data is the subject of the message
		54h 'T' Trail of Reply/Forwards
01h	BYTE	subcommand
02h	DWORD	length of associated data

40-7 Format of message header buffer:

Offset	Size	Description
00h	30 BYTEs	subject line
1Eh	24 BYTEs	To
36h	24 BYTEs	From
4Eh	DWORD	Time
	BYTE	00h
	BYTE	hour
	BYTE	minute
	BYTE	second
52h	DWORD	Date
	BYTE	00h
	BYTE	year
	BYTE	month
	BYTE	day
56h	DWORD	serial number (00000000h)
5Ah	WORD	mail types (see Table 40-8)
5Ch	WORD	special types (0)

INT 92h Function E108h

40-8 Bitfields for mail types:

bit 7   blind carbon copy
bit 6   carbon copy
bit 5   priority
bit 4   confidential
bit 3   certified
bit 2   bulk
bits 1-0   class (first, second, third, bulk)

INT 92h Function E109h   *Da Vinci eMail Dispatcher*
"NetErrorFix" (UNUSED)

Registers at call:
AX = E109h
BX = 0001h (size of parameter block in words)
CX:DX -> parameter block (see Table 40-9)
Conflicts: Sangoma X.25 interface (Chapter 37), IBM ROM BASIC (PCI-54)
See also: Functions E107h and E180h

Return Registers:
AX = FF97h
(ERS_NOT_AVAILABLE)
(see also Table 40-1)

40-9 Format of parameter block:

Offset	Size	Description
00h	WORD	*unknown*

INT 92h Function E10Ah   *Da Vinci eMail Dispatcher*
"NetClose" - CLOSE DISPATCHER HANDLE

Registers at call:
AX = E10Ah
BX = 0001h (size of parameter block in words)
CX:DX -> parameter block (see Table 40-10)
Conflicts: Sangoma X.25 interface (Chapter 37), IBM ROM BASIC (PCI-54)
See also: Function E105h

Return Registers:
AX = 0001h

40-10 Format of parameter block:

Offset	Size	Description
00h	WORD	handle from NetOpen

INT 92h Function E10Bh   *Da Vinci eMail Dispatcher*
"NetCheckQueue"

Registers at call:
AX = E10Bh
BX = size of parameter block in words (0004h)
CX:DX -> parameter block (see Table 40-11)
Conflicts: Sangoma X.25 interface (Chapter 37), IBM ROM BASIC (PCI-54)
See also: Functions E102h and E10Ch

Return Registers:
AX = 0001h

40-11 Format of parameter block:

Offset	Size	Description
00h	WORD	segment of 24-byte username buffer
02h	WORD	offset of 24-byte username buffer
04h	WORD	segment of 24-byte protocol buffer
06h	WORD	offset of 24-byte protocol buffer

INT 92h Function E10Ch
"NetReadQueue"
Da Vinci eMail Dispatcher

Registers at call:
AX = E10Ch
BX = 0002h (size of parameter block in words)
CX:DX -> parameter block (see Table 40-12)
Conflicts: Sangoma X.25 interface (Chapter 37), IBM ROM BASIC (PCI-54)
See also: Function E10Bh

Return Registers:
AX = 0001h

40-12 Format of parameter block:

Offset	Size	Description
00h	WORD	Segment of 128 byte node address buffer
02h	WORD	Offset of 128 byte node address buffer

INT 92h Function E10Dh
"NetSubmitName" - VERIFY USERNAME/PASSWORD
Da Vinci eMail Dispatcher

Registers at call:
AX = E10Dh
BX = 0006h (size of parameter block in words)
CX:DX -> parameter block (see Table 40-13)
Conflicts: Sangoma X.25 interface (Chapter 37), IBM ROM BASIC (PCI-54)
See also: Function E10Eh

Return Registers:
AX = status (see Table 40-1)

40-13 Format of parameter block:

Offset	Size	Description
00h	WORD	segment of uppercase password string
02h	WORD	offset of uppercase password string
04h	WORD	segment of uppercase username string
06h	WORD	offset of uppercase username string
08h	WORD	segment of signature "DVSEMAIL"
0Ah	WORD	offset of signature "DVSEMAIL"

INT 92h Function E10Eh
"NetRemoveName" - REMOVE A USERNAME
Da Vinci eMail Dispatcher

Registers at call:
AX = E10Eh
BX = 0004h (size of parameter block in words)
CX:DX -> parameter block (see Table 40-14)
Conflicts: Sangoma X.25 interface (Chapter 37), IBM ROM BASIC (PCI-54)
See also: Function E10Dh

Return Registers:
AX = 0001h

40-14 Format of parameter block:

Offset	Type	Description
00h	WORD	segment of uppercase username
02h	WORD	offset of uppercase username
04h	WORD	segment of signature "DVSEMAIL"
06h	WORD	offset of signature "DVSEMAIL"

INT 92h Function E10Fh
Da Vinci eMail Dispatcher
IS ANYONE THERE? QUERY

Registers at call:
AX = E10Fh
BX = 0000h
CX:DX ignored
Conflicts: Sangoma X.25 interface (Chapter 37), IBM ROM BASIC (PCI-54)
See also: Function E180h

Return Registers:
AX = 0001h

INT 92h Function E110h
Da Vinci eMail Dispatcher
"NetGetAltRoute"

Registers at call:
AX = E110h
BX = 0006h (size of parameter block in words)
CX:DX -> parameter block (see Table 40-15)
Conflicts: Sangoma X.25 interface (Chapter 37), IBM ROM BASIC (PCI-54)
See also: Functions E111h and E113h

Return Registers:
AX = 0001h

40-15 Format of parameter block:

Offset	Size	Description
00h	6 WORDs	*unknown*

INT 92h Function E111h
Da Vinci eMail Dispatcher
"NetDeleteAltRoutes"

Registers at call:
AX = E111h
BX = 0004h (size of parameter block in words)
CX:DX -> parameter block (see Table 40-16)
Conflicts: Sangoma X.25 interface (Chapter 37), IBM ROM BASIC (PCI-54)
See also: Functions E110h and E113h

Return Registers:
AX = 0001h

40-16 Format of parameter block:

Offset	Size	Description
00h	4 WORDs	*unknown*

INT 92h Function E112h
Da Vinci eMail Dispatcher
"NetChangePassword"

Registers at call:
AX = E112h
BX = 0008h (size of parameter block in words)
CX:DX -> parameter block (see Table 40-17)
Conflicts: Sangoma X.25 interface (Chapter 37), IBM ROM BASIC (PCI-54)
See also: Function E180h

Return Registers:
AX = 0001h

40-17 Format of parameter block:

Offset	Size	Description
00h	8 WORDs	*unknown* (probably two words each for username, old password, new password, and "DVSEMAIL" signature)

INT 92h Function E113h
Da Vinci eMail Dispatcher
"NetSetAltRoute"

Registers at call:
AX = E113h

BX = 0008h (size of parameter block in words)
CX:DX -> parameter block (see Table 40-18)

Return Registers:
AX = 0001h

Conflicts: Sangoma X.25 interface (Chapter 37), IBM ROM BASIC (PCI-54)
See also: Functions E110h and E111h

40-18 Format of parameter block:

Offset	Size	Description
00h	8 WORDs	*unknown*

INT 92h Function E175h
BECOME MICRO TSR
Da Vinci eMail Dispatcher

Registers at call:
AX = E175h

Return Registers:
AX = 0012h
BX = PSP segment

Conflicts: Sangoma X.25 interface (Chapter 37), IBM ROM BASIC (PCI-54)
See also: Function E180h

INT 92h Function E180h
INSTALLATION CHECK
Da Vinci eMail Dispatcher

Registers at call:
AX = E180h

Return Registers:
AX = 0012h if installed
ES:DX -> '$'-terminated driver information string

Conflicts: Sangoma X.25 interface (Chapter 37), IBM ROM BASIC (PCI-54)
See also: Functions E102h, E105h, E10Fh, and E175h

CHAPTER 41

Other Electronic Mail Software

This chapter describes additional E-mail products, including that from Shamrock Software, Microsoft Mail's MICRO.EXE TSR interface, and the predecessor of Microsoft's product, Network Courier.

Shamrock Software EMAIL

INT 16h Function 4500h
GET STATUS

Registers at call:
AX = 4500h
DL = port number (01h = COM1)
ES:BX -> 13-byte buffer for ASCIZ name

Return Registers:
AX = 4D00h if EMAIL installed on specified port
    ES:BX -> user name
        ("" if no connection, "*" if connection
          but caller has not identified name)
    CX = version (CH = major, CL = minor)
    DL = privilege level of user (00h = guest)
    DH = chosen language (00h German, 01h English)

See also: Functions 4501h and 4502h

INT 16h Function 4501h
GET ELAPSED ONLINE TIME AND MAXIMUM TIME

Registers at call:
AX = 4501h
DL = port number (01h = COM1)

Return Registers:
AX = 4D00h if EMAIL installed on specified port
    BX = maximum connect time in clock ticks
    CX = maximum connect time for guests
    (without name) in clock ticks
    DX = elapsed connect time of current user in
    clock ticks

See also: Function 4500h

INT 16h Function 4502h
GET CURRENT COMMUNICATIONS PARAMETERS

Registers at call:
AX = 4502h
DL = port number (01h = COM1)

Return Registers:
AX = 4D00h if EMAIL installed on specified port
    BL = current value of serial port's Line
    Control Register
    BH = flags
        bit 0: ISO code
        bit 1: pause

                                              bit 2: linefeed
                                              bit 3: ANSI sequences
                                    CX = selected country code (33 = France,
                                       49 = Germany, etc)
                                    DX = baudrate divisor (115200/DX = baudrate)

See also: Function 4500h

INT 16h Function 4503h
SPECIFY COMMAND-WORD FOR USER FUNCTION
Shamrock Software EMAIL

Registers at call: **Return Registers:**
AX = 4503h   AX = 4D00h if EMAIL installed on specified port
DL = port number (01h = COM1)
DH = maximum execution time in
  clock ticks (00h = 5 seconds)
ES:BX -> ASCIZ string with new user
  command-word

Details: A single user command (consisting of only uppercase letters and digits) may be defined, and remains valid until it is overwritten or the EMAIL program terminates; the user command must be activated by calling Function 4504h at least once.

  An existing command word may be redefined with this function.

See also: Functions 4504h and 4505h

INT 16h Function 4504h
CHECK FOR USER FUNCTION COMMAND-WORD
Shamrock Software EMAIL

Registers at call: **Return Registers:**
AX = 4504h   AX = 4D00h if EMAIL installed on specified port
DL = port number (01h = COM1)   DL = flags
ES:BX -> 80-byte buffer for ASCIZ   bit 0: user function supported (always set)
  user input line   bit 1: user entered user-function command word
                                          if DL bit 1 set,
                                              ES:BX buffer contains line entered by
                                                user which begins with the defined
                                                command word and has been converted
                                                to all caps

Details: The caller must process the returned commandline and invoke Function 4505h within five seconds with the result of that processing.

See also: Functions 4503h and 4505h

INT 16h Function 4505h
SEND RESULT OF USER FUNCTION
Shamrock Software EMAIL

Registers at call: **Return Registers:**
AX = 4505h   AH = 4Dh if EMAIL installed on specified port
DL = port number (01h = COM1)   AL = status
DH = error flag   00h successful
    bit 3: set on error   02h unable to perform function (timeout,
ES:BX -> ASCIZ text to return to   prev call not complete)
  user, max 1024 bytes   other error

Details: If the error flag in DH is set, the string is not sent and an error message is generated instead; if this function is not called within five seconds of Function 4504h, EMAIL automatically generates an error message.

  The string is copied into an internal buffer, allowing this function's caller to continue immediately.

See also: Functions 4503h and 4504h, NET.24 INT 17h Function 2400h (Chapter 31)

INT 16h Function 4503h

INT 16h Function 4506h
MONITOR XMODEM DOWNLOAD

Registers at call:
AX = 4506h
DL = port number (01h = COM1)
ES:BX -> 13-byte buffer for ASCIZ filename

Return Registers:
AX = 4D00h if EMAIL installed on specified port
DH = Xmodem status
    00h no XGET command given
    01h XGET in progress
    02h XGET completed successfully
    ES:BX buffer filled with last filename given to
        XGET command
        (without path)

Details: DH=02h will only be returned once per XGET; subsequent calls will return DH=00h.
See also: Function 4500h, INT 17h Function 2408h

Workgroup Connection MICRO.EXE

MICRO.EXE is a TSR of the Microsoft Mail part of Workgroup Connection. It is based on the TSR of the same name described in the next section under "Network Courier." In 1991, Microsoft purchased the Network Courier product and renamed it Microsoft Mail Version 3.0.

MICRO.EXE

INT 2Fh Function 9400h
INSTALLATION CHECK

Registers at call:
AX = 9400h
Conflicts: none known, but see Table 2-2
See also: Functions 9401h, 9402h, 9403h, and 9404h; INT 21h Function 3Fh

Return Registers:
AL = 07h or 08h if installed

MICRO.EXE

INT 2Fh Function 9401h
SET UNKNOWN FLAG

Registers at call:
AX = 9401h
Conflicts: none known, but see Table 2-2
See also: Functions 9400h and 9403h

Return Registers:
none

MICRO.EXE

INT 2Fh Function 9402h
UNDETERMINED FUNCTION

Registers at call:
AX = 9402h
unknown
Conflicts: none known, but see Table 2-2
See also: Function 9400h

Return Registers:
unknown

MICRO.EXE

INT 2Fh Function 9403h
SET UNKNOWN FLAG

Registers at call:
AX = 9403h
Conflicts: none known, but see Table 2-2
See also: Functions 9400h and 9404h

Return Registers:

INT 2Fh Function 9404h
CLEAR UNKNOWN FLAG   *MICRO.EXE*
Registers at call:
AX = 9404h
ES:DI -> name of executable from which MICRO.EXE was started
Details: If the specified name is identical to the name of the program file from which MICRO was
started, the *unknown* flag is cleared; otherwise, it is left unchanged.
Conflicts: none known, but see Table 2-2
See also: Functions 9400h and 9403h

Network Courier E-Mail

The Network Courier, an E-mail package developed by Consumers Software Inc. of Vancouver,
BC, was reputed to have the widest range of gateways to other systems of any available product at
the time Microsoft purchased the company and renamed the product to Microsoft Mail Version
3.0 in 1991. This section describes the API used by Network Courier in its original incarnation.

INT 2Fh Function 92h
API   *Network Courier E-Mail*
Registers at call: **Return Registers:**
AH = 92h   *unknown*
AL = function
    00h installation check
    01h uninstall
    02h pop down MICRO.EXE notification window
    03h *unknown*
    04h *unknown*
    05h *unknown*
See also: Function 9Ch

INT 2Fh Function 9Ch
OPERATOR.EXE - API   *Network Courier E-Mail*
Registers at call: **Return Registers:**
AH = 9Ch   *unknown*
AL = subfunction
    01h uninstall
See also: Function 92h

CHAPTER 42

Miscellaneous Networking Calls

This final chapter describes those functions which do not neatly fit into any of the other chapters. These include the License Service API, General Software's Embedded DOS (and its STARLITE architecture), QPC Software's PKTINT.COM, and other calls that did not fit elsewhere.

License Service

The License Service API is being maintained by Microsoft but is being supported by a large number of companies including Apple, Banyan, DEC, HP, Lotus, Microsoft, Novell, Software Publishers Association, and Wordperfect (not a complete list!).

License Service

INT 2Fh Function 7000h
INSTALLATION CHECK

Registers at call:
AX = 7000h
CX = license server index (0000h to 001Fh)

Return Registers:
AL = status
    00h not installed
    FFh installed

Details: Each license service provider must search for the next free index slot to use.
Conflicts: none known, but see also Table 2-2
See also: Functions 7001h, 7003h, 7004h, and 7005h

License Service

INT 2Fh Function 7001h
REQUEST LICENSE

Registers at call:
AX = 7001h
CX = license server index (0000h to 001Fh)
DS:DX -> SLSREQUEST structure (see Table 42-1)

Return Registers:
AX = status
    0000h success
    else provider error code
ES:BX = provider specific handle for the license context

Conflicts: none known, but see also Table 2-2
See also: Functions 7002h, 7004h, and 7005h

42-1 Format of SLSREQUEST structure:

Offset	Size	Description
00h	DWORD	(return) status code
04h	DWORD	(return) handle identifying context
08h	DWORD	(call) address of Publisher string
0Ch	DWORD	(call) address of Product string
10h	DWORD	(call) address of Version string
14h	DWORD	units required

| 18h | DWORD | address of comment string |
| 1Ch | DWORD | address of SLSCHALLENGE structure (see Table 42-2) |

42-2 Format of SLSCHALLENGE structure:

Offset	Size	Description
00h	DWORD	algorithm (currently always 1)
04h	DWORD	secret to be challenged (1-255)
08h	DWORD	size of challenge in bytes (1-255)
0Ch	N BYTEs	challenge data

INT 2Fh Function 7002h
RELEASE LICENSE
License Service

Registers at call:
AX = 7002h
CX = license server index (0000h to 001Fh)
DS:DX -> SLSRELEASE structure (see Table 42-3)
ES:BX = provider specific handle for the license context
Conflicts: none known, but see also Table 2-2
See also: Functions 7001h and 7005h

Return Registers:
AL = status
   00h not installed
   FFh installed

42-3 Format of SLSRELEASE structure:

Offset	Size	Description
00h	DWORD	handle indentifying license context
04h	DWORD	total units consumed
08h	DWORD	address of comment string

INT 2Fh Function 7003h
UPDATE
License Service

Registers at call:
AX = 7003h
CX = license server index (0000h to 001Fh)
DS:DX -> SLSUPDATE structure (see Table 42-4)
ES:BX = provider specific handle for the license context
Conflicts: none known, but see also Table 2-2
See also: Functions 7004h and 7005h

Return Registers:
AL = status
   00h not installed
   FFh installed

42-4 Format of SLSUPDATE structure:

Offset	Size	Description
00h	DWORD	(return) status code
04h	DWORD	(call) handle identifying license context
08h	DWORD	(call) total units consumed
0Ch	DWORD	additional units required
10h	DWORD	address of comment string
14h	DWORD	address of SLSCHALLENGE structure (see Table 42-2)

INT 2Fh Function 7004h
GET ERROR
License Service

Registers at call:
AX = 7004h
CX = license server index (0000h to 001Fh)
DS:DX -> SLSGETERROR structure (see Table 42-5)
ES:BX = provider specific handle for the license context
Conflicts: none known, but see also Table 2-2
See also: Functions 7000h and 7001h

Return Registers:
AL = status
   00h not installed
   FFh installed

42-5 Format of SLSGETERROR structure:

Offset	Size	Description
00h	DWORD	(return) status code
04h	DWORD	handle identifying license context
08h	DWORD	error code
0Ch	DWORD	buffer size in bytes
10h	N BYTEs	data buffer

License Service

INT 2Fh Function 7005h
QUERY LICENSE

Registers at call:
AX = 7005h
CX = license server index (0000h to 001Fh)
DS:DX -> SLSQUERY structure (see Table 42-6)
ES:BX = provider specific handle for the license context
Conflicts: none known, but see also Table 2-2
See also: Functions 7001h and 7002h

Return Registers:
AL = status
　00h not installed
　FFh installed

42-6 Format of SLSQUERY structure:

Offset	Size	Description
00h	DWORD	(return) status code
04h	DWORD	handle identifying license context
08h	DWORD	information index
0Ch	DWORD	buffer size in bytes
10h	N BYTEs	data buffer

Embedded DOS (STARLITE Architecture)

The STARLITE interfaces described in this section permit a system using General Software's Embedded DOS (a replacement for MS-DOS) to connect to several networks simultaneously.

STARLITE architecture

INT 21h Function 5F05h
MAP LOCAL DRIVE LETTER TO REMOTE FILE SYSTEM

Registers at call:
AX = 5F05h
DL = drive number (0=A:)
DS:SI -> ASCIZ name of the object to
which to map the drive
Conflicts: MS-DOS (Chapter 3)
See also: Function 5F06h

Return Registers:
CF set on error
　AX = error code (see Table 3-1)
CF clear if successful

STARLITE architecture

INT 21h Function 5F06h
UNMAP DRIVE LETTER

Registers at call:
AX = 5F06h
DL = drive to be unmapped (0=A:)

Conflicts: MS-DOS (Chapter 3)
See also: Function 5F05h

Return Registers:
CF set on error
　AX = error code (see Table 3-1)
CF clear if successful

INT 21h Function 5F07h
MAKE NAMED OBJECT AVAILABLE ON NETWORK

STARLITE architecture

Registers at call:
AX = 5F07h
DS:SI -> ASCIZ name of object to
  offer to network
ES:DI -> ASCIZ name under which
  object will be known on the network
    (*must* begin with three slashes)
Conflicts: MS-DOS (Chapter 3)
See also: Function 5F08h

Return Registers:
CF set on error
  AX = error code (see Table 3-1)
CF clear if successful

INT 21h Function 5F08h
REMOVE GLOBAL NETWORK NAME OF OBJECT

STARLITE architecture

Registers at call:
AX = 5F08h
DS:SI -> ASCIZ network name
  (not local name) of object to unshare
Conflicts: MS-DOS (Chapter 3)
See also: Function 5F07h

Return Registers:
CF set on error
  AX = error code (see Table 3-1)
CF clear if successful

INT 21h Function 5F09h
BIND TO NETWORK DEVICE

STARLITE architecture

Registers at call:
AX = 5F09h
DS:DX -> ASCIZ name of the device
  driver to which to attach
Details: The STARLITE distributed file system can attach to multiple networks simultaneously.
See also: Function 5F0Ah

Return Registers:
CF set on error
  AX = error code (see Table 3-1)
CF clear if successful

INT 21h Function 5F0Ah
DETACH FROM NETWORK DEVICE

STARLITE architecture

Registers at call:
AX = 5F0Ah
DS:DX -> ASCIZ name of device
  driver to detach from
See also: Function 5F09h

Return Registers:
CF set on error
  AX = error code (see Table 3-1)
CF clear if successful

QPC Software PKTINT

QPC Software's PKTINT.COM provides support for using packet drivers under MS Windows.

INT 80h Function 01h
INITIALIZE

QPC Software PKTINT.COM

Registers at call:
AH = 01h

Return Registers:
AX = 0000h
CX = FFFFh
DX = FFFFh

Details: This interrupt is the WinQVTNet protected mode interface to Windows 3.0.
  All buffer pointers are reset back to 0.
Conflicts: SoundBlaster SBFM driver (PCI-22), IBM ROM BASIC (PCI-54), Q-PRO (PCI-66)

INT 80h Function 02h
GET BUFFER ADDRESSES

QPC Software PKTINT.COM

Registers at call:
AH = 02h
BX = extra bytes to allocate per packet

Return Registers:
AX = segment address of 10K buffer (*for receives*)
BX = segment address of 2K buffer (*for sends*)

Conflicts: SoundBlaster SBFM driver (PCI-22), IBM ROM BASIC (PCI-54), Q-PRO (PCI-66)
See also: Function 05h

INT 80h Function 03h
GET ENTRY POINT

QPC Software PKTINT.COM

Registers at call:
AH = 03h

Return Registers:
CX:DX -> receive call address

Details: The returned address can be used in the packet driver calls since it will be a valid address in all DOS boxes.
Conflicts: SoundBlaster SBFM driver (PCI-22), IBM ROM BASIC (PCI-54), Q-PRO (PCI-66)
See also: Function 06h

INT 80h Function 04h
ENABLE

QPC Software PKTINT.COM

Registers at call:
AH = 04h
BX = *unknown*

Return Registers:
unknown

Conflicts: SoundBlaster SBFM driver (PCI-22), IBM ROM BASIC (PCI-54), Q-PRO (PCI-66)
See also: Function 01h

INT 80h Function 05h
GET RECEIVE STATISTICS

QPC Software PKTINT.COM

Registers at call:
AH = 05h

Return Registers:
AX = amount of buffer currently in use
BX = current offset in buffer
CX = number of times receive has been called

Conflicts: SoundBlaster SBFM driver (PCI-22), IBM ROM BASIC (PCI-54), Q-PRO (PCI-66)
See also: Function 02h

INT 80h Function 06h
REMOVE RECEIVED PACKET

QPC Software PKTINT.COM

Registers at call:
AH = 06h

Return Registers:
BX = next packet offset
CX = number of bytes still buffered
DX = size of packet released back into buffer pool

Conflicts: SoundBlaster SBFM driver (PCI-22), IBM ROM BASIC (PCI-54), Q-PRO (PCI-66)
See also: Function 03h

Miscellaneous

In a chapter totally dedicated to describing "those functions which do not neatly fit into any of the other chapters", this section holds the messiest misfits of them all. That's not to say that the programs discussed in this section are "misfits" but simply that their use of interrupts did not fit into the classification technique we chose in our efforts to bring some semblance of order into the chaos of reality. If you can't find what you're looking for elsewhere in this book, it's probably in this section.

INT 2Fh Functions 7F24h and 7F26h
UNDETERMINED FUNCTIONS

Multiplex
Undocumented

Registers at call:
AX = 7F24h and 7F26h
unknown

Return Registers:
unknown

Details: These functions are called by PC/370, an IBM 370 emulator by Donald S. Higgins.
Conflicts: CD-ROM redirector (PCI-11); see also Table 2-2

INT 48h
DATA POINTER 1

Watstar PC Network

Conflicts: Acorn BBC Master and Z100 (PCI-7), Western Digital SuperBIOS (PCI-10), PCjr (PCI-13), Compaq UILIB.EXE (PCI-54)
See also: INT 49h

INT 49h
DATA POINTER 2

Watstar PC Network

Conflicts: Acorn BBC Master and Z100 (PCI-7), Texas Instruments PC (PCI-8), PCjr (PCI-13), MAGic (PCI-23)
See also: INT 48h

INT 50h
API

TIL Xpert AIM (X.25)

Registers at call:
AH = function
others as appropriate

Return Registers:
unknown

Conflicts: IBM 3278 emulation program (Chapter 37), OS/2 v1.x IRQ0 (PCI-26), DESQview IRQ0 (PCI-44), Vanderaart Text Windows and PC-Thuis Shell (PCI-66)

INT 5Ah
BIOS ENTRY ADDRESS

Cluster adapter

Conflicts: DESQview IRQ10 (PCI-44), DoubleDOS IRQ2 (PCI-49)

INT 5Bh
UNDETERMINED FUNCTION

Used by cluster adapter

Conflicts: Microsoft Network Transport Layer Interface below, AT&T Starlan NetBIOS (Chapter 8), Alloy NTNX (Chapter 12), ISOLAN Multi-Protocol Software (Chapter 31), DESQview IRQ11 (PCI-44), DoubleDOS IRQ3 (PCI-49), SitBack (PCI-66)

INT 5Bh
NETWORK COMMANDS

Microsoft Network Transport Layer Interface

Details: This interrupt is used by MS-NET for executing network commands.
Conflicts: Cluster Adapter above, AT&T Starlan NetBIOS (Chapter 8), Alloy NTNX (Chapter 12), ISOLAN Multi-Protocol Software (Chapter 31), DESQview IRQ11 (PCI-44), DoubleDOS IRQ3 (PCI-49), SitBack (PCI-66)
See also: NetBIOS INT 5Ch (Chapter 8)

INT 60h
UNDETERMINED FUNCTION

PC/370 v4.2
Undocumented

Program: PC/370 is an IBM 370 emulator by Donald S. Higgins.
Details: This is the default interrupt; the documentation includes instructions for patching the system for another interrupt.
Conflicts: see Table 2-3
See also: INT 2Fh Function 7F24h, INT DCh

INT 7Ah   *X.PC Packet software interface*
API
Registers at call: **Return Registers:**
ES:BX -> parameter block   none
Conflicts: Novell NetWare IPX/SPX drivers (Chapter 5), TopWare (Chapter 28), IBM 3270
Workstation Program (Chapter 37), IBM PC/3270 (Chapter 37), IBM 3270 Emulation Program
(Chapter 37), PRINDIR (PCI-15), GO32 (PCI-37), AutoCAD Device Interface (PCI-66)
See also: Packet Driver INT 60h Function 01FFh (Chapter 11)

INT 81h   *IBM TOKEN RING ADAPTER*
UNDETERMINED FUNCTION
Conflicts: BASIC (PCI-54)
See also: INT 82h, INT 91h

INT 82h   *IBM TOKEN RING ADAPTER*
UNDETERMINED FUNCTION
Registers at call: **Return Registers:**
AH = function   *unknown*
    00h *display message*
        DS:BX -> string
unknown
Conflicts: BASIC (PCI-54)
See also: INT 81h, INT 91h

INT 91h and INT 93h   *IBM TOKEN RING ADAPTER*
UNDETERMINED FUNCTIONS
Conflicts: BASIC (PCI-54)
See also: INT 81h, INT 82h

INT DCh   *PC/370 until v4.1*
API
Conflicts: STSC APL*PLUS/PC (PCI-53), IBM ROM BASIC (PCI-54), Screen Thief IRQ4
(PCI-66)
See also: PC/370 INT 60h

Bibliography

Julie Anderson, "Irresistible DOS 3.0", *PC Tech Journal*, volume 3 number 12, December 1984, p. 74-87.

Steven Armbrust and Ted Forgeron, ".OBJ Lessons", *PC Tech Journal*, volume 4 number 10, October 1985, p. 62-81.

AST Research, Quadram Inc., and Ashton-Tate, *Enhanced Expaneded Memory Specification (Enhanced EMS)*, version 2.0, (020022-001 A), July 1986.

Douglas Boling, "Strategies for Writing State-of-the-Art TSRs that Exploit MS-DOS", *Microsoft Systems Journal*, volume 7 number 1.

Penn Brumm and Don Brumm, *80386: A Programming and Design Handbook* (2nd ed). TAB Books, 1989. ISBN 0-8306-3237-9.

Banyan Systems, Inc., *VINES Programmer's Interface (DOS)*. Banyan Systems, Inc. 2 Jun 1988.

Borland International, *MANUAL.TNT* for Borland C++ 2.0.

Turbo Debugger hardware breakpoint interface.

Borland International, *Open Architecture Handbook.*

Borland debug information.

Byte Magazine, Volume 1 number 12 (1987 Extra Edition).

Ken W. Christopher, Jr., Barry A. Feigenbaum, and Shon O. Saliga, *Developing Applications Using DOS*, John Wiley and Sons 1990, 573pp. ISBN 0-471-52231-7.

DOS 4.0 internals and various undocumented functions.

Cirrus Logic, *Cirrus Logic CL-GD542X Technical Reference Manual*, April 1993.

Cirrus Logic, *V542X (Super VGA) User Manual.*

CL-GD 5420/5422/5426 video modes.

Computer and Business Equipment Manufacturers Association (CBEMA), "SCSI-2 Common Access Method, Transport and SCSI Interface Module, Revision 2.3", February 25, 1991. Available from the SCSI BBS, (316) 636-8700.

Computer Language Magazine, March 1990 (special issue on Windows).

Comtrol Corporation, *COMTROL HOSTESS i/ISA Programmer's Reference*, First Edition, December 1991, product number 6978-12/96/91.

Cornerstone Technology, *PG1600 Display Adapter, Installation and Reference*, First Edition, November 1987, 0010216-101A.

Ralph Davis, "Developing for NetWare", *PC Tech Journal*, volume 6 number 8, August 1988, p. 108-129.

Digital Communications Associates, Inc. and Intel Corporation, *DCA/Intel Communicating Applications Specification, version 1.2*, 27 Sep 1990. Intel Corporation, part number 301812-004 (supercedes *DCA/Intel Communicating Applications Specification, Version 1.0A*, Sep 1988),

Digital Equipment Corporation, *DECnet DOS Programmer's Reference Manual*, AA-EB46C-TV.

Digital Research Inc., DR DOS 6.0 TaskMAX API document.

The DPMI Committee, *DOS Protected Mode Interface (DPMI) Specification, Version 0.9*. Intel Corporation, 15 May 1990, order number 240763-001.

The DPMI Committee, *DOS Protected Mode Interface (DPMI) Specification, Version 1.0*. Intel Corporation, 12 March 1991, order number 240977-001.

Ray Duncan, *Advanced MSDOS* (1st edition), Microsoft Press 1986, 468pp. ISBN 0-914845-77-2.

Ray Duncan, *Advanced MSDOS Programming: the Microsoft Guide for Assembly Language and C Programmers* (2nd ed), Microsoft Press 1988.

Ray Duncan, "DOS Extenders Old and New: Protected-Mode Programming in DOS", *PC*, volume 10 number 4, 26 February 1991, p. 385-391.

Ray Duncan (ed), *Extending DOS*, Addison-Wesley 1990, 432pp. ISBN 0-201-55053-9.

Ray Duncan, *IBM ROM BIOS*, Microsoft Press 1988, 126pp. ISBN 1-55615-135-7.

Ray Duncan (ed), *The MS-DOS Encyclopedia*, Microsoft Press 1988, 1570pp. ISBN 1-55615-174-8.

Bo Ericsson, "VESA VGA BIOS Extensions", *Dr. Dobb's Journal* #163, April 1990, p. 65H-70.

Ted Forgeron, "We Interrupt This Program", *PC Tech Journal*, volume 4 number 4, April 1985, p. 42. *Tech Notebook on trapping control-break.*

Susan Glinert-Cole, "A Network for All Reasons", *PC Tech Journal*, volume 3 number 12, December 1984, p. 90-106. *Discussion of the IBM PC Network, and brief looks at INT 2Ah and INT 5Ch.*

Augie Hansen, "Detecting Display Systems", *PC Tech Journal*, volume 5 number 7, July 1987, p. 174-182.

J. Axorr Haugdahl, "The DOS-LAN Juncture", *PC Tech Journal*, volume 5 number 7, July 1987, p 78-90. Includes a detailed description of file-sharing modes.

Helix Software, CLOAKAPI.INC and RMFUNCS.DOC on Netroom Supplemental Disk.

Thomas V. Hoffmann, "Graphic Enhancement", *PC Tech Journal*, volume 4 number 4, April 1985, p. 58-71.

Michael Holmes and Bob Flanders, "PCSPOOL Lets You Get Back to Work While You Print", *PC*, volume 10 number 1, 15 January 1991, p. 419-433.

Intel Corporation, *80286 and 80287 Programmer's Reference Manual*. Intel Corporation 1987, order number 210498-004. ISBN 1-55512-055-5.

Intel Corporation, *i486 (tm) Microprocessor Programmer's Reference Manual*. McGraw-Hill 1990. ISBN 0-07-881674-2.

Intel Corporation and Microsoft Corporation, *Advanced Power Management: The Next Generation*, version 1.0.

Stephen E. Jones, *General Software Project STARLITE: Architecture Specification, 1 October 1990*.

Art Krumrey, "NetWare in Control", *PC Tech Journal*, volume 4 number 11, November 1985, p. 102-119. *Briefly covers NetWare interrupt calls.*

Richard Kryszak, "Multiuser DOS for Control Systems: Part I", *Dr. Dobb's Journal*, April 1992.

John A. Lefor and Karen Lund, "Reaching into Expanded Memory", *PC Tech Journal*, volume 5 number 5, May 1987, p. 100-124.

Pete Maclean, "1STCLASS and COURIERS Make Binary MCI Transfers Easy", *PC*, volume 8 number 19, 14 November 1989, p. 399-408.

Teddy Matsumoto, "DIET APPLICATION INTERFACE version 1.43e" (DIETAPI.DOC).

Microsoft Corporation, "Errors in the VDS API in Enhanced Mode Windows", KnowledgeBase article Q77998, November 8, 1991.

Microsoft Corporation, *eXtended Memory Specification (XMS), version 2.0*, July 19, 1988.

Microsoft Corporation, *Microsoft MS-DOS CD-ROM Extensions Function Requests*, 28 May 1988. *MSCDEX v2.00 documentation.*

Microsoft Corporation, *Microsoft MS-DOS CD-ROM Extensions Function Requests Specification*, 29 March 1989. *MSCDEX v2.10 documentation.*

Microsoft Corporation, *Microsoft MS-DOS CD-ROM Extensions Hardware-Dependent Device Driver Specification*, 17 March 1989. Document number 000080010-100-O00-1186.

Microsoft Corporation, "Using Auto-Initialize DMA under Windows", KnowledgeBase article Q83012, April 17, 1992.

Microsoft Corporation, *Virtual DMA Services (VDS), Version 1.00*, July 16, 1990.

Microsoft Press, *Microsoft MS-DOS(r) Programmer's Reference*, version 5, ISBN 1-55615-329-5.

Stan Mitchell, "Building Device Drivers", *PC Tech Journal*, volume 4 number 5, May 1985, p. 76-87.

Bob Montgomery, VPIC version 4.6 and 5.0 configuration files.

Rick Moore, "Fundamentals of FOSSIL Implementation and Use, Version 5", Fidonet document FSC-0015, 11 February 1988.

Rick Moore, "VFOSSIL - An OS/2-Subset Video FOSSIL Appendage, Version 1.00", Fidonet document FSC-0021, 23 May 1988.

Nanosoft, Inc., MultiDOS Plus on-line manual, available from Nanosoft BBS (508) 650-9552.

John G. Nelson, "Japanese Double Byte Character Processing", *Windows/DOS Developer's Journal*, January 1992.

John G. Nelson, "Uncovering the NEC-9801 PC", *Windows/DOS Developer's Journal*, January 1992.

Novell, Inc., "API/HLLAPI Information", *SNA Note 3-133*, March 7, 1991.

Novell, Inc., *Btrieve Reference Manual, Rev. 2.00, For Btrieve Version 5.0 and above.* Novell Development Products Division, 6034 W. Courtyard Suite 220, Austin TX 78370, October 1988. Novell P/N 100-410000-410.

Novell, Inc., *NetWare Access Server Driver Specification",* Version 1.0, November 17, 1992. Part number 107-000018-002.

Novell, Inc., *NetWare(r) System Calls, Rev. 1.00.* Novell Development Products Division, #917, P.O.Box 9802, Austin TX 78766, April 1989. Novell P/N 100-000571-001. (supercedes Advanced NetWare 2.0 Reference, Novell, and NetWare Function Call Reference)

Novell, Inc., *NetWare(r) System Calls—DOS*, Volume I and Volume II (item numbers 100-00571-002 and 100-000572-002), 1989.

Novell, Inc., *NetWare(r) System Interface Technical Overview.* Addison-Wesley 1990, 346+xvi pp. ISBN 0-201-57027-0.

Novell, Inc., *ODI Developer's Guide for DOS Protocol Stacks*, Revision 1.1 3/18/92. Available for anonymous FTP from sjf-lwp.novell.com.

Novell, Inc., NOVLIB file SC3X04.EXE.

Vincent E. Perriello, "Fundamentals of FOSSIL Implementation and Use, Draft Version 4", Fidonet document FSC-0008, 10 August 1987.

Phar Lap Software, *Virtual Control Program Interface, Version 1.0.* 12 June 1989.

Phoenix Technologies, *PCMCIA Socket Services Interface Specification*, Revision A.00, June 20, 1991.

Phoenix Technologies, *System BIOS for IBM(r) PC/XT(tm)/AT(r) Computers and Compatibles*, Addison-Wesley 1989, 524pp. ISBN 0-201-51806-6.

Paul Pierce, "The Dashed Cursor", *PC Tech Journal*, volume 4 number 12, December 1985, p. 47.
Discusses a bug in the EGA BIOS which turns underline cursor into dash.

"Programmer's Workbench", *Dr. Dobb's Journal*, January 1992.
Discusses SMARTDRV API.

Jeff Prosise, "Mouse Software: See How They Run", *PC*, volume 6 number 13, July 1987, p. 411-428.

Quarterdeck Office Systems, *DESQview API Reference Guide*, 232pp.

Quarterdeck Office Systems, QDMEM.DOC and QPI.DOC, June 15, 1993.

Que Corporation, *DOS and BIOS Functions Quick Reference.* Que Corporation 1989, 154pp. ISBN 0-88022-426-6.

Guy Quedens and Gary Webb, "Switching Modes", *PC Tech Journal*, volume 4 number 8, August 1985, p. 163-173.
Switching the 286 into and out of protected mode.

John W. Ratcliff, "Examining PC Audio, welcome to the wild and wooly world of PC sound", *Dr. Dobb's Journal* #198, March 1993.
IBMSND driver API.

Glen F. Roberts, "Finding Disk Parameters", *PC Tech Journal*, volume 4 number 5, May 1986, p. 112-150.

Robin Rodabaugh, "Accelerating 2.1", *PC Tech Journal*, volume 5 number 4, April 1986, p. 43.
Reducing floppy head-settling time for faster throughput.

Leo J. Scanlon, "An Alarm for the AT", *PC Tech Journal*, volume 5 number 4, April 1986, p. 179-182.
Introduces the real-time clock's alarm and INT 4Ah.

Andrew Schulman, Raymond J. Michels, Jim Kyle, Tim Paterson, David Maxey, and Ralf Brown, *Undocumented DOS: A Programmer's Guide to Reserved MS-DOS(r) Functions and Data Structures.* Addison-Wesley 1990, 694+xviii pp. ISBN 0-201-57064-5.

W. David Schwaderer, "Exploiting NetBIOS", *Programmer's Journal*, volume 8.1, Jan/Feb 1990, p. 39-45.

W. David Schwaderer, *C Programmer's Guide to NetBIOS.* Howard Sams 1988. ISBN 0-672-22638-3.

Seiko Epson Corp., *SOLLEX Super VGA Standard (Smos videO controLLer EXtensions)*, No. S03-SP-001-01, September 23, 1991.

Softwarehouse Corporation, *The Connection Manager User's Guide*,
Third Edition, February 1993.

Paul Somerson, "DOS Lives", *PC*, volume 6 number 13, July 1987, p. 175-188.
Overview of DOS 3.3.

Robert B. Stam, "Environmental Excavations", *PC Tech Journal*, volume 4 number 2, February 1985, p. 90-98.
Getting at the DOS environment from Turbo Pascal.

George Adam Stanislav, "AVATAR: Advanced Video Attribute Terminal Assembler and Recreator", Fidonet document FSC-0025, 23 August 1988.
Describes AVATAR level 0 codes as used in the Opus BBS software.

George Adam Stanislav, "AVATAR: Advanced Video Attribute Terminal Assembler and Recreator", Fidonet document FSC-0037, 1 May 1989 (revised 25 November 1989).
Describes the additional codes made available in AVATAR level 0+.

Pawel Szczerbina, "The NetWare Core Protocol (NCP)", *Dr. Dobb's* Journal, November 1993.

Tiara Computer Systems, "10NET Implementation Specification".

Michael Triner, "The High Road to Host Connectivity", *PC Tech Journal*, volume 7 number 1, January 1989, p. 85-94.

V Communications, Inc. "RSIS: Relocated Screen Interface Specification".

John Vanderaart, "The Golden Btriever", *LAN Magazine*, July 1990.
Vanderaart Text-Windows API.

John Vanderaart, "Voorheen Methode Vanderaart", *PC Thuis Power* magazine, June/July 1990.
Vanderaart PC Thuis Shell.

Video Electronics Standards Association, *Super VGA BIOS Extension*, Standard #VS900602, 2 June 1990.

Video Electronics Standards Association, *Super VGA BIOS Extension*, Standard #VS911022, 22 October 1991.
Version 1.2.

Richard Wilton, "DOS Marches On", *PC Tech Journal*, volume 7 number 1, January 1989, p. 99-108.
Description of new DOS 4.0 features.

Additional References

Many of the reference materials from which information in the interrupt list forming the basis of this volume were extracted have been lost in the mists of time, or were never indicated by contributors in the first place. The following is a list of the materials for which we have only partial references.

10-Net Reference Manual v2.0.

Advanced Program-to-Program Communication for the IBM Personal Computer, Programming Guide (2nd ed), Dec 1986.

Carbon Copy Plus user's manual.

Compaq DeskPro 386 Technical Reference Guide.

Da Vinci Systems Dispatcher Development Toolkit (Revision 2), June 20, 1990.

Dr. Dobbs' Journal, May 1986 (BIOS Window Extensions).

Everex Viewpoint Owner's Manual and Reference Guide, version 1.0, Everex Corp.

FaxBios sample source code dated October 1, 1991.

FTP Software Professional Development Series Bulletins, v2n5 (June 1990).

Hercules GraphX manual, edition 2.1, Aug 1986.

IBM 3270 Workstation Program Version 1.10, Programming Guide, Dec 1987.

IBM VGA-Compatible Video Graphics Controller User's Manual.

Inset Systems, *Inset Extended Specification*, 23 Nov 1988.

Intel Image Processing Interface Specification, Version 1.0, 1989.

LAN-Magazine, issue #1.

LANtastic (tm) Network Operating System Technical Reference Manual.

LANtastic (tm) Network Operating System Technical Reference Manual, version 3.0, 6/13/90.

MS-DOS Extensions Quick Reference, Ray Duncan Microsoft Systems Journal, 9/87.

Microsoft Windows 3.0 Device Driver Kit.

Novell Network Driver Interface Specification 2.01, May 18, 1990.

Networking Software, ed. Colin B. Ungaro, McGraw Hill, p265.

PC Magazine, February 26, 1991. Windows 3.0 DOSX.

PC Mouse Reference Manual v4.00.

PC/TCP Packet Driver Specification, version 1.09.

Programmer's Guide to EGA and VGA Programming, second edition.

Tseng Labs, *ET4000 Graphics Controller Data Book.*

Video Seven VGA Technical Reference Manual.

pcANYWHERE v2.10 User's Guide.

ABNORMAL EXIT (INT 2Fh Function 7A80h), 419
ABORT SERVICING QUEUE JOB/FILE (INT 21h Function E3h Subfunction 73h), 394
ABORT SPX CONNECTION (INT 7Ah Function 0014h), 100-101
ABORT TRANSACTION (INT 21h Function C703h), 405
ABSOLUTE DISK READ (INT 2Fh Function 1508h), 242
ABSOLUTE DISK WRITE (INT 2Fh Function 1509h), 243
ACCEPT (SOCKET API Function 0013h), 264-265
access server, NetWare, 427-430
ACCESS TYPE (INT 60h Function), 151
ACCESS VECTOR (INT 7Fh), 524
accounting services, NetWare, 316-318
ACKNOWLEDGE DATAGRAM (INT 7Fh Function 12h), 176
ACTIVATE DLC (INT 68h, Function 01h, Subfunction 2B00h), 200
ACTIVATE USER-WRITTEN PRINTER DRIVER (INT 17h Function 8Ah), 162
ADD BINDERY OBJECT TO SET (INT 21h Function E3h Subfunction 41h), 326-327
ADD DIAGNOSTIC ELEMENT (INT 7Ah Function 0018h), 102
ADD PRINTER TO SPOOLER (INT 17h Function 89h), 161
ADD TRUSTEE TO DIRECTORY (INT 21h Function E2h Subfunction 0Dh), 340
ADD UNKNOWN ITEM
(INT 62h Function 0Bh), 528
(INT 64h Function 03h), 527-528
ALLOCATE (INT 68h, Function 02h, Subfunction 0100h), 200-202
ALLOCATE A VIRTUAL CIRCUIT (INT 6Bh Function 11h), 661
ALLOCATE FREE CLUSTER ON SHARED DRIVE (INT 7Fh Function 06h), 171
ALLOCATE GLOBAL DESCRIPTOR (INT 61h Function 29h), 555
ALLOCATE NETWORK DESCRIPTOR (INT 61h Function 22h), 554
ALLOCATE PERMANENT DIRECTORY HANDLE (INT 21h Function E2h Subfunction 12h), 341
ALLOCATE RESOURCE (INT 21h Function D8h), 411
ALLOCATE SPECIAL TEMP DIRECTORY HANDLE (INT 21h Function E2h Subfunction 16h), 343
ALLOCATE TEMPORARY DIRECTORY HANDLE (INT 21h Function E2h Subfunction 13h), 342
ALLOCATE UNKNOWN (INT 6Ah Function 0004h), 569

ALLOCATE/MAP EMS FOR DRIVER (INT 62h Function 18h), 530
Alloy Computer Products, Inc, 157-193
Alloy multiuser/network systems, 157-193
Alternate Multiplex Interrupt Specification (AMIS), 7
ANSK (Alloy NetWare Support Kit), 157-193
API
(INT 16h Function FF70h), 275
(INT 21h Function 4402h), 563
(INT 21h Function 44E0h), 566
(INT 2Fh Function 92h), 680
(INT 50h), 686
(INT 53h), 502
(INT 5Bh), 519
(INT 5Ch), 519, 522-523
(INT 60h), 508-510
(INT 61h), 570
(INT 6Ch), 254
(INT 7Ah), 687
(INT 7Bh), 644
(INT 7Fh), 664-665
(INT 92h), 643
(INT DCh), 687
OVERVIEW (INT 92h Function E1h), 669
POINTER (INT 0Ch), 635
APPC/PC protocol, 195-214
AppleTalk INTERFACE (INT 5Ch), 520-522
APT (INT 60h), 643
ARM MODIFIED LOCATION TRIGGER (INT 6Fh Function 002Bh), 642
ArtiCom interrupts, 645-649
ASSIGN DIRECTORY TO GROUP (INT 7Fh Function F1h), 192
ASSIGN GROUP NAME (INT 7Fh Function FBh), 193
ASSIGN USER TO GROUP (INT 7Fh Function F8h), 192
ASYNCHRONOUS SEND PACKET
(INT 60h Function 0Bh), 153
(INT 60h Function 0Ch), 153-154
ATTACH OR RELEASE DRIVE FOR LOW-LEVEL WRITE ACCESS (INT 7Fh Function 24h), 180
ATTACH ASYNCHRONOUS RESOURCE (INT 14h Function 8004h), 646-647
ATTACH DEVICE FOR USER (INT 7Fh Function 81h), 185
ATTACH LOGICAL COMMUNICATIONS PORT TO PHYSICAL PORT (INT 14h Function 20h), 158
ATTACH LOGICAL UNIT (INT 68h, Function 01h, Subfunction 2100h), 197-199
ATTACH PHYSICAL UNIT (INT 68h, Function 01h, Subfunction 2000h), 196-197

ATTACH QUEUE SERVER TO QUEUE (INT 21h Function E3h Subfunction 6Fh), 392
ATTACH/DETACH PRINTER (INT 6Fh Function 10h), 472
ATTACH/RELEASE HOST PROCESSOR (INT 7Fh Function 24h), 180
AttachHandle (INT 21h Function B4h), 409-410
Attachmate Extra! interrupts, 622-624
AUDIT
(INT 6Fh Function 19h), 474
(INT 6Fh Function 99h), 478
AUTOSELECT TRANSCEIVER (INT 60h Function E9h), 156

Banyan interrupt handler, 215
Banyan VINES, 215-240
BAPI (Bridge Application Program Interface) functions, 87-90
BASIC interpreter, 7-8
BASIC.COM file, 8
BASICA.COM file, 8
Beame & Whiteside BWCOM14 interrupts, 650 software, 525-539
BECOME MICRO TSR (INT 92h Function E175h), 676
BEGIN BACKGROUND PRINTING (INT 2Ah Function 8700h), 63
BEGIN CRITICAL SECTION (INT 62h Function 0Eh), 529
BEGIN DOS CRITICAL SECTION (INT 2Ah Function 80h), 62
BEGIN LOGICAL FILE LOCKING (INT 21h Function C8h), 400
BEGIN TRANSACTION (INT 21h Function C700h), 404-405
BIND (SOCKET API Function 0011h), 264
BIND TO NETWORK DEVICE (INT 21h, Function 5F09h), 684
bindery services, NetWare, 318-329
BIOS ENTRY ADDRESS (INT 5Ah), 686
BROADCAST INFORM (INT 2Fh Function 7A85h), 419
BROADCAST TO CONSOLE (INT 21h Function E1h Subfunction 09h), 378
BSD 4.x Unix Sockets, 575-593
BUFFERED READ
(INT 14h Function E2h), 572
(INT 6Bh Function 0100h), 660
BUFFERED WRITE
(INT 14h Function E3h), 572
(INT 6Bh Function 000h), 660
BUG (INT 2Fh Function 9200h), 275
BUILD CURRENT DIRECTORY STRUCTURE (INT 2Fh Function 121Fh), 69
BULL (INT 6Fh Function 1Ah), 474
BW-NFS, 525-539
BW-TCP, 525-539
BWCOM14 interrupts, 650

CALL ETHDEV.SYS (INT 64h Function 10h), 538

CALL TopLook FUNCTION (INT 21h Function FFCCFh), 491-492

CALL TopShow FUNCTION (INT 21h Function FF8Dh), 485

calls, networking, 681-687

CANCEL ALL JOBS FOR CURRENT USER (INT 17h Function 82h), 160

CANCEL DIAGNOSTIC ELEMENT (INT 7Ah Function 0019h), 102-103

CANCEL EVENT (INT 7Ah Function 0006h), 96

CANCEL FLUSH OR WRITE (INT 7Fh Function 26h, Subfunction 06h), 181

CANCEL JOBS FOR CURRENT USER (INT 17h Function 81h), 159-160

CANCEL LPT CAPTURE (INT 21h Function DFh Subfunction 02h), 382

CANCEL REDIRECTION (INT 21h Function 5F04h), 59

CANCEL SERVER SHUTDOWN (INT 21h Function 5FC9h), 306-307

CANCEL SPECIFIC LPT CAPTURE (INT 21h Function DFh Subfunction 06h), 383

CANCEL TopShow FUNCTION (INT 21h Function FF8Eh), 485 (INT 21h Function FFBCh), 487

CANONICALIZE FILE NAME (INT 2Fh Function 1221h), 70 (SOCKET API Function 0024h), 270

CCPOP 3270 interrupts, 643

CD-ROM, 241-245

Central Point Software (PC Tools), 275-280

CHANGE BINDERY OBJECT PASSWORD (INT 21h Function E3h Subfunction 40h), 326

CHANGE BINDERY OBJECT SECURITY (INT 21h Function E3h Subfunction 38h), 322

CHANGE CONSOLE MODE (INT 7Fh Function C5h), 188

CHANGE DRIVER ADDRESS (INT 7Ch Function 0003h), 442

CHANGE LOGICAL UNIT (INT 68h, Function 03h, Subfunction 2A00h), 210-211

CHANGE NAME OF DOS TASK (INT 7Fh Function E3h), 190

CHANGE NUMBER OF SESSIONS (INT 68h, Function 06h), 212

CHANGE PASSWORD (INT 21h Function 5F85h), 296

CHANGE PHYSICAL PORT PARAMETERS (INT 14h Function 24h), 159

CHANGE PROPERTY SECURITY (INT 21h Function E3h Subfunction 38h), 323

CHANGE QUEUE JOB ENTRY (INT 21h Function E3h Subfunction 6Dh), 391-392

CHANGE QUEUE JOB POSITION (INT 21h Function E3h Subfunction 63h), 392

CHANGE TEMPORARY SPOOL DRIVE (INT 17h Function A9h), 167

CHANGE TO CLIENT RIGHTS (INT 21h Function E3h Subfunction 74h), 394-295

Channel Control functions, 173-175

CHAT (INT 6Fh Function 0Ah), 468 (INT 6Fh Function 8Ah), 476

CHDIR (INT 2Fh Function 1105h), 124-125

CHECK CONSOLE PRIVILEGES (INT 21h Function E3h Subfunction C8h), 349

CHECK DIRECT I/O (INT 2Ah Function 0300H), 61

CHECK FOR USER FUNCTION COMMAND WORD (INT 16h Function 5404h), 678

CHECK IF CHARACTER DEVICE (INT 2Fh Function 1223h), 70

CHECK IF CONNECTION ALIVE (INT 5Ch Function 04h), 523

CHECK IF MAPPED DRIVE (INT 2Fh Function 9201h), 276

CHECK IF NETWORK DESCRIPTOR VALID (INT 61h Function 0Dh), 548

CHECK IF REDIRECTED DRIVE (INT 2Fh Function 5601h), 511

CHECK PIPE STATUS (INT 21h Function E1h Subfunction 08h), 378

CHECK PORT ASSIGNMENT (INT 7Fh Function 31h), 182

CHECK PRINTER DRIVER (INT 17h Function 92h), 163

CHECK SERVICE (INT 61h, Function 01h), 240

CHECK SPOOLER (INT 17h Function AFh), 168

CHECKSUM MEMORY (INT 2Fh Function 121Ch), 69

CLEAR CONNECTION NUMBER (INT 21h Function E3h Subfunction D2h), 353

CLEAR FILE (FCB) (INT 21h Function CEh), 401-402

CLEAR FILE (INT 21h Function EDh), 404

CLEAR FILE SET (INT 21h Function CFh), 402

CLEAR LOGICAL RECORD (INT 21h Function D4h), 403

CLEAR LOGICAL RECORD SET (INT 21h Function D5h), 403

CLEAR PHYSICAL RECORD (INT 21h Function BEh), 397

CLEAR PHYSICAL RECORD SET (INT 21h Function C4h), 398

CLEAR RECORD (FCB) (INT 21h Function C1h), 398

CLEAR UNKNOWN FLAG (INT 2Fh Function 9404h), 680

CLIENT - INCREMENT UNKNOWN COUNTER (INT 2Ah Function D850h), 421

CLIENT - RESET UNKNOWN COUNTER (INT 2Ah Function D851h), 421

CLIENT HOOK (INT 7Ch Function 0010h), 448

CLIENT UNHOOK (INT 7Ch Function 0011h), 448

CLIENT.EXE - INSTALLATION CHECK (INT 2Fh Function D800h), 421 424

CLOSE A NETWORK DESCRIPTOR (INT 61h Function 08h), 545

CLOSE A SOCKET (INT 61h, Function 0001h, Subfunction 0004h), 220

CLOSE ALL CHANNELS (INT 7Fh Function 10h, Subfunction 05h), 174

CLOSE ALL FILES FOR GIVEN COMPUTER (INT 21h Function 5D03h), 47

CLOSE ALL FILES FOR GIVEN PROCESS (INT 21h Function 5D04h), 47

CLOSE ALL FILES FOR PROCESS (INT 2Fh Function 112Ah), 134

CLOSE ALL NON-GLOBAL DESCRIPTORS, (INT 61h Function 09h), 545

CLOSE ALL REMOTE FILES FOR PROCESS (INT 2Fh Function 111Dh), 131

CLOSE BINDERY (INT 21h Function E3h Subfunction 44h), 328

CLOSE CHANNEL (INT 7Fh Function 10h, Subfunction 01h), 173

CLOSE COMMUNICATION (INT 14h Function 05h), 655

CLOSE CURRENT FILE (INT 2Fh Function 1201h), 64

CLOSE FILE (INT 2Fh Function 1227h), 71

CLOSE FILE AND START QUEUE JOB (INT 21h Function E3h Subfunction 69h), 389

CLOSE FILE BY NAME (INT 21h, Function 5D02h), 47

CLOSE MESSAGE PIPE (INT 21h Function E1h Subfunction 07h), 377

CLOSE NETWORK DESCRIPTOR (INT 63h Function 0Eh), 533

CLOSE REMOTE FILE (INT 2Fh Function 1106h), 125

CLOSE SEMAPHORE (INT 21h Function C504h), 399-400

CLOSE SESSION (INT 69h Function 0106h), 248 (INT 6Ah Function D000h), 252

CLOSE SOCKET (INT 7Ah Function 0001h), 92 (SOCKET API Function 0006h), 260-261

CLOSE SPOOL FILES/START PRINTING (INT 2Fh Function FF23h), 495

CLOSE TRANSMIT SIDE OF CONNECTION (INT 61h Function 18h), 550

codes, extended MS-DOS error, 21-23

COMMIT ALL FILES (INT 21h Function 5D01h), 46-47

COMMIT REMOTE FILE (INT 2Fh Function 1107h), 125

COMPARE FAR POINTERS (INT 2Fh Function 1214h), 67

COMPARE FILENAMES (INT 2Fh Function 121Eh), 69

CONFIGURE RUNNING KERNEL (INT 61h Function Subfunction 000h), 544

CONFIRM (INT 68h, Function 02h, Subfunction 0300h), 202-203

CONFIRMED (INT 68h, Function 02h, Subfunction 0400h), 203

conflicts, probability of, 7

CONNECT (SOCKET API Function 0008h), 261

CONNECT TO PORT (NT 14h Function A0h), 87

CONNECT TO X SERVER (SOCKET API Function 0014h), 265

CONNECTION CONTROL
(INT 14h Function A9h), 571-572
(INT 14h Function E4h), 572-573
(INT 21h Function E3h), 329-331

Connection controls, 200-210

CONNECTION INFORMATION (INT 14h Function A8h), 571

Connection Manager interrupts, 650-658

connection services, NetWare, 329-334

CONTROL (INT 6Bh Function 0600h), 660

CONTROL MONITOR (INT 61h Function 0003h, Subfunction 02h), 229-230

CONTROL QUEUE (INT 21h Function 5FA2h), 300-301

CONVERT (INT 68h, Function FBh), 213

CONVERT CURSOR POSITION TO ROW/COLUMN (INT 6Fh Function 001Ah), 640

CONVERT ROW/COLUMN TO CURSOR POSITON (INT 6Fh Function 0019h), 639

COPY FILE (INT 21h Function 5F97h), 297

COPY FILE TO FILE (FCB) (INT 21h Function E6h), 412

COPY LAT COUNTERS (INT 6Ah Function D400h), 253

COPY SERVICE (INT 7Ah Function 09h), 632

CREATE A QUEUE (INT 7Ah Function 04h), 629

CREATE BINDERY OBJECT (INT 21h Function E3h Subfunction 32h), 319

CREATE DIRECTORY (INT 21h Function E2h Subfunction 0Ah), 338-339

CREATE DOS TASK (INT 7Fh Function 30h), 189-190

CREATE INDIRECT FILE (INT 21h Function 5FB4h), 305

CREATE NEW SOCKET (SOCKET API Function 000Ah), 262

CREATE PROPERTY (INT 21h Function E3h Subfunction 39h), 322-323

CREATE QUEUE (INT 21h Function E3h Subfunction 64h), 386

CREATE QUEUE JOB AND FILE (INT 21h Function E3h Subfunction 68h), 388-389

CREATE USER AUDIT ENTRY (INT 21h Function 5FA7h), 302

CREATE/TRUNCATE FILE WITHOUT CDS (INT 2Fh Function 1118h), 129

CREATE/TRUNCATE REMOTE FIELD (INT 2Fh Function 1117h), 129

CRITICAL SECTION (INT 2Fh Function 9212h), 278

Da Vinci eMail interrupts, 669-676

DATA LINK LAYER (INT 69h Function 0Ah), 249-250

DATA LINK LAYER PROGRAM (INT 6Dh), 254

DATA POINTER 1 (INT 48h), 686

DATA POINTER 2 (INT 49h), 686

data structures, MS-DOS, 75-86

DCA 10Net, 457-482

DEALLOCATE (INT 68h, Function 02h, Subfunction 0500h), 203-204

DEALLOCATE DIRECTORY HANDLE (INT 21h Function E2h Subfunction 14h), 342

DEALLOCATE RESOURCE (INT 21h Function D9h), 411

DECnet DOS, 247-254

DECnet NETWORK PROCESS API (INT 6Eh), 254

DECnet STATUS (INT 69h Function 0104h), 248

DECREMENT SFT REFERENCE COUNT (INT 2Fh Function 1208h), 65

DEFINE TEMPORARY FILENAME (INT 17h Function A8h), 167

DEINSTALL CTERM (INT 69h Function 010Fh), 249

DELETE A QUEUE (INT 7Ah Function 06h), 629

DELETE BINDERY OBJECT (INT 21h Function E3h Subfunction 33h), 319-320

DELETE BINDERY OBJECT FROM SET (INT 21h Function E3h Subfunction 42h), 327

DELETE DIRECTORY (INT 21h Function E2h Subfunction 0Bh), 339

DELETE FILE FROM SPOOLING QUEUE (INT 21h Function FFC8h), 490

DELETE PROPERTY (INT 21h Function E3h Subfunction 3Ah), 323

DELETE REMOTE FILE
(INT 2Fh Function 1113h), 128
(INT 2Fh Function 1114h), 128

DELETE SHARED DEVICE (INT 6Fh Function 9503h), 478

DELETE SHARED DEVICE ENTRY (INT 6Fh Function 1503h), 473

DELETE TRUSTEE FROM DIRECTORY (INT 21h Function E2h Subfunction 0Eh), 340

DESQview/X, 255-274

DESQview/X Socket API functions, 258-274

DESQview/X socket interrupts, 255-258

DESTROY QUEUE (INT 21h Function E3h Subfunction 65h), 386

DETACH ASYNCHRONOUS RESOURCE (INT 14h Function 8005h), 647

DETACH FROM NETWORK DEVICE (INT 21h, Function 5F0Ah), 684

DETACH LOGICAL UNIT (INT 68h, Function 01h, Subfunction 2200h), 199-200

DETACH PHYSICAL UNIT (INT 68h, Function 01h, Subfunction 2700h), 200

DETACH QUEUE SERVER FROM QUEUE (INT 21h Function E3h Subfunction 70h), 393

DETACH SOCKET (SOCKET API Function 0020h), 269

DETECT READINESS OF NETWORK (INT 61h Function 0Eh), 548

Digital Equipment Corporation (DECnet), 247-254

DIRECT MEMORY TRANSFER (INT 7Fh Function 16h), 179

directory services, NetWare, 334-347

DISABLE ACCOUNT (INT 21h Function 5F86h), 296

DISABLE ASYNCHRONOUS HANDLERS (INT 61h Function 11h), 548-549

DISABLE BUFFER UPDATES (INT 21h Function B8h), 624

DISABLE DRIVE (INT 21h Function 5F08h), 60

DISABLE FILE SERVER LOGIN (INT 21h Function E3h Subfunction CBh), 350

DISABLE MULTICAST (INT 7Ch Function 000Ah), 446

DISABLE PROTOCOL (INT 7Ch Function 0008h), 445

DISABLE TRANSACTION TRACKING (INT 21h Function E3h Subfunction CFh), 351 352

DISCONNECT A VIRTUAL CIRCUIT (INT 6Bh Function 17h), 662

DISCONNECT FROM PORT (INT 14h Function A1h), 87

DISCONNECT FROM TARGET (INT 7Ah Function 000Bh), 97-98

Disk Server Information (INT E1h), 524

DISPLAY (INT 68h, Function 01h, Subfunction 1B00h), 195-196

DO REDIRECTION (INT 2Fh Function 111Eh), 131-132

DOS TASK DELAY (INT 7Fh Function E8h), 191

DOS
embedded interrupts, 683-684
parameter list, 46

DosCallNmPipe (INT 21h Function 5F37h), 106-107

DosDeleteMailSlot (INT 21h Function 5F4Eh), 289

DosMailSlotInfo (INT 21h Function 5F4Fh), 289
DosMakeMailSlot (INT 21h Function 5F4Dh), 289
DosPeekMailslot (INT 21h Function 5F51h), 290
DosReadAsynchNmPipe
    (INT 2Fh Function 1186h), 292
    (INT 2Fh Function 1190h), 293
DosReadMailslot (INT 21h Function 5F50h), 289
DosWriteAsynchNmPipe
    (INT 2Fh Function 118Fh), 292
    (INT 2Fh Function 1191h), 293
DosWriteMailslot (INT 21h Function 5F52h), 290
DOWN (UNINSTALL) DRIVER (INT 7Ch Function 0001h), 441-442
DOWN FILE SERVER (INT 21h Function E3h Subfunction D3h), 353
DRIVE CHECK (INT 2Fh Function 150Bh), 243
DRIVEMAP, 275-280
DRIVER I/O CONTROL (INT 7Ch Function 0016h), 450
drivers, old-style configuration, 558-560
DROP A SESSION (INT 14h Function A6h), 659
DROP PACKET FROM QUEUE (INT 60h Function 0Dh), 154
DUMP STRING TO TERMINAL (INT 7Fh Function 37h), 182

electronic mail interrupts, 677-679
Embedded DOS interrupts, 683-684
EN/DISABLE (ECM) CHARACTER (INT 14h Function B0h), 89
ENABLE (INT 80h Function 04h), 685
ENABLE ASYNCHRONOUS HAN-DLERS (INT 61h Function 12h), 549
ENABLE DRIVE INT (21h Function 5F07h), 60
ENABLE FILE SERVER LOGIN (INT 21h Function E3h Subfunction CCh), 351
ENABLE TRANSACTION TRACK-ING (INT 21h Function E3h Sub-function D0h), 352
ENABLE/DISABLE
    API FUNCTIONS (INT 17h Function 2400h), 513-514
    API VERB TRACING (INT 68h, Function FDh), 214
    APPC (INT 68h, Function FAh), 213
    AUTOBAND DETECT (INT 7Fh Function 3Ch), 183
    BANNER PAGE (INT 17h Function A6h), 167
    BRAODCAST MESSAGES (INT 21h Function E1h Subfunc-tion 02h/03h), 375
    FORM FEED (INT 17h Function A4h), 166
    KEYBOARD (INT 6Fh Function 0027h), 642
    MESSAGE TRACING (INT 68h, Function FCh), 213
    MUD FILE CHECKING (INT 7Fh Function 09h), 172

TopTerm SERVICE (INT 21h Function FF9Fh), 486
END ACCESS TO SPECIFIC PACKET TYPE (INT 21h Func-tion FFE3h, Subfunction 01h), 493
END ACTIVE SESSION (INT 61h Function 0003h, Subfunction 04h), 230
END BACKGROUND PRINTING (INT 2Ah Function 8701h), 63
END BACKGROUND RECEIVE VIDEO DATA (INT 2Fh Func-tion FF15h), 494
END CHARACTER-ORIENTED TRANSMIT (INT 17h Function 240Ch), 515
END CRITICAL SECTION (INT 62h Function 0Fh), 529
END DOS CRITICAL SECTION (INT 2Ah Function 81h), 62
END DOS CRITICAL SECTIONS 0 THROUGH 7 (INT 2Ah Func-tion 82h), 62-63
END LOGICAL FILE LOCKING (INT 21h Function C9h), 400
END LPT CAPTURE (INT 21h Func-tion DFh Subfunction 01h), 382
END OF JOB (INT 21h Function D6h), 407
END SPECIFIC LPT CAPTURE (INT 21h Function DFh Subfunction 05h), 383
END TRANSACTION (INT 21h Func-tion C701h), 405
END VIRTUAL MACHINE (INT 21h Function B501h), 434
ENTER COMMAND MODE (INT 14h Function B1h), 89
ENTER CONSOLE MODE (INT 7Fh), 419
ENTER LOGIN AREA (INT 21h Function E3h, Subfunction 0Ah), 331
ENTER TERMINAL MODE (INT 6Fh Function 0000h), 636
ENUMERATE Streetalk NAMES (INT 61h, Function 0007h, Subfunc-tion 0008h), 238-239
ENUMERATE USERS OF SHARED DEVICE (INT 6Fh Function 9504h), 478
ENUMERATE USERS ON NET-WORK (INT 6Fh Function 0Dh), 469-470
ERASE FILES (INT 21h Function F244h), 373
error codes, exended MS-DOS, 21-23
ERROR INTO ASCII STRING (INT 61h, Function 0006h, Subfunc-tion 0006h), 237
ESTABLISH SPX CONNECTION (INT 7Ah Function 0011h), 99-100
EXAMINE SEMAPHORE (INT 21h Function C501h), 399
Excelan LAN Workplace for DOS, 508-510
EXCHANGE TWO NETWORK DESCRIPTORS (INT 61h Func-tion 28h), 555

EXECUTE NetBIOS REQUEST (INT 2Ah Function 04h), 117-118
EXECUTE NetBIOS REQUEST, NO ERROR RETRY (INT 2Ah Func-tion 01h), 117
EXIT EMULATION (INT 61h Func-tion 0003h, Subfunction 0Dh), 233
EXPAND ERROR INTO STRING (INT 2Fh Function 05h), 64
EXTENDED ATTRIBUTES (INT 2Fh Function 112Dh), 134-135
EXTENDED FILE ATTRIBUTES (INT 21h Function B6h), 369-370
extended MS-DOS error codes, 21-23
EXTENDED OPEN/CREATE FILE (INT 2Fh Function 112Eh), 135
external device interrupts, 2
EXTERNAL STATUS (INT 6Bh Func-tion 1Fh), 664

FEED BACK BUFFER (INT 7Ch Func-tion 000Fh), 448
FETCH RAW BYTES RECEIVED (INT 60h Function 1Ch), 156
FILE SERVER CONNECTION (INT 21h Function F1h), 333-334
FILE SERVER FILE COPY (INT 21h Function F3h), 373
file server, NetWare, 347-369
file services, NetWare, 369-373
FILE/RECORD LOCKING (INT 6Fh Function 0Fh), 471-472
files
    BASIC.COM, 8
    BASICA.COM, 8
    closing, 47
    commiting all, 46-47
    deleting, 24-25
    opening existing, 23-24
    renaming, 45
FIND FIELD LENGTH (INT 6Fh Function 0023h), 641
FIND FIRST FILE WITHOUT CDS (INT 2Fh Function 1119h), 130
FIND NEXT FIELD (INT 6Fh Func-tion 001Bh), 640
FIND NEXT FILE WITHOUT CDS (INT 2Fh Function 111Ah), 130
FIND NEXT PROTECTED FIELD (INT 6Fh Function 001Fh), 640
FIND NEXT UNPROTECTED FIELD (INT 6Fh Function 001Dh), 640
FIND PREVIOUS FIELD (INT 6Fh Function 001Ch), 640
FIND PREVIOUS PROTECTED FIELD (INT 6Fh Function 0020h), 640-641
FIND PREVIOUS UNPROTECTED FIELD (INT 6Fh Function 001Eh), 640
FIND UNREFERENCED DISK BUFF-ER (INT 2Fh Function 121 0h), 67
FINDFIRST (INT 2Fh Function 111Bh), 130
FINDNEXT (INT 2Fh Function 111Ch), 130
FINISH SERVICING QUEUE JOB/FILE (INT 21h Function E3h Subfunction 72h), 393-394

FLOCK (INT 21h Function 56h), 45-46

FLOW CONTROL DATA (INT 61h Function 0003h, Subfunction 03h), 230

FLUSH (INT 68h, Function 02h, Subfunction 0600h), 204

FLUSH ALL DISK BUFFERS (INT 2Fh Function 1120h), 132

FLUSH AND FREE DISK BUFFER (INT 2Fh Function 1209h), 65

FLUSH BUFFER (INT 2Fh Function 1215h), 68

FLUSH DISK BUFFERS (INT 7Fh Function D8h), 189

FLUSH LPT CAPTURE (INT 21h Function DFh Subfunction 03h), 382

FLUSH PENDING DATA (INT 61h Function 1Eh), 552

FLUSH RAW BYTES RECEIVED (INT 60h Function 1Bh), 155-156

FLUSH REDIRECTED PRINTER OUTPUT (INT 21h Function 5D09h), 52

FLUSH SERVER CACHES (INT 21h Function 5FCDh), 307-308

FLUSH SPECIFIC LPT CAPTURE (INT 21h Function DFh Subfunction 07h), 383

FORCE WORKSTATION SCREEN UPDATE (INT 10h Function 8Bh), 157

FREE/CLOSE ALL UNKNOWN (INT 6Ah Function 000Fh), 570

FREE/CLOSE UNKNOWN (INT 6Ah Function 0005h), 569

FTP Software PC/TCP, 541-562

functions
BAPI, 87-90
Channel Control, 173-175
DESQview/X Socket API, 258-274
internal network support, 63-75
NetWare, 311-419
NetWare Lite, 421-426

general functions, NetWare, 409-419

GENERATE PRINT BREAK (INT 17h Function 84h), 160-161

GENERIC IOCTL (INT 2Fh Function 112Bh), 134

generic network support, 505-508

GET 3270 DISPLAY STATE (INT 21h Function A0h), 622-623

GET ABSTRACT FILE NAME (INT 2Fh Function 1503h), 241-242

GET ACCOUNT (INT 21h Function 5F87h), 296-297

GET ACCOUNT STATUS (INT 21h Function E3h Subfunction 96h), 316-317

GET ACKNOWLEDGE ISR (INT 7Fh Function 14h, Subfunction 04h), 177

GET ACTIVE USER INFORMATION (INT 21h Function 5FB0h), 302-304

GET ADDRESS (INT 60h Function 06h), 152

GET ADDRESS OF CONFIGURATION TABLE (INT 6Fh Function 03h), 465-467

GET ADDRESS, OF DOS SWAPPABLE DATA AREA (INT 21h Function 5D06h), 48-51

GET ADDRESS OF SYSTEM FILE TABLE ENTRY (INT 2Fh Function 1216h), 68

GET ALLOCATE (INT 68h, Function 03h, Subfunction 2800h), 210

GET ALTERNATE INTERRUPT (INT 7Fh Function 09h, Subfunction 03h), 172

GET AND CLEAR ACKNOWLEDGE STATUS (INT 7Fh Function 15h, Subfunction 04h), 179

GET API ENTRY POINT (INT 21h Function 4402h), 503-504

GET APPLICATION THRESHOLDS (INT 21h Function C705h), 405-406

GET ASYNCHRONOUS REDIRECTOR STATUS (INT 14h Function 8002h), 645-646

GET ATTRIBUTES (INT 68h, Function 02h, Subfunction 0700h), 204-205

GET AUTO-LOGIN DEFAULTS (INT 21h Function 5FB7h), 305-306

GET AVAILABLE SERVER NAME (INT 14h Function 8008h), 648-649

GET BANNER USER NAME (INT 21h Function B808h), 381

GET BANV INTERRUPT NUMBER (INT 2Fh Function D701h, Subfunction 0000h), 216

GET BIBLIOGRAPHIC DOCUMENT FILE NAME (INT 2Fh Function 1504h), 242

GET BINDERY ACCESS LEVEL (INT 21h Function E3h Subfunction 46h), 328-329

GET BINDERY OBJECT DISK SPACE LEFT (INT 21h Function E3h Subfunction E6h), 367

GET BINDERY OBJECT ID (INT 21h Function E3h Subfunction 35h), 320-321

GET BINDERY OBJECT NAME (INT 21h Function E3h Subfunction 36h), 321

GET BROADCAST MESSAGE (INT 21h Function E1h Subfunction 01h), 375

GET BUFFER ADDRESS (INT 80h Function 02h), 685

GET BUSY POINTER (INT 7Fh Function 14h, Subfunction 05h), 177

GET CALL ADDRESS (INT 2Fh Function 7A20h, Subfunction 0000h), 417

GET CALLER'S REGISTERS (INT 2Fh Function 1218h), 68

GET CD-ROM DRIVE LETTERS (INT 2Fh Function 150Dh), 243

GET CHANNEL STATUS (INT 7Fh Function 15h, Subfunction 00h), 178

GET CHARACTER FROM DEVICE BUFFER (INT 6Fh Function 0005h), 637

GET COMPLETION RESULTS (INT 7Ah Function 83h), 633

GET CONFIGURATION INFORMATION (INT 61h Function 2Ah), 556

GET CONFIGURATION STRINGS (INT 2Ah Function FF95h), 561

GET CONNECTION ID TABLE (INT 21h Function 3F03h), 408

GET CONNECTION INFO (INT 14h Function EAh), 573

GET CONNECTION INFORMATION
(INT 21h Function E3h Subfunction 16h), 333
(INT 61h Function 0003h, Subfunction 12h), 235

GET CONNECTION NUMBER (INT 21h Function DCh), 329

GET CONNECTION STATISTICS (INT 61h Function 0Ch), 546-547

GET CONNECTION'S
OPEN FILES (INT 21h Function E3h Subfunction D8h), 359-360
SEMAPHORES (INT 21h Function E3h Subfunction E1h), 364-365
TASK INFORMATION (INT 21h Function E3h Subfunction DAh), 358-359
USAGE STATISTICS (INT 21h Function E3h Subfunction E5h), 366-367
USING A FILE (INT 21h Function E3h Subfunction DCh), 361

GET CONTROL PROGRAM VERSION (INT 6Fh Function 000Eh), 638

GET CONVERSATION TYPE (INT 68h, Function 02h, Subfunction 0800h), 205

GET COPYRIGHT FILE NAME (INT 2Fh Function 1502h), 241

GET CURRENT AUTOPRINT TIME (INT 21h Function FFBDh), 487-488

GET CURRENT COMMUNICATIONS PARAMETERS (INT 16h Function 4502h), 677

GET CURRENT DEVICE BUFFER SIZE (INT 6Fh Function 002Ah), 642

GET CURRENT DIRECTORY STRUCTURE FOR DRIVE (INT 2Fh Function 1217h), 68

GET CURRENT PRINTER (INT 17h Function 95h), 164

GET DATA AREA (INT 2Fh Function D002h), 245

GET DATA FROM A QUEUE (INT 7Ah Function 13h), 633

GET DATA ON REMOTE PEER (INT 61h Function 16h), 550

GET DATE AND TIME (INT 2Fh Function 120Dh), 66

GET DEBUG INFORMATION (INT 61h Function 00h), 543

GET DECnet SOCKET (INT 69h Function 010Bh), 249

GET DEFAULT CAPTURE FLAGS (INT 21h Function B800h), 379-380

GET DEFAULT CONNECTION ID (INT 21h Function 002h), 409

GET DEFAULT COPIES OF SPOOLING FILE (INT 21h Function FFC2h), 489

GET DEFAULT END-OF-JOB FORMFEED STATUS (INT 21h Function FFC0h), 488

GET DEFAULT LOCAL PRINTER (INT 21h Function B804h), 380

GET DEFAULT PRINT FILE HEADER STATUS (INT 21h Function FFC8h), 490

GET DEFAULT START-OF-JOB FORMFEED STATUS (INT 21h Function FFB3h), 487

GET DESQview DIRECTORY (SOCKET API Function 0021h), 269

GET DEVICE NAME FROM PHYSICAL DEVICE NUMBER (INT 17h Function 8Ch), 162

GET DEVICE CHAIN (INT 2Fh Function 122Ch), 73

GET DIAGNOSTICS INFORMATION (INT 2Fh Function 7A1Bh), 431

GET DIRECT-WRITE CURSOR POSITION (INT 6Fh Function 0018h), 639

GET DIRECTORY ENTRY (INT 2Fh Function 150Fh), 244-245

GET DIRECTORY HANDLE (INT 21h Function E900h), 346

GET DIRECTORY PATH (INT 21h Function E2h Subfunction 01h), 335

GET DISK CACHE STATISTICS (INT 21h Function E3h Subfunction D6h), 355-356

GET DISK CHANNEL STATISTICS (INT 21h Function E3h Subfunction D9h), 357 358

GET DISK UTILIZATION (INT 21h Function E3h Subfunction 0Eh), 348

GET DOS DATA SEGMENT (INT 2Fh Function 1203h), 64

GET DOS INTERCEPT ENTRY POINT (INT 17h Function 8Fh), 162

GET DOS SERVICE VECTOR (INT 21h Function 5FE0h), 308

GET DOS SWAPPABLE DATA AREAS (INT 21h Function 5D08h), 52-56

GET DOS TASK PID FROM CREATE ID (INT 7Fh Function E1h), 190

GET DRIVE CONNECTION ID TABLE (INT 21h Function EF02h), 408

GET DRIVE DEVICE LIST (INT 2Fh Function 1501h), 241

GET DRIVE FLAG TABLE (INT 21h Function EF01h), 407-408

GET DRIVE HANDLE TABLE (INT 21h Function EF00h), 407

GET DRIVE MAPPING TABLE (INT 21h Function E3h Subfunction D7h), 356

GET DRIVE TYPE (INT 2Fh Function 9200h), 277-278

GET DRIVER INFO (INT 21h Function 3Fh), 525-526

GET DRIVER INFO (INT 60h Function 01FFh), 147-151

GET DRIVER INFORMATION (INT 7Ch Function 000Eh), 447-448

GET DRIVER PACKET SIZE LIMIT (INT 7Ah Function 001Ah), 103

GET DRIVER STATISTICS (INT 7Ch Function 000Dh), 446-447

GET DRIVER STATUS (INT 7Ch Function 0002h), 442

GET ECM WATCH STATE (INT 14h Function B2h), 89

GET EFFECTIVE DIRECTORY RIGHTS (INT 21h Function E2h Subfunction 03h), 336 337

GET ENTRY POINT (INT 21h Function 3Fh), 503

GET ENTRY POINT (INT 80h Function 03h), 685

GET ERROR (INT 2Fh, Function 7004h), 682-683

GET EXTENDED ERROR CODE (INT 2Fh Function 122Dh), 73

GET EXTENDED FILE ATTRIBUTES (INT 21h Function 4310h), 215

GET EXTENDED REDIRECTION LIST ENTRY (INT 21h Function 5F05h), 59

GET FILE SERVER DATE/TIME (INT 21h, Function E7h), 216

GET FILE SERVER DESCRIPTION STRINGS (INT 21h Function E3h Subfunction C9h), 349-350

GET FILE SERVER INFORMATION (INT 21h Function E3h Subfunction 11h), 348 349

GET FILE SERVER LAN I/O STATISTICS (INT 21h Function E3h Subfunction E7h), 367-368

GET FILE SERVER LOGIN STATUS (INT 21h Function E3h Subfunction CDh), 351

GET FILE SERVER MISCELLANEOUS INFORMATION (INT 21h Function E3h Subfunction E8h), 368-369

GET FILE SERVER NAME TABLE (INT 21h Function EF04h), 408-409

GET FILE SERVER STATION NUMBER (INT 21h Function FF91h), 485

GET FILE TRANSFER PARAMETERS (INT 61h Function 0003h, Subfunction 11h), 234

GET FILE'S DRIVE (INT 2Fh Function 121Ah), 68

GET FULL REDIRECTION LIST (INT 21h Function 5F06h), 60

GET GROUP NAME (INT 7Fh Function FCh), 193

GET HOST BUFFER ADDRESS (INT 2Fh Function B401h), 634

GET HOST INFORMATION (SOCKET API Function 0015h), 265-266

GET HOST NAME (SOCKET API Function 0001h), 258-259

GET HOST NAME FROM DNS (INT 61h Function 27h), 555

GET HOST NAME FROM LOCAL TABLE (INT 61h Function 26h), 555

GET HOST NAME GIVEN ADDRESS (INT 61h Function 25h), 554-555

GET HOST WINDOW BUFFER ADDRESS (INT 21h Function A4h), 624

GET HOST WINDOW CURSOR POSITION (INT 21h Function A5h), 624

GET IFSFUNC SEGMENT (INT 2Fh Function 1130h), 136

GET INACTIVE SERVER ENTRY (INT 21h Function 5F84h), 296

GET INDIRECT FILE CONTENTS (INT 21h Function 5FB5h), 305

GET INFORMATION (SOCKET API Function 000Ch), 262-263

GET INFORMATION ABOUT A SERVICE (SOCKET API Function 0018h), 266

GET INFORMATION ABOUT A SERVICE (SOCKET API Function 0019h), 266-267

GET INFORMATION HANDLE (INT 21h Function 5F33h), 105-106

GET INSTANCE DATA (INT 21h Function B500h), 434

GET INT 08h HANDLERS (INT 2Fh Function 7A19h), 431

GET INT 28h ENTRY POINT (INT 17h Function 8Eh), 162

GET INT 2Fh HANDLERS (INT 2Fh Function 7A11h), 432

GET INT 2Fh HANDLERS (INT 2Fh Function 7A1Ah), 431

GET INT 64h HANDLERS (INT 2Fh Function 7A12h), 432

GET INT 7Ah HANDLERS (INT 2Fh Function 7A13h), 432

GET INTERFACE STATISTICS (INT 61h Function 06h), 544-545

GET INTERNAL SEND/RECEIVE VECTOR (INT 14h Function 8035h), 649

GET INTERNET ADDRESS (INT 21h Function E3h Subfunction 13h), 331

GET INTERNET ADDRESS (INT 63h Function 25h), 536

GET INTERNET ADDRESS OF NETWORK DESCRIPTOR (INT 61h Function 05h), 544

GET INTERNETWORK ADDRESS (INT 7Ah Function 0009h), 97

GET INTERRUPT ADDRESS (INT 2Fh Function 1202h), 64

GET INTERRUPT VECTORS (INT 7Fh Function 08h), 171

GET INTERVAL MARKER (INT 7Ah Function 0008h), 97

GET IP ADDRESS (INT 63h Function 03h), 531

GET IP ADDRESS (INT 64h Function 07h), 538

GET JOB FILE TABLE ENTRY (INT 2Fh Function 1220h), 69-70

GET KEYCARD SERIAL NUMBER/MAXIMUM USERS (INT 21h Function FFD6h), 492

GET LAN DRIVER'S CONFIGURATION INFORMATION (INT 21h Function E3h Subfunction E3h), 366

GET LAST RECEIVED UNSOLICITED MESSAGE (INT 21h Function 5F99h), 298

GET LENGTH OF ASCIZ STRING (INT 2Fh Function 1212h), 67

GET LENGTH OF ASCIZ STRING (INT 2Fh Function 1225h), 71

GET LIST OF SERVER NAMES (INT 14h Function A2h), 659

GET LIST OF SESSIONS WITH STATUS (INT 14h Function A1h), 658

GET LIST OF SHARED DRIVES (INT 7Fh Function 07h), 171

GET LOCAL NETWORK INTERFACE ADDRESS (INT 21h Function FFE3h, Subfunction 03h), 493

GET LOCAL TARGET (INT 7Ah Function 0002h), 92-93

GET LOGGED ON USER NAME (INT 2Ah Function 7802h), 437

GET LOGICAL RECORDS BY CONNECTION (INT 21h Function E3h Subfunction DFh), 363-364

GET LOGIN ENTRY (INT 21h Function 5F80h), 295

GET LOGIN LIST (INT 6Fh Function 1Ch), 475

GET LOGIN LIST (INT 6Fh Function 9Ch), 478

GET LOGON USER INFORMATION (INT 21h Function FFBFh), 488

GET LPT CAPTURE STATUS (INT 21h Function F003h), 385

GET LPT TYPE (INT 2Fh Function 9218h), 279

GET MACHINE NAME (INT 21h Function 5E00h), 56-57, 457

GET MACHINE NAME (INT 2Fh Function 8103h), 512

GET MACHINE, USER, AND PROCESS NUMBER (INT 7Fh Function A1h), 185

GET MAXIMUM FILE NUMBER (INT 21h Function FF98h), 485

GET MAXIMUM NUMBER OF CHANNELS (INT 7Fh Function 15h, Subfunction 02h), 178

GET MAXIMUM PACKET SIZE (INT 7Fh Function 15h, Subfunction 03h), 178-179

GET MAXIMUM STATION NUMBER (INT 21h Function FF97h), 485

GET MEDIA STATISTICS (INT 7Ch Function 0015h), 449-450

GET MESSAGE (INT 7Fh Function 22h), 180

GET MESSAGE PROCESSING FLAGS (INT 21h Function 5F9Ah), 298

GET MESSAGE SERVICE VECTOR (INT 21h Function 5FE2h), 308

GET MICROCODE VERSION (INT 6Fh Function 000Fh), 638

GET MISCELLANEOUS LOCAL INFO (INT 61h Function 02h), 544

GET MSCDEX.EXE VERSION (INT 2Fh Function 150Ch), 243

GET MULTICAST LIST (INT 60h Function 17h), 155

GET MULTICAST LIST (INT 7Ch Function 0014h), 448-449

GET MW386 INVOCATION DRIVE (INT 7Fh Function DBh), 189

GET NetBIOS NAME NUMBER/MACHINE NAME (INT 2Fh Function B807h), 506

GET NETWORK EVENT POST HANDLER (INT 2Fh Function B803h), 505

GET NETWORK EXECUTIVE TYPE (INT 7Fh Function 25h, Subfunction 01h), 181

GET NETWORK EXECUTIVE VERSION (INT 7Fh Function 25h, Subfunction 00h), 180

GET NETWORK PRINTER SETUP STRING (INT 21h Function 5E03h), 57

GET NETWORK PROTECTION ATTRIBUTES STATUS (INT 21h Function FFD7h), 492

GET NETWORK PROTOCOL INFORMATION (SOCKET API Function 0016h), 266

GET NETWORK PROTOCOL INFORMATION (SOCKET API Function 0017h), 266

GET NETWORK RESOURCE AVAILABILITY (INT 2Ah Function 0500h), 118

GET NETWORK SERIAL NUMBER (INT 21h Function E3h, Subfunction 12h), 412

GET NEXT FULL CHANNEL (INT 7Fh Function 15h, Subfunction 01h), 178

GET NEXT LAT SERVICE NAME (INT 6Ah Function D500h), 253

GET NTNX FILE MODE (INT 7Fh Function 26h, Subfunction 00h), 181

GET NUMBER OF AVAILABLE USER TASKS (INT 7Fh Function E6h), 191

GET NUMBER OF LOCAL DRIVES (INT 21h Function DBh), 407

GET NUMBER OF USERS (INT 7Fh Function 04h), 169

GET OBJECT CONNECTION NUMBERS (INT 21h Function E3h Subfunction 15h), 332

GET ONLINE TIME/MAXIMUM TIME (INT 16h Function 4501h), 677

GET OPEN FILE LIST ENTRY (INT 21h Function 5D05h), 47-48

GET OPTIONS APPLIED TO NET DESCR (INT 61h Function 21h), 553-554

GET OR SET ERROR TABLE ADDRESS (INT 2Fh Function 122Eh), 73-75

GET OR SET LOCK MODE (INT 21h Function C6h), 400

GET PARAMETERS (INT 60h Function 0Ah), 152-153

GET PATH FROM DIRECTORY ENTRY (INT 21h Function E2h Subfunction 1Ah), 347 348

GET PEER NAME (SOCKET API Function 001Bh), 267

GET PERSONAL MESSAGE (INT 21h Function E1h Subfunction 05h), 376

GET PHYSICAL DEVICE NUMBER FROM NAME (INT 17h Function 8Bh), 152

GET PHYSICAL DISK STATISTICS (INT 21h Function E3h Subfunction D8h), 356 357

GET PHYSICAL HARDWARE ADRESS (INT 62h Function 00h), 526

GET PHYSICAL RECORD LOCKS BY CONNECTION AND FILE (INT 21h Function E3h Subfunction DDh), 361-362

GET PHYSICAL RECORD LOCKS BY FILE (INT 21h Function E3h Subfunction DEh), 362-363

GET PHYSICAL STATION ADDRESS (INT 21h Function EEh), 333

GET PHYSICAL WORKSTATION ADAPTER TYPE (INT 10h Function 91h), 157-158

GET PHYSICAL WORKSTATION DISPLAY MODE (INT 10h Function 90h), 157

GET PORT INFORMATION (INT 7Fh Function 30h), 182

GET PORT NUMBER FROM LOGICAL PORT ID (INT 14h Function 23h), 158-159

GET PORTS FOR SERVICE (INT 61h, Function 0007h, Subfunction 0002h), 236 237

GET PREFERRED CONNECTION ID (INT 21h Function F001h), 409

GET PRIMARY CONNECTION ID (INT 21h Function F005h), 409

GET PRINT JOB TERMINATION CONFIGURATION (INT 2Ah Function FF97h), 561

GET PRINT SERVER'S SPOOLING QUEUE STATUS (INT 21h Function FFCCh), 491

GET PRINTER MODE (INT 21h Function 5E05h), 58

GET PRINTER SERVER STATION ADDRESS (INT 21h Function FFBBh), 487

GET PRINTER STATUS (INT 21h Function E0h Subfunction 06h), 384

GET PRINTER STATUS (INT 21h Function 5FA3h), 301

GET PROCESS IDENTIFIER (SOCKET API Function 000Fh), 263

GET PROCESS NUMBER FROM TASK NAME (INT 7Fh Function E5h), 191

GET PROTOCOL LIST (INT 7Ch Function 000Bh), 446

GET PROTOCOL STATUS (INT 7Ch Function 000Ch), 446

GET QUEUE ENTRY (INT 21h Function 5FA0h), 299-300

GET QUEUE JOB LIST (INT 21h Function E3h Subfunction 6Bh), 390

GET QUEUE JOB'S FILE SIZE (INT 21h Function E3h Subfunction 78h), 396

GET REAL IP ADDRESS (INT 62h Function 03h), 527

GET REAL-TIME PRINTER STATUS (INT 17h Function AAh), 167-168

GET RECEIVE ISR (INT 7Fh Function 14h, Subfunction 03h), 177

GET RECEIVE MODE (INT 60h Function 15h), 154

GET RECEIVE STATISTICS (INT 80h Function 05h), 685

GET RECEIVER.COM INT 2Fh HANDLER ADDRESS (INT 2Fh Function B901h), 439

GET RECEIVER.COM POST ADDRESS (INT 2Fh Function B903h), 439

GET REDIRECTED PORT INFORMATION (INT 14h Function 8007h), 647-648

GET REDIRECTED PRINTER MODE (INT 21h Function 5D07h), 51

GET REDIRECTED PRINTER TIMEOUT (INT 21h Function 5FD0h), 308

GET REDIRECTION LIST ENTRY (INT 21h Function 5F02h), 58

GET REDIRECTION MODE (INT 21h Function 5F00h), 58

GET REDIRECTOR CONTROL BITS (INT 21h Function 5F9Dh), 299

GET REMOTE CONFIGURATION TABLE ADDRESS (INT 6Fh Function 13h), 472

GET REMOTE FILE'S ATTRIBUTES AND SIZE (INT 2Fh Function 110Fh), 127

GET REMOTE FILE'S ATTRIBUTES/SIZE (INT 2Fh Function 1110h), 127-128

GET REMOTE MEMORY (INT 6Fh Function 14h), 473

GET RESOURCE INFORMATION (INT 14h Function 8006h), 647

GET REVISION NUMBER (INT 61h, Function 02h), 240

GET RUNTIME PARAMETER (INT 2Fh Function 4E53h Subfunction 01h), 516-517

GET SEMAPHORE INFORMATION (INT 21h Function E3h Subfunction E2h), 365-366

GET SEMAPHORE TABLE (INT 7Fh Function 37h), 182

GET SERVER SERIAL NUMBER (INT 61h Function 0004h), 236

GET SESSION CONTROL BLOCK SIZE (INT 69h Function 010Ah), 249

GET SESSION PARAMETER (INT 61h Function 0003h, Subfunction 06h), 231

GET SHARED DEVICE ENTRY (INT 6Fh Function 1501h), 473

GET SHARED DEVICE ENTRY (INT 6Fh Function 9501h), 477-478

GET SHARED DIRECTORY INFORMATION (INT 21h Function 5FB1h), 304

GET SHARED DRIVE INFO (INT 7Fh Function 06h), 170-171

GET SHARING STATUS OF PRINTER SERVER (INT 21h Function FFC3h), 489

GET SHOW TYPE (INT 2Fh Function FF27h), 495

GET SOCKET (INT 63h Function 24h), 536

GET SOCKET NAME (SOCKET API Function 001Ah), 267

GET SOFTWARE VERSION (INT 61h Function 0Fh), 548

GET SPECIFIC CAPTURE FLAGS (INT 21h Function B802h), 380

GET SPOOLER PRINTING PRIORITY (INT 21h Function FFB0h), 486

GET SPX CONNECTION STATUS (INT 7Ah Function 0015h), 101

GET START PARAMETERS (INT 2Fh Function B80Fh), 507-508

GET STATION ADDRESS (INT 21h Function FF82h), 484

GET STATION ADDRESS (INT 60h, Function 0Ch), 217

GET STATION NUMBER (INT 21h, Function DCh), 216

GET STATISTICS (INT 2Fh Function 7A14h), 432-433

GET STATISTICS (INT 60h Function 18h), 155

GET STATUS
(INT 16h Function 4500h), 677
(INT 6Bh Function 0700h), 661
(INT 6Bh Function 10h), 661

GET STATUS OF ALL PRINT SERVERS (INT 21h Function FFCDh), 491

GET STATUS OF TopShow/Emulated FUNCTION (INT 21h Function FF8Ch), 484

GET STATUS/TRANSMISSION BUFFER (INT 17h Function 2403h), 514

GET STREAM INFORMATION (INT 21h Function 5FA4h), 301

GET SYSTEM FLAGS (INT 7Fh Function 0Ah Subfunction 00h), 172

GET SYSTEM INFORMATION (INT 21h Function FF00h), 483

GET TAB SETTINGS (INT 61h Function 0003h, Subfunction 08h), 231-232

GET TASK NAME FROM PROCESS NUMBER (INT 7Fh Function E4h), 190

GET TBMI STATUS (INT 2Fh Function 7A10h), 431

GET TERMINAL PARAMETERS (INT 7Fh Function 3Ah), 183

GET TIME FROM SERVER (INT 21h Function 5FC0h), 306

GET TIME OF DAY (SOCKET API Function 0010h), 264

GET TopNet VERSION STRING (INT 2Fh Function FF02h), 494

GET TRANSACTION TRACKING STATISTICS (INT 21h Function E3h Subfunction D5h), 354-355

GET TRANSLATE TABLE ADDRESS (INT 21h Function AFh), 624

GET UNKNOWN (INT 2Fh Function 7A20h, Subfunction 0003h), 418

GET UNKNOWN DATA
(INT 2Fh Function 7A20h, Subfunction 0002h), 418
(INT 2Fh Function 7A20h, Subfunction 0004h), 418
(INT 2Fh Function 920Fh), 278
(INT 2Fh Function 9211h), 278
(INT 2Fh Function 9214h), 279
(INT 2Fh Function 9215h), 279

GET UNKNOWN DATA AREA (INT 6Ah Function 0003h), 569

GET UNKNOWN ENTRY POINT
(INT 2Fh Function 7A20h, Subfunction 0080h-0082h), 418
(INT 2Fh Function 7A20h, Subfunction 0001h), 417
(INT 2Fh Function 7A20h, Subfunction 0006h-0008h), 418
(INT 2Fh Function 7A20h, Subfunction 0005h), 418
(INT 2Fh Function 7A42h), 565

GET UNKNOWN ITEM
(INT 14h Function E7h), 573
(INT 14h Function EBh), 573
(INT 21h Function 4402h), 562
(INT 2Fh Function FE08h), 566
(INT 62h Function 15h), 530

GET UNKNOWN VALUE
(INT 2Fh Function 5602h), 511
(INT 2Fh Function 7A4Ch), 565
(INT 2Fh Function 9207h), 277
(INT 2Fh Function 921Dh), 280
(INT 62h Function 12h), 529

GET USER GROUP LIST (INT 7Fh Function FAh), 193

GET USER LOGIN STATE (INT 7Fh Function A3h), 186

GET USER NAME (INT 61h, Function 0007h, Subfunction 0005h), 237

GET USER NAME (INT 7Fh Function A0h), 185

GET USER NUMBER (INT 7Fh Function 03h), 169

GET USER NUMBER AND CURRENT PRINTER (INT 17h Function 91h), 163

GET USER PARAMETERS (INT 7Fh Function 05h), 170

GET USER PRIVILEGE LEVEL (INT 7Fh Function A2h), 186

GET USER STATUS (INT 7Fh Function A500h), 186

GET USERNAME ENTRY (INT 21h Function 5F83h), 295-296

GET USERNAME FROM ACCOUNT FILE (INT 21h Function 5FB2h), 304

GET USERS (INT 6Fh Function 16h), 474

GET VERSION (INT 2Fh Function 9203h), 276

GET VERSION (INT 2Fh Function FF01h), 493

GET VIRTUAL MACHINE SUPPORT LEVEL (INT 21h Function B506h), 435

GET VOLUME INFORMATION (INT 21h Function E3h Subfunction E9h), 345

GET VOLUME INFORMATION WITH HANDLE (INT 21h Function E2h Subfunction 15h), 342-343

GET VOLUME INFORMATION WITH NUMBER (INT 21h Function DAh), 334-335

GET VOLUME NAME (INT 21h Function E2h Subfunction 06h), 338

GET VOLUME NUMBER (INT 21h Function E2h Subfunction 05h), 337-338

GET WORKSTATION THRESHOLDS (INT 21h Function C707h), 406

GET/SET
  10NET WORKSTATION PRINTER SETUP STRUCTURE (INT 21h Function 5E06h), 462
  CONFIGURATION INFO (INT 14h Function B3h), 90
  DEFAULT FILE PROTECTION ATTRIBUTES (INT 21h Function FF04h), 483-484
  LPT PORT ON PRINT SERVER (INT 21h Function FFC4h), 489
  PRINTER MODE (INT 17h Function 99h), 165
  SERVER CONTROL BITS (INT 21h Function 5FCCh), 307
  SOCKET HANDLER (INT 15h Function 112Dh), 255
  SOCKET HANDLER (INT 15h Function DED2h), 255
  SOCKET OPTIONS (SOCKET API Function 001Ch), 267-268
  SPOOL FLAGS (INT 17h Function A7h), 167
  VOLUME DESCRIPTOR PREFERENCE (INT 2Fh Function 150Eh), 243-244

GETLOCAL 10NET CONFIGURATION TABLE (INT 21h Function 5E01h), 457-461

GMOUNT (INT 6Fh Function 1Bh), 474

HIGH-LEVEL LANGUAGE API (INT 44h), 419

HLLAPI interrupts, 625-628

HOLD CURRENTLY ACTIVE SESSION (INT 14h Function A4h), 659

HoldFileModeSet (INT 21h Function B7h), 410

HOOK TIMER INTERRUPT (INT 62h Function 09h), 528

HOST SERVICES (INT 7Ah Function 09h), 632-633

HTONS (SOCKET API Function 0004h), 260

IBM 3270 High-level Language API/Rabbit Low Level API (INT 7Fh Function 0104h), 625-628

IBM 3270 Workstation program interrupts, 629-633

IBM PC 3270 Emulation program interrupts, 633-635

IBM System 36/38 Workstation Emulation interrupts, 635-636

IFS IOCTL (INT 2Fh Function 112Fh), 135

INDIRECT INT 15h CALL (SOCKET API Function 0025h), 270

INHIBIT WORKSTATION SCREEN UPDATES (INT 10h Function 92h), 158

INITIALIZE
  (INT 14h Function 57h), 650
  (INT 62h Function 02h), 527
  (INT 80h Function 01h), 684

INITIALIZE DISPATCHER (INT 92h Function E100h), 669-670

INITIALIZE NETWORK ADDRESS (INT 7Ah Function 000Ch), 98

INITIALIZE SOCKET (SOCKET API Function 000h), 258

INITIALIZE USER BUFFER POINTER INFO (INT 61h Function 0003h, Subfunction 00h), 227-228

INITIATE ACCESS TO SPECIFIC PACKET TYPE (INT 21h Function FFE3h Subfunction 00h), 492-493

INITIATE OUTPUT EVENT (INT 61h, Function 0001h, Subfunction 0002h), 218 219

INITIATE PRINT JOB (INT 21h Function 5E04h), 461

INSTALL DEFAULT UNKNOWN HANDLER (INT 63h Function 0Dh), 533

INSTALL SERVICE (INT 2Fh Function 1182h), 291

INSTALL UNKNOWN HANDLERS (INT 63h Function 09h), 532

INSTALLATION CHECK
  (INT 13h Function 4257h), 525
  (INT 14h Function 6Fh Subfunction FFFFh), 658
  (INT 14h Function 56h), 650

(INT 14h Function 8000h), 645
(INT 14h Function AF00h), 89
(INT 14h Function FF00h), 574
(INT 21h Function C702h), 405
(INT 2Ah Function 0000h), 117
(INT 2Ah Function 00h), 61
(INT 2Ah Function FF92h), 560
(INT 2Fh Function 4E53h Subfunction 00h), 516
(INT 2Fh Function 7A4Fh, Subfunction 0001h), 565
(INT 2Fh Function 7AFFh Subfunction 0000h), 434
(INT 2Fh Function 7AFFH Subfunction 0001h), 434
(INT 2Fh Function FE00h, Subfunction 4454h), 566
(INT 2Fh Function 0500h), 63
(INT 2Fh Function 1100h), 123
(INT 2Fh Function 1200h), 64
(INT 2Fh Function 1500h), 241
(INT 2Fh Function 4100h), 293
(INT 2Fh Function 5600h), 511
(INT 2Fh Function 7A18h), 430
(INT 2Fh Function 7A40h), 564
(INT 2Fh Function 7A4Fh), 565
(INT 2Fh Function 7A90h), 435
(INT 2Fh Function 7AF0h), 435
(INT 2Fh Function 7AF1h), 427-430
(INT 2Fh Function 7AFEh), 435
(INT 2Fh Function 8000h), 511, 519
(INT 2Fh Function 8100h), 512
(INT 2Fh Function 9204h), 276
(INT 2Fh Function 9400h), 679
(INT 2Fh Function B400h), 634
(INT 2Fh Function B800h), 462, 505
(INT 2Fh Function C000h), 137-146
(INT 2Fh Function D000h), 245
(INT 2Fh Function DAB2h), 526
(INT 2Fh Function EE00h), 497
(INT 2Fh Function FF00h), 493
(INT 2Fh, Function 7000h), 681
(INT 5Ch), 523
(INT 69h Function 0100h), 247
(INT 6Ah Function 0000h), 566-567
(INT 6Bh Function 02h), 660
(INT 7Ah Function 0010h), 99
(INT 7Ah Function FDCBh), 643-644
(INT 92h Function E180h), 676
(INT7Fh), 168

INSTALLATION CHECK/STATUS REPORT (INT 14h Function A0h), 658

INT 05h (print-screen), 2

INT 0Ch (API POINTER), 635

INT 10h
  Function 90h (GET PHYSICAL WORKSTATION DISPLAY MODE), 157
  Function 91h (GET PHYSICAL WORKSTATION ADAPTER TYPE), 157-158
  Function 3000h (LOCATE 3270PC CONFIGURATION TABLE), 621-622

Function 8Bh (FORCE WORK-STATION SCREEN UPDATE), 157
Function 92h (INHIBIT WORK-STATION SCREEN UPDATES), 158
Function 93h (REDRAW SCREEN), 158
INT 13h, Function 4257h (INSTALLATION CHECK), 525
INT 14h
    Function 20h (ATTACH LOGICAL COMMUNICATION PORT TO PHYSICAL PORT), 158
    Function 21h (RELEASE PHYSICAL COMMUNICATIONS PORT), 158
    Function 23h (GET PORT NUMBER FROM LOGICAL PORT ID), 158-159
    Function 6Fh, Subfunction FFFEh (UNDETERMINED FUNCTION), 658
    Function 6Fh, Subfunction FFFFh (INSTALLATION CHECK), 658
    Function 00h (MODIFY DEFAULT CONNECTION PARAMETERS), 650
    Function 01h (SEND CHARACTER), 651
    Function 02h (RECEIVE CHARACTER), 651
    Function 03h (RETURN COMMUNICATION PORT STATUS), 651
    Function 04h (OPEN COMMUNICATION), 651-655
    Function 05h (CLOSE COMMUNICATION), 655
    Function 06h (SEND CHARACTER BLOCK), 655
    Function 06h (WRITE), 571
    Function 07h (RECEIVE CHARACTER BLOCK), 655
    Function 07h (WRITE), 571
    Function 08h (RETURN DEFAULT CONNECTION PARAMETERS), 656
    Function 09h (SEND BREAK), 656
    Function 0Ah (MODIFY ACTIVE CONNECTION PARAMETERS), 656
    Function 0Bh (PREPARE FOR INBOUND CONNECTION), 656
    Function 0Ch (TEST FOR INBOUND CONNECTION REQUEST), 657
    Function 0Dh (TERMINATE CONNECTION CLIENT ACTIVITY), 657
    Function 0Eh (SET HARDWARE FLOW STATE), 657
    Function 0Fh (RETURN ACTIVE CONNECTION PARAMETERS), 657
    Function 10h (QUERY SERVICE NAMES), 657-658

Function 22h (RELEASE LOGICAL COMMUNICATIONS PORT), 158
Function 24h (CHANGE PHYSICAL PORT PARAMETERS), 159
Function 56h (INSTALLATION CHECK), 650
Function 57h (INITIALIZE), 650
Function 58h (SHUTDOWN), 650
Function 8000h (INSTALLATION CHECK), 645
Function 8001h (UNLOAD ASYNCHRONOUS REDIRECTOR FROM MEMORY), 645
Function 8002h (GET ASYNCHRONOUS REDIRECTOR STATUS), 645-646
Function 8003h (TRANSLATE ERROR CODE TO ERROR STRING), 646
Function 8004h (ATTACH ASYNCHRONOUS RESOURCE), 646-647
Function 8005h (DETACH ASYNCHRONOUS RESOURCE), 647
Function 8006h (GET RESOURCE INFORMATION), 647
Function 8007h (GET REDIRECTED PORT INFORMATION), 647-648
Function 8008h (GET AVAILABLE SERVER NAME), 648-649
Function 8009h (SET SEND/RECEIVE TIMEOUTS), 649
Function 800Ah (MODIFY FLOW CONTROL), 649
Function 8025h (SET INTERNAL SEND/RECEIVE VECTOR), 649
Function 8035h (GET INTERNAL SEND/RECEIVE VECTOR), 649
Function A0h (CONNECT TO PORT), 87
Function A0h (INSTALLATION CHECK/STATUS REPORT), 658
Function A1h (DISCONNECT FROM PORT), 87
Function A1h (GET LIST OF SESSIONS WITH STATUS), 658
Function A2h (GET LIST OF SERVER NAMES), 659
Function A2h (WRITE CHARACTER), 88
Function A3h (READ CHARACTER), 88
Function A3h (START A NEW SESSION), 659
Function A4h (HOLD CURRENTLY ACTIVE SESSION), 659
Function A4h (WRITE BLOCK), 88

Function A5h (READ BLOCK), 88
Function A5h (RESUME A SESSION), 659
Function A6h (DROP A SESSION), 659
Function A6h (SEND SHORT BREAK), 88-89
Function A7h (READ STATUS), 89
Function A7h (SWITCH TO NEXT ACTIVE SESSION), 659
Function A8h (CONNECTION INFORMATION), 571
Function A8h (SEND STRING TO COMMAND INTERPRETER), 660
Function A9h (CONNECTION CONTROL), 571-572
Function AF00h (INSTALLATION CHECK), 89
Function B0h (EN/DISABLE [ECM] CHARACTER), 89
Function B1h (ENTER COMMAND MODE), 89
Function B2h (GET ECM WATCH STATE), 89
Function B3h (GET/SET CONFIGURATION INFO), 90
Function E0h (UNDETERMINED FUNCTION), 572
Function E1h (UNDETERMINED FUNCTION), 572
Function E2h (BUFFERED READ), 572
Function E3h (BUFFERED WRITE), 572
Function E4h (CONNECTION CONTROL), 572-573
Function E5h/36h (UNDETERMINED FUNCTION), 573
Function E7h (GET UNKNOWN ITEM), 573
Function E8h (SET UNKNOWN ITEM), 573
Function E9h (UNDETERMINED FUNCTION), 573
Function EAh (GET CONNECTION INFO), 573
Function EBh (GET UNKNOWN ITEM), 573
Function ECh (UNDETERMINED FUNCTION), 573-574
Function EDh (UNDETERMINED FUNCTION), 574
Function FF00h (INSTALLATION CHECK), 574
INT 15h
    Function 112Dh (GET/SET SOCKET HANDLER), 255
    Function 112Eh (SOCKET API), 255
    Function DE2Dh (GET/SET SOCKET HANDLER), 255
    Function DE2Eh (SOCKET API), 255-258
INT 16h
    Function 4500h (GET STATUS), 677

Function 4501h (GET ONLINE TIME/MAXIMUM TIME), 677
Function 4502h (GET CURRENT COMMUNICATIONS PARAMETERS), 677
Function 4503h (SPECIFY COMMAND WORD FOR USER FUNCTION), 678
Function 4504h (CHECK FOR USER FUNCTION COMMAND WORD), 678
Function 4505h (SEND RESULT OF USER FUNCTION), 678
Function 4506h (MONITOR XMODEM DOWNLOAD), 679
Function FF70h (API), 275

INT 17h
Function 8Ah (ACTIVATE USER-WRITTEN PRINTER DRIVER), 162
Function 8Bh (GET PHYSICAL DEVICE NUMBER FROM NAME), 162
Function 8Ch (GET DEVICE NAME FROM PHYSICAL DEVICE NUMBER), 162
Function 2400h (ENABLE/DISABLE API FUNCTIONS), 513-514
Function 2401h (RECEIVE BLOCK, NO HANDSHAKE), 514
Function 2402h (TRANSMIT BLOCK, NO HANDSHAKE), 514
Function 2403h (GET STATUS/TRANSMISSION BUFFER), 514
Function 2405h (SEND NAK BLOCK), 514
Function 2406h (PREPARE CHARACTER-ORIENTED RECEIVE), 514
Function 2407h (RECEIVE CHARACTER FROM REMOTE), 515
Function 2408h (RECEIVE BLOCK, WITH HANDSHAKE), 515
Function 2409h (TRANSMIT COMMAND, WITH HANDSHAKE), 515
Function 240Ah (PREPARE CHARACTER-ORIENTED TRANSMIT), 515
Function 240Bh (TRANSMIT SINGLE CHARACTER TO REMOTE), 515
Function 240Ch (END CHARFACTER-ORIENTED TRANSMIT), 515
Function 81h (CANCEL JOBS FOR CURRENT USER), 159-160
Function 82h (CANCEL ALL JOBS FOR CURRENT USER), 160

Function 83h (SET NUMBER OF COPIES), 160
Function 84h (GENERATE PRINT BREAK), 160-161
Function 87h (SET INDOS POINTER), 161
Function 88h (REMOVE PRINTER FROM SPOOLER), 161
Function 89h (ADD PRINTER TO SPOOLER), 161
Function 8Dh (RESET SPOOLER), 162
Function 8Eh (GET INT 28h ENTRY POINT), 162
Function 8Fh (GET DOS INTERCEPT ENTRY POINT), 162
Function 90h (SPOOL FILE BY NAME), 163
Function 91h (GET USER NUMBER AND CURRENT PRINTER), 163
Function 92h (CHECK PRINTER DRIVER), 163
Function 94h (SELECT PRINTER), 163-164
Function 95h (GET CURRENT PRINTER), 164
Function 96h (SET SERIAL PORT PARAMETERS), 164
Function 97h (SET DATA DRIVER PRINT BREAK), 164-165
Function 98h (RESTART PRINTER), 165
Function 99h (GET/SET PRINTER MODE), 165
Function 9Ah (SET TAB EXPANSION), 165
Function 9Bh (SET PRINT BREAK TIMEOUT), 166
Function A0h (SPOOL COPY OF FILE), 166
Function A4h (ENABLE/DISABLE FORM FEED), 166
Function A6h (ENABLE/DISABLE BANNER PAGE), 167
Function A7h (GET/SET SPOOL FLAGS), 167
Function A8h (DEFINE TEMPORARY FILENAME), 167
Function A9h (CHANGE TEMPORARY SPOOL DRIVE), 167
Function AAh (GET REAL-TIME PRINTER STATUS), 167-168
Function AFh (CHECK SPOOLER), 168

INT 1Ah
Function 6108h (SNAP_SENDWITHREPLY), 451-452
Function 6205h (SNAP_SENDNOREPLY), 452
Function 6308h (SNAP_BEGINCONV), 452
Function 6405h (SNAP_ENDCONV), 452

Function 6900h (SNAP_DATASEG), 453
Function 6B01h (SNAP_FREE), 453
Function 6C04h (SNAP_COPYTO), 453
Function 6D04h (SNAP_COPYFROM), 453
Function 6E01h (SNAP_SETDEBUG), 453
Function 6F01h (SNAP_CHKINSTALL), 454
Function 7002h (SNAP_SETANCHOR), 454
Function 7101h (SNAP_GETANCHOR), 454
Function 7302h (SNAP_CLIENTVERSION), 454
Function 7400h (SNAP_VERSION), 454
Function 75h (SNAP_NOP), 455
Function 76h (SNAP_802_5), 455
Function 77h (UNDETERMINED FUNCTION), 455
Function 7802h (UNDETERMINED FUNCTION), 455

INT 21h
Function 002h (GET DEFAULT CONNECTION ID), 409
Function 3306h (NETWORK REDIRECTOR), 518
Function 3Dh (OPEN), 23-24
Function 3Fh
    (GET DRIVER INFO), 525-526
    (GET ENTRY POINT), 503
    (READ CONFIGURATION DATA), 558-560
Function 40h (WRITE CONFIGURATION DATA), 560
Function 41h (UNLINK), 24-25
Function 4310h (GET EXTENDED FILE ATTRIBUTES), 215
Function 4311h (SET EXTENDED FILE ATTRIBUTES), 215
Function 4402h
    (10BEUI.DOS - API), 479
    (10MEMMGR.SYS - API), 479-480
    (API), 563
    (GET API ENTRY POINT), 503-504
    (GET UNKNOWN ITEM), 562
    (PROTOCOL MANAGER), 109-115
    (VDI.SYS - GET UNKNOWN DATA), 636
Function 44E0h (API), 566
Function 52h (SYSVARS), 25-45
Function 56h (RENAME), 45
Function 5Ch (FLOCK), 45-46
INT 21h (continued)

Function 5D-6h (GET ADDRESS OF DOS SWAPPABLE DATA AREA), 48-51

Function 5D00h (SERVER FUNCTION CALL), 46

Function 5D01h (COMMIT ALL FILES), 46-47

Function 5D02h (CLOSE FILE BY NAME), 47

Function 5D03h (CLOSE ALL FILES FOR GIVEN COMPUTER), 47

Function 5D04h (CLOSE ALL FILES FOR GIVEN PROCESS), 47

Function 5D05h (GET OPEN FILE LIST ENTRY), 47-48

Function 5D06h (GET ADDRESS OF DOS 3 SWAPPABLE DATA AREA), 48-51

Function 5D07h (GET REDIRECTED PRINTER MODE), 51

Function 5D08h (GET ADDRESS OF DOS 4 SWAPPABLE DATA AREA), 53
(GET ADDRESS OF DOS 5 SWAPPABLE DATA AREA), 53-56
(GET ADDRESS OF DOS 6 SWAPPABLE DATA AREA), 53-56
(SET REDIRECTED PRINTER MODE), 52

Function 5D09h (FLUSH REDIRECTED PRINTER OUTPUT), 52

Function 5D0Ah (SET EXTENDED ERROR INFORMATION), 52

Function 5D0Bh (GET DOS SWAPPABLE DATA AREAS), 52-56

Function 5E00h (GET MACHINE NAME), 56-57, 457

Function 5E01h (GETLOCAL 10NET CONFIGURATION TABLE), 457-461

Function 5E01h (SET MACHINE NAME), 57

Function 5E02h (SET NETWORK PRINTER SETUP STRING), 57

Function 5E03h (GET NETWORK PRINTER SETUP STRING), 57

Function 5E04h (INITIATE PRINT JOB), 461

Function 5E04h (SET PRINTER MODE), 57

Function 5E05h (GET PRINTER MODE), 58

Function 5E05h (TERMINATE PRINT JOB), 462

Function 5E06h (GET/SET 10NET WORKSTATION PRINTER SETUP STRUCTURE), 462

Function 5F00h (GET REDIRECTION MODE), 58

Function 5F01h (SET REDIRECTION MODE), 58

Function 5F02h (GET REDIRECTION LIST ENTRY), 58

Function 5F03h (REDIRECT DEVICE), 59

Function 5F04h (CANCEL REDIRECTION), 59

Function 5F05h (GET EXTENDED REDIRECTION LIST ENTRY), 59

Function 5F05h (MAP LOCAL DRIVE LETTER), 683

Function 5F06h (GET FULL REDIRECTION LIST), 60

Function 5F06h (UNMAP DRIVE LETTER), 683

Function 5F07h (ENABLE DRIVE), 60

Function 5F07h (MAKE NAMED OBJECT AVAILABLE), 684

Function 5F08h (DISABLE DRIVE), 60

Function 5F08h (REMOVE GLOBAL NETWORK NAME), 684

Function 5F09h (BIND TO NETWORK DEVICE), 684

Function 5F0Ah (DETACH FROM NETWORK DEVICE), 684

Function 5F30h (UNDETERMINED FUNCTION), 281

Function 5F32h (QUERY NAMED PIPE INFORMATION), 105

Function 5F33h (GET INFORMATION HANDLE), 105-106

Function 5F34h (SET STATE FOR PIPE HANDLE), 106

Function 5F35h (PEEK AT PENDING INPUT FOR PIPE), 106

Function 5F36h (LOCAL DosTransactNmPipe), 106

Function 5F37h (DosCallNmPipe), 106-107

Function 5F38h (WAIT UNTIL PIPE INSTANCE AVAILABLE), 107

Function 5F39h (RAW INPUT FROM PIPE), 107

Function 5F3Ah (RAW OUTPUT TO PIPE), 107

Function 5F3Bh (NET HANDLE SET INFO), 281

Function 5F3Ch (NET HANDLE GET INFO), 282

Function 5F3Dh (WRITE MAILSLOT), 282

Function 5F3Eh (LOCAL NetSpecialSMB), 282

Function 5F3Fh (REMOTE API CALL), 282

Function 5F40h LOCAL NetMessageBufferSend), 282

Function 5F41h (LOCAL NetServiceEnum), 283-284

Function 5F42h (LOCAL NetServiceControl), 284

Function 5F43h (LOCAL DosPrintJobGetId), 285

Function 5F44h (LOCAL NetWkstaGetInfo), 285

Function 5F45h (LOCAL NetWkstaSetInfo), 285

Function 5F46h (LOCAL NetUseEnum), 285-286

Function 5F47h (LOCAL NetUseAdd), 286

Function 5F48h (LOCAL NetUseDel), 286

Function 5F49h (NetUseGetInfo), 286

Function 5F4Ah (LOCAL NetRemoteCopy), 287

Function 5F4Bh (LOCAL NetRemoteMove), 287-288

Function 5F4Ch (LOCAL NetServerEnum), 288

Function 5F4Dh (DosMakeMailslot), 289

Function 5F4Eh (DosDeleteMailslot), 289

Function 5F4Fh (DosMailslotInfo), 289

Function 5F50h (DosReadMailslot), 289

Function 5F51h (DosPeekMailslot), 290

Function 5F52h (DosWriteMailslot), 290

Function 5F53h (NetServerEnum2), 290-291

Function 5F55h (KILL ALL CONNECTIONS), 291

Function 5F80h (GET LOGIN ENTRY), 295

Function 5F81h (LOGIN TO SERVER), 295

Function 5F82h (LOGOUT FROM SERVER), 295

Function 5F83h (GET USERNAME ENTRY), 295-296

Function 5F84h (GET INACTIVE SERVER ENTRY), 296

Function 5F85h (CHANGE PASSWORD), 296

Function 5F86h (DISABLE ACCOUNT), 296

Function 5F87h (GET ACCOUNT), 296-297

Function 5F88h (LOGOUT FROM ALL SERVERS), 297

Function 5F97h (COPY FILE), 297

Function 5F98h (SEND UNSOLICITED MESSAGE), 297-298

Function 5F99h (GET LAST RECEIVED UNSOLICITED MESSAE), 298

INT 21h (continued)

Function 5F9Ah (GET MES-SAGE PROCESSING FLAGS), 298
Function 5F9Bh (SET MESSAGE PROCESSING FLAGS), 298
Function 5F9Ch (POP UP LAST RECEIVED MESSAGE), 298-299
Function 5F9Dh (GET REDIRECTOR CONTROL BITS), 299
Function 5F9Eh (SET REDIREC-TOR CONTROL BITS), 299
Function 5FA0h (GET QUEUE ENTRY), 299-300
Function 5FA1h (SET QUEUE ENTRY), 300
Function 5FA2h (CONTROL QUEUE), 300-301
Function 5FA3h (GET PRINTER STATUS), 301
Function 5FA4h (GET STREAM INFORMATION), 301
Function 5FA5h (SET STREAM INFO), 301-302
Function 5FA7h (CREATE USER AUDIT ENTRY), 302
Function 5FA9h (SET EXTENDED QUEUE ENTRY), 302
Function 5FB0h (GET ACTIVE USER INFORMATION), 302-304
Function 5FB1h (GET SHARED DIRECTORY INFORMA-TION), 304
Function 5FB2h (GET USERNAME FROM ACCOUNT FILE), 304
Function 5FB3h (TRANSLATE PATH), 304-305
Function 5FB4h (CREATE INDI-RECT FILE), 305
Function 5FB5h (GET INDI-RECT FILE CONTENTS), 305
Function 5FB6h (SET AUTO-LOGIN DEFAULTS), 305
Function 5FB7h (GET AUTO-LOGIN DEFAULTS), 305-306
Function 5FC0h (GET TIME FROM SERVER), 306
Function 5FC8h (SCHEDULE SERVER SHUTDOWN), 306
Function 5FC9h (CANCEL SERVER SHUTDOWN), 306-307
Function 5FCAh (STUFF SERV-ER KEYBOARD BUFFER), 307
Function 5FCBh (TERMINATE USER), 307
Function 5FCCh (GET/SET SERVER CONTROL BITS), 307
Function 5FCDh (FLUSH SERV-ER CACHES), 307-308

Function 5FD0h (GET REDI-RECTED PRINTER TIMEOUT), 308
Function 5FD1h (SET REDI-RECTED PRINTER TIMEOUT), 308
Function 5FE0h (GET DOS SER-VICE VECTOR), 308
Function 5FE1h (SET DOS SER-VICE VECTOR), 308
Function 5FE2h (GET MESSAGE SERVICE VECTOR), 308
Function 5FE3h (SET MESSAGE SERVICE VECTOR), 309
Function 60h (TRUENAME), 60-61
Function A0h (GET 3270 DIS-PLAY STATE), 622-623
Function A1h (SET 3270 DIS-PLAY STATE), 623
Function A2h (SET HOST WIN-DOW STATE), 623
Function A3h (SEND KEY-STROKES TO HOST WIN-DOW), 623-624
Function A4h (GET HOST WIN-DOW BUFFER ADDRESS), 624
Function A5h (GET HOST WIN-DOW CURSOR POSI-TION), 624
Function AFh (GET TRANS-LATE TABLE ADDRESS), 624
Function B4h (AttachHandle), 409-410
Function B500h (GET INSTANCE DATA), 434
Function B501h (END VIR-TUAL MACHINE), 434
Function B502h (START VIR-TUAL MACHINE), 435
Function B505h (SET VIRTUAL MACHINE ID), 435
Function B506h (GET VIRTUAL MACHINE SUPPORT LEVEL), 435
Function B5h (TASK MODE CONTROL), 410
Function B6h (EXTENDED FILE ATTRIBUTES), 369-370
Function B7h (Hold-FileModeSet), 410
Function B800h (GET DEFAULT CAPTURE FLAGS), 379-380
Function B801h (SET DEFAULT CAPTURE FLAGS), 380
Function B802h (GET SPECIFIC CAPTURE FLAGS), 380
Function B803h (SET SPECIFIC CAPTURE FLAGS), 380
Function B804h (GET DEFAULT LOCAL PRINTER), 380
Function B805h (SET DEFAULT LOCAL PRINTER), 381
Function B806h (SET CAPTURE PRINT QUEUE), 381
Function B807h (SET CAPTURE PRINT JOB), 381

Function B808h (GET BANNER USER NAME), 381
Function B809h (SET BANNER USER NAME), 381
Function B8h (DISABLE HOST BUFFER UPDATES), 624
Function B9h (SpecialAttachableFunction), 410
Function BAh (ReturnCommandComPointers), 410
Function BBh (SET END OF JOB STATUS), 406-407
Function BCh (LOG PHYSICAL RECORD), 397
Function BDh (RELEASE PHYSI-CAL RECORD), 397
Function BEh (CLEAR PHYSI-CAL RECORD), 397
Function BFh (LOG/LOCK RECORD (FCB)), 397
Function C0h (RELEASE RECORD (FCB)), 398
Function C1h (CLEAR RECORD (FCB)), 398
Function C2h (LOCK PHYSI-CAL RECORD SET), 398
Function C3h (RELEASE PHYSI-CAL RECORD SET), 398
Function C4h (CLEAR PHYSI-CAL RECORD SET), 398
Function C500h (OPEN SEMA-PHORE), 399
Function C501h (EXAMINE SEMAPHORE), 399
Function C502h (WAIT ON SEMAPHORE), 399
Function C503h (SIGNAL SEMA-PHORE), 399
Function C504h (CLOSE SEMA-PHORE), 399-400
Function C6h (GET OR SET LOCK MODE), 400
Function C700h (BEGIN TRANS-ACTION), 404-405
Function C701h (END TRANS-ACTION), 405
Function C702h (INSTALLA-TION CHECK), 405
Function C703h (ABORT TRANSACTION), 405
Function C704h (TRANSAC-TION STATUS), 405
Function C705h (GET APPLICA-TION THRESHOLDS), 405-406
Function C706h (SET APPLICA-TION THRESHOLDS), 406
Function C707h (GET WORK-STATION THRESH-OLDS), 406
Function C708h (SET WORK-STATION THRESH-OLDS), 406
Function C8h (BEGIN LOGI-CAL FILE LOCKING), 400
Function C9h (END LOGICAL FILE LOCKING), 400
Function CAh (LOG/LOCK PERSONAL FILE (FCB)), 400-401

INT 21h (continued)
Function CBh (LOCK FILE SET), 401
Function CCh (RELEASE FILE (FCB)), 401
Function CDh (RELEASE FILE SET), 401
Function CEh (CLEAR FILE (FCB)), 401-402
Function CFh (CLEAR FILE SET), 402
Function CFh (UNDETERMINED FUNCTION), 518
Function D0h (LOG LOGICAL RECORD), 402
Function D0h to D5h (LOGICAL RECORD LOCK/UNLOCK), 216
Function D1h (LOCK LOGICAL RECORD SET), 402
Function D2h (RELEASE LOGICAL RECORD), 403
Function D3h (RELEASE LOGICAL RECORD SET), 403
Function D4h (CLEAR LOGICAL RECORD), 403
Function D5h (CLEAR LOGICAL RECORD SET), 403
Function D6h (END OF JOB), 407
Function D7h (SYSTEM LOGOUT), 329
Function D8h (ALLOCATE RESOURCE), 411
Function D8h and D9h (RESOURCE ALLOCATION), 216
Function D9h (DEALLOCATE RESOURCE), 411
Function DAh (GET VOLUME INFORMATION WITH NUMBER), 334-335
Function DBh (GET NUMBER OF LOCAL DRIVES), 407
Function DCh (GET CONNECTION NUMBER), 329
Function DCh (GET STATION NUMBER), 216
Function DDh (SET NetWare ERROR MODE), 407
Function DEh (SET BROADCAST MODE), 374
Function DEh, Subfunction 05h/06h (SHELL TIMER INTERRUPT CHECKS), 411
Function DFh
    Subfunction 00h (START LPT CAPTURE), 382
    Subfunction 01h (END LPT CAPTURE), 382
    Subfunction 02h (CANCEL LPT CAPTURE), 382
    Subfunction 03h (FLUSH LPT CAPTURE), 382
    Subfunction 04h (START SPE-

CIFIC LPT CAPTURE), 383
    Subfunction 05h (END SPECIFIC LPT CAPTURE), 383
    Subfunction 06h (CANCEL SPECIFIC LPT CAPTURE), 383
    Subfunction 07h (FLUSH SPECIFIC LPT CAPTURE), 383
Function E0h (PRINT SPOOLING), 383-384
    Subfunction 06h (GET PRINTER STATUS), 384
    Subfunction 09h (SPECIFY CAPTURE FILE), 384-385
Function E1h
    Subfunction 00h (SEND BROADCAST MESSAGE), 374
    Subfunction 01h (GET BROADCAST MESSAGE), 375
    Subfunction 02h/03h (ENABLE/DISABLE BROADCAST MESSAGES), 375
    Subfunction 04h (SEND PERSONAL MESSAGE), 375-376
    Subfunction 05h (GET PERSONAL MESSAGE), 376
    Subfunction 06h (OPEN MESSAGE PIPE), 377
    Subfunction 07h (CLOSE MESSAGE PIPE), 377
    Subfunction 08h (CHECK PIPE STATUS), 378
    Subfunction 09h (BROADCAST TO CONSOLE), 378
Function E2h
    Subfunction 00h (SET DIRECTORY HANDLE), 335
    Subfunction 01h (GET DIRECTORY PATH), 335
    Subfunction 02h (SCAN DIRECTORY INFORMATION), 336
    Subfunction 03h (GET EFFECTIVE DIRECTORY RIGHTS), 336-337
    Subfunction 04h (MODIFY MAXIMUM RIGHTS MASK), 337

    Subfunction 05h (GET VOLUME NUMBER), 337-338
    Subfunction 06h (GET VOLUME NAME), 338
    Subfunction 0Ah (CREATE DIRECTORY), 338-339
    Subfunction 0Bh (DELETE DIRECTORY), 339
    Subfunction 0Ch (SCAN DIRECTORY FOR TRUSTEES), 339 340
    Subfunction 0Dh (ADD TRUSTEE TO DIRECTORY), 340
    Subfunction 0Eh (DELETE TRUSTEE FROM DIRECTORY), 340
    Subfunction 0Fh (RENAME DIRECTORY), 341
    Subfunction 11h (RESTORE ERASED FILE), 370-371
    Subfunction 12h (ALLOCATE PERMANENT DIRECTORY HANDLE), 341
    Subfunction 13h (ALLOCATE TEMPORARY DIRECTORY HANDLE), 342
    Subfunction 14h (DEALLOCATE DIRECTORY HANDLE), 342
    Subfunction 15h (GET VOLUME INFORMATION WITH HANDLE), 342-343
    Subfunction 16h (ALLOCATE SPECIAL TEMP DIRECTORY HANDLE), 343
    Subfunction 17h (SAVE DIRECTORY HANDLE), 343
    Subfunction 18h (RESTORE DIRECTORY HANDLE), 344
    Subfunction 19h (SET DIRECTORY INFORMATION), 344
    Subfunction 1Ah (GET PATH FROM DIRECTORY ENTRY), 347-348
Function E3h (CONNECTION CONTROL), 329-331

Subfunction 0Ah (ENTER LOGIN AREA), 331

Subfunction 0Ch (VERIFY NETWORK SERIAL NUMBER), 411

Subfunction 0Dh (LOG NETWORK MESSAGE), 378-379

Subfunction 0Eh (GET DISK UTILIZATION), 348

Subfunction 0Fh (SCAN FILE INFORMATION), 371-372

Subfunction 10h (SET FILE INFORMATION), 372

Subfunction 11h (GET FILE SERVER INFORMATION), 348-349

Subfunction 12h (GET NETWORK SERIAL NUMBER), 412

Subfunction 13h (GET INTERNET ADDRESS), 331

Subfunction 14h (LOGIN TO FILE SERVER), 332

Subfunction 15h (GET OBJECT CONNECTION NUMBERS), 332

Subfunction 16h (GET CONNECTION INFORMATION), 333

Subfunction 32h (CREATE BINDERY OBJECT), 319

Subfunction 33h (DELETE BINDERY OBJECT), 319-320

Subfunction 34h (RENAME BINDERY OBJECT), 320

Subfunction 35h (GET BINDERY OBJECT ID), 320-321

Subfunction 36h (GET BINDERY OBJECT NAME), 321

Subfunction 37h (SCAN BINDERY OBJECT), 321-322

Subfunction 38h (CHANGE BINDERY OBJECT SECURITY), 322

Subfunction 39h (CREATE PROPERTY), 322-323

Subfunction 3Ah (DELETE PROPERTY), 323

Subfunction 3Bh (CHANGE PROPERTY SECURITY), 323

Subfunction 3Ch (SCAN PROPERTY), 324

Subfunction 3Dh (READ PROPERTY VALUE), 324-325

Subfunction 3Eh (WRITE PROPERTY VALUE), 325

Subfunction 3Fh (VERIFY BINDERY OBJECT PASSWORD), 325-326

Subfunction 40h (CHANGE BINDERY OBJECT PASSWORD), 326

Subfunction 41h (ADD BINDERY OBJECT TO SET), 326-327

Subfunction 42h (DELETE BINDERY OBJECT FROM SET), 327

Subfunction 43h (IS BINDERY OBJECT IN SET), 327-328

Subfunction 44h (CLOSE BINDERY), 328

Subfunction 45h (OPEN BINDERY), 328

Subfunction 46h (GET BINDERY ACCESS LEVEL), 328-329

Subfunction 47h (SCAN BINDERY OBJECT TRUSTEE PATHS), 344-345

Subfunction 63h (CHANGE QUEUE JOB POSITION), 392

Subfunction 64h (CREATE QUEUE), 386

Subfunction 65h (DESTROY QUEUE), 386

Subfunction 66h (READ QUEUE CURRENT STATUS), 387

Subfunction 67h (SET QUEUE CURRENT STATUS), 387-388

Subfunction 68h (CREATE QUEUE JOB AND FILE), 388-389

Subfunction 69h (CLOSE FILE AND START QUEUE JOB), 389

Subfunction 6Ah (REMOVE JOB FROM QUEUE), 389

Subfunction 6Bh (GET QUEUE JOB LIST), 389-390

Subfunction 6Ch (READ QUEUE JOB ENTRY), 390-391

Subfunction 6Dh (CHANGE QUEUE JOB ENTRY), 391-392

Subfunction 6Fh (ATTACH QUEUE SERVER TO QUEUE), 392

Subfunction 70h (DETACH QUEUE SERVER FROM QUEUE), 393

Subfunction 71h (SERVICE QUEUE JOB AND OPEN FILE), 393

Subfunction 72h (FINISH SERVICING QUEUE JOB/FILE), 393-394

Subfunction 73h (ABORT SERVICING QUEUE JOB/FILE), 394

Subfunction 74h (CHANGE TO CLIENT RIGHTS), 394-395

Subfunction 75h (RESTORE QUEUE SERVER RIGHTS), 395

Subfunction 76h (READ QUEUE SERVER CURRENT STATUS), 395

Subfunction 77h (SET QUEUE SERVER CURRENT STATUS), 395-396

Subfunction 78h (GET QUEUE JOB'S FILE SIZE), 396

Subfunction 96h (GET ACCOUNT STATUS), 316-317

Subfunction 97h (SUBMIT ACCOUNT CHARGE), 317

Subfunction 99h (SUBMIT ACCOUNT NOTE), 318

Subfunction C8h (CHECK CONSOLE PRIVILEGES), 349

Subfunction C9h (GET FILE SERVER DESCRIPTION STRINGS), 349-350

Subfunction CBh (DISABLE FILE SERVER LOGIN), 350

Subfunction CCh (ENABLE FILE SERVER LOGIN), 351

Subfunction CDh (GET FILE SERVER LOGIN STATUS), 351

Subfunction CEh (PURGE ALL ERASED FILES), 372-373

Subfunction CFh (DISABLE TRANSACTION TRACKING), 351-352

Subfunction D0h (ENABLE TRANSACTION TRACKING), 352

Subfunction D1h (SEND CONSOLE BROADCAST), 352

Subfunction D2h (CLEAR CONNECTION NUMBER), 353

Subfunction D3h (DOWN FILE SERVER), 353

Subfunction D4h (GET FILE SYSTEM STATISTICS), 353-354

Subfunction D5h (GET TRANSACTION TRACKING STATISTICS), 354-355

Subfunction D6h (GET DISK CACHE STATISTICS), 355-356

Subfunction D7h (GET DRIVE MAPPING TABLE), 356

Subfunction D8h (GET PHYSICAL DISK STATISTICS), 356-357

Subfunction D9h (GET DISK CHANNEL STATISTICS), 357-358

Subfunction DAh (GET CONNECTION'S TASK INFORMATION), 358-359

Subfunction DBh (GET CONNECTION'S OPEN FILES), 359-360

Subfunction DCh (GET CONNECTIONS USING A FILE), 361

Subfunction DDh (GET PHYSICAL RECORD LOCKS BY CONNECTION AND FILE), 361-362

Subfunction DEh (GET PHYSICAL RECORD LOCKS BY FILE), 362-363

Subfunction DFh (GET LOGICAL RECORDS BY CONNECTION), 363-364

Subfunction E1h (GET CONNECTION'S SEMAPHORES), 364-365

Subfunction E2h (GET SEMAPHORE INFORMATION), 365-366

Subfunction E3h (GET LAN DRIVER'S CONFIGURATION INFO), 366

Subfunction E5h (GET CONNECTION'S USAGE STATISTICS), 366-367

Subfunction E6h (GET BINDERY OBJECT DISK SPACE LEFT), 367

Subfunction E7h (GET FILE SERVER LAN I/O STATISTICS), 367-368

Subfunction E8h (GET FILE SERVER MISCELLANEOUS INFO), 368-369

Subfunction E9h (GET VOLUME INFORMATION), 345

Function E4h (SET FILE ATTRIBUTES (FCB)), 346

Function E5h (UPDATE FILE SIZE (FCB)), 346

Function E6h (COPY FILE TO FILE (FCB)), 412

Function E7h (GET FILE SERVER DATE/TIME), 216

Function E8h (SET FCB REOPEN MODE), 412

Function E900h (GET DIRECTORY HANDLE), 346

Function E905h (MAP A FAKE ROOT DIRECTORY), 346

Function EAh (RETURN SHELL VERSION), 412-413

Function EBh (LOG FILE), 403-404

Function ECh (RELEASE FILE), 404

Function EDh (CLEAR FILE), 404

Function EEh (GET PHYSICAL STATION ADDRESS), 333

Function EF00h (GET DRIVE HANDLE TABLE), 407

Function EF01h (GET DRIVE FLAG TABLE), 407-408

Function EF02h (GET DRIVE CONNECTION ID TABLE), 408

Function EF03h (GET CONNECTION ID TABLE), 408

Function EF04h (GET FILE SERVER NAME TABLE), 408-409

Function F000h (SET PREFERRED CONNECTION ID), 409

Function F001h (GET PREFERRED CONNECTION ID), 409

Function F003h (GET LPT CAPTURE STATUS), 385

Function F004h (SET PRIMARY CONNECTION ID), 409

Function F005h (GET PRIMARY CONNECTION ID), 409

Function F1h (FILE SERVER CONNECTION), 333-334

Function F244h (ERASE FILES), 373

Function F2h (MULTIPLEXOR), 413-417

Function F3h (FILE SERVER FILE COPY), 373

Function FF00h (GET SYSTEM INFORMATION), 483

Function FF04h (GET/SET DEFAULT FILE PROTECTION ATTRIBUTES), 483-484

Function FF80h, Subfunction FFh (SEND MESSAGE), 484

Function FF82h (GET STATION ADDRESS), 484

Function FF8Ch (GET STATUS OF TopShow/Emulated FUNCTION), 484

Function FF8Dh (CALL TopShow FUNCTION), 485

Function FF8Eh (CANCEL TopShow FUNCTION), 485

Function FF91h (GET FILE SERVER STATION NUMBER), 485

Function FF97h (GET MAXIMUM STATION NUMBER), 485

Function FF98h (GET MAXIMUM FILE NUMBER), 485

Function FF9Ah (RECEIVE USER-DEFINED PACKETS), 486

Function FF9Fh (ENABLE/DISABLE TopTerm SERVICE), 486

Function FFB0h (GET SPOOLER PRINTING PRIORITY), 486

Function FFB1h (SET SPOOLER PRINTING PRIORITY), 486

Function FFB3h (GET DEFAULT START-OF-JOB FORMFEED STATUS), 487

Function FFBBh (GET PRINTER SERVER STATION ADDRESS), 487

Function FFBCh (CANCEL TopShow FUNCTION), 487

Function FFBDh (GET CURRENT AUTOPRINT TIME), 487-488

Function FFBEh (SET AUTOPRINT TIME), 488

Function FFBFh (GET LOGON USER INFORMATION), 488

Function FFBRh (SET DEFAULT START-OF-JOB FORMFEED STATUS), 487

Function FFC0h (GET DEFAULT END-OF-JOB FORMFEED STATUS), 488

Function FFC1h (SET DEFAULT END-OF-JOB FORMFEED STATUS), 488

Function FFC2h (GET DEFAULT COPIES OF SPOOLING FILE), 489

Function FFC3h (GET SHARING STATUS OF PRINTER SERVER), 489

Function FFC4h (GET/SET LPT PORT ON PRINT SERVER), 489

Function FFC6h (SET DEFAULT PRINT FILE HEADER), 489

Function FFC7h (SET DEFAULT PRINT COPIES), 489-490

Function FFC8h (GET DEFAULT PRINT FILE HEADER STATUS), 490

Function FFC9h (SET PRINTER SHARING), 490

Function FFCAh (MOVE FILE FROM ONE PRINT SERVER TO ANOTHER), 490

Function FFCBh (DELETE FILE FROM SPOOLING QUEUE), 490

Function FFCCh (GET PRINT SERVER'S SPOOLING QUEUE STATUS), 491

Function FFCDh (GET STATUS OF ALL PRINT SERVERS), 491

Function FFCFh (CALL TopLook FUNCTION), 491-492

Function FFD6h (GET KEYCARD SERIAL NUMBER/MAXIMUM USERS), 492

Function FFD7h (GET NETWORK PROTECTION ATTRIBUTES STATUS), 492

INT 2Ah

Function 01h (EXECUTE NetBIOS REQUEST, NO ERROR RETRY), 117

Function 82h (END DOS CRITICAL SECTIONS 0 THROUGH 7), 62-63

Function 0000h (INSTALLATION CHECK), 117

Function 00h (INSTALLATION CHECK), 61

Function 02h (SET NET PRINTER MODE), 117

Function 0300h (CHECK DIRECT I/O), 61

Function 04h (EXECUTE NetBIOS REQUEST), 117-118

Function 0500h (GET NETWORK RESOURCE AVAILABILITY), 118

Function 06h (NETWORK PRINT-STREAM CONTROL), 62

Function 07h (RECEIVER.COM), 437

Function 2001h (UNDETERMINED FUNCTION), 518

Function 2002h/2003h (UNDETERMINED FUNCTION), 518

Function 7802h (GET LOGGED ON USER NAME), 437

Function 80h (BEGIN DOS CRITICAL SECTION), 62

Function 81h (END DOS CRITICAL SECTION), 62

Function 84h (KEYBOARD BUSY LOOP), 63

Function 86h (RECEIVER.COM), 437

Function 8700h (BEGIN BACKGROUND PRINTING), 63

Function 8701h (END BACKGROUND PRINTING), 63

Function 89h (RECEIVER.COM), 437

Function 90h (UNDETERMINED FUNCTION), 633

Function C2h (UNDETERMINED FUNCTION), 518

Function C4h (RECEIVER.COM), 437-438

Function D800h/D801h (SERVER - SET/RESET UNKNOWN FLAG), 421

Function D850h (CLIENT - INCREMENT UNKNOWN COUNTER), 421

Function D851h (CLIENT - RESET UNKNOWN COUNTER), 421

Function E0h (UNDETERMINED FUNCTION), 438

Function FF90h (UNDETERMINED FUNCTION), 560

Function FF91h (UNDETERMINED FUNCTION), 560

Function FF92h (INSTALLATION CHECK), 560

Function FF93h (UNDETERMINED FUNCTION), 561

Function FF94h (UNDETERMINED FUNCTION), 561

Function FF95h (GET CONFIGURATION STRINGS), 561

Function FF96h (SET PRINT JOB TERMINATION CONFIGURATION), 561

Function FF97h (GET PRINT JOB TERMINATION CONFIGURATION), 561

INT 2Fh

(multiplex interrupt), 7

Function 110Fh (GET REMOTE FILE'S ATTRIBUTES AND SIZE), 127

Function 1110h (GET REMOTE FILE'S ATTRIBUTES/SIZE), 127-128

Function 111Dh (CLOSE ALL REMOTE FILES FOR PROCESS), 131

Function 1205h (OUTPUT CHARACTER TO STANDARD OUTPUT), 65

Function 1207h (MAKE DISK BUFFER MOST-RECENTLY USED), 65

Function 1216h (GET ADDRESS OF SYSTEM FILE TABLE ENTRY), 68

Function 1217h (GET CURRENT DIRECTORY STRUCTURE FOR DRIVE), 68

Function 4E53h
    Subfunction 00h (INSTALLATION CHECK), 516
    Subfunction 01h (GET RUNTIME PARAMETER), 516-517
    Subfunction 02h (SET RUNTIME PARAMETERS), 517

Function 7000h (INSTALLATION CHECK), 681

Function 7001h (REQUEST LICENSE), 681-682

Function 7002h (RELEASE LICENSE), 682

Function 7003h (UPDATE), 682

Function 7004h (GET ERROR), 682-683

Function 7005h (QUERY LICENSE), 683

Function 7A20h
    Subfunction 0000h (GET CALL ADDRESS), 417
    Subfunction 0001h (GET UNKNOWN ENTRY POINT), 417

Subfunction 0002h (GET UNKNOWN DATA), 418

Subfunction 0003h (GET UNKNOWN), 418

Subfunction 0004h (GET UNKNOWN DATA), 418

Subfunction 0005h (GET UNKNOWN ENTRY POINT), 418

Subfunction 0006h-0008h (GET UNKNOWN ENTRY POINTS), 418

Subfunction 0080h-0082h (GET UNKNOWN ENTRY POINT), 418

Function 7A4Fh, Subfunction 0001h (INSTALLATION CHECK), 565

Function 7A4Fh, Subfunction 0002h (UNDETERMINED FUNCTION), 565

Function 7AFFh, Subfunction 0000h (INSTALLATION CHECK), 434

Function 7AFFh, Subfunction 0001h (INSTALLATION CHECK), 434

Function D702h (PCPRINT Interface), 216

Function D703h (MAIL Interface), 216

Function D704h (Streetalk Directory Assistance Interface), 216

Function FE00h, Subfunction 4454h (INSTALLATION CHECK), 566

Function 0200h (REDIR/REDIRIFS - INSTALLATION CHECK), 438

Function 0201h (REDIR/REDIRIFS - UNDETERMINED FUNCTION), 438

Function 0202h (REDIR/REDIRIFS - UNDETERMINED FUNCTION), 438

Function 0203h (UNDETERMINED FUNCTION), 438

Function 0204h (UNDETERMINED FUNCTION), 438-439

Function 02xxh (UNDETERMINED FUNCTION), 439

Function 0500h (INSTALLATION CHECK), 63

Function 05h (EXPAND ERROR INTO STRING), 64

Function 1100h (INSTALLATION CHECK), 123

Function 1101h (REMOVE REMOTE DIRECTORY), 123-124

Function 1102h (REMOVE REMOTE DIRECTORY), 124

Function 1103h (MAKE REMOTE DIRECTORY), 124

Function 1104h (MAKE REMOTE DIRECTORY), 124

Function 1105h (CHDIR), 124-125

Function 1106h (CLOSE REMOTE FILE), 125

Function 1107h (COMMIT REMOTE FILE), 125

Function 1108h (READ FROM REMOTE FILE), 125

Function 1109h (WRITE TO REMOTE FILE), 125-126

Function 110Ah (LOCK REGION OF FILE), 126

Function 110Ah (LOCK/UNLOCK REGION OF FILE), 126

Function 110Bh (UNLOCK REGION OF FILE), 126-127

Function 110Dh (SET REMOTE FILE'S ATTRIBUTES), 127

Function 110Eh (SET REMOTE FILE'S ATTRIBUTES), 127

Function 1112h (RENAME REMOTE FILE), 128

Function 1113h (DELETE REMOTE FILE), 128

Function 1114h (DELETE REMOTE FILE), 128

Function 1115h (OPEN REMOTE FILE), 128-129

Function 1116h (OPEN EXISTING REMOTE FILE), 129

Function 1117h (CREATE/TRUNCATE REMOTE FILE), 129

Function 1118h (CREATE/TRUNCATE FILE WITHOUT CDS), 129

Function 1119h (FIND FIRST FILE WITHOUT CDS), 130

Function 111Ah (FIND NEXT FILE WITHOUT CDS), 130

Function 111Bh (FINDFIRST), 130

Function 111Ch (FINDNEXT), 130

Function 111Eh (DO REDIRECTION), 131-132

Function 111h (RENAME REMOTE FILE), 128

Function 1120h (FLUSH ALL DISK BUFFERS), 132

Function 1121h (SEEK FROM END OF REMOTE FILE), 133

Function 1122h (PROCESS TERMINATIN HOOK), 133

Function 1123h (QUALIFY REMOTE FILENAME), 133

Function 1124h (TURN OFF REMOTE PRINTER), 133

Function 1125h (REDIRECTED PRINTER MODE), 133

Function 1126h (REMOTE PRINTER ECHO ON/OFF), 134

Function 1127h (UNUSED FUNCTION), 134

Function 1128h (UNUSED FUNCTION), 134

Function 1129h (UNUSED FUNCTION), 134

Function 112Ah (CLOSE ALL FILES FOR PROCESS), 134

Function 112Bh (GENERIC IOCTL), 134

Function 112Ch (UPDATE CB), 134

Function 112Dh (EXTENDED ATTRIBUTES), 134-135

Function 112Eh (EXTENDED OPEN/CREATE FILE), 135

Function 112Fh (IFS IOCTL), 135

Function 1130h (GET IFSFUNC SEGMENT), 136

Function 1180h (UNDETERMINED FUNCTION), 291

Function 1182h (INSTALL SERVICE), 291

Function 1184h (UNDETERMINED FUNCTION), 291

Function 1186h (DosReadAsynchNmPipe), 292

Function 118Ah (STREAM ENCRYPTION SERVICE), 292

Function 118Bh (UNDETERMINED FUNCTION), 292

Function 118Ch (UNDETERMINED FUNCTION), 292

Function 118Eh (UNDETERMINED FUNCTION), 292

Function 118Fh (DosWriteAsynchNmPipe), 292

Function 1190h (DosReadAsynchNmPipe2), 293

Function 1191h (DosWriteAsynchNmPipe2), 293

Function 11xxh (NETWORK REDIRECTOR INTERFACE), 64

Function 1200h (INSTALLATION CHECK), 64

Function 1201h (CLOSE CURRENT FILE), 64

Function 1202h (GET INTERRUPT ADDRESS), 64

Function 1203h (GET DOS DATA SEGMENT), 64

Function 1204h (NORMALIZE PATH SEPARATOR), 65

Function 1206h (INVOKE CRITICAL ERROR), 65

INT 2Fh (continued)

Function 1208h (DECREMENT SFT REFERENCE COUNT), 65

Function 1209h (FLUSH AND FREE DISK BUFFER), 65

Function 120Ah (PERFORM CRITICAL ERROR INTERRUPT), 66

Function 120Bh (SIGNAL SHARING VIOLATION TO USER), 66

Function 120Ch (OPEN DEVICE AND SET SFT OWNER/MODE), 66

Function 120Dh (GET DATE AND TIME), 66

Function 120Eh (MARK ALL DISK BUFFERS UNREFERENCED), 66

Function 120Fh (MAKE BUFFER MOST RECENTLY USED), 67

Function 121 0h (FIND UNREFERENCED DISK BUFFER), 67

Function 1211h (NORMALIZE ASCIZ FILENAME), 67

Function 1212h (GET LENGTH OF ASCIZ STRING), 67

Function 1213h (UPPERCASE CHARACTER), 67

Function 1214h (COMPARE FAR POINTERS), 67

Function 1215h (FLUSH BUFFER), 68

Function 1218h (GET CALLER'S REGISTERS), 68

Function 1219h (SET DRIVE), 68

Function 121Ah (GET FILE'S DRIVE), 68

Function 121Bh (SET YEAR/LENGTH OF FEBRUARY), 69

Function 121Ch (CHECKSUM MEMORY), 69

Function 121Dh (SUM MEMORY), 69

Function 121Eh (COMPARE FILENAMES), 69

Function 121Fh (BUILD CURRENT DIRECTORY STRUCTURE), 69

Function 1220h (GET JOB FILE TABLE ENTRY), 69-70

Function 1221h (CANONICALIZE FILE NAME), 70

Function 1222h (SET EXTENDED ERROR INFORMATION), 70

Function 1223h (CHECK IF CHARACTER DEVICE), 70

Function 1224h (SHARING RETRY DELAY), 70

Function 1225h (GET LENGTH OF ASCIZ STRING), 71

Function 1226h (OPEN FILE), 71

Function 1227h (CLOSE FILE), 71

Function 1228h (MOVE FILE POINTER), 71

Function 1229h (READ FROM FILE), 72

Function 122Ah (SET FASTOPEN ENTRY POINT), 72

Function 122Bh (IOCTL), 73

Function 122Ch (GET DEVICE CHAIN), 73

Function 122Dh (GET EXTENDED ERROR CODE), 73

Function 122Eh (GET OR SET ERROR TABLE ADDRESS), 73-75

Function 13h (UNDETERMINED FUNCTION), 518

Function 1500H (INSTALLATION CHECK), 241

Function 1501h (GET DRIVE DEVICE LIST), 241

Function 1502h (GET COPYRIGHT FILE NAME), 241

Function 1503h (GET ABSTRACT FILE NAME), 241-242

Function 1504h (GET BIBLIOGRAPHIC DOCUMENT FILE NAME), 242

Function 1505h (READ VTOC), 242

Function 1506h (TURN DEBUGGING ON), 242

Function 1507h (TURN DEBUGGING OFF), 242

Function 1508h (ABSOLUTE DISK READ), 242

Function 1509h (ABSOLUTE DISK WRITE), 243

Function 150Ah (RESERVED), 243

Function 150Bh (DRIVE CHECK), 243

Function 150Ch (GET MSCDEX.EXE VERSION), 243

Function 150Dh (GET CD-ROM DRIVE LETTERS), 243

Function 150Eh (GET/SET VOLUME DESCRIPTOR PREFERENCE), 243-244

Function 150Fh (GET DIRECTORY ENTRY), 244-245

Function 1510h (SEND DEVICE DRIVER REQUEST), 245

Function 4100h (INSTALLATION CHECK), 293

Function 4103h (UNDETERMINED FUNCTION), 293

Function 4104h (UNDETERMINED FUNCTION), 293

Function 42h (MESSENGER SERVICE), 294

Function 4Bh (NETWORK WORKSTATION REDIRECTOR), 294

Function 5600h (INSTALLATION CHECK), 511

Function 5601h (CHECK IF REDIRECTED DRIVE), 511

Function 5602h (GET UNKNOWN VALUE), 511

Function 7A00h (LOW-LEVEL [IPX] INSTALLATION CHECK), 91

Function 7A10h (GET TBMI STATUS), 431

Function 7A11h (GET INT 2Fh HANDLERS), 432

Function 7A12h (GET INT 64h HANDLERS), 432

Function 7A13h (GET INT 7Ah HANDLERS), 432

Function 7A14h (GET STATISTICS), 432-433

Function 7A15h (RESET UNKNOWN VARIABLE), 433

Function 7A16h (UNDETERMINED FUNCTION), 433

Function 7A17h (UNDETERMINED FUNCTION), 433

Function 7A18h (INSTALLATION CHECK), 430

Function 7A19h (GET INT 08h HANDLERS), 431

Function 7A1Ah (GET INT 2Fh HANDLERS), 431

Function 7A1Bh (GET DIAGNOSTICS INFORMATION), 431

Function 7A1Ch (UNDETERMINED FUNCTION), 433

Function 7A1Dh (UNDETERMINED FUNCTION), 433

Function 7A1Eh (UNDETERMINED FUNCTION), 433

Function 7A40h (INSTALLATION CHECK), 564

Function 7A41h (WINDOWS SUPPORT), 564

Function 7A42h (GET UNKNOWN ENTRY POINT), 565

Function 7A43h (UNDETERMINED FUNCTION), 565

Function 7A44h (UNDETERMINED FUNCTION), 565

Function 7A4Ch (GET UNKNOWN VALUES), 565

Function 7A4Dh (UNDETERMINED FUNCTION), 434

Function 7A4Fh (INSTALLATION CHECK), 565

Function 7A80h (ABNORMAL EXIT), 419

Function 7A81h (SET SHELL INT 21h HANDLER), 419

Function 7A85h (BROADCAST INFORM), 419

Function 7A90h (INSTALLATION CHECK), 435

Function 7AC1h (LHR - DISABLE), 667

Function 7AC2h (LHR - SYNCHRONIZE SHIFT STATES), 667

Function 7AC3h (LHR - CLEAR UNKNOWN FLAG), 667

Function 7AC8h (LHR - ENABLE FUNCTIONS), 667-668

Function 7AC9h (LHR - DISABLE FUNCTIONS), 668

INT 2Fh (continued)
Function 7ACAh (LHJ - UNDE-
TERMINED FUNCTION),
668
Function 7ACBh/7ACCh (LHJ -
UNDETERMINED FUNC-
TION), 668
Function 7ACFh (LHR -
INSTALLATION CHECK),
668
Function 7AF0h (INSTALLA-
TION CHECK), 435
Function 7AF1h (INSTALLA-
TION CHECK), 427-430
Function 7AFEh (INSTALLA-
TION CHECK), 435
Function 8000h (INSTALLA-
TION CHECK), 511
Function 8000h (INSTALLA-
TION CHECK), 519
Function 8001h (UNDETER-
MINED FUNCTION), 511
Function 8100h (INSTALLA-
TION CHECK), 512
Function 8101h (UNDETER-
MINED FUNCTION), 512
Function 8103h (GET
MACHINE NAME), 512
Function 8104h (UNDETER-
MINED FUNCTION), 512
Function 8105h (UNDETER-
MINED FUNCTION), 512
Function 9200h (BUG), 275
Function 9201h (CHECK IF
MAPPED DRIVE), 276
Function 9202h (UNINSTALL),
276
Function 9203h (GET VER-
SION), 276
Function 9204h (INSTALLA-
TION CHECK), 276
Function 9205h (SET
UNKNOWN VALUE), 276
Function 9206h (UNDETER-
MINED FUNCTION), 276
Function 9207h (GET
UNKNOWN VALUE), 277
Function 9208h (UNDETER-
MINED FUNCTION), 277
Function 9209h (UNDETER-
MINED FUNCTION), 277
Function 920Ah (UNDETER-
MINED FUNCTION), 277
Function 920Bh (SET DRIVE
MAPPING), 277
Function 920Ch (UNDETER-
MINED FUNCTION), 277
Function 920Dh (GET DRIVE
TYPE), 277-278
Function 920Eh (SET LPT MAP-
PING), 278
Function 920Fh (GET
UNKNOWN DATA), 278
Function 9210h (UNDETER-
MINED FUNCTION), 278
Function 9211h (GET
UNKNOWN DATA), 278
Function 9212h (CRITICAL SEC-
TION), 278
Function 9213h (UNDETER-
MINED FUNCTION), 278

Function 9214h (GET
UNKNOWN DATA), 279
Function 9215h (GET
UNKNOWN DATA), 279
Function 9216h (UNDETER-
MINED FUNCTION), 279
Function 9217h (UNDETER-
MINED FUNCTION), 279
Function 9218h (GET LPT
TYPE), 279
Function 9219h (UNDETER-
MINED FUNCTION), 279
Function 921Ah (UNDETER-
MINED FUNCTION), 279
Function 921Bh (UNDETER-
MINED FUNCTION), 280
Function 921Ch (UNDETER-
MINED FUNCTION), 280
Function 921Dh (GET
UNKNOWN VALUE), 280
Function 921Eh (UNDETER-
MINED FUNCTION), 280
Function 92h (API), 680
Function 9400h (INSTALLA-
TION CHECK), 679
Function 9401h (SET
UNKNOWN FLAG), 679
Function 9402h (UNDETER-
MINED FUNCTION), 679
Function 9403h (SET
UNKNOWN FLAG), 679
Function 9404h (CLEAR
UNKNOWN FLAG), 680
Function 9Ch (OPERATOR), 680
Function B400h (INSTALLA-
TION CHECK), 634
Function B401h (GET HOST
BUFFER ADDRESS), 634
Function B402h-B405h (UNDE-
TERMINED FUNCTION),
634
Function B800h (INSTALLA-
TION CHECK), 462
Function B800h (INSTALLA-
TION CHECK), 505
Function B803h (GET NET-
WORK EVENT POST
HANDLER), 505
Function B804h (SET NET-
WORK EVENT POST
HANDLER), 506
Function B807h (GET NetBIOS
NAME NUM-
BER/MACHINE NAME),
506
Function B808h (RELINK KEY-
BOARD HANDLER), 507
Function B809h (VERSION
CHECK), 507
Function B80Ah (UNDETER-
MINED FUNCTION), 439
Function B80Fh (GET START
PARAMETERS), 507-508
Function B900h
(RECEIVER.COM -
INSTALLATION CHECK),
439
Function B901h (GET
RECEIVER.COM INT 2Fh
HANDLER ADDRESS),
439

Function B903h (GET
RECEIVER.COM POST
ADDRESS), 439
Function B904h (SET
RECEIVER.COM POST
ADDRESS), 439
Function B905h
(RECEIVER.COM - GET
FILENAME), 440
Function B906h
(RECEIVER.COM - SET
FILENAME), 440
Function B908h
(RECEIVER.COM -
UNLINK KEYBOARD
HANDLER), 440
Function BF00h (REDIRIFS.EXE
- UNDETERMINED
FUNCTION), 440
Function BF01h (REDIRIFS.EXE
- UNDETERMINED
FUNCTION), 440
Function BF80h (REDIR.SYS -
SET REDIRIFS ENTRY
POINT), 440
Function C000h (INSTALLA-
TION CHECK), 137-146
Function D000h (INSTALLA-
TION CHECK), 245
Function D002h (GET DATA
AREA), 245
Function D701h, Subfunction
0000h (GET BANV INTER-
RUPT NUMBER), 216
Function D800h (CLIENT.EXE -
INSTALLATION CHECK),
421-424
Function D856h (SERVER - GET
UNKNOWN VALUES), 424
Function D880h (SERVER -
INSTALLATION CHECK),
424-425
Function D8C0h (NLCACHE -
INSTALLATION CHECK),
425
Function DAB2h (INSTALLA-
TION CHECK), 526
Function EE00h (INSTALLA-
TION CHECK), 497
Function EE0h (WEB GENERAL
NOTIFICATION), 502
Function EExx0h (WEB MOD-
ULE INSTALLATION
CHECK), 497-502
Function FE08h (GET
UNKNOWN ITEM), 566
Function FF00h (INSTALLA-
TION CHECK), 493
Function FF01h (GET VER-
SION), 493
Function FF02h (GET TopNet
VERSION STRING), 494
Function FF10h (TopTerm -
INSTALLATION CHECK),
494
Function FF11h (TopTerm -
ENABLE KEYBOARD SER-
VICE), 494
Function FF12h (TopTerm - DIS-
ABLE KEYBOARD SER-
VICE), 494

Function FF13h (TopTerm - SET INSTALLATION FLAG), 494
Function FF14h (START BACK-GROUND RECEIVE VIDEO DATA), 494
Function FF15h (END BACK-GROUND RECEIVE VIDEO DATA), 494
Function FF16h (SET CONTROL NUMBER OF SHOW SCREEN), 495
Function FF18h (SEND FULL SCREEN OF DATA FOR TopShow), 495
Function FF23h (CLOSE SPOOL FILES/START PRINTING), 495
Function FF27h (GET SHOW TYPE), 495
Functions 7F24h and 7F26h (UNDETERMINED FUNCTION), 686
INT 44h (HIGH-LEVEL LANGUAGE API), 419
INT 48h (DATA POINTER 1), 686
INT 49h (DATA POINTER 2), 686
INT 50h (API), 686
INT 50h-INT 57h (RELOCATED IRQ0 THROUGH IRQ7), 643
INT 53h (API), 502
INT 5Ah (BIOS ENTRY ADDRESS), 686
INT 5Bh
    (API), 519
    (INTERFACE), 118-119
    (NETWORK COMMANDS), 686
    (UNDETERMINED FUNCTION), 686
    (UNKNOWN), 168
INT 5Ch
    (API), 519, 522-523
    (AppleTalk INTERFACE), 520-522
    Function 04h (CHECK IF CONNECTION ALIVE), 523
    (INSTALLATION CHECK), 523
    (NetBIOS INTERFACE), 119-122
INT 60h
    (API), 508-510, 643
    (UNDETERMINED FUNCTION), 686
    Function 0Ch (GET STATION ADDRESS), 217
    Function 11h to 13h (SEMAPHORE LOCKING/UNLOCKING), 217
    Function 01FFh (GET DRIVER INFO), 147-151
    Function 02h (ACCESS TYPE), 151
    Function 03h (RELEASE TYPE), 152
    Function 04h (SEND PACKET), 152
    Function 05h (TERMINATE DRIVER FOR HANDLE), 152
    Function 06h (GET ADDRESS), 152

Function 07h (RESET INTERFACE), 152
Function 0Ah (GET PARAMETERS), 152-153
Function 0Bh (ASYNCHRONOUS SEND PACKET), 153
Function 0Ch (ASYNCHRONOUS SEND PACKET), 153-154
Function 0Dh (DROP PACKET FROM QUEUE), 154
Function 11h (LOCK AND WAIT), 523
Function 12h (LOCK), 523
Function 13h (UNLOCK), 524
Function 14h (SET RECEIVE MODE), 154
Function 15h (GET RECEIVE MODE), 154
Function 16h (SET MULTICAST LIST), 154
Function 17h (GET MULTICAST LIST), 155
Function 18h (GET STATISTICS), 155
Function 19h (SET NETWORK ADDRESS), 155
Function 1Ah (SEND RAW BYTES), 155
Function 1Bh (FLUSH RAW BYTES RECEIVED), 155-156
Function 1Ch (FETCH RAW BYTES RECEIVED), 156
Function E9h (AUTOSELECT TRANSCEIVER), 156
INT 60h-INT 67h (user interrupts), 7
INT 61h
    (API), 570
    (INTERFACE), 643
    (TCP/IP TSR System Call interface), 541-543
    Function 0001h
        Subfunction 0001h (OPEN COMMUNICATION SOCKET), 217-218
        Subfunction 0002h (INITIATE OUTPUT EVENT), 218-219
        Subfunction 0003h (SOREC), 219-220
        Subfunction 0004h (CLOSE A SOCKET), 220
        Subfunction 0005h (SOWAIT), 220-221
        Subfunction 0008h (SOSESSION), 221
        Subfunction 000Bh (SOINT), 221
    Function 0002h (3270 INTERFACE), 222-226
    Function 0003h
        Subfunction 00h (INITIALIZE USER BUFFER POINTER INFO), 227-228

Subfunction 01h (SEND TO HOST), 228-229
Subfunction 02h (CONTROL MONITOR), 229-230
Subfunction 03h (FLOW CONTROL DATA), 230
Subfunction 04h (END ACTIVE SESSION), 230
Subfunction 05h (SET SESSION PARAMETER), 230-231
Subfunction 06h (GET SESSION PARAMETER), 231
Subfunction 07h (SET TAB SETTINGS), 231
Subfunction 08h (GET TAB SETTINGS), 231-232
Subfunction 09h (REFRESH EMULATION SCREEN), 232
Subfunction 0Ah (SUSPEND SESSION TEMPORARILY), 232
Subfunction 0Bh (RESUME SUSPENDED SESSION), 232
Subfunction 0Ch (SET SCROLL LOCK CHECKING), 233
Subfunction 0Dh (EXIT EMULATION), 233
Subfunction 0Eh (INTERRRUPT ON CHARACTER FROM HOST), 233
Subfunction 0Fh (START SESSION), 233-234
Subfunction 10h (START/STOP PRINTING), 234
Subfunction 11h (GET FILE TRANSFER PARAMETER), 234
Subfunction 12h (GET CONNECTION INFORMATION), 235
Subfunction 13h (START/STOP TRACING TRAFFIC), 235
Subfunction 14h (INTERRUPT ON HOST MESSAGE), 235
Subfunction 15h (RESET ERROR), 236

INT 61h
   Function 0004h (GET SERVER SERIAL NUMBER), 236
   Function 0005h (PRINTER CONTROL), 236
   Function 0007h
      Subfunction 0002h (GET PORTS SERVICE), 236 237
      Subfunction 0004h (SET PORTS FOR A SERVICE), 237
      Subfunction 0005h (GET USER NAME), 237
      Subfunction 0006h (ERROR INTO ASCII STRING), 237
      Subfunction 0007h (VERIFY EXISTANCE), 238
      Subfunction 0008h (ENUMERATE Streetalk NAMES), 238-239
   Function 0008h, Subfunction 0002h (POST MESSAGE ON LOCAL DISPLAY), 239
   Function 0008h, Subfunction 0003h (INTERCEPT VINES), 239-240
   Function 000Ah (SECONDARY 3270 INTERFACE), 240
   Function 01h (CHECK SERVICE), 240
   Function 01h, Subfunction 000h (CONFIGURE RUNNING KERNEL), 544
   Function 02h (GET REVISION NUMBER), 240
   Function 00h (GET DEBUG INFORMATION), 543
   Function 02h (GET MISCELLANEOUS LOCAL INFO), 544
   Function 05h (GET INTERNET ADDRESS OF NETWORK DESCRIPTOR), 544
   Function 06h (GET INTERFACE STATISTICS), 544-545
   Function 07h (MAKE NET DESCRIPTOR GLOBAL), 545
   Function 08h (CLOSE A NETWORK DESCRIPTOR), 545
   Function 09h (CLOSE ALL NON-GLOBAL DESCRIPTORS), 545
   Function 0Ah (UNDETERMINED FUNCTION), 546
   Function 0Bh (UNDETERMINED FUNCTION), 546
   Function 0Ch (GET CONNECTION STATISTICS), 546-547
   Function 0Dh (CHECK IF NETWORK DESCRIPTOR VALID), 548
   Function 0Eh (DETECT READINESS OF NETWORK), 548

   Function 0Fh (GET SOFTWARE VERSION), 548
   Function 10h (UNINSTALL), 548
   Function 11h (DISABLE ASYNCHRONOUS HANDLERS), 548-549
   Function 12h (ENABLE ASYNCHRONOUS HANDLERS), 549
   Function 13h (OPEN A NETWORK CONNECTION), 549
   Function 14h (NO LONGER SUPPORTED), 549-550
   Function 15h (UNDETERMINED FUNCTION), 550
   Function 16h (GET DATA ON REMOTE PEER), 550
   Function 17h (RE-READ KERNEL CONFIGURATION), 550
   Function 18h (CLOSE TRANSMIT SIDE OF CONNECTION), 550
   Function 19h (RESET A NETWORK CONNECTION), 550-551
   Function 1Ah (WRITE TO THE NETWORK), 551
   Function 1Bh (READ FROM THE NETWORK), 551
   Function 1Ch (WRITE A DATAGRAM), 551-552
   Function 1Dh (READ A DATAGRAM), 552
   Function 1Eh (FLUSH PENDING DATA), 552
   Function 1Fh (SET UP ASYNCHRONOUS CALLBACK), 552-553
   Function 20h (SET AN OPTION ON A DESCRIPTOR), 553
   Function 21h (GET OPTIONS APPLIED TO NET DESCR), 553-554
   Function 22h (ALLOCATE NETWORK DESCRIPTOR), 554
   Function 23h (LISTEN FOR INCOMING CONNECTIONS), 554
   Function 24h (RESET ALL NETWORK CONNECTIONS), 554
   Function 25h (GET HOST NAME GIVEN ADDRESS), 554-555
   Function 26h (GET HOST NAME FROM LOCAL TABLE), 555
   Function 27h (GET HOST NAME FROM DNS), 555
   Function 28h (EXCHANGE TWO NETWORK DESCRIPTORS), 555
   Function 29h (ALLOCATE GLOBAL DESCRIPTOR), 555
   Function 2Ah (GET CONFIGURATION INFORMATION), 556

   Function 2Bh (SET TIMED ASYNCHRONOUS EVENT), 556
   Function 30h (SEND ICMP ECHO REQUEST), 556-557
   Function 31h-33h (NOP for SLIP kernel), 557
   Function 34h (UNDETERMINED FUNCTION) 557
   Function 50h (TRANSLATE NUMERICAL IP ADDRESS), 557
   Function 51h (RESOLVE NAME USING HOST TABLE), 557
   Function 52h (RESOLVE NAME USING DNS), 558
   Function 53h (RESLOVE HOST NAME USING IEN116), 558
   Function 54h (RESOLVE HOST NAME), 558
INT 62h
   Function 00h (GET PHYSICAL HARDWARE ADRESS), 526
   Function 01h (NOP for ETHDEV.ODI), 527
   Function 02h (INITIALIZE), 527
   Function 03h (GET REAL IP ADDRESS), 527
   Function 04h (SET UNKNOWN POINTER), 527
   Function 05h/06h (UNDETERMINED FUNCTION), 527
   Function 07h (UNDETERMINED FUNCTION), 527
   Function 08h (UNDETERMINED FUNCTION), 527-528
   Function 09h (HOOK TIMER INTERRUPT), 528
   Function 0Ah (UNHOOK TIMER INTERRUPT), 528
   Function 0Bh (ADD UNKNOWN ITEM), 528
   Function 0Ch (REMOVE UNKNOWN ITEM), 528
   Function 0Dh (NOP for ETHDEV.ODI), 528
   Function 0Eh (BEGIN CRITICAL SECTION), 529
   Function 0Fh (END CRITICAL SECTION), 529
   Function 10h (QUERY CRITICAL SECTION), 529
   Function 11h (SET UNKNOWN POINTER), 529
   Function 12h (GET UNKNOWN VALUE), 529
   Function 13h (UNDETERMINED FUNCTION), 529
   Function 14h (UNDETERMINED FUNCTION), 530
   Function 15h (GET UNKNOWN ITEM), 530
   Function 16h (UNDETERMINED FUNCTION), 530
   Function 17h (UNDETERMINED FUNCTION), 530

Function 18h (ALLO-CATE/MAP EMS FOR DRIVER), 530
Function FEh (MAP EMS), 530
INT 63h (SOCKET API), 258
Function 00h (SET IP ADDRESS), 531
Function 01h (UNDETER-MINED FUNCTION), 531
Function 02h (UNDETER-MINED FUNCTION), 531
Function 03h (GET IP ADDRESS), 531
Function 04h (UNDETER-MINED FUNCTION), 531
Function 05h (UNDETER-MINED FUNCTION), 531
Function 06h (UNDETER-MINED FUNCTION), 532
Function 07h (UNDETER-MINED FUNCTION), 532
Function 08h (SET DEFAULT UNKNOWN HANDLER), 532
Function 09h (INSTALL UNKNOWN HANDLERS), 532
Function 0Bh (UNDETER-MINED FUNCTION), 532
Function 0Ch (UNDETER-MINED FUNCTION), 533
Function 0Dh (INSTALL DEFAULT UNKNWON HANDLER), 533
Function 0Eh (CLOSE NET-WORK DESCRIPTOR), 533
Function 0Fh (UNDETER-MINED FUNCTION), 533
Function 10h (UNDETER-MINED FUNCTION), 533
Function 11h (UNDETER-MINED FUNCTION), 533
Function 12h (LISTEN FOR INCOMING CONNEC-TIONS), 533-534
Function 13h (NOP), 534
Function 14h (OPEN NET-WORK CONNECTION), 534
Function 15h (UNDETER-MINED FUNCTION), 534
Function 16h (RESET NET-WORK CONNECTION), 534
Function 17h (UNDETER-MINED FUNCTION), 534
Function 18h (UNDETER-MINED FUNCTION), 534
Function 19h (WRITE TO THE NETWORK), 535
Function 1Ah (READ FROM THE NETWORK), 535
Function 1Bh (UNDETER-MINED FUNCTION), 535
Function 1Ch (UNDETER-MINED FUNCTION), 535
Function 1Dh (UNDETER-MINED FUNCTION), 535
Function 1Eh (UNDETER-MINED FUNCTION), 535

Function 1Fh (SET SOCKET UNKNOWN HANDLER), 536
Function 20h (REMOVE SOCKET UNKNWON HANDLER), 536
Function 21h (UNDETER-MINED FUNCTION), 536
Function 22h (REMOVE UNKNOWN HANDLER), 536
Function 23h (UNDETER-MINED FUNCTION), 536
Function 24h (GET SOCKET), 536
Function 25h (GET INTERNET ADDRESS), 536
Function 26h (SET INTERNET ADDRESS), 537
Function 27h (SET UNKNOWN ITEM), 537
Function 28h/29h (UNDETER-MINED FUNCTION), 537
INT 64h (LOW-LEVEL API), 91
Function 02h (UNDETER-MINED FUNCTION), 537
Function 03h (ADD UNKNOWN ITEM), 527-528
Function 04h (REMOVE UNKNOWN ITEM), 538
Function 05h (UNDETER-MINED FUNCTION), 538
Function 06h (UNDETER-MINED FUNCTION), 538
Function 07h (GET IP ADDRESS), 538
Function 10h (CALL ETHDEV.SYS), 538
Function 11h (NOP), 539
Function FEh (MAP EMS PAGE FRAME), 539
INT 65h (POST PROCESSING INTERRUPT), 115
INT 66h (NETWORK PROCESS-ING), 512
INT 67h (UNDETERMINED USE), 643
Function 00h (LOCK SEMA-PHORE AND WAIT), 513
Function 01h (LOCK SEMA-PHORE), 513
Function 02h (UNLOCK SEMA-PHORE), 513
INT 68h (UNDETERMINED USE), 643
Function 01h
    Subfunction 2000h (ATTACH PHYSI-CAL UNIT), 196-197
    Subfunction 2200h (DETACH LOGI-CAL UNIT), 199-200
    Subfunction 2700h (DETACH PHYSI-CAL UNIT), 200
    Subfunction 2B00h (ACTIVATE DLC), 200

    Subfunction 2100h (ATACH LOGI-CAL UNIT), 197-199
Function 02h
    Subfunction 0100h (ALLOCATE), 200-202
    Subfunction 0300h (CONFIRM), 202-203
    Subfunction 0400h (CONFIRMED), 203
    Subfunction 0500h (DEALLOCATE), 203-204
    Subfunction 0600h (FLUSH), 204
    Subfunction 0700h (GET ATTRI-BUTES), 204-205
    Subfunction 0800h (GET CONVERSA-TION TYPE), 205
    Subfunction 0900h (POST ON RECEIPT), 205
    Subfunction 0A00h (PREPARE TO RECEIVE), 206
    Subfunction 0B00h (RECEIVE AND WAIT), 206-207
    Subfunction 0C00h (RECEIVE IMME-DIATE), 207
    Subfunction 0E00h (REQUEST TO SEND), 207
    Subfunction 0F00h (SEND DATA), 208
    Subfunction 1000h (SEND ERROR), 208
    Subfunction 1200h (TEST), 209
    Subfunction 1300h (WAIT), 209
Function 03h
    Subfunction 2400h (TP STARTED), 209-210
    Subfunction 2800h (GET ALLO-CATE), 210
    Subfunction 2A00h (CHANGE LOGI-CAL UNIT), 210-211
Function 04h (TRANSACTION PROCESSING), 211
Function 05h (TRANSFER MES-SAGE DATA), 211
Function 06h (CHANGE NUM-BER OF SESSIONS), 212
Function 07h (PASSTHROUGH), 213
Function FAh (ENABLE/DIS-ABLE APPC), 213

Function FBh (CONVERT), 213
Function FCh (ENBALE/DISABLE MESSAGE TRACING), 213
Function FDh (ENABLE/DISABLE API VERB TRACING) 214
Function FEh (SET TRACE DESTINATION), 214
Function FFh (SET PASSTHROUGH), 214
Function 01h, Subfunction 1B00h (DISPLAY), 195-196

INT 69h
Function 0100h (INSTALLATION CHECK), 247
Function 0101h (SEND BYTE), 247
Function 0102h (READ BYTE), 247
Function 0103h (STATUS), 247-248
Function 0104h (DECnet STATUS), 248
Function 0105h (OPEN SESSION), 248
Function 0106h (CLOSE SESSION), 248
Function 010Ah (GET SESSION CONTROL BLOCK SIZE), 249
Function 010Bh (GET DECnet SOCKET), 249
Function 010Fh (DEINSTALL CTERM), 249
Function 0Ah (DATA LINK LAYER), 249-250
Function 4001h (SYSSVC.COM), 480
Function 4002h (SYSSVC.COM), 480
Function 4101h (SYSSVC.COM), 480
Function 4102h-4104h (SYSSVC.COM), 480
Function 42h (SYSSVC.COM), 480
Function 43h (SYSSVC.COM), 480
Function 44h (SYSSVC.COM), 481
Function 49h (SYSSVC.COM - BUG), 481
Function FFh (SYSSVC.COM - SIGNAL SYSTEM ERROR), 481

INT 6Ah
(LOCAL AREA TRANSPORT PROGRAM), 251
Function 0000h (INSTALLATION CHECK), 566-567
Function 0001h (UNDETERMINED FUNCTION), 567-569
Function 0002h (UNDETERMINED FUNCTION), 569
Function 0003h (GET UNKNOWN DATA AREA), 569
Function 0004h (ALLOCATE UNKNOWN), 569

Function 0005h (FREE/CLOSE UNKNOWN), 569
Function 000Fh (FREE/CLOSE ALL UNKNOWN), 570
Function 0010h (UNINSTALL), 570
Function 01h (SEND BYTE), 251
Function 02h (READ BYTE), 251
Function 03h (STATUS), 251
Function D000h (CLOSE SESSION), 252
Function D0h (OPEN SESSION), 251-252
Function D100h (SEND BREAK), 253
Function D300h (RESET LAT COUNTERS), 253
Function D400h (COPY LAT COUNTERS), 253
Function D500h (GET NEXT LAT SERVICE NAME), 253
Function D600h (LAT SERVICE TABLE RESET), 253

INT 6Bh
(PORT DRIVER), 253-254
Function 000h (BUFFERED WRITE), 660
Function 0100h (BUFFERED READ), 660
Function 02h (INSTALLATION CHECK), 660
Function 0600h (CONTROL), 660
Function 0700h (GET STATUS), 661
Function 08H (UNDETERMINED FUNCTION), 574
Function 10h (GET STATUS), 661
Function 11h (ALLOCATE A VIRTUAL CIRCUIT), 661
Function 12h (VIRTUAL CIRCUIT STATUS), 661
Function 13h (SET/RETRIEVE REQUEST/REPLY SERVICE NAME), 661-662
Function 14h (SET/RETRIEVE SERVICE ADDRESS), 662
Function 15h (SET/RETRIEVE VIRTUAL CIRCUIT CONFIGURATION), 662
Function 16h (LOG/OR INITIALIZE VIRTUAL CIRCUIT), 662
Function 17h (DISCONNECT A VIRTUAL CIRCUIT), 662
Function 18h (WRITE DATA ON A VIRTUAL CIRCUIT), 662-663
Function 19h (READ DATA ON A VIRTUAL CIRCUIT), 663
Function 1Ah (RECEIVE STATUS), 663
Function 1Bh (TRANSMIT STATUS), 663
Function 1Ch (RECEIVE BUFFER CONTROL), 663
Function 1Dh (TRANSMIT BUFFER CONTROL), 663
Function 1Eh (ISSUE CONTROL REQUEST), 663

Function 1Fh (EXTERNAL STATUS), 664
Function 21h (QUERY NAME SERVICE), 664
INT 6Ch (API), 254
INT 6Dh (DATA LINK LAYER PROGRAM), 254
INT 6Eh (DECnet NETWORK PROCESS API), 254
INT 6Fh
Function 00h (LOGIN), 462-464
Function 0000h (ENTER TERMINAL MODE), 636
Function 0001h (RESET INTERFACE), 636
Function 0002h (SET DISPLAY PARAMETERS), 636
Function 0003h (READ STATUS), 636
Function 0004h (READ CURSOR POSITION), 636
Function 0005h (GET CHARACTER FROM DEVICE BUFFER), 637
Function 0006h (SEND CHARACTER), 637
Function 0007h (SET TIMEOUT), 637
Function 0008h (WAIT FOR LOCATION TO BE MODIFIED), 637
Function 0009h (NOP), 637
Function 000Ah (RESTORE DISPLAY), 637
Function 000Bh (UPDATE DEVICE BUFFER), 637
Function 000Ch (WRITE STRING TO ADD INFORMATION AREA), 637
Function 000Dh (MAINTENANCE OPERATIONS), 638
Function 000Eh (GET CONTROL PROGRAM VERSION), 638
Function 000Fh (GET MICROCODE VERSION), 638
Function 0010h (SAVE/DISPLAY GRAPHICS), 638
Function 0011h (PERFORM STRUCTURED FIELD OPERATION), 638
Function 0012h (SET CURSOR POSITION FOR DIRECT WRITE BUFFER), 638
Function 0013h (WRITE DIRECT TO BUFFER), 638-639
Function 0014h (WRITE DIRECT TO BUFFER WITHOUT ECHO), 639
Function 0016h (WRITE STRING DIRECT TO BUFFER), 639
Function 0017h (WRITE STRING DIRECT TO BUFFER), 639
Function 0018h (GET DIRECT-WRITE CURSOR POSITION), 639

Function 0019h (CONVERT ROW/COLUMN TO CURSOR POSITION), 639

Function 001Ah (CONVERT CURSOR POSITION TO ROW/COLUMN), 640

Function 001Bh (FIND NEXT FIELD), 640

Function 001Ch (FIND PREVIOUS FIELD), 640

Function 001Dh (FIND NEXT UNPROTECTED FIELD), 640

Function 001Eh (FIND PREVIOUS UNPROTECTED FIELD), 640

Function 001Fh (FIND NEXT PROTECTED FIELD), 640

Function 0020h (FIND PREVIOUS PROTECTED FIELD), 640-641

Function 0021h (MASKED SEARCH FORWARD), 641

Function 0022h (MASKED SEARCH BACKWARD), 641

Function 0023h (FIND FIELD LENGTH), 641

Function 0024h (READ FIELD), 641

Function 0025h (READ SCREEN), 641

Function 0026h (READ BUFFER UNTRANSLATED), 641

Function 0027h (ENABLE/DISABLE KEYBOARD), 642

Function 0028h (SELECT HOST SESSION), 642

Function 0029h (RETRIEVE HOST SESSION NAME), 642

Function 002Ah (GET CURRENT DEVICE BUFFER SIZE), 642

Function 002Bh (ARM MODIFIED LOCATION TRIGGER), 642

Function 015h (SET DIRECT WRITE STRING LENGTH), 639

Function 01h (LOGOFF), 464

Function 02h (STATUS OF NODE), 464-465

Function 03h (GET ADDRESS OF CONFIGURATION TABLE), 465-467

Function 05h (RECEIVE), 467

Function 07h (LOCK HANDLE), 467

Function 08h (UNLOCK HANDLE), 468

Function 09h (SUBMIT), 468

Function 0Ah (CHAT), 468

Function 0Bh (LOCK SEMAPHORE, RETURN IMMEDIATELY), 468 469

Function 0Ch (UNLOCK SEMAPHORE), 469

Function 0Dh (ENUMERATE USERS ON NETWORK), 469-470

Function 0Eh (SPOOL/PRINT), 470-471

Function 0Fh (FILE/RECORD LOCKING), 471-472

Function 10h (ATTACH/DETACH PRINTER), 472

Function 11h (LOCK FCB), 472

Function 12h (UNLOCK FCB), 472

Function 13h (GET REMOTE CONFIGURATION TABLE ADDRESS), 472

Function 14h (GET REMOTE MEMORY), 473

Function 1501h (GET SHARED DEVICE ENTRY), 473

Function 1502h (SET SHARED DEVICE ENTRY), 473

Function 1503h (DELETE SHARED DEVICE ENTRY), 473

Function 16h (GET USERS), 474

Function 17h (MOUNT), 474

Function 18h (UNMOUNT), 474

Function 19h (AUDIT), 474

Function 1Ah (BULL), 474

Function 1Bh (GMOUNT), 474

Function 1Ch (GET LOGIN LIST), 475

Function 1Dh (TABDATA), 475

Function 1Eh (SCHED), 475

Function 1Fh (WHOAMI), 475

Function 20h (UNDETERMINED FUNCTION), 475

Function 21h (UNDETERMINED FUNCTION), 475

Function 22h (UNDETERMINED FUNCTION), 475

Function 80h (LOGIN), 475-476

Function 81h (LOGOUT), 476

Function 8Ah (CHAT), 476

Function 8Dh (WHO), 476-477

Function 9501h (GET SHARED DEVICE ENTRY), 477-478

Function 9502h (SET SHARED DEVICE ENTRY), 478

Function 9503h (DELETE SHARED DEVICE), 478

Function 9504h (ENUMERATE USERS OF SHARED DEVICE), 478

Function 99h (AUDIT), 478

Function 9Ch (GET LOGIN LIST), 478

INT 7AH

(API), 687

(UNDETERMINED FUNCTION), 495

(LOW-LEVEL API), 91

Function 0000h (OPEN SOCKET), 91

Function 0001h (CLOSE SOCKET), 92

Function 0002h (GET LOCAL TARGET), 92-93

Function 0003h (SEND PACKET), 93-95

Function 0004h (LISTEN FOR PACKET), 95-96

Function 0005h (SCHEDULE IPX EVENT), 96

Function 0006h (CANCEL EVENT), 96

Function 0007h (SCHEDULE SPECIAL EVENT), 96

Function 0008h (GET INTERVAL MARKER), 97

Function 0009h (GET INTERNETWORK ADDRESS), 97

Function 000Ah (RELINQUISH CONTROL), 97

Function 000Bh (DISCONNECT FROM TARGET), 97-98

Function 000Ch (INITIALIZE NETWORK ADDRESS), 98

Function 000Dh (IPX GET PACKET SIZE), 98

Function 000Eh (TERMINATE SOCKETS), 98

Function 000Fh (SEND PACKET), 98-99

Function 0010h (INSTALLATION CHECK), 99

Function 0011h (ESTABLISH SPX CONNECTION), 99-100

Function 0012h (LISTEN FOR SPX CONNECTION), 100

Function 0013h (TERMINATE SPX CONNECTION), 100

Function 0014h (ABORT SPX CONNECTION), 100-101

Function 0015h (GET SPX CONNECTION STATUS), 101

Function 0016h (SEND SPX PACKET), 102

Function 0017h (LISTEN FOR SPX PACKET), 102

Function 0018h (ADD DIAGNOSTIC ELEMENT), 102

Function 0019h (CANCEL DIAGNOSTIC ELEMENT), 102-103

Function 001Ah (GET DRIVER PACKET SIZE LIMIT), 103

Function 001Bh (UNKNOWN FUNCTION), 103

Function 04h (CREATE A QUEUE), 629

Function 06h (DELETE A QUEUE), 629

Function 09h

(3270 EMULATION), 631

(COPY SERVICE), 632

(HOST SERVICES), 632-633

(KEYBOARD SERVICES), 629-630

(Multi-DOS), 632

(OPERATOR INFORMATION AREA), 631

(PRESENTATION SPACE SERVICES), 631

(SESSION SERVICES), 629

(TRANSLATE DATA), 631-632

(WINDOW SERVICES), 630

Function 13h (GET DATA FROM A QUEUE), 633

Function 81h (RESOLVE A GATE NAME), 633

Function 83h (GET COMPLETION RESULTS), 633

Function FDCBh (INSTALLATION CHECK), 643-644

Function FE01h/FE02h (INTERNAL SEND/RECEIVE), 634

Function FF01h (INTERNAL API INITIALIZATION), 634

Function FF02h (INTERNAL API TERMINATION), 634

Function FF03h (INTERNAL API INITIALIZATION), 634

Function FF04h (UNDETERMINED FUNCTION), 635

INT 7Bh (API), 644

INT 7Ch

Function 0001h (DOWN (UNINSTALL) DRIVER), 441-442

Function 0002h (GET DRIVER STATUS), 442

Function 0003h (CHANGE DRIVER ADDRESS), 442

Function 0004h (REQUEST BUFFER), 442-443

Function 0005h (RELEASE BUFFER), 443

Function 0006h (TRANSMIT FRAME), 443

Function 0007h (REGISTER PROTOCOL), 443-445

Function 0008h (DISABLE PROTOCOL), 445

Function 0009h (REGISTER MULTICAST), 446

Function 000Ah (DISABLE MULTICAST), 446

Function 000Bh (GET PROTOCOL LIST), 446

Function 000Ch (GET PROTOCOL STATUS), 446

Function 000Dh (GET DRIVER STATISTICS), 446-447

Function 000Eh (GET DRIVER INFORMATION), 447-448

Function 000Fh (FEED BACK BUFFER), 448

Function 0010h (CLIENT HOOK), 448

Function 0011h (CLIENT UNHOOK), 448

Function 0012h (SYNC REQUEST BUFFER), 448

Function 0013h (TRANSMIT FRAME RELEASE), 448

Function 0014h (GET MULTICAST LIST), 448-449

Function 0015h (GET MEDIA STATISTICS), 449-450

Function 0016h (DRIVER I/O CONTROL), 450

Function 0017h (INTERRUPT REQUEST), 450

INT 7Fh

(ACCESS VECTOR), 524

(API), 664-665

(ENTER CONSOLE MODE), 419

(INSTALLATION CHECK), 168

Function 06h (ALLOCATE FREE CLUSTER ON SHARED DRIVE), 171

Function 08h, Subfunction 02h (SET MESSAGE DISPLAY TIMEOUT), 172

Function 09h, Subfunction 02h (SWITCH HOST TO DEDICATED MODE), 172

Function 09h, Subfunction 03h (GET ALTERNATE INTERRUPT), 172

Function 0Ah Subfunction 00h (GET SYSTEM FLAGS), 172

Function 0Bh, Subfunction 02h (SET/RESET GRAPHICS DOS ON SLAVE), 173

Function 10h

Subfunction 01h (CLOSE CHANNEL), 173

Subfunction 02h (LOCK CHANNEL), 173

Subfunction 03h (UNLOCK CHANNEL), 174

Subfunction 04h (RELEASE BUFFER), 174

Subfunction 05h (CLOSE ALL CHANNELS), 174

Subfunction 06h (LOCK ALL OPEN CHANNELS), 174

Subfunction 07h (UNLOCK ALL LOCKED IDLE CHANNELS), 174

Subfunction 08h (LOCK MULTIPLE CHANNELS), 175

Function 13h, Subfunction 00h (RESET USER DATAGRAMS), 176

Function 14h

Subfunction, 00h (SET RECEIVE ISR), 176

Subfunction 01h (SET ACKNOWLEDGE ISR), 177

Subfunction 02h (SET CHANNEL BUFFER POINTER), 177

Subfunction 03h (GET RECEIVE ISR), 177

Subfunction 04h (GET ACKNOWLEDGE ISR), 177

Subfunction 05h (GET BUSY POINTER), 177

Function 15h

Subfunction 00h (GET CHANNEL STATUS), 178

Subfunction 01h (GET NEXT FULL CHANNEL), 178

Subfunction 02h (GET MAXIMUM NUMBER OF CHANNELS), 178

Subfunction 03h (GET MAXIMUM PACKET SIZE), 178-179

Subfunction 04h (GET AND CLEAR ACKNOWLEDGE STATUS), 179

Function 25h, Subfunction 00h (GET NETWORK EXECUTIVE VERSION), 180

Function 25h, Subfunction 01h (GET NETWORK EXECUTIVE TYPE), 181

Function 26h

Subfunction 00h (GET NTNX FILE MODE), 181

Subfunction 01h-05h (SET FILE I/O CHECKING LEVEL), 181

Subfunction 06h (CANCEL FLUSH OR WRITE), 181

Function B1h, Subfunction 00h (RELEASE NORMAL SEMAPHORES FOR USER), 187

Function B2h, Subfunction 01h (RELEASE MESSAGES FOR USER), 187

Function B3h, Subfunction 02h (RELEASE FILES FOR USER), 187

Function 00h (SEMAPHORE LOCK AND WAIT), 168

Function 0104h (IBM 3270 High-level Language API/Rabbit Low Level API), 625-628

Function 01h (SEMAPHORE LOCK), 169

Function 02h (RELEASE SEMAPHORE), 169

Function 03h (GET USER NUMBER), 169

Function 04h (GET NUMBER OF USERS), 169

Function 05h (GET USER PARAMETERS), 170

Function 05h (LOCK/UNLOCK SYSTEM, SPOOLER CONTROL), 169

Function 06h (GET SHARED DRIVE INFO), 170-171

Function 07h (GET LIST OF SHARED DRIVES), 171

Function 08h (GET INTERRUPT VECTORS), 171

Function 09h (ENABLE/DISABLE MUD FILE CHECKING), 172

Function 11h (SEND DATAGRAM), 175

Function 12h (ACKNOWLEDGE DATAGRAM), 176

Function 16h (DIRECT MEMORY TRANSFER), 179

Function 21h (SEND MESSAGE OR COMMAND TO USER(S)), 179 180

Function 22h (GET MESSAGE), 180

Function 24h (ATTACH OR RELEASE DRIVE FOR LOW-LEVEL WRITE ACCESS), 180

Function 24h (ATTACH/RELEASE HOST PROCESSOR), 180

Function 30h (GET PORT INFORMATION), 182

Function 31h (CHECK PORT ASSIGNMENT), 182

Function 37h (DUMP STRING TO TERMINAL), 182

Function 37h (GET SEMAPHORE TABLE), 182

Function 38h (SET NEW TERMINAL DRIVER), 182

Function 39h (SET TERMINAL DRIVER FOR ANOTHER USER), 182-183

Function 3Ah (GET TERMINAL PARAMETERS), 183

Function 3Bh (SET TERMINAL PARAMETERS), 183

Function 3Ch (ENABLE/DISABLE AUTOBAND DETECT), 183

Function 3Dh (POST TERMINAL CONFIGURATION CHANGES), 183

Function 41h (LOCK FILE FOR USER), 184

Function 41h (LOCK SEMAPHORE FOR USER), 184

Function 42h (UNLOCK FILE FOR USER), 184

Function 42h (UNLOCK SEMAPHORE FOR USER), 184

Function 4Eh (SET ERROR MODE), 184-185

Function 4Fh (SET FCB MODE), 185

Function 81h (ATTACH DEVICE FOR USER), 185

Function 82h (RELEASE DEVICE FOR USER), 185

Function A0h (GET USER NAME), 185

Function A1h (GET MACHINE, USER, AND PROCESS NUMBER), 185

Function A2h (GET USER PRIVILEGE LEVEL), 186

Function A3h (GET USER LOGIN STATE), 186

Function A4h (VERIFY USER PASSWORD), 186

Function A500h (GET USER STATUS), 186

Function A501h (SET USER STATUS), 186-187

Function B0h (RELEASE ALL SEMAPHORES FOR USER), 187

Function B4h (RELEASE DEVICES FOR USER), 187

Function C3h (WRITE BYTE TO TERMINAL AUX PORT), 188

Function C5h (CHANGE CONSOLE MODE), 188

Function C6h (WRITE BYTE TO CONSOLE PORT), 188

Function C7h (READ CONSOLE DATA BYTE), 188

Function C8h (READ CONSOLE DATA INTO BUFFER), 188-189

Function CFh (REBOOT USER PROCESSOR), 189

Function D6h (RESET NETWORK EXECUTIVE), 189

Function D7h (POST EVENT), 189

Function D8h (FLUSH DISK BUFFERS), 189

Function DBh (GET MW386 INVOCATION DRIVE), 189

Function E0h (CREATE DOS TASK), 189-190

Function E1h (GET DOS TASK PID FROM CREATE ID), 190

Function E2h (SWITCH TO NEW DOS TASK), 190

Function E3h (CHANGE NAME OF DOS TASK), 190

Function E4h (GET TASK NAME FROM PROCESS NUMBER), 190

Function E5h (GET PROCESS NUMBER FROM TASK NAME), 191

Function E6h (GET NUMBER OF AVAILABLE USER TASKS), 191

Function E7h (REMOVE DOS TASK), 191

Function E8h (DOS TASK DELAY), 191

Function F0h (RESTRICT DIRECTORY TO GROUP), 191

Function F1h (ASSIGN DIRECTORY TO GROUP), 192

Function F2h (READ RESTRICTED DIRECTORY ENTRY), 192

Function F8h (ASSIGN USER TO GROUP), 192

Function F9h (REMOVE USER FROM GROUP), 192

Function FAh (GET USER GROUP LIST), 193

Function FBh (ASSIGN GROUP NAME), 193

Function FCh (GET GROUP NAME), 193

INT 80h

Function 01h (INITIALIZE), 684

Function 02h (GET BUFFER ADDRESS), 685

Function 03h (GET ENTRY POINT), 685

Function 04h (ENABLE), 685

Function 05h (GET RECEIVE STATISTICS), 685

Function 06h (REMOVE RECEIVED PACKET), 685

INT 81h (UNDETERMINED FUNCTION), 687

INT 82h (UNDETERMINED FUNCTION), 687

INT 86h, (ORIGINAL INT 18h), 122

INT 91h (UNDETERMINED FUNCTION), 687

INT 92h

(API), 643

Function E100h (INITIALIZE DISPATCHER), 669-670

(NetGetAltRoute), 675

Function E101h (NetInitCheck), 670

Function E102h (NetCheckDriver), 670

Function E103h (NetTerminate), 670

Function E104Ah (NetClose), 673

Function E104h (NetWhereIs), 670

Function E105h (NetOpen), 671

Function E106h (NetRead), 671

Function E107h (NetGetError), 671

Function E108h (NetWrite), 671-673

Function E109h (NetErrorFix), 673

Function E10Bh (NetCheckQueue), 673

Function E10Ch (NetReadQueue), 674

Function E10Dh (NetSubmitName), 674

Function E10Eh (NetRemoveName), 674

Function E10Fh (IS ANYONE THERE? QUERY), 675

Function E111h (NetDeleteAltRoutes), 675

Function E112h (NetChangePassword), 675

Function E113h (NetSetAltRoute), 675-676

Function E175h (BECOME MICRO TSR), 676

Function E180h (INSTALLATION CHECK), 676

Function E1h (API OVERVIEW), 669

INT 93h (UNDETERMINED FUNCTION), 687

INT DCh (API), 687

INT E1h (Disk Server Information),
    524
INT E2h (UNDETERMINED
    USAGE), 524
INT ECh (UNKNOWN), 193
Intel 80186 CPU, 2
Intel 80286 CPU, 2
Intel 80x86 CPU, interrupts with, 2
INTERCEPT VINES (INT 61h Func-
    tion 0008h, Subfunction 0003h),
    239-240
Interconnections Inc. TES interrupts,
    658-660
INTERFACE (INT 5Bh), 118-119
INTERFACE (INT 61h), 643
INTERLINK, 510-511
INTERNAL API INITIALIZATION
    (INT 7Ah Function FF01h), 634
INTERNAL API INITIALIZATION
    (INT 7Ah Function FF03h), 634
INTERNAL API TERMINATION
    (INT 7Ah Function FF02h), 634
internal data areas, 21
internal network support functions, 63-
    75
INTERNAL SEND/RECEIVE (INT
    7Ah Function FE01h/FE01h),
    634
internal support calls, 21
INTERRRUPT ON CHARACTER
    FROM HOST (INT 61h Func-
    tion 0003h, Subfunction 0Eh),
    233
interrupt handler, 215
INTERRUPT ON HOST MESSAGE
    (INT 61h Function 0003h, Sub-
    function 14h), 235
INTERRUPT REQUEST (INT 7Ch
    Function 0017h), 450
interrupt request signal (INTR), 2
interrupt vectors, 2
interrupts
    10NET, 457-482
    3270PC, 621-622
    ArtiCom, 645-649
    Attachmate Extra!, 622-624
    Beame & Whiteside BWCOM14,
        650
    CCPOP 3270, 643
    concepts of, 2
    Connection Manager, 650-658
    Da Vinci eMail, 669-676
    DCA 10Net, 457-482
    DESQview/X, 255-258
    electronic mail, 677-679
    Excelan LAN Workplace for DOS,
        508-510
    generic network support, 505-508
    HLLAPI, 625-628
    IBM 3270 Workstation program,
        629-633
    IBM PC 3270 Emulation pro-
        gram, 633-635
    IBM System 36/38 Workstation
        Emulation, 635-636
    INT 7Fh, 20
    Intel 80x86 CPU, 2
    Interconnections Inc. TES, 658-
        660
    INTERLINK, 510-511
    LAN HiJack, 667-668
    Lanera TCPOpen, 570

License Service API, 681-683
Microsoft LAN Manager TCP/IP,
    563
miscellaneous, 518-524, 562, 643-
    644
multiplex, 7, 14-18
NACS, 660-661
Nanosoft TurboNET, 511-512
NASI, 660-661
Network Courier E-Mail, 680
Network Kernel, 541-558
network remote control software,
    667-668
Network serial I/O emulation,
    645-668
Novell NASI/NACS, 660-661
Novell NetWare TCP/IP, 563-565
Novell PCOX 3270 PC Terminal
    Interface, 636-642
NPC NCSI extended serial I/O,
    661-664
old-style configuration, 558-560
overview, 7-20
PC LAN program, 437-440
PC-NET, 513
printer redirection, 560-561
QPC software PKTINT, 684-685
Sangoma X.25, 643
Shamrock Software
        EMAIL, 677-679
        NET.24, 513-515
SilverNET, 515-517
SK-UPPS Data Link Interface,
    441-450
SNAP (Simple Network Access
    Protocol), 451-455
Sun PC-NFS, 566
Super-TCP, 566-570
TCP/IP, 541-562, 563-574
TEIAPI, 571-574
Telebit ACS serial I/O, 664-665
TES, 658-660
TopWare Network Operating Sys-
    tem, 483-496
user, 7, 18-20
Web for DOS, 497-502
Workgroup Connection, 503-504
    MICRO.EXE, 679-680
INVOKE CRITICAL ERROR (INT
    2Fh Function 1206h), 65
IOCTL
    (SOCKET API Function 002h),
        259
    (INT 2Fh Function 122Bh), 73
IPX (Internetwork Packet Exchange)
    protocols, 91
IPX GET PACKET SIZE (INT 7Ah
    Function 000Dh), 98
IPX/SPX protocols, 91-103
IS ANYONE THERE? QUERY (INT
    92h Function E10Fh), 675
IS BINDERY OBJECT IN SET (INT
    21h Function E3h Subfunction
    43h), 327-328
ISSUE CONTROL REQUEST (INT
    6Bh Function 1Eh), 663

KEYBOARD BUSY LOOP (INT 2Ah
    Function 84h), 63
KEYBOARD SERVICES (INT 7Ah
    Function 09h), 629-630

KILL ALL CONNECTIONS (INT
    21h Function 5F55h), 291

LAN HiJack interrupts, 667-668
LAN Manager, 281-294
Lanera TCPOpen interrupts, 570
LANtastic network operating system,
    295-309
LAT SERVICE TABLE RESET (INT
    6Ah Function D600h), 253
LHJ - UNDETERMINED FUNC-
    TION (INT 2Fh Function
    7ACAh), 668
LHJ - UNDETERMINED FUNC-
    TION (INT 2Fh Function
    7ACBh/7ACCh), 668
LHR
    CLEAR UNKNOWN FLAG
        (INT 2Fh Function 7AC3h),
        667
    DISABLE (INT 2Fh Function
        7AC1h), 667
    DISABLE FUNCTIONS (INT
        2Fh Function 7AC9h), 668
    ENABLE FUNCTIONS (INT
        2Fh Function 7AC8h), 667-
        668
    INSTALLATION CHECK (INT
        2Fh Function 7ACFh), 668
    SYNCHRONIZE SHIFT
        STATES (INT 2Fh Function
        7AC2h), 667
License Service API, 681-683
LINKUP (SOCKET API Function
    0023h), 269-270
LISTEN (SOCKET API Function
    0012h), 264
LISTEN FOR INCOMING CONNEC-
    TIONS (INT 61h Function 23h),
    554
LISTEN FOR INCOMING CONNEC-
    TIONS (INT 63h Function 12h),
    533-534
LISTEN FOR PACKET (INT 7Ah
    Function 0004h), 95-96
LISTEN FOR SPX CONNECTION
    (INT 7Ah Function 0012h), 100
LISTEN FOR SPX PACKET (INT 7Ah
    Function 0017h), 102
lists, getting, 25-45
LOCAL AREA TRANSPORT PRO-
    GRAM (INT 6Ah), 251
LOCAL DosPrintJobGetId (INT 21h
    Function 5F43h), 285
LOCAL DosTransactNmPipe (INT 21h
    Function 5F36h), 106
LOCAL NetMessageBufferSend (INT
    21h Function 5F40h), 282
LOCAL NetRemoteCopy (INT 21h
    Function 5F4Ah), 287
LOCAL NetRemoteMove (INT 21h
    Function 5F4Bh), 287-288
LOCAL NetServerEnum (INT 21h
    Function 5F4Ch), 288
LOCAL NetServiceControl (INT 21h
    Function 5F42h), 284
LOCAL NetServiceEnum (INT 21h
    Function 5F41h), 283-284
LOCAL NetSpecialSMB (INT 21h
    Function 5F3Eh), 282
LOCAL NetUseAdd (INT 21h Func-
    tion 5F47h), 286

LOCAL NetUseDel (INT 21h Function 5F48h), 286

LOCAL NetUseEnum (INT 21h Function 5F46h), 285-286

LOCAL NetWkstaGetInfo (INT 21h Function 5F44h), 285

LOCAL NetWkstaSetInfo (INT 21h Function 5F45h), 285

LOCATE 3270PC CONFIGURATION TABLE (INT 10h Function 3000h), 621-622

LOCK (INT 60h Function 12h), 523

LOCK ALL OPEN CHANNELS (INT 7Fh Function 10h, Subfunction 06h), 174

LOCK AND WAIT (INT 60h Function 60h), 523

LOCK CHANNEL (INT 7Fh Function 10h, Subfunction 02h), 173

LOCK FCB (INT 6Fh Function 11h), 472

LOCK FILE FOR USER (INT 7Fh Function 41h), 184

LOCK FILE SET (INT 21h Function CBh), 401

LOCK HANDLE (INT 6Fh Function 07h), 467

LOCK LOGICAL RECORD SET (INT 21h Function D1h), 402

LOCK MULTIPLE CHANNELS (INT 7Fh Function 10h, Subfunction 08h) 175

LOCK PHYSICAL RECORD SET (INT 21h Function C2h), 398

LOCK REGION OF FILE (INT 2Fh Function 110Ah), 126

LOCK SEMAPHORE (INT 67h Function 01h), 513

LOCK SEMAPHORE AND WAIT (INT 67h Function 00h), 513

LOCK SEMAPHORE FOR USER (INT 7Fh Function 41h), 184

LOCK SEMAPHORE, RETURN IMMEDIATELY (INT 6Fh Function 08h), 468-469

LOCK/UNLOCK REGION OF FILE (INT 2Fh Function 110Ah), 126

LOCK/UNLOCK SYSTEM, SPOOLER CONTROL (INT 7Fh Function 05h), 169

LOG FILE (INT 21h Function EBh), 403-404

LOG LOGICAL RECORD (INT 21h Function D0h), 402

LOG NETWORK MESSAGE (INT 21h Function E3h Subfunction 0Dh), 378-379

LOG PHYSICAL RECORD (INT 21h Function BCh), 397

LOG/LOCK PERSONAL FILE (FCB) (INT 21h Function CAh), 400-401

LOG/LOCK RECORD (FCB) (INT 21h Function BFh), 397

LOG/OR INITIALIZE VIRTUAL CIRCUIT (INT 6Bh Function 16h), 662

LOGICAL RECORD LOCK/UNLOCK (INT 21h Function D0h to D5h), 216

LOGIN (INT 6Fh Function 00h), 462-464

LOGIN (INT 6Fh Function 80h), 475-476

LOGIN TO FILE SERVER (INT 21h Function E3h Subfunction 14h), 332

LOGIN TO SERVER (INT 21h Function 5F81h), 295

LOGOFF (INT 6Fh Function 01h0, 464

LOGOUT (INT 6Fh Function 81h), 476

LOGOUT FROM ALL SERVERS (INT 21h Function 5F88h), 297

LOW-LEVEL (IPX) INSTALLATION CHECK (INT 2Fh Function 7A00h), 91

LOW-LEVEL API (INT 64h), 91

LOW-LEVEL API (INT 7Ah), 91

MAIL Interface (INT 2Fh Function D703h), 216

MAINTENANCE OPERATIONS (INT 6Fh Function 000Dh), 638

MAKE BUFFER MOST RECENTLY USED (INT 2Fh Function 120Fh), 67

MAKE DISK BUFFER MOST-RECENTLY USED (INT 2Fh Function 1207h), 65

MAKE NAMED OBJECT AVAILABLE (INT 21h Function 5F07h), 684

MAKE NET DESCRIPTOR GLOBAL (INT 61h Function 07h), 545

MAKE REMOTE DIRECTORY (INT 2Fh Function 1103h), 124

MAKE REMOTE DIRECTORY (INT 2Fh Function 1104h), 124

MAP A FAKE ROOT DIRECTORY (INT 21h Function E905h), 346

MAP EMS (INT 62h Function FEh), 530

MAP EMS PAGE FRAME (INT 64h Function FEh), 539

MAP LOCAL DRIVE LETTER (Function 5F05h), 683

MARK ALL DISK BUFFERS UNREFERENCED (INT 2Fh Function 120Eh), 66

MASKED SEARCH BACKWARD (INT 6Fh Function 0022h), 641

MASKED SEARCH FORWARD (INT 6Fh Function 0021h), 641

message services, NetWare, 373-379

MESSENGER SERVICE (INT 2Fh Function 42h), 294

Microsoft LAN Manager TCP/IP interrupts, 563

miscellaneous interrupts, 518-524, 562, 643-644

miscellaneous NetWare, 435

MODIFY ACTIVE CONNECTION PARAMETERS (INT 14h Function 0Ah), 656

MODIFY DEFAULT CONNECTION PARAMETERS (INT 14h Function 00h), 650

MODIFY FLOW CONTROL (INT 14h Function 800Ah), 649

MODIFY MAXIMUM RIGHTS MASK (INT 21h Function E2h Subfunction 04h), 337

MONITOR XMODEM DOWNLOAD (INT 16h Function 4506h), 679

MOUNT (INT 6Fh Function 17h), 474

MOVE FILE FROM ONE PRINT SERVER TO ANOTHER (INT 21h Function FFCAh), 490

MOVE FILE POINTER (INT 2Fh Function 1228h), 71

MS-DOS operating system, 1
built-in networking support, 21
data structures, 75-86
extended error codes, 21-23
network support, 21-86

MSCDEX (Microsoft CD Extensions), 241-245

Multi-DOS (INT 7Ah Function 09h), 632

multiplex interrupts (INT 2Fh), 7

MULTIPLEXOR (INT 21h Function F2h), 413-417

MW386 (386/MultiWare), 157-193

NACS (NetWare Asynchronous Communications Services) interrupts, 660-661

named pipes, 105-107

Nanosoft TurboNET, 511-512

NASI (NetWare Asynchronous Services Interface) interrupts, 660-661

NDIS (Network Device Interface Specification), 109-115

NET HANDLE GET INFO (INT 21h Function 5F3Ch), 282

NET HANDLE SET INFO (INT 21h Function 5F3Bh), 281

NetBIOS (Network Basic Input/Output System), 117-122

NetBIOS INTERFACE (INT 5Ch), 119-122

NetChangePassword (INT 92h Function E112h), 675

NetCheckDriver (INT 92h Function E102h), 670

NetCheckQueue (INT 92h Function E10Bh), 673

NetClose (INT 92h Function E104Ah), 673

NetDeleteAltRoutes (INT 92h Function E111h), 675

NetErrorFix (INT 92h Function E109h), 673

NetGetAltRoute (INT 92h Function E110h), 675

NetGetError (INT 92h Function E107h), 671

NetInitCheck (INT 92h Function E101h), 670

NetOpen (INT 92h Function E105h), 671

NetRead (INT 92h Function E106h), 671

NetReadQueue (INT 92h Function E10Ch), 674

NetRemoveName (INT 92h Function E10Eh), 674

NetServerEnum2 (INT 21h Function 5F53h), 290-291

NetSetAltRoute (INT 92h Function E113h), 675-676

NetSubmitName (INT 92h Function E100h), 674

NetTerminate (INT 92h Function E103h), 670

NetUseGetInfo (INT 21h Function 5F49h), 286

NetWare functions, 311-419
    access server, 427-430
    accounting services, 316-318
    bindery services, 318-329
    connection services, 329-334
    directory services, 334-337
    file server, 347-369
    file services, 369-373
    general, 409-419
    message services, 373-379
    miscellaneous, 435
    overview, 311-316
    print services, 379-385
    queue services, 385-396
    synchronization services, 396-404
    TASKID 430-431
    TBMI, 431-434
    transaction tracking system, 404-406
    VNETWARE.386, 434-435
    workstation, 406-409

NetWhereIs (INT 92h Function E104h), 670

NETWORK COMMANDS (INT 5Bh), 686

Network Courier E-Mail interrupts, 680

Network Device controls, 195-200

network overview, 7-20

network reasons for, 1-2

Network Manager Interface (SOCKET API Function 0026H), 270-273

NETWORK PRINT-STREAM CONTROL (INT 2Ah Function 06h), 62

NETWORK PROCESSING (INT 66h), 512

NETWORK REDIRECTOR (INT 21h Function 3306h), 518

network redirector interface, 21, 123-136

NETWORK REDIRECTOR INTERFACE (INT 2Fh Function 11xxh), 64

network remote control software interrupts, 667-668

Network serial I/O emulation interrupts, 645-668

network support, 21-86

NETWORK WORKSTATION REDIRECTOR (INT 2Fh Function 4Bh), 294

networking calls, 681-687

NetWrite (INT 92h Function E108h), 671-673

NETX (Novell NetWare Shell), 311-419

NLCACHE - INSTALLATION CHECK (INT 2Fh Function D8C0h), 425

NO LONGER SUPPORTED (INT 61h Function 14h), 549-550

NOP
    (INT 63h Function 13h), 534
    (INT 64h Function 11h), 539
    (INT 6Fh Function 0009h), 637

NOP for ETHDEV.ODI (INT 62h Function 01h), 527

NOP for ETHDEV.ODI (INT 62h Function 0Dh), 528

NOP for SLIP kernel (INT 61h Function 31h-33h), 557

NORMALIZE ASCIZ FILENAME (INT 2Fh Function 1211h), 67

NORMALIZE PATH SEPARATOR (INT 2Fh Function 1204h), 65

Novell NetWare Lite, 421-426

Novell NetWare
    NASI/NACS interrupts, 660-661
    PCOX 3270 PC Terminal Interface interrupts, 636-642
    TCP/IP interrupts, 563-565
    utilities, 427-435

NPC NCSI extended serial I/O interrupts, 661-664

NTNX (Novell-Type Network Executive), 157-193

ODI (Open Data-Link Interface), 137-146

old-style configuration drivers, 558-560

OPEN (INT 21h Function 3Dh), 23-24

OPEN A NETWORK CONNECTION (INT 61h Function 13h), 549

OPEN BINDERY (INT 21h Function E3h Subfunction 45h), 328

OPEN COMMUNICATION (INT 14h Function 04h), 651-655

OPEN COMMUNICATION SOCKET (INT 61h Function 0001h, Subfunction 0001h), 217 218

OPEN DEVICE AND SET SFT OWNER/MODE (INT 2Fh Function 120Ch), 66

OPEN EXISTING REMOTE FILE (INT 2Fh Function 1116h), 129

OPEN FILE (INT 2Fh Function 1226h), 71

OPEN MESSAGE PIPE (INT 21h Function E1h Subfunction 06h), 377

OPEN NETWORK CONNECTION (INT 63h Function 14h), 534

OPEN REMOTE FILE (INT 2Fh Function 1115h), 128-129

OPEN SEMAPHORE (INT 21h Function C500h), 399

OPEN SESSION (INT 69h Function 0105h), 248

OPEN SESSION (INT 6Ah Function D0h), 251-252

OPEN SOCKET (INT 7Ah Function 0000h), 91

OPERATOR (INT 2Fh Function 9Ch), 680

OPERATOR INFORMATION AREA (INT 7Ah Function 09h), 631

ORIGINAL INT 18h (INT 86h), 122

OUTPUT CHARACTER TO STANDARD OUTPUT (INT 2Fh Function 1205h), 65

packet driver specification, 147-156

PASSTHROUGH (INT 68h Function 07h), 213

PC LAN program interrupts, 437-440

PC-NET, 513

PCPRINT Interface (Function D702h), 216

PEEK AT PENDING INPUT FOR PIPE (INT 21h Function 5F35h), 106

PERFORM CRITICAL ERROR INTERRUPT (INT 2Fh Function 120Ah), 66

PERFORM STRUCTURED FIELD OPERATION (INT 6Fh Function 0011h), 638

pipes, named, 105-107

PKTINT interrupts, 684-685

POP UP LAST RECEIVED MESSAGE (INT 21h Function 5F9Ch), 298-299

PORT DRIVER (INT 6Bh), 253-254

POST EVENT (INT 7Fh Function D7h), 189

POST MESSSAGE ON LOCAL DISPLAY (INT 61h, Function 0008h, Subfunction 0002h), 239

POST ON RECEIPT (INT 68h, Function 02h, Subfunction 0900h), 205

POST PROCESSING INTERRUPT (INT 65h), 115

POST TERMINAL CONFIGURATION CHANGES (INT 7Fh Function 3Dh), 183

PREPARE CHARACTER-ORIENTED RECEIVE (INT 17h Function 2406h), 514

PREPARE CHARACTER-ORIENTED TRANSMIT (INT 17h Function 240Ah), 515

PREPARE FOR INBOUND CONNECTION (INT 14h Function 0Bh), 656

PREPARE TO RECEIVE (INT 68h, Function 02h, Subfunction 0A00h), 206

PRESENTATION SPACE SERVICES (INT 7Ah Function 09h), 631

print services, NetWare, 379-385

PRINT SPOOLING (INT 21h Function E0h), 383-384

print-screen (INT 05h), 2

PRINTER CONTROL (INT 61h Function 0005h), 236

printer redirection, 560-561

PROCESS TERMINATION HOOK (INT 2Fh Function 1122h), 133

programs, BASIC, 7-8

PROTOCOL MANAGER (INT 21h Function 4402h), 109-115

protocols, APPC/PC, 195-214

PURGE ALL ERASED FILES (INT 21h Function E3h Subfunction CEh), 372-373

QPC Software PKTINT interrupts, 684-685

QUALIFY REMOTE FILENAME (INT 2Fh Function 1123h), 133

QUERY CRITICAL SECTION (INT 62h Function 10h), 529

QUERY LICENSE (Function 7005h), 683

QUERY NAME SERVICE (INT 6Bh Function 21h), 664

QUERY NAMED PIPE INFORMA-TION (INT 21h Function 5F32h), 105
QUERY SERVICE NAMES (INT 14h Function 10h), 657-658
queue services, NetWare, 385-396

RAISE/LOWER PRIORITY (SOCKET API Function 0028h/0029h), 273-274
RAW INPUT FROM PIPE (INT 21h Function 5F39h), 107
RAW OUTPUT TO PIPE (INT 21h Function 5F3Ah), 107
RE-READ KERNEL CONFIGURA-TION (INT 61h Function 17h), 550
READ A DATAGRAM (INT 61h Func-tion 1Dh), 552
READ BLOCK (INT 14h Function A5h), 88
READ BUFFER UNTRANSLATED (INT 6Fh Function 0026h), 641
READ BYTE (INT 69h Function 0102h), 247
READ BYTE (INT 6Ah Function 02h), 251
READ CHARACTER (INT 14h Func-tion A3h), 88
READ CONFIGURATION DATA (INT 21h Function 3Fh), 558-560
READ CONSOLE DATA BYTE (INT 7Fh Function C7h), 188
READ CONSOLE DATA INTO BUFFER (INT 7Fh Function C8h), 188-189
READ CURSOR POSITION (INT 6Fh Function 0004h), 636
READ DATA ON A VIRTUAL CIR-CUIT (INT 6Bh Function 19h), 663
READ FIELD (INT 6Fh Function 0024h), 641
READ FROM FILE (INT 2Fh Func-tion 1229h), 72
READ FROM REMOTE FILE (INT 2Fh Function 1108h), 125
READ FROM SOCKET (SOCKET API Function 0009h), 261-262
READ FROM THE NETWORK (INT 61h Function 1Bh), 551
READ FROM THE NETWORK (INT 63h Function 1Ah), 535
READ PROPERTY VALUE (INT 21h Function E3h Subfunction 3Dh) 324-325
READ QUEUE CURRENT STATUS (INT 21h Function E3h Subfunc-tion 66h), 387
READ QUEUE JOB ENTRY (INT 21h Function E3h Subfunction 6Ch), 390-391
READ QUEUE SERVER CURRENT STATUS (INT 21h Function E3h Subfunction 76h), 395
READ RESTRICTED DIRECTORY ENTRY (INT 7Fh Function F2h), 192
READ SCREEN (INT 6Fh Function 0025h), 641
READ STATUS (INT 14h Function A7h), 89

READ STATUS (INT 6Fh Function 0003h), 636
READ VTOC (INT 2Fh Function 1505h), 242
REATTACH SOCKET (SOCKET API Function 001Fh), 268
REBOOT USER PROCESSOR (INT 7Fh Function CFh), 189
RECEIVE (INT 6Fh Function 05h), 467
RECEIVE AND WAIT (INT 68h, Function 02h, Subfunction 0B00h), 206-207
RECEIVE BLOCK, NO HAND-SHAKE (INT 17h Function 2401h), 514
RECEIVE BLOCK, WITH HAND-SHAKE (INT 17h Function 2408h), 515
RECEIVE BUFFER CONTROL (INT 6Bh Function 1Ch), 663
RECEIVE CHARACTER (INT 14h Function 02h), 651
RECEIVE CHARACTER BLOCK (INT 14h Function 07h), 655
RECEIVE CHARACTER FROM REMOTE (INT 17h Function 2407h), 515
RECEIVE IMMEDIATE (INT 68h, Function 02h, Subfunction 0C00h), 207
RECEIVE STATUS (INT 6Bh Func-tion 1Ah), 663
RECEIVER USER-DEFINED PACK-ETS (INT 21h Function FF9Ah), 486
RECEIVER.COM
    (INT 2Ah Function 07h), 437
    (INT 2Ah Function 86h), 437
    (INT 2Ah Function 89h), 437
    (INT 2Ah Function C4h), 437-438
    GET FILENAME (INT 2Fh Func-tion B905h), 440
    INSTALLATION CHECK (INT 2Fh Function B900h), 439
    SET FILENAME (INT 2Fh Func-tion B906h), 440
    UNLINK KEYBOARD HAN-DLER (INT 2Fh Function B900h), 440
records, locking, 45-46
REDIR.SYS - SET REDIRIFS ENTRY POINT (INT 2Fh Function BF80h), 440
REDIR/REDIRIFS
    INSTALLATION CHECK (INT 2Fh Function 0200h), 438
    UNDETERMINED FUNCTION (INT 2Fh Function 0201h), 438
    UNDETERMINED FUNCTION (INT 2Fh Function 0202h), 438
REDIRECT DEVICE (INT 21h Func-tion 5F03h), 59
REDIRECTED PRINTER MODE (INT 2Fh Function 1125h), 133
redirectors, 505-525
REDIRIFS.EXE - UNDETERMINED FUNCTION (INT 2Fh Function BF00h), 440

REDIRIFS.EXE - UNDETERMINED FUNCTION (INT 2Fh Function BF01h), 440
REDRAW SCREEN (INT 10h Func-tion 93h), 158
REFRESH EMULATION SCREEN (INT 61h Function 0003h, Sub-function 09h), 232
REGISTER MULTICAST (INT 7Ch Function 0009h), 446
REGISTER PROTOCOL (INT 7Ch Function 0007h), 443-445
RELEASE ALL SEMAPHORES FOR USER (INT 7Fh Function B0h), 187
RELEASE BUFFER (INT 7Ch Func-tion 0005h), 443
RELEASE BUFFER (INT 7Fh Func-tion 10h, Subfunction 04h), 174
RELEASE DEVICE FOR USER (INT 7Fh Function 82h), 185
RELEASE DEVICES FOR USER (INT 7Fh Function B4h), 187
RELEASE FILE (FCB) (INT 21h Func-tion CCh), 401
RELEASE FILE (INT 21h Function ECh), 404
RELEASE FILE FOR USER (INT 7Fh Function B3h, Subfunction 02h), 187
RELEASE FILE SET (INT 21h Func-tion CDh), 401
RELEASE LICENSE (UNT 2Fh Func-tion 7002h), 682
RELEASE LOGICAL COMMUNICA-TIONS PORT (INT 14h Func-tion 22h), 158
RELEASE LOGICAL RECORD (INT 21h Function D2h), 403
RELEASE LOGICAL RECORD SET (INT 21h Function D3h), 403
RELEASE MESSAGES FOR USER (INT 7Fh Function B2h, Subfunc-tion 01h), 187
RELEASE NORMAL SEMAPHORES FOR USER (INT 7Fh Function B1h, Subfunction 00h), 187
RELEASE PHYSICAL COMMUNICA-TIONS PORT (INT 14h Func-tion 21h), 158
RELEASE PHYSICAL RECORD (INT 21h Function BDh), 397
RELEASE PHYSICAL RECORD SET (INT 21h Function C3h), 398
RELEASE RECORD (FCB) (INT 21h Function C0h), 398
RELEASE SEMAPHORE (INT 7Fh Function 02h), 169
RELEASE TYPE (INT 60h Function 03h), 152
RELINK KEYBOARD HANDLER (INT 2Fh Function B808h), 507
RELINQUISH CONTROL (INT 7Ah Function 000Ah), 97
RELOCATED IRQ0 THROUGH IRQ7 (INT 50h-INT 57h), 643
REMOTE API CALL (INT 21h Func-tion 5F3Fh), 282
REMOTE PRINTER ECHO ON/OFF (INT 2Fh Function 1126h), 134

REMOVE DOS TASK (INT 7Fh Function E7h), 191

REMOVE GLOBAL NETWORK NAME (INT 21h Function 5F08h), 684

REMOVE JOB FROM QUEUE (INT 21h Function E3h Subfunction 6Ah), 389

REMOVE PRINTER FROM SPOOLER (INT 17h Function 88h), 161

REMOVE RECEIVED PACKET (INT 80h Function 06h), 685

REMOVE REMOTE DIRECTORY (INT 2Fh Function 1101h), 123-124

REMOVE SOCKET UNKNOWN HANDLER (INT 63h Function 20h), 536

REMOVE UNKKNOW NANDLER (INT 63h Function 22h), 536

REMOVE UNKNOWN ITEM (INT 62h Function 0Ch), 528

REMOVE UNKNOWN ITEM (INT 64h Function 04h), 538

REMOVE USER FROM GROUP (INT 7Fh Function F9h), 192

RENAME (INT21h Function 56h), 45

RENAME BINDERY OBJECT (INT 21h Function E3h Subfunction 34h), 320

RENAME DIRECTORY (INT 21h Function E2h Subfunction 0Fh), 341

RENAME REMOTE FILE (INT 2Fh Function 1112h), 128

RENAME REMOTE FILE (INT 2Fh Function 111h), 128

REQUEST BUFFER (INT 7Ch Function 0004h), 442-443

REQUEST LICENSE (INT 2Fh, Function 7001h), 681-682

REQUEST TO SEND (INT 68h, Function 02h, Subfunction 0E00h), 207

RESERVED (INT 2Fh Function 150Ah), 243

RESET A NETWORK CONNECTION (INT 61h Function 19h), 550-551

RESET ALL NETWORK CONNECTIONS (INT 61h Function 24h), 554

RESET ERROR (INT 61h Function 0003h, Subfunction 15h), 236

RESET INTERFACE (INT 60h Function 07h), 152

RESET INTERFACE (INT 6Fh Function 0001h), 636

RESET LAT COUNTERS (INT 6Ah Function D300h), 253

RESET NETWORK CONNECTION (INT 63h Function 16h), 534

RESET NETWORK EXECUTIVE (INT 7Fh Function D6h), 189

RESET SPOOLER (INT 17h Function 8Dh), 162

RESET UNKNOWN VARIABLE (INT 2Fh Function 7A15h), 433

RESET USER DATAGRAMS (INT 7Fh Function 13h, Subfunction 00h), 176

RESLOVE HOST NAME USING IEN116 (INT 61h Function 53h), 558

RESOLVE A GATE NAME (INT 7Ah Function 81h), 633

RESOLVE HOST NAME (INT 61h Function 54h), 558

RESOLVE NAME USING DNS (INT 61h Function 52h), 558

RESOLVE NAME USING HOST TABLE (INT 61h Function 51h), 557

RESOURCE ALLOCATION (INT 21h, Function D8h and D9h), 216

RESTART PRINTER (INT 17h Function 98h), 165

RESTORE DIRECTORY HANDLE (INT 21h Function E2h Subfunction 18h), 344

RESTORE DISPLAY (INT 6Fh Function 000Ah), 637

RESTORE ERASED FILE (INT 21h Function E2h Subfunction 11h), 370-371

RESTORE QUEUE SERVER RIGHTS (INT 21h Function E3h Subfunction 75h), 395

RESTRICT DIRECTORY TO GROUP (INT 7Fh Function F0h), 191

RESUME A SESSION (INT 14h Function A5h), 659

RESUME SUSPENDED SESSION (INT 61h Function 0003h, Subfunction 0Bh), 232

RETRIEVE HOST SESSION NAME (INT 6Fh Function 0029h), 642

RETURN ACTIVE CONNECTION PARAMETERS (INT 14h Function 0Fh), 657

RETURN COMMUNICATION PORT STATUS (INT 14h Function 03h), 651

RETURN DEFAULT CONNECTION PARAMETERS (INT 14h Function 08h), 656

RETURN SHELL VERSION (INT 21h Function EAh), 412-413

ReturnCommandComPointers (INT 21h Function BAh), 410

ROM BIOS, 1

ROM Cassette BASSIC, 8

Sangoma X.25 interrupts, 643

SAVE DIRECTORY HANDLE (INT 21h Function E2h Subfunction 17h), 343

SAVE/DISPLAY GRAPHICS (INT 6Fh Function 0010h), 638

SCAN BINDERY OBJECT (INT 21H Function E3h Subfunction 37h), 321-322

SCAN BINDERY OBJECT TRUSTEE PATHS (INT 21h Function E3h Subfunction 47h), 344-345

SCAN DIRECTORY FOR TRUSTEES (INT 21h Function E2h Subfunction 0Ch), 339 340

SCAN DIRECTORY INFORMATION (INT 21h Function E2h Subfunction 02h), 336

SCAN FILE INFORMATION (INT 21h Function E3h Subfunction 0Fh), 371-372

SCAN PROPERTY (INT 21h Function E3h Subfunction 3Ch), 324

SCHED (INT 6Fh Function 1Eh), 475

SCHEDULE IPX EVENT (INT 7Ah Function 0005h), 96

SCHEDULE SERVER SHUTDOWN (INT 21h Function 5FC8h), 306

SCHEDULE SPECIAL EVENT (INT 7Ah Function 0007h), 96

SECONDARY 3270 INTERFACE (INT 61h, Function 000Ah), 240

SEEK FROM END OF REMOTE FILE (INT 2Fh Function 1121h), 133

Segment:Offset format, 2

SELECT (SOCKET API Function 0005h), 260

SELECT HOST SESSION (INT 6Fh Function 0028h), 642

SELECT PRINTER (INT 17h Function 94h), 163-174

SEMAPHORE LOCK (INT 7Fh Function 01h), 169

SEMAPHORE LOCK AND WAIT (INT 7Fh Function 00h), 168

SEMAPHORE LOCKING/UNLOCKING (INT 60h, Function 11h to 13h), 217

SEND BREAK (INT 14h Function 09h), 656

SEND BREAK (INT 6Ah Function D100h), 253

SEND BROADCAST MESSAGE (INT 21h Function E1h Subfunction 00h), 374

SEND BYTE (INT 69h Function 0101h), 247

SEND BYTE (INT 6Ah Function 01h), 251

SEND CHARACTER (INT 14h Function 01h), 651

SEND CHARACTER (INT 6Fh Function 0006h), 637

SEND CHARACTER BLOCK (INT 14h Function 06h), 655

SEND CONSOLE BROADCOAST (INT 21h Function E3h Subfunction D1h), 352

SEND DATA (INT 68h, Function 02h, Subfunction 0F00h), 208

SEND DATAGRAM (INT 7Fh Function 11h), 175

SEND DEVICE DRIVER REQUEST (INT 2Fh Function 1510h), 245

SEND ERROR (INT 68h, Function 02h, Subfunction 1000h), 208

SEND FULL SCREEN OF DATA FOR TopShow (INT 2Fh Function FF18h), 195

SEND ICMP ECHO REQUEST (INT 61h Function 30h), 556-557

SEND KEYSTROKES TO HOST WINDOW (INT 21h Function A3h), 623-624

SEND MESSAGE (INT 21h Function FF80h Subfunction FFh), 484

SEND MESSAGE OR COMMAND TO USER(S) (INT 7Fh Function 21h, 179-180

SEND NAK BLOCK (INT 17h Function 2405h), 514
SEND PACKET
 (INT 21h Function FFE3h, Subfunction 02h), 493
 (INT 60h Function 04h), 152
 (INT 7Ah Function 0003h), 93-95
 (INT 7Ah Function 000Fh), 98-99
SEND PERSONAL MESSAGE (INT 21h Function E1h Subfunction 04h), 375-376
SEND RAW BYTES (INT 60h Function 1Ah), 155
SEND RESULT OF USER FUNCTION (INT 16h Function 4505h), 678
SEND SHORT BREAK (INT 14h Function A6h), 88-89
SEND SPX PACKET (INT 7Ah Function 0016h), 102
SEND STRING TO COMMAND INTERPRETER (INT 14h Function A8h), 660
SEND TO HOST (INT 61h Function 0003h, Subfunction 01h), 118-229
SEND UNSOLICITED MESSAGE (INT 21h Function 5F98h), 297-298
SERVER
 GET UNKNOWN VALUES (INT 2Fh Function D856h), 424
 INSTALLATION CHECK (INT 2Fh Function D880h), 424-425
 SET/RESET UNKNOWN FLAG(INT 2Ah Function D800h/D801h), 421
SERVER FUNCTION CALL (INT 21h Function 5D00h), 46
SERVICE QUEUE JOB AND OPEN FILE (INT 21h Function E3h Subfunction 71h), 393
SESSION SERVICES (INT 7Ah Function 09h), 629
SET 3270 DISPLAY STATE (INT 21h Function A1h), 623
SET ACKNOWLEDGE ISR (INT 7Fh Function 14h, Subfunction 01h), 177
SET AN OPTION ON A DESCRIPTOR (INT 61h Function 20h), 553
SET APPLICATION THRESHOLDS (INT 21h Function C706h), 406
SET AUTO-LOGIN DEFAULTS (INT 21h Function 5FB6h), 305
SET AUTOPRINT TIME (INT 21h Function FFBEh), 488
SET BANNER USER NAME (INT 21h Function B809h), 381
SET BROADCAST MODE (INT 21h Function DEh), 374
SET CAPTURE PRINT JOB (INT 21h Function B807h), 381
SET CAPTURE PRINT QUEUE (INT 21h Function B806h), 381
SET CHANNEL BUFFER POINTER (INT 7Fh Function 14h, Subfunction 02h), 177

SET CONTROL NUMBER OF SHOW SCREEN (INT 2Fh Function FF16h), 495
SET CURSOR POSITION FOR DIRECT WRITE BUFFER (INT 6Fh Function 0012h), 638
SET DATA DRIVER PRINT BREAK (INT 17h Function 97h), 164-165
SET DEFAULT
 CAPTURE FLAGS (INT 21h Function B801h), 380
 END-OF-JOB FORMFEED STATUS (INT 21h Function FFC1h), 488
 LOCAL PRINTER (INT 21h Function B805h), 381
 PRINT COPIES (INT 21h Function FFC7h), 489-490
 PRINT FILE HEADER (INT 21h Function FFC6h), 489
 START-OF-JOB FORMFEED STATUS (INT 21h Function FFB3h), 487
 UNKNOWN HANDLER (INT 63h Function 08h), 532
SET DIRECT WRITE STRING LENGTH (INT 6Fh Function 015h), 639
SET DIRECTORY HANDLE (INT 21h Function E2h Subfunction 00h), 335
SET DIRECTORY INFORMATION (INT 21h Function E2h Subfunction 19h), 344
SET DISPLAY PARAMETERS (INT 6Fh Function 0002h), 636
SET DOS SERVICE VECTOR (INT 21h Function 5FE1h), 308
SET DRIVE (INT 2Fh Function 1219h), 68
SET DRIVE MAPPING (INT 2Fh Function 920Bh), 277
SET END OF JOB STATUS (INT 21h Function BBh), 406-407
SET ERROR MODE (INT 7Fh Function 4Eh), 184-185
SET EXTENDED ERROR INFORMATION (INT 21h Function 5D0Ah), 52
SET EXTENDED ERROR INFORMATION (INT 2Fh Function 1222h), 70
SET EXTENDED FILE ATTRIBUTES (INT 21h Function 4311h), 215
SET EXTENDED QUEUE ENTRY (INT 21h Function 5FA9h), 302
SET FASTOPEN ENTRY POINT (INT 2Fh Function 122Ah), 72
SET FCB MODE (INT 7Fh Function 4Fh), 185
SET FCB RE-OPEN MODE (INT 21h Function E8h), 412
SET FILE ATTRIBUTES (FCB) (INT 21h Function E4h), 346
SET FILE I/O CHECKING LEVEL (INT 7Fh Function 26h, Subfunction 01h-05h), 181
SET FILE INFORMATION (INT 21h Function E3h Subfunction 10h), 372
SET HARDWARE FLOW STATE (INT 14h Function 0Eh), 657

SET HOST WINDOW STATE (INT 21h Function A2h), 623
SET INDOS POINTER (INT 17h Function 87h), 161
SET INTERNAL SEND/RECEIVE VECTOR (INT 14h Function 8025h), 649
SET INTERNET ADDRESS (INT 63h Function 26h), 537
SET IP ADDRESS (INT 63h Function 00h), 531
SET LPT MAPPING (INT 2Fh Function 920Eh), 278
SET MACHINE NAME (INT 21h Function 5E01h), 57
SET MESSAGE DISPLAY TIMEOUT (INT 7Fh Function 08h Subfunction 02h), 172
SET MESSAGE PROCESSING FLAGS (INT 21h Function 5F9Bh), 298
SET MESSAGE SERVICE VECTOR (INT 21h Function 5FE3h), 309
SET MULTICAST LIST (INT 60h Function 16h), 154
SET NET PRINTER MODE (INT 2Ah Function 02h), 117
SET NetWare ERROR MODE (INT 21h Function DDh), 407
SET NETWORK ADDRESS (INT 60h Function 19h), 155
SET NETWORK EVENT POST HANDLER (INT 2Fh Function B804h), 506
SET NETWORK PRINTER SETUP STRING (INT 21h Function 5E02h), 57
SET NEW TERMINAL DRIVER (INT 7Fh Function 38h), 182
SET NUMBER OF COPIES (INT 17h Function 83h), 160
SET PASSTHROUGH (INT 68h, Function FFh), 214
SET PORTS FOR A SERVICE (INT 61h, Function 0007h, Subfunction 0004h), 237
SET PREFERRED CONNECTION ID (INT 21h Function F000h), 409
SET PRIMARY CONNECTION ID (INT 21h Function F004h), 409
SET PRINT BREAK TIMEOUT (INT 17h Function 9Bh), 166
SET PRINT JOB TERMINATION CONFIGURATION, (INT 2Ah Function FF96h), 561
SET PRINTER MODE (INT 21h Function 5E04h), 57
SET PRINTER SHARING (INT 21h Function FFC9h), 490
SET QUEUE CURRENT STATUS (INT 21h Function E3h Subfunction 67h), 387-388
SET QUEUE ENTRY (INT 21h Function 5FA1h), 300
SET QUEUE SERVER CURRENT STATUS (INT 21h Function E3h Subfunction 77h), 395-396
SET RECEIVE ISR (INT 7Fh Function 14h, Subfunction 00h), 176
SET RECEIVE MODE (INT 60h Function 14h), 154

SET RECEIVER.COM POST ADDRESS (INT 2Fh Function B904h0, 439

SET REDIRECTED PRINTER MODE (INT 21h Function 5D08h), 52

SET REDIRECTED PRINTER TIMEOUT (INT 21h Function 5FD1h), 308

SET REDIRECTION MODE (INT 21h Function 5F01h), 58

SET REDIRECTOR CONTROL BITS (INT 21h Function 5F9Eh), 299

SET REMOTE FILE'S ATTRIBUTES (INT 2Fh Function 110Dh), 127

SET REMOTE FILE'S ATTRIBUTES (INT 2Fh Function 110Eh), 127

SET RUNTIME PARAMETERS (INT 2Fh Function 4E53h Subfunction 02h), 517

SET SCROLL LOCK CHECKING (INT 61h Function 0003h, Subfunction 0Ch), 233

SET SEND/RECEIVE TIMEOUTS (INT 14h Function 8009h), 649

SET SERIAL PORT PARAMETERS (INT 17h Function 96h), 164

SET SESSION PARAMETER (INT 61h Function 0003h, Subfunction 05h), 230-231

SET SHARED DEVICE ENTRY (INT 6Fh Function 1502h), 473

SET SHARED DEVICE ENTRY (INT 6Fh Function 9502h), 478

SET SHELL INT 21h HANDLER (INT 2Fh Function 7A81h), 419

SET SOCKET UNKNOWN HANDLER (INT 63h Function 1Fh), 536

SET SPECIFIC CAPTURE FLAGS (INT 21h Function B803h), 380

SET SPOOLER PRINTING PRIORITY (INT 21h Function FFB1h), 486

SET STATE FOR PIPE HANDLE (INT 21h Function 5F34h), 106

SET STREAM INFO (INT 21h Function 5FA5h), 301-302

SET TAB EXPANSION (INT 17h Function 9Ah), 165

SET TAB SETTINGS (INT 61h Function 0003h, Subfunction 07h), 231

SET TERMINAL DRIVER FOR ANOTHER USER (INT 7Fh Function 39h), 182-183

SET TERMINAL PARAMETERS (INT 7Fh Function 3Bh), 183

SET TIMED ASYNCHRONOUS EVENT (INT 61h Function 2Bh), 556

SET TIMEOUT (INT 6Fh Function 0007h), 637

SET TRACE DESTINATION (INT 68h, Function FEh), 214

SET UNKNOWN FLAG (INT 2Fh Function 9401h), 679

SET UNKNOWN FLAG (INT 2Fh Function 9403h), 679

SET UNKNOWN ITEM (INT 14h Function E8h), 573

SET UNKNOWN ITEM (INT 63h Function 27h), 537

SET UNKNOWN POINTER (INT 62h Function 04h), 527

SET UNKNOWN POINTER (INT 62h Function 11h), 529

SET UNKNOWN VALUE (INT 2Fh Function 9205h), 276

SET UP ASYNCHRONOUS CALL-BACK (INT 61h Function 1Fh), 552-553

SET USER STATUS (INT 7Fh Function A501h), 186-187

SET VIRTUAL MACHINE ID (INT 21h Function B505h), 435

SET WORKSTATION THRESHOLDS (INT 21h Function C708h), 406

SET YEAR/LENGTH OF FEBRUARY (INT 2Fh Function 121Bh), 69

SET/RESET GRAPHICS DOS ON SLAVE (INT 7Fh Function 0Bh, Subfunction 02h), 173

SET/RETRIEVE REQUEST/REPLY SERVICE NAME (INT 6Bh Function 13h), 661-662

SET/RETRIEVE SERVICE ADDRESS (INT 6Bh Function 14h), 662

SET/REVTIEVE VIRTUAL CIRCUIT CONFIGURATION (INT 6Bh Function 15h), 662

Shamrock Software
EMAIL interrupts, 677-679
NET.24, 513-515

SHARE.EXE, closing files, 47-48

SHARING RETRY DELAY (INT 2Fh Function 1224h), 70

SHELL TIMER INTERRUPT CHECKS (INT 21h Function DEh, Subfunction 05h/06h), 411

shells, 505-525

SHUTDOWN (INT 14h Function 58h), 650

SIGNAL SEMAPHORE (INT 21h Function C503h), 399

SIGNAL SHARING VIOLATION TO USER (INT 2Fh Function 1208h), 66

SilverNET, 515-517

SK-UPPS Data Link Interface, 441-450

SLEEP (SOCKET API Function 003h), 259-260

SNAP (Simple Network Access Protocol), 451-455

SNAP_802_5 (INT 1Ah Function 76h), 455

SNAP_BEGINCONV (INT 1Ah Function 6308h), 452

SNAP_CHKINSTALL (INT 1Ah Function 6F01h), 454

SNAP_CLIENTVERSION (INT 1Ah Function 7302h), 454

SNAP_COPYFROM (INT 1Ah Function 6D04h), 453

SNAP_COPYTO (INT 1Ah Function 6C04h), 453

SNAP_DATASEG (INT 1Ah Function 6900h), 453

SNAP_ENDCONV (INT 1Ah Function 6405h), 452

SNAP_FREE (INT 1Ah Function 6B01h), 453

SNAP_GETANCHOR (INT 1Ah Function 7101h), 454

SNAP_NOP (INT 1Ah Function 75h), 455

SNAP_SENDNOREPLY (INT 1Ah Function 6205h), 452

SNAP_SENDWITHREPLY (INT 1Ah Function 6108h), 451-452

SNAP_SETANCHOR (INT 1Ah Function 7002h), 454

SNAP_SETDEBUG (INT 1Ah Function 6E01h), 453

SNAP_VERSION (INT 1Ah Function 7400h), 454

SOCKET API
(INT 15h Function 112Eh), 255
(INT 15h Function DE2Eh), 255-258
(INT 63h), 258
Function 0001h (GET HOST NAME), 258-259
Function 0004h (HTONS), 260
Function 0006h (CLOSE SOCKET), 260-261
Function 0008h (CONNECT), 261
Function 0009h (READ FROM SOCKET), 261-262
Function 000Ah (CREATE NEW SOCKET), 262
Function 000Bh (UNDETERMINED FUNCTION), 262
Function 000Ch (GET INFORMATION), 262-263
Function 000Dh (WRITE DATA TO SOCKET), 263
Function 000Eh (UNDETERMINED FUNCTION), 263
Function 000Fh (GET PROCESS IDENTIFIER), 263
Function 000h (INITIALIZE SOCKET), 258
Function 0010h (GET TIME OF DAY), 264
Function 0011h (BIND), 264
Function 0012h (LISTEN), 264
Function 0013h (ACCEPT), 264-265
Function 0014h (CONNECT TO X SERVER), 265
Function 0015h (GET HOST INFORMATION), 265-266
Function 0016h (GET NETWORK PROTOCOL INFORMATION), 266
Function 0017h (GET NETWORK PROTOCOL INFORMATION), 266
Function 0018h (GET INFORMATION ABOUT A SERVICE), 266
Function 0019h (GET INFORMATION ABOUT A SERVICE), 266-267
Function 001Ah (GET SOCKET NAME), 267
Function 001Bh (GET PEER NAME), 267

Function 001Ch (GET/SET SOCKET OPTIONS), 267-268

Function 001Dh (SOCKET EXIT), 268

Function 001Eh (SOCKET FILE HANDLE REFERENCE), 268

Function 001Fh (REATTACH SOCKET), 268

Function 0020h (DETACH SOCKET), 269

Function 0021h (GET DESQview DIRECTORY), 269

Function 0022h (START NEW APPLICATION), 269

Function 0023h (LINKUP), 269-270

Function 0024h (CANONICAL-IZE FILENAME), 270

Function 0025h (INDIRECT INT 15h CALL), 270

Function 0026h (Network Manager Interface), 270-273

Function 0027h (SOCKET UNLINK), 273

Function 0028h/0029h (RAISE/LOWER PRIORITY), 273-274

Function 002Ah (UNDETERMINED FUNCTION), 274

Function 002h (IOCTL), 259

Function 003h (SLEEP), 259-260

Function 00509h (SELECT), 260

SOCKET EXIT (SOCKET API Function 001Dh), 268

SOCKET FILE HANDLE REFERENCE (SOCKET API Function 001Eh), 268

socket functions
Unix, 575-593
Windows, 595-619

SOCKET UNLINK (SOCKET API Function 0027h), 273

software interrupt instruction (INT), 2

SOINT (INT 61h, Function 0001h, Subfunction 000Bh), 221

SOREC (INT 61h, Function 0001h, Subfunction 0003h), 219-220

SOSESSION (INT 61h, Function 0001h, Subfunction 0008h), 221

SOWAIT (INT 61h, Function 0001h, Subfunction 0005h), 220-221

SpecialAttachableFunction (INT 21h Function B9h), 410

SPECIFY CAPTURE FILE (INT 21h Function E0h Subfunction 09h), 384-385

SPECIFY COMMAND WORD FOR USER FUNCTION (INT 16h Function 4503h), 678

SPOOL COPY OF FILE (INT 17h Function A0h), 166

SPOOL FILE BY NAME (INT 17h Function 90h), 163

SPOOL/PRINT (INT 6Fh Function 0Eh), 470-471

SPX (Specified Packet Exchange), 91

STARLITE Architecture (embedded DOS interrupts), 683-684

START A NEW SESSION (INT 14h Function A3h), 659

START BACKGROUND RECEIVE VIDEO DATA (INT 2Fh Function FF14h), 494

START LPT CAPTURE (INT 21h Function DFh Subfunction 00h), 382

START NEW APPLICATION (SOCKET API Function 0022h), 269

START SESSION (INT 61h Function 0003h, Subfunction 0Fh), 233-234

START SPECIFIC LPT CAPTURE (INT 21h Function DFh Subfunction 04h), 383

START VIRTUAL MACHINE (INT 21h Function B502h), 435

START/STOP PRINTING (INT 61h Function 0003h, Subfunction 10h), 234

START/STOP TRACING TRAFFIC (INT 61h Function 0003h, Subfunction 13h), 235

STATUS (INT 69h Function 0103h), 247-248

STATUS (INT 6Ah Function 03h), 251

STATUS OF NODE (INT 6Fh Function 02h), 464-465

STREAM ENCRYPTION SERVICE (INT 2Fh Function 118Ah), 292

Streetalk Directory Assistance Interface (INT 2Fh, Function D704h), 216

STUFF SERVER KEYBOARD BUFFER (INT 21h Function 5FCAh), 307

SUBMIT (INT 6Fh Function 09h), 468

SUBMIT ACCOUNT CHARGE (INT 21h FunctionE3h Subfunction 97h), 317

SUBMIT ACCOUNT NOTE (INT 21h FunctionE3h Subfunction 99h), 318

SUM MEMORY (INT 2Fh Function 121Dh), 69

Sun PC-NFS interrupts, 566

Super-TCP interrupts, 566-570

SUSPEND SESSION TEMPORARILY (INT 61h Function 0003h, Subfunction 0Ah), 232

SWITCH HOST TO DEDICATED MODE (INT 7Fh Function 09h Subfunction 02h), 172

SWITCH TO NEW DOS TASK (INT 7Fh Function E2h), 190

SWITCH TO NEXT ACTIVE SESSION (INT 14h Function A7h), 659

SYNC REQUEST BUFFER (INT 7Ch Function 0012h), 448

synchronization services, NetWare, 396-404

SYSSVC.COM
(INT 69h Function 4001h), 480
(INT 69h Function 4002h), 480
(INT 69h Function 4101h), 480
(INT 69h Function 4102h-4104h), 480
(INT 69h Function 42h), 480
(INT 69h Function 43h), 480
(INT 69h Function 44h), 481
BUG (INT 69h Function 49h), 481

SIGNAL SYSTEM ERROR (INT 69h Function FFh), 481

SYSTEM LOGOUT (INT 21h Function D7h), 329

SYVARS (INT 21h Function 52h), 25-45

TABDATA (INT 6Fh Function 1Dh), 475

TASK MODE CONTROL (INT 21h Function B5h), 410

TASKID, NetWare, 430-431

TBMI, NetWare, 431-434

TCP/IP, 541-562
software interrupts, 563-574
TSR System Call interface (INT 61h), 541-543

TelAPI interrupts, 571-574

Telebit ACS serial I/O interrupts, 664-665

Terminate and Stay Resident (TSR), AMIS compliant, 7

TERMINATE CONNECTION CLIENT ACTIVITY (INT 14h Function 0Dh), 657

TERMINATE DRIVER FOR HANDLE (INT 60h Function 05h), 152

TERMINATE PRINT JOB (INT 21h Function 5E05h), 462

TERMINATE SOCKETS (INT 7Ah Function 000Eh), 98

TERMINATE SPX CONNECTION (INT 7Ah Function 0013h), 100

TERMINATE USER (INT 21h Function 5FCBh), 307

TES interrupts, 658-660

TEST (INT 68h, Function 02h, Subfunction 1200h), 209

TEST FOR INBOUND CONNECTION REQUEST (INT 14h Function 0Ch), 657

TopTerm
DISABLE KEYBOARD SERVICE (INT 2Fh Function FF12h), 494

ENABLE KEYBOARD SERVICE (INT 2Fh Function FF11h), 494

INSTALLATION CHECK (INT 2Fh Function FF10h), 494

SET INSTALLATION FLAG ((INT 2Fh Function FF13h), 494

TopWare Network Operating System, 483-496

TP STARTED (INT 68h, Function 03h, Subfunction 2400h), 209-210

TRANSACTION PROCESSING (INT 68h, Function 04h), 211

TRANSACTION STATUS (INT 21h Function C704h), 405

transaction tracking system, NetWare, 404-406

TRANSFER MESSAGE DATA (INT 68h, Function 05h), 211

TRANSLATE DATA (INT 7Ah Function 09h), 631-632

TRANSLATE ERROR CODE TO ERROR STRING (INT 14h Function 8003h), 646

TRANSLATE NUMERICAL IP ADDRESS (INT 61h Function 50h), 557
TRANSLATE PATH (INT 21h Function 5FB3h), 304-305
TRANSMIT BLOCK, NO HANDSHAKE (INT 17h Function 2402h), 514
TRANSMIT BUFFER CONTROL (INT 6Bh Function 1Dh), 663
TRANSMIT COMMAND, WITH HANDSHAKE (INT 17h Function 2409h), 515
TRANSMIT FRAME (INT 7Ch Function 0006h), 443
TRANSMIT FRAME RELEASE (INT 7Ch Function 0013h), 448
TRANSMIT SINGLE CHARACTER TO REMOTE (INT 17h Function 240Bh), 515
TRANSMIT STATUS (INT 6Bh Function 1Bh), 663
TRUENAME (INT 21h Function 60h), 60-61
TURN DEBUGGING OFF (INT 2Fh Function 1507h), 242
TURN DEBUGGING ON (INT 2Fh Function 1506h), 242
TURN OFF REMOTE PRINTER (INT 2Fh Function 1124h), 133

UNDETERMINED FUNCTION
(INT 14h Function 6Fh Subfunction FFFEh), 658
(INT 14h Function E0h), 572
(INT 14h Function E1h), 572
(INT 14h Function E5h/E6h), 573
(INT 14h Function E9h), 573
(INT 14h Function ECh), 573-574
(INT 14h Function EDh), 574
(INT 1Ah Function 77h), 455
(INT 1Ah Function 7802h), 455
(INT 21h Function 5F30h), 281
(INT 21h Function CFh), 518
(INT 2Ah Function 2001h), 518
(INT 2Ah Function 2002h/2003h), 518
(INT 2Ah Function 90h), 633
(INT 2Ah Function C2h), 518
(INT 2Ah Function E0h), 438
(INT 2Ah Function FF90h), 560
(INT 2Ah Function FF91h), 560
(INT 2Ah Function FF93h), 561
(INT 2Ah Function FF94h), 561
(INT 2Fh Function 7A4Fh, Subfunction 0002h), 565
(INT 2Fh Function 0203h), 438
(INT 2Fh Function 0204h), 438-439
(INT 2Fh Function 02xxh), 439
(INT 2Fh Function 1180h), 291
(INT 2Fh Function 1184h), 291
(INT 2Fh Function 118Bh), 292
(INT 2Fh Function 118Ch), 292
(INT 2Fh Function 118Eh), 292
(INT 2Fh Function 13h), 518
(INT 2Fh Function 4103h), 293
(INT 2Fh Function 4104h), 293
(INT 2Fh Function 7A16h), 433
(INT 2Fh Function 7A17h), 433

(INT 2Fh Function 7A1Ch), 433
(INT 2Fh Function 7A1Dh), 433
(INT 2Fh Function 7A1Eh), 433
(INT 2Fh Function 7A43h), 565
(INT 2Fh Function 7A44h), 565
(INT 2Fh Function 7A4Dh), 434
(INT 2Fh Function 8001h), 511
(INT 2Fh Function 8102h), 512
(INT 2Fh Function 8104h), 512
(INT 2Fh Function 8105h), 512
(INT 2Fh Function 9206h), 276
(INT 2Fh Function 9208h), 277
(INT 2Fh Function 9209h), 277
(INT 2Fh Function 920Ah), 277
(INT 2Fh Function 920Ch), 277
(INT 2Fh Function 9210h), 278
(INT 2Fh Function 9213h), 278
(INT 2Fh Function 9216h), 279
(INT 2Fh Function 9217h), 279
(INT 2Fh Function 9219h), 279
(INT 2Fh Function 921Ah), 279
(INT 2Fh Function 921Bh), 280
(INT 2Fh Function 921Ch), 280
(INT 2Fh Function 921Eh), 280
(INT 2Fh Function 9402h), 679
(INT 2Fh Function B402h-B405h), 634
(INT 2Fh Function B80Ah), 439
(INT 2Fh, Functions 7F24h and 7F26h), 686
(INT 5Bh), 686
(INT 60h), 686
(INT 61h Function 0Ah), 546
(INT 61h Function 0Bh), 546
(INT 61h Function 15h), 550
(INT 61h Function 34h), 557
(INT 62h Function 05h/06h), 527
(INT 62h Function 07h), 527
(INT 62h Function 08h), 527-528
(INT 62h Function 13h), 529
(INT 62h Function 14h), 530
(INT 62h Function 16h), 530
(INT 62h Function 17h), 530
(INT 63h Function 01h), 531
(INT 63h Function 02h), 531
(INT 63h Function 04h), 531
(INT 63h Function 05h), 531
(INT 63h Function 06h), 532
(INT 63h Function 07h), 532
(INT 63h Function 0Bh), 532
(INT 63h Function 0Ch), 533
(INT 63h Function 0Fh), 533
(INT 63h Function 10h), 533
(INT 63h Function 11h), 533
(INT 63h Function 15h), 534
(INT 63h Function 17h), 534
(INT 63h Function 18h), 534
(INT 63h Function 1Bh), 535
(INT 63h Function 1Ch), 535
(INT 63h Function 1Dh), 535
(INT 63h Function 1Eh), 535
(INT 63h Function 21h), 536
(INT 63h Function 23h), 536
(INT 63h Function 28h/29h), 537
(INT 64h Function 02h), 537
(INT 64h Function 05h), 538
(INT 64h Function 06h), 538
(INT 6Ah Function 0001h), 567-569
(INT 6Ah Function 0002h), 569

(INT 6Bh Function 08h), 574
(INT 6Fh Function 20h), 475
(INT 6Fh Function 21h), 475
(INT 6Fh Function 22h), 475
(INT 7Ah Function FF04h), 635
(INT 7Ah), 495
(INT 81h), 687
(INT 82h), 687
(INT 91h), 687
(INT 93h), 687
(SOCKET API Function 0008h), 262
(SOCKET API Function 000Eh), 263
(SOCKET API Function 002Ah), 274
UNDETERMINED USAGE (INT E2h), 524
UNDETERMINED USE (INT 67h), 643
UNDETERMINED USE (INT 68h), 643
UNHOOK TIMER INTERRUPT (INT 62h Function 0Ah), 528
UNINSTALL (INT 2Fh Function 9202h), 276
UNINSTALL (INT 61h Function 10h), 548
UNINSTALL (INT 6Ah Function 0010h), 570
Unix socket functions, 575-593
  accept, 579
  bind, 579
  close, 579
  connect, 579-590
  endhostent, 580
  endnetent, 580
  endprotoent, 580
  endservent, 580
  gethostbyaddr, 580-581
  gethostbyname, 581
  gethostent, 581
  gethostid, 581
  gethostname, 581-582
  getnetbyaddr, 582
  getnetbyname, 582
  getnetent, 582
  getpeername, 582-583
  getprotobyanme, 583
  getprotobynumber, 583
  getprotoent, 583
  getservbyname, 583-584
  getservbynumber, 584
  getservent, 584
  getsockname, 584
  getsockopt, 585
  htonl, 585
  htons, 585
  inet_addr, 585-586
  inet_lnaof, 586
  inet_makeaddr, 586
  inet_netof, 586
  inet_ntoa, 587
  inetnetwork, 586-587
  ioctl, 587
  listen, 587-588
  ntohl, 588
  ntohs, 588
  overview, 575-578
  recv, 588
  recvfrom, 588-589
  recvmsg, 589

select, 589-590
send, 590
sendmsg, 590
sendto, 590
sethostent, 590-591
sethostid, 591
sethostname, 591
setnetent, 591
setprotoent, 591
setservent, 592
setsockopt, 592
shutdown, 592-593
socket, 593
socketpair, 593
UNKNOWN (INT 5Bh), 168
UNKNOWN (INT ECh), 193
UNKNOWN FUNCTION (INT 7Ah Function 001Bh), 103
UNLINK (INT 21h Function 41h), 24-25
UNLOAD ASYNCHRONOUS REDIRECTOR FROM MEMORY (INT 14h Function 8001h), 645
UNLOCK (INT 60h Function 13h), 524
UNLOCK ALL LOCKED IDLE CHANNELS (INT 7Fh Function 10h, Subfunction 07h), 174
UNLOCK CHANNEL (INT 7Fh Function 10h, Subfunction 03h), 174
UNLOCK FCB (INT 6Fh Function 12h), 472
UNLOCK FILE FOR USER (INT 7Fh Function 42h), 184
UNLOCK HANDLE (INT 6Fh Function 08h), 468
UNLOCK REGION OF FILE (INT 2Fh Function 1108h), 126-127
UNLOCK SEMAPHORE (INT 67h Function 02h), 513
UNLOCK SEMAPHORE (INT 6Fh Function 0Ch), 469
UNLOCK SEMAPHORE FOR USER (INT 7Fh Function 42h), 184
UNMAP DRIVE LETTER (INT 21h, Function 5F06h), 683
UNMOUNT (INT 6Fh Function 18h), 474
UNUSED FUNCTION
(INT 2Fh Function 1127h), 134
(INT 2Fh Function 1128h), 134
(INT 2Fh Function 1129h), 134
UPDATE (INT 2Fh, Function 7003h), 682
UPDATE CB (INT 2Fh Function 112Ch), 134
UPDATE DEVICE BUFFER (INT 6Fh Function 000Bh), 637
UPDATE FILE SIZE (FCB) (INT 21h Function E5h), 346
UPPERCASE CHARACTER (INT 2Fh Function 1213h), 67
user interrupts
INT 60h-INT 67h, 7
usage, 18-20
user-levbel DOS calls, 21
utilities
10NET, 479-481
Novell NetWare, 427-435

VDI.SYS - GET UNKNOWN DATA (INT 21h Function 4402h), 636
VERIFY BINDERY OBJECT PASSWORD (INT 21h Function E3h Subfunction 3Fh), 325 326
VERIFY EXISTANCE OF NAME AND RETURN CANONICAL FORM (INT 61h, Function 0007h, Subfunction 0007h), 238
VERIFY NETWORK SERIAL NUMBER (INT 21h Function E3h, Subfunction 0Ch), 411
VERIFY USER PASSWORD (INT 7Fh Function A4h), 186
VERSION CHECK (INT 2Fh Function B809h), 507
VINES, Banyan, 215-240
VIRTUAL CIRCUIT STATUS (INT 6Bh Function 12h), 661
VNETWARE.E86, NetWare, 434-435

WAIT (INT 68h, Function 02h, Subfunction 1200h), 209
WAIT FOR LOCATION TO BE MODIFIED (INT 6Fh Function 0008h), 637
WAIT ON SEMAPHORE (INT 21h Function C502h), 399
WAIT UNTIL PIPE INSTANCE AVAILABLE (INT 21h Function 5F38h), 107
Web for DOS, 497-502
WEB GENERAL NOTIFICATION (INT 2Fh Function EE0h), 502
WEB MODULE INSTALLATION CHECK (INT 2Fh Function EExx0h), 497-502
Webcorp (Web for DOS), 497-502
WHO (INT 6Fh Function 8Dh), 476-477
WHOAMI (INT 6Fh Function 1Fh), 475
WINDOW SERVICES (INT 7Ah Function 09h), 630
Windows socket functions, 595-619
accept, 599-600
bind, 600
closesocket, 600
connect, 601
gethostbyaddr, 601
gethostbyname, 601-602
gethostname, 602
getpeername, 602
getprotobyname, 602-603
getprotobynumber, 603
getservbyname, 603
getservbyport, 604
getsockname, 604
getsockopt, 604-605
htonl, 605
htons, 605-606
inet_addr, 606
inet_ntoa, 606
ioctlsocket, 606-607
listen, 607
ntohl, 607
ntohs, 607-608
overview, 595-599
recv, 608
recvfrom, 608-609

select, 609
send, 610
sendto, 610
setsockopt, 610-611
shutdown, 611
socket, 611-612
WSAAsyncGetHostByAddr, 612
WSAAsyncGetHostByName, 612-613
WSAAsyncGetProtoByName, 613
WSAAsyncGetProtoByNumber, 613-614
WSAAsyncGetServByName, 614
WSAAsyncGetServByPort, 614-615
WSAAsyncSelect, 615
WSACancelAsyncRequest, 616
WSACancelBlockingCall, 616
WSACleanup, 616
WSAGetLastError, 617
WSAIsBlocking, 617
WSASetBlockingHook, 617
WSASetLastError, 617-618
WSAStartup, 618-619
WSAUnhookBlockingHook, 619
WNDOWS SUPPORT (INT 2Fh Function 7A41h), 564
Workgroup Connection interrupts, 503-504
Workgroup Connection MICRO.EXE interrupts, 679-680
workstation functions, NetWare, 406-409
WRITE (INT 14h Function 06h), 571
WRITE (INT 14h Function 07H), 571
WRITE A DATAGRAM (INT 61h Function 1Ch), 551-552
WRITE BLOCK(INT 14h Function A4h), 88
WRITE BYTE TO CONSOLE PORT (INT 7Fh Function C6h), 188
WRITE BYTE TO TERMINAL AUX PORT (INT 7Fh Function C3h), 188
WRITE CHARACTER (INT 14h Function A2h), 88
WRITE CONFIGURATION DATA (INT 21h Function 40h), 560
WRITE DATA ON A VIRTUAL CIRCUIT (INT 6Bh Function 18h), 662-663
WRITE DATA TO SOCKET (SOCKET API Function 000Dh), 263
WRITE DIRECT TO BUFFER (INT 6Fh Function 0013h), 638-639
WRITE DIRECT TO BUFFER WITHOUT ECHO (INT 6Fh Function 0014h), 639
WRITE MAILSLOT (INT 21h Function 5F3Dh), 282
WRITE PROPERTY VALUE (INT 21h Function E3h Subfunction 3Eh), 325
WRITE STRING DIRECT TO BUFFER (INT 6Fh Function 0016h), 639
WRITE STRING DIRECT TO BUFFER, UNTRANSLATED (INT 6Fh Function 0017h), 639

WRITE STRING TO ADD INFOR-
    MATION AREA (INT 6Fh Func-
    tion 000Ch), 637
WRITE TO REMOTE FILE (INT 2Fh
    Function 1109h), 125-126
WRITE TO THE NETWORK (INT
    61h Function 1Ah), 551
WRITE TO THE NETWORK (INT
    63h Function 19h), 535